I0010746

# SQL Server 2000 Fast Answers

## for DBAs and Developers

Joseph Sack

Apress®

# SQL Server 2000 Fast Answers
## for DBAs and Developers


(This book was originally published by Curlingstone in 2003.)



ISBN (pbk): 1-59059-592-0

Printed and bound in the United States of America 9 8 7 6 5 4 3 2 1



Distributed to the book trade in the United States by Springer-Verlag New York, Inc., 233 Spring Street, 6th Floor, New York, NY 10013, and outside the United States by Springer-Verlag GmbH & Co. KG, Tiergartenstr. 17, 69112 Heidelberg, Germany.

In the United States: phone 1-800-SPRINGER, fax 201-348-4505, e-mail `orders@springer-ny.com`, or visit `http://www.springer-ny.com`. Outside the United States: fax +49 6221 345229, e-mail `orders@springer.de`, or visit `http://www.springer.de`.

For information on translations, please contact Apress directly at 2560 Ninth Street, Suite 219, Berkeley, CA 94710. Phone 510-549-5930, fax 510-549-5939, e-mail `info@apress.com`, or visit `http://www.apress.com`.



The source code for this book is available to readers at `http://www.apress.com` in the Downloads section.

# Credits

**Author**
Joseph Sack

**Publisher**
Fiona McParland

**Commissioning Editor**
Timothy Briggs

**Technical Editors**
Duncan Black
Justin Crozier
Matthew Moodie

**Indexer**
Bill Johncocks

**Proofreader**
Pauline Briggs

**Cover Design**
Dawn Chellingworth
Natalie O'Donnell
Corey Stewart

**Technical Reviewers**
Chris Barnwell
Glen Berry
Greg Feirer
Terry Hickman
Narayana Vyas Kondreddi
Jeff Mason
Brian Moran
Paul Morris
Craig Mullins
Massimo Nardone
Alexzander Nepomnjashiy
Baya Pavliashvili

**Production Manager**
Zuned Kasu

**Figures**
Rachel Taylor
Pip Wonson

**Production Coordinators**
Rachel Taylor
Pip Wonson

# About the Author

Joseph Sack is a database administrator and consultant based in Minneapolis, Minnesota. Since 1997, he has been developing and supporting SQL Server environments for clients in financial services, IT consulting, and manufacturing. He is a Microsoft Certified Database Administrator (MCDBA). Joe has a BA in Psychology from the University of Minnesota, and so is somewhat qualified to listen to what troubles you. You can visit him at http://www.joesack.com.

## Acknowledgments


Thank you to David Hatch, for your advice, encouragement, and patience in hearing me discuss the book constantly.

Thank you to Barb Sorensen, who gave me my first break at becoming a DBA and developer. Barb sent me to Seattle for SQL Server training six years ago, and gave me plenty of fun SQL Server projects to work on.

Thank you to Earl Fultz and Andrée Abecassis, for your initial advice and suggestions.

Lastly, I am very grateful to the great big team of editors here at Curlingstone. Your excellent suggestions and careful review have really made this book what it is! Thank you to Tim Briggs, Duncan Black, Matthew Moodie, Justin Crozier, Terry Hickman, Baya Pavliashvili, Narayana Vyas Kondreddi, Massimo Nardone, Glenn Berry, Jeff Mason, Chris Barnwell, Craig S Mullins, Brian Moran, Greg Feirer, Paul Morris, and Sasha Nepomnjashiy. Your feedback was critical and much appreciated.

# Table of Contents

# Preface

Over the last five years, I have got into the habit of carrying around what I call "The Green Folder". This folder contains useful Transact-SQL tricks, rare error code definitions, complicated syntax examples, bug reports, and things I just cannot seem to remember without looking them up first.

My fellow SQL Server database administrators and developers soon found out about the folder, and asked me for copies of the contents. Some co-workers complained when I threw away articles that I no longer thought I needed, as they wanted to see if it was something they too should learn or commit to memory.

One day it occurred to me that "The Green Folder" would be much more useful if I migrated it to a reference manual format, organized by topic and question.

As SQL Server professionals we require continuous learning and hands-on experience in order to remain effective in our jobs. We must continually refine our craft by learning new technologies, as well as keeping a firm grasp on core administration and development topics. No one will be impressed if we are experts in using DTS or XML, but cannot remember how to rebuild an index or add a new login.

I have written this book with the following goals in mind:

- To provide succinct answers to SQL Server 2000 database administration *and* development questions –for both new and experienced DBAs.
- To provide intuitive and concise syntax examples.
- To review basic and advanced SQL Server topics, covering the "critical inch" of each subject.

My hope is that this book will be a helpful day-to-day reference, letting you revisit the bits of SQL Server about which you need to jog your memory, and showing you new SQL Server concepts, technologies, and best practices.

Joseph Sack

# Introduction

Welcome to *SQL Server 2000 Fast Answers for DBAs and Developers*.

In this book, we have assumed that you have a basic working knowledge of relational databases; that you know *what* you need to do as a DBA or a developer, but you want to know *how* to do it with SQL Server 2000.

To follow the text of the book, you'll need:

- Sysadmin rights to a PC running Windows, on which you can install SQL Server 2000
- A copy of SQL Server 2000 Personal, Standard, Developer or Enterprise Edition
- A database account with DBA rights

Some chapters need extra, or more specific, hardware (for example, Chapters 9, 10, and 12) or more than one database (for example, Chapters 8 and 11), but the requirements in each chapter are made clear.

The complete source code from the book is available for download at http://www.apress.com.

# Conventions

To help you understand what's going on, and in order to maintain consistency, we've used a number of conventions throughout the book:

> **These boxes hold key information.**

*Reminders and background information are presented like this.*

Syntax definitions are shown like this:

```
CREATE TABLE <database_name.owner.table_name> (
  <column_name_1> <datatype_for_column_1> nullability,
  <column_name_N> <datatype_for_column_N> nullability)
```

Examples are introduced with headings like this:

### Example 14.1.1: Creating a table

and example code is shown like this:

```
In our code examples, the code foreground style shows new, important, and
pertinent code.
Code background shows code that's less important in the present context, or code
that has been seen before.
```

The first time a key word or concept is discussed, or defined, it will be typed in bold, for example, **nullability**.

Words that appear on the screen in menus like the File or Window menu are in a similar font to what you see on screen. URLs are also displayed in this font.

In the book text, we use a fixed-width font when we talk about databases, fields, values, and other objects that may appear in code; for example, the `Customer` table and the `Customer_id` field. The same font is used for files, for example, `query.sql`. Keystrokes are shown like this: *Ctrl-I.*

# Customer Support

We value feedback from our readers, and we want to know what you think about this book: what you liked, what you didn't like, and what you think we can do better next time. You can send us your comments by e-mailing support@apress.com. Please be sure to mention the book's ISBN and title in your message.

## Errata

We have made every effort to make sure that there are no errors in the text or in the code. However, no one is perfect and mistakes do occur. If you find an error in this book, like a spelling mistake or a faulty piece of code, we would be very grateful to hear about it. By sending in errata, you may save another reader hours of frustration, and of course, you will be helping us provide even higher quality information.
To find known errata and submit new errata, simply go to the appropriate book page on the Apress website at http://www.apress.com.

## forums.apress.com

For author and peer discussion, join the Apress discussion groups. If you post a query to our forums, you can be confident that many Apress authors, editors, and industry experts are examining it. At forums.apress.com you will find a number of different lists that will help you, not only while you read this book, but also as you develop your own applications.

To sign up for the Apress forums, go to forums.apress.com and select the New User link.

# 1

# Installation, Upgrades, Service Packs, and Database Migration

This chapter provides an overview of how to install SQL Server 2000, upgrade from earlier versions of SQL Server, install service packs, apply security patches, and move databases between SQL Server implementations.

If you haven't already purchased the hardware, operating system, and SQL Server software, now may be a good time for you to assess your business and application needs.

When planning your SQL Server implementation, you should consider the following:

- Do you understand the strategic implications of your SQL Server implementation? Specifically, which individuals or groups in your organization will be using this database server? How will they be using it? How visible is it to those within your organization, or to your customers? Do you foresee rapid growth? Without understanding these questions, you risk implementing SQL Server in a non-scalable manner (under powered hardware, under staffed support, incorrect editions and licensing).
- Understand the tactical details of your implementation. Make sure you know who the key support employees are. This includes networking support, Windows NT/2000 administrators, application developers, and project managers. Of course, in a small organization, your position may comprise all these roles.
- Understand how SQL Server will be integrated with other applications. For example, will SQL Server be a back-end to your software packages? The core of your transaction-processing environment? The repository for your data warehouse?
- Understand Microsoft licensing options before you make the purchase. See the section *Selecting the Correct Edition and Licensing Option* later in the chapter. Also read Microsoft's licensing FAQ, which includes important information on both licensing and pricing, at http://www.microsoft.com/sql/howtobuy/faq.asp.
- What kind of availability does your SQL Server implementation require? Must the application be available 365 days a year, 24 hours a day? For high-availability solutions, investigate failover clustering (see Chapter 10), replication of data (see Chapter 8), or 'warm' standbys (see Chapter 12).

- What about the recoverability of your data in the event of a disaster? How much data loss can your organization tolerate? Make sure you have a data recovery plan before you move your SQL Server implementation into production. After your plan is formulated, test it thoroughly. See Chapter 6 for more on formulating your recovery strategy.
- Document your SQL Server implementation's requirements. Write down what decisions you have made, and how you came to them. Some day, you may be asked to account for your decisions regarding the hardware, licensing, and operating system.

# Common Installation Problems

It is tempting for SQL Server professionals to move quickly through the installation and configuration process. Without careful planning, however, you could end up having to correct several easily avoided problems in your production environment. Some common problems include:

- Incorrect file placement
- Incorrect server setting

## Incorrect File Placement

- Placing data and log files on an array that is not fault-tolerant (cannot be recovered). RAID (Redundant Arrays of Independent Disks), described later, not only assists with I/O activity, but also provides fault-tolerance. Physical disks can fail, and you should assume that it is a matter of when, rather than if, this will happen. Failures on drives not configured with RAID can render the database irrecoverable (except from backup).
- For small-scale, lower-budget operations, placing data and log files on the same partition. If you do not plan on buying hardware RAID, consider optimizing I/O performance by distributing data across multiple partitions defined on the server. Do this by using files and filegroups to distribute activity across partitions (discussed in Chapter 3).
- Putting data and log files on a partition that will not scale. Let's say you have a 20GB database; your business requires two full database backups held on the server; you estimate your array will be 60GB. You fail to plan for heavy transaction processing and realize that your transaction log backups take up an additional 2GB a day.
- Not using the correct RAID type for the data or log files. Different RAID types include:

| RAID Level | Description |
|---|---|
| RAID level 0 | RAID level 0 is geared towards performance by striping storage blocks in a regular sequence to all of an array's disks. The result is high I/O performance at low cost. RAID 0 has no data redundancy, regeneration, or rebuilding capabilities. |
| RAID level 1 | RAID level 1 is mirroring. Mirrored arrays have two or more disks. Each disk holds an exact image of the opposite disk's user data. RAID 1 can use parallel access to both disks, resulting in excellent read performance. Write operations suffer, as these operations are doubled (one update per mirrored disk – that is, two writes per update). |
| RAID level 5 | RAID level 5 stripes data across multiple disks and also uses parity to allow for data recovery if one disk fails. Space available in a RAID 5 array is equal to total drive space, less one entire drive (for parity). The parity and striping incurs a high I/O cost when write operations are performed. Read operations perform well on this RAID type due to the striping. |

| RAID Level | Description |
|---|---|
| RAID level 10 (1+0, 0+1) | RAID level 10 uses a RAID 0 striped array, and adds mirroring (RAID 1). This combination produces superior I/O performance (due to striping) along with fault-tolerance (mirroring). |

- Placing data and log files, or binaries, on the installation or boot partition (typically the C: drive).

## Incorrect Server Settings

- You set the server to the default collation (see Chapter 2 for an overview of collations). You realize that this collation is different from your remote sites, making data exchange much more complicated.

Before looking at pre-installation best practices, let's examine requirements.

# Hardware and Operating System Requirements for SQL Server 2000

The following are the minimum hardware requirements for running SQL Server 2000. Don't confuse the minimum with the **recommended** configuration:

| | |
|---|---|
| **Processor** | Intel Pentium 166Mhz or compatible minimum |
| **Memory** | Personal Edition on Windows XP, Desktop Engine on Windows XP 128MB<br>Enterprise Edition, Standard Edition, Desktop Engine on Windows 2000, Developer Edition, Personal Edition on Windows 2000 64MB<br>Personal Edition, Desktop Engine on non-Windows 2000 OS 32MB |
| **Disk space** | SQL Server database components:<br>95 to 270MB, 250MB for typical installation<br>Desktop Engine only:<br>44MB<br>Analysis Services:<br>130MB typical install, 50MB minimum<br>English Query:<br>80MB |
| **Accessories** | A VGA or higher resolution monitor with 800x600 or better if you want to use SQL Server graphical tools (and you do!)<br>A mouse<br>A CD-ROM drive |

Operating system requirements are less flexible and, thus, less complicated. Although Windows NT Server 4.0 is allowed, it is advisable to use Windows 2000 Server edition at the very least. Microsoft improved the Plug and Play support, reduced OS functions that require reboots, improved application performance, and included DBA-friendly utilities, such as Terminal Services and Windows Scripting Host. Also remember that if you plan on installing SQL Server Enterprise Edition, some features that it offers are only available in Windows 2000 Advanced Server and Data Center Server:

| SQL Server Editions | Supported on the Following Operating Systems |
|---|---|
| SQL Server Standard Edition<br>SQL Server Enterprise Edition | Windows NT Server 4.0 with Service Pack 5<br>Microsoft Windows NT Server Enterprise Edition<br>Windows 2000 Server<br>Windows 2000 Advanced Server<br>Windows 2000 Data Center Server |
| SQL Server 2000 Trial Software<br>SQL Server Developer Edition | Windows NT Server 4.0 with Service Pack 5<br>Microsoft Windows NT Server Enterprise Edition<br>Windows 2000 Server<br>Windows 2000 Advanced Server<br>Windows 2000 Data Center Server<br>Windows XP Professional<br>Windows XP Home Edition<br>Windows 2000 Professional<br>Windows NT Workstation 4.0 with Service Pack 5 or later |
| Personal Edition<br>Desktop Engine<br>Client Tools Only<br>Connectivity Only | Microsoft Windows ME<br>Windows 98 (with a network card)<br>Windows 98 Second Edition<br>Windows NT Workstation 4.0 with Service Pack 5 or later<br>Windows NT Server 4.0 with Service Pack 5 or later<br>Microsoft Windows NT Server Enterprise Edition<br>Windows 2000 Professional<br>Windows XP Professional<br>Windows XP Home Edition<br>Windows 2000 Server<br>Windows 2000 Advanced Server<br>Windows 2000 Data Center Server |

Other requirements worth noting are:

- Microsoft Internet Explorer 5.0 (minimal install) unless installing as connectivity-only, in which case Microsoft Internet Explorer 4.01 with Service Pack 2.

- Network software is required if using Banyan Vines or AppleTalk ADSP.
- Clients supported are Windows NT Workstation, Windows 2000 Professional, Windows XP Professional, Windows XP Home Edition, Windows 95, and Windows 98. Apple Macintosh, OS/2, and Unix are supported but have no graphical tools and require that you install third-party ODBC client connectivity software.

# Pre-Installation Best Practices

The following recommendations should be considered before installing SQL Server 2000.

## Hardware Configuration Recommendations

As stated earlier, prior to purchasing the server or servers, you should have an idea of what your database server needs are. Software applications that need SQL Server back-end support usually document their hardware sizing requirements. If the database schema or hardware requirements have not yet been defined, however, you must make estimates. When estimating needs, ask these questions:

- How much database storage is needed? How much storage will be needed a year (or two years) from now?
- How many backups will you plan on keeping on the server? Estimate that your full backups will be of similar size to your database data (note that the size is estimated by the actual data storage, not the file allocation size). Estimate the transaction log sizing according to the amount of activity you expect your transaction log to contain. So, if your transaction log contains 100MB of completed transactions, expect a similar size for the transaction log backup. The same goes for differential backups, except that the size is determined by the number of changes to data since the last full database backup. For more information on backups, see Chapter 6.
- Are these reporting or transaction processing databases, OLTP or OLAP? OLTP stands for Online Transaction Processing, and is commonly used to describe a database environment used for transaction processing (for example, a database used to place orders for a product). OLAP stands for Online Analytical Processing, which is used to describe database environments and applications used for analyzing stored data in a database. If you expect heavy transaction processing activity (OLTP), make sure to factor in transaction log growth and transaction log backups. For OLAP environments, the database may have more indexes (used to facilitate reporting), but will require smaller transaction logs, as very little transaction logging will be performed.
- How many users will be connecting? 100? 1000? User connections take up memory and CPU cycles.
- Will this be a dedicated SQL Server box or will other applications be installed on this server? It is highly recommended that you implement dedicated SQL Server boxes.

Knowing the answers to these questions will help you determine how much money needs to be invested in CPU, physical disks and controllers, memory, tape backups, off-site storage facilities, and your network card(s).

## CPU Recommendations

- SQL Server 2000 uses multiple CPUs. Standard and Enterprise Editions can take advantage of parallelism when generating query plans. Enterprise Edition can run parallel `DBCC` and `CREATE INDEX` operations. Each user connection consumes a thread (unit of work), which takes up CPU and memory resources.
- Standard Edition supports 4 processors on Microsoft Windows 2000 Data Center, Windows 2000 Advanced Server, Windows 2000 Server, and Windows NT 4.0 Server. On Windows NT 4.0 Server Enterprise Edition, 8 processors are supported.

- Enterprise Edition supports 32 processors on Microsoft Windows 2000 Data Center, 8 processors on Windows 2000 Advanced Server and Microsoft Windows NT 4.0 Server Enterprise Edition, and 4 processors on Windows 2000 Server and Windows NT 4.0 Server.
- The higher the L2 (Level 2) cache the better. L2 cache memory is memory external to the processor chip; it lowers wait time during CPU reads from and writes to memory.
- Choose the fastest processor(s) available. If you do not have the funds for a multi-processor system, buy a system that allows future processor additions.

## Memory (RAM) Recommendations

- SQL Server loves memory. If your application database is memory-intensive, invest in RAM. Each **lock** in SQL Server takes up 64 bytes plus 32 bytes per owner. Locks are used within SQL Server to restrict access to a resource in a multiuser (or multiconnection) database. (For more information on locks and locking, see Chapter 5).
- Open databases also consume memory, taking up 3924 bytes, plus 1640 bytes per file, and 336 bytes per filegroup. An open database **object** takes up 256 bytes plus 1724 bytes per index opened on the object. Each user connection takes up 12KB plus three times the network packet size (the default network packet size is 4KB).
- Enterprise Edition supports 64GB of memory on Windows 2000 Data Center, 8GB on Windows 2000 Advanced Server, 4GB on Windows 2000 Server, 3GB on Windows NT 4.0 Server Enterprise Edition, and 2GB on Windows NT 4.0 Server.
- Standard Edition supports 2GB on Windows 2000 Data Center, Windows 2000 Advanced Server, Windows 2000 Server, Windows NT 4.0 Server Enterprise Edition, and Windows NT 4.0 Server.

## Physical Disk and Disk Array Recommendations

- Plan your database file placement strategy before purchasing your system. Determine what you can afford, and prioritize in the following order: memory, CPU, physical disks.
- Get the fastest disk drives you can afford (look at RPM – Rotations Per Minute).
- Get the best I/O controller you can afford.
- Use hardware-based RAID only. Avoid software-based RAID. If you cannot afford RAID technologies, try to purchase multiple small or mid-size drives, rather than a few large drives. You can then stripe your database files across multiple drives, distributing I/O over multiple partitions.
- Avoid using RAID 0, as it is not fault-tolerant.

### File Placement Strategy

The following tables describe file placement strategies. The first table describes a Tier 1, or best-case, configuration, which also happens to be the most expensive (no surprise). The second table describes a Tier 2 file placement strategy; this will most likely cover the average database server implementation (and budget). Although the cost is greater, RAID is strongly recommended, because disk drives fail, and RAID solutions can help keep your database up and running. A single disk drive partition means a single point of failure.

*Tier 1 File Placement Strategy*

| File Type | RAID Type |
|---|---|
| Binary SQL Server files | RAID 1 – mirroring provides fault tolerance for your executable files. |
| `tempdb` system database | RAID 10 – on its own array, as SQL Server uses `tempdb` as a work area for serving specific types of user requests (queries). |
| Database data files (`*.mdf` and `*.ndf`) files | RAID 10 – databases with heavy write activity will benefit most. |
| Transaction log files (`*.ldf`) | RAID 10 – if possible, choose one array per transaction log. These files are written to sequentially and ideally should not be mixed on the same array as other transaction logs or database files (forcing non-sequential activity). |
| Backups (full, transaction log, differential) | RAID 1 – good fault tolerance for your backup files. |

*Tier 2 File Placement Strategy*

| File Type | RAID Type |
|---|---|
| Binary SQL Server files | RAID 1 – mirroring provides fault tolerance for your executable files. |
| `tempdb` system database | RAID 1 – write performance is better than RAID 5. `tempdb` should be on its own array. |
| Database data files (`*.mdf` and `*.ndf`) files | RAID 5 – good for reads and fault tolerance, not so good for heavy transaction processing environments (every update generates two reads and two writes for parity). |
| Transaction log files (`*.ldf`) | RAID 1 – mirroring provides fault tolerance for your executable files. Should be one transaction log file per array (but this is cost-prohibitive if you have many databases). |
| Backups (full, transaction log, differential) | RAID 1 – mirroring provides fault tolerance for your executable files. |

You should measure the recommendations for disk arrays against your actual needs. If you have just two or three small databases, placing both your data and log files on a RAID 5 array may suit you just fine. The previous recommendations are based on database servers that need to run at top performance with heavy activity.

# Backup Storage Recommendations

Plan on purchasing enough disk space for at least one day's worth of database backups (or more depending on your requirements). However, do not depend solely on performing backups to the local server. Backups should be archived to tape (via a tape drive), over the network to an off-site server, or burned to CD (a slow option, but an option nonetheless). Off-site data storage is critical to recovery in the event of a disaster at your site. You can purchase archiving and media storage services, where tape backups will be taken periodically off-site. If you cannot afford such solutions, at the very least purchase a fireproof safe to store your removable backup media (tapes and CDs).

# Network Card Recommendations

- ❑ Choose a 100Mb network card for local disk arrays.
- ❑ Two cards are better than one. Dual connections provide higher availability and performance.
- ❑ Fiber Channel network cards are required for Storage Area Network (SAN) connectivity.

## SAN and NAS Systems

Storage Area Network (SAN) and Network Attached Storage (NAS) technology is being adopted rapidly in the IT database world. SANs allow data transfer from your server to an external data storage array. The Fiber Channel network card is the key to this high-speed transfer. SAN technology is supported by SQL Server Enterprise and Developer editions. The advantage of SANs is their ability to scale storage for large databases. Caching controllers of some SAN products introduce sophisticated caching algorithms, improving I/O performance over regular local RAID arrays. SANs, in conjunction with purchased software packages, can improve availability of the databases on the server with high-speed snapshot backup and restore operations.

Network Attached Storage (NAS) allows a server to attach to a storage area via a regular network card. In general, NAS performance is not as good as SAN performance and, as a result, Microsoft does not recommend using NAS for databases.

# Selecting the Correct Edition and Licensing Option

It is common for administrators to buy editions of SQL Server that under-utilize the purchased server hardware. Expectations are often dashed when functionality is not included with the purchased edition. The following table reviews the features supported by each edition (note that support for SQL Server CE, used for data storage on Windows CE devices, is not discussed here, and is beyond the scope of this book):

| Feature | Description | Supported Editions |
|---|---|---|
| Failover clustering (up to four nodes) | Failover clustering provides high availability for your SQL Server instances. See Chapter 10 for more details. | Enterprise Edition<br>Developer Edition<br>Enterprise Evaluation Edition |
| Log shipping | Log shipping is the process of copying and loading transaction log backups to a 'warm' standby server. See Chapter 12 for more details. | Enterprise Edition<br>Developer Edition<br>Enterprise Evaluation Edition |
| Parallel `DBCC` and parallel `CREATE INDEX` | `DBCC` (database consistency checker) and `CREATE INDEX` commands can now take advantage of multiple CPUs on the SQL Server instance, thus increasing the efficiency of the operation. For information on DBCC commands, see Chapter 6. For more information on index creation, see Chapter 14. | Enterprise Edition<br>Developer Edition<br>Enterprise Evaluation Edition |
| Enhanced read-ahead and scan | Dynamically adjust the amount of memory allocated for read-ahead and scan activities (both operations grab data blocks for use in read operations). | Enterprise Edition<br>Developer Edition<br>Enterprise Evaluation Edition |

| Feature | Description | Supported Editions |
| --- | --- | --- |
| Indexed views | Indexed views are views that have a clustered index (see Chapter 14 for a description of indexes) and, potentially, multiple non-clustered indexes. Indexed views are **persistent**; the view data is physically stored and updated in the database. This translates to potentially faster query performance. | Enterprise Edition<br>Developer Edition<br>Enterprise Evaluation Edition |
| Federated database server | Federated database server refers to a union of views, defined across a set of SQL Server instances. The data is partitioned across tables spread over multiple servers, and joined in a view (essentially looking like one table). These are also called **distributed partitioned views**. This scaling-out of data can result in performance improvements. See Chapter 14 for more information. | Enterprise Edition<br>Developer Edition<br>Enterprise Evaluation Edition |
| System Area Network (SAN) support | SANs allow data transfer from your server to an external data storage array. | Enterprise Edition<br>Developer Edition<br>Enterprise Evaluation Edition |
| Graphical DBA and developer utilities, wizards | The graphical (non-command line) tools include Enterprise Manager, Query Analyzer, SQL Profiler, Server Manager, Client Network Utility, Server Network Utility, Books Online, and DTS Wizard and Designer. | All editions except Desktop Engine |
| Full-text search | Full-text search is a service that allows high-performance querying of text columns within a table. For more information on full-text search, see Chapter 13. | Enterprise Edition<br>Standard Edition<br>Personal Edition (but not on Windows 98)<br>Developer Edition<br>Enterprise Evaluation Edition |
| Transactional replication | Replication allows the distribution of data to other databases on the same server, or remote SQL Server instances. Transactional replication is one of three types of replication reviewed in detail in Chapter 8. | All editions; however, Personal Edition and Desktop Engine support the subscriber mode only (no transactional publications allowed). |

For Analysis Services features supported by the editions of SQL Server 2000, see Microsoft's web site, http://msdn.microsoft.com/library/default.asp?url=/library/en-us/architec/8_ar_ts_1cdv.asp.

You have two licensing choices – per processor or per seat. Per processor allows you to install one instance of SQL Server; an **instance** is a copy of SQL Server to be run on your server. You must purchase a per processor license for each processor on the server that you intend SQL Server to use (four CPUs = four per processor licenses). For SQL Server Enterprise Edition, you are allowed to install multiple instances (covered under the per processor licenses you purchase). No other licenses are needed for SQL Server under this licensing type. This licensing is required if you have anonymous users connecting to your server (Internet users).

Per seat requires a Client Access License (CAL) for each device accessing your SQL Server 2000 instance.

The following table helps clarify this murky subject:

| Use Per Seat if... | Use Per Processor if... |
|---|---|
| You and your users are inside the firewall | You have Internet or anonymous users |
| You have a small number of users | The cost of CALs is more expensive than the cost of per processor (many users) |

In either case, price out the cost of CALs against per processor, as costs sometimes are negotiated and can vary.

## Pre-Installation Checklist

Before beginning the installation process, make sure the following items are completed or prepared:

- ❑ Your operating system has the latest service packs and security patches installed.
- ❑ Your disk arrays are partitioned and ready to use.
- ❑ Your network card is up and running and able to connect to a domain controller.
- ❑ Your ODBC drivers and OLE providers for running heterogeneous DBMS queries or data extractions (Sybase, Teradata, DB2, Oracle) are installed. These drivers usually require a reboot, so finish this now to minimize downtime once SQL Server is installed. Also, make sure such driver product functions do not interact badly with SQL Server (test in your development/test environment).
- ❑ If you plan on having SQL Server communicate with other machines on the network, you will need a domain account for your SQL Server service account. Have this account ready and make sure it has administrative privileges on the server.
- ❑ Make sure your server meets the hardware and operating system requirements mentioned above.
- ❑ Decide your server default collation beforehand. See Chapter 2 for more information.
- ❑ Decide your file placement plan now.
- ❑ When you log on to the server for installation purposes, use an account with local administrative permissions.
- ❑ Shut down all services and applications that use ODBC drivers or file resources, as they may cause the installation to fail. Also, shut down Windows 2000 Event Viewer and registry viewers.
- ❑ Decide ahead of time if you will be using mixed or Windows authentication security mode. Windows authentication mode allows NT users and groups only, and is much more secure. Mixed allows NT users and groups as well as SQL logins.

# 1.1 How to... Install SQL Server 2000

- Log on to the server with an account with local administrative permissions.
- Insert your SQL Server 2000 CD, or map a drive on the operating system to a CD shared on the network. If making your CD drive a share, make sure you grant appropriate permissions to your domain login (read access). You can also copy the contents of your installation CD to a network drive, map a drive to the network path containing the files, and begin setup from this drive.
- If the main splash screen doesn't automatically start up in a few seconds, double-click `autorun.exe` in the root directory of the CD. Make sure the splash screen shows the edition you intend to install; for example Standard, Enterprise, or Developer.
- Select SQL Server 2000 Components.
- Select Install Database Server.
- Select Next at the Welcome screen.
- Select Next for a local computer installation. We'll deal with remote installations later in this chapter and virtual servers in Chapter 10.
- Select Create a new instance of SQL Server, or install Client Tools. With SQL Server 2000, you can install multiple instances of SQL Server on the same server. For more information, see *SQL Server Instances* later in the chapter. Select the Next button.
- Enter the administrator and company names. Select Next.
- Read the Software License Agreement. If you agree, select Next.
- Enter the CD-Key. Select Next.
- Select Server and Client Tools. Select Next.
- The Instance Name dialog box selects either the **default instance** or a **named instance** for installation. A default instance is a copy of SQL Server that adopts the same name as the server name. For example, if your server name is `ServerA`, the default instance will also be named `ServerA`. The default instance is the only instance that can use the default TCP/IP port 1433 (more on this later on in the chapter). A named instance is a copy of SQL Server that adopts a different name from the default and other named instances. This name is formed from the computer name and instance name (the instance name being designated at installation time). Named instances are described in more detail further on in the chapter.

  The checkbox will not be available if you have already installed a default instance. Leave Default selected if installing a default instance. Un-check and type in an instance name if installing a new named instance. SQL Server can support multiple named instances on one server, but whether or not you should take advantage of this feature is addressed further on in the chapter.
- Select the setup type – Typical, Minimum, or Custom. In this example, we are using Custom, which allows us to select settings for collation, network libraries, and subcomponents. Change your Program Files setting to point to a partition other than the C: drive; ideally, this should be a RAID 1 partition (mirrored set). You should also change your Data Files location to your planned partition, which designates where your system databases will be located. Please note that you can change the location of your `tempdb` database after installation. Select Next when finished.
- Select the components you wish to install. If you have no space restrictions, include them all; but install Books Online no matter what. This is an extremely valuable resource, which you will find useful more often than you may expect. Select Next.

- Configure services for SQL Server. Either designate the same accounts for SQL Server service and SQL Agent service, or select Customize to configure them differently. Remember that if you want SQL Server to communicate with other servers on the network, these service accounts should be configured with a domain user account. Also remember that you can change the service account for the SQL Server Service and SQL Agent Service after installation (if you do not have domain connectivity at the time, or the account isn't created yet). Select Next when finished.
- Next select the **authentication** mode. The mode you select determines how your users connect to your new SQL Server installation.

  When Windows Authentication Mode is selected, only Windows NT groups and users may access the SQL Server instance. This mode implies a high level of security, as SQL Server access also presumes Windows NT local machine or domain authority.

  Mixed Mode, however, allows both Windows authentication and SQL Server authentication. SQL Server authentication requires a user to specify a login defined for the SQL Server instance, along with a password (always define passwords!). Unlike Windows authentication mode, a SQL Server login can be stolen, shared, or used by multiple users (thus you do not know who is actually accessing the data). Nonetheless, many applications still use mixed mode. If using mixed mode, select a password for the sysadmin (`sa`) account.
- In Collation Settings, select your collation within either the Collation designator, or the SQL Collations section. SQL Collations use compatible names from previous SQL Server versions. The Collation designator uses a drop-down box to select Windows Locale. This should not be changed unless your installation is required to match the collation settings of another SQL Server 2000 implementation (one with a different Windows locale). When using Collation designator, you can also designate the sorting style, which is determined by the checkboxes described next:

  a. **Binary**
  When selected, sorts and comparisons of data in the database are based on bit patterns defined for each character. This is the fastest sort order, but requires that the case-sensitive and accent-sensitive be used.

  b. **Case-sensitive**
  This option specifies that SQL Server will distinguish between uppercase and lowercase characters, having lowercase characters precede uppercase. This option requires meticulous Transact-SQL coding, as any stored procedures or object references must always use the correct case.

  c. **Accent-sensitive**
  Forces SQL Server to distinguish between accented and unaccented characters.

  d. **Kana-sensitive**
  When enabled, SQL Server will distinguish two types of Japanese kana characters, hiragana and katakana.

  e. **Width-sensitive**
  When enabled, SQL Server differentiates between a single-byte character, and the same character stored as a double-byte character.

  For in-depth coverage of collations, see Chapter 2. Do not make your decision lightly if you perform frequent server-to-server migrations, exchange data with international applications, or recover to other servers. This setting determines the sort order for Unicode datatypes, sort order for non-Unicode datatypes, and the code page used to store non-Unicode data. Select Next when finished.

- Select which Network Libraries are to be installed with your SQL Server instance. Network libraries are used to communicate with SQL Server, necessitating that the libraries exist on both SQL Server and the client. The TCP/IP and Named Pipes protocols are both included by default. The TCP/IP default port setting for SQL Server is 1433. Do not change this default port value. You will see the value 0 when installing a named instance of SQL Server; this means that the port will be dynamically chosen during the installation. This will be discussed further in *How to...* 1.10.

  The Named Pipes protocol should be kept in your installation, unless you have a good reason for removing it. The Named Pipes and TCP/IP protocols have roughly equivalent performance over fast LAN networks; however, Named Pipes under-performs over slower networks (WANS) in comparison to TCP/IP.

  Add additional protocols only as needed (NWLink, AppleTalk, Banyan Vines, Multi-Protocol). Note that the Multi-Protocol doesn't support connections to a named SQL Server instance.
- In the Start Copying Files screen, select Next.
- Select your Licensing Mode. For per seat, enter the number of device client access licenses you purchased for this instance. Press the Continue button. For Per Processor, select the number of processor licenses you have purchased.
- Once the installation is complete, press Finish at the final screen. It is recommended you reboot after completion, although you may not be prompted to do so.

Later on in this chapter we will discuss troubleshooting a failed installation.

# 1.2 How to... Install Analysis Services

Microsoft SQL Server 2000 Analysis Services allows you to create OLAP (Online Analytical Processing) cubes, and perform data mining and queries against them. The hardware and software required for installation of Analysis Services is as follows:

- Intel compatible, Pentium 133 MHz or higher, Pentium PRO, Pentium II or III.
- 32MB minimum of RAM – but with Analysis Services you want as much memory as possible.
- 50-90 MB hard disk space minimum, 130MB for all components, 12MB disk space for the client only.
- Windows 2000 Server (not to be installed on a domain controller), or Windows NT Server 4.0 with SP5 or later. Client components may be installed on Windows 2000 Professional, Windows NT Workstation 4.0 with SP5, Windows 98, Windows 95 DCOM95, and Windows 95 OSR2 +DCOM95.
- Clients must have the TCP/IP network protocol.
- Microsoft Internet Explorer version 5.0 or later is required to view product documentation. For Windows NT 4.0, make sure that NT 4.0 SP5 (Service Pack 5) is installed prior to installing Internet Explorer 5.0.

To install Analysis Services follow these steps:

- Log on to the server with an account with local administrative permissions.
- Insert your SQL Server 2000 CD or map a drive on the operating system to a CD shared on the network.
- If the main splash screen doesn't automatically start up in a few seconds, double-click `autorun.exe` in the root directory of the CD.
- Select SQL Server 2000 Components.
- Select Install Analysis Services.

- Select Next.
- Read the license agreement and, if you agree, select Yes.
- Select the components you wish to install. Change the C: directory to your selected binary directory. Select Next. (As with SQL Server installation, choose a different partition from your Windows OS partition; do not put all your eggs in one basket.). Placing the executables on a mirrored RAID 1 array is recommended.
- Select Program folder name default or change it to your preference. Some administrators prefer smaller folder names, particularly if they script the directory paths.
- The installation process begins, starting with an installation of Microsoft Data Access Components (MDAC). The installer then begins installing the binaries.
- When the process is complete, press the Finish button.
- If you are prompted to reboot your server, do so.

# 1.3 How to... Install English Query

English Query allows you to pose questions in English instead of Transact-SQL to return result sets from relational databases or OLAP cubes.

Installation requirements are as follows:

- Windows 95, 98, NT 4.0 (SP6 or later), or Windows 2000
- 40MB of disk space
- Internet Explorer version 5.0 or later

Because English Query is installed within Microsoft Visual Studio version 6.0, this product is not considered to be eligible for the Windows 2000 logo. This means that this product does not meet the feature and quality goals defined by Microsoft as criteria for such certification. It is hoped that a future version will be compliant with the next release of SQL Server.

Prior to installing English Query, make sure to check out the *Installation Requirements and Considerations* topic in *SQL Server Books Online*.

To install a standard installation of English Query:

- Log on to the server with an account with local administrative permissions.
- Insert your SQL Server 2000 CD or map a drive on the operating system to a CD shared on the network.
- If the main splash screen doesn't automatically start up in a few seconds, double-click `autorun.exe` in the root directory of the CD.
- Select SQL Server 2000 Components.
- Select Install English Query. A prompt will show that Microsoft Data Access Components are being installed.
- Select Continue.
- Read the license agreement, and, if satisfied, select I Agree.
- Select either Complete or Run-time Only components. Run-time only components install just the necessary run-time DLLs (dynamic link libraries), which contain the programmatic components and capabilities of the English Query application.

- Select Change folder if you wish to change the default file location.
- File installation and configuration begins.
- Once complete, select OK.

# 1.4 How to... Perform an Unattended Installation

Unattended installations allow you to perform a SQL Server installation with all install screen options automatically selected. This can reduce user error when performing multiple installations or when walking an inexperienced administrator through the install process. For large companies, this process is very helpful for installing just the client tools or connectivity only.

You cannot use this process to perform a failover clustering or modification of installed optional components. The first step in allowing an unattended installation to take place is to record a simulated setup. Recording an unattended setup generates a `setup.iss` file. The process is as follows:

- Insert your SQL Server 2000 CD or map a drive on the operating system to a CD shared on the network.
- If the main splash screen doesn't automatically start up in a few seconds, double-click `autorun.exe` in the root directory of the CD. Make sure the splash screen shows the Edition you intend to install, for example Standard, Enterprise, or Developer.
- Select SQL Server 2000 Components.
- Select Install Database Server.
- Select Next at the Welcome screen.
- Select Next for a local computer installation.
- Select Advanced options, then Next.
- Select Record Unattended .ISS file. Select Next.
- Go through each of the regular setting screens as you would during a regular SQL Server installation.
- Once you have finished, look under your %windir% (Windows system directory) location for the `setup.iss` file. This file can then be used to perform an unattended installation.

You can now run an unattended installation from the command prompt on the server on which you wish to install SQL Server. Copy the `setup.iss` to the server prior to performing these steps.

In the root of the SQL Server installation CD directory you will find sample `.bat` files, which are used to begin the installation. You can copy these and use them for your own installations. You can also run the same commands via a command prompt, but it is recommended that you use a `.bat` file if you plan multiple unattended installations (save yourself some time).

Both the `.bat` file and command prompt methods run the `setupsql.exe` executable, which is located in the `\x86\setup` directory from your installation CD. `setupsql.exe` takes the following parameters:

- **-s**
  Directs the setup to occur in 'silent' mode, with no user interface.
- **-f1**
  Designates the location of the `setup.iss` file.

- **-SMS**
  Returns control at the command line back after the setup has completed. This is used with the start/wait commands within a `.bat` file.

The example files included in the root directory of the installation CD are:

- **sqlins.bat**
  Standard unattended installation
- **sqlins.iss**
  Standard unattended installation settings file
- **sqlcli.bat**
  Client-only unattended installation
- **sqlcli.iss**
  Client-only unattended installation settings file
- **sqlcst.bat**
  Custom unattended installation
- **sqlcst.iss**
  Custom unattended installation settings file

The following displays the `sqlins.iss` file; key values commonly changed are highlighted in bold. Make sure, however, to check out the *SQL Server Books Online* document, *Creating a Setup File Manually*, for a review of the meaning of each key in the `iss` file:

```
[InstallShield Silent]
Version=v5.00.000
File=Response File

...

[SdRegisterUser-0]
szName=MSEmployee
Result=1

...

[DlgInstanceName-0]
InstanceName=MSSQLSERVER
Result=1

...

[SetupTypeSQL-0]
szDir=%PROGRAMFILES%\Microsoft SQL Server
Result=301
szDataDir=%PROGRAMFILES%\Microsoft SQL Server

...

[DlgCollation-0]
collation_name=' '
Result=1

...
```

The following table reviews iss keys that are commonly configured:

| Section | Key | Description |
|---|---|---|
| [SdRegisterUser-0] | szName | Name of the user performing the install |
| [CDKEYDialog-0] | svCDKey | CD Key |
| [DlgInstanceName-0] | InstanceName | MSSQLSERVER when the default instance; otherwise, a unique name for a named instance |
| [SetupTypeSQL-0] | szDir | Directory where SQL Server program files are installed |
| [SetupTypeSQL-0] | szDataDir | Directory where data files are installed |
| [DlgSQLSecurity-0] | LoginMode | The type of security mode: 1 for Windows authentication and 2 for SQL authentication (mixed) |
| [DlgSQLSecurity-0] | szPwd | sa password, when mixed mode is chosen |
| [DlgCollation-0] | collation_name | Name of collation (if blank, the system default is used) |

To perform an unattended installation using the setup.iss file and command prompt (no .bat file), perform these steps:

- Go to Start | Run and type cmd
- Select OK
- Go to the x86\setup directory, where setupsql.exe is, for example, D:\>cd x86\setup
- For an unattended installation with no user interface, type in the following (assuming your CD is on the D: drive and setup.iss in the C:\winnt directory):

```
D:\x86\setup>setupsql.exe -f1 "c:\winnt\setup.iss" -s
```

# 1.5 How to... Perform a Remote Installation

With remote installation, you can install SQL Server on a remote server from your local workstation or server. To do this, you must use an account that has administrative permissions for the remote server. The remote server must meet the same hardware and operating system requirements as a regular installation of SQL Server 2000.

The installation is the same as a regular install, with the following exceptions:

- In the Computer Name screen, select Remote Computer and type in the server name.
- In the Remote Installation Setup screen, enter the user account that is to be used to install SQL Server, the target path to where the program files should be installed, and the source setup file locations (using UNC naming conventions).

# 1.6 How to... Install Only the Client Utilities

Often you will want to install just the client utilities to make SQL Server utilities available for developers or DBAs. This includes tools such as Enterprise Manager, Query Analyzer, Profiler, Books Online, and the Client Network Utility. To install only the client utilities:

- ❑ Follow steps 1 through 12 of the regular SQL Server installation process (*How to...* 1.1)
- ❑ On reaching the Installation Definition screen, select Client Tools Only, then Next
- ❑ Select the client components you want and uncheck those that you don't, then select Next to begin the installation

# 1.7 How to... Install Only Client Connectivity

Client connectivity components include Microsoft Data Access Components (MDAC), DB-Library, ODBC, and OLE DB. If you require only connectivity capabilities:

- ❑ Follow steps 1 through 12 of the regular SQL Server installation process (*How to...* 1.1)
- ❑ At the Installation Definition screen, select Connectivity Only
- ❑ Select Next again in the Start Copying Files dialog box

# 1.8 How to... Uninstall SQL Server

You can uninstall SQL Server in three different ways; the first two are the easier methods.

## Method 1: Control Panel

- ❑ First make sure that the SQL Server service is not running. Do this by going to Start | Programs | Microsoft SQL Server | Service Manager. If the service is running (green arrow), select the Stop button (red square) to stop the SQL Server service. You should also close any registry edit tools or NT event viewer tools that are currently open on your desktop. If you have other applications that you know are dependent on SQL Server, close these as well.
- ❑ Select Start | Settings | Control Panel.
- ❑ Select Add/Remove Programs.
- ❑ Click the instance of SQL Server 2000 you wish to uninstall, and click the Remove button.

## Method 2: Installation CD

- ❑ First make sure that the SQL Server service, registry edit tools, NT event viewer, and any other open applications that use SQL Server components are not running.
- ❑ Log in to the server with an account with local administrative permissions.
- ❑ Insert your SQL Server 2000 CD or map a drive on the operating system to a CD shared on the network.
- ❑ If the main splash screen doesn't automatically start up in a few seconds, double-click `autorun.exe` in the root directory of the CD. Make sure the splash screen shows the edition you intend to install, for example Standard, Enterprise, or Developer.
- ❑ Select SQL Server 2000 Components.
- ❑ Select Install Database Server.
- ❑ Select Next at the Welcome screen.
- ❑ Select Upgrade, remove, or add components to an existing instance of SQL Server. Select Next.
- ❑ Select the instance of SQL Server or default you wish to remove.
- ❑ Select Uninstall your existing installation. Select Next.

- In the Uninstalling dialog box, select Next.
- In the Setup Complete dialog box, select Finish.

## Method 3: Manual Uninstall

Sometimes, SQL Server will not uninstall properly. The causes vary, but some reasons are:

- Original files are missing or corrupted.
- A previous installation was interrupted.
- Older components were added to the server in error.
- The full details and latest documents on performing a manual uninstall can be found on Microsoft's web site, http://www.msdn.microsoft.com/default.asp. Check this site for support articles, also called Knowledge Base articles. The article specific to manual uninstalls, Knowledge Base article Q290991, is titled *HOW TO: Manually Remove SQL Server 2000 Default, Named or Virtual Instance*.

It is strongly suggested that you follow Microsoft's version of the procedure, as registry edits are involved and can lead to major problems if you do not modify or remove the correct registry keys. Do not use methods listed on message boards or non-Microsoft sites.

# 1.9 How to... Troubleshoot a Failed Installation

You can install SQL Server 300 times and not encounter a single failed installation. SQL Server 2000's installation process is significantly more robust (including failover clustering installation) than previous versions. Nonetheless, problems do occur. Here are the basic areas to check when you begin troubleshooting a failed installation:

- Write down any errors you see. Get the exact wording. You can troubleshoot most problems quickly if you have this information. Typing this into the search engine on http://support.microsoft.com/ usually turns up a Knowledge Base article. If you cannot find a match there, try non-Microsoft search engines, such as http://www.google.com/. Microsoft SQL Server newsgroups (microsoft.public.sqlserver.setup) sometimes turn up valuable information too. A complete newsgroup archive is available for search at http://groups.google.com/.
- For detailed errors that occur during installation, view the `sqlstp.log` and `setup.log` files located in the `\WinNT` directory. Also check out the `Errorlog` file located under your `<install path>\Log` directory or, for a named instance, `<install path>\log` directory.
- Verify that your hardware and operating system supports SQL Server 2000.
- Do you have any applications installed on the server that use connectivity components? If so, you should cross-reference your application with any problems regarding installation failure. Better yet, make your server a dedicated database server. Introducing application programming complexities and interrelationships on your server can cause major headaches for the SQL Server professional. Keeping SQL Server on its own server can improve performance, not to mention the security benefits of keeping access limited to the database server.

# SQL Server Instances: Overview and Best Practice

Microsoft introduced multiple instance functionality in SQL Server 2000. Essentially, you are able to install multiple copies (instances) of SQL Server on one machine. Each **named instance** operates as an entity, with its own potential collation, server settings, database, `sa` password, and so on. You can have up to 16 SQL Server instances on one machine.

Only one instance is the **default instance**, meaning its behavior and name is the same as previous versions of SQL Server. For example, if the server were named `FIREWORKS`, then the default instance name would also be `FIREWORKS`.

Named instances, on the other hand, require a second name. So if you created a named instance with the name `SQL2` on the `FIREWORKS` server, the full name would be `FIREWORKS\SQL2`. Instance names are limited to 32 Unicode characters. This is the name to which you would connect via Enterprise Manager, OSQL, Query Analyzer, SQL Profiler, or any other SQL Server 2000 connectivity tools.

Since you may only have one instance per server port, the default port 1433 is no longer available and a new port is determined upon instance installation. To verify the port used for your SQL Server instance, follow these steps:

- During installation of a named instance, you'll notice the port is set to 0, which allows it to find an unused port dynamically.
- After installation, you can find out which port was taken for use by the instance, via the Server Network Utility (see this chapter's section *Determine the Port Number for a Named Instance*).

Instances also have different directory structures and different service names from the default instance. Based on the `FIREWORKS\SQL2` example above, your SQL Server service name would be configured as `MSSQL$SQL2` and the SQL Server Agent service configured as `SQLAGENT$SQL2`. Registry keys also have named instance key names. Named instance file directories have their own executables, data, log, and backup directories. For example:

```
f:\Program Files\Microsoft SQL Server\MSSQL$SQL2
```

# SQL Server 2000 Performance Considerations when Using Named Instances

- Set maximum memory limits for each SQL Server instance running on your server, otherwise the instances will compete for memory as user activity increases. If you have the Address Windowing Extensions (AWE) enabled option set, you must set a maximum as this option uses fixed memory (non-paged memory that cannot be swapped out).
- Each named instance has its own overhead, consuming not only memory but also CPU cycles, adding I/O activity, and network bandwidth. You also increase your outage exposure if issues occur at the server level. If a RAID array loses disks, a network card goes bad, or a power outage occurs, you have multiple instances affected instead of just one (the same applies to reboot).

There are differing opinions in the SQL Server world regarding multiple instances on a production server. Multiple instances are undoubtedly an excellent choice for a development environment and even a QA or staging environment. If you have large, under-utilized servers, multiple instances can provide you with a better cost/benefit. You should test whether or not this makes sense for your environment before using this functionality in a mission-critical environment. From a recovery standpoint, using multiple production SQL Server instances on a single box increases your risk by creating a single point of failure (your server hardware). Mission-critical SQL Server instances may be better off spread across multiple servers.

## SQL Server 2000 Named Instance Connectivity Issues

- ISQL cannot connect to a named instance because it uses DB-Library. Use the `osql.exe` utility instead (the workaround is to add an alias in the Client Network Utility and use that name with ISQL, instead of the instance name).
- MDAC versions prior to 2.6 cannot connect directly to a SQL Server named instance. If your client connectivity must stay at version 2.5, you can use the Client Network Utility to create an alias to the instance.
- See Microsoft's Knowledge Base article Q313225, *HOWTO: Connect to a SQL Server 2000 Named Instance with JDBC* if you are programming connectivity with Java.
- If you connect to a named instance from the server itself, you will notice that there is only one set of tools. The same Enterprise Manager, Query Analyzer, and SQL Profiler are used for both the default and all named instances. Applying a service pack to one instance on your server actually updates MDAC and your tools for the entire machine.

There are two other points regarding SQL Server named instances:

- You cannot rename a named instance. If you need to rename an instance, install a new instance, copy all the databases over, then uninstall the old instance.
- However many instances you install, there will be only one MS Search service.

# 1.10 How to... Install a Named Instance of SQL Server

There is substantial overlap between a regular installation of SQL Server and that of a named instance. There are two differences in the installation of a named instance:

- At the Instance Name dialog box, after clearing the Default check box (it will be grayed out if a default instance is already installed), type in the instance name.
- The other difference is in the Network Libraries dialog box. The TCP/IP Sockets port number is 0 instead of 1433, meaning that a port will be chosen automatically. You can decide this port for yourself. Be sure, however, that it is not reserved by other applications. If you have external Internet connections, make sure this port can be accessed through the firewall.

The remaining options are exactly the same as a default instance installation.

# 1.11 How to... Register Your Named Instance in SQL Server Enterprise Manager

- To register your new SQL Server named instance, right-click Server Group and select New SQL Server Registration.
- Select From now on, I want to perform this task without using a wizard to bypass the wizard in the future (and go straight to the Server Registration dialog box).
- In the Registered SQL Server Properties dialog box, put in your server name followed by \ and the named instance. Select the Server Group under which you wish to register it, and decide whether to use SQL or Windows authentication. Press OK when finished.

# 1.12 How to... Determine the Port Number for a Named Instance

To determine the port number of your named instance (Java developers love to know this), follow these steps:

- In SQL Server Enterprise Manager, expand your SQL Server Group and right-click the SQL Server registration for the named instance. Select Properties.
- In the SQL Server Properties dialog box, select Network Configuration.
- In the SQL Server Network Utility dialog box, select TCP/IP in the Enabled Protocols window. Select the Properties button.
- You will see the named instance port in the Port text box.

Keep in mind that you can find the same information on the server itself by accessing the Server Network Utility from Start | Programs | Microsoft SQL Server | Server Network Utility.

# Microsoft Data Access Components (MDAC) Defined

Microsoft Data Access Components (MDAC) installs connectivity components for ActiveX Data Objects (ADO), Remote Data Service (RDS), OLE DB (open standard data interface, the next generation beyond ODBC), default SQL Server client Net-Libraries, and ODBC.

MDAC version 2.6 is the version installed with SQL Server 2000 and is necessary to connect to named instances of SQL Server. SQL Server Service Pack 3 installs MDAC version 2.7 Service Pack 1. This latest version does not have feature modifications, but does include fixes and security enhancements. MDAC is installed in the following ways:

- During Server and Client Tools full server installation
- During Connectivity Only installation
- During Client Tools Only installation
- By running the MDAC redist file, `mdac_typ.exe`, which is included in the SQL Server 2000 installation CD, in the `\MSEQ\x86\odbc` folder
- Downloading from the Microsoft web site (http://microsoft.com/data)
- Installed as part of SQL Server 2000 Service Pack 3
- As part of Microsoft products, such as Microsoft Office, Microsoft Back Office and Microsoft Visual Studio

# 1.13 How to... Troubleshoot MDAC Installation

With so many methods for installing MDAC, it is common for incorrect versions to be installed on your client or server. Microsoft has created a utility called Component Checker, which helps you determine which MDAC version is installed. You can also diagnose MDAC problems, and reconfigure as necessary.

For more information, see Microsoft's Knowledge Base article Q307255, *INFO: Component Checker: Diagnose Problems and Reconfigure MDAC Installations*.

You may also encounter problems with the MDAC installation itself. Microsoft has an excellent article on troubleshooting failed installations, Knowledge Base article Q232060 *HOWTO: MDAC Setup Troubleshooting Guide*.

# Ensuring Client Connectivity to Your Server

Clients can connect to SQL Server using OLE DB, ODBC, or DB-Library. Having MDAC version 2.5 will be sufficient for connecting to default instances of SQL Server. For named instances, MDAC 2.6 is required.

Client connectivity requires that a matching pair of SQL Server Net-Libraries exists, one library on the client and the other on the server. Net-Library allows SQL Server to utilize various network protocols. Network requests from the client and server are sent to a Net-Library and translated to the protocol in use.

Correct network protocols (such as TCP/IP) are needed for the SQL Server Net-Library to work properly. These are not included with the SQL Server setup but, rather, are included in the client and server operating system installations.

If you have problems connecting, consider the following:

- Rule out the obvious. Is the client connected to the network? Is the server properly connected to the network (check the cable)? Is the network card faulty or configured incorrectly?
- Do you have the correct version of MDAC installed?
- Do you have the necessary protocols installed? For example, if the server is set to use TCP/IP, do you have this protocol on your client?
- Are you connecting over the Internet or through a firewall? If so, there may be special considerations that you need to discuss with the network administrator.
- Do you have proper access to the server?
- Are you able to connect through the SQL Server tools such as Query Analyzer and Enterprise Manager, but not the application? Find out what methods the application is using to connect to SQL Server.

Use the tools `makepipe`, `readpipe`, and `odbcping` to assist in troubleshooting connectivity issues. All three command-line utilities can be found on the SQL Server 2000 installation CD, under `x:\x86\Binn`. Copy them to the SQL Server install directory on the SQL Server instance you are testing, under `x:\Program Files\Microsoft SQL Server\80\Tools\Binn`. You should also copy these to the client workstations from which you will be testing connectivity.

`makepipe` and `readpipe` work in conjunction to test connectivity to a SQL Server instance. To use, follow these steps:

- From the server you wish to connect to, open a command prompt. Change the directory to the location of the `makepipe` utility. Type `makepipe` and press *ENTER* (for other options, see the *SQL Server Books Online* topic, *makepipe Utility*):

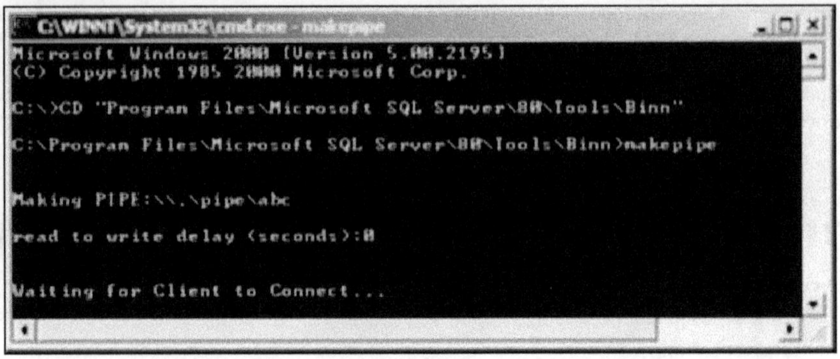


- From the workstation from which you are testing connectivity, open a command prompt. Change the directory to the location of `readpipe`. Type in `readpipe`, and `/S` with the name of the server you wish to connect to, for example:

```
C:\Program Files\Microsoft SQL Server\80\Tools\Binn>readpipe /SDOPEY
```

If the connection is successful, `readpipe` will connect to `makepipe`, and will close `makepipe` down.

The `odbcping` utility is used to check if ODBC is properly installed on the workstation or server, by connecting to a SQL Server instance using the ODBC SQL Server driver.

To use `odbcping`, open a command prompt for the server or workstation on which you are testing ODBC driver connectivity. Navigate to the location of your `odbcping` utility.

`odbcping` takes the following parameters:

| Parameter | Description |
|---|---|
| `/?` | Displays `odbcping` syntax |
| `-S` | SQL Server instance name you are attempting to connect to |
| `-D` | Data source name (DSN) you wish to use for connecting (if not connecting directly to a SQL Server instance) |
| `-U` | Login ID for connecting |
| `-P` | Password used for connecting |

The following example shows an `odbcping` connection to the server named `DOPEY`:

If the connection was successful, your SQL Server instance version information will be returned:

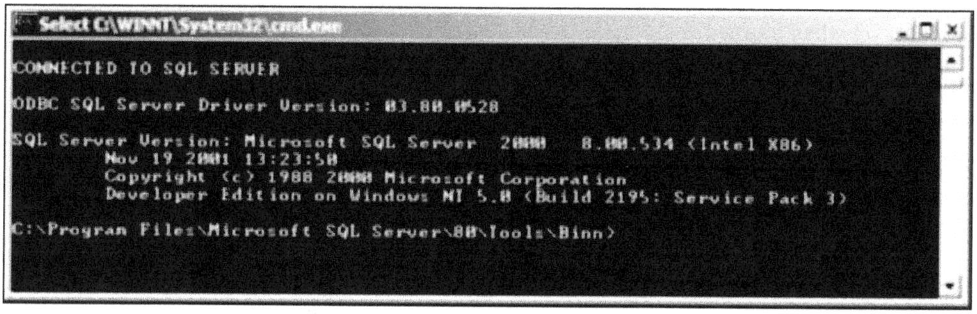


# Upgrading to SQL Server 2000 from SQL Server 6.5 and 7.0

The best resource for instructions on upgrading to SQL Server 2000 is found on http://www.msdn.microsoft.com/default.asp, in Knowledge Base article Q322620 *INF: How to Upgrade SQL Server 6.5 and 7.0 to SQL Server 2000*. This 52-page document reviews the upgrade hardware and software requirements, preparation steps, upgrade step-by-step procedure, replication considerations, details for upgrading to a failover cluster, and backward compatibility considerations.

You should also review Knowledge Base article Q261334 *INF: Frequently Asked Questions – SQL Server 2000 – Upgrade*. This gives good information on estimated upgrade run-time based on database size, and also covers a few common errors you may get during the upgrade.

You should also be aware that a number of upgrade errors were fixed in the SQL Server 2000 service packs. Cross-reference any upgrade errors you encounter with the fix lists located in the service pack documentation.

# Database Compatibility Settings

Database compatibility level impacts how Transact-SQL and queries behave in your database. In SQL Server 2000 you can set the level to:

- 80 – SQL Server 2000
- 70 – SQL Server 7.0
- 65 – SQL Server 6.5
- 60 – SQL Server 6.0

This does not mean you can restore a SQL Server 2000 database with a setting of 70 on to a SQL Server 7.0 server. The compatibility level impacts only the behavior of the SQL Server version. This helps recently upgraded databases avoid errors involving outdated syntax or rules.

To set database compatibility level:

- In Enterprise Manager, expand SQL Server Group, and the SQL Server node for the database you wish to view.
- Expand the Databases folder.

- Right-click the database you wish to view and select Properties.
- In the Options tab, view the Compatibility section. To change this, select from the drop-down menu. Select OK when finished.

You are allowed to revert to earlier compatibility levels, assuming that you have not added higher version functionality to your database (such as user-defined functions or indexed views).

Also, you can set this option with the `sp_dbcmtlevel` stored procedure. For example, to change the `Northwind` compatibility level to 80 (SQL Server 2000), you would run the following syntax in Query Analyzer:

```
sp_dbcmptlevel 'Northwind', 80
```

Also check out the *Books Online* reference on `sp_dbcmptlevel` for tables describing the exact differences between each compatibility level.

# Service Packs and Security Patches

Service packs and security patches are provided by Microsoft to fix bugs in SQL Server. New service packs and security patches are available from time to time, and can be downloaded from Microsoft's SQL Server site, http://www.microsoft.com/sql

## Preparation for the Service Pack or Security Patch

Testing is imperative before considering an upgrade to the latest service pack or security patch. SQL Server implementations can differ drastically. You should not only test SQL Server functionality, but also the functionality of the application referencing your database.

This presumes that you have a test environment set up for your databases. Having a test environment is critical for important databases in your organization. If you do not have a test environment, you have no safe way of implementing major changes, such as service pack or security patch upgrades.

In preparation for your service pack or security patch installation, remember the following:

- Read the documentation. It may be over 30 pages long, but important information is included from beginning to end.
- Test the installation in your test environment. Do thorough regression testing, not only of SQL Server's functionality, but also of the application's functionality. Can the application connect to the database after the upgrade? Can it still print a report, run a query and return the right results, and submit a new order? This can be quite a bit of work, but it is absolutely necessary.
- Service packs usually update all technologies included with SQL Server, not just the core engine. If you are using Analysis Services, English Query, or applications that use MDAC on the server, test each of these elements as well as the installation.
- Security patches often fix a specific security flaw. Microsoft will include a recommendation as to who should install the patch, and a rating indicating how critical it is.
- Some SQL Server DBAs wait a few months after the release of a service pack or security patch; the reason for this is that any problems with the patch itself will be made public by the time they get around to applying it. In the past, service packs have added undocumented bugs or problems. Security patches, however, should be tested and installed on your production servers as soon as possible, to protect your mission-critical data from attacks.

# 1.14 How to... Find the Latest SQL Server Service Packs and Security Patches

To keep up with the latest service pack and security patches, check out the Downloads section for Microsoft's SQL Server site, http://www.microsoft.com/sql/. The latest service packs and security patches are listed here. For more immediate notification of new security patches, register your e-mail address with Microsoft's HotFix & Security Bulletin Service (http://www.microsoft.com/technet/treeview/default.asp?url=/technet/security/current.asp/).

# 1.15 How to... Install a Service Pack

At the time of publication, most service pack install procedures have had similar, if not uniform, instructions. Remember to use the instructions included with the particular service pack that you are installing. Use the following instructions, based on Service Pack 3 for Microsoft SQL Server, as a framework:

- Go to Microsoft's SQL Server site, and their associated downloads section. You can usually order the CD or download the executables from the site (Microsoft recommends the CD, as there have been problems in the past with the downloaded version of the service packs). A CD will be useful if you do not have Internet connectivity directly from the server. When downloading the executables, you must specify a language. Microsoft broke down SQL Server 2000 Service Pack 3 into three downloads: database components (`SQL2KSP3.exe`), Analysis Services components (`SQL2KASP3.exe`), and SQL Server 2000 Desktop Engine MSDE (`SQL2KdeskSP3.exe`).
- Assuming that you wish to implement a service pack upgrade to database components, and that you downloaded the files from the Microsoft site, double-click `SQL2kSP3.exe` and select an extraction folder.
- Select Finish to extract. You will see a progress bar.
- When complete, navigate to the install directory and read `sp3readme.htm` if you have not done so already.
- Service Pack 3's installation will fail if you have security policies set to Do not allow installation for the Windows XP local security policy Devices: Unsigned driver installation behavior, or for the Windows 2000 local security policy Unsigned non-driver installation behavior. These policy settings must be changed instead to Silently Succeed prior to installing SP3.
- Prior to beginning the installation, back up all your databases. The service pack only makes changes to your `master`, `msdb`, and `model` databases (and databases involved in replication). It is a good idea, however, to have everything backed up within the same timeframe. Also, copy your backup files to tape or onto another server on the network. Having multiple recovery options is always a good idea in case something happens to the server itself. A disaster recovery plan is vital to your organization, and performing a service pack installation may test parts of your plan.
- Make sure that you have tested the service pack on a test server, and that you have carried out regression testing for the applications connecting to the test server.
- Back up your Analysis Services databases (if you have them).
- Verify that the autogrow option has been set for your system databases. Also, verify that you have at least 500KB of free space available for them to use.
- Stop the SQL Server service, the SQL Server Agent service, and Microsoft Distributed Transaction Coordinator (MS DTC).
- Other tools you may be using that should also be disabled are Microsoft Search, Microsoft Component Services, MSMQ (Microsoft Message Queuing), Microsoft COM Transaction Integrator, and MSSQLServerOLAPService services.

- Close all applications, including Control Panel.
- To install the regular database component upgrade run the `setup.bat` file in the CD-ROM base directory or directory from your extracted folder. If you are installing the service pack over the network, it is advisable to copy the install directory to your local machine, as installation may be speedier this way. If you must install over the network, make sure you use a mapped letter drive and not just a UNC path to the `setup.bat` file.
- At the Welcome screen select Next.
- Read the license agreement and, if you agree, select Yes.
- Select the instance you wish to upgrade. Uncheck Default and select a named instance if you are not upgrading the default instance.
- Next select your connection method to SQL Server. This account must have `sysadmin` permissions.
- The Backward Compatibility Checklist dialog box presents you with the following three options, two of them required:
    - Enable cross-database ownership chaining for all databases. Cross-database ownership chaining occurs when a source database object depends on objects in other databases. When the source database object and the target objects in the target databases are owned by the same login account, and cross-database ownership chaining is enabled, SQL Server will not check permissions on the target objects. This has various security implications, which is why Microsoft does not recommend enabling this option in most circumstances. You can enable this option later if you need, using the Server Properties dialog box in Enterprise Manager, on the Security tab.
    - Upgrade Microsoft Search and apply SQL Server 2000 SP3. This is a required checkbox, warning you that the Microsoft Search service will be upgraded.
    - I have created a master server account on the master server will be seen for those SQL Server Instances configured as a master multiserver administration server. For such SQL Server Instances, you must complete several steps detailed in the sp3readme.htm file prior to applying SP3. This is because there are features introduced in SP3 that are not compatible with instances not running SP3.

  Select the Continue button.
- The Error reporting dialog box allows you to enable automatic error reporting for your SQL Server instance, when a fatal error occurs. The data is sent to Microsoft over a secure connection, or to a Corporate Error Reporting server. If you do not select this option during the service pack installation, you can enable it later the in the Server Properties dialog box in Enterprise Manager, on the General tab. Select OK.
- Select Next for the Start Copying Files dialog box. Click Next to begin copying.
- You will see the file installations run, followed by the scripts. Once finished, you will be told to back up your system databases. Select Finish at the dialog box.
- Start up the SQL Server service and test your application functionality. Back up your system databases.

Keep in mind that SQL Server service packs should be reinstalled whenever new SQL Server components are added. If you have any read-only databases or filegroups as part of a replication topology that is no longer read-only, you should reapply the service pack. Reapplying the service pack involves the same steps as an initial installation.

View the `sp3readme.htm` file for detailed information on:

- Installing the service pack for Analysis Services
- Installing the service pack for MSDE (Microsoft Desktop Engine)
- Installing the service pack in unattended mode
- Installing the service pack on a failover cluster
- Installing the service pack on replicated servers. SQL Server 2000 Service Pack 3 should be deployed on the distributor (if separate from the publisher) first, then the publisher followed by the subscriber.
- Changes to master/target server configurations, and the ordering of installation for master and target servers.

# 1.16 How to... Uninstall a SQL Server Service Pack

Unfortunately there is no elegant way of removing a SQL Server service pack once it has been applied. This is why you must back up your system and user databases prior to the upgrade. Follow these instructions to uninstall a SQL Server service pack (referencing Service Pack 3).

If you have databases involved in replication, all of these must have publishing disabled. To disable publishing:

- Expand Server Group and registration in Enterprise Manager, and right-click the Replication folder. Select Disable Publishing.
- Select Next at the Disabling Publishing and Distribution Wizard screen.
- Select Yes, disable publishing on 'servername'. Select Next. If successful, you should see a dialog box with the following message:

  SQL Server Enterprise Manager successfully disabled 'servername' as a Publisher and Distributor.
- Click OK.

The next step is to detach all user databases. Detaching databases can be done using Enterprise Manager or Transact-SQL. In this example we will use Enterprise Manager:

- Expand Server Group, registration, and the Databases folder.
- Right-click the database you wish to detach and select All Tasks | Detach Database...
- Select OK in the Detach Database dialog box.
- When finished, you should see a dialog box with the following message:

  Detaching database has completed successfully

Repeat this process with each user database.

The next steps are as follows:

- Uninstall your SQL Server Instance (see *How to...* 1.8).
- Reinstall SQL Server 2000 (see *How to*...1.1), placing system databases and executables in the same directories in which they were originally installed.

- Restore the `master`, `msdb`, and `model` databases from the pre-service pack backups you performed prior to the upgrade. See Chapter 6 for different database recovery techniques and scenarios. We will review restoring the `master` database from a backup called `preSP3_master.bak`. To restore the `master` database:

  **a.** Stop the SQL Server service.

  **b.** Start up SQL Server in Single User mode.

  **c.** For a default instance, run the following in a command prompt at the directory where the `sqlservr.exe` executable exists:

  ```
  C:\Program Files\MMSQL\Binn>sqlservr -c -m
  ```

  **d.** If you are starting a named instance, run the following:

  ```
  sqlservr.exe -c -m -s {instancename}
  ```

  where `instancename` is the name of your server's named instance.

  **e.** Once you press *ENTER* at the `sqlservr` execution, you will see startup messages like the following:

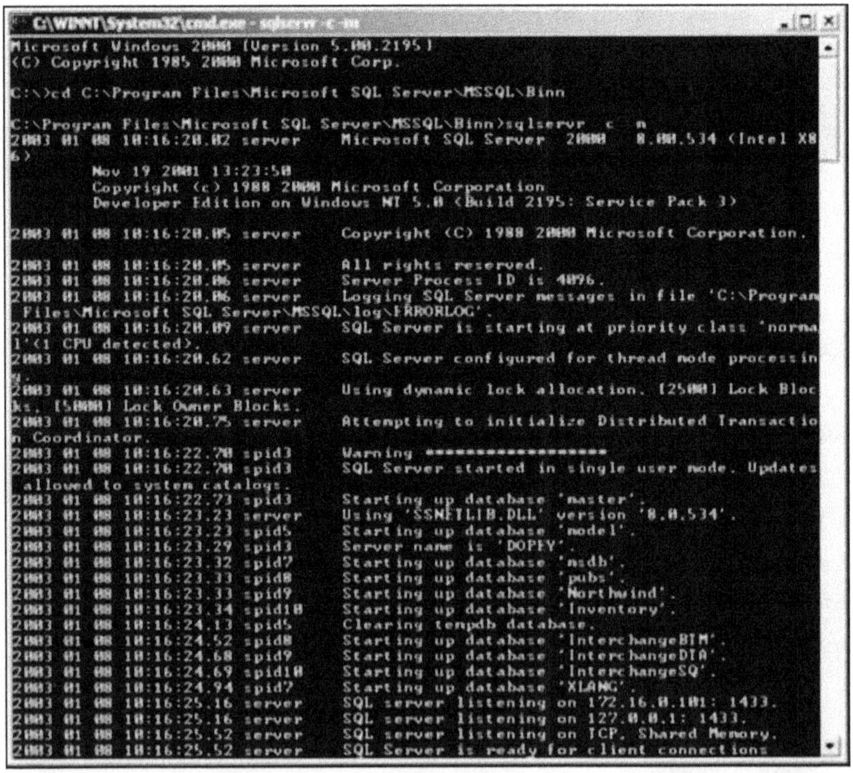


  Leave this command window open.

## Restoring the master Database

In this example, we will restore the `master` database from the `preSP3_master.bak` device:

- ❑ Open Query Analyzer. Beware – if your Object Browser pane opens with Query Analyzer, this will attempt to consume an additional connection! Your query window should be the first to grab a free window, so simply close the Object Browser in Query Analyzer by selecting the menu Tools | Object Browser | Show/hide.
- ❑ Type the following in Query Analyzer:

```
USE master
GO
RESTORE DATABASE master
FROM DISK = 'e:\mssql\mssql\backup\presp3_master.bak'
```

- ❑ Execute the query by selecting *F5*. After a few seconds you should get the message:

The master database has been successfully restored. Shutting down SQL Server. SQL Server is terminating this process.

- ❑ Close down your command prompt window and start up SQL Server as normal.

## Restoring the msdb and model Databases

- ❑ Open Query Analyzer and type the following:

```
USE master
GO
RESTORE DATABASE msdb
FROM DISK = 'e:\mssql\mssql\backup\presp3_msdb.bak'
GO

RESTORE DATABASE model
FROM DISK = 'e:mssql\mssql\backup\presp3_model.bak'
```

- ❑ Select *F5* to execute. You should see something like the following:

```
Processed [illegible] pages for database 'msdb', file 'MSDBData' on file 1.
Processed 1 pages for database 'msdb', file 'MSDBLog' on file 1.
RESTORE DATABASE successfully processed [illegible] pages in [illegible] seconds ([illegible] MB/sec).
Processed [illegible] pages for database 'model', file 'modeldev' on file 1.
Processed 1 pages for database 'model', file 'modellog' on file 1.
RESTORE DATABASE successfully processed [illegible] pages in [illegible] seconds ([illegible] MB/sec).
```

## Reattaching the User Databases

Lastly, open up Enterprise Manager and reattach the user databases (this can be done via Transact-SQL too):

- ❑ Expand Server Group and registration, and right-click the Databases folder.
- ❑ Select All Tasks | Attach Database...
- ❑ Select the `.mdf` file of the database you wish to attach. The remaining settings will auto-fill.

- ❑ Select OK. You should see a dialog box with the message:

  Attaching database has completed successfully.

- ❑ Repeat for each user database.

After restoring your user databases, do a full backup of all system and user databases.

# 1.17 How to... Install a Security Patch

This section covers the installation of a security patch for SQL Server. Security patch installation procedures will change frequently over time, so please make sure to download the latest version, and follow the latest instructions. Security patches are often *cumulative*, so you only need to install the latest one. The exceptions are patches for add-on technologies for SQL Server, such as SQLXML, which may then require a separate patch for the SQLXML utilities.

As with service packs, you should test the installation of security patches very carefully on a test server. Do not roll out into a production server until you have done full regression testing.

The following example describes the installation of the MS02-020 security patch. This patch helps protect SQL Server from a buffer overrun attack (a flaw that exploits an unchecked buffer in a program and allows code injection). Code injections occur when Transact-SQL (or another programming language) is used to execute under the security context of a SQL Server process, via a procedure or call not intended to be executed by the application developer (in this case Microsoft). This means that an insecure (vulnerable) procedure, for example, could be used to do harm to the database or the server itself.

To install the security patch:

- ❑ Download the `.exe` file from the Microsoft site. In this case, we are installing a security update requiring Service Pack 2 (reference Knowledge Base article Q316333).
- ❑ Double-click the downloaded `.exe` file to extract the security update patch.
- ❑ Read the `readme.txt` file.
- ❑ Make sure Microsoft SQL Server 2000 Service Pack 2 is installed. If it is not, the files you replace will be incompatible with the system databases (`master`, `msdb`), which may cause various SQL Server functionality problems.
- ❑ Shut down the SQL Server and SQL Server Agent services.
- ❑ Make backup copies of the following files located in the `<sql server install path>\binn` folder:

  **a.** `sqlservr.exe`

  **b.** `odsole70.dll`

  **c.** `xpqueue.dll`

  **d.** `xprepl.dll`

  **e.** `xpweb70.dll`

  **f.** `xplog70.dll`

  **g.** `xpstar.dll`

- ❑ Also make backups of the following file in the `<sql server install path>\binn\exe` folder:

  **h.** `sqlservr.pdb`

- Copy the `sqlservr.exe`, `odsole70.dll`, `xpqueue.dll`, `xprepl.dll`, `xpweb70.dll`, `xplog70.dll`, and `xpstar.dll` files from the patch self-extracting directory into the `<sql server install path>\binn` directory. This will copy over the existing files, so make sure the original files are backed up!
- Copy the `sqlservr.pdb` file from the patch self-extracting directory into the `<sql server install path>\binn\exe folder`. This too will copy over the existing files, so make sure the original files are backed up.
- Start the SQL Server and SQL Server Agent services.
- Open Query Analyzer while logged in with `sysadmin` permissions.
- Open the file `qfe356326.sql` from the extracted patch directory and press *F5* to execute.
- Open the file `qfe356938.sql` from the extracted patch directory and press *F5* to execute.
- Do regression testing for your default or SQL Server named instance, to make sure that your application(s) do not have any side effects from the patch upgrade.

# 1.18 How to... Roll Back a Security Patch

This section will review specifically how to roll back the MS02-020 security patch that we installed in the previous section. You may decide you need to uninstall (roll back) this patch if you encounter unexpected problems (such as application functionality breaking). To uninstall the MS02-020 security patch:

- Stop the SQL Server and SQL Server Agent service accounts.
- Copy over the files mentioned in the last section with the original files you backed up prior to the patch overlay.
- Connect to Query Analyzer with `sysadmin` permissions and execute the `uninstall.sql` script from the patch directory.

# Post-Installation Best Practices

After installing SQL Server, and before your database server goes into production, you should take the opportunity to perform a security, hardware, operating system, and SQL Server setting audit. Now is your chance to gather information about your server and fix problems *before* users start connecting.

## Security

- If you are using mixed mode security, make sure your `sa` password is set. A blank `sa` password is, unfortunately, quite common. Many virus attacks utilize this vulnerability (see Chapter 7 for how to change a password).
- Have you applied all the necessary operating system security patches? SQL Server security rollups and service packs? Avoid production outages by installing these now.
- Check Windows 2000 user and group accounts. Check their privileges. When SQL Server is installed, the `BUILTIN\Administrators` group is, by default, granted SQL Server `sysadmin` permissions. Review those users and groups with administrator membership on the server. Ensure that everyone who has `sysadmin` permissions *should* have `sysadmin` permissions.
- Check Window 2000 folder shares defined on your server. On the server, go to Start | Settings | Control Panel | Administrative Tools | Computer Management. Expand the Shared Folders node, and select Shares. The right-hand pane will display all shares defined on the server. Those with the $ sign are called **administrative shares**, and are only open to administrators on the server. Other shares should be explored to verify the configured permissions and individuals or groups with access to the share. Double-click the share you wish to explore, and check out the Security and Share Permissions tabs:

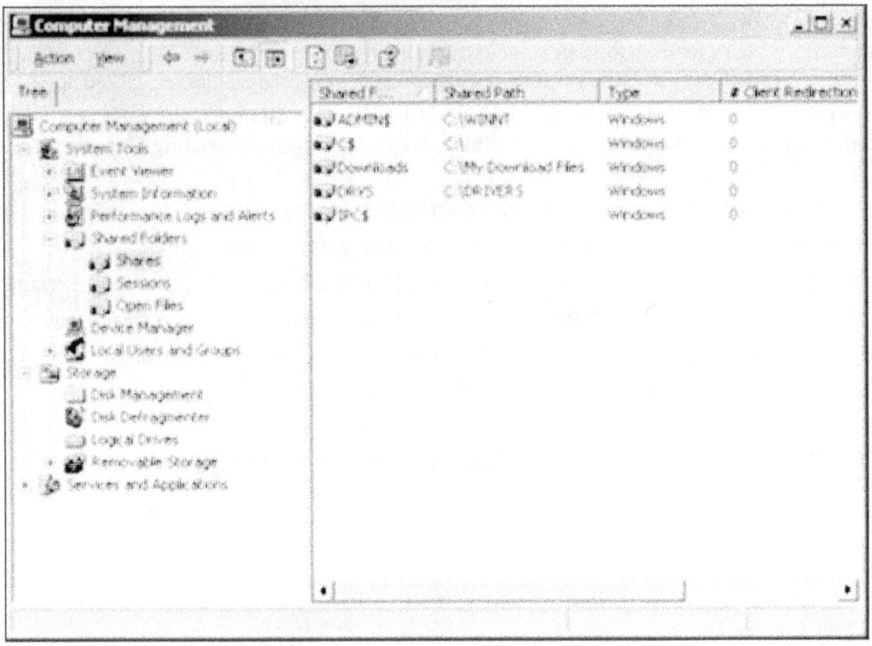


- ❑ Shares containing the entire SQL Server program file directory, open to 'Full Control' by all users, are more common than you would suspect. Look for permissions that seem inappropriate, or excessive.

# SQL Server Settings

- ❑ Is the proper collation set? We'll discuss collation considerations, including changing the server default collation and database collation, later in this chapter.
- ❑ Are the program files (binaries) and system database file locations where you want them to be? See *File Placement Strategy* earlier in this chapter for best practices.
- ❑ Do you have more than 3GB of memory, and are you running SQL Server Enterprise Edition? If so, there are steps you must take to utilize this extra memory. For information on what steps to take, see the *SQL Server Books Online* topic *Managing AWE Memory*. Also, if you are sharing your database server with other applications (not recommended!), you may decide to configure memory limits (see the *Configure Server Options* section later in Chapter 2).
- ❑ Set your default database file locations in the SQL Server Properties | Database Settings tab. You are able to set the default location for your log and data files when creating a new database in Enterprise Manager. It is good practice to keep your data and log files in consistent locations. To do this follow these steps:

**a.** In Enterprise Manager, expand the server you wish to configure.

**b.** Right-click the server and select Properties.

**c.** Go to the Database Settings tab.

**d.** Configure the new default location for the data and log directory values:

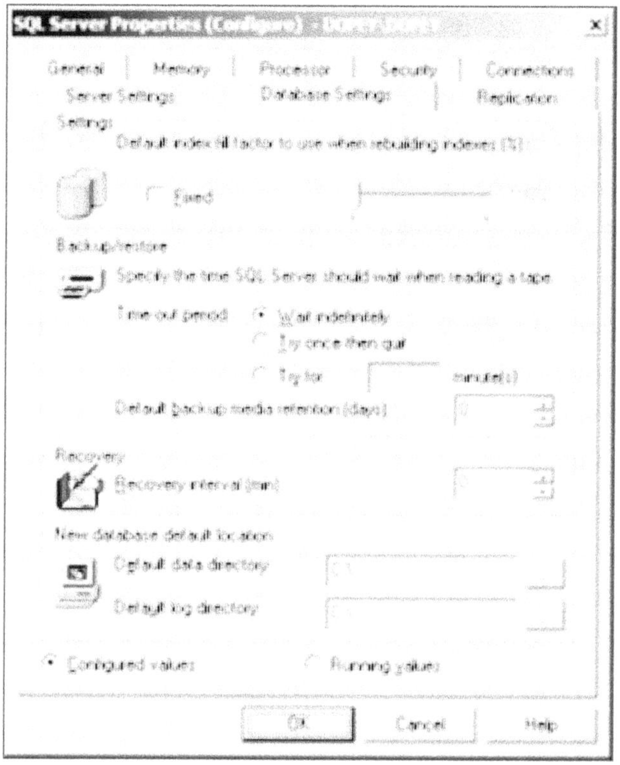


e. Verify that the SQL Server and SQL Server Agent are both set to autostart in the SQL Server Properties | General tab. If your server will be referenced as a linked server by another SQL Server instance, or if your SQL Server instance will be participating in distributed transactions, make sure MSDTC is also set to autostart.

- ❑ How about your SQL Server log? Do you see any warnings or unusual errors?
- ❑ Establish your backup and recovery plan *before* rolling out your new server (see Chapter 6). Not only should you establish your backup and recovery plan, but also you should test it several times.

# Operating System and Hardware

- ❑ Check the Application and System event logs – do you see anything strange? Any driver errors? If you check Computer Management's Device Manager, do you see any red Xs?
  - ❑ Make sure that Windows 2000 is configured to maximize throughput for network applications (reserves minimal memory for file caching, leaving the rest for SQL Server). To do this, follow these steps:

a. Go to Start | Settings | Network and Dial-up connections.

b. Right-click Local Area Connection and select Properties.

c. Select File and Printer Sharing for Microsoft Networks.

d. Click Properties. Select Maximize data throughput for network applications, and select OK.

- Your virus scanning software should not check the database files on your SQL Server instance (`*.mdf`, `*.ldf`, and `*.ndf` files). Some virus-scanning software can create intense I/O activity or, worse, open your database files while SQL Server is starting up, forcing a database into 'suspect' status (meaning a file necessary to operate a database is missing or unavailable). If the database option `AUTOCLOSE` is enabled (which is *not* recommended), you could also run into trouble if the virus scan software were to grab the file during a scan and SQL Server attempted to open the database at the same time.
- Although SQL Server does not make heavy use of the paging file when your memory available is sufficient, place the `Pagefile.sys` file on a drive without SQL Server files if possible.
- The sizing of the paging file should also be considered. The general rule-of-thumb for paging file size is 1.5 times the size of physical memory available on the server. See Microsoft's topic, *Configuring Virtual Memory*, at http://msdn.microsoft.com/library/default.asp?url=/library/en-us/optimsql/odp_tun_1a_2rqx.asp, for more details.
- Double-check that Windows 2000 is set to optimize performance for background services, and not applications. SQL Server services are, by definition, background services. Make sure that foreground applications do not take priority. To configure, right-click and select properties for My Computer on the server desktop. In System Properties, select the Advanced tab. Press the Performance Options... button. Select Optimize performance for: Background services:

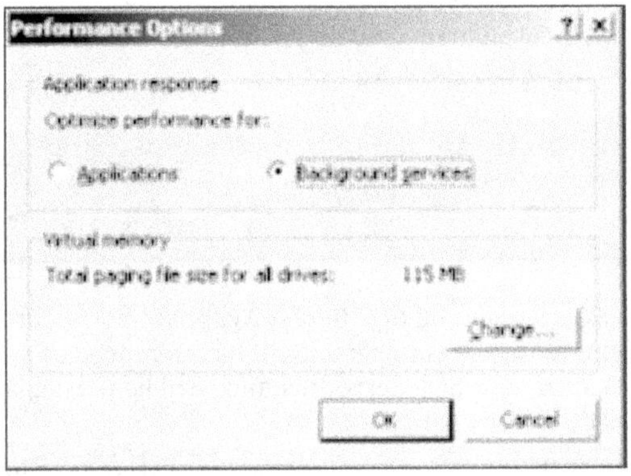


- Enable System Monitor's Logical Disk object counters. System Monitor allows you to track details about your server environment (details such as CPU utilization, memory, and other hardware and software measurements). The Logical Disk object counters measure information about disk activity for logical drives (such as drives C:, E:, and F:). The Physical Disk object counters are enabled on Windows 2000 by default, and measure disk activity at the physical level (for example DISK 0 could be a disk that is separated into three logical drives, but Physical Disk counters measure activity for just DISK 0). Logical Disk counters are turned off by default in Windows 2000. To enable the Logical Disk object counter, open a command prompt. At the command prompt, type `diskperf -yv`. Counters will be set on reboot.
- Check your hardware documentation to make sure your write caching controller has a battery backup (most new systems do). If it does not, disable the write caching function (if possible). UPS (uninterruptible power supply) systems are not good substitutes for battery backups.
- If you plan on using DTS or linked servers with other relational database management systems, avoid having to reboot an actively used database server by installing the necessary drivers now. Sybase and DB2 Connect drivers usually require a reboot. Other vendors, like Teradata, may not. As with any application installation, test the driver interactions with SQL Server before rolling this out to a production environment. I've encountered problems installing Sybase Open Client drivers on a SQL Server failover cluster. An MDAC (see the *Microsoft Data Access Components* section earlier in this chapter) `.dll` file was overwritten, and MDAC had to be reinstalled.

- Plan on using tape backup or network backup utilities. Make sure the utilities work and are installed properly. Enterprise backup software and drivers often require reboots, so save yourself and your end-users from unnecessary downtime. Make sure you also know how to use your tape backup software. Practice backing up files to tape (or the network), and then restoring back to disk.
- Disable unnecessary services. Make sure you first know what the service does before you disable it. Microsoft provides a glossary of services, on the following web page: http://www.microsoft.com/windows2000/techinfo/howitworks/management/w2kservices.asp.
- Verify that your network cards are configured to use the current network bandwidth available. For example, go to Start | Network and Dial-up Connections. Double-click the LAN connection you wish to configure. Select Properties. In the Properties dialog box, select the Configure button. On the Advanced tab, verify the property settings, such as Link Speed & Duplex. Check that the value for each property is appropriate for the card, and the network backbone.

# Database Migration Techniques

Now that your server is upgraded with the latest service packs and patched up with the latest security fixes, this next section covers migration techniques for bringing databases on to your SQL Server instance.

# 1.19 How to... Move Logins

Before moving or copying databases from other SQL Server instances, you should first move over the logins that have associated users in the databases. SQL Server holds logins in the `syslogins` table (actually this is really a view that references the `sysxlogins` table) in the master database.

To move logins and passwords from SQL Server 7.0 to SQL Server 2000, see Knowledge Base article Q246133 *INF: How to Transfer Logins and Passwords Between SQL Servers*. There are three different options for transferring logins between SQL Server servers, as detailed below.

## Option 1: Transact-SQL Script

The first option is available if you have kept a Transact-SQL script of all login additions to your SQL Server 7.0 server. For example, the following script adds users (with passwords), along with Windows-authenticated domain users:

```
-- Script of SQL Authentication and
-- Windows Authentication users

sp_addlogin @loginame     = N'JaneDoe',
         @passwd       = '123#$',
         @defdb        = N'pubs',
         @deflanguage = N'English'

sp_addlogin @loginame     = N'JackSmith',
         @passwd       = 'MeowMix1',
         @defdb        = N'pubs',
         @deflanguage = N'English'

GO

sp_grantlogin @loginame = N'JOEDOMAIN\joey'
GO

sp_grantlogin @loginame = N'JOEDOMAIN\marcy'
GO
```

Most DBAs will not have a complete script of login additions, so we shall move on to options 2 and 3.

## Option 2: DTS Package Transfer Logins Task

You can transfer logins and passwords using the new SQL Server 2000 Data Transformation Services DTS Package Transfer Logins Task. In this example, we will transfer all logins associated with users in the Northwind database:

- In Enterprise Manager, expand Server Group and the registration from which you wish to transfer logins. This assumes you are using the SQL Server 2000 Enterprise Manager. Expand the Data Transformation Services folder and right-click Local Packages. Select New Package.
- In DTS Designer, select Task | Transfer Logins Task…:

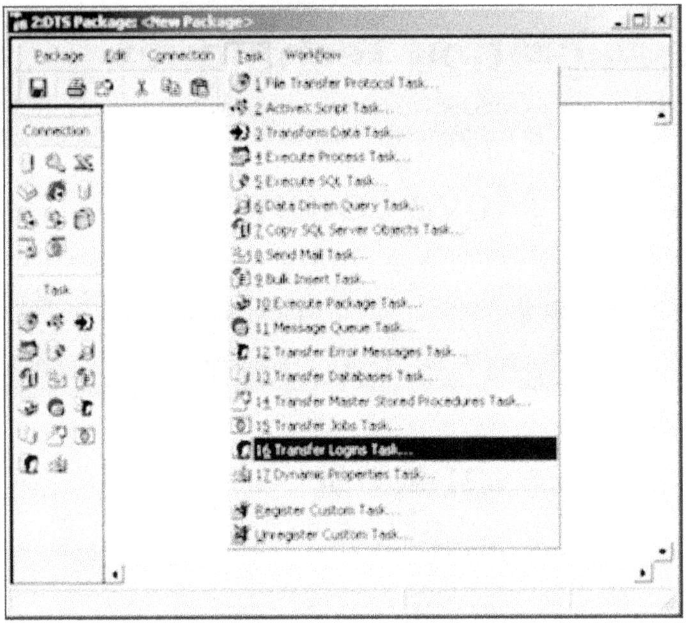

- Select the source server from which you wish to transfer logins:

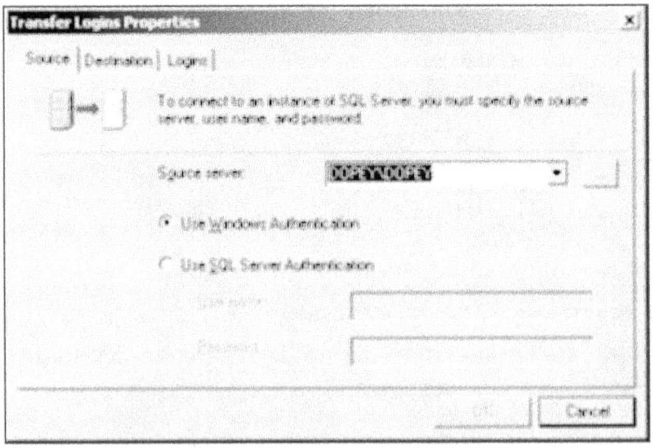

- Go to the Destination tab and type in the server to which you wish to transfer the logins and passwords:

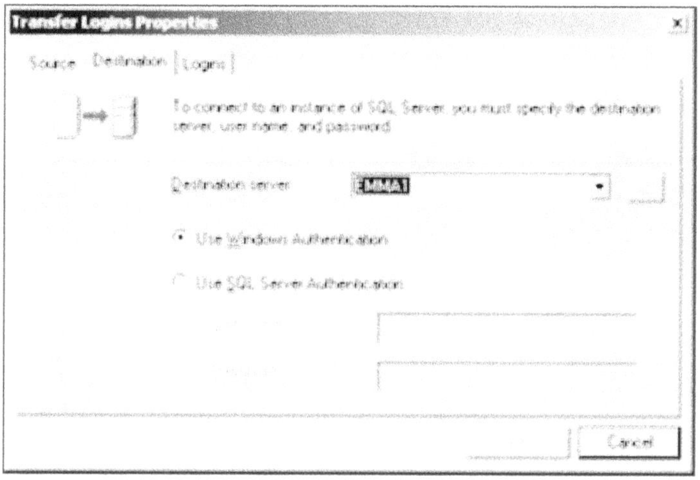


- Select the logins for the selected databases; otherwise, *all* logins will be transferred. Check Northwind and select OK:

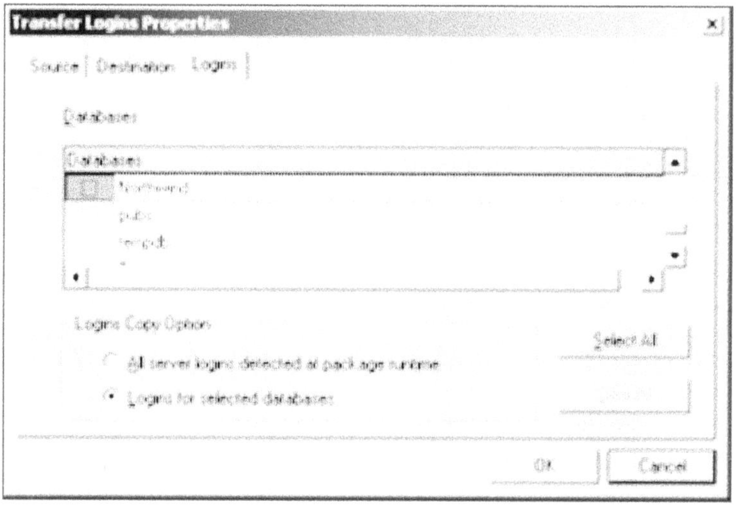


- From the Package menu, select Execute:

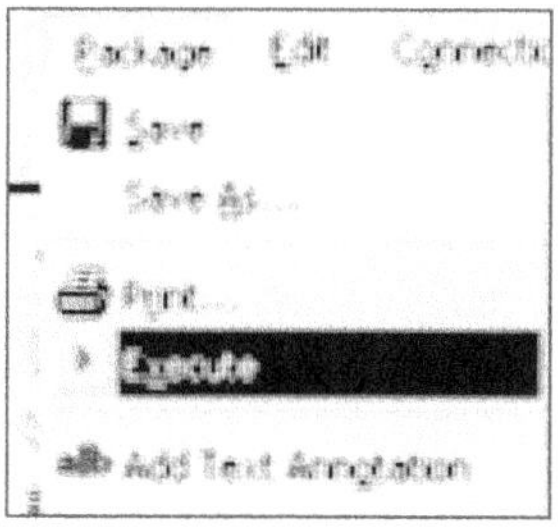

- After running, you should see a dialog box indicating success. Select OK.

## Some Details to Note About Using This Method

- Using this DTS method transfers passwords but not the original SID. You still must fix orphaned login\database associations.
- This method works for both SQL Server 7.0 to 2000, and SQL Server 2000 to 2000 login transfers.
- `sysadmin` permissions are required to use this method.

# Option 3: Scripting Out Logins and Passwords

This method scripts out all logins and passwords on a SQL Server 7.0 or SQL Server 2000 box while retaining the SID (security identifier ), assuming the same domain. Reference the Knowledge Base article Q246133 *INF: How to Transfer Logins and Passwords Between SQL Servers* for the code for the procedures, and follow these general steps:

- Compile the `sp_hexadecimal` and `sp_help_revlogin` stored procedures from the Q246133 article in the source server's master database using Query Analyzer.
- In Query Analyzer run the following to generate a script of all logins and associated passwords (if a SQL login) on the source server:

```
EXEC master..sp_help_revlogin
```

- Review the output of the procedure to make sure it looks correct. You can then take this output and run it in Query Analyzer on the destination server to generate logins. Remove those logins you do not wish to transfer from the script.

Some details to note about using this method:

- Run this procedure using `sysadmin` permissions.
- Default database info is not transferred in this script.
- If the source is **case-insensitive** and the destination is **case-sensitive**, this procedure will not work unless the original password contains no alphabetic characters or all alphabetic characters in the original password are uppercase characters. If both sides have the same case-sensitivity this is not a problem.
- The script will not overlay existing logins.
- The script will not overlay logins with different names but the same `SID`.

What about SQL Server 6.5 logins, you ask? One method is to:

- `BCP OUT` the `syslogins` table on SQL Server 6.5
- `BCP IN` the `syslogins` table into SQL Server 2000, and into a new table name
- Do an import into the `master.dbo.syslogins` table on SQL Server 2000 from the imported table of logins you wish to use

It isn't recommended that you do this as many things can go wrong. You could import a duplicate `SID`, attempt to bring in another `sa`, or the encrypted fields may not transfer as expected. Pounding data directly into system databases, particularly one as important as `syslogins`, is not a good idea.

Your best bet is to script out the logins and reset the passwords.

# 1.20 How to... Fix Orphaned Logins

Each user database holds a `sysusers` table containing one row for each Windows user, group, SQL user, or SQL role with access to the database. The `master` database contains the `syslogins` table that holds all logins for the SQL Server instance.

Both `sysusers` and `syslogins` contain the `SID` column. This unique identifier is what defines the relationship between the two tables. This allows you to change a login name without losing all the database access permissions, as the `SID` remains the same.

When you migrate a database to a new server, the `sysusers` table's `SID` relationship is broken. For example, on the original source server you have the following settings:

## Source Server

```
Login name - 'TestUser', SID 0003948
Database user name - 'Test User', SID 0003948
```

Let's say you migrate the database to a new server. This server also has a login named `TestUser`. The settings are as follows:

## Destination Server

```
Login name - 'TestUser', SID 1044444
Database user name - 'TestUser', SID 0003948
```

Although `syslogins` and `sysusers` both have a row with the name `TestUser`, SQL Server does not recognize these as the same user. This is because the `SID` is not the same.

To fix this relationship you can run the `sp_change_users_login`. This procedure can fix the above scenario by re-associating relationships between the `syslogins` and `sysusers` table. First run this procedure to get a listing of users that will be altered:

```
EXEC sp_change_users_login 'Report'
```

Next, for those users needing to be fixed, run the procedure as follows for each login:

```
USE databasename
GO
EXEC sp_change_users_login 'Update_One', 'TestUser', 'TestUser'
```

The above procedure tells SQL Server to re-associate the user with the login. This login must already exist.

For more detailed information on this subject, see Knowledge Base article Q240872 *INF: How to Resolve Permission Issues When a Database is Moved Between SQL Servers*, article Q168001 *PRB: User Logon and / or Permission Errors After Restoring Dump*, and Q298897 *SAMPLE: Mapsids.exe Helps Map SIDs Between User and Master Databases When Database Is Moved.*

# 1.21 How to... Restore Another SQL Server's Database from Backup to SQL Server 2000

One method of migrating databases from server to server is to back up the source database and restore it on the destination server. This method works for 7.0 to 2000 and 2000 to 2000 transfers. You cannot restore SQL Server 6.5 databases into SQL Server 2000.

There are different methods you can use to back up and restore databases. See Chapter 6 for more details. In the following example, we will use Query Analyzer to back up a database on the source and restore the database on the destination:

- Open Query Analyzer for the source server and run the following command in the master database:

```
BACKUP DATABASE SofaOrders
TO DISK = 'E:\MSSQL\backups\sofaorders_migrate.bak'
```

  Replace `SofaOrders` with your own database name to migrate, and the disk device with the name of your backup directory on the source server.

- Move the `*.bak` file to the destination server.
- Make sure you have the logins migrated over first (see the previous section on login migration).
- Open Query Analyzer for the destination server and run the following command in the `master` database:

```
RESTORE FILELISTONLY
FROM DISK = 'E:\MSSQL\backup\sofaorders_migrate.bak'
```

  The directory is the location to which you copied the `*.bak` file. `FILELISTONLY` returns a result set with a list of database and log files contained in the `*.bak` file.

- Once you know the logical database and log file names, you can execute a `RESTORE` operation, as in the following example:

```
RESTORE DATABASE SofaOrders
FROM DISK = 'E:\MSSQL\backups\sofaorders_migrate.bak'
WITH MOVE 'SofaOrders_Data' TO 'E:\MSSQL\Data\SofaOrders_Data.mdf',
MOVE 'SofaOrders_Log' TO 'E:\MSSQL\Data\SofaOrders_log.ldf'
GO
```

  See Chapter 6 for more syntax details and a review of the `RESTORE` command.

- Once the restore is complete, re-link any orphaned users in the database by using `sp_change_users_login` (see previous section).

## Detaching and Reattaching Databases

You can move databases by using the **detach** and **reattach** methods. This presumes that you wish to bring the database offline in the source server and copy it to the destination server. There are two methods for doing this, through Enterprise Manager and through Transact-SQL in Query Analyzer.

Since we showed you the Enterprise Manager method of detaching databases in *How to...* 1.16, in this example we will use Transact-SQL:

- Open up Query Analyzer on your source server.
- You must have exclusive access to the database that is to be detached. If this is a SQL Server 7.0 server, run sp_who to see who is currently using the database. Ask users to log out, or run KILL for each SPID in sp_who that is referencing the database. Use this with caution if you do not want transactions to be cancelled. Plan for the downtime properly.
- If you are transferring this server from SQL Server 2000, you have the option of setting the database to SINGLE_USER by running the following command:

```
ALTER DATABASE SofaOrders SET SINGLE_USER
WITH ROLLBACK IMMEDIATE
```

  This sets the database to SINGLE_USER mode and kills all connections immediately. You also have the option of ROLLBACK *integer* (which designates seconds to allow transactions to finish running), where *integer* is the number of seconds.

- Once the database users have been removed, run the following command to detach the database, where SofaOrders is the name of your database:

```
sp_detach_db 'SofaOrders', 'true'
```

  The second parameter is true or false depending on whether you want to skip an UPDATE STATISTICS prior to detaching the database. This is useful when you plan on re-attaching the database in READ ONLY mode. Designating true makes the detach operation skip UPDATE STATISTICS.

- Copy the *.ldf and *.mdf files of the database you detached to the destination server.
- Open up Query Analyzer on the destination server.
- From the master database, run the following command, where @dbname is your database name and the @filename1 and @filename2 are the locations of your *.mdf and *.ldf files:

```
EXEC sp_attach_db @dbname = N'SofaOrders',
@filename1 = N'c:\Program Files\MSSQL\Data\SofaOrders_Data.mdf',
 @filename2 = N'c:\Program Files\MSSQL\Data\SofaOrders_Log.ldf'
```

- As with all migrations from server to server, take care of any orphaned users you have in your destination database.

# DTS Wizard

DTS Wizard allows you to import and export schemas and data from selected source and destination databases. The following example will go through the screen options:

- To load DTS Wizard, go to Start | Programs | Microsoft SQL Server | Import and Export Data.
- Select Next at the DTS Import/Export Wizard dialog box.
- Select the data source for your source data. You can reference another SQL Server data source, such as ODBC data source, Sybase, or Teradata.

> **Your data source choices depend on what drivers are installed on the client machine where you are running DTS Wizard. This is the same for all DTS utilities. If you create a package and schedule it on the server, make sure that the server has the same drivers and data sources set up as the client on which you created the package.**

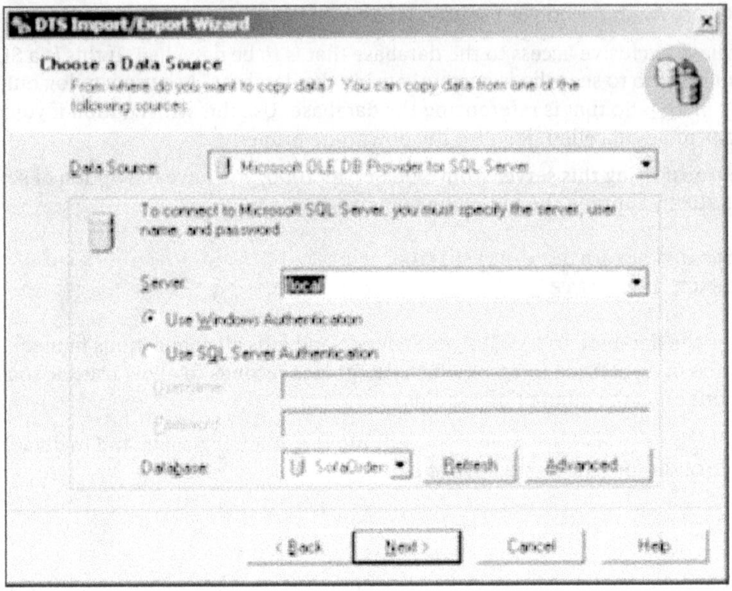


- ❑ In this example, we will select Microsoft OLE DB Provider for SQL Server, the local server (we are running DTS Wizard on the server itself), using Windows authentication. The database we want to transfer is `SofaOrders`. Select Next when finished.
- ❑ Next we select the destination settings, choosing the server, the connection method, and the destination database. In this case, we will transfer the database and call it `SofaOrders2`. Under the Database dropdown select <new>:

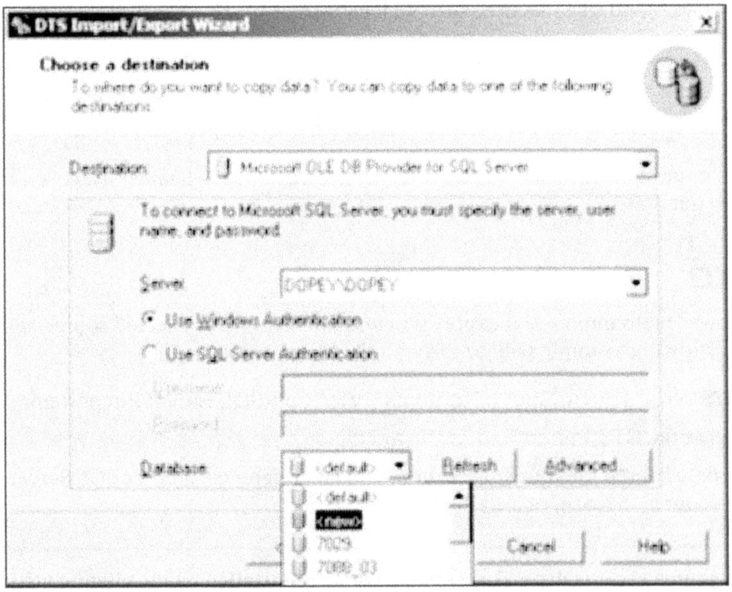

- We can create a new destination in the Create Database window. Select the new name and file sizes:

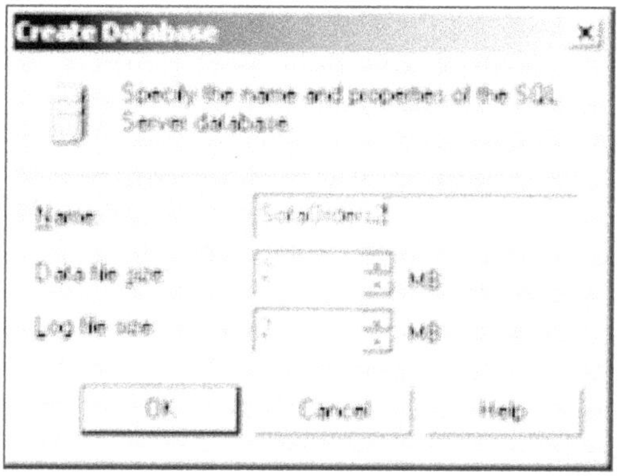


- Select OK when finished and then select Next at the Destination dialog box.
- Select the method for copying objects. If your data source is not SQL Server 7.0 or greater, you must select either of the first two options. Otherwise, if you have a SQL Server implementation, you can select any of the three options. Copy objects and data between SQL Server databases is the option that offers the most control. Select Next:

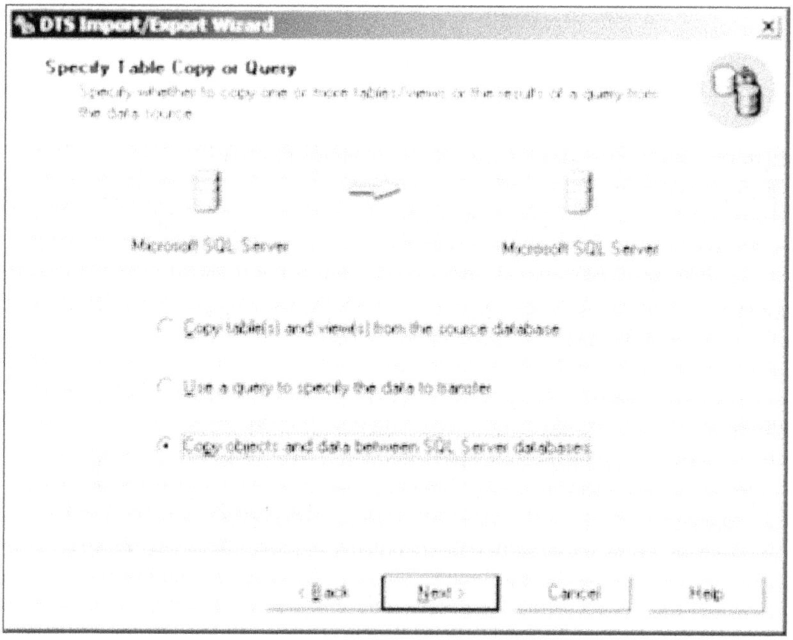

- You have several options on the next screen:

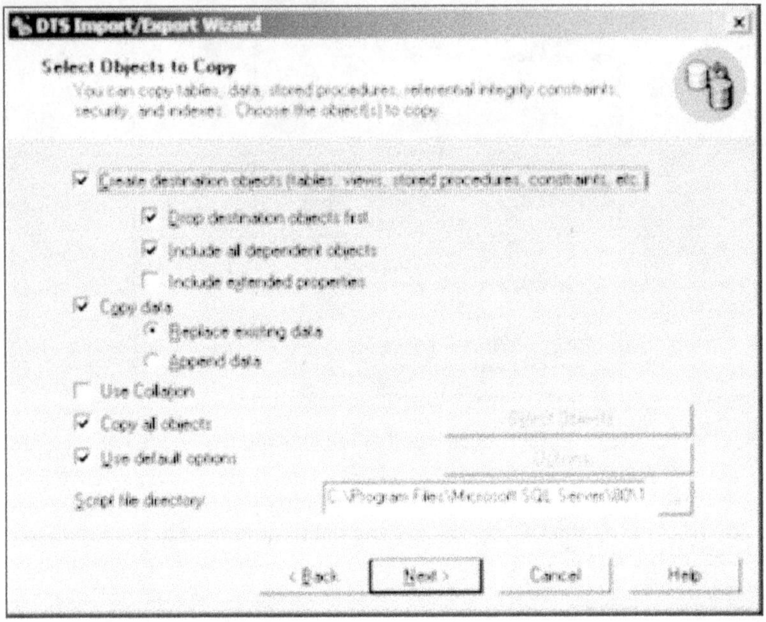


The following table shows options and descriptions:

| Option | Description |
|---|---|
| Create destination objects | Creates schema to be transferred to destination. |
| Drop destination objects first | Drops the destination objects if the same object names exist. **Caution**: make sure this is something you want to do. |
| Include all dependent objects | Dependent objects, for example, are tables supporting a view |
| Include all extended properties | New to SQL Server 2000, extended properties are user-supplied definitions associated with database objects. |
| Copy data | Copies data from source to destination. |
| Replace existing data | Overwrites existing data on the destination. |
| Append data | Adds data and does not overwrite existing data on destination. |
| Use Collation | Allows the copying of data between different collations. |
| Copy all objects | Transfers all schema objects. If unchecked, you must press the Select Objects button and select which objects to transfer. Do not forget to press the Check button for objects you wish to transfer. People often forget this, and nothing gets transferred. |
| Use default options | If unchecked, you can select your own settings by pressing the Options button.<br>By default, SQL Server logins are not transferred, and scripts are not generated in Unicode. **Warning**: if you select Transfer SQL Logins, the wizard transfers *all* logins on the datasource, without any regard to which database you want to transfer. This is not very helpful if you have hundreds of logins that should not be moved. |

| Option | Description |
|---|---|
| Script directory | Specifies the directory, local to your client or server where you run the DTS Wizard, where script and log files are created. The SQL and data files for each object are written to this directory. |

- ❑ For the Script directory option, make sure the client or server from which you are running this has enough space. This also highlights a benefit of running DTS Wizard from the source or destination server instead of a remote client, as one less hub is involved in sending the data.
- ❑ When done setting options, select Next.
- ❑ The Save, schedule, and replicate package dialog box contains a When section and a Save section. The When options are as follows:

| Option | Description |
|---|---|
| Run immediately | Executes the DTS package immediately. |
| Use replication to publish destination data | When selected, the Create Publication Wizard is launched after the DTS Import/Export Wizard is completed. |
| Schedule DTS Packages for later execution | Creates a SQL Server agent job, used to execute the package at a scheduled time. See Chapter 4, for more information on jobs. |

The Save settings are as follows:

| Option | Description |
|---|---|
| Save DTS Package | Options for saving the package to the msdb database, Meta Data Services, as a COM file, or as a Microsoft Visual Basic file. See Chapter 11 for more information on these settings. |

In this example, we will select Run immediately. Select Next:

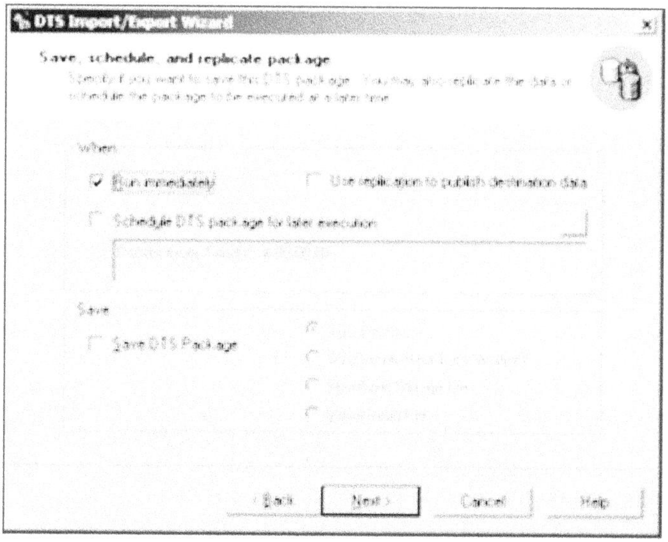

Select Finish, and the package will begin executing:

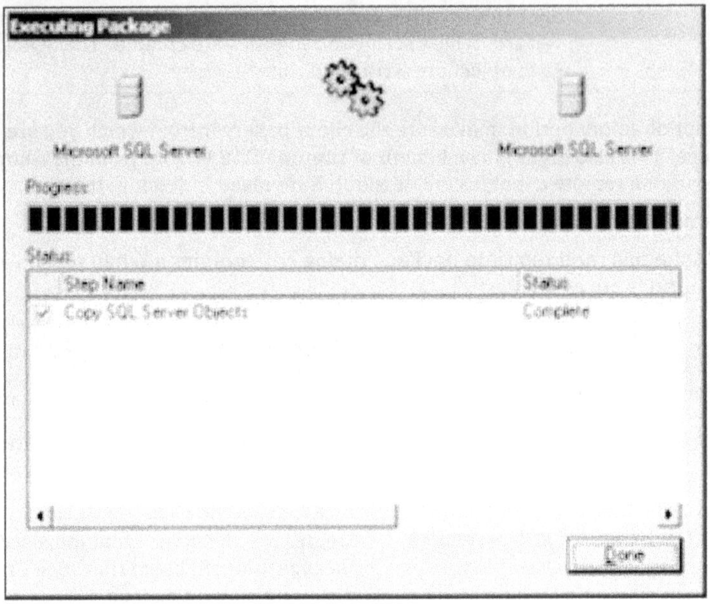


- ❑ When the process is complete, select OK.

We will review other examples of using DTS Wizard to import data from Access, Excel, and SQL Server 6.5 later in the chapter.

# Enterprise Manager SQL Scripting

If you just want to transfer the schema from an existing SQL Server 7.0 or 2000 database, you can use the SQL scripting functionality. SQL Server 6.5 also has a scripting utility.

To work with SQL scripting in SQL Server 7.0:

- ❑ Open Enterprise Manager and expand Server Group, registration, and the Databases folder.
- ❑ Right-click the database you wish to script in Transact-SQL and select All Tasks | Generate SQL Scripts.
- ❑ On the General tab, select which tables, views, stored procedures, defaults, rules, and user-defined data types you wish to script. Move selected objects to the right-hand pane, Objects to be scripted.
- ❑ Go to the Formatting tab and confirm the scripting options. You can select whether to generate the `CREATE <object>` command, `DROP <object>` command, script out dependent database objects, and include descriptive headers in the script file.
- ❑ Go to the Options tab and select the options you would like included in the script. Decide whether to script out users and roles, SQL logins, object-level permissions, indexes, full-text indexes, triggers, and constraints. Select file format from MS-DOS text, Windows Text, and Unicode text. Be aware that the Unicode format may have some unintended effects on Visual Source Safe. When Unicode files are stored in VSS, they are treated as binary files; because of this, VSS will not be able to identify differences between versions of a file. This invalidates one of the most important uses of VSS; so think carefully about saving files in Unicode format for this purpose.

- Lastly, decide if you would like to generate one file, or one file per object. Select OK when you have finished selecting options.
- The Save As dialog box appears. Select the directory in which you wish to save the script file or files.
- SQL Server will now generate the script and you should get a dialog box indicating that scripting was completed successfully.

The scripting functionality is almost exactly the same for SQL Server 2000, except for the following:

- The General tab in Generate SQL Scripts includes a new option, All user-defined functions, since user-defined functions are new to SQL Server 2000.
- The Formatting tab allows the inclusion of extended properties (new to SQL Server 2000) and gives the option to script only 7.0-compatible features.

To script in SQL Server 6.5, follow these steps:

- Expand Server Group, registration, and Databases folder.
- Click the database you wish to script.
- Go to Object | Generate SQL Scripts.
- Select the objects that you wish to script in the Generate SQL Scripts dialog box. In Scripting options, decide on `CREATE` and `DROP` options, inclusion of indexes, triggers, constraints (Keys/DRI), and whether to use quoted identifiers. Decide on security options and whether there should be a single file or multiple files per object.
- Select Script when ready.
- Select your file(s) location when the Save As dialog appears.
- You will receive a dialog box on completion, indicating success.

Scripting out your databases is often good practice, whether or not you plan on migrating the schema to a new server. It is a good backup in the event that you have to recreate your database from scratch.

You can also script out the schema as a separate task, and then use other tools to bring over the data itself (such as `BCP` and `BULK INSERT`).

# Copy Database Wizard

You can use the Copy Database Wizard to copy or move databases between SQL Server 7.0 and SQL Server 2000, and between SQL Server 2000 instances. Keep in mind that you cannot move or copy system databases or databases involved with replication. If any of the databases are in single-user mode, Copy Database Wizard will fail. For more information on Copy Database Wizard bugs, see Knowledge Base article Q299452, *BUG: Copy Database Wizard Exits Without Error if any of the Source Databases are in Single User Mode.* Other points to keep in mind are:

- Copy Database Wizard does not work if identical database names exist on the source and destination.
- You must be logged in with `sysadmin` privileges on both servers.
- Databases are moved sequentially and not simultaneously, even if you select multiple databases in one operation.

To use Copy Database Wizard to migrate databases from 7.0 to 2000, follow these steps:

- From a SQL Server 2000 Enterprise Manager console, expand Server Group and registration for the SQL Server 7.0 databases you wish to migrate.
- Go to Tools | Wizards.
- Expand the Management node.
- Select Copy Database Wizard from the Select Wizard dialog box. Select OK.
- Select Next at the Copy Database Wizard dialog box.
- Select the source server and connection method. Select Next.
- Select the destination server and connection method. Select Next.
- Select the database you wish to Copy or Move to the new server. You will see in the Destination column if it is possible to migrate the selected databases.
- Select Next.
- You will see Database File Location statuses letting you know if files are ready to be moved or copied. If you see a red x, there are databases on the destination with the same name, or there is insufficient free disk space.
- If you want to modify the file settings or destinations on the destination server, click the Modify button to implement changes. Select OK when you have finished the changes.
- Select Next.
- At the Select Related Objects dialog box, select login options associated with the databases, shared stored procedures in the `master` database, jobs from `msdb`, and user-defined error messages. If you select any of the User-selected options you will get another dialog box allowing you to select defined logins, `master` database stored procedures, selected jobs, and selected error messages.
- In the Schedule the DTS Package dialog, you can choose to run immediately, run at a scheduled date, or schedule the DTS package to run later. Select Next when finished.
- At the Completing the Copy Wizard dialog, select Finish.
- You will get a progress screen for each step.
- Make sure that no user connections are being made to the database while the copy is in progress, otherwise the database extraction will fail.

# 1.22 How to... Use BCP

For those who think that real DBAs don't use GUIs, SQL Server offers the `BCP` (Bulk Copy Program) utility. Once you have scripted out your schema and migrated it to the destination database, `BCP` is a great choice for extracting and loading data.

The full syntax and switches are detailed in *Books Online*. The following example will detail how to export the data from the `pubs.dbo.jobs` table and import into the `SofaOrders.dbo.jobs` table. This presumes you have extracted the required table schema to the `SofaOrders` database already, using SQL scripting.

You can run `BCP` in a command prompt or using `xp_cmdshell` in Query Analyzer. In the following examples, we will use a command prompt to run BCP.

To export the data out of a specific table follow these steps:

- Open a command prompt.
- Navigate to your `<sql server installation path>\binn` directory.
- To `BCP OUT` the `pubs.dbo.jobs` table, implement the following syntax:

```
BCP "pubs.dbo.jobs" OUT C:\jobs.txt -T -SDOPEY\DOPEY -c
```

- Press Enter to run. You should see feedback regarding the number of rows copied.

Here is a table describing the elements of this statement:

| Switch | Description |
|---|---|
| `bcp` | Command executable |
| `'pubs.dbo.jobs'` | Name of table from which to export data |
| `out` | Specifies direction of data (data exported out) |
| `c:\jobs.txt` | Output text file |
| `-T` | Uses trusted connection to connect to database |
| `-SJOEDEV` | `-S` specifies the server name, which in this example is `JOEDEV` |
| `-c` | Specifies that data is exported as `char`, with no prefixes, `\t tab` character for the field separator and `\n` for the row terminator |

Now that we have the `jobs.txt` data file, we can import this data into the `SofaOrders.dbo.jobs` table. To use `BCP` to import in data, follow these steps:

- In a command prompt, type:

```
BCP "SofaOrders.dbo.jobs" IN C:\jobs.txt -T -SDOPEY\DOPEY -c
```

- Select Enter.
- You should receive feedback on the number of rows copied. Check the table in SQL Server to verify that the rows were copied in.

When using `BCP IN`, the table reference becomes the destination and the data file becomes the source.

## Creating a Format File for BCP

The previous example shows a very simple `BCP OUT` and `IN` procedure; usually a production `BCP OUT` or `IN` will be more complicated. Enter the **BCP format file**. The format file gives default information used in either a `BCP IN` or `OUT` operation, designating how data is stored and what columns each data column belongs to.

SQL Server includes a method for generating a format file automatically, saving you time compared with having to generate this file column by column. To generate a `BCP` format file, follow these steps:

- First, make sure you have a data file to import in to the table for which we wish to generate a format file. If you have run the previous `BCP OUT` example, you can use the `C:\jobs.txt` file and `pubs.dbo.jobs` table to generate a format file.
- In Enterprise Manager, expand SQL Server Group and registration. Expand the Data Transformation Services folder.
- Right-click Local Packages and select New Package.
- In DTS Designer, click the Connection menu and select Microsoft OLE DB Provider for SQL Server.
- In the Connection Properties window, type in the server name, login method, and database you wish to access. Select OK when finished:

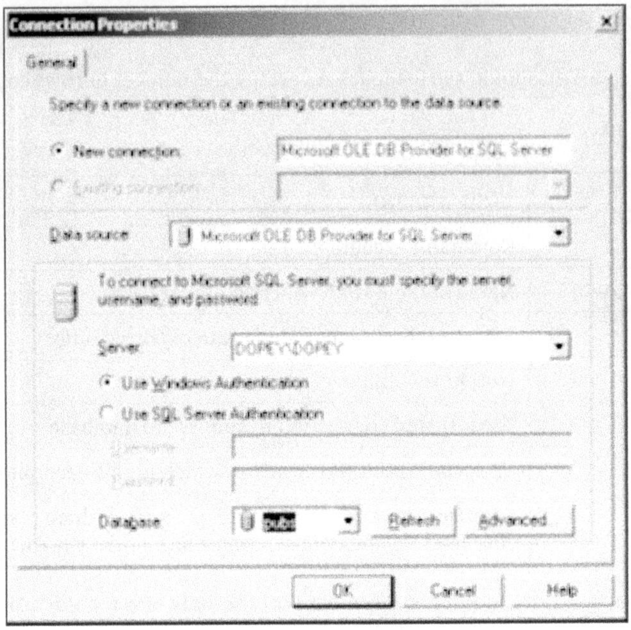


- In DTS Designer, select the Task menu and select Bulk Insert Task.
- We are interested in using this task to generate a format file. Under Destination table, select the table for which you wish to create a format file. Select Use Format File in the lower section.
- Click the button for the Source data file and select the `c:\jobs.txt` data file. Under the Use format file, type in a format file name, such as `c:\jobs_fmt.txt`:

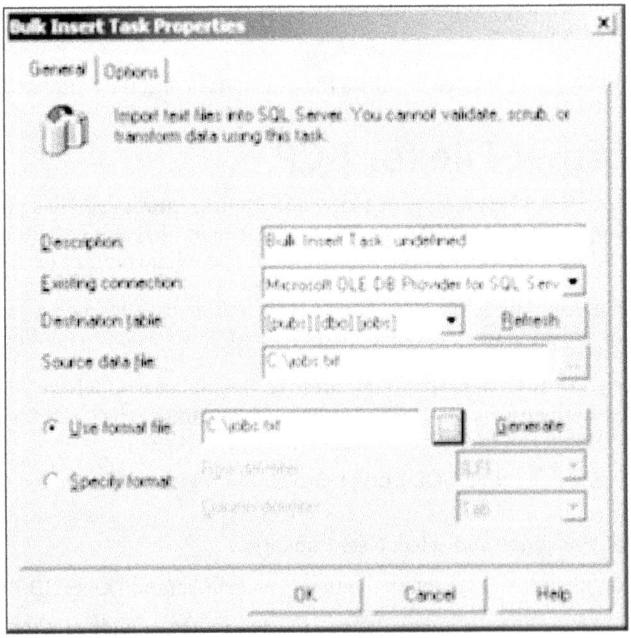

- Click the Generate button. Verify that the proper data and format files are selected. By the end of this exercise, the format file will be populated. Select Next:

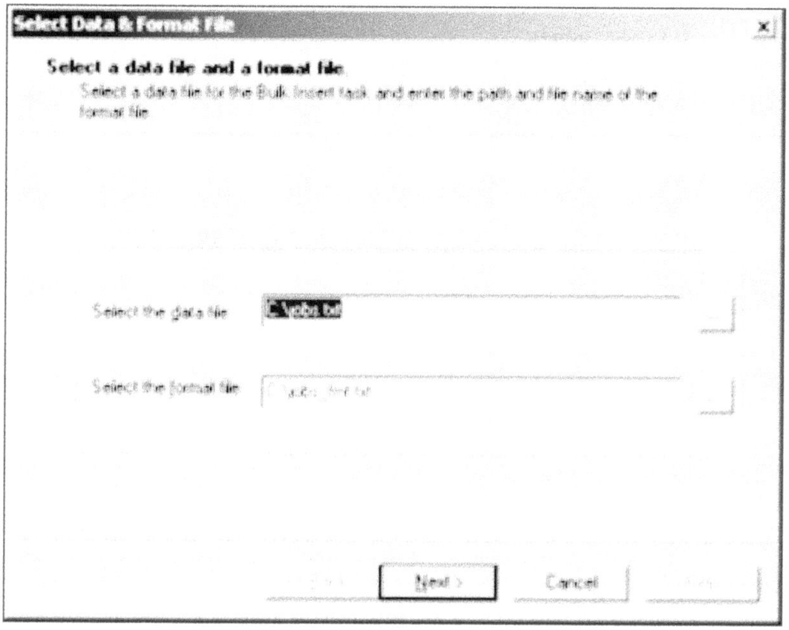

- Select the Text File Properties defaults. Select Next:

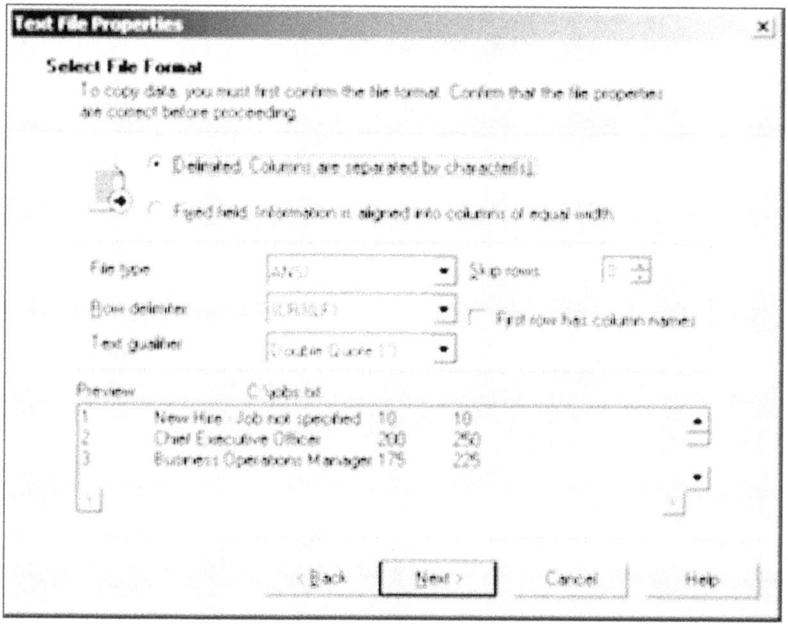

❑ Select the Tab delimiter type and press the Finish button:

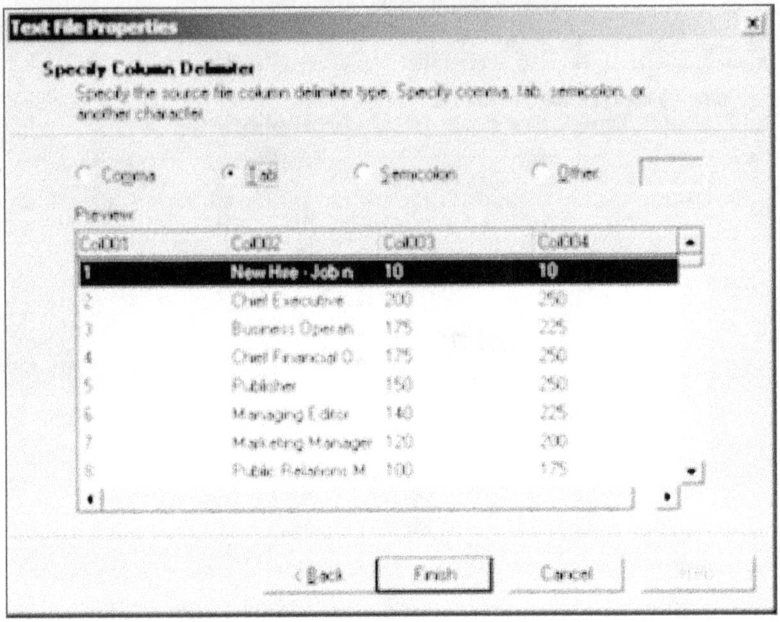


❑ Press OK at the Bulk Insert task and open up the `c:\jobs_fmt.txt` file. You will see it has been populated according to your choices:

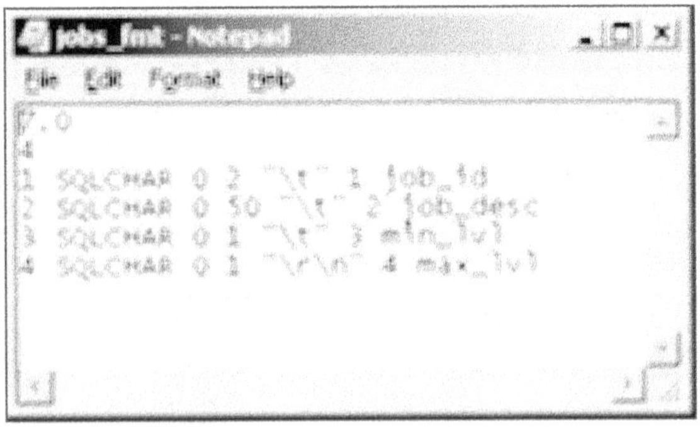


This file can now be reused for future `BCP IN` and `OUT` procedures for the `jobs` table.

# 1.23 How to... Use BULK INSERT

`BULK INSERT` is like `BCP`, in that you can use it to copy a data file into a database table (though you cannot use it to export data from SQL Server to a text file). `BULK INSERT` performs very well as it executes within the SQL Server process, whereas `BCP` and DTS execute within their own processes. If you are aiming to import data using the fastest method, you should test using `BULK INSERT`, DTS, and `BCP` to decide which works best.

We will be going over an example of how to import table data using `BULK INSERT`. As with the previous examples, we will attempt to import data from the `c:\jobs.txt` data file into the `SofaOrders.dbo.jobs` table:

- In Query Analyzer, connect to the server and select the database containing the table into which you wish to import data. In this example we are importing data into the `SofaOrders.dbo.jobs` table.
- In the Query Analyzer query window, type the following:

```
USE SofaOrders

BULK INSERT SofaOrders.dbo.jobs
FROM 'c:\jobs.txt'
WITH
( FORMATFILE = 'c:\jobs_fmt.txt' )
```

  Notice that we are using the BCP data file from the original `BCP OUT` example, and the format file generated in the previous example.

- Press *F5* to execute. You should get a prompt showing the number of rows inserted.

# Database Migration – Bringing It All Together

Now that we have reviewed the data migration technologies, we will tie together these technologies into best practices for specific tasks.

# 1.24 How to... Migrate Databases from SQL Server 6.5 to SQL Server 2000

There are two options when moving databases from 6.5 to 2000.

## Option 1: Using the Upgrade Wizard

If you decide to upgrade your SQL Server 6.5 instance, one option is the **SQL Server Upgrade Wizard**. As a prerequisite to upgrading any SQL Server 6.5 server, make sure to read the Knowledge Base article Q322620 *INF: How to Upgrade SQL Server 6.5 and 7.0 to SQL Server 2000*, as substantial planning is required.

You have the choice of installing SQL Server 2000 either on the same server as your SQL Server 6.5 instance, or on a different server. If using the same server, only one version of SQL Server can be running at any one time (assuming you installed a default instance of SQL Server 2000).

If using a new server, you have the opportunity of upgrading to the latest and greatest OS and hardware. This allows you to keep your old SQL Server 6.5 server running until you are sure that the SQL Server 2000 version is ready for production. Make sure that the SQL Server 2000 service and SQL Server agent service accounts use a domain account with administrator permissions for the SQL Server 6.5 server, as these permissions will be required during the upgrade process.

You have two data transfer options when using the Upgrade Wizard, **named pipe** and **tape**. Named pipe transfers will generally run faster but require more space above and beyond that used by the SQL Server 6.5 databases (which can be a problem if you are upgrading on a single server). The tape option involves backing up all SQL Server 6.5 databases to tape. You can then choose to delete version 6.5 devices, freeing up space for the new SQL Server 2000 data files. Beware – the wizard deletes all 6.5 databases, not just those upgraded.

> **It is extremely important to read the Microsoft Knowledge Base article before initiating the SQL Server Upgrade Wizard. There are several important differences between 6.5 and 2000 that demand careful thought and planning.**

To initiate the SQL Server Upgrade Wizard from the server with the SQL Server 2000 instance (which can be the 6.5 server or a different server), go to Start | Programs | Microsoft SQL Server – Switch | SQL Server Upgrade Wizard. This opens the SQL Server Upgrade Wizard dialog boxes, which take you step by step through the upgrade process.

## Option 2: Scripting Out the Objects and Transferring the Data

If you decide you do not want to use the Upgrade Wizard, the alternative is to script out all your database objects (see *How to...* 1.21). Remember that passwords will not be retained, and some of your objects may not be compatible in SQL Server 2000.

Your options for transferring data out are `BCP OUT`, and DTS.

Your options for transferring data in are `BCP IN`, DTS, and `BULK INSERT`.

If you have many tables, DTS is certainly your best option. Follow this example to transfer data from your SQL Server 6.5 database to SQL Server 2000:

- Script out all the objects in the database(s) you wish to transfer on SQL Server 6.5.
- Create a system or user DSN for the SQL Server 6.5 server. This DSN should be on the box from which you will be running DTS. To create a DSN:
    - **a.** Select Start | Settings | Control Panel.
    - **b.** Select Administrative Tools | Data Sources (ODBC).
    - **c.** Go to the System DSN tab and select the Add button.
    - **d.** Select SQL Server for the driver type, and click Finish.
    - **e.** Enter the name of the data source and the name of the server. Select Next.
    - **f.** Decide your connection properties. Select a login with enough permissions to read rows from the database (for transfer). Select Next.
    - **g.** Select the default database you wish to migrate, and select Next.
    - **h.** Take the defaults in this next screen and select Finish.
    - **i.** Test the connection and make sure you get this feedback:

j. Select OK, and then OK again to exit the Data Sources Dialog box.

- Open Enterprise Manager. Expand Server Group and registration for your destination database.
- Expand the Database folder and select the database to which you wish to import the data.
- Right-click this database and select All Tasks | Import Data.
- Select Next at the DTS Wizard dialog box.
- In the Choose a Data Source dialog box, select Other (ODBC Data Source) from the dropdown list. Enter a user name with proper permissions to read from the database. Select the database to migrate data from. Select Next.

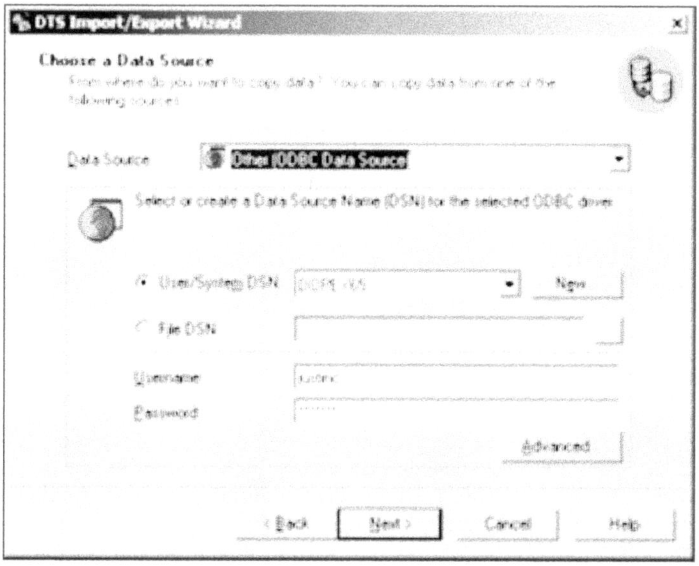

- Type in the destination server, and select the connection method and database to which the data is to be imported. Select Next:

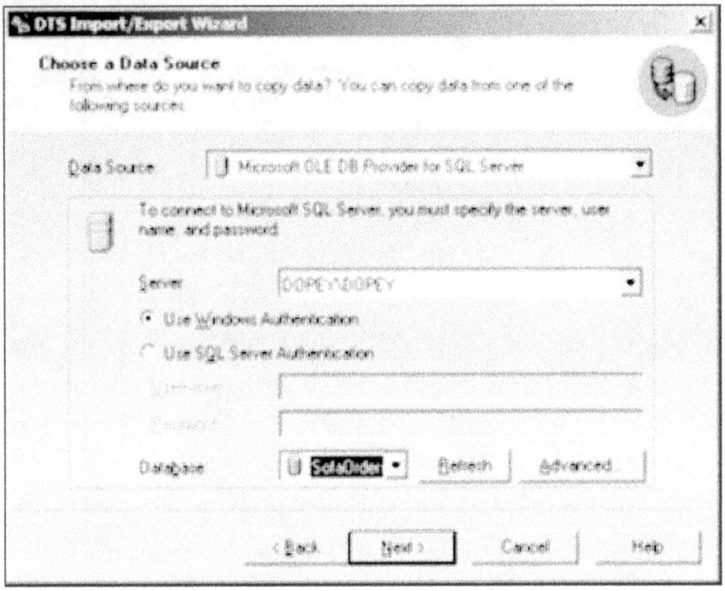


- Select Copy table(s) and view(s) from the source database. Select Next:

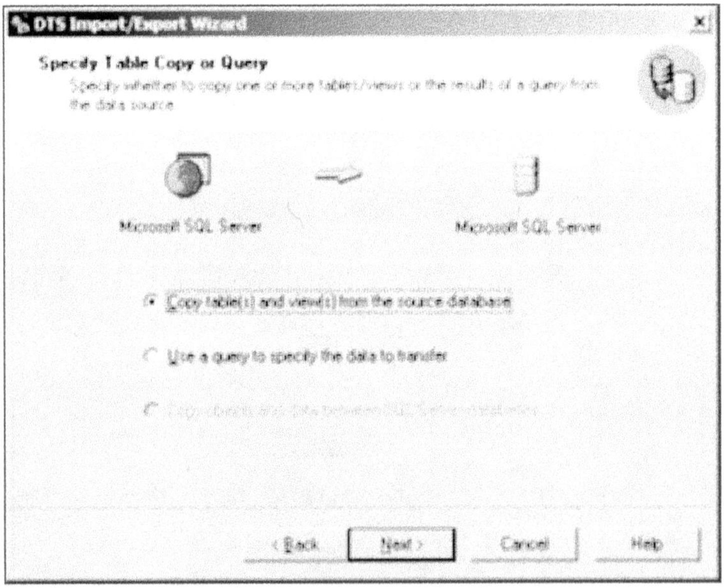


- Select each table or view from which you wish to transfer. Unlike SQL Server 7.0/2000 transfers to SQL Server 2000, there are no advanced options for bringing over schemas for your tables. In addition to this, your tables will be overlaid by the process of migrating data, so you should recreate from your original scripted database any triggers, constraints, indexes, and the like, that may have been dropped during the transfer. Select Next:

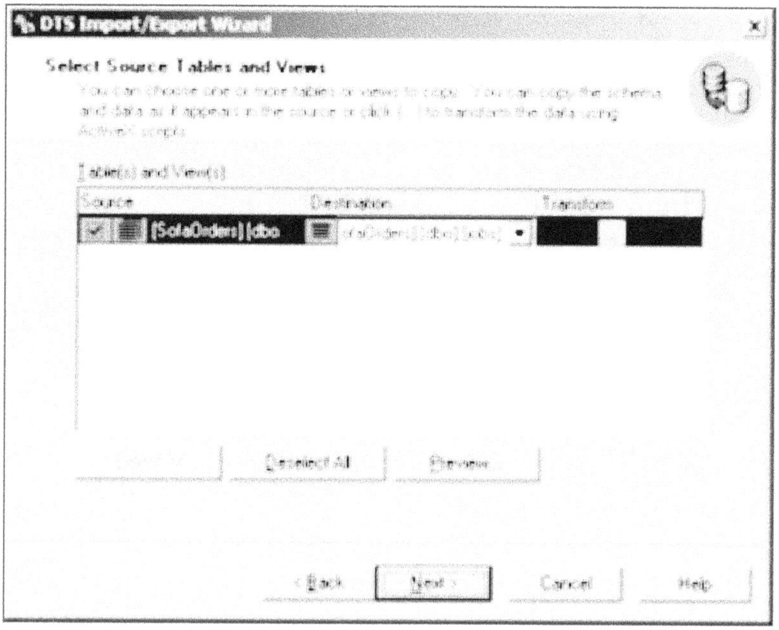


- ❑ Select Run Immediately, then Next:

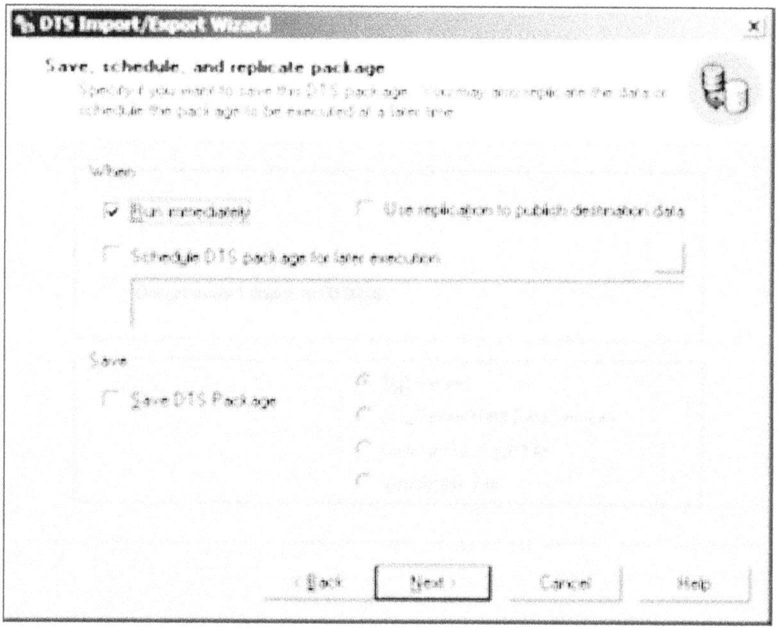


- ❑ Select Finish to start the transfer.
- ❑ You should see a dialog box upon completion indicating success, and green check marks by each table transferred:

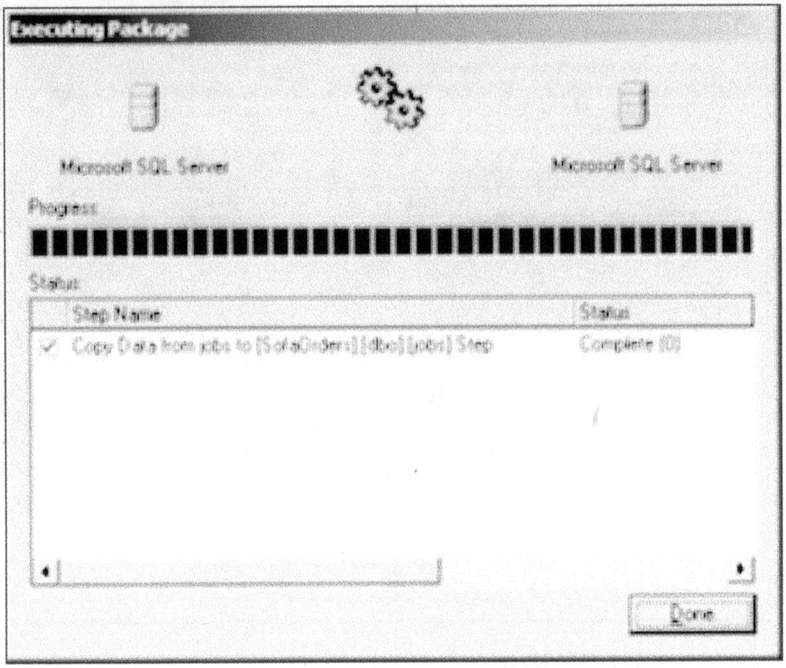

- Apply the remaining scripts you generated from SQL Server 6.5 to your SQL Server 2000 database. Be careful not to drop the tables you transferred over; rather just apply the remaining objects, including the objects dependent on those data tables. Test your logins and users to make sure they have the proper permissions to the database and objects.

# 1.25 How to... Migrate Data from Microsoft Access

DTS makes it easy to extract from several OLE DB and ODBC data sources. Microsoft Access is no exception.

To import data from Microsoft Access, follow these steps:

- In Enterprise Manager, expand Server Group and registration for the destination server.
- Expand the Databases folder and right-click the database into which you are importing data.
- Select All Tasks | Import Data.
- Select Next at the DTS Import/Export Wizard screen.
- For Data Source, select Microsoft Access. For file name, select the `*.mdb` source database. Before selecting Next, make sure **no one else** is using this database. Select Next:

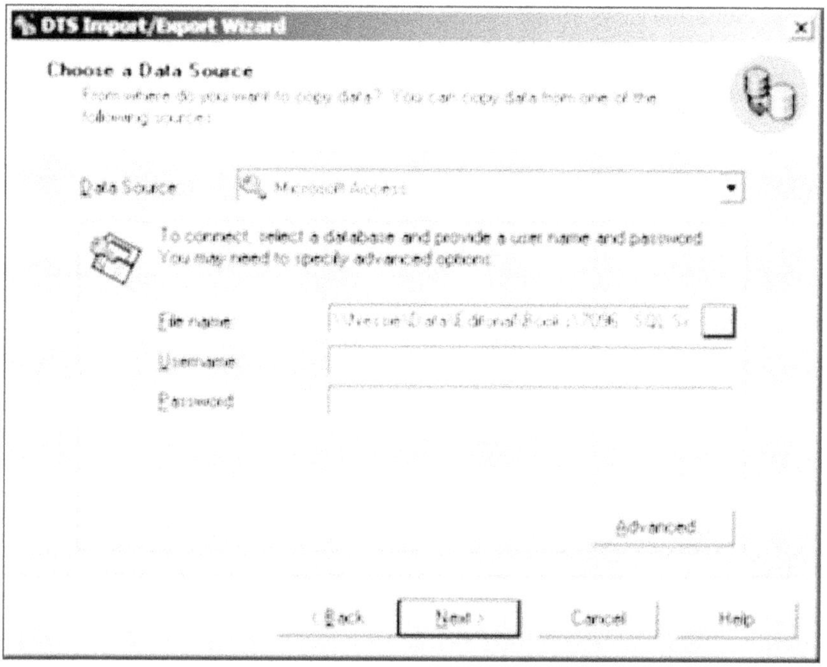


- Select your destination server, login, and database. Select Next:

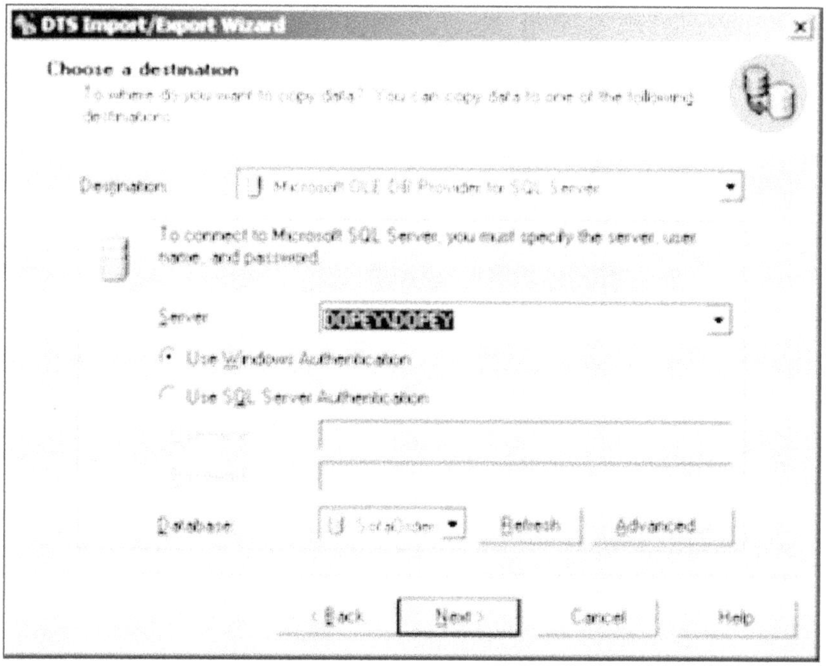

- Select copy tables and views from the source database. Select Next:

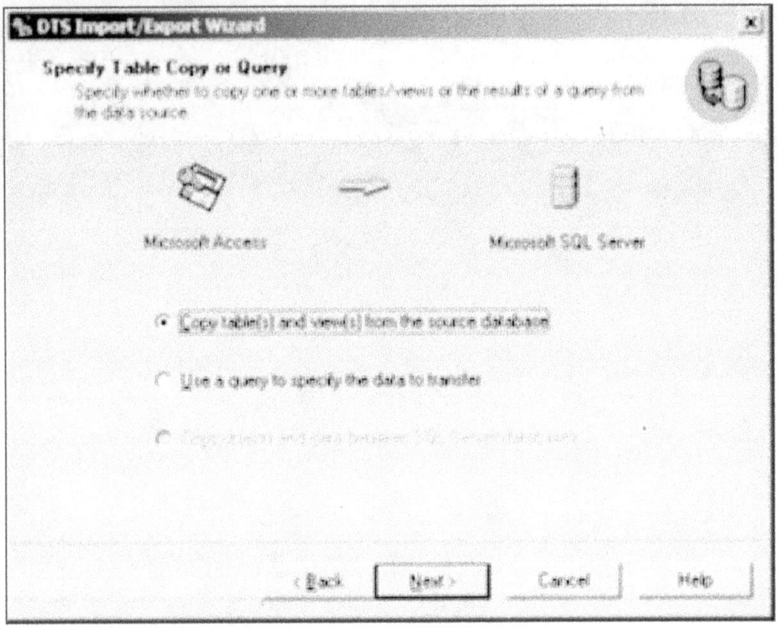


- Select the tables you wish to import, and the associated destination tables. If you press the Transform button, you have more advanced options for mapping data types, and columns:

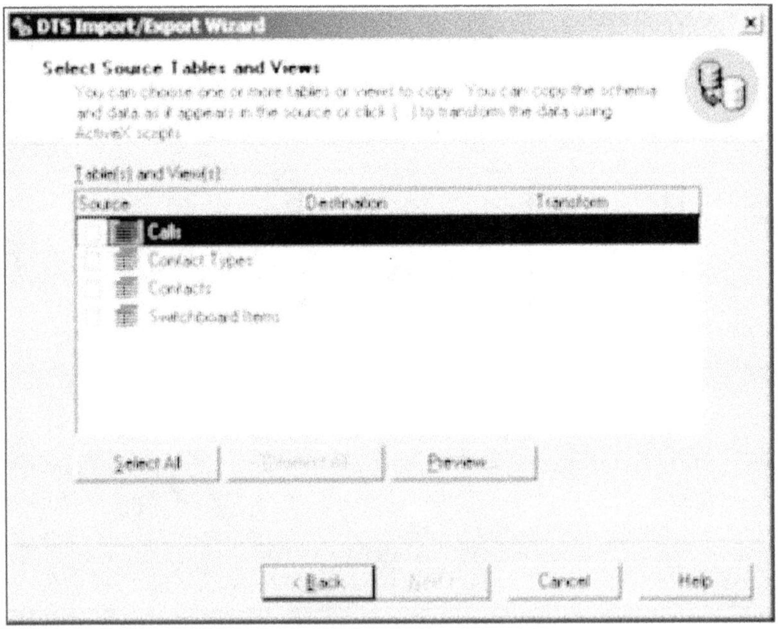


You can also choose whether to append the rows to the table, to delete the table rows in the destination table, or to create a new table altogether:

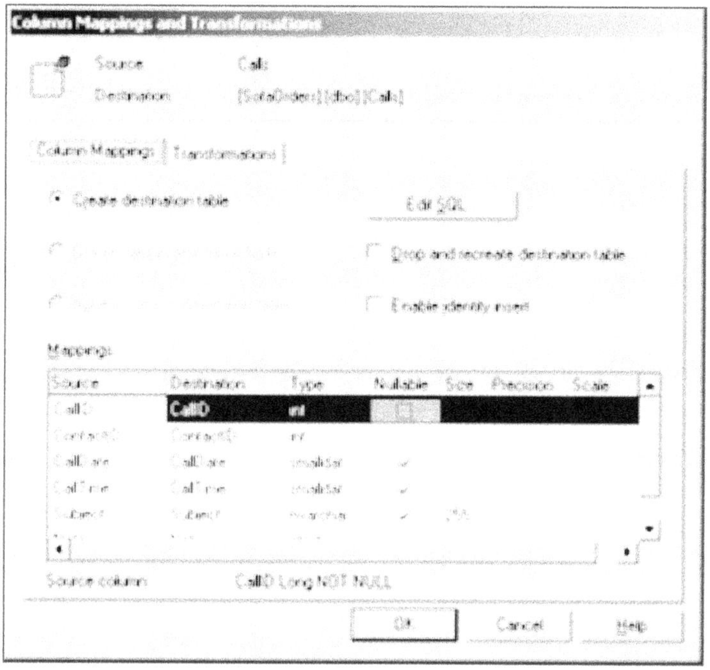


- You can also create Visual Basic transformation scripts in the Transformations tab if you need to do data cleansing prior to importing the rows. This means you can use the VBScript programming language (PerlScript or JScript if you prefer), to modify the data as it is transferred from the source to the destination:

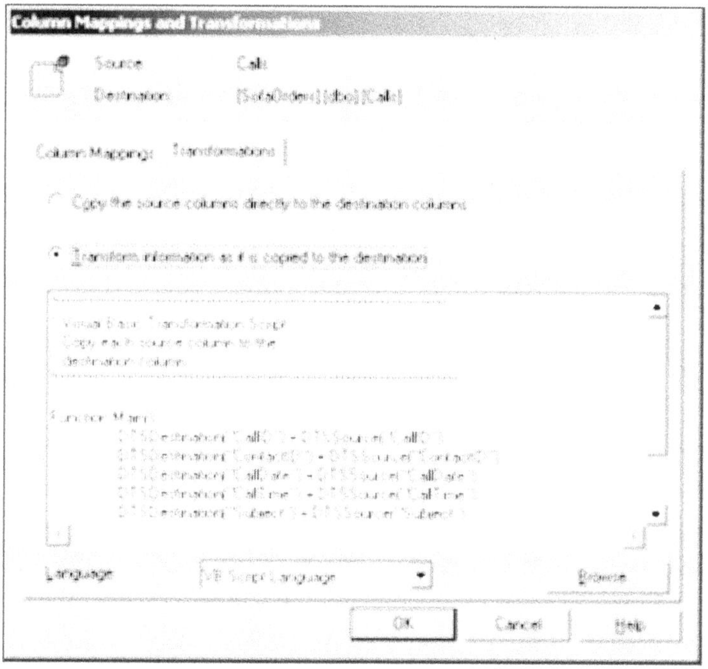

- After verifying (or modifying) the VB Script transformation code, select Next.
- Select Run Immediately, then Next.
- Select Finish to begin the transfer.
- Once the transfer has finished you should be told whether the transfer was a success. You will also see green check marks by each successful table transfer.

# 1.26 How to... Migrate Data from Microsoft Excel

To import data from a Microsoft Excel file, follow these steps:

- In Enterprise Manager, expand Server Group and registration for the destination server.
- Expand the Databases folder and right-click the database into which you are importing data.
- Select All Tasks | Import Data.
- Select Next at the DTS Import/Export Wizard screen.
- Select Microsoft Excel 97-2000 for the Data Source, and the location of the File name you wish to import. Select Next:

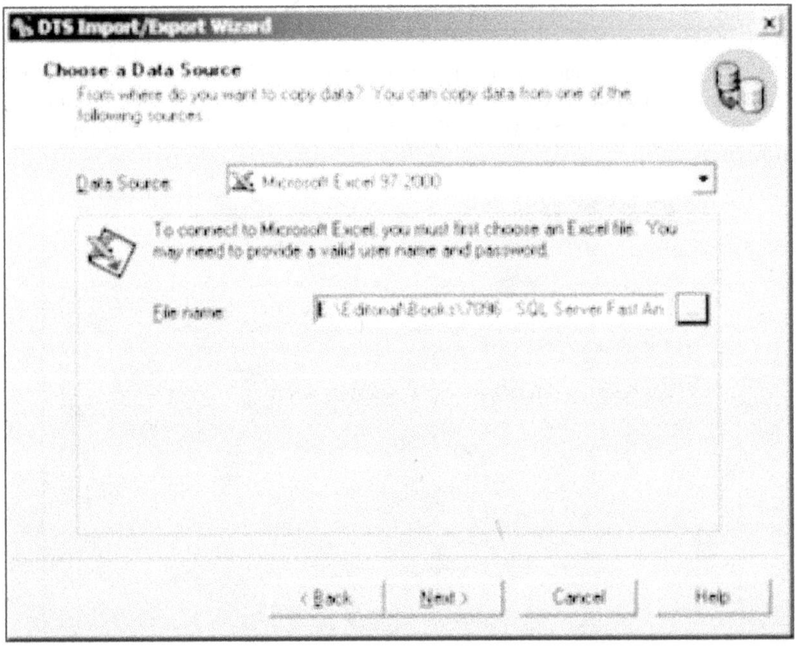


- Select the destination server, connection login, and database. Select Next.
- Select copy tables and views from the source database. Select Next.
- Each sheet in a spreadsheet is treated like a table. Select the sheets you wish to import. For the destination table name, you can overwrite Sheet1 with a more user-friendly entity name:

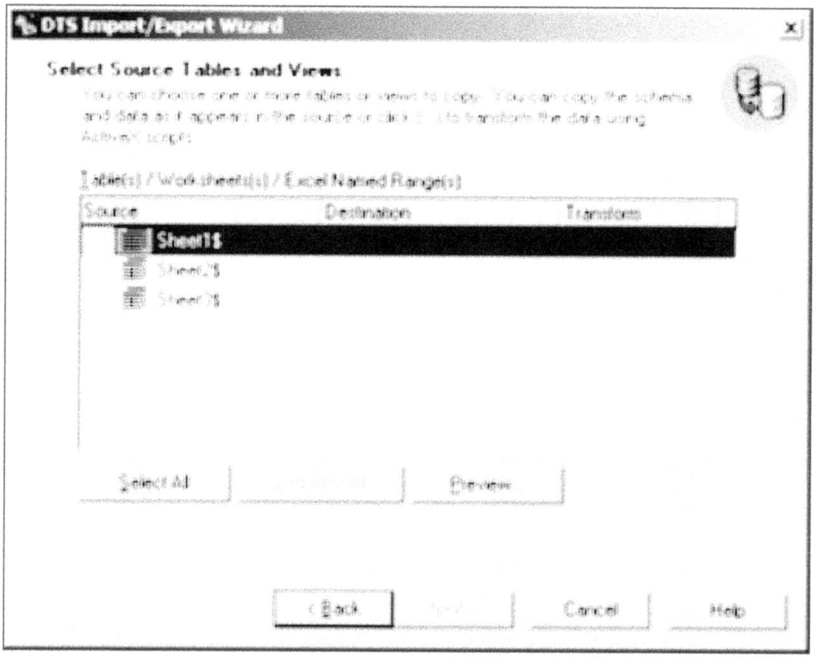

- As with Microsoft Access, you can use the Transform button to modify the behavior of the import (do column mapping, apply extraction transformations in Visual Basic, and so on). Select Next when you have finished.
- Select Run immediately.
- Select Finish.
- Execute a query in Query Analyzer to verify if the data imported properly. For example:

```
SELECT *
FROM dbo.USPresidents
```

You may encounter a problem when importing data from Excel for columns exceeding 255 characters in length. Microsoft Knowledge Base Article Q28157, *PRB: Transfer of Data from Jet 4.0LEDB Source Fails with Buffer Overflow Error*, examines this issue and workaround in more detail.

# 2

# Configuring SQL Server

This chapter explains how to view, understand, and modify the various SQL Server configurable settings. Collations, often a source of confusion for new and seasoned DBAs alike, will also be reviewed in detail.

## 2.1 How to... Configure Server Options with Enterprise Manager

- Begin by clicking Start | Programs | Microsoft SQL Server | Enterprise Manager.
- Expand the SQL Server Group containing the server you wish to configure.
- Right-click and select Properties for the server you wish to configure.
- The SQL Server Properties dialog box appears with tabs General, Memory, Processor, Security, Connections, Server Settings, Database Settings, and Replication. These tabs contain a subset of the available server configurations:

# 2.2 How to... Configure and View Server Options with sp_configure

I recommend you memorize the `sp_configure` stored procedure and the `RECONFIGURE` command. Although you can configure **some** server options in Enterprise Manager, **all** configurable server options may be set with `sp_configure`. We will review each configuration and its associated syntax later in this chapter. The basic syntax for `sp_configure` is as follows:

## Syntax

```
sp_configure  @configname = 'name'  ,  @configvalue = 'value'
```

## Arguments

`@configname` is the name of the server option. Its data type is `VARCHAR(35)`. We'll be reviewing each server option later on.

`@configvalue` is the **new** configuration value for the setting referenced in `@configname`. Its data type is `INT`.

Both arguments have a default of `NULL`. When `sp_configure` is run without arguments, an alphabetical list of server configurations is returned, as displayed in the following diagram:

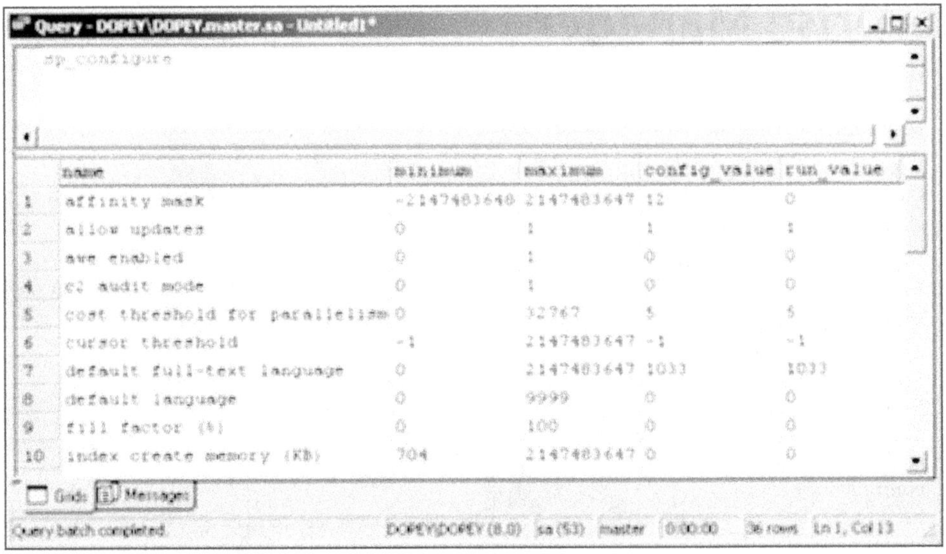

The output is broken down thus:

| Column | Description |
|---|---|
| `name` | The name of the server configuration. |
| `minimum` | The minimum value of the configuration option. |
| `maximum` | The maximum value of the configuration option. |
| `config_value` | The value to which the server configuration was last set. |
| `run_value` | The run-time value of the configuration. Some server configurations do not take effect until the SQL Server service has been restarted. Therefore, if you see a `config_value` that is different from the `run_value`, this indicates that the SQL Server service must be restarted in order for the new value to take effect. |

Executing `sp_configure` with the `run_value` equal to 0, means that only basic server options will be returned. To display advanced server options, type the following into Query Analyzer:

```
USE master
EXEC sp_configure 'show advanced option', 1
RECONFIGURE WITH OVERRIDE
EXEC sp_configure
```

This query returns:

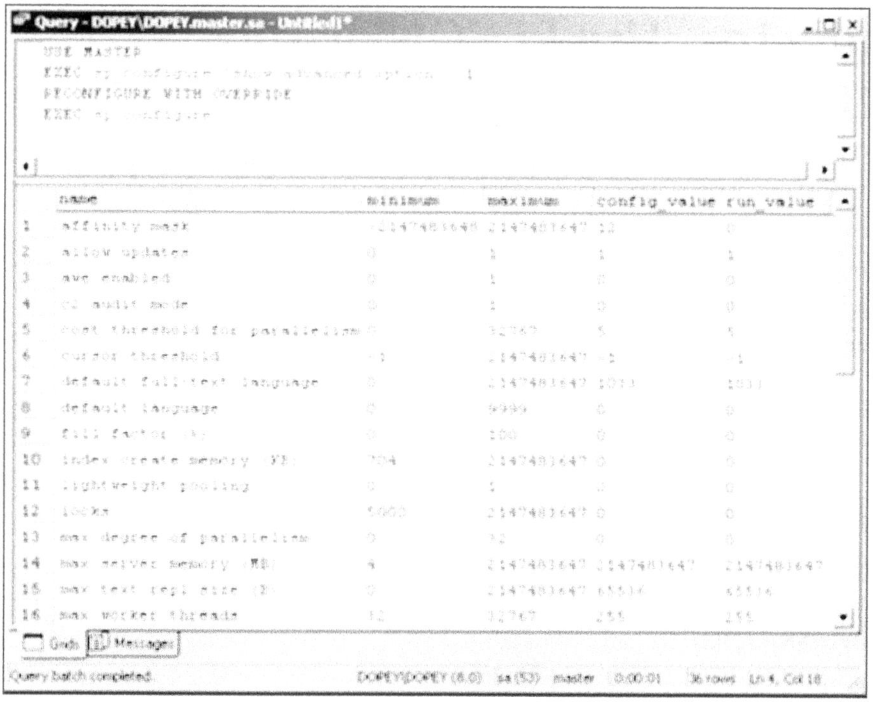

The full list of server options will be displayed. I prefer outputting these results to grid format as they can be copied easily to a spreadsheet. Rows are output more quickly in grid mode than in text mode, as text mode requires Query Analyzer to align and pad each column prior to outputting the results. To set your results to grid format, go to the Query menu and select Results in Grid. To copy the results, click the top-left box of the results (between the name column header and the row 1 boxes). This will select the results that you can then copy and paste to a spreadsheet application, such as Microsoft Excel.

Remember to set off advanced options by typing the following into Query Analyzer:

```
USE master
EXEC sp_configure 'show advanced option', 0
RECONFIGURE WITH OVERRIDE
```

Important facts on `sp_configure`:

- All users by default can run `sp_configure` with no parameters or just the `name` parameter. A good reason to disable `show advanced option` is to keep server configuration details private from the power users. If you wish to disable this access, enter and execute the following command in Query Analyzer:

```
DENY EXEC ON sp_configure TO public
```

- Executing `sp_configure` with both parameters by default is only allowed for the `sysadmin` and `serveradmin` fixed server roles. The same applies to the `RECONFIGURE` command.

# 2.3 How to... Use RECONFIGURE WITH OVERRIDE

`RECONFIGURE WITH OVERRIDE` is used to set runtime values to the new configuration value. This option disables configuration value checking (for invalid or values that aren't recommended) for the following options:

- Allow updates
- Recovery interval
- Time slice

Using `RECONFIGURE WITH OVERRIDE` with other server options will not cause value checking to be disabled (that is, invalid values will still return an error).

# 2.4 How to... Configure Server Options

This section describes the various options available when configuring your server.

## Affinity Mask Option

The affinity mask option allows you to set the number of processors that SQL Server can use. This is an advanced option, and requires a server restart to take effect.

### *Recommendations*

Under very busy conditions, a thread (activity) in a process may move from processor to processor, reloading the processor cache each time, which produces overhead. This is called **context switching**.

To identify context switching on your SQL Server instance, use Windows Performance Monitor (for information on **how** to use Performance Monitor, see Chapter 17 and Microsoft's MSDN site article *Collecting Performance Data*, found on http://msdn.microsoft.com/library/default.asp?url=/library/en-us/dnduwon/html/d5collection.asp).

View the Performance object `System`, and the counter `Context Switches/sec`. Prolonged values of more than 5000 switches/sec may indicate a problem.

By binding a processor to a thread (processor affinity), you can decrease the reloading of the processor cache. However, it is **not** recommended that you use this option, as it decreases the operating system's flexibility to select the most available processor for scheduling threads. If you do decide to configure this option, do extensive load testing and observe the overall performance of the system under peak loads. This should reveal the most suitable configuration for your environment.

### *Enterprise Manager SQL Server Properties*

- In the SQL Server Properties dialog box go to the Processor tab.
- In the Processor control section, select which processors SQL Server can use.

You will be prompted that the changes will not take effect until the SQL Server service has been restarted. Select Yes or No, based on when you wish to implement the change.

### *Command Syntax*

First decide what sort of binding you wish to perform. Your choices are:

| Decimal Value | SQL Server Threads Bound to Processors |
|---|---|
| 1 | 0 (first processor) |
| 3 | 0 and 1 |
| 7 | 0, 1, and 2 |
| 15 | 0, 1, 2, and 3 |
| 31 | 0, 1, 2, 3, and 4 |
| 63 | 0, 1, 2, 3, 4, and 5 |
| 127 | 0, 1, 2, 3, 4, 5, and 6 |

As an example, if we had a 4-processor system and wished to restrict use of SQL Server to the first three processors, we would run:

```
sp_configure 'show advanced options', 1
RECONFIGURE WITH OVERRIDE
GO
```

```
USE master
EXEC sp_configure 'affinity mask', 7
RECONFIGURE
GO
```

If you then run `sp_configure` you will see the `config_value` as 7 and `run_value` as 0 (assuming the default configuration). You must restart SQL Server to instantiate this change.

## Allow Updates Option

This option allows users with proper permissions to modify the system tables. The default is 0, which means system table updates are not allowed. This is a basic option and does not require the SQL Server service to be restarted.

### *Recommendations*

Only enable this option under limited circumstances and **always** disable it after completion of your system table modifications. A lot of damage can be done if users have permissions to modify the system tables.

### *Enterprise Manager SQL Server Properties*

In the SQL Server Properties dialog box, go to the Server Settings tab.

In the Server behavior section, check Allow modifications to be made directly to the system catalogs to enable, and uncheck it again to disable.

### *Command Syntax*

```
sp_configure 'allow updates', '1'
RECONFIGURE WITH OVERRIDE
GO
```

## AWE Enabled Option

AWE stands for Address Windowing Extensions and allows applications to use physical memory beyond 4GB. It is supported on SQL Server 2000 Enterprise Edition, and allows memory support of up to 8GB on Windows 2000 Advanced Server and 64 GB on Windows 2000 Datacenter Server. By enabling AWE, SQL Server will use almost all the available memory on your system up to the limit specified for maximum server memory (if configured). This is an advanced option, and requires a SQL Server service restart.

### *Recommendations*

If you have more than 4GB of RAM and are not sharing the server with other memory-hungry applications (I would **always** recommend a dedicated database server), then it is recommended that you set AWE enabled to 1. Important items to remember:

- You must add `/PAE` to your `boot.ini` file if your OS uses between 4GB and 16GB of RAM.
- To reserve 1GB of virtual memory for the operating system, add the `/3GB` flag, so append `/3GB /PAE` to `boot.ini` as shown below; otherwise the operating system takes 2GB:

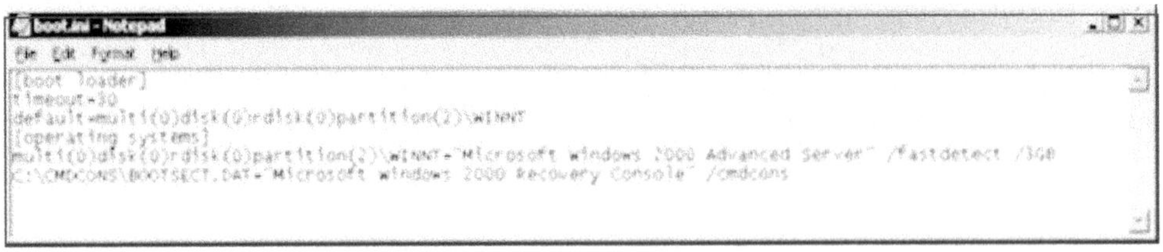

- Above 16GB, **do not** use the `/3GB` switch because Windows 2000 needs to reserve 2 GB for memory above 16GB. Use the `/PAE` switch.
- The `awe enabled` option will be ignored if set for systems with less than 3GB available.
- Only enable this option with SQL Server 2000 SP2 onwards. Bugs were fixed with regard to latch timeout warnings, slow response time, and `autoexec` stored procedures not executing at startup as they should.
- For AWE to be enabled for SQL Server use, the SQL Server Service account must have permissions to lock pages in memory. This is given automatically if you assign the Service account in Enterprise Manager; however if you start up SQL Server in a command prompt that was not assigned this way, you must explicitly assign this privilege using the Group Policy tool. For a review of how to use the Group Policy snap-in, see Microsoft's article *Step-by-Step Guide to Understanding the Group Policy Feature Set*, at http://www.microsoft.com/windows2000/techinfo/planning/management/groupsteps.asp.
- Each instance on your server must have maximum server memory set. The sum of all SQL Server instances' maximum server memory should ideally leave a minimum of 128MB of RAM for the operating system, assuming this is a dedicated SQL Server implementation. If you are sharing your server with other applications (not recommended), reserve more memory based on the needs of the application; the same goes for failover clusters. For example, an active/active failover cluster has one instance staying on each node. However, in a failover situation with AWE enabled, the sum of the two instances' max server memory **must** be less than the total physical memory available on one node (less the OS memory needs and other applications). See Chapter 10 for more information on failover clustering.
- Do review Microsoft's Knowledge base article *Q274750, HOW TO: Configure Memory for More Than 2 GB in SQL Server.*

### Enterprise Manager SQL Server Properties

Not configurable in Enterprise Manager.

### Command Syntax

```
sp_configure 'show advanced options', 1
RECONFIGURE WITH OVERRIDE
GO

sp_configure 'awe enabled', 1
RECONFIGURE
GO
```

## C2 Audit Mode Option

This option enables monitoring of all access attempts on database objects and is based on a certified government rating ensuring that resources are secured and have sufficient auditing enabled. The auditing information is written to a trace file located in the `\mssql\data` directory for default SQL Server instances, and the `\mssql$instancename\data` for named instances. This file grows quite rapidly with even minor activity. The trace files are rolled over to a new file every 200MB, and new files are created on each SQL Server restart. SQL Server shuts down if physical space runs out for the trace file. If this occurs, you must either free up space prior to restarting the SQL Server service, or restart SQL Server in minimal mode (using the command prompt, designating `sqlservr -c -f -s {instancename}`). Once logged in, you can then remove C2 auditing until you can free up the required space.

This is an advanced option, and requires a SQL Server service restart.

### Recommendations

If your database server requires C2 certified security, you must enable this option, otherwise the physical disk space required for even minor OLTP databases may be cost-prohibitive. The logging itself can produce significant performance impact.

### Enterprise Manager SQL Server Properties

Not configurable in Enterprise Manager.

### Command Syntax

```
sp_configure 'show advanced options', 1
RECONFIGURE WITH OVERRIDE
GO

sp_configure 'c2 audit mode', 1
RECONFIGURE
GO
```

## Cost threshold for Parallelism Option

This option sets in seconds the cost threshold used by SQL Server when determining whether to use a serial or parallel execution plan. This option is used only if your server has multiple processors and parallelism is enabled (see the *Max Degree of Parallelism Option* section later on). You may set this threshold from 0 to 32767 seconds. The default is 5 seconds. This is an advanced option, and does not require a restart of the SQL Server service.

### Recommendations

You may want to consider increasing this number if you find that a few complex and long-running queries are tying up your server's processors. Test changes to this configuration in your development or test server first. For your test to be valid, your test environment's database(s), hardware, and SQL Server configurations should be **exactly** the same as those in your production environment.

### Enterprise Manager SQL Server Properties

- In the SQL Server Properties dialog box go to the Processor tab.
- In the Parallelism section, adjust the number beside the Minimum query plan threshold for considering queries for parallel execution (cost estimate): label.

### Command Syntax

```
sp_configure 'show advanced options', 1
RECONFIGURE WITH OVERRIDE
GO

sp_configure 'cost threshold for parallelism', 6
RECONFIGURE WITH OVERRIDE
GO
```

## Cross DB Ownership Chaining

The Cross DB Ownership Chaining option has been introduced in SQL Server 2000 Service pack 3, to enable you to use cross-database security. Cross-database ownership chaining occurs when a source database object depends on objects in other databases. When the source database object and the target objects in the target databases are owned by the same login account, and cross-database ownership chaining is enabled, SQL Server will not check permissions on the target objects. The database user names can be different; if the login mapped to the user is the same, security is not re-verified.

When this option is on, cross-database ownership chaining is enabled for all databases. If it is disabled, you can still enable this option for individual user databases.

### *Recommendations*

Microsoft does not recommend this option because of its security implications. When this option is enabled, database owners (`dbo` users or members of `db_owner`), members of the `db_ddladmin` role, or those with `CREATE DATABASE` permissions should only be highly trusted individuals, as they can potentially reference objects in other databases should they create objects owned by other users, or create or attach database. Roles such as `db_owner` and `db_ddladmin`, as well as permissions are discussed in detail in Chapter 7.

### *Enterprise Manager SQL Server Properties*

- In the SQL Server Properties dialog box go to the Security tab.
- In the Ownership chaining section, select the checkbox next to Allow cross-database ownership chaining, to enable this option.

### *Command Syntax*

```
sp_configure 'show advanced options', 1
RECONFIGURE WITH OVERRIDE
GO


sp_configure 'Cross DB Ownership Chaining', 1
RECONFIGURE WITH OVERRIDE
GO
```

## Cursor Threshold Option

This option controls whether SQL Server allows the user to fetch rows from a cursor while it populates, or makes the user wait until all rows are populated. The default is -1, and means users must wait until all rows are returned to the cursor. Setting this option to 0 lets the user pre-fetch rows before the cursor row population is finished. Setting to any other positive integer value indicates a row count threshold. If the number of returned rows is greater than this number, users may pre-fetch rows asynchronously (before the query is finished):

| Integer Value | Cursor Type |
|---|---|
| -1 | Synchronous (you must wait) |
| 0 | Asynchronous (you can see results prior to completion) |
| > 1 to 2,147,483,647 | Row threshold which, if exceeded, will trigger an asynchronous setting |

This is an advanced option, and does not require a restart of the SQL Server service.

### Recommendations

Large result sets benefit from asynchronous cursor population. Experiment in a test environment to see what setting provides the best performance. Adding a row value may provide some benefit over the all or nothing -1 and 0 settings.

### Enterprise Manager SQL Server Properties

Not configurable in Enterprise Manager.

### Command Syntax

The following is an example of setting the cursor threshold to 50,000 rows. If the cursor exceeds this row count, asynchronous reads will be allowed:

```
sp_configure 'show advanced options', 1
RECONFIGURE WITH OVERRIDE
GO

sp_configure 'cursor threshold', 50000
RECONFIGURE WITH OVERRIDE
GO
```

## Default Full-Text Language Option

This option designates the default language used for full-text indexed columns when no language has been specified with `sp_fulltext_column` (procedure that adds columns to the table's full-text index). The option itself defaults to the language of the server.

This is an advanced option, and does not require a restart of the SQL Server service.

### Enterprise Manager SQL Server Properties

Not configurable in Enterprise Manager.

### Command Syntax

Linguistic options included with SQL Server 2000 are:

| Language | Setting |
|---|---|
| Neutral | 0 |
| Chinese Traditional | 1028 |
| German | 1031 |
| English US | 1033 |
| French | 1036 |
| Italian | 1040 |
| Japanese | 1041 |

| Language | Setting |
|---|---|
| Korean | 1042 |
| Dutch | 1043 |
| Swedish Default | 1053 |
| Chinese Simplified | 2052 |
| English UK | 2057 |
| Spanish Modern | 3082 |

If you wanted to change the default full-text language to Korean, you would use the following syntax:

```
sp_configure 'show advanced options', '1',
RECONFIGURE WITH OVERRIDE
GO

sp_configure 'default full-text language', 1042
RECONFIGURE WITH OVERRIDE
GO
```

## Default Language Option

This option sets the default language for all new logins if not explicitly designated using `sp_addlogin` or `sp_defaultlanguage`. The default language of a login connection dictates what language is used to return SQL Server error messages stored in `master.dbo.sysmessages`. This is a basic option, and does not require a restart of the SQL Server service.

### *Enterprise Manager SQL Server Properties*

- In the SQL Server Properties configuration dialog box, go to the Server Settings tab.
- In the Default language section, select the default language for users from the drop-down box.

### *Command Syntax*

The language ID used to configure this option is found in the `syslanguages` table in the master database. Run the following query to show `langid` and associated language:

```
SELECT langid, alias, name FROM master.dbo.syslanguages ORDER BY alias
```

So the Finnish language, for example, has a `langid` of 10, a US English name of `Finnish`, and actual language name of `Suomi`.

If you wanted to set the language to Finnish, you would use the following syntax:

```
sp_configure 'default full-text language', 10
RECONFIGURE WITH OVERRIDE
GO
```

## Error Reporting

The error reporting server option allows you to enable automatic error reporting for your SQL Server instance when a fatal error occurs. The data is sent to Microsoft over a secure connection, or to your Corporate Error Reporting server. (See http://oca.microsoft.com/en/Cerintro.asp for more information on setting up such a server for your enterprise.)

### Recommendations

Microsoft does not use this functionality to collect personal information, but rather for product improvement purposes. Data collected includes the condition of SQL Server at the time of the error, operating system and hardware information, digital product ID, the computer's IP address, and information from memory or files regarding the process that caused the error.

### Enterprise Manager SQL Server Properties

- In the SQL Server Properties dialog box go to the General tab.
- In the Error Reporting section, select Enable the error reporting feature checkbox to enable.

This option is not configurable using the `sp_configure` system stored procedure.

## Fill Factor Option

Fill factor determines how full each 8k leaf level page should be when a new index is created with existing data rows (see Chapter 3 for a discussion of pages and extents). Leaf level pages belong to the index node containing a **pointer** to the row data or the **actual** row data.

This is an advanced option and requires a restart of the SQL Server service.

### Recommendations

For every fill factor advantage, there is an associated disadvantage. Potential advantages of a higher fill factor are:

- High fill factors take up less space (less index storage).
- Less storage means less I/O activity as it takes fewer reads to extract rows.
- Excellent for low-write activity databases.

Potential disadvantages of a higher fill factor are:

- Page splits. Page splitting occurs when there is no more room for data in the index pages. When a new row must be inserted, SQL Server will relocate half the rows to a new index page to make room. This new page will most likely not be contiguous (located near the same extent) and, therefore, cause non-sequential I/O access when referencing the index pages.

Potential advantages of a lower fill factor are:

- Less page splitting, which benefits write activity.
- Benefits tables with high-write ratios in general.

Potential disadvantages to a lower fill factor are:

- Extra storage overhead. If you have 1 million rows on a wide column and decrease your fill factor to 50 from 100, your data file space usage will increase significantly.
- Non-contiguous data pages cause non-sequential I/O activity.
- Higher space usage translates to more data pages used in the buffer cache, potentially knocking other data pages out.

The best way to determine fill factor is to become familiar with your database schema, activity, hot spots (most active tables), and indexes. Do not assume that performance will benefit without testing the fill factor in your development environment. Here are some guidelines:

- Monitor page splits per second in Performance Monitor, using the counter SQL Server:Access Methods Page Splits/sec. This counter is only meaningful in the context of your environment. A disadvantage to this counter is that it measures activity at the server level, which means one large table could be responsible for the averages you see.

  This counter, however, can be used in the context of others, such as the SQLServer:SQL Statistics Batch Requests/sec counter, which monitors how much activity is hitting your server. You can then correlate this number to your Page Splits/sec to see whether page splits are widespread or centered around a certain time period or data load.
- Determine your read/write ratio by monitoring PhysicalDisk % Disk Read Time, and % Disk Write time.
- Keep in mind table size; a larger table encountering page splits has more of an I/O performance drag than high page splits on a small table.
- If you decide to change fill factor, then monitor total server performance, not just page splits per second; this is necessary because a lower fill factor may slow down query response time but decrease page splits. A higher fill factor may increase page splits but increase query performance.

To summarize in a table:

| Fill Factor Setting | Less I/O | Higher I/O | Better Reads | Better Writes |
|---|---|---|---|---|
| Lower fill factor | | X | | X |
| Higher fill factor | X | | X | |

Information on value settings:

| Fill Factor Setting | Description |
|---|---|
| 0 | This is the default. Leaf pages of the index are full. Some room is left in the upper level of the index tree. |
| 100 | All index node levels are filled 100%. Best for read-only tables. |
| 1 - 99 | Percentage full for leaf node level. |

Set the fill factor with this option only if you believe there will be uniformity in table structure across the database. Otherwise, keep the default, and set individual fill factors when creating the indexes.

Be careful with your optimization job in the Database Maintenance plans. You are given the option of reorganizing pages with the original amount of free space, or changing to a free space percentage designated in the Change free space per page percentage to: field.

If you explicitly designated a fill factor when creating your indexes, selecting Change free space per page percentage to: will invalidate your original settings. In either case, plan on selecting one of the options provided by Reorganize data and index pages on the Optimizations tab. See section in Chapter 6 on database maintenance plans. Below is a screenshot of the Optimizations tab:

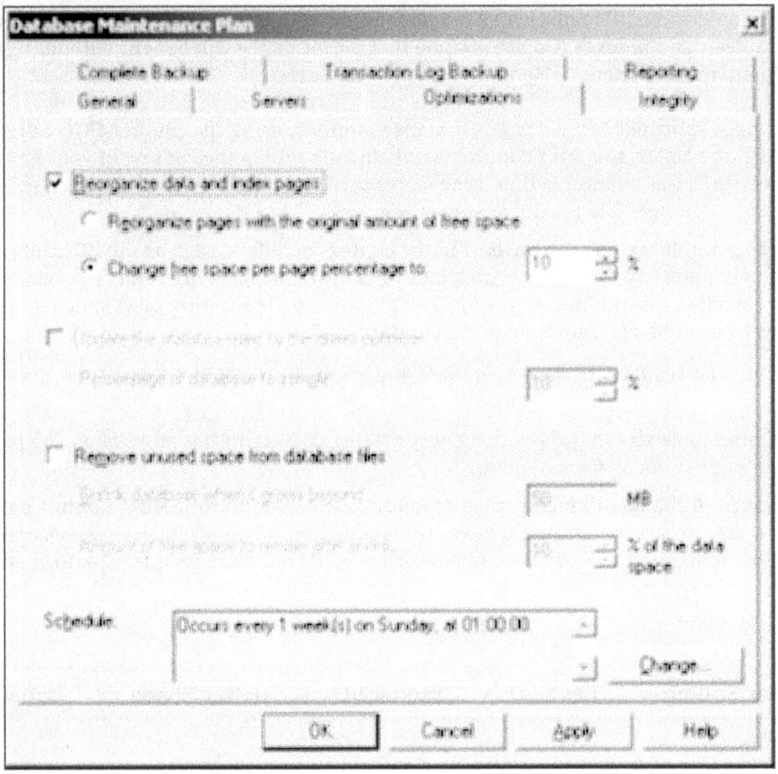


### *Enterprise Manager SQL Server Properties*

- ❑ In the SQL Server Properties configuration dialog box, go to the Database Settings tab.
- ❑ In the Settings section, select the checkbox Fixed and choose a percentage default index fill factor on the slider for use when rebuilding indexes.

### *Command Syntax*

The following is an example of setting the fill factor option to 70%:

```
sp_configure 'show advanced options', '1'
RECONFIGURE WITH OVERRIDE
GO
```

```
sp_configure 'fill factor', '70'
RECONFIGURE WITH OVERRIDE
GO
```

## Index Create Memory Option

This option allows you to set the number of kilobytes reserved for index creation sorts.

This is an advanced option which does not require a restart of the SQL Server service, and is self-configuring.

### *Recommendations*

Leave this alone unless you have a compelling reason to adjust it. The default for this option is 0, which means it configures itself. Microsoft recommends increasing this if you have index creation problems (involving very large indexes).

### *Enterprise Manager SQL Server Properties*

Not configurable in Enterprise Manager.

### *Command Syntax*

In this example we will change the index create memory reserved to 1000KB or 1MB.

```
sp_configure 'show advanced options', '1'
RECONFIGURE WITH OVERRIDE
GO

sp_configure 'index create memory', 1000
RECONFIGURE WITH OVERRIDE
GO
```

## Lightweight Pooling Option

When this option is enabled on multiprocessor systems, SQL Server switches to **fiber mode** scheduling, which can reduce context switches (a costly operation where one thread/process moves from one processor to another). Fibers are less costly as they do not need to change from system kernel mode (basic system operations) to user mode.

This is an advanced option, and requires a restart of the SQL Server service.

### *Recommendations*

This is recommended for servers with excessive context switching and four or more processors. However, as of the time of writing, Microsoft has published two articles detailing circumstances where lightweight pooling should not be used; the conditions are:

- Using Distributed Transaction Coordinator; Microsoft strongly recommends you disable this option. For more details, see Microsoft Knowledge Base article *Q303287, BUG: DTC Transactions May Fail When SQL Server Is Running in Lightweight Pooling Mode.*
- MAPI and SQLMail are not supported if you have lightweight pooling enabled. The thread scheduling of these two technologies causes SQLMail to hang. For more details, see Microsoft Knowledge Base article *Q308604, PRB: SQLMail Is Not Supported When You Run the Server in Fiber Mode.*

To identify context switching, use Performance Monitor and the System:Context Switches/sec counter (see the *Affinity Mask option* description for a reference to this counter). If you also have a high CPU processor time % (greater than 70% average) and context switches/sec exceeds 5000-8000, then you most probably have a context-switching problem. Explore lightweight pooling only if you do not use DTC, SQLMail, or MAPI functionality.

### *Enterprise Manager SQL Server Properties*

Not configurable in Enterprise Manager.

### *Command Syntax*

To enable lightweight pooling:

```
sp_configure 'show advanced options', '1'
RECONFIGURE WITH OVERRIDE
GO

sp_configure 'lightweight pooling', '1'
RECONFIGURE WITH OVERRIDE
GO
```

## Locks Option

This option determines the maximum number of locks (96 bytes per lock) allowed on the SQL Server instance. The default is 0, which means locks are dynamically allocated and de-allocated. The default works as follows:

| Scenario | Action |
|---|---|
| SQL Server startup | 2% of allocated memory is reserved for the lock pool. |
| The initial pool is exhausted | The lock pool allocates up to 40% of available memory. |
| More memory is required than available but max server memory **has not** been reached | SQL Server allocates the memory to fulfill the lock requests. |
| More memory is required than available but max server memory **has** been reached | SQL Server does not allocate more memory to the lock pool. If this occurs, you may receive Error 1204, 'The SQL Server cannot obtain a LOCK resource at this time. Rerun your statement when there are fewer active users or ask the system administrator to check the SQL Server lock and memory configuration'. |

This is an advanced option, requires a restart of the SQL Server service, and is self-configuring (meaning in most cases it should be left alone).

### *Recommendations*

SQL Server should manage the number of locks allowed. If you get errors warning that you have run out of locks, increasing their number may help you. You may see more of a benefit, however, from understanding what is causing so many locks; increasing available memory and looking at your locking strategy may be a better long-term solution.

### *Enterprise Manager SQL Server Properties*

Not configurable in Enterprise Manager.

### *Command Syntax*

In this example we will allow a maximum of 500MB worth of locks. If there are 96 bytes for each lock, this will result in 5,461,333 locks. Let's bring this down to a clean 5,000,000 locks allowed.

```
sp_configure 'show advanced options', '1'
RECONFIGURE WITH OVERRIDE
GO

sp_configure 'locks', 5000000
RECONFIGURE WITH OVERRIDE
GO
```

## Max Degree of Parallelism Option

This option allows you to limit the number of processors used in parallel plan execution. The value settings are as follows:

| Setting | Description |
|---|---|
| Set to 0 | All available processors (up to 32) are used |
| Set to 1 | Parallelism is disabled |
| Set 2 to 32 | Number of processors involved in parallelism |
| Set beyond number of processors you actually have... | All available processors are used (up to 32) |
| If the affinity mask option is enabled... | This restricts the number of CPUs available |

This is an advanced option, and does not require a restart of the SQL Server service.

### *Recommendations*

If your server primarily receives OLTP short-term queries that run in a serial fashion, you may find some benefit in disabling parallelism. By doing so, you reduce the overhead of evaluating the Cost threshold for parallelism option.

If your server often uses parallel query plans, you will want to keep this enabled. Also, if you have 8 or more CPUs on your server you may want to consider setting parallelism to 4 CPUs. This means that although all CPUs can participate in parallelism, only a maximum of 4 CPUs can participate in a query plan. This prevents too many CPUs from participating in one query and slowing down other activity. This option is definitely something that should be tested in a development environment, as each system and application is different. If you encounter parallelism focusing too many CPUs on one query, however, it is worth exploring.

### *Enterprise Manager SQL Server Properties*

- In the SQL Server Properties configuration dialog box, go to the Processor tab.
- In the Parallelism section, the default is Use all available processors. To specify 1 or more processors, select Use and the associated number to the right.

### *Command Syntax*

In this example, a 4-processor limit will be imposed for parallel execution of queries:

```
sp_configure 'show advanced options', '1'
RECONFIGURE WITH OVERRIDE
GO

sp_configure 'max degree of parallelism', 4
RECONFIGURE WITH OVERRIDE
GO
```

## Min and Max Server Memory Options

The min server memory option designates the amount of minimum memory SQL Server's buffer pool may reserve. The max server memory option designates the maximum amount that may be reserved. To summarize how these memory options work:

| Setting | Min Server Memory | Max Server Memory |
|---|---|---|
| Default setting | 0MB | 2147483647MB |
| Minimum allowed setting | 0MB | 4MB |
| Min and Max the same | Translates to fixed memory allocated to buffer pool. Will only take memory needed, but will not relinquish memory once threshold is reached. Set working set size option must be configured afterwards to 1. | Translates to fixed memory allocated to buffer pool. Will only take memory needed, but will not relinquish memory once threshold is reached. Set working set size option must be configured afterwards to 1. |
| Min and max span range of values | Buffer pool only filled to minimum once needed, but once minimum is reached, min memory is not returned to the operating system. | Once minimum server memory threshold is reached, free memory is taken when needed but cannot exceed maximum. |
| AWE enabled instance | | Buffer pool is fully allocated to max server memory threshold on startup. |
| Multiple instances with AWE enabled | | Sum of max memory for all instances must not exceed total physical memory (less OS memory and other application memory needs). |

| Setting | Min Server Memory | Max Server Memory |
|---|---|---|
| Active/Active Failover Clustering | | Sum of max memory for all instances in the active/active cluster must not exceed total physical memory (less OS memory and other application memory needs). |

Min and max server memory are advanced options, do not require a restart of the SQL Server service, and are self-configuring.

### *Recommendations*

Keep memory allocation dynamic if you have a dedicated SQL Server database server. If you **must** share your servers with other applications, here are some suggestions:

| Scenario | Solution | Potential Drawbacks |
|---|---|---|
| If SQL Server is being starved of memory... | Setting min server memory may help. This value set should be based on testing in a development environment. Make sure to conduct a load or stress test that simulates the production environment.<br><br>Several load simulation tools are available, such as Mercury LoadRunner (http://www-svca.mercuryinteractive.com/products/testcenter/supported/), the Database Hammer (included with the SQL Server 2000 Resource Kit), and SQL Profiler (which is free, comes with SQL Server, and can capture loads for later replay). | Setting min server memory could cause other applications to **page**. Paging occurs when an application requires a data page that is not in memory, and is forced to copy the required page into memory then copy another page back to the disk. Paging negatively impacts system performance. |
| If SQL Server is crowding out memory for other applications ... | Setting max server memory may help. Determine memory requirements for other applications to function and factor in average needed for SQL Server. | SQL Server may legitimately need the memory it was taking from those other applications. |

In either case, consider:

- Making your server a dedicated box with only SQL Server on it. SQL Server loves RAM; let it have as much as possible.
- If you must share, add more RAM to the server.

### *Enterprise Manager SQL Server Properties*

- In the SQL Server Properties configuration dialog box, go to the Memory tab.
- In the Memory section move the Minimum (MB) and Maximum (MB) sliders to the values you desire.

### Command Syntax

In this example, we will set the minimum server memory to 128MB and max server memory to 256MB:

```
sp_configure 'show advanced options', '1'
RECONFIGURE WITH OVERRIDE
GO

sp_configure 'min server memory', 128
RECONFIGURE WITH OVERRIDE
GO

sp_configure 'max server memory', 256
RECONFIGURE WITH OVERRIDE
GO
```

## Max Text Repl Size Option

This option sets the maximum bytes of text or image data that can be replicated to a column using `INSERT`, `UPDATE`, `WRITETEXT`, or `UPDATETEXT`. The default value is 65536 bytes, which is 64KB.

This is a basic option, and does not require a restart of the SQL Server service.

### Recommendations

Set this to the largest size you expect to replicate from the publisher. Large text or image chunks can be network bandwidth hogs, so beware!

### Enterprise Manager SQL Server Properties

Not configurable in Enterprise Manager.

### Command Syntax

In this example, we will set the maximum text or image-replicated data to 128KB (128KB * 1024 bytes = 131072 bytes).

```
sp_configure 'max text repl size', 131072
RECONFIGURE WITH OVERRIDE
GO
```

## Max Worker Threads Option

This option designates the maximum worker threads allowed for use by SQL Server; the default is 255. You should understand what threads are, and what their context is in Windows 2000 before thinking about configuring this value. The following points should help you understand threads and their context:

- A **process** is an instance of an application or executable and is a collection of one or more threads.
- A **thread** is a unit of work that can operate in parallel with other units of work. It is an executable part of a process.
- **Threads** can spawn other threads.

- The more **threads**, the more overhead (memory, CPU utilization).
- **Fibers** (see *Lightweight Pooling Option*) share a thread and minimize system overhead. This sharing can cause contention with SQL Server users (SQL Server performance hit).

The following table shows how this setting works with the 255 default:

| Scenario | Action |
|---|---|
| There are 80 user connections. | 80 threads are allocated. |
| New connections are added and await a free thread. | More threads are added, up to the max worker threads option (default 255). |
| 255 connections are exceeded and all available threads are being used. | Thread pooling (sharing the thread) is used, which means that new connections will wait for some of the currently running threads to finish (and become available). |

This is an advanced option, and requires a restart of the SQL Server service.

### Recommendations

You should generally leave this option alone.

Even if you have several user connections, in most implementations not all connections run commands concurrently. So a server with 5000 connections may actually be using 200 threads with concurrent transactions.

Additional threads mean more system resources are used up. Thread pooling means fewer system resources are taken up but there is more potential user contention. You must measure the trade-offs and make sure to implement any changes to your test environment first. Use load testing tools to simulate production on your test environment (Mercury LoadRunner, SQL Server Resource Kit's Database Hammer, or SQL Profiler). Applications should be designed to create connections to SQL Server in a parsimonious fashion, opening connections only when needed, and closing them as soon as possible.

| Scenario | Pros | Cons |
|---|---|---|
| Increasing worker threads | Increases resources for user processes within SQL Server | Takes up extra system resources |
| Limiting worker threads and causing thread pooling | Frees up system resources for other processes | Can cause user query contention and performance hits |

### Enterprise Manager SQL Server Properties

- In the SQL Server Properties configuration dialog box, go to the Processor tab.
- In the Processor control section, modify the Maximum worker threads value.

### Command Syntax

In this example, we will set max worker threads to 200:

```
sp_configure 'show advanced options', 1
RECONFIGURE WITH OVERRIDE
GO

sp_configure 'max worker threads', 200
RECONFIGURE WITH OVERRIDE
GO
```

## Media Retention Option

This option designates the server default for retention time on backup media after they are used in a database or transaction log backup. The default value is 0.

This is an advanced option, and requires a restart of the SQL Server service.

### Recommendations

This setting is excellent for ensuring that your backups do not get overlaid by accident. If you try to overwrite a device, you will get the message, 'The medium on device ['test'] expires on [datetime] and cannot be overwritten'.

### Enterprise Manager SQL Server Properties

- In the SQL Server Properties configuration dialog box, go to the Database Settings tab.
- In the Backup/restore section, modify the number next to the Default backup media retention (days) field.

### Command Syntax

In this example, we set the default backup media retention for 2 days:

```
sp_configure 'show advanced options', 1
RECONFIGURE WITH OVERRIDE
GO

sp_configure 'media retention', 2
RECONFIGURE WITH OVERRIDE
GO
```

## Min Memory Per Query Option

This option designates the minimum amount of memory in kilobytes allocated per query execution. The default value is 1024KB.

This is an advanced option, and does not require a restart of the SQL Server service.

### Recommendations

If your server runs queries that make heavy use of sort and hash operations (sort operations sort all rows in a query, hash operations build in-memory table structures) on large tables, you may see some benefit from increasing this minimum. Be aware that setting this incorrectly can cause query performance issues if SQL Server cannot allocate the memory needed (too many queries taking up too much memory). Experiment with this value in your test environment first.

### *Enterprise Manager SQL Server Properties*

- In the SQL Server Properties configuration dialog box, go to the Memory tab.
- In the bottom of the Memory section, configure the Minimum query memory (KB) number.

### *Command Syntax*

In this example, we will reconfigure the memory to 2MB (2048KB):

```
sp_configure 'show advanced options', 1
RECONFIGURE WITH OVERRIDE
GO

sp_configure 'min memory per query', 2048
RECONFIGURE WITH OVERRIDE
GO
```

## Using Nested Triggers Option

This option designates whether or not triggers can be fired that fire other triggers. The default is 1, which means triggers can cascade fire up to 32 iterations. This is a basic option, and does not require a restart of the SQL Server service.

### *Recommendations*

Even when this option is enabled, a trigger cannot run in an infinite loop. Leaving this enabled provides you with flexibility in using triggers to provide referential integrity, auditing capabilities, data backup (saving deleted rows, for example), updates against views (using **instead of** triggers), and enforcement of business rules. It is recommended that you not disable this functionality, but rather program your triggers bearing in mind their interrelationships.

### *Enterprise Manager SQL Server Properties*

- In the SQL Server Properties configuration dialog box, go to the Server Settings tab.
- In the Server behavior section, select the checkbox Allow triggers to be fired which fire other triggers (nested triggers) to enable or disable.

### *Command Syntax*

In this example, we disable nested triggers:

```
sp_configure 'nested triggers', 0
RECONFIGURE WITH OVERRIDE
GO
```

## Network Packet Size Option

This option determines the size of packets (in bytes) received and sent by SQL Server. The default is 4096 bytes.

This is an advanced option, and does not require a restart of the SQL Server service.

### *Recommendations*

In general, the default is the optimal configuration, satisfying small to large packet deliveries and receipts. You must have a good understanding of the network protocols used, the network's topology, and network specifics, such as routers. For example, you could increase your network packet size, just to have it broken up into smaller chunks by the router.

If you are sure that the data sent and received will always be small (for example 1024 bytes on average) setting this option lower could improve performance. If the data sent and received is on average larger than the default, setting this option could improve performance by reducing the number of network packets sent. In either case, unless your server is near capacity, you may see no impact from your changes at all. Also, keep in mind that each user connection takes up 12KB + (3 * network packet size); so, increasing the network packet size adds significant overhead if you have many user connections.

If you decide to configure this option, be sure to test the configuration first in a test environment.

### *Enterprise Manager SQL Server Properties*

This step differs from other server options in that you do not change the server side through Enterprise Manager. In Enterprise Manager, you configure the packet size for client connections; this applies to **all** servers to which you connect from Enterprise Manager.

- ❑ In Enterprise Manager, go to Tools | Options.
- ❑ Go to the Advanced tab.
- ❑ Enter the desired value in Packet size (bytes). After pressing OK, you will be warned that 'The change in Packet Size will not take effect for connected servers. You must reconnect'.

### *Command Syntax*

Setting this option with `sp_configure` sets the **server** setting, not the client setting (as it does in Enterprise Manager). The following example sets the bytes to 8192 bytes (8K):

```
sp_configure 'show advanced options', 1
RECONFIGURE WITH OVERRIDE
GO

sp_configure 'network packet size', 8192
RECONFIGURE WITH OVERRIDE
GO
```

## Open Objects Option

This option sets a limit on the number of database objects that can be opened (referenced by connections) at one time. Anything defined in the `sysobjects` table counts as an object. The default value is 0, which means SQL Server will configure this value based on current activity.

This is an advanced option, requires a restart of the SQL Server service, and is self-configuring (meaning in most cases it should be left alone).

### *Recommendations*

Prior to SQL Server 7.0, this option designated a maximum value and did not autoconfigure based on system conditions. If you estimated incorrectly how many objects would be open concurrently, you would often see error messages (especially in large schema/user databases). In the current Version, with the setting 0 (autoconfigure) as the default, you should not consider changing this option unless you see errors related to open object limits reached.

Also note that open objects take up memory; each open object takes up 276 bytes. Add 1724 bytes for each index on the table object.

### *Enterprise Manager SQL Server Properties*

Not configurable in Enterprise Manager.

### *Command Syntax*

In this example, we will set the open objects option to allow a maximum of 100,000 database objects:

```
sp_configure 'show advanced options', 1
RECONFIGURE WITH OVERRIDE
GO

sp_configure 'open objects', 100000
RECONFIGURE WITH OVERRIDE
GO
```

## Priority Boost Option

By enabling this option, you force SQL Server to run at a higher priority than the system default. The default priority boost option value is 0, which means it is disabled.

This is an advanced option, and requires a restart of the SQL Server service.

### *Recommendations*

It is strongly recommended that you do not enable this option; SQL Server rarely faces priority contention when on a dedicated box. Enabling this option can starve the operating system of resources. This can cause Error 17824, which describes a network connection problem but is usually an indication that priority boost is enabled. If you are seeking to boost priority because SQL Server shares the server with other applications and is encountering performance difficulties, it is strongly suggested that you seek solutions to the individual problems (CPU, Memory, I/O, Network) or consider placing the instance on a dedicated box. See Chapter 17 for more details.

### *Enterprise Manager SQL Server Properties*

- In the SQL Server Properties configuration dialog box, go to the Processor tab.
- Select the check box in the Processor control area, Boost SQL Server priority on Windows.

### *Command Syntax*

The following example enables this option:

```
sp_configure 'show advanced options', 1
RECONFIGURE WITH OVERRIDE
GO

sp_configure 'priority boost', 1
RECONFIGURE WITH OVERRIDE
GO
```

## Query Governor Cost Limit Option

This option puts a limit on how long (in seconds) a query can run. The "seconds" are based on Microsoft's specific hardware, database and server settings that are used to originally define the value. These seconds translate to estimated cost as calculated by the query optimizer (so cost is relative to your hardware, database, and server settings) and this setting will most likely not map to seconds for YOUR SQL Server instances (lessening the usefulness of the setting). The query optimizer determines if a query will exceed the time limit designated and aborts the query if the estimate exceeds this value. This value impacts **all SQL Server users.** The default is 0 and no limit is configured.

This is an advanced option, and does not require a restart of the SQL Server service.

### *Recommendations*

You should only set this option if you are confident that queries exceeding a certain threshold are superfluous or detrimental to performance. An example of when you could use this is as follows:

You have a transaction processing database server that performs inserts, updates, and deletes to an order center. You know the application never takes longer than 1 second to perform data changes and that `SELECT` queries do not exceed 5 seconds. You turn on SQL Profiler to monitor activity, and see that some users are performing long-running queries against your transaction processing database, causing long-term blocking and eating up CPU cycles with their large result sets.

Aside from keeping these users off your OLTP database or directing them to a reporting server, you can also set the query governor cost limit to 10 seconds to keep them from tying up the transaction processing.

Keep in mind that this option limits a single query's capability to exceed 10 seconds. It does not prevent transactions with infinite loops. Using a simple example:

```
WHILE 1<>0
BEGIN
SELECT *
FROM sysobjects
END
```

Since `1` is never equal to `0`, this `SELECT` statement will keep running until you kill the process or the user stops the query.

### *Enterprise Manager SQL Server Properties*

- In the SQL Server Properties configuration dialog box, go to the Server Settings tab.
- Check the checkbox next to Use query governor to prevent queries exceeding specified cost: and enter a value.

### *Command Syntax*

Below is an example of setting the query governor cost limit to 10 seconds:

```
sp_configure 'show advanced options', 1
RECONFIGURE WITH OVERRIDE
GO
```

```
sp_configure 'query governor cost limit', 10
RECONFIGURE WITH OVERRIDE
GO
```

## Query Wait Option

This option sets a limit on how long a query waits for memory to generate a sorting or hashing operation. This option works as follows:

| Scenario | Action |
|---|---|
| Option set to `-1` (default) | Query times out at 25 times the estimated query cost determined by the query optimizer. |
| Option set to `0` through `2147483647` | Number of seconds to wait for memory resources. |

This is an advanced option, and does not require a restart of the SQL Server service.

### *Recommendations*

This setting is relevant if your SQL Server instance runs out of memory and you receive error 8645 A time out occurred while waiting for memory resources to execute the query. Re-run the query. At this point you should investigate memory configurations – asking questions such as:

- Are you running min and max server memory settings? Dynamic or fixed SQL Server memory?
- Is the paging file big enough?
- Do you have enough memory?
- Is existing memory being used efficiently?

Investigate available memory with Performance Monitor (Memory:Available Mbytes, Pages/Sec).

For in-depth detail on troubleshooting memory bottlenecks see Chapter 17.

Changing this value to a higher setting may remove your memory error messages, while you track down the memory availability issues.

Here is a table clarifying the impact of setting this option:

| Scenario | Action |
|---|---|
| Setting a lower query wait time | Minimizes time for which locks on objects are held while the query waits for memory. |
| Setting a higher query wait time | If the query is holding locks on resources, these will be held for the duration of the wait and may still be terminated on reaching the threshold. |

### *Enterprise Manager SQL Server Properties*

Not configurable in Enterprise Manager.

### *Command Syntax*

In this example, we will set the query wait time to 60 seconds:

```
sp_configure 'show advanced options', 1
RECONFIGURE WITH OVERRIDE
GO
```

```
sp_configure 'query wait', 60
RECONFIGURE WITH OVERRIDE
GO
```

## Recovery Interval Option

To better understand this option, you should understand the checkpoint event.

When a checkpoint occurs, dirty pages of committed transactions are written to disk. Checkpoints also write a record to the transaction log. This record shows all active transactions as of run time. Checkpoints run with the following frequency:

- Based on the `minute` value in the Recovery Interval setting.
- When a database option is changed with `ALTER DATABASE`.
- When the SQL Server service is stopped (by an administrator). A checkpoint does not happen in a crash situation (hard reboot, blue screen, and so on). Checkpoints also **do not** happen if you issue `SHUTDOWN WITH NOWAIT` (this command allows you to stop SQL Server from a SQL client).
- When the database is in `SIMPLE` recovery mode, a checkpoint is issued if a database log reaches 70% of the total log file limit.
- The `CHECKPOINT` command is issued.

The recovery interval setting designates the maximum database recovery time. When SQL Server starts up, the process of recovery occurs for each database; recovery involves the following two processes:

- If the server is stopped after a transaction was committed but not yet written to disk by a checkpoint, this is now 'rolled forward' (written to disk).
- If the server is stopped before a transaction was committed, the transaction is rolled back (changes to the database done by this transaction are undone).

The recovery interval option designates the maximum time (in minutes) allowed for the database recovery process. SQL Server then evaluates this number to make sure checkpoints are issued frequently enough to avoid recovery times exceeding this threshold. Although this option's unit of measurement is minutes, SQL Server estimates a ratio of transactions loosely correlating to minutes. The default for this option is 0, which means SQL Server autoconfigures the checkpoint frequency (generally selecting one minute or less, depending on transaction activity).

This option is an advanced option, and does not require a SQL Server service to be restarted.

### *Recommendations*

Leaving this option at the default of 0 is generally good practice. For databases with intense transaction activity, you may find that checkpoints are occurring too frequently. Checkpoints also get their own worker threads, which can add to server resource overhead. If this is the case, you may consider setting the option value to smaller increments. To monitor checkpoint activity use Performance Monitor to view SQLServer:Buffer Manager Checkpoint pages/sec.

### *Enterprise Manager SQL Server Properties*

- In the SQL Server Properties configuration dialog box, go to the Database Settings tab.
- In the Recovery section type in the recovery interval (in minutes).

### Command Syntax

In this example, we will set the recovery interval to 5 minutes:

```
sp_configure 'show advanced options', 1
RECONFIGURE WITH OVERRIDE
GO

sp_configure 'recovery interval', 5
RECONFIGURE WITH OVERRIDE
GO
```

## Remote Access Option

Set this option to 0 if you want to deny access from remote servers running instances of SQL Server; this applies to remote procedure calls. The default is 1, which means access is enabled.

This is a basic option, and requires a restart of the SQL Server service.

### Recommendations

For servers wanting to restrict access to RPCs, disable this option. If you attempt to execute a procedure on a remote server with this option disabled, you will get the error 'Msg 7201, Level 17, State 4, Line 1 Could not execute procedure on remote server 'servername' because SQL Server is not configured for remote access. Ask your system administrator to reconfigure SQL Server to allow remote access'.

### Enterprise Manager SQL Server Properties

- In the SQL Server Properties configuration dialog box, go to the Connections tab.
- Under the Remote server connections section, uncheck Allow other SQL Servers to connect remotely to this SQL Server using RPC to disable access.

### Command Syntax

In this example, we will disable RPC access from other SQL Server instances:

```
sp_configure 'remote access', 0
RECONFIGURE WITH OVERRIDE
GO
```

## Remote Login Timeout Option

If a remote server is currently unavailable, setting Remote Login Timeout will specify the maximum time (in seconds) a connection attempt will wait prior to returning an error message. If the value is set to 0, the connection will wait indefinitely. This default is 20, which is usually sufficient. This option impacts all OLE DB connections from your server.

This is a basic option, and does not require a restart of the SQL Server service.

### Recommendations

This is a good setting to configure if you know the OLE DB connection takes longer than 20 seconds to connect, or never connects within 20 seconds. Just remember this setting impacts all OLE DB connections from your server.

### Enterprise Manager SQL Server Properties

Not configurable in Enterprise Manager.

### Command Syntax

The following example sets the timeout to 15 seconds rather than the default of 20:

```
sp_configure 'remote access', 15
RECONFIGURE WITH OVERRIDE
GO
```

## Remote Proc Trans Option

When enabled, this option forces every distributed transaction to run as a transaction managed by the MS DTC service (distributed transaction coordinator). This ensures data integrity by implementing a two-phase commit. Two-phase commit refers to a method of handling transactions that involve more than one server; it ensures that transactions completed or rolled back apply either to all servers or none. The default is for the Remote Proc Trans option to be disabled (value 0).

This is a basic option, and does not require a restart of the SQL Server service.

### Recommendations

This option is a good choice to enforce integrity of distributed transactions via procedures. When this option is enabled the two-phase commit is enforced (phase 1 locks the necessary resources, phase 2 does the commit), dictating that a distributed transaction either commits as a whole unit or aborts.

### Enterprise Manager SQL Server Properties

- In the SQL Server Properties configuration dialog box, go to the Connections tab.
- In the Remote server connections section, check Enforce distributed transactions to enable this option.

### Command Syntax

In this example, we will enable this option:

```
sp_configure 'remote proc trans', 1
RECONFIGURE WITH OVERRIDE
GO
```

## Remote Query Timeout Option

This option designates the maximum duration of a remote query; this includes heterogeneous queries (non-SQL Server distributed queries) and remote procedure queries to other SQL Server servers. The default is 600 seconds (ten minutes).

This is a basic option, and does not require a restart of the SQL Server service.

### Recommendations

Modify this timeout based on your knowledge of the remote query. If it is common to have long-running queries (from daily data extraction, slow network connection) that exceed ten minutes, increase this timeout to the appropriate value. If your distributed (remote) queries are always short in duration, then decrease the timeout value. Doing so will ensure that bad queries do not take up resources on the distributed and local servers (both can be affected, especially if the query uses joins between table/views on the distributed **and** local server).

### *Enterprise Manager SQL Server Properties*

- In the **SQL Server Properties** configuration dialog box, go to the **Connections** tab.
- In the **Remote server connections** section, adjust the **Query time-out** number to the desired value (in seconds).

### *Command Syntax*

In this example, we will increase the remote query timeout value to 900 (15 minutes):

```
sp_configure 'remote query timeout', 900
RECONFIGURE WITH OVERRIDE
GO
```

## Scan for Startup Procs Option

This option determines whether SQL Server will search for autoexec stored procedures to execute upon startup of the SQL Server Service. Autoexec stored procedures are those enabled by the stored procedure `sp_procoption` to run upon SQL Server startup. The default is 0, which means this behavior is disabled. By running `sp_procoption` to enable or disable autoexec for a stored procedure, the scan for startup procs option gets configured automatically (see Chapter 14 for more details).

This is an advanced option, and requires a restart of the SQL Server service.

### *Recommendations*

Do not configure this option. Let `sp_procoption` handle the enabling and disabling of this option.

### *Enterprise Manager SQL Server Properties*

Not configurable in Enterprise Manager.

### *Command Syntax*

The following example enables this option:

```
sp_configure 'show advanced options', 1
RECONFIGURE WITH OVERRIDE
GO

sp_configure 'scan for startup procs', 1
RECONFIGURE WITH OVERRIDE
GO
```

## Set Working Set Size Option

This option changes memory management to a fixed setting and disables dynamic memory configuration. Prior to setting this option, the min and max server memory options must be the same value. This value is the amount SQL Server will reserve at startup (so choose carefully).

This is an advanced option, and requires a restart of the SQL Server service.

### Recommendations

By setting fixed memory for SQL Server you deny it the opportunity to allocate or de-allocate memory based on actual database activity. This dynamic behavior is beneficial and SQL Server usually makes intelligent decisions regarding your most precious SQL Server commodity – RAM.

### Enterprise Manager SQL Server Properties

- In the SQL Server Properties configuration dialog box, go to the Memory tab.
- Click the option Use a fixed memory size (MB).
- Check the Reserve physical memory for SQL Server box.

### Command Syntax

In this example, we will set the fixed SQL Server memory to 500MB:

```
sp_configure 'show advanced options', 1
RECONFIGURE WITH OVERRIDE
GO

sp_configure 'min server memory', 500
RECONFIGURE WITH OVERRIDE
GO

sp_configure 'max server memory', 500
RECONFIGURE WITH OVERRIDE
GO

sp_configure 'set working set size', 1
RECONFIGURE WITH OVERRIDE
GO
```

## Two Digit Year Cutoff Option

This option determines which century to use for two-digit years. The default value for this option is 2049. This causes the following behavior when interpreting `datetime` values with two-digit years:

| Two-digit Year Entered | Interpretation |
|---|---|
| 0 to 49 | 2000 to 2049 |
| 50 to 99 | 1950 to 1999 |

This is an advanced option, and does not require a restart of the SQL Server service.

### Recommendations

It is best to leave this option alone if you are extracting data from other SQL Server implementations; this will keep backward compatibility with previous versions of SQL Server.

**Always use the four-digit year to avoid ambiguity.**

### Enterprise Manager SQL Server Properties

- In the SQL Server Properties configuration dialog box, go to the Server Settings tab.
- In the two-digit year support section, update the end range if you wish to change the year interpretation. This will automatically impact the bottom range.

### Command Syntax

In this example we will set the two-year cutoff range to 1931-2030, which is the OLE automation object default. OLE objects expose their classes (functionality) to be utilized within a programming language. Notice that only the upper range year needs to be changed. The lower range is configured automatically, based on your new value.

```
sp_configure 'show advanced options', 1
RECONFIGURE WITH OVERRIDE
GO

sp_configure 'two digit year cutoff', 2030
RECONFIGURE WITH OVERRIDE
GO
```

## User Connections Option

This option sets the maximum user connections allowed on the SQL Server instance. The default value is 0, which means SQL Server manages the number dynamically. The upper limit of connections is 32,767. Whether the maximum number of user connections is left dynamic or set to a specific value, SQL Server does not pre-allocate memory for the connections, but rather adds and removes them as needed. Each user connection takes up 12KB + (3 * the network packet size). The typical network packet size is 4KB; so, based on this calculation, each user connection takes up 24KB.

This is an advanced option, requires a restart of the SQL Server service, and is self-configuring (meaning, in most cases, it should be left alone).

### Recommendations

It is best **not** to configure this option. Setting the limit low may keep user connections out unnecessarily. You may also underestimate the number of connections needed, as your application may spawn multiple connections for a single user. Connection pooling (sharing a user connection among different users) must also be considered, without which you may designate too high a limit. This does no harm, but proves that configuring this option is unnecessary.

One of the few valid reasons to configure this option would be if you had a very small amount of memory to allocate to SQL Server. Limiting the number of connections would ensure multiple connections did not consume the limited memory resources.

### Enterprise Manager SQL Server Properties

- In the SQL Server Properties configuration dialog box, go to the Connections tab.
- In the Connections section, configure the number labeled Maximum concurrent user connections (0=unlimited).

### *Command Syntax*

The following example sets the maximum user connections to 500:

```
sp_configure 'show advanced options', 1
RECONFIGURE WITH OVERRIDE
GO

sp_configure 'user connections', 500
RECONFIGURE WITH OVERRIDE
GO
```

## User Options Option

This option allows you to configure user connection defaults for the duration of a user's connection time. Users can still override the defaults.

This is a basic option, and does not require a restart of the SQL Server service. Changes are only adopted by **new** connections after changing the value of this option. The default for this option is 0, which means no user options are configured.

Values are as follows:

| Value | Configuration Name | Description |
|---|---|---|
| 1 | DISABLE_DEF_CNST_CHK | This option is provided for backward compatibility only. This functionality was used in SQL Server version 6.x for deferred constraint checking. |
| 2 | IMPLICIT_TRANSACTIONS | This option allows connections to treat several DDL and DML statements as a part of a transaction without specifying BEGIN TRANSACTION. The drawback of this option is that all statements submitted must end with a COMMIT TRAN statement, otherwise work will be rolled back. The default is to keep this off. |
| 4 | CURSOR_CLOSE_ON_COMMIT | When this option is enabled, all open cursors are closed when the transaction they belong to is committed. The default is to keep this off, thus the cursor may only be closed explicitly or when the connection is closed. |
| 8 | ANSI_WARNINGS | See the next table for details on how this works. |
| 16 | ANSI_PADDING | Controls column storage when values are shorter than fixed length size or contain trailing blanks. When set on CHAR or BINARY columns, trailing blanks are appended to values with lengths shorter than the column definition. A VARCHAR and VARBINARY column that contains trailing blanks does not trim them. The ANSI standard is to have this option set on. |
| 32 | ANSI_NULLS | When set on, a SELECT statement using a '=Null' WHERE clause will return zero rows, even if a NULL value exists in the column. Comparisons against a null value return UNKNOWN. |

| Value | Configuration Name | Description |
|---|---|---|
| 64 | ARITHABORT | When on, a query with an overflow or division by zero will terminate and return an error. If within a transaction, that transaction gets rolled back. |
| 128 | ARITHIGNORE | When on, an overflow or division by zero error returns NULL. This is overridden if SET ANSI_WARNINGS is on. |
| 256 | QUOTED_IDENTIFIER | When set on, identifiers can be delimited by double quotation marks and literals with single quotation marks. When off, identifiers may not have quotes but literals may be delimited by either single or double quotes. |
| 512 | NOCOUNT | When set on, this turns off the rows affected message. This can produce a **small performance boost** if set in stored procedures that perform several row set operations. |
| 1024 | ANSI_NULL_DFLT_ON | When set on, columns not explicitly defined with a NULL or NOT NULL in a CREATE or ALTER table statement will default to allow NULLs. This setting is mutually exclusive with ANSI_NULL_DFLT_OFF. If one option is on, the other option is set off. |
| 2048 | ANSI_NULL_DFLT_OFF | When set on, columns not explicitly defined with a NULL or NOT NULL in a CREATE or ALTER table statement will default to **not** allow NULLs. This setting is mutually exclusive with ANSI_NULL_DFLT_ON. If one option is on, the other option is set off. |
| 4096 | CONCAT_NULL_YIELDS_NULL | When set on, concatenating a NULL value with a string produces a NULL value. |
| 8192 | NUMERIC_ROUNDABORT | When set on, an error is produced if a loss of precision occurs in an expression. If ARITHABORT is off while NUMERIC_ROUNDABORT is on, a warning is produced instead of an error, and a NULL is returned. |
| 16384 | XACT_ABORT | When set on, a transaction is rolled back if a runtime error is encountered. This must be set on for data modification statements (implicit and explicit transactions) for OLE DB and ODBC provider connections. |

The following table clarifies the ANSI_WARNINGS option:

| Event | ANSI_WARNINGS ON | ANSI_WARNINGS OFF |
|---|---|---|
| NULL value in an aggregate function | Warning message given | No warning message |

*Table continued on following page*

| Event | ANSI_WARNINGS ON | ANSI_WARNINGS OFF |
|---|---|---|
| Division by zero or arithmetic overflow | Statement is rolled back and error is generated | Statement is rolled back and error is generated |
| String or binary data value size limit is exceeded by `INSERT` or `UPDATE` statement | Warning is given and statement is rolled back | `Truncated value` is inserted or updated |

### *Recommendations*

To understand the impact of setting these options you must consider the following:

- `SET` options by the user overrule this option.
- Database options overrule this option.

Also, the following settings must be on if working with indexes on computed columns or indexed views. They are as follows:

- `ANSI_NULLS`
- `ANSI_PADDING`
- `ANSI_WARNINGS`
- `ARITHABORT`
- `QUOTED_IDENTIFIER`
- `CONCAT_NULL_YIELDS_NULL`

The following must be off to work with indexes on computed columns or indexed views:

- `NUMERIC_ROUNDABORT`

*See Chapter 3 for more details on database options.*

### *Enterprise Manager SQL Server Properties*

- In the SQL Server Properties configuration dialog box, go to the Connections tab.
- In the Default connection options window, check each option that you would like enabled.

### *Command Syntax*

The following example enables the Quoted Identifier and Implicit Transactions settings.

See the above table for the values for each option. In this case, Quoted Identifier has a value of 256 and Implicit Transactions a value of 2; therefore total value should be 258:

```
sp_configure 'user options', 258
RECONFIGURE WITH OVERRIDE
GO
```

# 2.5 How to... View Server Property Information with SERVERPROPERTY

This is a useful function that outputs server properties and configurations as a `SQL_VARIANT` data type (one that can contain any SQL Server data type except for `TEXT`, `NTEXT`, and `IMAGE`). The syntax is as follows:

```
SERVERPROPERTY ( propertyname )
```

The following `SELECT` statement executed in the Query Analyzer returns SQL Server instance name, edition, and version:

```
SELECT SERVERPROPERTY('ServerName') as 'Instance Name',
       SERVERPROPERTY('Edition') as 'Edition',
       SERVERPROPERTY('ProductLevel')as 'Version'
```

Outputs:

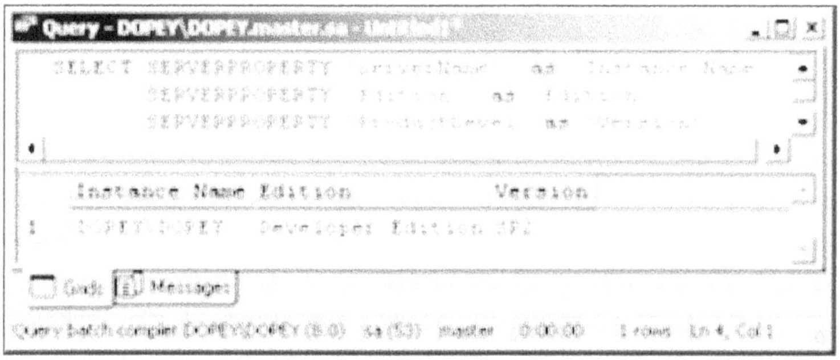

The `propertyname` options are as follows:

| Property | Returns |
|---|---|
| `Collation` | Server default collation. |
| `Edition` | Edition of the SQL Server instance installed on the server: one of Desktop Engine, Developer, Enterprise, Enterprise Evaluation, Personal, and Standard. |
| `Engine Edition` | Engine edition of the SQL Server instance:<br>1 = Personal or Desktop Engine<br>2 = Standard<br>3 = Enterprise (returned for Enterprise, Enterprise Evaluation, and Developer) |
| `InstanceName` | Instance name. |

*Table continued on following page*

| Property | Returns |
|---|---|
| IsClustered | Designates if instance is clustered:<br>1 = Clustered<br>0 = Not clustered |
| IsFullTextInstalled | Designates if full-text indexing is installed:<br>1 = Full-text is installed<br>0 = Full-text is not installed |
| IsIntegratedSecurityOnly | Designates if only integrated security is enabled (if not, SQL logins are allowed):<br>1 = Integrated security<br>0 = Not integrated security |
| IsSingleUser | Reports if the SQL Server instance is in single-user mode (started with option -m):<br>1 = Single user<br>0 = Not single user |
| LicenseType | License mode of the SQL Server Instance:<br>PER_SEAT = Per-seat licensing<br>PER_PROCESSOR = Per-processor licensing<br>DISABLED = Licensing is disabled |
| MachineName | Name of the Windows 2000 (or NT) computer on which SQL Server is running (useful for virtual servers on failover clusters). See Chapter 10 for more information. |
| NumLicenses | If per-seat licensing, the number of client licenses registered for the SQL Server instance. If per-processor licensing, the number of licensed processors for the SQL Server instance. |
| ProcessID | The process ID of the SQL Server instance (associated with the sqlservr.exe executable). |
| ProductVersion | The version of the SQL Server instance. |
| ProductLevel | The version of the SQL Server instance, for example SP3 (service pack 3). |
| ServerName | The default or full named instance name (servername\instancename format) of the SQL Server Instance. |

# 2.6 How to... Show Version Information for Your Server – xp_msver

xp_msver is an extended stored procedure that returns version and build information for the queried SQL Server instance in a similar way to sp_server_info and SERVERPROPERTY. Some useful information not included in sp_server_info or SERVERPROPERTY is:

- **WindowsVersion**
  Reports the operating system build number.
- **ProcessorCount**
  Reports the number of processors.
- **PhysicalMemory**
  Reports the amount of RAM installed on the server in megabytes.

The syntax is as follows:

```
xp_msver [option name]
```

The option name parameter is optional.

An example of running this extended stored procedure to return just RAM is as follows:

```
EXEC master.dbo.xp_msver 'PhysicalMemory'
```

This outputs:

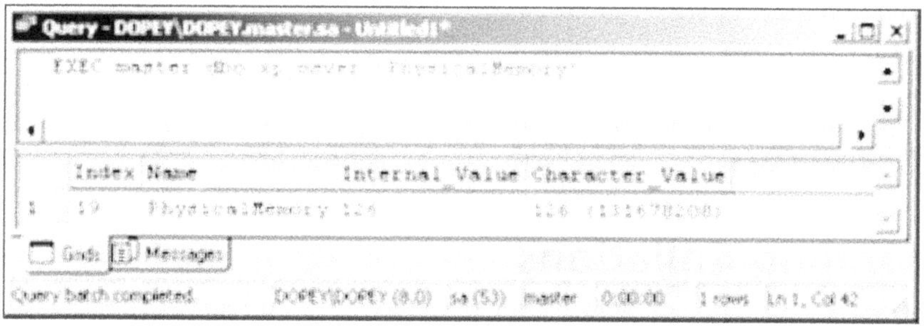


Notice that this also shows bytes in parenthesis next to megabytes.

An example of running this extended stored procedure to return all options is as follows:

```
EXEC master.dbo.xp_msver
```

This outputs:

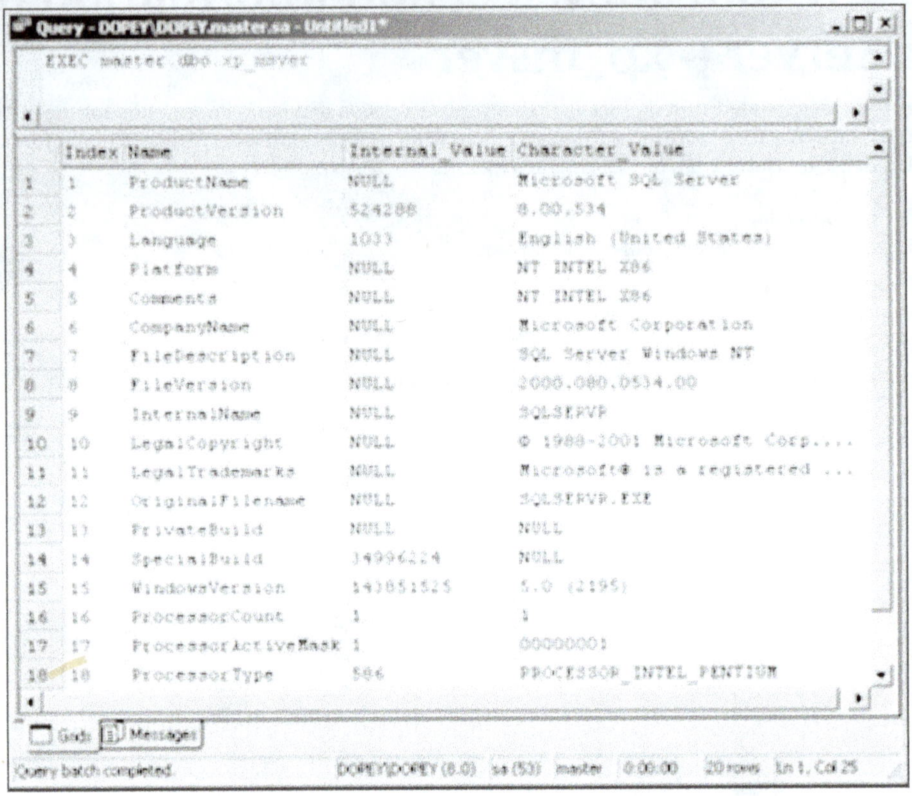
Query - DOPEY\DOPEY.master.sa - Untitled1*

EXEC master.dbo.xp_msver

| | Index | Name | Internal_Value | Character_Value |
|---|---|---|---|---|
| 1 | 1 | ProductName | NULL | Microsoft SQL Server |
| 2 | 2 | ProductVersion | 524288 | 8.00.534 |
| 3 | 3 | Language | 1033 | English (United States) |
| 4 | 4 | Platform | NULL | NT INTEL X86 |
| 5 | 5 | Comments | NULL | NT INTEL X86 |
| 6 | 6 | CompanyName | NULL | Microsoft Corporation |
| 7 | 7 | FileDescription | NULL | SQL Server Windows NT |
| 8 | 8 | FileVersion | NULL | 2000.080.0534.00 |
| 9 | 9 | InternalName | NULL | SQLSERVR |
| 10 | 10 | LegalCopyright | NULL | © 1988-2001 Microsoft Corp.... |
| 11 | 11 | LegalTrademarks | NULL | Microsoft® is a registered ... |
| 12 | 12 | OriginalFilename | NULL | SQLSERVR.EXE |
| 13 | 13 | PrivateBuild | NULL | NULL |
| 14 | 14 | SpecialBuild | 34996224 | NULL |
| 15 | 15 | WindowsVersion | 143851525 | 5.0 (2195) |
| 16 | 16 | ProcessorCount | 1 | 1 |
| 17 | 17 | ProcessorActiveMask | 1 | 00000001 |
| 18 | 18 | ProcessorType | 586 | PROCESSOR_INTEL_PENTIUM |

Grids | Messages

Query batch completed. DOPEY\DOPEY (8.0) sa (53) master 0:00:00 20 rows Ln 1, Col 25

**Notice that we use the three-part name to execute this extended stored procedure. This differs from the system stored procedures, as extended stored procedures must be referenced in the database where they exist, either by `USE MASTER` or the two part prefix '`master.dbo.`'.**

# Understanding Collations

For many SQL Server professionals, the subject of **collations** can be a bit confusing. Below, we will review the basics of SQL Server 2000 collations.

## What are Collations?

SQL Server 2000 collations determine how data is sorted, compared, presented, and stored.

Collations are used to define three settings:

- A code page used to store non-Unicode character data types (`CHAR`, `VARCHAR`, and `TEXT`)
- The sort order for non-Unicode character data types
- The sort order for Unicode data types (`NCHAR`, `NVARCHAR`, and `NTEXT`)

## What is a Code Page?

A code page defines language and country characters using a 1-byte or 2-byte per character format. 1-byte per character code pages can define up to 256 unique patterns. 2-byte per character code pages can define up to 65,536 unique patterns. Below is a table listing the code page IDs and associated code page names supported in SQL Server.

| Code Page | Description |
|---|---|
| 1256 | Arabic |
| 1257 | Baltic |
| 1250 | Central European |
| 936 | Chinese (Simplified) |
| 950 | Chinese (Traditional) |
| 1251 | Cyrillic |
| 1253 | Greek |
| 1255 | Hebrew |
| 932 | Japanese |
| 949 | Korean |
| 1252 | Latin1 (ANSI) |
| 437 | MS-DOS US English |
| 850 | Multilingual (MS-DOS Latin1) |
| 874 | Thai |
| 1254 | Turkish |
| 1258 | Vietnamese |

## What is Sort Order?

First of all, sort order is defined within a collation separately for Unicode and non-Unicode data. Sort order determines how data is interpreted, compared, and ordered. Choices for sort order are:

- Binary sorting order behavior
- Accent-sensitive or accent-insensitive behavior
- Case-insensitive or case-sensitive behavior
- For 2-byte code pages, width sensitivity or insensitivity must be decided (that is, whether 1- or 2- byte characters that are equivalent are treated the same or differently)
- For Japanese sort order, you must determine kana sensitivity and designate katakana characters as equal or unequal to hiragana characters

**Case sensitivity** determines whether or not your SQL Server instance or database distinguishes between uppercase and lowercase letters. For example, is 'Y' = 'y'?

**Accent sensitivity** determines if an accented character is equivalent to an unaccented character. For example, is 'e' = 'é'?

**Binary sorting** determines how data is ordered. If binary is selected, sorting is case-sensitive and data in tables is sorted based on the bit pattern. This has performance benefits compared to dictionary-based sorting (alphabet standard sorting), but does not always sort intuitively for the end user.

## What is Unicode Data?

Unicode data provides a way for different SQL Server instances to exchange data from different languages and regions without implementing data conversion. This avoids the complexities involved in transferring data between different code pages.

Unicode data types in SQL Server are `NCHAR`, `NVARCHAR`, and `NTEXT`. Unicode data types use 2 bytes per character and 65,536 patterns are available, meaning most world languages are covered. Unicode data types do not require conversion from one language's SQL Server instance to another, as Unicode always uses the same code page. One drawback of using Unicode data types is that they need more space and allow fewer characters (4000 characters is the limit for `NCHAR` and `NVARCHAR` as opposed to 8000 for their non-Unicode equivalent). Also, all Unicode constants must be preceded by an N, for example `N'stringtoinsert'`.

## Collation Compatibility Issues

If data is exchanged between SQL Server instances using different code pages, you must make sure that the source data is converted properly, either by the sending or the receiving party. Extended characters (characters beyond the first 128 patterns defined in a 1-byte code page) can be lost or misinterpreted. Processing overhead from converting millions of rows can be a huge performance drain. If your data must be shared across languages and regions, moving to Unicode data types is recommended.

## SQL Collation vs. Windows Collation

You will notice when installing SQL Server that you have two options for setting collation: **SQL collation** and **Windows collation**.

SQL collation names are used for backward compatibility with previous versions of SQL Server. You must use SQL collations if you plan to replicate using SQL Server 6.5 or SQL Server 7.0, or have application code dependent on SQL collation names.

Windows collations, however, allow you to specify case, accent, (Japanese) kana, width sensitivity, and binary sorts.

For a complete listing of all SQL and Windows collation names, run the following query in Query Analyzer:

```
SELECT * FROM ::fn_helpcollations()
```

This returns all collation names along with user-friendly descriptions. If you want to see a description for a specific Windows or SQL collation name, for example `Latin1_General_CI_AS`, execute the following statement in Query Analyzer:

```
SELECT * FROM ::fn_helpcollations()
WHERE name = 'Latin1_General_CI_AS'
```

The output is:

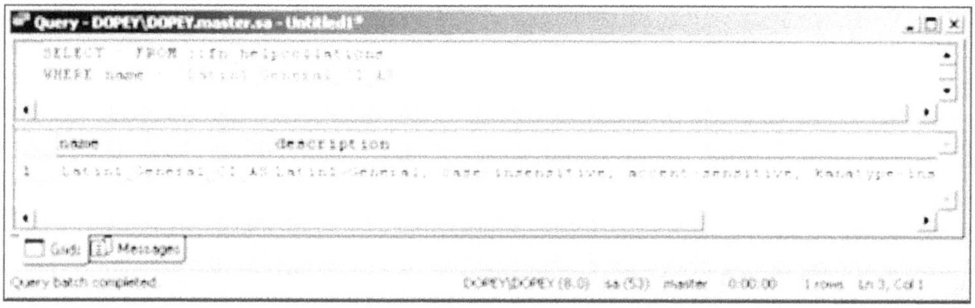


Collation is determined during your SQL Server instance installation. The collation designated during installation will determine that of any new databases created, unless you explicitly create the database using a non-default collation. You can also set a different collation for your database, table column, or literal strings; we'll be reviewing how to do this and more in the next section.

# 2.7 How to... View Server Default Collation using SELECT SERVERPROPERTY

In Query Analyzer, run the following statement to check default server collation:

```
SELECT SERVERPROPERTY ('collation')
```

In this example, the output is:

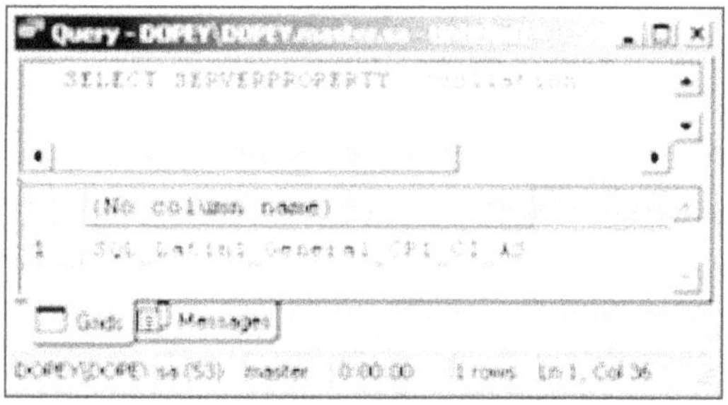


# 2.8 How to... View Server Default Collation using sp_helpsort

The following example lists the default server collation using `sp_helpsort`. Notice the difference in format compared to `SERVERPROPERTY('collation')`. The syntax is as follows:

```
EXEC sp_helpsort
```

This outputs:

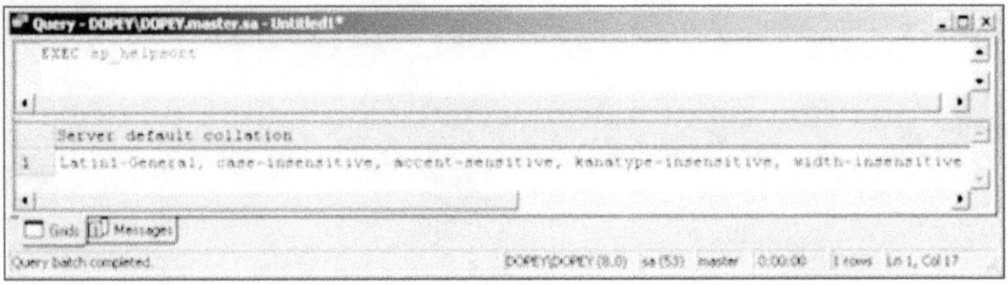


# 2.9 How to... Create a Database with a Collation Different from the Server Default

To create a new database with a collation that differs from the server default using Transact-SQL, follow these steps.

Example setup:

| Setting | Value |
|---|---|
| Database name | FrenchProducts |
| Data file logical name | frprod_data |
| Data file physical name | e:\mssql\data\frprod_data.mdf |
| Initial size | 5MB |
| Maxsize and growth increment | 50MB, 5MB |
| Log file logical name | frprod_log |
| Log file physical name | g:\mssql\data\frprod_log.ldf |
| Initial size | 2MB |
| Maxsize and growth increment | 10MB, 1MB |
| Collation | French case insensitive, accent insensitive |

In Query Analyzer run the following command:

```
USE master
GO
CREATE DATABASE FrenchProducts ON
    (NAME = frprod_data,
     FILENAME = 'e:\mssql\data\frprod_data.mdf',
     SIZE=5,
     MAXSIZE=50,
     FILEGROWTH=5)
LOG ON
```

```
    (NAME=frprod_log,
     FILENAME='g:\mssql\data\frprod_log.ldf',
     SIZE=2,
     MAXSIZE=10,
     FILEGROWTH=1)
COLLATE French_CI_AI
```

To create a new database with a collation that differs from the server default using Enterprise Manager, follow these steps:

- In Enterprise Manager, expand the server node where you wish to add a new database.
- Right-click the databases folder and select New Database.
- In the General tab, type in the new database name.
- At the bottom of the General tab, select the Collation name you wish to use.
- Continue with the regular database creation procedure in the Data Files and Transaction Log tabs.

# 2.10 How to... Change Database Collation

Database collation cannot be changed in Enterprise Manager, but it can be modified using the `ALTER DATABASE` Transact-SQL statement. Changing the collation of the database will impact **new** tables created, but will not convert the collation of **existing** table columns. To do this, you must use `ALTER TABLE` (shown in a later section).

Be aware that, depending on the change, stored data differences (such as accent sensitivity) can be lost.

This example changes the `FrenchProducts` database from the French case-insensitive, accent-insensitive to Greek case-insensitive, accent-insensitive:

```
ALTER DATABASE FrenchProducts
COLLATE Greek_CI_AI
```

# 2.11 How to... Create a Table with a Column using a Non-Default Collation

Below is a Transact-SQL example creating a table called `BjorkAlbums`. This table has one field called `vchAlbumName` with the collation set to Icelandic case-insensitive and accent-insensitive. The data type of this column is `VARCHAR`, with a 50-character limit and no nulls allowed:

```
CREATE TABLE dbo.BjorkAlbums (
    vchAlbumName varchar (50)
    COLLATE Icelandic_CI_AI NOT NULL)
    ON [PRIMARY]
GO
```

To perform this same action in Enterprise Manager:

- Expand the server node for which you wish to add the table.

- ❑ Expand the database.
- ❑ Right-click Tables and select New Table.
- ❑ In Column Name, type `vchAlbumName`.
- ❑ For data type, select `varchar` with length 50.
- ❑ Uncheck Allow Nulls.
- ❑ In the Columns tab below, click collation field and click the ellipsis button to the right.
- ❑ Under Windows Collation, select Icelandic. Leave Dictionary sort selected and do not select Case Sensitive or Accent Sensitive.

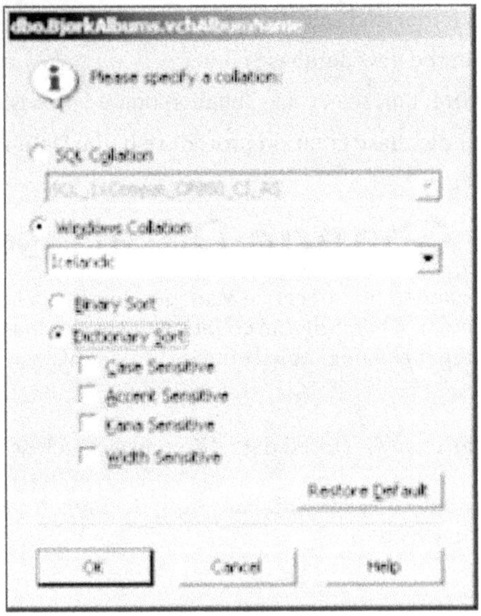


- ❑ Press OK.
- ❑ Press the Save button.

# 2.12 How to... Change a Column's Collation

In this example, we will change a column's existing collation using the `ALTER TABLE` and `ALTER COLUMN` syntax. We will change the `BjorkAlbums` column `vchAlbumName` to be Icelandic case-sensitive instead of case-insensitive:

```
ALTER TABLE BjorkAlbums
ALTER COLUMN vchAlbumName varchar(50) COLLATE Icelandic_CS_AI NOT NULL
GO
```

# 2.13 How to... Use the COLLATE Statement in a Transact-SQL Statement

The COLLATE statement can be used in several places in a Transact-SQL batch or statement.

Here is an example of using COLLATE with a SQL batch comparing names. We will compare the names 'Joe' and 'JOE' to measure equality, first using a case-sensitive collation:

```
IF (SELECT 'JOE' COLLATE SQL_Latin1_General_Cp1_CS_AS)
 = (SELECT 'Joe' COLLATE SQL_Latin1_General_Cp1_CS_AS)
    PRINT 'Yup, same name'
ELSE
    PRINT 'Nope, this name is not the same.'
```

The output for this statement will be 'Nope, this name is not the same'.

Next we can run the same statement, this time changing the collation to case-insensitive

```
IF (SELECT 'JOE' COLLATE SQL_Latin1_General_Cp1_CI_AS)
 = (SELECT 'Joe' COLLATE SQL_Latin1_General_Cp1_CI_AS)
    PRINT 'Yup, same name'
ELSE
    PRINT 'Nope, this name is not the same.'
```

The output changes to 'Yup, same name', because 'Joe' and 'JOE' are the same in a case -insensitive collation.

COLLATE can also be used within an ORDER BY statement. For example:

```
SELECT * FROM Alpha ORDER BY chAlphabet COLLATE Latin1_General_CS_AI
```

# 2.14 How to... Use COLLATIONPROPERTY

This function returns collation property information. For example, returning non-Unicode code page for a collation:

```
SELECT COLLATIONPROPERTY( 'Latin1_General_CI_AS', 'CodePage' )
```

This returns a value of 1252.

Returning the Windows LCID (locale id) for the collation:

```
SELECT COLLATIONPROPERTY( 'Latin1_General_CI_AS', 'LCID' )
```

This returns 1033.

The remaining available property for this function is ComparisonStyle which returns the Windows comparison style of the collation.

# 2.15 How to... Change Default Server Collation with the Rebuild Master Utility

The only way to change the server default collation is to re-install SQL Server or use the Rebuild Master utility, also called `rebuildm.exe`. This utility can also be used to fix a corrupted `master` database.

## Before You Use This Utility

Rebuild Master wipes your configurations clean; so, if you have existing databases that you wish to preserve, detach them first. You can re-attach them after rebuilding the master. See Chapter 1 for a review of how to attach or detach a database.

If you have any logins, jobs, alerts, operators, DTS packages, or custom objects kept in the system databases, script these out now (in the case of DTS packages, save them as files or export to another server).

If you are running replication, script out all publications and subscriptions and delete them. You can run the script in query analyzer once master is rebuilt. See Chapter 8 for instructions on how to do this.

**Another warning:** at the time of writing, there is a reported bug that causes the Rebuild Master utility to stop responding when referencing files from the local CD-ROM. See Microsoft Knowledge Base article *Q273572, 'BUG: Rebuildm.exe Utility Stops Responding When Source Directory is on a CD'*, for more information. The workaround is to copy the contents of the `\x86\data` folder from the CD-ROM to the network and use the network as the source directory. The read-only attribute on the directory and files must be removed (right-click the files, select Properties, and clear Read-only).

## Rebuilding the Master Database

To rebuild the master database and change the collation:

- Stop the instance of SQL Server 2000 you wish to rebuild.
- Run `rebuildm.exe`, which is located in `Program Files\Microsoft SQL Server\80\Tools\Binn` directory.
- Select the server instance you wish to rebuild in the Server dropdown.
- Select the network source directory containing the data files. Do not point to your CD-ROM until Microsoft has fixed this bug:

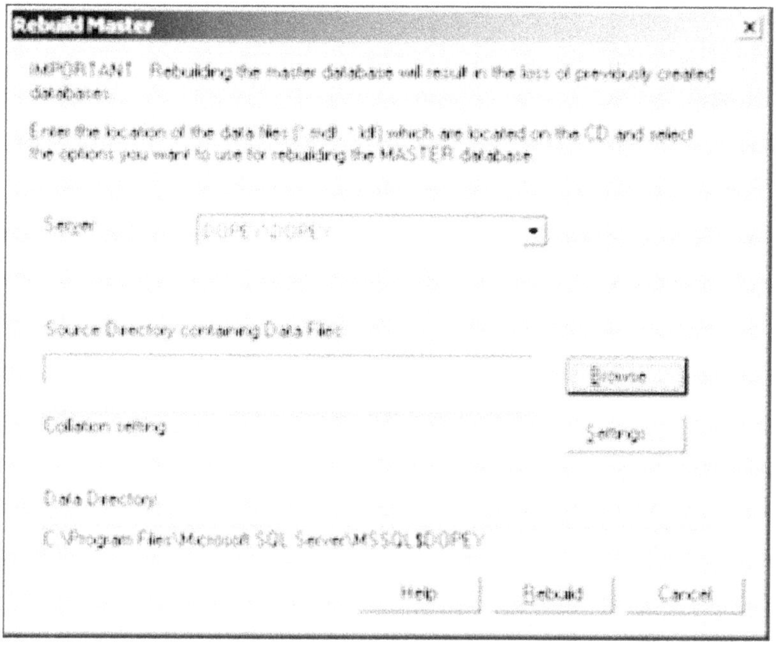


- Click the Settings button for the collation field. Select either Collation designator or SQL Collations (use SQL Collations if replicating to 7.0 or 6.5 boxes or if you have application programming dependencies on SQL collation names):

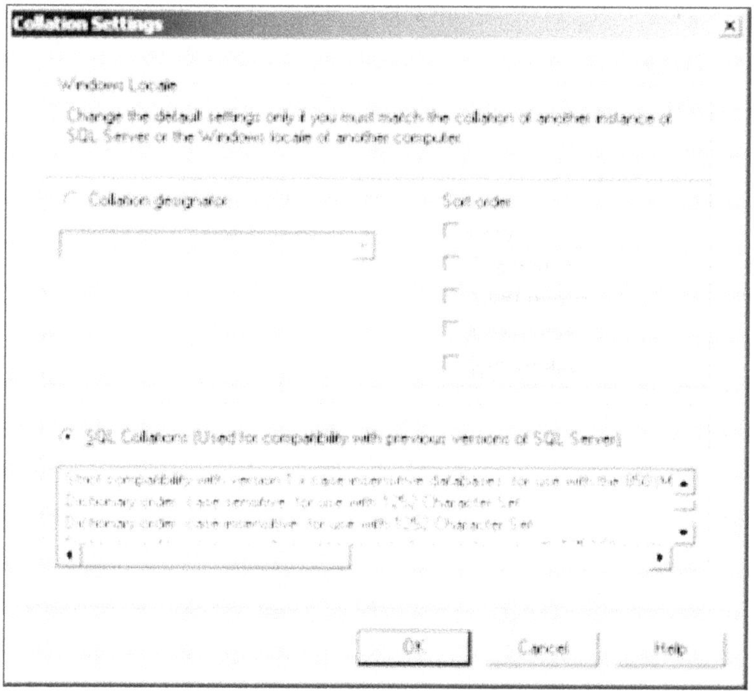

- Press OK to exit to the main screen. Press the Rebuild button. You will be see this message:

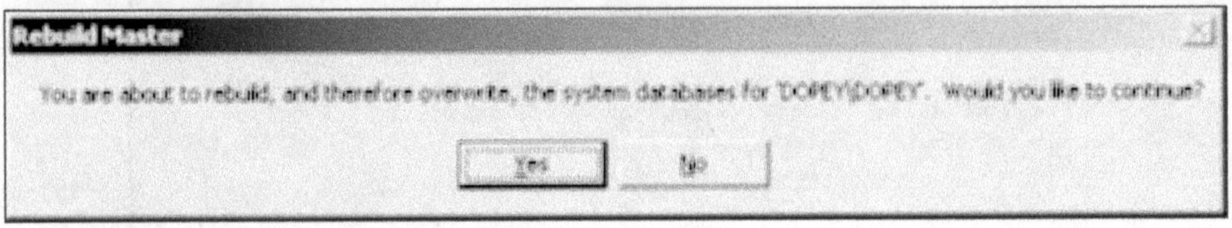


- If you understand this and have taken the necessary precautions to preserve logins, DTS packages, jobs, operators, alerts, and system database objects, press Yes.

If you receive a failure error, check the following items:

- Are the data files read-only? If so, disable this property.
- Are you reading from a network drive?
- Is your SQL Server service stopped?

If the rebuild succeeded you will see a dialog box with a message Rebuild Master completed successfully!.

Start the SQL Server instance and run the following command in Query Analyzer:

```
SELECT SERVERPROPERTY ('collation')
```

If the collation is what you intended, you have successfully rebuilt master. Now attach your databases, run your scripts, and import your DTS packages (if you had them prior to the rebuild).

# 3

# Creating and Configuring Databases

This chapter begins by examining SQL Server database storage concepts and database sizing considerations. We will also review how to create, change, and configure a database, as well as providing a brief overview of creating database objects using Enterprise Manager.

# SQL Server Storage Internals

Before creating and configuring a database, you should have a basic understanding of how SQL Server manages internal storage.

Tables are used to store data in the database, and provide the foundation on which most other database objects depend. Tables are defined with one or more columns. Each table column has a defined **data type**, which determines what kind of data is stored within the table.

## Data Types

What determines how many bytes are in a row? Each column has a data type attribute, which defines how much space it utilizes and what data it can store. The following table details each data type, and its associated byte size, showing logically what data can be stored, and how much physical space each data type uses:

| Data Type | Value Range | Physical Storage |
|---|---|---|
| `BIGINT` | Whole number from -2 ^ 63 (-9,223,372,036,854,775,808) through (2 ^ 63)-1 (9,223,372,036,854,775,807). | 8 bytes. |

*Table continued on following page*

| Data Type | Value Range | Physical Storage |
|---|---|---|
| INT | Whole number from -2^31 (-2,147,483,648) through (2^31)-1 (2,147,483,647). | 4 bytes. |
| SMALLINT | Whole number from -32768 through 32767. | 2 bytes. |
| TINYINT | Whole number from 0 through 255. | 1 byte. |
| BIT | Whole number either 0 or 1. | Bits columns are stored as *bits* in a byte (8 bits per byte), with one byte allocated per eight bits. |
| DECIMAL or NUMERIC (no real difference between the two) | Range from -10^38 +1 through 10^38-1. Decimal uses precision and scale. Precision determines maximum total number of decimal digits both left and right of the decimal point. Scale determines maximum decimal digits to the right of the decimal point. | Size depends on precision.<br>Precision of 1 through 9 = 5 bytes.<br>Precision of 10 through 19 = 9 bytes.<br>Precision of 20 through 28 = 13 bytes.<br>Precision of 29 through 38 = 17 bytes. |
| MONEY | Monetary value between -2^63 (-922,377,203,685,477.5808) through 2^63-1 (+922,337,203,685,477.5807). | 8 bytes. |
| SMALLMONEY | Monetary value between -214,748.3648 through +214,748.3647. | 4 bytes |
| FLOAT | Floating precision number from -1.79E + 308 through 1.79E +308. | If mantissa of float is:<br>1 through 24 = 4 bytes<br>25 through 53 = 8 bytes. |
| REAL | Floating precision number from -3.40E + 38 through 3.40E +38. | If mantissa of float is:<br>1 through 24 = 4 bytes<br>25 through 53 = 8 bytes. |
| DATETIME | Date and time from January 1, 1753 through December 31, 9999, with accuracy to one three-hundredth of a second (3.33 milliseconds). | 8 bytes. |
| SMALLDATETIME | Date and time from January 1, 1900, through June 6, 2079, with accuracy to the minute. Values with lower than 29.998 seconds are rounded down to the nearest minute, and values 29.999 seconds or higher are rounded up to the nearest minute. | 4 bytes. |

| Data Type | Value Range | Physical Storage |
|---|---|---|
| CHAR | Fixed-length character data with maximum length of 8000 characters. | 1 to 8000 bytes, matching the number of characters you designate. |
| VARCHAR | Variable-length character data with a maximum length of 8000 characters. | 1 to 8000 bytes, but based on actual data entered. So, if you select VARCHAR(50), but type in a 25 character name, only 25 bytes are used. |
| TEXT | Variable-length data with maximum length of 2,147,483,647 characters. | Maximum of 2,147,483,647 bytes. One byte for each character. |
| IMAGE | Variable-length binary data from 0 through 2^31-1. | Maximum of 2,147,483,647 bytes. |
| NCHAR | Fixed-length Unicode character data with a maximum length of 4000 characters. | Multiply fixed length number by 2 to calculate number of bytes required. |
| NVARCHAR | Variable-length Unicode character data with maximum length of 4000 characters. | Multiply number of characters entered by 2 to calculate number of bytes required. |
| NTEXT | Variable-length Unicode character data with a maximum length of 1,073,741,823 characters. | Maximum of 2,147,483,647 bytes. Multiply number of characters entered by 2 to calculate number of bytes required. |
| BINARY | Fixed-length binary data with a maximum of 8000 bytes. | Maximum 8000 bytes. Storage is value of length specified (n) + 4 bytes. |
| VARBINARY | Variable-length data with a maximum of 8000 bytes. | Storage is actual length of data + 4 bytes. 8000 byte maximum. |
| SQL_VARIANT | A data type that can store all data types except TEXT, NTEXT, TIMESTAMP, and another sql_variant. | Depends on the data type it is holding, but has a maximum of 8016 bytes. |
| TIMESTAMP | Database-wide unique number that is updated when a row gets updated. | 8 bytes. TIMESTAMP is equivalent to BINARY(8) or VARBINARY(8) with nulls. |
| UNIQUEIDENTIFIER | Stores a GUID (Globally Unique Identifier). | 16 bytes. |
| TABLE | Data type used to store a result set (from a SELECT statement for example). | Depends on columns and column data types defined. |

In addition to columns, tables can contain zero or more **rows**, each of which represents a horizontal line in the table, like a spreadsheet row. Rows are stored within a **page**. Pages are on-disk structures, 8KB in size, which contain data rows. Pages also contain **header** and **row offset** areas. Headers, 96 bytes in size, store information about the page type, amount of free space on the page, and object `ID` of the table storing rows in it. The row offset table holds one entry for each row on the page.

Although a page takes up 8K of storage, or 8192 bytes, the actual space that can be used after the header and row offset storage is **8060 bytes**.

There are different types of pages. **Data pages** are used to hold all table data, except `TEXT`, `NTEXT`, and `IMAGE` data types. **Index pages** are used for clustered and nonclustered index storage. **Text/Image** pages contain `TEXT`, image, and `NTEXT` data. **Free space** pages track free space available in pages allocated.

Pages are allocated within blocks, called **extents**. Extents contain eight contiguous 8KB pages, which are allocated to data files. There are two types of extents, **uniform** and **mixed**. Mixed extents share up to eight objects (one object per 8KB page). Once an object is big enough to contain eight 8KB pages, the pages are switched to a uniform extent. Uniform extents contain a single object. All eight 8KB pages are dedicated to this object.

Extents also have data pages, which are used to manage **meta data** – data about the extents themselves.

**Global Allocation Map** (GAM) and **Secondary Global Allocation Map** (SGAM) pages contain meta data about extents. **Index Allocation Map** pages store data about extents used by tables or indexes. **Bulk Changed Map** pages list extents changed by bulk operations since the last transaction log backup was performed. **Differential Changed Map** pages track extents that have changed since the last full database backup.

# Data Files

As mentioned earlier, extents are allocated to data files. A database requires a minimum of **one data file** and **one log file**. The primary data file uses the `*.mdf` extension. Optional secondary data files use the `*.ndf` extension. Log files use the `*.ldf` file extension. These are the standard file extensions; using them, however, is not mandatory. You *can* use different file extensions if you prefer.

Extents are not allocated to **transaction logs**. Transaction logs are sequential files made up of **virtual log files** (VLFs). VLFs are truncation units, meaning that the space can be used for new transactions once it no longer contains log records for active transactions. The minimum VLF size is 256KB, with a minimum of 2 VLFs per log file.

# Filegroups

Data files belong to **filegroups**. Every database has a primary filegroup, which contains startup information for the database; you may also create secondary filegroups. Filegroups are useful for grouping files logically, easing administration (for example, you can back up individual filegroups). Filegroups are often used for **very large databases** (VLDB). We will cover these in more detail later in this chapter. Transaction logs are not placed in filegroups.

## Bringing It All Together

The table below summarizes storage allocation from the smallest unit to the largest:

| | |
|---|---|
| Page | A fixed-length 8KB block is the basic storage unit for SQL Server data files. |
| Extent | Eight contiguous 8KB pages = One extent = 64KB. Extents store data and index pages. |
| Files | Files contain extents. |
| File groups | File groups contain files. |

## Storage Limits

SQL Server has the following storage limitations:

| | |
|---|---|
| Filegroups per database | 256 |
| Files per database | 32,767 |
| File size (data) | 32TB |
| File size (log) | 32TB |

# Estimating Growth

Database size is determined by data file and transaction log sizes. Data file size is dictated by object storage in the database. To estimate data file size, you must first define each object in your database. Most storage overhead in a database is comprised of tables and indexes.

If you are planning for a VLDB (very large database) implementation, or if physical disk space is limited, it may be important for you to calculate a *very* accurate estimate. For this, see the *SQL Server Books Online* topics, *Estimating the Size of a Table*, *Estimating the Size of a Table with a Clustered Index*, and *Estimating the Size of a Table Without a Clustered Index*. These topics include several lengthy and involved calculations.

Most DBAs use a spreadsheet to perform the calculations listed in *SQL Server Books Online*. The Microsoft BackOffice 4.5 Resource Kit includes a Data Sizer spreadsheet, originally created for SQL Server 7.0, but still applicable to SQL Server 2000 database size estimates.

For most DBAs, a rough estimate is usually sufficient for planning purposes. If you are looking for a simpler, generalized estimate of base table disk space required, the guidelines below provide this (this example does not include index sizing):

- Determine how many bytes each table row consumes. Use the data type table in the previous section to determine the total number of bytes. Remember that a row cannot exceed 8060 bytes in length.
- For this example, we will estimate bytes per row for a table with the following columns:

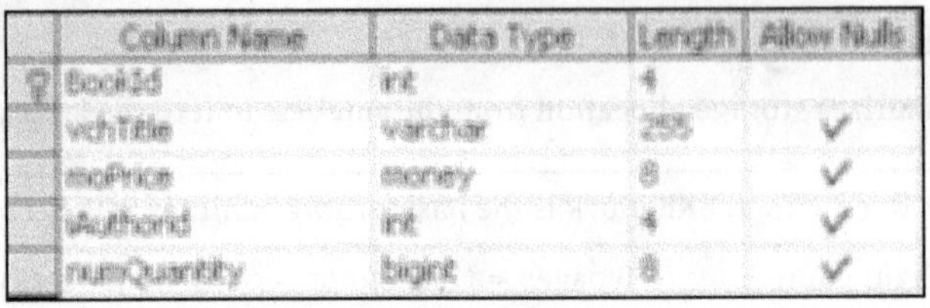

Column Name
Data Type
Length
Allow Nulls
BookId
int
4
vchTitle
varchar
255
moPrice
money
8
iAuthorId
int
4
numQuantity
bigint
8


In this case, the bytes would be calculated as follows:

`BookId` = 4 bytes

`vchTitle` = 178 bytes (because of variable length, we are assuming a 70% column usage, instead of the max usage of 255 bytes)

`moPrice` = 8 bytes

`iAuthorID` = 4 bytes

`numQuantity` = 8 bytes

Total bytes per row = 202 bytes

- ❑ Determine how many rows your table will have. This is your **number of estimated rows** value. For our example, we will estimate an initial 100,000 rows.
- ❑ Calculate the number of rows that can fit on an 8K data page. The calculation is:

  8060 / bytes per row = rows per page

  So for our example, 8060 / 202 = 39 rows per page (rounded **down** from 39.9, since a row cannot traverse a data page).
- ❑ Calculate the number of data pages needed, based on the estimated table rows. The calculation is:

  **Number of estimated rows / rows per page = data pages needed**

  For our example, 100,000 / 39 = 2565 data pages needed (rounded up)
- ❑ Multiply this number by 8192 to get the total bytes needed for the base table:

  **8192 * data pages needed = Total bytes**

  For our example, 8192 * 2565 = 21,012,480 bytes
- ❑ To calculate total KB needed:

  **Total bytes / 1024 = Total KB**

  For our example, 21,012,480 / 1024 = 20520KB
- ❑ To calculate total MB needed:

  **Total KB / 1024 = Total MB**

  For our example, 20520 / 1024 = 20MB (rounded)

If you wish to avoid calculations altogether, an informal way to estimate database size is to create the database schema in your test environment first. As you configure each table (and associated indexes), you can monitor space usage with the `sp_spaceused` stored procedure. Load the estimated number of rows your production environment will have, and then measure the results using this procedure:

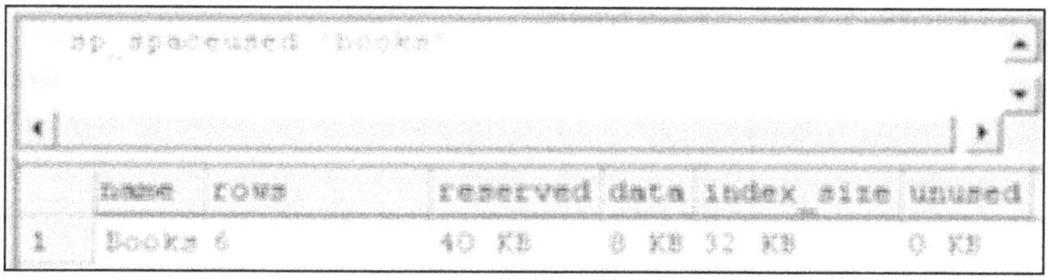


The data returned by this procedure tends to get out-of-date, particularly after an index is dropped. Run the procedure with the `@updateusage` parameter, to ensure accuracy. For example, the following stored procedure updates space usage information, and also returns total size for the `BookRepository` database:

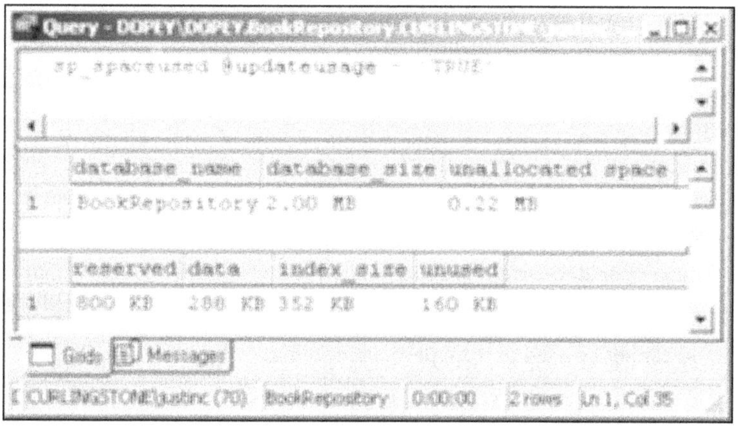


# Transaction Log Size

Log file size is dictated by the frequency, volume, and type of transaction activity in your database. In general, size your transaction log in the following proportions to the data file:

| Activity Type | Transaction Log Size |
|---|---|
| No activity (read-only database) | Minimum size possible. |
| Light activity | 5-10% of the data file(s) size. If the data file is under 100MB, assign 25MB. |
| Medium activity | 10%-50% of the data file(s) size. If the data file is under 100MB, allocate 50MB. |
| Heavy activity | > 50% of the data file(s) size. If the data file is under 100MB, assign the same space as the data file. |

These estimates are a good starting point; monitor your transaction log size, however, to make sure that you have not assigned too much or too little. Recoverability models (simple, bulk-logged, full), reviewed later on in the chapter, can also have an impact on the size of your transaction log.

# The System Databases

Before reviewing how to create and configure a database, let's first review the databases that come with SQL Server. The following table details each of the system databases, and their roles in the SQL Server environment:

| Table | Description |
|---|---|
| `master` | This is your most critical database, and is the core of your SQL Server implementation. Limit changes and access to this database as much as possible. Without the `master` database, your SQL Server instance will not start up. |
| `msdb` | This database contains tables that control and track the elements of the SQL Server Agent, as well as replication, log shipping (Enterprise Edition), database backup and restore history, database maintenance plan configurations and history, and a subset of tables participating in replication status and jobs. DTS packages saved to SQL Server are also stored within this database. |
| `model` | The model database is a **template** database, which, when modified, will affect the default values of databases that are created in the future. For example, if a table is added to the `model` database, future databases created for the SQL Server instance will include this table. |
| `tempdb` | The `tempdb` database is used to hold all temporary tables and temporary stored procedures. SQL Server also uses it for internal sorting and query operations (called work tables, or spooling). This database is re-created each time SQL Server is started, and cannot be used to store permanent tables. |

# Creating, Configuring, and Modifying Your Database

We will now examine the process of creating databases, and methods of configuring and modifying databases once they exist.

# 3.1 How To... Create a Database in SQL Server 2000

To create a database using Enterprise Manager:

- Start Enterprise Manager. Expand Server Group and registration. Expand the Databases folder.
- Right-click the Databases folder and select New Database...
- In the General tab, designate the database name. If this database has a collation other than the default collation, designate it (see Chapter 2 for collations). Otherwise leave it as the default:

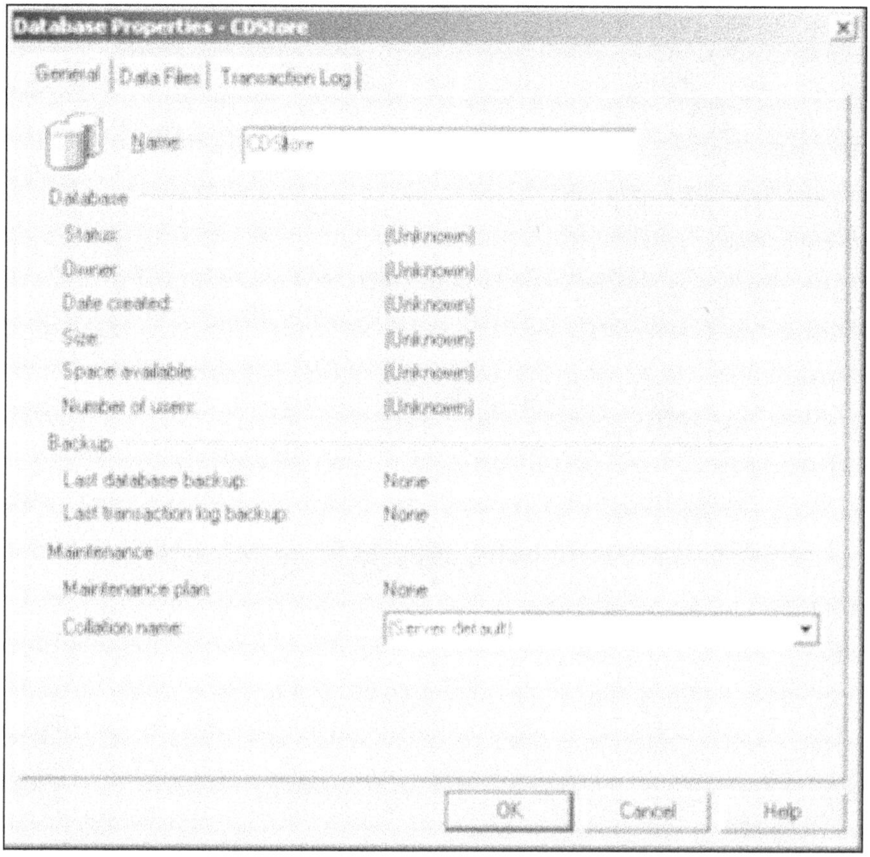


- If you plan on extracting data from other databases, or will be performing multi-database queries (queries that reference tables or views from two or more databases on the server), you may encounter issues if the other database or databases have a different collation. For example, if attempting to join two table columns with **different** collations, you may receive the following error message:

  ```
  Server: Msg 446, Level 16, State 9, Line 1
  Cannot resolve collation conflict for equal to operation.
  ```

  You may also encounter issues involving `tempdb`, if `tempdb` also has a different collation from the new database you are creating.
- Select the Data Files tab.
- Change the logical file name or leave it at its default.
- You can change the location of the file by either typing it in or pressing the ellipsis (...) button. This will generate a file search directory where you can specify the location.
- Select the initial size of the data file and the default filegroup that it belongs to.

  When the data file row is selected, you can set that file's growth and file size properties. You can set whether the file grows automatically, and if so by what increment. If the file autogrows, then you can specify whether or not a maximum file size should be defined.

- If you have plentiful disk space, there is no harm in setting autogrow for your database. Make sure, however, that the growth increment is large enough to minimize frequent file expansions, as file expansions can disrupt performance for the users of the database. Even with plentiful disk space, it is still a very good idea to set maximum thresholds for file sizes, *particularly* `tempdb`. It is much too easy for developers and end users to create runaway transactions that fill up your entire transaction log (and your drive, if autogrow is enabled).

  If space is at a premium, you can still specify autogrow; but make sure to set maximum file sizes for each of your databases as well.

- If you wish to add multiple data files, simply type into the blank row beneath the first data file. Fill out File Name, Location, Initial size, and Filegroup. This file can have autogrow and max settings determined as well:

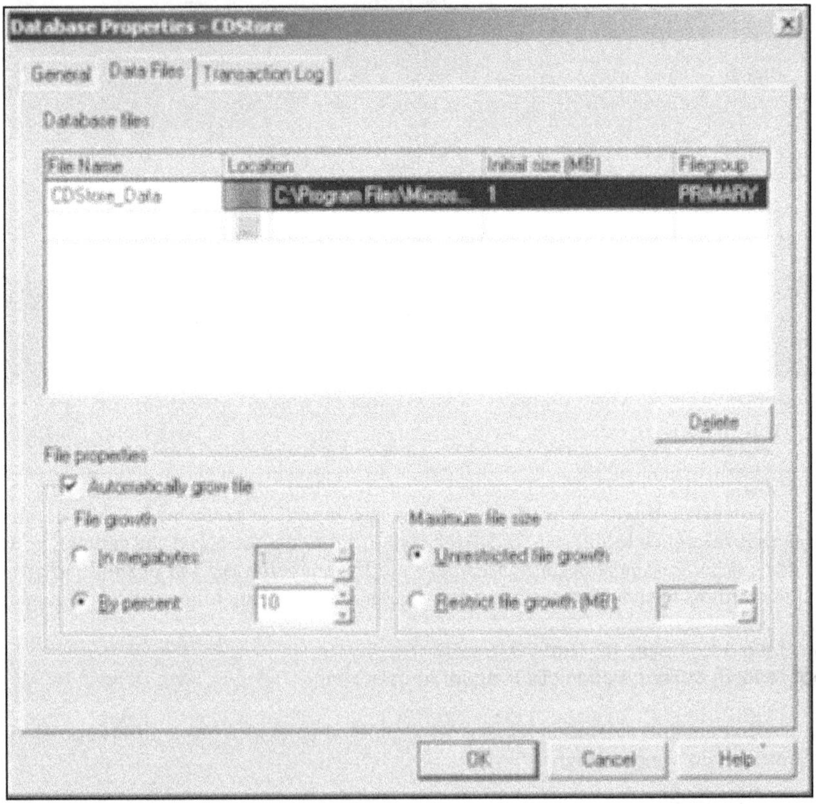


- Select the Transaction Log tab. This tab works much the same as the Data Files tab, where you can designate file name, location, and initial file size. You can also specify autogrow and maximum file size properties, or add new transaction log files. Notice that we do not specify a filegroup; only data files are placed in file groups.
- Select OK when finished.

This example created a database on a local disk drive on the server. Microsoft does not recommend creating databases on a network drive; you cannot do so unless you utilize a trace flag documented in Microsoft's Knowledge Base article Q304261, *INF: Support for Network Database Files*.

# Creating a Database using Transact-SQL

To create a database using Transact-SQL:

- Open Query Analyzer and connect to the server to which you wish to add a database.
- Run the CREATE DATABASE command with the specified values (we will see examples shortly).

The following is the CREATE DATABASE syntax from *SQL Server Books Online* and a table describing each parameter and option:

```
CREATE DATABASE database_name
[ ON
  [ < filespec > [ ,...n ] ]
  [ , < filegroup > [ ,...n ] ]
]
[ LOG ON { < filespec > [ ,...n ] } ]
[ COLLATE collation_name ]
[ FOR LOAD | FOR ATTACH ]

< filespec > ::=

[ PRIMARY ]
( [ NAME = logical_file_name , ]
  FILENAME = 'os_file_name'
  [ , SIZE = size ]
  [ , MAXSIZE = { max_size | UNLIMITED } ]
  [ , FILEGROWTH = growth_increment ] ) [ ,...n ]

< filegroup > ::=

FILEGROUP filegroup_name < filespec > [ ,...n ]
```

| Parameter or Option | Description |
|---|---|
| `database_name` | Name of database to be created. |
| `[ ON [ < filespec > [ ,...n ] ] [ , < filegroup > [ ,...n ] ] ]` | Designates disk files and, optionally, a comma-separated list of filegroup and associated files. |
| `[ LOG ON { < filespec > [ ,...n ] } ]` | Designates files used to store the database transaction log. If not designated, a single log file is created with a system-generated name and size that is 25% of total data file size. |
| `[ COLLATE collation_name ]` | Designates default collation for the database; uses Windows collation or SQL collation. See Chapter 2 for a detailed review of collations. |

*Table continued on following page*

<table>
<tr><th>Parameter or Option</th><th>Description</th></tr>
<tr><td>[ FOR LOAD | FOR ATTACH ]</td><td>FOR LOAD is a backward compatibility option used for earlier versions of SQL Server, setting database to dbo use only and a status of loading.<br><br>FOR ATTACH is used to denote that an existing set of operating system files should be included.</td></tr>
<tr><td>< filespec > ::= [ PRIMARY ]</td><td>Designates the primary filegroup, which contains all database system tables and objects not assigned to user-defined filegroups. The first <filespec> entry becomes the primary file in the primary filegroup.</td></tr>
<tr><td>[ NAME = logical_file_name , ]</td><td>Logical name for the file in the <filespec>.</td></tr>
<tr><td>FILENAME = 'os_file_name'</td><td>Operating system file name for the file in the <filespec>.</td></tr>
<tr><td>[ , SIZE = size ]</td><td>Size of file in <filespec> in MB. If not specified, the model database size of the primary file is used.</td></tr>
<tr><td>[ , MAXSIZE = { max_size | UNLIMITED } ]</td><td>Maximum size in KB, MB, GB or TB for file in <filespec>. The default is megabyte (MB) and must be a whole number. The default is unlimited.</td></tr>
<tr><td>[ , FILEGROWTH = growth_increment ] ) [ ,...n ]</td><td>Designates a growth increment in MB, KB, GB, TB, or %. The default is 10% and minimum value is 64KB.</td></tr>
<tr><td>< filegroup > ::=<br><br>FILEGROUP filegroup_name < filespec > [ ,...n ]</td><td>Designates user-defined filegroup in which files are to be placed.</td></tr>
</table>

## Example 3.1.1: Creating a simple database based on the model database

You can create a database with settings identical to the model database, with only the name and file names being different:

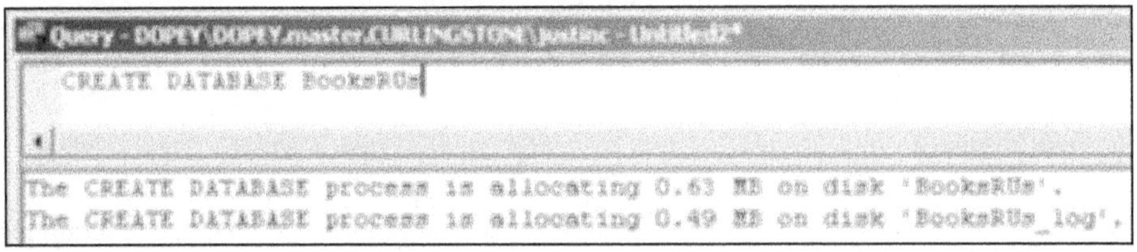

If you look at `sp_helpfile` for `model` and your new database `BooksRUs`, you will see the similar settings:

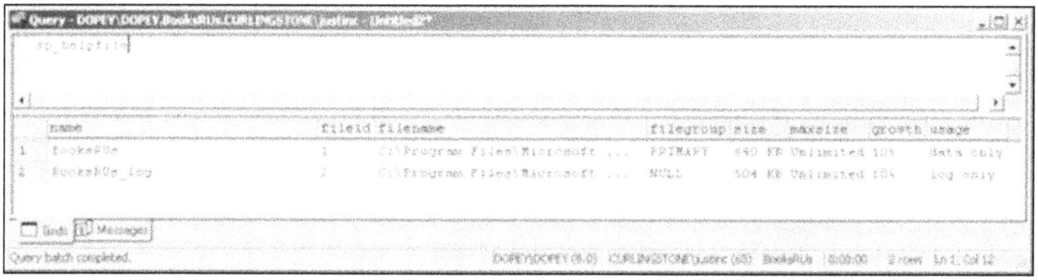

## Example 3.1.2: Creating a database with the data and log file on separate partitions

In this example, we create a database called `BookRepository` that places the data file on the G: drive and the transaction log on the H: drive. Because we do not explicitly designate file sizes and autogrowth options, these are created according to the `model` database:

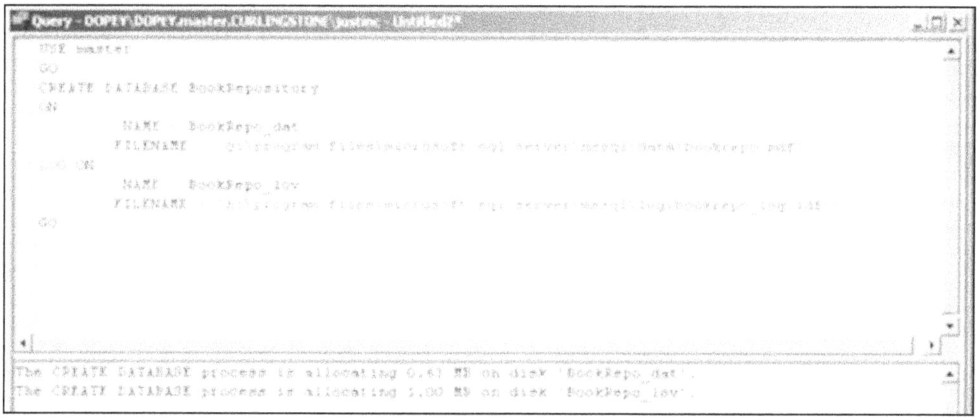

## Example 3.1.3: Creating a database with SIZE, MAXSIZE, and FILEGROWTH

In this example, we will create the `BookRepository` database with the following settings:

- Initial data file size = 2MB
- Initial log file size = 1MB
- Data file maximum size = 100MB
- Log file maximum size = 25MB
- Data file growth = 10% increments
- Log file growth = 1MB increments

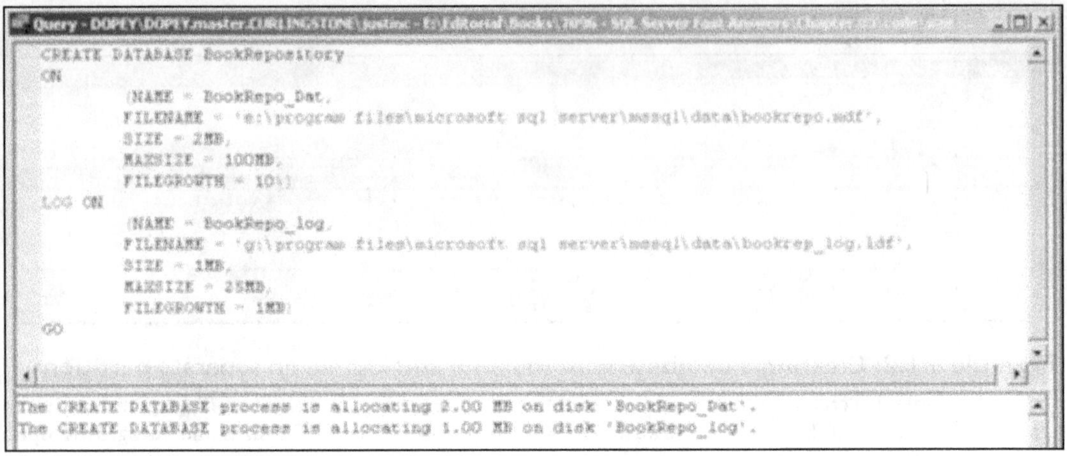
Query - DOPEY\DOPEY.master.CURLINGSTONE\justinc
CREATE DATABASE BookRepository
ON
(NAME = BookRepo_Dat,
FILENAME = 'e:\program files\microsoft sql server\mssql\data\bookrepo.mdf',
SIZE = 2MB,
MAXSIZE = 100MB,
FILEGROWTH = 10%)
LOG ON
(NAME = BookRepo_log,
FILENAME = 'g:\program files\microsoft sql server\mssql\data\bookrep_log.ldf',
SIZE = 1MB,
MAXSIZE = 25MB,
FILEGROWTH = 1MB)
GO
The CREATE DATABASE process is allocating 2.00 MB on disk 'BookRepo_Dat'.
The CREATE DATABASE process is allocating 1.00 MB on disk 'BookRepo_log'.

## Example 3.1.4: Creating a database with multiple data and log files

In this example, we will create the database `BookRepositoryUK`, which will have two data and two log files. Notice the `PRIMARY` keyword being used with the first data file, and note that the secondary data file uses the `*.ndf` extension instead of `*.mdf`. We will use sizing based on the model database (meaning we do not have explicitly to include the syntax in the `CREATE DATABASE` statement):

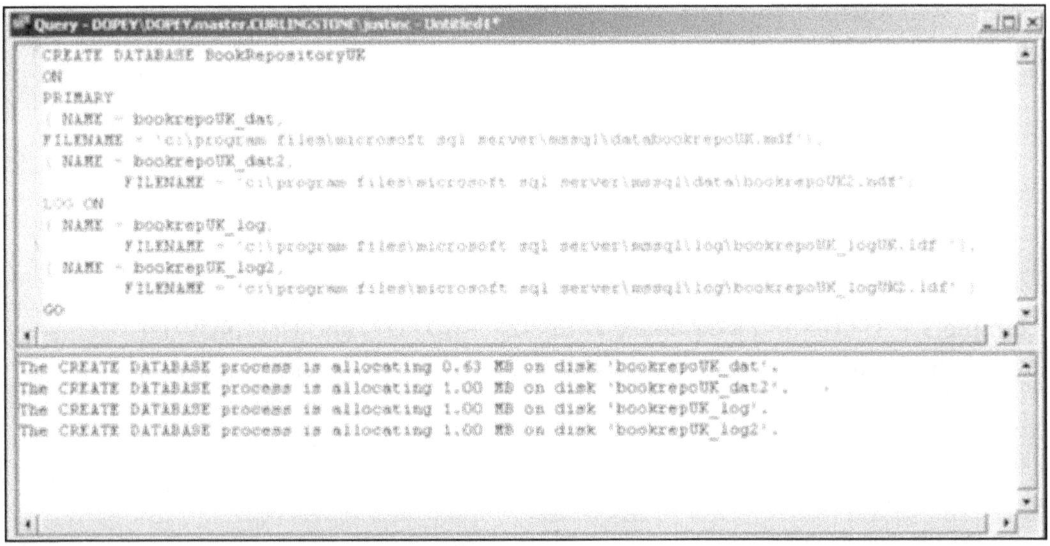
Query - DOPEY\DOPEY.master.CURLINGSTONE\justinc - Untitled1*
CREATE DATABASE BookRepositoryUK
ON
PRIMARY
( NAME = bookrepoUK_dat,
FILENAME = 'c:\program files\microsoft sql server\mssql\databookrepoUK.mdf'),
( NAME = bookrepoUK_dat2,
FILENAME = 'c:\program files\microsoft sql server\mssql\data\bookrepoUK2.ndf')
LOG ON
( NAME = bookrepUK_log,
FILENAME = 'c:\program files\microsoft sql server\mssql\log\bookrepoUK_logUK.ldf'),
( NAME = bookrepUK_log2,
FILENAME = 'c:\program files\microsoft sql server\mssql\log\bookrepoUK_logUK2.ldf')
GO
The CREATE DATABASE process is allocating 0.63 MB on disk 'bookrepoUK_dat'.
The CREATE DATABASE process is allocating 1.00 MB on disk 'bookrepoUK_dat2'.
The CREATE DATABASE process is allocating 1.00 MB on disk 'bookrepUK_log'.
The CREATE DATABASE process is allocating 1.00 MB on disk 'bookrepUK_log2'.

## Example 3.1.5: Creating a database using a filegroup

In this example, we will recreate the `BookRepositoryUK` database, this time placing the secondary data file into its own filegroup, named `FG2`. We'll also place the `.mdf`, `.ndf`, and log files on their own partitions:

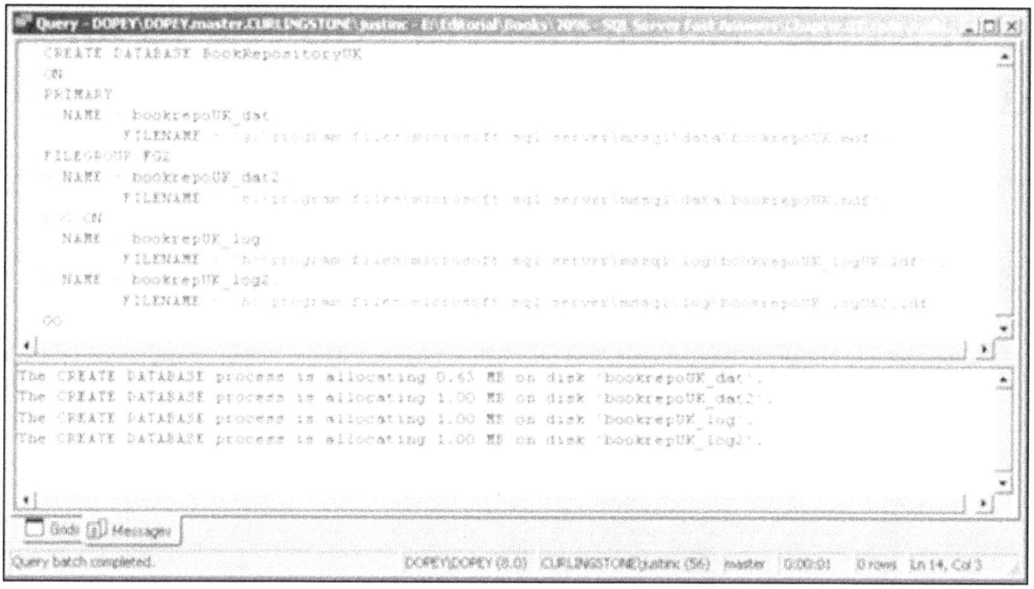


## Example 3.1.6: Creating a database with a different collation using COLLATE

In this example, we will create a database using a French collation, which is accent-insensitive and case-sensitive. We will use the `model` database defaults:

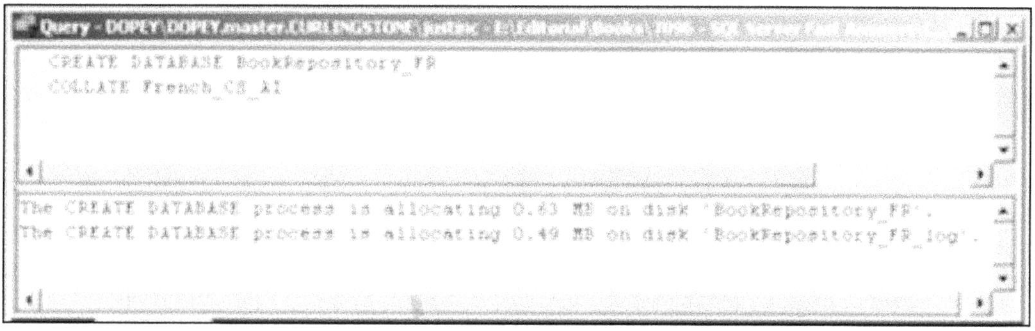


To confirm your changes, you can run DATABASEPROPERTYEX, as shown below:

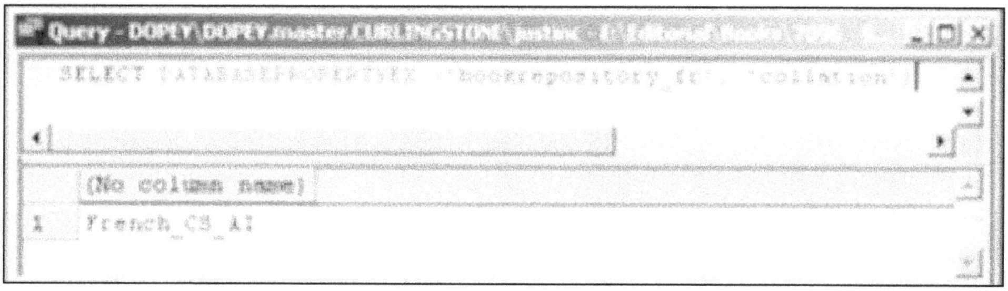


We will investigate this property later in the chapter.

# 3.2 How to... Add a Data or Log File to an Existing Database

To add a new data or log file to an existing database using Enterprise Manager:

- Expand Server Group and registration.
- Expand the Databases folder.
- Right-click the database to which you wish to add a data or log file. Select Properties.
- In the Properties dialog box, to add a new data file, click the Data Files tab.
- Click the row under the last data file, and type in file name, file location and name, megabytes to be allocated, and the filegroup to which it belongs. Designate automatic growth options and maximum file size allowed:

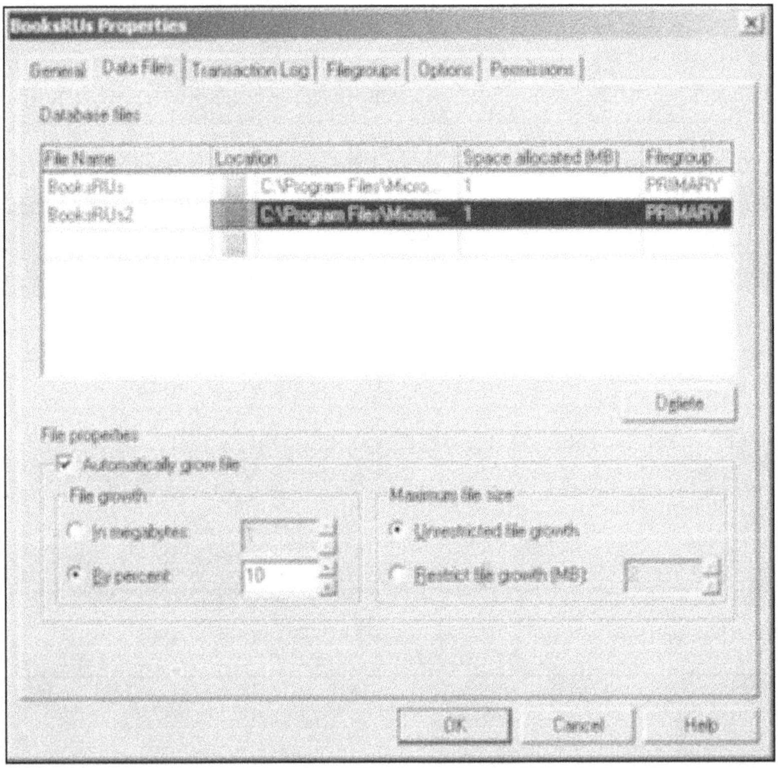


- To add a new transaction log file, select the Transaction Log tab and follow the same steps as for Data Files.
- Select OK when finished.

The following example adds a new data file to the `Inventory_UK` database using Transact-SQL:

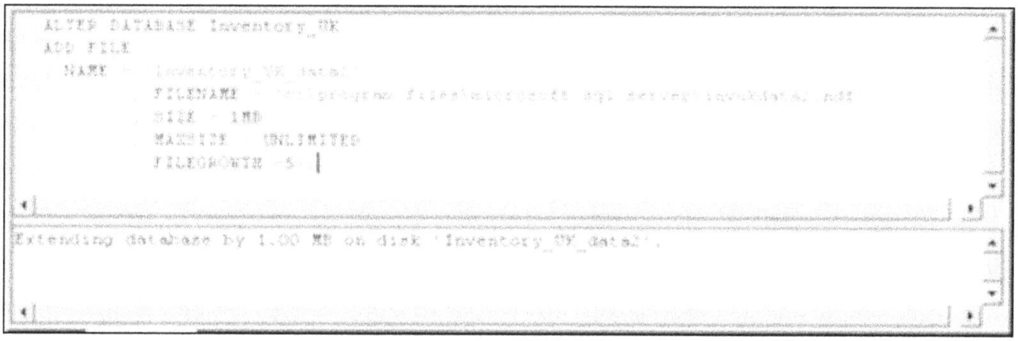
ALTER DATABASE Inventory_UK
ADD FILE
SIZE = 1MB
MAXSIZE = UNLIMITED

If we wanted to add an additional transaction log to `Inventory_UK`, we could use the following syntax:

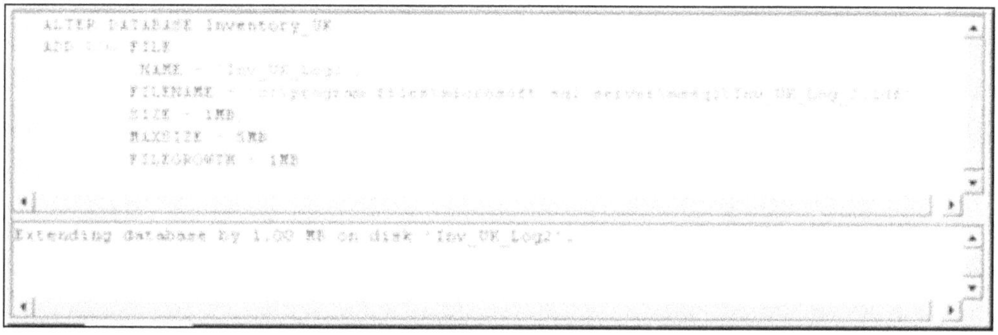
ALTER DATABASE Inventory_UK
SIZE = 1MB

# 3.3 How to... Remove a Data or Log File from a Database

To remove a data or log file in Enterprise Manager:

- Expand the **Server** group and registration.
- Expand the **Databases** folder.
- Right-click the database from which you wish to delete data or log file.
- Select Properties then the **Data File** tab to delete a data file. The data file should not contain data; if it does, issue a `DBCC SHRINKFILE` (filename, `EMPTYFILE`) command. See further on in this chapter for more details. Click the file you wish to delete and press the **Delete** button:

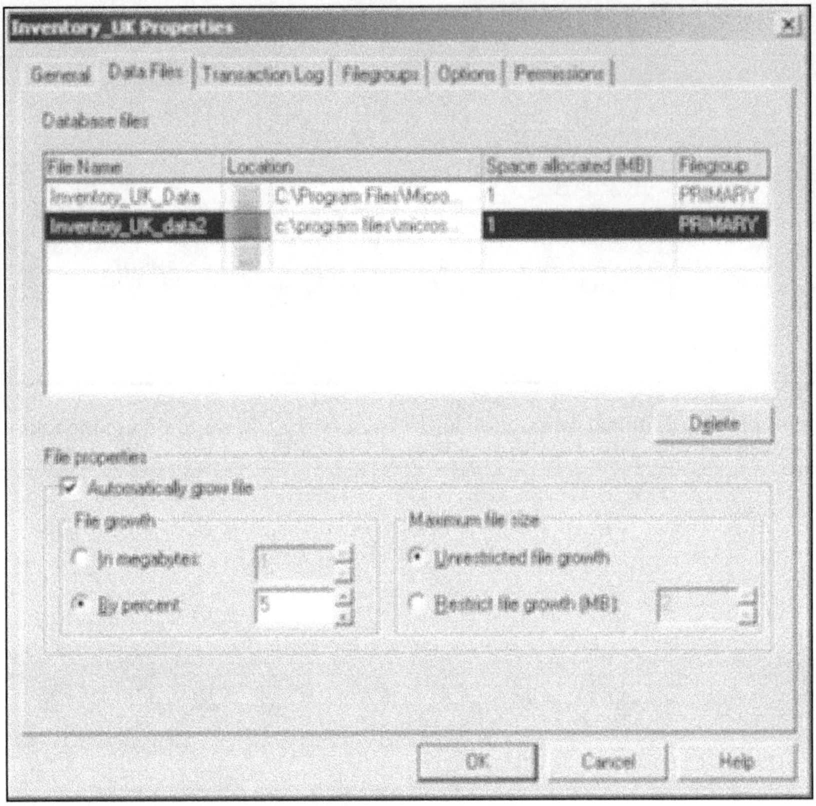


- To delete a transaction log file, select the Transaction Log tab.
- Click the transaction log you wish to delete. You cannot delete a transaction log that contains an active virtual log. See *How to...* 3.16 for a discussion of the logical and physical behavior of the transaction log. You must backup or truncate the log until the active portion is no longer on the file you wish to delete. If the transaction log is not in use, click Delete.

In both scenarios, there must be at least one data file and one transaction log. The primary data file cannot be deleted.

In the following example, we will delete a data file using Transact-SQL:

- First, verify the logical file name with `sp_helpfile`:

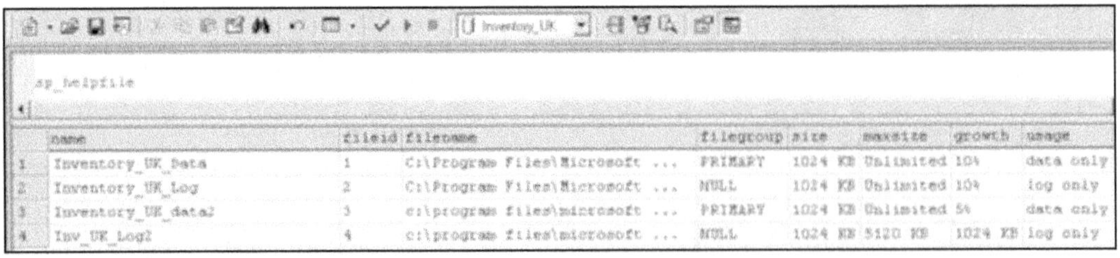

```
sp_helpfile
```

| | name | fileid | filename | filegroup | size | maxsize | growth | usage |
|---|---|---|---|---|---|---|---|---|
| 1 | Inventory_UK_Data | 1 | C:\Program Files\Microsoft ... | PRIMARY | 1024 KB | Unlimited | 10% | data only |
| 2 | Inventory_UK_Log | 2 | C:\Program Files\Microsoft ... | NULL | 1024 KB | Unlimited | 10% | log only |
| 3 | Inventory_UK_data2 | 3 | c:\program files\microsoft ... | PRIMARY | 1024 KB | Unlimited | 5% | data only |
| 4 | Inv_UK_Log2 | 4 | c:\program files\microsoft ... | NULL | 1024 KB | 5120 KB | 1024 KB | log only |

- ❑ Run the ALTER DATABASE command:

```
ALTER DATABASE Inventory_UK
REMOVE FILE Inventory_data2
```

- ❑ Removing a transaction log file uses the same syntax:

```
ALTER DATABASE Inventory_UK
REMOVE FILE Inventory_Log2
```

# 3.4 How to... Change a File's Logical Name

The following is an example of changing the logical name of a file. In this case, we will change the `Inventory_UK` database's data file from the logical name `Inventory_Data`, to `Inventory_UK_Data`:

```
ALTER DATABASE Inventory_UK
MODIFY FILE
(NAME = Inventory_Data,
NEWNAME = Inventory_UK_Data)
```

You cannot change the physical file name using `ALTER DATABASE`. The `*.mdf` file can be renamed if you detach the database, rename the file, and reattach.

# 3.5 How to... Change a Database Owner

The database owner (or `dbo`) can perform all database functions. This is not to be confused with the `db_owner` fixed database role, which has the same permissions but can allow one or more members. The distinction is that `dbo` is a user and not a group, and only one login can be associated with `dbo` (although `sysadmin` is implicitly associated with `dbo`).

To change the login that is linked to `dbo`, use `sp_changedbowner`.

> **Beginning with SQL Server 2000 Service Pack 3, only members of the `sysadmin` fixed server role may use the `sp_changedbowner` system stored procedure.**

Below is an example of changing the database owner to `sa`:

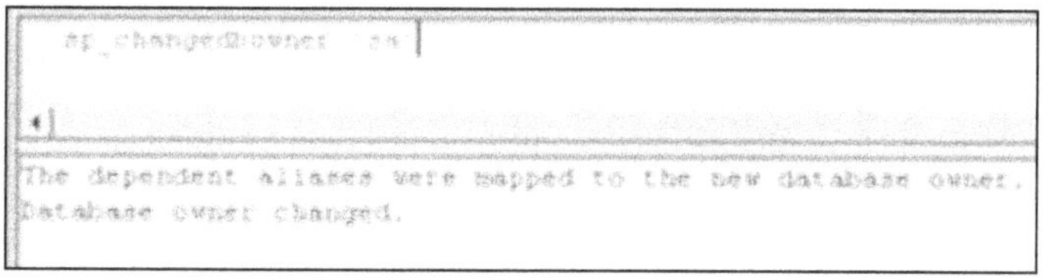

# Database Options

Database options can be categorized under the following groupings:

- State options
- Auto options
- Cursor options
- Recovery options
- ANSI SQL options

Database options can be configured in Enterprise Manager, using ALTER DATABASE, and with the stored procedure sp_dboption. We will not review sp_dboption in detail, as this is included in SQL Server 2000 for backward compatibility only. All options except one that can be configured with sp_dboption, can also be configured with ALTER DATABASE. For other options, get in the habit of using ALTER DATABASE, as sp_dboption may be removed in future versions of SQL Server.

## DB Chaining with sp_dboption

The one option that must be configured using sp_dboption is **db chaining** and was introduced in SQL Server 2000 Service Pack 3. In Chapter 2, we reviewed the Cross DB Ownership Chaining server option. This option allows you to use cross-database security within your SQL Server instance. Cross-database ownership chaining occurs when a source database object depends on objects in other databases. When the source database object and the target objects in the target databases are owned by the same login account, and cross-database ownership chaining is enabled, SQL Server will not check permissions on the target objects. The database user names owning the objects can be different; provided the login mapped to the user is the same, permissions are not re-checked.

If this server level option is disabled, you can enable this option for individual user databases using sp_dboption. If the server level option is disabled, all participants in a cross database ownership chain must have the db chaining database option enabled. This option can only be set for user databases. If the server level option is enabled, the database level options are ignored. You must be a member of the sysadmin fixed server role to change this option.

The following is an example of using sp_dboption to enable cross-database ownership chaining for the Northwind database. Keep in mind that the same syntax is used for both the source and target databases:

```
EXEC sp_dboption 'Northwind', 'db chaining', true
GO
```

The first parameter is the database for which you wish to enable the option. The second parameter is the name of the database option to configure, in this case 'db chaining'. The last parameter is the value to set the database option, in this case true.

For each of the other options, we will review: what it configures; whether it can be configured using Enterprise Manager; and the ALTER DATABASE syntax.

# State Options

State options define the status of the database.

## OFFLINE | ONLINE

When a database is in OFFLINE status, it is completely shut down and cannot be modified or accessed (no SELECT, INSERT, UPDATE, DELETE, EXEC). To give a database OFFLINE status in Enterprise Manager:

- ❑ Expand Server Group and registration.
- ❑ Expand the Databases folder.
- ❑ Right-click the database you wish to take OFFLINE or ONLINE.
- ❑ Select All Tasks, and Take Offline (if database is online) or Bring Online (if the database is offline).

### *ALTER DATABASE Syntax Examples*

To take a database offline:

```
USE master
GO
ALTER DATABASE Inventory
SET OFFLINE
```

To bring a database online:

```
USE master
GO
ALTER DATABASE Inventory
SET ONLINE
```

## READ_ONLY | READ_WRITE

When READ_ONLY is set for a database, users can only retrieve data and cannot modify it. READ_ONLY removes locking overhead and automatic recovery options. READ_ONLY can provide significant performance benefits to large or frequently accessed databases that do not require updates. Prior to marking your database as READ_ONLY, make sure to update statistics, rebuild or add the appropriate indexes, add users and permissions, and to implement any other required database modifications. Such modifications are **not** allowed once the database is READ_ONLY.

The database cannot have connections to it when changing the mode to READ_ONLY. Remove all connections, or set the database to SINGLE_USER (see next section). READ_WRITE is the reverse of READ_ONLY. To change a database to READ_ONLY or READ_WRITE in Enterprise Manager:

- ❑ Expand Server Group and registration.
- ❑ Expand the Databases folder and right-click the chosen database.
- ❑ Select Properties.
- ❑ In the Database Properties dialog box select the Options tab.
- ❑ In the Access section, select or de-select Read-only.

### *ALTER DATABASE Syntax Examples*

To enable READ_ONLY:

```
USE master
GO
ALTER DATABASE Inventory
SET READ_ONLY
```

To enable READ_WRITE (disable READ_ONLY):

```
USE master
GO
ALTER DATABASE Inventory
SET READ_WRITE
```

## SINGLE_USER | RESTRICTED_USER | MULTI_USER

SINGLE_USER mode restricts database access to **one** user connection. SINGLE_USER mode cannot be granted if other users are connected to the database, unless the WITH ROLLBACK clause is included with your modification (described in the next section). WITH ROLLBACK will roll back any existing connections to the database. All other connections except the one changing this option are broken. SINGLE_USER is often needed to fix database issues, such as running DBCC CHECKDB (with fix options included), or when changing a database to READ_ONLY mode, and back again.

RESTRICTED_USER mode restricts database access to db_owner, dbcreator, and sysadmin roles. All other users are disconnected. You may need to perform this action when dealing with problems where user activity may interrupt your activities (changing tables, options, etc).

MULTI_USER mode lets all users with proper access connect to the database.

To change the access mode in Enterprise Manager:

- Expand the Server Group and registration.
- Expand the Databases folder and right-click the chosen database.
- Select Properties.
- In the Database Properties dialog box select the Options tab.
- Check the Restrict access check box in the ~ section to enable either SINGLE_USER or RESTRICTED_USER modes. Select the bullet to choose between the two. To disable, uncheck Restrict access.

### *ALTER DATABASE Syntax Examples*

With the ALTER DATABASE syntax you can use the WITH clause to specify how to terminate incomplete transactions during state modifications:

- WITH ROLLBACK AFTER *integer* gives users a set amount of time before incomplete transactions are rolled back and connections are broken.
- WITH ROLLBACK IMMEDIATE breaks all connections (except the one running the ALTER DATABASE statement) immediately.

- WITH NO_WAIT will cancel the ALTER DATABASE if any connections exist during a SINGLE_USER mode option setting. ALTER DATABASE will also be cancelled during a RESTRICTED_USER mode setting if regular users (without dbo or sa permissions) are in the database.

To enable SINGLE_USER mode:

```
USE master
GO
ALTER DATABASE Inventory
SET SINGLE_USER
```

To disable SINGLE_USER mode:

```
USE master
GO
ALTER DATABASE Inventory
SET MULTI_USER
```

To enable SINGLE_USER mode and rollback incomplete transactions after 10 seconds:

```
USE master
GO
ALTER DATABASE Inventory
SET SINGLE_USER
WITH ROLLBACK AFTER 10
```

To enable SINGLE_USER mode and rollback incomplete transactions immediately:

```
USE master
GO
ALTER DATABASE Inventory
SET SINGLE_USER
WITH ROLLBACK IMMEDIATE
```

To enable SINGLE_USER mode and cancel the ALTER DATABASE if any users are still connected:

```
USE master
GO
ALTER DATABASE Inventory
SET SINGLE_USER
WITH NO_WAIT
```

To enable RESTRICTED_USER mode:

```
USE master
GO
ALTER DATABASE Inventory
SET RESTRICTED_USER
```

To disable RESTRICTED_USER mode:

```
USE master
GO
ALTER DATABASE Inventory
SET MULTI_USER
```

To enable RESTRICTED_USER mode and rollback incomplete transactions after 10 seconds:

```
USE master
GO
ALTER DATABASE Inventory
SET RESTRICTED_USER
WITH ROLLBACK AFTER 10
```

To enable RESTRICTED_USER mode and rollback incomplete transactions immediately:

```
USE master
GO
ALTER DATABASE Inventory
SET RESTRICTED_USER
WITH ROLLBACK IMMEDIATE
```

The next example sets the database to RESTRICTED_USER mode. If any users are still connected, the statement will be cancelled because of the WITH NO_WAIT clause:

```
USE master
GO
ALTER DATABASE Inventory
SET RESTRICTED_USER
WITH NO_WAIT
```

# Auto Options

Auto options designate automatic behaviors for the database.

## AUTO_CLOSE

When AUTO_CLOSE is enabled, the database is closed and shut down when the last user connection exits and all processes are completed. This is good for personal databases (databases on Microsoft SQL Server Personal Edition, or Desktop Engine), but not for databases with multiple user activity, as the overhead of shutting down and starting up the database is too significant.

To enable AUTO_CLOSE with Enterprise Manager:

- Expand Server Group and registration.
- Expand the Databases folder and right-click the appropriate database.
- Select Properties.
- In the Database Properties dialog box select the Options tab.
- In the Settings section, check Auto shrink to enable, or uncheck to disable.

### *ALTER DATABASE Syntax Examples*

To enable AUTO_CLOSE:

```
USE master
GO
ALTER DATABASE Inventory
SET AUTO_CLOSE ON
```

To disable AUTO_CLOSE:

```
USE master
GO
ALTER DATABASE Inventory
SET AUTO_CLOSE OFF
```

## AUTO_CREATE_STATISTICS

When AUTO_CREATE_STATISTICS is enabled, SQL Server automatically generates statistical information about the distribution of values in a column. This information assists the query processor with generating an acceptable query execution plan (the internal plan for returning the result set requested by the query).

This option should be enabled, as the performance cost is not significant, and the benefits of having the statistics are great. Only consider disabling this option if server resources (CPU, memory) are at a premium. Do, however, update statistics manually, after data updates and over time, if you decide to disable this option. See Chapter 17 instructions on how to update statistics manually.

To enable AUTO_CREATE_STATISTICS in Enterprise Manager:

- ❑ Expand Server Group and registration.
- ❑ Expand the Databases folder and right-click the database.
- ❑ Select Properties.
- ❑ Select the Options tab.
- ❑ In the Settings section, check Auto create statistics to enable, and uncheck to disable automatic statistics.

### *ALTER DATABASE Syntax Example*

To enable AUTO_CREATE_STATISTICS:

```
USE master
GO
ALTER DATABASE Inventory
SET AUTO_CREATE_STATISTICS ON
```

To disable AUTO_CREATE_STATISTICS:

```
USE master
GO
ALTER DATABASE Inventory
SET AUTO_CREATE_STATISTICS OFF
```

## AUTO_UPDATE_STATISTICS

When enabled, this option automatically updates statistics already created for your tables. It is important to keep statistics up-to-date, especially if your tables have frequent data INSERT, UPDATE, or DELETE operations. Updated statistics increase the likelihood of the SQL Server query processor making informed decisions, translating to better query performance. As with AUTO_CREATE_STATISTICS, the cost/benefit of keeping this option enabled is significant.

To enable AUTO_UPDATE_STATISTICS in Enterprise Manager:

- Expand Server Group and registration.
- Expand the Databases folder and right-click the appropriate database.
- Select Properties.
- Select the Options tab.
- In the Settings section, check Auto update statistics to enable, and uncheck to disable automatic updating of statistics.

### *ALTER DATABASE Syntax Examples*

To enable AUTO_UPDATE_STATISTICS:

```
USE master
GO
ALTER DATABASE Inventory
SET AUTO_UPDATE_STATISTICS ON
```

To disable AUTO_UPDATE_STATISTICS:

```
USE master
GO
ALTER DATABASE Inventory
SET AUTO_UPDATE_STATISTICS OFF
```

## AUTO_SHRINK

When AUTO_SHRINK is enabled, SQL Server shrinks data and log files automatically. Shrinking will only occur when more than 25 percent of the file has unused space. The database is then shrunk to either 25% free, or the original data or log file size. For example, if you defined your primary data file to be 100MB, a shrink operation would be unable to decrease the file size below 100MB.

This option can have a dreadful impact on performance. Shrinking files takes up system resources, and having unplanned shrink events can slow down your production performance significantly. It is best, therefore, to leave this disabled and manage your file space manually.

To enable or disable AUTO_SHRINK in Enterprise Manager:

- Expand Server Group and registration.
- Expand the Databases folder and right-click the database.
- Select Properties.
- Select the Options tab.
- In the Settings section, check Auto shrink to enable, and uncheck to disable, automatic shrinking of the data and log files.

### *ALTER DATABASE Syntax Examples*

To enable AUTO_SHRINK:

```
USE master
GO
ALTER DATABASE Inventory
SET AUTO_SHRINK ON
```

To disable AUTO_SHRINK:

```
USE master
GO
ALTER DATABASE Inventory
SET AUTO_SHRINK OFF
```

# Cursor Options

Cursor options designate Transact-SQL cursor behaviors within the database.

## CURSOR_CLOSE_ON_COMMIT

When CURSOR_CLOSE_ON_COMMIT is enabled, Transact-SQL cursors automatically close once a transaction is committed. Connection level SET options override this setting, if set. The default is OFF, meaning that cursors stay open until they are explicitly closed or the connection is closed. Keeping cursors open until explicitly closed allows you to refresh and continue working with the cursor when necessary. The danger of keeping too many cursors open is that you depend on the application or developer to close cursors when they are finished with them. Cursors take up memory, and can place locks on database resources, thus potentially reducing concurrency and performance.

CURSOR_CLOSE_ON_COMMIT is not configurable in Enterprise Manager.

### *ALTER DATABASE Syntax Examples*

To enable CURSOR_CLOSE_ON_COMMIT:

```
USE master
GO
ALTER DATABASE Inventory
SET CURSOR_CLOSE_ON_COMMIT ON
```

To disable CURSOR_CLOSE_ON_COMMIT:

```
USE master
GO
ALTER DATABASE Inventory
SET CURSOR_CLOSE_ON_COMMIT OFF
```

## CURSOR_DEFAULT LOCAL | GLOBAL

If CURSOR_DEFAULT LOCAL is enabled, cursors created without explicitly setting scope as GLOBAL will default to local access. If CURSOR_DEFAULT GLOBAL is enabled, cursors created without explicitly setting scope as LOCAL will default to GLOBAL access.

LOCAL cursors can only be read by the local batch, stored procedure, or trigger for the created cursor connection. GLOBAL cursors can be referenced from any connection. GLOBAL is the default setting. Changing the default setting to LOCAL will reduce the chances of cursor naming conflicts (two connections trying to open the same cursor, using the same cursor name).

CURSOR_DEFAULT is not configurable in Enterprise Manager.

### *ALTER DATABASE Syntax Examples*

To enable CURSOR_DEFAULT LOCAL:

```
USE master
GO
ALTER DATABASE Inventory
SET CURSOR_DEFAULT LOCAL
```

To enable CURSOR_DEFAULT GLOBAL:

```
USE master
GO
ALTER DATABASE Inventory
SET CURSOR_DEFAULT GLOBAL
```

# Recovery Options

These options allow you to configure the recoverability of your database.

## RECOVERY FULL | BULK_LOGGED | SIMPLE

SQL Server 2000 introduced the concept of recovery options. Prior to 2000, individual database options defined the behaviors now aggregated in the recovery model.

FULL recovery mode ensures full recoverability from database and transaction log backups. Bulk operations (SELECT INTO, CREATE INDEX, bulk loading) are fully logged. Use this option when you must ensure point-in-time recovery, via a combination of full database backups, and transaction log backups.

BULK_LOGGED recovery mode minimally logs bulk operations, resulting in less log space used. The trade-off is that you cannot issue a point-in-time recovery from a transaction log backup (STOPAT command). Instead, you can only recover to the end of the log backup. If point-in-time recovery is not necessary, use this option. See Chapter 6 for more detail on how restore operations work.

SIMPLE recovery mode does not allow backups of the transaction log, and bulk operations are not logged. Transaction logs are frequently truncated, removing committed transactions. Although you cannot perform transaction log backups, you can still perform full and differential backups with this recovery mode. Do not select this mode if you want the advantages that a transaction log backup gives you.

To implement RECOVERY operations in Enterprise Manager:

- ❑ Expand Server Group and registration.
- ❑ Expand the Databases folder and right-click the database.
- ❑ Select Properties.

- Select the Options tab.
- In the Recovery section, select the Model from the dropdown box.

### *ALTER DATABASE Syntax Examples*

To set the recovery model to `FULL`:

```
USE master
GO
ALTER DATABASE Inventory
SET RECOVERY FULL
```

To set the recovery model to `BULK_LOGGED`:

```
USE master
GO
ALTER DATABASE Inventory
SET RECOVERY BULK_LOGGED
```

To set the recovery model to `SIMPLE`:

```
USE master
GO
ALTER DATABASE Inventory
SET RECOVERY SIMPLE
```

## TORN_PAGE_DETECTION

SQL Server pages are 8KB. Windows 2000 disk I/O operations, however, use 512 byte sectors. If an unexpected outage or power failure occurs, a 'torn' page can result, with the 8KB-page write not completely written. Enabling the `TORN_PAGE_DETECTION` option allows SQL Server to detect incomplete I/O operations.

If a torn page occurs when the database is online, an I/O error is raised and the connection is killed; if discovered during database recovery, the database assumes 'suspect' status. SQL Server gives a database 'suspect' status when it is unable to recover the database. Recovery is the process SQL Server goes through prior to making a database available; when SQL Server first starts up, each database is recovered. Recovery completes transactions that were committed prior to the previous shutdown, but not yet written to disk. Recovery also 'rolls back' transactions that were not committed prior to shutdown, and, therefore, must be 'undone' (see Chapter 5 for more information on transactions).

Suspect status is triggered when SQL Server cannot finish the recovery process. This could be caused by a missing or corrupt file, or by insufficient space on the drive or array to complete the recovery process.

To enable `TORN_PAGE_DETECTION` in Enterprise Manager:

- Expand Server Group and registration.
- Expand the Databases folder and right-click the appropriate database.
- Select Properties.
- Select the Options tab.
- In the Settings section, check Torn page detection to enable, and uncheck to disable.

### *ALTER DATABASE Syntax Examples*

To enable TORN_PAGE_DETECTION:

```
USE master
GO
ALTER DATABASE Inventory
SET TORN_PAGE_DETECTION ON
```

To disable TORN_PAGE_DETECTION:

```
USE master
GO
ALTER DATABASE Inventory
SET TORN_PAGE_DETECTION OFF
```

# ANSI SQL Options

ANSI SQL options define the behavior of Transact-SQL within the database as it relates to ANSI standards.

## ANSI_NULL_DEFAULT

When ANSI_NULL_DEFAULT is set to ON, columns not explicitly defined with a NULL or NOT NULL in a CREATE or ALTER table statement will default to allow NULL values. Connection level settings can override this option. Generally, NULL should be avoided whenever possible. When possible, try to define columns with default values or deferred values (values that will be changed later on).

To enable ANSI_NULL_DEFAULT in Enterprise Manager:

- Expand Server Group and registration.
- Expand the Databases folder and right-click the appropriate database.
- Select Properties.
- Select the Options tab.
- In the Settings section, check the ANSI NULL default checkbox to enable ANSI_NULL_DEFAULT settings. Disable by unchecking the checkbox.

### *ALTER DATABASE Syntax Example*

To enable ANSI_NULL_DEFAULT:

```
USE master
GO
ALTER DATABASE Inventory
SET ANSI_NULL_DEFAULT ON
```

To disable ANSI_NULL_DEFAULT:

```
USE master
GO
ALTER DATABASE Inventory
SET ANSI_NULL_DEFAULT OFF
```

# ANSI_NULLS

When ANSI_NULLS are enabled, a SELECT statement using '=NULL' in a WHERE clause will return zero rows even if a NULL value exists in the column. Comparisons against a NULL value return UNKNOWN. (Comparisons against NULL are done using the IS NULL or IS NOT NULL syntax.) Connection settings override this option. This option must be ON when creating or manipulating indexes on computed columns or indexed views. Unless you have a compelling reason to do so, this option should be enabled, as it complies with ANSI standards and is the behavior that most developers expect to see with SQL Server.

ANSI_NULLS is not configurable in Enterprise Manager.

### *ALTER DATABASE Syntax Examples*

To enable ANSI_NULLS:

```
USE master
GO
ALTER DATABASE Inventory
SET ANSI_NULLS ON
```

To disable ANSI_NULLS:

```
USE master
GO
ALTER DATABASE Inventory
SET ANSI_NULLS OFF
```

# ANSI_PADDING

ANSI_PADDING controls column storage when values are shorter than fixed length size, or contain trailing blanks. When set ON for CHAR or BINARY columns, trailing blanks are appended to column storage. This trimming does not take place with VARCHAR and VARBINARY columns. The ANSI standard is to have this option set ON. This option must be ON for creation and manipulation of indexes on computed columns or indexed views. This option is set ON when connected to by the SQL Server ODBC and OLE DB drivers.

ANSI_PADDING is not configurable in Enterprise Manager.

### *ALTER DATABASE Syntax Examples*

To enable ANSI_PADDING:

```
USE master
GO
ALTER DATABASE Inventory
SET ANSI_PADDING ON
```

To disable ANSI_PADDING:

```
USE master
GO
ALTER DATABASE Inventory
SET ANSI_PADDING OFF
```

## ANSI_WARNINGS

ANSI_WARNINGS impacts query behavior as follows:

| Query Behavior | ANSI_WARNINGS ON | ANSI_WARNINGS OFF |
|---|---|---|
| NULL value in an aggregate function. | Warning message given. | No warning message. |
| Division by zero or arithmetic overflow. | Statement is rolled back and error is generated. | Statement is rolled back and error is generated. |
| String or binary data value size limit is exceeded by INSERT or UPDATE statement. | Warning is given and statement is rolled back. | The truncated value will be inserted or updated. |

Connection level settings can override this option. This option must be ON for creation and manipulation of indexes on computed columns or indexed views and, aside from this, is generally recommended.

ANSI_WARNINGS is not configurable in Enterprise Manager.

### *ALTER DATABASE Syntax Examples*

To enable ANSI_WARNINGS:

```
USE master
GO
ALTER DATABASE Inventory
SET ANSI_WARNINGS ON
```

To disable ANSI_WARNINGS:

```
USE master
GO
ALTER DATABASE Inventory
SET ANSI_WARNINGS OFF
```

## ARITHABORT

When ARITHABORT is set to ON, a query with an overflow or division by zero will terminate the query and return an error. If this occurs within a transaction, then that transaction gets rolled back. This option must be ON to create or manipulate indexes on computed columns or indexed views. Keep this option enabled, unless you have a good reason not to do so.

ARITHABORT is not configurable in Enterprise Manager.

### *ALTER DATABASE Syntax Examples*

To enable ARITHABORT:

```
USE master
GO
ALTER DATABASE Inventory
SET ARITHABORT ON
```

To disable ARITHABORT:

```
USE master
GO
ALTER DATABASE Inventory
SET ARITHABORT OFF
```

# NUMERIC_ROUNDABORT

When NUMERIC_ROUNDABORT is set to ON, an error is produced when a loss of precision occurs in an expression. If ARITHABORT is OFF while NUMERIC_ROUNDABORT is ON, a warning is produced instead of an error, and a NULL is returned. This option must be ON in order to create or manipulate indexes on computed columns or indexed views. Keep this option enabled, unless you have a good reason not to do so.

NUMERIC_ROUNDABORT is not configurable in Enterprise Manager.

## *ALTER DATABASE Syntax Examples*

To enable NUMERIC_ROUNDABORT:

```
USE master
GO
ALTER DATABASE Inventory
SET NUMERIC_ROUNDABORT ON
```

To disable NUMERIC_ROUNDABORT:

```
USE master
GO
ALTER DATABASE Inventory
SET NUMERIC_ROUNDABORT OFF
```

# CONCAT_NULL_YIELDS_NULL

When CONCAT_NULL_YIELDS_NULL is set to ON, concatenating a NULL value with a string produces a NULL value. This option must be ON in order to create or manipulate indexes on computed columns or indexed views. Keep this option enabled, unless you have a good reason not to do so. Connection level settings override this option.

CONCAT_NULL_YIELDS_NULL is not configurable in Enterprise Manager.

## *ALTER DATABASE Syntax Examples*

To enable CONCAT_NULL_YIELDS_NULL:

```
USE master
GO
ALTER DATABASE Inventory
SET CONCAT_NULL_YIELDS_NULL ON
```

To disable CONCAT_NULL_YIELDS_NULL:

```
USE master
GO
ALTER DATABASE Inventory
SET CONCAT_NULL_YIELDS_NULL OFF
```

## QUOTED_IDENTIFIER

When QUOTED_IDENTIFIER is set to ON, identifiers can be delimited by double quotation marks, and literals with single quotation marks. When OFF, identifiers may not have quotes, but literals may be delimited by either single or double quotes.

In SQL Server 7.0, Query Analyzer had this option turned OFF by default, so programmers were able to use double quotes for representing string values.

For example, the following query was valid in SQL Server 7.0, by default:

```
SELECT *
FROM Books
WHERE vchBookName = "SQL Server Fast Answers for DBA and Developer"
```

In SQL Server 2000, by default, you would receive the following error when running this example query with quotations, instead of single quotes:

```
Server: Msg 207, Level 16, State 3, Line 1
Invalid column name 'SQL Server Fast Answers for DBA and Developer'.
```

In SQL Server 2000 the behavior has been changed, and this option is ON by default. As a best practice, use single quotes for representing strings.

QUOTED_IDENTIFIERS must be ON in order to create or manipulate indexes on computed columns or indexed views. Connection level settings override this option.

To configure QUOTED_IDENTIFIERS in Enterprise Manager:

- Expand Server Group and registration.
- Expand the Databases folder and right-click the database.
- Select Properties.
- Select the Options tab.
- In the Settings section, check Use quoted identifiers to enable (or uncheck to disable) this option.

### *ALTER DATABASE Syntax Examples*

To enable QUOTED_IDENTIFIER:

```
USE master
GO
ALTER DATABASE Inventory
SET QUOTED_IDENTIFIER ON
```

To disable QUOTED_IDENTIFIER:

```
USE master
GO
ALTER DATABASE Inventory
SET QUOTED_IDENTIFIER OFF
```

## RECURSIVE_TRIGGERS

When the RECURSIVE_TRIGGERS option is enabled, triggers can fire recursively (trigger 1 fires trigger 2, which fires trigger 1 again). When enabled, a chain of trigger firing can be nested up to 32 levels, meaning that recursion is limited to 32 trigger firings.

To enable RECURSIVE_TRIGGERS in Enterprise Manager:

- Expand Server Group and registration.
- Expand the Databases folder and right-click the appropriate database.
- Select Properties.
- Select the Options tab.
- In the Settings section, check Recursive triggers to enable (or uncheck to disable) this option.

### *ALTER DATABASE Syntax Example*

To enable RECURSIVE_TRIGGERS:

```
USE master
GO
ALTER DATABASE Inventory
SET RECURSIVE_TRIGGERS ON
```

To disable RECURSIVE_TRIGGERS:

```
USE master
GO
ALTER DATABASE Inventory
SET RECURSIVE_TRIGGERS OFF
```

# 3.6 How to... View Database Options with DATABASEPROPERTYEX

One easy way to view the database properties we examined in the previous section is by using DATABASEPROPERTYEX.

The syntax is DATABASEPROPERTYEX (databasename, propertyname).

To find out if ANSI_PADDING is enabled for your database, you would execute the following syntax in Query Analyzer:

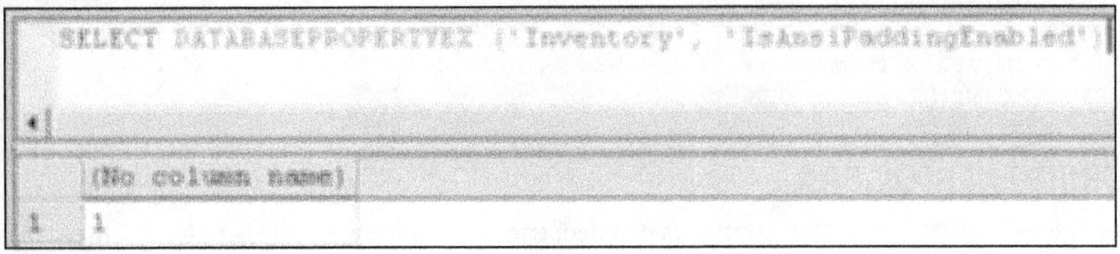
SELECT DATABASEPROPERTYEX ('Inventory', 'IsAnsiPaddingEnabled')
(No column name)
1
1

The return code of 1 indicates Yes. A value of 0 means No, and a NULL value indicates an invalid input. String values can also be returned for other properties, such as Collation, which returns a sql_variant data type.

The following are properties you can reference with DATBASEPROPERTYEX and their associated database properties from the previous section. If there is no associated database property, a short description is included:

| Property | Associated DB Option or Description |
|---|---|
| Collation | Default collation for the database. |
| IsAnsiNullDefault | ANSI_NULL_DEFAULT |
| IsAnsiNullsEnabled | ANSI_NULLS |
| IsAnsiPaddingEnabled | ANSI_PADDING |
| IsAnsiWarningsEnabled | ANSI_WARNINGS |
| IsArithmeticAbortEnabled | ARITHABORT |
| IsAutoClose | AUTO_CLOSE |
| IsAutoCreateStatistics | AUTO_CREATE_STATISTICS |
| IsAutoShrink | AUTO_SHRINK |
| IsAutoUpdateStatistics | AUTO_UPDATE_STATISTICS |
| IsCloseCursorsOnCommit Enabled | CURSOR_CLOSE_ON_COMMIT |
| IsFulltextEnabled | Designates if database is full-text enabled. |
| IsInStandBy | Designates if the database is in Stand By mode, where database can have read-only activity only, and may apply additional RESTORE LOG operations. |
| IsLocalCursorsDefault | CURSOR_DEFAULT LOCAL |
| IsMergePublished | Designates that tables can be published for merge publication. |
| IsNullConcat | CONCAT_NULL_YIELDS_NULL |
| IsNumericRoundAbortEnabled | NUMERIC_ROUNDABORT |
| IsQuotedIdentifiersEnabled | QUOTED_IDENTIFIER |

| Property | Associated DB Option or Description |
|---|---|
| IsRecursiveTriggersEnabled | RECURSIVE_TRIGGERS |
| IsSubscribed | Indicates that database can subscribe to publications. |
| IsTornPageDetectionEnabled | TORN_PAGE_DETECTION |
| Recovery | RECOVERY FULL \| BULK_LOGGED \| SIMPLE |
| SQLSortOrder | SQL Collation Sort Order ID (Pre SQL Server 2000). |
| Status | Online or offline database. |
| Updateability | READ_ONLY \| READ_WRITE |
| UserAccess | SINGLE_USER \| RESTRICTED_USER \| MULTI_USER |
| Version | SQL Server version number used by SQL Server for upgrades. |

# 3.7 How to... View User Options for the Current Connection with DBCC USEROPTIONS

Some database options can in effect be overridden by user options for a user connection; execute DBCC USEROPTIONS to see what user options are in effect. Below is an example of running DBCC USEROPTIONS in Query Analyzer:

This DBCC command shows options that are enabled. If you run the command SET ANSI_PADDING ON, and rerun DBCC USEROPTIONS you will see ansi_padding added to the DBCC result set:

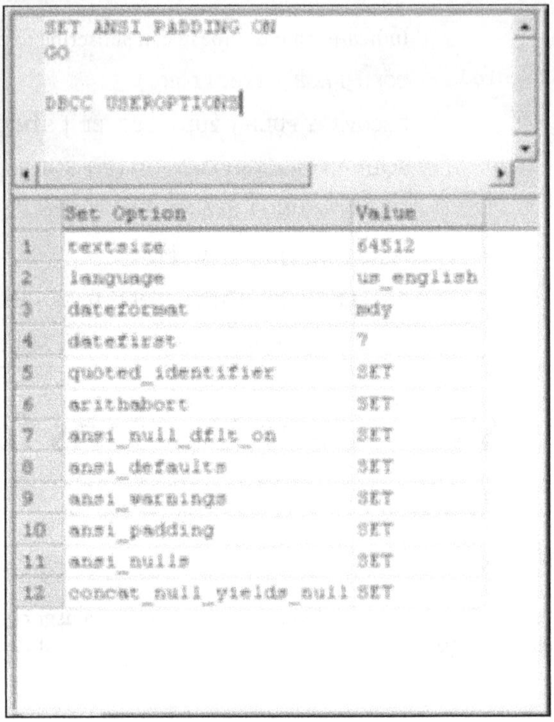


# 3.8 How to... Set User Options in Query Analyzer

You saw a preview in the last example on how to use the SET command to enable database options. The syntax is:

```
SET optionname ON
```

optionname is the value you want to have enabled. You are not limited to database options, but can use other connection properties as well.

For example, the following SET option, NOCOUNT, is used to stop messages from being returned in your query results. Such messages include the number of rows affected by your Transact-SQL statements:

```
SET NOCOUNT ON
```

If your Transact-SQL statement, batch, or procedure produces many row changes, setting NOCOUNT ON can reduce the amount of network traffic, by saving SQL Server from having to update the client as to the status of row changes.

Other SET options not already mentioned in the *Database Option* sections (ARITHABORT, ANSI_NULLS, etc) are:

# SET DATEFIRST

SET DATEFIRST assigns the first day of a week to a number ranging from 1 through 7. For example, to set the first day of the week to Monday:

```
SET DATEFIRST 1
```

To set first day of week to Sunday:

```
SET DATEFIRST 7
```

## SET DEADLOCK_PRIORITY

This option lets you increase the likelihood of a transaction being chosen as the deadlock victim. Your options are:

```
SET DEADLOCK_PRIORITY LOW
```

LOW designates the transaction as a preferred deadlock victim:

```
SET DEADLOCK_PRIORITY NORMAL
```

NORMAL indicates default deadlock handling.

## SET FMTONLY

SET FMTONLY is useful for preventing rows from being processed or sent to the client. When enabled, you only receive meta data. To enable:

```
SET FMTONLY ON
```

If you ran the following query, you would see only the column headers:

```
SELECT *
FROM sysobjects
```

## SET FORCEPLAN

This option forces the query optimizer to process a join in the same order as tables in the FROM clause of your SELECT statements. To enable:

```
SET FORCEPLAN ON
```

It isn't recommended that you use this unless you have a very good reason; the query optimizer should be left to make this sort of decision.

## SET IDENTITY_INSERT

This option allows explicit values to be inserted into an identity column. To enable:

```
SET IDENTITY_INSERT databasename.owner.tablename ON
```

## SET IMPLICIT_TRANSACTIONS

This option enables implicit transactions for the connection, meaning that ALTER TABLE, FETCH, REVOKE, CREATE, GRANT, SELECT, DELETE, INSERT, TRUNCATE TABLE, DROP, OPEN, and UPDATE statements are treated as transactions if no BEGIN TRAN statement is used. Users must commit implicit transactions before closing the database connection, or else the changes will be rolled back. To enable:

```
SET IMPLICIT_TRANSACTIONS ON
```

## SET LANGUAGE

SET LANGUAGE sets the language environment for a connection session and determines datetime formats and system messages.

To enable:

```
SET LANGUAGE N'language or @languagevar
```

For example:

```
SET LANGUAGE French
```

This returns:

Changed language setting to Français

## SET LOCK_TIMEOUT

This setting specifies how long to wait for a lock to be released on a resource. To enable:

```
SET LOCK_TIMEOUT milleseconds
```

The following example sets lock timeouts for 4 seconds:

```
SET LOCK_TIMEOUT 4000
```

## SET NOEXEC

When enabled, SET NOEXEC allows you to compile, but not execute, a query. This enables syntax checking, verification of object names, and debugging. To enable:

```
SET NOEXEC ON
```

## SET PARSEONLY

PARSEONLY checks the syntax of Transact-SQL statements, returning error messages if syntax problems are encountered. The Transact-SQL statement or statements being parsed are not compiled or executed. To enable:

```
SET PARSEONLY ON
```

## SET QUERY_GOVERNOR_COST_LIMIT

Like the server option, this connection level setting limits a query from running if its estimated time exceeds the value designated in:

```
SET QUERY_GOVERNOR_COST_LIMIT seconds
```

This example limits the time to 1 second:

```
SET QUERY_GOVERNOR_COST_LIMIT 1
SELECT * FROM sysobjects,
sysobjects b,
sysobjects c
```

This returns the error:

Server: Msg 8649, Level 17, State 1, Line 3
The query has been canceled because the estimated cost of this query (8450) exceeds the configured threshold of 1. Contact the system administrator.

## SET TRANSACTION ISOLATION LEVEL

This option controls the locking behavior for the connection for SELECT statements. The options are:

- READ COMMITTED
- READ UNCOMMITTED
- REPEATABLE READ
- SERIALIZABLE

To enable READ COMMITTED, for example, run:

```
SET TRANSACTION ISOLATION LEVEL READ COMMITTED
```

See Chapter 5 for an overview of the isolation levels. We have not discussed the SET SHOWPLAN, SHOWPLAN_ALL, SHOWPLAN_TEXT, STATISTICS IO, STATISTICS PROFILE, and STATISTICS TIME options, but will do so in Chapter 17.

# 3.9 How to... Rename a Database with sp_renamedb

If you wish to give a database a new name, follow these steps:

- In Query Analyzer set the database to SINGLE_USER mode. In this example, we are setting the Inventory database to SINGLE_USER mode:

```
ALTER DATABASE Inventory
SET SINGLE_USER
WITH ROLLBACK IMMEDIATE
```

This returns:

The command(s) completed successfully.

- Next, we rename the Inventory database to Inventory_UK. Make sure to use the same window to execute sp_rename, as this is SINGLE_USER mode, or close the existing window prior to opening a new window:

```
sp_renamedb 'Inventory', 'Inventory_UK'
```

This returns:

The database name 'Inventory_UK' has been set.

- Do not forget to return the database to MULTI_USER mode:

```
ALTER DATABASE Inventory_UK
SET MULTI_USER
```

# 3.10 How to... Show Database Information with sp_helpdb

The stored procedure sp_helpdb shows all databases, database size in megabytes, database owner, database ID, date created, compatibility level, and the value of several database options. To execute, use the following syntax in Query Analyzer:

```
EXEC sp_helpdb
```

For example:

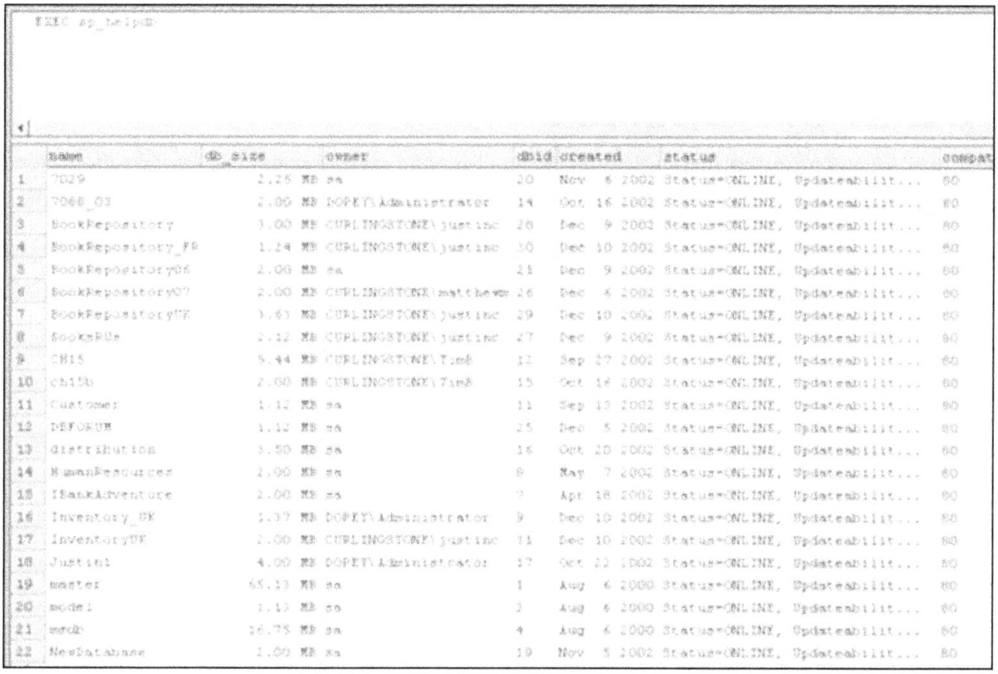


| | name | db_size | owner | dbid | created | status | compat |
|---|---|---|---|---|---|---|---|
| 1 | 7029 | 2.25 MB | sa | 20 | Nov 6 2002 | Status=ONLINE, Updateabilit... | 80 |
| 2 | 7068_03 | 2.00 MB | DOPEY\Administrator | 14 | Oct 16 2002 | Status=ONLINE, Updateabilit... | 80 |
| 3 | BookRepository | 3.00 MB | CURLINGSTONE\justinc | 28 | Dec 9 2002 | Status=ONLINE, Updateabilit... | 80 |
| 4 | BookRepository_FR | 1.24 MB | CURLINGSTONE\justinc | 30 | Dec 10 2002 | Status=ONLINE, Updateabilit... | 80 |
| 5 | BookRepository06 | 2.00 MB | sa | 21 | Dec 9 2002 | Status=ONLINE, Updateabilit... | 80 |
| 6 | BookRepository07 | 2.00 MB | CURLINGSTONE\matthewm | 26 | Dec 6 2002 | Status=ONLINE, Updateabilit... | 80 |
| 7 | BookRepositoryUK | 3.63 MB | CURLINGSTONE\justinc | 29 | Dec 10 2002 | Status=ONLINE, Updateabilit... | 80 |
| 8 | BooksRUs | 2.12 MB | CURLINGSTONE\justinc | 27 | Dec 9 2002 | Status=ONLINE, Updateabilit... | 80 |
| 9 | CH15 | 5.44 MB | CURLINGSTONE\Tim8 | 12 | Sep 27 2002 | Status=ONLINE, Updateabilit... | 80 |
| 10 | ch15b | 2.00 MB | CURLINGSTONE\Tim8 | 15 | Oct 16 2002 | Status=ONLINE, Updateabilit... | 80 |
| 11 | Customer | 1.12 MB | sa | 11 | Sep 13 2002 | Status=ONLINE, Updateabilit... | 80 |
| 12 | DBFORUM | 1.12 MB | sa | 25 | Dec 5 2002 | Status=ONLINE, Updateabilit... | 80 |
| 13 | distribution | 3.50 MB | sa | 16 | Oct 20 2002 | Status=ONLINE, Updateabilit... | 80 |
| 14 | HumanResources | 2.00 MB | sa | 8 | May 7 2002 | Status=ONLINE, Updateabilit... | 80 |
| 15 | IBankAdventure | 2.00 MB | sa | 7 | Apr 18 2002 | Status=ONLINE, Updateabilit... | 80 |
| 16 | Inventory_UK | 1.37 MB | DOPEY\Administrator | 9 | Dec 10 2002 | Status=ONLINE, Updateabilit... | 80 |
| 17 | InventoryUK | 2.00 MB | CURLINGSTONE\justinc | 31 | Dec 10 2002 | Status=ONLINE, Updateabilit... | 80 |
| 18 | Justin1 | 4.00 MB | DOPEY\Administrator | 17 | Oct 22 2002 | Status=ONLINE, Updateabilit... | 80 |
| 19 | master | 65.13 MB | sa | 1 | Aug 6 2000 | Status=ONLINE, Updateabilit... | 80 |
| 20 | model | 1.13 MB | sa | 3 | Aug 6 2000 | Status=ONLINE, Updateabilit... | 80 |
| 21 | msdb | 16.75 MB | sa | 4 | Aug 6 2000 | Status=ONLINE, Updateabilit... | 80 |
| 22 | NewDatabase | 2.00 MB | sa | 19 | Nov 5 2002 | Status=ONLINE, Updateabilit... | 80 |

# 3.11 How to... Show Log Size and % Space Used for Each Database

To show log size in megabytes (total) and percentage of the log space used (total) for each database, run the following command in Query Analyzer:

```
DBCC SQLPERF(LOGSPACE)
```

For example:

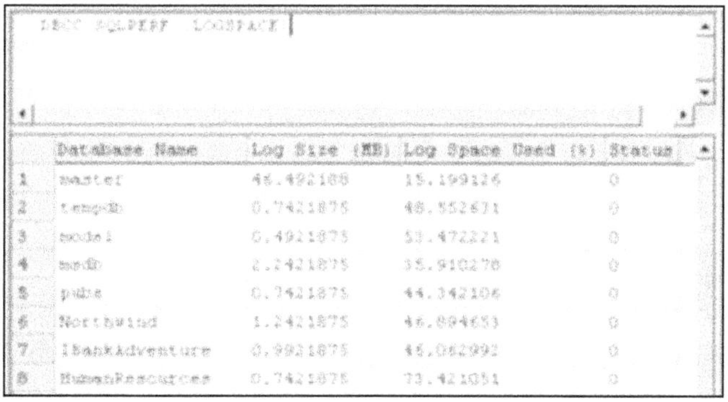


| | Database Name | Log Size (MB) | Log Space Used (%) | Status |
|---|---|---|---|---|
| 1 | master | 46.492188 | 15.199126 | 0 |
| 2 | tempdb | 0.7421875 | 48.552631 | 0 |
| 3 | model | 0.4921875 | 53.472221 | 0 |
| 4 | msdb | 2.2421875 | 35.910278 | 0 |
| 5 | pubs | 0.7421875 | 44.342106 | 0 |
| 6 | Northwind | 1.2421875 | 46.894653 | 0 |
| 7 | IBankAdventure | 0.9921875 | 45.062992 | 0 |
| 8 | HumanResources | 0.7421875 | 73.421051 | 0 |

# 3.12 How to... Report and Correct Inaccuracies in the sysindexes Table with DBCC UPDATEUSAGE

Run UPDATEUSAGE to correct inaccuracies in the sysindexes table. If you run sp_spaceused (next section), you may sometimes see inaccurate numbers. Running DBCC UPDATEUSAGE will correct the sysindexes table for tables and clustered indexes.

In this example, we are running DBCC UPDATEUSAGE for all tables and clustered indexes in the Inventory_UK database:

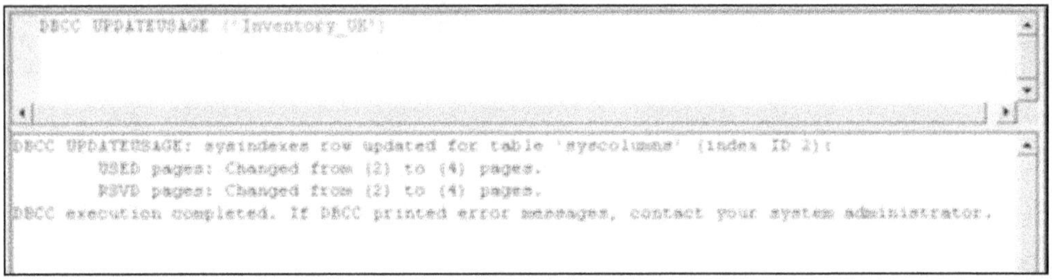
DBCC UPDATEUSAGE ('Inventory_UK')
DBCC UPDATEUSAGE: sysindexes row updated for table 'syscolumns' (index ID 2):
USED pages: Changed from (2) to (4) pages.
RSVD pages: Changed from (2) to (4) pages.
DBCC execution completed. If DBCC printed error messages, contact your system administrator.

Notice that the results output page information that was fixed in the sysindexes table. You will not see messages if the data is accurate.

You can also run DBCC UPDATEUSAGE for a single table, indexed view, or clustered index. For example, to run DBCC UPDATEUSAGE for just the Books table in the Inventory_UK database:

```
DBCC UPDATEUSAGE ('Inventory_UK','dbo.Books')
```

To run this command for the clustered index IX_iAuthorid in the Books table:

```
DBCC UPDATEUSAGE ('Inventory_UK','dbo.Books', 'IX_iAuthorid')
```

This command also has two WITH options: COUNT_ROWS and NO_INFOMSGS. COUNT_ROWS specifies that the rows column of sysindexes receive the approximate value of rows in the table or indexed view. With huge tables, running this command can have a negative impact on performance while it executes:

```
DBCC UPDATEUSAGE ('Inventory_UK','dbo.Books', 'IX_iAuthorid')
WITH COUNT_ROWS
```

NO_INFOMSGS keeps data from being returned by the command:

```
DBCC UPDATEUSAGE ('Inventory_UK','dbo.Books', 'IX_iAuthorid')
WITH NO_INFOMSGS
```

# 3.13 How to... View Space Usage with sp_spaceused

The system stored procedure sp_spaceused reports:

- Database name
- Size in megabytes
- Unallocated space
- Reserved kilobytes
- Data kilobytes
- Total index size in kilobytes
- Total unused size in kilobytes

The index size is particularly useful when adding new indexes, as you can estimate if the index size usage is worth the performance your index was added for.

Remember that the information in sysindexes gets out-of-date and should be updated prior to running sp_spaceused with DBCC UPDATEUSAGE. You can also skip a step and run:

```
EXEC sp_spaceused @updateusage = 'TRUE'
```

This is the same as running DBCC UPDATEUSAGE, and will report the information after the update:

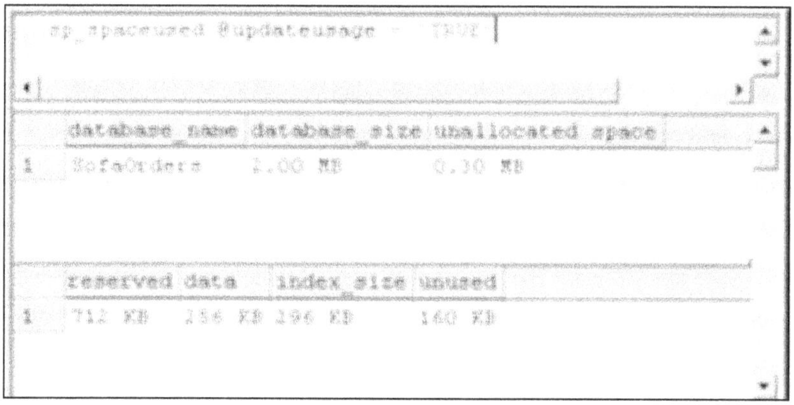


You can also run this stored procedure for a specific object. In this example, we check the space used for the books table in the Inventory_UK database:

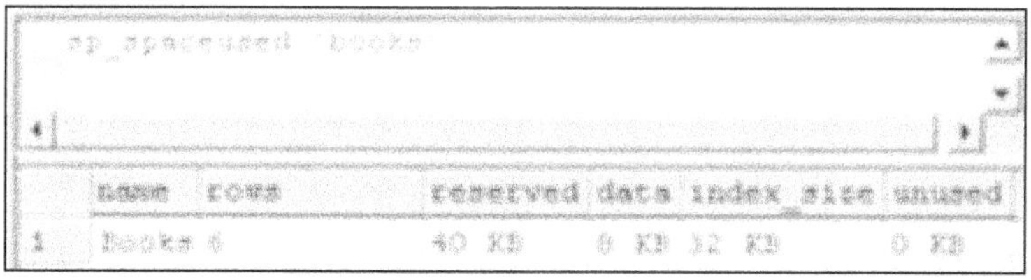

# 3.14 How to... Shrink Data and Log Files in a Database with DBCC SHRINKDATABASE

DBCC SHRINKDATABASE shrinks the data and log files in your database. The behavior of this DBCC command is deceptively simple; however, there are many details you should be aware of.

First off, the syntax is:

```
DBCC SHRINKDATABASE (databasename,
target percentage (optional),
NOTRUNCATE or TRUNCATEONLY (both optional))
```

The target percentage designates the free space remaining in the database file after shrinking.

NOTRUNCATE keeps the freed file space. If NOTRUNCATE is not designated, the free file space is released to the operating system.

TRUNCATEONLY frees up space without relocating rows to unallocated pages. If not designated, rows are reallocated to free up space, which can lead to extensive I/O.

## DBCC SHRINKDATABASE Behaviors

- DBCC SHRINKDATABASE shrinks each data file on a per-file basis, but treats the transaction log or logs as a single entity.
- The database can never shrink smaller than the model database, so keep the model database small.
- Do not run this command during busy periods in production, as it has a negative impact on I/O and user concurrency.
- You cannot shrink a database past the target percentage specified.
- You cannot shrink a file past the original file creation size, or size used in an ALTER DATABASE statement.

In this table we will show what happens to a database according to the command options used:

| Command | Result |
|---|---|
| DBCC SHRINKDATABASE (Inventory) | The database is shrunk to its minimum size. Pages are reallocated to free space, and freed space is given back to the operating system. |
| DBCC SHRINKDATABASE (Inventory, 10) | Depending on data file usage and current size, a shrink will be attempted in order to reduce the free space to 10%. Pages are reallocated to free space, and freed space above and beyond 10% is reclaimed by the operating system. |

| Command | Result |
|---|---|
| DBCC SHRINKDATABASE (SofaOrders, TRUNCATEONLY) | Available free space is reclaimed from the **end** of the file to the operating system, meaning that data pages are not rearranged in the process. This is the least invasive DBCC SHRINKDATABASE format; it may, however, result in less space being reclaimed. If you designate a target percentage, it is ignored. |
| DBCC SHRINKDATABASE (SofaOrders, NOTRUNCATE) | The NOTRUNCATE option moves allocated pages from the end of the data file, and unused pages to the front of the file, but does **not** give the freed space back to the operating system |

When DBCC SHRINKDATABASE executes, a result set is returned. For example:

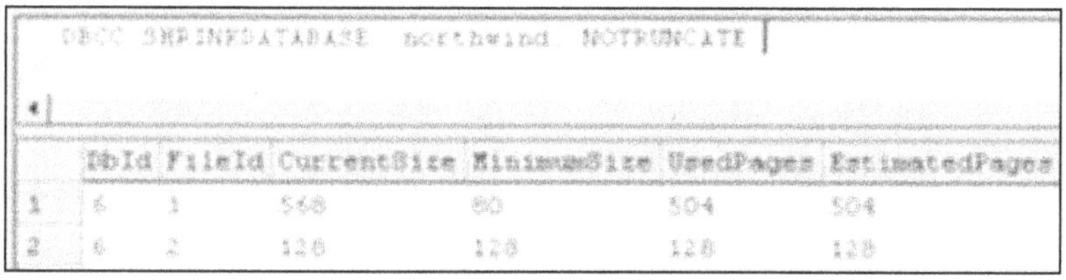


This returns:

- The database ID
- File ID(s) shrunk
- Current 8KB pages the file is using
- Minimum number of 8KB pages the file could use
- Number of in-use pages
- Estimated post-shrink pages

If no shrink operation takes place, you will not see a result set.

# 3.15 How to... Shrink Data Files in a Database using Enterprise Manager

To shrink a database using Enterprise Manager, follow these steps:

- Expand Server Group and registration.
- Expand the Databases folder.
- Right-click the database you wish to shrink and select All Tasks | Shrink Database.

- In the Shrink Database dialog box, choose whether you wish to leave 0% or more free in your database. Also, check Move pages to beginning of file before shrinking, to free up more space than that at the end of the file. Notice this is unchecked by default, which is the opposite behavior to `DBCC SHRINKFILE`. By checking this box you incur a higher performance cost, as pages will be rearranged in order to free up space.

  You can also choose to schedule the shrink operation by selecting the check box Shrink the database based on this schedule.

- Selecting OK will start the shrink process, and Cancel will stop it. The larger the database size and fragmentation, the longer the process will take. Some prefer running `DBCC SHRINKDATABASE` for the simple reason that Enterprise Manager 'hangs' until the process is completed:

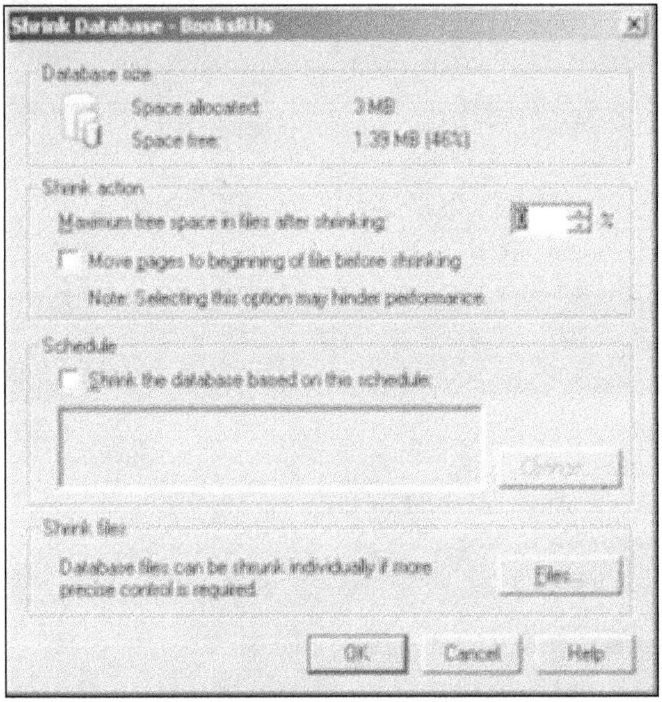

- Click the Files button in the Shrink files section if you wish to shrink individual files. This dialog box calls the `DBCC SHRINKFILE` command, which we will review in the next section. You have the option of:

  **a.** Compressing pages and then truncating free space from the file.

  **b.** Truncating free space from the end of the file only (less I/O overhead).

  **c.** Emptying the data file.

  **d.** Shrinking it to a specific size in megabytes.

  As with the previous dialog, you can also specify a schedule by selecting Shrink the file later:

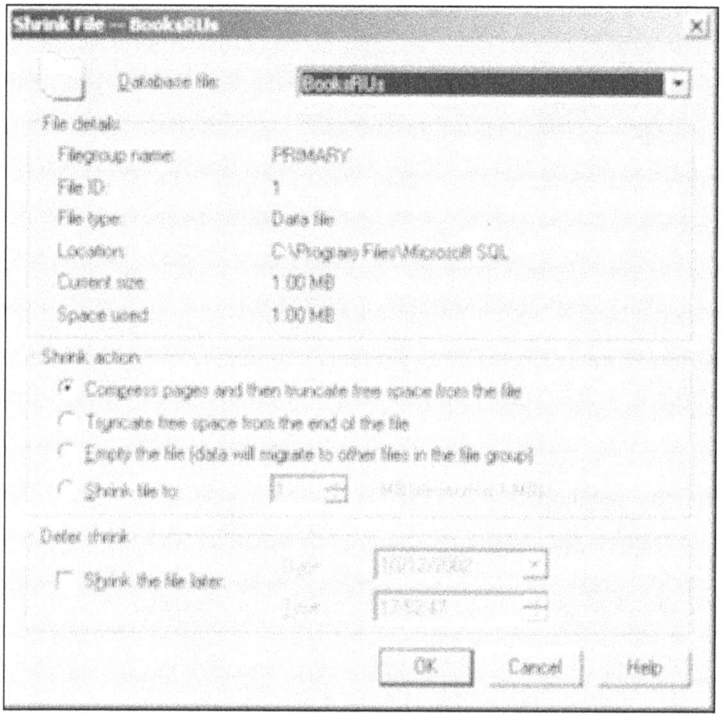


- ❑ Select OK when ready to commence file shrinkage or Cancel if you wish to avoid a shrink operation. Pressing OK will generate a dialog box with the message:

```
The database has been shrunk successfully.
```

# 3.16 How to... Shrink a Specific Data Or Log File using DBCC SHRINKFILE

`DBCC SHRINKFILE` allows you to shrink individual data and log files.

The syntax is:

```
DBCC SHRINKFILE
(logical file name or file id,
target file size (optional),
EMPTYFILE or NOTRUNCATE or TRUNCATEONLY)
```

The logical file name or file ID can be gathered by running `sp_helpfile` in the context of the database where you wish to shrink files. For example, running `sp_helpfile` in the `Inventory_UK` database returns the following output:

Either the name or `fileid` column can be used from these result sets. For example:

`DBCC SHRINKFILE (Inventory_Data)` or `DBCC SHRINKFILE (1)` will both work to shrink the `Inventory_Data.mdf` database file to its minimum potential size.

The target file size option works just like `DBCC SHRINKDATABASE`, in that it designates the percentage you would like free; `SHRINKFILE`, however, only applies the target percent to a single file. This is an optional integer value, and, if not designated, the file will be shrunk to its smallest potential size.

Options `EMPTYFILE`, `NOTRUNCATE`, and `TRUNCATEONLY` are all mutually exclusive (you may only specify one out of the three options, or none at all).

`EMPTYFILE` is used to migrate the contents of one data file to others. The emptied file is then not allowed to receive any data, and can be deleted using `ALTER DATABASE`. For example, if we had a second datafile in the `Inventory_UK` database that we wanted to delete, we would follow these steps:

- ❑ In Query Analyzer, run `sp_helpfile` for the `Inventory_UK` database to retrieve the file name or ID:

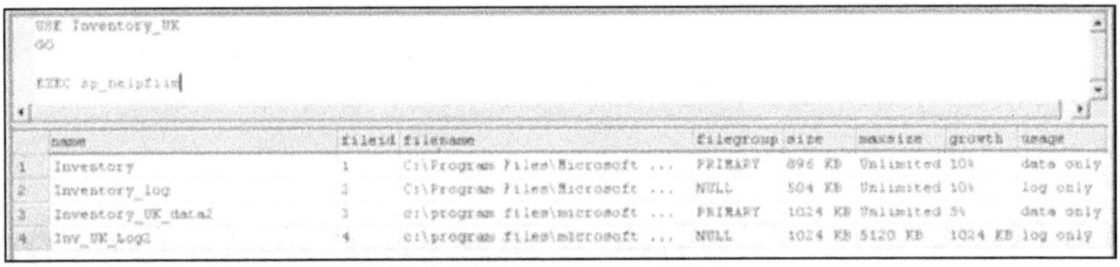


- ❑ Next, run the `DBCC SHRINKFILE (Inventory_Data2, EMPTYFILE)` command:

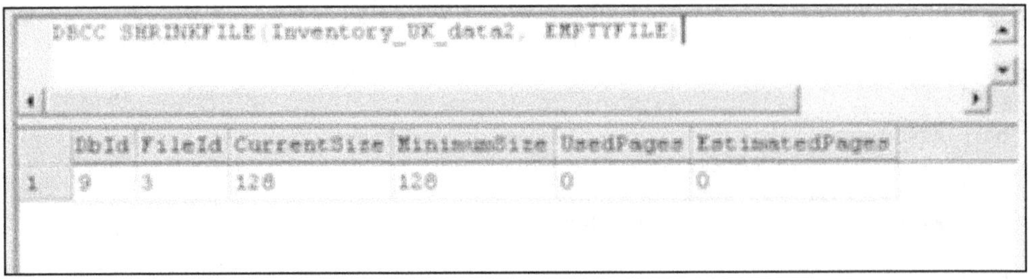


Notice that the `EstimatedPages` column is 0.

- ❑ To remove the file, execute:

```
ALTER DATABASE Inventory_UK
REMOVE FILE Inventory_Data2
```

This returns:

```
The file 'Inventory_Data2' has been removed.
```

The `NOTRUNCATE` and `TRUNCATEONLY` options work just the same as they do in `DBCC SHRINKDATABASE`, except that `SHRINKFILE` impacts the file instead of the entire database.

`NOTRUNCATE` relocates allocated pages from within the file to the front of the file, but does not free the space to the operating system. Target size is ignored when using `NOTRUNCATE`.

`TRUNCATEONLY` causes unused space in the file to be released to the operating system, but only does so with free space at the end of the file. No pages are moved to the beginning of the file. Target size is also ignored with the `TRUNCATEONLY` option. Use this option if you must free up space on the database file and want minimal impact on database performance (rearranging pages on an actively utilized production database can cause performance problems, such as slow query response time).

Shrinking transaction log files involves different underlying methods from shrinking data files. A physical log file is actually made up of **Virtual Log Files**, or VLFs; these VLFs allocate space dynamically when SQL Server is creating and extending log files.

The physical transaction log file should not be confused with the **logical** or **active** portion of the transaction log file. Whenever log records are truncated from the log file, the logical beginning of the log file starts at this truncation end point. When you initially create a log file, the active portion starts at the physical beginning of the file. The following diagram demonstrates this.

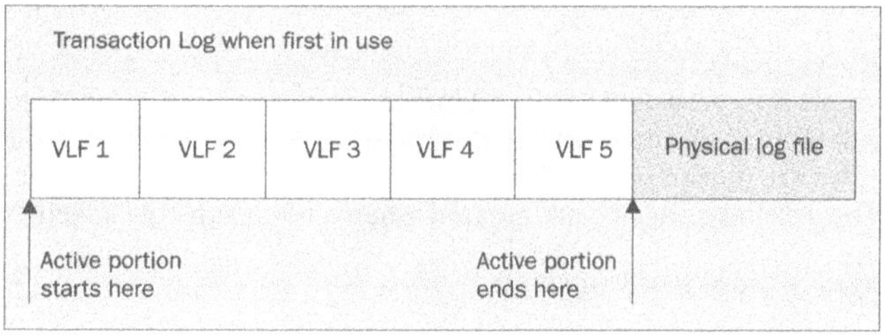


As the log records get truncated, the active portion is reset to any potential point in the physical file. The active portion can also wrap around the end and beginning of a physical file. For example:

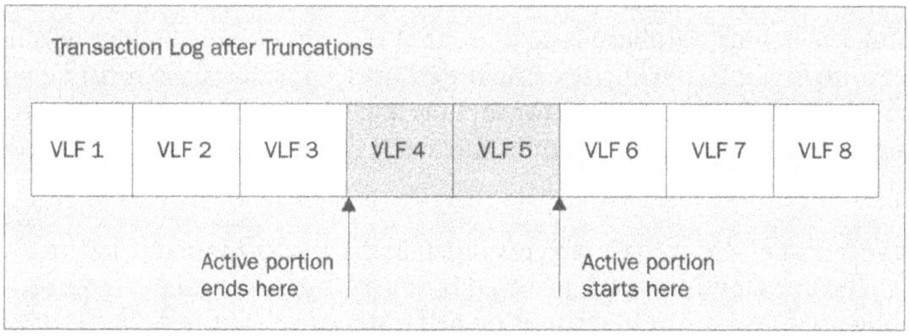


In the scenario above, how would you truncate the transaction log if the active portion took up the end of the file? In SQL Server 7.0, one would have to create enough transaction activity to move this active portion to the beginning of the file so the VLFs could be truncated.

This would be difficult if your VLFs were too large (as too many transactions would be needed to move the active portion), or if the transaction activity were so busy that the active portion traversed the file too quickly (trying to shrink the file when it was just right).

SQL Server 2000 introduced features to force the truncation of a transaction log with `DBCC SHRINKDATABASE` and `SHRINKFILE`. SQL Server adds dummy log entries to pad the last VLF file until a virtual log is filled (this is why large VLFs were more difficult to truncate), and moves the start of the active (logical) transaction log to the beginning of the physical file.

After this, issuing a `BACKUP LOG` frees up the inactive portion of the log. You must sometimes repeat the `DBCC SHRINKFILE` and `BACKUP LOG` statements until you reach the desired transaction log size.

You may not have to run `BACKUP LOG` at all, as in SQL Server 2000 running `DBCC SHRINKDATABASE` and `SHRINKFILE` attempts to truncate as many VLFs at the end of the file as possible to reach the designated target size.

With all these methods of shrinking your database, remember that production servers **should not** require frequent shrink operations. You should size your database appropriately, and filter out potential problems that can cause unnecessary expansion (runaway updates) in your development (or QA) environment. With that said, test environments often require frequent shrink operations, due to the trial and error nature of development databases.

# Filegroups

Database files reside in **filegroups**. The two types of filegroups are:

- Primary
- User-defined

A **primary filegroup** exists for every database, and includes your primary `*.mdf` data file. The primary filegroup is also your default filegroup until you designate another. Default filegroups designate the filegroup into which new data files are placed when a filegroup is not explicitly designated. Default filegroups are where tables, and other database objects, are created when a filegroup isn't specified.

**User-defined filegroups** are those that you create.

## Using Filegroups for Performance and Very Large Databases (VLDB)

Filegroups are useful when your database is so large that it cannot be backed up within an acceptable amount of time. SQL Server allows you to backup specific filegroups. Your database must be using either a `FULL` or `BULK_LOGGED` recovery model, as restoring transaction logs is part of the filegroup recovery process. Backing up filegroups allows you to restore a filegroup in the event that the array on which your filegroup exists is corrupted or requires data recovery.

Filegroups also let you organize database objects logically for performance benefits. For example, you can place a table on `FileGroupA` and the nonclustered index for the same table on `FileGroupB`. For very large and active tables, placing files within filegroups on separate arrays can benefit performance.

SQL Server 2000 allows very large databases (VLDB) with a potential maximum size of 1,048,516TB. For VLDB implementations, it is most likely that you will use filegroups to manage your database. You are allowed up to 256 filegroups per database. Filegroup usage comes with extra complexities, so make sure your performance or backup/recovery benefits outweigh the extra administration time needed for the database.

# 3.17 How to... Add a User-Defined Filegroup

To add a user-defined filegroup to a new database using Enterprise Manager:

- ❑ Expand Server Group and registration.
- ❑ Right-click the Databases folder and select New Database.
- ❑ Filegroup is designated on the Data Files tab. You cannot change the primary data file's filegroup. You can, however, designate a different filegroup for new files (`*.ndf` extension files, or your preferred file extension) added to the database after the primary. In the example below, we create a new filegroup by typing over `PRIMARY` with the name of your filegroup, in this case `FG2`:

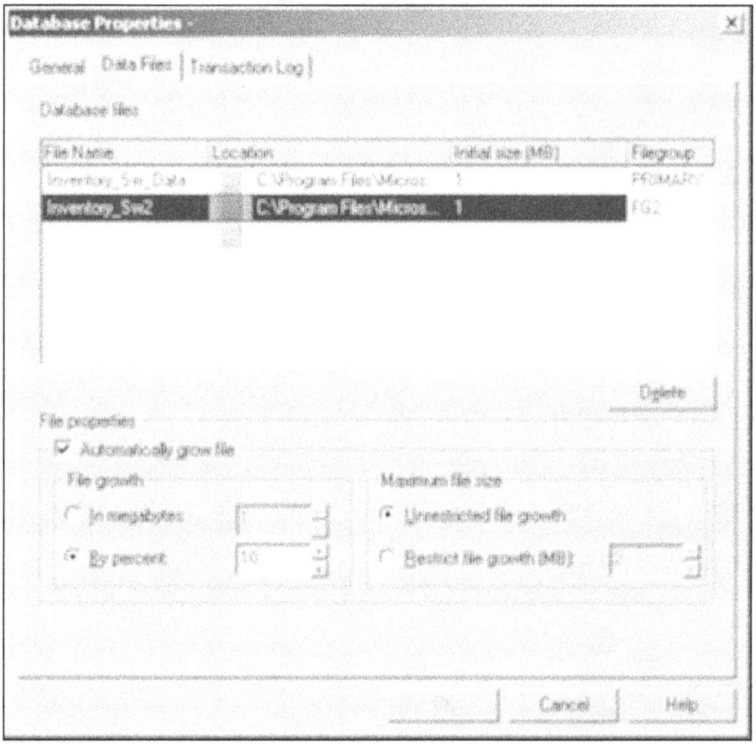


- ❑ Configure your database options as usual, and select OK to finish.
- ❑ In this next example, we create a database called `Inventory_IT` using Transact-SQL. We create two data files. Notice that the second data file is placed on filegroup `Inventory_FG2`, by using the `FILEGROUP Inventory_FG` statement:

```
USE master
GO

CREATE DATABASE Inventory_IT
ON PRIMARY
        (NAME = 'Inventory_Data1',
        FILENAME = 'c:\program files\microsoft sql server\mssql\data\inv_it_data1.mdf',
        SIZE = 1,
        MAXSIZE = 10,
        FILEGROWTH = 1),
FILEGROUP Inventory_FG2
        (NAME = 'Inventory_Data2',
        FILENAME = 'c:\program files\microsoft sql server\mssql\data\inv_it_data2.ndf',
        SIZE = 1,
        MAXSIZE = 10,
        FILEGROWTH = 1)
```

```
The CREATE DATABASE process is allocating 1.00 MB on disk 'Inventory_Data1'.
The CREATE DATABASE process is allocating 1.00 MB on disk 'Inventory_Data2'.
The CREATE DATABASE process is allocating 0.50 MB on disk 'Inventory_IT_log'.
```

To add a user-defined filegroup to an existing database using Enterprise Manager:

- Expand Server Group and registration.
- Expand the Databases folder and right-click the database to which you wish to add the new filegroup. Select Properties.
- In the Data Files tab, you can add a new filegroup within the context of adding a new file. You cannot change the filegroup of an existing secondary file.

You can add a filegroup using Transact-SQL without having to add a new file to the database, unlike in Enterprise Manager. The example below shows how to add a user-defined filegroup to an existing database. In this example, we add the filegroup `FG2` to the `Inventory_UK` database using the `ADD FILEGROUP` extension to the `ALTER DATABASE` command:

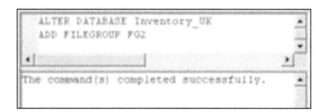

```
ALTER DATABASE Inventory_UK
ADD FILEGROUP FG2
```

```
The command(s) completed successfully.
```

# 3.18 How to... Make a User-Defined Filegroup the Default Filegroup

Making your user-defined filegroup the default means that objects created in your database will reside there unless explicitly placed on another filegroup. You cannot change the default filegroup using Enterprise Manager. Furthermore, you cannot designate a filegroup as default until it contains files.

- In this example, we change the `Inventory_FG2` filegroup in the `Inventory_IT` database to the default filegroup using the `MODIFY FILEGROUP` extension of the `ALTER DATABASE` command:

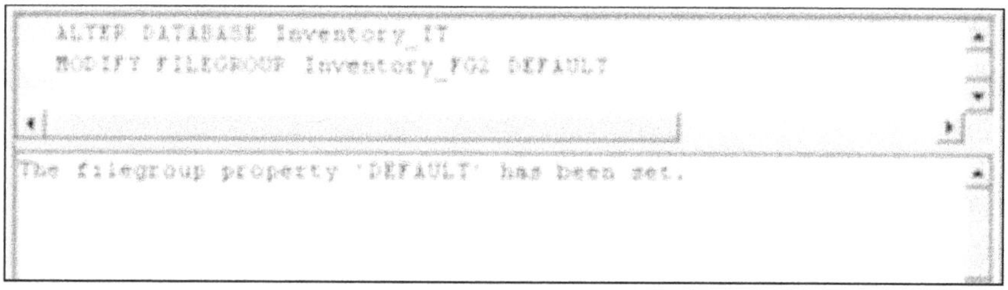


**Default warning: a filegroup must contain files if it is to be set as the default.**

- To test whether new objects will be placed in the `FG2` filegroup, we will create the table `Books_IT` with no filegroup explicitly designated:

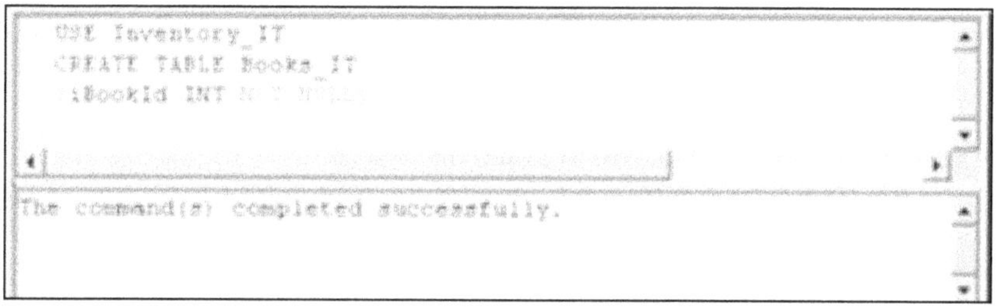


- Next we run `EXEC sp_help` for the Books_UK table. Notice the last row designates that `FG2` is the filegroup for the table:

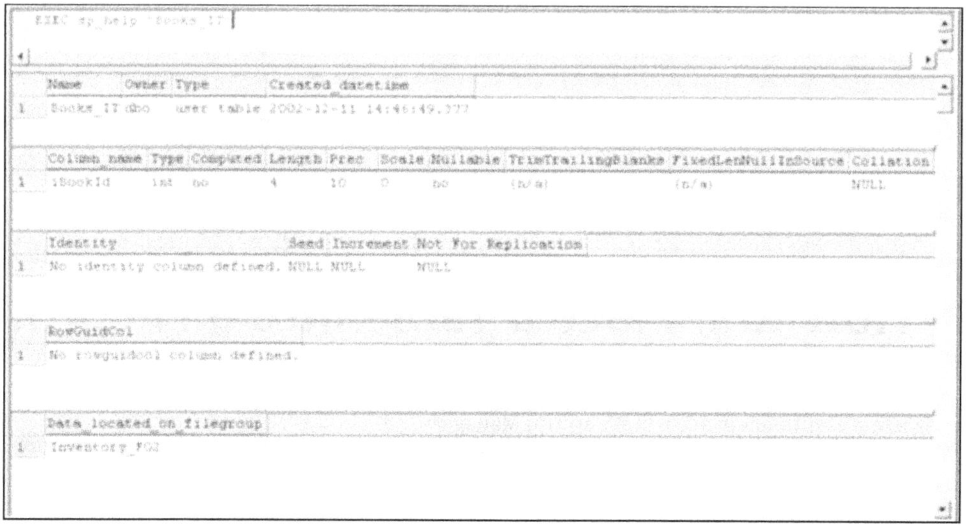

# 3.19 How to... Make a Filegroup Read-Only

If you have specific tables that do not require updates, you can place them on a filegroup that is read-only. You must have exclusive access to your database.

In this example, we will designate `Inventory_FG2` in the `Inventory_IT` database as read-only:

```
ALTER DATABASE Inventory_IT
SET SINGLE_USER
WITH ROLLBACK IMMEDIATE
GO

ALTER DATABASE Inventory_IT
MODIFY FILEGROUP Inventory_FG2 READONLY
GO

ALTER DATABASE Inventory_IT
SET MULTI_USER
WITH ROLLBACK IMMEDIATE
GO
```

```
The filegroup property 'READONLY' has been set.
```

To allow the filegroup to accept update activity again, run:

```
ALTER DATABASE Inventory_IT
SET SINGLE_USER
WITH ROLLBACK IMMEDIATE
GO

ALTER DATABASE Inventory_IT
MODIFY FILEGROUP Inventory_FG2 READWRITE
GO

ALTER DATABASE Inventory_IT
SET MULTI_USER
WITH ROLLBACK IMMEDIATE
GO
```

```
The filegroup property 'READWRITE' has been set.
```

# 3.20 How to... Place a Table into a Filegroup

In the next example, we will specify a table's filegroup (user-defined filegroup).

To designate a user-defined group in Enterprise Manager:

- Expand Server Group and registration.
- Expand Databases.

- ❑ Expand the database to which you wish to add a table.
- ❑ Right-click Tables and select New Table.
- ❑ After designating your columns, select the Table and Index Properties button. 
- ❑ Under the Table Filegroup drop-down box, select the filegroup for your table. If you have text or image data types, you can also use the Text Filegroup drop-down box to determine in which filegroups these datatypes store data:

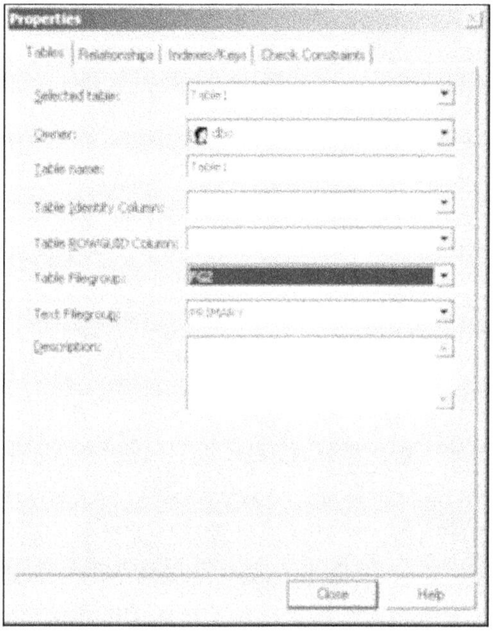


- ❑ Select the Close button when finished. Save and close the Tables dialog box as usual. Also, you can use this same property window to move existing tables to a new filegroup.

Next, is an example of placing a new table in a filegroup using Transact-SQL. We will add the table `Books_USA` to the `Inventory_IT` database and Inventory_`FG2` user-defined filegroup:

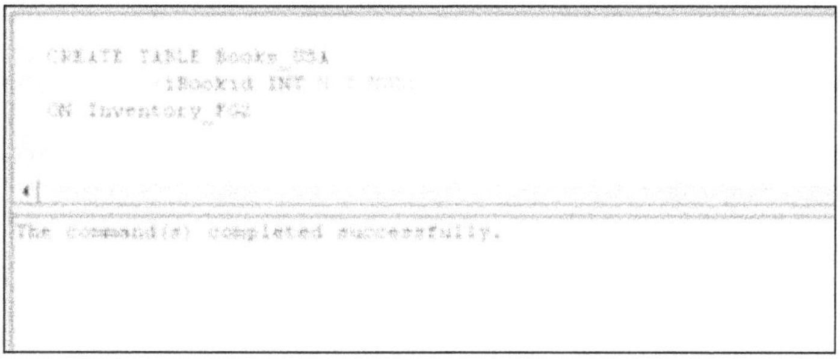

In this next example, we designate a separate filegroup for a nonclustered index using Transact-SQL:

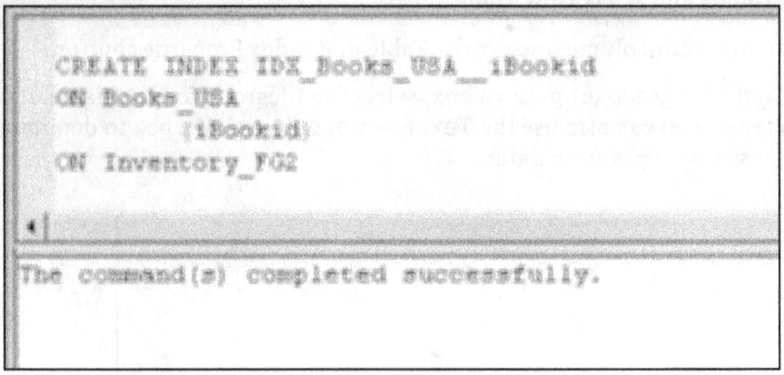
CREATE INDEX IDX_Books_USA__iBookid
ON Books_USA
(iBookid)
ON Inventory_FG2
The command(s) completed successfully.

To place an index in a user-defined group using Enterprise Manager:

- Expand Server Group and registration.
- Expand the Database folder, and the database to which you wish to add an index.
- Click on Tables.
- Right-click the table to which you wish to add an index. Select All Tasks | Manage Indexes.
- Select the New button:

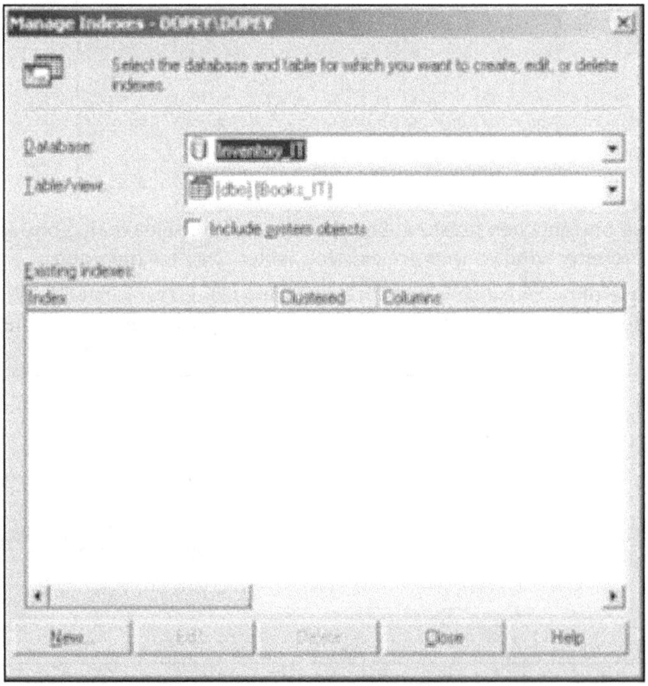

- We will review the different index options in more detail in Chapter 14, but to designate the filegroup in this example, check the File group checkbox, and select the group from the drop-down box:

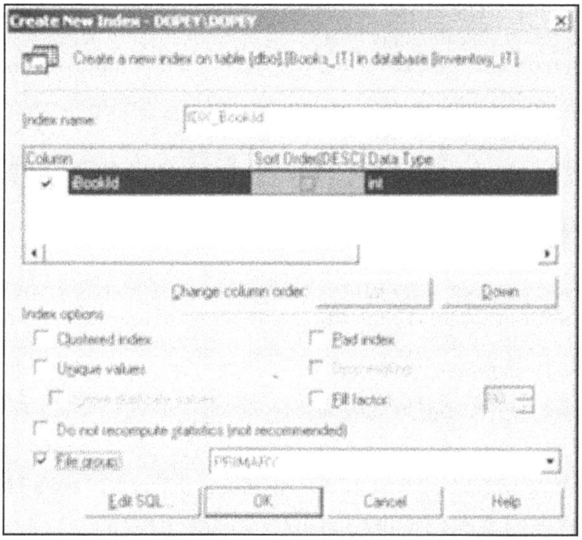


# 3.21 How to... Change a Filegroup for an Existing Table

- To change the filegroup of an existing table, right-click on the table in the right-hand pane of Enterprise Manager. Select Design Table.
- Open the Table and Index Properties dialog box (second from the left at the top of the screen):

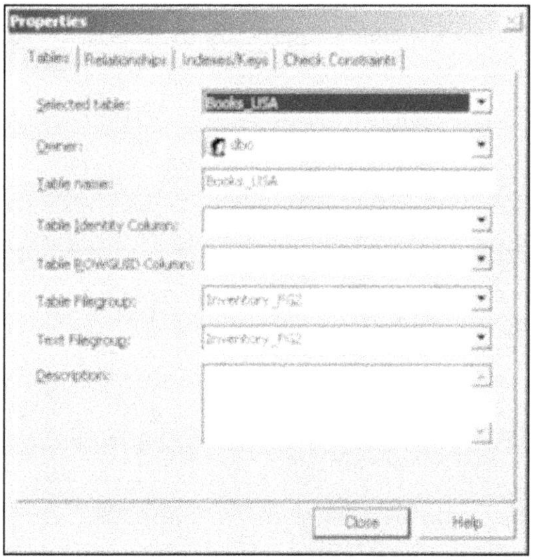

- ❑ Select Table or Text Filegroup and press Close when finished.

There is no ALTER TABLE statement to change the filegroup in Transact-SQL. When updating via Enterprise Manager, the table is actually dropped and recreated in a new filegroup. If you have an extra-large table, be careful, as dropping and recreating this may be a very time-consuming process. Also, if the table has a clustered index, you can rebuild the index on another filegroup. For more details on creating indexes, see Chapter 14.

# 3.22 How to... Change a Filegroup for an Existing Index

Changing a filegroup for an existing index is possible in Enterprise Manager but not in a Transact-SQL statement (as with the previous topic). To modify the filegroup of an existing index, follow these steps:

- ❑ Expand Server Group and registration.
- ❑ Expand the Database folder, and the database to which you wish to add an index.
- ❑ Click on Tables.
- ❑ Right-click the table to which you wish to add an index. Select All Tasks | Manage Indexes.
- ❑ Highlight the index you wish to modify and press the Edit button:

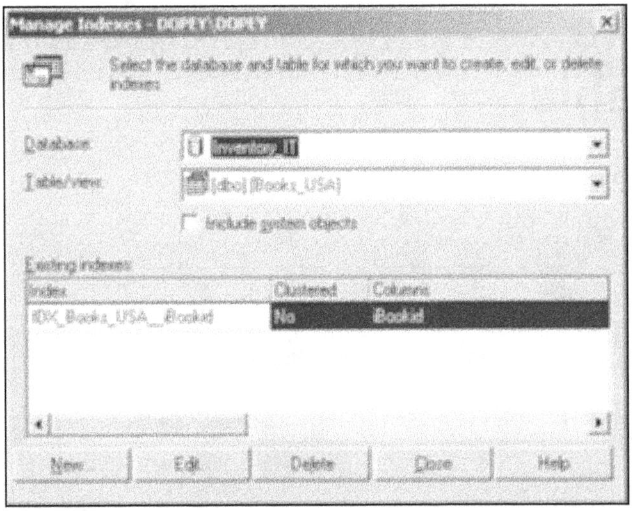


- ❑ In the Edit Existing Index dialog box, change to the desired filegroup from the drop-down box. Select OK when finished:

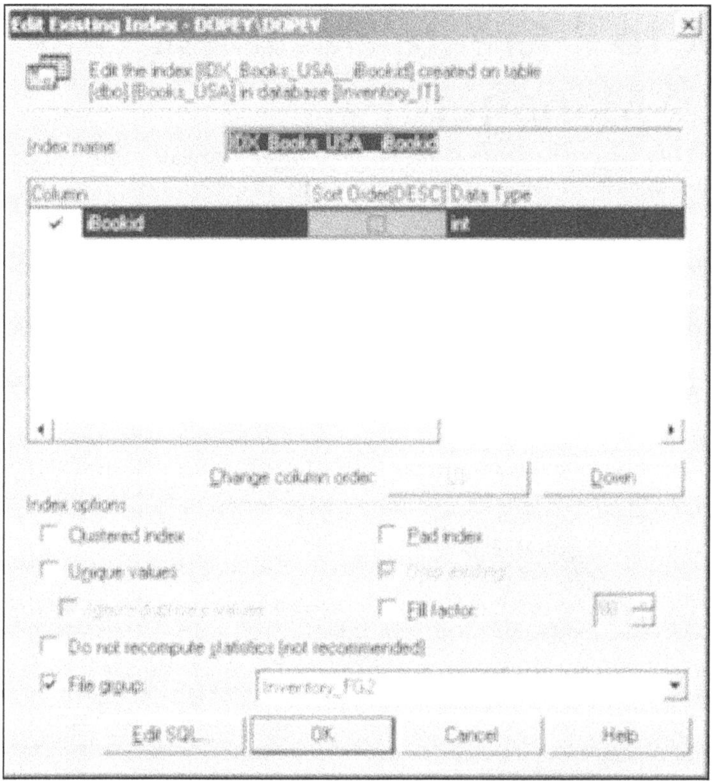


If you run SQL Profiler, you will see that the index is actually recreated, rather than altered. For the above example, the following Transact-SQL is executed in the background:

```
CREATE
INDEX [IDX_NC_Books_USA_iBookId] ON [dbo].[Books_USA] ([iBookId])
WITH
DROP_EXISTING
ON [FG2]
```

# 3.23 How to... Remove a Filegroup

You can only remove a filegroup if it contains no files. In this example, we will remove the FG3 filegroup from the Inventory_UK database using the REMOVE FILEGROUP clause in the ALTER DATABASE statement:

```
ALTER DATABASE Inventory_UK
REMOVE FILEGROUP FG3
```

# 3.24 How to... Create Database Objects using Enterprise Manager

Enterprise Manager allows you to create all the database objects provided with SQL Server 2000. Chapter 14 will examine how each of these objects is used, and how to create database objects using the Transact-SQL language.

The following is a brief review of how to create database objects using Enterprise Manager. Refer to Chapter 14 for in-depth coverage of this area. As a DBA or developer, you should be familiar with database object creation and manipulation using both Enterprise Manager and Transact-SQL.

## Creating Tables

**Tables** are used to store data in the database, and provide the foundation for most other databases. Tables are defined with one or more columns. Each column for the table has a defined data type, which determines what kind of data is stored within the table.

To create a table using Enterprise Manager:

- Expand Server Group, the server node, the Databases folder, and the appropriate database. Right-click the Tables node, and select New Table.
- The New Table dialog box allows you to add and modify columns for your defined table. The following table describes the configurable fields:

| Value | Description |
|---|---|
| Column Name | Designates the unique name of the column. |
| Data Type | Designates the data type of the column. |
| Length | Is configurable for the BINARY, CHAR, NCHAR, VARBINARY, VARCHAR, or NVARCHAR data types. |
| Allow Nulls | When checked, NULL values are allowed. |

- Your total row width (total number of columns per row), is limited to 8,060 bytes:

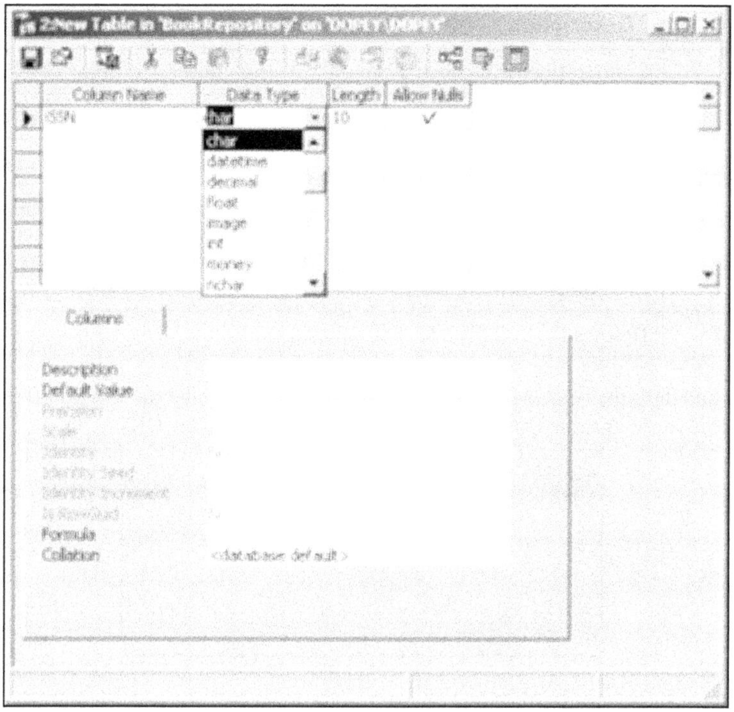

- The lower half of the new table designer allows modification of the following column properties, and is applied to the column currently selected in the designer:

| Property | Description |
|---|---|
| Description | User-friendly description of the column, good for describing cryptic or confusing column names. |
| Default Value | Defines a default value for the column. For example, if 90% of employees in the `Employee` table live in Minnesota, you can create a `Minnesota` default value. |
| Precision | Applies to the numeric and decimal data types. Precision determines maximum total number of decimal digits both left and right of the decimal point. |
| Scale | Applies to the numeric and decimal data types. Scale determines maximum decimal digits to the right of the decimal point. |
| Identity | The Identity property allows you to define an automatically incrementing numeric value for a specific column or columns. When a new row is inserted into a table with an identity column, the column is inserted with a unique incremented value. The data type for an identity column can be `INT`, `TINYINT`, `SMALLINT`, `BIGINT`, `DECIMAL`, or `NUMERIC`. Tables may only have one identity column defined, and the defined identity column cannot have a default or rule settings associated with it. Check Yes, to enable the property. Selecting Yes (Not for Replication) allows published data to override the incrementing of the identity column and original values, as preserved from the publisher on the subscriber. |

*Table continued on following page*

| Property | Description |
|---|---|
| Identity Seed | Seed defines the starting number for the identity column. |
| Identity Increment | Increment defines the value for each consecutive row added to the table. |
| Is RowGuid | Designates the column as a ROWGUID data type column. |
| Formula | This property is used to define a computed column. A computed column is defined by a **computation**, which can be a freestanding calculation (such as `1+1`) or can involve other columns defined in the table (multiplying the `rate` column by the `mortgage` column, for example). |
| Collation | Defines the collation for the column values. |

- When finished defining one or more columns for your table, select the Save button to save the table. Select a name for your table (maximum 128 characters), and click OK:

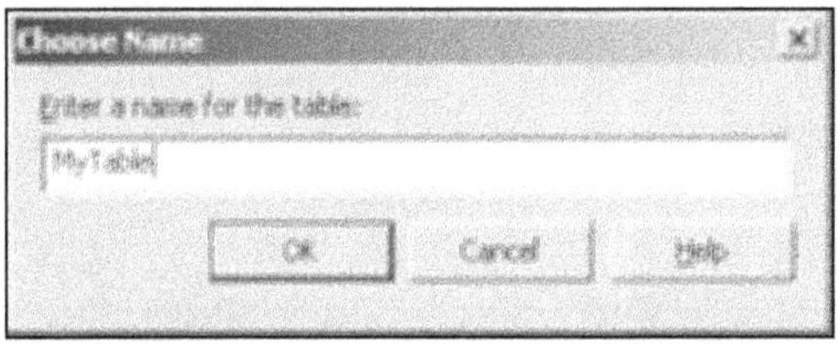


- Once you have saved your table, you can exit the designer by selecting the button, and selecting Close, or simply clicking the X in the upper right-hand corner

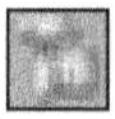

To modify an existing table:

- Expand Server Group, server node, Databases folder and selected database, and click Tables.
- Right-click the table you wish to edit and select Design Table. This will return you to the Table designer seen in the previous section.

## Primary Keys

A primary key defines a column or set of columns that uniquely identifies all rows in the table. To create a primary key in Enterprise Manager:

- From the Table designer, select the column or columns you wish to make the primary key.
- If selecting multiple columns, hold the *Ctrl* key down when selecting. Click the key icon to define the key.

  The following example shows the key icon next to the two columns making up the primary key:

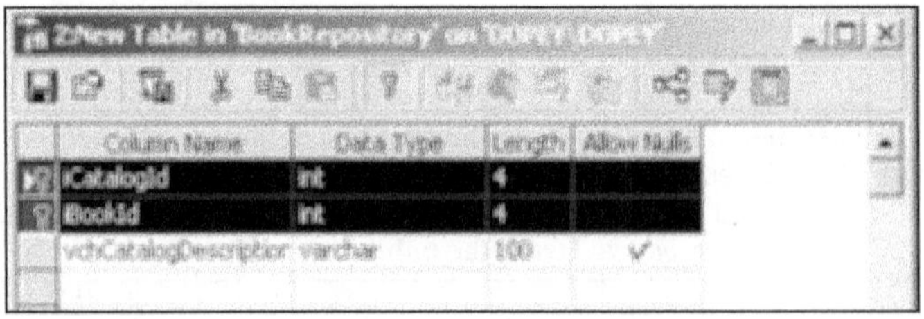

- Select the Save button to save the new primary key.

## Views

Views allow you to create a virtual representation of a table using a `SELECT` statement as a definition. The view can then be referenced with a `SELECT` query in the same way as you would with a table. The `SELECT` statement can join one or more tables, and can include one or more returned columns.

To create a view using Enterprise Manager:

- Expand Server Group, Server node, the Databases folder, and the selected database. Right-click Views, and select New View.
- The New View dialog box allows you to generate a view by using Transact-SQL (see Chapter 14) or by adding tables or view references graphically, by clicking the Add Table button:

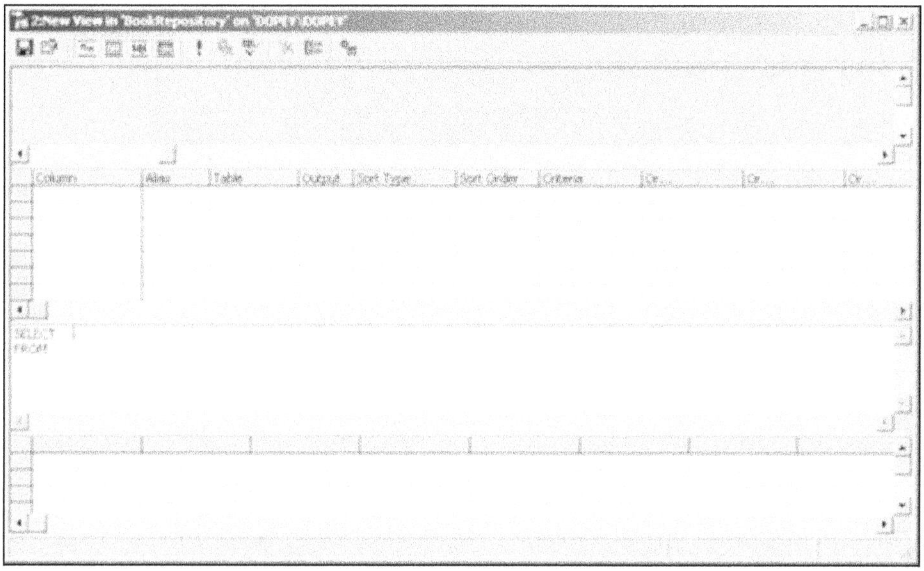


- Click the  button. You can select Tables, Views, or Functions for use in your view. Press the Add button after selecting each object you wish to use. Press the Close button when finished:

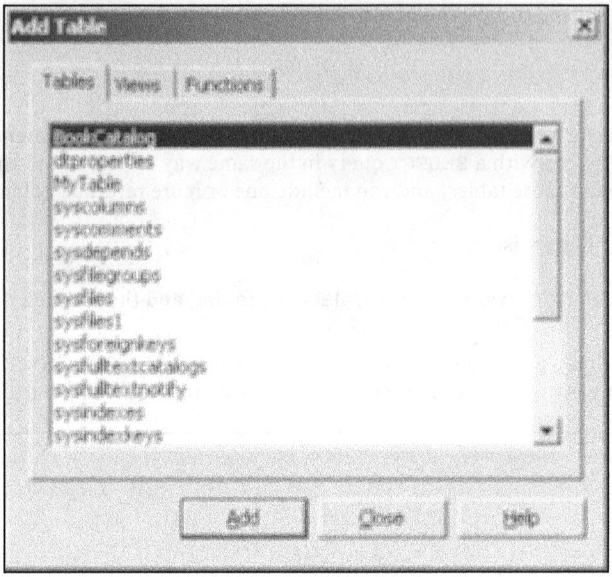


- Any foreign key references between the selected tables will be reflected in the graphical workspace, and join operations will be generated automatically:

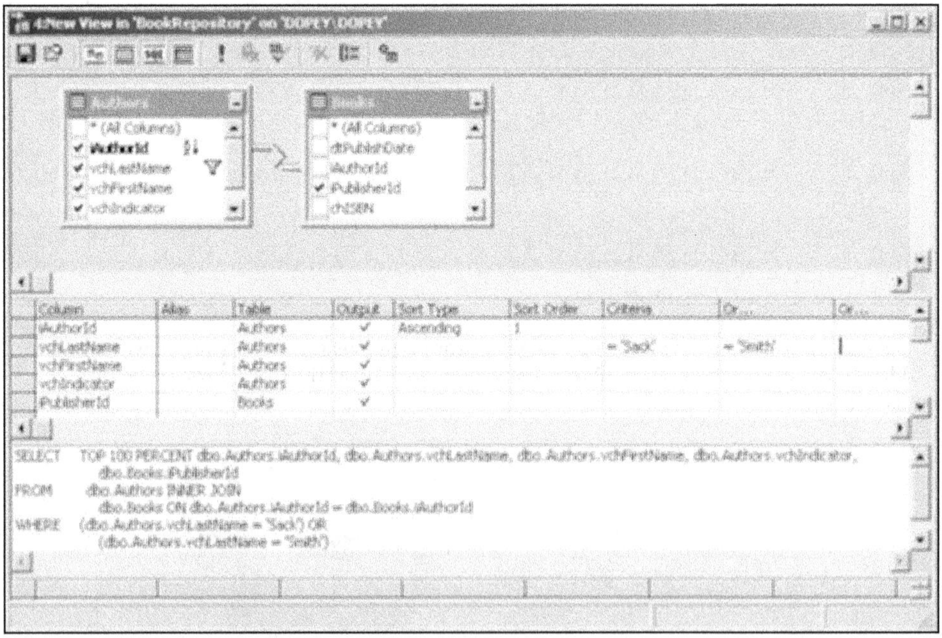

- Click the checkbox next to each column you wish to see for each table. You can also create joins between columns, by clicking a column and dragging it to the other table column to which you wish to join:

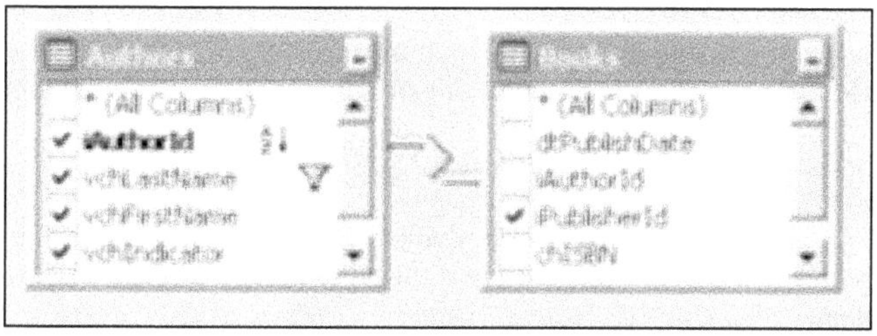

- You can define column Sort Order by selecting the number from the drop-down, and also add criteria (`WHERE` clauses) for each column. Use the `OR` columns to add `WHERE` clauses with the `OR` operator. See Chapter 15 for more information on `SELECT` statements and `WHERE` clauses:

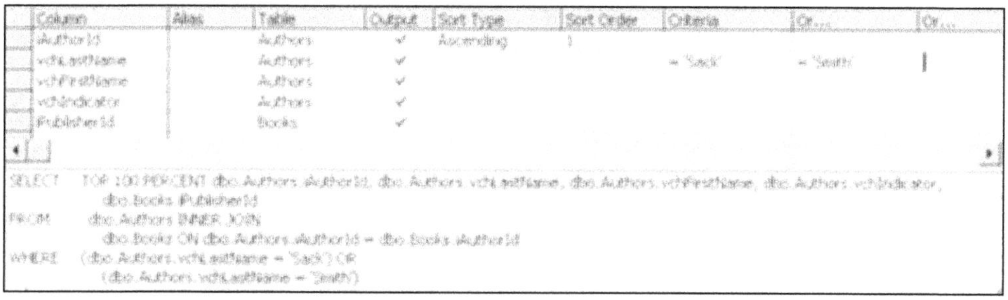

- Select the Properties button to configure advanced properties of the view. This will translate to `CREATE VIEW` options, which are reviewed in more detail in Chapter 14. `GROUP BY` and the `TOP` keywords are reviewed in Chapter 15:

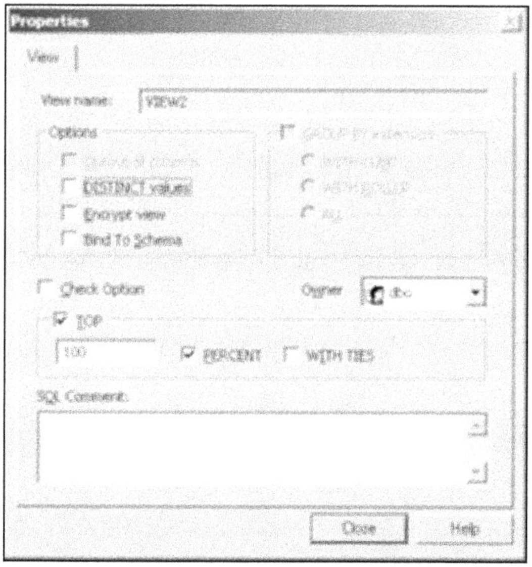

- ❑ At the main View designer, click the Run (!) button to execute the query (to test the results). Press the Save button to save the view.

## Indexes

Indexes assist with query processing by speeding up data access against tables and views. Indexes are defined by designating an index key, which is made up of one or more columns from the table or view.

To create an index for tables in Enterprise Manager:

- ❑ Expand Server Group, and the server node. Expand the Databases folder and the appropriate database, and select the Tables node. In the right-hand pane, right-click the table and select All Tasks | Manage Indexes.
- ❑ In the Manage Indexes dialog box, select Edit to edit an existing index, Delete to remove an index, and New to add a new index:

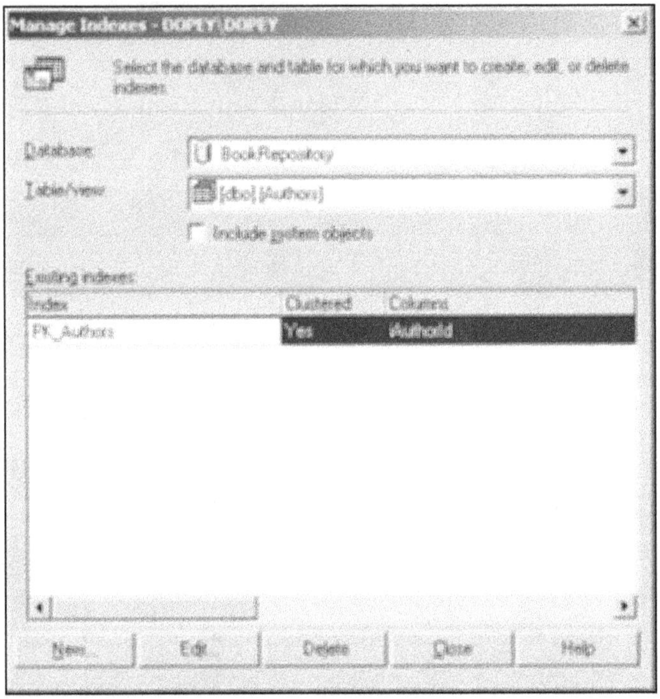


- ❑ If selecting New, you will be presented with the Create New Index dialog box. The following fields are configurable:

| Field | Description |
|---|---|
| Index name | The name of the index, which must be unique to the database. |
| Column | This is the list of columns to include in the index. Click the checkbox to select the columns you wish to index. |
| Sort order<br><br>Data type | When selected, this sorts the data in descending order. Otherwise, the default is ascending.<br><br>Information on the column's data type. |
| Change column order | Select the Up and Down buttons to move columns in the order they should be within the index (for multi-column indexes). |
| Clustered index | Check clustered index if the index is clustered (one clustered index is allowed per table). If this is not selected, the index will be nonclustered. |
| Unique values | Check this option to form a unique index. |
| Ignore duplicate values | When selected, initial table values will be ignored for the unique constraint. |
| Pad index | When specified, the fill factor percentage is applied to the interior node of the index. |
| Drop existing | Deletes the existing index with the same name, prior to creating the new index. |
| Fill factor | Determines how full each leaf level page is left during the index creation. |
| Do not recompute statistics (not recommended) | When selected, statistics are not regenerated for the index. |
| File group | If you wish to create the index on a non-default filegroup. |
| Edit SQL | The Edit SQL button allows you to modify the actual `CREATE INDEX` statement. |

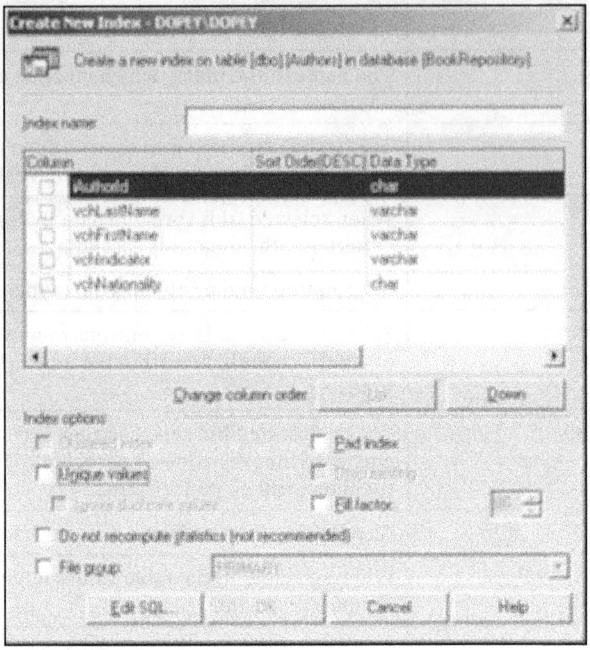

- When you have finished configuring the options, select OK to create the index, or Cancel to exit without an update.
- Select Close at the Manage Indexes dialog box.

Indexes can also be managed and created from the Design view of the Table editor. To do so:

- Select the Properties button in Table editor.
- Select the Indexes/Keys tab. From here, select an existing index to modify from the Selected Index drop-down box; select the New button to add new indexes, and Delete to remove indexes:

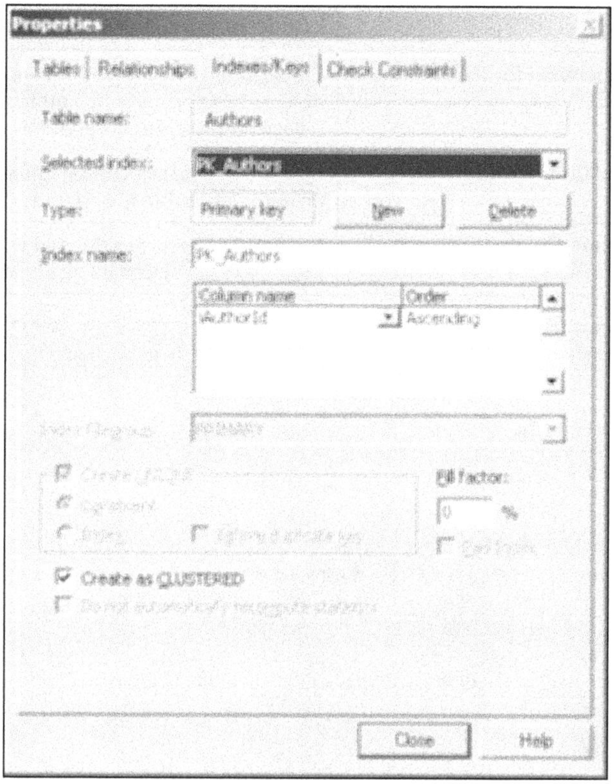

## Foreign Keys

Foreign key constraints establish relationships between tables. This relationship is defined in order to maintain referential integrity, which means that every value in the column must exist in the corresponding column for the referenced table.

To create a foreign key reference in Enterprise Manager:

- From the previous example's Properties dialog box, select the Relationships tab. Select New to add a new foreign key relationship, Delete to remove a foreign key, or choose an existing foreign key relationship to configure from the Selected relationship dialog box.

| Field | Description |
|---|---|
| Primary key table | Primary key table drop-down, followed by the primary key columns. |
| Foreign key table | Foreign key table, followed by columns that can make up the foreign key. |
| Check existing data on creation | Applies foreign key relationship to existing data. |
| Enforce relationship for replication | Foreign key constraint is enforced when copied to a different database. |

*Table continued on following page*

| Field | Description |
|---|---|
| Enforce relationship for INSERTS and UPDATEs | Constraints are enforced for Inserts, updates, and deletes (and primary key table rows cannot be deleted if matching foreign key rows exist). |
| Cascade Update Related Fields | Foreign-key values will be updated when the primary-key value is updated. |
| Cascade Delete Related Records | Foreign-key rows are deleted when primary-key table rows are deleted. |

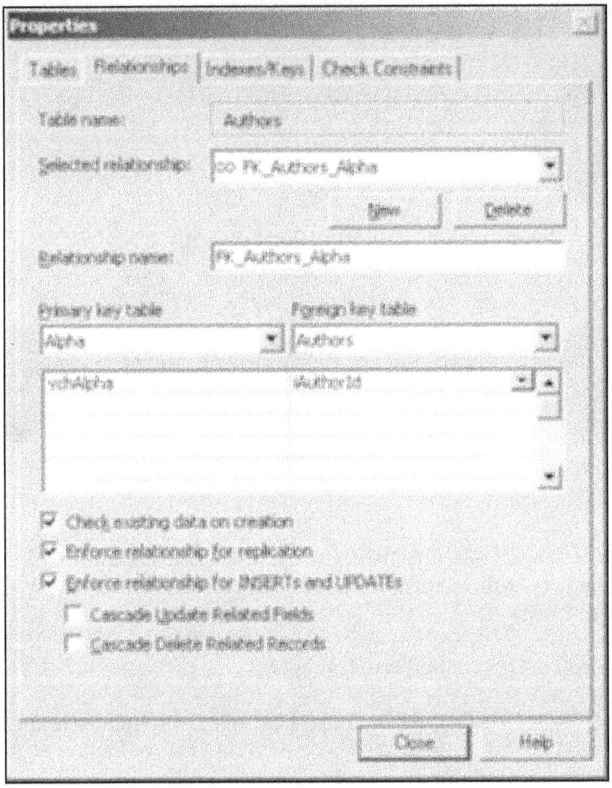


- ❑ Select Close after you have finished configuring foreign keys. Select the Save button in the Table design window.

## Triggers

Triggers respond to user INSERT, UPDATE, or DELETE operations against a table or a view. When a data modification event occurs, the trigger 'fires', and performs a set of actions defined within the trigger. Triggers are defined via Transact-SQL, and allow a full range of activities to be performed, much like a stored procedure. Triggers are useful for complicated data validation routines and cleanup.

To create a trigger in Enterprise Manager:

- Expand Server Group, the server node, and the Databases folder. Expand the appropriate database, and select the Tables node. In the right-hand pane, right-click the table, select All Tasks | Manage Triggers.
- In the Trigger Properties dialog box, enter the trigger logic for a new trigger in the Text window (see Chapter 14 for the Transact-SQL reference on Triggers). Otherwise, modify an existing trigger by selecting it from the Name drop-down box. Select Delete to remove a trigger, Check Syntax to check the validity of the trigger, and Apply to save the trigger. Save as Template saves the text in your Text window as the initial Transact-SQL you will see when creating a new trigger. Select Close to exit Trigger Properties:

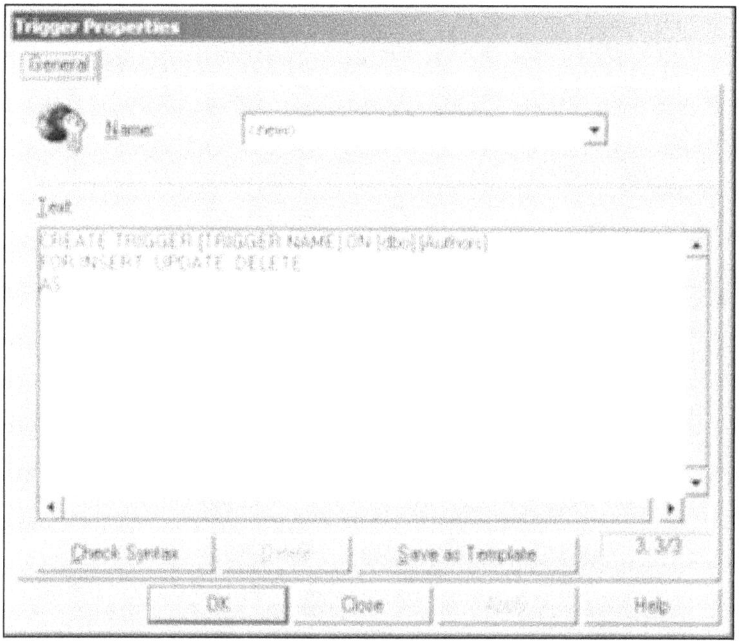

## Stored Procedures

A stored procedure allows you to group one or more statements as a logical unit, and store this unit as an object in a SQL Server database. Stored procedures are used to execute Transact-SQL commands, and can often produce faster execution times than ad hoc calls from a workstation.

To create a stored procedure in Enterprise Manager:

- Expand Server Group, the server node, and the Databases folder. Expand the appropriate database, right-click the Stored Procedures node, and select New Stored Procedure:
- From Stored Procedure Properties, use the Transact-SQL syntax reviewed in Chapter 14 to check the validity of the stored procedure, and OK to save the stored procedure. Save as Template saves the text in your Text window as the initial Transact-SQL you will see when creating a new stored procedure:

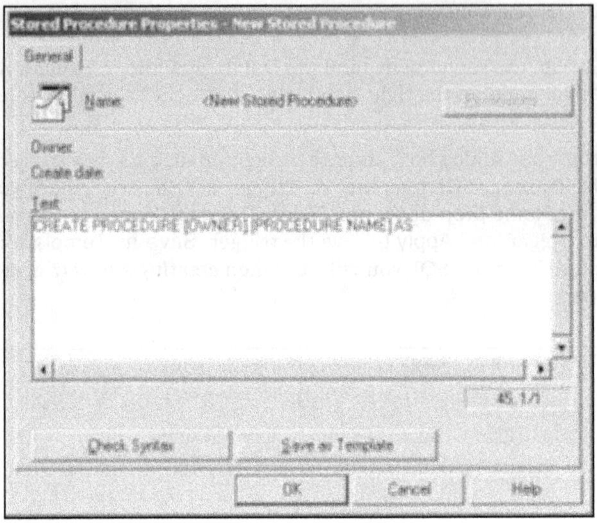


## User-Defined Functions

User-defined functions (UDFs) allow you to encapsulate logic and subroutines, to be used within your queries and DML (Data Manipulation Language) statements.

To create a user-defined function in Enterprise Manager:

- Expand Server Group, the server node, and the Databases folder. Expand the database, right-click the User-defined Functions node, and select New User-defined Function...
- From the User-defined Function Properties dialog box, use the Transact-SQL syntax reviewed in Chapter 14. Use Check Syntax to check the validity of the user-defined function, and OK to save the user-defined function. Save as Template saves the text in your Text window as the initial Transact-SQL you will see when creating a new user-defined function:

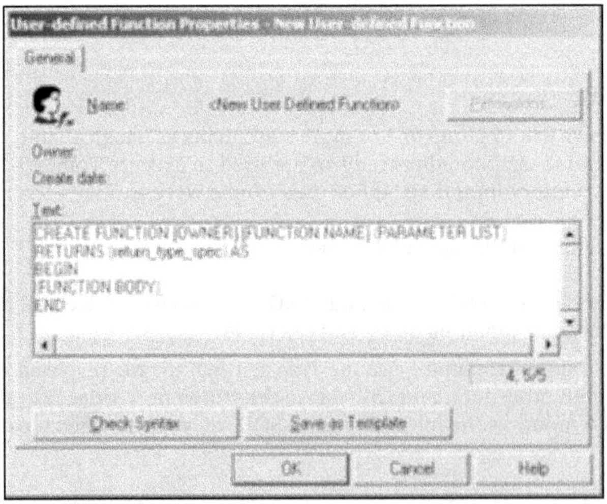

## Defaults

Defaults are used to define values for a column when a value is not specified. Defaults can be defined when a table is created or altered (see Chapter 14), or can be created independently for re-use across multiple tables, to which they are bound.

To create a default with Enterprise Manager:

- Expand Server Group, server node, and the Databases folder. Expand the database, right-click the Defaults node, and select New Default...
- Select the name of the default (which must be unique to the database) and the associated default value. Select OK:

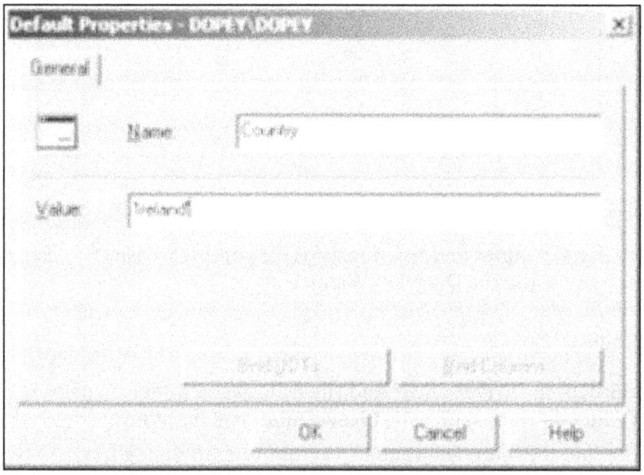


- To bind the default to user-defined data types, or columns, double-click the new default in the right-hand pane of Enterprise Manager. In the Default Properties dialog box, the Bind UDTs and Bind Columns buttons will no longer be grayed out. Use these dialog boxes to associate the new default with existing user-defined data types or table columns.

## User-Defined Data Types

User-defined data types enable you to create a data type template, for re-using and enforcing similar data type structures, based on underlying system data types. For example, you could create a user-defined data type called SSN, which would be used for social security numbers. Such a user-defined data type can ensure consistency for similar columns across tables within the database.

To create a user-defined data type in Enterprise Manager:

- Expand Server Group, the server node, and the Databases folder. Expand the appropriate database, right-click the User-defined Data Types node, and select New User-defined Data Type...
- In the User-Defined Data Type Properties dialog box, select the name of the new data type, data type, length, and whether or not the data type allows NULL values. You can also apply rules or defaults if defined for the database. Rules are provided for backward compatibility purposes (use constraints instead) :

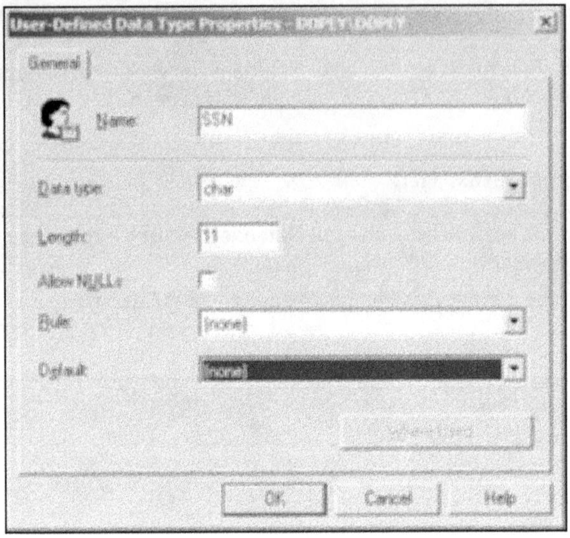


## Diagrams

Diagrams allow you to display tables and relationships for your database. You can create diagrams manually via the Diagram pane, or by using the Diagram Wizard.

To create a new diagram:

- Expand Server Group, the server node, and the Databases folder. Expand the appropriate database, right-click the Diagrams node, and select New Database Diagram...
- Select Next at the initial Create Database Diagram Wizard dialog box.
- Select which tables you would like to see in the diagram by selecting them from the Available tables pane, and selecting the Add button. Select Remove to move tables off the diagram, and select Add related tables automatically to include tables related by foreign keys. You can keep the chain of related tables to a specified limit, by selecting a number in the How many levels of related tables field. Select Next:

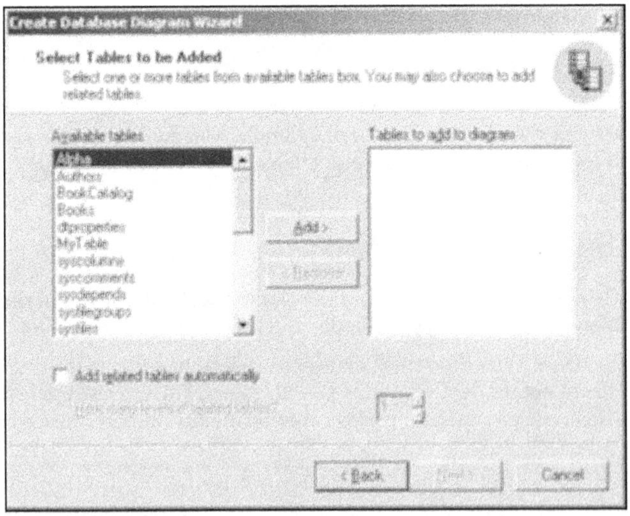

- On the completion screen, confirm the tables you selected, and select Finish. A diagram showing the relationships of the tables will be generated automatically. Select the Save button to save the diagram. You can add additional tables by selecting the Add table on Diagram button, add text comments using the New text annotation button, and print via the printer icon. Modify the table properties themselves by selecting the Properties button, and change the level of detail for the diagram using the Show… button (for example, showing table names only, or including data types and nullability information):

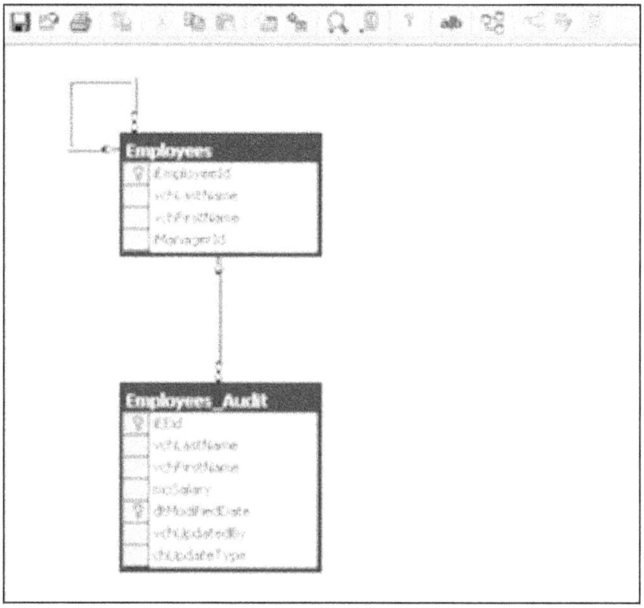

# 4

# SQL Server Agent and SQL Logs

The SQL Server Agent is a service that executes scheduled jobs, monitors server performance conditions and thresholds, and sends alerts notifications via e-mail, paging, or Net send. This combination of technologies allows the DBA to be notified about problems as they occur, which is important for mission-critical 24/7 applications.

The table below describes the SQL Server Agent's three primary functions:

| Function | Description |
|---|---|
| Jobs | SQL Server Agent allows you to schedule and execute jobs. Jobs can contain one or more steps, which can be Transact-SQL scripts, replication operations, ActiveX scripts (using Visual Basic Script, Jscript, PerlScript, or any other scripting language you have installed on your machine), and operating system commands. Tasks include success and failure flow, allowing you to run other tasks or stop the job based on the outcome of the task. |
| Alerts | Alerts allow you to monitor SQL Server events and performance conditions. SQL Server Alerts can fire for specific errors or severity levels. SQL Server performance conditions can be monitored for threshold values that fall below, rise above, or match a specific value. You can configure responses to Alerts, such as executing a job or notifying an operator via e-mail, pager, or Net send. |
| Operators | Operators are contacts that are notified when job outcomes require action or alerts have been fired. Operators can be contacted via e-mail, pager, or Net send. You can also configure schedules for when operators can and cannot be contacted. |

SQL Server Agent is a Windows Service named `SQLServerAgent` for the default instance of SQL Server, and `SQLAgent$Instancename` for a named instance of SQL Server. This service should be set to start automatically, so that jobs will continue to run according to their schedules. You can configure this with the Services manager in Windows 2000 or with Enterprise Manager. To configure in Enterprise Manager:

- Expand Server Group and right-click the server registration, selecting Properties.

- Make sure that Autostart SQL Server Agent is selected. You should also ensure that the SQL Server service and SQL Server Agent services are restarted if they are stopped unexpectedly.
- Click OK.
- Expand the Management folder.
- Right click the SQL Server Agent icon and select Properties.
- Select the Advanced tab. Check both Autostart SQL Server if it stops unexpectedly and Autostart SQL Server Agent if it stops unexpectedly.

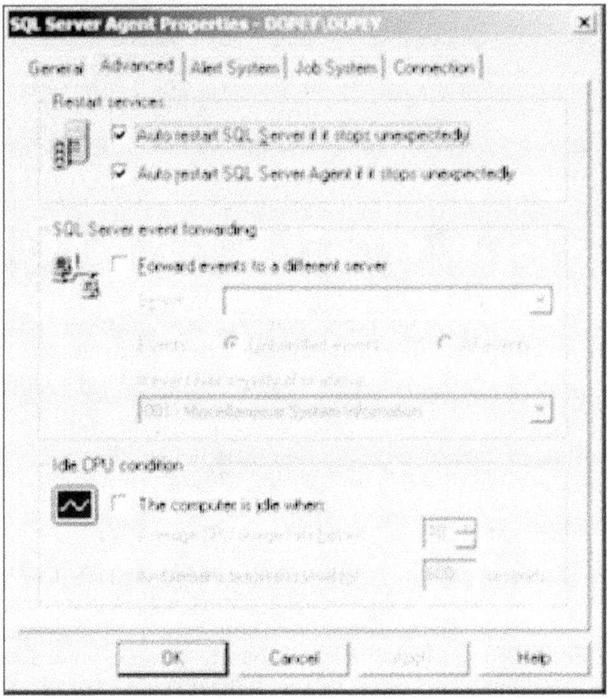


In a production environment, having these options selected is recommended. When these options are not selected, you may be unaware that your jobs or alerts have not been running.

# 4.1 How to... Configure SQL Server Agent Properties

Before setting up jobs, alerts, and operators, let's review the properties of the SQL Server Agent service. In the previous section, we saw how to bring up the SQL Server Agent dialog box. We'll begin by reviewing the General tab within this dialog box.

The General tab allows you to configure the SQL Server Agent service account. If you choose the System account, you are limited to running jobs that access local server resources only. If you want to run jobs (such as replication) that communicate with other servers, or if you wish to notify operators through e-mail or Net send (the Net send command sends messages to other users, computers, or messaging names on the Windows network), you must use a domain account. This domain account must have permissions appropriate to the server or servers you wish to use:

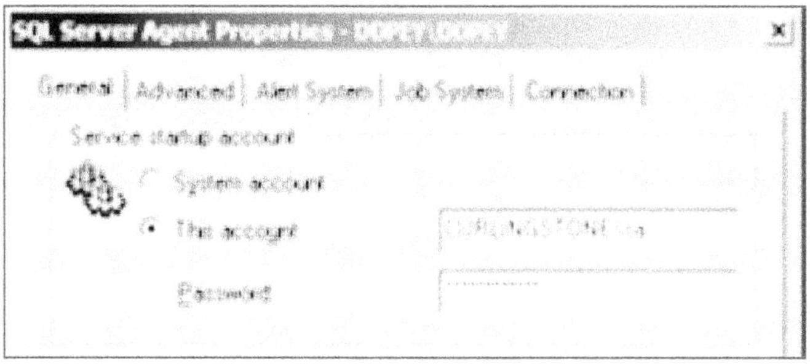


The mail profile is also designated in the General tab. We will go into more detail about this later in the chapter.

The SQL Server Agent has an error log, with error messages specific to its own functions (for example, recording if a job was deleted during execution, or if SQL Mail functionality was misconfigured). You can view the name and location of the file in the Error log section of the General tab. You can view the error log by clicking the View button, and set a Net send recipient for whenever an error appears in the log.

You can also choose whether execution trace messages should be enabled; trace messages are essentially advanced and detailed logging of SQL Server agent activity. If you enable this option, be careful, as trace messages can result in huge log files. Enable this functionality only if there are issues with the SQL Server Agent that require in-depth investigation:

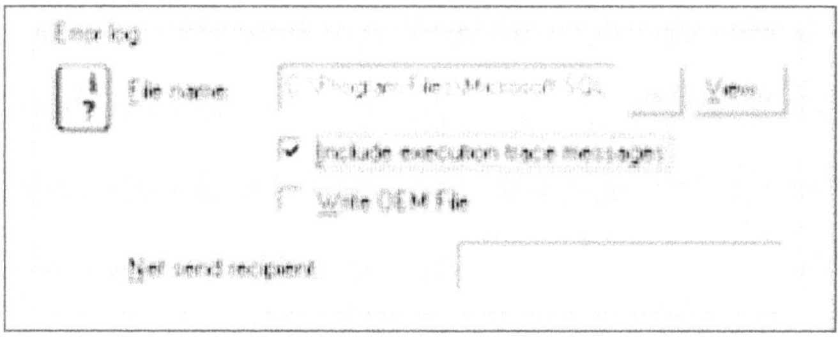


In the Advanced tab, as well as setting auto restarts for the SQL Server and SQL Server Agent services, you can also forward events to another server if you prefer to manage servers from a centralized location:

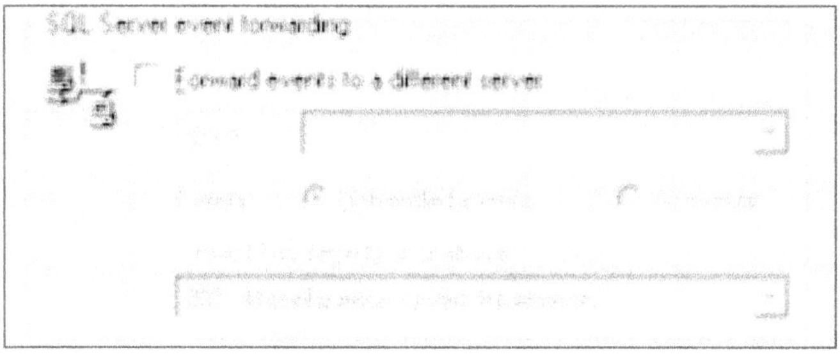

Lastly, on the Advanced tab, you can specify what constitutes an idle CPU level on your server. You may decide that some jobs should only be run during these idle times:

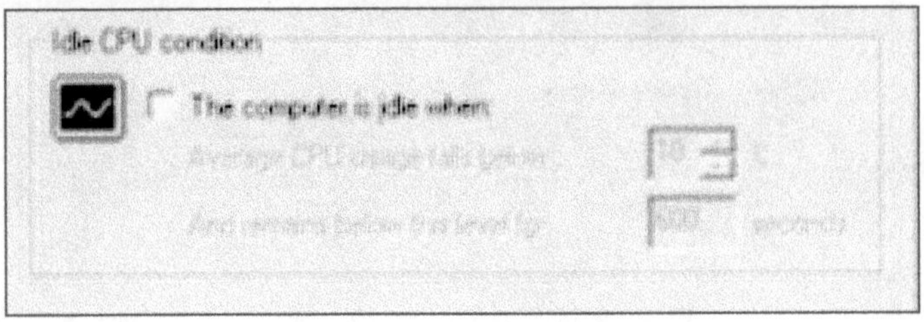

The Alert System tab allows you to configure header information for pager e-mails. You can also choose a Fail-safe operator in the event that an error occurs during attempts to notify the designated operator:

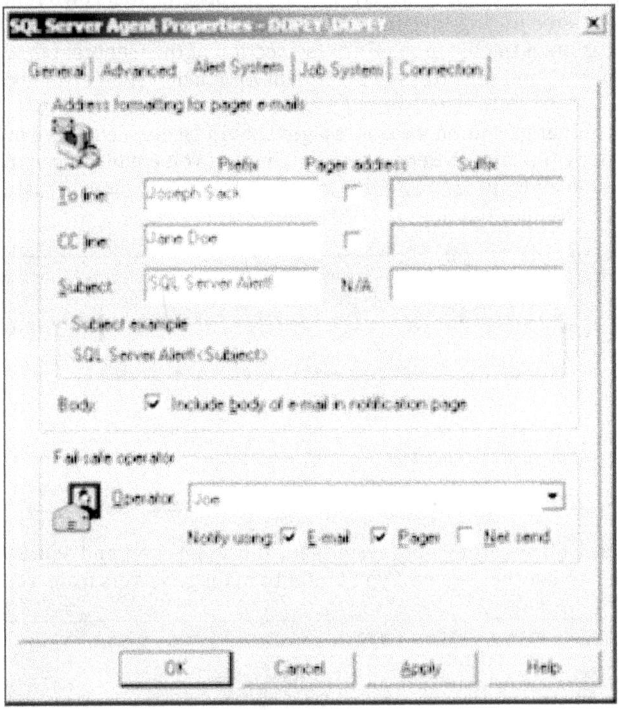

The Job System tab allows you to set the maximum size of the job log history. If you have many jobs and you wish to keep an eye on history, it is recommended that you configure this section. When troubleshooting, it is important to remember that frequently executed jobs can leave you with very little history, as the turnover of log messages is high. You should clear the job history log as part of your weekly database maintenance activities. How much history you keep depends on the capacity and speed of your server. On most systems, 100,000 rows or more of history can amount to a long wait time:

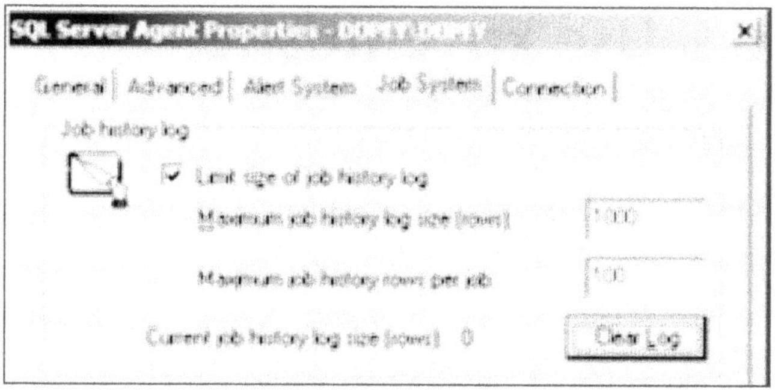

In the Job System tab, you can specify a shutdown time-out interval; this configures the maximum time that SQL Server Agent will wait for a job to finish executing before it shuts down. Increase this interval for jobs that **must** finish, ensuring that the interval is long enough for the job to run.

This section also shows if another server is acting as the master SQL Server Agent. You can designate an MSX server for the purpose of controlling jobs across multiple SQL Server instances from a centralized location. We will show you how to do this later in the chapter:

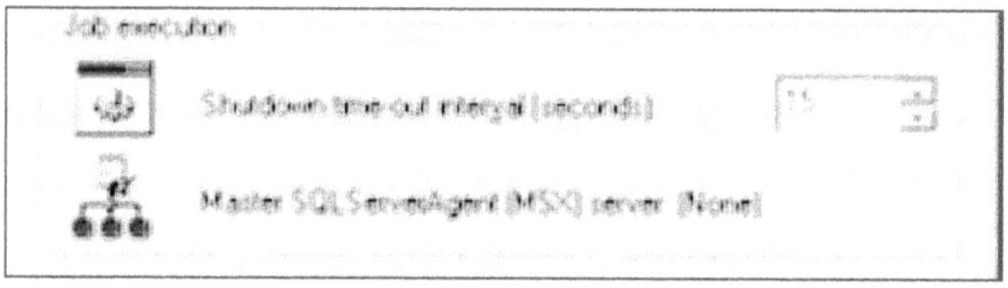

The last section on the Job System tab is the Non-SysAdmin job step proxy account configuration. This will be reviewed in more detail later on in the chapter.

The Connection tab controls SQL Server Agent security when connecting to an instance of SQL Server. You can select whether to use Windows authentication or SQL Server authentication. You can also define a login time-out that determines how long SQL Server Agent will wait for a connection to the instance before timing out:

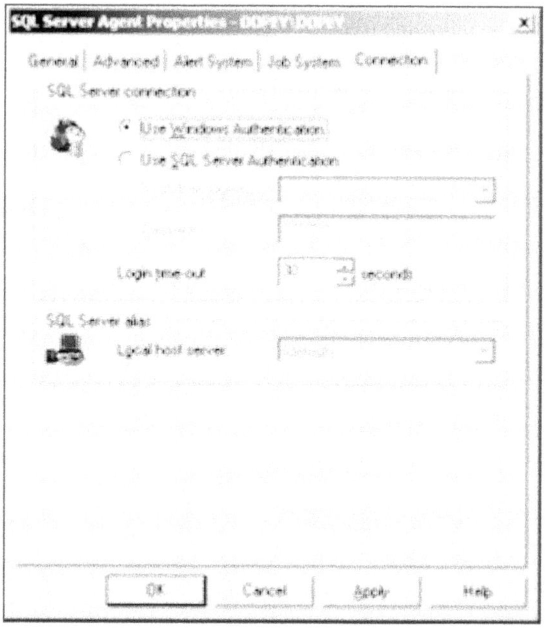

# 4.2 How to... Use xp_cmdshell

Before we move on to the subject of the proxy account, let's review the syntax and usage of xp_cmdshell. The syntax from SQL Server Books Online is as follows:

```
xp_cmdshell {'command_string'} [, no_output]
```

xp_cmdshell allows you to execute an operating system command. xp_cmdshell is an extended stored procedure, and resides in the master database. If you are referencing this command within the context of a different database, make sure to fully qualify the execution of the procedure using master..xp_cmdshell. Extended stored procedures are discussed in more detail in Chapter 14.

The command_string for xp_cmdshell can be either the VARCHAR(255) or the NVARCHAR(4000) data type. Use a single pair of quotation marks if spaces are embedded in file paths and names. The no_output parameter is optional, and specifies that no output from the command should be returned to the client.

Sysadmins can run the xp_cmdshell stored procedure; however, non-sysadmins must be granted explicit permissions to execute the extended stored procedure. For example:

```
GRANT EXEC ON xp_cmdshell TO janedoe
```

The following is an example of using xp_cmdshell to copy a file to a new directory:

```
EXEC xp_cmdshell 'copy C:\WINNT\system32\original.txt C:\WINNT\system32\new.txt'
```

Almost anything you can do with a command prompt, you can do with xp_cmdshell. For particularly difficult DOS statements, statements that exceed NVARCHAR(4000) or VARCHAR(255), or statements with quotes, embed the commands in a .cmd or .bat file.

The following is an example of running a *.bat file that copies a file. The text of the batch file is as follows:

```
copy c:\winnt\temp\original.txt c:\winnt\temp\new.txt
```

Next, we execute the batch file using xp_cmdshell:

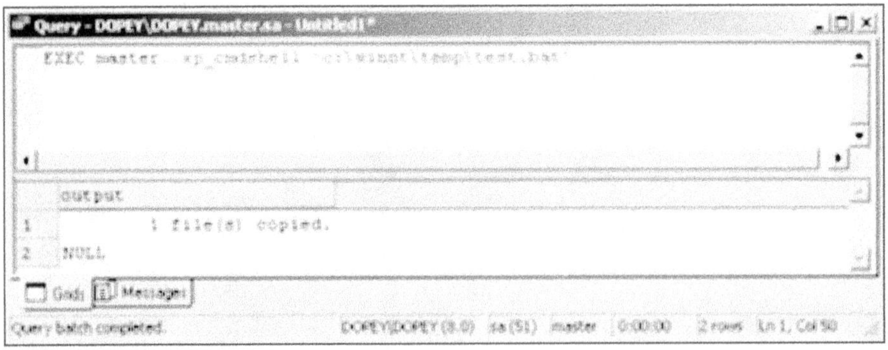

Beware of xp_cmdshell calls to applications or processes that require user feedback. Processes initiated by xp_cmdshell should not have user interfaces. xp_cmdshell runs within the context of SQL Server, and you can, therefore, hang your process if any user or application feedback is required to proceed. DOS failures or syntax issues with non-interactive xp_cmdshell calls do not usually have these problems. When an error occurs with a non-interactive command, the xp_cmdshell call will return an error, and terminate the process.

Lastly, aside from configuring the proxy account in Enterprise Manager, you can also use the xp_sqlagent_proxy_account to configure and report information on the proxy account.

The syntax is as follows, from SQL Server Books Online:

```
xp_sqlagent_proxy_account {N'GET' | N'SET' | N'DEL', N'agent_domain_name',
                           N'agent_username', N'agent_password'}
```

To show current proxy account configuration run:

```
EXEC master.dbo.xp_sqlagent_proxy_account N'GET'
```

The following is an example of changing the proxy account:

```
EXEC master.dbo.xp_sqlagent_proxy_account N'SET', N'JOEDOMAIN',
                                           N'JOEUSER', N'JOEPASSWORD'
```

You can also delete the account with:

```
EXEC master.dbo.xp_sqlagent_proxy_account 'DEL'
```

The xp_sqlagent_proxy_account will configure the account itself, but will not necessarily enable xp_cmdsehell permissions. To enable, you can run:

```
EXEC msdb.dbo.sp_set_sqlagent_properties @sysadmin_only = 0
```

This translates to the setting in SQL Server Agent Properties.

To disable this with Transact-SQL:

```
EXEC msdb.dbo.sp_set_sqlagent_properties @sysadmin_only = 1
```

Since this is undocumented, be aware that this behavior may change. Use the user interface if possible.

# 4.3 How to... Set up the Proxy Account

The proxy account determines whether non-sysadmin SQL Server users can:

- Execute CmdExec steps in a job or run xp_cmdshell
- Run ActiveScripting job steps
- Interact with the local server or remote servers

If you have sysadmin permissions, you have the ability to run `CmdExec` and ActiveScripting steps in a job. If the SQL Server service account is configured to use the system account, then you have administrator permissions to the local box only. If the SQL Server service is running under a domain account, the sysadmin role will adopt whatever permissions are associated with that account. If you assign a domain account with administrator permissions to multiple servers, sysadmin members will have access to these servers as well.

We are not discussing SQL Server object security, but rather security of the server itself. For example, a sysadmin can run the following command in Query Analyzer and receive output:

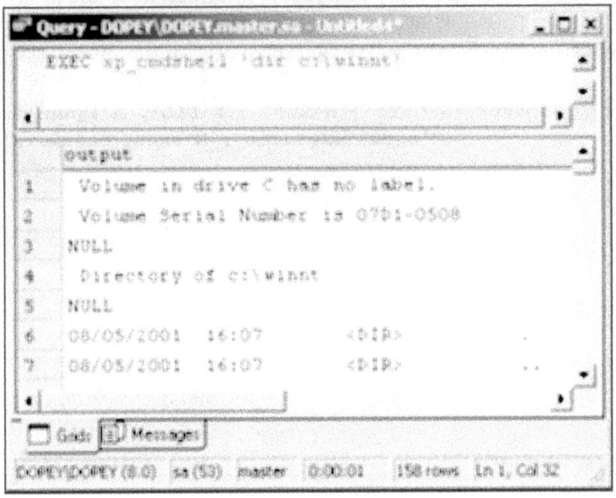


The `xp_cmdshell` extended stored procedure allows you to run DOS commands on the database server. In this case, we are running the DIR command to list the contents of directories.

What if you do not have sysadmin permissions? If the proxy account is not set and does not have execute permissions to `xp_cmdshell`, you will receive the following error for the same command as above:

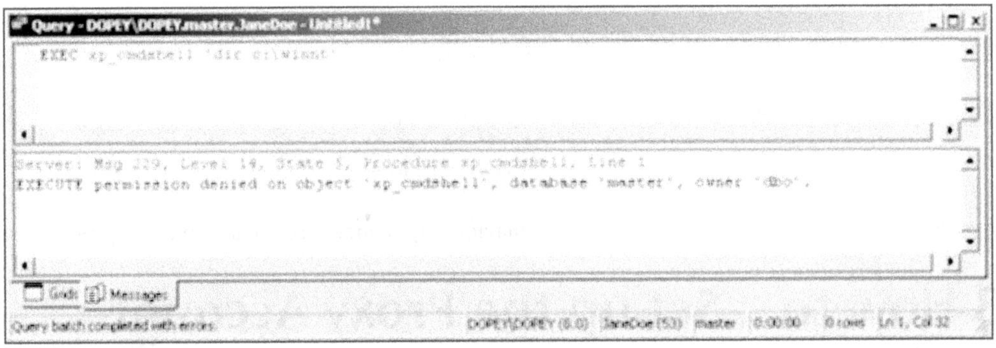


Even if you grant `xp_cmdshell` access to the non-sysadmin user, if the proxy account is not enabled, you will receive the following error:

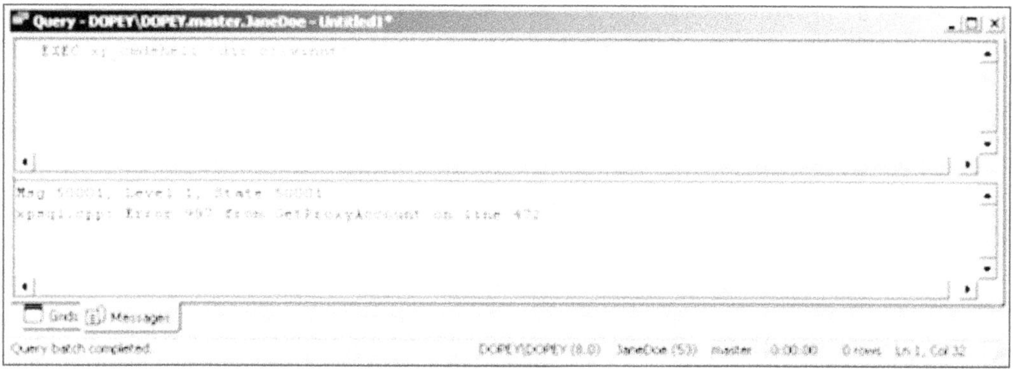


- To configure the proxy account, go to the Job System tab in the SQL Server Agent properties.
- Uncheck Only users with SysAdmin privileges can execute CmdExec and ActiveScripting job steps. You will be prompted for the username, password, and domain you wish to act as the proxy account.
- Select OK when finished.

Assuming you entered in a domain account with proper permissions, you should be able to run the `DIR` command for non-sysadmin users.

There are some drawbacks to configuring this account:

- By configuring the proxy account, you open up access to the local server, and possibly others, to non-sysadmin users.
- You may configure only **one** proxy account per SQL Server instance. For a single application, this is fine; however, if multiple applications have a need for the proxy account you may have problems. Let's say Application A needs access to Server X, and Application B needs access to Server Y, and only one proxy account can be assigned. Do you use a proxy account with access to both X and Y? If so, you open up access to both applications for servers they should use. If you assign a proxy account to just X or Y, then you do not meet the business requirements.

Why would you configure the proxy account in the first place?

- If you want non-sysadmin users to be able to read, write, or manipulate files using ActiveX scripting or `cmdexec`. This is NOT recommended. Such file manipulation activities should be managed by an application, or via sysadmin-owned jobs. The security risk, and risk of bad operations (moving, reading, changing files incorrectly) is too high.
- Some applications search for files on remote servers, and when the file becomes available, a DTS package or job loads the file. Without the proxy account set, only sysadmin job owners can run such a process.
- Some applications like to run executables based on relational table data in the database. You cannot call an executable on the local or remote server if you are not sysadmin and a proxy account is not configured. To avoid this kind of problem, the application should be programmed in such a way as to control the executables from the Web or Application tier, not the database tier.
- Beginning with SQL Server 2000 Service Pack 3, a proxy account is required if you wish non-sysadmin users to have the ability to create a publication or subscription for replication. (See Chapter 8 for more information on replication.)

- ❑ If you want non-sysadmins SQL Server users to own jobs that write output to a file, the proxy account must be configured with write permissions to the output file (described later on in *How to...* 4.6).

SQL Server 2000 introduced the concept of a domain account for the proxy account. SQL Server 7.0 only allowed proxy access to the local server. With this flexibility comes an increased security risk, so configure the proxy account with care.

# 4.4 How to... Add Alerts

To add an alert using Enterprise Manager:

- ❑ Expand the server group and server registration.
- ❑ Expand the Management folder.
- ❑ Expand the SQL Server Agent node, right-click Alerts, and select New Alert.
- ❑ In the General tab of the New Alert Properties dialog box, enter the name and select the type from the dropdown box. The type choices are:
    - ❑ SQL Server event alert
    - ❑ SQL Server performance condition alert
- ❑ The dialog box for SQL Server event alert allows you to select a specific error number or severity level. You may also specify a specific database to monitor:

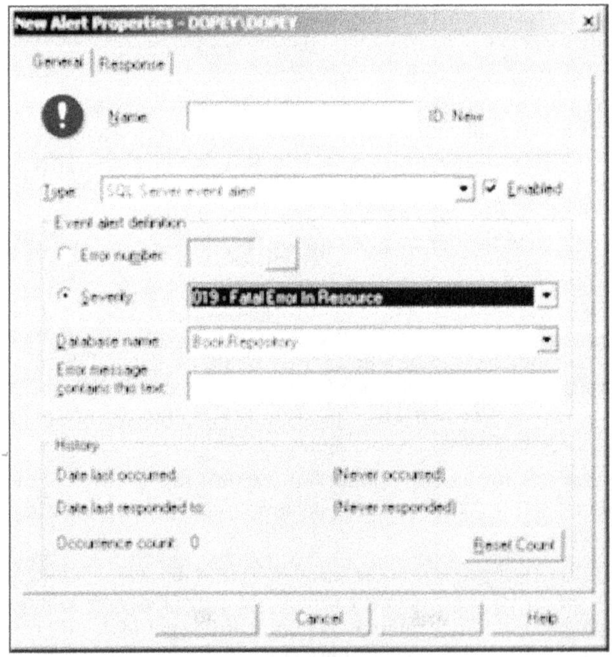


- ❑ The SQL Server performance condition alert allows you to select Object, Counter and, when applicable, SQL Server Instance. You may configure the alert to fire if the value falls below, rises above, or meets a certain threshold:

- In the Response tab, you may select a job to execute in response to an alert firing. For example, if an alert fires when a transaction log becomes full, you can trigger a job to back up the transaction log for the database.

The Response tab also allows you to select which operator or operators should be contacted when an alert is fired, and choose whether to e-mail, page, or Net send the notification. You can also specify additional text to send to the operator.

Lastly, you can configure the delay between responses of the alert. This is an important number to configure, as some alerts can fire many times in a short time period. Prevent getting thirty e-mails for the same event by increasing the Delay between responses value.

- When finished configuring the alert, select OK to create the alert.

# Checklist... Recommended Alerts – What to Monitor

There are hundreds of performance conditions and errors you could potentially monitor. Below is a list of basic alerts you should be concerned with as a SQL Server DBA. You can always add new alerts as new issues present themselves.

Performance conditions vary based on your server hardware and application requirements. You should experiment with certain thresholds before assuming that they necessarily indicate a problem. Below are performance conditions that you should keep an eye on:

| Object | Counter | Definition and Recommended Threshold |
|---|---|---|
| `SQLServer: Buffer Manager` | `Buffer cache hit ratio` | This counter shows the percentage of pages found in the buffer cache compared with SQL Server reading pages from the physical disk. This number should be as close to 100% as possible. A lower number can indicate that SQL Server has insufficient memory available and must perform excessive physical reads to retrieve data.<br><br>Set up an alert to fire when the value drops under 95%. You may decide to increase or decrease this value based on your server configuration and database sizes (extremely complex queries on large tables can take up more of the buffer and push older data out of the buffer cache). |
| `SQL Server:Locks` | `Number of Deadlocks/sec` | This counter measures lock requests per second that result in a deadlock. A deadlock occurs when multiple threads have a cyclical dependency on the same resources. For example, connection A is holding a lock on table `Orders` and also needs to update table `Customers`; connection B is holding a lock on table `Customers` but needs to update table `Orders`.<br><br>SQL Server recognizes that this is a no-win situation and thus decides to kill one of the connections, called a **deadlock victim**. We will review this in more detail in Chapter 5. Deadlocks should and can be avoided, so set this threshold to 1 or greater. |
| `SQL Server: Access Methods` | `Full Scans/sec` | This counter measures the number of full scans performed against a table or index. Scans on larger tables or indexes are not desirable in comparison to seek operations, so you may wish to monitor this counter. Check beforehand in Performance Monitor to determine what is 'normal' for your server. Your threshold should be based on what is excessive for your server and databases. |

| Object | Counter | Definition and Recommended Threshold |
|---|---|---|
| SQL Server: Access Methods | Page Splits/sec | This counter measures the number of page splits per second. Page splits occur when INSERTs are done against a table and SQL Server decides to move half the inserted rows in a data or index page to two new pages, to make room for the new row. Excessive page splitting can negatively impact performance on your server. Formatting an appropriate fill factor can reduce page splitting. Monitor this counter beforehand in Performance Monitor to determine what is 'normal' for your server. Your threshold should be based on what is excessive for your server and databases. |
| SQL Server: Buffer Manager | Free Pages | This counter shows the number of free buffer pages for the server. If this number gets too low, or reaches 0, investigate your memory configuration and determine if there is an issue (such as too little memory). |

The following is a list of recommended Error number and Severity levels to add as alerts:

| Error Number or Severity Level | Description |
|---|---|
| Severity levels 19-25 | Setting alerts to fire for all fatal errors with a severity level of 19 and higher is generally good practice. Severity level descriptions are as follows:<br>Level 19: Fatal error in resource<br>Level 20: Fatal error in current process<br>Level 21: Fatal error in database processes<br>Level 22: Table integrity suspect<br>Level 23: Database integrity suspect<br>Level 24: Hardware error<br>Level 25: Fatal error |
| Error 9002: 'The log file for database % is full'. | You can specify this for all databases or a single database; it will inform you when the transaction log has filled up. |
| Error 8645: 'A time out occurred while waiting for memory resources to execute the query. Re-run the query'. | If you see this error, it means SQL Server waited 25 times the estimated query cost for the memory needed to run the query. If the query wait server configuration is set to a number other than -1, then SQL Server waited for this amount of time instead. This error suggests potential memory issues that should be investigated. |

*Table continued on following page*

| Error Number or Severity Level | Description |
|---|---|
| Replication Errors:<br>Error 20578: Replication: agent custom shutdown.<br>Error 20536: Replication: agent failure.<br>Error 14157: The subscription created by Subscriber to publication has expired and has been dropped.<br>Error 20574:Subscriber subscription to article in publication failed data validation. | If you are using replication, you may want to enable alerts for replication errors. There are several replication errors available; however, the ones listed here are a good start. |

# 4.5 How to... Add Operators

To add a new operator using Enterprise Manager:

- Expand the server group and server registration.
- Expand the Management folder.
- Expand the SQL Server Agent node, right-click Operators, and select New Operator.
- Enter the name of the operator, e-mail name, pager e-mail name, and Net send address. You must have SQLAgentMail (this is reviewed later on in the chapter) configured to use the e-mail and pager e-mail functionality. If this is set up, you can press the Test button to make sure the address is valid. You can also test the Net send address, which does not require SQLAgentMail (Many paging or cell phone providers allow e-mail text messages or alerts. You can utilize pager alerts by using the provider's addressing standard, for example 999887777@pagername.com, to send notification to pagers or cell phones.).

You can also define the pager on duty schedule, which allows you to pick time periods when operators can be reached:

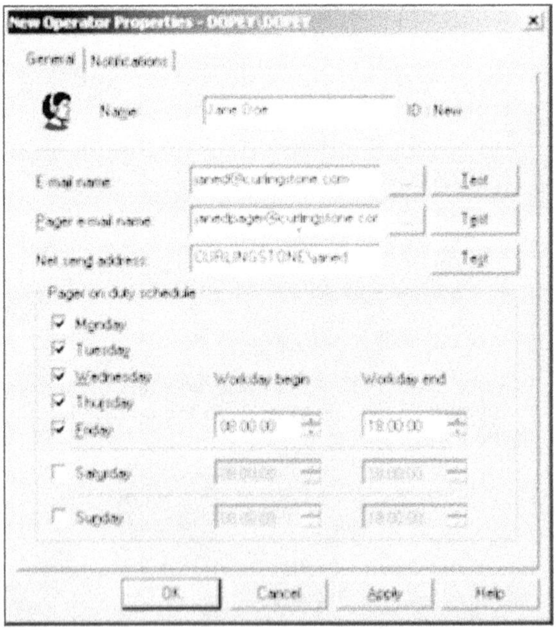

- In the Notifications tab, you can configure and view what alerts the operator will receive. You can also view what jobs send notifications by clicking Jobs in the option bullet. Unlike the alerts view, however, you can only view jobs set up to notify the operator, but cannot edit them.

  You can also view the most recent notification attempts in the bottom section of the Notifications tab.
- Select OK when finished.

# 4.6 How to... Add and Configure Jobs

To add a job using Enterprise Manager:

- Expand the server group and server registration.
- Expand the Management folder.
- Expand the SQL Server Agent node and right-click Jobs and select New Job.
- In the General tab, choose the job name, category, owner, and description:

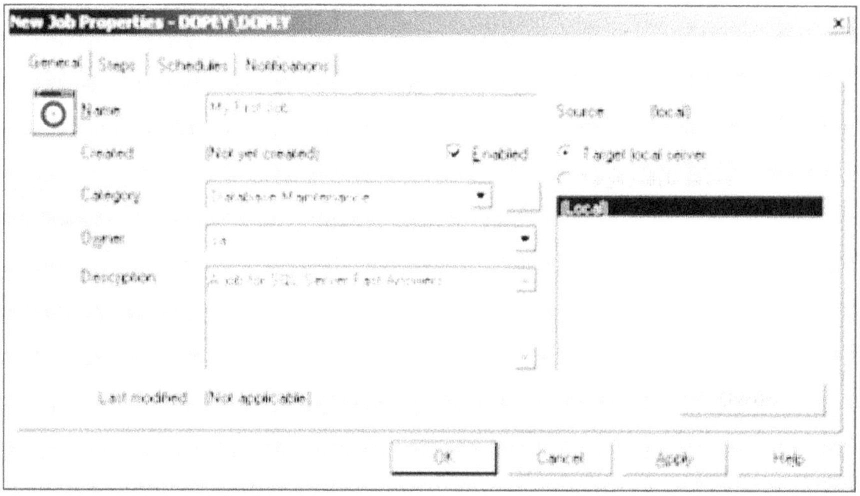

If yours is an MSX server, you have the option to run this job on multiple servers. We will review this functionality later in the chapter.

It is good practice to use a category for your jobs if your server is accessed by multiple projects or applications. If you need to migrate a specific application to a new server, having a category designated for your jobs will make it easier to determine what jobs (if any) should move with the application's databases. See the next section for instructions on creating your own job categories.

- The Steps tab allows you to create one or more job steps. When you have more then one step, you can use the Move step arrows to rearrange steps, and the Start step dropdown box to select the beginning step for the job. Click on the New button to add a new step.
- In the New Job Step dialog box, select a name, type, database (when type is Transact-SQL), and the command to run. The choices for job types are:
  - **Transact-SQL Script**
    Run any type of Transact-SQL command, up to 3200 characters. For example, the following script performs a full backup of the `BookRepository` database:

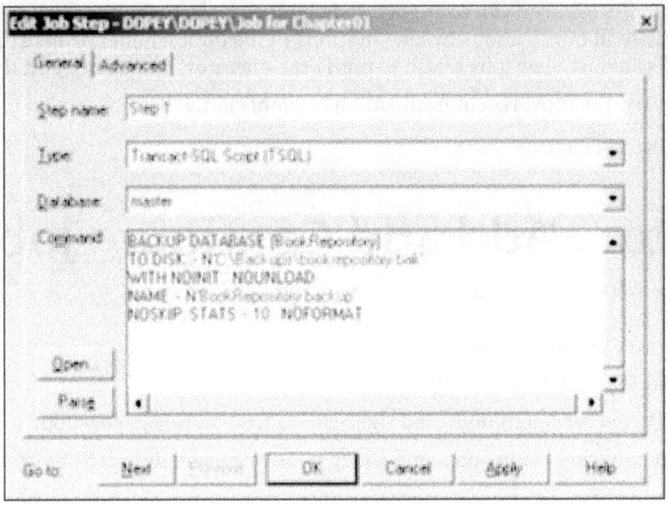

- **ActiveX Script**
  Allows you to run a script in the VB Script language, JScript, or PerlScript.
- **Operating System Command** (`CmdExec`)
  Allows you to run operating system commands or execute .bat, .cmd, .com, or .exe programs.
- **Replication Job Steps**
  These include Replication Distributor, Replication Transaction-Log Reader, Replication Merge, Replication Queue Reader, and Replication Snapshot. These are designated automatically when you set up replication. The Command window takes a combination of keywords and switches. See Chapter 8 for details on how to set up replication.

- Once you have decided on the type, you can enter the command to be run, using the Command field.
- In the Advanced tab of the New Job Step dialog box, you can set On success / failure flow and specify Transact-SQL command options when applicable.

  For the On success action, you can set whether the next step should be run or the job should stop. You can also set retry attempts and the interval of minutes between each attempt. This can be useful if you have a task that looks for a flat file or other external output, and that file is available at variable times. Having a retry will allow your task to keep looking for the file or output until it arrives.

  The On failure action allows you to choose if the job should quit or if a step should be run in response to the failure.

  The option Output file allows you to output any return data from your Transact-SQL step. For example, if your step were to run `sp_who`, the text file you enter for the output would show the `sp_who` output of the server processes. You can decide if this file should be appended to or overwritten each time the job runs.

  Beginning with SQL Server 2000 Service Pack 3, permission to append or overwrite the output log file has changed. The owner of the job determines whether or not the file can be appended or overwritten:

  - If the owner is a member of the sysadmin role, the file can be appended or overwritten.
  - If the owner is a Windows Authentication user, SQL Server will verify that the account has write permission on the specific output file.

- If the job owner is a SQL Server user account, the SQL Server Agent proxy account requires write permissions to the output file. If the account does not have these permissions, the job may still run, but the history will show an error like:

  *Executed as user: [Username]. Warning: cannot write logfile [C:\temp\output.txt]. Error 1332: No mapping between account names and security IDs was done. The step succeeded.*

Once you initially execute the job, you can select the View button to view the actual text file output:

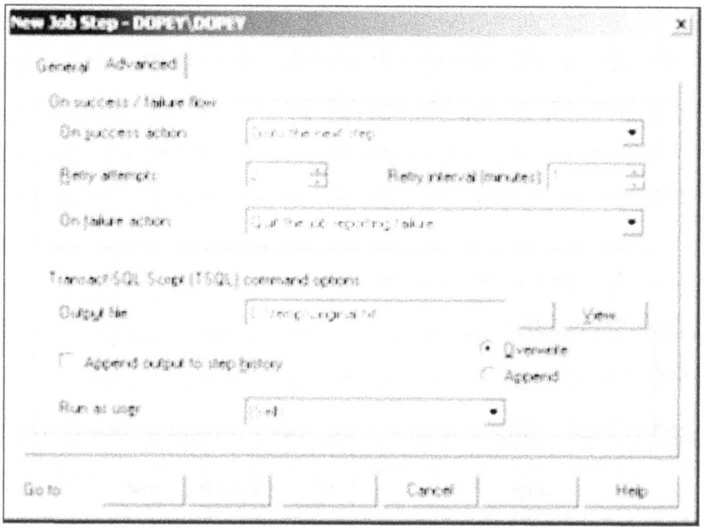


The option Append output to step history allows you to append the output of your Transact-SQL step to the history of the job. The normal output when viewing job history is as follows:

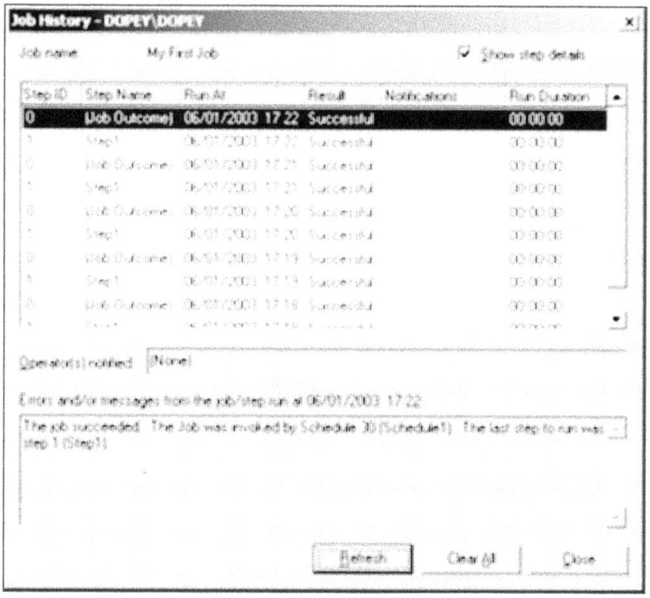

However (as there is a limit on characters), if we took the example of running sp_who, you would see the first few lines of this stored procedure's output in the step history instead:

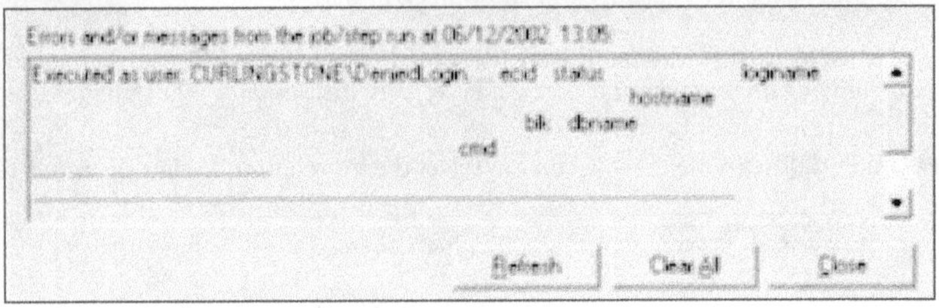

The Transact-SQL script command option Run as user allows you to designate what user context the Transact-SQL script runs under, if different from the job owner.

- When you have finished configuring the General and Advanced tabs of the New Job Step dialog box, select OK to exit.
- You should then see any steps you created in the steps list:

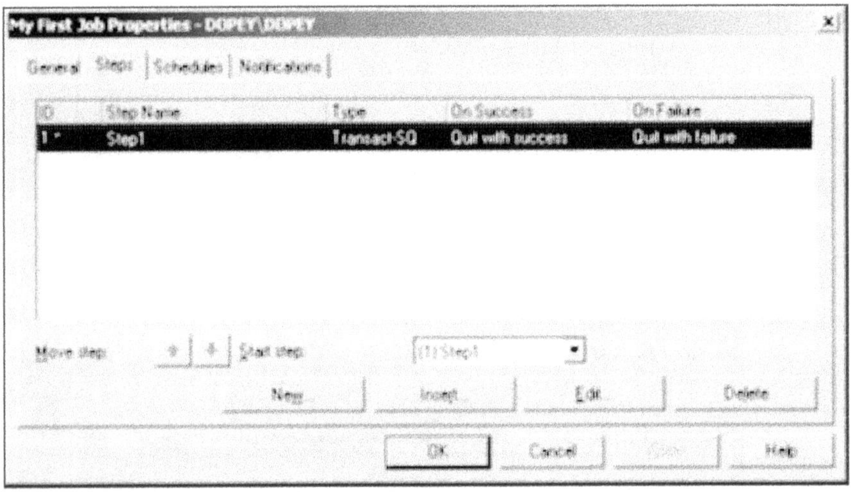

- In the Schedules tab, you can specify a schedule or schedules for your job to run. To create a new schedule, select the New Schedule button.
- In the New Job Schedule dialog box, you can determine whether the job starts automatically when the SQL Server Agent starts, starts when the CPU becomes idle (remember that the idle threshold can be configured in the SQL Server Agent properties), runs one time on a specific date and time, or runs on a recurring schedule.

  Type in the name of the schedule and uncheck the Enabled checkbox if you do not want it to go into effect right away.

  If you want a recurring schedule, click the Change... button to define the frequency.

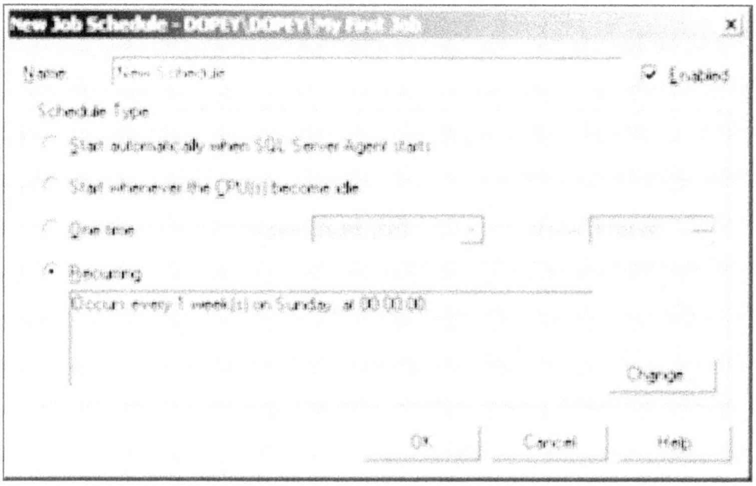


- The Edit Recurring Job Schedule dialog box allows you to select a daily, weekly, or monthly frequency. You can also specify specific dates, times, and frequency by the hour or minute. You can define a start date and end date for this recurring schedule in the bottom section. When finished configuring the schedule, select OK.
- Select OK at the New Job Schedule to add the schedule.
- Lastly, in the Notifications tab, you can define e-mail, pager, and Net send operators that should be contacted in the event that the job fails, completes, or succeeds.

  You can also write entries to the Windows application event log on job failure, completion, or success.

  Lastly, you can have the job deleted when it succeeds, fails, or completes. This is useful when you are creating jobs that are intended to run only once, or jobs that are dynamically created for data loads and must be recreated with varying schedules and tasks that are applicable only one time.
- Select OK when finished configuring the job.

# 4.7 How to... Create Job Categories

You can create your own custom categories by following these steps:

- Right-click Jobs, select All Tasks | Manage Job Categories.
- In the Job Categories dialog box, select the Add button to create a new job category.
- In the New Job Category Properties dialog box, type in the name of your new project. Select the Show all jobs checkbox to include specific jobs as members of this new category. Select OK when finished.
- You will see your new category in the main dialog box. Expand the folder to the view jobs that are members of this new category. Select Close when finished:

# Configuring SQL Mail and SQLAgentMail

SQL Server 2000 provides e-mail integration with the SQL Server and SQL Server Agent services.

**SQL Mail** is the name of the mail session used by the MSSQLServer service. SQL Mail allows you to send e-mails from your scripts, stored procedures, and batches using the extended stored procedure `xp_sendmail`. This stored procedure can send a message or result set to one or more recipients.

**SQLAgentMail** is the name of the mail session used by the SQL Server Agent service for sending e-mail notifications to operators.

SQL Mail and SQLAgentMail require a mail profile to function. If the SQL Server and SQL Server Agent domain accounts are different, two separate profiles are required (unless you change them to the same domain account). Otherwise, only one profile is needed. SQL Mail and SQLAgentMail can connect with either Microsoft Exchange Server or a Post Office Protocol 3 (POP3) server.

If you are using Lotus Notes, Lotus cc:Mail, Novell GroupWise, or other third-party mail server products, these must be configured as POP3 servers. The third-party mail server must also be MAPI compliant.

Consumer web-based mail services (such as Yahoo, AOL, Compuserve) are not officially supported, and may not be licensed for business utilization. Another reason web-based mail services should not be used is that if SQL Mail is unable to connect to the web-based POP3 server, SQL Mail will hang and the SQL Server service must **restart** before it can be used again.

Also, be aware that SQL Mail is not fully supported on a SQL Server Failover cluster. The SQL Mail service is not cluster-aware, meaning it cannot act as a cluster resource, nor be controlled by the Cluster Administrator. Since it is not a resource, it cannot reside on a shared disk and, therefore, cannot failover or failback between cluster nodes. For more information on this bug, see Microsoft's Knowledge Base article Q298723, *BUG: SQL Mail Not Fully Supported for Use in Conjunction with Cluster Virtual SQL Servers*. See Chapter 10 for more information on failover clustering.

## Pre-Configuration Checklist

- ❑ If you are using Microsoft Exchange Server, SQL Mail requires that your SQL Server Service account use a domain account. It cannot be a local system account.
- ❑ If you are using Microsoft Exchange Server, SQLAgentMail requires that your SQL Server Agent service account use a domain account. It cannot be a local system account.
- ❑ If you are using a third-party mail server application, this product must be configured as a POP3 mail server. Since these mail servers often use a login and password (not Windows authentication), your service account can be a local system or a domain account.

## Setting up SQL Mail and SQLAgentMail for Exchange

### Setting up the Profile

- ❑ Set up a mailbox on Exchange Server for use by the SQL Server and SQL Server Agent service accounts. You can create one mailbox for both SQL Mail and SQLAgentMail to use, or one mailbox each. If they both use the same domain account, create one mailbox.
- ❑ When configuring SQL Mail, log on to the SQL Server server using the same domain account as that used to run the SQL Server service.

- Install the Microsoft Outlook 2000 or Outlook 2002 client on the SQL Server server. A disadvantage to using Outlook 2002 is that it must have the client running at all times (for SQL Server 2000). Outlook 98 can be used if you have SQL Server Service Pack 1 or greater installed. Start up Microsoft Outlook and connect to the Microsoft Exchange server and mailbox you designated in step 1.
- Test that you can send and receive mail from this mailbox. Do not proceed until you are sure you can.

## Setting up SQL Mail

- Expand the server group and server registration in Enterprise Manager.
- Expand the Support Services folder.
- Right-click SQL Mail and select Properties.
- Select the profile name you configured when testing Outlook. Click the Test button and check the mailbox to confirm that a message is received regarding SQL Mail.
- Select OK. SQL Server 2000 starts the SQL Mail service automatically when `xp_sendmail` is invoked.

## Setting up SQLAgentMail

Once SQLAgentMail is configured for SQL Server, you will be able to send e-mails in response to alerts or jobs. If your mail server allows e-mails that can communicate with pagers, you will also be able to page in response to alerts or jobs.

To enable SQLAgentMail:

- Decide beforehand if you will use the same profile as SQL Mail or a separate profile. If separate, create the new profile with Microsoft Outlook.
- Log in to the server with the domain account used to run the SQL Server Agent.
- In Enterprise Manager, expand server groups and server registration.
- Expand the Management folder and right-click SQL Server Agent. Select Properties.
- In the General tab, under the Mail session section, select the mail profile you created for SQLAgentMail. Click the Test button and check the mailbox for this profile to make sure the test succeeded. Check Save copies of the messages in the 'Sent Items' folder if you wish to do so. If you anticipate many e-mails being sent out, you may wish to leave this unchecked.
- Select OK, and say Yes to restart the SQL Server Agent service (necessary for this mail profile to take effect).

# 4.8 How to... Troubleshoot SQL Mail and SQLAgentMail

Unfortunately, SQL Mail and SQLAgentMail can be difficult to configure, and even more difficult to keep running. Check the Knowledge Base article Q311231, *INF: Frequently Asked Questions-SQL Server-SQL Mail*. This article reviews several common issues and references to bugs.

Two important bugs to note are:

- There is a bug that causes `xp_sendmail` to fail if you send mail to a personal distribution list. See Knowledge Base article Q315666, *BUG: XP_Sendmail Fails to send mail to Personal Distribution List*. The workaround is to use the SQLAgentMail functionality instead or run through the list of individuals instead of using a group.

- SQL Mail will not work with Windows Messaging, Outlook Express, and Outlook 97. Outlook 98 is supported only if SQL Server 2000 Service Pack 1 or greater is installed, and must be configured with the corporate or workgroup option enabled.

# 4.9 How to... Configure SQL Mail for a Valid POP3 Server

These steps apply to any valid POP3 server. This includes Lotus Notes or other third-party e-mail servers set up as POP3 servers:

- Set up the e-mail account on the POP3 server. This account must allow incoming and outgoing mail.
- Log on to the SQL Server server using the SQL Server service domain account.
- Install Microsoft Outlook 2000 or 2002 for your Windows 2000 server. Outlook 2002 must remain open at all times, and, therefore, is less robust than Outlook 2000. Outlook 98 is accepted if running SQL Server Service Pack 1 or greater.
- Start Outlook and configure the profile to connect to the POP3/SMTP server. Test this account to make sure inbound and outbound e-mail is functioning.
- Expand the server group and server registration in Enterprise Manager.
- Expand the Support Services folder.
- Right-click SQL Mail and select Properties.
- Select the profile name you configured when testing Outlook. Click the Test button and check the mailbox to confirm that a message is received. Test this several times to confirm that no dialog boxes appear that require feedback to the POP3 server. If any dialog boxes or feedback is needed, SQL Mail will hang and SQL Server will need to be restarted. If you cannot avoid a dialog box, then you should not use the POP3 mail server for SQL Mail.

# 4.10 How to... Use Alternative E-Mail Solutions

If you cannot meet the requirements for configuring SQL Mail and SQLAgentMail functionality, Microsoft has provided a method for e-mailing from SQL Server through Collaboration Data Objects for Windows 2000 (CDOSYS). The `sp_OA` stored procedures used for invoking OLE Automation call these objects and allow you to e-mail if you have a valid Internet mail server on your network. This is good news for those who do not like installing extra software on the database server.

This CDOSYS object model is included with Windows 2000. For details on how to install it, see Knowledge Base article Q312839, *HOW TO: Send E-Mail Without Using SQL Mail in SQL Server*.

Keep in mind that this functionality does not integrate with SQL Mail or SQLAgentMail, but allows custom notification from your own Transact-SQL statements. A word of caution regarding `sp_OA` procedures: although able to expand functionality available to SQL Server, these procedures are sometimes resource-intensive and do not provide the flexibility available in COM compliant languages. The `sp_OA` procedures are reviewed in more detail in Chapter 16.

# 4.11 How to... Use xp_sendmail

The stored procedure `xp_sendmail` uses the SQL Mail functionality to send a message or a query result set attachment to recipients you specify. The syntax from SQL Server Books Online is:

```
xp_sendmail {[@recipients =] 'recipients [;...n]'}
     [,[@message =] 'message']
     [,[@query =] 'query']
     [,[@attachments =] 'attachments [;...n]']
     [,[@copy_recipients =] 'copy_recipients [;...n]'
     [,[@blind_copy_recipients =] 'blind_copy_recipients [;...n]'
     [,[@subject =] 'subject']
     [,[@type =] 'type']
     [,[@attach_results =] 'attach_value']
     [,[@no_output =] 'output_value']
     [,[@no_header =] 'header_value']
     [,[@width =] width]
     [,[@separator =] 'separator']
     [,[@echo_error =] 'echo_value']
     [,[@set_user =] 'user']
     [,[@dbuse =] 'database']
```

| Parameter | Description |
|---|---|
| `@recipients` | Designates one or more e-mail recipients. |
| `@message` | Designates the e-mail message body. |
| `@query` | Designates a valid Transact-SQL query, which is then sent in the e-mail. |
| `@attachments` | Indicates file or files to be attached to the e-mail. |
| `@copy_recipients` | Cc: recipients. |
| `@blind_copy_recipients` | Bcc: recipients. |
| `@subject` | Subject line. |
| `@type` | The input message type for MAPI mail definition. |
| `@attach_results` | Indicates that the `@query` results should be attached as results to the e-mail if set to `TRUE`. Default is `FALSE`. |
| `@no_output` | Optional parameter, which sends the mail but does not return any output to the sending client session. |
| `@no_header` | Optional parameter, which sends query results but not column headers. |
| `@width` | Optional parameter, which designates the line width of output text. |
| `@separator` | Designates the column separator string. The default is to use blank space. |

*Table continued on following page*

| Parameter | Description |
| --- | --- |
| @echo_error | If set to TRUE, this will send the e-mail recipient any server or DB-Library errors generated while running the query and will show a row count. |
| @set_user | User context under which the @query runs. |
| @dbuse | Database context under which the @query runs. |

The following is an example of sending both a message and a query to janedoe@curlingstone.com:

```
xp_sendmail
  @recipients = 'janedoe@curlingstone.com',
  @subject = 'Failed Book rows',
  @message = 'Jane, here are the books that failed to be scrubbed by our Data
Scrub job.',
  @query = 'SELECT * from BookRepository.dbo.FailedBooks'
```

This procedure also lets you attach files, copy and blind-copy recipients, specify user and database context, set column width and separator for the query output, and return errors received when errors are encountered running the query.

Some bugs to note regarding xp_sendmail:

- Using @query will leave temporary files in your System32 directory; therefore, you should clean up this directory or specify a preferred directory to place these files. See Microsoft Knowledge Base article Q151545, *BUG: Xp_sendmail With @query Leaves Temporary Files on Server*.
- Large query result set attachments can cause problems if the rows returned are greater than 2,000 bytes, the @width parameter is greater than 2,000, and the results are not attached to a file. The workaround is to attach the results to a file or to choose a value of @width less than 2,000 characters. See Knowledge Base article Q169641, *BUG: Xp_sendmail with Large Row Results May Cause Error 35909*.
- xp_sendmail will break text data into 4,096 byte chunks, even if @width is set to a greater value. The workaround is to send the query as an attachment. See Knowledge Base article Q221981, *BUG: Xp_sendmail Sends Text Data in 4 KB Chunks*.
- Stored procedure calls or PRINT statements in the @query parameter may cause missing results in an attachment. See Knowledge Base article Q317797, *BUG: Xp_sendmail with Attachment Option Does Not Include All Results in Attachment*.
- SQLMail is not supported in a failover cluster, or when the server is set to run in Fiber Mode. See Knowledge Base article Q308604, *PRB: SQLMAil is Not Supported When you Run the Server in Fiber Mode*.

If you wish to start a mail session other than the default set in Enterprise Manager, you can use the xp_startmail extended stored procedure. For example, the following opens up a mail session for the user janedoe:

```
USE master
GO
EXEC xp_startmail 'janedoe', 'password'
GO
```

Then you can use xp_sendmail.

A gotcha with xp_startmail – if your SQLAgentMail and SQL Mail processes are running under the same profile, you cannot switch client profiles using xp_startmail; you are stuck with the same one for both processes.

Run the following to end the mail session:

```
EXEC xp_stopmail
GO
```

Always run xp_stopmail when you have finished running xp_sendmail, as new xp_sendmail calls cannot share the same mailbox DLL resources, and only **one** active session can be running at a time.

# 4.12 How to... Process Incoming E-Mails with SQL Mail Procedures

In addition to sending e-mails, you can also receive, process, and take action on e-mails sent to the SQL Mail profile mailbox. The full syntax for each of these extended stored procedures is in Microsoft Books Online; however, we will review examples of each.

The sp_processmail extended stored procedure allows you to process incoming mail messages from the inbox configured for the SQL Mail profile. sp_processmail actually uses multiple extended stored procedures to do its job:

- **xp_findnextmsg**
  Takes a message ID for input and returns the message ID for output, and helps sp_processmail.
- **xp_readmail**
  Reads a mail message from the SQL Mail profile mail inbox.
- **xp_sendmail**
  Sends back the result sets if a query request is embedded in the inbox message or messages.
- **xp_deletemail**
  Deletes the message from the SQL Mail profile mail inbox.

sp_processmail takes incoming mail messages (for single query requests only) and returns the result set to the mail sender. The original inbox e-mail is then deleted. The syntax for sp_processmail from SQL Server Books Online is as follows:

```
sp_processmail [ [ @subject = ] 'subject' ]
               [ , [ @filetype = ] 'filetype' ]
               [ , [ @separator = ] 'separator' ]
               [ , [ @set_user = ] 'user' ]
               [ , [ @dbuse = ] 'dbname' ]
```

The @subject parameter looks at the 'subject' line of an incoming mail message. If the subject line contains the @subject value, the message is processed by sp_processmail. The @filetype parameter gives the file extension to be used when sending the result set back to the sender. @separator specifies the column separator for each result set column. @set_user defines the security context of the query. Note that SQL Server Books Online states that @set_user is a SYSNAME data type (which is functionally equivalent to NVARCHAR(128)), when actually the data type is VARCHAR (132). See Knowledge Base article Q303665, *BUG: BOL Incorrectly States That Data Type for @set_user in sp_processmail is Sysname.*

One bug affecting sp_processmail involves the @set_user parameter defaulting to the guest account of the master database, instead of to the current user's security context. If the guest account is disabled for the master database, you will see an error when running sp_processmail. See Knowledge Base article Q303666, *BUG: SP_Processmail @set_user Parameter Defaults to Guest Instead of the Security Context of the Current User*.

The @dbuse parameter sets the database context where the query runs.

You should schedule sp_processmail in a SQL Server Agent job if you want to process inbox mail periodically.

An example of running the sp_processmail procedure:

```
sp_processmail @subject = 'SQL:DBA',
               @filetype = 'TXT',
               @separator = ',',
               @set_user = 'janedba',
               @dbuse = 'master'
```

This sp_processmail will search for inbox messages with SQL:DBA in the subject line, and will return results in .TXT format in comma separated columns. Keep your subject lines secret if you intend to have sensitive information or permissions available. E-mail is processed based on this @subject line and it doesn't matter who sent the e-mail. Be careful.

One last note; the query or stored procedure call you send to the SQL Mail mailbox must be in the message text, and can be a single valid SQL Server query only. Also note that Chapter 11 reviews the Send Mail Task, which allows you to send e-mail from a DTS package.

# 4.13 How to… Configure Multi-Server Administration

Multi-server administration allows you to centralize the location of SQL Server Agent jobs on one master server. The master server, or MSX server, then runs the jobs on other target servers on the network. You can run the same job on multiple servers and view the history for all target servers from the master server. The master jobs cannot be modified on the target. This functionality is only available for SQL Server Standard and Enterprise Edition.

Multi-server administration eases the burden of DBAs who must manage many SQL Server instances, by centralizing job administration.

An example of using multi-server jobs; you could create a multi-server job that periodically ensures updates against system tables in the master database are NOT allowed (in case someone forgot to disable this option):

```
EXEC sp_configure 'allow updates', 0
```

Instead of having to create a job twenty times, one for each SQL Server instance you support (assuming you support twenty SQL Server instances), you only have to define this **once** on the master server, and define those servers against which it will execute.

> **If you have upgraded to SQL Server 2000 Service Pack 3, your SQL Server instance can only be a target or master server in association with other servers also running SQL Server 2000 SP3.**

# 4.14 How to... Configure the Master Server

- In Enterprise Manager, expand server group and the server registration.
- Expand the Management folder.
- Right-click SQL Server Agent and select Multi Server Administration and Make this a Master.
- Select Next at the dialog box.
- The Create 'MSXOperator' dialog box allows you to specify a SQL Server Agent operator that should receive notifications regarding multi-server job completion. Select Next when you have finished the configuration (you do not need to select an operator, this is optional).
- Next, select which target servers (TSX) to enlist. These are the servers where your jobs will run. You can add additional target servers later too. Check which servers you wish to enlist. Select the Properties button to configure how you connect to the TSX server or select the Register Server button to add new servers to the list. Select Next when finished.
- Next, you can provide a description for each target server if you wish. Select Next when finished.
- Select the Finish button in the Completing the Make MSX Wizard.
- Press the Close button when finished.

Your master server (MSX) should now show the following icon for SQL Server Agent:

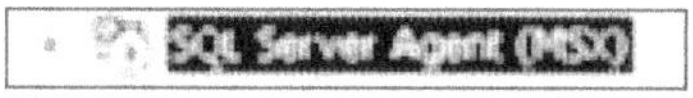


# 4.15 How to... Set up Target Servers

To set up additional target servers, follow these steps:

- Right-click the SQL Server Agent on your MSX server and select Multi Server Administration and Add Target Servers.
- In the Enlist Registered Servers Into This MSX dialog box, select the new target servers. Click the Enlist button when finished.
- You should then see a dialog box saying 'Successfully Enlisted N servers', where N = number of servers.

You can also enlist a target server from the target server registration itself:

- In Enterprise Manager, right-click SQL Server Agent, select Multi Server Administration and Make this a Target.
- Select Next in the Make TSX Wizard dialog box.
- Select the master server for which this server will be a target server. Select Next.
- Select Finish. After adding the target server, you should see a dialog box indicating success.

# 4.16 How to... Create a Multi Server Job

- Expand the SQL Server Group and SQL Server registration for the MSX server.
- Expand the Management folder, expand SQL Server Agent, Jobs, and select Multi Server Jobs.

- ❑ Right-click Multi Server Jobs and select Add Job.
- ❑ The New Job dialog box is just as for a regular job, except that the Category is Uncategorized (Multi-Server), and the Target multiple servers bullet point is selected:

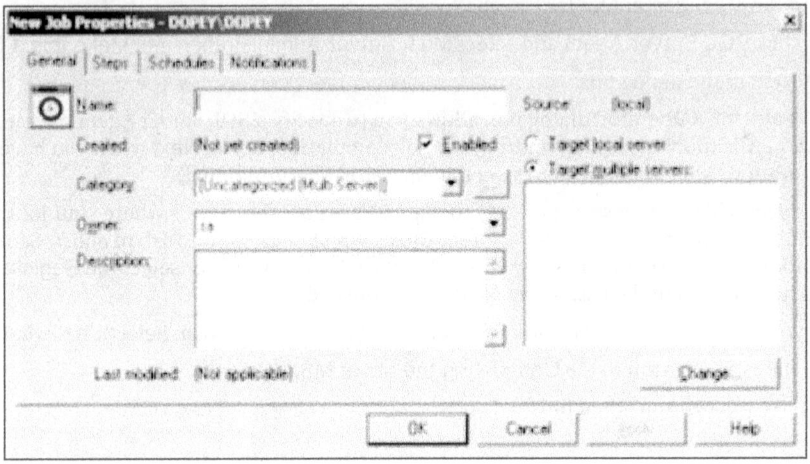


- ❑ Click the Change button to add target servers for your job. Select servers on which you wish to run the job by selecting them in the target server in the left pane and clicking the arrow to move it to the Selected target servers pane. Selecting Properties for the target server will show the time zone and polling properties for the target server. When finished, select OK.
- ❑ Configure your job as you would a regular job. The only difference is that you should avoid running multi-server jobs that reference unique attributes which are not the same on all target servers, such as databases that only exist on one target server but not others. Note that the Notifications tab only allows the MSXOperator:

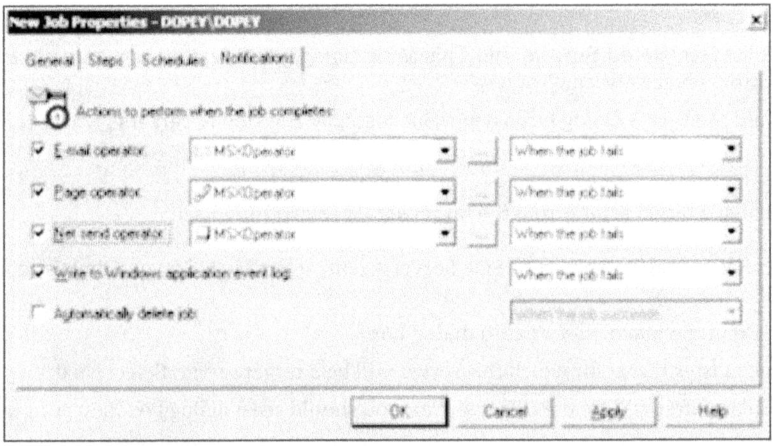


You can run it manually by following these steps:

- ❑ Expand SQL Server Agent on the MSX server. Expand Jobs and select Multi Server Jobs.
- ❑ Right-click the job you wish to start, and select Start Job, and either Start on all targeted servers or Start on specific target servers.

# 4.17 How to... View Multi-Server Job History

- ❑ You can view job history by right-clicking the job and selecting Job Status.
- ❑ The Job Execution Status tab allows you to view remote job history and target server status. You can also synchronize jobs from this dialog box. Synchronization updates the target servers with any changes made to the master server's job definitions. You can view status by job or server by selecting the bullet point under the Show status by section:

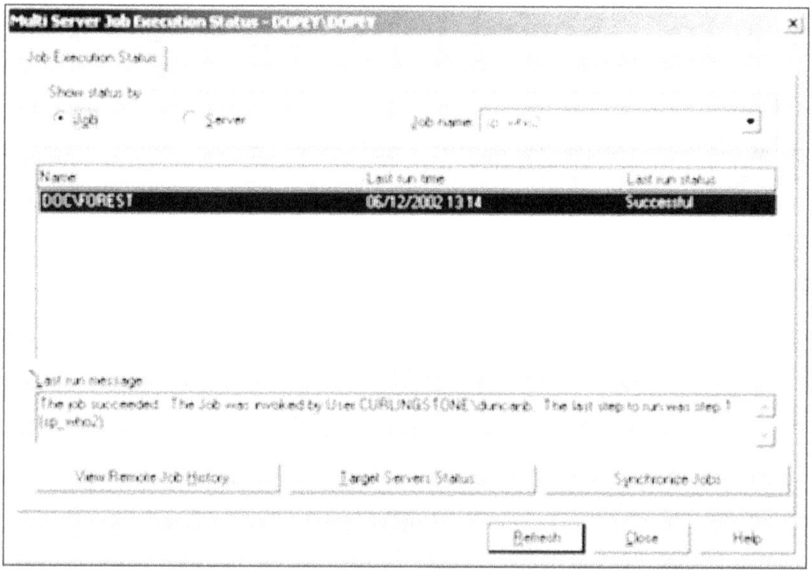


Click View Remote Job History... to view history for the specified job or server.

Clicking the Target Servers Status... button allows you to poll the target server (check to see if the MSX server can reach the target server), post instructions (run a job, synchronize clocks, defect from MSX), and force defection (which we will cover in the next section).

# 4.18 How to... Defect a Target Server

Defecting a target server means that it will no longer participate in multi-server administration; that is, the target server will no longer receive jobs from the master server. To defect the target server:

- ❑ In Enterprise Manager, expand server group and server registration.
- ❑ Expand the Management folder and right-click SQL Server Agent. Select Multi Server Administration and Defect from MSX.
- ❑ Click Force defection **only** if you know that the MSX server is somehow corrupted or unavailable. Otherwise, for a normal defection, select the Yes button.

You can also defect a target server from the MSX server:

- ❑ In Enterprise Manager, expand server group and server registration.

- Expand the Management folder and right-click SQL Server Agent. Select Multi Server Administration and Manage Target Servers.
- Click the server you wish to defect and select the Force Defection button. You will be asked if you wish to try a normal defection first; select Yes.

Note that your MSX server will no longer show MSX in the SQL Server Agent icon if there are no target servers. You implicitly remove MSX functionality by removing all target servers.

# 4.19 How to... Script Jobs, Operators, and Alerts

You can script out SQL Server Agent jobs, operators, and alerts using SQL Server Enterprise Manager. You can then run this script on other servers to recreate them. Be aware that if jobs reference objects that do not exist on the new server, they may fail when executed, or otherwise not work as expected. Note that the GO keyword can cause issues if used within a Transact-SQL task in a job, because GO delimits one batch or statements from the rest.

To script jobs in Enterprise Manager:

- Expand the server group and server registration.
- Expand the Management folder and expand SQL Server Agent.
- Select Jobs.
- To script one job, right-click the job and select All Tasks | Generate SQL Script.
- To script **all** jobs, right-click Jobs and select All Tasks | Generate SQL Script.
- In the Generate SQL Script dialog box, enter the filename of the script you wish to generate and give the file format. Choose whether or not to add Transact-SQL that replaces the job if the job exists. If you do not select this option, the job creation will fail if a job with the same name exists on the server. Also, specify the T-SQL batch separator (which is GO by default):

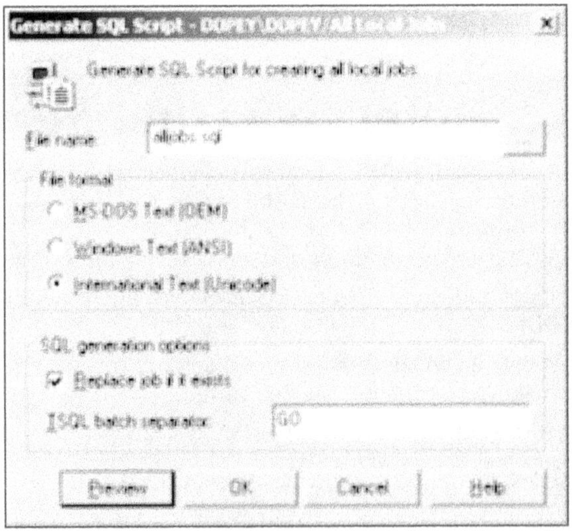

Remember that you will get a warning if any GO statements are used within your Transact-SQL steps. Remove them temporarily (or comment them out) prior to scripting. You can also choose a different batch separator, such as MYBATCH, or a word that is meaningful to you, and then modify the batch separator temporarily in Query Analyzer. To do this, in Query Analyzer, select the Tools and Options menu. Select the Connections tab, and change the Batch separator value from GO to your new batch separator. Make sure to change this back to GO when finished compiling the script:

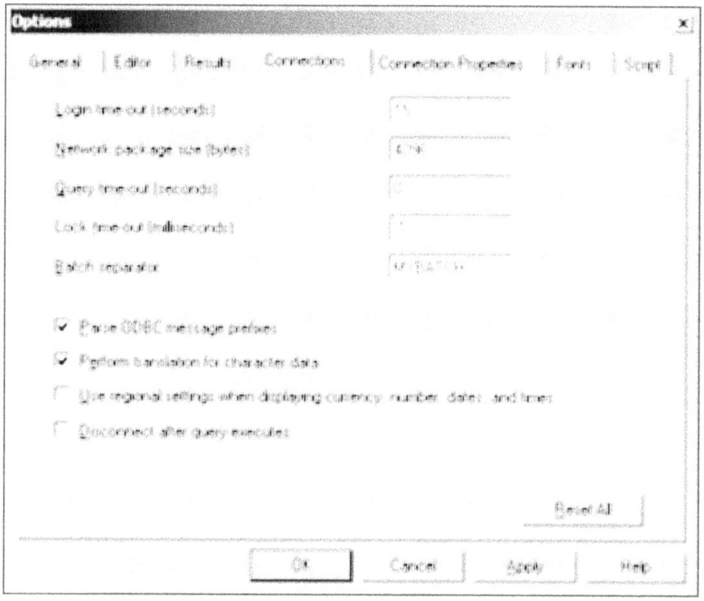

- Select Preview to see the script or OK to generate the script. This script can be run in Query Analyzer on the remote server to generate the jobs.

# 4.20 How to... Transfer Jobs using DTS

Chapter 11 reviews DTS in detail, but, in the meantime, we will review how to transfer jobs using the Transfer Jobs DTS task:

- In Enterprise Manager, expand the server group and server registration.
- Expand the Data Transformation Services folder.
- Right-click the Local Packages node and select New Package.
- In the DTS Package Designer, go to the Task menu and select Transfer Jobs Task...
- In the Transfer Msdb Jobs Property dialog box enter the source server and method for connection, Windows authentication or SQL Server authentication.
- Select the Destination tab and select the destination server for your jobs, as well as connection method.
- Select the Jobs tab. In the Job Copy Option, select whether you wish to transfer all jobs or selected jobs. If selected jobs, check the jobs you wish to transfer after switching the option bullet to Selected jobs. Select OK when finished:
- Go to the Package menu and select Execute.

- You should see the transfer in progress, and then the success dialog box.

  Check the destination server to make sure the jobs were created. You can save the DTS package if you plan on transferring the jobs again, or can exit and say 'No' to saving the package.

# 4.21 How to... Delete or Re-Assign Jobs Belonging to a Specified Login using sp_manage_jobs_by_login

Sometimes, when a DBA or developer leaves the company, project, or department, you need to remove that person's logins and reassign object and job owners. In this example, we reassign all jobs belonging to `JaneDoe`, to the new DBA `JohnDeer`.

In Query Analyzer, execute:

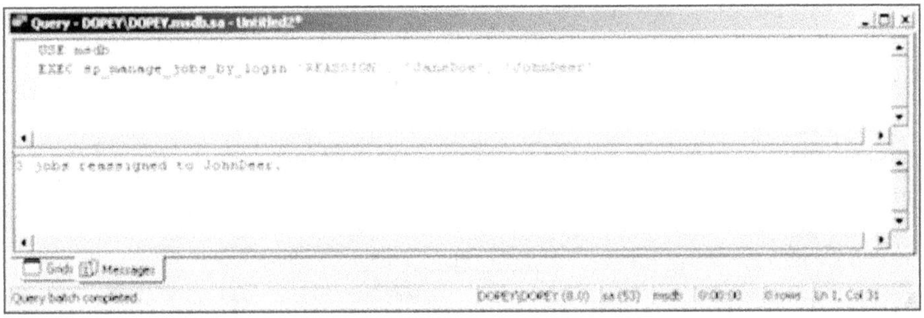

Let's say we decide to get rid of `JohnDeer` too, but this time we would like to remove the jobs he owns rather then reassign them to a new owner. To remove jobs for a specific login, in Query Analyzer, execute:

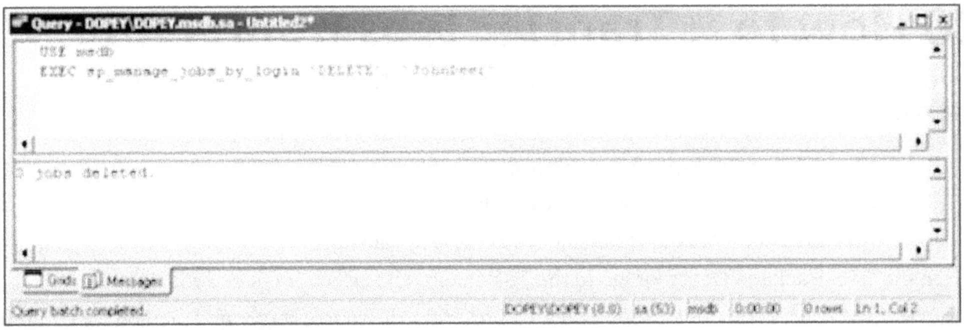

# 4.22 How to... Purge Job History Rows with sp_purge_jobhistory

If you have many jobs and a high job history threshold set in SQL Server Agent, the `sp_purge_jobhistory` is a handy stored procedure to learn. This removes rows from the `sysjobhistory` table.

In this example, we will purge the job history for the job `Data Feed`. In Query Analyzer, execute:

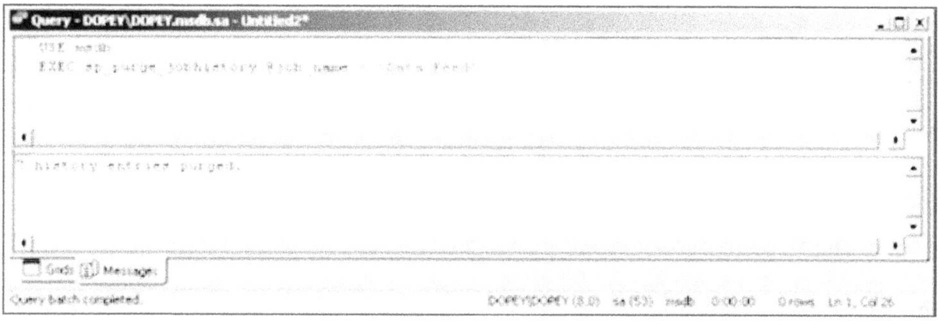


If you decide you want to purge all history for all jobs, in Query Analyzer execute:

```
EXEC msdb..sp_purge_jobhistory
```

Notice that you do not choose a job name when purging all history.

# 4.23 How to... Start and Stop a Job with Transact-SQL Stored Procedures sp_start_job and sp_stop_job

Sometimes, you need to start or stop a job programmatically, rather than as scheduled in the job's properties. For example, you could have code in a stored procedure that starts a job when certain table row criteria are met.

In this example, we will start the Data Scrub job if a `bScrub` column has a false value (indicating that the book row has not been data scrubbed). The job being executed, for example, could be a set of Transact-SQL statements that update information, and then set the `bScrub` column to 1 when complete:

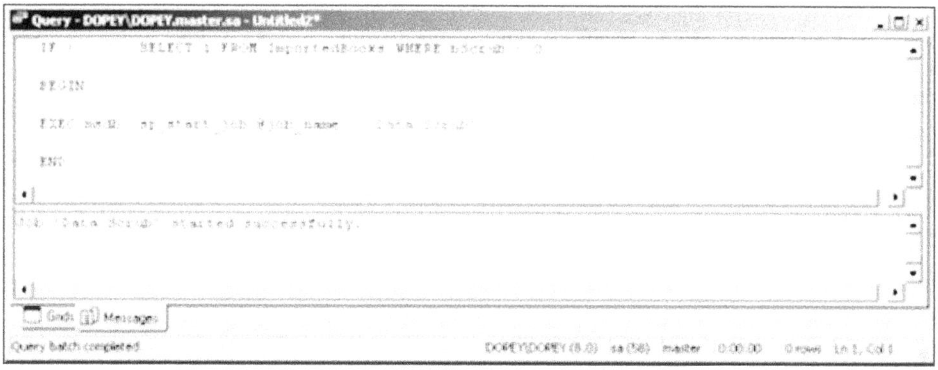


Walking through the code:

```
IF EXISTS(SELECT 1 FROM ImportedBooks WHERE bScrub = 0)
BEGIN
```

The above code looks for records where `bScrub = 0`, which for this table means the row has not been scrubbed yet. If the row count is greater than 0, the batch will begin:

```
EXEC msdb..sp_start_job @job_name = 'Data Scrub'

END
```

The `EXEC sp_start_job` starts the job `Data Scrub`.

In the next example, we will `STOP` a running job called `Data Feed` if an error table contains more than five error rows, by using the `sp_stop_job` procedure:

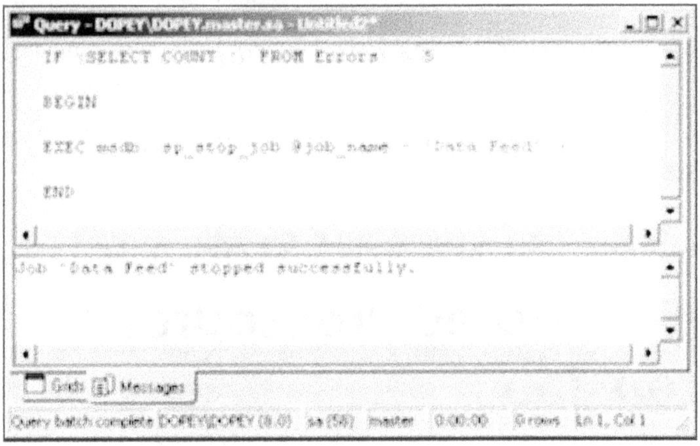


# 4.24 How to... View and Interpret SQL Server Agent Error Logs

The SQL Server Agent error log tracks errors related to the SQL Server Agent functionality. This includes errors and warnings about failed jobs, alerts, SQLAgentMail, and other SQL Server Agent properties.

To view the SQL Server Agent error log:

- Expand server group and server registration.
- Expand the Management folder.
- Right-click the SQL Server Agent icon and select Display Error Log....
- The SQL Server Agent error log allows you to filter errors by type. Types include error, warning, and information.

Entering a value for the Containing text field filters the returned rows further. Select Apply Filter to refresh the output based on your text filter.

Double-click a row to view more data about the warning, error, or information entry. If it is unclear what the error message indicates, cross-reference the error text on http://support.microsoft.com/ or http://groups.google.com, where all the Microsoft SQL Server public newsgroups are archived.

# 4.25 How to... Change the Name or Location of the SQL Server Agent Error Log

The SQL Server Agent service must be stopped to change the name or location of the SQL Server Agent error log:

- Expand the SQL Server group and SQL Server registration.
- Expand the Management folder.
- Right-click the SQL Server Agent icon and select Properties.
- In the General tab, type in the new file name or location in the File name field, or select the ellipsis button to select a directory.
- By default, the file name is `SQLAgent.OUT`. In addition to this, nine archived files are kept in the `Program Files\Microsoft SQL Server\MSSQL\Log` directory (`SQLAGENT.1-SQLAGENT.9`).
- Select OK when finished selecting the file name and location, and start the SQL Agent service to begin logging to the new location or file name.

# SQL Server Agent Stored Procedures

Almost all the SQL Server Agent functionality in Enterprise Manager has an associated system stored procedure that can perform the same task. You may decide to script out jobs and job steps programmatically within a stored procedure or a DTS package. Such functionality provides endless possibilities. Below are groupings of SQL Server Agent stored procedures. For more information on usage, see SQL Server Books Online:

## Alert System Stored Procedures

| Stored Procedure | Description |
|---|---|
| `sp_add_alert` | Creates an alert. |
| `sp_add_notification` | Adds notification for an alert. |
| `sp_delete_alert` | Deletes an alert. |
| `sp_delete_notification` | Removes all notifications sent to a specified operator in response to an alert. |
| `sp_help_alert` | Provides help information regarding an alert. |
| `sp_help_notification` | Reports a list of alerts for a selected operator or a list of operators for a selected alert (very useful for helpdesk representatives, who need to know who is responsible for certain alerts). |
| `sp_update_alert` | Updates an alert. |
| `sp_update_notification` | Updates notification method of an alert notification. |

# Operator System Stored Procedures

| Stored Procedure | Description |
|---|---|
| sp_add_operator | Creates an operator. |
| sp_delete_operator | Deletes an operator. |
| sp_help_notification | Reports a list of alerts for a selected operator or a list of operators for a selected alert. |
| sp_help_operator | Lists operators for the SQL Server instance. |
| sp_update_operator | Updates operator information. |

# Job System Stored Procedures

| Stored Procedure | Description |
|---|---|
| sp_add_category | Adds a new job, alert, or operator category. |
| sp_add_job | Adds a new job. |
| sp_add_jobschedule | Adds a new job schedule. |
| sp_add_jobserver | Targets a job to a specified server (multi-server administration). |
| sp_add_jobstep | Adds a new step to a job. |
| sp_add_targetservergroup | Creates a server group (multi-server administration). |
| sp_add_targetsvrgrp_member | Adds a specified target server to the server group (multi-server administration). |
| sp_apply_job_to_targets | Applies a job to one or more target servers (multi-server administration). |
| sp_delete_category | Removes a job, alert, or operator category on the SQL Server instance. |
| sp_delete_job | Deletes a job. |
| sp_delete_jobschedule | Deletes a job schedule. |
| sp_delete_jobserver | Removes a job from the target server (multi-server administration). |
| sp_delete_jobstep | Deletes a job step from a job. |
| sp_delete_targetserver | Removes a target server from the list of available target servers (multi-server administration). |
| sp_delete_targetservergroup | Deletes the target server group specified (multi-server administration). |
| sp_delete_targetsvrgrp_member | Removes a target server from the target server group (multi-server administration). |

| Stored Procedure | Description |
| --- | --- |
| sp_help_category | Provides list of categories for jobs, alerts, and operators. |
| sp_help_downloadlist | Shows all rows for sysdownloadlist for a specific job or all jobs (multi-server administration). |
| sp_help_job | Provides information on a job or jobs. |
| sp_help_jobhistory | Returns report of history for specified schedule jobs or all scheduled jobs. |
| sp_help_jobschedule | Returns job schedule information. |
| sp_help_jobserver | Returns target server information (multi-server administration). |
| sp_help_jobstep | Returns job step information. |
| sp_help_targetserver | Returns all target servers. |
| sp_help_targetservergroup | Returns all target server groups, or servers, for a specified group. |
| sp_manage_jobs_by_login | Removes or reassigns jobs that belong to a specific login. |
| sp_msx_defect | Removes server from multiserver operations (multi-server administration). |
| sp_msx_enlist | Adds server to list of target servers (multi-server administration). |
| sp_post_msx_operation | Inserts operations into `sysdownloadlist` for target servers to download and execute (multi-server administration). |
| sp_purge_jobhistory | Removes history records from a selected job or all jobs. |
| sp_remove_job_from_targets | Removes a job from the target servers or server groups (multi-server administration). |
| sp_resync_targetserver | Deletes all current instructions on target server and posts new set for target server to download and execute (multi-server administrator). |
| sp_start_job | Starts a job. |
| sp_stop_job | Stops a job. |
| sp_update_category | Changes the category name. |
| sp_update_job | Changes job attributes. |
| sp_update_jobschedule | Changes schedule attributes. |
| sp_update_jobstep | Changes job step attributes. |
| sp_update_targetservergroup | Changes the target server group name (multi-server administration). |

# SQL Server Error Log

The SQL Server error log should be checked frequently. The name `SQL Server error log` is something of a misnomer, as it tracks errors, warnings, **and** information events. Some events that are logged to the SQL Server error log include:

- Database recovery status
- CHECKDB execution
- Backups (full, transaction log, differential)
- Processes deadlocked
- Processes killed
- Errors – multiple severity errors from low to high
- Notification when DBCC TRACEON or TRACEOFF is run

The SQL Server error log is your best resource for identifying issues. The Internet community often posts common error messages, so take advantage of http://support.microsoft.com/, search engines like http://www.google.com, and news group web sites like http://communities2.microsoft.com/home/msnewsgroups.aspx or http://www.devx.com/.

Proactively checking the SQL Server error log will ensure faster issue identification.

# 4.26 How to... Read the SQL Server Error Log

The SQL Server error log is saved by default to the `Program Files\Microsoft SQL Server\MSSQL\Log` directory, and is saved under the name `ERRORLOG`. You can open it with Notepad or any text editor.

You can also read the SQL log or any archived log by following these steps in Enterprise Manager:

- Expand server group and server registration.
- Expand the Management folder.
- Expand SQL Server Logs and select the Current log to view the active log, or view previous logs (Archive #1, #2, and so on). The error log entries will appear in the right pane:

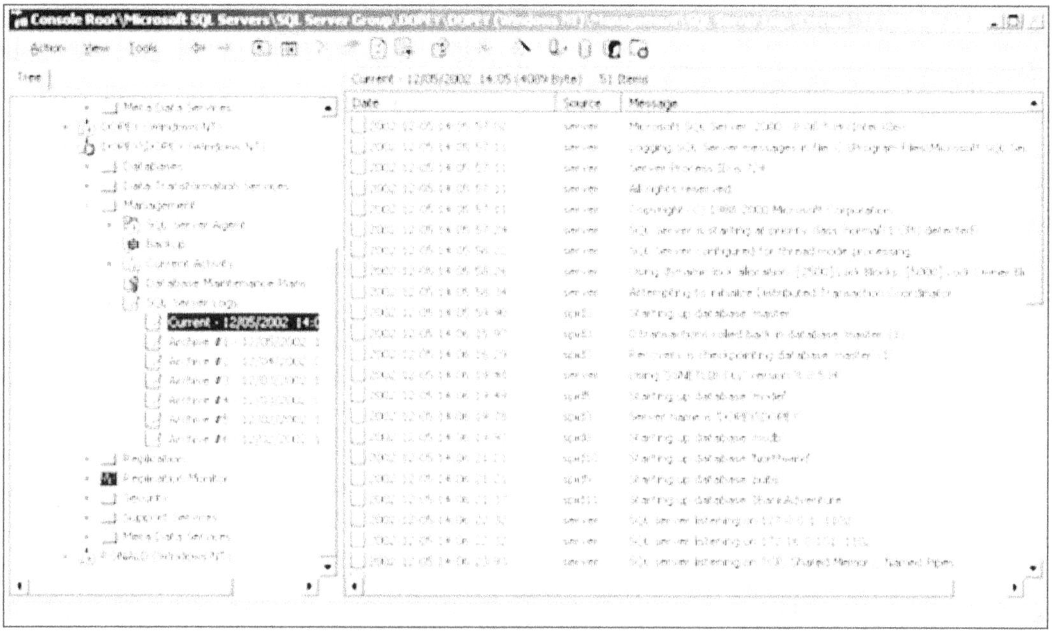

# 4.27 How to... Setting the Number of SQL Server Error Logs to Keep

You can have multiple archived error logs, each named `ERRORLOG.N`, where N=1 to the number chosen. To set the number of SQL Error logs to keep, in Enterprise Manager:

- Expand server group and server registration.
- Expand the Management folder.
- Right click the SQL Server Logs icon and select Configure.
- Select the checkbox to limit the number of error logs to keep on the server and set the number; if you do not, the default is six archived error logs. Select OK when finished.

# 4.28 How to... Start up a New SQL Server Error Log without Restarting the SQL Server Service

The SQL Server error log starts afresh on the restart of the SQL Server service. If you have a stable environment, it could be several months before the log is cycled. If you have normal activity on your server, this can really add to the size of the error log, which slows down its access time.

If you would like to start a new log without restarting the SQL Server service, follow these steps in Query Analyzer:

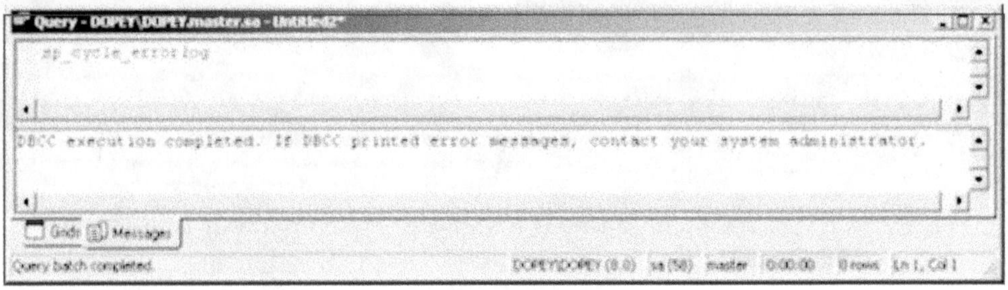


When checking your SQL Server error log, you will see a message stating 'Errorlog has been reinitialised. See previous log for older entries.' after running this command.

# 4.29 How to... Change the Logging Status of an Error Message with sp_altermessage

The `sysmessages` table contains error and warning messages and descriptions that are used by SQL Server. Several warnings and error messages are written to the Windows NT event log by default; however, a good many are not. Using `sp_altermessage`, you can enable logging for a message so that it is written to the Windows NT Application event log.

For example, let's say we want to log whenever someone references an invalid object name:

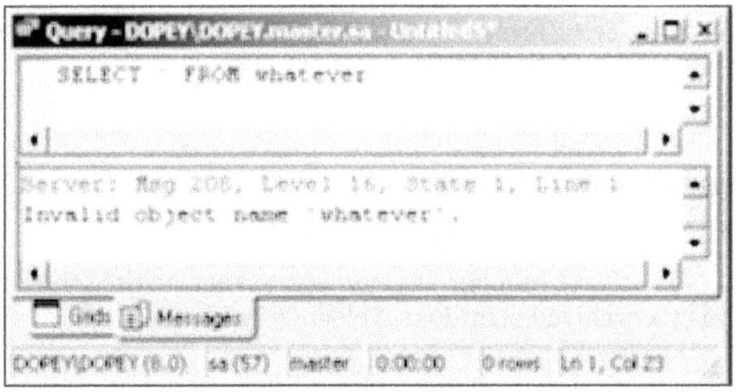


To add logging for `Msg 208`, run the following in Query Analyzer:

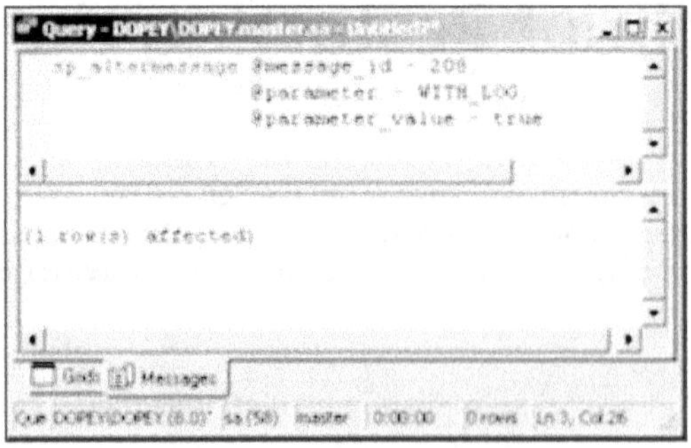

To verify that it creates an application log entry in the Windows Event Viewer, run the bad `SELECT` statement again to generate the error. Next:

- ❑ Select Start | Run.
- ❑ Type in `eventvwr` and select OK.
- ❑ In the left pane select the Application Log node:

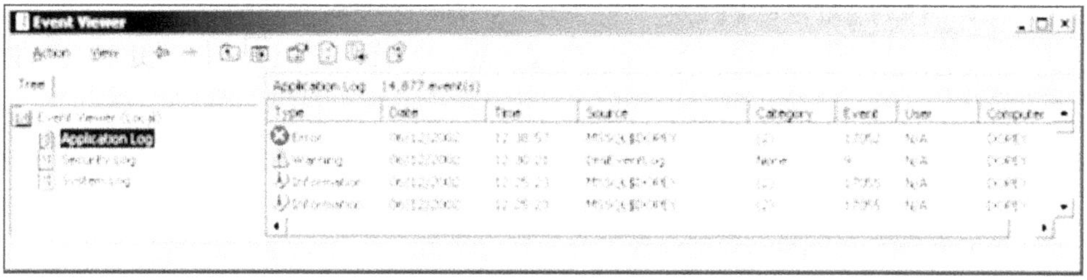

- ❑ Double-click the error for MSSQLServer to see the detailed message:

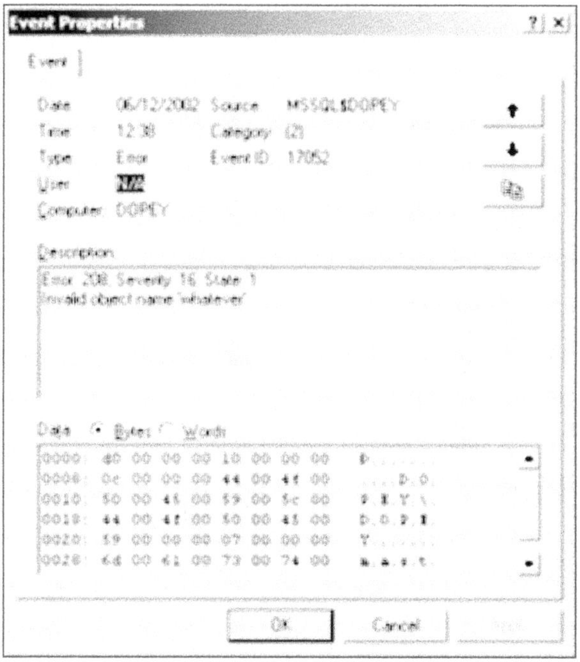

Also, this logging will carry over to your SQL Server Error log in Enterprise Manager, and you will see a similar error message description to that in Event Properties.

To disable logging for an error:

- ❑ In Query Analyzer, run the following:

```
sp_altermessage @message_id = 208,
                @parameter = WITH_LOG,
                @parameter_value = false
```

# 4.30 How to... Log a User-Defined Message with xp_logevent

Using `xp_logevent`, you can write your own custom error message to the SQL Server error log and Windows 2000 Event Viewer. This is an excellent way to log custom messages without having to add them to `sysmessages` permanently or mark them as logged with `sp_altermessage`. `xp_logevent` also has an advantage over `RAISERROR...WITH LOG` (reviewed in Chapter 16), as `xp_logevent` does not require sysadmin role permissions. `xp_logevent` execution can be granted to users or role members, without sysadmin role membership.

In this example, we will log the event 'Warning, your data scrub job found rows that could not be scrubbed!'.

In Query Analyzer, we will verify that if any row has a 1 in the `scruberror` column, that the previously mentioned error will be generated:

```
USE BookRepository
IF (SELECT COUNT(*) FROM ImportedBooks WHERE bScrubError = 1) > 0
BEGIN

USE master
EXEC xp_logevent 55000,
      'Warning, your data scrub job found rows that could not be scrubbed!',
      informational
END
```

If the `COUNT(*)` returns greater than 0 records, we execute `xp_logevent`. `xp_logevent` takes three parameters: error number (must be greater than 50,000 and less than 1,073,741,823), message (limited to 8,000 characters), and a severity of Informational, Warning, or Error.

You will see the logged error in the Windows 2000 Event Viewer application log and the SQL Server error log:

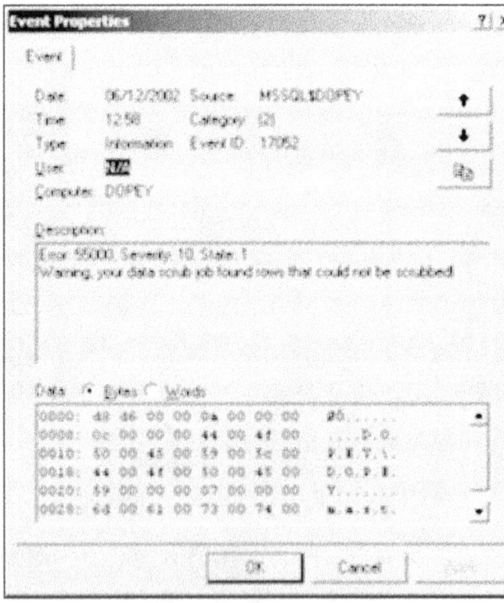

# 5

# Transactions, Locking, Blocking, and Deadlocking

This chapter explores the concepts of transactions and locking. You will learn how transactions work, and how they are managed and used. Locking is also examined, covering the different types of locks in a database and how they interact with each other (lock compatibility). Locking issues, such as long-term locking (called blocking), and deadlocking are explained. You will learn techniques for identifying and troubleshooting blocking and deadlocking problems.

## Understanding Transactions

Transactions are an integral part of a relational database system. A transaction defines a single unit of work; this unit of work can include one or more Transact-SQL statements. In a transaction, all statements are applied, or none at all. Let's review an example of a book inventory system; in this scenario, when a book is purchased, two tables are impacted: `BookInventory` and `BookSales`:

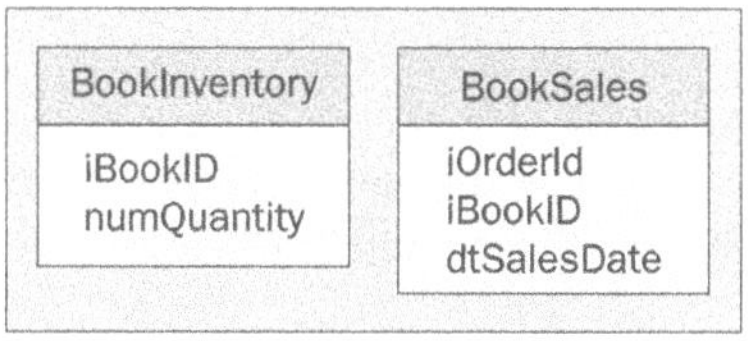


If a book is sold, `numQuantity` is reduced in the `BookInventory` table. A new entry is also made to the `BookSales` table, documenting order number, ID of the book sold, and the date of the sale:

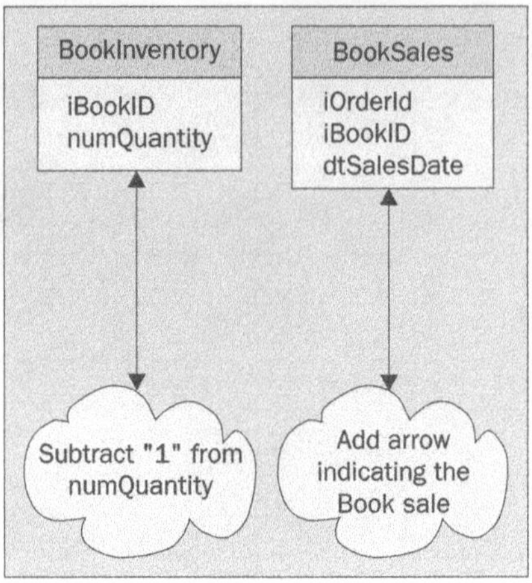


Transactions are used within SQL Server to prevent partial updates. A partial update occurs when one part of an interrelated process is rolled back or cancelled without rolling back **all** logically necessary updates:

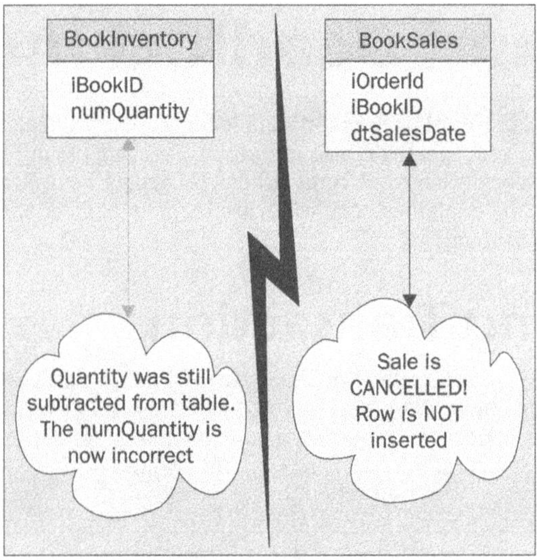


A transaction protects a unit of work from partial updates; if one data modification operation is unsuccessful, or is cancelled, the **entire** transaction (all data modifications) is rolled back. This ensures database consistency.

At the beginning of a transaction, SQL Server writes any changes that the Transact-SQL statements issue to the transaction log file. If any statement fails, then the entire transaction is rolled back and none of the data modifications are made. If the transaction succeeds, the transaction is committed and modifications are made.

A transaction is bound by the **ACID** test. ACID stands for Atomicity, Consistency, Isolation (or Independence), and Durability:

- **Atomicity**
  An atomic transaction is an all-or-nothing entity, which carries out all its steps or none at all.
- **Consistency**
  In a consistent transaction, no data modifications should break the structural or design rules of the database.
- **Isolation** (or **Independence**)
  Isolated (or independent) transactions do not depend on other transactions being run concurrently.
- **Durability**
  A durable transaction has permanent effect after it has been committed; its changes should survive system failures.

# Implicit Transactions

Transactions can be **explicit** or **implicit**. Implicit transactions occur when the SQL Server session is in **implicit transaction mode**. While a session is in implicit transaction mode, a new transaction is created automatically after any of the following statements are executed:

- `ALTER TABLE`
- `CREATE`
- `DELETE`
- `DROP`
- `FETCH`
- `GRANT`
- `INSERT`
- `REVOKE`
- `SELECT`
- `TRUNCATE TABLE`
- `UPDATE`

The transaction does not complete until a `COMMIT` or `ROLLBACK` statement is issued. After one of these keywords is issued, a new transaction begins when any of the aforementioned statements is executed.

Implicit transaction mode is enabled when `SET IMPLICIT_TRANSACTIONS ON` is executed. The default is `OFF`. If `ANSI_DEFAULTS` is `ON`, however, `SET IMPLICIT_TRANSACTIONS` is enabled. Got that? Let's organize it in a table:

| State | Implicit Transactions Enabled? |
|---|---|
| SQL Server default | No |
| `SET IMPLICIT_TRANSACTIONS ON` | Yes |
| `SET ANSI_DEFAULTS ON` | Yes |

You can see which user options are enabled by running DBCC USEROPTIONS; if the SET ANSI_DEFAULTS or IMPLICIT_TRANSACTIONS options appear in the result set, then the option is ON:

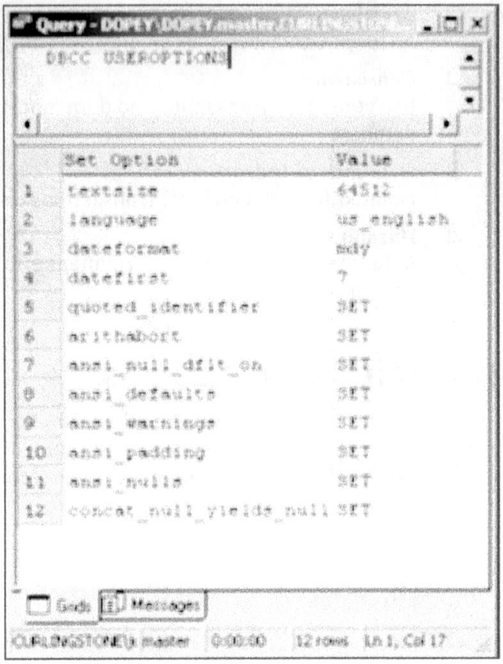


In the following example, we SET IMPLICIT_TRANSACTIONS ON, and create a table called t_TranExample:

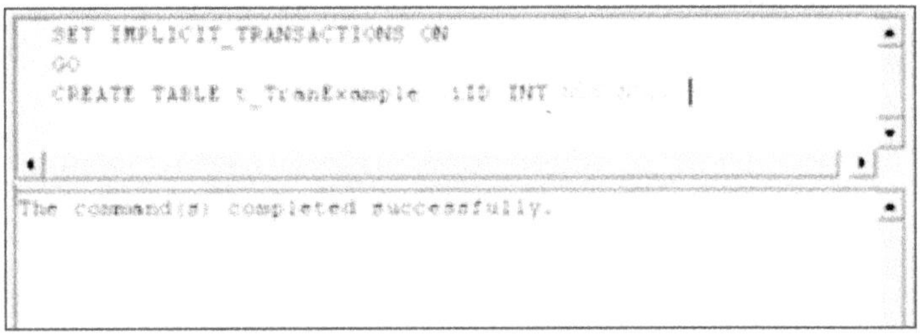


The command completes successfully. This message is misleading, however, as the transaction itself has not been committed. If you try closing the Query Analyzer window, you will see the following warning:

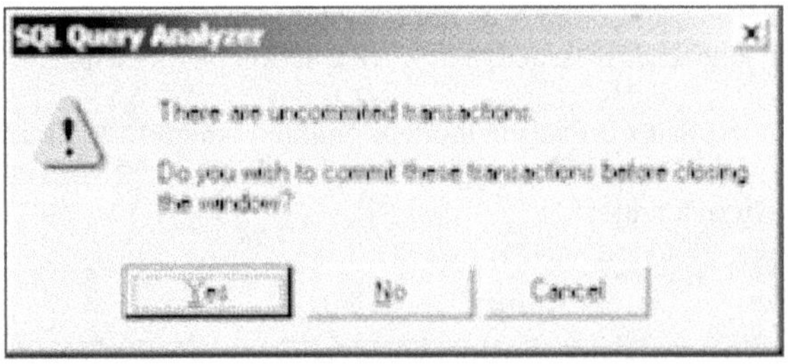


You can select Yes to commit the transaction, or No to rollback. If you select No, the transaction's updates will be undone.

Avoid using implicit transactions if possible, as they make it easier for connections to leave uncommitted transactions out in the database, holding locks on resources and reducing concurrency Implicit transactions **are** useful for ensuring that database users are sure of any changes they make to the database; the user must make a decision as to committing or rolling back their transaction(s).

# Explicit Transactions

Explicit transactions are those that you define yourself. Explicit transactions use the following Transact-SQL commands and keywords:

| | |
|---|---|
| BEGIN TRANSACTION | Sets the starting point of an explicit transaction. |
| ROLLBACK TRANSACTION | Restores original data modified by a transaction, to the state it was in at the start of the transaction. Resources held by the transaction are freed. |
| COMMIT TRANSACTION | Ends the transaction if no errors were encountered and makes changes permanent. Resources held by the transaction are freed. |
| BEGIN DISTRIBUTED TRANSACTION | Allows you to define the beginning of a distributed transaction to be managed by Microsoft Distributed Transaction Coordinator (MS DTC). MS DTC must be running locally and remotely. |
| SAVE TRANSACTION | SAVE TRANSACTION issues a savepoint within a transaction, which allows you to define a location to which a transaction can return if part of the transaction is cancelled. A transaction must be rolled back or committed immediately after rolling back to a savepoint. |
| @@TRANCOUNT | Returns the number of active transactions for the connection. BEGIN TRANSACTION increments @@TRANCOUNT by 1, and ROLLBACK TRANSACTION and COMMIT TRANSACTION decrements @@TRANCOUNT by 1. ROLLBACK TRANSACTION to a savepoint has no impact. |

### Example: Simple explicit transaction

The following is an example of a simple transaction using BEGIN TRANSACTION and COMMIT TRANSACTION. We include two INSERT statements, one to the t_Orders table, and the other to the t_OrdersHistory table. This activity benefits from an explicit transaction, as both statements have a logical dependency on each other. If there is a system failure after the first INSERT occurs but before the second, the first INSERT will be rolled back on database recovery:

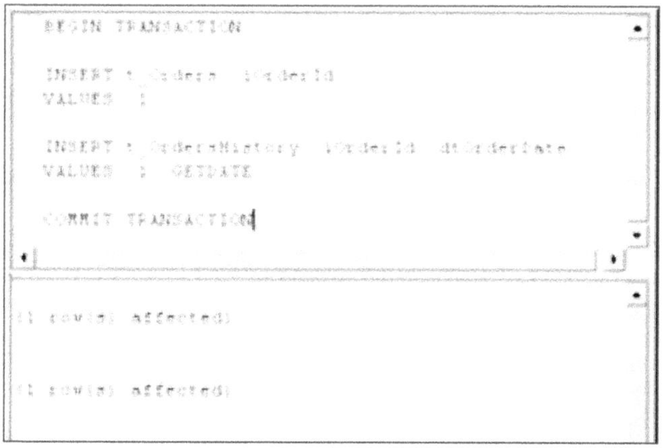

## Example: Named transaction

Naming a transaction improves code readability and helps clarify nested transactions. The syntax for BEGIN TRANSACTION from *SQL Server Books Online* is as follows:

```
BEGIN TRAN [ SACTION ] [ transaction_name | @tran_name_variable
  [ WITH MARK [ 'description' ] ] ]
```

| Parameter | Description |
|---|---|
| BEGIN TRAN [ SACTION ] | You can use either BEGIN TRAN or BEGIN TRANSACTION. |
| transaction_name \| @tran_name_variable | transaction_name is the name of the transaction, and can be up to 32 characters in length. @tran_name_variable is the option of using a valid local variable (CHAR, VARCHAR, NCHAR, NVARCHAR). |
| WITH MARK 'description' | WITH MARK is used to mark a specific point in the transaction log. When used, a transaction log restoration can be recovered to the point prior to the MARK. |

This example begins a transaction called update_orders. A new value is inserted into the t_Orders and t_OrdersHistory tables. After this, another transaction, called update_lastorder is created. Within the update_lastorder transaction, the t_LastOrder table is updated, and the transaction is committed. The outer transaction, update_orders, is also committed:

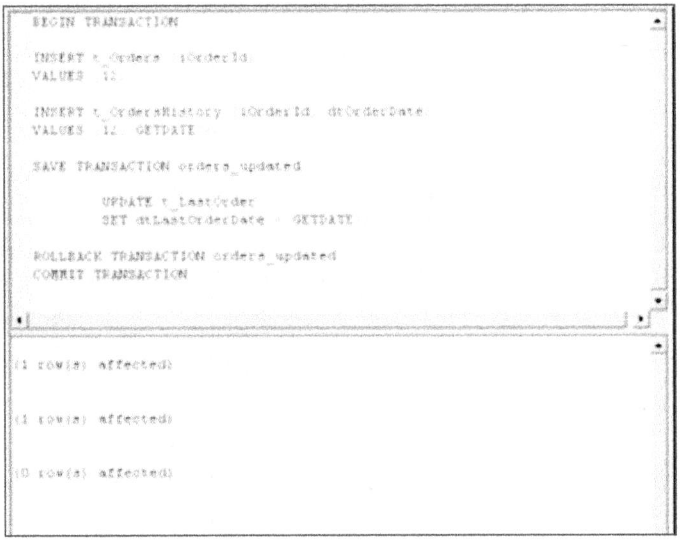


The above example shows how to use named and **nested transactions**; when a transaction is used within another named transaction, it is called a nested transaction.

It is important to note that SQL Server mostly ignores nested transactions. If the first or outer transaction is committed, then the inner nested transactions are committed too. If a COMMIT that is not at the outermost level is called, the COMMIT is ignored. However, if the outer transaction is rolled back, all inner transactions roll back too, even if they were committed.

### Example: SAVEPOINT and ROLLBACK

This example does the following:

- Inserts a row into the `t_Orders` and `t_OrdersHistory` table.
- Issues a `SAVE TRANSACTION`
- Makes an `UPDATE` to the `t_LastOrder`
- We then decide against this update, and issue a `ROLLBACK TRANSACTION` for the named savepoint.

Both the `t_Orders` and `t_OrdersHistory` changes are committed, but the `t_LastOrder` change is not:

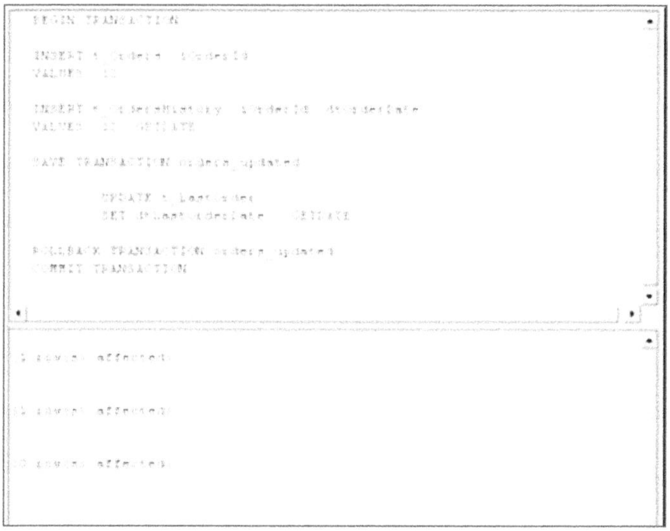

### Example: @@Errors

You can use `@@Errors` to roll back a transaction if errors occur within it. This prevents partial updates and having to `SET XACT_ABORT ON`.

In this example, if either `INSERT` statement produces an error (in this case a primary key constraint error), the transaction rolls back:

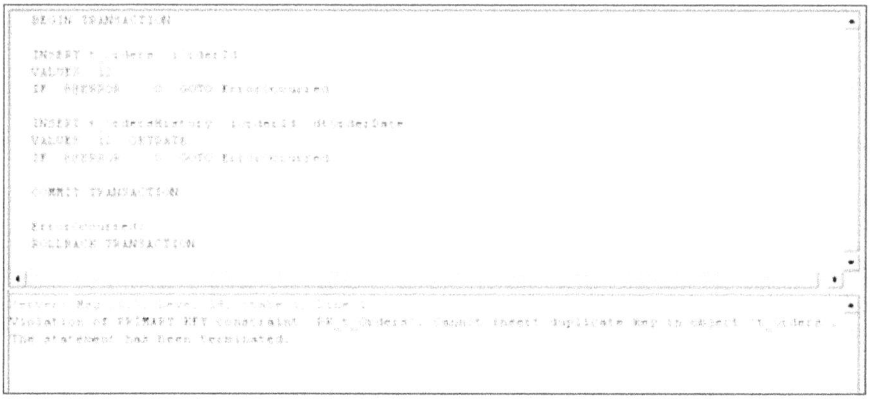

GOTO is a Transact-SQL keyword that helps you control the flow of statement execution. In this example, ErrorOccured is a **label**. You define a label by using a text word followed by a colon. For example:

```
jumptohere:
```

You can then execute:

```
GOTO jumptohere
```

The code will then jump to that code section. GOTO is a throwback from the file-oriented programming languages, and is most often used for jumping to error handling placed towards the end of a batch.

# 5.1 How to... Use a Transaction Mark

Using the WITH MARK command with the BEGIN TRANSACTION statement places a named mark in the transaction log, allowing you to restore your log to this point. The transaction must contain at least one data modification for the mark to be placed in the log. You should use this functionality for transactions that are prone to causing problems, where you may need to recover or undo the transaction to a point before the modification. We will review backup and restore techniques in the next chapter; the following, however, is an example of setting a mark:

```
BEGIN TRAN bookorderupdate WITH MARK
UPDATE BookRepository.dbo.Books
SET dtReceived = GETDATE()
COMMIT TRAN bookorderupdate
```

The following query shows the results of the update:

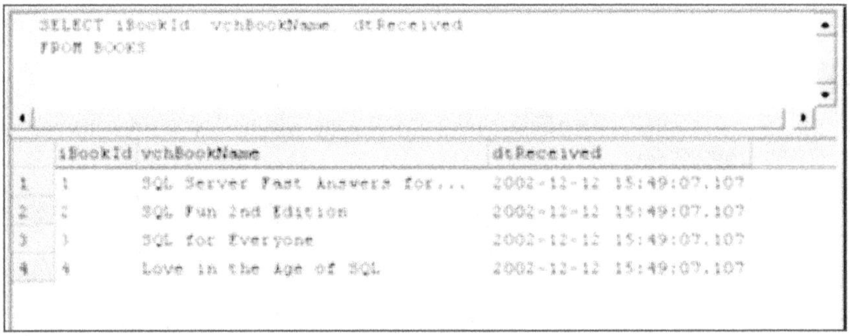


If this update is a mistake, you can restore the data up to the mark point. This assumes that you have already completed a full backup and transaction log backup before the transaction committed.

To restore the full backup (more details in the next chapter):

```
RESTORE DATABASE BookRepository
FROM DISK= 'J:\MSSQL\Backup\bookrepo_jul_17.bak' WITH NORECOVERY

RESTORE LOG BookRepository
FROM DISK = 'J:\MSSQL\Backup\bookrepo_jul_17_3pm.trn' WITH RECOVERY,
STOPATMARK=' bookorderupdate'
```

After the restore, the original `dtReceived` for each book is restored to the value it had prior to the change:

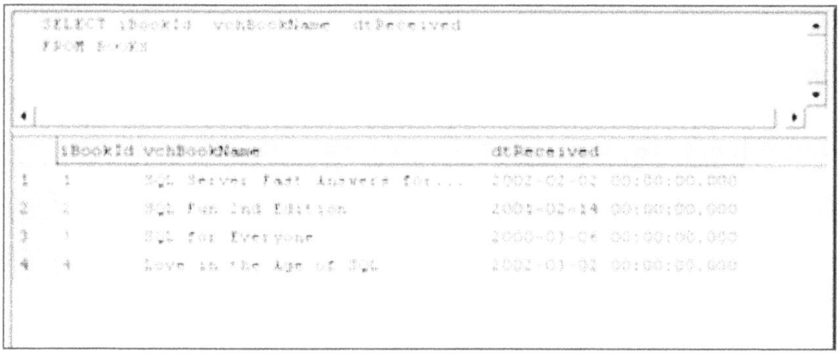


# Best Practices for using Transactions

- Keep transaction time short.
- Minimize resources locked by the transaction. Narrow down rows impacted by `INSERT`, `UPDATE`, and `DELETE` statements.
- Add Transact-SQL statements to a transaction where they are relevant to that transaction **only**.
- Do not open new transactions that require user feedback within the transaction. Open transactions can hold locks on resources, and user feedback can take an indefinite length of time to receive. Gather user feedback before issuing an explicit transaction.
- Check `@@ERROR` after issuing a DML (Data Manipulation Language) statement. If there was an error, you can roll back the transaction.
- The database option `SET XACT_ABORT` affects how errors are handled within a transaction. When set `ON`, DML statements within a transaction that raise a run-time error cause the entire transaction to roll back and terminate. When `OFF`, only the DML statement that raised the error is rolled back, and the rest of the transaction continues. Keep this option `ON` to ensure data consistency.
- If possible, do not open a transaction when browsing data.
- Use and understand the correct isolation levels. We will review isolation levels further on in this chapter.

# 5.2 How to... Display the Oldest Active Transaction with DBCC OPENTRAN

`DBCC OPENTRAN` is a Transact-SQL command that is used to view the oldest running transaction for the selected database. The `DBCC` command is very useful for troubleshooting orphaned connections (connections still open on the database but disconnected from the application or client), and identification of transactions missing a `COMMIT` or `ROLLBACK`.

This command also returns the oldest distributed and undistributed replicated transactions, if any exist within the database. If there are no active transactions, no data will be returned.

If you are having problems with your transaction log not truncating inactive portions, `DBCC OPENTRAN` can show whether an open transaction is to blame.

The syntax for DBCC OPENTRAN from *SQL Server Books Online* is as follows:

```
DBCC OPENTRAN
  ( { 'database_name' | database_id} )
   [ WITH TABLERESULTS
     [ , NO_INFOMSGS ]
   ]
```

| Parameter | Description |
|---|---|
| database_name \| database_id | Use either the database name or the database ID. If left blank, the DBCC command will run for the current database context. |
| WITH TABLERESULTS | When specified, this returns data in tabular format, meaning it can be output to a table. |
| NO_INFOMSGS | Disables the return of informational messages. |

In this example, we run DBCC OPENTRAN for the BookRepository database using WITH TABLERESULTS:

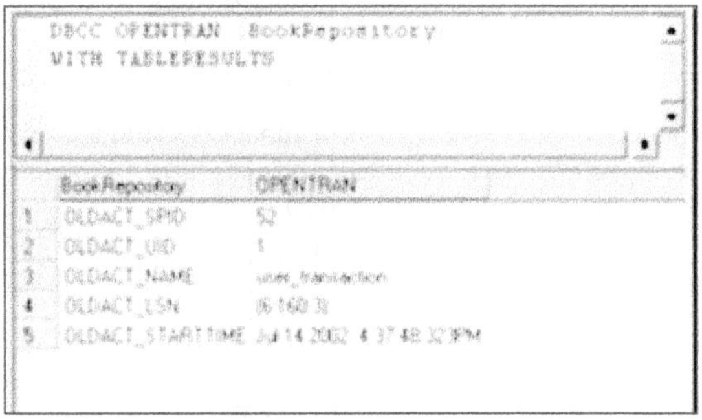


Since you now have the **SPID**, you can see what command is currently in the input buffer using DBCC INPUTBUFFER (SPID). The SPID is a process identifier that is assigned to each user connection when a connection to SQL Server is made The DBCC INPUTBUFFER command is used to view the last statement sent by the client connection to SQL Server. DBCC INPUTBUFFER takes one parameter, the SPID:

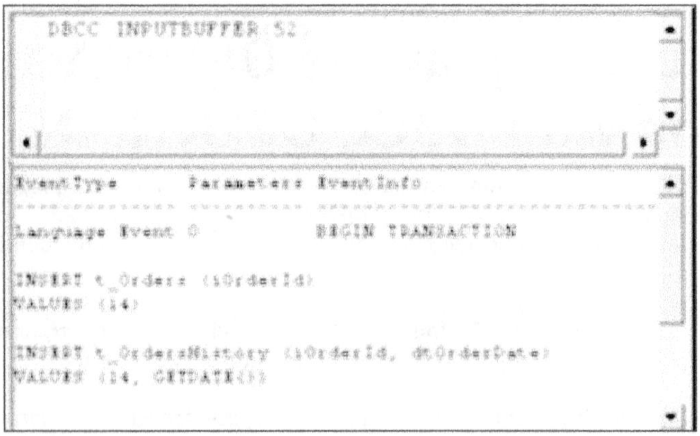

# 5.3 How to... Use SET TRANSACTION ISOLATION LEVEL

This section touches on the topic of locking, which will be discussed in more detail later in this chapter.

Transactions and locking go hand in hand. Depending on your application design, your transactions can significantly impact database concurrency (the number of people that can access and modify the database and database objects at the same time); this can have a significant effect on performance and scalability.

The following statement sets the default transaction locking behavior for `SELECT` statements used in a connection; you may only have one level set at a time. Isolation level does not change unless explicitly `SET`. The syntax for `SET TRANSACTION ISOLATION LEVEL` from *SQL Server Books Online* is as follows:

```
SET TRANSACTION ISOLATION LEVEL
 {READ COMMITTED
  | READ UNCOMMITTED
  | REPEATABLE READ
  | SERIALIZABLE
 }
```

| Option | Description |
|---|---|
| `READ COMMITTED`<br>(this is the default value) | Shared locks are held for the duration of the transaction; the data cannot be changed. Data inserts and modifications to the same table by other transactions **are** allowed, so long as the rows involved are not locked by the first transaction. |
| `READ UNCOMMITTED` | This is the least restrictive isolation level, issuing no locks on the data selected by the transaction. This provides the highest concurrency but the lowest level of data integrity, as the data that you read can be changed while you read it (these reads are known as **dirty reads**), or new data can be added or removed that would change your original query results. |
| `REPEATABLE READ` | Dirty and nonrepeatable reads are not allowed. New rows can still be inserted by other transactions. |
| `SERIALIZABLE` | This is the most restrictive setting. Ranges of shared locks are held on the data, disallowing insertion of new rows, deletion of existing rows, and modification of rows within the selected range. |

Later on in the chapter we will discuss the pros and cons of the different locking isolation levels.

In this example, we will set the isolation level to SERIALIZABLE:

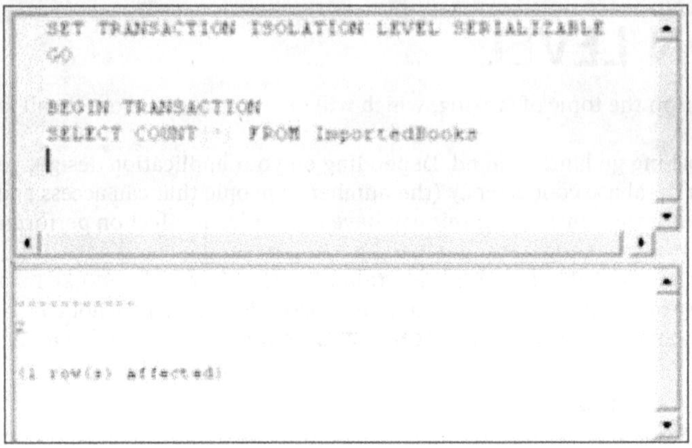


This example begins a transaction that selects the row count of the `ImportedBooks` table. Since we did not commit the transactions, range locks will be held on the table's rows. If you attempt to insert rows within the range of the `ImportedBooks` table, you will wait indefinitely; the little Query Analyzer globe will spin until the original transaction commits or rolls back:

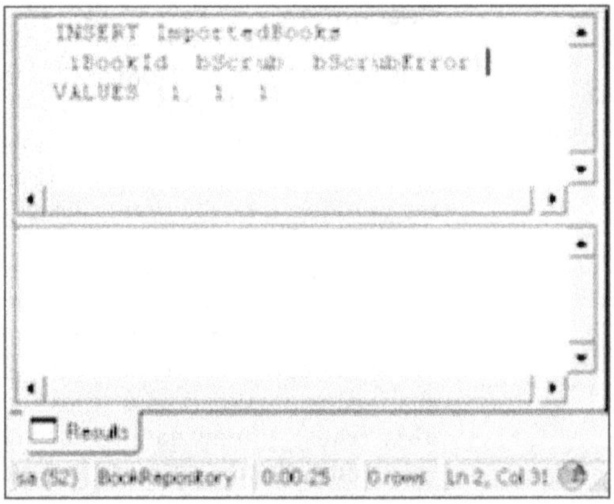


# 5.4 How to... Use SET CURSOR_CLOSE_ON_COMMIT

This option specifies whether a cursor is closed or open when a transaction is committed. We will cover Transact-SQL cursors in more detail in Chapter 16.

When this option is set to `ON`, cursors created within a transaction are no longer available once the transaction is committed or rolled back. This is an ANSI SQL-92 standard. When `OFF` (which is the default for SQL Server), the cursor is not closed when a transaction commits.

Below is an example that creates a cursor on the `ImportedBooks` table within a transaction. Because we have set `CURSOR_CLOSE_ON_COMMIT ON`, the cursor `FETCH` statement after the transaction commit will fail:

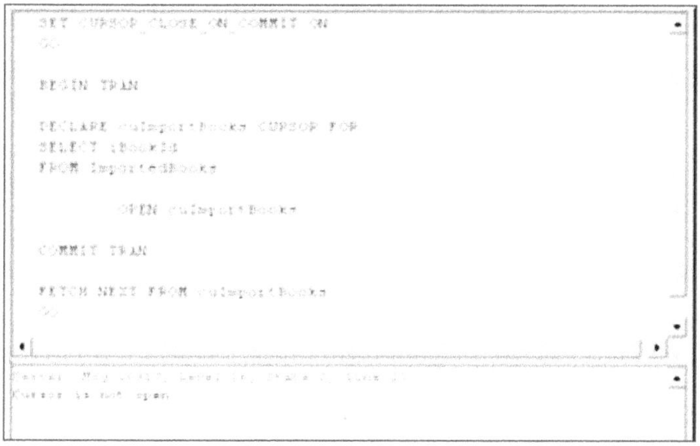


# 5.5 How to... Use SET REMOTE_PROC_TRANSACTIONS

If `SET REMOTE_PROC_TRANSACTIONS` is `ON`, a distributed transaction is started when a remote stored procedure is called from a local server transaction. This remote procedure call (RPC) uses Microsoft Distributed Transaction Coordinator (MS DTC) to manage the transaction. This is a Windows service that can be found in Service Manager, or under the Support Services folder in Enterprise Manager. MS DTC is used to handle distributed transactions, acting as the manager of the transaction. This means that MS DTC is responsible for the `COMMIT` or `ROLLBACK` phase of a transaction that traverses two SQL Server instances. MS DTC ensures **all or nothing** transaction behavior, even though the transaction traverses two servers.

Both the local and distributed servers must have MS DTC running to control the procedure call. This `SET` option overrides the `sp_configure REMOTE_PROC_TRANS` option. When the option is `OFF`, a distributed transaction is not used.

You can also start distributed transactions by using `BEGIN DISTRIBUTED TRANSACTION`. Note that `REMOTE_PROC_TRANSACTIONS` only covers remote stored procedure calls.

The following is an example of enabling the `REMOTE_PROC_TRANSACTIONS SET` option:

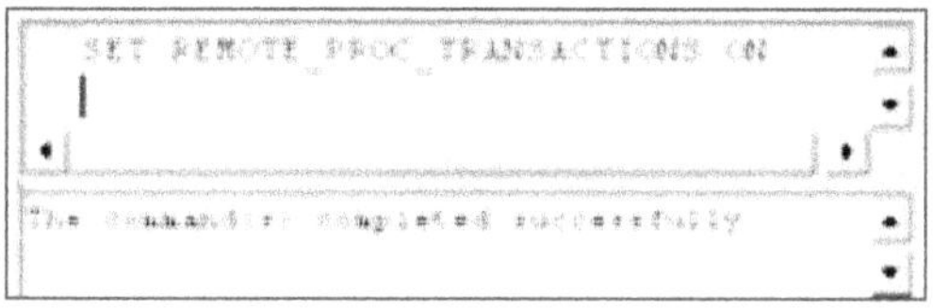

# Lock Types, Compatibility, Isolation Levels, and Hints

Locking ensures that multiple users do not modify data at the same time. Depending on your lock type and isolation level, locking can also prevent users from reading data while it is being updated.

Application design and use of isolation levels can have a significant impact on database concurrency (the ability of users to access the data) and data consistency (the ability of users to read the correct data). Isolation levels can also have an impact on scalability and performance. The more users you have, the more resource locking can occur, potentially impacting query performance.

## The 'Famous Four' Concurrency Problems

The 'famous four' database concurrency problems occur when more than one user attempts to:

- Read data that another is modifying.
- Modify data that another is reading.
- Modify data that another transaction is trying to modify.

The 'famous four' are as follows:

- **Dirty reads**
  Dirty reads occur while a transaction is updating a row, and a second transaction reads the row before the first transaction is committed. If the original update rolls back, the data read by the second transaction is not the same, hence a dirty read has occurred.
- **Nonrepeatable reads**
  These occur when a transaction is updating data while a second transaction is reading the same data, both before and after a change. Data retrieved from the first query does not match the second query (this presumes that the second transaction reads the data twice; once before and once after).
- **Phantom reads**
  These occur when a transaction retrieves a set of rows once, another transaction inserts or deletes a row from that same table, and the first transaction looks at the query again. The **phantom** is the missing or new row.
- **Lost updates**
  Lost updates occur when two transactions update a row's value, and the transaction that **last** updates the row 'wins'; thus the first update is lost.

Locks help alleviate these problems when applied appropriately. The following table displays the types of lock that SQL Server 2000 can issue:

| Name | Initial | Description |
|---|---|---|
| Intent Lock | `I` | Intent locks effectively create a lock queue, designating the order of connections and their associated right to update or read resources. SQL Server uses intent locks to show future intention of acquiring locks on a specific resource. |
| Intent Shared | `IS` | Intent to read some (but not all) of the resources in the table or page using shared locks. Used for read-only operations. |

| Name | Initial | Description |
|---|---|---|
| Intent Exclusive | `IX` | Intent to modify some (but not all) resources in the table or page using an exclusive lock. Used for data-modification purposes. |
| Shared with Intent Exclusive | `SIX` | Intent to read all resources and modify some. A combination of shared locks and exclusive locks will be placed. One lock is held for the resource, and multiple `IX` and `IS` locks can be placed. |
| Update Lock | `U` | Update locks are acquired prior to modifying the data. When the row is modified, this lock is escalated to an exclusive lock. If not modified, it is downgraded to a shared lock. This lock type prevents deadlocks if two connections hold a shared (`S`) lock on a resource, and attempt to convert to an exclusive (`X`) lock, but cannot because they are each waiting for the other transaction to release the shared (`S`) lock. |
| Exclusive Lock | `X` | Lock on the resource that bars any kind of access (reads or writes). Issued during `INSERT`, `UPDATE`, or `DELETE` statements. |
| Schema Modification | `Sch-M` | Issued when a DDL statement is executed. |
| Schema Stability | `Sch-S` | Issued when a query is being compiled. Keeps DDL operations from being performed on the table. |
| Bulk Update | `BU` | This type of lock is issued during a bulk-copy operation. Performance is increased for the bulk-copy operation, but table concurrency is reduced. Used when either `TABLOCK` hint or `sp_tableoption 'table lock on bulk load'` is enabled. |

The following are resources to which SQL Server can apply locks:

| Resource | Description |
|---|---|
| `RID` | Row identifier, designating a single table row. |
| `Key` | Index row lock, helping prevent phantom reads. Also called key-range lock, this lock type uses both a range and a row component. The range represents the range of index keys between two consecutive index keys. The row component represents the lock type on the index entry. Range types are as follows:<br>`RangeS_S` mode – Shared range, shared resource lock.<br>`RangeS_U` mode – Shared range, update resource lock.<br>`RangeI_N` mode – Insert range, null resource lock (row doesn't exist yet).<br>`RangeX_X` mode – Exclusive range, exclusive resource lock. |
| `Page` | Referring to a 8KB data or index page. |

*Table continued on following page*

| Resource | Description |
|---|---|
| Extent | Allocation unit of eight 8KB data or index pages. |
| Table | Entire table, data, and indexes locked. |
| DB | Entire database lock. |

Not all lock types are compatible with each other; for lock types to be compatible, SQL Server must be able to place a lock on a table that has a lock already in place. Lock types must be compatible with any existing lock currently placed on a resource.

The following table lists the lock types, and their associated compatibility types:

| Lock Type | Compatible With... |
|---|---|
| Shared (S) locks | Compatible with intent shared (IS), other shared (S), and update (U) locks. |
| Update (U) locks | Compatible with intent shared (IS) and shared (S) locks. |
| Exclusive (X) locks | Compatible with **any** other lock types. |
| Intent Shared (IS) locks | Compatible with all locks **except** exclusive (X) locks. |
| Shared with Intent Exclusive (SIX) locks | Compatible with intent shared (IS) locks. |
| Intent Exclusive (IX) locks | Compatible with intent shared (IS) and intent exclusive (IX) locks. This is because IX intends to update **some** rows, but not all. |
| Schema Stability (Sch-S) locks | Compatible with all lock modes **except** schema modification (Sch-M). |
| Schema Modification (Sch-M) locks | Incompatible with **all** locks. |
| Bulk Update (BU) locks | Compatible only with schema stability (Sch-S) and other bulk update (BU) locks. |
| RangeS_S mode | Compatible with shared (S), rangeS_S, and rangeS_U locks. |
| RangeS_U mode | Compatible with shared (S) and RangeS_S locks. |
| RangeI_N mode | Compatible with shared, update, exclusive, and RangeI_N locks; this is because the inserted rows do not yet exist. |
| RangeX_X mode | Compatible with any other lock type. |

Locks are allocated and escalated automatically by SQL Server; escalation means that finer grain locks (row and page locks) are converted into coarse-grain table locks. Locks take up system memory, so converting many locks into one larger lock can free up memory resources. Row level locking (versus page or table locking) does increase database concurrency, but at a cost of memory overhead.

Although you cannot control lock escalation, you **do** have control over locking isolation levels and locking hints in your queries. Below is a review of each isolation level, this time including what type of issue the isolation level resolves:

| Option | Description | What Does It Solve? |
|---|---|---|
| READ COMMITTED | While READ COMMITTED is set, shared locks are held for the duration of the transaction. The data cannot be changed. Data inserts and modifications to the same table **are** allowed by other transactions, so long as the rows involved are not locked by the first transaction. | **This is the default isolation level for SQL Server.** Remember this always; it means that your SELECT statements, unless otherwise specified, cannot read uncommitted data. Dirty reads are prevented. |
| READ UNCOMMITTED | This is the least restrictive isolation level, issuing no locks on the data selected by the transaction. This provides the highest concurrency but the lowest amount of data integrity. Data that you read can be changed while you read it (dirty reads), or new data can be added or removed that would change your original query results. | It does not solve concurrency problems, but it does help with locking contention difficulties. You can read data while it is being updated or selected, so you do not have to wait to retrieve the data. If this is used with static data, or data that doesn't require exact approximations, READ UNCOMMITTED may make sense for your query. |
| REPEATABLE READ | Dirty and nonrepeatable reads are not allowed. New rows can still be inserted by other transactions. | Prevents nonrepeatable and dirty reads. |
| SERIALIZABLE | This is the most restrictive setting. Ranges of shared locks are held on the data, preventing insertion of new rows, deletion of existing rows, and modification of rows within the selected range. | Prevents phantom, nonrepeatable, and dirty reads. |

Locking hints are another weapon in your locking strategy arsenal, and bypass SQL Server's dynamic locking behavior. SQL Server cannot always guess your intentions, so adding locking hints can help SQL Server make the best locking decision. For example, if you have a table with static data that can use the NOLOCK hint without risk of dirty data, doing so will lower the overhead of the locking that SQL Server would use by default.

On the other hand, hints can also do more harm than good. Using ROWLOCK, for example, on a million-row table could cause outrageous memory overhead, as opposed to SQL Server dynamically escalating a rowlock to a page or table lock. It is best to use hints carefully, and not forget where you placed them in your application. Schemas and data distribution can change over time, and your previously well-performing query could suffer from the use of a hint.

Locking hints are used with the SELECT, INSERT, UPDATE, and DELETE statements; not all hints can be used with each DML type (SELECT, INSERT, UPDATE, and DELETE). Keep in mind that locking hints override the default or specified isolation level for the user session.

The syntax for locking hint usage from *SQL Server Books Online* is as follows:

```
FROM
< table_source > ::=
 table_name [ [ AS ] table_alias ] [ WITH ( < table_hint > [ ,...n ] ) ]
< table_hint > ::=
 { INDEX ( index_val [ ,...n ] )
   | FASTFIRSTROW
   | HOLDLOCK
   | NOLOCK
   | PAGLOCK
   | READCOMMITTED
   | READPAST
   | READUNCOMMITTED
   | REPEATABLEREAD
   | ROWLOCK
   | SERIALIZABLE
   | TABLOCK
   | TABLOCKX
   | UPDLOCK
   | XLOCK
 }
```

There are two categories of lock hints: **granularity hints** and **isolation-level hints**. Granularity hints impact the resource locking used by a query; isolation-level hints impact the lock types used on the locked resource.

The granularity hints are:

| Granularity Hint | Description |
|---|---|
| PAGLOCK | Tells SQL Server to use page locks instead of a single table lock. Use this hint if you are seeing a table lock being used unnecessarily by SQL Server (where page locks would be more efficient). |
| NOLOCK | Same behavior as UNCOMMITTED READ isolation level. No locks of any kind are issued, but dirty reads are possible. Only usable with SELECT statement. Use this hint when you feel confident that locks will be unnecessary (read-only databases, or updates to data that are on off-periods). |
| ROWLOCK | Issues row-level locks instead of page and table-level locks. Be careful about applying this to too many rows (to avoid memory problems). |
| TABLOCK | Issues a table lock instead of a row or page lock. Lock is held until the end of the statement, not the transaction. Use this if page locks are granted, but you intend to lock the entire table. |
| TABLOCKX | Issues an exclusive lock on a table. No reads or updates are allowed by other connections until the end of the statement or transaction. |

The isolation-level hints are as follows (notice some are considered both granularity and isolation hints):

| Isolation Level Hint | Description |
|---|---|
| HOLDLOCK | Issues a shared lock until completion of the transaction. Does **not** release lock after table, row, or data page has been modified. Same behavior as SERIALIZABLE isolation level. |
| NOLOCK | Same behavior as uncommitted read isolation level. No locks of any kind are issued, but dirty reads are possible. Only useable with SELECT statements. |
| READCOMMITTED | SQL Server 2000 default isolation level of READ COMMITTED. |
| READPAST | Within a SELECT statement, designating READPAST will cause the query to skip any locked rows. Applies to transactions using READ COMMITTED isolation level. Only reads past row level locks. |
| READUNCOMMITTED | Same as NOLOCK hint. |
| REPEATABLEREAD | Same behavior as REPEATABLE READ isolation level. |
| SERIALIZABLE | Same as HOLDLOCK. Uses SERIALIZABLE isolation level. |
| UPDLOCK | With UPDLOCK, you can read data without blocking other readers, and update the data later knowing that data has not been changed since the last read. |
| XLOCK | Issues an exclusive lock that will be held until the end of the transaction for all data processed. Can be included with the PAGLOCK or TABLOCK hints. |

The following is an example of using the SERIALIZABLE locking hint:

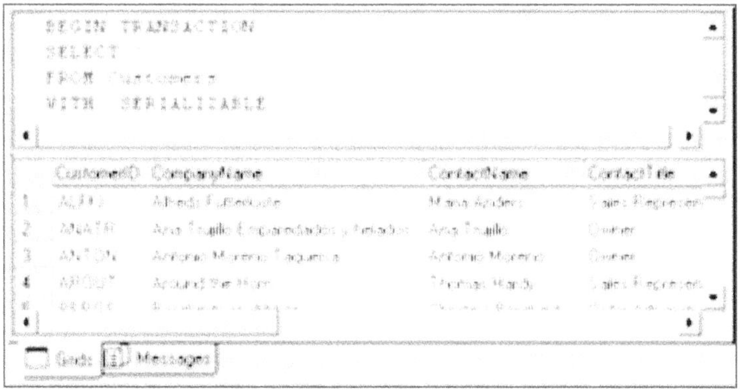


Using sp_lock, you can see that the query (since it is not committed yet) holds key locks on all the rows in the range. sp_lock is a system stored procedure that reports information on locks held within the SQL Server instance:

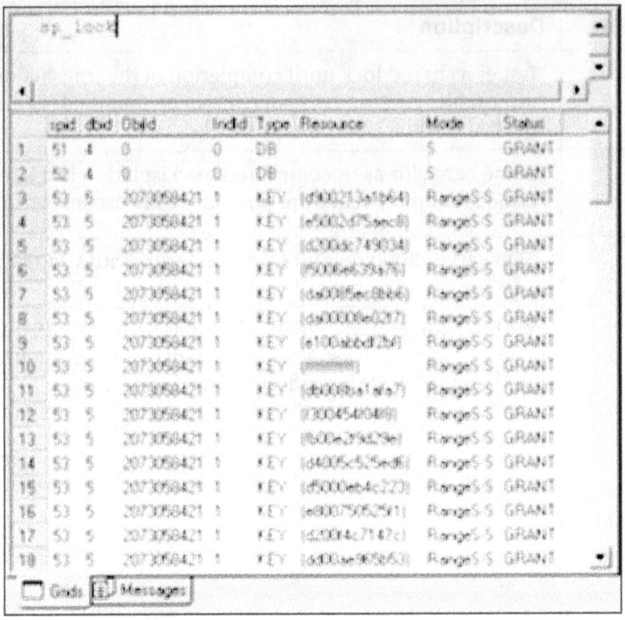


The ObjId in the results output is the object ID of the resource being locked. To view the object name, run the following command with the integer value from `sp_lock`:

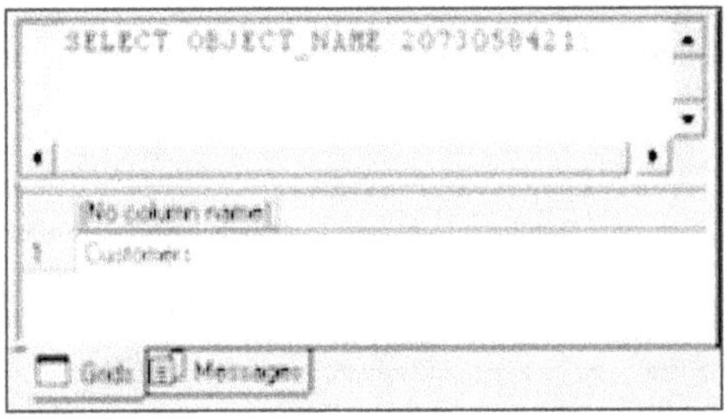


We will go into more detail on `sp_lock` later in the chapter.

In the next example, we run the same query, but this time with the `NOLOCK` hint:

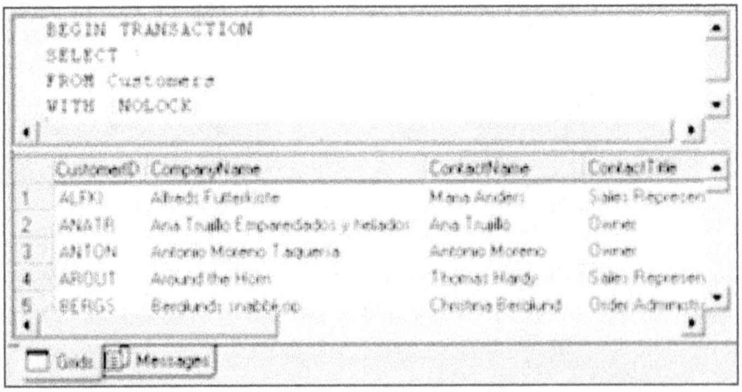

Looking at sp_lock, you will not see any locks held on the Customers table:

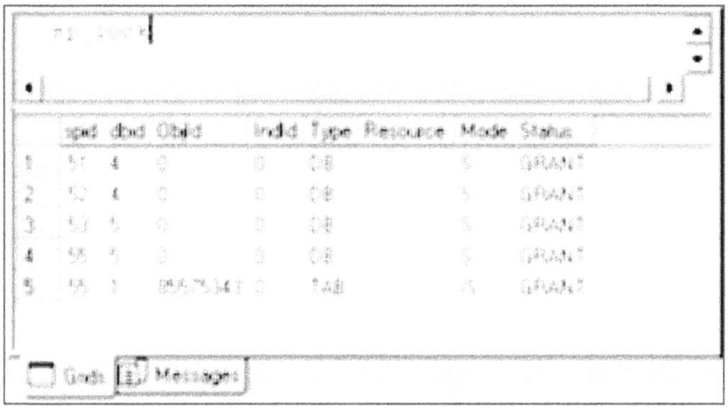


In the next example, we want to update the Customers table's update date for **all** rows. We run the following statement:

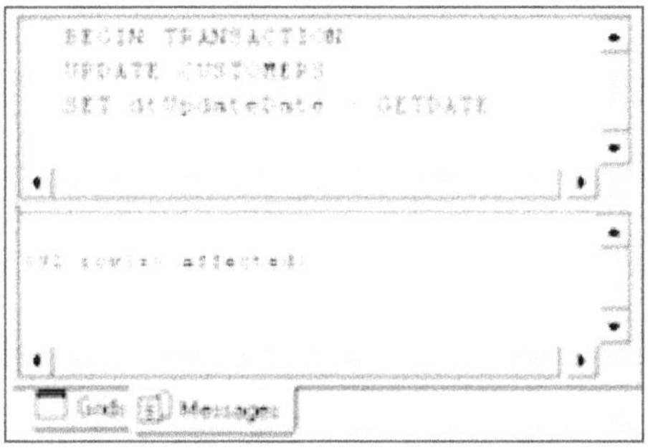

The statement has not committed, so by running sp_lock, we see that exclusive locks have been placed on the key resources:

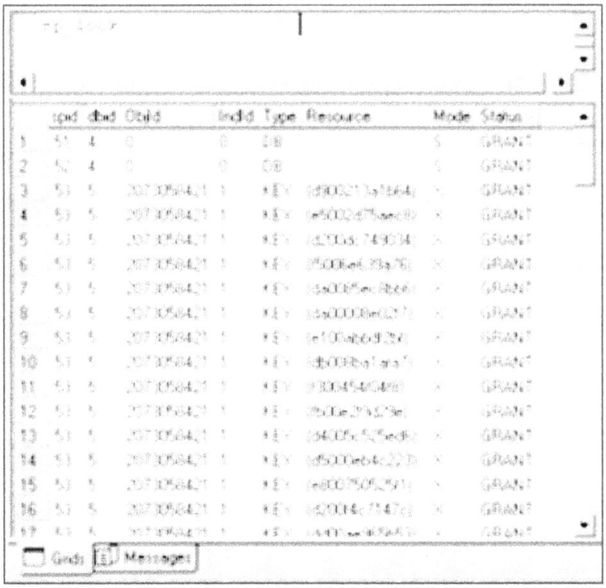

This is a case where SQL Server decides to place key locks when a table lock would have worked just as well. If you know that all rows must be updated, you can use a coarser-grained resource lock, like the following:

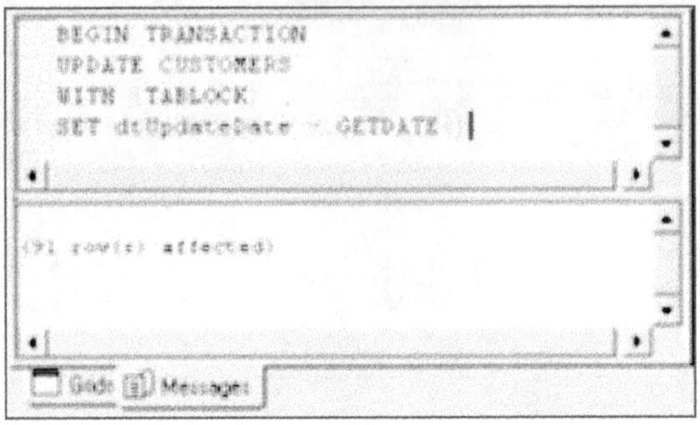


The result of sp_lock after using the WITH (TABLOCK) statement is as follows:

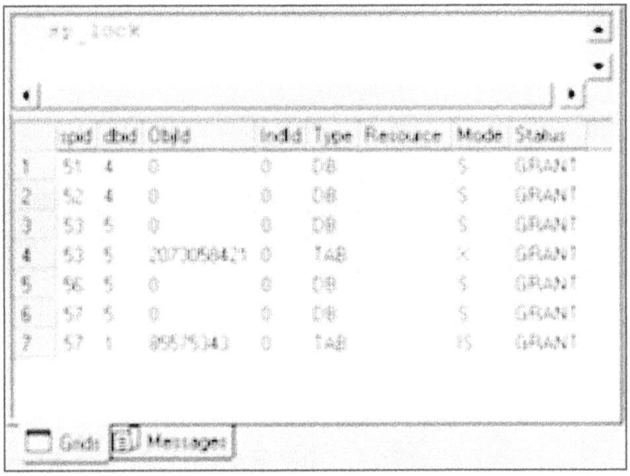


Instead of multiple key locks being issued, **one** exclusive table lock is created. For multiple rows in a large table (if you know that you will be updating all rows), it may make more sense to issue a table lock upfront, rather than issue hundreds of key locks (which consume memory).

# 5.6 How to... View Locking Activity in Enterprise Manager

Enterprise Manager allows you to view locking activity by SPID (process ID) and by database object. You can also view the process info (host, last batch time, login, database) and locking activity by object. To view locking activity in Enterprise Manger:

- ❑ Expand Server Group and registration.
- ❑ Expand the Management folder.
- ❑ Expand the Current Activity node.
- ❑ Click Process Info to see SPIDs (process IDs) in the database.

- In the right pane, double-click a process ID to view the last command that it ran. From this window, you can also send the connection a message, or `KILL` the process. Select Close when finished with the Process Details dialog box:

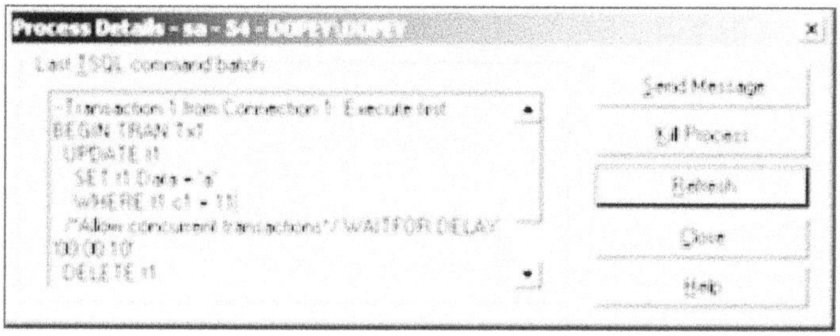

- To see locked resources by process ID, expand the Locks / Process ID node. Click a specific SPID to see what objects are being locked, the lock type, mode, status, owner, Index, and resource.
- Expand the Locks / Object node to view locks by object resource. Click a specific object to view associated process IDs issuing locks.
- When a blocking situation is in progress, the locks by process id view will display the process IDs being blocked, and the process ID doing the blocking. For example:

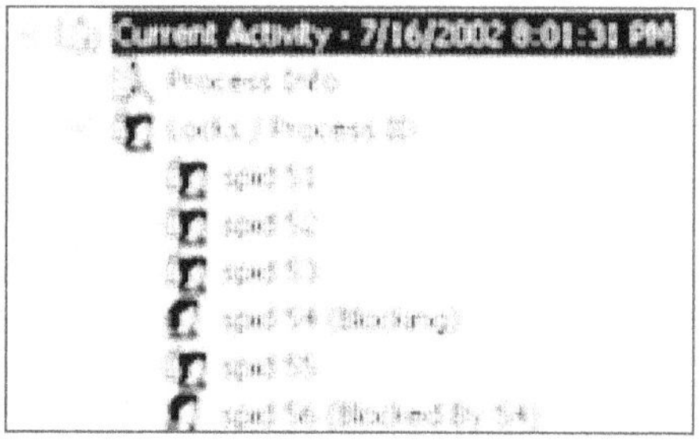


- To refresh the activity to reflect the current activity of the server, right-click the Current Activity node and select Refresh.

Remember that you are looking at past history, and should refresh this view often, particularly if you plan on killing any process IDs.

# 5.7 How to... Use sp_who

Stored procedure `sp_who` displays information on current users and processes. `sp_who` returns:

- System process ID
- Execution context ID
- Status
- Login name
- Host or computer name
- Whether or not the process is currently blocked by another process

- Database name
- Transact-SQL command type

To display all processes on the server in Query Analyzer, run:

```
EXEC sp_who
```

For example:

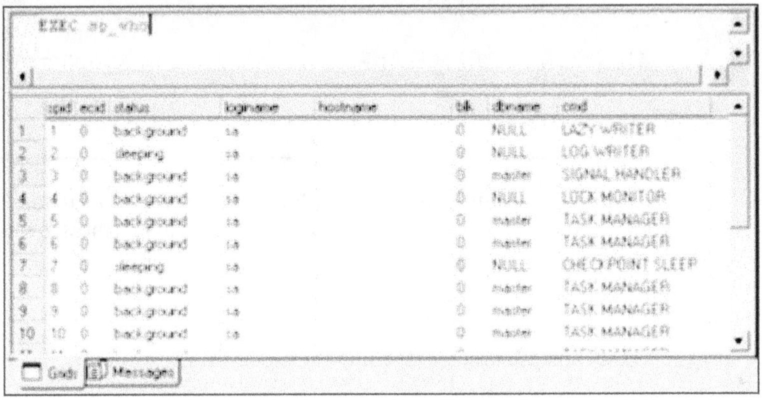


To specify activity for a specific process ID, execute:

```
EXEC sp_who SPID
```

For example:

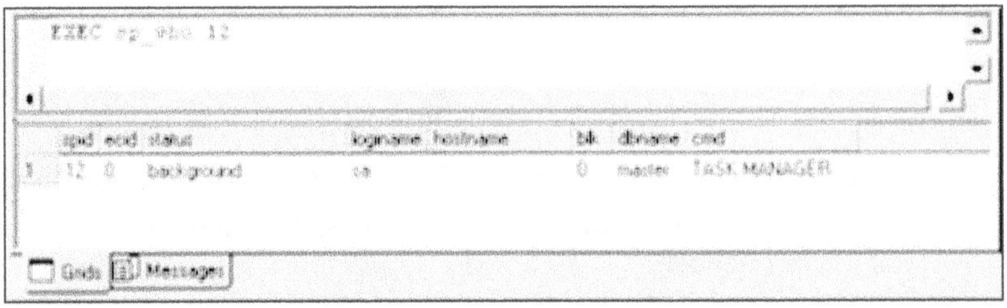


To specify only active processes, execute:

```
EXEC sp_who 'active'
```

For example:

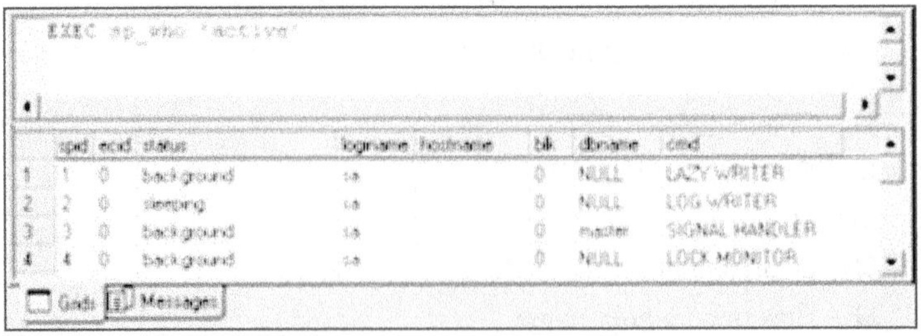

# 5.8 How to... Use DBCC INPUTBUFFER and DBCC OUTPUTBUFFER

The `DBCC INPUTBUFFER` command is used to view the last statement sent by the client connection to SQL Server. The syntax for `DBCC INPUTBUFFER` is:

```
DBCC INPUTBUFFER (SPID)
```

`SPID` is the process ID, which you can get from viewing current activity in Enterprise Manager or executing `sp_who`. The output from `DBCC INPUTBUFFER` is good information to note when you encounter a blocking situation. We will review blocking and deadlocking in the next section, but it is important to be aware that identification of the blocking statement will assist you when troubleshooting the issue.

The following example of running `DBCC INPUTBUFFER` shows the Event Type, Parameters, and Event Info columns. For Event Type, the values RPC, Language, or No Event are returned. Parameters show either 0 for text, or an integer for the number of parameters. Event Info for an RPC (remote procedure call) will contain the procedure name. Event Type for a language or No Event will contain the first 255 characters of the text sent by the client:

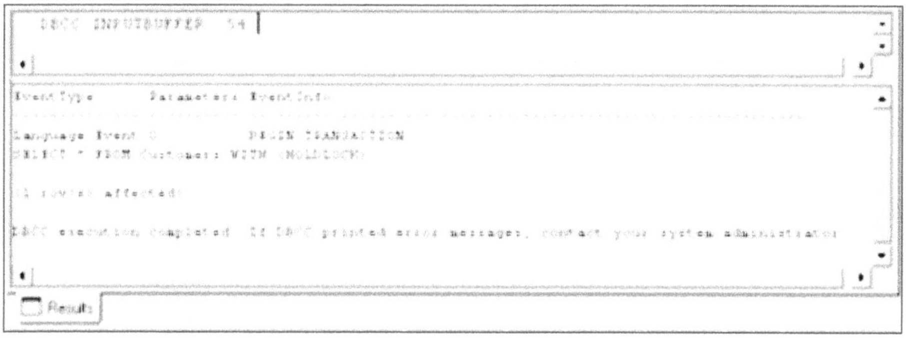

`DBCC OUTPUTBUFFER` shows the information sent to the client in hexadecimal and ASCII format for the process ID specified. For example, for a SPID requesting all rows from the `Customers` table:

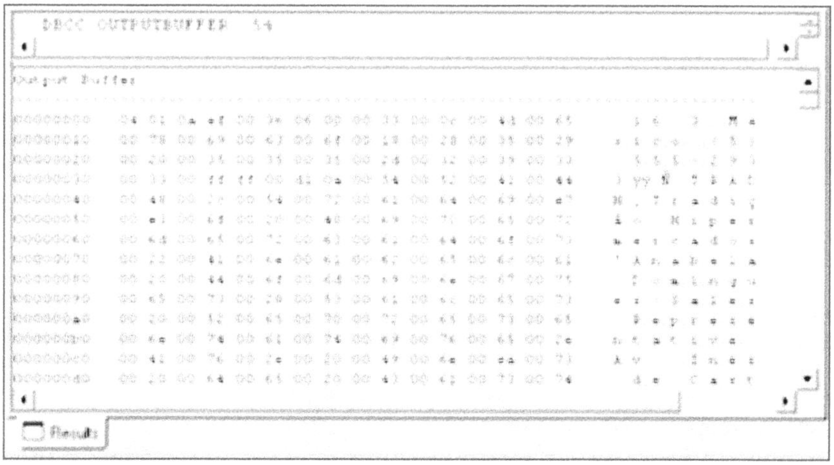

If you look carefully, you will see words in the third column. For greater legibility, there are stored procedures on the Internet and referenced in SQL Server message boards that allow you to decipher the ASCII format and view the actual query results returned to the client. This is useful if you are trying to see what sort or amount of data is being returned to the client. This command can only be run by members of the `sysadmin` group.

# 5.9 How to... Use fn_get_sql

SQL Server 2000 Service Pack 3 has introduced a new function called `fn_get_sql`. Like `DBCC INPUTBUFFER`, this function is used to return the SQL string for an active connection. Unlike `DBCC INPUTBUFFER`, `fn_get_sql` is able to return SQL strings greater than 255 characters.

One drawback of this function is that it won't usually return SQL strings for zero cost query plans. These are basic ad-hoc queries or calls that SQL Server usually does not cache because they have low overhead. The function also cannot return bulk copy statements or those statements with string literals exceeding 8KB, because these are not cached either.

The syntax for `fn_get_sql` is:

```
::fn_get_sql ( @SqlHandle )
```

The `@SqlHandle` parameter refers to the new column added in SP3 to `sysprocesses`, the `sql_handle` column. This new column represents the current executing batch, and is a `binary(20)` data type.

The following example query populates the `@Handle` parameter via a query to `sysprocesses`. (You must be sysadmin to execute this function):

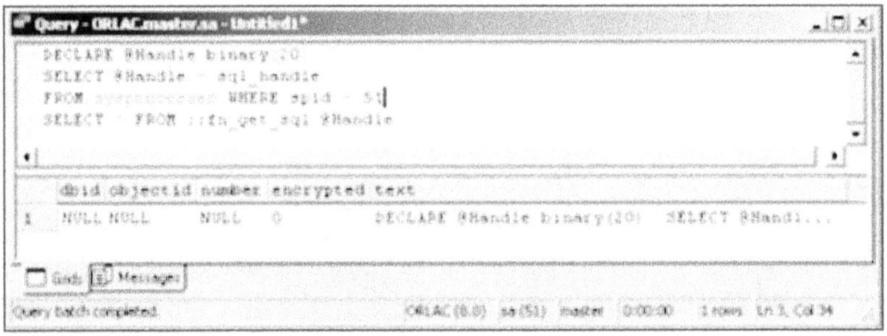

In this example, a variable was used to hold the `sql_handle` for the `spid 51`. This variable was then fed to the `fn_get_sql` function, returning the text of the query in the `text` column.

The encrypted field returns `0` if not encrypted, and `1` if encrypted. The `dbid` and `objectid` fields will return `NULL` if the SQL Statement is an ad hoc SQL statement. If the procedure captured is grouped, the `number` column is the number of the stored procedure group. Otherwise the `number` column is `NULL` for ad hoc SQL statements or `0` for statements that are not procedures.

# 5.10 How to... Use SET LOCK_TIMEOUT

When a transaction or statement is blocked, it is waiting for a lock on a resource to be released. SQL Server offers the `SET LOCK_TIMEOUT` option to specify how long a statement should wait for a lock to be released. The syntax from *SQL Server Books Online* is as follows:

```
SET LOCK_TIMEOUT timeout_period
```

`timeout_period` is the number of milliseconds the statement should wait. For example, setting the timeout to five seconds (5000 milliseconds):

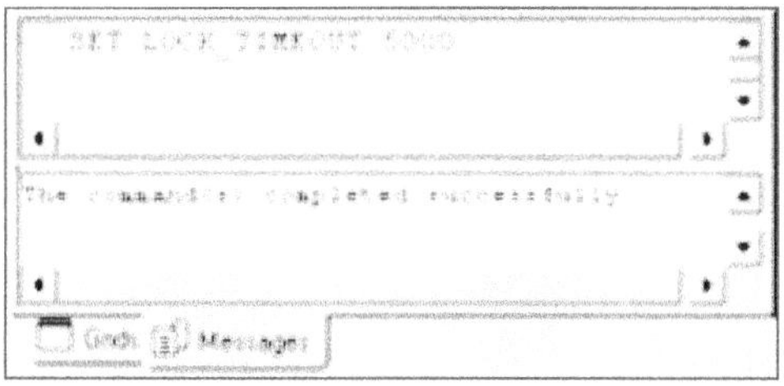

This setting doesn't impact how long a resource can be held by a process, only how long it has to wait for another process to give up the goods. Rather than setting this lock timeout, you may be better off examining why inappropriate locking is occurring.

# Blocking and Deadlocking Defined

**Blocking** occurs when a transaction is locking resources that one or more other transactions want to read or modify. Short-term blocking is usually okay, depending on your application requirements. Poorly-designed applications can cause long-term blocking, unnecessarily holding locks on resources and keeping other sessions from reading or updating those resources. A blocked process can wait indefinitely, until:

- It times out (based on `SET LOCK_TIMEOUT`)
- The server goes down
- The connection finishes its updates
- Something happens to the original transaction to cause it to release its locks on the resource

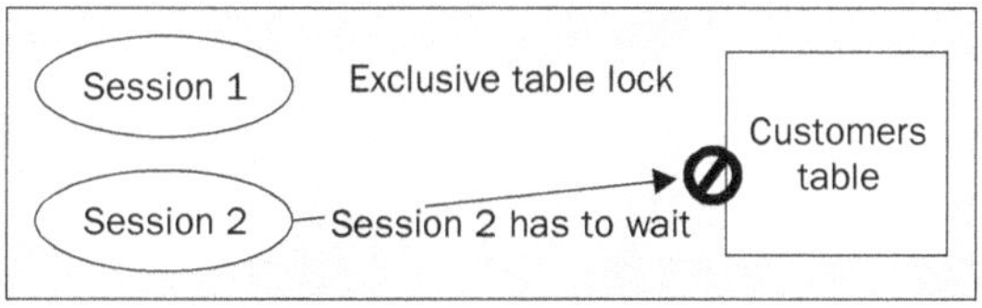


**Deadlocking** occurs when one user session (let's call it Session 1) has locks on a resource that another user session (let's call it Session 2) wants to modify, and Session 2 has locks on resources that Session 1 needs to modify. Neither Session 1 nor Session 2 can continue until the other releases the locks, so SQL Server chooses one of the sessions in the deadlock as the **deadlock victim**. This deadlock victim has its session killed and transactions rolled back:

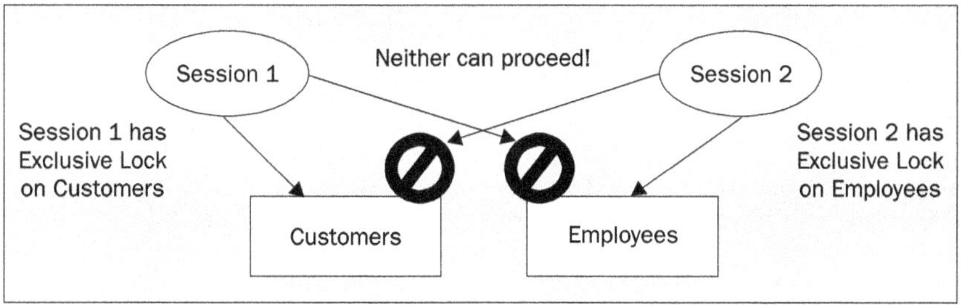

# Why Blocking and Deadlocking Happen

Before trying to troubleshoot blocking and deadlocking, we should understand why they happen in the first place. There are various reasons for why long-term blocking occurs:

- The issue may be normal database blocking or excessive long-term blocking. If users are waiting long periods of time, system processes are standing still, and you see long-standing blocks, or numerous blocks in a short period of time, investigate further.
- Without proper indexing, blocking issues can grow. Row locks on a table without an index can cause SQL Server to acquire a table lock, blocking out other transactions.
- Badly written applications can cause blocking. This is a broad category, so let's deal with it in more detail:
    - Transactions that `BEGIN` and then request user feedback or interaction. This is usually when an end user is allowed to enter data in a GUI while a transaction remains open. While open, any resources referenced by the transaction may be held with locks.
    - Transactions that `BEGIN` and then look up data that could have been referenced prior to the transaction starting.
    - Using locking hints inappropriately; for example, if the application only needs one row, but uses a table lock instead.
    - The application uses long-running transactions, updating many rows or many tables within one transaction.

Reasons why deadlocks occur:

- The application accesses tables in different orders. For example, Session A updates `Customers` and then `Orders`, whereas Session B updates `Orders` and then `Customers`. This increases the chance of two processes deadlocking, rather then accessing and updating a table in a serialized fashion.
- The application uses long-running transactions, updating many rows or many tables within one transaction.
- In some situations, SQL Server issues several row locks, which it later decides must be escalated to page or table locks. If these rows exist on the same data pages, and two sessions are both trying to escalate the lock granularity on the same page, a deadlock can occur.

# 5.11 How to... Identify and Resolve Blocking

First we will review resolution of blocking issues on your server, keeping in mind that we are talking about short-term resolution. This means identification of the offending session and, if possible, stopping the session or transaction. If this is not possible, we could issue a `KILL` statement to get rid of the blocking process. This often does not solve the original problem of why the blocking occurred, so check *Troubleshooting Blocking and Deadlocking Problems* later in the chapter.

- In Query Analyzer, run `sp_who`.
- Look at the `BlkBy` column. When a number exists in this column, this identifies the SPID that is blocking that current row's process. You could have a chain of blocking (numerous blocked or blocking processes), so you may need to run through this process many times. In order to solve the long-term issue that may be causing the blocking, track the SPID doing the blocking, and also the login, host, database name, command, program name, and last batch columns.

- Run sp_lock, including the SPID that is blocking other processes. For example:

```
EXEC sp_lock 53
```

This returns:

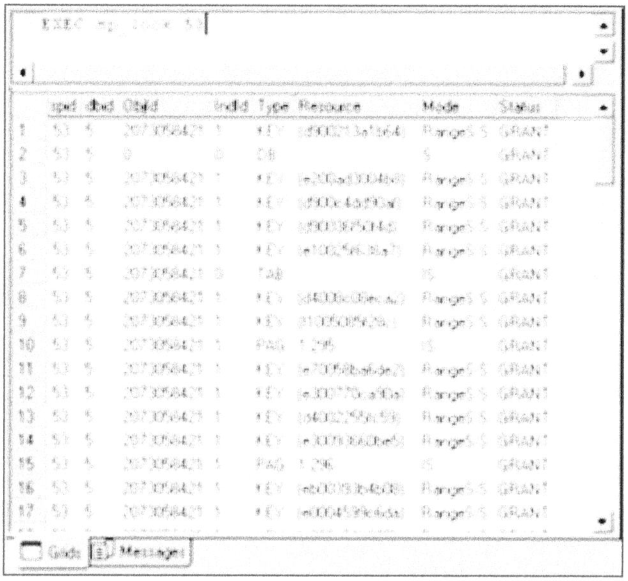


- From the results, you should track the type of locks, lock mode, and objects impacted. The options for status are GRANT (lock was obtained), WAIT (blocking is occurring), or CNVT (lock is converting to another lock). To see the object name from the ObjId integer, execute:

```
SELECT OBJECT_NAME (integer)
```

This returns:

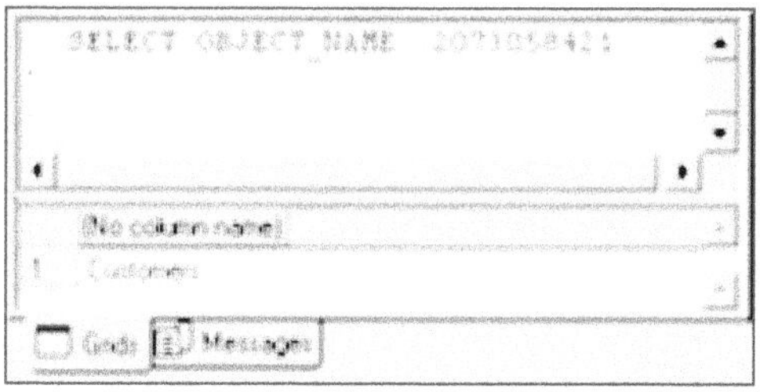


- Now that you know which statement is blocking the resources, and which resources are being blocked, it is time to take a look at the statement issuing the block, by running DBCC INPUTBUFFER (SPID):

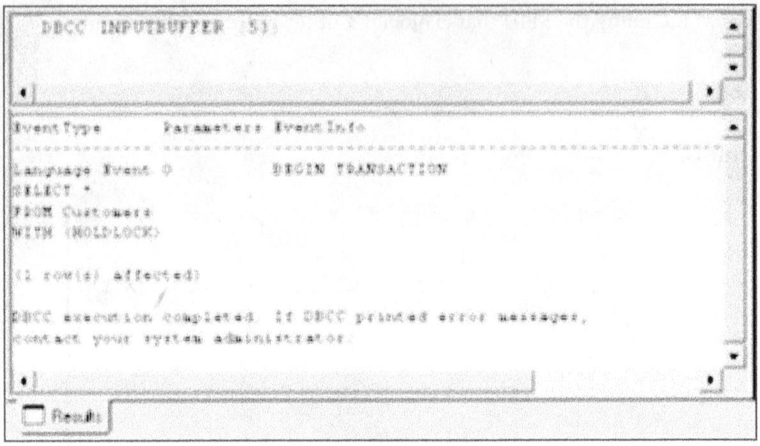


- ❑ If possible, ask your client or application contact to stop the transaction blocking the resources. Make sure that this is not a long-running transaction that is critical to the business (you do not want to stop a payroll process midstream). In that case, you may want to let it run and attempt to fix the problem later. In either case, if you cannot stop the process in an elegant way, you can run the `KILL` process to stop the blocking:

```
KILL SPID
```

For example:

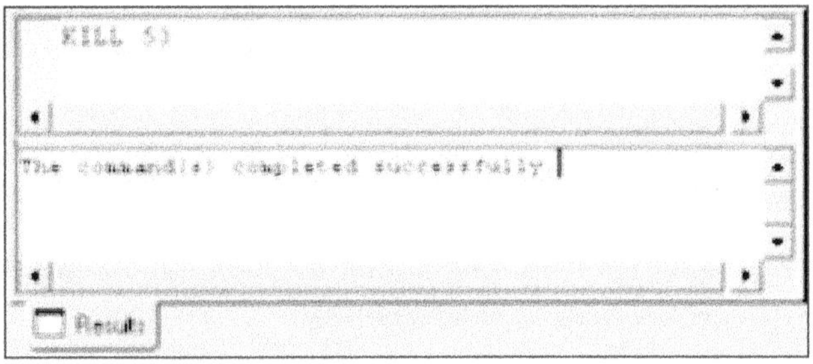


While we are on the topic of the `KILL` keyword, it is important to understand that some `KILL` statements take longer to roll back a transaction than others. SQL Server 2000 added the ability to check the status of the `KILL` rollback by running `KILL SPID WITH STATUSONLY`:

```
KILL 54 WITH STATUSONLY
```

For example:

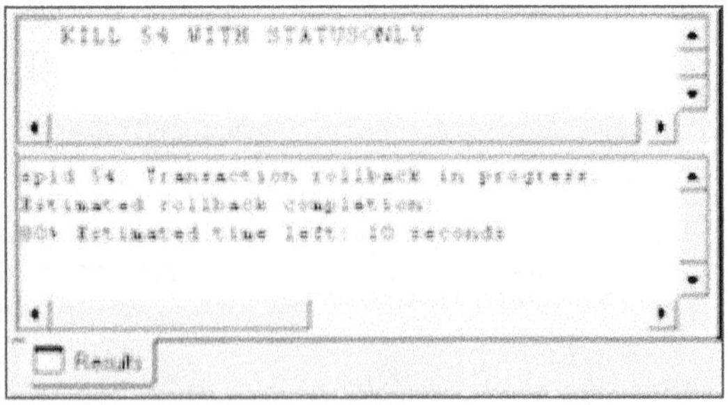

Regarding block troubleshooting in Enterprise Manager, we reviewed functionality of the Current Activity node in a previous section. To troubleshoot blocking, follow these steps:

- Expand Server Group and registration.
- Expand the Management folder.
- Expand Current Activity.
- Expand Locks / Process ID.
- Click the blocking SPID to see which locks are being held on which resources in the right-hand pane:
- Click the Process Info node and check the right-hand pane for details on the blocking SPID.
- Inform the user, application, or process that is causing the blocking – giving them an opportunity to either finish the process, or shut the process down. If this is a process that has no owner and can be removed, right-click the SPID and select Kill Process.
- Select YES in the dialog box to kill the process.
- Right-click and select Refresh to see a new view of the processes.

# 5.12 How to... Identify Deadlocks with Trace Flag 1204

When a deadlock occurs, the deadlock victim will receive an error like this:

```
Server: Msg 1205, Level 13, State 50, Line 6
Transaction (Process ID 60) was deadlocked on lock resources with another process and has been
chosen as the deadlock victim. Rerun the transaction.
```

You will also see a message in the SQL error log something like this:

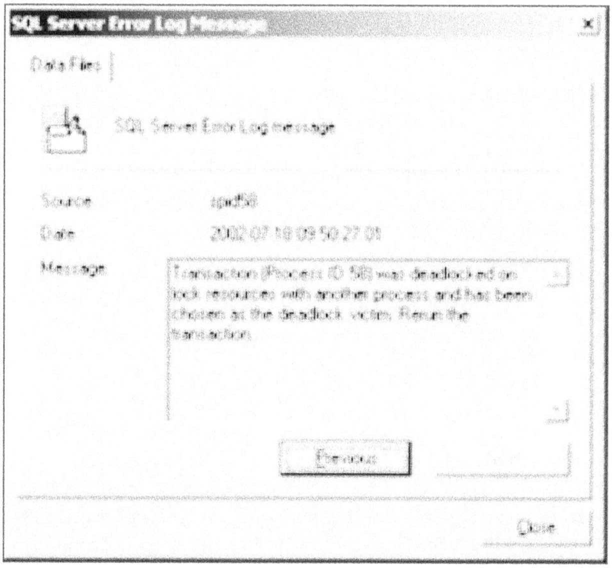

Unfortunately, the default message does not include detailed information on the resources involved and the commands being run.

In Query Analyzer, you can activate **trace flag** number 1204 to show more information on deadlocking errors. Trace flags are used within SQL Server to enable or disable specific SQL Server instance characteristics temporarily. Traces are enabled using the `DBCC TRACEON` command, and disabled using `DBCC TRACEOFF`.

When trace flag 1204 is enabled, it returns the types of lock participating in the deadlock and the statements involved. Trace flag 1204 is often coupled with trace flag 3605, which writes the results of flag 1204 to the SQL error log. Including trace flag -1 means that the traces will apply to all sessions, and not just the current user session where the trace is activated.

> **Beginning in SQL Server 2000 Service Pack 3, the trace flag 1204 will automatically write the results of the flag to the SQL error log. This means that with SP3, you need not enable the trace flag 3605.**

Trace flags -1 and 3605 are undocumented, so there are no guarantees that these will be available in future service packs or versions of SQL Server. Below is an example of enabling all three trace flags with `DBCC TRACEON`:

```
DBCC TRACEON (3605,1204, -1)
```

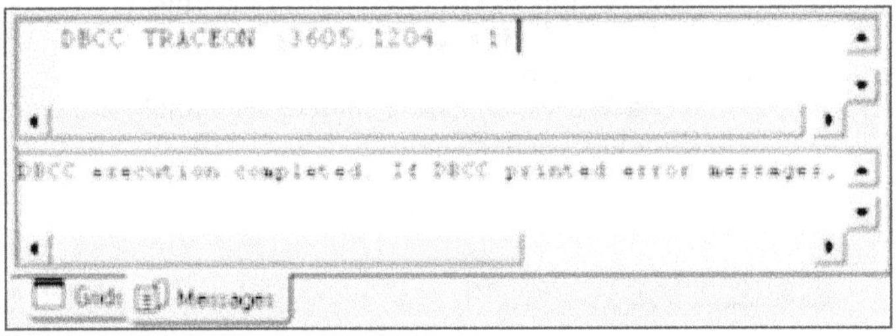


To check currently enabled flags for all sessions, run:

```
DBCC TRACESTATUS (-1)
```

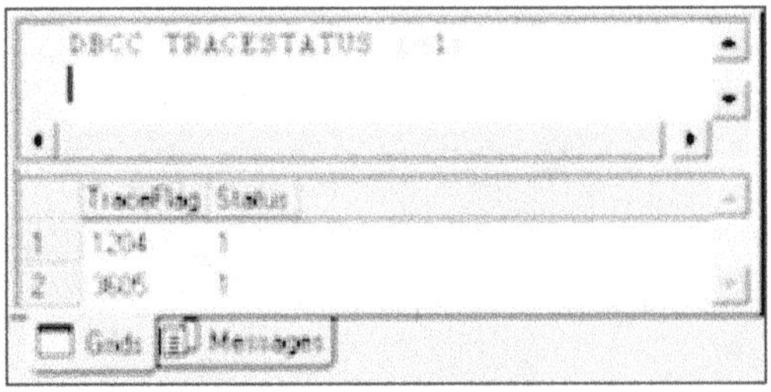


You will not see `-1` as one of the trace flags, but you can test to see if it worked by opening a new window and running `DBCC TRACESTATUS (-1)`. If you see the other two trace flags, you know that it worked, as trace flag `-1` applies `TRACEON` settings to all sessions.

If a deadlock occurs after enabling these flags, you will see output like the following in the SQL error log:

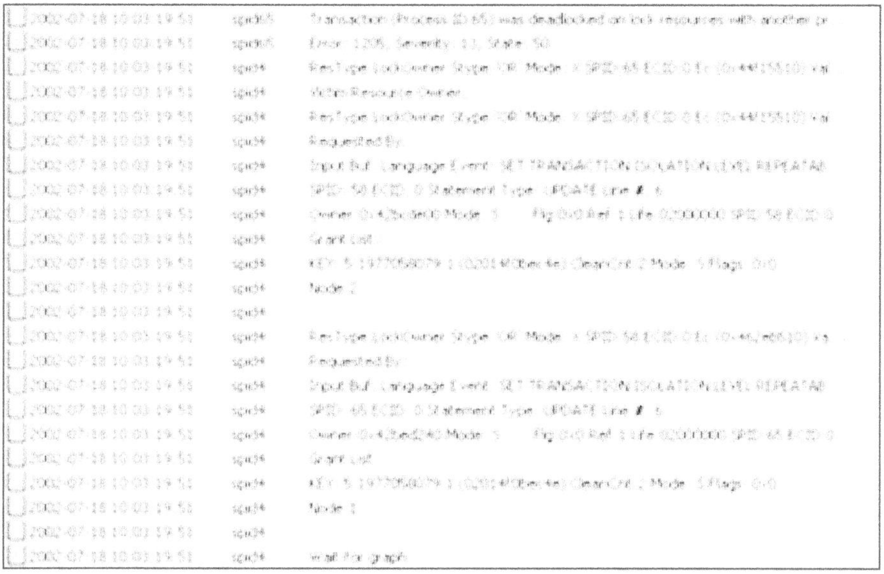

This SQL error log output shows the `DBCC INPUTBUFFER` results for the deadlock victim, `DBCC INPUTBUFFER` for the surviving process, and lock types held on the participating resources. Deadlock error log output depends on the type of deadlock that occurred. For an in-depth review of interpreting the SQL error log trace 1204 output, see the *SQL Server Books Online* topics, *Deadlocks Involving Locks*, *Deadlocks Involving Parallelism*, and *Deadlocks Involving Threads*.

When you have finished troubleshooting a deadlocking situation, make sure to disable the trace flags as follows. If you keep flags running, you risk increasing the overhead of SQL Server, and potentially reducing the SQL Server instance performance:

```
DBCC TRACEOFF (3605, 1204)
```

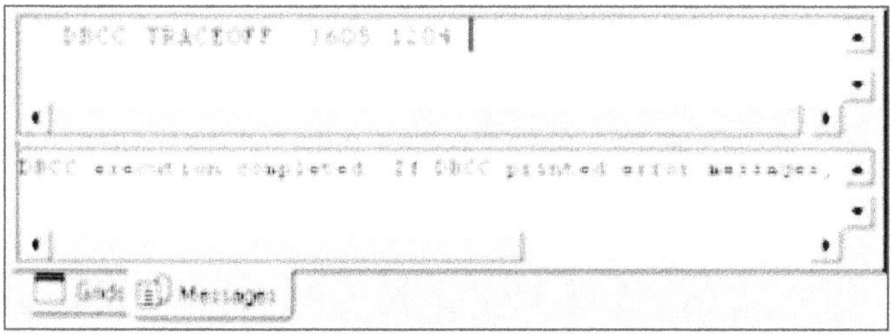

# 5.13 How to... Enable Trace Flags at SQL Server Startup

You can also set trace flags to start when SQL Server is restarted, using startup parameters. For example:

- ❑ Expand Server Group, right-click the registration and select Properties.

- At the SQL Server Properties window, select the Startup Parameters button.
- For each startup parameter you wish to have, type -Tnumber and press the Add button, where Tnumber is the letter T and the trace flag number:

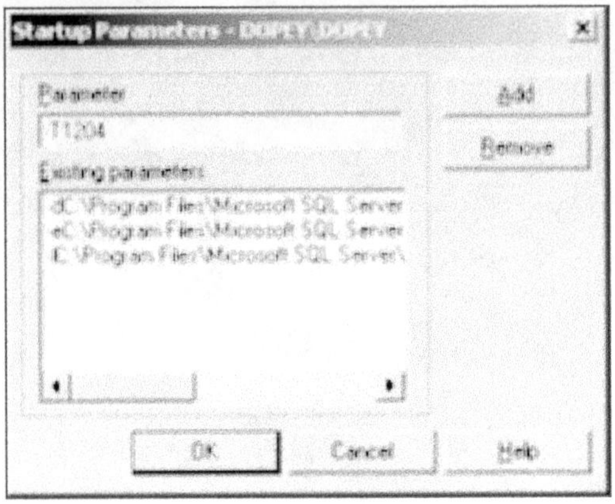

- If you wanted both trace flags 1204 and 3605, your startup parameters should look something like this:

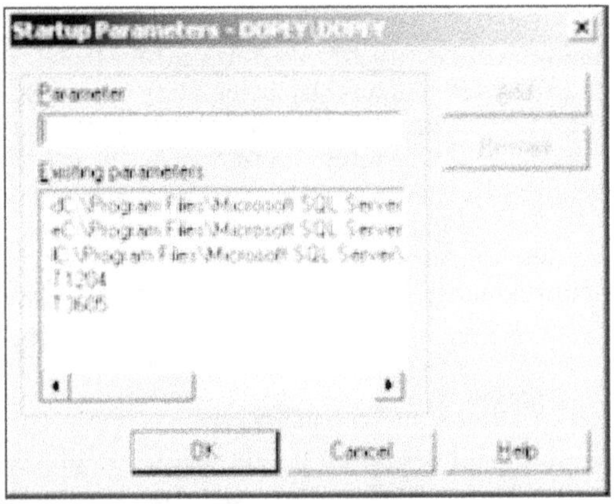

- Select OK when finished. Select OK at the SQL Server properties window. The service must restart for these trace flags to take effect. To remove them, you must go back to Startup Parameters, select Remove for each trace flag, and restart the SQL Server service.

# 5.14 How to... SET DEADLOCK_PRIORITY

You can increase the likelihood of a session being chosen as a deadlock victim by using the `SET DEADLOCK_PRIORITY` statement.

The syntax from *SQL Server Books Online* is:

```
SET DEADLOCK_PRIORITY { LOW | NORMAL | @deadlock_var }
```

LOW identifies the session to be the preferred deadlock victim, and NORMAL returns the session to the default deadlock-handling method. @deadlock_var has the character value 3 for LOW and 6 for NORMAL. Notice that there is not a HIGH (a deadlock always involves two processes; therefore, designating LOW will be enough to ensure the other session has the higher priority).

In the following example, we set the priority to LOW for our query:

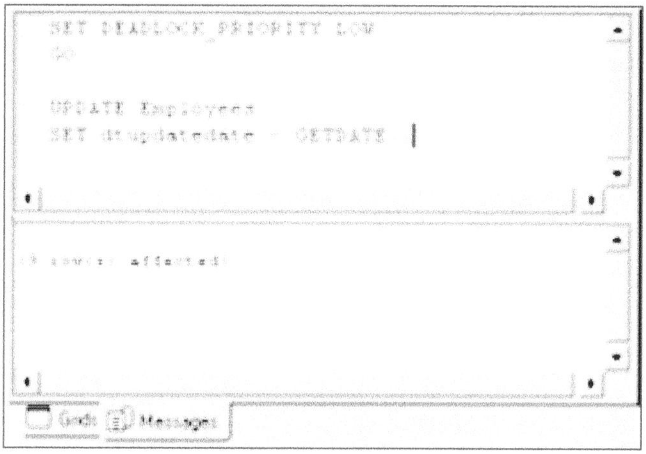

# 5.15 How to... Capture Deadlock Activity using SQL Profiler

All DBAs and developers should become familiar with SQL Profiler, as it is an excellent tool for capturing activity on your SQL Server instance.

SQL Profiler is able to capture data on the following deadlock-related events:

- Lock:Deadlock – captures deadlock event.
- Lock:Deadlock Chain – captures events leading up to deadlock.

Because you can see when a deadlock occurs by activating trace 1204, the first piece of information is less impressive. Where SQL Profiler excels, however, is in its ability to capture SQL events leading up to the deadlock. Unlike DBCC INPUTBUFFER, where you are limited to 255 characters, SQL Profiler can capture the entire statement. It can also capture the starting class of events, showing SQL statements that ran, but may not complete (because one of them was chosen as a deadlock victim).

Events to capture, depending on your SQL activity:

- SQL:BatchStarting – TSQL batch has started.
- SQL:StmtStarting – TSQL statement has started (lowest granularity).
- RPC:Starting – remote procedure call started.
- SP:Starting – stored procedure call started.
- SP:StmtStarting – statement within a stored procedure call started (lowest granularity).

Some of these events may show duplicate information, as statements vary in granularity, and `stmt` type events are smaller than batch and `sp` or `rpc` events. Batch and `stmt` types may capture the same statement (if one batch consists of one statement, for example); however, this will not hinder your ability to identify the deadlocked query.

To create a trace to capture deadlock activity and the statements leading up to it:

- Go to Start | Programs | Microsoft SQL Server | Profiler.
- Click the New Trace button:

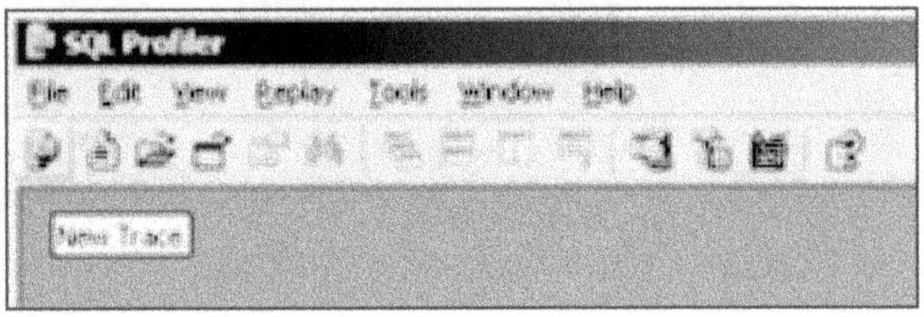


- Enter the server and login information. Select OK.
- Type in a trace name if you wish, and select a file or table to which you will save your output. If saving to a file, you can enable file rollover at a maximum file size in megabytes. If you save your data to a table, you can set the maximum number of rows (in the thousands). Alternatively, you can decide to save the trace file later, after you have captured the necessary data. You can also enable a trace stop time if you prefer:

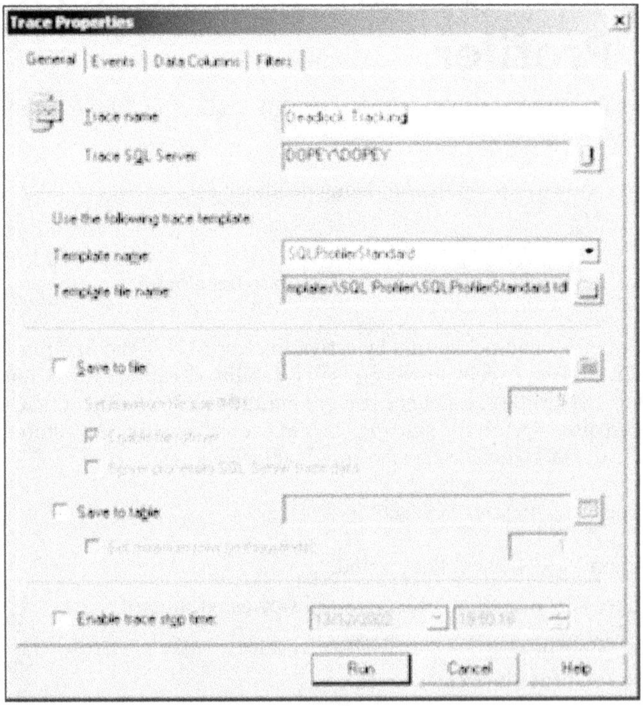

- ❑ In the Event tab select the existing event classes and remove them by clicking the Remove button. Expand the Locks, Stored Procedures, and T-SQL event classes, and select the events we discussed earlier. Your screen should look like the example below:

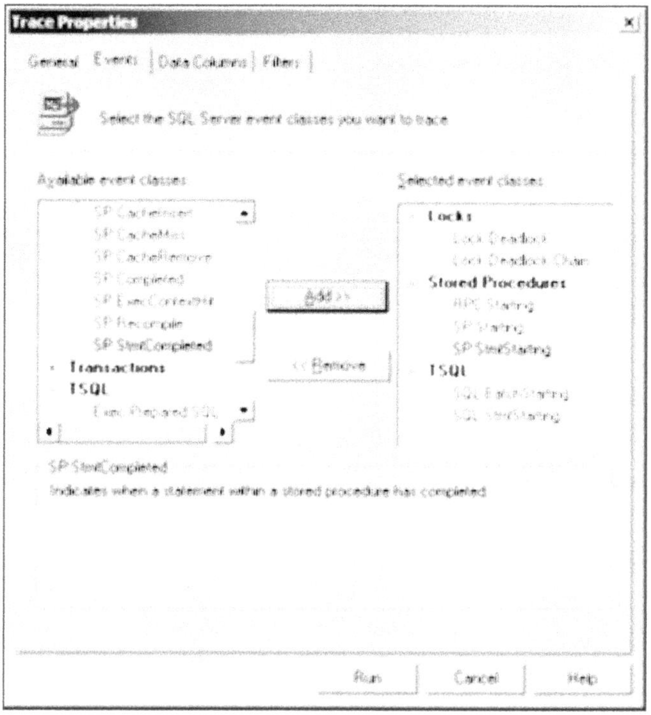


- ❑ Select the Data Columns tab. Click the Remove button to remove fields you do not need (such as duration, CPU, Reads, Writes), and add data columns you do need by selecting them in the left pane and clicking the Add button. Select only the fields that you will be interested in using, as each field adds to the size of the resulting trace file. Use the Up and Down buttons to rearrange the order of columns in your output:

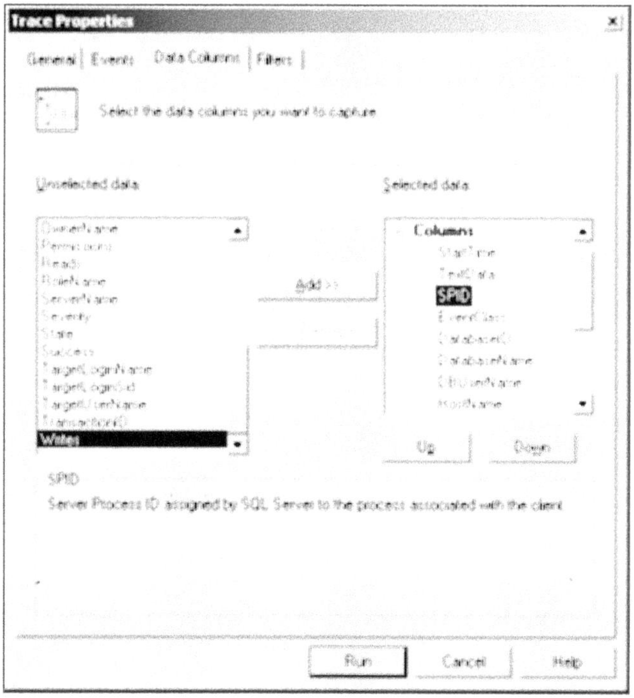

- Click the **Filters** tab. If you have a tremendous amount of activity on your server, you may want to filter database ID, login, or host name. You can also exclude system IDs by clicking the **Exclude system IDs** checkbox. Be careful not to filter out any activities that may be causing the deadlocking:

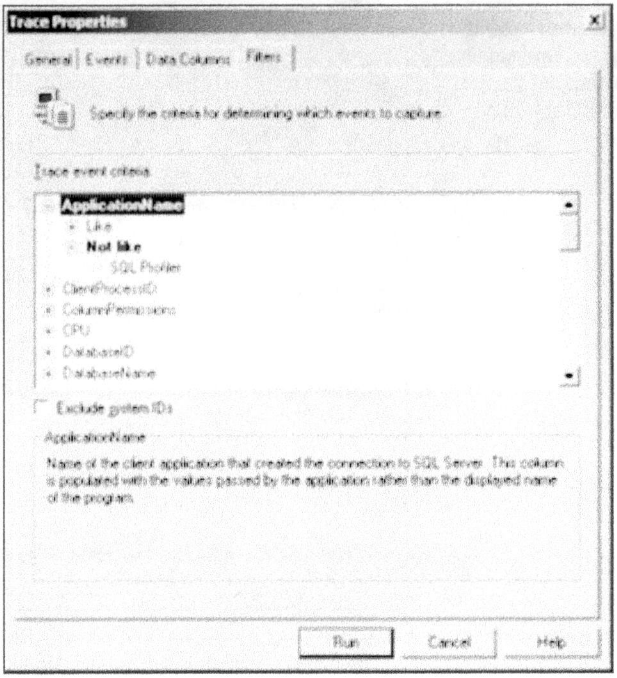


- Click the **Run** button to begin.

Once a deadlock occurs, you can track the order of events. Here is an example of trace output:

| StartTime | TextData | SPID | EventClass |
|---|---|---|---|
| 2002-07-18 15:18... | | | TraceStart |
| 2002-07-18 15:18... | SET TRANSACTION ISOLATION LEVEL SER... | 51 | SQL:BatchStarting |
| 2002-07-18 15:18... | SET TRANSACTION ISOLATION LEVEL SER... | 51 | SQL:StmtStarting |
| 2002-07-18 15:18... | BEGIN TRAN | 51 | SQL:StmtStarting |
| 2002-07-18 15:18... | SELECT * FROM FactoryParts WHERE pa... | 51 | SQL:StmtStarting |
| 2002-07-18 15:18... | WAITFOR DELAY '00:00:05' | 51 | SQL:StmtStarting |
| 2002-07-18 15:18... | SET TRANSACTION ISOLATION LEVEL SER... | 54 | SQL:BatchStarting |
| 2002-07-18 15:18... | SET TRANSACTION ISOLATION LEVEL SER... | 54 | SQL:StmtStarting |
| 2002-07-18 15:18... | BEGIN TRAN | 54 | SQL:StmtStarting |
| 2002-07-18 15:18... | SELECT * FROM FactoryParts WHERE pa... | 54 | SQL:StmtStarting |
| 2002-07-18 15:18... | WAITFOR DELAY '00:00:05' | 54 | SQL:StmtStarting |
| 2002-07-18 15:18... | UPDATE FactoryParts SET vendor_id=... | 51 | SQL:StmtStarting |
| 2002-07-18 15:18... | UPDATE FactoryParts SET vendor_id=... | 54 | SQL:StmtStarting |
| 2002-07-18 15:18... | Deadlock Chain SPID = 51 | 4 | Lock:Deadlock Chain |
| 2002-07-18 15:18... | Deadlock Chain SPID = 54 | 4 | Lock:Deadlock Chain |
| 2002-07-18 15:18... | | 54 | Lock:Deadlock |
| 2002-07-18 15:18... | COMMIT TRAN | 51 | SQL:StmtStarting |

Notice the last few rows showing the deadlock chain – designating SPIDs 51 and 54 as members of the deadlock:

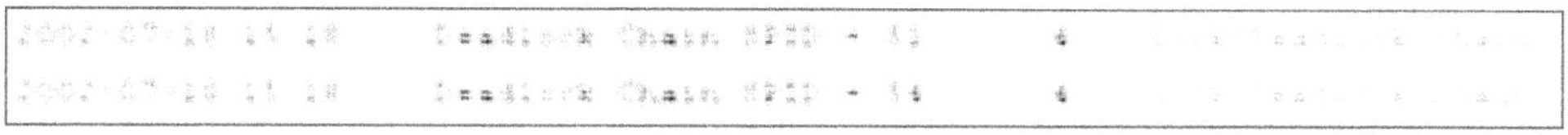

Next notice the Lock:Deadlock event, with a SPID of 54, meaning this was the deadlock victim:

If you look at the last SQL:StmtStarting event prior to the deadlock for SPID 54, you will see:

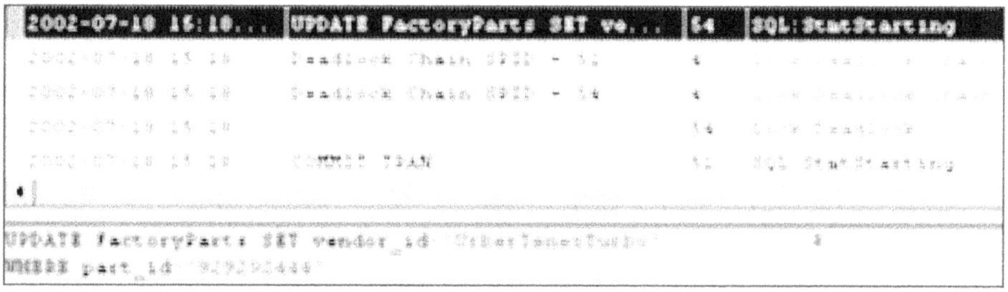


The lower gray pane will show the entire query (no 255 character limitation), designating the part of the statement that became a deadlock victim.

From here you can troubleshoot the application calls (see the next section for tips).

If you would like to save this trace file:

- In the File menu, select Save As | Trace File to save as a file.
- In the Save As window, select the file name and location of your `.trc` file. Select the Save button:

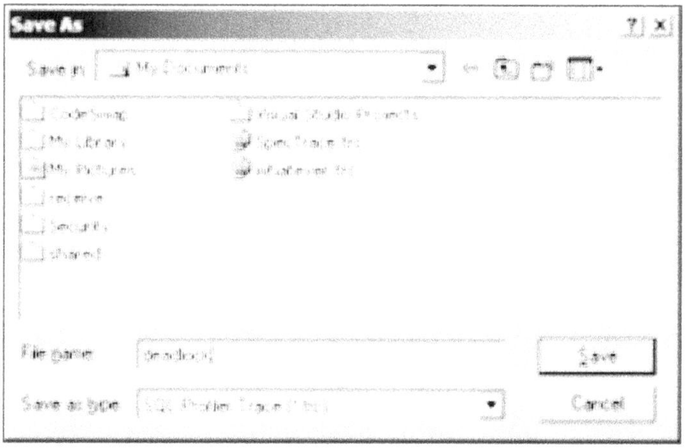

To save the trace to a table:

- ❑ Select File | Save As | Trace Table.
- ❑ Select the server and connection login. Select OK.
- ❑ Select the database and type in or select the destination table to which you wish to save the trace file. Select OK:

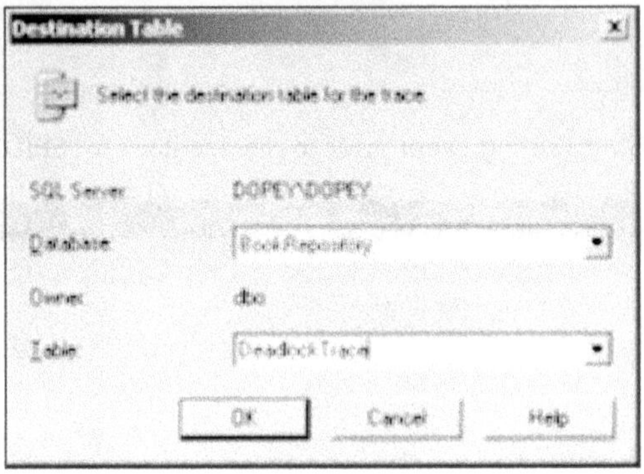


To save the template (thus saving your events, filters, and data columns so you can re-use the settings in future traces):

- ❑ Select File | Save As | Trace Template.
- ❑ Name your template something indicative of what it traces, such as Deadlock Detection. Select Save when finished:

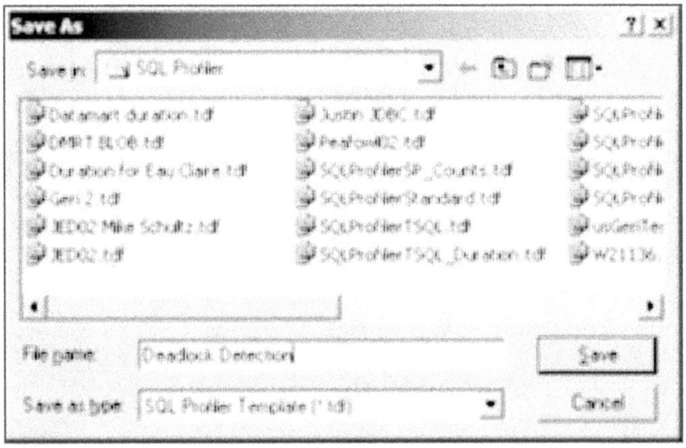


- ❑ You will see the following dialog box:

To re-use your template when creating a new trace, select it from the Template Name drop-down:

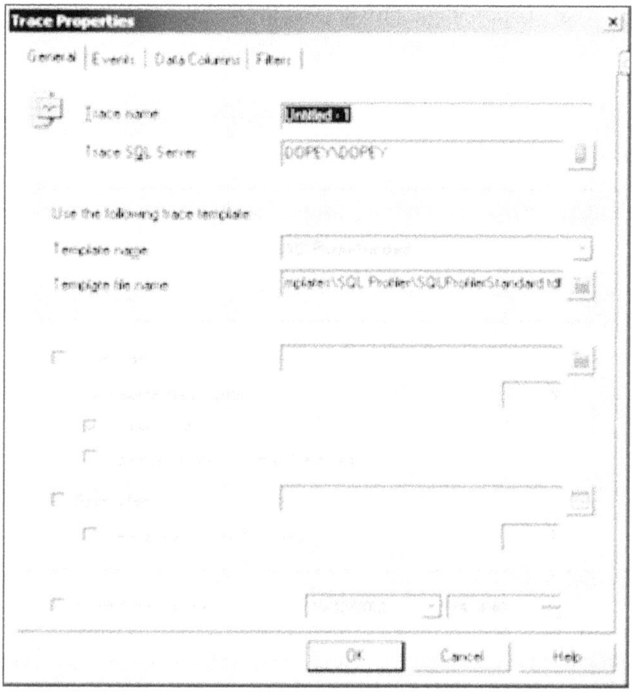

# Troubleshooting Blocking and Deadlocking Problems

We will now bring together all the technologies we have discussed in the three following deadlock troubleshooting scenarios.

## Scenario 1: Out of Order Updates

In this first scenario, you notice deadlock error messages appearing in the SQL log throughout the day. You decide to turn on trace flags 1204, 3605, and -1 to get more detail about which process ends up being the deadlock victim, and which one survives (remember that beginning with SQL Server 2000 Service Pack 3, the trace flag 3605 is no longer necessary). A deadlock occurs again, and this time you have more detailed information (because of the trace flags).

You see in the `INPUTBUFFER` output in the SQL Log that the deadlock victim is a stored procedure call (execution) that updates the `Orders` and `OrderDetails` tables. The 'winner' is a different stored procedure, which updates the `OrderDetails`, and then `Orders` tables.

You check the stored procedures, and see that they are both updating the same tables, but in a different order. You decide to redesign the stored procedures to update the tables in the same order.

# Scenario 2: Conflicting Updates During Busy Periods

During the evening, you download several million rows of data to an `Orders` table. Later, you notice that deadlocks are appearing in your SQL log. You decide to enable the trace flags 1204, 3605, and -1. You also decide to turn on SQL Profiler to trace the events as they occur, since they seem to occur predictably (every evening).

When the deadlocks occur again, you see that the victim is sometimes an `UPDATE` statement, and sometimes a `SELECT` statement. You have the exact time that these deadlocks occurred in the SQL error log, so you check the SQL Profiler for the activity that was running around this time.

You see that certain users are running reports against the data as it is being loaded. To reduce contention and deadlocking, you create a read-only copy of the table for reporting purposes, using transactional replication (see Chapter 8). This allows the data load to proceed without interruption, and reporting against the data to continue.

# Scenario 3: JDBC Driver Settings

You have a new Web application running against your SQL Server instance. The database is very small, but has many users. The Web application is Java-based, and uses the Microsoft JDBC driver to connect.

As activity increases, you sometimes see long-term blocking. Every so often you see deadlocking. You turn on the trace flags and SQL Profiler.

The deadlock victims vary, sometimes being `INSERT` statements, sometimes `UPDATE` statements, and sometimes `SELECT` statements. You notice that the long-term blocking almost always precedes the deadlocks, and you ask the Java developer why this is happening.

She tells you that the user connections and updates should be taking no longer than 1 second. After much digging, she finds out that the autocommit function of her JDBC call is not enabled. The autocommit JDBC setting determines whether or not a transaction is explicitly committed. If `FALSE`, transactions that are not explicitly committed or rolled back may hold on to resources until the connection is closed.

As you have seen, SQL Server tools were insufficient to solve this problem. Sometimes you must look at the entire picture, asking other people questions about how the application is designed.

# Tips for Avoiding and Minimizing Deadlocks

The following tips will help you to avoid or minimize deadlocks in your database:

- Keep transaction time short.
- Minimize resources locked.
- Update your tables in the same order.
- If you have relatively static data, or data that is loaded only periodically, consider placing your database into a read-only state. This removes the locking problem entirely.
- Watch SQL Server's lock escalation behavior. If you see frequent escalations from row or page locks to table locks, consider adding locking hints to force either finer or coarser grain locks. SQL Profiler has the Lock:Escalation event to help you keep an eye on this.
- If the data is static or not updated frequently, consider using the `NOLOCK` hint, which places no locks on the resource. Do not use this if you need the data for mission-critical and accuracy-critical tasks.
- Do not allow user input during an open transaction. Also, make sure to pull data needed for the transaction `BEFORE` the transaction begins.

- Make sure to program mission-critical processes to restart or redo any transactions that were chosen as deadlock victims. This should be done only if you cannot solve the deadlocking problem.
- Use the `UPDLOCK` hint to prevent shared locks on data you are likely, but not certain, to update. This is better than an exclusive lock, as users can still read the data, but cannot put a lock on the data and risk a deadlock situation.
- SQL Server 2000 excels at set processing rather than cursor processing. Set processing works with blocks of rows at the same time, whereas cursor processing works with one row at a time. Transact-SQL cursors have a well-deserved reputation for causing blocking and performance issues. The reason is that, depending on the cursor fetch option, a cursor can hold many locks while it runs a row-by-row processing routine.
- The lower the isolation level you are able to use, the better.
- Using **bound connections** allows two or more connections to act as if they are part of the same connection, allowing them to update resources held by one another.
- Normalized databases are suggested for transaction processing environments. Databases that are normalized well by design help improve concurrency and reduce blocking and deadlocking, although a bad query can still be enough to cause major blocking or deadlocking problems.

# 6

# Backup, Recovery, and Maintenance

This chapter investigates the core of a DBA's job. The top priority of a database administrator is to have a database recovery plan for all of your SQL Server installations; not only should you have a plan, you should be able to *carry it out*. This means knowing the recovery process inside and out, and testing the plan. This chapter will review considerations for generating a recovery plan, and consider the SQL Server tools and methods used to help you *implement* your plan. Database commands, tools, and maintenance tasks are also reviewed. You will learn how to check the integrity of your database, rebuild indexes, and set up database maintenance plans.

## Creating a Backup and Recovery Plan

Before generating a database recovery plan, ask yourself the following questions:

- What data is important? Is this a 'crash and burn' server or a mission-critical order center?

  Business-critical databases must be backed up. If you cannot afford to lose or reproduce the data, or would incur a large cost to re-enter it, you should be performing backups. We will review each backup type available for SQL Server in this chapter.

  In addition to this, backups should be archived to another server on the network or to a tape. If your server is destroyed, you need backups from an off-site source. There are archive services that can be used to store your tape backups.

- How much data can you afford to lose? Can you lose a day's worth of work? An hour? None at all?

  Once you have identified what databases should be backed up, you should next decide the frequency and type of backups. If you can afford to lose 24 hours of data, then, depending on the database size, a full database backup may be acceptable. If you cannot lose more than 30 minutes of updates, then you should be running transaction log backups every 30 minutes. If you absolutely cannot lose any data, then you should investigate such solutions as log shipping, RAID mirroring, or vendor solutions like storage area networks (SAN) coupled with third-party split mirror software.

- ❑ What is the maximum downtime for your server and databases? Aside from what data can be lost once you are down, how much time do you have to get everything up and running?

  Once the server is down, how much time do you have to bring it back up? If the answer is 'very little', you need to investigate how long it would take to recover your databases from a backup. If a restore operation for one database takes eight hours, you need to investigate other options. Using log shipping from one server to a remote server will allow you to recover within minutes. Replication is also a viable option for transporting a copy of a database to another database on the same, or different, server. Depending on the network throughput capabilities and hardware, data changes to the publication database can be moved to the subscriber within seconds. Failover clustering will help you with your server availability, but not necessarily in the event of a database failure (corruption or file loss); and availability may suffer if a database restoration takes several hours.

  If your hardware goes bad, you must know where to get new equipment and how long it will take you to replace your defunct machines. Do you have replacement memory, disks for arrays, and network cards? Are they the right kind for your database servers?

Your strategy should flow from the answers to these questions. You have many tools at your disposal, ranging from no cost to very high cost. We will be reviewing each question and possible solution in this chapter.

# Checklist... When Problems Occur...

Disaster recovery is a rather large topic, so we will focus on disaster recovery at the database-server level. Whether you are the only technical contact in your business or part of a team of hundreds, as DBA you should know:

- ❑ Who in the organization needs to be involved when there is a hardware or server failure?
- ❑ Who on the application side needs to be contacted? Do you have a list of application contacts for the databases? Who will contact your user base? If you have a 'warm standby' server (one that is available to use in the event of a hardware failure on the original server), which people need to change the settings to point to a new server (property files, code, DSN names, and so on)?
- ❑ Do you have a support plan with your hardware and server vendors? What are the phone and account numbers for your company? If you have no support, what budget do you have to pay for on-phone or on-site support?
- ❑ Do you have spare parts or an available spare server?
- ❑ Do you have a paging distribution list? An e-mail distribution list? A list of key contact phone numbers? A list of vendor hotlines?
- ❑ If your site is down, do you have an alternative site? Do you have a documented process for moving to this alternate site?

# Checklist... If You Have to Rebuild Your Server...

- ❑ Who is your host master or domain administrator? Are they available at 3 in the morning? If you have to create a server from scratch and give it the same server name, you will need this person to be available.

- Where are your backups kept? When was the last good backup? Were you using full, transaction log, differential, or offline backups?
- Were there any other applications installed or configured on this server?
- Was the operating system backed up?
- What was the drive configuration (size and drive letters, disk type) and operating system version, what service packs or third-party software were installed?
- Regarding reinstalling SQL Server, what version were you running? What service packs or security patches were installed? What was your SQL Server collation? Where was SQL Server installed (what drive), where were the data and log files placed?
- What jobs did you have running under the SQL Server Agent? Do you have them scripted somewhere? Do you use DTS packages? If so, are they saved anywhere else? (DTS packages can be saved as files outside SQL Server) Are the DTS packages scheduled to run via jobs?
- Do you have a warm standby or another server to which to restore databases? Does the application have a way to point to this new server?
- Where are your backups located? Can you run a last transaction log backup on the database and recover to a point prior to the failure?
- Where are your installation CDs and CD keys kept?
- Where will you keep the answers to these questions? (At the very least, keep a copy by your server, on the network, and off-site.)

# Database Backup Methods

You have five backup methods available with SQL Server 2000.

## Full Backups

A full backup copies your entire database; a full backup allows you to restore your entire database from the latest full backup. This is the most time-consuming backup option. Since the database is online when it is backed up, the backup includes changes and log file entries from the point the backup began to the point that it is completed.

## Transaction Log Backups

Transaction log backups back up the transaction log from the previous full backup or transaction log backup. When the backup completes, SQL Server truncates the inactive portion of the log (the virtual log files, or VLFs, that are no longer part of an active transaction or transactions).

Transaction log backups have low resource overhead and can be run frequently. The size of the transaction log backup depends on the level of activity and whether or not you are using a full or bulk-logged recovery model. The `SIMPLE` recovery model does not allow transaction log backups (except if issuing a `TRUNCATE_ONLY` statement, shown in *How to...* 6.4). Transaction log backups allow point-in-time and transaction mark recovery.

To recover the database using transaction logs, you must first restore from the full database backup and all transaction log backups that have occurred from that point. Transaction logs are cumulative, meaning each backup is part of a sequential line of transaction log backups. You cannot, for example, restore a full database backup and the third transaction log backup, skipping the first two transaction log backups. A database also should not be **recovered** (brought online and available for use), until you have finished applying ALL the transaction logs that you wish to apply. Recovery is handled by the `RECOVERY` and `NORECOVERY` clauses of the `RESTORE` command, reviewed later in the chapter.

## Backup Sequence

| Time | Backup |
|---|---|
| 8am | Full backup |
| 10am | Tran log backup |
| 1pm | Tran log backup |

## Incorrect RESTORE Sequence

| Restore |
|---|
| Full backup from 8am |
| Tran log backup from 1pm |

## Correct RESTORE Sequence

| Restore |
|---|
| Full backup from 8am |
| Tran log backup from 10am |
| Tran log backup from 1pm |

If using differential backups, you must restore the full backup, differential backup, and **then** transaction log backups run after the differential backup.

## Backup Sequence

| Time | Backup |
|---|---|
| 8am | Full backup |
| 9am | Differential backup |
| 10am | Tran log backup |
| 1pm | Tran log backup |

## Correct RESTORE Sequence

| Restore |
|---|
| Full backup from 8am |
| Differential backup from 9am |
| Tran log backup from 10am |
| Tran log backup from 1pm |

## Differential Backups

Differential backups copy all changed pages since the last full backup. They are:

- Smaller than full database backups
- Faster in backup time then full backups
- Slower in total restore time (full plus differential restore)

Differential backups, unlike transaction log backups, are self-contained and only require the latest full backup from which to restore. For example, if you run a full backup at 8am, a differential backup at 10am, and an additional differential backup at 1pm, this 1pm differential backup will include all changes since 8am:

| Time | Backup |
|---|---|
| 8am | Full backup |
| 10am | Differential backup (changes from 8am – 10am) |
| 1pm | Differential backup (changes from 8am – 1pm) |

Differential backups work side-by-side with transaction log backups.

Transaction log backups cannot be restored until any full and differential backups have first been restored. Since the database is online when it is being backed up, the backup includes changes and log file entries from the point the backup began to its completion.

## Offline Backups

Offline backups take your database offline, either by shutting down the SQL Server service or detaching the database. Once the database files are no longer in use, you may:

- Copy them to a remote server
- Use a third-party backup utility
- Back up using Window 2000's backup tool

Offline backups are not always the best option for most databases, as they do not make the database highly available. Caching for stored procedures and prepared statements also suffers, as the database has to begin from scratch when it is reattached or SQL Server is restarted. This is not an option you should consider for most databases.

## Snapshot Backups

SQL Server 2000 Enterprise Edition supports **snapshot backups**, also called **split mirroring**. Third-party hardware and software must be purchased; but for very large databases, this may be your best backup solution. At best, backups and restores of a very large database can be performed in seconds; this is achieved by splitting a mirrored set of disks, or producing a copy of a disk block as it is written while keeping the original.

## Recovery Models

Beginning with SQL Server 2000, Microsoft introduced the concept of recovery models. Prior to SQL Server 2000, such options were controlled by separate database options. In essence, the recovery model setting of your database determines the amount of logging that occurs on your transaction log. The recovery models are as follows:

- Full
- Bulk-logged
- Simple

## Full

This model allows full, differential, and transaction log backups. All operations are fully logged; this means that your transaction log can quickly grow large during bulk loading, `SELECT INTO`, and `CREATE INDEX` operations. The trade-off is that you can recover from a transaction log to a specific point in time or transaction mark (more on this later).

## Bulk-Logged

This model allows full, differential, and transaction log backups. The transaction log backups, however, will include minimal logging for:

- Bulk processes
- `SELECT INTO`
- `CREATE INDEX`
- Text/image operations

This model is similar to SQL Server 7.0's `select into/bulkcopy` database option. This minimal logging will help keep your transaction log at a reasonable size, but the trade-off is inability to restore a transaction log using point-in-time recovery. Also, if the data file is damaged, minimally logged operations will need to be redone; this is because in bulk-logged mode, a transaction log backup requires access to the database data files. If SQL Server cannot reach the corrupted files, the database cannot be backed up.

## SIMPLE

This recovery model allows for full and differential backups. It does not allow transaction log backups, unless you are issuing a `TRUNCATE_ONLY` backup. The `SIMPLE` model is equivalent to the `trunc log on checkpoint` database option in SQL Server 7.0 and prior versions. This model does not log:

- Bulk load operations
- `SELECT INTO` operation
- `CREATE INDEX`
- Text/image operations

The advantage is that log space used is kept to a minimum. The disadvantage is you can only recover from a full or differential backup.

# Understanding the Transaction Log

Before reviewing how to back up databases, let's take a quick detour and review the architecture of the transaction log.

A SQL Server database requires at least one data file and one transaction log file. Even if you are using the `SIMPLE` recovery model, you need a transaction log, which is used to recover the database. SQL Server writes the following activity to the database transaction log:

- The start and end of each transaction in the database. These are written sequentially.
- Images of data **before** and **after** a modification.
- Every extent (eight 8KB pages) allocation or de-allocation.
- `CREATE TABLE`, `CREATE INDEX` (if full or bulk-logged recovery model), `DROP TABLE`, and `DROP INDEX`.
- If full recovery model, `SELECT INTO`, bcp operations, text or image modifications.
- If bulk-logged recovery model, limited logging of `SELECT INTO`, bcp operations, text or image modifications.

SQL Server writes this information to the transaction log in sequential order. Data modifications are written to the physical disk periodically, based on **checkpoint** operations (reviewed in the next section). Transaction logs allow for consistent recovery of a database. When SQL Server starts up (either after a crash or a regular shutdown), all databases go through the recovery process. SQL Server analyzes the transaction log for committed and uncommitted transactions in each database. Committed transactions not yet written to disk are then written; uncommitted transactions (no `COMMIT` or `ROLLBACK`) are rolled back.

In versions prior to SQL Server 7.0, the transaction log was actually a table stored on a segment in a log device (physical file). Beginning with SQL Server 7.0, the transaction log is now a sequential file and not a table. The transaction log can be made up of several files; however, it will be treated logically as one sequential file.

The physical log file or files are actually made up of smaller segments, called virtual log files, or VLFs. These virtual log files are created when the transaction log is initially created, and a new VLF is created each time the transaction log physically expands.

Too many VLFs can slow down your database recovery, so make sure your automatic file growth setting for the transaction log is not too small. Try to scale your transaction log close to the final size needed, with a relatively large growth increment value. See Chapter 3 for a review of transaction log size estimates (when you are unsure of the initial size).

As we reviewed in the `DBCC SHRINKFILE` section of Chapter 3, the physical transaction log file should not be confused with the **logical** or **active** portion of the transaction log file. Whenever log records are truncated from the log file, the logical beginning of the log file begins at this truncation end point. When you initially create a log file, the active portion starts at the physical beginning of the file. As the transaction log is backed up, the logical portion of the transaction log gets reset to the end of the log truncation point.

The logical transaction log can actually wrap around the physical transaction log, for example:

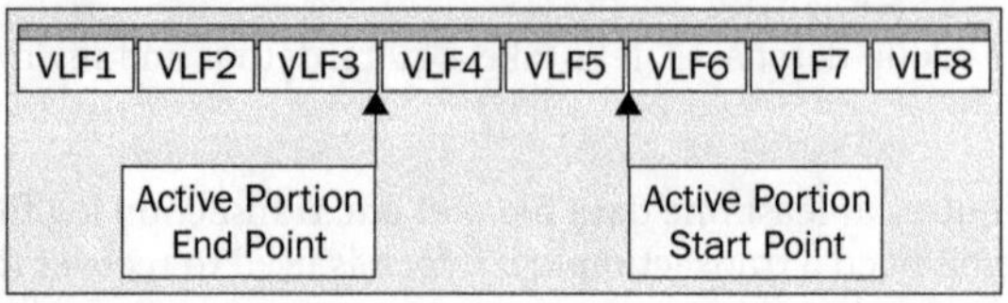


If the logical end of the file reaches the logical beginning of the file, your transaction log will fill up (if your transaction log isn't set to auto expand, or no physical disk space remains).

You can view the number of virtual log files in your physical transaction log or logs by running `DBCC LOGINFO`. This `DBCC` command will also show you what VLFs are active. Below is an example of the `DBCC LOGINFO` output. Each row signifies a VLF, and those rows with a `Status` column of 2 indicate the active portion of the transaction log:

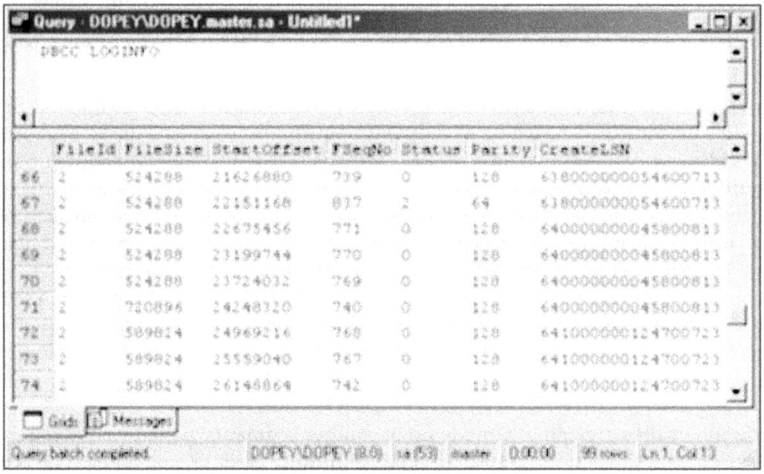


| | FileId | FileSize | StartOffset | FSeqNo | Status | Parity | CreateLSN |
|---|---|---|---|---|---|---|---|
| 66 | 2 | 524288 | 21626880 | 739 | 0 | 128 | 630000000054600713 |
| 67 | 2 | 524288 | 22151168 | 817 | 2 | 64 | 630000000054600713 |
| 68 | 2 | 524288 | 22675456 | 771 | 0 | 128 | 640000000045800813 |
| 69 | 2 | 524288 | 23199744 | 770 | 0 | 128 | 640000000045800813 |
| 70 | 2 | 524288 | 23724032 | 769 | 0 | 128 | 640000000045800813 |
| 71 | 2 | 720896 | 24248320 | 740 | 0 | 128 | 640000000045800813 |
| 72 | 2 | 589824 | 24969216 | 768 | 0 | 128 | 641000000124700723 |
| 73 | 2 | 589824 | 25559040 | 767 | 0 | 128 | 641000000124700723 |
| 74 | 2 | 589824 | 26148864 | 742 | 0 | 128 | 641000000124700723 |

Backing up the transaction log truncates the log records that are not part of the active portion of the log. VLFs are truncated prior to the VLF containing the oldest outstanding transaction. To view the oldest outstanding transaction for your database, you can run `DBCC OPENTRAN` for the current database context.

The logical log (as opposed to the physical) contains transactions begun since the last checkpoint, or had active transactions during the prior checkpoint. This leads us to the topic of checkpoints...

# Checkpoints

Checkpoints:

- Minimize the amount of time a database takes to recover.
- Write dirty buffer pages (modified data pages) to the physical disk.
- Write a list to the transaction log identifying active transactions that were running during the checkpoint.
- Write a 'start of checkpoint' and 'end of checkpoint' record to the transaction log.

The time your database takes to recover depends on the frequency of checkpoints in the database and the amount of transaction activity since the last checkpoint.

Checkpoints run under the following circumstances:

- Based on the value set for the recovery interval server setting.
- Issued after an `ALTER DATABASE` command is executed.
- Issued after a `CHECKPOINT` command is executed.
- When SQL Server is shutdown (manually, not crashed).
- If the database is in `SIMPLE` mode and the log becomes 70% full.
- If the database is in `SIMPLE` mode and both `BACKUP LOG` with `TRUNCATE_ONLY` is issued, and a nonlogged operation is performed in the database.

You may see a negative performance impact if checkpoints are run too frequently, resulting in heavy I/O activity. Configure your recovery interval appropriately, based on your database activity. If you are concerned that you may have an I/O bottleneck, use Performance Monitor's PhysicalDisk: Avg. Disk Queue Length counter, to see whether read or write requests are being queued excessively. Excessive values are those that exceed 2 times the number of physical disks making up the partition.

# 6.1 How to... Perform Full, Differential, File, Filegroup, and Transaction Log Backups with Enterprise Manager

Microsoft makes database backups a breeze with the Enterprise Manager utility; however, before we review the Enterprise Manager way, let's state immediately that you should know the hard and the easy way.

The 'hard way' (using Transact-SQL `BACKUP` syntax) isn't so hard if you keep brushed up on the syntax. As you step through the process of backing up your database using Enterprise Manager, remember that there may be a day you need to back up or restore a database using OSQL or Query Analyzer. Do not depend 100% on Enterprise Manager. Brushing up on Transact-SQL syntax during a crisis is quite unpleasant, so learn both methods.

To back up your database through Enterprise Manager:

- Expand the server group and server registration
- Expand the Databases folder
- Click the database you wish to back up
- Go to the Tools menu and select Backup Database (or right click the database, and select All Tasks, and Backup Database)...
- In the SQL Server Backup dialog box, you will see the following fields:
    - Database
      Name of database to back up. If you clicked the wrong database initially in Enterprise Manager, you can select a different database to back up from the dropdown menu.
    - Name
      Logical name of your backup set.

- ❑ Description
  Free-text description of your backup.
- ❑ Backup
  - ❑ Database – complete
    Performs a full database backup.
  - ❑ Database – differential
    Performs a differential backup.
  - ❑ Transaction log
    Performs a transaction log backup.
  - ❑ File and filegroup
    Performs a file or filegroup backup.

❑ Destination
Defined device, disk directory and file, or tape destination for the backup.

❑ Overwrite

- ❑ Append to media
  Appends backup to existing destination media.
- ❑ Overwrite existing media
  Overwrites all backups with existing backup on destination media.

❑ Schedule
Schedules define backup as a job

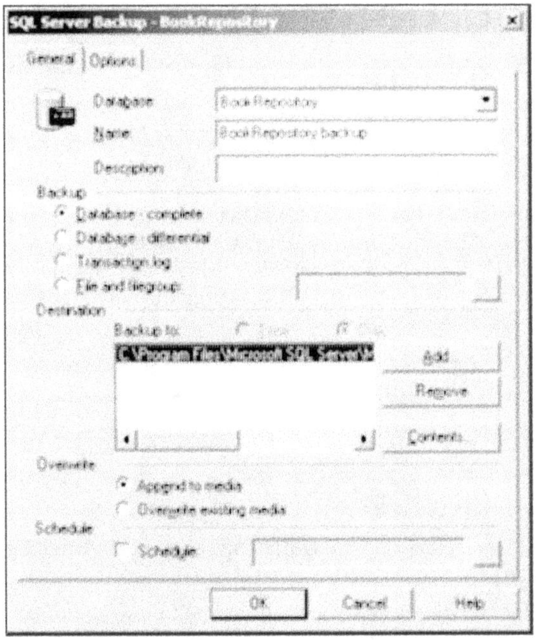


❑ To change the existing destination, select the Remove button. To review the contents of the current backup destination, select the Contents button. Backup media contents with the date of operation will be shown. Select Close when you have finished.

❑ Select the Add button to add one or more backup destinations (one backup with multiple backup destinations is called a **striped** backup):

Select either a file name or a backup device.

If you select the file name, select the ellipsis button to select a directory and file name. You can select an existing device or type in a new name in the File name text box. Select OK when finished.

If you are using a backup device, select an existing device or create a new one by selecting New Backup Device:

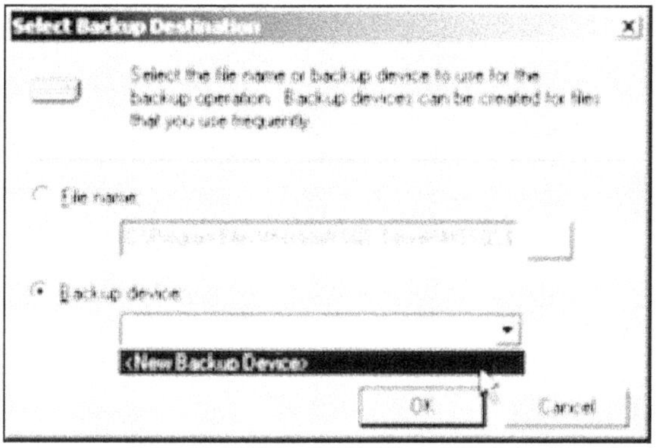


If you are creating a new backup device, select a logical device name and the physical file location:

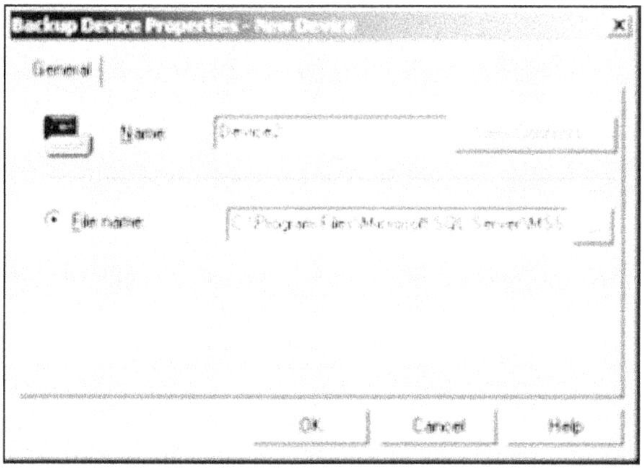


Select OK when finished.

Select OK at the Select Backup Destination dialog box.

- At the main dialog, select the Options tab. You will see the following settings:
    - Verify backup upon completion
      Checks integrity after completion.
    - Eject tape after backup
      Eject the backup media tape after backup completion.
    - Remove inactive entries from transaction log
      Truncates inactive entries from the transaction log after backup completion.
    - Media set name
      Name of media set that is verified in order for the media to be overwritten.

- Backup set will expire
  Conditions for backup expiration; meaning when the backup can overwrite existing backups on the media set.
  - After X days: backup expires after set number of days.
  - On MM/DD/YYYY: backup expires on a specific day.
- Initialize and label media
  A Microsoft Tape Format header is written to the beginning of the media. This erases all tape contents and previous media header information.
- Media set name
  Media name as part of Microsoft Tape Format header.
- Media set description
  Media description as part of the Microsoft Tape Format header.

When finished selecting options, select OK to begin the backup, or return to the General tab and select the checkbox for Schedule, to create a job and schedule the backup for another time.

The scheduling window:

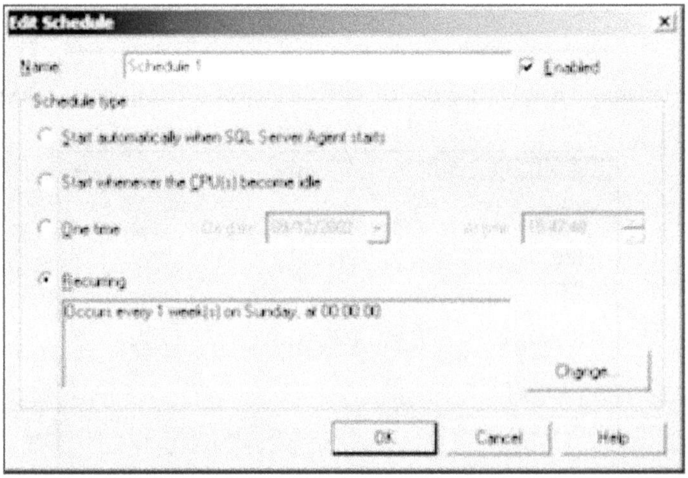


Total backup time depends on the size of the database. You will see a progress bar during the backup, and will be informed if it is successful.

# 6.2 How to... Create a Named Backup Device

Backup devices make your job a little easier by using a logical name in your Transact-SQL code in place of a file and path name.

You can also create a backup device with Enterprise Manager or Transact-SQL.

To create a backup device in Enterprise Manager:

- Expand the server group and server registration.
- Expand the Management folder.
- Right-click the Backup icon and select New Backup Device....

- ❑ In the Backup Device dialog box, select the device name and tape drive or file name. Select OK when finished.
- ❑ You will then see your new device in the right-hand pane of Enterprise Manager. This can be used in your Backup in Enterprise Manager, or in your Transact-SQL BACKUP command:

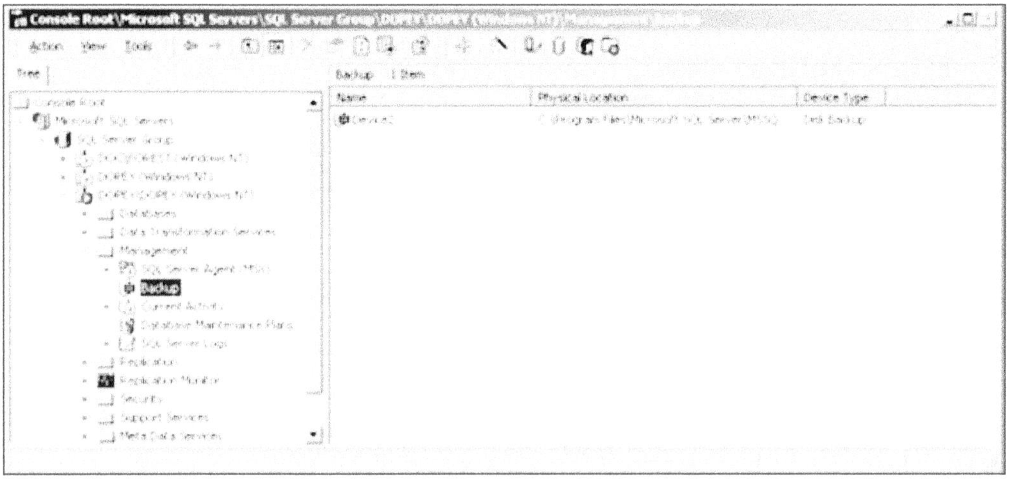


To create a new device using Transact-SQL, in Query Analyzer, you can use the following command:

```
sp_addumpdevice [ @devtype = ] 'device_type' ,
                [ @logicalname = ] 'logical_name' ,
                [ @physicalname = ] 'physical_name'
                [ , { [ @cntrltype = ] controller_type
                    | [ @devstatus = ] 'device_status'}
                ]
```

| Parameter | Description |
|---|---|
| Device_type | For the device type you can specify disk, pipe, or tape. |
| logical_name | Name of the backup device used in the BACKUP and RESTORE syntax. |
| physical_name | Operating system file name, universal naming convention (UNC) name, or tape path. |
| controller_type | This is **not** a required field: 2 = disk, 5 = tape, 6 = pipe. |
| device_status | This option determines whether ANSI tape labels are read (noskip) or ignored (skip) prior to usage. noskip is the default for type tape. Either this option or controller_type can be specified, but not both. |

Example of adding a regular physical disk device:

```
USE master
EXEC sp_addumpdevice 'disk', 'BookRepository_Backups', 'c:\backups\bookrepo.bak'
```

Adding a tape device:

```
USE master
EXEC sp_addumpdevice 'tape', 'BookRepository_Backups', '\\.\tape0':
```

Referencing a share on a UNC (Universal Naming Convention) path:

```
USE master
EXEC sp_addumpdevice 'disk', 'BookRepository_Backups',
'\\DOPEY\Backups\bookrepo.bak'
```

# 6.3 How to... Perform a Full Database Backup with Transact-SQL

The syntax for performing a backup from SQL Server Books Online is as follows:

```
BACKUP DATABASE { database_name | @database_name_var }
TO < backup_device > ::=
    {
        { logical_backup_device_name | @logical_backup_device_name_var }
        |
        { DISK | TAPE } =
            { 'physical_backup_device_name' | @physical_backup_device_name_var }
[ WITH
    [ BLOCKSIZE = { blocksize | @blocksize_variable } ]
    [ [ , ] DESCRIPTION = { 'text' | @text_variable } ]
    [ [ , ] EXPIREDATE = { date | @date_var }
        | RETAINDAYS = { days | @days_var } ]
    [ [ , ] PASSWORD = { password | @password_variable } ]
    [ [ , ] FORMAT | NOFORMAT ]
    [ [ , ] { INIT | NOINIT } ]
    [ [ , ] MEDIADESCRIPTION = { 'text' | @text_variable } ]
    [ [ , ] MEDIANAME = { media_name | @media_name_variable } ]
    [ [ , ] MEDIAPASSWORD = { mediapassword | @mediapassword_variable } ]
    [ [ , ] NAME = { backup_set_name | @backup_set_name_var } ]
    [ [ , ] { NOSKIP | SKIP } ]
    [ [ , ] { NOREWIND | REWIND } ]
    [ [ , ] { NOUNLOAD | UNLOAD } ]
    [ [ , ] RESTART ]
    [ [ , ] STATS [ = percentage ] ]
]
```

| Parameter | Description |
|---|---|
| `database_name \| @database_name_var` | Database name or character string variable designating which database to back up. |
| `< backup_device > [ ,...n ]` | Logical or physical device on which to place the backup. |
| `logical_backup_device_name \| @logical_backup_device_name_var` | A logical device (created by `ap_addumpdevice`) to which to backup. Can be a logical device name or a character string data type. |

| Parameter | Description |
|---|---|
| DISK \| TAPE = 'physical_backup_device_name' \| @physical_backup_device_name_var | If not using a logical dump device, specify DISK or TAPE. You must then specify path and file name for TO DISK option, and tape volume for the TO TAPE. If the file does not exist, it will be created dynamically. |
| [ BLOCKSIZE = { blocksize \| @blocksize_variable } ] | Default blocksize is 64KB and is the limit for SQL Server. This option specifies physical block size in bytes. SQL Server will choose the appropriate block size for the device, so designating this is not necessary unless a vendor requires it. |
| DESCRIPTION = { 'text' \| @text_variable } | Free-form text describing the backup set, helping identify the contents of the backup device. |
| EXPIREDATE = { date \| @date_var } \| RETAINDAYS = { days \| @days_var } | EXPIREDATE indicates the date when the backup set expires and can be overwritten.<br><br>RETAINDAYS specifies the days before the backup media set can be overwritten. |
| PASSWORD = { password \| @password_variable } | If a password is specified, it must be supplied to restore from the backup set. |
| FORMAT \| NOFORMAT | FORMAT generates a media header to all volumes used for the backup; existing headers are overwritten. This renders a backup set unusable if a stripe exists on the device.<br><br>NOFORMAT indicates that a media header should **not** be written on all volumes. |
| INIT \| NOINIT | INIT overwrites existing backup sets, but preserves the media header. Backup sets are not overwritten if they have not expired yet, or the name set in the BACKUP statement doesn't match the name on the backup media.<br><br>NOINIT appends the backup set to the disk or tape device. NOINIT is the default option. |
| MEDIADESCRIPTION = { 'text' \| @text_variable } | Free-form text description of media set, helping identify the contents of the media. |
| MEDIANAME = { media_name \| @media_name_variable } | Name of entire backup media set, limited to 128 characters. |
| MEDIAPASSWORD = { mediapassword \| @mediapassword_variable } | If specified, password must be supplied to create a backup on the media set. |
| NAME = { backup_set_name \| @backup_set_name_var } | Name of backup set. |
| { NOSKIP \| SKIP } | SKIP does not check expiration and name verification. NOSKIP checks the date and name, and is an extra safeguard to ensure the backup is not overwritten improperly. |

*Table continued on following page*

| Parameter | Description |
|---|---|
| { NOREWIND \| REWIND } | NOREWIND prevents applications from using the tape until SQL Server issues a BACKUP or RESTORE command. Sometimes not supported by the tape device. REWIND makes SQL Server rewind the tape and release control. |
| { NOUNLOAD \| UNLOAD } | UNLOAD specifies that the tape is automatically rewound and unloaded after the backup.<br>NOUNLOAD means that the tape is not unloaded from the tape drive after backup, and can be used by other backup operations. |
| RESTART | Restarts a backup operation that has previously failed. |
| STATS [ = percentage ] | Returns feedback to the client on backup progress. Default is 10% update increments. |

We will review several examples of using the BACKUP command:

### Example 6.3.1: Backup erasing file contents

- Full database backup.
- Erasing current backup file contents.
- Updating progress of backup at the 20% mark:

```
BACKUP DATABASE BookRepository
TO DISK = N'C:\Backups\bookrepo_July24.bak'
WITH INIT, STATS = 20
```

### Example 6.3.2: Backup appending to file contents

- Full database backup.
- Backing up to two backup files (striped backup).
- Updating progress of backup at the 25% mark.
- Appending backup to the backup files, not overlaying current backup sets:

```
BACKUP DATABASE BookRepository
TO DISK = N'C:\Backups\bookrepo_dev1.bak',
   DISK =  N'C:\Backups\bookrepo_dev2.bak'
WITH NOINIT, STATS = 25
```

Notice that 'DISK =' is specified for each file in the striped backup set.

### Example 6.3.3: Backup to a disk device

- Full database backup to a disk device:

```
USE master
EXEC sp_addumpdevice 'disk', 'BookRepobackups', 'c:\backups\bookrep.bak'
GO

BACKUP DATABASE BookRepository
TO BookRepobackups
WITH NOINIT
```

# 6.4 How to... Perform a Transaction Log Backup using Transact-SQL

The following is syntax for performing a transaction log backup. Many of the key words have the exact same usage as a BACKUP DATABASE command. The new options are highlighted:

```
BACKUP LOG { database_name | @database_name_var }
{
    TO < backup_device > [ ,...n ]
    [ WITH
        [ BLOCKSIZE = { blocksize | @blocksize_variable } ]
        [ [ , ] DESCRIPTION = { 'text' | @text_variable } ]
        [ [ ,] EXPIREDATE = { date | @date_var }
            | RETAINDAYS = { days | @days_var } ]
        [ [ , ] PASSWORD = { password | @password_variable } ]
        [ [ , ] FORMAT | NOFORMAT ]
        [ [ , ] { INIT | NOINIT } ]
        [ [ , ] MEDIADESCRIPTION = { 'text' | @text_variable } ]
        [ [ , ] MEDIANAME = { media_name | @media_name_variable } ]
        [ [ , ] MEDIAPASSWORD = { mediapassword | @mediapassword_variable } ]
        [ [ , ] NAME = { backup_set_name | @backup_set_name_var } ]
        [ [ , ] NO_TRUNCATE ]
        { NO_LOG | TRUNCATE_ONLY } ]
        [ [ , ] { NORECOVERY | STANDBY = undo_file_name } ]
        [ [ , ] { NOREWIND | REWIND } ]
        [ [ , ] { NOSKIP | SKIP } ]
        [ [ , ] { NOUNLOAD | UNLOAD } ]
        [ [ , ] RESTART ]
        [ [ , ] STATS [ = percentage ] ]
    ]
}
< backup_device > ::=
    {
        { logical_backup_device_name | @logical_backup_device_name_var }
        |
        { DISK | TAPE } =
            { 'physical_backup_device_name' | @physical_backup_device_name_var }
    }
```

| Parameter | Description |
|---|---|
| NO_TRUNCATE | If the database is damaged, NO_TRUNCATE allows you to back up the transaction log without truncating the inactive portion. Do not run this on a long-term basis, as your log file size will keep expanding. |
| NO_LOG \| TRUNCATE_ONLY | These two commands are the same, and will truncate the transaction log without backing it up. Avoid running this with full or bulk-logged recovery model, as it breaks the sequential chain of transaction log backups. |

Remember that your database must be in full or bulk-logged mode to back up the transaction log; otherwise, you will see the error:

```
Server: Msg 4208, Level 16, State 1, Line 1
The statement BACKUP LOG is not allowed while the recovery model is SIMPLE. Use BACKUP
DATABASE or change the recovery model using ALTER DATABASE.
Server: Msg 3013, Level 16, State 1, Line 1
BACKUP LOG is terminating abnormally.
```

Also, one full database backup is required prior to running your initial transaction log backup; otherwise, you will see the error:

```
There is no current database backup. This log backup cannot be used to roll forward a preceding database
backup.
```

### Example 6.4.1: Backup transaction log to a file

- Backing up transaction log to one file.
- Updating progress at the 25% mark.
- Erasing existing contents of the backup file:

```
BACKUP LOG BookRepository TO
DISK = 'C:\backups\bookrepo_log.trn'
WITH INIT, STATS = 25
```

### Example 6.4.2: Backup transaction log to a disk device

- Backing up transaction log to a disk device:

```
BACKUP LOG BookRepository TO
BookRepoBackups
```

### Example 6.4.3: Backup log without truncating inactive portion

- Backing up log without truncating the inactive portion (used for emergency backups when the data file is corrupted):

```
BACKUP LOG BookRepository TO
DISK = 'C:\backups\emergencybookrepo.trn'
WITH NO_TRUNCATE
```

### Example 6.4.4: Truncate inactive portion

- Truncating the inactive portions of the transaction log.
- No physical backup file produced:

```
BACKUP LOG BookRepository
WITH TRUNCATE_ONLY
```

# 6.5 How to... Perform a Differential Backup using Transact-SQL

Differential backups have the same syntax as regular full database backups, only the `DIFFERENTIAL` keyword is included. Differential backups should be run after a full database backup. For a new database, they cannot be the initial backup method:

### Example 6.5.1: Differential backup to a file

- Differential backup to a single file.
- Appending to the file without overlaying existing backup sets.
- Updating progress at the 25% mark:

```
BACKUP DATABASE BookRepository
TO DISK = N'C:\Backups\bookrepo_July24.bak'
WITH DIFFERENTIAL, NOINIT, STATS = 25
```

### Example 6.5.2: Differential backup to a device

- Differential backup to a device.
- Overlaying any backup sets on the device:

```
BACKUP DATABASE BookRepository
TO BookRepobackups
WITH DIFFERENTIAL, INIT
```

# 6.6 How to... Backup Individual Files or Filegroups using Transact-SQL

Backing up a file or filegroup uses virtually the same syntax as a full database backup, except you use the `FILEGROUP` or `FILE` keywords. You should reserve these backup types for use on VLDBs (very large databases), or for special circumstances that require individual filegroup or file backups. If your backup window (time that you have to perform a backup) is exceeded by a full backup, you may decide to back up specific filegroups one night, and the rest of the filegroup(s) on the next night. This allows recovery in the event of lost files or filegroups. You must be using FULL or bulk-logged recovery models, as transaction log backups must be applied after restoring a file or filegroup backup:

### Example 6.6.1: Filegroup backup to a file

- Filegroup backup to a backup file:

```
BACKUP DATABASE BookRepository
FILEGROUP = 'FG2'
TO DISK = 'C:\backups\bookrepo_fg2.bak'
```

### Example 6.6.2: File backup to a file

- File backup to a backup file.
- Overlaying existing backup sets on the backup file:

```
BACKUP DATABASE BookRepository
FILE = 'BookRepo_Dat2'
TO DISK = 'C:\backups\bookrepo_fg2.bak'
WITH INIT
```

Note that the previous example uses the logical file name, which can be retrieved using:

```
EXEC sp_helpfile
```

## Tape Backups

Regarding backing up to tape, you may see the error:

```
Server: Msg 3266, Level 16, State 1, Line 1
The backup data in 'devicename' is incorrectly formatted. Backups cannot be appended, but existing
backup sets may still be usable.
Server: Msg 3013, Level 16, State 1, Line 1
BACKUP DATABASE is terminating abnormally.
```

This is due to a 'filemark' error, and basically means you must run a backup with the `FORMAT` keyword to delete or erase the device to which you are backing up. For more detail, see Knowledge Base article Q290787, *PRB: Error Message 3266 Occurs When Microsoft Tape Backup Format Cannot be Read.*

# Checklist... Backup Reminders

- ❑ Back up to your server disk drive or array first, and then to tape. Backups directly to tape are often much slower than backups to disk.
- ❑ Full backups take longer to create, but less time to restore. Transaction logs on the other hand, have the lowest overhead to create, but are also the slowest to restore. This is because transaction logs must re-run transactions, as they are applied to the database.
- ❑ Run your system database backups (`master`, `msdb` databases) after your user database backups; then your `msdb` database will have the backup history from the latest user database backups.
- ❑ Striping your backup sets can sometimes pay excellent speed dividends. Depending on the type of array to which you are backing up, network card, and network capacity, striping a database backup across multiple devices can improve backup time significantly.
- ❑ This may seem obvious, but run your tape backup **after** your system and user databases have been backed up. It isn't unusual to find that nothing is backed up on your server or your backups are always one day old. This is something you do not want to discover when disaster strikes (this is where warm-standby servers come in handy).
- ❑ Transaction logs that get too large too quickly should be backed up more frequently. The cumulative sizes of the transaction logs (whether 3 large backups over the day or 20 smalle ones over the same time period) will be the same. Your physical transaction log file sizes will be smaller if truncated frequently enough.

# 6.7 How to... Restore a Database using Enterprise Manager

To restore from a backup using Enterprise Manager:

- Expand the server group and server registration.
- Click the Databases folder.
- Select Tools | Restore Database...
- In the General tab, you have the following options:
    - Restore as database
      Sets the new database to restore or the name of an existing database over which to restore.
    - Restore:
        - Database
          Restore an entire database
        - Filegroups or files
          Restore a specific file or filegroup
        - From device
          Restore from a device
    - Show backups of database
      Shows backups of a selected database (history of backups from `msdb` database)
    - First backup to restore
      The first full backup to restore (if you selected Database as the Restore type)
    - Point in time restore
      Allows point in time recovery when restoring from a transaction log or logs:

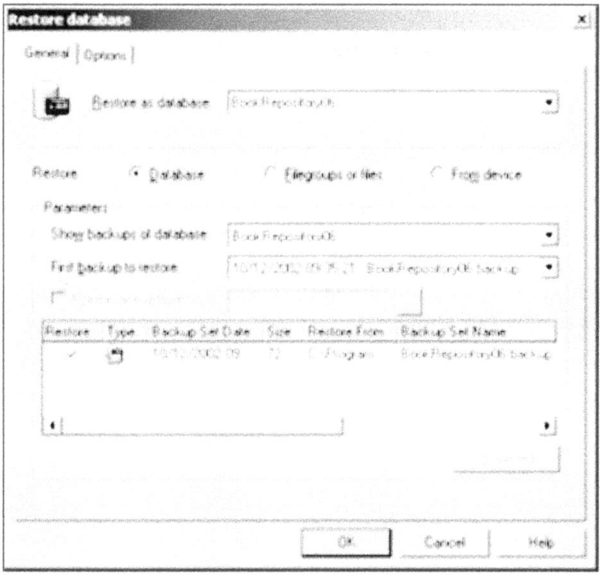

The list in the lower half of the dialog box shows backup sets for the database you specified. Select the checkbox for each backup from which you wish to restore. For example, below we select a full backup and the transaction log backup immediately after this (transaction logs must be restored sequentially):

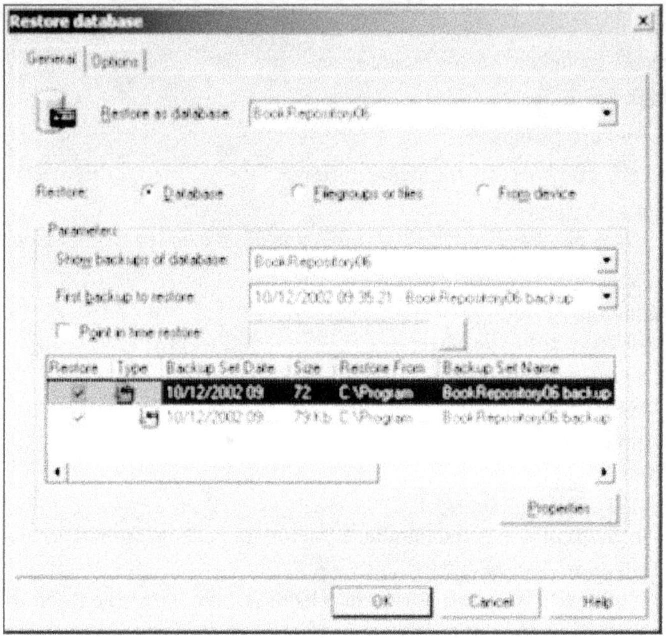


The Type column shows different icons for each backup type:

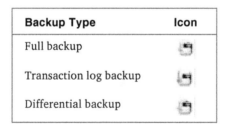

| Backup Type | Icon |
|---|---|
| Full backup | |
| Transaction log backup | |
| Differential backup | |

You can also see more information about the backup set by highlighting one of the backup set rows and clicking the Properties window.

- If you select Filegroups or files for your restore, you will see a listing of backups by file or filegroup:

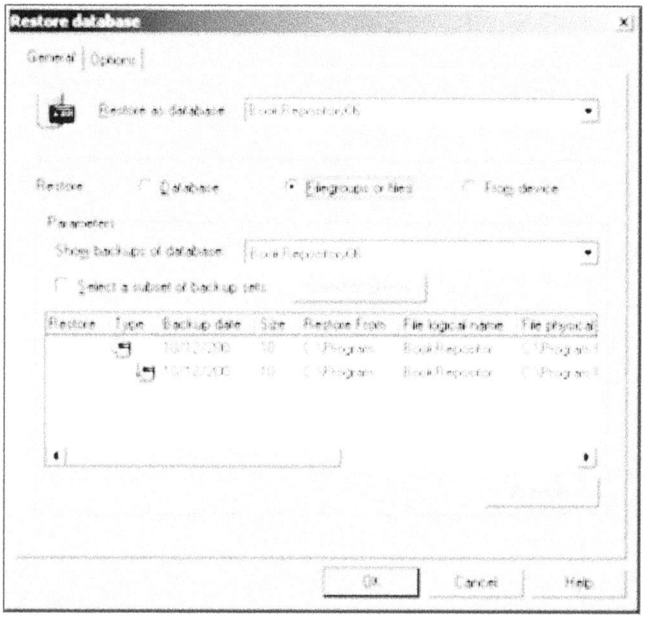


- ❑ If you select From device for your restore, you need explicitly to select your device or devices. Click the Select Devices... button. In Choose Restore Devices, select the Add... button to add new backup devices from which to restore:

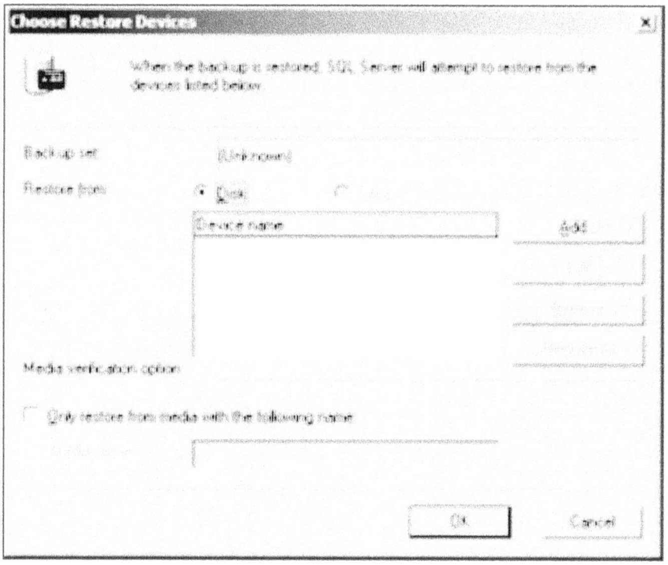

Select either a file name or device:

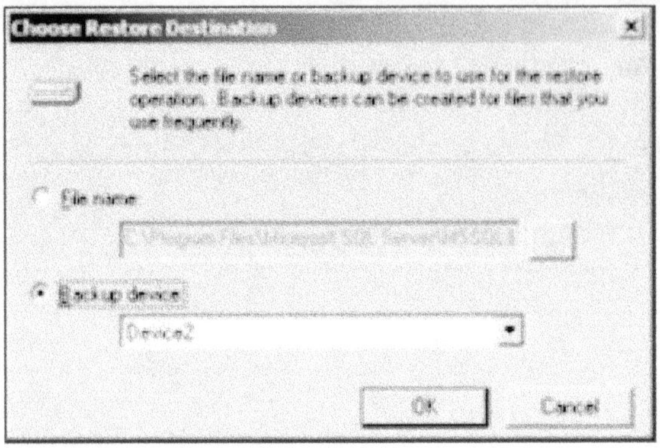

When finished, select OK, and then OK at the Choose Restore Devices.

- When finished with the restore selections on the General tab, click the Options tab. The options are as follows:
  - Eject tapes (if any) after restoring each backup
    Does just that, ejects tape after the restore is finished.
  - Prompt before restoring each backup
    Prompts user before restoring.
  - Force restore over existing database
    Forces restore over an existing database. This must be checked if you are restoring a database to its previous state, and the database is still on the server (or the `.ldf` and `.mdf` files still exist).
  - Restore database files as
    Shows original file name and restore as file name. You can change the destination directory for the restored files and the file name.
  - Recovery completion state
    - Leave database operational
      No additional transaction logs can be restored. Data is available and online.
    - Leave database nonoperational but able to restore additional transaction logs
      Database is not online and transaction logs can still be restored.
    - Leave database read-only and able to restore additional transaction logs
      Database can be read from only. Additional logs can be applied:

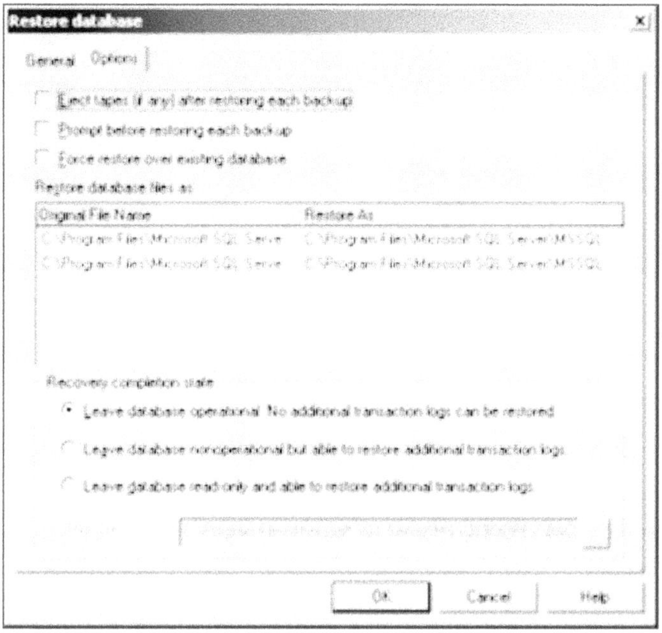


Select OK to start the restore. For each backup set from which you are restoring, you will see a separate sequential progress bar. When the process is complete, you will see a dialog box indicating success.

Also, you will get an error if you try to restore a database over an existing database when there are still user sessions connected to it. Your connection should be the only connection:

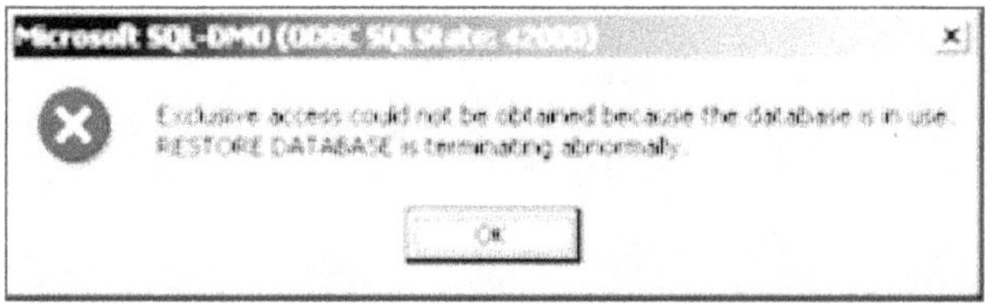


# 6.8 How to... Use RESTORE FILELISTONLY

Before looking at restoring databases using Transact-SQL, there are a few commands you should be familiar with. These are information commands that will make your life easier: `RESTORE FILELISTONLY`, `HEADERONLY`, and `LABELONLY`.

`RESTORE FILELISTONLY` lists the database and log files in your backup set; this is useful for gathering the logical name of the files, and physical locations of the original files.

An example of using RESTORE FILELISTONLY:

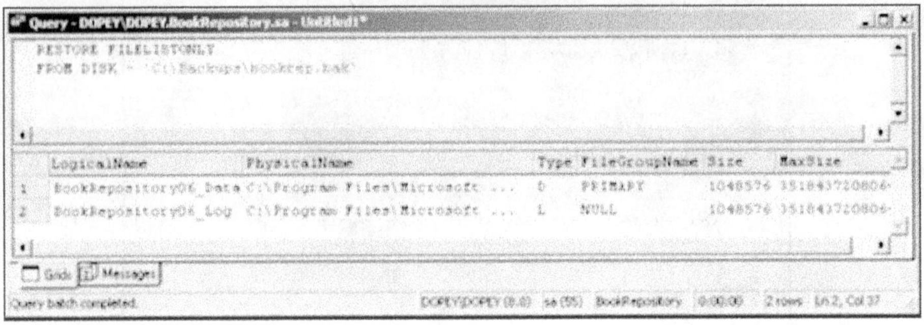


This command returns:

- Logical file name
- Physical file name
- File type (D for data and L for log)
- File group name
- Size in bytes
- Maximum size setting in bytes

# 6.9 How to... Use RESTORE HEADERONLY

RESTORE HEADERONLY returns header information for all backup sets on the specified device. For example:

```
RESTORE HEADERONLY
FROM DISK = 'C:\backups\bookrep.bak'
```

This returns the following information (the table below shows a subset of the information provided by SQL Server Books Online):

| Column Name | Description |
|---|---|
| BackupName | Backup set name. |
| BackupDescription | Backup set description. |
| BackupType | Backup type:<br>1 = Database<br>2 = Transaction Log<br>4 = File<br>5 = Differential Database<br>6 = Differential File |
| ExpirationDate | Expiration date for the backup set. |

| Column Name | Description |
|---|---|
| `Compressed` | 0 = No. SQL Server does not support software compression. |
| `Position` | Position of the backup set in the volume (for use with the `FILE=` option). |
| `DeviceType` | Number corresponding to the device used for the backup operation: |
| | Disk |
| | 2 = Logical |
| | 102 = Physical |
| | Tape |
| | 5 = Logical |
| | 105 = Physical |
| | Pipe |
| | 6 = Logical |
| | 106 = Physical |
| | Virtual Device |
| | 7 = Logical |
| | 107 = Physical |
| `UserName` | Username that performed the backup operation. |
| `ServerName` | Name of the server that wrote the backup set. |
| `DatabaseName` | Name of the database that was backed up. |
| `DatabaseVersion` | Version of the database from which the backup was created. |
| `DatabaseCreationDate` | Date and time the database was created. |
| `BackupSize` | Size of the backup, in bytes. |
| `FirstLSN` | Log sequence number of the first transaction in the backup set. `NULL` for file backups. |
| `LastLSN` | Log sequence number of the last transaction in the backup set. `NULL` for file backups. |
| `CheckpointLSN` | Log sequence number of the most recent checkpoint at the time the backup was created. |
| `DatabaseBackupLSN` | Log sequence number of the most recent full database backup. |
| `BackupStartDate` | Date and time that the backup operation began. |
| `BackupFinishDate` | Date and time that the backup operation finished. |

*Table continued on following page*

| Column Name | Description |
|---|---|
| SortOrder | Server sort order. This column is valid for database backups only. Provided for backward compatibility. |
| CodePage | Server code page or character set used by the server. |
| UnicodeLocaleId | Server Unicode locale ID configuration option used for Unicode character data sorting. Provided for backward compatibility. |
| UnicodeComparisonStyle | Server Unicode comparison style configuration option, which provides additional control over the sorting of Unicode data. Provided for backward compatibility. |
| CompatibilityLevel | Compatibility level setting of the database from which the backup was created. |
| SoftwareVendorId | Software vendor identification number. For SQL Server, this number is 4608 (or hexadecimal 0x1200). |
| SoftwareVersionMajor | Major version number of the server that created the backup set. |
| SoftwareVersionMinor | Server minor version number that did the backup. |
| SoftwareVersionBuild | Server build number that did the backup. |
| MachineName | Server that performed the backup. |
| Flags | Bit 0 (X1) is returned if bulk-logged data is captured in the log backup. |
| BindingID | Database binding ID. |
| RecoveryForkID | Recovery fork ID. |
| Collation | Database collation. |

# 6.10 How to... Use RESTORE LABELONLY

RESTORE LABELONLY returns information about the backup media for the selected backup device. For example:

```
RESTORE LABELONLY
FROM DISK = 'C:\backups\bookrep.bak'
```

This returns the following information (the table below shows a subset of the information provided by SQL Server Books Online):

| Column Name | Description |
|---|---|
| MediaName | Media name. |
| MediaSetId | If more than one media set, specifies a unique identification number of the media set. |
| FamilyCount | Media family total in the media set. |

| Column Name | Description |
|---|---|
| FamilySequenceNumber | The ordinal position of the family within the media set. |
| MediaFamilyId | Unique identification number for the media family. |
| MediaSequenceNumber | Sequence number in the media family. |
| MediaLabelPresent | Whether the media description contains:<br>1 = Microsoft Tape Format media label<br>0 = Media description |
| MediaDescription | Media description in free-form text, or the Microsoft Tape Format media label. |
| SoftwareName | Name of the backup software that wrote the label. |

In summary, use RESTORE FILELISTONLY to list the database and log files in the backup set, and to retrieve logical file names and physical locations of the original files backed up.

Use RESTORE HEADERONLY to return information on the backups held on the device (configuration and type).

Finally, use RESTORE LABELONLY to return information about the backup media held on the backup device.

# 6.11 How to... Restore a Database from a Full Backup using Transact-SQL

The following is syntax from SQL Server Books Online for running the RESTORE DATABASE command:

```
RESTORE DATABASE { database_name | @database_name_var }
[ FROM < backup_device > [ ,...n ] ]
[ WITH
    [ RESTRICTED_USER ]
    [PARTIAL]
    [ [ , ] FILE = { file_number | @file_number } ]
    [ [ , ] PASSWORD = { password | @password_variable } ]
    [ [ , ] MEDIANAME = { media_name | @media_name_variable } ]
    [ [ , ] MEDIAPASSWORD = { mediapassword | @mediapassword_variable } ]
    [ [ , ] MOVE 'logical_file_name' TO 'operating_system_file_name' ]
            [ ,...n ]
    [ [ , ] KEEP_REPLICATION ]
    [ [ , ] { NORECOVERY | RECOVERY | STANDBY = undo_file_name } ]
    [ [ , ] { NOREWIND | REWIND } ]
    [ [ , ] { NOUNLOAD | UNLOAD } ]
    [ [ , ] REPLACE ]
    [ [ , ] RESTART ]
    [ [ , ] STATS [ = percentage ] ]
]
```

| Option | Description |
|---|---|
| `{ database_name \| @database_name_var }` | Database name or character variable to restore the database as (can be a new database name or overlay of an existing database). |
| `[ FROM < backup_device > [ ,...n ] ]` | Name of backup device. |
| `[ RESTRICTED_USER ]` | Only `db_owner`, `dbcreator`, and `sysadmin` may have access to the newly restored database. |
| `[ PARTIAL ]` | The `PARTIAL` command can be used with `RESTORE` to restore a specific filegroup to a new database on the current or remote SQL Server instance. |
| `[ [ , ] FILE = { file_number \| @file_number } ]` | File number from the backup set from which to restore. |
| `[ [ , ] PASSWORD = { password \| @password_variable } ]` | Password needed if chosen when the restore was created. |
| `[ [ , ] MEDIANAME = { media_name \| @media_name_variable } ]` | If given, must match media name on backup volume; otherwise the check is not performed. |
| `[ [ , ] MEDIAPASSWORD = { mediapassword \| @mediapassword_variable } ]` | If a password was chosen for the media set, this password is required to restore from that media set. |
| `[ [ , ] MOVE 'logical_file_name' TO 'operating_system_file_name' ] [ ,...n ]` | `MOVE` allows you to restore the database to a different filename and/or path. |
| `[ [ , ] KEEP_REPLICATION ]` | Prevents replication settings from being removed on restore. Used for replication set up for log shipping. |
| `[ [ , ] { NORECOVERY \| RECOVERY \| STANDBY = undo_file_name } ]` | `NORECOVERY` keeps the database in a restored state that allows more differential or transaction log backups to be applied.<br>`RECOVERY` specifies that no further differential or transaction logs need to be applied. Default is `RECOVERY`. |
| `[ [ , ] { NOREWIND \| REWIND } ]` | `NOREWIND` indicates that after the restore, the tape is not rewound.<br>`REWIND` rewinds the tape at the end of the restore. |
| `[ [ , ] { NOUNLOAD \| UNLOAD } ]` | `NOUNLOAD` does not eject the tape after the restore.<br>`UNLOAD` ejects the tape at the end of the restore. |

| Option | Description |
|---|---|
| `[ [ , ] REPLACE ]` | Overlays an existing database with the database name defined in RESTORE DATABASE. |
| `[ [ , ] RESTART ]` | If a RESTORE stops prematurely, RESTART allows you to continue with the operation. Recommended for long RESTORE operations. |
| `[ [ , ] STATS [ = percentage ] ]` | Returns progress percentage of RESTORE operation. |

## Example 6.11.1: Restore from a device

- Restoring database from a device.
- Updating progress in 10% completion increments.
- Database set to fully recovered:

```
RESTORE DATABASE BookRepository
FROM BRDevice
WITH STATS = 10, RECOVERY
```

## Example 6.11.2: Restore from a file

- Recovering the database from a file.
- Leaving the database in a loading status, so additional differential or transaction logs can be applied:

```
RESTORE DATABASE BookRepository
FROM DISK = 'c:\backups\bookrep.bak'
WITH NORECOVERY
```

If you look in Enterprise Manager after setting a database to NORECOVERY, you will see the following status:

If you decide that you have no transaction logs or differential backups to apply, you can run this command to put it in RECOVERY status:

```
RESTORE DATABASE BookRepository
WITH RECOVERY
```

Notice that the FROM clause is not set.

## Example 6.11.3: Restore and move logs

- Restoring the database from a device.
- Moving the data and log files to a new location.

First retrieve the file lists from the device:

```
RESTORE FILELISTONLY
FROM BrDevice
```

Next, we will restore the Book Repository database; only this time, placing the files in the `C:\MSSQL\DB` directory:

```
RESTORE DATABASE BookRepository
FROM BrDevice
WITH MOVE 'BookRepo_Dat' TO 'C:\MSSQL\DB\bookrepo.mdf',
MOVE 'BookRepo_Dat2' TO 'C:\MSSQL\DB\bookrepo_dat2_data.ndf',
MOVE 'BookRepo_Log' TO 'C:\MSSQL\DB\bookrep_log.ldf'
```

### Example 6.11.4: Restore from file with multiple backups

- Restoring a database from a backup file containing multiple backups.
- Designating a restore from the third backup set on the device:

```
RESTORE DATABASE BookRepository
FROM BrDevice
WITH FILE = 3
```

Note that with these previous examples, if you do not specify `WITH RECOVERY` or `NORECOVERY`, `RECOVERY` is the default.

## 6.12 How to... Restore a Database from a Differential Backup using Transact-SQL

The syntax for differential database restores is identical to full database restores; however, full database restores must be performed prior to applying differential backups.

### Example 6.12.1: Restore full and differential backups

- Performing a full database restore and applying a differential backup:

```
-- First the full backup restore
RESTORE DATABASE BookRepository
FROM DISK = 'C:\Backups\bookrepo_full.bak'
WITH NORECOVERY

-- Now backup from the differential
RESTORE DATABASE BookRepository
FROM DISK = 'C:\Backups\bookrepo_dif.diff'
WITH RECOVERY
```

# 6.13 How to... Restore a Database from a Transaction Log Backup using Transact-SQL

The command for restoring transaction logs is RESTORE LOG instead of RESTORE DATABASE; otherwise, the syntax and options are the same. The exceptions are the STOPAT, STOPATMARK, and STOPBEFOREMARK keywords:

| Keyword | Description |
|---|---|
| STOPAT | Allows you to recover to a specific point-in-time from the transaction log backup. |
| STOPATMARK | Recovers to the first instance of a marked transaction, and **includes** the updates made within this transaction. Designating STOPATMARK = 'mark_name' AFTER datetime recovers to the first instance of the marked transaction **on** or after the specified datetime. |
| STOPBEFOREMARK | STOPBEFOREMARK restores the database up to the first instance of the marked transaction, **excluding** any activity within this transaction. STOPBEFOREMARK ... AFTER datetime will restore the database up to the first instance of the marked transaction **on** or **after** the specified datetime, **excluding** this transaction. |

Transaction log restores require an initial full database restore. If applying multiple transaction logs, you must apply them in order. Applying transaction logs out of order, or with gaps between backups, will not be allowed.

### Example 6.13.1: Restore backup from a file

- Restoring full database backup from a backup file.
- Restoring a transaction log backup from a backup file:

```
RESTORE DATABASE BookRepository
FROM DISK = 'C:\Backups\bookrepo_full.bak'
WITH NORECOVERY

RESTORE LOG BookRepository
FROM DISK = 'C:\Backups\bookrepo809PM_log.trn'
WITH RECOVERY
```

### Example 6.13.2: Restore backup from a file, apply two log backups

- Restoring from a full database backup file
- Applying two transaction log backups

```
RESTORE DATABASE BookRepository
FROM DISK = 'C:\Backups\bookrepo_full.bak'
WITH NORECOVERY

RESTORE LOG BookRepository
FROM DISK = 'C:\Backups\bookrepo809PM_log.trn'
```

```
WITH NORECOVERY

RESTORE LOG BookRepository
FROM DISK = 'C:\Backups\bookrepo814PM_log.trn'
WITH RECOVERY
```

Notice that the last RESTORE LOG statement has the RECOVERY option specified instead of NORECOVERY.

### Example 6.13.3: Restore full and differential backups, apply backup log

- Restoring a full database backup from a backup file.
- Restoring a differential backup from a backup file.
- Applying a transaction log from a backup file:

```
RESTORE DATABASE BookRepository
FROM DISK = 'C:\Backups\bookrepo_full.bak'
WITH NORECOVERY

RESTORE DATABASE BookRepository
FROM DISK = 'C:\Backups\bookrepo_dif.diff'
WITH NORECOVERY

RESTORE LOG BookRepository
FROM DISK = 'C:\Backups\bookrepo_tran.trn'
WITH RECOVERY
```

### Example 6.13.4: Restore to specified time

- Restoring the database from a full backup file.
- Restoring database from a transaction log to July 24, 2002 8:40PM:

```
RESTORE DATABASE BookRepository
FROM DISK = 'C:\Backups\bookrepo_full.bak'
WITH NORECOVERY

RESTORE LOG BookRepository
FROM DISK = 'C:\Backups\bookrepo_tran.trn'
WITH STOPAT = 'July 24, 2002 8:40PM' , RECOVERY
```

### Example 6.13.5: Restore using STOPATMARK

This example shows how to restore a database from a transaction mark using the STOPATMARK keyword. Let's say you ran the following marked transactions to create two tables:

```
USE BookRepository
BEGIN TRANSACTION WITH MARK 'TableMark'

CREATE TABLE mark1 (iID int NOT NULL)
CREATE TABLE mark2(iID int NOT NULL)

COMMIT TRANSACTION
```

Prior to this marked transaction, a full backup was performed. After this transaction, you perform a transaction log backup:

- Restore the database from a full database backup file.
- Restore from a transaction log backup to the first instance of the transaction mark, including changes within this mark:

```
RESTORE DATABASE BookRepository
FROM DISK = 'C:\backups\bookrepo_full.bak'
WITH NORECOVERY

RESTORE LOG BookRepository
FROM DISK = 'C:\backups\bookrepotran.trn'
WITH STOPATMARK = 'TableMark'
```

- The database will still be in `NORECOVERY` state, so we perform the following last step:

```
RESTORE DATABASE BookRepository WITH RECOVERY
```

If you were to select from either the `mark1` or `mark2` tables created in the marked transactions, you would see that they both exist; this is because the above `STOPATMARK` includes the contents of the marked transaction.

### Example 6.13.6: Restore using STOPBEFOREMARK

This example assumes that the Example 5 marked transaction was run, only this time we will recover using `STOPBEFOREMARK`:

- Restoring the database from a full database backup.
- Restoring from the transaction log to the first instance of the marked transaction, stopping right before this transaction is begun.
- Recovering the database:

```
RESTORE DATABASE BookRepository
FROM DISK = 'C:\Backups\bookrepo_full.bak'
WITH NORECOVERY

RESTORE LOG BookRepository
FROM DISK = 'C:\Backups\bookrepotran.trn'
WITH STOPBEFOREMARK = 'TableMark'

RESTORE DATABASE BookRepository WITH RECOVERY
```

If you were to now try to select from either table made in the TableMark transaction, you would get the error:

```
Server: Msg 208, Level 16, State 1, Line 1
Invalid object name 'mark1'.
```

This is because the `STOPBEFOREMARK` restores the transaction log right UP TO the first occurrence of the marked transaction.

# 6.14 How to... Restore a File or Filegroup

Restoring a file or filegroup uses virtually the same syntax as a full database restore, except you use the `FILEGROUP` or `FILE` keywords. To perform a restore of a specific file or filegroup, you must be using full or bulk-logged recovery models for your database; this is because transaction log backups must be applied after restoring a file or filegroup backup.

### Example 6.14.1: Restore file from backup file

- ❑ Restoring the database file from a backup file.
- ❑ Applying the transaction log (required):

```
RESTORE DATABASE BookRepository FILE = 'BookRepo_Dat2'
FROM DISK = 'C:\backups\bookrepo_fg2.bak'
WITH NORECOVERY

RESTORE LOG BookRepository
FROM DISK = 'C:\backups\bookrepo_trandump.trn'
WITH RECOVERY
```

### Example 6.14.2: Restore filegroup from backup file

- ❑ Restoring the database filegroup from a backup file.
- ❑ Applying the transaction log (required):

```
RESTORE DATABASE BookRepository FILEGROUP = 'PRIMARY'
FROM DISK = 'C:\backups\bookrepo_primaryfg.bak'
WITH NORECOVERY

RESTORE LOG BookRepository
FROM DISK = 'C:\backups\bookrepo_tranprimary.trn'
WITH RECOVERY
```

# 6.15 How to... Do a PARTIAL Restore to a New Database

The `PARTIAL` command can be used with `RESTORE` to restore a specific filegroup to a new database on the current or remote SQL Server instance. If you have a corrupt table in the filegroup, you can restore the filegroup to a new database and then export the corrupted table's data back to the original database (after dropping and recreating the original table on the original database).

### Example 6.15.1: Restore filegroup to a new database

- ❑ Restoring the filegroup to a new database.
- ❑ Making sure the database file names are different from the original database file names:

```
RESTORE DATABASE tempFG2
FILEGROUP = 'FG2'
FROM DISK = 'C:\backups\bookrepo_full.bak'
WITH PARTIAL,
```

```
MOVE 'BookRepo_Dat' TO 'C:\MSSQL\DB\bookrepo_tmp.mdf',
MOVE 'BookRepo_Dat2' TO 'C:\MSSQL\DB\bookrepodat2_tmp.ndf',
MOVE 'BookRepo_log' TO 'C:\MSSQL\DB\bookrepo_log.ldf'
```

Keep in mind that the primary filegroup will also be restored with this `PARTIAL` restore; however, other user-defined filegroups will not. Make sure that you have enough space for both the user-defined filegroup and the primary filegroup on the destination database or server.

Also, you may still see filegroups and files referenced in your `PARTIAL` restored database properties; but user-defined groups not restored explicitly are **not** available. For example, if you try to select from a table in this `PARTIAL` database that belongs to another user-defined filegroup that has not been restored, you will get the following error:

```
Server: Msg 8653, Level 16, State 1, Line 1
Warning: The query processor is unable to produce a plan because the table 'tempfg2.dbo.tempwhatever'
is marked OFFLINE.
```

Use the `PARTIAL` keyword as a means of saving your data to a new location, dropping the corrupted tables from the original database, and importing the database tables and data from the `PARTIAL` database to your original database.

# 6.16 How to... Recover from File Loss or Database Corruption

There are many events that can corrupt your database or cause it to disappear:

- Power outages or surges can corrupt your database (anything that results in an incomplete or interrupted I/O operation can potentially cause corruption).
- Physical disks have a limited lifetime. Using array types, like mirroring RAID 1 or striping with parity RAID 5, can lessen your exposure.
- Users can inadvertently delete database files when the SQL Server service is shut down, or the database is offline. This is a good reason to restrict access to data and log file drives to trusted administrators and DBAs only.
- If virus-scanning utilities are running on the server while the databases are recovering, virus scans can lock the database files, which sometimes results in corruption.
- Application-side updates have the potential to corrupt data. Also, if system catalog updates are allowed, the system tables can be corrupted. Make sure periodically to check that system catalog updates are **not** allowed.

## Losing Data and Log Files

Let's first review what would happen if we lost a user-defined database; we'll talk about system database restores later.

If you lost both the data and log files, you need, at the very least, to have a full database backup. If you have been performing offline backups, then you need a copy of the `.mdf`, `.ldf`, and `.ndf` files:

- Make sure your original problem is solved; that is, missing disks are identified, rogue end-users are banished, and virus scanning on database files is filtered out.

- Restore your database from the latest full database backup.
- If there are any, apply your latest differential database backup.
- Apply your transaction log backups in sequential order from the last full or differential backup, if any.

Any changes made between the last transaction log backup (if full or bulk-logged) or full database backup (`SIMPLE`) will be lost. This is another good reason to back up your transaction logs frequently.

If you perform offline backups of your database files, restore these from tape or your third-party backup software, and place them in the original file directories. Attach them using `sp_attach_db`.

# Losing Data and Log Files for Your System Databases

This example assumes your system databases are destroyed, and would work for a corrupt `master` database too. If you have been backing up your system databases, you can restore your system databases as follows:

- Run `rebuildm.exe` located in `Program Files\Microsoft SQL Server\80\Tools\Binn` directory.
- Select the server instance you wish to rebuild in the Server dropdown.
- Select the Network source directory containing the data files. Do not point to your CD-ROM until Microsoft has fixed a bug that causes `rebuildm` to hang (see Microsoft Knowledge Base article Q273572, *BUG: Rebuildm.exe Utility Stops Responding When Source Directory is on a CD*, for more information).
- Click the Settings button for the Collation field; set it to your **current** master database settings. These must match the settings of your original default collation!
- Press OK to exit to the main screen. Press the Rebuild button. You will be prompted that you are about to rebuild and, therefore overwrite, your system databases. If you understand this and have taken the necessary precautions to preserve logins, DTS packages, jobs, operators, alerts, and system database objects, press Yes. Once your `master` database is rebuilt, you can restore it from the backup:
- Open a command prompt.
- For a default instance, run the following in a command prompt at the directory where the `sqlservr.exe` executable exists (the `-c` switch starts SQL Server independently of the Windows NT Service Control Manager, and the `-m` switch starts SQL Server in single-user mode):

```
> sqlservr -c -m
```

If you are starting a Named Instance, run the following:

```
sqlservr.exe -c -m -s {instancename}
```

Where `instancename` is the name of the instance you wish to start.

Once you press Enter at the `sqlservr` execution, you will see startup messages. Leave this command window open.

- Next, open Query Analyzer and RESTORE the master database from the backup:

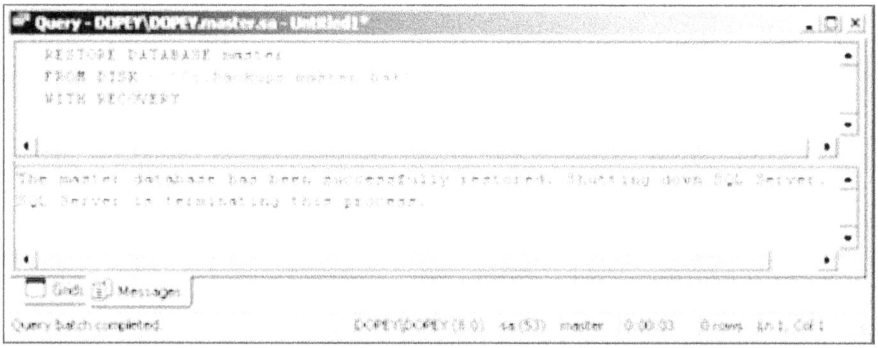


- Close out your command prompt window and start up SQL Server as normal.
- Restore the msdb database (and model database if you made modifications):

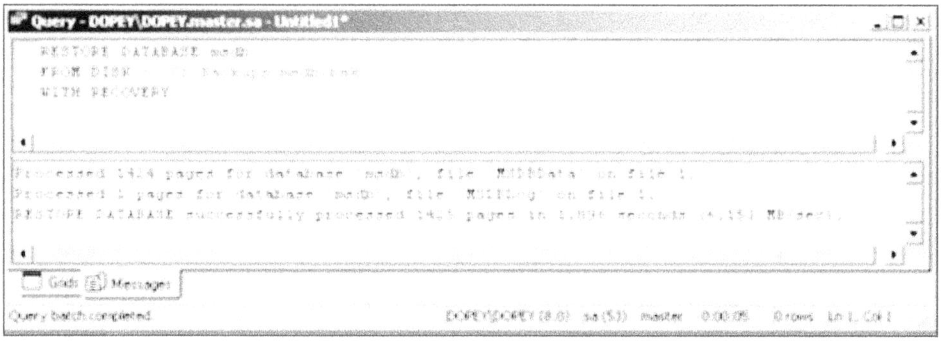


Any changes made to your system databases after the latest full backup will be lost. This includes logins (master), jobs, and DTS packages (both saved in the msdb database).

# Corrupted Binary Files

If you have lost more than just your system databases, you may need to reinstall SQL Server and any service packs you originally applied. If you have system database backups, you can restore them as described in the previous example.

After a reinstall, if you have the original .ldf and .mdf files for the system databases, you can stop the SQL Server service and overlay the newly installed system database files with your older, pre-corruption files. This assumes that you backed them up elsewhere prior to reinstalling SQL Server. This also assumes that when you reinstalled SQL Server, you placed the system databases and binaries in **exactly** the same location as the original installation.

## Losing System and User Databases

If you have lost both your system and user databases:

- Follow the previous steps for rebuilding the `master` database, restoring `msdb`, and `model`.
- Restore each user database from backup.

Remember that any modifications made to your databases since the last backups will be lost.

## Losing Data Files but not Log Files

If your database files have become corrupted or are missing, but your log file is still available and you have a full backup from which to restore (and any transaction log backups from that point), it is recommended that you get one last transaction log backup prior to a recovery attempt.

For completely corrupted data files, assuming you have a full backup from which to restore later on, run the command:

```
BACKUP LOG databasename to DISK = <device name> WITH NO_TRUNCATE
```

For example:

```
BACKUP LOG BookStore
TO DISK = 'C:\backups\bookstore_tran.trn'
WITH NO_TRUNCATE
```

Then restore the full backup and any transaction log backups since the full backup in order. For example:

```
DROP DATABASE BookStore

RESTORE DATABASE BookStore
FROM DISK = 'C:\backups\bookstore.bak'
WITH NORECOVERY

RESTORE LOG BookStore
FROM DISK = 'C:\backups\bookstore_tran.trn'
WITH RECOVERY
```

# 6.17 How to... Reset a Suspect Database with sp_resetstatus

SQL Server will set a database into `suspect` status for various reasons:

- The disk or array where the database files are located is unavailable.
- Data files have become corrupted (for example, by a power failure or problem with the disk).
- If the database is recovering during SQL Server startup, but the data or log file is grabbed by another process (virus scanning software, for example), the status will be set to `suspect`. Stopping and restarting SQL Server after stopping the process that has taken the file will usually take the database out of `suspect` status.

Check the SQL error log and your Windows Event application and system logs to search for clues as to what happened. If the problem is with a disk or array that can be repaired, carry out the repair and try running sp_resetstatus. If the problem is database corruption, you may have to restore your database from the last good backup.

The syntax for sp_resetstatus from SQL Server Books Online is as follows:

```
sp_resetstatus [ @DBName = ] 'database'
```

For example, to run sp_resetstatus on the pubs database, enter:

```
EXEC sp_resetstatus 'pubs'
```

# The Database has Suspect Status and sp_resetstatus does not Work

If you have made sure all the data and log files are in their place, and physical disk issues taken care of, then you may need to restore your database from a backup, or export its data to a new database.

To access a database for bulk copying the data, the database must be placed into **emergency mode**:

```
EXEC sp_configure 'allow updates', 1
RECONFIGURE WITH OVERRIDE

UPDATE SYSDATABASES SET STATUS=-32768 WHERE NAME='databasename'
```

The status value 32768, is used to set the database into emergency mode in sysdatabases. For example:

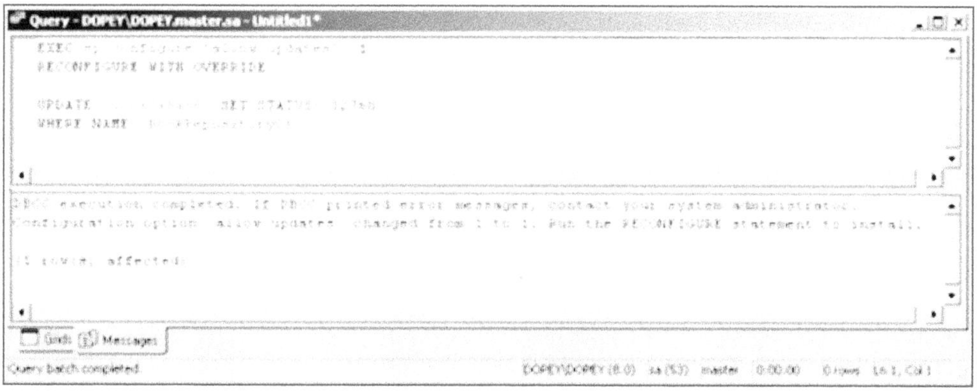


From this point, you can bulk copy tables out or even export them with Transact-SQL. For example, below we use the SELECT * INTO syntax to place a table into a new database that holds the contents of the corrupted sysusers table:

```
SELECT * INTO BookRepository.dbo.TempUsers FROM sysusers
```

# 6.18 How to... Rebuild the Registry

If your registry is corrupted, you can rebuild the SQL Server installation registry entries (and reinstall MDAC and MS DTC) by following these steps. (**WARNING** – any registry modifications, manual or otherwise, should be performed as a last resort. Make sure to reapply service packs and security hotfixes you may have installed for the SQL Server instance, after performing this operation.):

- Click `autorun.exe` from your install CD or network SQL Server installation directory.
- Select the SQL Server 2000 Components option.
- Select Install Database Server.
- Select Next at the Installation Wizard dialog box.
- Select Next at the Computer Name dialog box.
- Select Advanced options in the Installation Selection dialog box.
- Click Registry Rebuild in the Advanced Options dialog box.
- Select Next.
- You will be warned that the registry will be rebuilt based on the settings you select.
- Select **exactly** the same options you selected during the original installation, otherwise the registry rebuild may fail, or may apply incorrect settings that will cause your SQL Server Instance to encounter errors.

# 6.19 How to... Start SQL Server in Single-User Mode

To start a SQL Server instance in single-user mode, follow these steps:

- Open up a command prompt.
- Navigate to your `sql_server_home\binn` directory.
- Enter the following to connect to your default instance:

```
> sqlservr.exe -c -m
```

- For multiple instances, execute:

```
> sqlservr.exe -c -s instancename -m
```

- Open up Query Analyzer or Enterprise Manager with your single connection and perform the work you need to do (for example, recover the master database).

# 6.20 How to... Set Up a Database Maintenance Plan

Microsoft added **database maintenance plans** to SQL Server from version 7.0. Maintenance plans are an excellent means of providing consistent user and system database maintenance. Maintenance plans allow you to:

- Perform full database backups.
- Perform transaction log backups.
- Check database integrity.
- Rebuild indexes and update statistics.
- With Enterprise Edition, set up Log Shipping (See Chapter 12 for more details).

SQL Server provides a wizard to create the plan, but there are some tips and issues that you should be aware of. For the part-time DBA with little time to spare, maintenance plans can be quite helpful, but you should still understand exactly what it is you are scheduling; although Microsoft makes it easy, you can still make poor decisions if you do not understand the process.

To set up a new database maintenance plan:

- In Enterprise Manager, expand the SQL Server group and SQL Server registration.
- Expand the Management folder and right-click Database Maintenance Plans. Select New Maintenance Plan.
- Select Next.
- Select which databases this maintenance plan should manage. You can select:
    - All databases
    - All system databases (`master`, `model`, and `msdb`)
    - All user databases (not `master`, `model`, and `msdb`)
    - Specific databases – checking the boxes of those you wish to be managed by the maintenance plan:

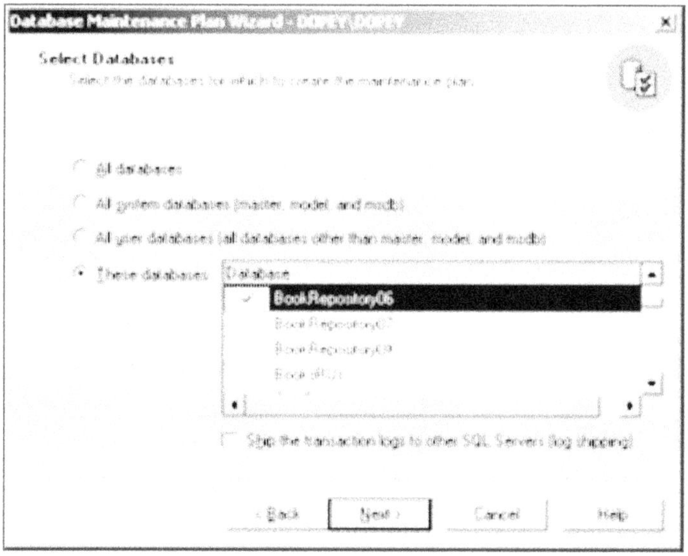

- Select Next.
- In the Update Data Optimization Information dialog box, you can select:
  - Reorganize data and index pages
    This option runs a DBCC DBREINDEX for each table in the selected databases. This rebuilds each index, lowering fragmentation, but sometimes taking a long time depending on the base table size and number of indexes. Running this once a week is usually good for most applications; however, running it more frequently may be necessary for tables with large numbers of updates.
  - Reorganize pages with the original amount of free space
    When we talk about free space, we are actually discussing fill factor; this is the percentage of the index pages we should leave free for new rows. Lower fill factors can help prevent excessive page splitting (process of relocating half the rows in a full data page or index page to two new pages, making room for the new row or index entry). Select this option if you have taken care to specify the fill factor differently from the default value for your indexes. If you took the time to do this, but select the other option below, you will lose the intended fill factors you worked so hard to set.
  - Change free space per page percentage
    This option allows you to set a percentage of free space to leave across all indexes in the database. If you choose 10%, for example, this translates to a 90% fill factor. Only use this if you have not explicitly set index fill factors from values other than the default. The server default is 0, which means that SQL Server creates clustered and nonclustered indexes with full pages. This default leaves some space within the upper level of the index tree, and differs from a fill factor of 100 (which leaves no space). If you choose to reorganize the data and index pages, you cannot select this next option:
  - Update statistics used by query optimizer
    This is the equivalent of running the `UPDATE STATISTICS owner.tablename WITH all, SAMPLE 10 PERCENT` statement for each table in the database. You specify the sample percentage to the right of the checkbox.

    `UPDATE STATISTICS` helps the query processor decide which key values in an index to use by refreshing the statistics tracked on the distribution of the key values in each index. It is a good idea to run `UPDATE STATISTICS` after significant data changes.

    Rebuilding indexes automatically refreshes these statistics; however, you may consider using this option when you have large tables and indexes that would take up extreme amounts of time and system resources to rebuild. Updating statistics is not as invasive, and you can get the benefit of updating your statistics without an index rebuild.

    This option will affect all column, index, and existing statistics (created by you or the system). It will run a sample instead of a `FULLSCAN`, which reads all the rows in the table or indexed view. `SAMPLE` looks at the chosen percentage of rows, to generate useful statistics, and is usually quite accurate.
  - Remove unused space from database files
    Issues a `DBCC SHRINKDATABASE` based on the specifications of:
    - When it grows beyond XX MB (megabytes)
    - Amount of free space to remain after shrink (%).

For example, if we specified that we want to remove unused space from database files when it grows beyond 10MB of free space, when the job runs it would issue something like:

```
DBCC SHRINKDATABASE(N'DatabaseName', 10, TRUNCATEONLY)
```

The TRUNCATEONLY statement releases the free space at the end of the file to the operating system; rows are not relocated to the beginning of the file to produce unallocated pages towards the end of the file. This produces less overhead, but is also less effective in freeing up data file space.

In either case, this option is very invasive to a production environment. DBCC SHRINKFILES and DBCC SHRINKDATABASE operations should be planned and monitored; they can reduce database concurrency significantly.

> **Rather then add this option to your maintenance plan, instead add it to your checklist of weekly or monthly items to keep an eye on. Once space can be freed, you can pick a good time to run the DBCC operation.**

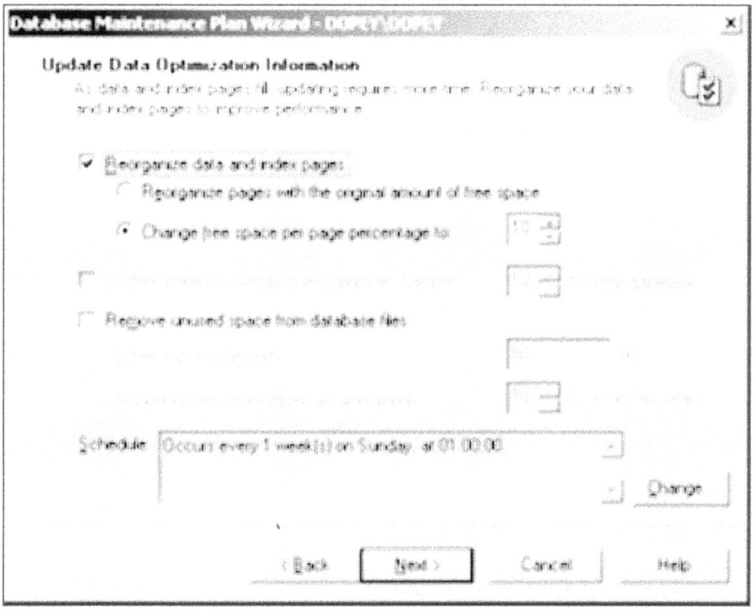


- All screens in the wizard have the Schedule box and the Change... button. Select the Change... button to decide on a schedule. Select OK when finished.
- Select Next to continue to the Integrity dialog box. The options are:
  - Check database integrity
    By selecting this option, you will be issuing DBCC CHECKDB WITH NO_INFOMSGS for each database. CHECKDB validates the integrity of all objects in the database. DBCC CHECKDB runs the same processes as DBCC CHECKALLOC and DBCC CHECKTABLE.
  - Include indexes
    If selected, this option will check both data and index pages.
  - Attempt to repair any minor problems
    This option will put your database in single user mode every time the job runs. For most production databases this is not a good idea, especially if you are running this job once or more often a week. It is better for you to set up your job to notify an operator (via pager) when a failure is found. The DBA can then inform the users that they should log out and can take the time and care that is needed when the database is corrupted.

- Exclude indexes
  This option checks just the data pages in the integrity tests; the advantage is that the DBCC command will run faster. However, if an index is corrupted, wouldn't you want to know?
- Perform these checks before doing backups
  This is another option that looks perfectly reasonable to select, but can impact your server performance significantly. This will run the DBCC command prior to every database and transaction log backup; for a large database with several user connections, this can be a problem. Avoid selecting this option:

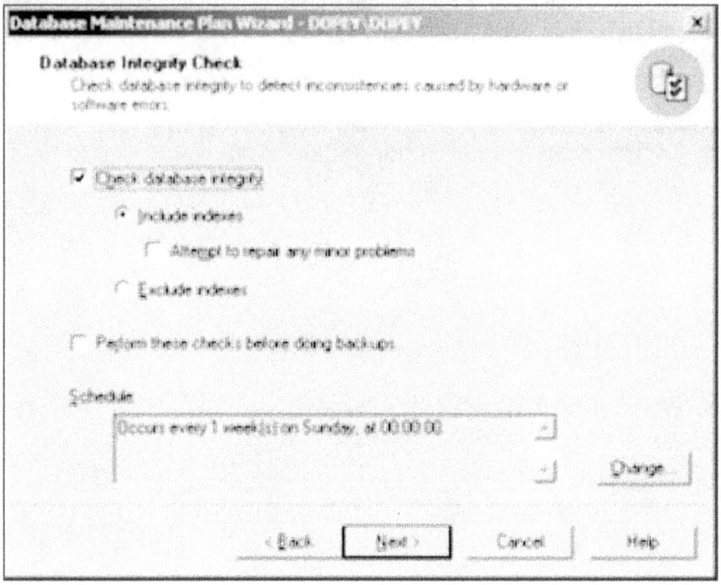


- Select your schedule for the Integrity Check job and select Next. This brings us to the Database Backup dialog box. Your options are:
  - Back up the database as part of the maintenance plan
    This will create a time-stamped full backup file for each database selected for your maintenance plan.
  - Verify the integrity of the backup when complete
    Not to be confused with running integrity checks prior to each database backup, this less invasive action will run RESTORE VERIFYONLY for each full backup. The command checks to make sure the backup is complete and readable.
  - Location to store the backup file
    - Tape
      If this option is set, you can select tape devices attached to your computer only.
    - Disk
      Allows you to specify a file directory in the next dialog box:

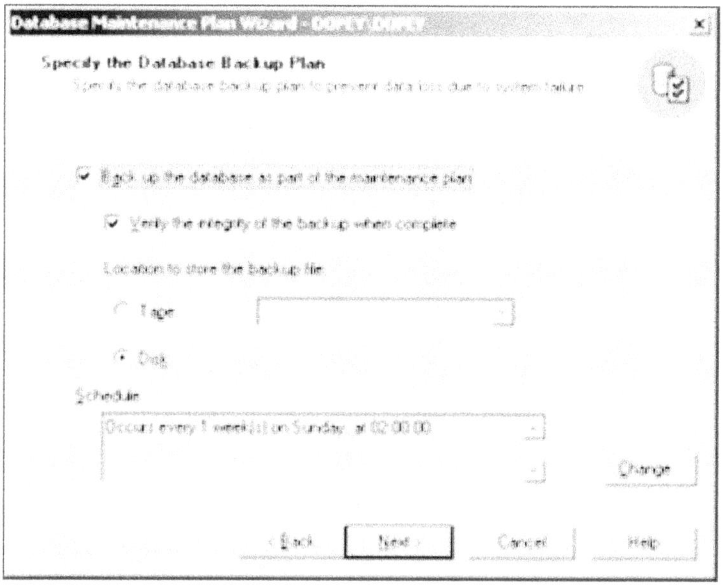

Configure your Schedule and select Next when finished.

- If you selected Disk, you will see the Backup Disk Directory dialog box. The options here are:
  - Directory in which to store the backup file
    - Use the default backup directory
      This places your backup files in the `\MSSQL\BACKUP` directory for default instances, and `\MSSQL$instancename\BACKUP` for named instances.
    - Use this directory
      This option allows you to choose a location other than the default for your backup disks. This only lists local database files. You should place these backup files on a fault-tolerant array, such as a RAID 1 array (mirroring), separately from the data and log files.
  - Create a subdirectory for each database
    Having subdirectories for each directory helps you locate your backup files faster, especially if you have numerous database backups with similar naming conventions.
  - Remove files older than
    This option removes your data files after a set number of minutes, hours, days, weeks, or months. For large databases, this is a necessary administrative task. One gotcha is that the cleanup occurs **after** your backups have run; this means that if you choose 2 days worth of backups, you actually must have room for 3 days. SQL Server will create the third backup and then remove the two oldest backups. Plan your backup space needs with this in mind.

One last note on backup retention: keep as many backups as the business considers necessary. Good recovery planning means that you will also archive these backup files to tape or another network server or facility. Make sure that you schedule your tape backups to occur **after** the user and system database backups. If your server is destroyed, you need an off-server or off-site option.

  - Backup file extension
    The default is `.bak`. Unless you have a compelling business reason to change it, leave this setting as it is:

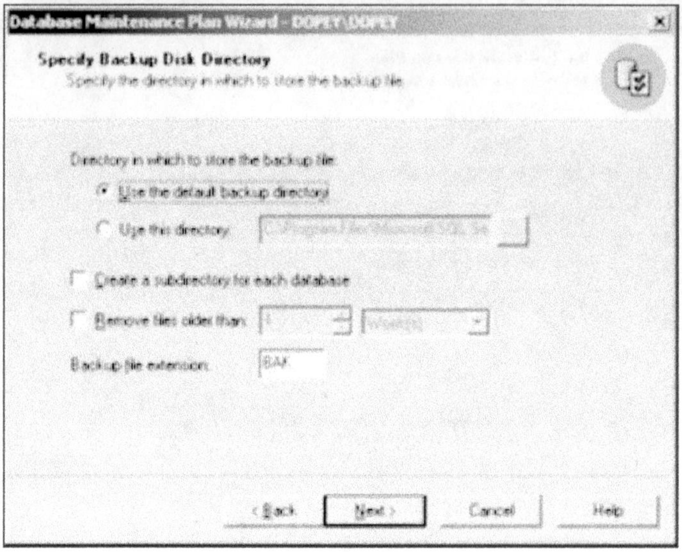

- Select Next.
- In the Transaction Log Backup dialog box, you have the following options:
    - Back up the transaction log as part of the maintenance plan
      If you select this option, a BACKUP LOG operation will be performed for each database in the maintenance plan. Make sure your database recovery modes are not set to Simple. For example, the databases pubs and Northwind come out of the box in Simple recovery mode. If you select all user databases or all databases, this means your transaction log backup will fail until you either change the recovery mode or remove them from the plan.
    - Verify the integrity of the backup when complete
      Runs RESTORE VERIFYONLY on the transaction log backup.
    - Location to store the backup file
        - Tape
          Can be a tape device attached to the server only.
        - Disk
          If selected, the next dialog will present you with further disk options:

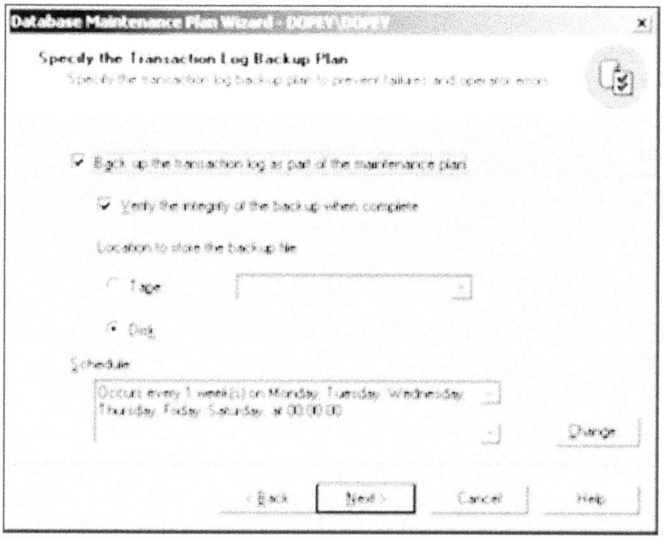

Select a schedule for your transaction log backups to run and select the Change... button.

The Transaction Log Backup Disk Directory dialog works just like the full Backup Disk Directory dialog, only applying to your transaction logs.

Select Next when finished.

- The Reports to Generate dialog box allows you to specify where to send reports, how long to keep the reports, and whether or not reports should be e-mailed to an operator. These reports return detailed information about any maintenance plan failures, such as the exact error messages encountered:

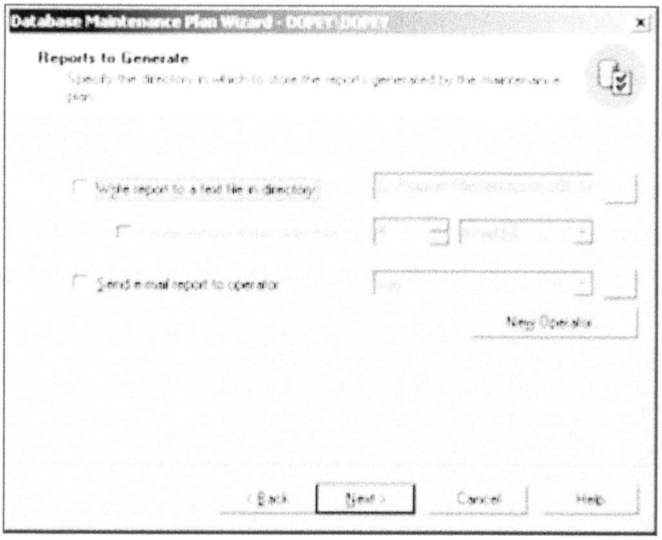

Select Next when finished.

- The Maintenance Plan History dialog allows you to store job and error history for the maintenance plan steps. You should limit the history of these jobs, as they have only short-term value. You can also write history to another server if you have limited space on the local server. Select Next when finished:

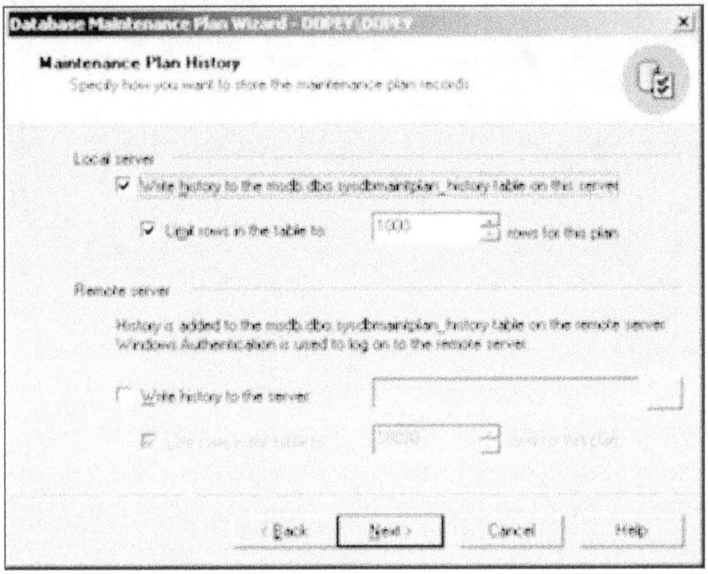


- The last dialog box allows you to confirm your selected database, schedule, and settings. Select a name for your maintenance plan; if it covers all databases, use a naming convention to denote this; if it covers just users or system databases, add this to the name. If it covers just one database, use this as the plan name as good practice. Select Finish.

  You will now see the maintenance plan listed in the right-hand pane:

  Notice that it lists what actions you selected above.

- Go to the Jobs node under SQL Server Agent.

  You will notice the jobs that the database maintenance plan created in the right-hand pane, after clicking the Jobs icon:

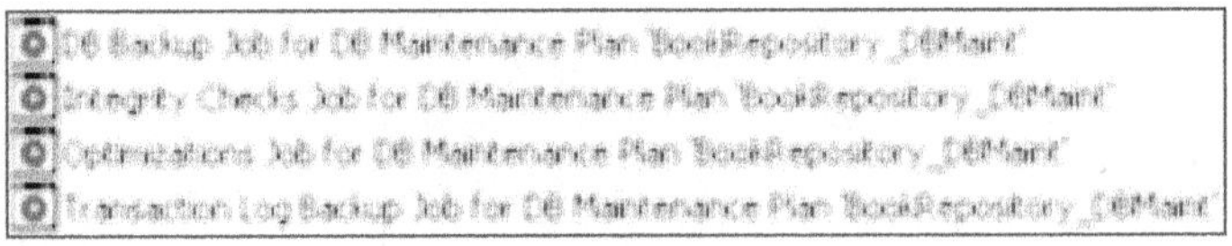

  Notice that these jobs have very long names. If you choose to have multiple maintenance plans, it may be a good idea to change the names to something shorter.

- Double-click on the first job in the plan to bring up the General tab in the Job properties.

- At this point, change the name to something more concise, like 'DatabaseName Full Backup'. A word of warning: if you are using Windows Authentication to register your server in Enterprise Manager; you may find that your domain account is the selected owner of the job. In some cases, if your login is not explicitly added to SQL Server as a login, your maintenance jobs will fail. A better practice would be to set your maintenance jobs to `sa`; then only sysadmins can see or modify the jobs.
- While you are here, look at the Steps tab to see what commands will run:

  Double click Step 1:

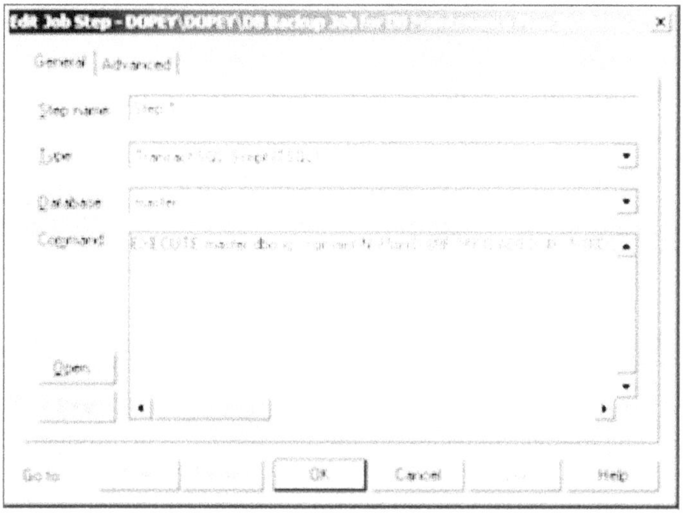

  The task is running `xp_sqlmaint`. You will see this statement, with various switches, later in the chapter when we cover it properly. Select OK when finished.

There are a few last notes on maintenance plans:

- You can change some details of your jobs, such as name and owner, without worrying about creating issues between your individual jobs and the maintenance plan. Some changes in the maintenance plan overlay your job settings, but job name and owner are not included among those fields. In addition to being able to change the job name and owner, you can also add extra steps to the job. This is not recommended, however, because a recreation of the maintenance plan will cause the extra steps to be removed.
- Do not select the Remove unused space from database files if you can avoid it. This option was intended for sites that have no DBA and need the bare minimum attention to let SQL Server run along without intervention.
- Another reminder, do not set the Attempt to repair any minor problems unless you have an excellent reason to do so; this places your database in single user mode. Also, do not enable Perform these tests before backing up the database or transaction log, as this adds unnecessary system overhead.

# 6.21 How to... Investigate Maintenance Plan Failures

When a job participating in a maintenance plan fails, you are able to view error details at two levels: the job and the database maintenance plan.

To show job history for the failed job:

- In Enterprise Manager, expand server group and server registration.
- Expand the Management folder and SQL Server Agent, then click Jobs.
- Right-click the failed job and select View Job History.
- In the Job History dialog box, click Show step details to show each step's detail:

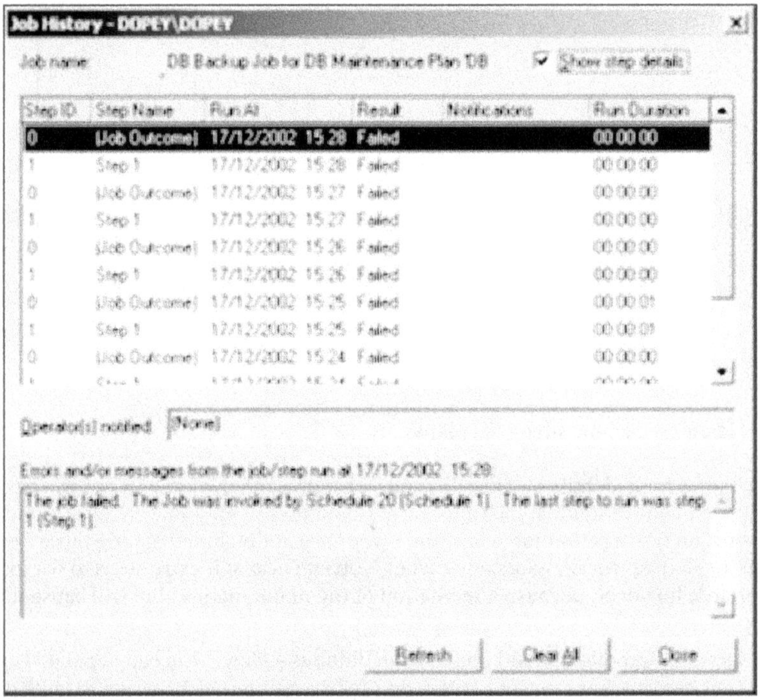


Click Step 1 to see the error description (in the lower-half of the window). You will notice that this description is not very helpful. Not all jobs will be this cryptic, but maintenance plans almost certainly will be.

To see better error detail, follow these steps:

- In Enterprise Manager, expand server group and server registration.
- Expand the Management folder and select Database Maintenance Plans.
- Right-click the maintenance plan that failed and select Maintenance Plan History.

- In the Maintenance Plan History dialog box, you can see the status of the plan and activity where the failure occurred. You can also filter criteria by plan name, server name, database, status, activity, or keywords.
- Double-click the failed row to see more detail. You will see that the Backup can not be performed on this database. Since this is a transaction log backup, you should check the recovery mode of your database to make sure it is either full- or bulk-logged mode.

This view of history is particularly helpful for troubleshooting maintenance plans that hit multiple databases. You can then pinpoint which database or databases are causing the issue.

# 6.22 How to... Use the xp_sqlmaint or SQLMaint Utility

As you saw in the previous section, maintenance plans generate jobs, which in turn run `xp_sqlmaint`. `xp_sqlmaint` in turn runs the `sqlmaint` command-line utility. If you would like to use this utility, you may do so directly. The syntax from SQL Server Books Online is as follows:

```
xp_sqlmaint 'switch_string'
```

The `switch_string` is the switches used by the `sqlmaint` utility. The syntax from SQL Server Books Online for sqlmaint is as follows:

```
sqlmaint
[-?] |
[
    [-S server_name[\instance_name]]
    [-U login_ID [-P password]]
    {
        [ -D database_name | -PlanName name | -PlanID guid ]
        [-Rpt text_file]
        [-To operator_name]
        [-HtmlRpt html_file [-DelHtmlRpt <time_period>] ]
        [-RmUnusedSpace threshold_percent free_percent]
        [-CkDB | -CkDBNoIdx]
        [-CkAl | -CkAlNoIdx]
        [-CkCat]
        [-UpdOptiStats sample_percent]
        [-RebldIdx free_space]
        [-WriteHistory]
        [
            {-BkUpDB [backup_path] | -BkUpLog [backup_path] }
            {-BkUpMedia
                {DISK [    [-DelBkUps <time_period>]
                            [-CrBkSubDir ] [ -UseDefDir ]
                      ]
                | TAPE
                }
            }
            [-BkUpOnlyIfClean]
            [-VrfyBackup]
        ]
    }
]
```

| Switch | Description |
|---|---|
| ? | Shows options and syntax. Use this alone with no other parameters. |
| -S server_name\instance_name | Server or instance name. |
| -U login_ID -P password | Login ID and password. If login is not supplied, sqlmaint will try to use Windows Authentication. Use double quotes if either the login_ID or password contain any special characters. |
| -D database_name \| -PlanName name \| -PlanID guid | Database name, database maintenance plan name, or plan globally unique identifier. |
| -Rpt text_file | Error log directory. |
| -To operator_name | Name of operator to e-mail the error report. |
| -HtmlRpt html_file<br>-DelHtmlRpt <time_period> | Path of the HTML report to be generated. This publishes an HTML version of the error report. The -DelHtmlReport indicates that the report should be deleted after the specified <time period>. |
| -RmUnusedSpace<br>threshold_percent<br>free_percent | Enables the task to remove unused space. Threshold_percent indicates in megabytes the size the database must reach before sqlmaint will try to remove the unused space. Free_percent indicates how much unused space must remain. |
| -CkDB \| -CkDBNoIdx | If -CkDB is specified, DBCC CHECKDB runs with checks to data and indexes. If -CKDBNoIdx is selected, indexes are skipped. |
| -CkAl \| -CkAlNoIdx | If -CkAl is specified, DBCC NEWALLOC is run for both data and indexes. If -CkAlNoIdx is specified, DBCC NEWALLOC skips indexes. DBCC NEWALLOC is actually included for backward compatibility, and is identical to DBCC CHECKALLOC. Outside this utility, use DBCC CHECKALLOC instead of DBCC NEWALLOC. Both DBCC CHECKALLOC and NEWALLOC check the consistency of disk space allocation structures. |
| -CkCat | When specified, DBCC CHECKCATALOG is run. This DBCC command checks for system table consistency. |

| Switch | Description |
|---|---|
| `-UpdOptiStats sample_percent` | Runs the `UPDATE STATISTICS` table `WITH SAMPLE sample_percent PERCENT` statement for each table in the database. |
| `-RebldIdx free_space` | Indicates fill factor for rebuilt indexes. |
| `-WriteHistory` | Enters history into `msdb.dbo.sysdbmaintplan_history`. |
| `-BkUpDB [backup_path] \| -BkUpLog [backup_path]`<br>`-BkUpMedia`<br>`DISK [`<br>[-DelBkUps <time_period>]<br>`[-CrBkSubDir ] [ -UseDefDir ] ]`<br>`\| TAPE` | `-BkUpDB` indicates backup path for full backup.<br>`-BkUpLog` indicates backup path for transaction log.<br>`backup_path` indicates the directory for the backup. If you indicate `-UseDefDir`, this isn't necessary. Default file naming for backups is `dbname_log_yyyymmddhhmm.BAK`.<br>`-BkUpMedia` indicates backup media type `DISK` or `TAPE`.<br>-DelBkUps <time period> indicates the time interval after which the backup file will be deleted.<br>`-CrBkSubDir` indicates that a subdirectory will be created in the backup path using a folder for each database, with the database name specified in the folder.<br>`-UseDefDir` specifies that the default backup directory be used. |
| `-BkUpOnlyIfClean` | This option checks the integrity of the database before running a backup. Just like the maintenance plan setup, this can be a costly operation, so avoid using it if possible. |
| `-VrfyBackup` | Runs a `RESTORE VERIFYONLY` after submitting the backup. |

In the example below, we run the following statement in Query Analyzer:

```
EXEC xp_sqlmaint '-S JOEPROD -D BookRepository -BkUpLog -UseDefDir
                 -BkUpMedia DISK -CrBkSubDir'
```

This statement runs a transaction log backup for the `BookRepository` database on the `DOPEY\DOPEY` server, using the default directory. It also creates a subdirectory for the backup. To run, the `xp_sqlmaint` procedure call requires either `db_owner` membership of the `master` database, or sysadmin permissions. This procedure can also be made available for use by other users (`GRANT EXEC` permissions, reviewed in Chapter 7):

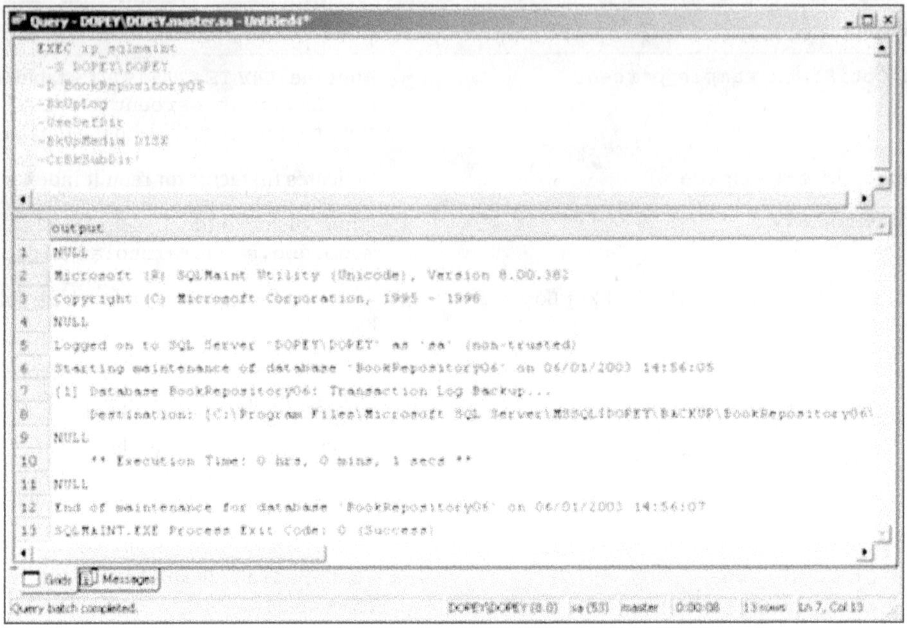


The subdirectory and file deletion options are the most useful functions of this utility. When `CrBkSubDir` is set, a new directory is created for each backed up database, if it does not already exist. If you do not use `xp_sqlmaint` for backups, you must create folders manually, or just output all backups to a central folder.

The `DelBkUps` switch allows you to remove backup files that exceed a certain age. If not using `xp_sqlmaint` for this functionality, you will need to explore using Transact-SQL (most likely `xp_cmdshell` and an OS deletion statement) to maintain the number of days' worth of backups to keep on your server.

`DBCC CHECKDB`, `BACKUP DATABASE`, `BACKUP LOG`, and `DBCC DBREINDEX` include more options than `sqlmaint` and `xp_sqlmaint`, but you will need to code them yourself instead of simply running the stored procedure.

# 6.23 How to... Check Consistency of the Disk Space Allocation Structures with DBCC CHECKALLOC

`DBCC CHECKALLOC` checks page usage and allocation in the database. Use this `DBCC` command if only allocation errors are found for the database. If you run `DBCC CHECKDB`, you do not need to run `DBCC CHECKALLOC`, as `DBCC CHECKDB` includes the same checks (and more) that `DBCC CHECKALLOC` performs.

The syntax from SQL Server Books Online is as follows:

```
DBCC CHECKALLOC
    ( 'database_name'
            [ , NOINDEX
                |
```

```
                { REPAIR_ALLOW_DATA_LOSS
                    | REPAIR_FAST
                    | REPAIR_REBUILD
                } ]
    )     [ WITH { [ ALL_ERRORMSGS | NO_INFOMSGS ]
                    [ , [ TABLOCK ] ]
                    [ , [ ESTIMATEONLY ] ]
                }
        ]
```

| Option | Description |
|---|---|
| database_name | The name of the database on which to perform allocation and page usage checks. Defaults to current database if not set. |
| NOINDEX | A backward compatibility option – do not use this. Originally used to skip nonclustered index for user tables. |
| REPAIR_ALLOW_DATA_LOSS<br><br>\| REPAIR_FAST \| REPAIR_REBUILD | REPAIR_ALLOW_DATA_LOSS is the most invasive option. Repairs can result in data loss, so embed this in a transaction so you can roll it back if problems occur. If you roll the transaction back, keep in mind that the problems will not be fixed.<br><br>REPAIR_FAST – does minor repair actions with no data loss.<br><br>REPAIR_REBUILD – does minor repairs done by REPAIR_FAST and some time-consuming repairs (rebuilding indexes). There is no risk of data loss. |
| ALL_ERRORMSGS | Shows every error from the command. When not included, SQL Server displays up to 200 error messages per object. |
| NO_INFOMSGS | No informational messages will be returned. |
| TABLOCK | Ignored for this command. |
| ESTIMATEONLY | Reports tempdb space required to run the command. |

The following example runs DBCC CHECKALLOC without any fixes if an issue is found. This will help you detect whether there are errors. If you do identify errors, you can then put the database into single user mode and run DBCC CHECKALLOC with one of the three fix options.

## Example 6.23.1: Run DBCC CHECKALLOC

We'll run DBCC CHECKALLOC on the BookRepository:

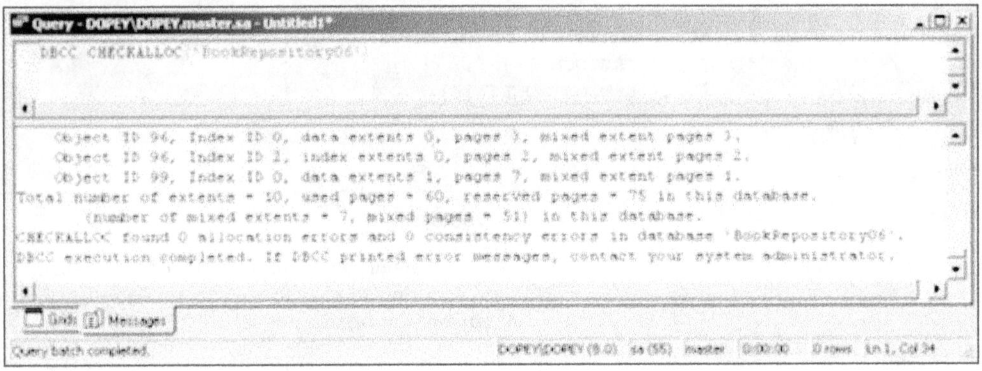


Look at the last few rows of the result set to see if any allocation or consistency errors are found in your database. For example:

CHECKALLOC found 0 allocation errors and 0 consistency errors in database 'BookRepository06'.

If you find errors, you should run the DBCC CHECKALLOC command using the least invasive repair option, REPAIR_FAST, first. If this doesn't fix the problem, next use REPAIR_REBUILD. Lastly, if REPAIR_REBUILD does not work, use REPAIR_ALLOW_DATA_LOSS.

## Example 6.23.2: Run DBCC CHECKALLOC with REPAIR_FAST

In the next example, we run the DBCC command with the REPAIR_FAST option, suppressing informational messages. We do not need an explicit transaction, as this will not risk any data loss. We do still need to be in single user mode:

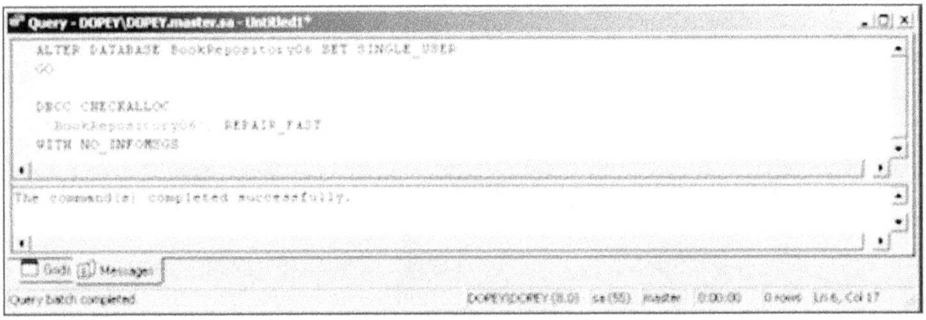


## Example 6.23.3: Run DBCC CHECKALLOC with REPAIR_REBUILD and ESTIMATEONLY

In the next example, we run DBCC CHECKALLOC with REPAIR_REBUILD and ESTIMATEONLY specified. Even when you are just estimating the tempdb space and not actually running the command, the database must be in single user mode:

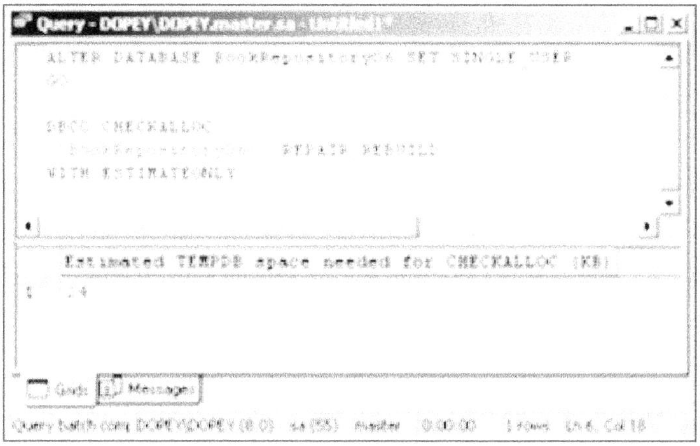

The report output shows that 28KB is required in the tempdb space. By removing WITH ESTIMATEONLY, you can then run this command for real.

### Example 6.23.4: Run DBCC with REPAIR_ALLOW_DATA_LOSS

The following is an example of running DBCC CHECKALLOC with REPAIR_ALLOW_DATA_LOSS. This example:

- Puts the database into single user mode (required).
- Creates BEGIN TRANSACTION, so we may roll it back if the database loses an unacceptable amount of data.
- Issues the DBCC CHECKALLOC statement:

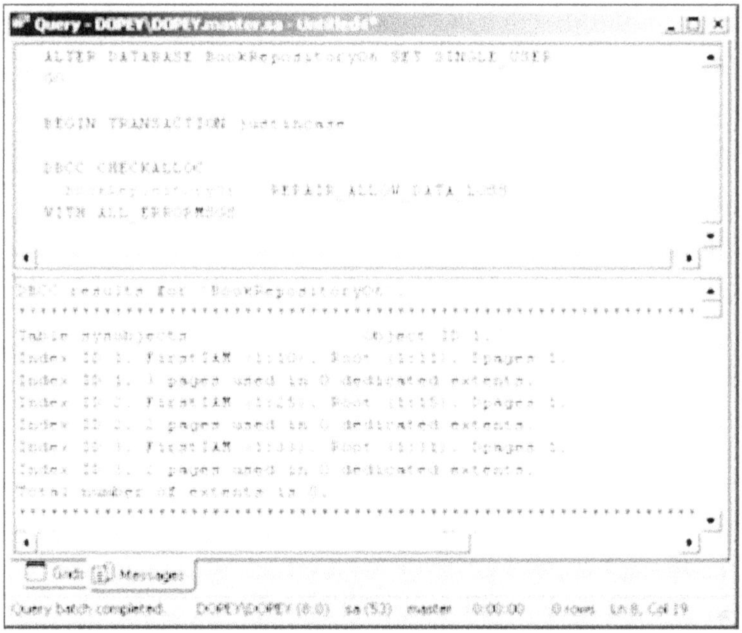

If your REPAIR_ALLOW_DATA_LOSS operation results in unacceptable data loss, you can roll back the transaction by issuing the following command:

```
ROLLBACK TRANSACTION justincase
GO
ALTER DATABASE BookRepository SET MULTI_USER
GO
```

# 6.24 How to... Check System Table Consistency with DBCC CHECKCATALOG

This command checks for consistency in and between system tables. This DBCC command is not covered by the DBCC CHECKDB command, so running it weekly is recommended.

The syntax from SQL Server Books Online is very straightforward:

```
DBCC CHECKCATALOG ( 'database_name' ) [ WITH NO_INFOMSGS ]
```

| Option | Description |
|---|---|
| database_name | Database to run the DBCC command. Uses the current database context if not specified. |
| WITH NO_INFOMSGS | Suppresses all information and space usage messages if they equal less than 200 rows. |

### Example 6.24.1: Run DBCC with CHECKCATALOG

The following example demonstrates execution of DBCC CHECKCATALOG against the BookRepository database:

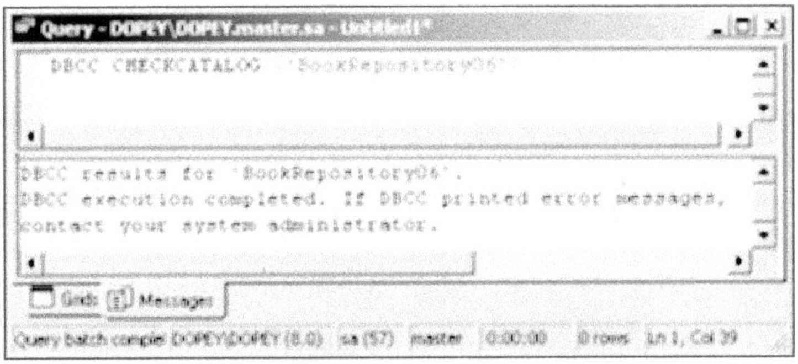
Query - DOPEY\DOPEY.master.sa - Untitled1*
DBCC CHECKCATALOG ('BookRepository06')
DBCC results for 'BookRepository06'.
DBCC execution completed. If DBCC printed error messages, contact your system administrator.
Grids
Messages

# 6.25 How to... Check Table Integrity with DBCC CHECKCONSTRAINTS

DBCC CHECKCONSTRAINTS alerts you to any CHECK or constraint violations. The syntax from SQL Server Books Online is as follows:

```
DBCC CHECKCONSTRAINTS
    [( 'table_name' | 'constraint_name'
    )]
    [ WITH { ALL_ERRORMSGS | ALL_CONSTRAINTS } ]
```

| Option | Description |
|---|---|
| 'table_name' \| 'constraint_name' | Defines which table or constraint to check for foreign key or CHECK constraint violations. If nothing is selected, all constraints on all tables in the database are checked. |
| ALL_ERRORMSGS \| ALL_CONSTRAINTS | ALL_ERRORMSGS returns all rows that violate constraints; otherwise, only the first 200 rows are returned.<br><br>ALL_CONSTRAINTS checks both enabled and disabled table constraints. Not valid if a constraint name is mentioned. |

Use DBCC CHECKCONSTRAINTS if you suspect that there are rows in your tables that do not meet the constraint or CHECK constraint rules. For example, if we have the following relationship between Books and Authors:

The Books table contains a foreign key reference to the Authors table for the iAuthorId column. We can check the integrity of this foreign key constraint using DBCC CHECKCONSTRAINTS:

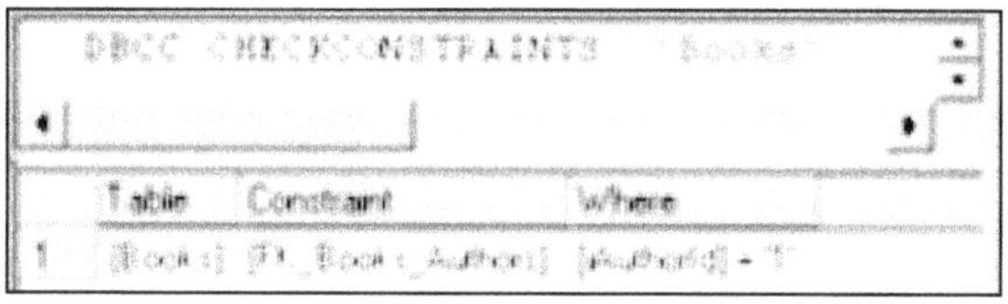

We see that the FK_Books_Authors constraint has been violated, where iAuthorId = '1'. If you check the Authors table, you will see that there is indeed no iAuthorId with the value '1'. This situation can occur when foreign key constraints are created with the option of **ignoring** existing values. This directs SQL Server to enforce foreign key relationships for **new** operations only. Foreign key violations can also occur when constraints have been disabled (but not deleted) from a table (see Chapter 14, for the section *Disabling constraints using ALTER TABLE*):

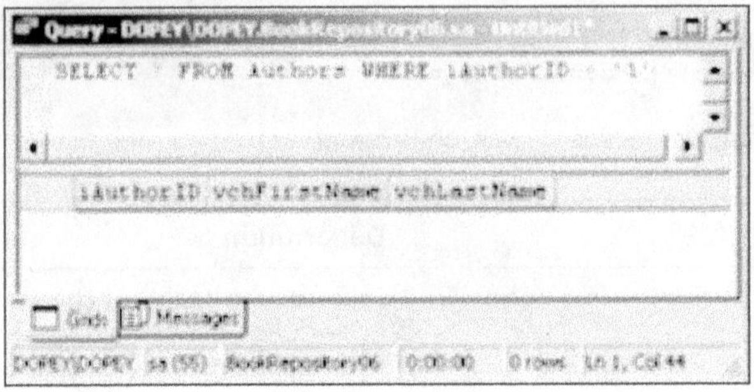


To remedy the situation, we can add an Author record to the Authors table:

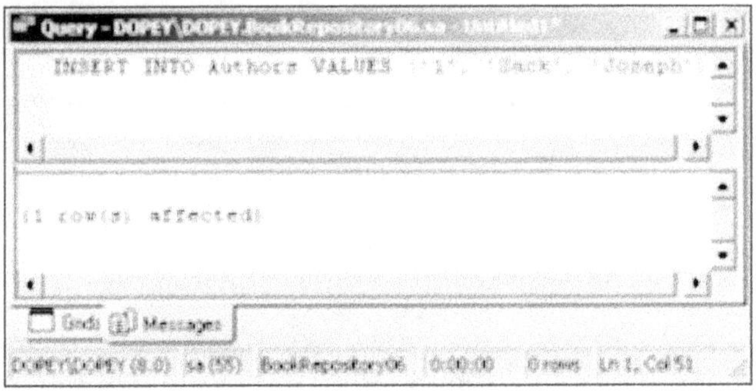


Rerunning the same DBCC CHECKCONSTRAINTS, you will find no errors appear:

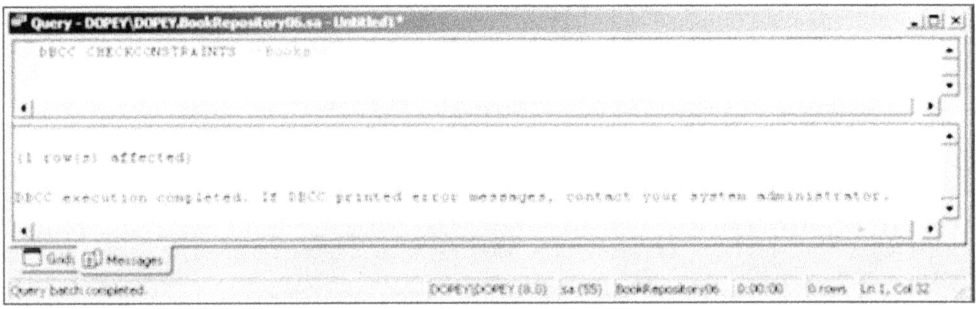


Remember that you do not need to run this table by table, but can run it for all tables in the database. For example:

```
DBCC CHECKCONSTRAINTS
```

# 6.26 How to... Check Allocation and Structural Integrity of All Database Objects with DBCC CHECKDB

DBCC CHECKDB should run on your SQL Server instance weekly. Although each release of SQL Server reduces occurrences of integrity or allocation errors, they still occur from time to time.

The DBCC CHECKDB syntax from SQL Server Books Online is as follows:

```
DBCC CHECKDB
    ( 'database_name'
            [ , NOINDEX
                | { REPAIR_ALLOW_DATA_LOSS
                    | REPAIR_FAST
                    | REPAIR_REBUILD
                    } ]
    )     [ WITH { [ ALL_ERRORMSGS ]
                    [ , [ NO_INFOMSGS ] ]
                    [ , [ TABLOCK ] ]
                    [ , [ ESTIMATEONLY ] ]
                    [ , [ PHYSICAL_ONLY ] ]
                    }
         ]
```

| Option | Description |
|---|---|
| database_name | Database for the integrity check. If not specified, the integrity check uses the current database context. |
| NOINDEX | Skips checks of nonclustered indexes for user tables. This option can decrease execution time significantly. Use this if your DBCC CHECKDB command takes too long. Make sure your indexes are rebuilt often enough to justify not checking them. |
| REPAIR_ALLOW_DATA_LOSS<br>\| REPAIR_FAST<br>\| REPAIR_REBUILD | REPAIR_ALLOW_DATA_LOSS is the most invasive fix option when errors exist. Some data loss could occur during the fix. Single user mode is required.<br>REPAIR_FAST performs minor fixes, without risk of data loss. This is the fastest repair option. Single user mode is required.<br>REPAIR_REBUILD performs minor fixes, and some time-consuming repairs (rebuilding indexes). No data loss is risked. Single user mode is required. |
| ALL_ERRORMSGS | Shows errors per object for all objects. If not specified, 200 is the limit of errors per object. |
| NO_INFOMSGS | Specifies that informational messages are not returned. |

*Table continued on following page*

| Option | Description |
|---|---|
| TABLOCK | Forces DBCC CHECKDB to obtain shared table locks. This makes DBCC CHECKDB run faster, but reduces concurrency. Other users will have more restricted resource-locking access. |
| ESTIMATEONLY | Shows how much tempdb space is needed to run with the options specified, but the actual DBCC command is not run. |
| PHYSICAL_ONLY | This option limits checking to the physical structures, torn pages, and consistency between page object ID, index ID, and allocation structure. This option cannot be used with repair options, and defaults to NO_INFOMSGS. |

DBCC CHECKDB includes the same checks as DBCC CHECKALLOC and DBCC CHECKTABLE.

Some behaviors to be aware of with DBCC CHECKDB:

- DBCC CHECKDB (and DBCC CHECKTABLE) may fail when checking a table with an index on a computed column. The error message is:

  "DBCC failed because the following SET options have incorrect settings: 'QUOTED_IDENTIFIER, ARITHABORT'"

  This happens when DBCC CHECKDB is scheduled from a job or a maintenance plan: this is not a bug, as computed columns require the settings in the error. To fix this, change any job you have scheduled that runs for indexed computed columns to include settings such as:

```
SET ARITHABORT ON
SET QUOTED_IDENTIFIER ON
DBCC CHECKDB(BookRepository)
GO
```

- After upgrading SQL Server 7 to SQL Server 2000, you may see an error when DBCC CHECKDB runs on your nonclustered indexes. Whenever you upgrade from 7.0 to 2000, drop and rebuild your indexes or run DBCC DBREINDEX for all your tables. SQL Server 2000 has a nonclustered index column that allows insertion of NULL values into the sysindexes.status; however, SQL Server 7.0 has different value (0), which can cause issues after an upgrade. For more information, see Microsoft's Knowledge Base article Q298806, *PRB: Index Corruption Occurs in a Database That Is Upgraded to SQL Server 2000*
- DBCC CHECKDB uses tempdb, so use the ESTIMATEONLY switch to ensure you have enough space. Also, using NO_INFOMSGS can reduce tempdb use.
- DBCC CHECKDB is rough on concurrency. Run this during quiet server times, but **do** run it at least once a week.

### Example 6.26.1: Run DBCC CHECKDB with ESTIMATEONLY

To verify how much `tempdb` space your `CHECKDB` operation will need, run:

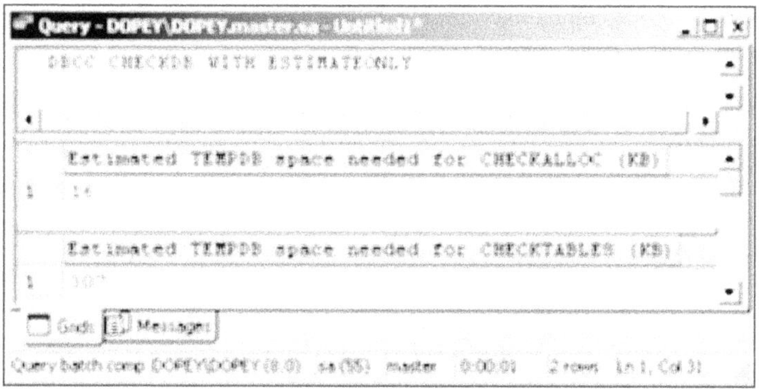


Notice that estimates are made for both `CHECKALLOC` and `CHECKTABLES`.

### Example 6.26.2: Check for errors using DBCC CHECKDB

To check for the existence of errors from your current database context in Query Analyzer, run:

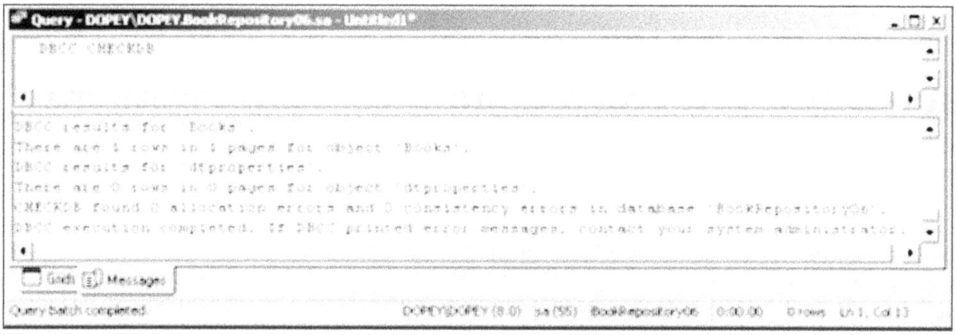


Check the final rows to confirm whether any allocation or consistency errors have been found.

### Example 6.26.3: Repair with REPAIR_FAST

If you found errors, run the least invasive repair statement first: `REPAIR_FAST`. This will require that your database is running in single user mode:

```
ALTER DATABASE BookRepository SET SINGLE_USER

DBCC CHECKDB ('BookRepository', REPAIR_FAST)
```

### Example 6.26.4: Repair with REPAIR_REBUILD

If this did not work, try the next level of repairs (no data loss, but more time-consuming), `REPAIR_REBUILD`:

```
ALTER DATABASE BookRepository SET SINGLE_USER

DBCC CHECKDB ('BookRepository', REPAIR_REBUILD)
```

### Example 6.26.5: Repair with REPAIR_ALLOW_DATA_LOSS

If this doesn't fix the errors, try the most invasive option, `REPAIR_ALLOW_DATA_LOSS`. Remember to embed this `DBCC` command within a `BEGIN TRANSACTION` statement, so that you can roll back the transaction should the data loss (if any) become unacceptable. It doesn't hurt to do a full backup of the database prior to running this, too:

```
ALTER DATABASE BookRepository SET SINGLE_USER

BEGIN TRANSACTION dbccrepair
DBCC CHECKDB ('BookRepository', REPAIR_ALLOW_DATA_LOSS)
```

If the database was fixed by this last option, do not forget to commit the transaction. You must do so from the same query session. Highlight the `COMMIT` statement you wish to execute, so the transaction is not rerun, but the existing transaction is committed:

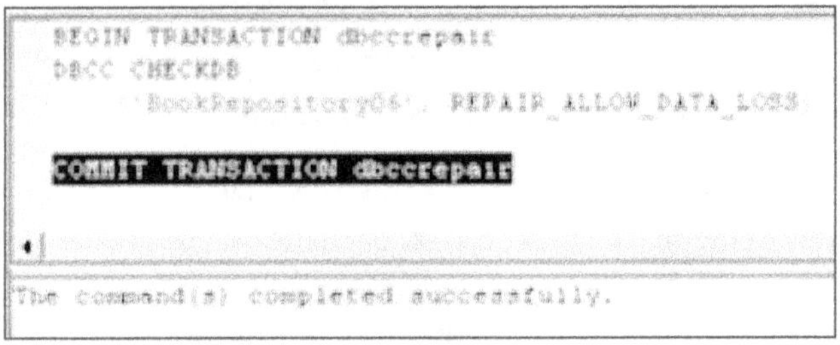


## What if DBCC CHECKDB Cannot Fix Your Problems?

If the integrity errors belong to specific tables, you can try exporting the data to a new table, dropping the existing table or tables, and renaming the new tables to the old names. Dropping and recreating the clustered index has also been known to work for table corruption.

If you are unable to retrieve any data from a corrupted table, then you must restore your database from the last good backup to a **new** database. You can then drop the corrupted tables and replace any tables that were corrupted from the last good backup. This may not be acceptable for your application, as you will lose any data updated since the last good backup.

If you cannot afford to lose the data that is currently corrupted, and a restore of data would cause unacceptable data loss, your last chance is to open a call with Microsoft. They may be able to fix your issue, but you may need to pay for such a call. Consider that the issue may be attributed to hardware problems (physical disk corruption), and may not be fixable.

# 6.27 How to... Check data, index, text, ntext, and image Pages for Tables or Indexed Views Using DBCC CHECKTABLE

`DBCC CHECKTABLE` is almost identical to `DBCC CHECKDB`, except that it is performed at the table, not the database, level. `DBCC CHECKTABLE` verifies index and data page links, index sort order, page pointers, index pointers, data page integrity, and page offsets. `DBCC CHECKTABLE` uses schema locks by default, but can use the `TABLOCK` option to acquire a shared table lock. `CHECKTABLE` also performs object checking using parallelism by default (if on a multi-CPU system).

The syntax from SQL Server Books Online is as follows:

```
DBCC CHECKTABLE
    ( 'table_name' | 'view_name'
        [ , NOINDEX
            | index_id
            | { REPAIR_ALLOW_DATA_LOSS
                | REPAIR_FAST
                | REPAIR_REBUILD }
        ]
    )    [ WITH { [ ALL_ERRORMSGS | NO_INFOMSGS ]
                    [ , [ TABLOCK ] ]
                    [ , [ ESTIMATEONLY ] ]
                    [ , [ PHYSICAL_ONLY ] ]
                }
        ]
```

| Option | Description |
|---|---|
| table_name \| view_name | Table or indexed view to check. |
| NOINDEX | Skips checks of nonclustered indexes. Can decrease execution time significantly. |
| REPAIR_ALLOW_DATA_LOSS<br>\| REPAIR_FAST<br>\| REPAIR_REBUILD | REPAIR_ALLOW_DATA_LOSS is the most invasive fix option when errors exist. Some data loss could occur during the fix. Single user mode is required.<br>REPAIR_FAST performs minor fixes, without risk of data loss. This is the fastest repair option. Single user mode is required.<br>REPAIR_REBUILD performs minor fixes, and some time-consuming repairs (rebuilding indexes). No data loss is risked. Single user mode is required. |
| ALL_ERRORMSGS | Shows errors per object for all objects. If not specified, 200 is the limit of errors per object. |
| NO_INFOMSGS | Specifies that informational messages are not returned. |
| TABLOCK | Forces DBCC CHECKTABLE to obtain shared table locks. This makes DBCC CHECKTABLE run faster, but reduces concurrency. Other users will have more restricted resource-locking access. |
| ESTIMATEONLY | Shows how much tempdb space is needed to run with the options specified, but the actual DBCC command is not run. |
| PHYSICAL_ONLY | This option limits checking to the physical structures, torn pages, and consistency between page object ID, index ID, and allocation structure. This option cannot be used with repair options, and defaults to NO_INFOMSGS. |

### Example 6.27.1: Run DBCC with CHECKTABLE

To estimate how much tempdb space you will need for your DBCC CHECKTABLE command, run:

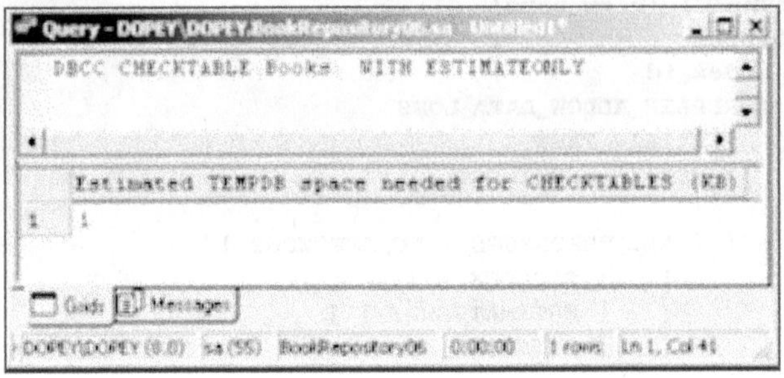


To run the command on a table:

```
DBCC CHECKTABLE(Books)
```

If you encounter an error, just like DBCC CHECKDB, you should try the following commands in the order of least to most invasive:

- DBCC CHECKTABLE (table or indexed view, REPAIR_FAST)
- DBCC CHECKTABLE (table or indexed view, REPAIR_REBUILD)
- DBCC CHECKTABLE (table or indexed view, REPAIR_ALLOW_DATA_LOSS)

You should wrap REPAIR_ALLOW_DATA_LOSS within a transaction, without a COMMIT statement, so you can roll the transaction back if an unacceptable amount of data is lost.

# 6.28 How to... Check Allocation and Structural Integrity of All Tables in a Filegroup using DBCC CHECKFILEGROUP

DBCC CHECKFILEGROUP works just like DBCC CHECKDB, only DBCC CHECKFILEGROUP checks the specified filegroup for allocation and structural issues.

If you have a very large database (this term is relative, and higher end systems may be more adept at performing well with multi-GB or TB systems), running DBCC CHECKDB can take far longer then you may have time for. If you have your database divided into user-defined filegroups, DBCC CHECKFILEGROUP will allow you to separate out your integrity checks, and stagger them over a number of days.

The syntax from SQL Server Books Online is as follows:

```
DBCC CHECKFILEGROUP
    ( [ { 'filegroup' | filegroup_id } ]
        [ , NOINDEX ]
    )    [ WITH { [ ALL_ERRORMSGS | NO_INFOMSGS ]
                    [ , [ TABLOCK ] ]
                    [ , [ ESTIMATEONLY ] ]
                    }
        ]
```

| Option | Description |
|---|---|
| filegroup \| filegroup_id | Filegroup or filegroup identification number for which to check allocation and structural integrity. |
| NOINDEX | Skips checks of nonclustered indexes. Can decrease execution time significantly if you have nonclustered indexes on very large tables. |
| ALL_ERRORMSGS \| NO_INFOMSGS | ALL_ERRORMSGS returns all error messages. When not set, a maximum of 200 error messages per table are returned.<br><br>NO_INFOMSGS suppresses all informational and space usage messages. |
| TABLOCK | A shared table lock is generated which speeds up the DBCC command but slows down database concurrency. |
| ESTIMATEONLY | Displays the space needed in tempdb to run the DBCC command. |

Conspicuously missing are the FIX commands that come with DBCC CHECKDB, DBCC CHECKTABLE, and DBCC CHECKALLOC. When errors occur, error fixes should be performed by CHECKDB, CHECKTABLE, or CHECKALLOC.

Filegroups are often used to separate tables from nonclustered indexes. The rules for checking objects that have relations in **other** filegroups depend on whether you are checking a table or a nonclustered index:

| Object | Related Object in Other Filegroup | Checked by DBCC? |
|---|---|---|
| Table (heap or clustered index) | Nonclustered index | Table, but not the nonclustered index in another filegroup. |
| Nonclustered index | Table | Both are checked, since nonclustered indexes have integrity based on table. |

## Example 6.28.1: Check user-defined filegroup for errors

The following is an example of running DBCC CHECKFILEGROUP for the BookRepository database's user-defined filegroup FG2:

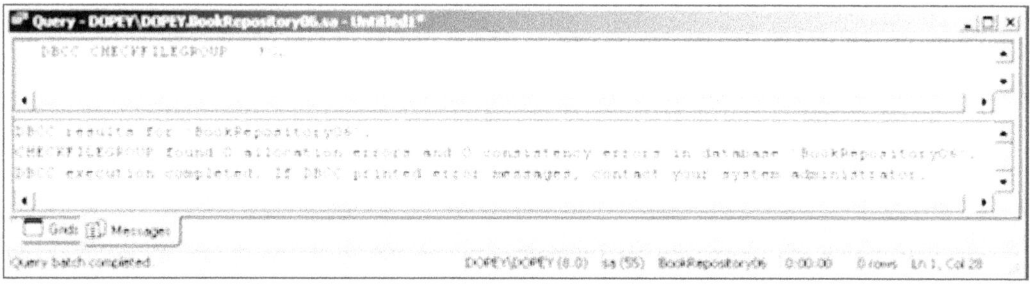

### Example 6.28.2: Check tempdb for errors

Next is an example of running this check with an estimate of `tempdb` only:

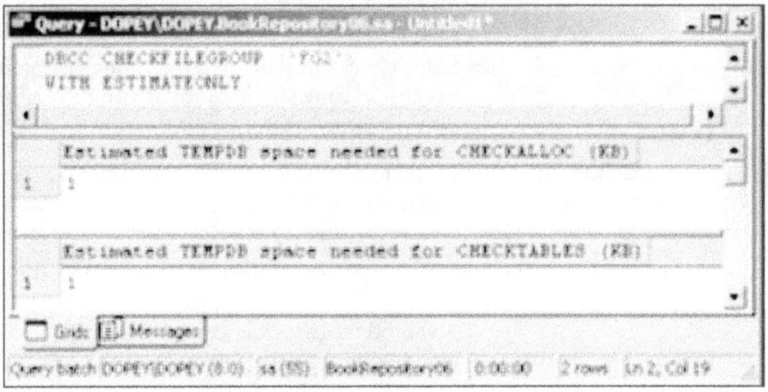


### Example 6.28.3: Run without nonclustered indexes check

Last is an example of running `CHECKFILEGROUP` with no checks of nonclustered indexes:

```
DBCC CHECKFILEGROUP ('FG2', NOINDEX)
```

# 6.29 How to... Disable Parallelism in DBCC CHECKDB, DBCC CHECKFILEGROUP, and DBCC CHECKTABLE

SQL Server 2000 performs parallel object checking for `DBCC CHECKDB`, `DBCC CHECKFILEGROUP`, and `DBCC CHECKTABLE` by default. The number of processors used to perform parallel operations is determined by the max degree of parallelism option.

Parallel processing is advantageous for the `DBCC` commands, but may reduce concurrency and resources for other processes running during the `DBCC` execution. Although you should run `DBCC CHECKDB` and the other commands during low usage periods, this is not always possible.

To disable parallel processing you can use trace flag 2528. The following is an example of disabling parallelism with `DBCC TRACEON(2528)`:

```
DBCC TRACEON(2528)
```

To disable this trace flag and re-enable parallelism for `DBCC` commands:

```
DBCC TRACEOFF(2528)
```

It is not generally recommended to disable parallel processing for the following reasons:

- Transaction log scanning by `DBCC` is increased
- Demand for `tempdb` space is increased
- When `TABLOCK` is enabled, the duration of the lock may be extended

# 6.30 How to... Output DBCC Data in Tabular Form using WITH TABLERESULTS

When writing your own custom maintenance scripts, you may need to capture the results of your `DBCC` commands. Some `DBCC` options provide you with the choice of returning informational and error messages in tabular format.

You can do this by specifying `WITH TABLERESULTS`. For many `DBCC` commands, this is not included in the regular syntax for SQL Server Books Online, but it is an option. For example, `DBCC CHECKDB` makes no mention of `WITH TABLERESULTS`; however, as you'll see in this example, it allows you to return results in column format:

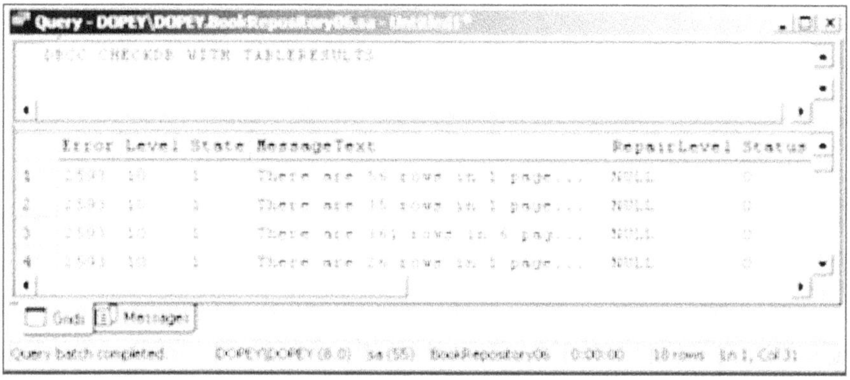


By returning results in tabular format, you can output them to a temporary or regular table, and process the results however you wish in your jobs or custom stored procedures.

### Example 6.30.1: Run DBCC ... WITH TABLERESULTS

In this example, we capture constraint violation data into a table.

- Create a table to capture violation data:

```
CREATE TABLE #ConstraintViolations
  (vchTable varchar(255),
   vchConstraint varchar(255),
   vchWhere varchar(255))
```

- Insert the data. We need to run the `DBCC` command using the `EXEC` function, and the command itself wrapped in single quotes:

```
INSERT #ConstraintViolations
EXEC('DBCC CHECKCONSTRAINTS WITH TABLERESULTS')
```

- Select the records from the table to confirm that something was captured. From here, you can process your table rows within your stored procedure or job:

```
SELECT * FROM #ConstraintViolations
```

# Index Fragmentation

Fragmentation is the natural byproduct of data modification. INSERT, UPDATE, and DELETE activity can cause table and index fragmentation over time. Fragmentation in SQL Server is categorized as either **internal** or **external**.

Internal fragmentation involves free space on the index pages. As data modifications occur, 8KB index pages will begin to produce row gaps. Depending on your level of database activity, fill factor, and indexing, fragmentation can happen slowly or very quickly; because gaps are left on the index pages, you will not necessarily see your data modification activity slow down. The biggest detriment caused by internal fragmentation is to your SELECT and read activity. Because fewer rows are stored over more pages, SQL Server must read more index or data pages to fulfill the same query request.

External fragmentation involves the order of the index pages themselves. The order of index pages may not be contiguous, which means that logical order doesn't match physical order. External fragmentation is usually caused by page splitting, when an index page is full and SQL Server must create two new pages and relocate rows to make room. This process can cause new pages that aren't physically contiguous. When requests are made for data to be logically ordered, and if external fragmentation exists, non-sequential disk access occurs. When index pages reflect the same logical and physical order, disk reads can pull the data in a continuous block (sequential read). If the logical and physical order is not the same, disk reads must scan the disk and move about to fulfill the same request, reducing performance.

Internal and external fragmentation are not the same as file-system fragmentation; physical file fragmentation can occur, as with any other file on a Windows operating system. The next section will not address issues of contiguous physical files and disk blocks. Physical fragmentation can reduce your I/O performance significantly, and there are third-party defragmentation utilities available (Executive Software's Diskeeper, Symantec's Norton SystemWorks), as well as the Windows 2000 defragmentation utilities. Although you can use Window 2000's defragmentation utility or other third-party utilities, your SQL Server services must still be **stopped** in order to perform defragmentation on .mdf and .ldf files. Because of this, defragmentation of the physical file may not be a viable option for your SQL Server instance.

We will now review how to handle internal and external SQL Server index fragmentation. For details on index architecture, see Chapter 14. For ways to identify index fragmentation, see Chapter 17.

# 6.31 How to... Rebuild Indexes with DBCC DBREINDEX

If your database allows modifications and has indexes, you should rebuild your indexes regularly. The frequency of your index rebuilds depends on the level of database activity, and how quickly your database and indexes become fragmented. For the average database that requires modifications, rebuilding indexes weekly is generally good practice. For read-only databases, you should build the indexes once prior to marking the database as read-only. From that point forward, index rebuilds for read-only databases will not be necessary, while they remain read-only.

DBCC DBREINDEX allows you to rebuild one index or all indexes for a table. Like DBCC CHECKDB, DBCC CHECKTABLE, and DBCC CHECKALLOC, running DBREINDEX during busy database times can reduce concurrency. The operation can be quite expensive in terms of concurrency and performance; and the duration for rebuilding the indexes could be significant depending on the table size and width of the index (how many columns make up the index). Also, note that rebuilding just the clustered index actually rebuilds all nonclustered indexes as well.

The syntax from SQL Server Books Online is as follows:

```
DBCC DBREINDEX
    (    [ 'database.owner.table_name'
            [ , index_name
                [ , fillfactor ]
            ]
        ]
    )    [ WITH NO_INFOMSGS ]
```

| Option | Description |
|---|---|
| database.owner.table_name | Table for which to rebuild all indexes or a selected index. |
| index_name | Name of the index to rebuild. If not specified, all indexes are rebuilt. |
| fillfactor | Percentage of space on the index page to be used to store data. For example, specifying 80 translates to 80% of the index page filled with rows, saving 20% for new inserts. Specifying 100% leaves no free space, and 0% indicates the original fillfactor specified during the CREATE INDEX statement. |
| WITH NO_INFOMSGS | Keeps informational messages from being returned. |

### Example 6.31.1: Rebuild indexes

In the following example, we will rebuild all indexes for the Books table with their original fill factor:

```
DBCC DBREINDEX ('BookRepository.dbo.Books', '', 0)
```

### Example 6.31.2: Rebuild a specific index

In this next example, we rebuild a specific index, IX_Books, with a fill factor of 80 by running:

```
DBCC DBREINDEX ('BookRepository.dbo.Books', 'IX_Books', 80)
```

Some behaviors to be aware of:

- Run DBCC DBREINDEX during low activity periods in the database. DBCC DBREINDEX can cause significant table blocking while it runs.
- Make sure automatic database shrinking is not enabled while you run DBCC DBREINDEX. Corruption errors can occur if a shrink operation is issued during a DBREINDEX operation.
- For running DBCC DBREINDEX on an indexed view, see Knowledge Base article Q310624, *BUG: DBCC DBREINDEX on Indexed View May Cause Handled Access Violation*. This bug affects Developer, Enterprise, and Enterprise Evaluation Editions.

You may be thinking 'DBCC DBREINDEX seems nice, but I have 400 tables; am I going to have to script this out for each one?' The answer is 'no'. There are many ways to do this, but here is one example of running DBCC DBREINDEX for all tables and indexes, using the default fill factor (note that this script can be downloaded from http://www.apress.com).

In the first section, we populate a temporary table with a list of all base tables from the informational schema view `information_schema.tables`:

```
SELECT table_name
INTO #tablestoindex
FROM information_schema.tables
WHERE table_type = 'base table'
```

Next, we create a variable to hold the table name:

```
DECLARE @Table sysname
```

Then we begin a loop that re-indexes each table until the table count is empty:

```
WHILE (SELECT COUNT(*) FROM #tablestoindex) > 0
BEGIN
```

We then populate the variable with the maximum table name from the temporary table. It really doesn't matter in what order these tables are re-indexed, so you could also use the aggregate function `MIN`:

```
SELECT @Table = MAX(table_name) FROM #tablestoindex
```

Next, we print the progress of the table for which we are rebuilding indexes and then run `DBCC DBREINDEX` for the table specified in the `@Table` variable:

```
PRINT 'Rebuilding index for ' + @Table
DBCC DBREINDEX(@Table,'',0 )
```

We then remove the `@table` name we just re-indexed from the temporary table:

```
DELETE #tablestoindex
WHERE table_name = @Table
```

This `END` statement marks the end of the `WHILE` loop. The `BEGIN...END` statement will only end when the `COUNT(*)` from `#tabletoindex` is no longer greater than `0`:

```
END
```

Lastly, we drop the temporary table we created:

```
DROP TABLE #tablestoindex
```

# 6.32 How to... Defragment Indexes with DBCC INDEXDEFRAG

Microsoft introduced the excellent `DBCC INDEXDEFRAG` statement with SQL Server 2000. This `DBCC` command, unlike `DBCC DBREINDEX`, does not hold long-term locks on indexes. Use `DBCC INDEXDEFRAG` for indexes that are not very fragmented, otherwise the time this operation takes will be far longer then running `DBCC DBREINDEX`. The ability to run `DBCC INDEXDEFRAG` during busy times makes this a good option for databases that cannot run `DBCC DBREINDEX` frequently.

The syntax from SQL Server Books Online is as follows:

```
DBCC INDEXDEFRAG
    ( { database_name | database_id | 0 }
        , { table_name | table_id | 'view_name' | view_id }
        , { index_name | index_id }
    )     [ WITH NO_INFOMSGS ]
```

| Option | Description |
|---|---|
| `database_name` \| `database_id` \| `0` | Database name or ID to defragment. If `0` is specified, `DBCC INDEXDEFRAG` uses the current database context. |
| `table_name` \| `table_id` \| `view_id` | The table or indexed view name, table ID, or indexed view ID to defragment. |
| `index_name` \| `index_id` | The index name or ID to defragment. |
| `NO_INFOMSGS` | Leaves out all information messages. |

An example of running `DBCC INDEXDEFRAG` for the `BookRepository` database and `BooksISBN` table:

Notice that the report output shows pages scanned, moved, and removed.

Some other behaviors to be aware of for `DBCC INDEXDEFRAG`:

- System tables are not defragmented.
- The original index fill factor is used for this operation.
- Pages are reorganized by file, not across files. Pages are not moved between files.
- If the `DBCC INDEXDEFRAG` runs for a long time, an update will be returned every five minutes to give an estimated percentage completed.
- If you encounter errors when issuing `DBCC INDEXDEFRAG` against indexes containing varchar columns, see the Microsoft Knowledge Base article Q324630, *FIX: DBCC INDEXDEFRAG May Cause an Assertion Failure If the Index Includes Variable-Length Columns*.

One strategy for index maintenance is to mix `DBCC INDEXDEFRAG` and `DBCC DBREINDEX`. For example, you run `DBCC` commands in the following schedule:

| When? | Command |
|---|---|
| First weekend of the month | DBCC DBREINDEX |
| Second weekend of the month | DBCC INDEXDEFRAG |
| Third weekend of the month | DBCC INDEXDEFRAG |
| Fourth weekend of the month | DBCC INDEXDEFRAG |

INDEXDEFRAG requires the database, table, and index name. The following is an example of running this command against the index idx_BookId of the BookRepository database's Book table:

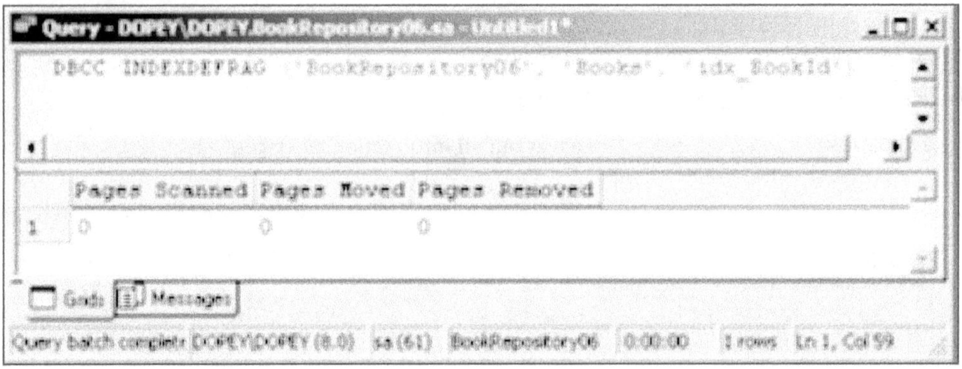


What if you want to run INDEXDEFRAG against all your user tables? If you have 300 tables, must you manually run this 300 times? SQL Server Books Online actually has a script example in the DBCC SHOWCONTIG topic (see Chapter 17). Their script allows you to run DBCC INDEXDEFRAG for all user tables that exceed a certain fragmentation threshold.

# 6.33 How to... Defragment Heaps

When rebuilding a clustered index, you are actually defragmenting the data pages of the table. A table may only have **one** clustered index; in a clustered index, data rows are stored in the order of the clustered index key. Running DBCC DBREINDEX or DBCC INDEXDEFRAG on a clustered index reduces fragmentation.

Tables without a clustered index are called heaps and data rows in a heap are stored in no particular order and, therefore, the data pages have no particular order.

Without a clustered index, there is no inherent way to reorganize and fix internal or external fragmentation.

Some tips for keeping heap fragmentation low:

- **Use a clustered index**
  There are differing opinions on this, but some say **every** table should have a clustered index no matter what. Others disagree; you don't need a clustered index on smaller tables or tables used for temporary data loads (as they slow down the INSERTs). One big advantage of having a clustered index is it can then be defragmented when accessed by regular DBCC DBREINDEX or DBCC INDEXDEFRAG jobs.

  By default, add a clustered index for **all** tables. If there are complaints about the performance that the clustered index is causing, carry out a test to see if this impact is real or imagined (see Chapter 17 for techniques for testing query performance).

- **Add a clustered index to your table temporarily**
  If your developers won't let you add a clustered index, you can use one temporarily, to defragment the table, and remove it when you're done.

# 6.34 How to… Reclaim Space after Dropping Variable Length or Text Columns with DBCC CLEANTABLE

Having run ALTER TABLE DROP COLUMN for a variable length or text column, SQL Server does not automatically reclaim space after performing this statement. To reclaim the space being wasted, you must run DBCC CLEANTABLE.

The syntax from SQL Server Books Online is as follows:

```
DBCC CLEANTABLE
    ( { 'database_name' | database_id }
        , { 'table_name' | table_id | 'view_name' | view_id }
        [ , batch_size ]
    )
```

| Option | Description |
|---|---|
| database_name \| database_id | Database name or ID. |
| table_name \| table_id \| view_name \| view_id | Table name or ID, indexed view name or ID. |
| batch_size | The number of rows to be processed for each transaction. If you have millions of rows, it is a good idea to make this a small number (1000 to 10,000 rows), as this operation is fully logged. If DBCC CLEANTABLE is treated as one giant transaction, rolling back updates in the recovery when there is a system failure would be quite time-consuming. |

The following is an example of removing a text field from the Books table and reclaiming the space with DBCC CLEANTABLE:

```
USE BookRepository

ALTER TABLE Books DROP COLUMN txtDescription
GO

DBCC CLEANTABLE ('BookRepository', 'Books')
```

# 7

# Security

In this chapter, we will discuss SQL Server 2000 security. This is a vital issue, as seemingly innocuous mistakes in securing SQL Server can create vulnerabilities throughout your entire network. When considering SQL Server security, we must look at the following areas:

- **SQL Server logins and users**
  Logins provide access to a SQL Server instance. Users provide access to the database or databases within the SQL Server instance. This chapter will discuss how to configure and manage logins and users. The different types of logins, Windows authentication and SQL authentication, will also be discussed.
- **SQL Server permissions**
  Permissions are actions that a user or login is allowed to perform within the database or SQL Server instance. Permissions can be granted to users, logins, or roles (discussed next). This chapter will review permissions in detail.
- **SQL Server roles**
  Roles allow us to group together multiple database users that must perform similar database activities and require the same permissions within the database. SQL Server comes with pre-defined (fixed) database and server roles. You can also create user-defined database roles and application roles. Each role type will be reviewed in this chapter.
- **SQL Server service accounts**
  The SQL Server service account can be run either as the local system account or as a domain user account. Let's say that a Windows 2000 administrator creates a domain account for use by all SQL Server service accounts. The administrator thinks this will minimize the total number of service accounts, saving time in password-change maintenance; however, the administrator has unknowingly placed all his SQL Server servers at risk. A potential problem with using one domain account for all SQL Server instances is that when someone logs in with `sysadmin` permissions, and uses `xp_cmdshell` to execute an operating system command shell, they now run by proxy under the SQL Server service account.

  If one of these SQL Server instances were lacking an `sa` password, or had a password that could easily be guessed, any malicious attack or targeted virus could affect not only that particular server, but **all** other servers running under the SQL Server service domain user account. If that service account had access to file servers (for use by DTS), the risk exposure would be even more widespread.

- **SQL Server security patches and service packs**
  Chapter 1 reviewed how to apply security patches and service packs. Security patches and service packs provide the latest protection against known security flaws within SQL Server. It is important that you keep up-to-date with these.
- **Operating system security**
  You must make sure that the file system of your SQL Server instance is also protected; this means securing file directories on the SQL Server machine from use by non-administrators. You should also avoid using your SQL Server machine for purposes unrelated to the database functionality; for example, avoid using your machine as an FTP server or as a file server. Not only does adding such components to your machine increase the risks of exposure of your sensitive files to malicious or inadvertent actions, but SQL Server performance can suffer as well. Audit your machine for all users that have access to the box, and make sure that such access is appropriate (for both the file system and defined shares).
- **Data transmission security**
  SQL Server 2000 allows you to use Secure Sockets Layer (SSL) to **encrypt** data sent between the client and SQL Server instance. To use SSL, the computer running SQL Server, as well as the application connecting to SQL Server, must have an assigned certificate from a public certification authority (for example, http://www.verisign.com/). The application client must also have the SQL Server 2000 client components installed. The "Force protocol encryption" must be enabled within Server Network Utility General tab, or enabled at the Client Network Utility of the client application. To access these utilities, go to the Start menu, select Programs | Microsoft SQL Server, and then select Server Network Utility (if configuring the server) or Client Network Utility (if configuring the application client). Be aware that SSL encryption slows down transmission performance, because of the extra encryption and decryption steps.

This chapter will review most of these concepts, beginning with a review of logins, users, and roles.

# SQL Server Logins, Users, Roles, and Permissions

The building blocks for security within SQL Server are:

- Logins
- Users
- Roles
- Permissions

## Logins

Logins are security accounts that allow access to a SQL Server instance. There are two types of logins: Windows NT/2000 user accounts or groups, and SQL Server standard logins.

When you first install SQL Server, you are asked to decide between Windows-only and mixed-mode (SQL Server and Windows) authentication. If you choose Windows-only authentication, you can change to mixed-mode later, and vice-versa, by reconfiguring SQL Server's properties in Enterprise Manager. Windows-only authentication allows tighter security, as no passwords are transmitted over the network and security is integrated with the operating system, local machine, or domain.

Windows NT/2000 user accounts or groups do not need a password to log on to the SQL Server instance, once they have been granted access to SQL Server. The only security login they need is at the operating system level.

There is a discrepancy between Microsoft's vision of Windows-only mode and the reality of what sites are using. Although there is no doubt that Windows-only authentication is much more secure than mixed-mode, many companies' still use mixed-mode security. This is partly due to the reliance of web and desktop application developers on SQL Server standard logins, the second type of login available in SQL Server if mixed-mode is selected. Web server sites that frequently access SQL Server use SQL authentication, as Internet sites (as opposed to intranet) often have anonymous logins that cannot use Windows authentication. Non-Microsoft web server products (for example IBM's Websphere) and programming technologies (Java) also do not integrate easily with Windows security.

Standard SQL Server logins have a user name and password combination created by a member of the SQL Server `sysadmin` or security administrator server role. This login has no relationship with the operating system authentication method.

The following security accounts can be added to SQL Server:

| Security Account | Description |
|---|---|
| Windows NT, 2000, .NET user | User account in the domain or local server. |
| Windows NT, 2000, .NET group | Domain local groups (single domain groups). Global group in the domain. Local group on the local server. |
| SQL Server standard login | A login name and password created by the system administrator for express use within SQL Server. No association with a Windows NT user or group. |

# Users

Once a login is granted access to SQL Server, and if it is not also a member of a server role with permissions to interact with databases, that login must become a **user** of a database to begin interacting with the database or databases.

Login information is held in the `sysxlogins` table of the `master` database. User information is held in `sysusers` for each database on the server. One login can have access to multiple databases, each with an entry for that login in `sysusers`.

A login maps to a user account, which can be an alias (such as `dbo`) or the same as the login.

To summarize, the relationship between logins and users is as follows:

- A login is granted access to SQL Server. That login can be added as a member to a fixed server role or roles.
- A login is added as a user to a database or to a server role that permits database access.
- That user name can be the same as the login name or an alias.
- Logins and users are linked by a security identifier (SID) in `sysxlogins` and `sysusers`.
- A login can be added as a user to multiple databases.

# Roles

One advantage of granting Windows NT/2000 groups access to SQL Server is the ability to organize database and server permissions more effectively for different individuals. For example, you can give a group, `BIGCO\AccountingDept`, `SELECT` access to all accounting-related tables and views.

Managing roles is more efficient then granting each individual in the NT group access to the server, and then adding each one of them as a user to the accounting database. Using roles makes it easier to remove users if they leave the company, change departments, or no longer require access. As a best practice, keep a document or log that records to which roles and groups a user belongs; this will reduce the time it takes to remove or move a user following an organizational change.

What if you are relying heavily on SQL Server standard logins instead of NT security accounts? One solution is to employ user-defined database roles. Roles are useful for grouping multiple database users that must perform similar database activities, and require the same permissions within the database. Rather than specifying permissions to database objects for multiple SQL users, you can assign permissions to a role instead, and add the users as members of this role. You can also assign Windows NT/2000 accounts to a role, which can save you time too. Database roles are equally effective for both SQL Server standard and Windows NT/2000 accounts.

There are three types of roles in SQL Server:

- Server roles
- Database roles
- Application roles

Server roles, also called **fixed server roles**, operate on the level of the entire server; membership of these roles grants server-level permissions. These fixed server roles include the `sysadmin` role, which gives all the permissions of `sa`. The fixed server roles are as follows:

| **Short Name (used for system stored procedures)** | **Full Name** | **Description** |
|---|---|---|
| `sysadmin` | System administrators | Performs **any** activity in SQL Server. This is the highest permission that you may grant within SQL Server. |
| `setupadmin` | Setup administrators | Allows you to configure linked servers and mark stored procedures as startup stored procedures (procedures that execute when SQL Server starts up). |
| `serveradmin` | Server administrators | Configures the server-wide settings, allowing you to execute `sp_configure` and `RECONFIGURE`. This role also allows you to execute the `sp_fulltext_service` and `sp_tableoption` procedures, as well as issue a `SHUTDOWN` command (shuts down SQL Server). |

| Short Name (used for system stored procedures) | Full Name | Description |
|---|---|---|
| securityadmin | Security administrators | Allows you to add logins, grant CREATE DATABASE permissions, set default language settings for a login, add and remove linked server logins, and change login passwords. |
| processadmin | Process administrators | Allows you to remove a server process with the KILL command. |
| diskadmin | Disk administrators | Allows you to add and manage backup devices with the sp_addumpdevice and sp_dropdevice procedures. |
| dbcreator | Database creators | Allows you to ALTER, CREATE, and DROP databases. This role also allows you to rename databases, back up the database, and apply transaction log backups. |
| bulkadmin | Bulk insert administrators | Allows you to issue the BULK INSERT command (which allows high speed imports into a table). |

SQL Server fixed database roles (which cannot be changed or removed) and user-defined roles (roles that you can create and to which you can assign permissions) allow for database-level permission grouping. The fixed database roles are as follows:

| Fixed Database Role Name | Description |
|---|---|
| public | Every user belongs to public. This role cannot be dropped, and cannot have users, groups, or roles assigned to it because these entities already belong to public. If all users must have certain permissions by default, assign them to public. |
| db_securityadmin | Manages statement and object database permissions. Manages roles and members of database roles. |
| db_accessadmin | Allowed to add logins to the database (any kind of login, be it NT user, NT group, or SQL login). |
| db_backupoperator | Allowed to back up the database. |
| db_datareader | Allowed to read from all database tables. |
| db_datawriter | Allowed to write to all database tables. |
| db_ddladmin | Allowed to add, modify, or drop new objects within the database. |
| db_denydatareader | Denies the ability to read from any tables in the database. |

*Table continued on following page*

| Mixed Database Role Name | Description |
|---|---|
| db_denydatawriter | Denies the ability to write to any tables in the database. |
| db_owner | The highest database power, allowing full control over the database and objects, as well as database operations. |

In addition to fixed database roles, you can also create your own database roles. These act in a similar manner to Windows groups, in that you add database users as members and assign permissions to the database role (group). Members of this role will inherit permissions assigned to your user-defined role.

Lastly, SQL Server offers application roles. You can assign object permissions to application roles in the same way as you can assign object permissions to user-defined roles. Application roles differ from database and server roles, however, in that application roles do not allow members.

Instead, an application role is activated like a user and password login. Because an application role has no members, it requires a password for the permissions to be enabled by a user. In addition to this, once a session's context is set to use an application role, any existing user or login permissions are nullified. **Only** the application role's permissions apply.

To use an application role:

- The application or user logs in to SQL Server with NT authentication or a SQL login.
- The application role is activated within the user session.
- Any permissions the original login had are now nullified, and the application role permissions take over.

Why use an application role? Very often an application developer will want to grant users access **only** through the application. Perceptive end users often figure out that their SQL login can also be used to connect to SQL Server with other applications, such as Microsoft Access or Query Analyzer. To prevent this, you can change the SQL login or authentication account to have minimal permissions for the databases, and then use an application role for the required permissions. This way, the user can only access the data through the application, which has to be programmed to use the application role.

# Permissions

Permissions determine what you can do within a database. There are three kinds of permissions:

- Statement
- Object
- Role

Statement permissions control database statements that a user can or cannot execute. For example:

- CREATE DATABASE
- BACKUP DATABASE
- BACKUP LOG
- CREATE TABLE
- CREATE VIEW

- CREATE PROCEDURE
- CREATE DEFAULT
- CREATE RULE
- CREATE FUNCTION
- BACKUP DB
- BACKUP LOG

Object permissions determine a user's control over database objects, such as tables, views, indexes, and stored procedures:

- SELECT
- INSERT
- UPDATE
- DELETE
- EXECUTE
- REFERENCES

Role permissions are those database or server activities only available to members of fixed server or database roles. For example, the `KILL` command, which allows you forcibly to remove a connection/process from the SQL Server instance, cannot be granted to a user; only members of the `sysadmin` or `processadmin` fixed server roles can execute the `KILL` command. This chapter will review how to implement each of these security components.

# 7.1 How to... Create Logins using Enterprise Manager and Transact-SQL

To create a login using Enterprise Manager:

- Expand the SQL Server Group and registration.
- Expand the Security folder.
- Right-click Logins, and select New Login.
- In the General tab, type in the name of the Windows NT/2000 account or group you wish to add. Alternatively, type the name of the new SQL Server standard login.
- In the Authentication section, select which mode you will be using, Windows Authentication or SQL Server Authentication. If you are using Windows Authentication, notice that you have the option to Grant or Deny access to the Windows NT/2000 account or group. If an NT account to which you wish to deny access is a member of an NT group that **has** access to your SQL Server instance, this account will have implicit permissions via the group membership. Adding the account or group explicitly to SQL Server to deny access will override any group membership that account may have.
- If you are selecting a SQL Server standard account, you should enter a password.
- In the Defaults selection, select the default database and language for the new login:

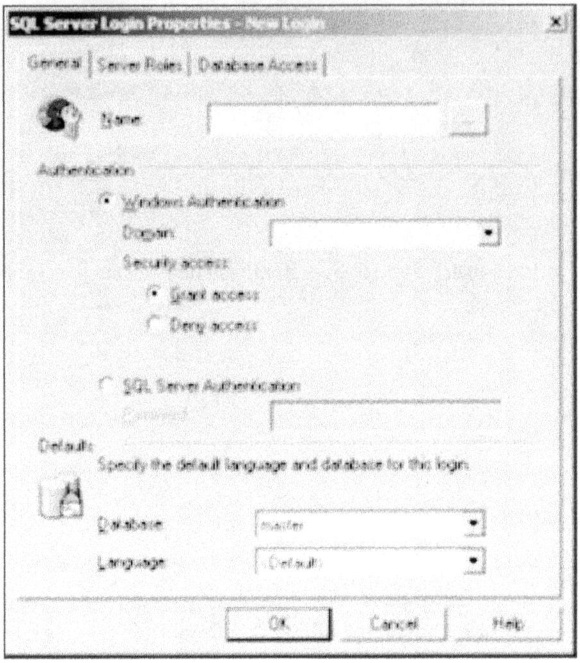


In the Server Roles tab, select any server roles of which this new login should be a member. Remember not to grant a login more permissions than it actually needs:

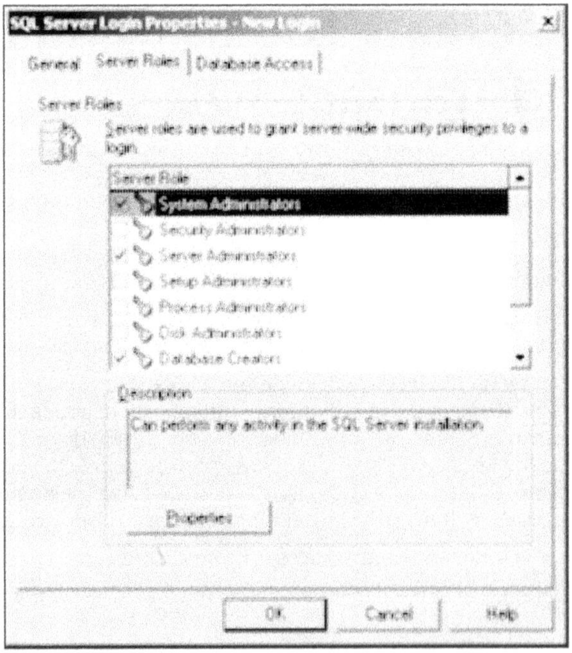

You can view the current role members and specific permissions of a fixed server role by clicking on the role and selecting the Properties button.

In the Database Access tab, select which databases this user login can access. You can also add the user to fixed database roles or user-defined roles specified for the database:

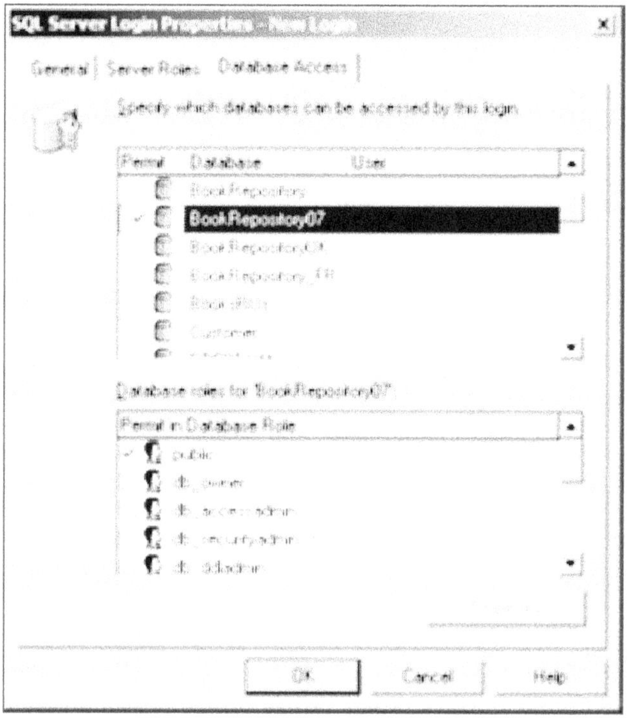


When you have finished configuring all three tabs, select OK. If selecting a standard SQL login, you will be prompted to confirm the password.

The system stored procedure `sp_addlogin` is used to add SQL Server standard logins. The syntax from *SQL Server Books Online* for adding a login is as follows:

```
sp_addlogin [ @loginame = ] 'login'
    [ , [ @passwd = ] 'password' ]
    [ , [ @defdb = ] 'database' ]
    [ , [ @deflanguage = ] 'language' ]
    [ , [ @sid = ] sid ]
    [ , [ @encryptopt = ] 'encryption_option' ]
```

| Parameter | Description |
|---|---|
| `[ @loginame = ]` | The standard SQL Server login name, allowing up to 128 characters, including letters, symbols, and numbers. The name cannot contain a backslash \, empty string, `NULL` value, or reserved login name (for example, `sa` or `public`). |

*Table continued on following page*

| Parameter | Description |
|---|---|
| [ @passwd = ] | In a standard SQL Server login, the password. |
| [ @defdb = ] | The default database. |
| [ @deflanguage = ] | The default language. |
| [ @sid = ] | The security identifier for the login (used in both sysxlogins and sysusers). This is useful if you are migrating databases to a new server, and want the syslogin SID to match the sysusers SID. |
| [ @encryptopt = ] 'encryption_option' ] | The encryption of the password when stored in the system tables; the default is NULL, which means the password is encrypted. Otherwise, skip_encryption tells SQL Server that the password is already encrypted, and should not be re-encrypted upon storage. The other option is skip_encryption_old, which means that the password was encrypted by an older version of SQL Server, and should not be re-encrypted. |

To grant a Windows NT/2000 user account or group access to SQL Server using Transact-SQL, you must use the system stored procedure sp_grantlogin. The syntax is:

```
sp_grantlogin 'loginname'
```

## Example 7.1.1: Adding a standard SQL Server login account

- Standard login name: BookUser
- Password: t0ughPassword$1
- Default database: BookRepository07
- Default language: English:

```
EXEC sp_addlogin
     'BookUser',
     't0ughPassword$1',
     'BookRepository07',
     'English'
```

Adding a Windows NT/2000 user account or group using Transact-SQL:

## Example 7.1.2: Adding an NT user account

```
EXEC sp_grantlogin
     'CURLINGSTONE\BookAdministrator'
```

## Example 7.1.3: Adding an NT group

```
EXEC sp_grantlogin
     'CURLINGSTONE\Accounting'
```

# 7.2 How to... Remove a SQL Server Login using Enterprise Manager or Transact-SQL

To remove a login in Enterprise Manager:

- Expand the SQL Server Group and registration.
- Expand the Security folder.
- Select Logins.
- In the right-hand pane, right-click the login you wish to delete, and select Delete.
- You will receive a dialog box asking you to confirm your choice.
- Select Yes to delete the login and associated users.

### Example 7.2.1: Removing a Windows NT/2000 login using sp_revokelogin

To remove a Windows NT/2000 login using Transact-SQL, execute `sp_revokelogin`:

```
sp_revokelogin 'CURLINGSTONE\SQLUser'
```

### Example 7.2.2: Removing a standard SQL Server login using sp_droplogin

To remove a standard SQL Server login, execute `sp_droplogin`:

```
sp_droplogin 'testuser'
```

If the user is `dbo` of any databases, you must assign another login to be `dbo` for each database (using the `sp_changedbowner` stored procedure). The following example changes the `dbo` of the `BookRepository07` database to `sa`:

```
USE BookRepository07
EXEC sp_changedbowner 'sa'
```

Also note that you must drop any database users associated with this login before running `sp_droplogin`, otherwise you will receive an error:

Server: Msg 15175, Level 16, State 1, Procedure sp_droplogin, Line 93
Login 'testuser' is aliased or mapped to a user in one or more database(s). Drop the user or alias before dropping the login.

# 7.3 How to... Change the Default Database for a Login with sp_defaultdb

The default database for a login determines the initial database context when a user first logs in to SQL Server. You can change the default database for a login using Enterprise Manager, or with the stored procedure `sp_defaultdb`.

**Example 7.3.1: Changing the default database for JaneDoe to the BookRepository07 database**

```
sp_defaultdb 'JaneDoe', 'BookRepository07'
```

The first parameter is the login name and the second parameter the new database default.

# 7.4 How to... Change the Default Login Language using sp_defaultlanguage

If not specified when you first created the login, the default language for your login will be the same as your server default (default server language is configured with `sp_configure` or Properties in Enterprise Manager).

**Example 7.4.1: Changing the default language for login JaneDoe to French**

```
sp_defaultlanguage 'JaneDoe', 'French'
```

The first parameter is the login, and the second parameter the language. For a list of languages, run `sp_helplanguage`.

# 7.5 How to... List Defunct NT Users or Groups with Access to SQL Server

Over time, employees, consultants, and contractors come and go. Best practice when an employee leaves the company is to remove their access from SQL Server immediately. In large implementations, Human Resources do not always keep the SQL Server DBAs up-to-date.

The system stored procedure `sp_validatelogins` allows you to analyze which NT security accounts or groups no longer exist in the NT world. The stored procedure will return SID and login name for the orphaned login:

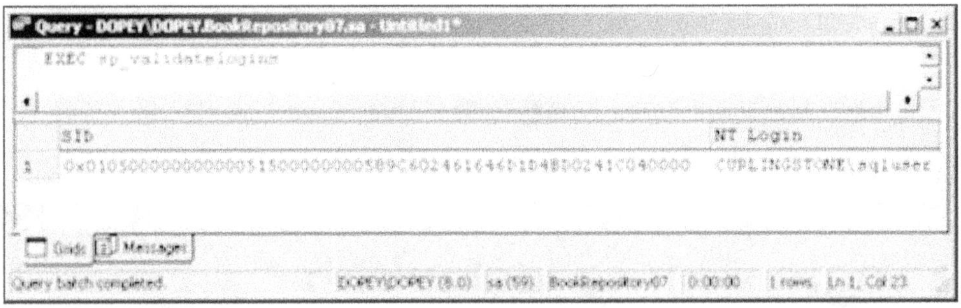


This is another good reason to use Windows authentication over a standard SQL Server login. With standard SQL Server logins, intruders or angry ex-employees can log in anonymously. Standard SQL Server login passwords can be shared and abused.

# 7.6 How to... Change or Add a Password in Enterprise Manager or Transact-SQL

To change or add a password in Enterprise Manager:

- Expand Server Group and registration.
- Expand the Security folder.
- Click Logins.
- Right-click the login of the user whose password you wish to change and select Properties.
- In the Properties dialog box, type in the password in the password box (type over the stars in the box):

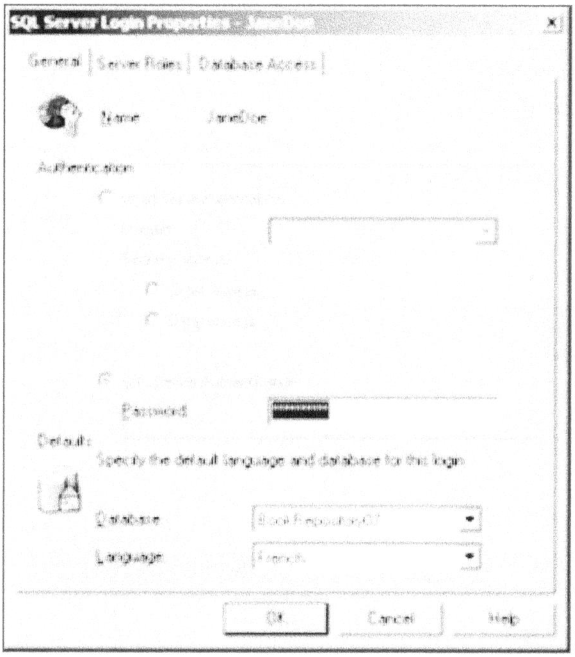


- Select OK.
- Type in the password for confirmation and select OK.

To change a password using Transact-SQL, use the `sp_password` system stored procedure. If there is an existing password, you must enter it correctly to change to the new password.

## Example 7.6.1: Changing an existing password

```
EXEC sp_password 'oldpassword', 'newpassword', 'JaneDoe'
```

The first parameter is the old password, the second parameter the new password, and the last parameter the standard SQL Server login name. You cannot reset an NT login using `sp_password`. If you are `sysadmin` and wish to change to a new password, but cannot remember the old one, you can place a `NULL` in the old password parameter.

**Example 7.6.2: Adding a new password or changing an existing password when you do not know the old one**

```
EXEC sp_password NULL, 'newpassword', 'JaneDoe'
```

Passwords have a 128-character limit and can use any letter, symbol, or number. Try to assign passwords that are difficult to guess. Using a combination of letters, numbers, and symbols provides the best security for standard SQL Server logins.

# 7.7 How to... Create Database Users in Enterprise Manager or Transact-SQL

To add a database user in Enterprise Manager:

- Expand Server Group and registration.
- Expand the Databases folder.
- Expand the database to which you wish to add the user.
- Right-click Users and select New Database User.
- Select Login name and associated User name (keep the names the same if you want to minimize confusion). You can also add this user to fixed or user-defined database roles:

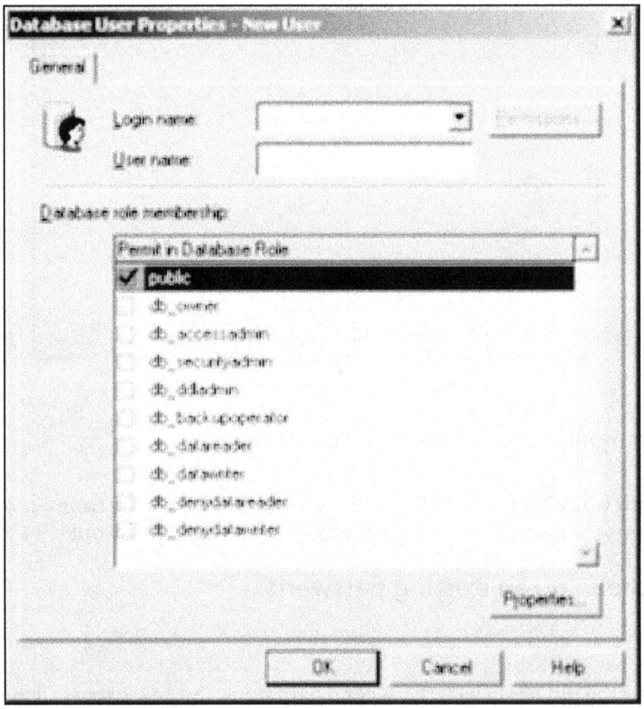


- Select OK when you have finished.

Another method for adding database users in Enterprise Manager:

- Expand SQL Server Group and registration.
- Expand the Security folder and select Logins.
- Double-click the login for which you wish to add database user access.
- In the Database Access tab, you can allow database access by clicking the Permit checkbox. The associated user name defaults to the same as the login name, but you can change it if you wish. You can also add this user to any fixed database or user-defined database roles for the specified database.
- Select OK when you have finished.

To grant database access and create a user in Transact-SQL, use the system stored procedure `sp_grantdbaccess`.

### Example 7.7.1: Adding an NT login access to the BookRepository07 database

```
USE BookRepository07
EXEC sp_grantdbaccess 'CURLINGSTONE\SallySue'
```

The first parameter is the login account. If you do not specify a user name, the default name is the same as the login name (not the domain name).

### Example 7.7.2: Adding an NT login access to BookRepository07, using a different database name

```
USE BookRepository07
EXEC sp_grantdbaccess 'CURLINGSTONE\SallySue', 'SallySue'
```

The second parameter is the user name in the database.

### Example 7.7.3: Adding a standard SQL Server login account access to a database

```
USE BookRepository07
EXEC sp_grantdbaccess 'JaneDoe'
```

A user name can have up to 128 characters, using letters, symbols, and numbers. You cannot use the backslash character, `NULL`, or empty string for SQL Server user names.

## 7.8 How to... Remove a User From the Database

To remove a user from a database using Enterprise Manager:

- Expand Server Group and registration.
- Expand the Databases folder.
- Expand the database.
- Click Users.
- Right-click the user you wish to remove and select Delete. When prompted to make sure, select Yes to continue.

Another method for removing a user in Enterprise Manager is as follows:

- Expand Server Group and registrations.
- Expand the Security folder.
- Select Logins.
- Double-click the login in the right-hand pane for the user you wish to remove.
- In the SQL Server Login Properties dialog box select the Database Access tab.
- Uncheck the Permit checkbox for each database from which you wish to remove the login association.
- Select OK when you have finished. If that user owns any objects in the database, you will get the following error:

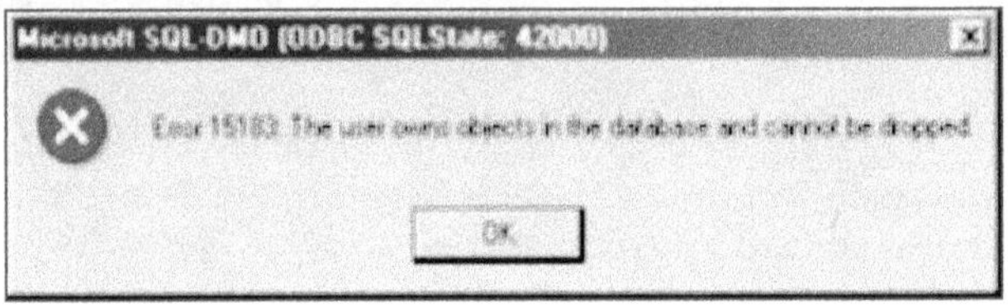


To change an object owner, use the `sp_changeobjectowner` procedure. This procedure takes two parameters, the first being the object name (a table or view, for example), and the second parameter the **new** owner. In this example, we change the `Test` table's owner to `dbo`:

```
EXEC sp_changeobjectowner 'janedoe.Test', 'dbo'
```

To remove a database user with Transact-SQL, use the `sp_revokedbaccess` system stored procedure.

## Example 7.8.1: Removing a database user from the database

```
USE BookRepository07
EXEC sp_revokedbaccess 'JaneDoe'
```

This stored procedure only takes one parameter or database user name to be dropped. If that user owns any object in the database, you will get an error, and a list of objects that user owns. For example, on the Query Analyzer Messages tab,

```
Server: Msg 15183, Level 16, State 1, Procedure sp_MScheck_uid_owns_anything, Line
17
The user owns objects in the database and cannot be dropped.
```

then on the Grids tab, a list of owned objects:

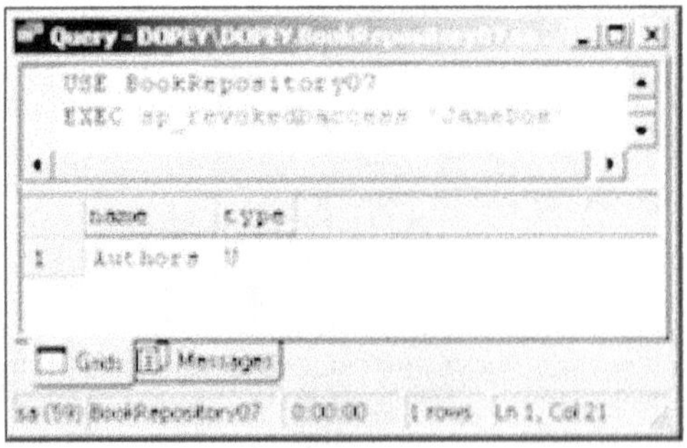

The syntax for removing a standard SQL Server user and a NT security account is the same. You may be familiar with `sp_dropuser` (used in previous versions of SQL Server); this was provided in SQL Server 2000 for backward compatibility. Microsoft now recommends that you use `sp_revokedbaccess` instead.

# 7.9 How to... Create and Manage User-Defined Database Roles

User-defined database roles allow you to manage database permissions more effectively. Instead of granting permissions across several database users, you can grant permissions to a user-defined database role instead. Then you can add users as members of the role.

To create a standard user-defined database role using Enterprise Manager:

- Expand SQL Server Group and registration.
- Expand Databases.
- Expand the database to which you wish to add a role.
- Right-click Roles and select New Database Role.
- In the Database Role Properties dialog box, type in the name of your new role. Select Standard Role. This means that the role can have members. We will review application roles in the next section. Select the Add button to add new users in the database to the role:

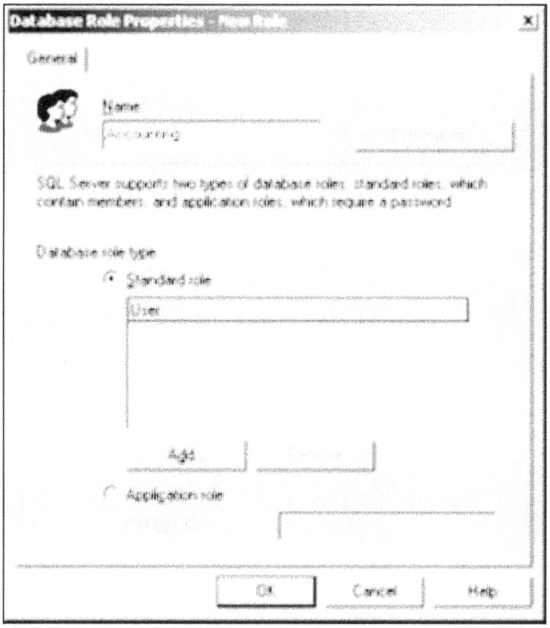


- The Permissions button is grayed out. You cannot modify the permissions unless you create the role first. Select OK to create the role.
- Double-click the new role that you created in the previous step (in the right-hand pane of Enterprise Manager).

- Click the Permissions button, which is no longer grayed out. Select the permissions that this role should have:

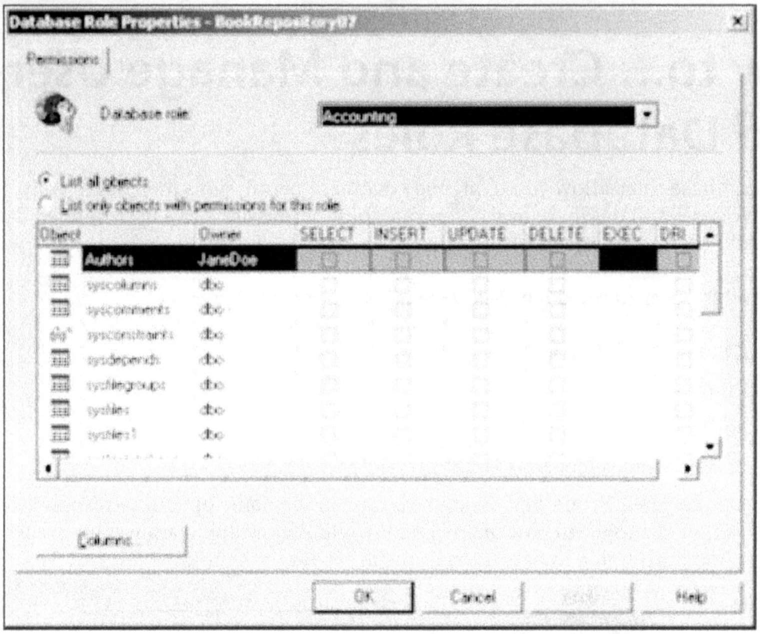


- For tables or views, you can select which columns have the associated permissions by clicking the Columns button:

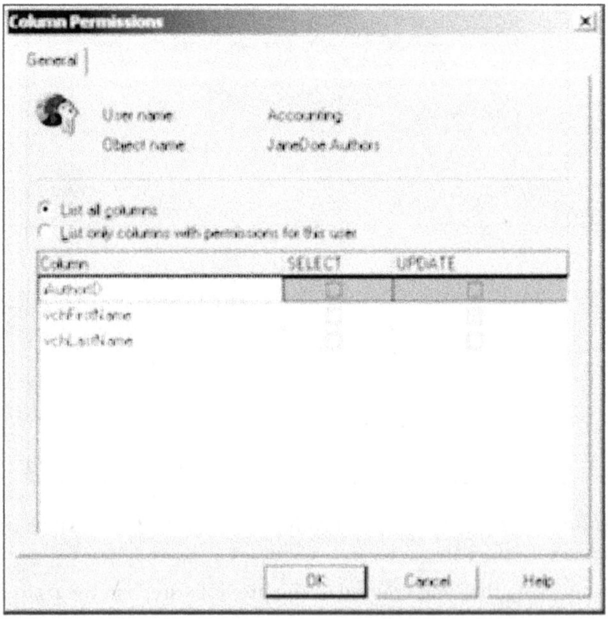

- Select OK at the column permissions for the columns you selected. Select OK at the permissions dialog box. Select OK at the main role properties dialog box.

Keep in mind that views are often a better alternative to managing column permissions, as you can define the columns that should be displayed within the view definition. You can then grant `SELECT` permissions to the view, instead of individual columns of a table. For more on views, see Chapter 14.

To delete the role in Enterprise Manager:

- Expand SQL Server Group and registration.
- Expand the Databases folder, and expand the database from which you wish to delete the role.
- Click the Roles icon.
- In the right-hand pane, right-click the role you wish to delete and select Delete.
- Select Yes at the warning dialog box to continue with the deletion.
- If your role has members, they must be deleted first.

To add or remove members to a role in Enterprise Manager:

- Expand SQL Server Group and registration.
- Expand the Databases folder, and expand the database from which you wish to delete the role.
- Click the Roles icon.
- Double-click the role you wish to modify (in the right-hand pane).
- In the Database Role Properties dialog box, click Add to add new members; or click a member and select the Remove button to remove a role member.
- Click the Apply or OK button for these changes to take effect.

You can also add role membership from the SQL Server Login Properties. The login must first be permitted for the database, and then for the associated database role:

To add a role using Transact-SQL, use the `sp_addrole` system stored procedure.

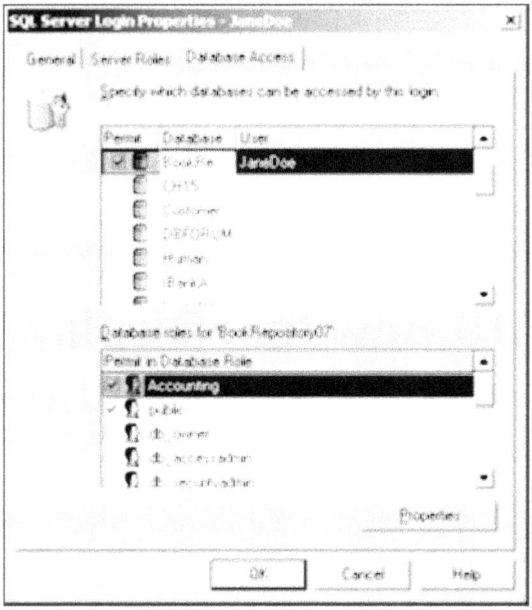

### Example 7.9.1: Adding a new standard database role

```
USE BookRepository07
EXEC sp_addrole 'BookReader'
```

The above example added the BookReader standard user-defined database role. The sp_addrole system stored procedure also takes a second parameter, owner, which determines which user owns the role. The default is dbo. Using an owner other than dbo allows the owner to grant membership to other users for the new role. To assign database permissions to the role, see the *SQL Server Permission Types* section later in this chapter. Roles are assigned permissions just like database users. For example:

```
GRANT SELECT ON Books TO BookReader
```

### Example 7.9.2: Adding a member to a database role

To add role members using Transact-SQL, use the sp_addrolemember system stored procedure:

```
USE BookRepository07
EXEC sp_addrolemember 'BookReader', 'JohnDeer'
```

The first parameter for sp_addrolemember is role name and the second parameter is the database user name.

### Example 7.9.3: Removing a member from a database role

To remove members from a role, execute the system stored procedure sp_droprolemember:

```
USE BookRepository07
EXEC sp_droprolemember 'BookReader', 'JohnDeer'
```

The first parameter for sp_droprolemember is role name, and second parameter database is user name.

### Example 7.9.4: Dropping a database role

After removing all members from a role, you can drop the standard user-defined database role:

```
USE BookRepository07
EXEC sp_droprole 'BookReader'
```

The procedure sp_droprole takes only one parameter, the role name to be dropped.

## 7.10 How to... Display User-Defined or Fixed Database Roles in the Current Database using sp_helprole

The stored procedure sp_helprole lists all user-defined and fixed database roles in the current database.

#### Example 7.10.1: Listing all user-defined and fixed database roles in the BookRepository07 database

If the role is an application role, the `IsAppRole` column will contain a `1` for that row.

## 7.11 How to... Display Members of a Specific Database Role using sp_helprolemember

The stored procedure `sp_helprolemember` displays members of a role in the current database context.

#### Example 7.11.1: Showing a member of the db_owner database role

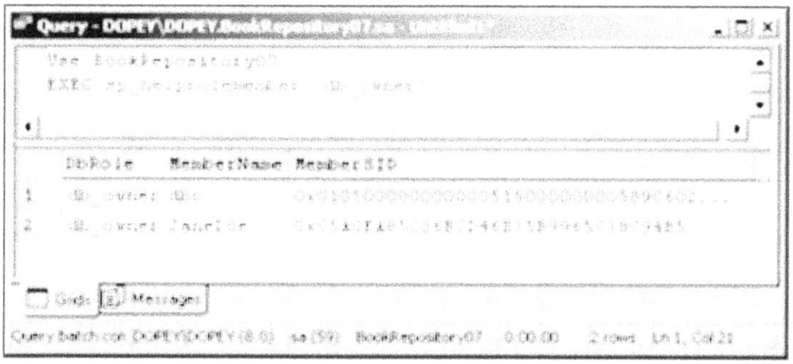


The stored procedure takes only one parameter, the role name. This can be a fixed database role or a user-defined database role – but it must exist in the database context you are using. The results return the role name, member (user) name, and security identifier (SID).

# 7.12 How to... Create, Manage, and Drop Application Roles

You can assign permissions to application roles just as you can assign permissions to standard user-defined database roles. Application roles, however, do not have members: SQL Server instantiates application roles after an application makes a login connection to the server and assigns the permissions of the application role to that application for the duration of its connection to the server.

To create an application role in Enterprise Manager, use the same process as for a standard user-defined database role, only select Application in the Database Role Properties dialog box. You also need to set an application role password:

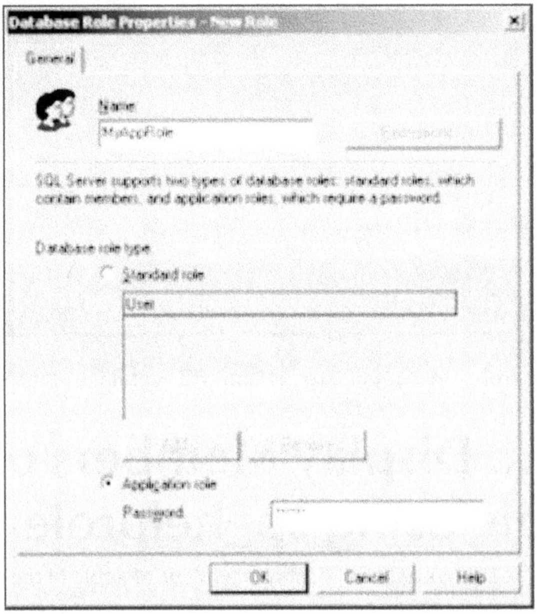


Select OK when you have finished. Just like standard roles, permissions can only be specified after the application role has been created. Application roles can also be deleted just like standard roles in Enterprise Manager. Since they have no members, you needn't worry about errors when attempting to delete them.

To use the application role, you must use the system stored procedure `sp_setapprole`:

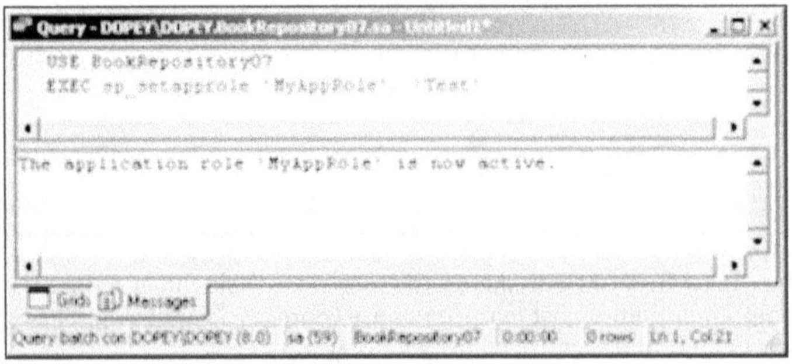

### Example 7.12.1: Activating the application role with encryption

So that your application role password does not transmit the password in clear text, you can use the encryption option of the sp_setapprole procedure. This will work for OLE DB and ODBC clients, but not DB-Library clients. If using DB-Library clients, consider using a non-application role solution; or consider encrypting the call some other way:

```
USE BookRepository07
EXEC sp_setapprole 'MyAppRole', {Encrypt N'Test'}, odbc
```

The first parameter is the application role name. The second parameter puts brackets around the Encrypt statement, and then passes the Unicode password string. The format is:

```
{Encrypt N'password'}
```

password is the password you wish to encrypt. The last parameter is odbc; if this is left blank, encryption is not used.

Remember that once you have set an application role context for a database, your existing permissions are nullified for the connection; you will only have the database permissions granted to the application role. Since an application role is defined for a single database, your only means of switching database context for the existing session is if the guest account is enabled in other databases, or if you **log off** and back in as your user login.

### Example 7.12.2: Adding an application role using sp_addapprole

To add an application role with Transact-SQL, use the following system stored procedure sp_addapprole:

```
USE BookRepository07
EXEC sp_addapprole 'BookWriter', 'D1fficultPass$word'
```

The first parameter is the application role name, which allows up to 128 characters, including letters, symbols, and numbers. The name cannot contain a backslash \, empty string, or NULL. The second parameter is the password.

### Example 7.12.3: Dropping an application role using sp_dropapprole

To drop an application role with Transact-SQL, log on to Query Analyzer with a SQL login or via Windows Authentication and execute the sp_dropappprole system stored procedure. Your login context requires sysadmin, db_owner, or db_securityadmin role membership to execute this stored procedure:

```
USE BookRepository07
EXEC sp_dropapprole 'BookWriter'
```

# 7.13 How to... Show Users and Roles with Access to the Current Database using sp_helpuser

Use `sp_helpuser` to retrieve a list of all SQL users, NT users, and database roles with access to the current database.

## Example 7.13.1: Displaying all users in the database

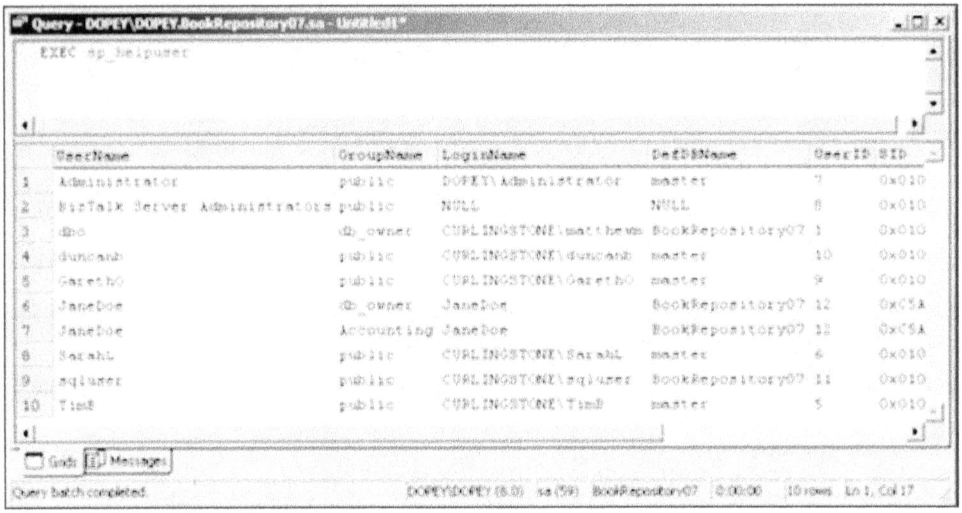


Notice that LoginName is included, in case the name differs from the database user name. Also included are default database name, user id, and security identifier (SID). GroupName shows the roles of which the user is a member. If a user is a member of multiple groups, this will be reflected in multiple rows.

## Example 7.13.2: Displaying information on one user

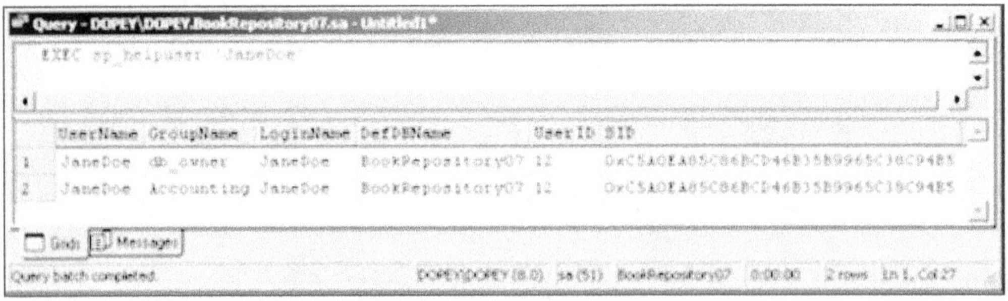


Notice `JaneDoe` appears twice, with one row for `db_owner` and one row for the `Accounting` role membership.

### Example 7.13.3: Displaying all user members of a role

To show all members of the db_datareader database role:

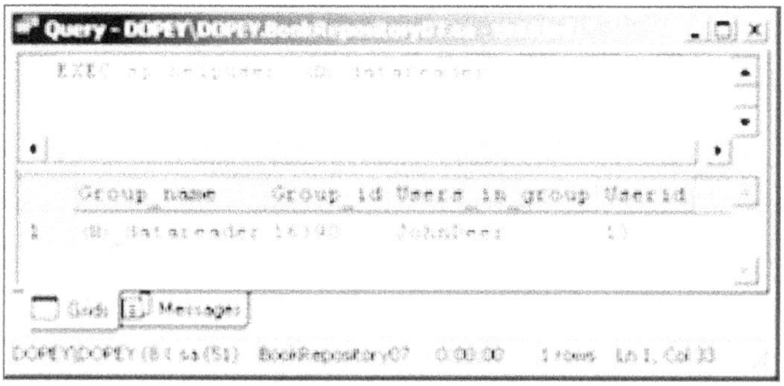


# 7.14 How to... Display Account Permissions and Permission Path using xp_logininfo

Sometimes it can become difficult to see how a particular login is inheriting the permissions that it is. For example, let's say you have a domain login called CURLINGSTONE\DeniedLogin; this account was added to SQL Server with minimal permissions, yet the user is accessing objects and performing tasks that are well beyond the assigned permission level.

By running xp_logininfo, you can figure out the "permission path" for the login. This extended stored procedure tells you if the login user or group is a member of a group with higher permissions. For example:

```
EXEC master..xp_logininfo 'CURLINGSTONE\DeniedLogin'
```

will return the following results, indicating that it is inheriting its permissions from BUILTIN\Administrators (member of the local server administrator group):

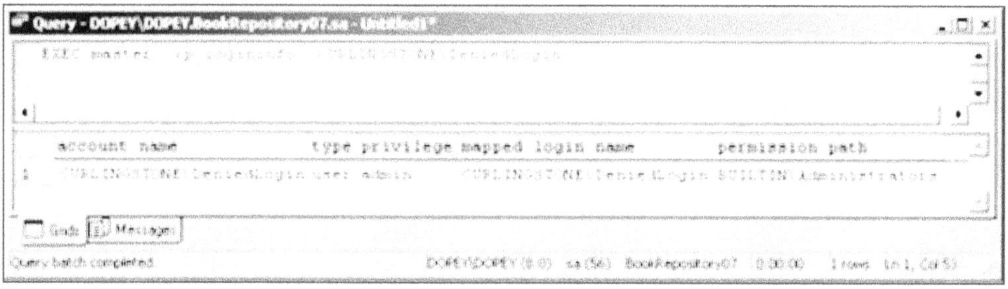

# 7.15 How to... Deny SQL Server Access to a Windows NT User or Group using sp_denylogin

Use the system stored procedure sp_denylogin to deny a Windows NT user or group access to SQL Server. This stored procedure can only be used with domain logins, domain groups, and local machine accounts, not SQL logins. Access can also be denied from local machine logins, for example BUILTIN\Administrators.

### Example 7.15.1: Denying access to a domain group

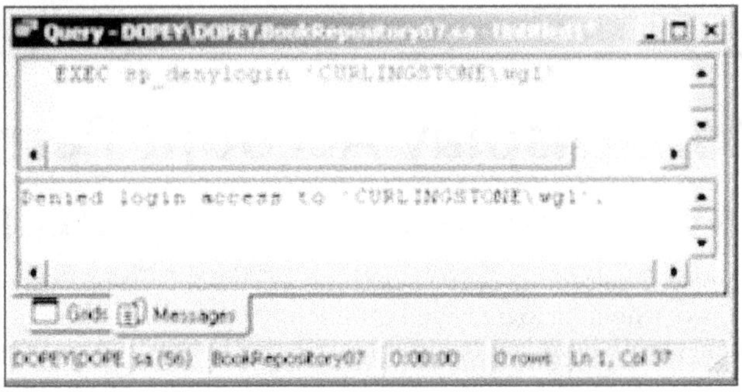


The syntax is identical for both users and groups, for example, in denying access to a specific domain user:

```
EXEC sp_denylogin 'CURLINGSTONE\MSAccessUser'
```

Note that this does not **drop** a login from the server, but rather denies access; dropping a login would clear out any permissions currently assigned to that user or group. But denying that login access could be used as a temporary stopgap against login permissions, until you perform whatever further action is required. Alternatively, if you want to give access to a group, **except** for that specific user, denying access in this manner would allow other members of the group to keep their permissions.

# 7.16 How to... Return a List of Fixed Server Roles with sp_helpsrvrole

You can return a list of the fixed server role names and user-friendly descriptions using sp_helpsrvrole. This list will never change (for SQL Server 2000 anyhow). This procedure is helpful when you need to remember the exact spelling of a server role name, prior to adding a member to the role, or when checking the role's current members or assigned permissions.

**Example 7.16.1: Returning a list of all fixed server roles**

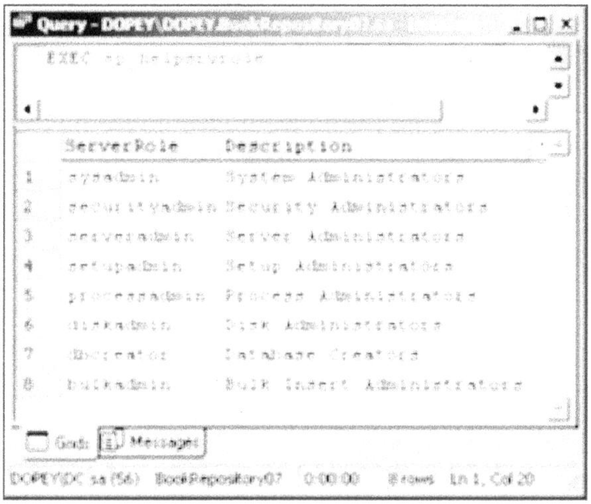


# 7.17 How to... Display Permissions for Fixed Server Roles with sp_srvrolepermission

If you would like to know exactly what permissions a fixed server role has, run the `sp_srvrolepermission` system stored procedure.

**Example 7.17.1: Returning all permissions for all fixed server roles**

### Example 7.17.2: Returning permissions owned by the processadmin fixed server role

```
EXEC sp_srvrolepermission 'processadmin'
```

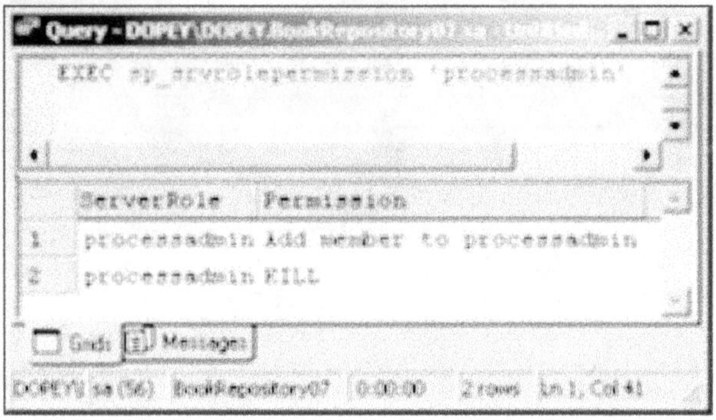


# 7.18 How to... List Members of a Fixed Server Role using sp_helpsrvrolemember

Use the system stored procedure sp_helpsrvrolemember to show all members of a fixed-server role, or all members in all fixed-server roles. The procedure takes one parameter: the fixed-server role name. If you do not supply the parameter, all members of all fixed-server roles will be returned.

### Example 7.18.1: Returning members of the security administrator role

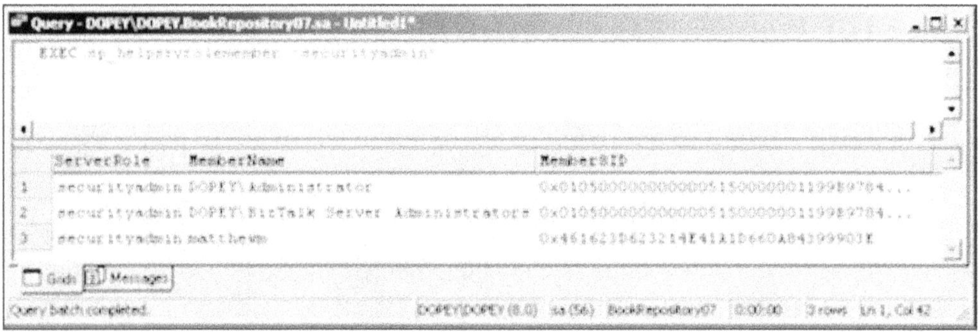


Notice that the database user name is returned, as well as the security identifier (SID).

### Example 7.18.2: Returning all members of all fixed security roles

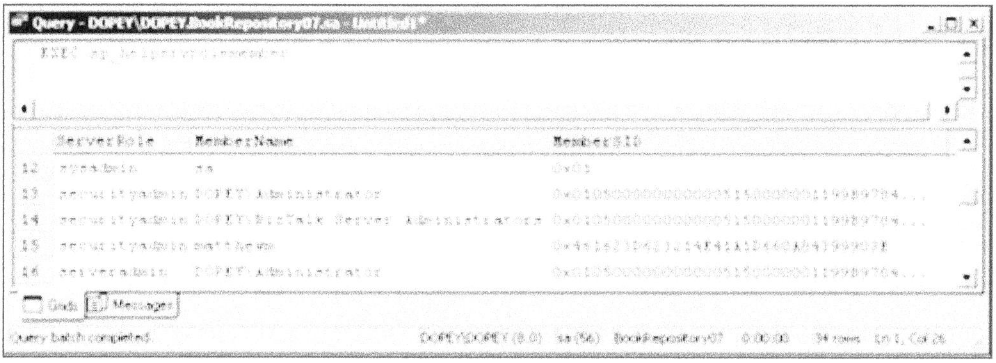

## 7.19 How to... Return a List of Fixed Database Roles with sp_helpdbfixedrole

The system stored procedure `sp_helpdbfixedrole` returns the list of SQL Server fixed database roles. This list will never change, and will display the role name and role user-friendly name. This procedure is helpful when you need to remember the exact spelling of a fixed database role name, prior to adding a member to the role, or when checking out the role's current members or assigned permissions.

### Example 7.19.1: Listing all fixed database roles

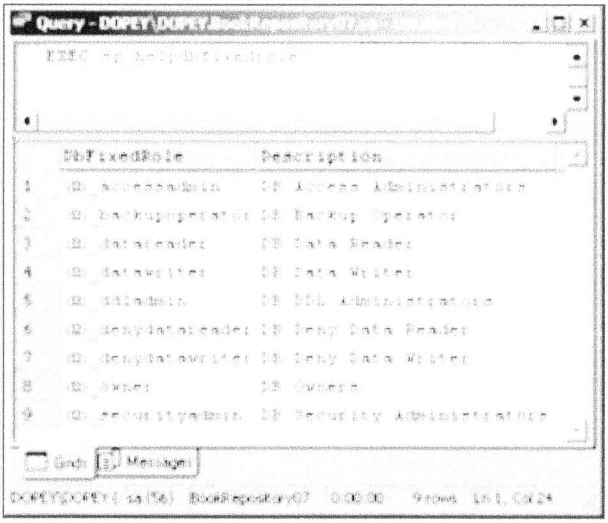

# 7.20 How to... Display Fixed Database Role Permissions

End users and application developers often ask, when told about database roles, "what does that role allow me to do?" To answer the question, run the system stored procedure `sp_dbfixedrolepermission`. It takes one parameter, the name of the fixed database role.

### Example 7.20.1: Listing permissions for the db_securityadmin role

```
EXEC sp_dbfixedrolepermission 'db_securityadmin'
```

# SQL Server Permission Types

SQL Server manages security for database objects and commands using three categories of permissions:

- **Object Permissions**
  Object permissions control in which databases users can execute a stored procedure, read data in a table or view, insert new data, update existing data, or delete data in a table. The object permissions are:
  - `SELECT`
  - `INSERT`
  - `UPDATE`
  - `DELETE`
  - `EXECUTE`
  - `REFERENCES`

- **Statement Permissions**
  Statement permissions control the execution of Data Definition Language and database management commands such as:
  - `CREATE DATABASE`
  - `BACKUP DATABASE`
  - `BACKUP LOG`
  - `CREATE TABLE`
  - `CREATE VIEW`
  - `CREATE PROCEDURE`
  - `CREATE DEFAULT`
  - `CREATE RULE`
  - `CREATE FUNCTION`
  - `BACKUP DB`
  - `BACKUP LOG`

  Note that statement permissions do not include **all** possible database management commands. Enter **role permissions**.
- **Role Permissions**
  Members of predefined server or database roles have certain permissions that cannot be explicitly granted to database users. Rather, you must grant a login membership to a server role or database user membership to a database role. Depending on the role, these un-grantable permissions include:
  - `ALTER DATABASE`
  - `CREATE DATABASE`
  - `BULK INSERT`
  - `DBCC`
  - `DENY`
  - `GRANT`
  - `KILL`
  - `RECONFIGURE`
  - `RESTORE`
  - `REVOKE`
  - `SHUTDOWN`

In this section, we will see how to grant and revoke statement and object permissions. Before we continue, here are a few tips to keep in mind when thinking about object and statement permissions:

- When assigning permissions to objects, assign permissions to a user-defined database role, rather than across separate database users. This will help you manage security more effectively as you can change permissions for a single role rather than for 50 users. Be careful to track what roles you assign to what users. You may need to remove a user or users quickly; and with role membership documented, this process will be easier.
- Protect your base tables as best you can. You can secure your database environment by restricting direct access to your base tables; users can instead read or modify data via views or stored procedures. Stored procedures can be used for `INSERT`, `UPDATE`, and `DELETE` activity, rather than direct updates to the base tables.

# 7.21 How to... GRANT, REVOKE, or DENY Statement and Object Permissions

Permissions are managed either by Transact-SQL commands or from within Enterprise Manager.

Transact-SQL uses the GRANT, REVOKE, and DENY commands to control statement permissions.

## GRANT Permissions for Statements

The GRANT keyword assigns permissions to a specific object or statement, to a user or role. The syntax for GRANT from *SQL Server Books Online* is as follows:

For statement permissions:

```
GRANT { ALL | statement [ ,...n ] }
TO security_account [ ,...n ]
```

| Parameter | Description |
|---|---|
| { ALL \| statement [ ,...n ] } | ALL grants all statement permissions, and can only be granted by members of the sysadmin role. Otherwise, the following statements can be granted:<br>BACKUP DATABASE<br>BACKUP LOG<br>CREATE DATABASE<br>CREATE DEFAULT<br>CREATE FUNCTION<br>CREATE PROCEDURE<br>CREATE RULE<br>CREATE TABLE<br>CREATE VIEW<br>One or more statements can be included in one GRANT statement. |
| security_account [ ,...n ] | This specifies the recipient of the granted statement permission(s). This can be a SQL Server login, NT login, NT group, or database role. |

### Example 7.21.1: Granting permissions to back up the database and transaction log to a user

```
GRANT BACKUP DATABASE, BACKUP LOG
TO JaneDoe
```

### Example 7.21.2: Granting all statement permissions to a user

```
GRANT ALL TO JaneDoe
```

### Example 7.21.3: Granting CREATE TABLE permissions to a user-defined database role

```
GRANT CREATE TABLE TO BookDistributor
```

# GRANT Permissions for Objects

For object permissions:

```
GRANT
    { ALL [ PRIVILEGES ] | permission [ ,...n ] }
    {
        [ ( column [ ,...n ] ) ] ON { table | view }
        | ON { table | view } [ ( column [ ,...n ] ) ]
        | ON { stored_procedure | extended_procedure }
        | ON { user_defined_function }
    }
TO security_account [ ,...n ]
[ WITH GRANT OPTION ]
[ AS { group | role } ]
```

| Parameter | Description |
|---|---|
| { ALL \| statement [ ,...n ] } | ALL grants all object permissions, and can only be granted by members of the sysadmin or db_owner roles. Database object owners can also use ALL for their owned objects.<br><br>Otherwise, individual object permissions that can be granted for a table, view, or table-valued function are:<br><br>SELECT<br>INSERT<br>UPDATE<br>DELETE<br><br>SELECT and UPDATE can define specific columns for which the permissions apply. If none are specified, all columns receive the granted SELECT or UPDATE permissions.<br><br>REFERENCES is used for permission to reference another table for a FOREIGN KEY constraint. REFERENCES is also required for the object specified in WITH SCHEMABINDING for functions or views.<br><br>EXECUTE is granted for permissions to execute a stored procedure or scalar-valued function.<br><br>One or more statements can be included in one GRANT statement. |

*Table continued on following page*

| Parameter | Description |
|---|---|
| [ ( column [ ,...n ] ) ] ON { table \| view } \| ON { table \| view } [ ( column [ ,...n ] ) ] \| ON { stored_procedure \| extended_procedure } \| ON { user_defined_function } | Column or columns for specific table or view having permissions granted. Otherwise, permissions can be granted at the table, view, stored procedure, extended stored procedure, or user-defined function levels. |
| security_account [ ,...n ] | This specifies the recipient of the granted object permission(s). This can be a SQL Server login, NT login, NT group, or database role. |
| [ WITH GRANT OPTION ] | Allows designated login, group, or database role to grant the specified object permission to other security accounts. |
| [ AS { group \| role } ] | Uses the security account that has authority to execute the GRANT statement. |

### Example 7.21.4: Granting SELECT permissions for a table to one user

```
GRANT SELECT ON Authors TO JaneDoe
```

### Example 7.21.5: Granting SELECT permissions for a table to one user using WITH GRANT

This example allows the user to grant the specified permissions to other security accounts:

```
GRANT SELECT ON Authors TO JaneDoe
   WITH GRANT OPTION
```

### Example 7.21.6: Granting INSERT, UPDATE, and DELETE permissions for a table to one user

```
GRANT INSERT, UPDATE, DELETE ON Authors
TO JaneDoe
```

### Example 7.21.7: Granting ALL permissions for a table to one user

```
GRANT ALL ON Authors
TO JaneDoe
```

### Example 7.21.8: Granting SELECT permissions for a table to multiple users

```
GRANT SELECT ON Books
TO JaneDoe, JohnDeer, JackSmith
```

### Example 7.21.9: Granting REFERENCES to a table for a user-defined role

```
GRANT REFERENCES ON Books TO BookDistributor
```

# DENY Permissions for Statements

The DENY keyword restricts permissions to a specific object or statement, for a user or role. DENY trumps any other permission granted implicitly by database role membership, unless you are a member of the sysadmin, db_owner, or db_securityadmin role. Users in the sysadmin role never have issues accessing objects, even with DENY statements in effect. Users in db_owner or db_securityadmin, if blocked by a DENY, can simply grant themselves access to the denied objects. The syntax for DENY from *SQL Server Books Online* is as follows:

For statement permissions:

```
DENY { ALL | statement [ ,...n ] }
TO security_account [ ,...n ]
```

| Parameter | Description |
|---|---|
| { ALL \| statement [ ,...n ] } | ALL denies all statement permissions, and can only be denied by members of the sysadmin role. Otherwise, the following statements can be denied:<br>BACKUP DATABASE<br>BACKUP LOG<br>CREATE DATABASE<br>CREATE DEFAULT<br>CREATE FUNCTION<br>CREATE PROCEDURE<br>CREATE RULE<br>CREATE TABLE<br>CREATE VIEW<br>One or more statements can be included in one DENY statement. |
| security_account [ ,...n ] | This specifies the recipient of the denied statement permission(s). This can be a SQL Server login, NT login, NT group, or database role. |

### Example 7.21.10: Denying permissions to back up the database and transaction log for a user

```
DENY BACKUP DATABASE, BACKUP LOG TO JaneDoe
```

### Example 7.21.11: Denying all statement permissions for a user

```
DENY ALL TO JaneDoe
```

### Example 7.21.12: Denying CREATE TABLE permissions to a user-defined database role

```
DENY CREATE TABLE TO BookDistributor
```

# DENY Permissions for Objects

For object permissions:

```
DENY
        { ALL [ PRIVILEGES ] | permission [ ,...n ] }
        {
                [ ( column [ ,...n ] ) ] ON { table | view }
                | ON { table | view } [ ( column [ ,...n ] ) ]
                | ON { stored_procedure | extended_procedure }
                | ON { user_defined_function }
        }
TO security_account [ ,...n ]
[ CASCADE ]
```

| Parameter | Description |
|---|---|
| { ALL \| statement [ ,...n ] } | ALL denies all object permissions, and can only be executed by members of the sysadmin or db_owner roles. Database object owners can also deny permissions for their owned objects.<br><br>Otherwise, individual object permissions that can be denied for a table, view, or table-valued function are:<br><br>SELECT<br>INSERT<br>UPDATE<br>DELETE<br><br>SELECT and UPDATE can define specific columns for which the permissions are denied. If none are specified, all columns are denied the SELECT or UPDATE permissions.<br><br>DENY REFERENCES is used to deny permission to reference another table for a FOREIGN KEY constraint, or deny objects referenced WITH SCHEMABINDING (functions or views).<br><br>EXECUTE is denied for permissions to execute a stored procedure or scalar-valued function.<br><br>One or more statements can be included in one DENY statement. |
| [ ( column [ ,...n ] ) ] ON { table \| view }<br><br>\| ON { table \| view } [ ( column [ ,...n ] ) ]<br><br>\| ON { stored_procedure \| extended_procedure }<br><br>\| ON { user_defined_function } | Column or columns for the specific table or view having permissions denied. Otherwise, permissions can be denied at the table, view, stored procedure, extended stored procedure, or user-defined function levels. |

| Parameter | Description |
|---|---|
| security_account [ ,...n ] | This specifies the recipient of the denied object permission(s). This can be a SQL Server login, NT login, NT group, or database role. |
| [ CASCADE ] | Will deny permissions to the security account, and any permissions that security account may have granted to other security accounts. |

### Example 7.21.13: Denying SELECT permissions for a table to one user

```
DENY SELECT ON Authors TO JaneDoe
```

### Example 7.21.14: Denying INSERT, UPDATE, and DELETE permissions for a table to one user

```
DENY INSERT, UPDATE, DELETE ON Authors TO JaneDoe
```

### Example 7.21.15: Denying ALL permissions for a table to one user

```
DENY ALL ON Authors TO JaneDoe
```

### Example 7.21.16: Denying SELECT permissions for a table to multiple users

```
DENY SELECT ON Books TO JaneDoe, JohnDeer, JackSmith
```

### Example 7.21.17: Denying REFERENCES to a table for a user-defined role

```
DENY REFERENCES ON Books TO BookDistributor
```

### Example 7.21.18: Denying SELECT to a table to a user, and any users to whom the original WITH GRANT OPTION user may have granted permissions

This example denies access to the `Authors` table for `JaneDoe`, and also anyone to whom `JaneDoe` may have granted `Authors SELECT` permissions:

```
DENY SELECT ON Authors TO JaneDoe CASCADE
```

# REVOKE Permissions for Statements

The `REVOKE` keyword removes both `GRANT` and `DENY` permissions from a specific object or statement, for a user or role. The syntax for `REVOKE` from *SQL Server Books Online* is as follows:

For statement permissions:

```
REVOKE { ALL | statement [ ,...n ] }
{TO | FROM} security_account [ ,...n]
```

| Parameter | Description |
|---|---|
| { ALL \| statement [ ,...n ] } | ALL removes all statement permissions, and can only be executed by members of the sysadmin role. Otherwise, the following statements can be revoked:<br><br>BACKUP DATABASE<br>BACKUP LOG<br>CREATE DATABASE<br>CREATE DEFAULT<br>CREATE FUNCTION<br>CREATE PROCEDURE<br>CREATE RULE<br>CREATE TABLE<br>CREATE VIEW<br><br>One or more statements can be included in one REVOKE statement. |
| security_account [ ,...n ] | This specifies the recipient of the revoked statement permission(s). This can be a SQL Server login, NT login, NT group, or database role. |

### Example 7.21.19: Revoking permissions to back up the database and transaction log from a user

```
REVOKE BACKUP DATABASE, BACKUP LOG FROM JaneDoe
```

### Example 7.21.20: Revoking all statement permissions from a user

```
REVOKE ALL FROM JaneDoe
```

### Example 7.21.21: Revoking CREATE TABLE permissions from a user-defined database role

```
REVOKE CREATE TABLE FROM BookDistributor
```

## REVOKE Permissions for Objects

For object permissions:

```
REVOKE [ GRANT OPTION FOR ]
    { ALL [ PRIVILEGES ] | permission [ ,...n ] }
    {
        [ ( column [ ,...n ] ) ] ON { table | view }
        | ON { table | view } [ ( column [ ,...n ] ) ]
        | ON { stored_procedure | extended_procedure }
        | ON { user_defined_function }
    }
{ TO | FROM }
    security_account [ ,...n ]
[ CASCADE ]
[ AS { group | role } ]
```

| Parameter | Description |
|---|---|
| `[ GRANT OPTION FOR ]` | Removes the `WITH GRANT OPTION` for the specified user and permissions. This switch is ignored if `WITH GRANT OPTION` wasn't originally granted. If originally granted, both `CASCADE` and `GRANT OPTION FOR` must be specified. |
| `{ ALL [ PRIVILEGES ] \| permission [ ,...n ] }` | `ALL` revokes all object permissions, and can only be executed by members of the `sysadmin` or `db_owner` roles. Database object owners can also revoke permissions for their owned objects.<br><br>Otherwise, individual object permissions that can be revoked for a table, view, or table-valued function are:<br><br>`SELECT`<br>`INSERT`<br>`UPDATE`<br>`DELETE`<br><br>`SELECT` and `UPDATE` can choose specific columns for which the permissions are revoked. If none are specified, all columns have `SELECT` or `UPDATE` permissions revoked.<br><br>`REVOKE REFERENCES` is used to revoke permission to reference another table for a `FOREIGN KEY` constraint, or revoke permissions for objects referenced `WITH SCHEMABINDING` (functions or views).<br><br>`EXECUTE` is revoked for permissions to execute a stored procedure or scalar-valued function.<br><br>One or more statements can be included in one `REVOKE` statement.<br><br>`PRIVILEGES` is used for SQL-92 compliance and is optional. |
| `{`<br>`[ ( column [ ,...n ] ) ]`<br>`ON { table \| view }`<br>`\| ON { table \| view }`<br>`[ ( column [ ,...n ] ) ]`<br>`\| ON { stored_procedure \| extended_procedure }`<br>`\| ON { user_defined_function }`<br>`}` | Column or columns for the specific table or view having permissions denied. Otherwise, permissions can be denied at the table, view, stored procedure, extended stored procedure, or user-defined function levels. |

*Table continued on following page*

| Parameter | Description |
|---|---|
| { TO \| FROM } security_account [ ,...n ] | This specifies the recipient of the revoked object permission(s). This can be a SQL Server login, NT login, NT group, or database role. TO and FROM can be used interchangeably. |
| [ CASCADE ] | Will revoke permissions to the security account and any permissions that security account may have granted to other security accounts. |
| [ AS { group \| role } ] | Uses the security account that has authority to execute the REVOKE statement. |

### Example 7.21.22: Revoking SELECT permissions for a table from one user

```
REVOKE SELECT ON Authors TO JaneDoe
```

### Example 7.21.23: Revoking SELECT permissions for a table from a user that was given WITH GRANT OPTION permissions

```
REVOKE SELECT ON Authors TO JaneDoe CASCADE
```

### Example 7.21.24: Revoking INSERT, UPDATE, and DELETE permissions for a table from one user

```
REVOKE INSERT, UPDATE, DELETE ON Authors TO JaneDoe
```

### Example 7.21.25: Revoking ALL permissions for a table to one user

```
REVOKE ALL ON Authors TO JaneDoe
```

### Example 7.21.26: Revoking SELECT permissions for a table to multiple users

```
REVOKE SELECT ON Books TO JaneDoe, JohnDeer, JackSmith
```

### Example 7.21.27: Revoking REFERENCES to a table for a user-defined role

```
REVOKE REFERENCES ON Books TO BookDistributor
```

# 7.22 How to... Report User Permissions and Statement Permissions using sp_helprotect

The system stored procedure sp_helprotect allows you to:

- View GRANT and DENY permissions applied to database users for both statement and object permissions, including:
    - REFERENCES
    - SELECT
    - INSERT

- DELETE
- UPDATE
- CREATE TABLE
- CREATE DATABASE
- CREATE FUNCTION
- CREATE DEFAULT
- CREATE RULE
- CREATE VIEW
- CREATE PROCEDURE
- EXECUTE
- BACKUP DATABASE
- CREATE DEFAULT
- BACKUP LOG

- Allows you to report permissions for the current database by object, permission granted, the user that was granted the permission, and the type of permission (designating "o" for object permissions, "s" for statement permissions, or "o s" for both).
- For statement permissions, both object-level and column-level permissions are reported.

The syntax from *SQL Server Books Online* is as follows:

```
sp_helprotect [ [ @name = ] 'object_statement' ]
    [ , [ @username = ] 'security_account' ]
    [ , [ @grantorname = ] 'grantor' ]
    [ , [ @permissionarea = ] 'type' ]
```

| Parameter | Description |
|---|---|
| `[ @name = ] 'object_statement'` | For this field, either use the name of an object (table, view, stored procedure, or extended stored procedure), or enter a name of an object permission statement (for example, `CREATE DEFAULT`). This field is optional, and defaults to `ALL` permissions. |
| `[ @username = ] 'security_account'` | The name of the account for which to report permissions; for example, display all permissions for `JaneDoe`. |
| `[ @grantorname = ] 'grantor'` | The name of the account that granted permissions; for example, display all permissions granted by `dbo`. |
| `[ @permissionarea = ] 'type'` | Use "o" for object permissions, "s" for statement permissions, or "o s" for both types of permissions. |

## Example 7.22.1: Displaying all permissions set for the database

```
USE BookRepository07
EXEC sp_helprotect
```

This returns permission information on the owner, object, grantee, grantor, permission type, action, and column(s) (when applicable) for all permissions in the database:

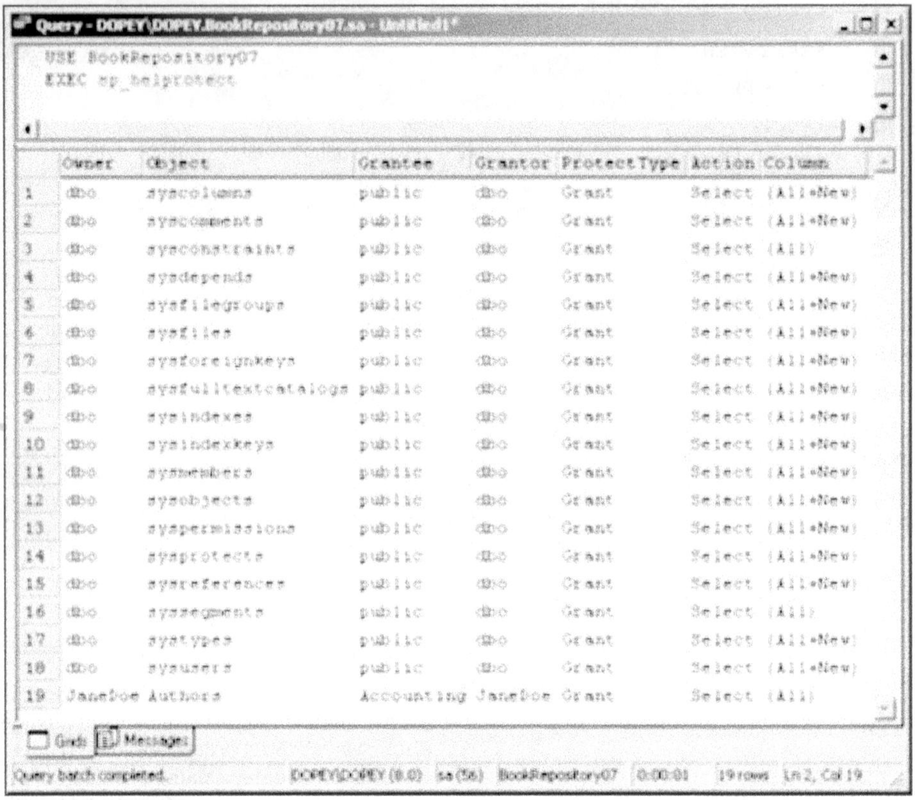


| | Owner | Object | Grantee | Grantor | ProtectType | Action | Column |
|---|---|---|---|---|---|---|---|
| 1 | dbo | syscolumns | public | dbo | Grant | Select | (All+New) |
| 2 | dbo | syscomments | public | dbo | Grant | Select | (All+New) |
| 3 | dbo | sysconstraints | public | dbo | Grant | Select | (All) |
| 4 | dbo | sysdepends | public | dbo | Grant | Select | (All+New) |
| 5 | dbo | sysfilegroups | public | dbo | Grant | Select | (All+New) |
| 6 | dbo | sysfiles | public | dbo | Grant | Select | (All+New) |
| 7 | dbo | sysforeignkeys | public | dbo | Grant | Select | (All+New) |
| 8 | dbo | sysfulltextcatalogs | public | dbo | Grant | Select | (All+New) |
| 9 | dbo | sysindexes | public | dbo | Grant | Select | (All+New) |
| 10 | dbo | sysindexkeys | public | dbo | Grant | Select | (All+New) |
| 11 | dbo | sysmembers | public | dbo | Grant | Select | (All+New) |
| 12 | dbo | sysobjects | public | dbo | Grant | Select | (All+New) |
| 13 | dbo | syspermissions | public | dbo | Grant | Select | (All+New) |
| 14 | dbo | sysprotects | public | dbo | Grant | Select | (All+New) |
| 15 | dbo | sysreferences | public | dbo | Grant | Select | (All+New) |
| 16 | dbo | syssegments | public | dbo | Grant | Select | (All) |
| 17 | dbo | systypes | public | dbo | Grant | Select | (All+New) |
| 18 | dbo | sysusers | public | dbo | Grant | Select | (All+New) |
| 19 | JaneDoe | Authors | Accounting | JaneDoe | Grant | Select | (All) |

## Example 7.22.2: Displaying all permissions for a specific user

The following example displays all permissions applied to the JaneDoe user, for the BookRepository07 database:

```
USE BookRepository07
EXEC sp_helprotect @username = 'JaneDoe'
```

Notice that both object and statement permissions are returned. Columns to which permissions are explicitly granted (txtDescription on the Books table, for example) are listed in the Column column. The ProtectType value of GRANT_WGO means that the WITH GRANT OPTION has been included with the permission (meaning JaneDoe can grant others permission to SELECT from the Employees table):

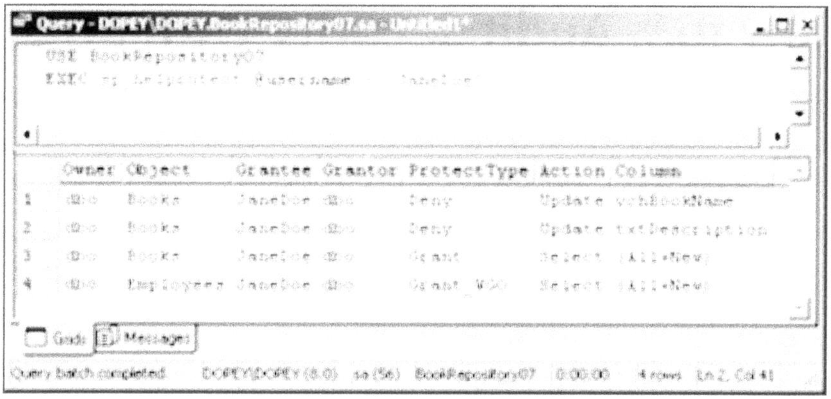


### Example 7.22.3: Displaying all permissions for a specific table

```
USE BookRepository07
EXEC sp_helprotect @name = 'Authors'
```

Returns all permissions explicitly granted for the `Authors` table:

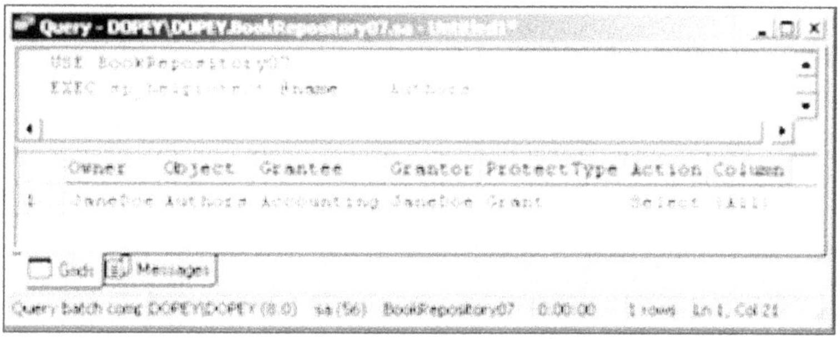


### Example 7.22.4: Displaying all users granted or denied a specific object permission

```
USE BookRepository07
EXEC sp_helprotect @name = 'CREATE DEFAULT'
```

Returns:

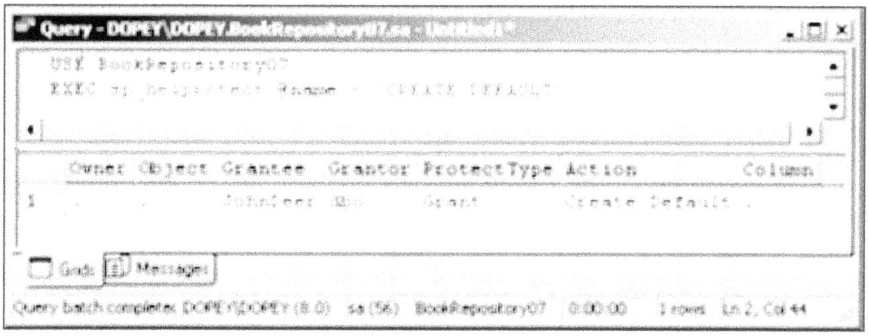

# 7.23 How to... Audit Security with SQL Profiler

Using SQL Profiler, you can audit an array of SQL Server events. Along with capturing every Transact-SQL command, beginning with SQL Server 2000, SQL Profiler can audit:

- The addition and removal of logins and database users
- Login password changes
- Default database or default language changes
- Failed login attempts
- The addition and removal of logins from a fixed server role
- The addition and removal of users from a database role
- The addition and removal of database roles themselves
- Changes to a password for an application role
- `BACKUP` and `RESTORE` operations
- DBCC operations
- `CREATE`, `ALTER`, and `DROP` operations
- `GRANT`, `DENY`, and `REVOKE` operations
- Object permission success or failure events
- SQL Server shut down, pause, or service startups
- Statement permission operations

Using SQL Profiler from your desktop means that you are using a **client-side trace**. Client-side traces do not run on the server, unless you run SQL Profiler from the server itself. Running SQL Profiler from your desktop means that if your system shuts down, your trace will stop running. In many cases, if you want ongoing security auditing, you should either consider running SQL Profiler from a dedicated box or create what is called a **server-side trace**.

Using a server-side trace, you can utilize a series of stored procedures to track events, choose fields, and set filters. You use stored procedures to begin this trace via Transact-SQL, and it will run as long as your SQL Server service stays up. Your output can be forwarded to a table or file. We will be going over how to create a server-side trace in Chapter 17.

In the meantime, setting up a client-side trace in SQL Profiler is functionally equivalent to a server-side trace, and is a little easier.

Before creating your trace, consider that running a trace adds *some* performance overhead to your server. Traces are excellent for short-term troubleshooting, or for auditing activity for databases containing sensitive data (employee salary information, trade secrets). Try to keep your traces as narrow as possible, by including only events and columns that you need, making liberal use of filters (events, columns, and filters are reviewed next), and running the trace only as long as needed.

To create a security auditing trace using SQL Profiler:

- Go to Start | Programs | Microsoft SQL Server | Profiler.
- Go to File | New | Trace.
- Select the server and login you wish to trace. The login you use must have enough permissions to run the SQL Profiler stored procedures; therefore, use either a `sysadmin` account or an account with `EXEC` permissions for the following extended stored procedures located in the master database:
    - `sp_trace_create`
    - `sp_trace_generateevent`
    - `sp_trace_setevent`
    - `sp_trace_setfilter`
    - `sp_trace_setstatus`
- In the General Tab, specify the:
    - Trace name: user-defined name.
    - Trace SQL Server: server for which you are tracing activity.
    - Template name: when creating SQL Profiler traces, you have the option to save your settings (events, data columns, filters) to a trace template. This allows you to save time and re-use templates. It is recommended that you save templates for future use.
    - Template file name: you can select either template name or point to a template file. Looks for the `*.tdf` file extension.
    - Save to file: allows you to save your results to a `*.trc` file.
    - Set maximum file size (MB): maximum size allowed for the `*.trc` file.
    - Enable file rollover: at a certain file size, allows a new `*.trc` file to start afresh; for very active servers, trace files can quickly get large. Opening a 200,000 row `*.trc` file can take a long time on an average laptop or desktop computer. This helps you keep the trace file size to a minimum, while still capturing data.
    - Server processes SQL Server trace data: the default SQL Profiler behavior is client-side processing of the trace, which means that under very busy trace activity, some events can be missed. By selecting the server processes option, the traced server will track the events on the server, meaning no events will be missed. The downside is that performance under high activity periods may be impacted by the trace.
    - Save to table: this allows you to save your trace activity to a table in SQL Server. This is a great option for archiving trace data, as well as granting you flexibility to aggregate information. For example, when tracing query events, you could calculate average duration or the total of all read and write activity.
    - Set maximum rows (in thousands): sets a maximum number of rows allowed in your trace table.
    - Enable trace stop time: enables you to stop the trace at a specific time so that it can run unattended from your client.

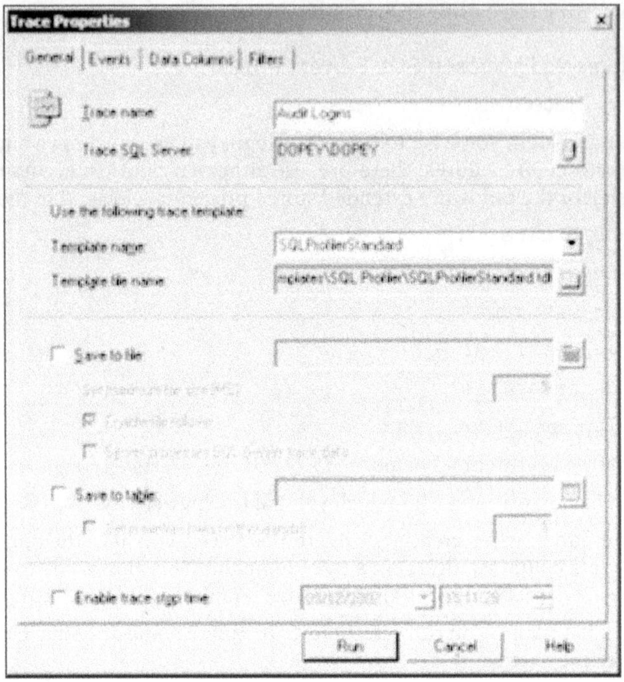


Note that you don't have to save the results to a file or table after the trace is finished running. You can also just close out the trace file without saving it.

A big gotcha in working with trace files, which you should be aware of, is the following:

> **Let's say you have been running a security audit trace for the last 12 hours. You stop the trace, and decide that you would like to take out some of the events, or filter out some of the rows of your existing data set. Watch out: to change the settings of an existing set of rows, you must save the file first, close out of the file, and reopen that file. After this, you can remove events, data columns, or add filters. Trying to make changes before the file is saved will cause the trace to restart, thus losing 12 hours of information.**

In the Events tab, use the Add or Remove button to select or deselect event classes. You'll notice that by clicking on a specific event, you can see the user-friendly description in the lower half of the window; you can select individual events, or an entire event class. In this example, we will be monitoring successful and failed login attempts.

Expand the Security Audit node and you will see the list of all possible security-related events. Choose Audit Login and Audit Login Failed and press Add:

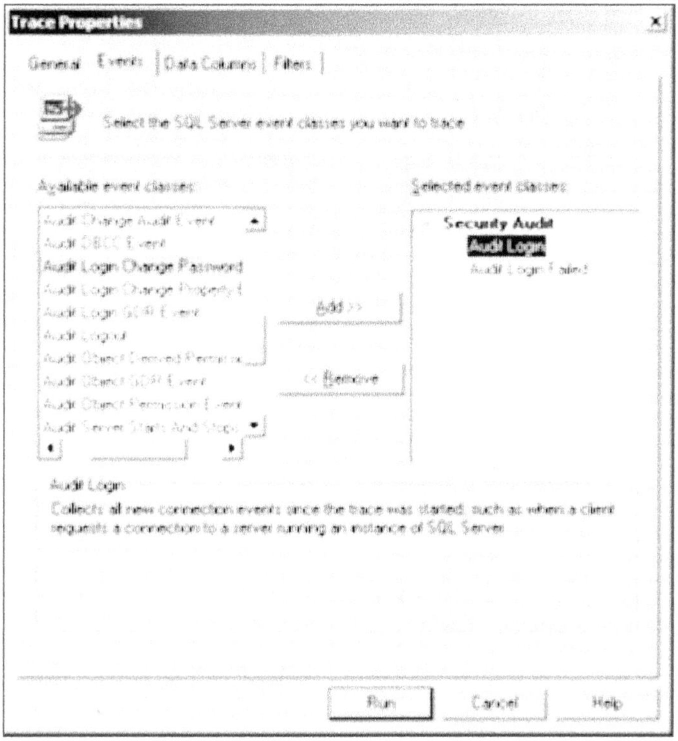


In the Data Columns tab, you can select which data columns to capture for your selected trace events. Note that not all data columns are used for each trace event. In addition to this, the output is not always entirely clear, as return codes are used rather than user-friendly descriptions. See *Security Audit Data Columns* in *SQL Server Books Online* for a comprehensive listing of data columns and descriptions for each event class.

In the following example, we will track EventClass (the type of event), SPID (the SPID of the user), TextData (a textual description of the event), BinaryData (any binary data that was sent as part of the event), and Success (a Boolean that shows whether the event was successful or not). These are the only columns used for the two login auditing events we chose in the Events tab. Note that you can click a column and select the Up button to reorder the event output. You can also move a data column up to the Groups section, which groups the events together in the trace output. Not all columns are allowed in the Groups section. In the following example we order by EventClass:

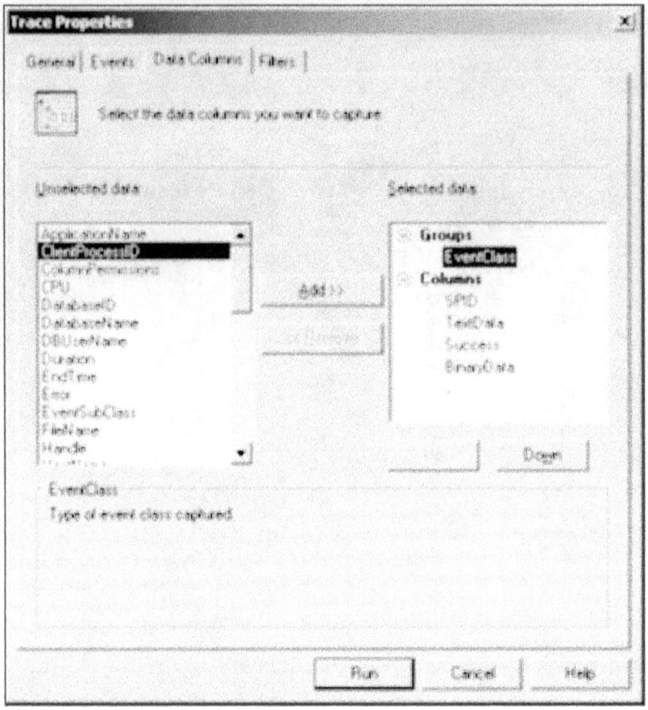


On the **Filters** tab, you can specify what rows appear in your trace. This tab is the equivalent of the `WHERE` clause in a `SELECT` statement.

Depending on the filtered column, you define a specification:

- Equals
- Not equal to
- Greater than or equal
- Less than or equal
- Like
- Not Like

Both the **Like** and **Not Like** filters can use the "`%`" wildcard character, for matches against any string of zero or more characters. The "`%`" character can be used as a prefix, suffix, or both. For example, if you wish to find occurrences of the word "`Authors`" in the `TextData` column, you could add a filter saying **Like %Authors%**:

Select the Run button to begin the trace. In our example, we will capture successful login attempts and failures. The Success column will show 1 for success and 0 for login failures:

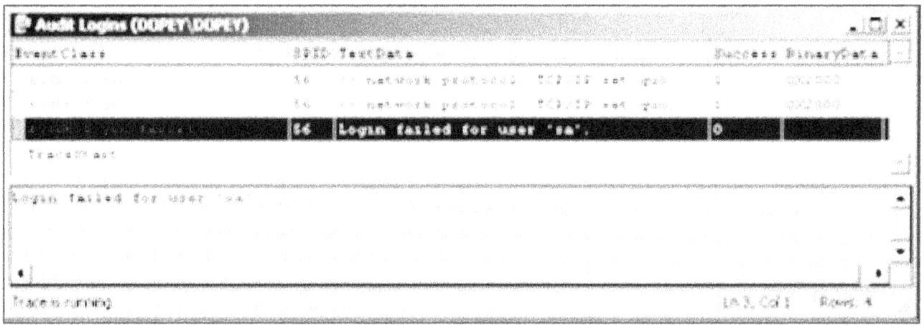


# 7.24 How to... Audit Logins at the OS Level

In addition to auditing your SQL Server security, you may also be curious about who is logging on to your server. To enable auditing of successful or unsuccessful login attempts:

- On the server, select Start | Programs | Administrative | Tools | Local Security Policy.
- In the Local Security Settings dialog box, expand the Local Policies folder and click Audit Policies.
- From this view, you can add auditing for logon events, account management, directory service access, logon events, object access, policy changes, privilege use, process tracking, and system events. Click Audit Logon Events to configure auditing of login success and failure.

To view logon attempts that end in failure, click the checkbox next to Failure. Select OK when you have finished:

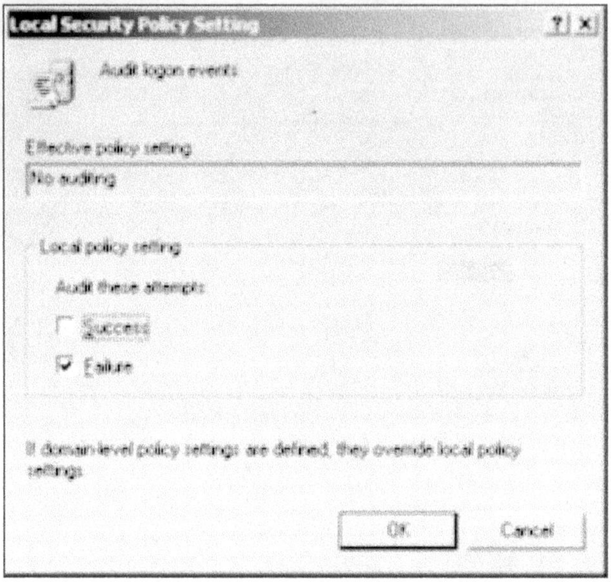


Remember that domain-level policy settings will override any local policy settings you define for the server.

Your security auditing will now be written to the Security Log in Event Viewer:

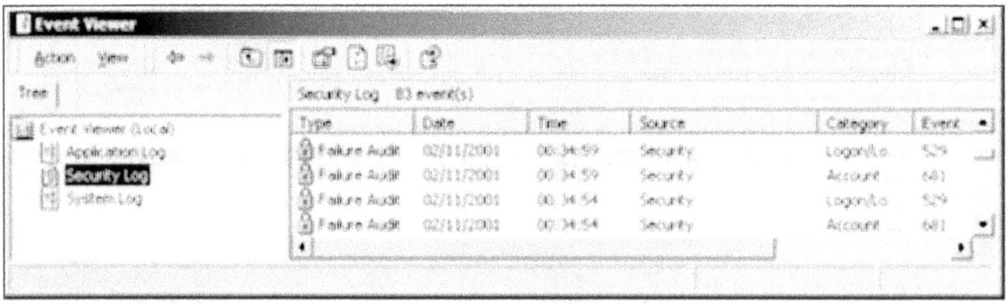


Double-clicking a specific audit event will show more information about the login attempt. Remember to limit your security auditing to necessary events and objects, as your security log can quickly get large.

# 7.25 How to... Monitor Updates with Triggers

A popular technique for monitoring data modifications to tables in a database is the creation of triggers. You can use triggers to generate audit information when updates to a table occur. You can use an audit table to track information such as the user making the update, the time of the update, data changed, data removed, and data inserted.

You should first determine the level of detail you wish to track. Audit tables can get quite large if you track every single update or every column being updated. You should address the following questions when investigating the use of audit tables:

- What information do you wish to track? Will you be using this audit to track every column and row modified, deleted, or inserted? Do you just want to know the type of event (INSERT, UPDATE, or DELETE) and the user responsible?
- What tables do you wish to audit?
- Do you want one central audit table (good for general information, but not for column-by-column changes across tables), or a single audit table per update table?

We will review two scenarios: trigger auditing for general update information and trigger auditing for specific row INSERT, UPDATE, and DELETE. In both scenarios, we will be auditing activity for the Employees table:

```
CREATE TABLE dbo.Employees (
    iEmployeeId int IDENTITY (1, 1) NOT NULL
      CONSTRAINT PK_Employees PRIMARY KEY CLUSTERED,
    vchLastName varchar (100),
    vchFirstName varchar (100),
    moSalary money NULL
)
```

### Scenario 7.25.1: Capturing general modification activity with triggers

For this scenario, we want to audit the following information:

- Employee ID modified
- Time data modification occurred
- User who made the modification
- Operation type – INSERT, UPDATE, or DELETE

To capture this data, we will make a table called Employees_Audit:

```
CREATE TABLE dbo.Employees_Audit (
    iEmployeeId int NOT NULL,
    dtModifiedDate datetime NOT NULL,
    vchUpdatedBy varchar (100),
    chUpdateType char (6)
    CONSTRAINT PK_Employees_Audit PRIMARY KEY CLUSTERED
    (iEmployeeId, dtModifiedDate)
)
```

Next, we will create a trigger on the Employees table to capture all INSERT, UPDATE, and DELETE activity (for an explanation of triggers, see Chapter 14):

```
CREATE TRIGGER dbo.TRG_Employees ON dbo.Employees
FOR INSERT, UPDATE, DELETE
AS
```

We will provide variables to hold counts of inserted and deleted values. The Type variable holds the type of operation that occurred (INSERT, UPDATE, or DELETE):

```
DECLARE @Inserted int,
        @Deleted int,
        @Type char (6)
```

Retrieve counts of rows in the `inserted` and `deleted` trigger tables:

```
SELECT @Inserted = COUNT(*) FROM inserted
SELECT @Deleted = COUNT(*) FROM deleted
```

If inserted row counts are greater than zero, and deleted rows are zero, then the trigger is of type `INSERT`. If inserted rows are greater than zero, and deleted rows also are greater than zero, then the trigger type is `UPDATE`. Lastly, if there are no inserted rows, but the row counts for deleted rows are greater than zero, the trigger type is `DELETE`:

```
SELECT @Type = CASE
    WHEN (@Inserted > 0) and (@Deleted = 0) THEN 'INSERT'
    WHEN (@Inserted > 0) and (@Deleted > 0) THEN 'UPDATE'
    WHEN (@Inserted = 0) and (@Deleted > 0) THEN 'DELETE'
END
```

If the type is `INSERT` or `DELETE`, insert the employee ID, current time, type, and user name into the `Employees_Audit` table:

```
IF (@Type IN ('INSERT', 'UPDATE'))
INSERT INTO dbo.Employees_Audit
SELECT iEmployeeId, current_timestamp, @Type ,suser_sname()
FROM inserted
ELSE
```

Otherwise, the type must be `DELETE`, so the employee ID, current time, type, and user name will be inserted into `Employees_Audit` from the `deleted` table:

```
INSERT INTO dbo.Employees_Audit
SELECT iEmployeeId, current_timestamp, @Type ,suser_sname()
FROM deleted

RETURN
```

With this trigger in place, perform the following `INSERT`:

```
INSERT Employees (vchLastName, vchFirstName, moSalary)
VALUES ('Schmoe', 'Joe', 43000.42)
GO
```

This will return the following results to the `Employees_Audit` table:

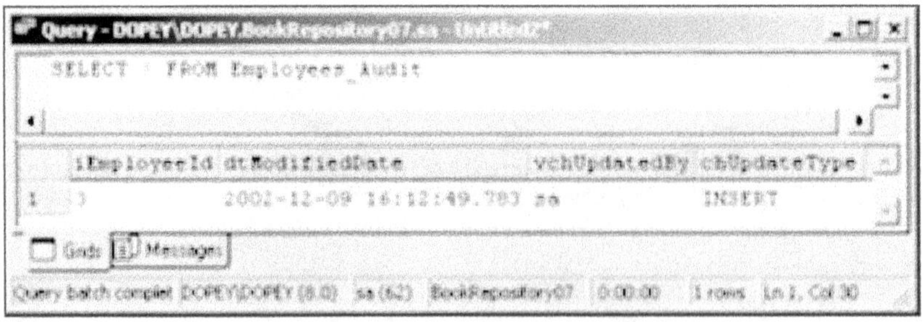

Next, perform an UPDATE operation:

```
UPDATE Employees
SET moSalary = 0.00
WHERE iEmployeeId = 1
```

This will return the following results to the Employees_Audit table:

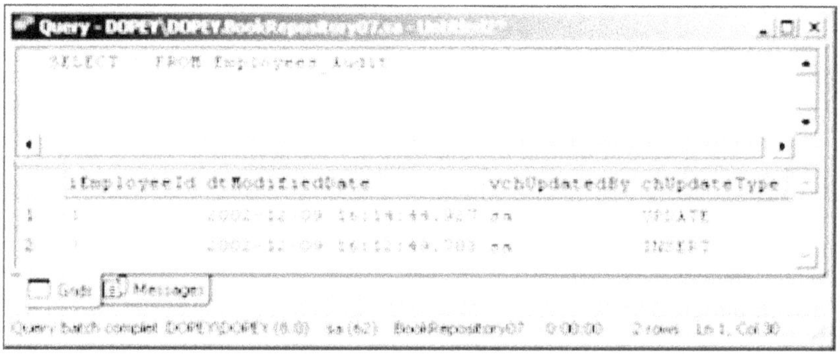


Lastly, perform a DELETE operation:

```
DELETE Employees
WHERE iEmployeeId = 1
```

This will return the following results to the Employees_Audit table:

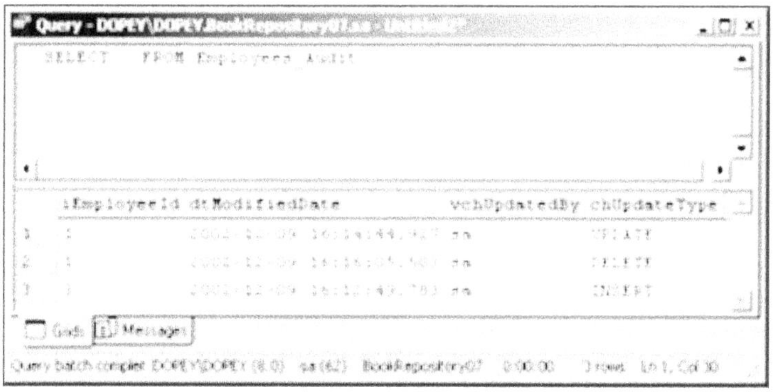


## Scenario 7.25.2: Capturing data modified with triggers

If you need the full ability to track exactly what data was modified, this scenario will review how to create a trigger that audits:

- Employee ID modified
- Time data modification occurred
- User who made the modification
- Operation type – INSERT, UPDATE, or DELETE
- Data inserted, deleted, or updated

This example also uses the Employees table; however we will need to modify the Employees_Audit table to track the additional column information:

```
CREATE TABLE dbo.Employees_Audit (
        iEmployeeId int NOT NULL,
        vchLastName varchar(100),
        vchFirstName varchar(100),
        moSalary money,
        dtModifiedDate datetime NOT NULL,
        vchUpdatedBy varchar (100),
        chUpdateType char (6)
    CONSTRAINT PK_Employees_Audit PRIMARY KEY CLUSTERED
      (iEmployeeId, dtModifiedDate)
)
```

The example trigger:

```
CREATE TRIGGER dbo.TRG_Employees2 ON dbo.Employees
FOR INSERT, UPDATE, DELETE
AS
DECLARE @Inserted int,
        @Deleted int,
        @Type char (6)

SELECT @Inserted = COUNT(*) FROM inserted
SELECT @Deleted = COUNT(*) FROM deleted

SELECT @Type = CASE
    WHEN (@Inserted > 0) and (@Deleted = 0) THEN 'INSERT'
    WHEN (@Inserted > 0) and (@Deleted > 0) THEN 'UPDATE'
    WHEN (@Inserted = 0) and (@Deleted > 0) THEN 'DELETE'
END

IF (@Type IN ('INSERT', 'UPDATE'))

INSERT INTO dbo.Employees_Audit
SELECT iEmployeeId,
       vchLastName,
       vchFirstName,
       moSalary,
       current_timestamp,
       suser_sname(),
       @Type
FROM inserted

ELSE

INSERT INTO dbo.Employees_Audit
SELECT iEmployeeId,
       vchLastName,
       vchFirstName,
       moSalary,
       current_timestamp,
       suser_sname(),
       @Type
FROM deleted

RETURN
```

Now, run the following INSERT:

```
INSERT Employees (vchLastName, vchFirstName, moSalary)
VALUES ('Schmoe', 'Sandy', 45000.00)
GO
```

We get the following row in the Employees_Audit table:

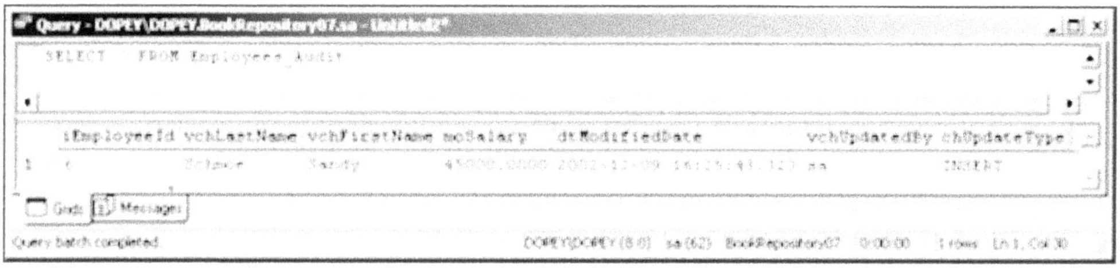

Notice that we can tell exactly what information was inserted.

If we issue an UPDATE to this new employee, giving them a salary of zero dollars:

```
UPDATE Employees
SET moSalary = 0
WHERE iEmployeeId = 6
```

We would get the following row in the Employees_Audit table:

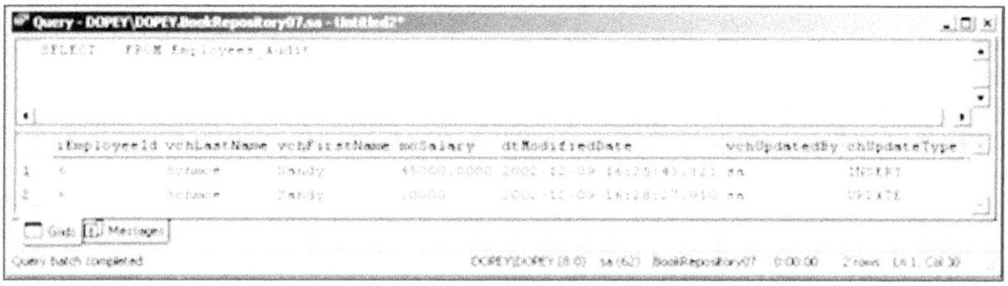

Lastly, if we issue a DELETE:

```
DELETE Employees WHERE iEmployeeId = 6
```

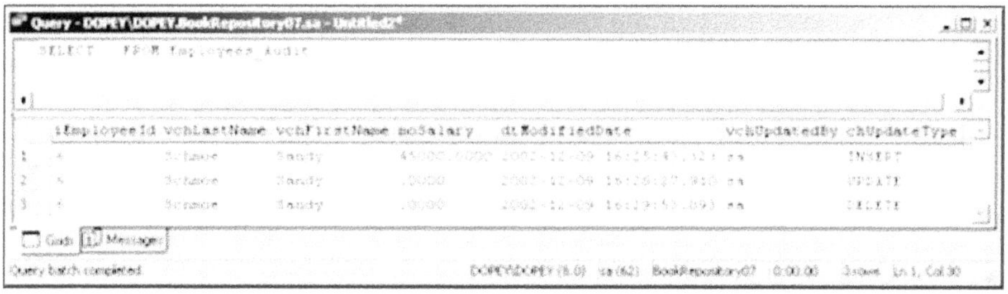

# 8

# Replication

SQL Server 2000 Replication allows you to distribute copies of data from one database to another, on the same SQL Server instance or between different instances. Replication allows data to be read and, depending on the replication type, updated from multiple locations.

Some uses for replication:

- Separating transaction processing from reporting activity, and replicating a read-only copy of the data to a different server or database.
- Splitting activity across two servers, allowing updates to both servers, and synchronizing the changes.
- Distributing data to remote employees working with data offline. Data can be modified offline, and the changes synchronized after reconnection to the network.
- Distributing multiple copies of data to remote sites.
- Replicating to a 'warm' standby database. If using a database as a warm standby, you must ensure that any database objects or permissions not migrated with replication are brought over manually.

If you are looking for a high availability solution, consider failover clustering rather than replication. With failover clusters, the SQL Server instance (or instances) is housed on a shared disk array, rather than a local disk array. Only one server maintains control of a single SQL Server instance at a time. If a failure or issue occurs to the server controlling the SQL Server instance, the second server can take control (fail over) from the first node. See Chapter 10 for more information on failover clusters.

Also consider log shipping as a method of keeping a warm standby database in the event of a problem on the primary database. Log shipping allows you to keep a closely synchronized copy of a selected database, by transferring and applying transaction log backups of the primary database to a secondary database on a different SQL Server instance. See Chapter 12 for more details. Log shipping does not allow continuous read access to the warm standby database; so, if you require this, consider using replication instead.

# Replication Topology

Replication topology defines what data is replicated (that is, published), who is tracking and managing the data changes and data movement (the distributor), and who is receiving the data (the subscriber). A replication topology also defines the servers that are available for replication, the data or database object to be replicated, and the servers requesting the data being replicated.

A replication topology is made up of at least one publisher, one distributor, and one subscriber.

The publisher holds the data that is distributed using replication, and organizes it in publications. A publication contains articles, which can include tables, stored procedure definitions, view definitions and data, indexed views, user-defined functions, and the actual execution of a stored procedure. The data itself can be partitioned to include specific columns (using a vertical filter) or rows (using a horizontal filter). All articles must be from the **same** database:

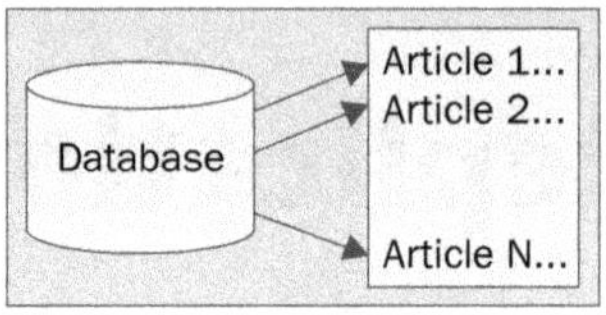


The distributor manages the process and tracks the history, transactions, and data that describe the state of replication. The distribution database is created when the distributor is set up, and the distributor process can exist on either the same or a different server from the publisher.

Subscribers subscribe to publications, which means they choose to receive data and synchronizations from a specific publication. When the publisher is responsible for distributing and synchronizing the data, this is called a **push subscription**. When the subscriber is responsible for the data distribution and synchronization, this is called a **pull subscription**. The type of subscription used does not restrict the location of the distribution database; the distribution database can exist on the publication server, subscribing server, or a separate distributor server. When subscribing to a publication, the subscriber will receive all articles in the publication, and cannot select a subset of available articles.

Replication topologies (also called **replication models**) are simply a framework for organizing your publications, distributors, and subscribers in a meaningful way. The common replication topologies are:

- **Central publisher, local distributor**
  One central server contains one or more publications. The distribution database is located on the same server, and the publications are pushed to one or more subscriber servers. This topology is excellent for situations where the data is updated in a central location, with many remote sites requiring copies. This is generally seen with snapshot and transactional replication (described later on).
- **Central publisher, remote distributor**
  One central server contains one or more publications. The distribution database is located on a remote server, and one or more subscribers subscribe to the central publisher publications. Offloading the distribution database to another server can increase the performance of the publisher, especially if the publisher server is heavily utilized. Remote distributors are beneficial when located closer to the subscribers geographically. Once again, this is generally seen with transactional and snapshot replication types.

- **Central subscriber, remote distributors**
  One central subscriber subscribes to multiple publications; in this scenario, each publication server uses its own distributor. Central subscription topologies are excellent when the publishers contain horizontally partitioned information (which means that the data is distinguished by rows). If you have multiple publishers from different departments or regions, code for the department or region can distinguish the rows, and the data can be combined at the subscriber. You will see this topology with transactional and snapshot replication types.
- **Publishing subscriber**
  A publishing subscriber topology involves publishing to a subscriber, and then the subscriber publishing that data to one or more different subscribers. This is beneficial for publications that must send data over slow or expensive LAN or WAN connections, assuming the republishing subscriber is more ideally located.
- **Hybrid**
  Two or more servers act as publisher, distributor, and subscriber. This is the most complicated topology, and would be based on complex application requirements for data exchange by the server. Note that one server can adopt all three replication topology roles.

The following table summarizes details on selecting the proper topology for your requirements:

| Topology | Best For... |
|---|---|
| Central publisher, local distributor | A database that is centrally updated and is used by multiple distributed SQL Server instances for reporting purposes. |
| Central publisher, remote distributor | Beneficial for overloaded publisher servers; distributes workload to the remote distributor. Ideal when the remote distributor server is in a better location in relation to the subscribers (faster connection, or closer geographically). |
| Central subscriber, remote distributors | Good for regional or department-based partitioned databases, where data exchange across sales or products is common. |
| Publishing subscriber | Beneficial when the publisher must publish to multiple sites, where the cost or speed of replicating directly from the publisher is not optimal. |
| Hybrid | Flexible solution. Requires potentially fewer servers, but imposes more performance overhead depending on the publication size and expected activity. |

# Replication Types

There are three types of replication available in SQL Server 2000: **snapshot**, **transactional**, and **merge**.

## Snapshot Replication

Snapshot replication copies articles from a publication to the target subscriber database. The articles reflect data as it exists at the moment the snapshot is started on the publisher; no monitoring for updates to the data is performed after this point. The snapshot also generates schema files and outputs the data using `BCP`. Schema files are applied to the subscriber, and data is imported into the subscriber database using `BCP`.

All replication types use various **agents** to perform replication tasks. Agents have configurable properties, located in a **profile**. Properties and profiles are reviewed later in this chapter.

Snapshot replication uses the following agents:

| Agent | Description |
|---|---|
| Snapshot agent | Creates schema and data files based on articles in the publication. |
| Distribution agent | Moves snapshot schema and data held in the distribution database to the subscribers. If using a push subscription, this runs from the Distributor. For pull subscriptions, this agent runs from the subscriber or subscribers. |
| Agent history clean up: distribution | Cleans up replication agent history on the distribution database. Default is for agent to run every 10 minutes. |
| Distribution clean up: distribution | Cleans up replication transactions in the distribution database. Default is for agent to run every 10 minutes. |
| Expired subscription clean up | Finds and removes expired subscriptions from the publication databases. Default is to run daily at 1:00AM. |
| Reinitialize subscriptions having data validation failures | Reinitializes subscriptions with data validation failures. This agent does not have a default schedule. |
| Replication agents checkup | Finds replication agents that are not actively logging history. Default is for agent to run every 10 minutes. |

## Snapshot Replication Reminders

- ❑ Use snapshot replication for data that does not need to be updated frequently. Also use snapshots to initialize the subscription for use by a transactional replication publication. Do not use snapshot replication if the data must be up-to-the-minute.
- ❑ Updates made at the subscriber are also allowed when using immediate updating subscriptions (covered later in the chapter).

# Transactional Replication

Transactional replication applies an initial snapshot of the data to the subscriber, and then moves any ongoing data changes at the publisher to the subscriber. This includes any `INSERT`, `UPDATE`, and `DELETE` statements against your selected articles in the publication.

You can configure transactional replication to propagate changes in real-time to the subscribers, or to perform the data changes on a scheduled basis. Transactional consistency is maintained, in that partial updates are not allowed within the publication; this means that when a batch of updates is carried across to the subscriber, the entire batch will be rolled back if some updates fail.

System-generated stored procedures are created automatically when a subscription is created, to update the subscription database for `INSERT`, `UPDATE`, and `DELETE` operations. This is done instead of using the original update statements used on the publisher. You will also see new system tables generated for the use of transactional replication.

Transactional replication uses the following agents:

| Agent | Description |
|---|---|
| Snapshot agent | Creates schema and data files based on articles in the publication. |
| Log reader agent | Moves transactions marked for replication from the transaction log of the publication database to the distribution database. Log reader agents are used exclusively for transactional replication. You will see one log reader agent for each published database. |
| Distribution agent | Moves snapshot schema and data and transactions held in the distribution database to the subscribers. You can choose to run this agent either at the distributor or subscriber. |
| Agent history clean up: distribution | Cleans up replication agent history on the distribution database. Default is for agent to run every 10 minutes. |
| Distribution clean up: distribution | Cleans up replication transactions in the distribution database. Default is for agent to run every 10 minutes. |
| Expired subscription clean up | Finds and removes expired subscriptions from the publication databases. Default is to run daily at 1:00AM. |
| Reinitialize subscriptions having data validation failures | Reinitializes subscriptions with data validation failures. This agent does not have a default schedule. |
| Replication agents checkup | Finds replication agents that are not actively logging history. Default is for agent to run every 10 minutes. |

## Transactional Replication Reminders

- Tables selected as articles in a transactional replication publication must have a primary key.
- Transaction log records for the publication database are not purged until they are moved to the distribution database. If the distribution database cannot be contacted, or the log reader agent has stopped running, the transaction log will continue to grow and cannot be truncated past the last transaction that was read by the log reader.
- Updates made at the subscriber are allowed if you have enabled queued or immediate updating within the publication. Subscriber updates for both snapshot and transactional replication will be covered later in the chapter.
- If your application uses `UPDATETEXT` or `WRITETEXT` to modify text or image data, you must use the `WITH LOG` option in order for these changes to be replicated.

# Merge Replication

Like transactional replication, merge replication begins by applying an initial snapshot to the subscriber. Merge replication then allows both the publisher and subscriber databases to be modified independently. The subscriber can disconnect from the publisher, make modifications, reconnect, and have changes and modifications on both the publisher and subscriber merged into one copy. If the publisher and subscriber stay connected, changes will be merged more frequently. When the same data is modified, merge replication allows you to set up rules determining which record will be the final update.

SQL Server uses a `uniqueidentifier` column to identify every row in a table. SQL Server also creates triggers to track changes to data rows and data columns. System-generated stored procedures are created to update the subscription database for `INSERT`, `UPDATE`, and `DELETE` operations, rather then the original update statements used on the publisher. You will see many new system tables generated for the exclusive use of merge replication.

It is also important to note that merge replication does not use the distribution database as much as transactional replication. Size the distribution database accordingly.

Merge replication uses the following agents:

| Agent | Description |
|---|---|
| Snapshot agent | Creates schema and data files based on articles in the publication, stores the files in the snapshot folder, and records synchronization jobs in the distribution database on the distributor. |
| Merge agent | The merge agent applies the snapshot to the subscriber, and is responsible for transferring and reconciling data changes between the publisher and subscriber. The merge agent is used exclusively with merge replication. One merge agent will exist for each subscriber. |
| Agent history clean up: distribution | Cleans up replication agent history on the distribution database. Default is for agent to run every 10 minutes. |
| Distribution clean up: distribution | Cleans up replication transactions in the distribution database. Default is for agent to run every 10 minutes. |
| Expired subscription clean up | Finds and removes expired subscriptions from the publication databases. Default is to run daily at 1:00AM. |
| Reinitialize subscriptions having data validation failures | Reinitializes subscriptions with data validation failures. This agent does not have a default schedule. |
| Replication agents checkup | Finds replication agents that are not actively logging history. Default is for agent to run every 10 minutes. |

## Merge Replication Reminders

- ❑ Remember to include primary and foreign key tables within the same publication to avoid lookup or integrity errors.
- ❑ Remember that `TIMESTAMP` columns are regenerated at the subscriber; the values do not stay the same when being propagated to the publisher.
- ❑ `TEXT` and `IMAGE` data is not replicated using the `UPDATETEXT` and `WRITETEXT` commands; you must use the `UPDATE` statement for these values to be replicated.
- ❑ If you do not have a `uniqueidentifier` data type column in your table, SQL Server will add it.

# Comparing Replication Types

| Replication Type | Advantages | Disadvantages |
|---|---|---|
| Snapshot | Excellent for read-only copies of the data. Good for small data sets, and for data that does not require frequent updates. | Not good when frequent data updates occur that subscribers need to see. Large articles in a publication can cause the snapshot replication to run for long periods. Network speed can impact the time it takes to apply the snapshot. |
| Transactional | Excellent for keeping subscribers up-to-date with changes made on the publisher. Maintains transactional consistency. (Near real time updates from the publisher. Good for both batch updates and single-row updates). | Can result in much network traffic if immediate updating is involved. Has more system resource overhead. Network speed can impact the time it takes to apply the initial snapshot. |
| Merge | Excellent where the site requires autonomy and the ability to modify the published data. Good for sales force operations when end users must take the data offline for reads and modifications. Good for single-row updates (rather than batch updates). | Data conflicts require more planning to prevent. Merge replication is the most complicated type of replication to manage. Excellent for distributing transaction processing (load balancing across servers). Network speed can impact the time it takes to apply the initial snapshot. |

Updates can be made at the subscriber for snapshot and transactional replication. This is achieved by using the replication option immediate-updating subscribers, queued updating, and immediate updating with queued updating as a failover. Enabling subscriber updates for transactional or snapshot replication is best used for databases requiring infrequent updates.

**Immediate updating** is used when there is a stable connection between the subscriber and publisher. If an update is made to the subscriber, the change is applied immediately to the publisher.

**Queued updating** allows modifications at the subscriber without an ongoing connection to the publisher. The changes are queued up until the subscriber connects to the publisher again, and are applied to the publisher and any other subscribers upon reconnection.

**Immediate updating with queued updating as a failover** is used to allow immediate updating **and** queued updating if a connection is broken between the subscriber and publisher.

In addition to agents included in snapshot or transactional replication, queued updates use the following agent:

| Agent | Description |
|---|---|
| Queue reader agent | The queue reader agent is responsible for queued updating and the immediate updating with queued updating as a failover option. Subscriber data changes are taken from a queue and applied to the publication. One queue reader agent is used to fulfill all queued update requests per distributor (multiple publications use one queue reader agent). |

### Queued Update Reminders

Like merge replication, queued updates require conflict resolution when conflicts occur. You should only use queued subscribers if you expect conflicts to be rare.

Tables being replicated for a snapshot publication should have a primary key or unique index. Tables used as articles in transactional replication must have a primary key.

If using an `IDENTITY` column for a primary key, be sure that the same identity values are not allocated at the subscriber or subscribers, causing a false conflict. See this chapter's section, *Data Type Considerations*, for more information on managing `IDENTITY`-type columns within replication.

# Replication Configuration Methods

SQL Server 2000 provides a set of replication wizards that guide you through the process of creating publications, adding a distribution database, pushing or pulling subscriptions, and removing replication. The wizards should meet 99% of most database administrators' needs. Enterprise Manager provides methods for monitoring replication activity, configuring properties of the publication or subscriber, and modifying agent profile properties.

If you are developing your own applications using Visual Basic or C++, you can use SQL-DMO to program your replication logic. SQL-DMO is a set of programming classes that allow you to configure much of the functionality available within SQL Server.

Also available for application developers are ActiveX replication controls, which are good for using a subset of the available replication functionality, specifically the functionality included with the snapshot, merge, and distribution agents.

Lastly, there are several system stored procedures in SQL Server that allow you to configure replication. You will see some of these stored procedures when scripting your replication topology (see later in the chapter, for instruction on scripting replication). Although you can script replication entirely from stored procedures, it is not a method that is recommended over using Enterprise Manager, or SQL-DMO. This chapter will focus primarily on how to set up replication using Enterprise manager and the replication wizards.

# Data Type Considerations

There are aspects of column data type that must be understood prior to configuring replication:

| Data Type | Replication Considerations |
|---|---|
| `TEXT` and `IMAGE` | Immediate updating and queued updating does not support updates of `TEXT` or `IMAGE` data type columns at the subscriber. |
| `TIMESTAMP` | The `TIMESTAMP` data type generates binary numbers that guarantee uniqueness within a database. The purpose of the `TIMESTAMP` data type is to distinguish the relative sequence of data modifications within a database. When replicating the `TIMESTAMP` column, merge and transactional replication with queued updating **regenerate** the `TIMESTAMP` value during the snapshot transfer. All other types of replication transfer the literal value (the same value will be transferred from publisher to subscriber) during the snapshot transfer. |

*Table continued on following page*

| Data Type | Replication Considerations |
|---|---|
| UNIQUEIDENTIFIER | A UNIQUEIDENTIFIER data type column is added to your table if you are using merge replication or queued updating (with snapshot or transactional) and your table does not already have a UNIQUEIDENTIFIER column. The UNIQUEIDENTIFIER data type holds a globally unique identifier (GUID), which no other server will contain. |
| IDENTITY | Although IDENTITY is a property applied to a data type, and not a data type itself, there are still special considerations to keep in mind. IDENTITY automatically creates a number (an integer, for example) based on a seed number and increment value. When using merge replication or queued updating subscriptions (snapshot or transactional), make sure to manage the ranges of IDENTITY values assigned by the subscriber, as conflicts can occur if the same values are assigned by the publisher and subscriber. |

# SQL Server Version Compatibility

Replication can be used across different SQL Server versions. The following table shows the possible replication topologies when using SQL Server 6.5, 7.0, and 2000; this table assumes that you are not using new publication or subscriber features included with SQL Server 2000. Functionality is equivalent to the earliest version in the topology, meaning that if you have 6.5 in your topology, only 6.5 features are available:

| Replication Types Allowed | Publisher Versions | Distributor Versions | Subscriber Versions |
|---|---|---|---|
| Snapshot | 6.5 SP4 | 6.5 SP4 | 6.0 (ODBC) |
| Transactional | | 7.0 SP1 | 6.5 SP4 |
| | | | 7.0 SP1 |
| | | | 2000 |
| Snapshot | 7.0 SP1 | 7.0 SP1 | 6.0 (ODBC) |
| Transactional | | 2000 | 6.5 SP4 |
| | | | 7.0 SP1 |
| | | | 2000 |
| Snapshot | 2000 | 2000 | 6.0 (ODBC) |
| Transactional | | | 6.5 SP4 |
| | | | 7.0 |
| | | | 2000 |
| Merge | 7.0 SP1 | 2000 | 7.0 SP1 or later |
| Merge | 2000 | 2000 | 6.5 SP4 or later, 7.0 SP1or later |

# Pre-Replication Checklist

Before you begin configuring replication, make sure that you have the proper permissions defined for setting up and executing replication. This includes the following considerations:

- You must be a member of the `sysadmin` role in order to enable replication for the server.
- You must be a member of the `db_owner` database role of the database you wish to publish, in order to create publications for this database.

> **Beginning with SQL Server 2000 Service Pack 3, a subscription or publication created by a user who is not a member of the `sysadmin` server role must either configure the SQL Server Agent proxy account with a login and password with sufficient privileges; or have the owner of the SQL Server Agent replication jobs (which run the agents) set to a member of the `sysadmin` server role.**

- The SQL Server Agent defines the security context of the snapshot, merge, and distribution agents. The local system account cannot be used for replication between two SQL Server instances; a Windows domain or standard account must be used. This SQL Server Agent service account should also have `db_owner` role permissions for the subscriber database or databases.
- For the snapshot folder share, assign **write** access to the SQL Server Agent on the publisher and distributor, and **read** permissions to the SQL Server Agent on the subscriber (for pull subscriptions).
- You can issue a pull subscription from a publication for which you are a member of the publication access list (described later).
- Decide on your replication topology in advance. Decide which servers will act as your publisher, distributor, and subscriber. Decide whether the distributor should be on the same server as the publisher or subscriber, or on its own server.
- Determine the location of your snapshot files.
- Decide if you will be using push or pull subscriptions.
- Know your row size limits. Merge replication has a row size limit of 6,000 characters and 246 columns. Transactional replication has a row size limit of 8,000 characters. `TEXT` and `IMAGE` data type columns are not counted towards this limit, unless they use **in row** storage. Snapshot replication is limited to 255 columns and 8,000 bytes.
- Replicate only rows and columns that are necessary to the subscriber. Do test to ensure that filtering does not incur more overhead than just letting all rows carry across to the subscriber(s). We will review horizontal and vertical partitioning later, in the *How to...* sections. Dynamic filters will also be reviewed, which allow you to partition rows by the recipient login or computer name. Minimizing data movement will have a lesser impact on your network and server performance.
- For all three types of replication, you will be asked to choose a default location for your snapshot files. Create an explicit folder share on your server that all subscriber servers will have access to, rather than using an administrative share (drive letter and $, for example Y$). To configure a share:
  - Right-click My Computer on the server desktop, and select Manage.
  - Under the System Tools node, expand the Shared Folders icon.
  - Right-click Shares, and select New File Share.
  - Select the folder to share, share name, and share description, then click Next.
  - Select the level of permissions, making sure that all subscriber server SQL Server Agent service accounts will have access to this share, and then select Finish. When creating your publication, you can now select the share you created.

- Use caution when replicating to servers with heterogeneous collations (or, for prior versions, character set, sort order, accent sensitivity, and case sensitivity). Replicated data is not converted, so data can be corrupted on the subscriber, or during synchronization (merge) to the publisher. It is highly recommended that you replicate only to servers with compatible collations or code page, sort orders, accent sensitivity, and case sensitivity. (For a review of collations, see the topic *Understanding Collations* in Chapter 2).
- You can add or remove columns from a published table while the publication still has subscribers (although this is not possible for immediate-updating subscribers). For a change to be replicated to subscribers, you must make the change through Publication Properties in Enterprise Manager, or use the `sp_repladdcolumn` to add a column or `sp_repldropcolumn` to remove a column. If adding a new column, you must either allow it to be `NULL` or specify a default value.
- SQL Server replication benefits significantly from fast network connections, 100mbps or higher. The larger the snapshot and transactional throughput, the more important the role of network speed becomes.

# 8.1 How to... Configure Snapshot Replication

To configure snapshot replication in Enterprise Manager:

- Expand Server Group and registration.
- Expand the Replication folder.
- Right-click Publications and select New Publication.
- In the Create Publication Wizard, click the checkbox to show advanced options, and select Next.
- If this is your first publication on the server, you will be asked to choose the distributor server for use by the publication. In this example, the publisher will also be the distributor, thus creating a distribution database on the server. Use this option if your publication server has enough capacity. Use a remote distributor if your publication server is already reaching its performance limit.
- If your SQL Server Agent is using a system account, you must replace the account with a domain account with access to the other servers in your replication topology. If you receive this dialog box, select OK:

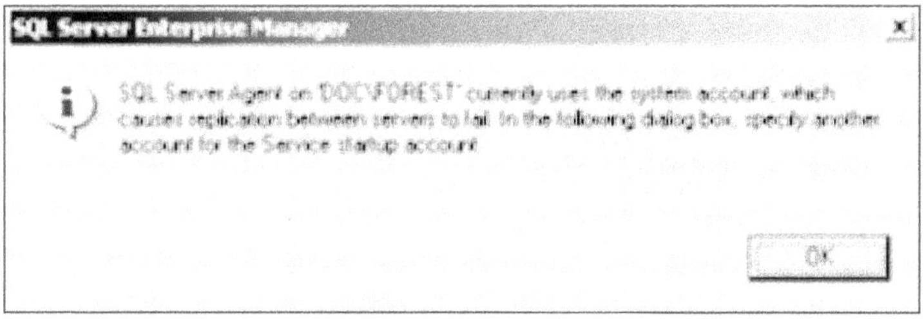


- Enter in your domain account for the SQL Server Agent service.
- Select the location of the snapshot folder. Select a predefined share, or the system share default. Make sure that the SQL Server Agent account configured for the publisher/distributor has write permissions to this directory. Make sure that the SQL Server Agent for the subscriber has read permissions to this directory:

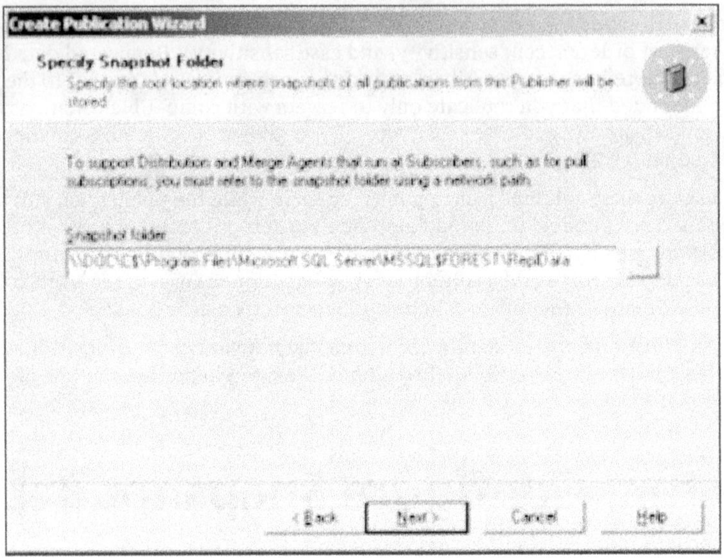


- ❑ You may be warned about the snapshot folder path if you use an administrative share, which means that only a login with administrative privileges on the server can access it. Select Yes to confirm the snapshot folder, or No to choose a predefined share.
- ❑ Select the database you wish to publish.
- ❑ Select the publication type. In this example, we are creating a snapshot publication:

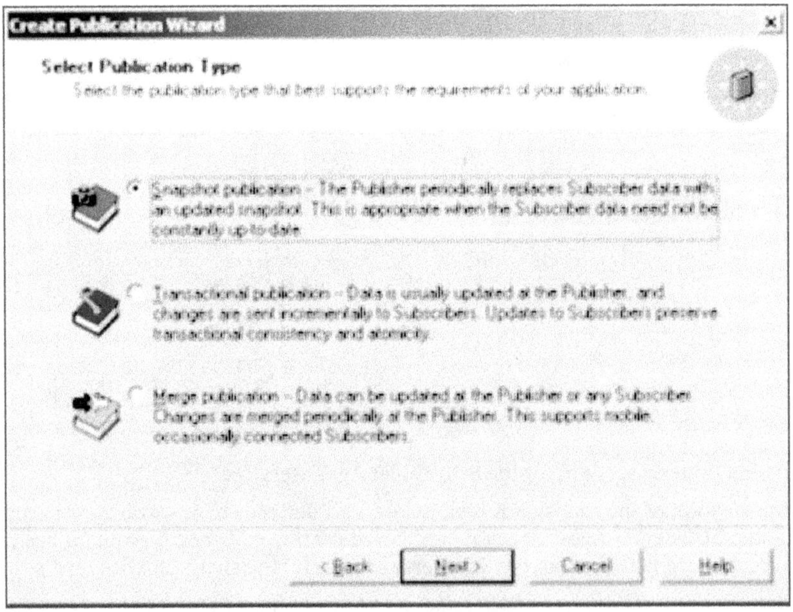


- ❑ In the Updatable Subscriptions dialog box, you can choose whether your subscribers will be allowed to have immediate or queued updating subscriptions. Notice that the MS DTC service has to be running on both servers (publisher and subscriber) for immediate updating subscriptions:

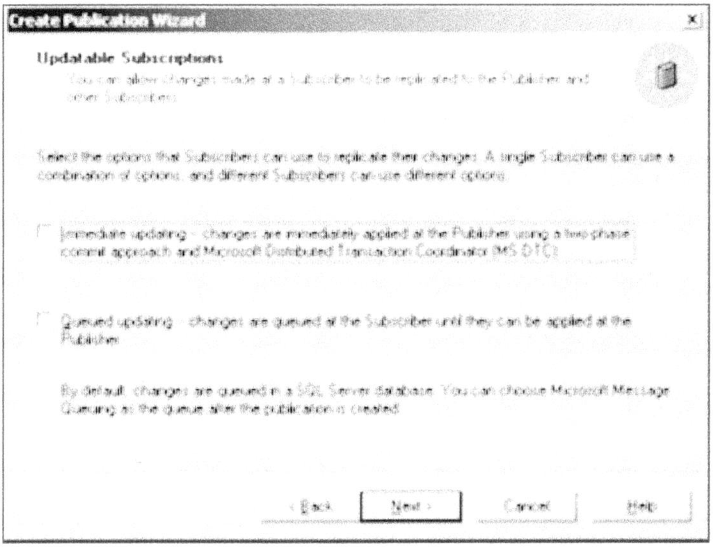


- Transform Published Data specifies whether you wish to use DTS to convert your published data prior to being pushed to subscribers. Keep in mind that this adds overhead, particularly if you have many rows, columns, and transformations you wish to apply. It may be better to transform the data in staging tables, and publish these staging tables after transformation, rather then tying up the process during replication. If you do decide to have transformation, after creating the publication, right-click it in Enterprise Manager and select Define Transformation of Published Data. The wizard will step you through the process, creating a DTS package that you can modify and configure.
- Select the types of subscribers that will be subscribing to the publication. If you enable Servers running SQL Server version 7.0, only replication options that are compatible with SQL Server 7.0 subscribers will be displayed. If you enable Heterogeneous data sources, versions of SQL Server prior to 7.0, Oracle and, potentially, other non-SQL Server data sources, will be able to subscribe to snapshot or transactional publications. Microsoft Access will be able to subscribe to snapshot, transactional, and merge publications:

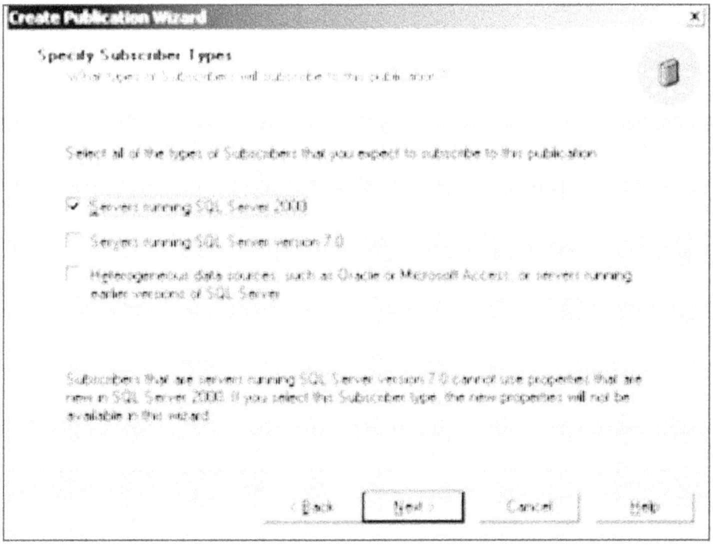

- Select the articles you wish to publish. Articles available for publication are tables, stored procedures, execution of a stored procedure, views, view definitions, indexed views, and user-defined functions. Check the box in the right-hand pane for each article that you wish to publish. Click Article Defaults to configure defaults for each article type:

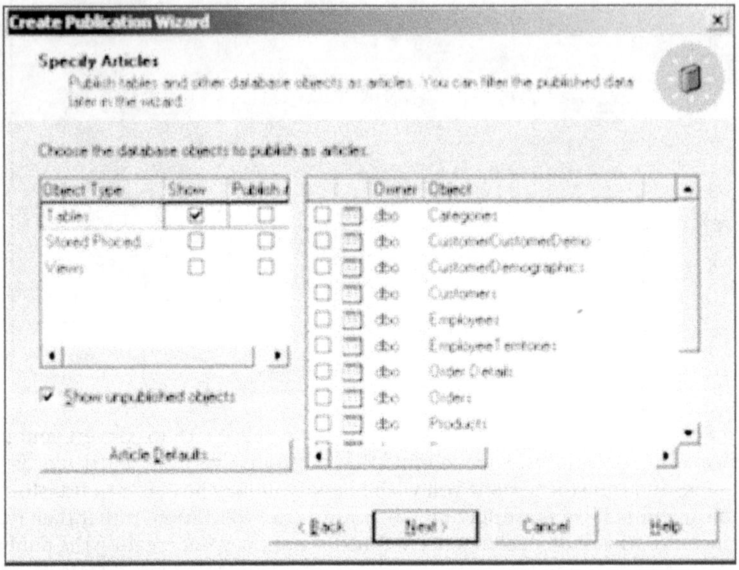

- Table defaults allow you to select a different destination (subscriber) owner name:

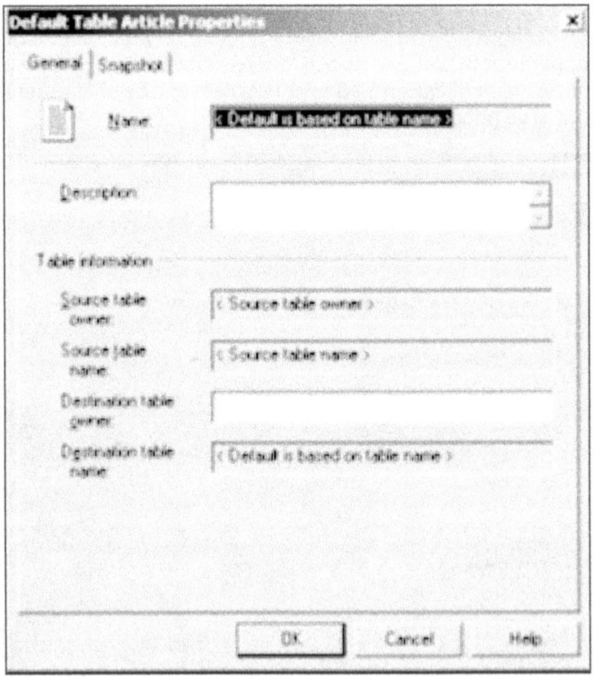

- In the Snapshot tab, you can configure what happens when a table with the same name exists at the subscriber. If you select Keep the existing table unchanged, and the destination table exists at the subscriber, it is not dropped and recreated. If you select Drop the existing table and re-create it, it will be dropped and recreated if the table exists on the subscriber. Delete data in the existing table that matches the row filter statement will delete a subset of the data if you are using row filters, and Delete all data in the existing table will delete all data, but will not drop and recreate the table itself.
- You can also choose which objects or properties are replicated with the table to the subscriber. You can select whether or not to include referential integrity (foreign key constraints), indexes, triggers, extended properties, and collation (based on publisher collation).
- You can also choose to convert user-defined data types to the appropriate SQL Server base data type, by selecting Convert user-defined to base data types. This means that the individual base data types making up the user-defined data type will be used on the subscriber, instead of the user-defined data type defined on the publisher:

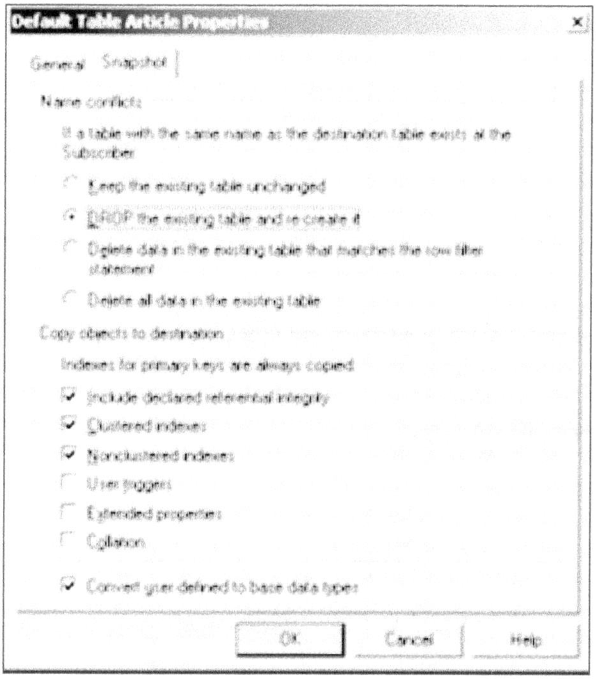


- In the Other tab of the Default Stored Procedure Article Properties dialog box, the stored procedure default options allow you to specify whether an existing object should be dropped, and whether extended properties should be included.
- In the Snapshot tab of the Default View Article Properties dialog box, there are also options for dropping the view if it exists on the subscriber, or replicating extended properties or triggers.
- In addition to article default properties, you can also configure **individual** article properties by clicking the ellipsis next to the selected article in the Article Selection dialog box.
- The General tab of the Table Article Properties dialog box lists configuration options for the destination table name, table owner, article name, and description. These extra field options are also included for views and stored procedure properties. The Snapshot tab is the same as the Default Article Properties dialog box Snapshot tab:

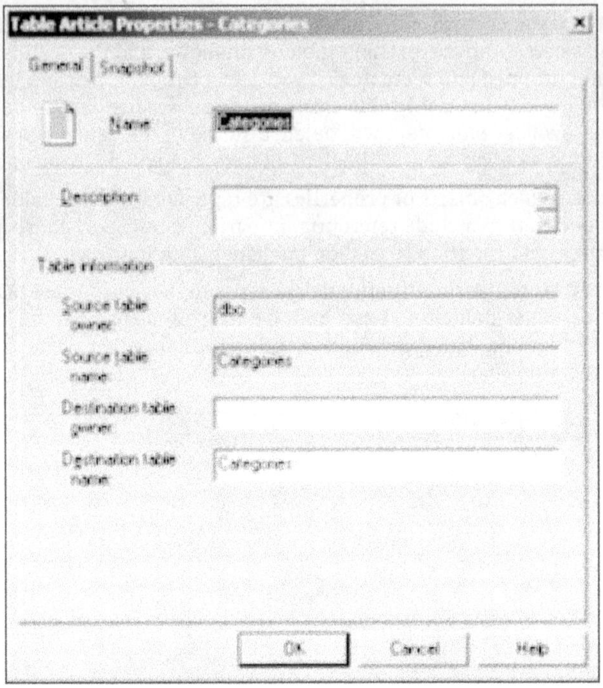


- ❑ Once you have selected articles, the next dialog box will list any warnings or issues regarding the articles you have chosen. For example, if you included a table that contains an `IDENTITY` column, you would get a warning like the following:

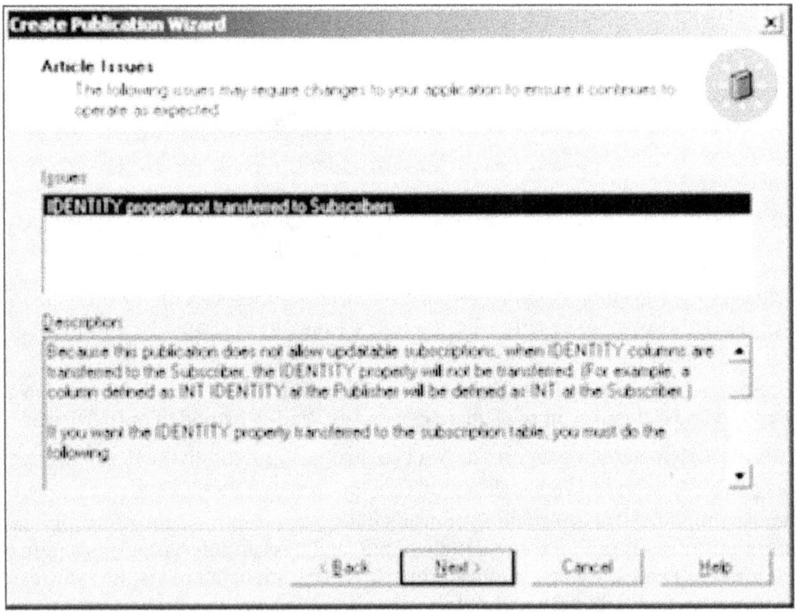

- In the Select Publication Name and Description dialog box, type in a publication name and description:

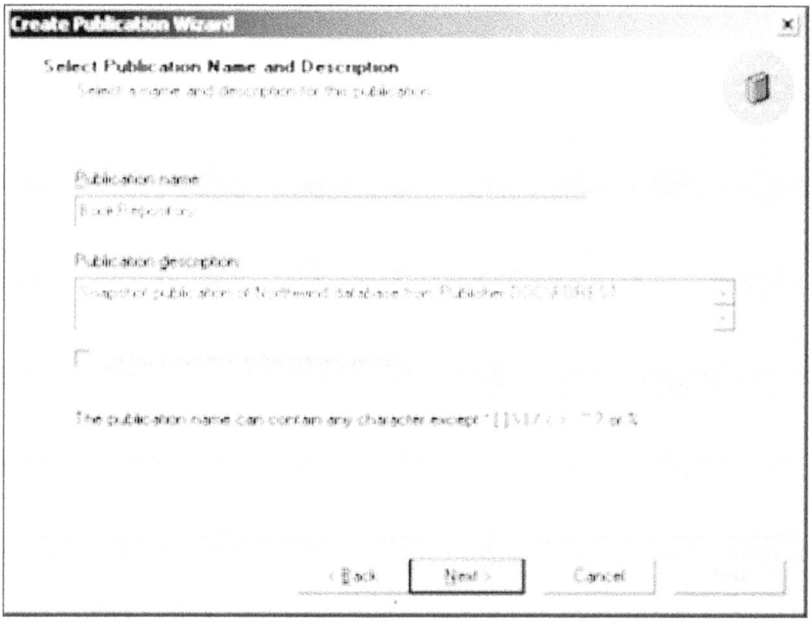


- Next, decide if you wish to define filters, anonymous subscriptions, or other properties for the publication. Select Yes to see how these are configured:

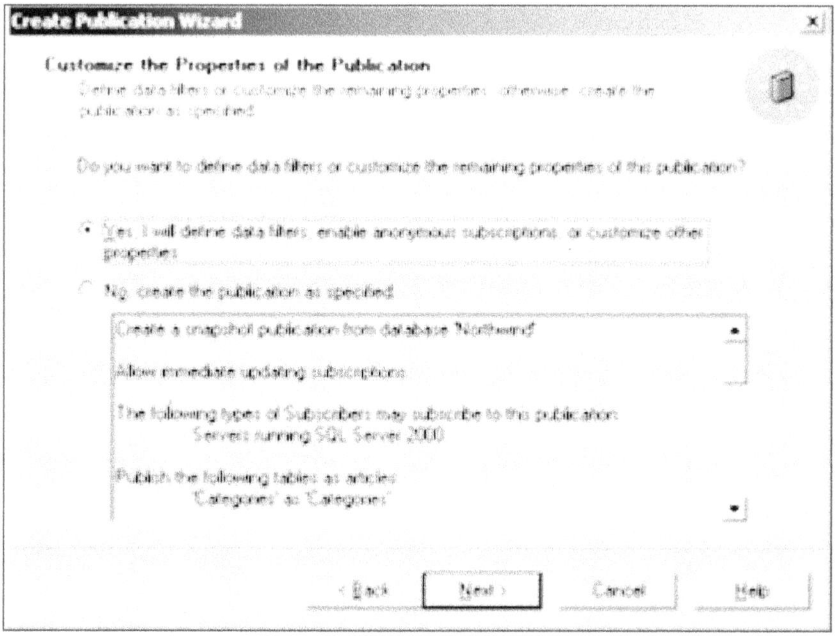

- If you are replicating tables, you can filter them vertically (filtering columns published) or horizontally (filtering rows published). Use filtering to remove columns or rows that are not necessary at the subscriber from the publication. This reduces publication-processing time and improves network bandwidth performance (by reducing data that needs to be synchronized).
- If you selected vertical filtering, you will be able to select and deselect columns that you do not wish to have replicated to the subscriber:

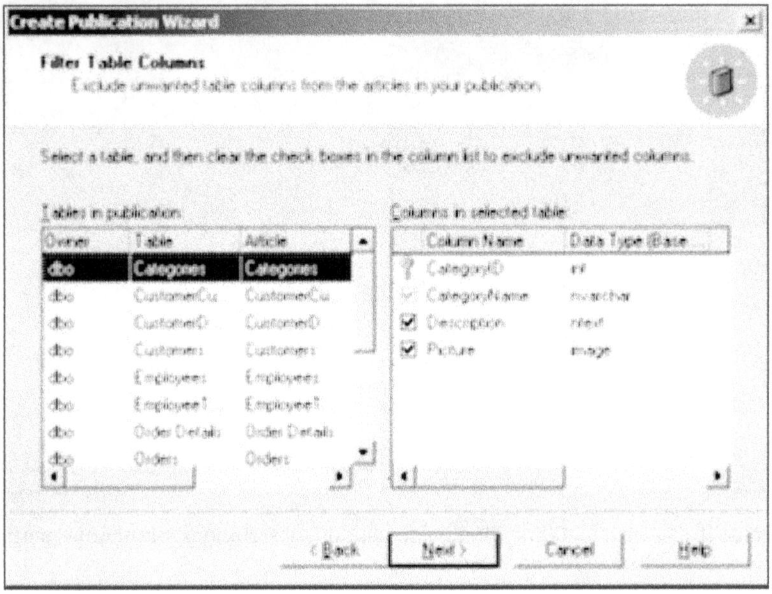


- If you have selected horizontal filtering, you will be presented with the Filter Table Rows dialog box. Click the ellipsis next to the table for which you wish to add row filters:

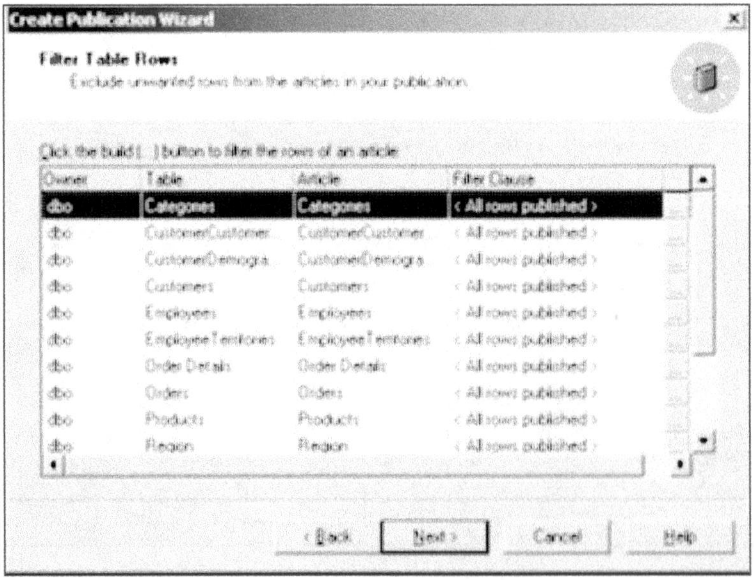

- Select the WHERE clause you wish to use to enable filtering for the publication by clicking the ellipsis to the right of the Filter Clause column. Remember to place indexes on columns used for filtering; otherwise, you may incur table scans during the filtering operation:

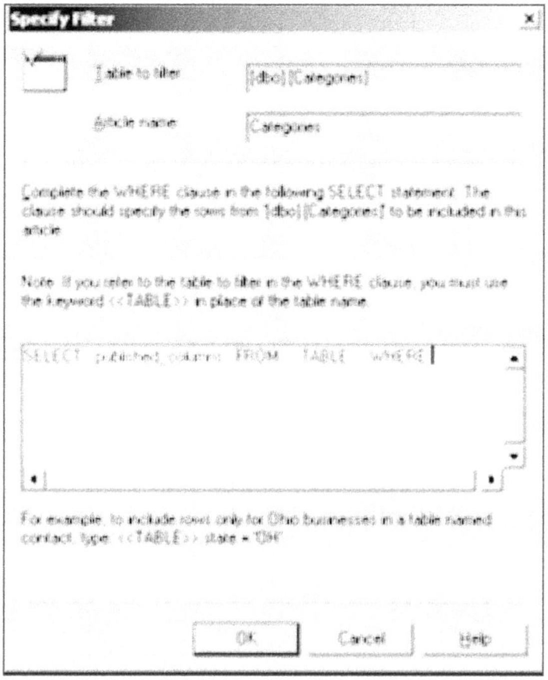


- Allow Anonymous Subscriptions enables your publication to be used in pull subscriptions without the awareness of the publisher; this reduces history records and the performance overhead of maintaining subscriber information in the distribution database and is beneficial when you have numerous subscribers, or when you are publishing over the Internet. You should consider this option very carefully before implementing it, as it may allow unintended subscribers to view the published data.

- Next, configure the schedule for creating the snapshot schema and data files. You can also specify whether the first snapshot should be created immediately:

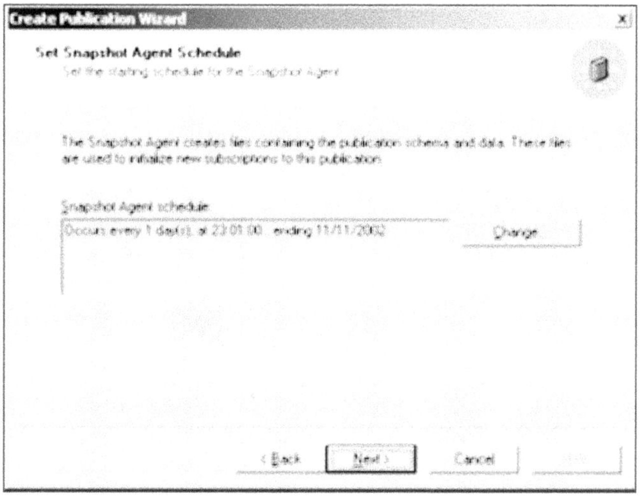

- ❑ Select Finish at the final dialog box.
- ❑ You will see a status screen for each phase of the publication creation:

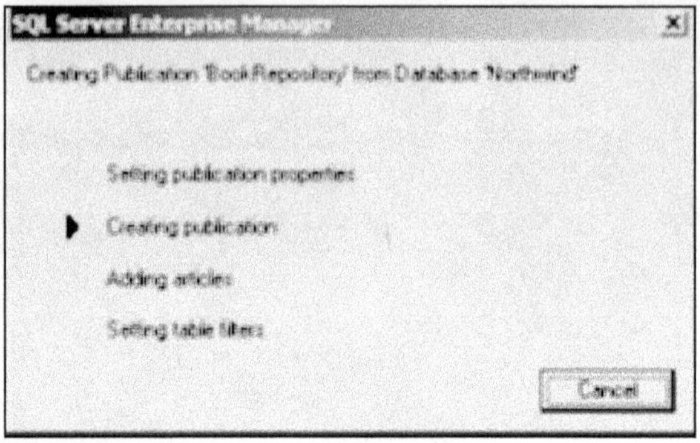


- ❑ Select Close to exit, or Publication Properties to view the properties of your new publication:

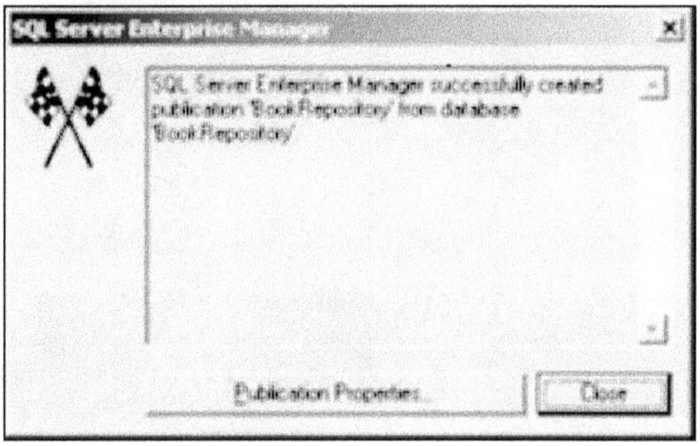


- ❑ If your server was not already set up as a distributor, you will see a dialog box describing Replication Monitor:

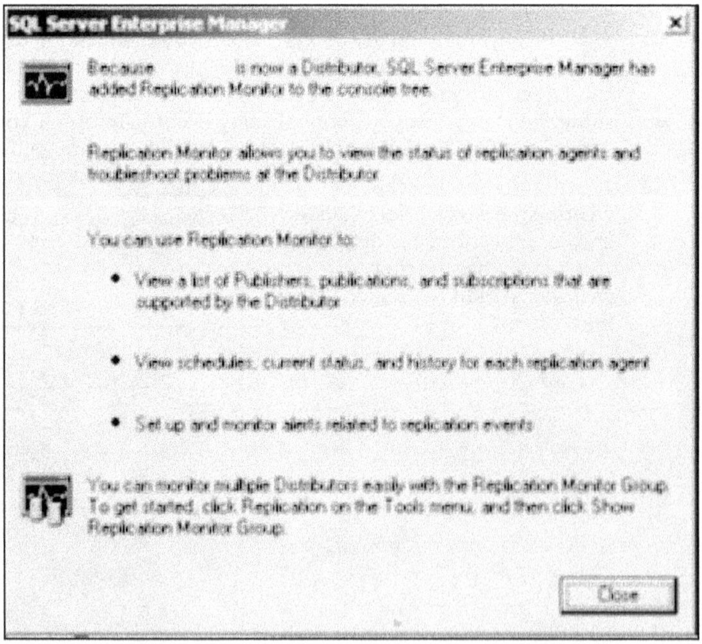

# Viewing Replication Monitor in Enterprise Manager

To view Replication Monitor in Enterprise Manager, expand the server registration, the Replication Monitor node, the Publisher folder, and the publication you wish to view. Replication Monitor is excellent for viewing the dynamic status of your replication jobs. Within this view of agents, you can:

- View agent history (right-click the agent and select Agent History).
- View or modify agent profiles (right-click the agent and select Agent Profile).
- View job properties (right-click the agent and select Agent Properties).
- Start or stop synchronizing (right-click the agent and select Start Synchronizing, or Stop Synchronizing). You will not see this for all agent types.
- For some agent types, start the agent by right-clicking the agent and selecting Start Agent.

To configure your refresh rate of the Replication Monitor (the level of update frequency for replication agent status), right-click the Replication Monitor icon and select Refresh Rate and Settings...:

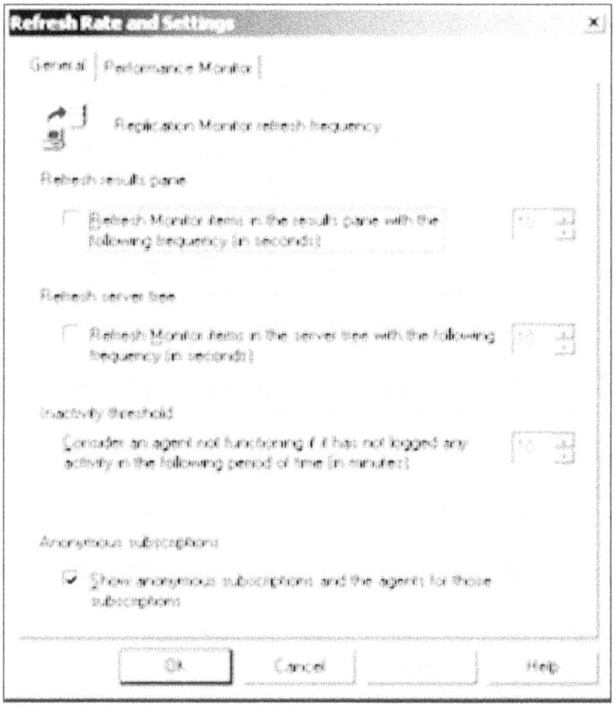


Configure your refresh rate according to how frequently you wish replication status to be updated. Keep in mind that Replication Monitor will perform constant polling on your server based on the increment you select. When running SQL Profiler, this background activity can be a nuisance; it does not incur a significant performance penalty, however.

# 8.2 How to... Create a Transactional Replication Publication

To configure transactional replication in Enterprise Manager:

- ❑ Expand Server Group and registration.
- ❑ Expand the Replication folder.
- ❑ Right-click Publications and select New Publication.
- ❑ In the Create Publication Wizard, click the checkbox to show advanced options (includes options for enabling immediate or queued updating subscriptions, and published data transformations), and select Next
- ❑ You will see the Select Distributor dialog box if the server is not already configured to point to another distributor or if it is its own distributor.
- ❑ If creating your own distribution database for the first time, you will be prompted for the snapshot folder location, and also warned if using an administrative share.
- ❑ In the Choose Publication dialog box, select the database you wish to publish for transactional replication.
- ❑ In the Select Publication Type, select Transactional publication:

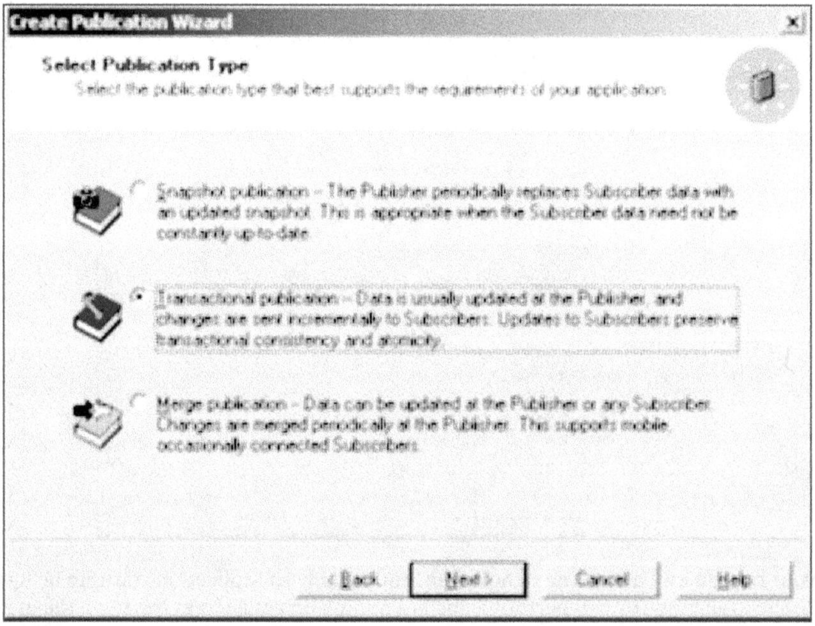


- ❑ In the Updatable Subscriptions dialog box, choose either immediate updating or queued updating for the subscribers.
- ❑ In the Transform Published Data dialog box, select whether or not you wish to add DTS transformations to your transactional replication publication. Remember that there is a performance overhead when adding such transformations as a step to your publication snapshot.

- In Specify Subscriber Types, select which versions of SQL Server your subscribers will be running. Remember that the lowest version of SQL Server determines the maximum functionality allowed at the publisher.
- The Specify Articles dialog box allows you to select which objects should be migrated to the subscriptions. Notice that in the example dialog box below there are keys with a red X; these are tables without primary keys, which means they cannot be replicated using transactional replication. If you must replicate them, cancel the publication wizard and select a primary key for the table or tables:

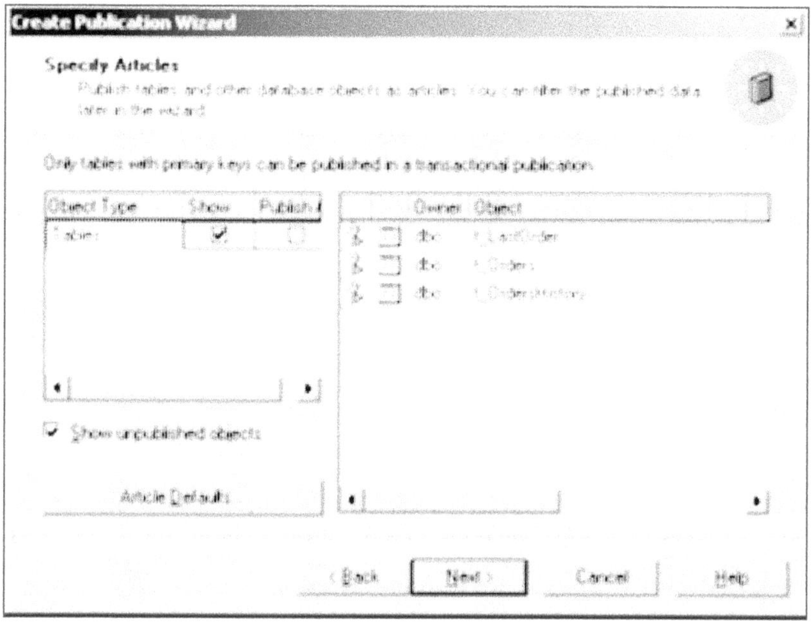


- Select Article Defaults if you wish to configure default publication behavior for articles.
- For table article properties, the General tab allows you to choose a different destination table owner on the subscriber; you can also add a description. These are the same options as for stored procedure defaults.
- The commands tab allows you to replace `INSERT`, `UPDATE`, and `DELETE` commands with stored procedures. The result is that transactional replication will call the stored procedures (using a remote procedure call) instead of sending the longer statements, thus improving performance. You can also select whether or not the stored procedures are created during the initial synchronization. If you wish the parameters of the stored procedure to be sent in binary format (for faster performance), keep the default checkbox selected:

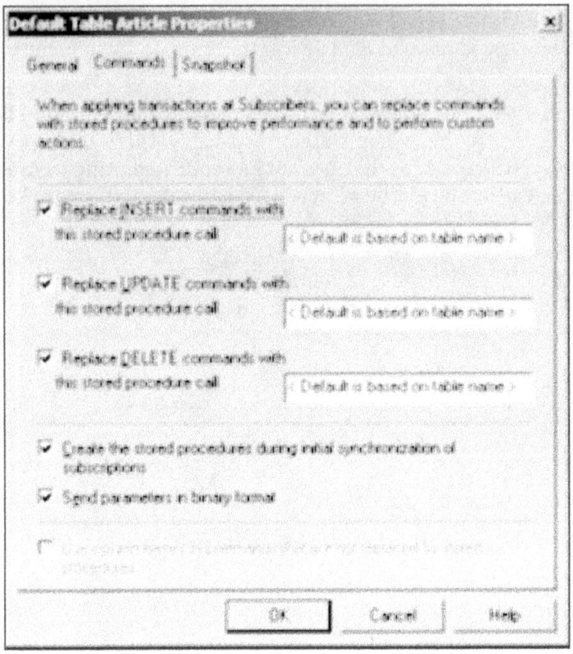

- The Snapshot tab specifies what action is taken if a table with the same name already exists on the subscriber. You can also choose whether referential integrity, indexes, triggers, properties, and table collation are migrated during the initial snapshot. If you do not intend to allow updates on the subscriber, these additional constraints and objects should not be migrated with the snapshot. Even if changes **are** allowed on the subscriber, triggers can cause unintended effects (firing the trigger on the subscriber could cause data duplication or inconsistency):

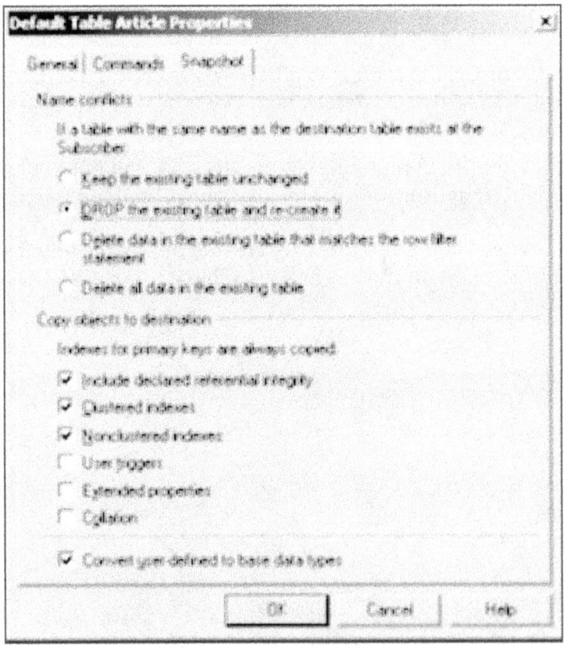

- For stored procedure article properties, the General tab lets you specify an owner and description on the subscriber database.
- In the Other tab for stored procedures, you can select what actions to take if a stored procedure with the same name already exists on the subscriber.
- Other important aspects of configuration include whether the stored procedure should have only its schema replicated, and whether the actual execution on the publisher should in turn be executed on the subscriber, or executed only if performed within a **serializable** transaction. *Serializable* means that the isolation level of the transaction should use the strictest possible locking strategy, thereby reducing database concurrency but ensuring consistent data. Replicating the execution of stored procedures requires thoughtful planning. Although performance improvements may be gained, if data consistency is a factor you must ensure that the stored procedure is running under the same conditions as the publisher.
- As the final step in this dialog box, you can decide whether extended properties should be copied to the destination server with the stored procedure:

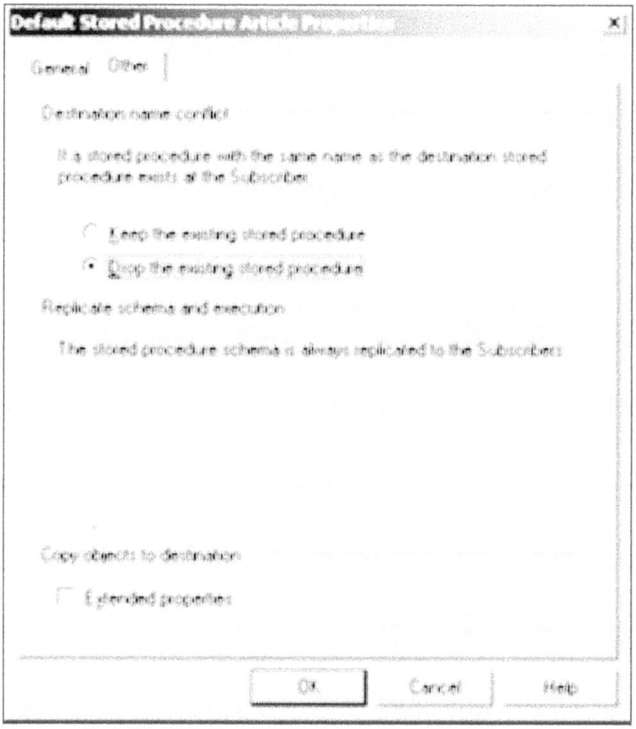


- For views, the Default View Article Properties also allow you to add destination owner and description. In the Snapshot tab for view article properties, you select what action to take if a destination view exists at the subscriber with the same name. You can also specify whether triggers and extended properties may be included with the snapshot schema:

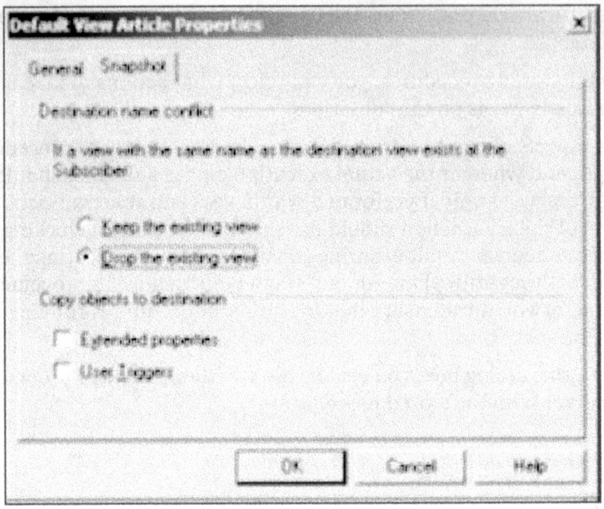


Configuration of article properties can also be done at the single article level. To configure the properties of a single article:

- Click the ellipsis next to the selected article.
- The Table Article Properties dialog box allows you to configure name, description, destination table owner, and destination table name. These fields are also available for individual stored procedures and views:

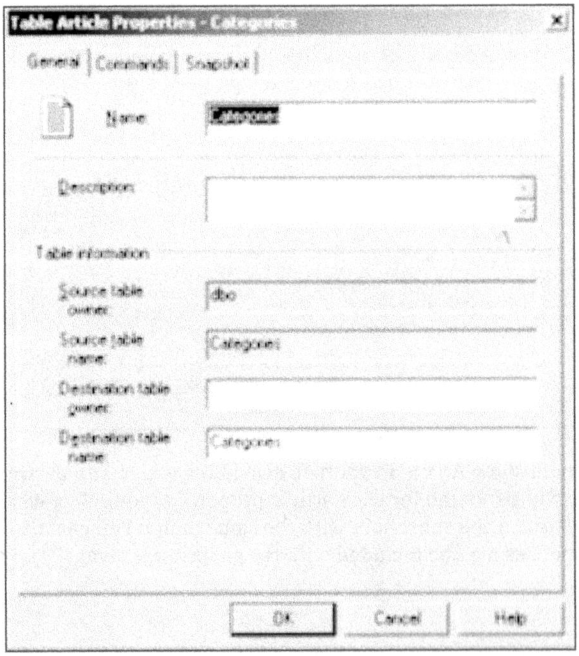

- The Commands tab lets you modify individual stored procedures. Leave the names at their default values unless you have a compelling reason to change them:

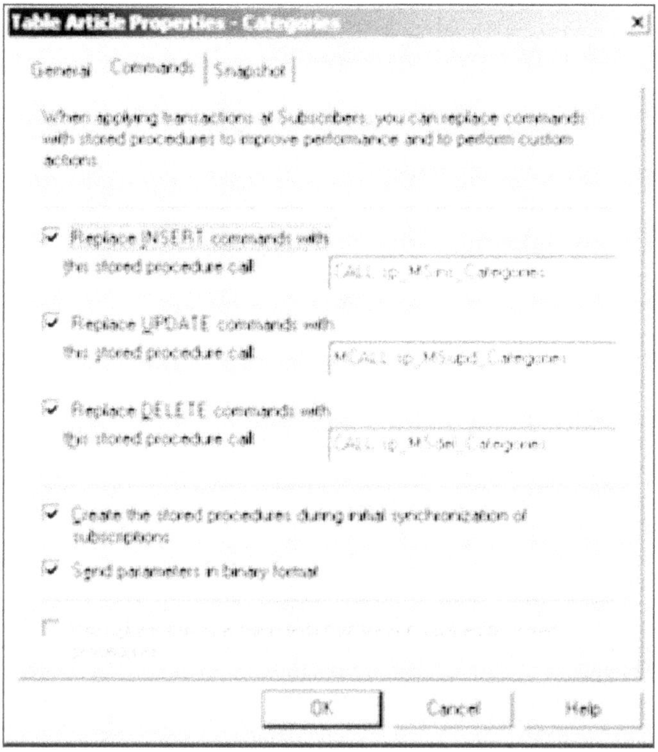


- The Snapshot tab has the same configurable values as the Default Article Properties dialog box.
- Finally, if you selected queued updating for your publication, and you have articles that use IDENTITY columns, you will see the Identity Range tab in Article Properties. The Identity Range tab allows you to define the range of values permitted for the IDENTITY column of each subscription article. You can select the range size at the publisher, subscriber, and assign a new range when the specified percentage of values is used. Queued updating necessitates identity value ranges, because new rows inserted on the Subscriber may not be updated directly to the publisher right away; this means that a value of 10 may be used for the IDENTITY value on the subscriber, and then used by a different transaction at the publisher around the same time. If an attempt to insert the value 10 occurs when the subscriber synchronizes queued updates to the publisher, the row will be rejected. Designating ranges allows you to avoid duplicate IDENTITY values for foreign keys:

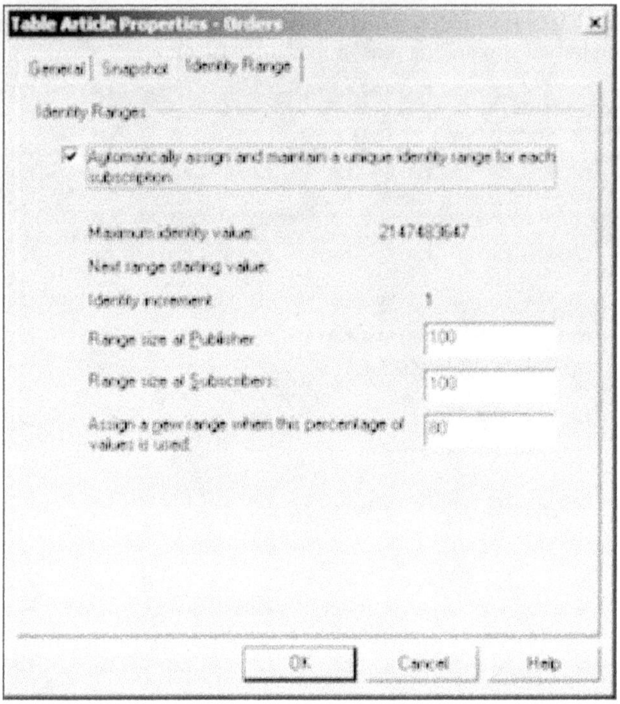


- The next dialog box after selecting articles will list any warnings or issues concerning the articles you selected. For example, if you included views or stored procedures that reference tables not included in the publication, these must be added. You will receive a warning like this:

  Because this publication does not allow updatable subscriptions, when IDENTITY columns are transferred to the Subscriber, the IDENTITY property will not be transferred. (For example, a column defined as INT IDENTITY at the Publisher will be defined as INT at the Subscriber.)

  If you want the IDENTITY property transferred to the subscription table, you must do the following:

  » Create the subscription table manually using the IDENTITY property and the NOT FOR REPLICATION option. You can have SQL Server execute a custom script to perform this action before the snapshot is applied. To specify a custom script, create the publication, create the script, and enter the script name on the Snapshot tab of the publication properties.

  » Set the name conflicts article property so that SQL Server does not drop an existing table when applying the snapshot at the Subscriber. This property is on the Snapshot tab of article properties.

  The following published tables contain IDENTITY columns:

  [dbo].[TableName]

  - If you do not allow updates on the subscriber, a literal value for the identity column will be transferred. The destination table on the subscriber will not include the `IDENTITY` property, which should have no impact if you are using the subscriber for read-only purposes:

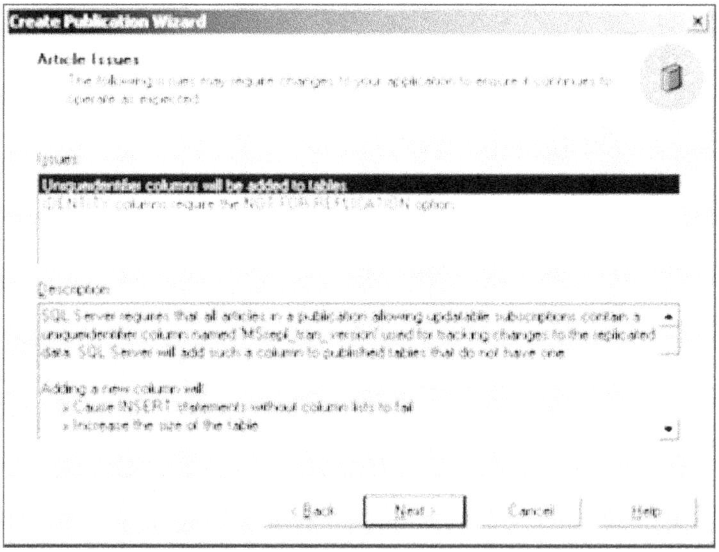


- Next, select the publication name and description:

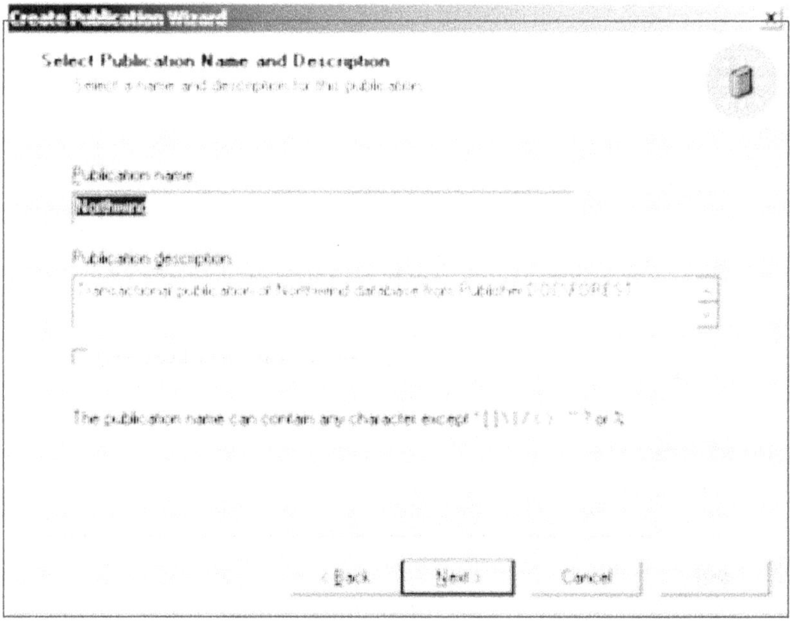


- In the Customize the Properties of the Publication dialog box, decide whether you wish to create the publication as you have already specified, or customize its properties:

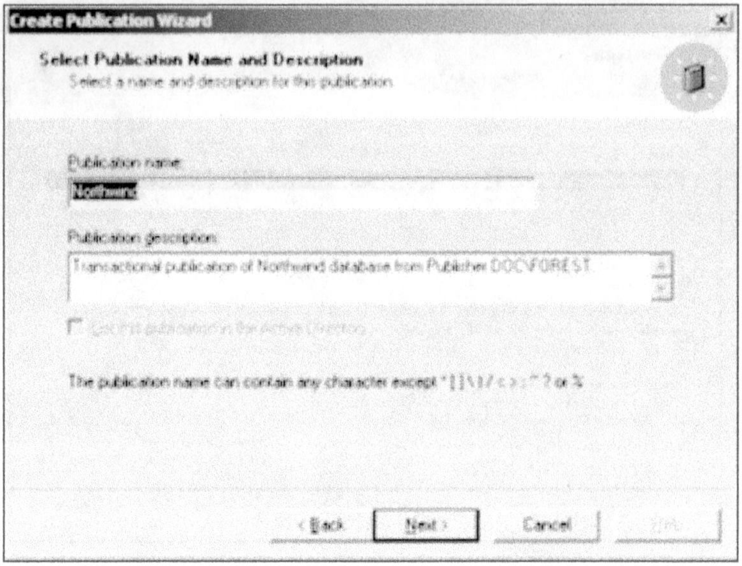


- ❑ If you select Yes to configure additional properties, decide whether you wish to add vertical or horizontal partitioning. You will receive the same dialog boxes as with the snapshot replication wizard, including an option to specify columns replicated and a WHERE clause for rows to be published, the option of allowing anonymous subscriptions, and the schedule of the snapshot agent.
- ❑ Select Finish to create the publication. You will see a status screen showing the distributor creation (if configuring a publication server for the first time), setting publication properties, creating the publication, and articles. Select Close to exit the process or Publication Properties to view or edit the publication immediately.

# 8.3 How to... Create a Merge Replication Publication

To configure merge replication in Enterprise Manager:

- ❑ Expand Server Group and registration.
- ❑ Expand the Replications folder.
- ❑ Right-click Publications and select New Publication.
- ❑ In the Create Publication Wizard dialog box, select Next.
- ❑ You will see the Select Distributor dialog box if the server is not already configured to point to another distributor or is its own distributor.
- ❑ If creating your own distribution database for the first time, you will be prompted for the snapshot folder location, as well as warned when using an administrative share.
- ❑ In the Choose Publication dialog box, select the database you wish to publish for merge replication.
- ❑ In the Select Publication Type dialog box, select Merge publication.

- In the Specify Subscriber Types dialog box, select the subscriber types intended for this publication. If you enable Servers running SQL Server version 7.0, only replication options that are compatible with SQL Server 7.0 subscribers will be displayed. If you enable Heterogeneous data sources, versions of SQL Server prior to 7.0, Oracle and, potentially, other non-SQL Server data sources will be able to subscribe to snapshot or transactional publications (so merge replication is not an option). Microsoft Access will be able to subscribe to snapshot, transactional, and merge publications.
- In the Specify Articles dialog box, select which objects will be replicated in the publication. Remember that SQL Server will automatically add a `uniqueidentifier` column to those tables without one:

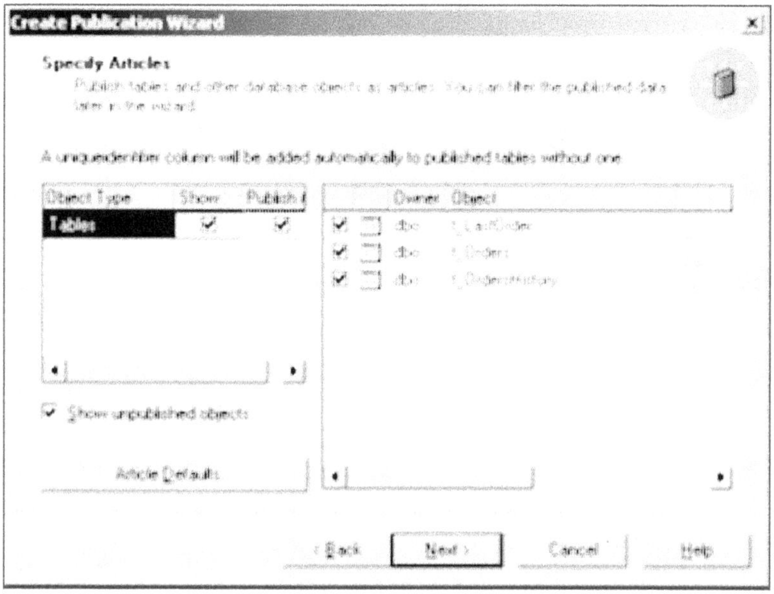

- Select the article defaults to specify Table, Stored Procedure, and View defaults for the articles. Pay careful attention to how these properties are set, as several merge replication specific features are included in the property dialog boxes.
- In the General tab of Table Article Properties, you can specify a description and destination table owner.

  You can also decide the level of granularity at which a merge conflict is determined. You can choose to treat any changes to the same row on both the publisher and subscriber as a conflict, or you can treat changes to only the same column as a conflict; if selecting column level conflicts, the publisher and subscriber can modify the same row, so long as the same column is not modified.

  For example, if Treat changes to the same row as a conflict were selected, the following two transactions to the same row would cause one change to be rejected (depending on the conflict resolver):

  Publisher modification:

```
UPDATE Books
SET iAuthorID = 2
WHERE iBookId = 1
```

Subscriber modification:

```
UPDATE Books
SET  dtUpdateDate = '11/2/02'
WHERE iBookId = 1
```

Both modifications affect the same row, but modify different columns. With Treat changes to the same row as a conflict, however, one of these UPDATE statements will be rejected. Otherwise, if Treat changes to same column as a conflict were selected, the two updates would both be allowed; the resulting merged row would have both a new iAuthorId and a new dtUpdateDate value:

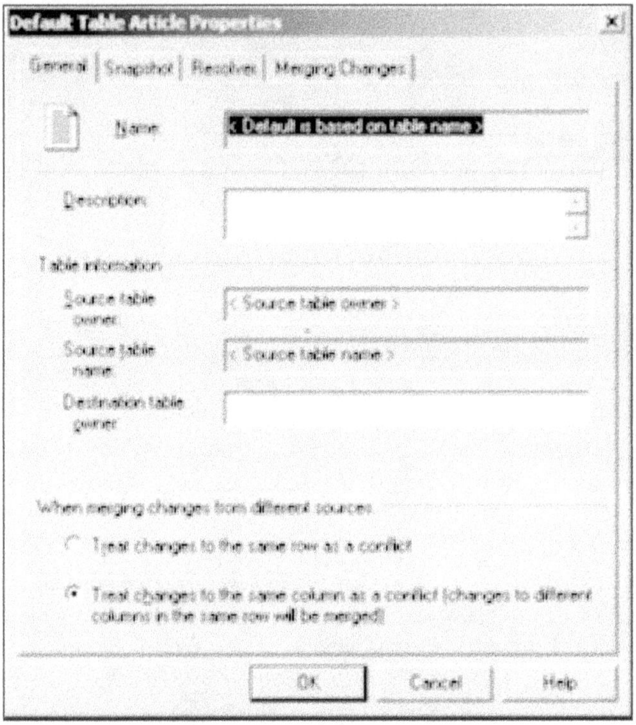


- The Snapshot tab contains the same options as snapshot and transactional replication. Be careful about de-selecting triggers and referential integrity (foreign keys), as changes are merged between the publisher and subscriber. The merging process assumes that the same data integrity features apply to **both** sides of the replication topology:

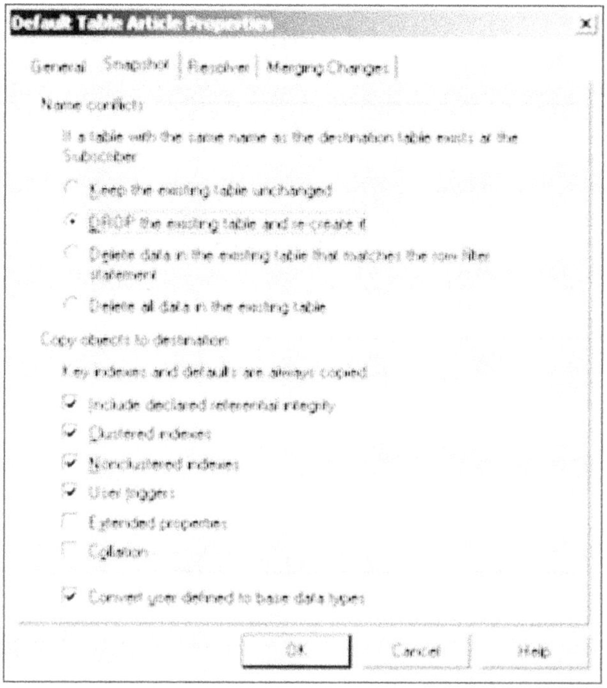


- The Resolver tab allows you to decide whether subscribers can resolve conflicts interactively during on-demand synchronizations; the resolver displays the conflicting data rows, and allows you to edit and resolve the conflicting data. The resolver is reviewed later on in the chapter:

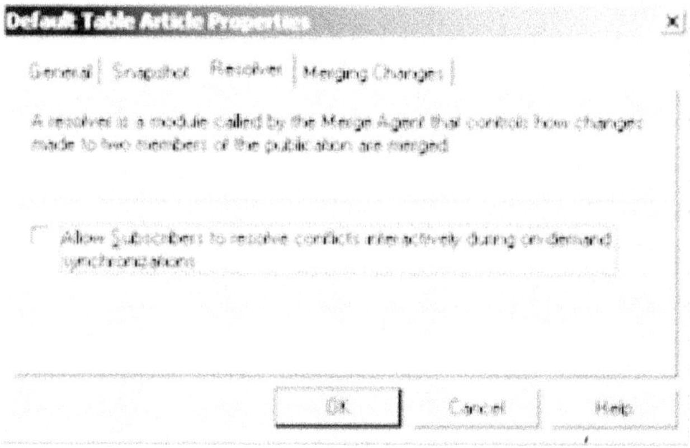


- In the Merging Changes tab, you can opt to give the Merge Agent login permissions to perform `INSERT`, `UPDATE`, and `DELETE` operations. There is also the option, selected by default, of applying multiple column changes for the same row into one `UPDATE` statement, instead of multiple statements. Unless you have a compelling reason to do so, do not de-select this option. For merge publications with significant updates, and depending on the application and schema, this option can reduce the number of statements required to change the same row:

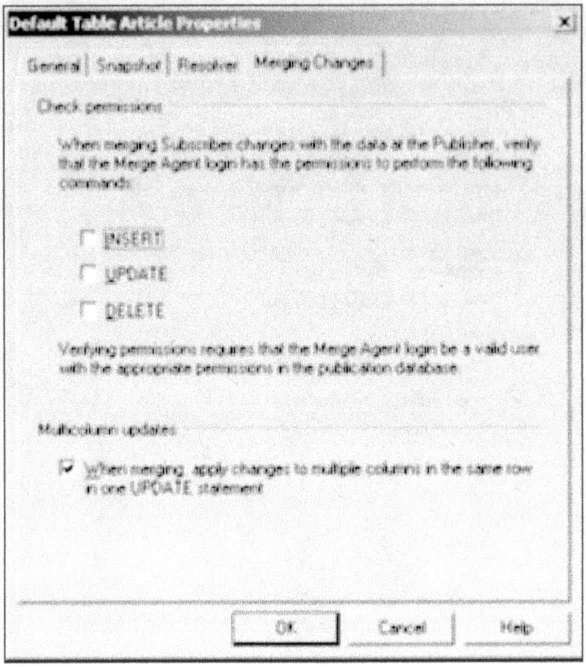


- You can specify article properties for a specific article; to do so, click the ellipsis button on the article row you wish to modify.
- In the General tab of Table Properties, notice that you can modify name, description, and object owner for the specific article on the subscriber:

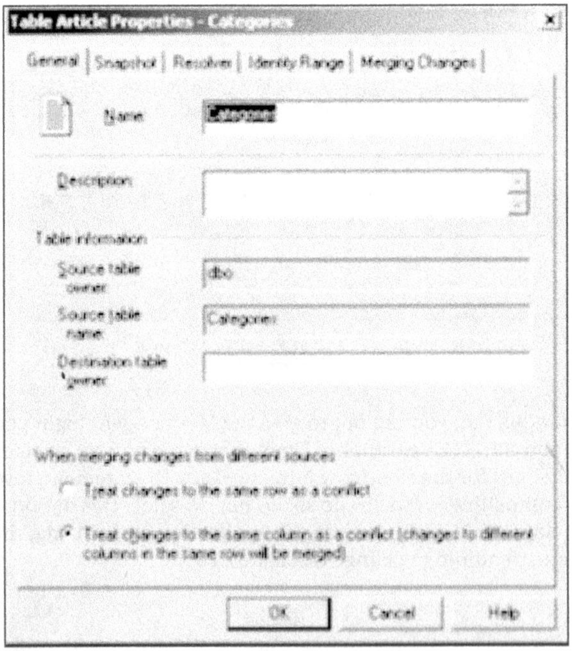

- The Snapshot tab offers the same options as the Article Defaults dialog box.

- The Resolver tab allows you to specify which resolver to run when data conflicts occur. Notice that this was not an option in the Article Defaults dialog box, as the resolver is determined by specific article. If you select the default resolver, conflicts will be resolved based on a priority value assigned to individual subscribers; the default is for the publisher's changes to take priority over subscribers. You can also choose one of the twelve other conflict resolvers. These resolvers include:

    - **Microsoft SQL Server Additive Conflict Resolver**
      This supports update conflicts to numeric columns. Winning updates are determined by a priority value. The resulting value is the sum of both numeric values from the publisher and subscriber columns.
    - **Microsoft SQL Server Averaging Conflict Resolver**
      This supports update conflicts to columns. Winning updates are determined by a priority value. The resulting value is an average of both the numeric values from the publisher and subscriber columns.
    - **Microsoft SQL Server DATETIME (Earlier Wins) Conflict Resolver**
      This supports update conflicts to rows and columns. Winning updates are based on the earlier row date. A datetime column is used to determine the conflict winner. A drawback to this resolver is that adjustments are not made by time zone.
    - **Microsoft SQL Server DATETIME (Later Wins) Conflict Resolver**
      This supports update conflicts to rows and columns. Winning updates are based on the later row date. A datetime column is used to determine the conflict winner. A drawback to this resolver is that adjustments are not made by time zone.
    - **Microsoft SQL Server Maximum Conflict Resolver**
      This supports row and column changes. You must choose an arithmetic data type, which will be used to evaluate which update has the larger numeric value. The larger numeric value wins.
    - **Microsoft SQL Server Merge Text Conflict Resolver**
      This supports row and column updates. The resolver takes text columns from both the updates and merges the values, separated by a linefeed and header. This is good for applications where multiple text updates are required, such as a help line ticketing system, or customer service application.
    - **Microsoft SQL Server Minimum Conflict Resolver**
      This supports row and column update conflicts. You must select an arithmetic data type to be used to evaluate which update has the smaller numeric value. The smaller value wins.
    - **Microsoft SQL Server Subscriber Always Wins Conflict Resolver**
      This lets the subscriber always win over a publisher update conflict.
    - **Microsoft SQL Server Stored Procedure Resolver**
      This allows you to create a custom resolver using a stored procedure. The procedure is executed from the publisher, and requires parameters for table owner, table name, row GUID, subscriber name, and subscriber database. Output values are also required for conflict resolution code and conflict resolution.

  You can also create your own custom resolver using Visual Basic.

- Some resolvers require further input in the Enter information needed by the resolver field:

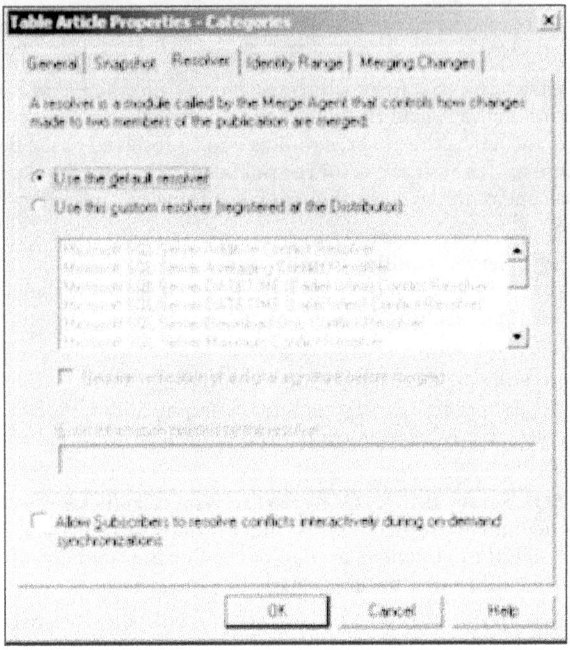


- The Identity Range tab for merge replication has the same options as that for queued updates for transactional replication, allowing you to define the range of values permitted for the `IDENTITY` column of each subscription article:

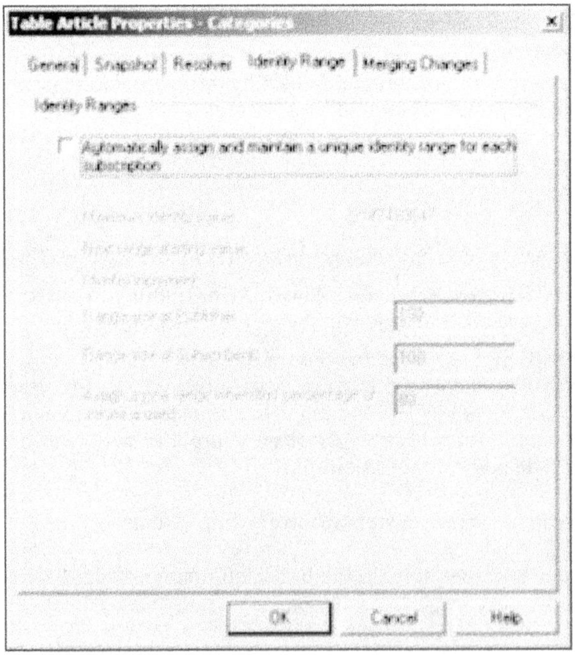

- The Merging Changes tab has the same settings as the Article Defaults dialog box.
- In the Article Issues dialog box, you will be warned about any issues relating to the use of selected articles in the publication. In the following example, SQL Server warns that some tables do not have a `uniqueidentifier` data type column, and that SQL Server will add these. Pay attention to the following warning about adding this column:

  Adding a new column will:

  » Cause INSERT statements without column lists to fail

  » Increase the size of the table

  » Increase the time required to generate the first snapshot

  Also, if you have `IDENTITY` columns, you may get the following warning:

  It is strongly recommended that all replicated IDENTITY columns use the NOT FOR REPLICATION option. When automatic identity range management is enabled for an article, SQL Server automatically adds the NOT FOR REPLICATION option to the IDENTITY column.

  The following published tables, for which automatic identity range management has not been enabled, contain IDENTITY columns without the NOT FOR REPLICATION option:

  [dbo].[tablename]

- The NOT FOR REPLICATION option will maintain the same `IDENTITY` values from the publisher on the subscriber. The seed value will not be reset to the highest number if automatic identity range management is used:

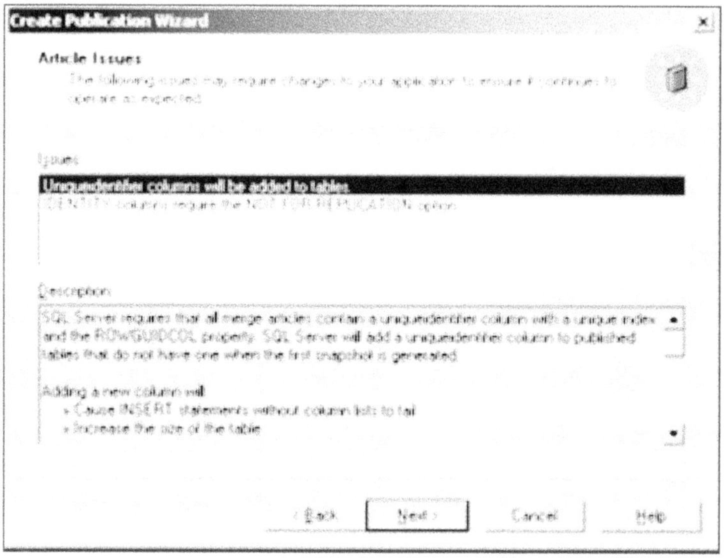


- In the Select Publication Name and Description dialog box, type in the publication name and description, or leave as the default.
- In the Customize the Properties of the Publication dialog box, decide whether you wish to define data filters, anonymous subscriptions, or a different snapshot schedule. Otherwise, select No to create the publication as specified.

- ❑ In the Completing the Create Publication Wizard, select Finish to begin the process of creating the publication. You will see the progress of the publication creation, and then will receive a dialog box designating the success or failure of the publication. Select Close, or Publication Properties to view and modify the new publication properties.

# 8.4 How to... Push a Subscription

To push a subscription in Enterprise Manager:

- ❑ Expand Server Group and registration.
- ❑ Expand the Replication folder and Publications folder.
- ❑ Right-click the appropriate publication and select Push New Subscription.
- ❑ Click Show advanced options (for this example). For transactional or snapshot replication, checking this box will allow you to set configuration options for immediate or queued updating. You will also receive a dialog box that allows you to set the location of the distribution agent. If you are performing a push of a merge subscription, you will see these options regardless of selecting Show advanced options. Select Next:

- ❑ Select one or more subscribers:

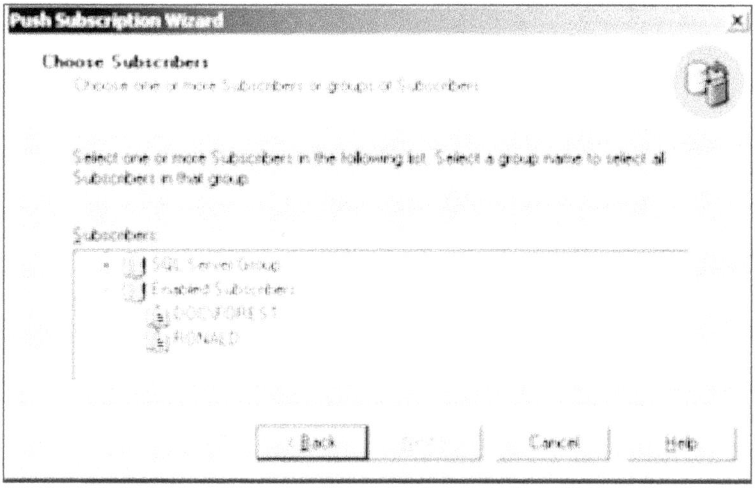


- Select the name of the subscription database. Select Browse or Create to select an existing database, or create a new database:

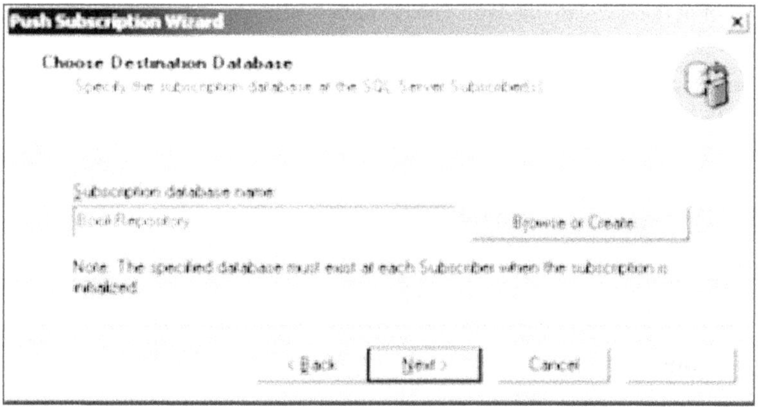


- Decide whether or not to run the agent at the distributor, or select an agent at the subscriber. By running the agent at the subscriber, you are able to offload processing overhead to a different server while still keeping control from the publisher and distributor. For snapshot and transactional replication, you will see the Distribution Agent Location dialog box.
- For merge replication, you will select the location of the merge agent. (If you wish to offload processing overhead to another server, select Run the agent at the Subscriber.)
- For snapshot and transactional replication, decide how often you wish the distribution agent to update the subscription. Select the Change button to change the schedule, take the default schedule, or select Continuously. If both continuous and scheduled update frequencies are an option for your topology, test both frequencies to see which performs better:

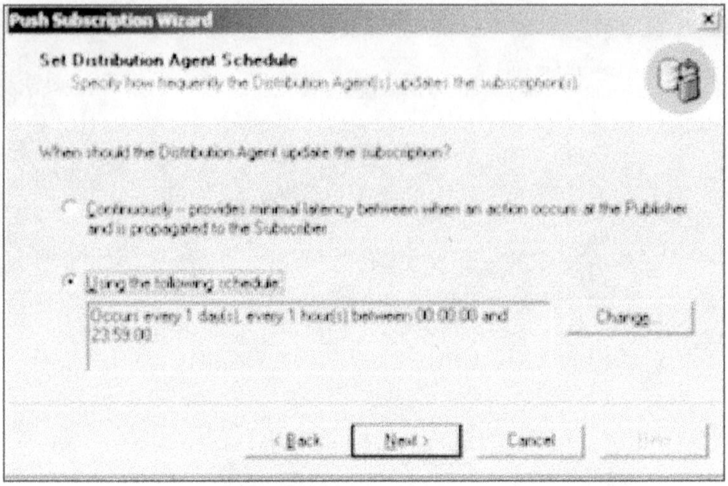


- For merge replication, the Set Merge Agent Schedule dialog box determines the schedule and frequency for the merge agent.
- Select the Start the Snapshot Agent to begin the initialization process immediately, and to kick off a new snapshot of the schema and data. The No option will be grayed out for snapshot replication:

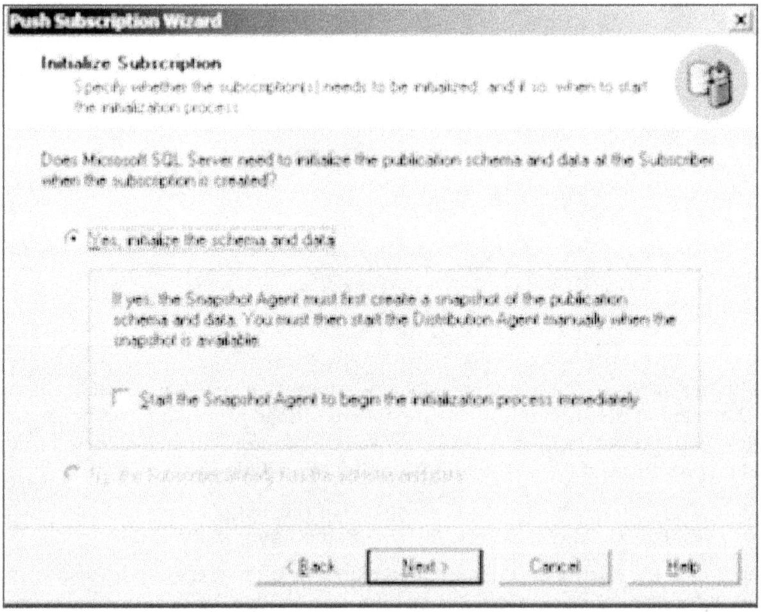


- In the Set Subscription Priority dialog box, you can designate the publisher as the proxy decision maker for resolving conflicts, or you can set a numeric priority for resolving row or column update conflicts. When setting a number, you are making the subscription **global**; meaning different subscribers have different assigned priorities. Selecting the publisher as a proxy means that the subscriber adopts the priority assigned by the publisher. This means that the first subscriber to make an update wins the conflict over other subscribers. You cannot set the publisher and subscriber with the same priority values.

- The Start Required Services dialog box is for checking the status of the required services for the subscriptions; in this case, SQL Server Agent. (The MS DTC service is required for transactional replication that allows immediate updating subscribers.):

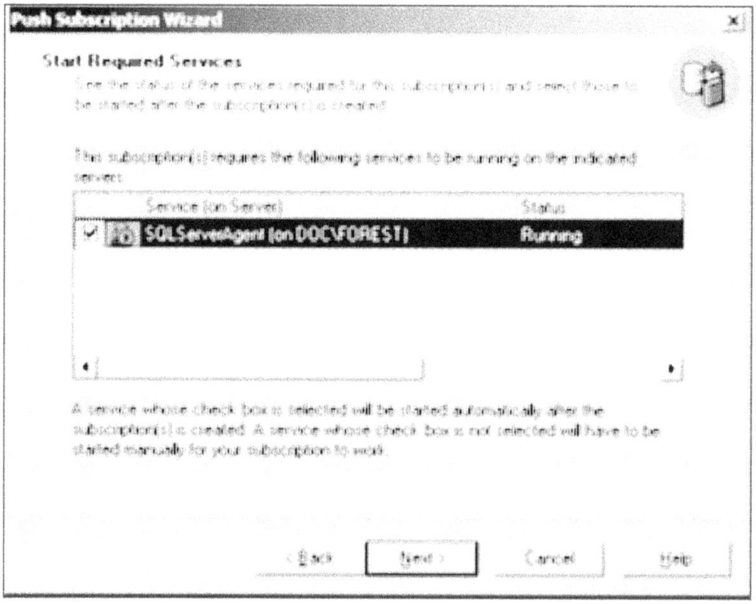


- Select Finish at the final dialog box.
- Select Close:

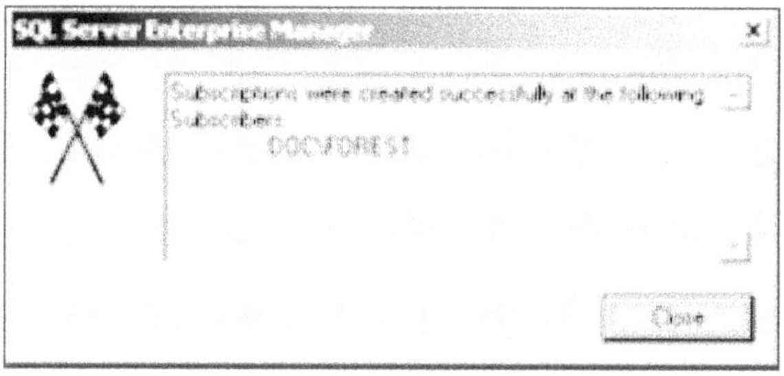


- Expand the Replication monitor directory. Expand the Publishers folder, and the publication node. Click the publication. The right-hand pane will show the publication agents. You can check the status of the last action for the replication agents. For transactional replication, the distribution agent will stop running if the snapshot has not yet completed. If you chose to have replication run continuously, the distribution agent will start up again once the snapshot has finished. Otherwise, you must manually start up the distribution agent, or wait until the scheduled start time:

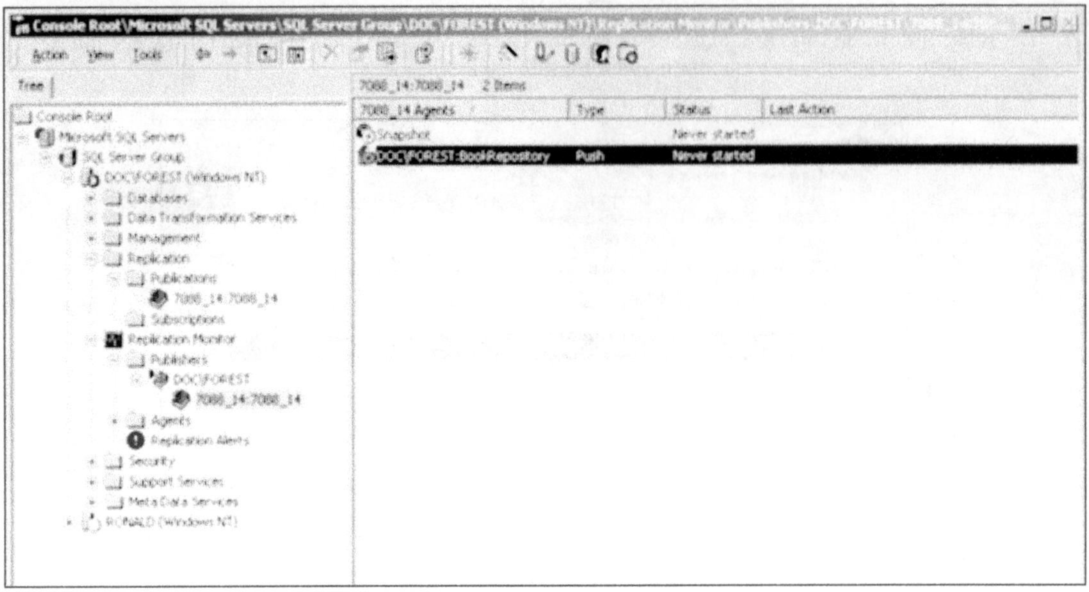

# 8.5 How to... Create a Pull Subscription

To create a pull subscription in Enterprise Manager:

- ❑ Expand the Server Group and registration.
- ❑ Expand the Replication folder and right-click Subscriptions. Select New Pull Subscription.
- ❑ In the Wizard dialog box, select the checkbox to show advanced options, then press Next.
- ❑ In the Look for Publications dialog box, decide whether or not to look for publications from registered servers, or through active directory or specification of publication information:

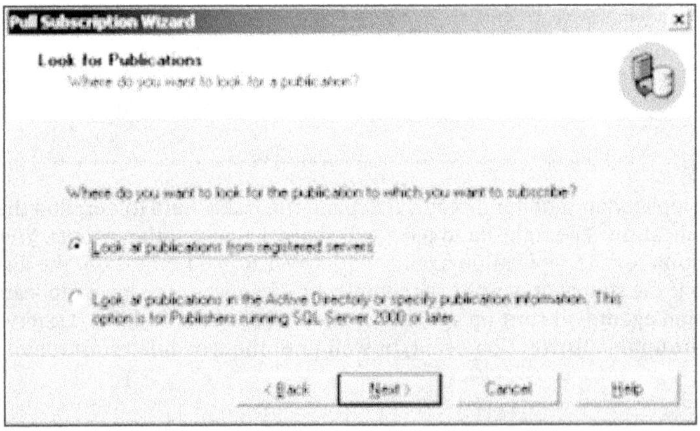


- ❑ If you selected registered servers, you will see the list of servers registered on your client. You can also select the Register Server button to register a new publication server. Expand the server and select the publication to which you wish to subscribe:

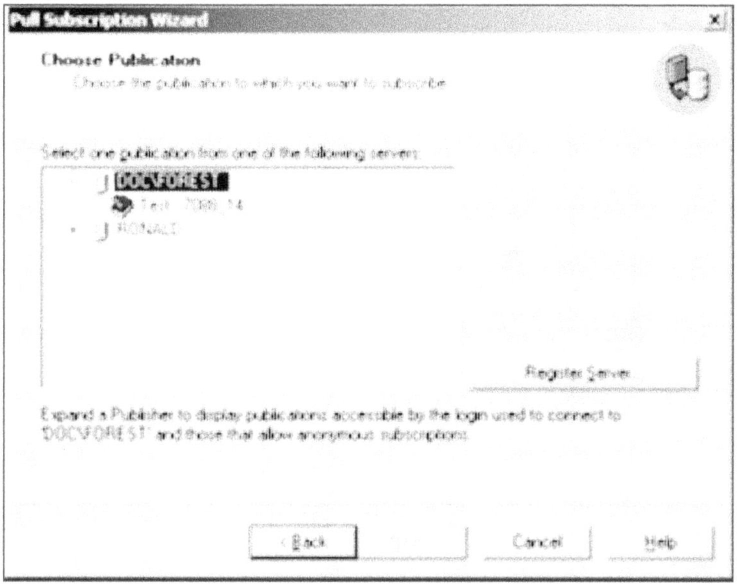


- If you selected active directory and publication specification, you will see the following dialog box to select your publisher server name, database, and publication name. You also must select a connection method; either Windows authentication, or SQL Server authentication. Select the Browse button to look up active directory-registered publications:

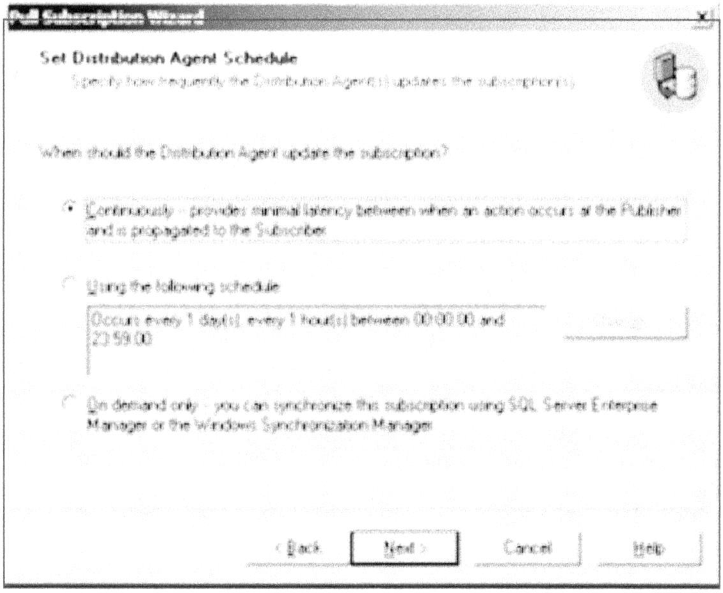


- In the Choose Destination Database dialog box, select the database where the subscription is created. Select the New button to create a new subscription database on the subscriber server.
- In the Initialize Subscription wizard, specify whether the subscription schema and data need to be created, or if the subscriber already has them:

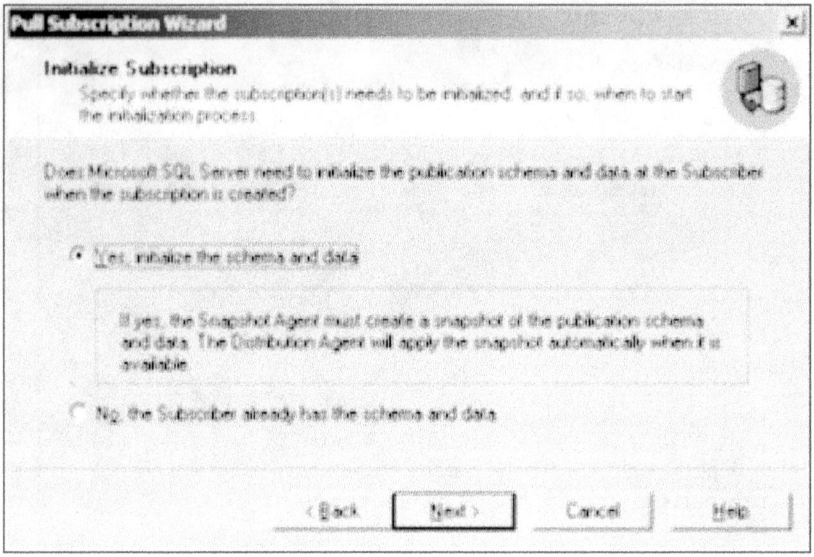


If you are just pulling a snapshot publication, the No, the Subscriber already has the schema and data option will be grayed out.

- In the Snapshot Delivery dialog box, select the default snapshot folder for the publication, or an alternative folder:

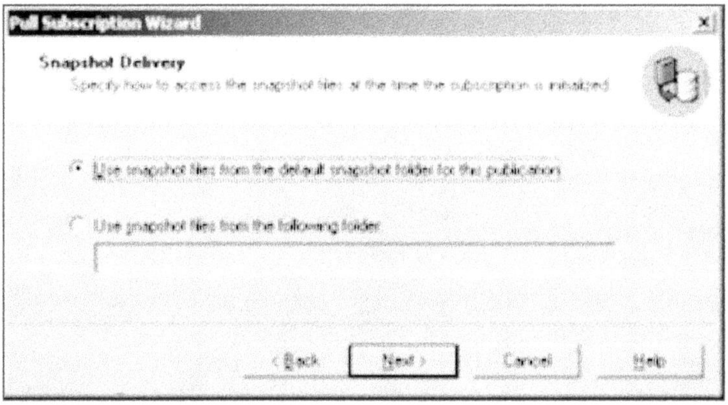


- In the Set Merge Agent Schedule (merge replication only) dialog box, select the frequency of the updates: continuously, scheduled, or on demand only (which means you start the synchronization process either through your application using ActiveX or Enterprise Manager, or through Windows Synchronization Manager):

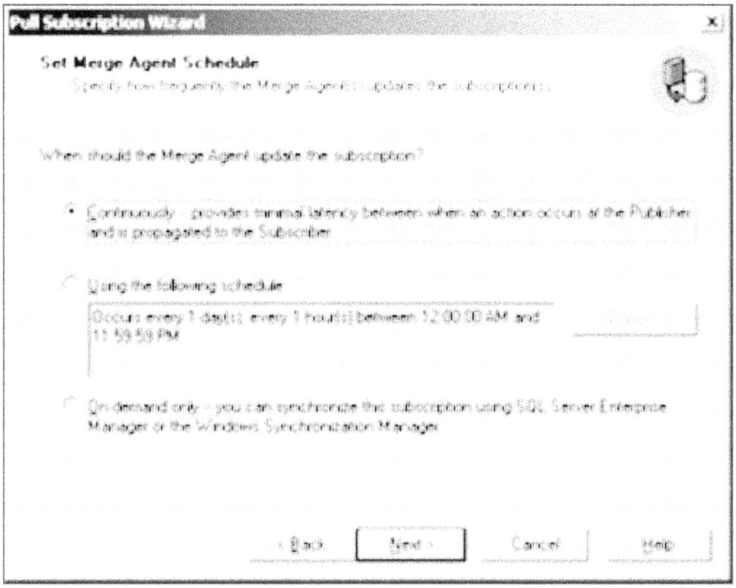


For transactional and snapshot replication, you will see the same options, but for the Distribution Agent Schedule:

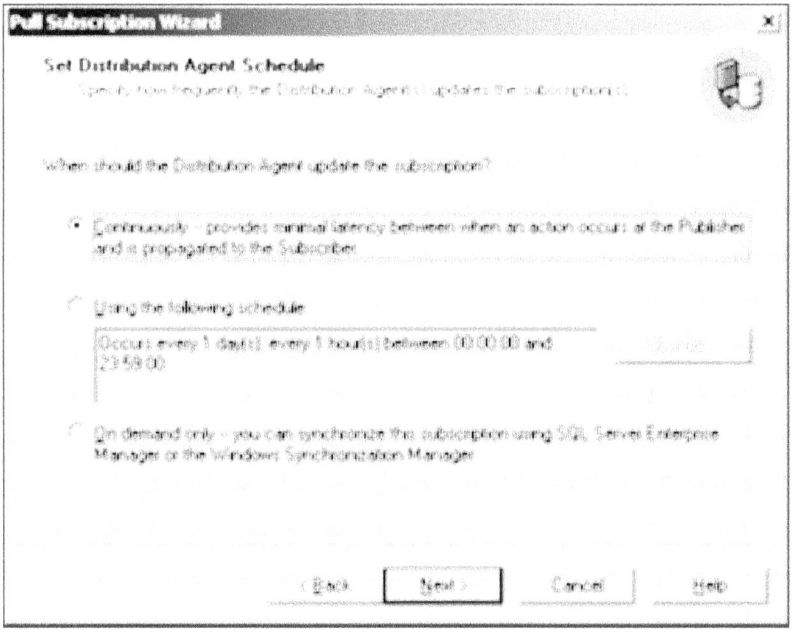


- If you are setting up a subscription for merge replication, you will see the Set Subscription Priority dialog box. In Set Subscription Priority, you can designate that the publisher is the proxy decision maker for resolving conflicts, or you can set a numeric priority for solving row or column update conflicts:

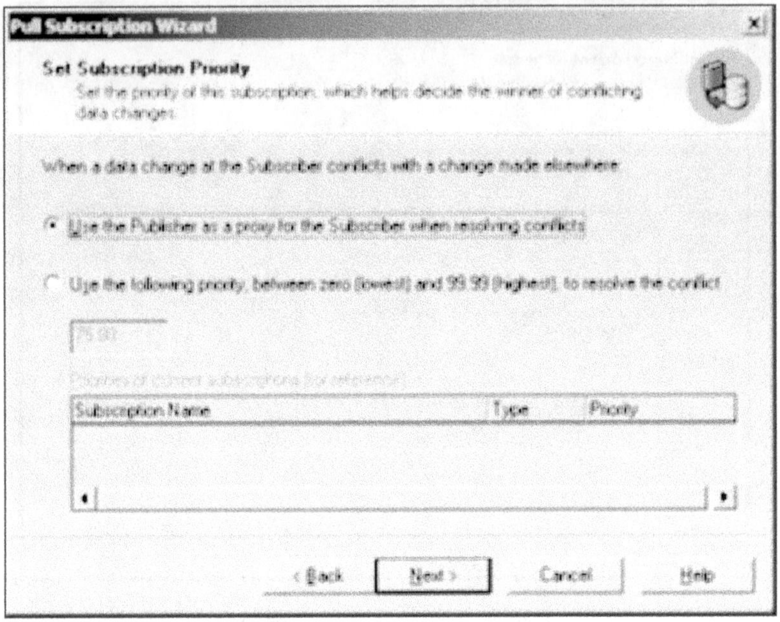


- In the Start Required Services dialog box, you are shown the status of required services on the subscriber server.
- Select Finish to begin pulling the subscription. You will be shown a status screen listing each step of the build process. Select Close when finished.

# 8.6 How to... Transform Data Within Your Publication

DTS transformations are allowed for snapshot or transactional publications. In order to take advantage of this functionality, the publication must have been configured initially to use transformations:

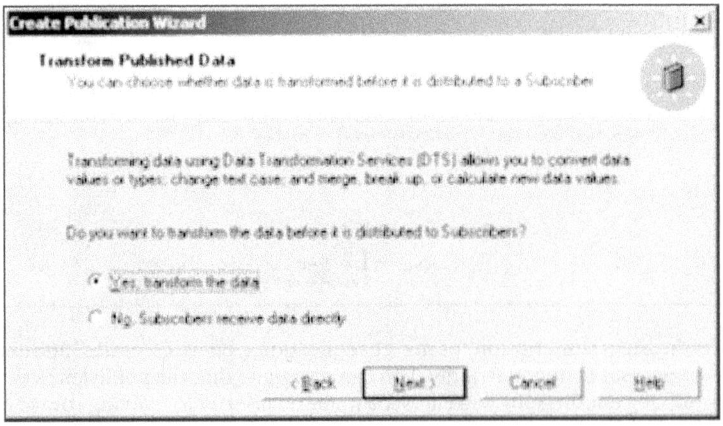

If you decided to include DTS transformations in your publication, you can follow these steps after completing the configuration of your publication prior to moving data to the subscriber:

- Expand Server Group and registration for the publication server.
- Expand the Replication folder and expand the Publications folder. Right-click the publication to which you wish to add DTS transformations. Select Define Transformation of Published Data (this option will not appear unless the publication was initially configured to allow transformations).
- In the Welcome screen, enter the publication name or keep the current name, and select Next.
- Select the subscriber server name, login method, and database.
- Select the ellipsis in the Transform column for the article you wish to transform, or leave transformation article defaults as they are currently defined:

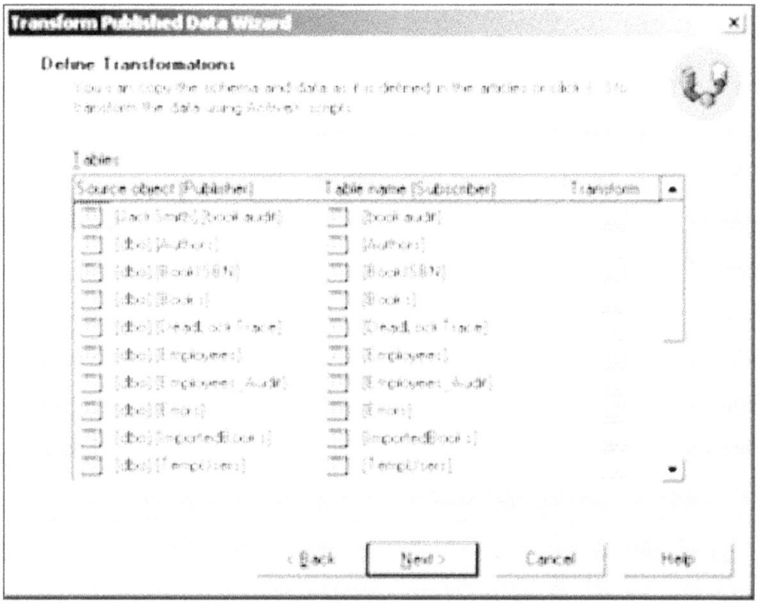


- If you selected the ellipsis button, you will be able to configure source and destination column mappings in the Column Mappings and Transformations tab:

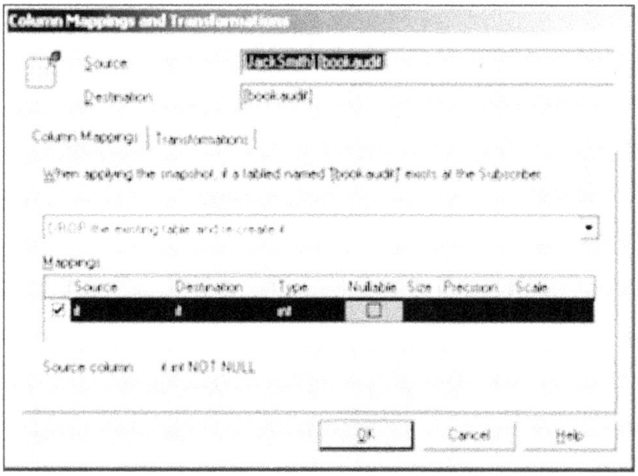

- In the Transformations tab, you can choose whether to copy the source columns directly, or use a scripting language, like VBScript, to transform the data prior to movement. Click the Advanced tab to configure advanced transformation properties:

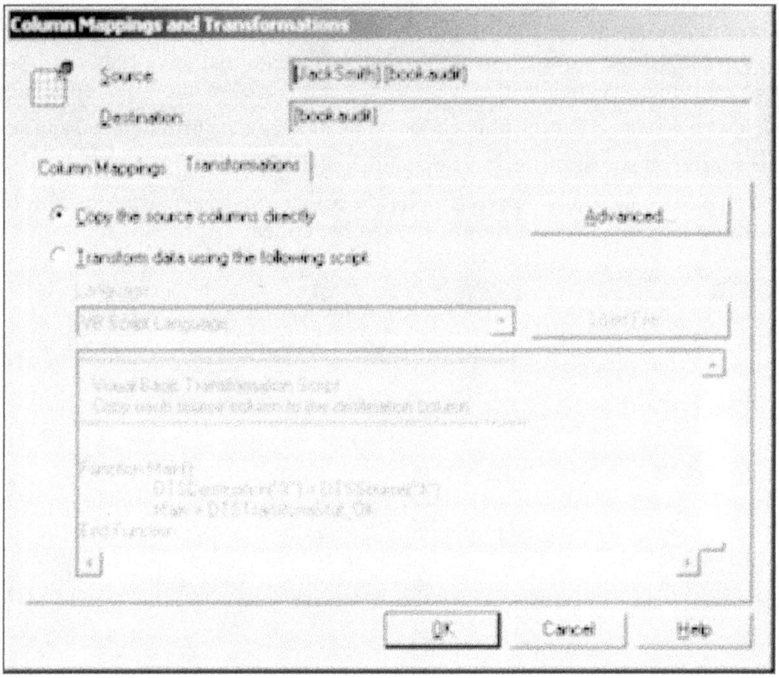


- In the Advanced Transformation Properties dialog box, decide whether all possible conversions are allowed, whether an exact match between source and destination is required, or whether any advanced data type promotion, demotion, or NULL conversions are allowed:

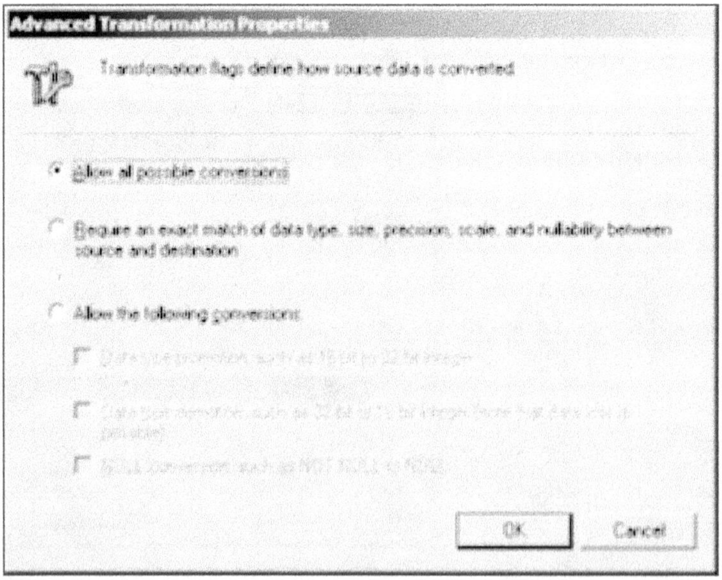

- In the DTS Package Location dialog, you will be asked if the DTS package should be saved to the distributor or subscriber server. Choose your preference if you have one. There should not be a significant performance differential between storing the package on the distributor versus the subscriber. You should also choose an authentication method:

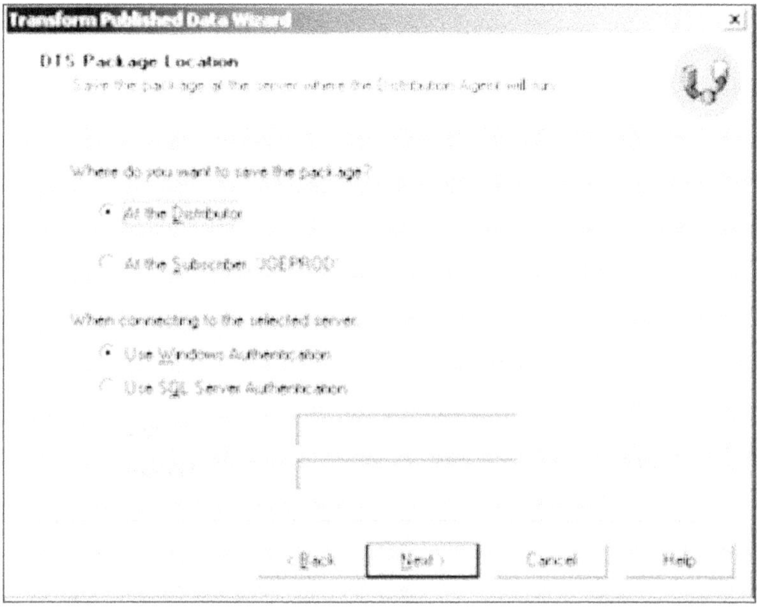


- The DTS Package Identification dialog box requires you to choose a package name, description, and an optional owner password for the DTS package:

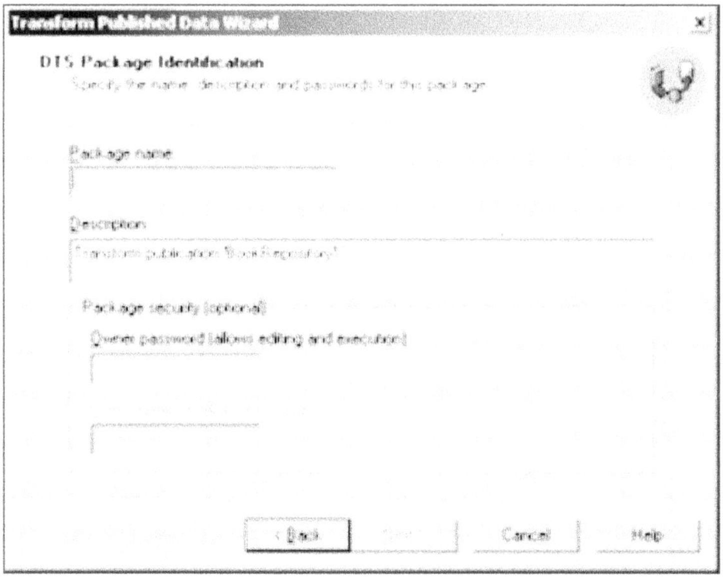

- Select Finish at the final dialog box to generate the transformation package. You will see a progress dialog box showing phases of the package creation:

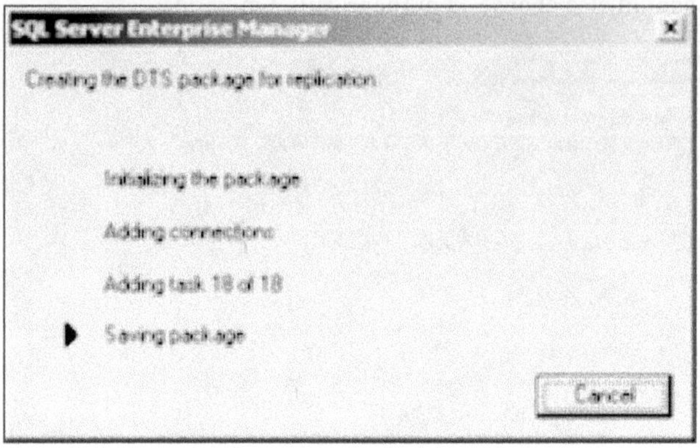


- You will receive the following dialog box when complete:

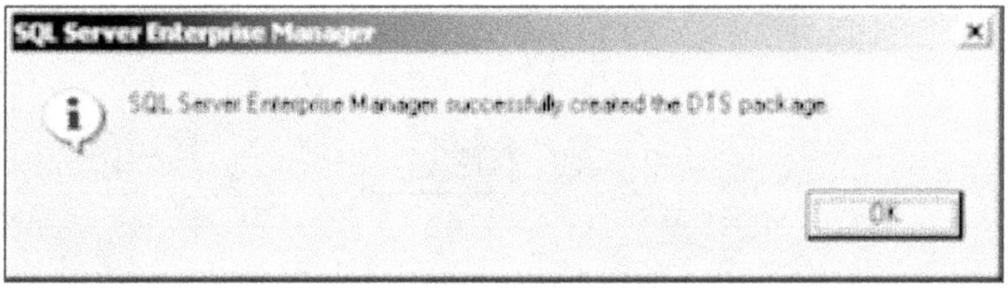


The resulting DTS package can then be further modified using DTS Designer. See Chapter 11 for more details on DTS and DTS Designer.

# 8.7 How to... Use Dynamic Filters and Dynamic Snapshots for a Merge Publication

Dynamic filters are actually article row filters (horizontal partitioning) that use system functions to narrow down rows based on the subscriber. For example, let's say you have a central merge publication topology, and the central database contains sales records by sales staff; the business requirement is to distribute only those records owned by each specific salesperson. If you had one hundred sales staff, you would need to create one hundred separate publications in order to partition the data horizontally by salesperson.

This can be avoided by using dynamic filters. For example, you can create one publication with the sales tables, and dynamically filter the row by `SUSER_SNAME()` or `HOST_NAME()`. `SUSER_SNAME()` returns the login ID of the user's security identification number. `HOST_NAME()` is useful for partitioning rows by the workstation ID.

Make sure to add indexes to columns used for filtering, to improve the performance of the filtering operation by avoiding table scan or index scan (as opposed to index seek) operations.

To add dynamic filters during the creation of a publication:

- ❑ While creating a new merge publication, at the Customize the Properties of the Publication dialog box, select Yes to define data filters:

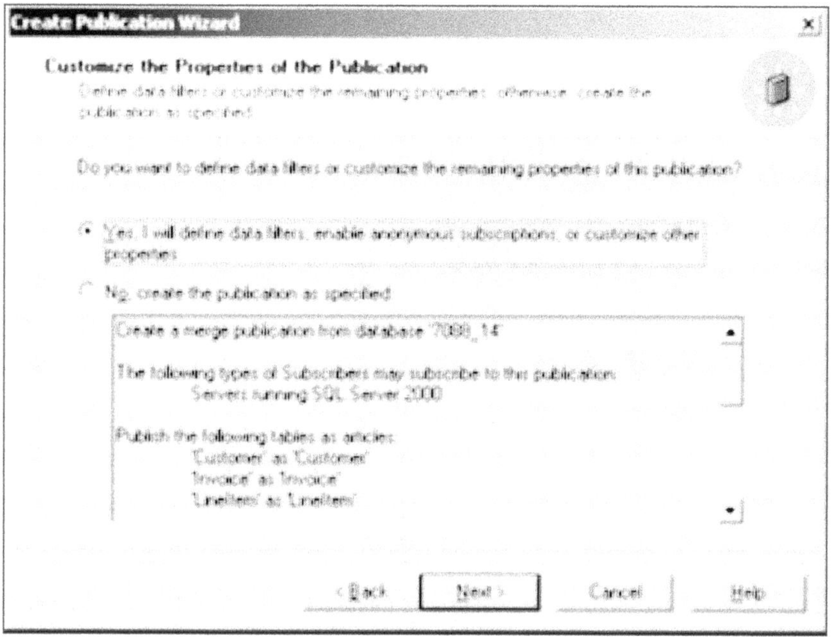


- ❑ Select the checkbox for horizontal filtering (row filtering):

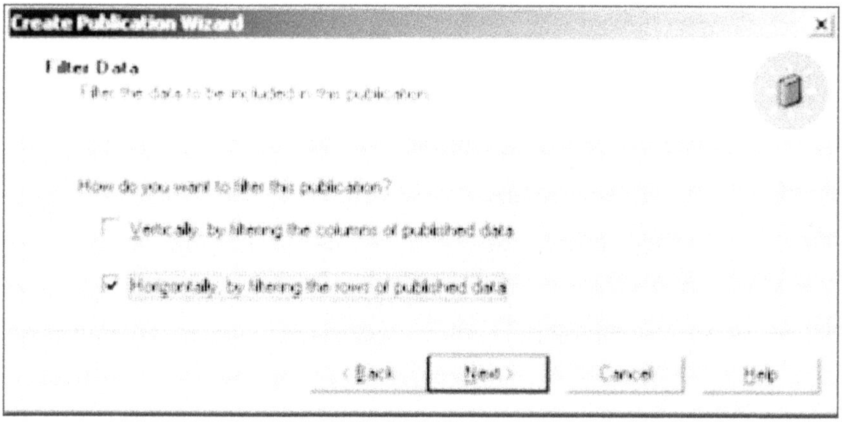

- Select Yes to enable dynamic filters:

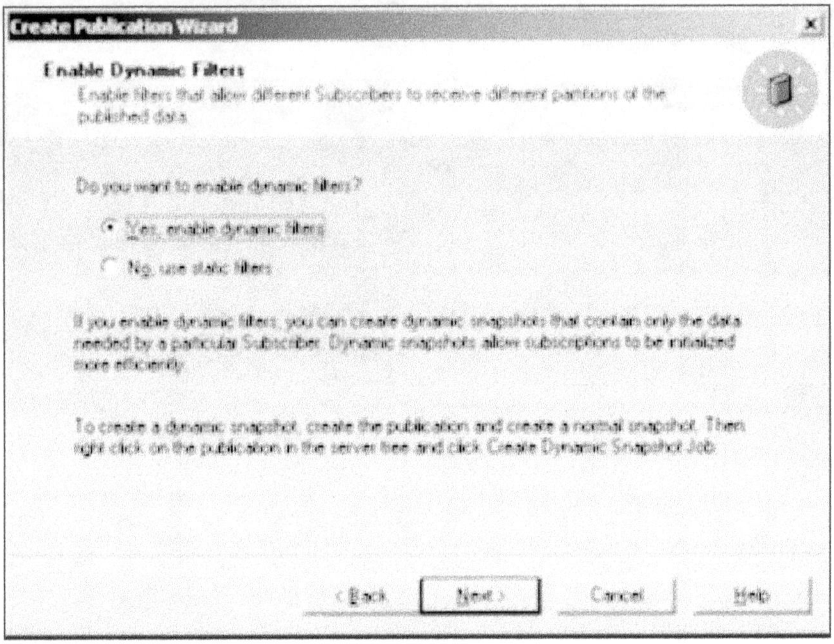


- Select the table to filter; SQL Server will extend this filtering based on existing table relationships. The example below uses `SUSER_SNAME()` to filter by the `chSalesPerson` column on the `SalesTerritory` table:

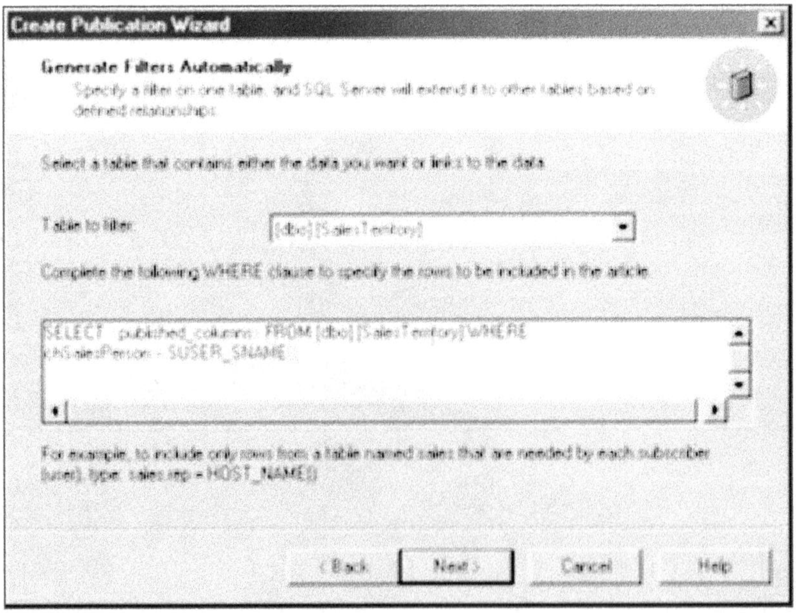

- You will then see a dialog box for dynamic filters to be created with similar tables:

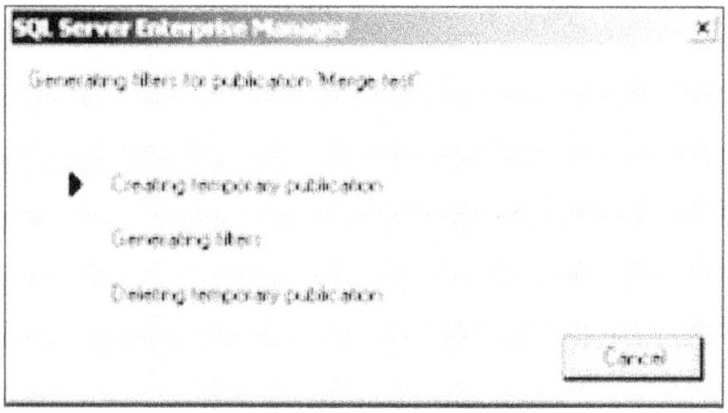


- Next, you will get a chance to add dynamic filters to other tables manually. Select the ellipsis button for each table you wish to filter. You can also extend filtering on a table to a related table by defining a join between the two filters (in the lower half of the dialog box). Remember to index your join filter columns just as you did with the column filters used for dynamic filtering:

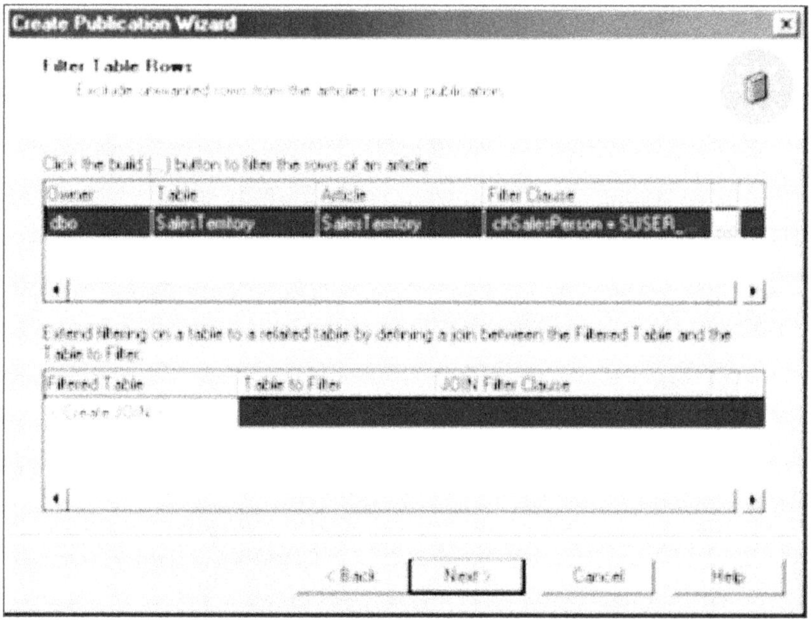


- In the Validate Subscriber Information screen, you can specify that if dynamic filters are changed at the subscriber, then the subscriber will be reinitialized. The text box should already list functions used for dynamic filters, separated by the concatenation (+) sign:

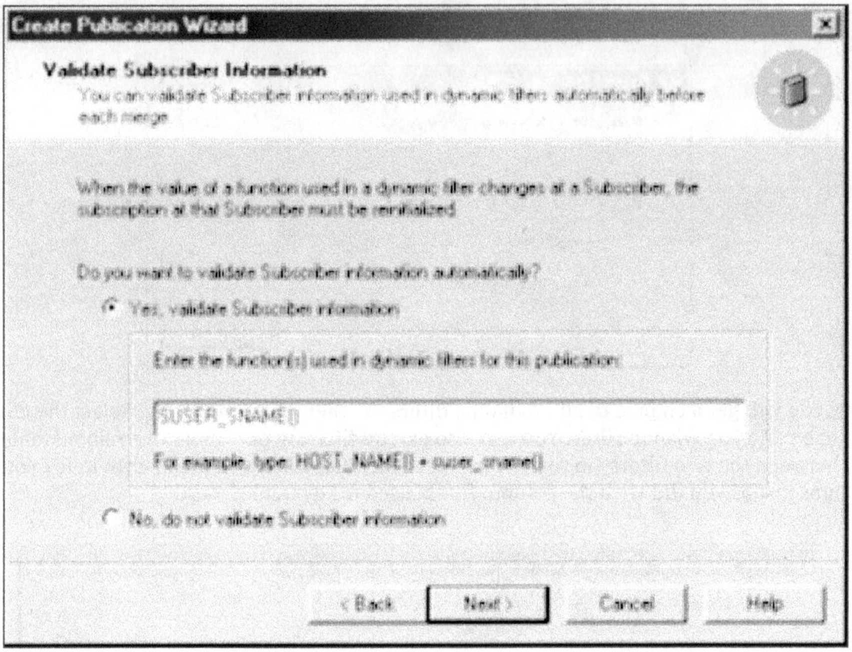


- The Optimize Synchronization dialog box is used to improve performance over a slow network connection, by storing more information at the publisher. This extra information stored on the publisher helps the distribution agent determine more efficiently whether row changes are required for each subscriber:

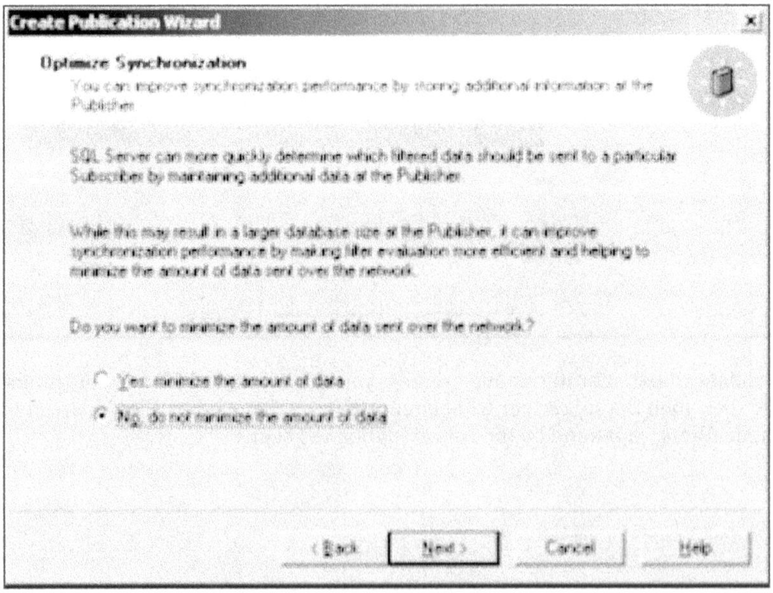


The remaining steps in the Create Publication Wizard are not specific to dynamic filters.

Dynamic filters should be used for multiple subscribers, not when there is only one. Also, remember that dynamic filters cause more performance overhead for distribution to the subscribers. The overhead can be significant, which is why SQL Server offers dynamic snapshots to address this problem.

Regular snapshots for merge replication process dynamic filters using `INSERT` statements, which migrate data to the subscriber during the initial snapshot synchronization. For large tables, the processing can be time-consuming, as well as having an impact on server performance.

Dynamic snapshots use bcp to migrate data to a subscriber for initial snapshot synchronization. There are various ways to generate a dynamic snapshot (using stored procedures, SQL-DMO, and ActiveX controls); this chapter will review the Enterprise Manager method. Dynamic snapshots are generated in Enterprise Manager as follows:

- After generating a dynamic publication, create a regular snapshot by starting the Snapshot Agent. You can start the snapshot agent by expanding the Replication Monitor node, expanding the Publishers folder, expanding the server name folder, and clicking the dynamic merge publication. In the right-hand pane, right-click Snapshot Agent and select Start Agent.

  You can also start the snapshot by starting the snapshot job in the SQL Server Agent jobs listing. You are ready to continue once your job succeeds, or your agent status shows a status of succeeded:

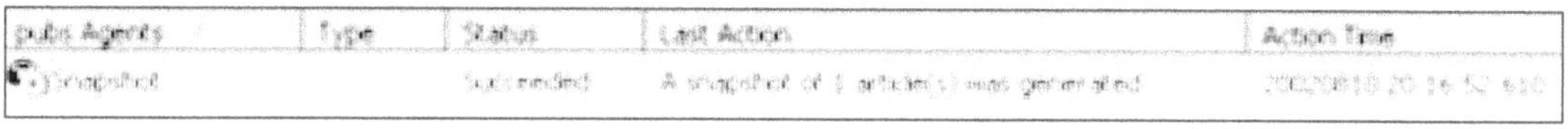


- Next, expand the Replication folder and Publications folder and right-click the dynamic merge publication. Select Create Dynamic Snapshot Job.
- Select Next at the Welcome screen of the Dynamic Snapshot Job wizard.
- In the Specify Filter Values dialog box, select the value of either the `HOST_NAME()`, `SUSER_SNAME()` or both:

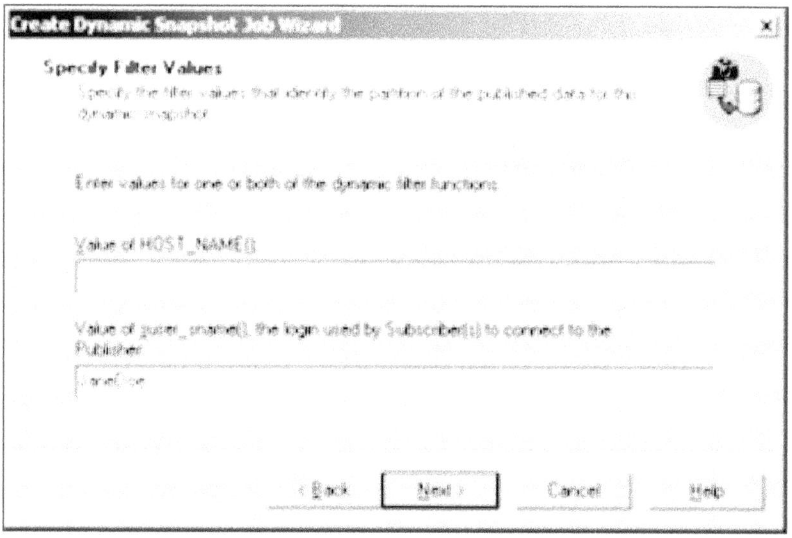

- ❑ Make sure that the login you select is a member of the publication access list for the publication. If not, you can configure it by canceling out of the publication, right-clicking the publication node, and selecting Properties.
- ❑ In the Publication Access List tab, add any logins that should have pull access to the publication:

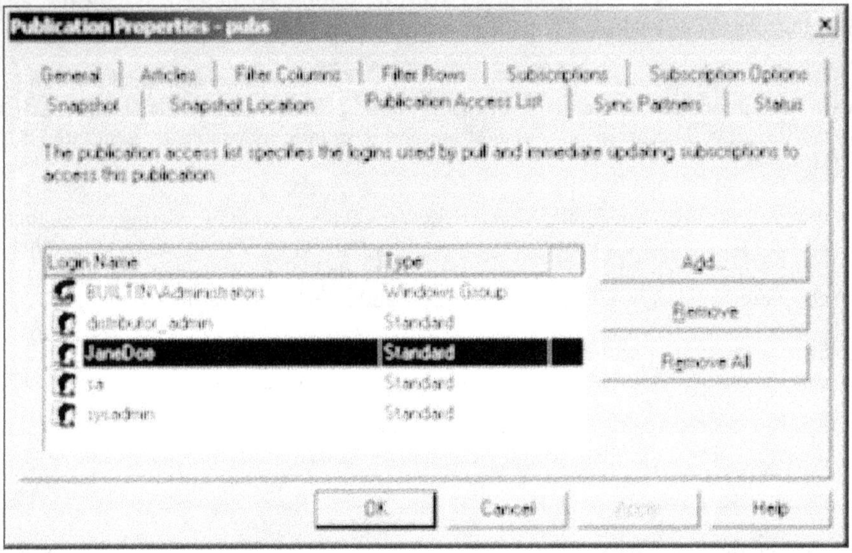


- ❑ Continuing with the Dynamic Snapshot wizard, select a network path for the snapshot folder:

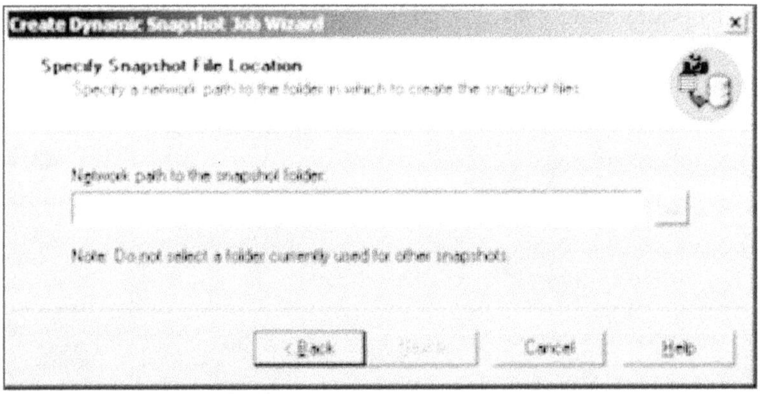


- ❑ In the Set Job Schedule dialog box, select a schedule for the dynamic snapshot job, or whether the job should be run on demand only. Also, select whether the first snapshot should be run immediately:

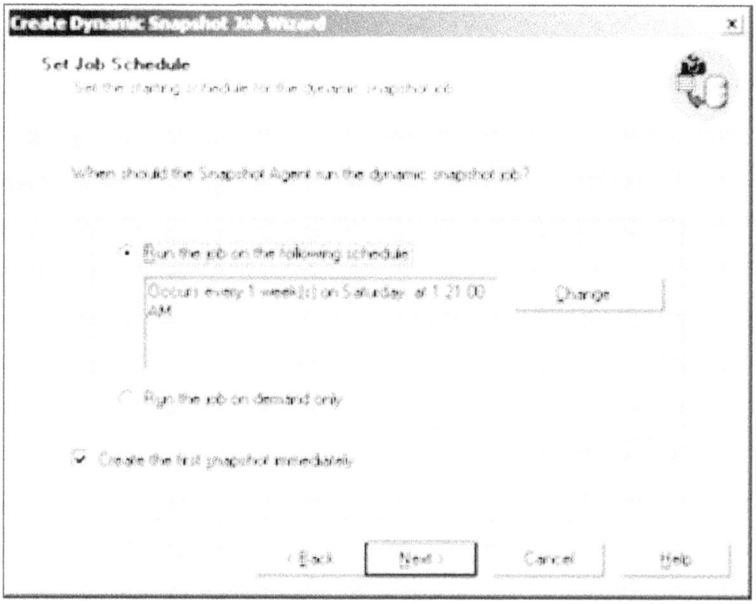


- ❑ Next, specify the job name for the dynamic snapshot job:

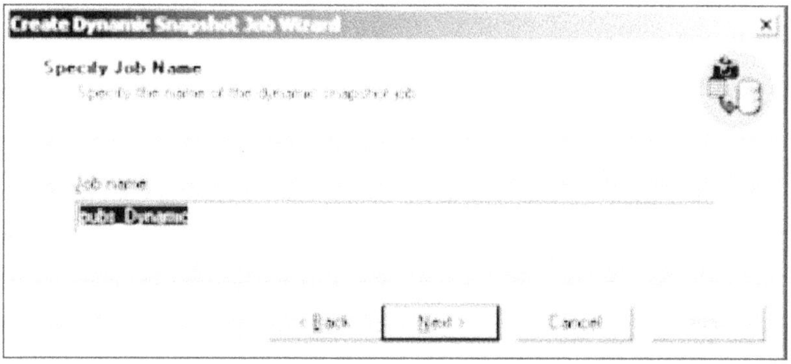


- ❑ Select Finish to create the job. You will receive notification if the job was created successfully. You are also notified that this job can only be monitored from the SQL Server Agent Jobs view, and not Replication Monitor.
- ❑ Follow your normal procedure for creating a pull subscription from the subscriber. When reaching the Snapshot Delivery dialog box, select the location of the dynamic snapshot files, and select the checkbox for This snapshot is for a dynamically filtered subscription.
- ❑ Go through the rest of the dialog boxes for pulling a subscription as normal. When finished, verify your tables after the merge agent has run.

Dynamic snapshots increase the speed of applying dynamic filters to the subscriber. If you have small publications, dynamic snapshots may not be necessary and may in fact add to the work needed to achieve the dynamic row filtering by subscriber. Use dynamic snapshots for large publications. Use dynamic filters to reduce information sent over the network, reduce space used at the subscriber, and reduce the number of publications needed.

# 8.8 How to... Use Windows Synchronization Manager

Windows Synchronization Manager is a tool included with Microsoft Windows 2000 and Microsoft Internet Explorer version 5.0, or above. It allows you to synchronize subscriptions to snapshot, transactional, and merge publications. This tool is very useful for those end users who take data offline, and synchronize changes or pull updates when reconnected with the network.

To start Windows Synchronization Manager:

- Go to Start | Programs | Accessories | Synchronize. You will then see any existing publications or offline web pages:

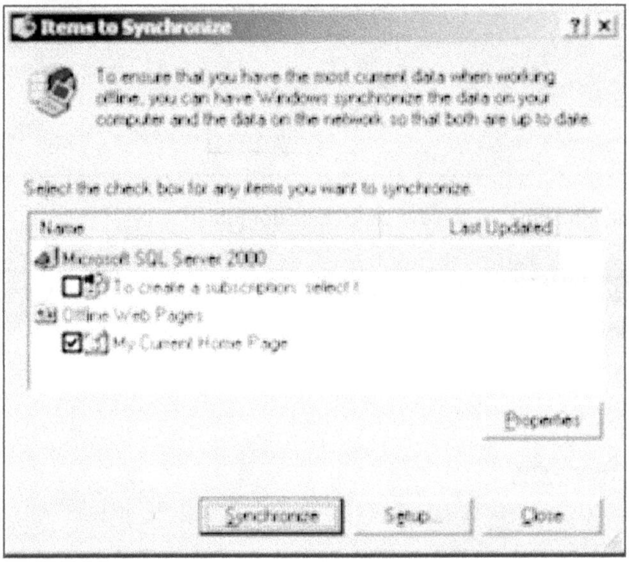


- To add a new subscription to your local subscriber server, click the first checkbox under the Microsoft SQL Server 2000 icon and select Properties.
- Select a method for creating a new subscription; you can browse Active Directory, attach a subscription database, or specify a publication and subscription manually. Follow the dialog boxes to create the new subscriptions.

> **After creating the new subscription, close the Windows Synchronization Manager, and re-open it in order to see the newly created subscription.**

Keep in mind that you can still use Enterprise Manager to create the subscriptions, and they will appear in the main Items to Synchronize dialog box.

You can also automate the synchronization of subscriptions by selecting the Setup button in the Items to Synchronize dialog box.

The Login/Logoff tab allows you to select items to be synchronized when you log on or off the network. You can also select prompting before performing synchronization:

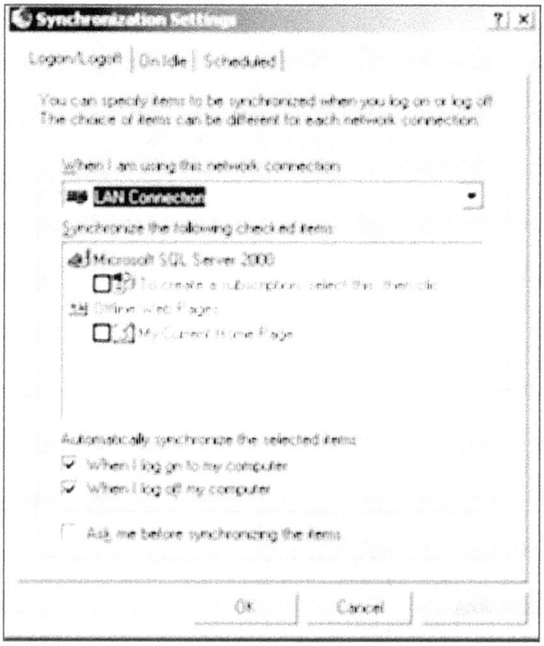


The On Idle tab allows you to synchronize specific subscriptions when the computer is idle. Select the checkbox to enable:

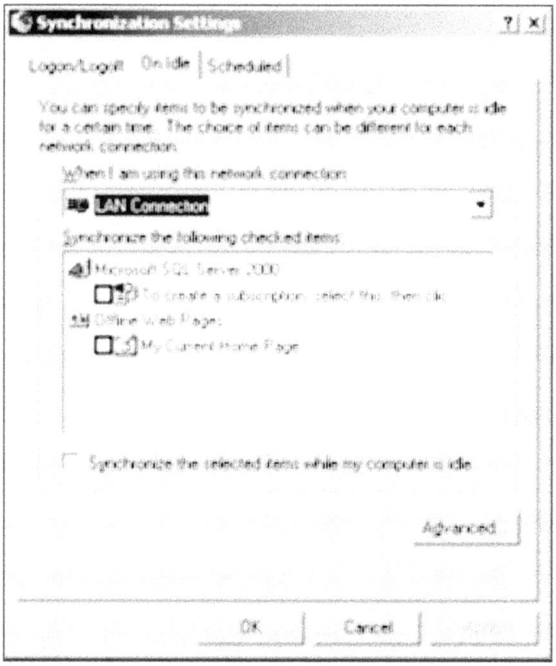

Click the Advanced button to define what constitutes idle time. You can also define the frequency of updates, and prevent synchronization when the computer is running on battery power:

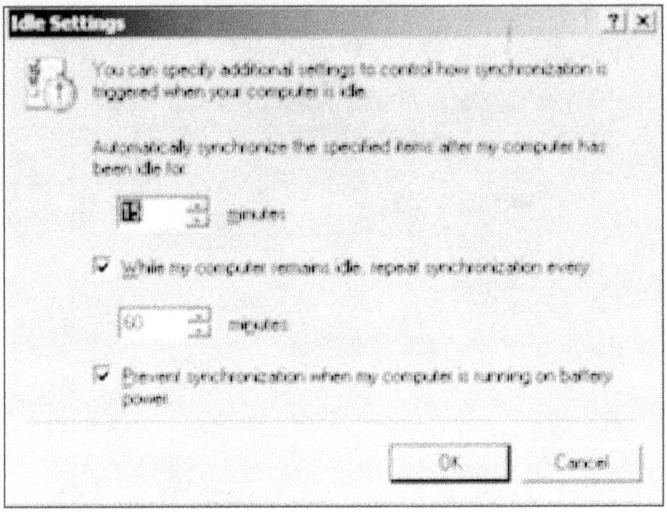


You can also define scheduled synchronization tasks to run:

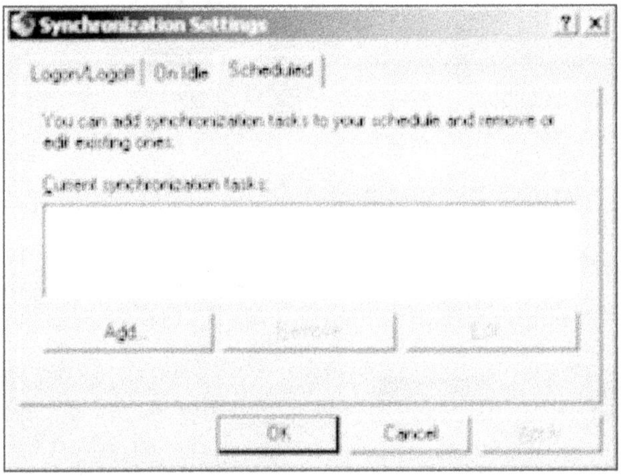


To create a new scheduled synchronization task:

- ❑ In the Schedule tab, select the Add button.
- ❑ Select Next at the wizard startup screen.
- ❑ Select the network connection used for the synchronization, subscriptions to be synchronized, and whether or not the task should automatically connect if not already connected to the network:

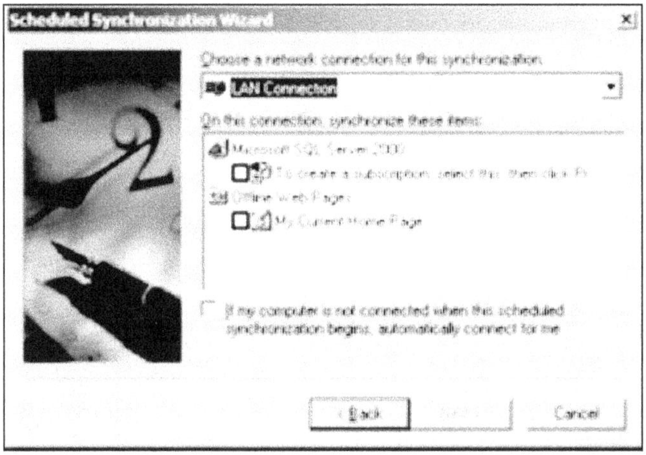


- Select the time and frequency of the synchronization task:

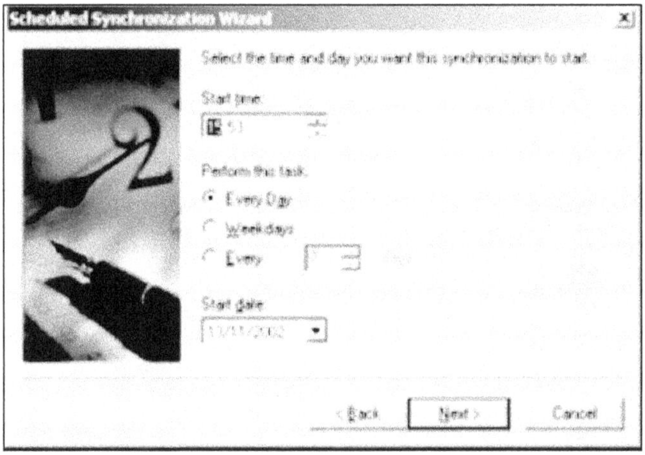


- Select the name of the task:

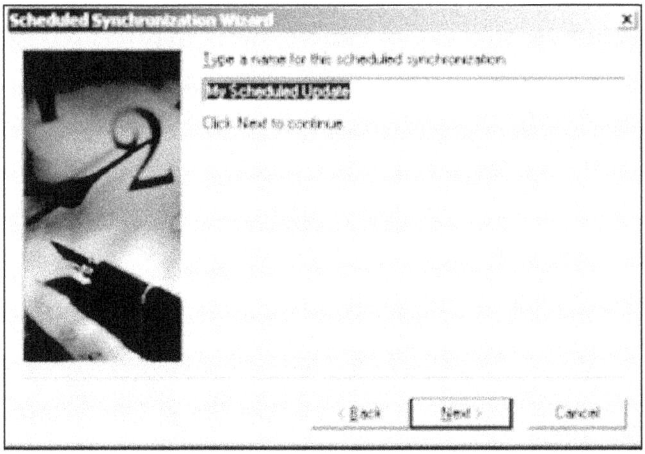

- ❑ Confirm the settings and select Finish.
- ❑ To remove a scheduled task, click the task and select Remove:

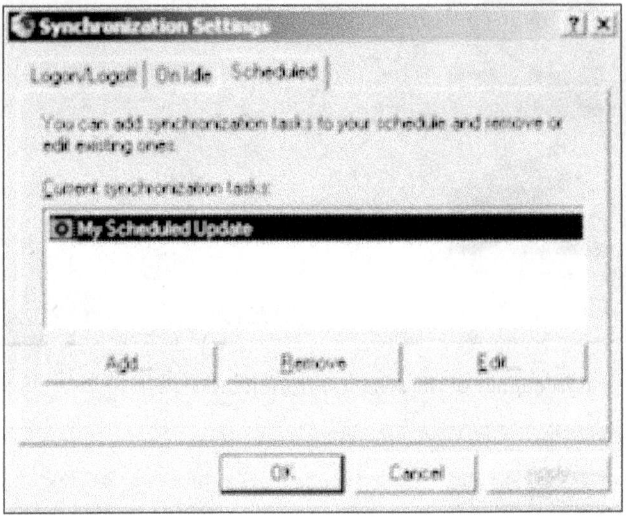


- ❑ To synchronize a subscription manually, check the box for the subscription and press the Synchronize button:

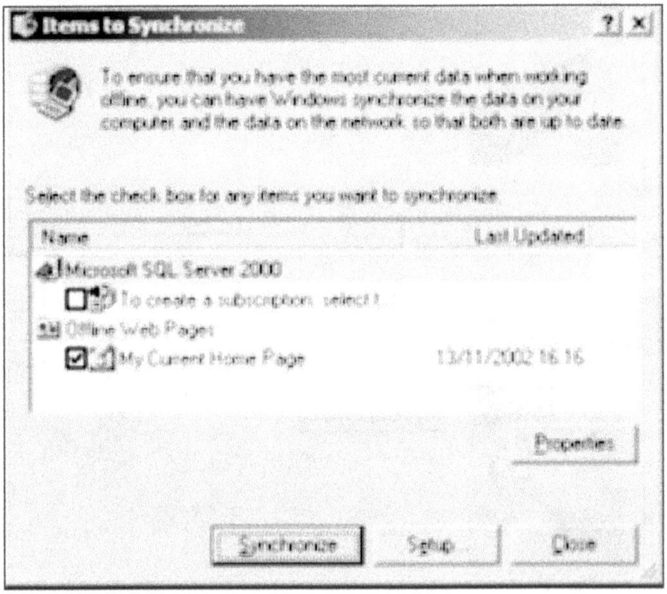


You will see a progress bar during the synchronization.

# 8.9 How to... Configure Publication Properties

After creating your publication, you may wish to make modifications to the publication (such as adding new articles, removing articles, changing article properties, and adding article filters). To do so via Enterprise Manager:

- Expand Server Group and registration.
- Expand the Replication and Publications folders and right-click the publication you wish to view or configure. Select Properties.
- You may be warned that many properties of the publication cannot be modified if the publication has subscriptions. Once all subscriptions are dropped for a publication, you can make most modifications to the publication properties:

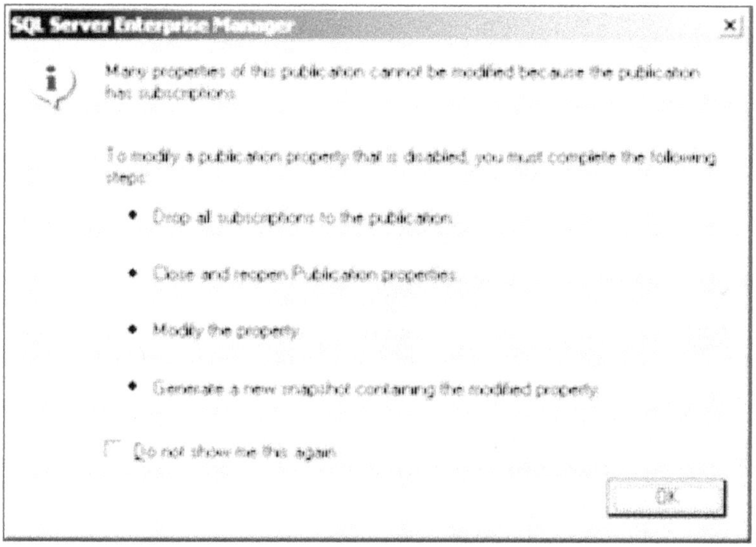


- For merge replication, in the General tab, you can configure the publication description and the number of **days** without synchronizing before a subscription is marked as expired and dropped.

  When a push subscription exceeds the expiry quota, the subscription is marked as expired and the distribution agent associated with the subscription is removed and must be recreated.

  When a pull subscription exceeds the expiry quota, the distribution agent on the subscriber will not be removed, but will encounter an error when it attempts to synchronize with the publication. When this occurs, you must then delete the pull subscription, and recreate it:

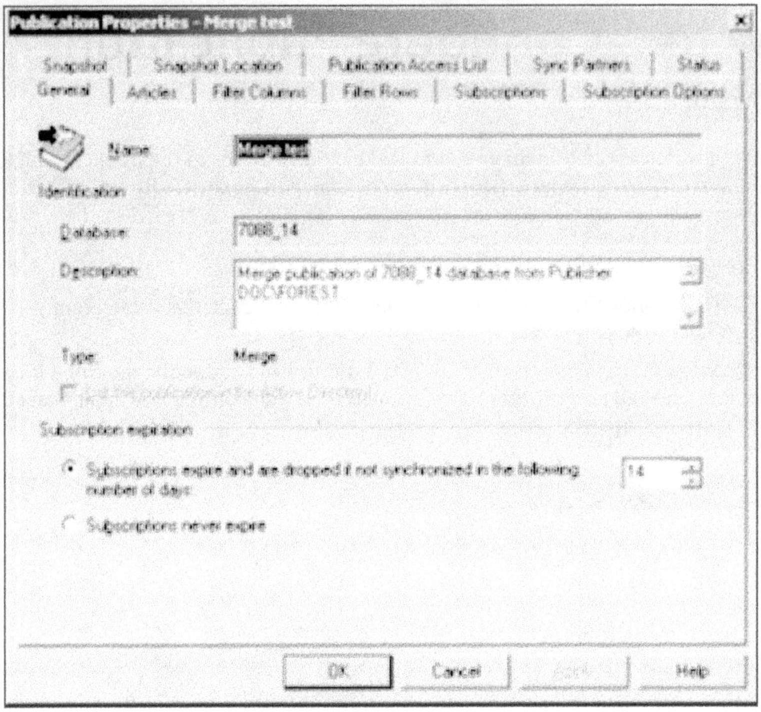


- For snapshot and transactional replication, you can specify the number of hours before subscriptions are expired and dropped. If you select the Subscriptions never expire option, subscriptions will be deactivated only after transactions have been kept in the distribution database for a maximum retention period (72 hour default for transactional replication) without being synchronized via the distribution agent.

  Once a subscription is deactivated, it will need to be reinitialized; meaning a new snapshot must be applied to the subscriber before replication can continue for the subscriber.

To reinitialize a subscription in Enterprise Manager:

- Expand the Replication and Publications folder and click the appropriate publication.
- Right-click the subscription to be reinitialized in the right-hand pane and select Reinitialize.
- In the Articles tab, you can configure article defaults and specify objects to publish or remove. To show articles not currently published, click the Show unpublished objects checkbox:

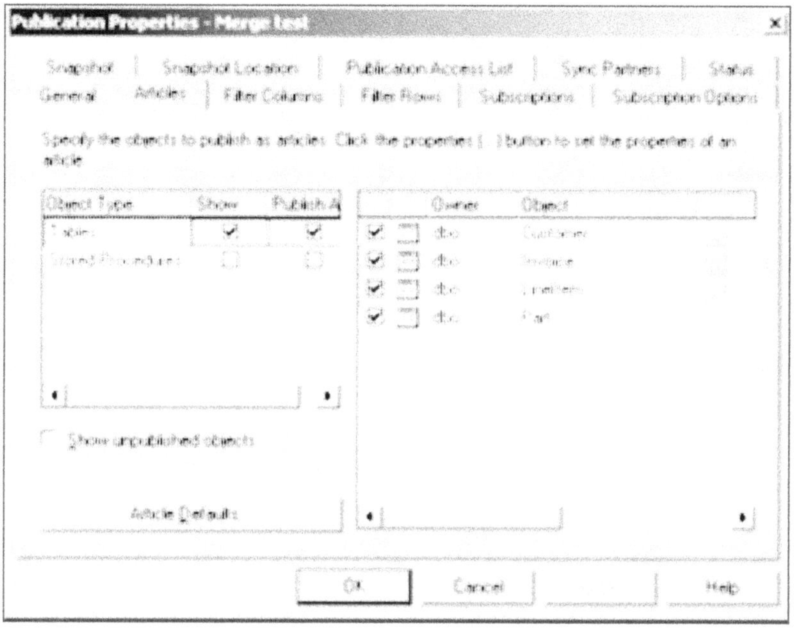

- You can add new articles to the publication by selecting Show unpublished objects, and selecting the articles you wish to add. Click Apply to initiate. You will be warned that this requires subscribers with SQL Server 2000 in order to propagate the change. Select Yes to continue, unless you have subscribers with previous versions of SQL Server:

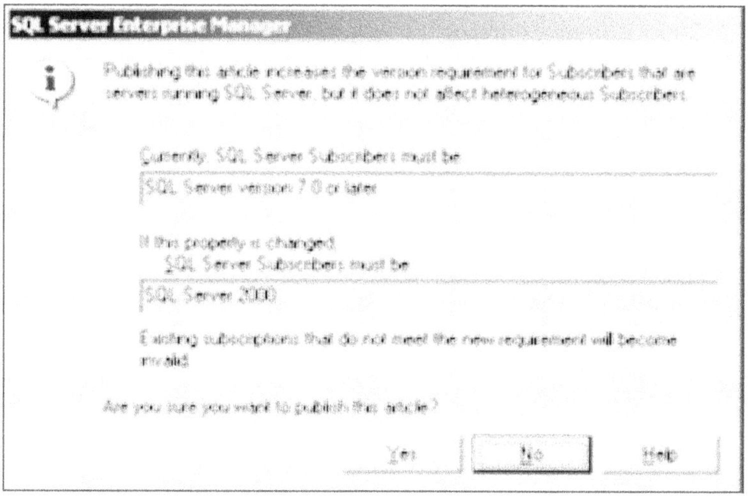

  The changes will be migrated after the snapshot is rerun, and the distribution or merge agent is started or picks up the changes.

- The Filter Columns tab allows you to add or remove columns to include in the publication:

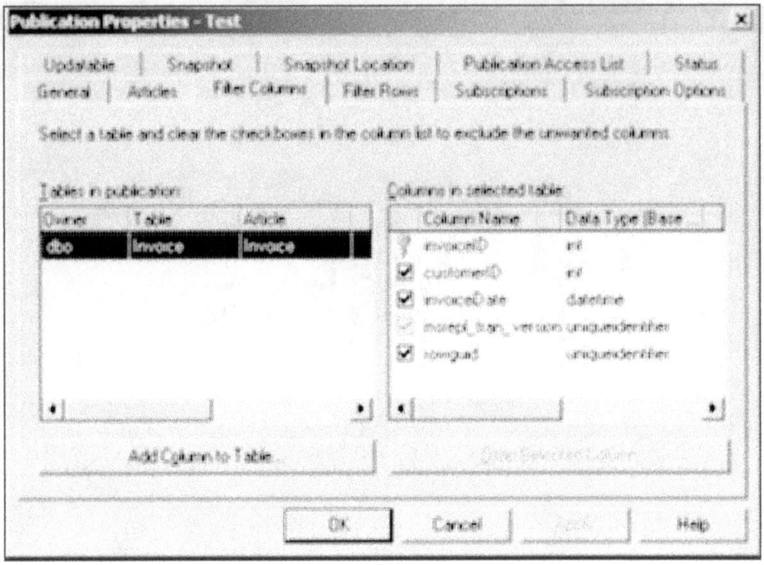


This is the tab where you can add a new column to a table, even when the publication still has subscribers. Click the Add Column to Table button.

You may be warned that subscribers must be running SQL Server 7.0 or greater in order to add new columns to existing subscribers. Type the new column name. Also enter the column definition, including data type, defaults (if any), `IDENTITY` properties, or other properties. Select OK to add to the article and table.

These changes will be propagated to the publisher and all subscribers. Prior to SQL Server 2000, it was necessary to drop all subscribers in order to add new columns or articles, and then re-push the subscriptions. For large publications, this was quite time-consuming:

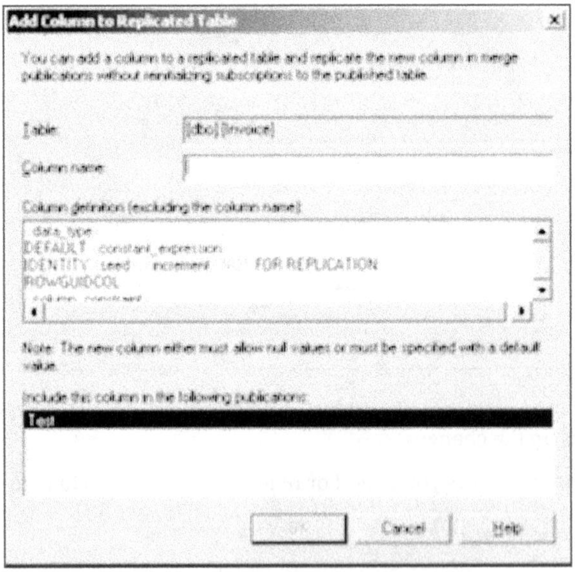

- By selecting a column, you can also click Drop Column to drop the base table column and propagate the change to the publisher and all subscribers. Keep in mind that you cannot drop columns with dependencies (such as default binding or foreign keys).
- The Filter Rows tab will show filters used to exclude unwanted rows for articles. The following example is for snapshot and transactional replication:

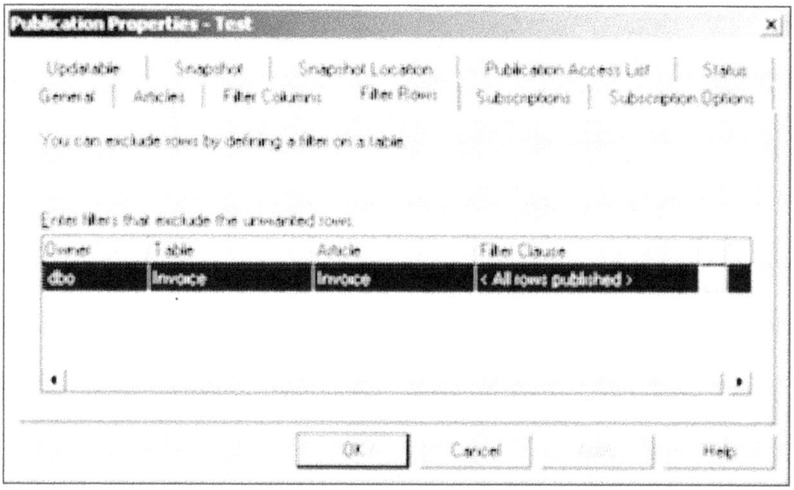


- For merge replication you also can extend filtering on a table by joining to a related table:

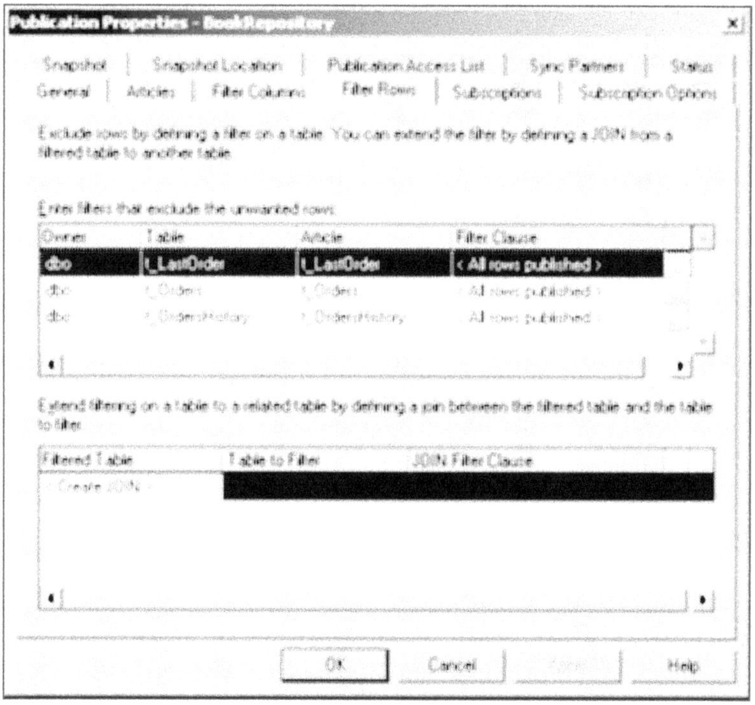

- For snapshot and transactional replication, the Subscriptions tab can control the pushing of new subscriptions, delete existing subscriptions, reinitialize individual or all subscriptions, and check subscription properties:

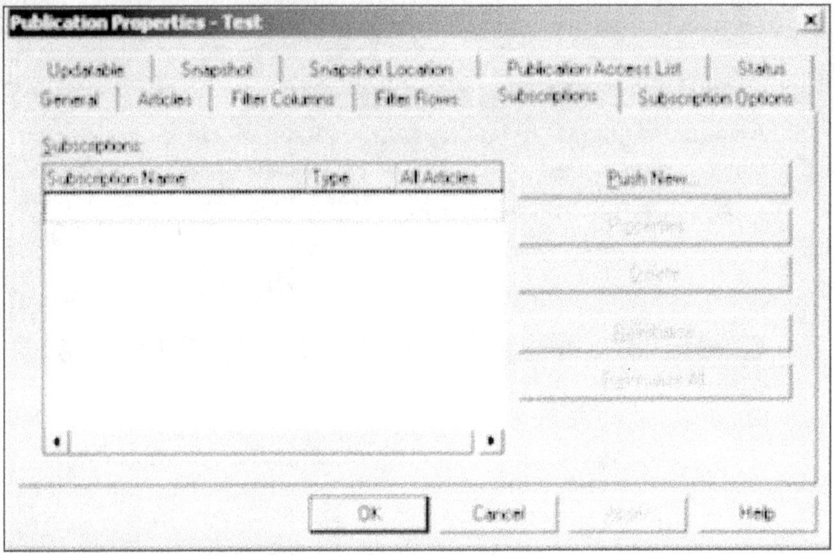


- For merge replication on the Subscriptions tab, you also have the options of viewing conflicts for a subscription or creating a dynamic snapshot job. You can limit the number of concurrent merge processes (if your system is under stress, and processing must be limited):

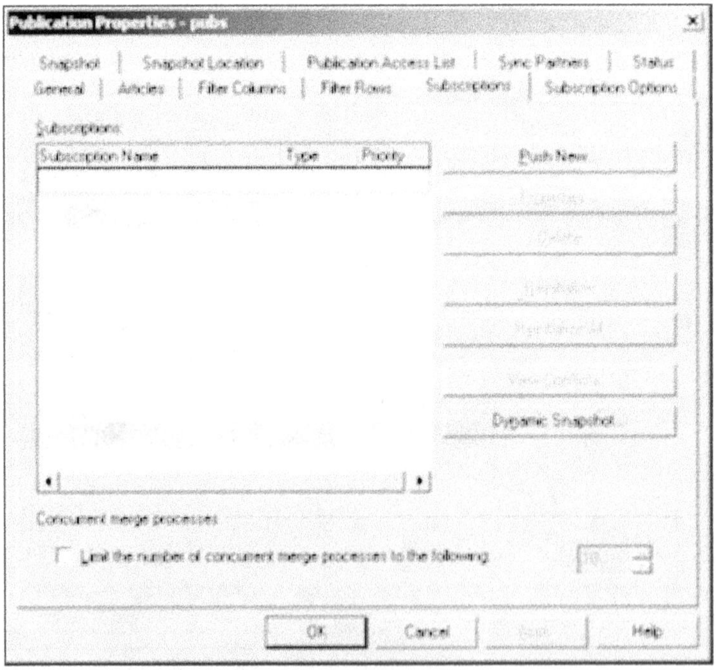

- For snapshot and transactional replication, you can specify whether or not to use a distribution agent independent of other publications in the database, and whether snapshot files are to be available to initialize new subscriptions. Sharing the distribution agent usually produces better performance. Independent distribution agents are used for anonymous or attachable database subscriptions for the publication. Also, if you are allowing anonymous or attachable database subscriptions, you must specify that snapshot files are always available to initialize new subscriptions; this means that your snapshot schema and data files will be maintained on the server for later use.

- You can also enable anonymous pull subscriptions, or create new subscriptions, by attaching a copy of the subscription database. You can enable or disable pull subscriptions for the publication from this tab. This tab also reports whether DTS is used to transform data before distributing to the subscriber:

- For merge replication, the Subscription Options tab allows you to specify whether conflict reporting is centralized at the publisher, and whether or not subscribers are validated with a system function (like HOST_NAME() or SUSER_SNAME()). This tab reports whether or not dynamic filters are used:

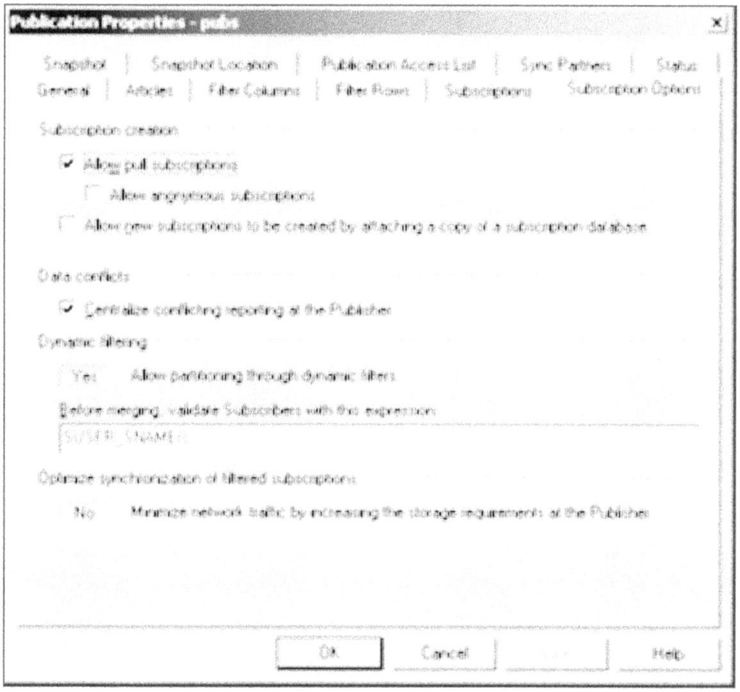

- For snapshot and transactional replication, the Updateable tab reports whether immediate updating or queued updating subscriptions are enabled:

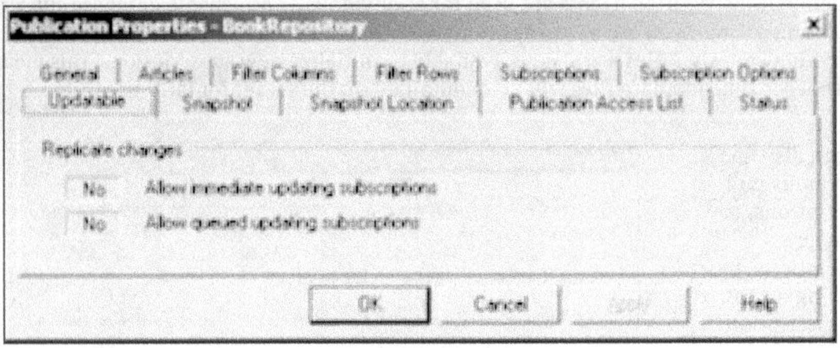


- For snapshot, transactional, and merge replication, the Snapshot folder specifies whether the snapshot data format is native (SQL Server only) or character mode format (heterogeneous subscribers). You can also select any scripts to apply before and after a snapshot is applied:

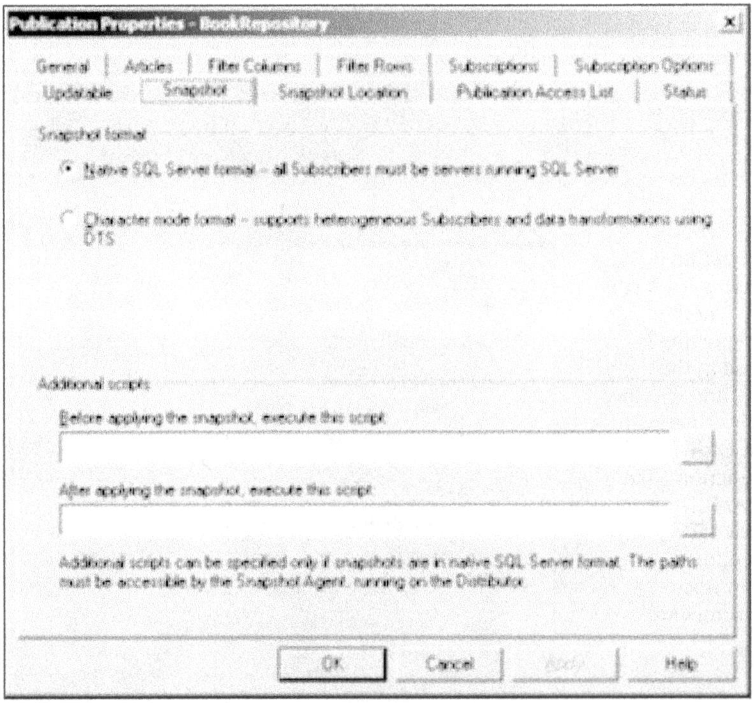


- For transactional replication, you have the additional option of not locking tables during snapshot generation. This requires that the publication be on SQL Server 2000, and the subscribers on version SQL Server 7.0 or later, and is definitely recommended for use in high traffic and concurrency environments:

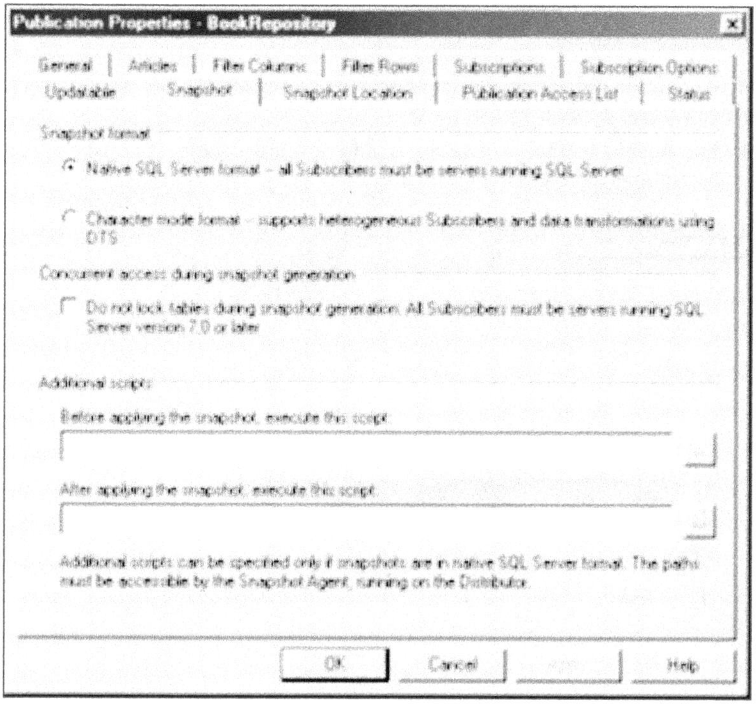


❑ The Snapshot location tab specifies whether or not the snapshot schema and data files are applied to the default snapshot folder or another location:

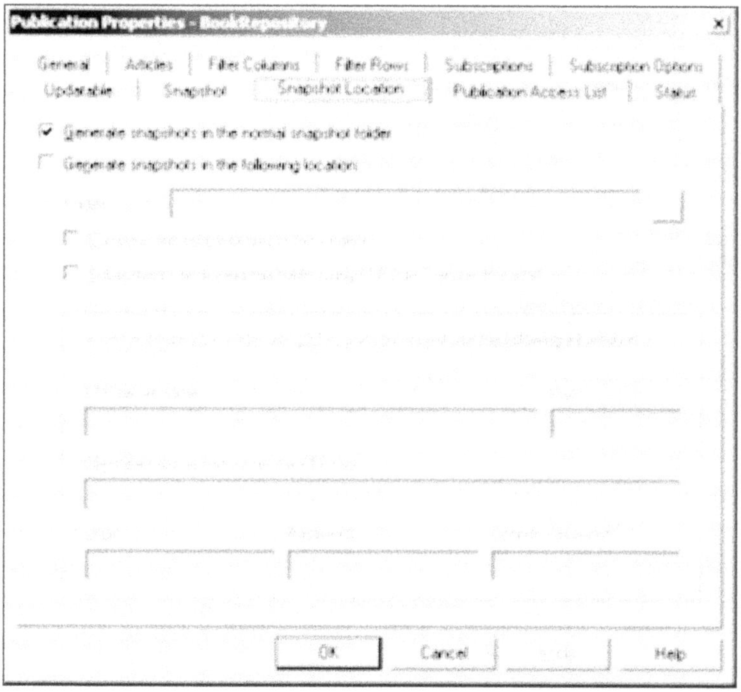

If you select another location, you will receive a dialog box warning that you are using SQL Server 2000 features exclusively.

- Select Yes to continue. After this, you can enable compression for snapshot files, and also specify that subscribers can access a folder by using FTP.
- The Publication Access List tab allows you to add or remove logins that use pull and immediate updating subscriptions to access the publication:

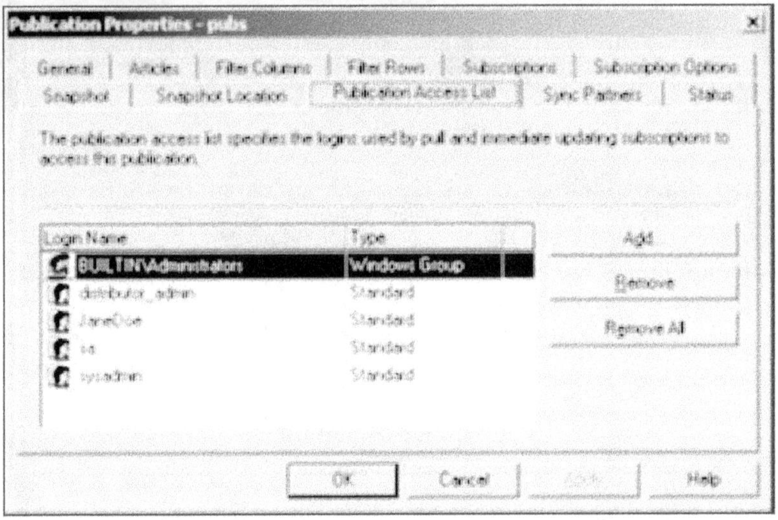


- For merge replication, the Sync Partners tab allows subscribers to synchronize with partners other than the publisher. This is useful for mobile users who may have faster access to another subscriber, or if the publication server is not available. To enable, click the checkbox:

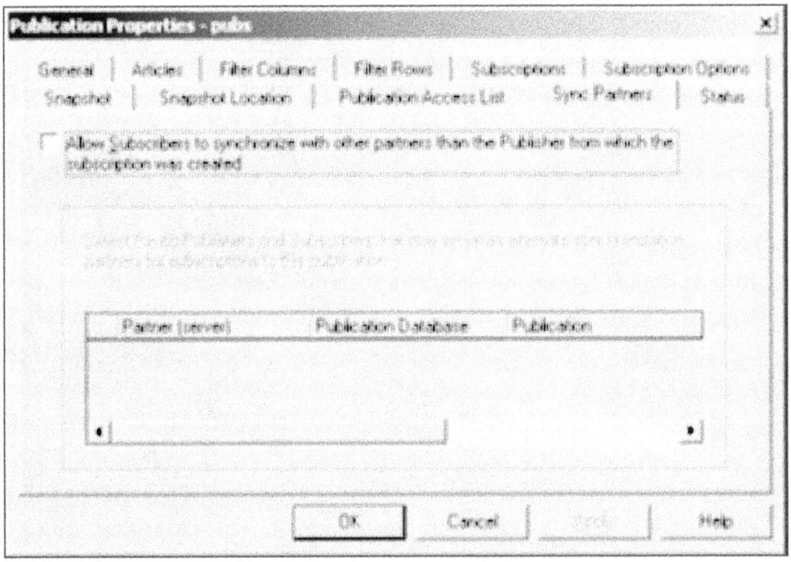

You may receive a dialog box warning that you are now using SQL Server 2000 features only.

- ❑ Select Yes to continue. You may then proceed with selecting sync partners.
- ❑ Finally, in the Status tab, you can run the snapshot agent, check agent job properties, or explore the snapshot files. You can also check the status of the SQL Server Agent service, either starting the agent or refreshing its status. This tab also reports the snapshot agent's last and next run times:

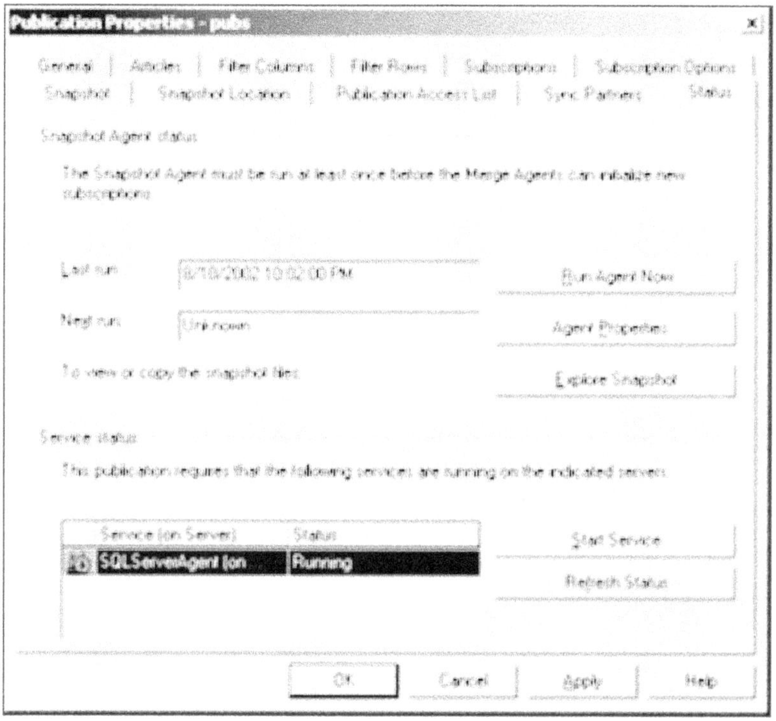


# 8.10 How to... Use Interactive Conflict Resolvers

Unlike the automatic behavior of the default and custom conflict resolvers, the interactive resolver allows you to resolve and view conflicts with merge replication manually. To allow the interactive resolver to work:

- ❑ When creating your publication, make sure Allow Subscribers to resolve conflicts interactively during on-demand synchronizations is selected in the Resolver tab of the Article Properties window:

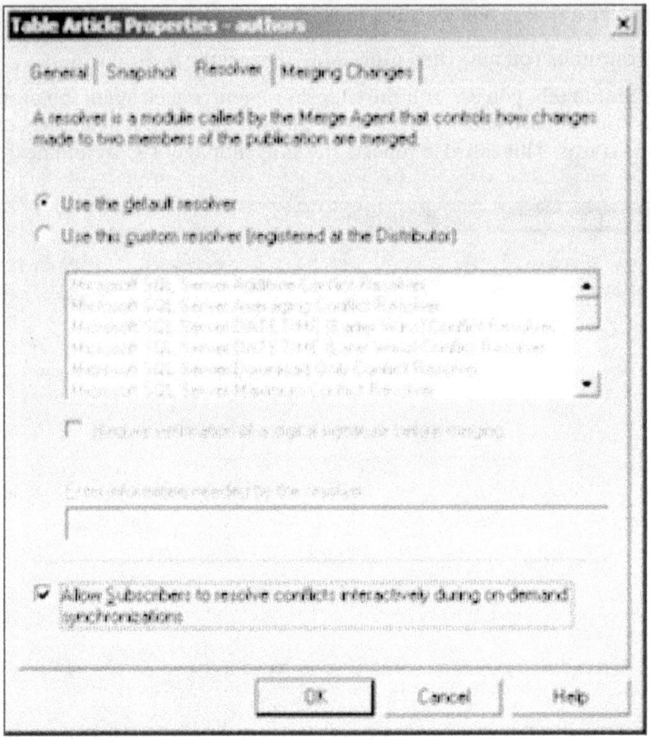


- ❑ In the Windows Synchronization Manager, select the pull subscription that you wish to have interactive resolver capabilities. Select Properties:

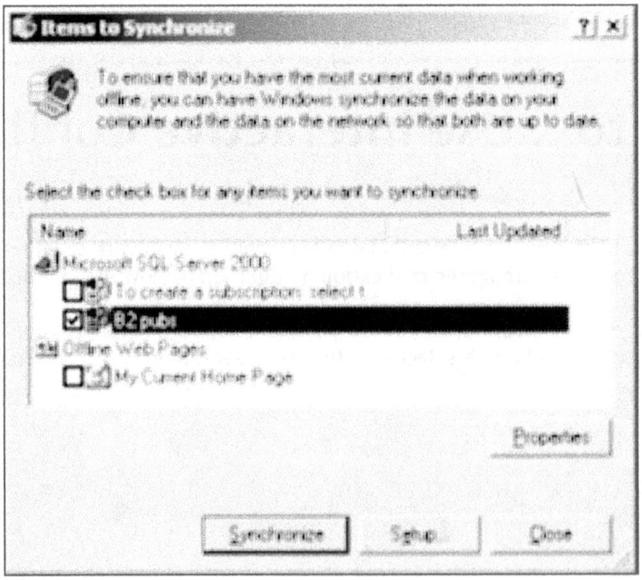

- In the Other tab, select Resolve conflicts interactively. Select Apply:

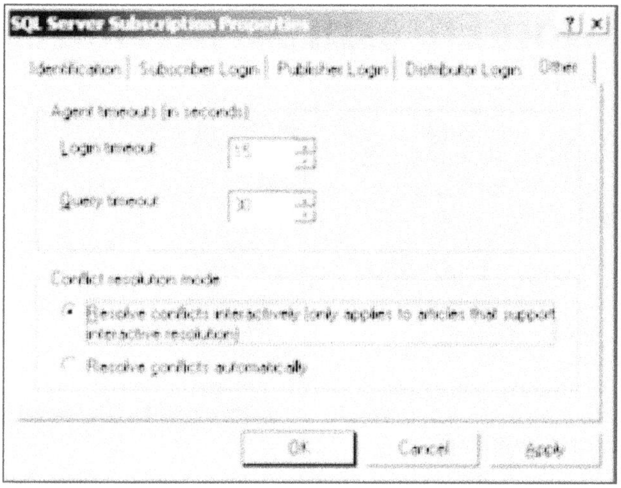


- Now, when you synchronize your pull subscription from the Windows Synchronizer, you will receive an interactive resolver dialog box when conflicts occur. For example:

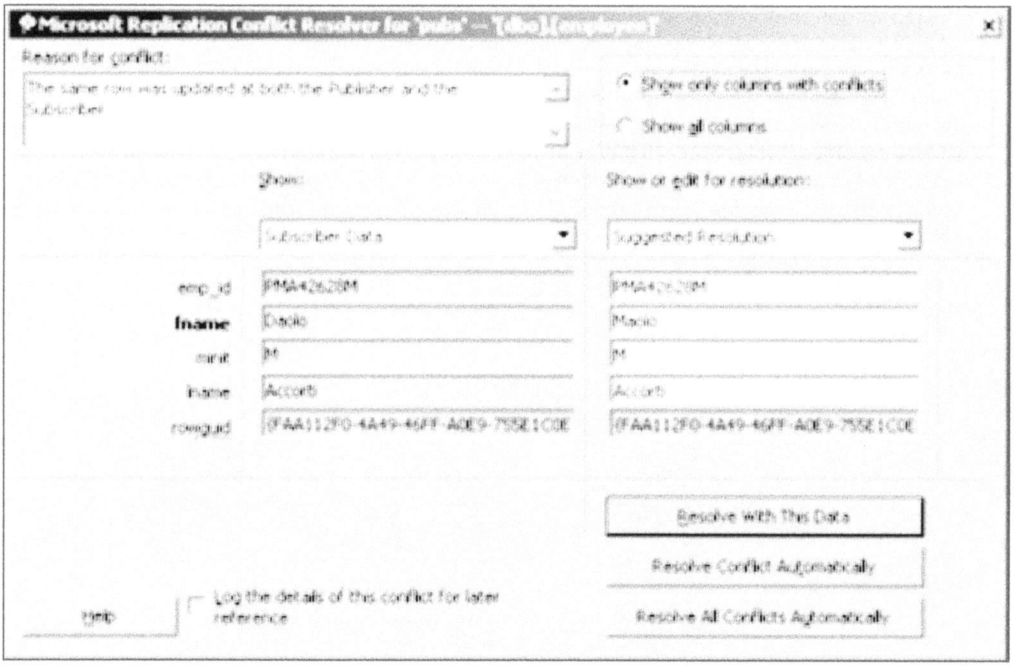


In this example, the subscriber and publisher have modified the `fname` column for the same row. Decide which row is the suggested solution and select the Resolve With This Data button. Keep in mind that you can modify the data too. You can also select to resolve this particular conflict automatically, or resolve all current conflicts automatically. If you want to keep a record of this conflict, click the checkbox for Log the details of this conflict for later reference.

# 8.11 How to... View Merge Replication Conflicts using Enterprise Manager

To view replication conflict history:

- In Enterprise Manager, expand the Replication and Publications folders, and right-click the publication for which you wish to view conflict history. Select View Conflicts...
- If any conflicts have occurred, they will be listed in the Table with conflicts screen. You can also select which publications to monitor in the Publications in 'publication name' drop-down. To view details of a conflict, select a table and click the View button:

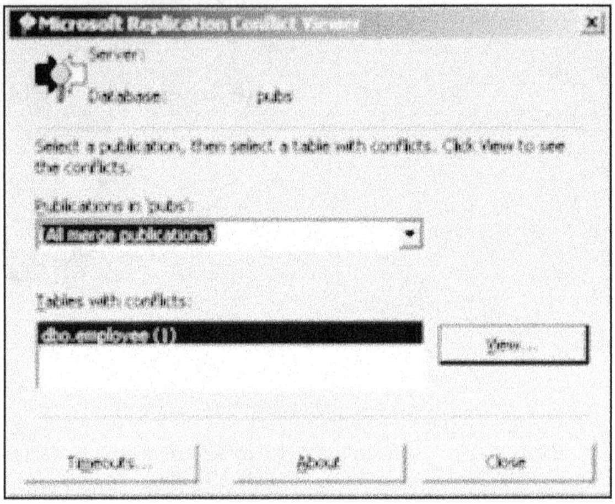


- The replication conflict viewer will display the conflict winner and loser. Within this screen, you can reverse a decision by selecting Resolve With this Data. You can modify the data in the Show or edit for resolution option, and also postpone a decision by selecting Postpone Resolution (although the winner will remain the winner until you decide otherwise). Select the checkbox, Log the details of this conflict for later, to keep this conflict history. Conflict information is held in SQL Server 2000 system-generated tables for each merge article (table). View the contents of `sysmergearticles` (specifically the `conflict_table` column) to see which table contains conflict information for each article. Also, the `msmerge_delete_conflicts` table contains information on rows that were deleted due to a lost conflict:

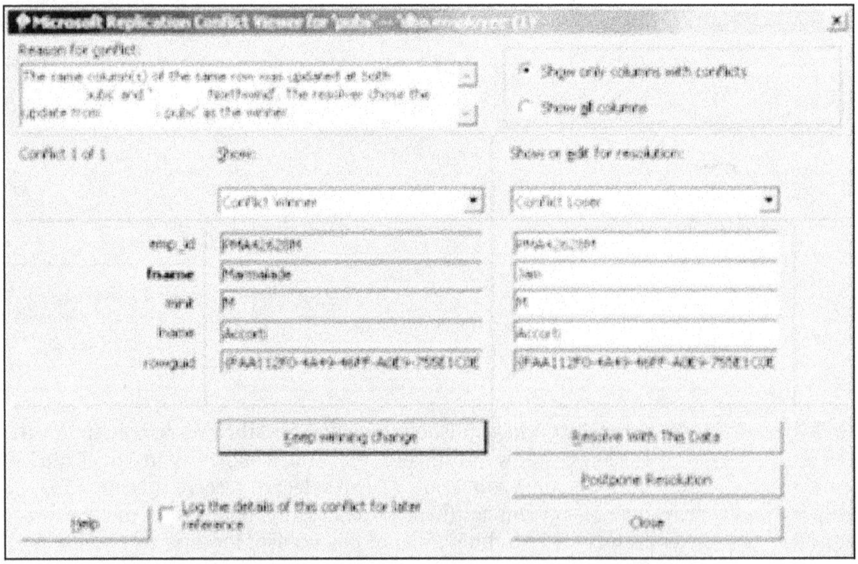

# 8.12 How to... Configure an Attachable Subscription Database

Attachable subscription databases are an excellent way to reduce network traffic and decrease the time taken to apply large snapshots. Attachable subscription databases can be used for snapshot, transactional, and merge publication types – but are only configurable for pull subscriptions. The attachable subscription functionality means that you transfer the database with existing published data and schema from one pull subscriber to another. Once the database is transferred, the pull subscription for the copied database will automatically take effect. To configure:

- ❑ In your publication properties on the Subscription Options tab, check the box for Allow new subscriptions to be created by attaching a copy of a subscription database:

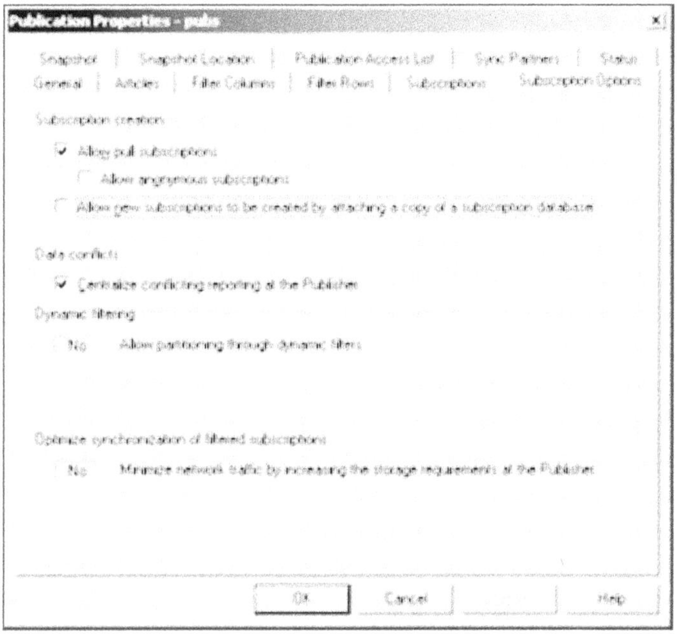

You will be warned that this functionality requires SQL Server 2000 or later at the subscribers.

- ❑ To copy a pull subscription, in Enterprise Manager expand the Replication folder, click the Subscriptions folder, right-click the pull subscription you wish to copy, and select Copy Subscription Database.
- ❑ A prompt will request where you wish to save your `*.msf` subscription file. Note that you cannot create the file until the pull subscription has been synchronized on the source subscriber.
- ❑ You will see a progress dialog box.
- ❑ To attach a new database based on the pull subscription copy, open Enterprise Manager on the new subscriber server, expand the Replication folder, right-click the Subscriptions folder, and select Attach Subscription Database.
- ❑ In the Attach Subscription Database dialog box, select the location of the `*.msf` file, the name of the new database, and the location of the new database files:

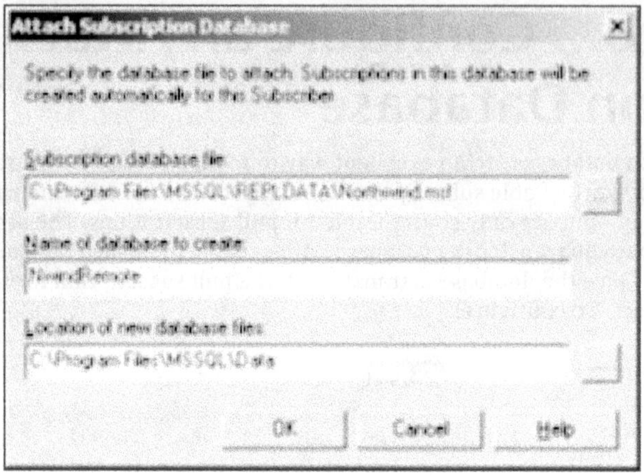


After creating the database, SQL Server will prompt you to execute `sp_addmergesubscription` at the publisher before running the merge agent for the first time:

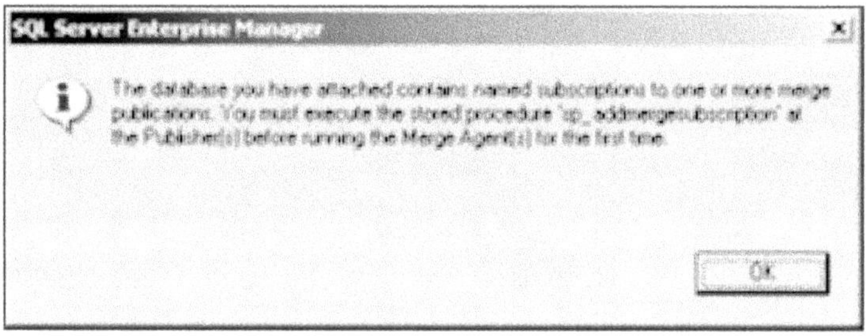


- ❑ Open Query Analyzer and connect to the publication server, set your session context to the published database, and run the suggested command from the previous step (differing according to the replication type). For example:

```
EXEC sp_addmergesubscription
@publication = N'pubs',
@subscriber = N'DOPEY\DOPEY',
@subscriber_db = N'N2',
@subscription_type = N'pull',
@subscriber_type = N'local',
@subscription_priority = 0.000000,
@sync_type = N'none'
GO
```

The following table reviews the parameters for the `sp_addmergesubscription` system stored procedure. This example includes a subset of the total available parameters. See *SQL Server Books Online* for descriptions of other options:

| Parameter | Description |
|---|---|
| @publication | The name of the publication. |
| @subscriber | The name of the subscriber SQL Server instance. |
| @subscriber_db | The name of the database subscribing to the publication. |
| @subscription_type | The type of subscription used, push or pull. |
| @subscriber_type | The type of subscriber, designating whether only the publisher, or all servers know the subscriber server. **Local** is the default; otherwise select **global**. |
| @subscription_priority | A number from 0.0 to 100.0 that indicates the priority of the subscription (for merge conflict resolution). |
| @sync_type | Sets the synchronization type of either **automatic** or **none**. If automatic, the schema and data are transferred to the subscriber prior to merge synchronization. If none, the subscriber is assumed to have the schema and initial data for the published table articles already. |

- Back at the subscriber, in Enterprise Manager, expand the Replication folder and click the Subscriptions folder. Right-click your new pull subscription, and select Start Synchronizing.

# 8.13 How to... Validate Replicated Data

If you are worried that data is not properly synchronized between the publisher and subscribers, you can validate data using either Enterprise Manager or the Transact-SQL stored procedures sp_publication_validation, sp_articlevalidation, sp_validatemergesubscription, or sp_validatemergepublication.

To validate merge replicated data via Enterprise Manager:

- Expand the Replication Monitor folder on the distributor server, and expand the Publishers folder, publisher name icon, and right-click the publication you wish to validate. Select Validate All Subscriptions.
- You will be prompted on which method to use for validation: verification of row counts only, row counts and checksums, or row counts and binary checksums (for a topology using only SQL Server 2000):
    - **Verify the row counts only**
      This validates data by calculating a rowcount at the publisher compared with the rowcount value at the subscriber.
    - **Verify the row counts and compare checksums to verify the row data**
      This validates data by comparing both a rowcount and checksum (a computed value that, although not perfect, ensures some level of uniqueness for row values) at the publisher and subscriber. This option incurs more overhead for larger publications.
    - **Verify the row counts and compare binary checksums to verify the row data (all Subscribers are servers running SQL Server 2000)**
      This validates data by calculating and comparing a binary checksum value at the publisher and subscriber. Binary checksum is similar to regular checksum, except that the value returned is more sensitive to differences in case sensitivity and collation differences:

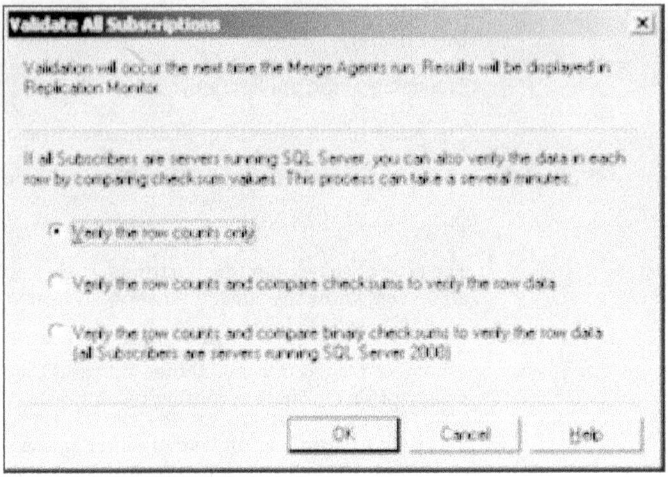


If selecting the last option, you will be warned that the subscribers must be running SQL Server 2000.

To validate transactional replication publications using Enterprise Manager:

- Expand the Replication Monitor folder on the distributor server, and expand the Publishers folder, publisher name icon, and right-click the publication you wish to validate. Select Validate Subscriptions.
- In the dialog box, decide whether to validate all subscriptions or a specific subscription.
- Click the Validation options button to specify validation methods:

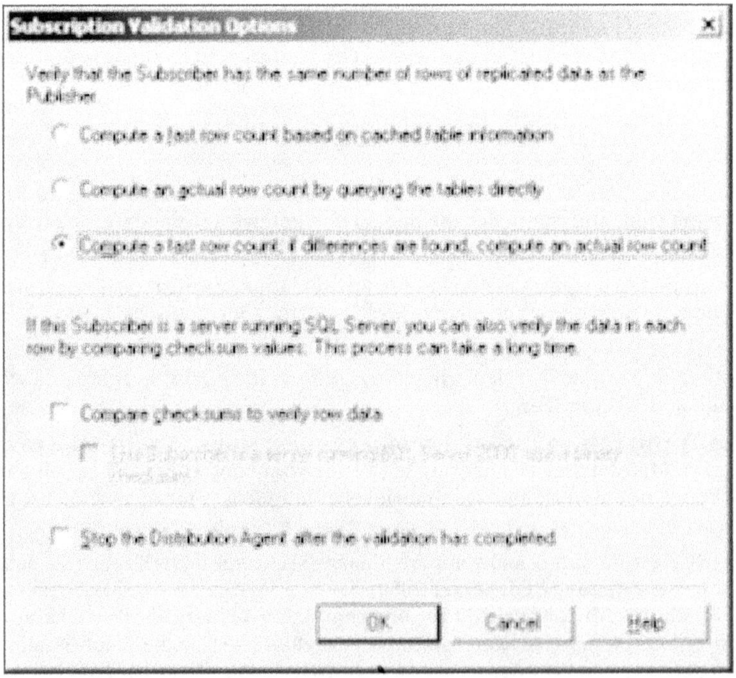

To validate transactional replication data with Transact-SQL system-stored procedures, use either sp_publication_validation or sp_article_validation.

The sp_publication_validation stored procedure is intended for use with transactional replication, and checks each article in the publication. Execute this within the context of the publication database. The syntax for sp_publication_validation from *SQL Server Books Online* is as follows:

```
sp_publication_validation [ @publication = ] 'publication'
  [ , [ @rowcount_only = ] type_of_check_requested ]
  [ , [ @full_or_fast = ] full_or_fast ]
  [ , [ @shutdown_agent = ] shutdown_agent ]
```

| Parameter | Description |
|---|---|
| @publication = | Publication name to validate. |
| @rowcount_only = | If equal to 1, returns the row count only. This is the default value. |
| | If equal to 0, performs a SQL Server 7.0 compatible checksum. |
| | If equal to 2, performs both a rowcount and checksum. |
| @full_or_fast = | If equal to 0, performs a full row count using COUNT(*). |
| | If equal to 1, performs a row count from sysindexes.rows (may be inaccurate). |
| | If equal to 2 (default), tries sysindexes.rows first. If any problems are identified, full row counts are used instead. |
| @shutdown_agent = | If equal to 1, the replication agent shuts down after validation. |
| | If equal to 0 (default), the distribution agent is not shut down. |

## Example 8.13.1: Validating a publication

To validate a transactional replication publication, Northwind, using rowcount, checksum and COUNT(*) rowcounts:

```
sp_publication_validation @publication ='Northwind'
  , @rowcount_only = 2
  , @full_or_fast = 0
  , @shutdown_agent = 0
```

In this example, you receive the rows stating whether or not expected results were generated:

Generated expected rowcount value of 226 and expected checksum value of 6715863886 for employees.
Generated expected rowcount value of 5 and expected checksum value of 14318298 for authors.
Generated expected rowcount value of 1 and expected checksum value of -65796633 for Books
Generated expected rowcount value of 5 and expected checksum value of -1675878485 for Timestamp.

The sp_article_validation stored procedure performs validation checks on a single article. This procedure is intended for transactional replication publications. The syntax from *SQL Server Books Online* is as follows:

```
sp_article_validation [ @publication = ] 'publication'
    [ , [ @article = ] 'article' ]
    [ , [ @rowcount_only = ] type_of_check_requested ]
    [ , [ @full_or_fast = ] full_or_fast ]
    [ , [ @shutdown_agent = ] shutdown_agent ]
    [ , [ @subscription_level = ] subscription_level ]
    [ , [ @reserved = ] reserved ]
```

| Parameter | Description |
|---|---|
| @publication = | Publication name to validate. |
| @article = | Article to validate. |
| @rowcount_only = | If equal to 1, returns the row count only. This is the default value. |
| | If equal to 0, performs a SQL Server 7.0 compatible checksum. |
| | If equal to 2, performs both a rowcount and checksum. |
| @full_or_fast = | If equal to 0, performs a full row count using COUNT(*). |
| | If equal to 1, performs a row count from sysindexes.rows (may be inaccurate). |
| | If equal to 2 (default), tries sysindexes.rows first. If any problems are identified, full row counts are used instead. |
| @shutdown_agent = | If equal to 1, the replication agent shuts down after validation. |
| | If equal to 0 (default), the distribution agent is not shut down. |
| @subscription_level = | If equal to 1, validation is only applied to subscribers specified by the sp_marksubscriptionvalidation call (this procedure marks an open transaction to be a subscription level validation transaction for a specific subscriber). |
| | If equal to 0 (default), all subscribers are validated. |
| @reserved = | Do not use. |

## Example 8.13.2: Validating an article

To validate the authors article from the Northwind database, validating checksum, full row using COUNT(*), shutting down the agent when complete (if there are validation issues, you may not want to have the distribution agent continue to run, until you resolve the problem), and validating all subscribers:

```
sp_article_validation @publication = 'Northwind'
    , @article = 'authors'
    , @rowcount_only = 0
    , @full_or_fast = 0
  , @shutdown_agent = 1
  , @subscription_level = 0
```

In this example, you receive one row reporting expected values for the authors table:

Generated expected rowcount value of 226 and expected checksum value of 21669620020 for authors.

To validate merge replication using Transact-SQL, use the `sp_validatemergesubscription` or `sp_validatemergepublication` system stored procedures.

The `sp_validatemergepublication` stored procedure validates data for all subscriptions to the publication. The stored procedure should be executed at the publication database, and only takes two parameters: publication name and validation level.

If selecting a validation level of 1, rowcount-only validation is performed. If selecting a validation level of 2, rowcount and checksum validation is performed. If selecting a validation level of 3, rowcount and binary checksum validation is run (can be used for SQL Server 2000 subscribers only).

### Example 8.13.3: Validating all subscribers

To validate all subscribers with a rowcount and binary checksum:

```
sp_validatemergepublication @publication = 'pubs' , @level = 3
```

The `sp_validatemergesubscription` performs merge replication data validation for a specific subscription. Like `sp_validatemergepublication`, this procedure should be run from the published database context. The syntax includes parameters to specify publisher, subscriber, subscriber database, and validation level (same value options as `sp_validatemergepublication`).

### Example 8.13.4: Validating a specific subscriber

To validate a specific subscriber with rowcount only:

```
sp_validatemergesubscription @publication = 'pubs'
  , @subscriber = 'JOEREMOTE'
  , @subscriber_db = 'Pubs2'
  , @level = 1
```

# 8.14 How to... Launch Replication Wizards from Enterprise Manager

To view a list of replication-related wizards in Enterprise Manager:

- Expand Server Group and registration.
- Click the Databases folder.
- Go to Tools | Wizards.
- Expand the Replication node to view all replication-related wizards:
- Click the wizard you would like to launch and select OK.

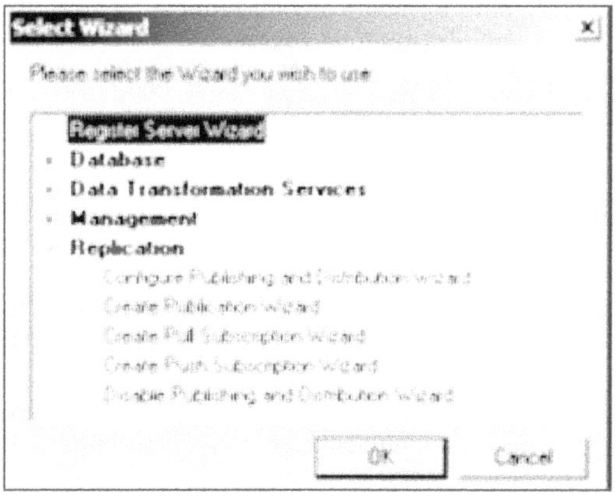

# 8.15 How to... Create and Manage Publications in Enterprise Manager

One method of creating and managing your server publications is to use the Create and Manage Publications dialog box in Enterprise Manager:

- ❑ Expand Server Group and registration.
- ❑ Click the Databases folder.
- ❑ Go to Tools | Replication | Create and Manage publications.
- ❑ From this dialog box, you can launch the Create Publication wizard, push a new subscription, open the publication properties dialog box, script the publication, or delete the publication:

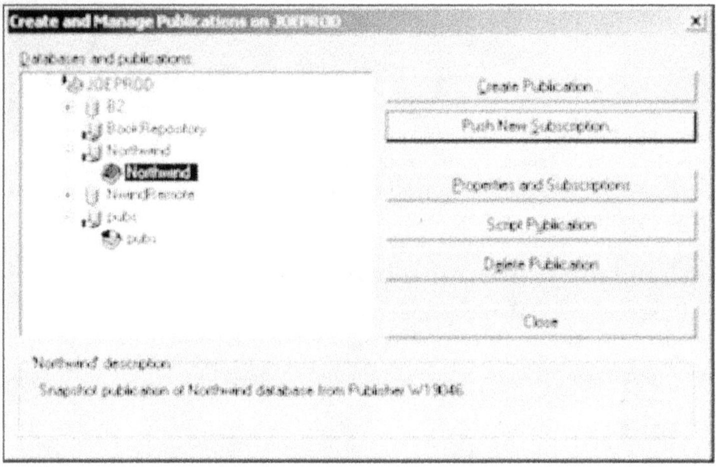


# 8.16 How to... Generate a Transact-SQL Script of Your Publication and Subscribers

Scripting a publication and subscribers allows you to:

- ❑ Keep a backup of your replication topology configuration, allowing you to rebuild the publication and subscribers if necessary.
- ❑ Save time when you need to delete your publication temporarily, or migrate it to a new server.

To script a publication and subscribers:

- ❑ Expand Server Group and registration.
- ❑ Click the Databases folder.
- ❑ Go to Tools | Replication | Generate SQL Script.
- ❑ In the General tab, you can choose whether distributor properties should be scripted, which publications to script, which pull subscriptions to include, and whether to script the creation or the dropping of the components. You can also script the creation of the replication jobs. Select the Preview button to see what is scripted:

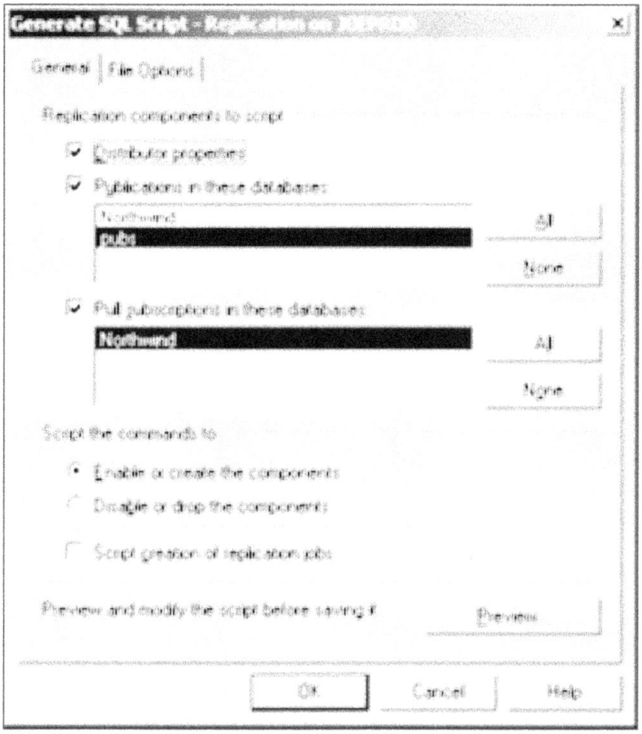


- In the File Options tab, choose the file format, and decide whether or not the script should be appended to an existing file. Select OK:

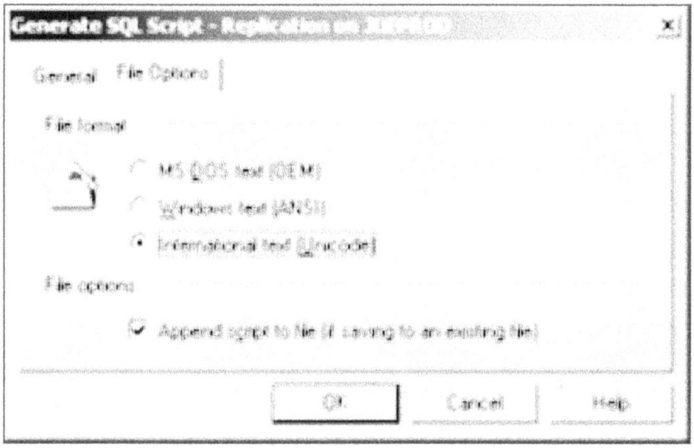


- You will be prompted for a file location.

# 8.17 How to... Configure Topology Roles from Enterprise Manager

To configure the topology roles of your server:

- Expand Server Group and Server registration.
- Click the Databases folder.
- Go to Tools | Replication menu | Configure Publishing, Subscribers, and Distribution...
- In the Distributor tab, you can configure the properties of the distribution database or databases. You can also configure **agent profiles** (see the next section):

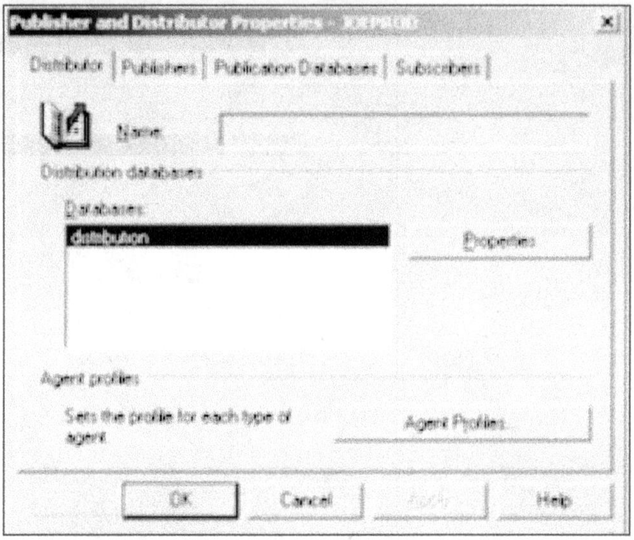


- The Distribution Database Properties dialog box allows you to specify how long transactional and historical replication history is retained in the database:

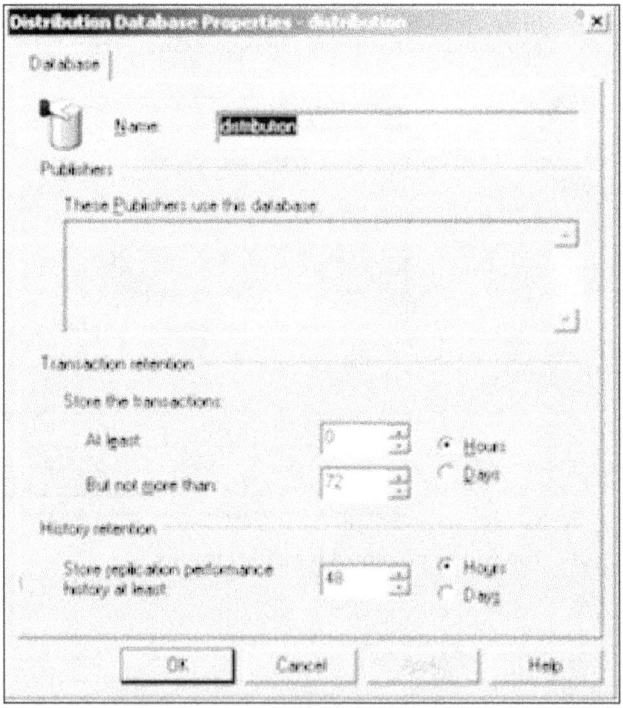

- The Publishers tab allows you to configure which servers use the current server as a distributor:

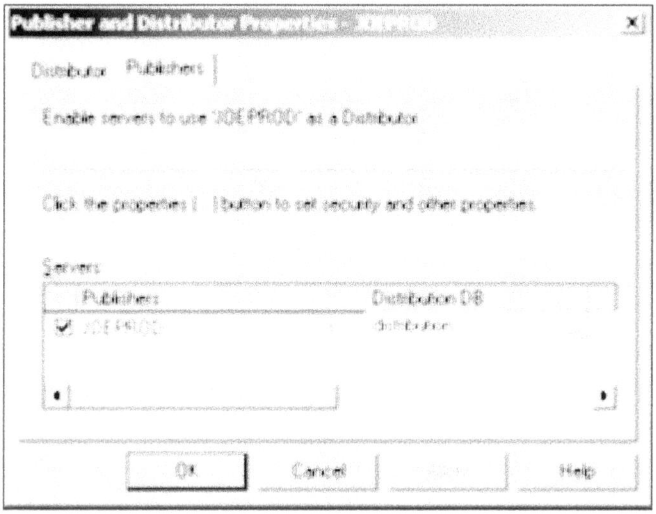

Selecting the ellipsis for the server row will show publisher properties, which includes information on the snapshot folder location and the login type for the replication agent connection.

- The Publication Database tab allows you to enable databases for transactional (which includes snapshot) replication, or merge replication:

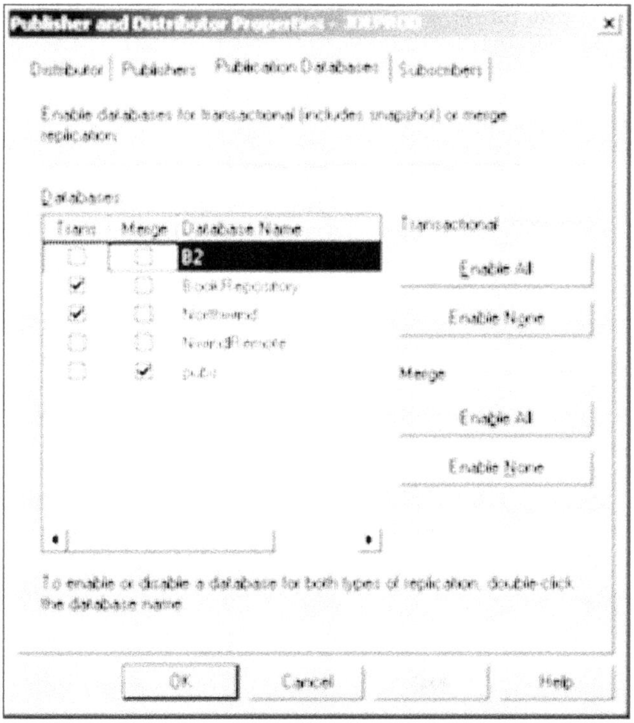

- In the Subscribers tab, enable servers that can subscribe to your publications

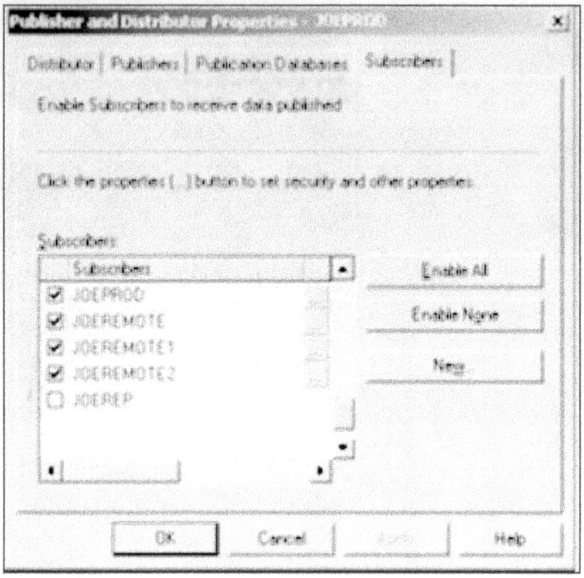


Select the ellipsis button to configure subscriber security options. The Subscriber Properties dialog box, on the General tab, allows you to define the publisher's agent (replication agent) connection method to the subscriber server. Selecting Impersonate the SQL Server Agent account on Distributor Server Name (trusted connection) means that the same Windows authentication account used by the distributor's SQL Server Agent is also used to connect to the subscriber.

- When selecting Use SQL Server Authentication, you select the login name and password of the account used to connect from the distributor to the subscriber SQL Server instance:

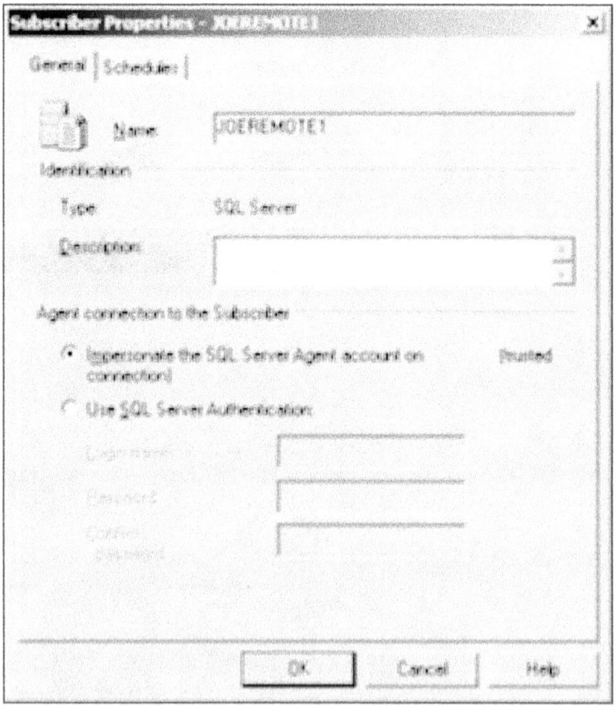

# 8.18 How to... Configure Agent Profiles

Replication agent profiles control the behavior of the distribution, merge, snapshot, log reader, and queue reader processes. A profile contains separate property settings, for which each agent type has unique options. You may find that you need to configure agent profile settings according to your environment or topology, or any unique problems that your network or servers may have.

One method of configuring agent profiles is as follows:

- ❑ Expand the Server Group and registration.
- ❑ Click the Databases folder.
- ❑ Select Tools | Replication | Configure Publishing, Subscribers, and Distribution...
- ❑ In the Publisher and Distributor Properties window, in the Distributor tab, click the Agent Profiles button.
- ❑ The Distribution tab shows profiles available, and the currently selected profile. There are also tabs for Merge, Snapshot, Log Reader, and Queue Reader profile settings. You can configure the agent to use a new profile by clicking the bullet point in the Default column. Create new profiles by clicking the New Profile button, or delete profiles by clicking the Delete button (user-created profiles only). To view the details of a specific profile, click the profile and the View Details button:

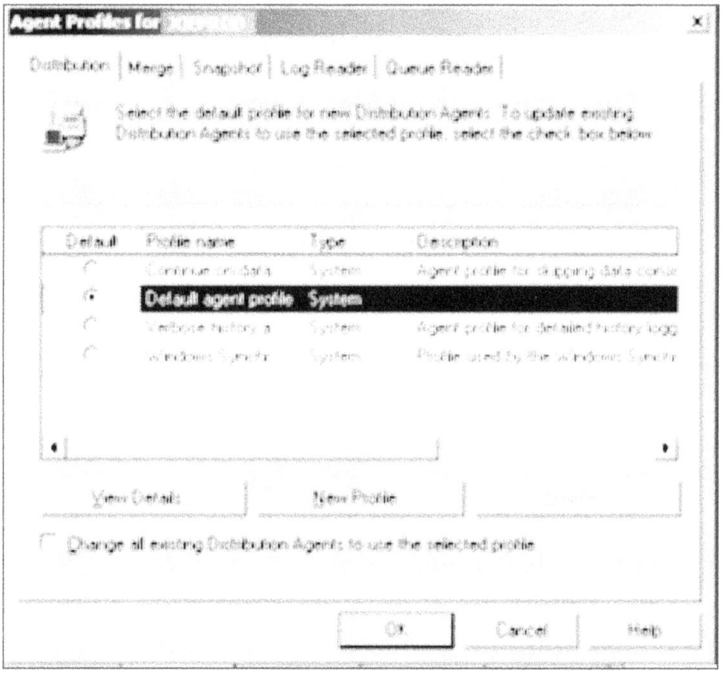

- The profile parameters and associated values are then listed, and can be modified:

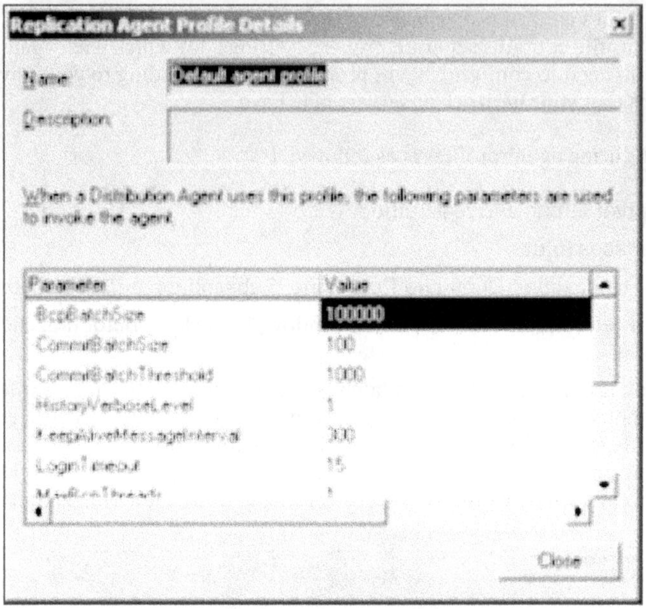


The following table sets out each agent's associated parameters and describes what each parameter configures:

| Agent Type | Parameter | Description |
|---|---|---|
| Distribution<br>Merge<br>Snapshot | `-BcpBatchSize` | Number of rows to send to a server in one transaction. If you have many updates to your publication or subscriber, consider increasing this number so round trips are reduced. The default value is 100,000. |
| Merge | `-ChangesPerHistory` | Transaction upload and download threshold before a message is logged to the SQL Server system replication tables. The default value is 100. |
| Distribution | `-CommitBatchSize` | Transactions issued before a `COMMIT` statement is generated on the subscriber. The default value is 100. |
| Distribution | `-CommitBatchThreshold` | Replication commands issued before a `COMMIT` statement is generated on the subscriber. The default value is 1000. |

| Agent Type | Parameter | Description |
|---|---|---|
| Merge | -DownloadGenerationsPerBatch | Number of generations per batch to be processed from the publisher to the subscriber (generation being a group of changes per article). Increasing this value can reduce the number of batches for publications or subscribers with heavy transaction updates. The default value is 100. |
| Merge | -DownloadReadChangesPerBatch | Changes read in one batch when download of changes from publisher to subscriber is in progress. The default value is 100. |
| Merge | -DownloadWriteChangesPerBatch | Changes to be applied to subscriber when downloaded from publisher. The default value is 100. |
| Merge | -FastRowCount | When set to 1, uses the fast method to calculate row counts (`syindexes.rows`). Otherwise, when set to 0, uses full `COUNT(*)` method. The default value is 1. |
| Distribution<br>Merge<br>Snapshot<br>Log Reader<br>Queue Reader | -HistoryVerboseLevel | If set to 1, updates a previous history message of the same status. If set to 2, inserts new history records for activities, but does not do so for idle messages or long-running jobs. These are updated on previous records. If set to 3, new records are inserted except for idle messages. The default value is 1. |
| Merge | -KeepAliveMessageInterval | Number of seconds before the agent will be marked as suspect by the checkup agent (increase this for long batches), due to existing connections waiting for a response. The default value is 300. |
| Distribution<br>Merge<br>Snapshot<br>Log Reader<br>Queue Reader | -LoginTimeOut | Number of seconds before a login attempt times out. The default value is 15. |

*Table continued on following page*

| Agent Type | Parameter | Description |
|---|---|---|
| Distribution<br>Snapshot | -MaxBcpThreads | Determines parallel bulk copy operations. Increasing this number may make the snapshot bulk copy operations run faster. One thread per article is usually sufficient, but watch your system resources to make sure you are not exceeding system capabilities. The default value is 1. |
| Distribution | -MaxDeliveredTransactions | Limits number of push or pull transactions applied to a subscriber in one synchronization. The default value is 0. |
| Merge | -MaxDownloadChanges | Maximum changes downloaded per merge session. The default value is 0. |
| Merge | -MaxUploadChanges | Maximum changes uploaded per merge session. The default value is 0. |
| Merge | -NumDeadlockRetries | Number of times the agent retries an operation after being deadlocked. The default value is 5. |
| Distribution<br>Merge<br>Log Reader<br>Queue Reader | -PollingInterval | Determines number of seconds the distribution database gets queried for replicated transactions. Increase this interval if you find that performance is suffering due to frequent polling. The default value is 60. |
| Distribution<br>Merge<br>Snapshot<br>Log Reader<br>Queue Reader | -QueryTimeout | The number of seconds before a query sent by the agent times out. Good to configure for large batch processing over slow network connections. The default value is 300. |
| Log Reader | -ReadBatchSize | Maximum transactions read from the transaction log by the log reader agent. The default value is 500. |
| Log Reader | -ReadBatchThreshold | Number of commands read from the transaction log before moving the updates to the subscriber. The default value is 100. |
| Distribution | -SkipErrors | Number of errors the distribution agent will skip before processing is stopped. The default value is NULL (not configured). |

| Agent Type | Parameter | Description |
|---|---|---|
| Distribution | -SkipFailureLevel | If set to 0, the distribution agent will not skip errors. If set to 1, errors will be skipped according to the -SkipErrors flagged. The default value is 1. |
| Merge | -StartQueueTimeout | Maximum number of seconds that the agent will wait for a free process thread (when processes are at the limit). The default value is 0. |
| Distribution | -TransactionsPerHistory | Defines at what number of transactions a history row is logged. The default value is 100. |
| Merge | -UploadGenerationsPerBatch | Number of generations processed in a batch during an upload from subscriber to publisher. Increase this number if you have excessive updates on the publisher and subscriber, and wish to reduce the number of batches. The default value is 100. |
| Merge | -UploadReadChangesPerBatch | Number of changes read in one batch during upload from subscriber to publisher. The default value is 100. |
| Merge | -UploadWriteChangesPerBatch | Number of changes applied in one batch during upload from subscriber to publisher. The default value is 100. |
| Merge<br>Distribution | -UseInprocLoader | The -UseInprocloader property uses the BULK INSERT command to load snapshot files to the subscriber, potentially increasing performance for larger snapshots significantly.<br><br>You will not find this setting in a profile, but rather you must add it manually to the distribution agent or merge agent step in the SQL Server job command text box. For example, the string of the job step would look something like this:<br><br>Publisher [DOPEY\|DOPEY] -UseInprocLoader [PublisherDB] BookRepository... |

*Table continued on following page*

| Agent Type | Parameter | Description |
|---|---|---|
| Merge | -Validate | If set to 0, no row validation is performed after the merge session finishes changes. If set to 1, rowcount-only is validated. If set to 2, rowcount and checksum validation is executed. If set to 3, binary checksum validation is executed (SQL Server 2000 only). The default value is 0. |
| Merge | -ValidateInterval | Frequency number of minutes before subscription is validated (continuous mode only). The default value is 60. |

# 8.19 How to... Disable Publishing and Distribution on Your Server

To disable publishing and distribution on your server:

- Expand Server Group and registration.
- Click the Databases folder.
- Select Tools | Replication | Disable Publishing...
- Select Next at the Disable Publishing and Distribution Wizard startup dialog box.
- Select Yes to disable publishing, associated subscriptions (for dropped publications), and to disable the distributor on the current server:

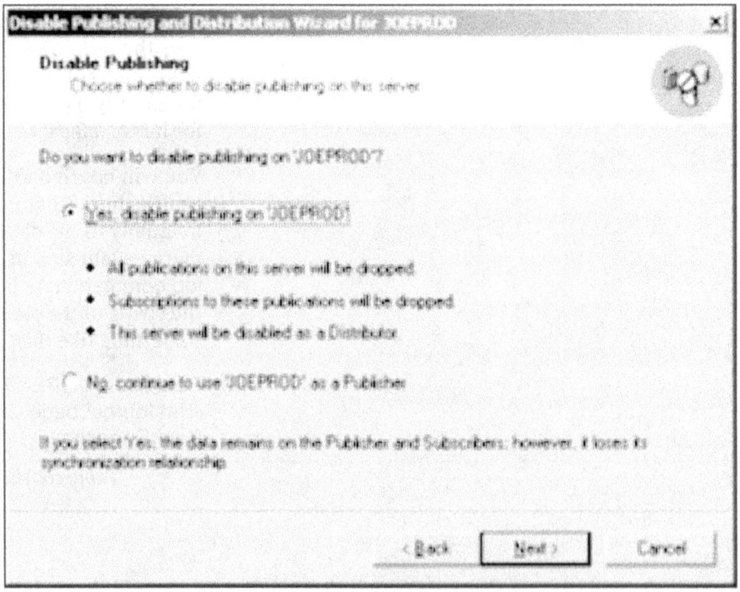

- You will receive a confirmation of publications and subscriptions to be dropped:

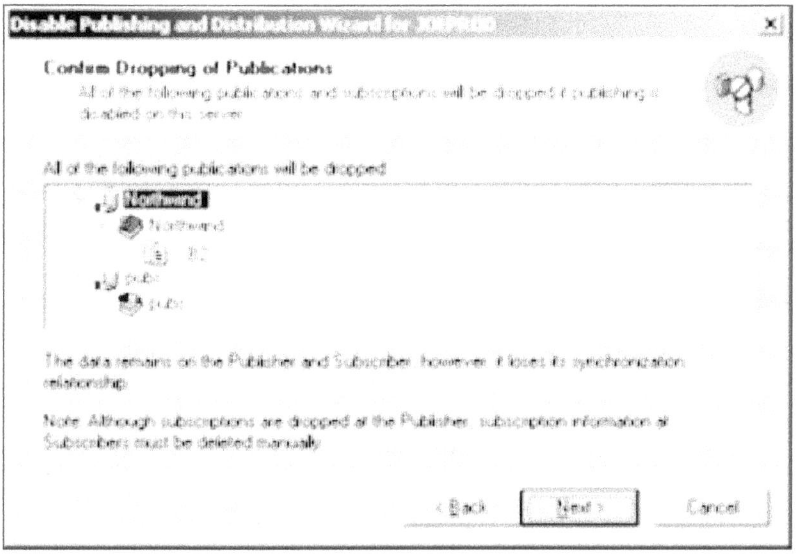

- Select Finish to initiate the removal.

# Replication System Tables

Before reviewing how to troubleshoot replication, it sometimes helps to understand where the replication configurations are stored within SQL Server.

For example, if you are unable to add a new publication because one with the same name already exists, you could check the `MSpublications` table in the distribution database to see if a row exists for the publication (problems can occur when replication has not been removed or added properly, due to an interruption or other issue).

The following table reviews each table that participates in replication, the database where it can be found, and a description of what it is used for. For detailed reviews of the columns in each table, see the associated replication system table name topic in *SQL Server Books Online*:

| Name | Database | Purpose |
|---|---|---|
| `MSagent_parameters` | distribution | Contains agent profile parameter settings. |
| `MSagent_profiles` | distribution | Contains one row for each replication agent profile. |
| `MSarticles` | distribution | Contains one row for each publication article. |
| `MSdistpublishers` | distribution | Contains one row for each publisher the local distributor supports. |

*Table continued on following page*

| Name | Database | Purpose |
|---|---|---|
| `MSdistribution_agents` | distribution | Contains one row for each distribution agent running on the local distributor. |
| `MSdistribution_history` | distribution | Contains execution history for the distribution agents. |
| `MSdistributiondbs` | distribution | Contains one row for each distribution database defined on the local distributor. |
| `MSdistributor` | distribution | Contains properties of the local distributor. |
| `MSlogreader_agents` | distribution | Contains a row for each log reader agent on the local distributor. |
| `MSlogreader_history` | distribution | Contains execution history for the log reader agents. |
| `MSmerge_agents` | distribution | Contains a row for each merge agent running on the local subscriber. |
| `MSmerge_contents` | publication and subscription databases | Has one row for each change made in the publication or subscription databases since they were published. |
| `MSmerge_delete_conflicts` | publication database (but can be subscriber too) | Lists rows deleted because of a merge conflict. |
| `MSmerge_genhistory` | publication subscription | Contains one row for each generation (batch of changes that must be applied) that a subscriber is aware of. This helps avoid sending redundant regenerations, or to trigger sending them when a subscriber needs to be resynchronized. |
| `MSmerge_history` | distribution | Contains execution history for updates made to the subscriber via merge replication. |
| `MSmerge_replinfo` | publication subscription | Tracks information on sent and received generations for each subscription, for merge replication. |
| `MSmerge_subscriptions` | distribution | Contains a row for each subscription replicated to via the local subscriber merge agent. |
| `MSmerge_tombstone` | publication subscription | Lists deleted rows, for tracking deletions that must be propagated to other subscribers. |

| Name | Database | Purpose |
|---|---|---|
| MSpublication_access | distribution | Contains a row for each SQL Server login with access to a specific publication or publisher. |
| Mspublications | distribution | Contains a row for each publication replicated by a publisher. |
| MSpublisher_databases | distribution | Contains a row for each publisher and its associated publication(s) serviced by the local distribution database. |
| MSrepl_commands | distribution | Contains rows of replicated commands. |
| MSrepl_errors | distribution | Contains expanded error information on distribution and merge agent failures. |
| MSrepl_originators | distribution | Contains a row for each updatable subscriber, name of the updating server, and updating database. |
| MSrepl_transactions | distribution | Contains a row for each replicated transaction (includes sequence and transaction time). |
| MSrepl_version | distribution | Contains information on the current version of replication installed (version of the distribution database, which can change with hotfixes and service packs). |
| MSreplication_objects | subscription | Contains a row for each table or trigger associated with replication for the subscriber database. |
| MSreplication_subscriptions | subscription | Contains one row for each distribution agent replicating to the local subscriber database. |
| MSsnapshot_agents | distribution | Contains one row for each snapshot agent on the local distributor. |
| MSsnapshot_history | distribution | Contains execution history for the snapshot agents on the local distributor. |
| MSsubscriber_info | distribution | Has a row for each publisher/subscriber pair being pushed from the local distributor. |
| MSsubscriber_schedule | distribution | Contains merge and transactional synchronization schedules for each publisher/subscriber serviced by the local distributor. |
| MSsubscription_properties | distribution | Contains rows for pull distribution agents (connection info, publication type). |

*Table continued on following page*

| Name | Database | Purpose |
|---|---|---|
| MSsubscriptions | distribution | Contains one row for each subscription serviced by the local distributor. |
| sysarticles | publication database | Contains one row for each article defined for the local database. |
| sysarticleupdates | publication database | Lists articles that support immediate-updating subscriptions. |
| sysdatabases | master | Has one row for each database for the SQL Server instance. The column category includes a value designating whether or not the database is published, subscribed, merge-published, or merge-subscribed. |
| sysmergearticles | publication database | Contains one row for each merge article in the local database. |
| sysmergepublications | publication database | Contains one row for each merge publication defined for the local database. |
| sysmergeschemachange | publication subscription | Tracks articles generated by the snapshot agent. |
| sysmergesubscriptions | publication subscription | Tracks each known subscriber to the merge publication. |
| sysmergesubsetfilters | publication subscription | Lists join filters for partitioned articles. |
| syspublications | publication database | Lists one row for each publication defined for the local database. |
| sysreplicationalerts | msdb | Has information about alerts related to replication. |
| sysservers | master | Has one row for each server that the SQL Server instance can access as an OLE DB data source. The pub column is a bit value that determines whether the data source is a publisher. The sub column is a bit value that determines whether the data source is a subscriber. The dist column determines whether the data source is a distributor. The dpub determines whether the data source is both a distributor and publisher. |
| syssubscriptions | publication database | Lists one row for each subscription for the local database. |

# 8.20 How to... Find Help Troubleshooting Replication Problems

With so much functionality comes a wide array of potential problems; most of these are configuration-based issues (the result of not planning ahead); some are caused by outside problems (such as slow network connection, network outage) and, on rare occasions, you may encounter bugs.

Knowing where to look is the key to troubleshooting a replication problem; when researching a failed replication, gather your information from the following resources:

- Use Replication Monitor to identify the failing components. When one agent out of several is failing, a visual red X indicator often points out the culprit.
- Examine your agent history. Do so by right clicking an agent in Replication Monitor and selecting Agent History. Look for items with red checkmarks:

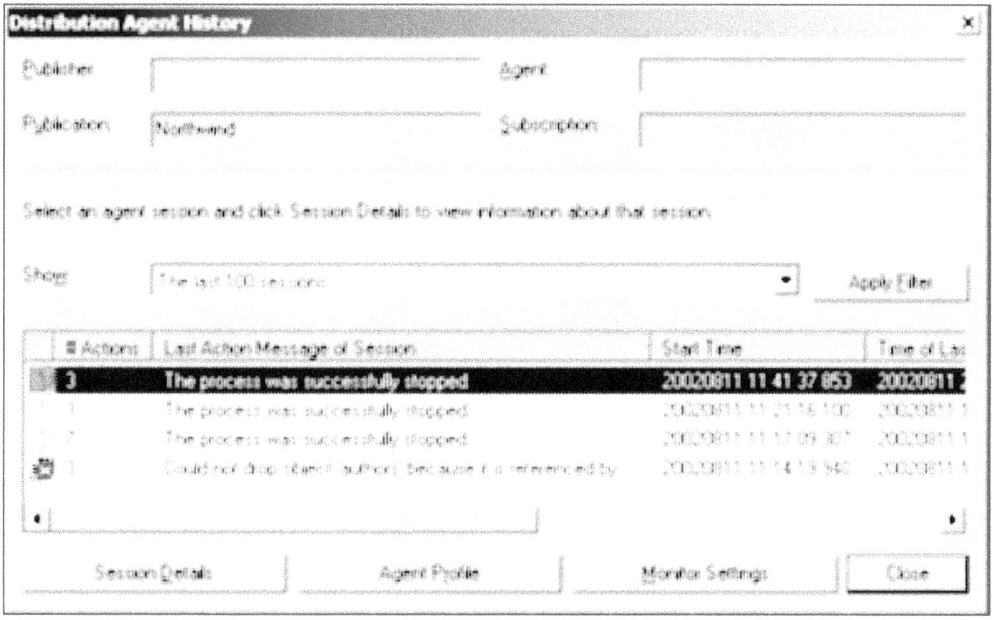


- View the job history for the SQL Server Agent jobs used to run the replication agents.
- View the SQL Log to examine server-related errors that may be impacting the replication process.
- Check your SQL Server Agent permissions. See the security guidelines in this chapter's section *Pre-Replication Checklist*.
- If you receive the error Length of text, ntext, or image data (%ld) to be replicated exceeds configured maximum %ld., use `sp_configure` to increase the max text repl size option.
- If you are having difficulty removing a subscription completely (receiving errors that the objects are already replicated on the subscriber), consider using the `sp_subscription_cleanup` (on the subscriber) for cleaning up dropped or orphaned subscription meta data. See *SQL Server Books Online* for the full syntax.

- For slow connections between the publisher and subscriber, or for very large publications, you may sometimes receive a distribution or merge agent timeout message such as Timeout Expired, or The agent is suspect. No activity reported within the last 10 minutes. Sometimes increasing the QueryTimeout profile setting can help reduce such errors. These errors do not always suggest a real problem, but often merely indicate that the replication agent is too busy to respond to SQL Server polling.
- If you are not seeing all expected transactions being moved from the publisher to the subscriber(s) for a transactional replication publication, use the `sp_replshowcmds` procedure. This procedure, when run from the publisher database, shows commands for transactions marked for replication waiting to be distributed. The distribution agent cannot be running when you execute this command; stop the agent prior to running this command, and restart the agent after you are finished.
- For immediate-updating subscribers, if you see error messages such as Rows do not match between Publisher and Subscriber. Refresh rows at Subscriber., Updatable Subscribers: RPC to Publisher failed., or Updatable Subscribers: Rolling back transaction., this is related to changes on the publisher that have not yet been updated on the subscriber. See Microsoft's Knowledge Base article 241511, *PRB: REPL: Msgs. 20515, 21054, or 20512 with Immediate-Updating Subscribers*.
- Once you have identified the error messages or clues for the issue, use these resources:
    - For specific error messages, search Microsoft's support site for error descriptions, http://support.microsoft.com/.
    - Have you overlooked the obvious? User error happens to the best of us; review the process to make sure you are implementing functionality correctly.
    - Seek advice from your colleagues, posting your questions and searching for answers in the Microsoft Community forum http://communities2.microsoft.com/home/default.asp.
    - Search engines, such as http://www.google.com/, do a great job of identifying exact error messages if they exist out on the web.
    - Other excellent sites for researching issues and getting free advice include SQL Server magazine, http://www.sqlmag.com/, SQL Team.com, http://www.sqlteam.com/, SQL Wire, http://www.sqlwire.com/, http://www.swynk.com/, and SQL Server Central.com, http://www.sqlservercentral.com/.

# 9

# Linked Servers

Linked servers provide SQL Server with access to data from remote data sources. Depending on the remote data source, you can issue queries, perform data modifications, and execute remote procedure calls. Remote data sources can be homogeneous (other SQL Server instances) or heterogeneous (other relational database products and data sources such as DB2, Access, Oracle, Excel, and text files). Cross-platform queries allow you to access legacy database systems, without the cost of merging or migrating existing data sources.

SQL Server connects to the remote data sources with an **OLE DB provider**. OLE DB, created by Microsoft, is a set of COM (component object model) interfaces used to access tabular data from varying data sources. An OLE DB provider is used to define a linked server on the local server. OLE DB providers are installed automatically with MDAC. The design of the OLE DB provider determines what kind of operations can be implemented through a distributed query (`SELECT`, `INSERT`, `UPDATE`, `DELETE`, stored procedure execution).

You can also run distributed queries without having to define linked servers, by using the Transact-SQL functions `OPENROWSET` and `OPENDATASOURCE`. Like linked servers, `OPENROWSET` and `OPENDATASOURCE` use OLE DB to connect to the remote data source; however, these functions do not encompass all the features included with linked servers, and should only be used for temporary or once-only queries.

When a Transact-SQL statement uses a linked server, the OLE DB provider for the linked server is loaded into the SQL Server memory address space, if it is not already loaded. SQL Server takes the Transact-SQL statement and calls the OLE DB interface. The OLE DB interface is then responsible for contacting the remote data source. The OLE DB provider processes the result set, and the output is then returned to the SQL Server client that made the initial call.

## Checklist

### Functionality and Performance Considerations for Linked Servers

- ❑ If you have another way to exchange or extract data, consider it. Linked servers require careful planning and have some performance drawbacks if used for heavy transaction processing or complicated decision-support reporting.

- Do not use linked servers instead of SQL Server replication. If you have two SQL Server instances that need to exchange data, consider replication over linked servers.
- Watch out for very large data sets and complicated queries. Do not assume that queries that run quickly on your local server will run as well in a distributed query to a linked server. Join operations, aggregate functions, `ORDER BY` clauses, and grouping can have harmful effects on your query response time.
- Read the fine print on your OLE DB provider. If the OLE DB provider for your database product is not supported, believe it. The fact that you can get one or two queries to work doesn't guarantee stability or extensibility down the road.
- Not all OLE DB providers, supported or otherwise, provide the same functionality. Understand what you can and cannot do with your heterogeneous OLE DB provider.
- Distributed queries require `ANSI_NULLS` and `ANSI_WARNINGS` connection settings to be set `ON`. Keep in mind that enabling these settings within a stored procedure will cause SQL Server to recompile the stored procedure, which may decrease some of the performance benefits of using a stored procedure.
- To use a specific OLE DB provider, you need to install the OLE DB provider drivers on your SQL Server computer.
- SQL Server will attempt to process certain relational database operations on the remote server side. This does not mean that it will use the most efficient method, or that certain operations (joins, aggregate functions, sorting, grouping) will always run on the remote server. Monitor very closely what behavior your distributed queries use, by checking the execution plan when performing initial testing.
- You cannot use query hints within distributed queries (see Chapter 15, for more details on query hints). If you do, you will get the error message "7277", "Cannot specify an index or locking hint for a remote data source".

# 9.1 How to... Add a Linked Server

To add a linked server using Enterprise Manager:

- Expand the SQL Server Group and registration.
- Expand the Security folder. Right-click Linked Server and select New Linked Server.
- Enter the remote server name in the Linked Server text box. For SQL Server instances, TCP/IP addresses can be used if TCP/IP is an enabled protocol for the remote data source and SQL Server instance. Select the Server type, either SQL Server or Other data source OLE DB provider.

  If you select SQL Server, the other text boxes will be grayed out. If you choose a different data source provider, the list of drop-down selections will be based on the drivers included with SQL Server, and any other OLE DB drivers on your server (from separately installed packages). SQL Server includes OLE DB providers for Microsoft Jet 4.0, DTS packages, Indexing Service, Internet Publishing, Microsoft Search, ODBC Drivers, OLAP Services 8.0, Oracle, Microsoft Directory Services, Simple Provider, and, of course, SQL Server. The OLE DB provider you select determines the values you choose for Product name, Data source, Provider string, Location, and Catalog:

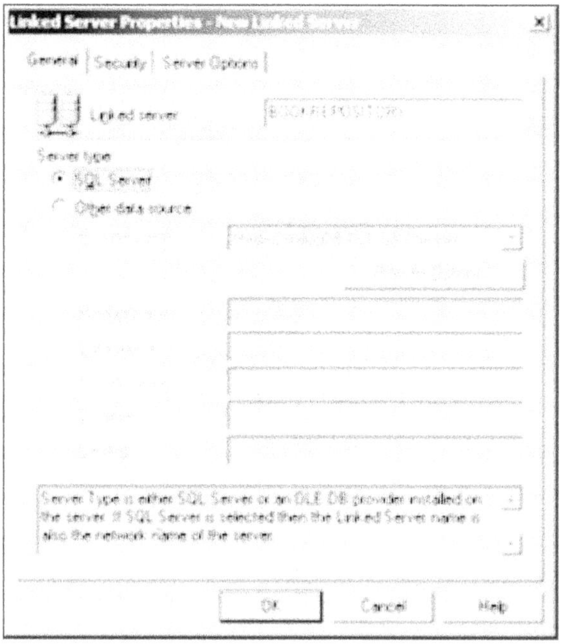


The Provider name shows the name of the OLE DB provider used to connect to the remote server. The Data source specifies the data source name property, which can be the server name, DSN name, or system path for the database. The Provider string may vary, based on the OLE DB provider used, and sets a unique data source string required by some OLE DB types. Location specifies the OLE DB provider location of the database, and is not required by all providers. The Catalog field sets the default database for the linked server connection. For a better understanding of what values to choose for different OLE DB providers, see the `sp_addlinkedsrvlogin` OLE DB provider options later in this section.

Selecting the Provider Options button will provide further configuration options:

| Parameter | Description |
|---|---|
| Dynamic parameters | If enabled, the parameter marker (`?`) sign is allowed. |
| Nested queries | If enabled, the OLE DB provider allows nested `SELECT` statements in the `FROM` clause. |
| Level zero only | If enabled, only **level 0** OLE DB interfaces are invoked against the provider. This means that the provider is responsible for executing, optimizing, and generating the rowset. The SQL Server instance making the linked server call is only responsible for making the initial call and receiving the rowset. |
| Allow InProcess | If enabled, the provider runs in process to the SQL Server process. This means that the OLE DB provider runs within the memory address space of SQL Server. This allows more functionality than out-of-process, but places the SQL Server process at risk if provider errors occur. |

*Table continued on following page*

| Parameter | Description |
|---|---|
| Non transacted updates | If enabled, provider updates are allowed, but are not supported as a transaction (and, therefore, SQL Server can't roll back or recover any data modifications if an error occurs). For example, you cannot use the `BEGIN TRAN`, `COMMIT`, or `ROLLBACK` commands. You would not be able to roll back a distributed update to a table, and partial updates would not necessarily be recovered. (For more information on transactions, see Chapter 5). |
| Index as access path | If enabled, SQL Server will utilize execution methods that use indexes on the data source. This may benefit performance of the distributed query (depending on the indexes on the data source, and the query construction). |
| Disallow ad hoc accesses | If enabled, no ad hoc access is allowed via the `OPENROWSET` or `OPENDATASOURCE` Transact-SQL functions. This will help you limit queries, by forcing them to use a defined linked server only. In SQL Server 2000 Service Pack 3, ad hoc access to OLE DB providers will not be allowed by default. If you want ad hoc access you must explicitly set this option to zero. |

Starting with SQL Server 2000 Service Pack 3, a new provider option called `SqlServerLike` has been introduced. When this option is non-zero, SQL Server can push queries that use the `LIKE` predicate to the provider for processing. In previous versions, if the provider was not a SQL Server OLE DB provider, any distributed queries using `LIKE` were evaluated and processed locally on the calling SQL Server instance. This option can potentially improve performance for queries that use the `LIKE` predicate.

You cannot configure the `SqlServerLike` option using Enterprise Manager. Instead, it must be enabled via a registry key modification. Use a registry editor to locate the registry key `HKEY_LOCAL_MACHINE\Software\Microsoft\MSSQLServer\Providers\<ProviderName>` for default instances, or `HKEY_LOCAL_MACHINE\Software\Microsoft\Microsoft SQL Server\<Instance Name>\Providers\<ProviderName>` for named instances. Under the specified provider `<ProviderName>` key, add a `DWORD` value, and name it `SQLServerLike`. Then set the value to `1` to enable, or `0` to disable it.

- In the Security tab, you can specify which login will be used for data access to the provider. In the Local server login to remote server login mappings: section, you can map one or more local logins to associated remote users. Specify the Local Login field for the local login to map. Select the Impersonate checkbox if the local ID matches the remote server ID and has the proper permissions. Select Remote User and Remote Password for the remote login and password to which to map the local login. Note that the remote login and password can't be a WinNT username and password.

  You can configure security for those connecting logins not found in the top section by setting the options in the For a login not defined in the list above, connections will: section. To restrict access only to those in the local server login list, select Not be made. For data sources that do not have a security context (for example, text files), select Be made without using a security context. If you wish the non-listed local login to impersonate a remote login (map to the same name and password on the remote server side), select Be made using the login's current security context. Select Be made using this security context: to select a remote login and password that will be used to connect to the remote data source for all unlisted local logins.

**When selecting logins for use with linked servers, choose a remote login with the lowest level of permissions that are needed to do the job.**

The Server Options tab allows you to set additional linked-server options:

| Parameter | Description |
|---|---|
| Collation compatible | Collation Compatible is used for SQL Server-to-SQL Server communication. Enable this setting if you are certain the local SQL Server instance has the **same collation** as the remote SQL Server instance. Doing so will improve performance, as SQL Server will no longer have to perform comparisons of character columns between the data sources, as the same collation is assumed. |
| Data access | If enabled, distributed query access is allowed. |
| RPC | Enables remote procedure calls from the server. |
| RPC out | Enables remote procedure calls to the server. |
| Use remote collation | Determines if remote server collation is used instead of the local server collation. |
| Collation name | If Use Remote Collation is enabled, you need to specify the name of the remote server collation. This name must be supported by SQL Server, and is used to associate a common and recognized SQL Server collation to the remote server. |

*Table continued on following page*

| Parameter | Description |
|---|---|
| Connection timeout | Specifies the number of seconds a connection attempt will be made to the linked server before a timeout occurs. |
| Query timeout | Determines the number of seconds after which a waiting query will time out. If this value is 0, then the `sp_configure` value configured for the **query wait** option will be used instead (see Chapter 2 for more details on this option). |

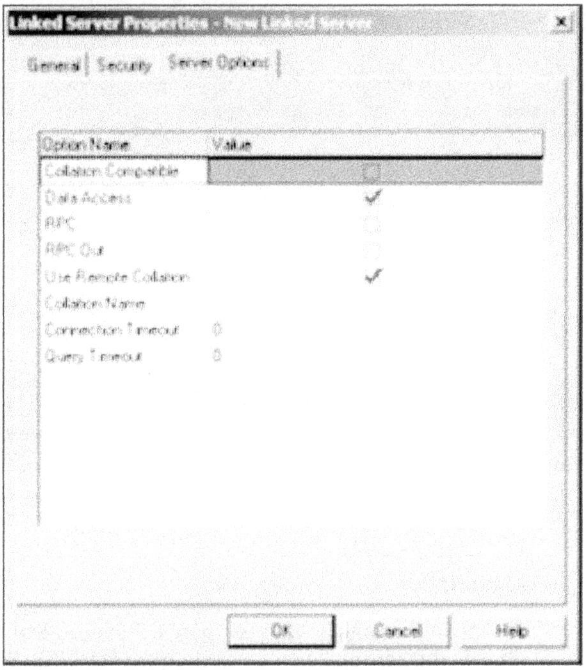

- Select OK to create the connection.
- Test the new linked server by expanding the server name node and clicking Tables or Views. Check the right-hand pane of Enterprise Manager to see what objects are listed (this will show default database objects based on the login).
- To remove a linked server entry, right-click the linked server, and select Delete.

  You will be prompted to check if you are sure about removing the linked server. If you have local logins associated with remote logins, you will receive an additional prompt:

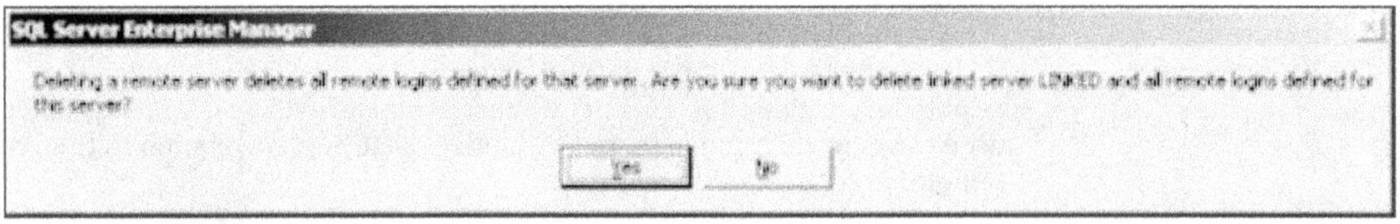

To add and configure a linked server using Transact-SQL, use the following stored procedures:

| Stored Procedure | Description |
|---|---|
| sp_addlinkedserver | Creates a linked server. |
| sp_addlinkedsrvlogin | Maps a local login to a remote login. |
| sp_droplinkedsrvlogin | Drops a login mapping for a linked server. |
| sp_serveroption | Sets server options for a linked server. |
| sp_dropserver | Drops a linked server definition. |

To add a new linked server, execute sp_addlinkedserver. The syntax from *SQL Server Books Online* is as follows:

```
sp_addlinkedserver [ @server = ] 'server'
                   [ , [ @srvproduct = ] 'product_name' ]
                   [ , [ @provider = ] 'provider_name' ]
                   [ , [ @datasrc = ] 'data_source' ]
                   [ , [ @location = ] 'location' ]
                   [ , [ @provstr = ] 'provider_string' ]
                   [ , [ @catalog = ] 'catalog' ]
```

The following are parameter descriptions; keep in mind that not all fields are required for each OLE DB provider type, and that they also vary according to the product as well. At the end of this section, we will review different connection types (including DB2, Jet, and Oracle):

| Parameter | Description |
|---|---|
| [ @server = ] 'server' | Local name used for linked server. Instance names are allowed, for example DOPEY\DOPEY. |
| [ @srvproduct = ] 'product_name' ] | Product name of OLE DB data source. |
| [ @provider = ] 'provider_name' ] | Unique programmatic identifier for the OLE DB provider. |
| [ @datasrc = ] 'data_source' ] | Data source as interpreted by the specified OLE DB provider. |
| [ @location = ] 'location' ] | Location as interpreted by the specified OLE DB provider. |
| [ @provstr = ] 'provider_string' ] | Connection string specific to the OLE DB provider. |
| [ @catalog = ] 'catalog' ] | catalog sometimes refers to database, but it can also be defined by OLE DB provider interpretation. |

Use the xp_enum_oledb_providers extended stored procedure to list all available OLE DB providers on your database server. This prevents you adding a linked server that references an OLE DB provider that is not on the database server. This is an undocumented stored procedure, so it should not be used within application code or procedures. Only use this procedure as a helpful ad hoc tool. To use the procedure, execute the following command in Query Analyzer:

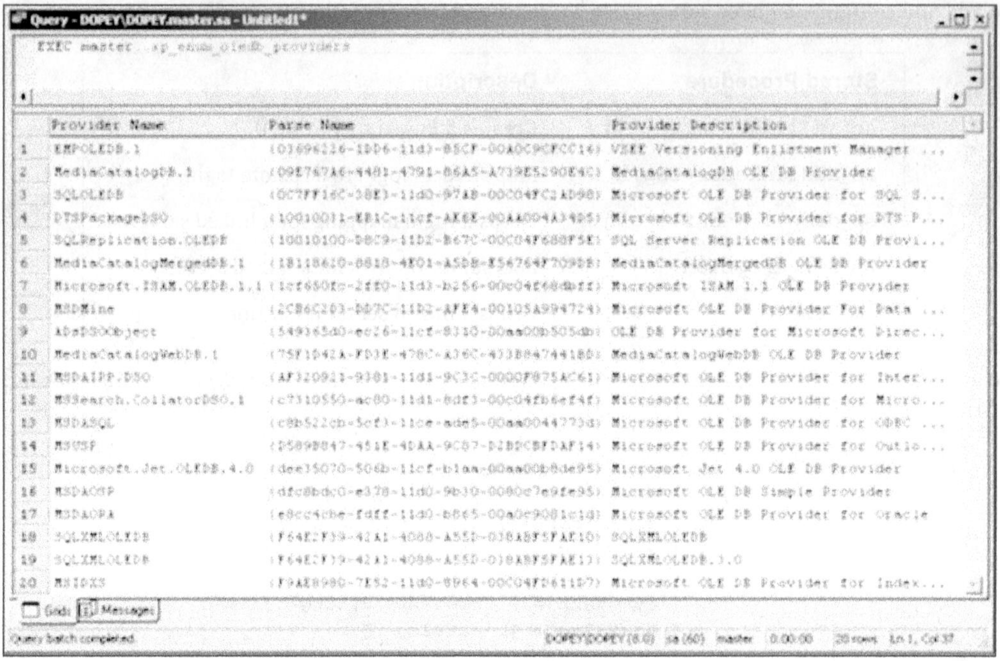


### Example 9.1.1: Adding a linked server

Adding a linked server referencing a SQL Server instance:

```
USE master
GO
EXEC sp_addlinkedserver 'BOOKREPOSITORY', N'SQL Server'
GO
```

### Example 9.1.2: Adding a linked server referencing a named instance

Adding a linked server referencing a SQL Server named instance:

```
USE master

GO
EXEC sp_addlinkedserver 'BOOKREPOSITORY\BOOKDB1', N'SQL Server'
GO
```

# OLE DB Provider Parameters

Other OLE DB providers require different parameters to create a linked server. The following section reviews required `sp_addlinkedserver` parameters for DB2, Jet, Oracle, ODBC valid system DSNs, and FoxPro.

## DB2

Install Windows NT Client for Host Integration Server 2000 on the SQL Server computer. Install the OLE DB Provider for DB2 and the proper network components for an SNA network.

You can also connect to DB2 via OLE DB for ODBC, by creating a system DSN with the DB2 Connect utility. Create the data source after installing DB2 Connect:

| Parameter | Value |
|---|---|
| server | Server name |
| product_name | Microsoft OLE DB |
| provider_name | DB2OLEDB |
| provider_string | Provider string example:<br>'NetLib=SNA;<br>NetAddr=;<br>NetPort=;<br>RemoteLU=XXXXXXX;<br>LocalLU=LOCAL;<br>ModeName=XXXXXX;<br>User ID=XXXXXX;<br>Password=XXXXXX;<br>InitCat=XXXXXXX;<br>DefaultSchema=XXXXXX;<br>PkgCol=XXXXXX;<br>TPName=;<br>Commit=YES;<br>IsoLvl=NC;<br>AccMode=;<br>CCSID=37;<br>PCCodePage=1252;<br>BinAsChar=NO;<br>Data Source=XXXXXXX' |
| catalog | DB2 catalog |

## Jet

In addition to Microsoft Access, the Jet provider can also be used to connect to an Excel spreadsheet or text file:

| Parameter | Value |
|---|---|
| server | Server name |
| product_name | Access |
| provider_name | Microsoft.Jet.OLEDB.4.0 |
| data_source | C:\path\databasename.mdb |

## OLE DB for ODBC

OLE DB for ODBC allows you to connect to most valid ODBC data sources configured on your server. If you do not have an OLE DB provider specific to the vendor product, try OLE DB for ODBC. Before adding a linked server, create a system data source on the SQL Server computer.

To add a data source, select the Start menu, Settings | Control Panel | Administrative Tools. Double-click Data Sources (ODBC) for a Windows NT 4.0 or Windows 2000 server. Select User DSN, System DSN, or File DSN tab, and select the Add button. Specify the type of data source you wish to set up, and any other user-defined options that may be required for that provider type:

| Parameter | Value |
|---|---|
| server | Server name |
| provider_name | MSDASQL |
| data_source | System data source name |

If you do not want to create a system data source on the SQL Server computer, you can create a DSN-less connection. For example:

| Parameter | Value |
|---|---|
| server | Server name |
| product_name | NULL |
| provider_name | MSDASQL |
| data_source | NULL |
| location | NULL |
| provider_string | A valid provider string. For SQL Server for example:<br>'Driver={SQL Server};<br>Database=databasename;<br>Server=ServerName;<br>UID=loginid;PWD=pwd;' |

## OLE DB for SQL Server 7.0 and 2000

Use OLE DB for SQL Server for versions SQL Server 7.0 and 2000. You can use OLE DB for ODBC, but it does not perform as well:

| Parameter | Value |
|---|---|
| server | Linked server name |
| provider_name | SQLOLEDB |
| data_source | Network server name |

## OLE DB for Oracle

Install Oracle client software on SQL Server computer. Make sure to reboot the server after installation:

| Parameter | Value |
|---|---|
| `server` | Server name |
| `product_name` | Oracle |
| `provider_name` | MSDAORA |
| `data_source` | SQL*Net alias name |

## FoxPro

FoxPro connections can be made via OLE DB for ODBC too. The following example details a connection with a DSN:

| Parameter | Value |
|---|---|
| `server` | Server name |
| `provider_name` | MSDASQL |
| `provider_string` | `'Driver={Microsoft Visual FoxPro Driver}; UID=; PWD=; SourceDB=<directory>\databasename.dbc; SourceType=DBC; Exclusive=No; BackgroundFetch=Yes; Collate=Machine;'` |

## Sybase

With Sybase being so much closer in the database family tree to SQL Server than, say, DB2, you would think that connectivity would be documented and supported via linked servers. Sybase does provide an OLE DB provider beginning with version 12, and can also be connected to via OLE DB for ODBC. At the time of writing, an **official** SQL Server 2000 provider test has not been blessed by either Sybase or Microsoft, so until then, you should think twice about staking your application on under-documented and ambiguously supported technologies.

## Active Directory

You can connect to Active Directory using the Microsoft OLE DB Provider for Microsoft Directory Services. Use `OPENQUERY` to send a command to the Active Directory Service. Use the values provided below for setting up the linked server Active Directory data source:

| Parameter | Value |
|---|---|
| `server` | User-defined name of the linked server |
| `product_name` | Active Directory Services 2.5 |
| `provider_name` | ADsDSOObject |
| `data_source` | adsdatasource |

## Adding Login Mappings to a Linked Server

Once you have added your linked server with sp_addlinkedserver, you can add login mappings from your local SQL Server instance to the linked server OLE DB provider.

The syntax for sp_addlinkedsrvlogin from *SQL Server Books Online* is as follows:

```
sp_addlinkedsrvlogin [ @rmtsrvname = ] 'rmtsrvname'
                     [ , [ @useself = ] 'useself' ]
                     [ , [ @locallogin = ] 'locallogin' ]
                     [ , [ @rmtuser = ] 'rmtuser' ]
                     [ , [ @rmtpassword = ] 'rmtpassword' ]
```

| Parameter | Description |
|---|---|
| [ @rmtsrvname = ] | Name of the linked server for the login mapping. |
| [ @useself = ] | If true (true is the default), SQL Server-authenticated logins use the same login credentials at the remote server. This will not work if account delegation and Windows authentication isn't supported on the provider server. Account delegation requires that all the servers that you connect to are running Windows 2000, use Microsoft Active Directory, and have Kerberos support enabled. Kerberos is a means of supporting mutual authentication and the ability to pass security credentials across servers and clients. |
| [ @locallogin = ] | Local login to map from the local SQL Server instance. |
| [ @rmtuser = ] | User name on remote server to map to. |
| [ @rmtpassword = ] | Password on remote server for a remote user. |

### Example 9.1.3: Allowing connections using local logins

```
EXEC sp_addlinkedsrvlogin @rmtsrvname = 'BOOKREPOSITORY',
                          @useself = 'true'
```

### Example 9.1.4: Mapping a domain login to a local user

```
EXEC sp_addlinkedsrvlogin @rmtsrvname = 'BOOKREPOSITORY',
                          @useself = 'false',
                          @locallogin='CURLINGSTONE\USR1',
                          @rmtuser='BookUsr',
                          @rmtpassword='BookFun'
```

A tip regarding sp_addlinkedsrvlogin: do not forget to include the @useself = 'false' for login mappings, otherwise your remote user and password parameters will be ignored, and SQL Server will attempt to use your local login on the remote server.

## Setting Server Options

To configure the options of a linked server, use the sp_serveroption procedure. The syntax from *SQL Server Books Online* is as follows:

```
sp_serveroption [@server =] 'server',
                [@optname =] 'option_name',
                [@optvalue =] 'option_value'
```

This procedure takes the linked server name as the first parameter, and then a name and value pair for the configurable properties, which are as follows:

| Property | Description |
|---|---|
| Collation compatible | For SQL Server-to-SQL Server communication. Enable this setting if you are certain the local SQL Server instance has the same collation as the remote SQL Server instance. |
| Collation name | If Use Remote Collation is enabled, specifies the name of the remote server collation. This name must be supported by SQL Server, and is used to associate a common and recognized SQL Server collation to the remote server. |
| Connect timeout | Sets the number of seconds a connection attempt will be made to the linked server before a timeout occurs. |
| Data access | If enabled, distributed query access is allowed. |
| Lazy schema validation | If set to `true`, the schema is not checked on remote tables at the beginning of the query. Although this reduces overhead for the remote query, if the schema has changed on the linked server data source after the query is compiled but before it is executed, an error could occur. |
| Query timeout | The number of seconds after which a waiting query will time out. |
| RPC | Enables remote procedure calls from the server. |
| RPC out | Enables remote procedure calls to the linked server data source. |
| Use remote collation | Determines whether the remote server collation is used instead of the local server collation. When this option is enabled, the remote data source column collation is used (for SQL Server linked servers), and the collation specified in the Collation Name option is then used for heterogeneous data sources. |

## Example 9.1.5: Designating that the collation is compatible

```
EXEC sp_serveroption 'BOOKREPOSITORY', 'collation compatible', 'true'
```

## Example 9.1.6: Enabling remote procedure calls to and from the server

```
EXEC sp_serveroption 'BOOKREPOSITORY', 'rpc', 'true'
EXEC sp_serveroption 'BOOKREPOSITORY', 'rpc out', 'true'
```

## Example 9.1.7: Disabling data access

```
EXEC sp_serveroption 'BOOKREPOSITORY', 'data access', 'false'
```

### Example 9.1.8: Dropping a linked server login

To drop a linked server entry from your local server, you must first drop associated login mappings. One method for dropping login mappings is to use sp_droplinkedsrvlogin. This stored procedure takes the linked server name for the first parameter, and the local login for the second parameter:

```
EXEC sp_droplinkedsrvlogin 'BOOKREPOSITORY', 'sa'
```

### Example 9.1.9: Dropping a linked server entry and associated logins

After you have finished dropping all login mappings, you can drop the linked server entry with the sp_dropserver stored procedure. This procedure takes two parameters: the first parameter uses the linked server name to drop and the second accepts either NULL or droplogins. This is an alternative method to dropping all logins associated with a linked server entry, if you didn't already do so with sp_droplinkedsrvlogin:

```
EXEC sp_dropserver 'BOOKREPOSITORY', 'droplogins'
```

# 9.2 How to... Execute Distributed Queries with a Linked Server

Distributed queries can reference one or more linked servers, performing either read or update operations against the individual linked servers. In general, Microsoft SQL Server requires distributed transactions support from the corresponding OLE DB provider whenever data from more than one linked server is likely to be updated in a transaction. The types of queries that are supported against linked servers depend on the level of support for transactions present in the OLE DB providers. You can run a distributed query referencing a linked server by using either a four-part name or the OPENQUERY Transact-SQL command.

The basic syntax for referencing a linked server using a four-part name is as follows:

```
linkedservername.databasename.owner.object
```

### Example 9.2.1: Querying a linked server using the four-part name

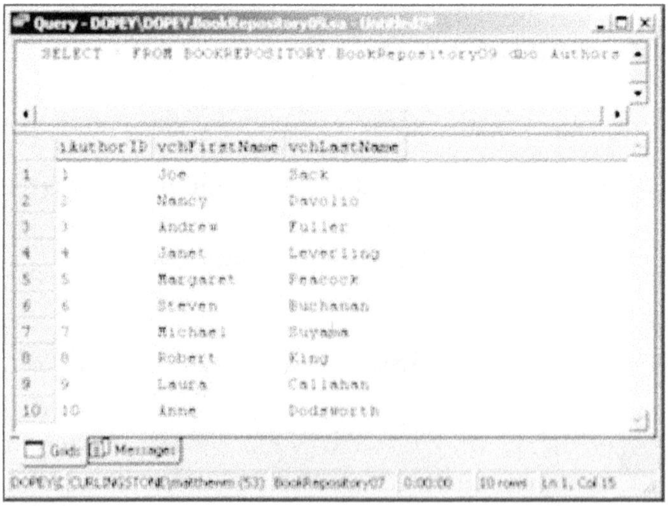

You can also query a linked server using the OPENQUERY function. The syntax is:

```
OPENQUERY (linked_server_name, 'query')
```

OPENQUERY acts like a table rowset, taking the linked server name as the first parameter and a valid query as the second parameter. No variables are allowed in the second parameter, and the types of queries allowed (SELECT, INSERT, UPDATE, and DELETE) depend on the OLE DB provider that is used. Note also that, although the query can return multiple result sets, only the first result set is displayed.

### Example 9.2.2: Querying a named instance linked server

To query a linked server that is also a named instance of SQL Server, you must put the server's name in square brackets:

```
SELECT * FROM [BOOKREPOSITORY\BOOKDB1].BookRepository09.dbo.Authors
```

### Example 9.2.3: Executing a stored procedure on the remote data source

The following example executes the sp_lock procedure on a linked server named BOOKREPOSITORY. The linked server must have RPC Out enabled, and the OLE DB provider must allow remote procedure calls. The security of the remote login used must also have the appropriate permissions:

```
EXEC BOOKREPOSITORY.master.dbo.sp_lock
```

### Example 9.2.4: Modifying data on the remote data source

The following examples show how to INSERT, UPDATE, and DELETE data on the remote data source. The OLE DB provider must allow data modifications. The security of the remote login used must also have the appropriate permissions:

```
INSERT BOOKREPOSITORY.BookRepository09.dbo.Authors
  (vchLastName, vchFirstName) VALUES ('Sack', 'Joe')

UPDATE BOOKREPOSITORY.BookRepository09.dbo.Authors
  SET vchFirstName = 'Joseph'
  WHERE vchLastName = 'Sack' AND vchFirstName = 'Joe'

DELETE BOOKREPOSITORY.BookRepository09.dbo.Authors
  WHERE vchLastName = 'Sack' AND vchFirstName = 'Joseph'
```

### Example 9.2.5: Querying a linked server with OPENQUERY

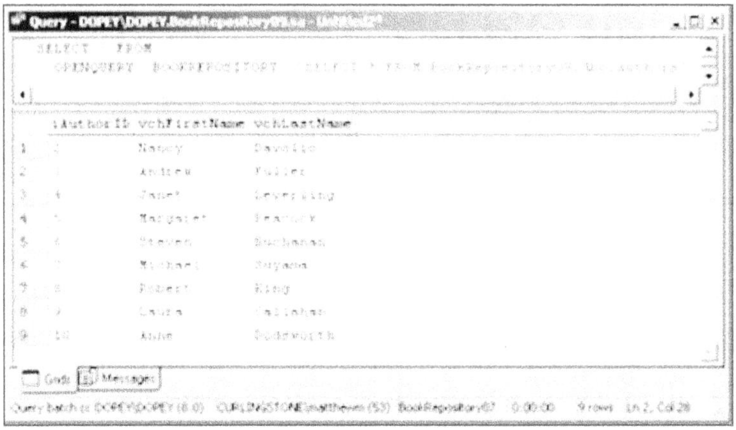

Remember that linked query behavior is not always predictable. SQL Server will attempt to have certain operations processed remotely but, depending on the operation and meta data available from the OLE DB provider, the best query plan may not always be selected.

### Example 9.2.6: Viewing a query plan for a distributed query

You can view the query execution plan to see where processes will take place. For example, the following query joins data from a remote table and a local table:

```
SELECT LocalPubs.* FROM
  OPENQUERY (BOOKREPOSITORY,
    'SELECT * FROM BookRepository09.dbo.Authors WHERE
      vchFirstName = ''Johnson''') AS RemotePubs,
  BookRepository09.dbo.Authors AS LocalPubs
  WHERE RemotePubs.iAuthorID = LocalPubs.iAuthorID
```

This query uses the RemotePubs alias for the OPENQUERY result set and the LocalPubs alias for the local table join (you can also join remote tables or views to local tables and views).

To view the query plan in Query Analyzer, go to the Query menu and select Show Execution Plan (you can also choose Show Estimated Execution Plan if you do not wish to run the actual query).

Execute the query and look at the Execution Plan tab:

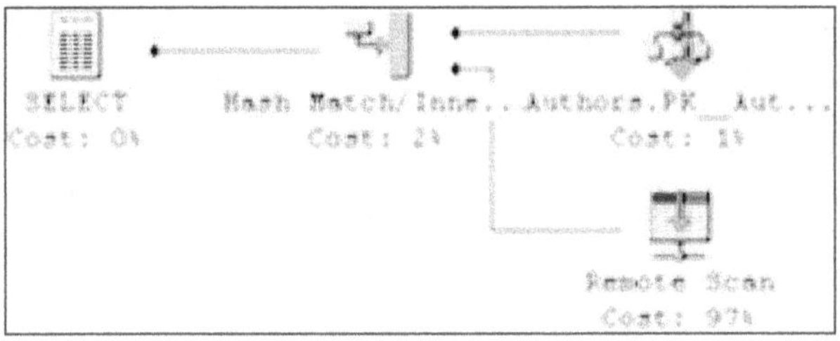

This execution plan tells us that 97% of the processing took place in a remote scan operation on the linked server. See Chapter 17 for more information on the graphical query plan tool.

# 9.3 How to... Execute Ad Hoc Distributed Queries using OPENROWSET and OPENDATASOURCE

If you only require a temporary method of accessing a remote server, SQL Server provides the Transact-SQL commands OPENROWSET and OPENDATASOURCE. These commands should be used as temporary or one-time use methods, as defined linked servers generally perform better.

OPENROWSET acts like a table in a SELECT statement, except that it takes OLE DB data source information and uses it to access a remote server. The syntax from *SQL Server Books Online* is as follows:

```
OPENROWSET ( 'provider_name',
             { 'datasource' ; 'user_id' ; 'password' | 'provider_string' },
             { [ catalog. ] [ schema. ] object | 'query' } )
```

| Parameter | Description |
|---|---|
| provider_name | Name describing the OLE DB provider. |
| datasource | OLE DB data source. |
| user_id | User ID on remote data source. |
| password | Password on remote data source. |
| provider_string | If you do not specify the first four parameters, you can use an OLE DB provider string instead. |
| { [ catalog. ] [ schema. ] object | Choose a specific catalog (database), schema (object owner), and object, or a specific query. The query is processed at the provider. |
| \| query } | |

OPENROWSET accepts the same OLE DB provider parameters as sp_addlinkedserver, so refer to the earlier *OLE DB Provider Parameters* section for more details.

> **Warning: Using rowset functions like OPENDATASOURCE in production code can be a security risk if you specify the password of a remote login in the call.**

The OPENDATASOURCE function, like OPENROWSET, also bypasses the linked server functionality. This function acts as a result set table and can be used with a SELECT query. The difference between OPENDATASOURCE and OPENROWSET, however, is that OPENDATASOURCE acts as the first part of a four-part name whereas OPENROWSET sits in place of the entire four-part name. The syntax from *SQL Server Books Online* is as follows:

```
OPENDATASOURCE ( provider_name, init_string )
```

| Parameter | Description |
|---|---|
| provider_name | Name of the registered ID for the OLE DB provider. |
| init_string | Specifies a connection string, using keyword-value pairs. |

### Example 9.3.1: Running a server-side query using OPENROWSET

In this example, we will run a server-side query using OPENROWSET, and return the top 10 rows:

```
SELECT TOP 10 *
FROM OPENROWSET
('SQLOLEDB', 'BOOKREPOSITORY';'sa';'xxxx',
 'SELECT * FROM BookRepository09.dbo.Authors')
```

### Example 9.3.2: Using Windows authentication with OPENROWSET

You can connect to other SQL Server instances using Windows authentication. To do so, use a name/value property setting of Trusted_Connection=Yes. For example:

```
SELECT TOP 10 *
FROM OPENROWSET
('SQLOLEDB',
 'SERVER=BOOKREPOSITORY;Trusted_Connection=yes',
 'SELECT * FROM BookRepository09.dbo.Authors')
```

### Example 9.3.3: Selecting data from a table using OPENDATASOURCE

```
SELECT TOP 10 *
FROM OPENDATASOURCE
('SQLOLEDB',
 'Data Source=BOOKREPOSITORY;User ID=sa;Password=xxxx'
).BookRepository09.dbo.Authors
```

### Example 9.3.4: Using Windows authentication with OPENDATASOURCE

You can connect to other SQL Server instances using Windows authentication. To do so, use a name/value property setting of `Integrated Security=SSPI`. For example:

```
SELECT *
FROM OPENDATASOURCE
('SQLOLEDB',
 'Data Source=BOOKREPOSITORY;Integrated Security=SSPI'
).BookRepository09.dbo.Authors
```

# 9.4 How to... List All Tables from a Linked Server using sp_tables_ex

To return information about a table on the linked server, run the procedure `sp_tables_ex`. The syntax from *SQL Server Books Online* is as follows:

```
sp_tables_ex [ @table_server = ] 'table_server'
             [ , [ @table_name = ] 'table_name' ]
             [ , [ @table_schema = ] 'table_schema' ]
             [ , [ @table_catalog = ] 'table_catalog' ]
             [ , [ @table_type = ] 'table_type' ]
```

| Parameter | Description |
|---|---|
| `[ @table_server = ]` | Name of linked server |
| `[ @table_name = ]` | Name of table on linked server |
| `[ @table_schema = ]` | Name of schema (usually object owner) |
| `[ @table_catalog = ]` | Name of catalog (usually database) |

| Parameter | Description |
|---|---|
| [ @table_type = ] | Type of table (default NULL), allowing values:<br>ALIAS<br>GLOBAL TEMPORARY (global temp table)<br>LOCAL TEMPORARY (local temp table)<br>SYNONYM<br>SYSTEM TABLE<br>TABLE (user table)<br>VIEW |

**Example 9.4.1: Listing all tables for a specific database on a linked server**

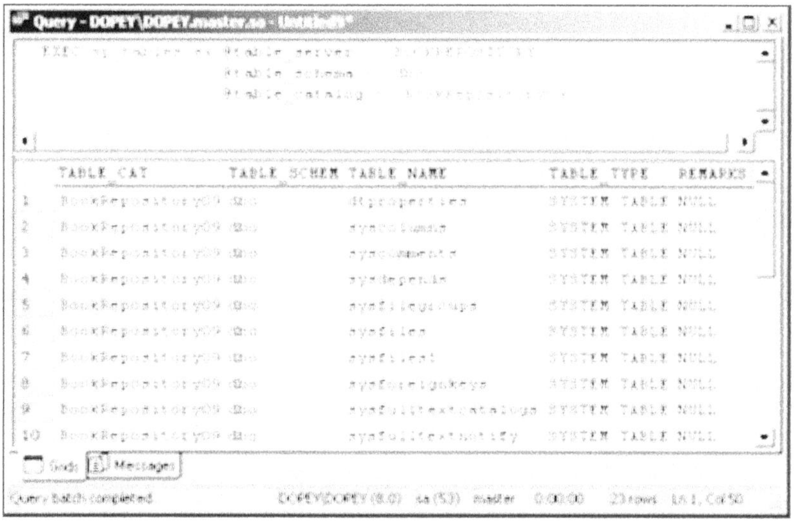


# 9.5 How to... Show Privilege Information about a Linked Server Table with sp_table_privileges_ex

To display table permissions for a linked server table, use the sp_table_privileges_ex stored procedure. The syntax from *SQL Server Books Online* is as follows:

```
sp_table_privileges_ex [ @table_server = ] 'table_server'
                       [ , [ @table_name = ] 'table_name' ]
                       [ , [ @table_schema = ] 'table_schema' ]
                       [ , [ @table_catalog = ] 'table_catalog' ]
```

| Parameter | Description |
|---|---|
| `[ @table_server = ]` | Linked server name |
| `[ @table_name = ]` | Specific table name |
| `[ @table_schema = ]` | Table schema (usually object owner) |
| `[ @table_catalog = ]` | Table catalog (usually database) |

**Example 9.5.1: Listing privileges for a specific table on a linked server**

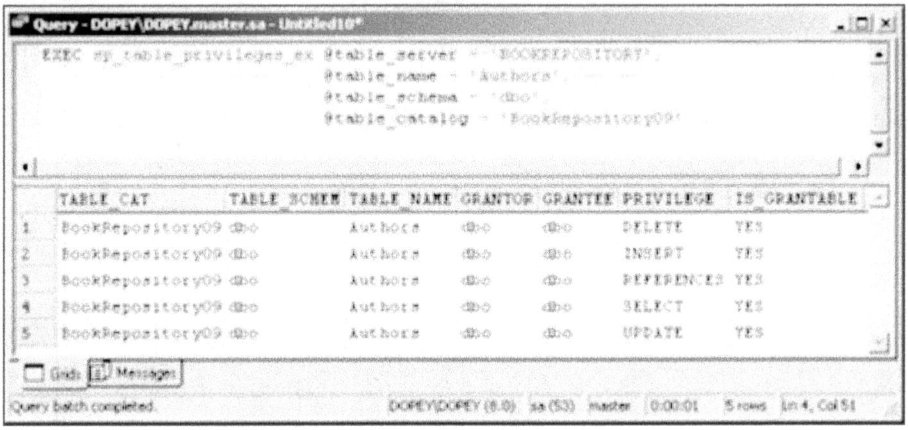


# 9.6 How to... Display Column Data for a Linked Server Table using sp_columns_ex

To return column information about a specific linked server table or tables, use the stored procedure `sp_columns_ex`. The syntax from *SQL Server Books Online* is as follows:

```
sp_columns_ex [ @table_server = ] 'table_server'
              [ , [ @table_name = ] 'table_name' ]
              [ , [ @table_schema = ] 'table_schema' ]
              [ , [ @table_catalog = ] 'table_catalog' ]
              [ , [ @column_name = ] 'column' ]
              [ , [ @ODBCVer = ] 'ODBCVer' ]
```

| Parameter | Description |
|---|---|
| `[ @table_server = ]` | Linked server name |
| `[ @table_name = ]` | Table name |
| `[ @table_schema = ]` | Schema name for table (usually relates to owner) |
| `[ @table_catalog = ]` | Catalog name for table (sometimes relates to database) |

| Parameter | Description |
|---|---|
| `[ @column_name = ]` | Column name |
| `[ @ODBCVer = ]` | Version of ODBC being used, either 2 or 3 |

**Example 9.6.1: Listing all columns for a specific table**

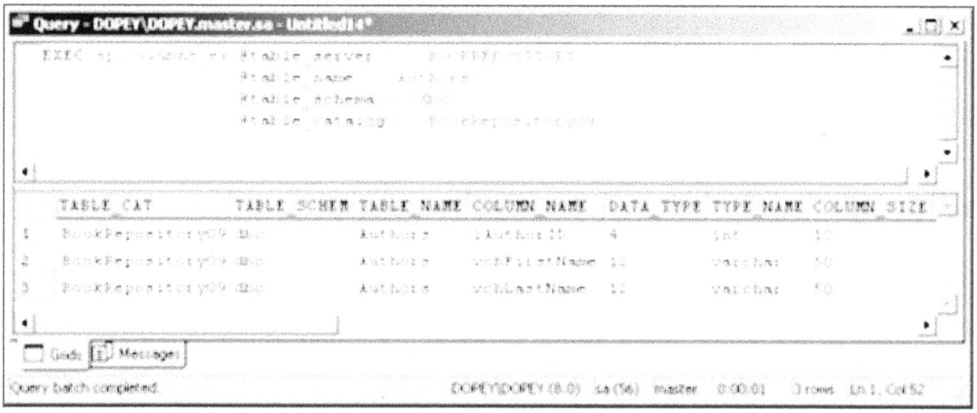


**Example 9.6.2: Listing data for one column**

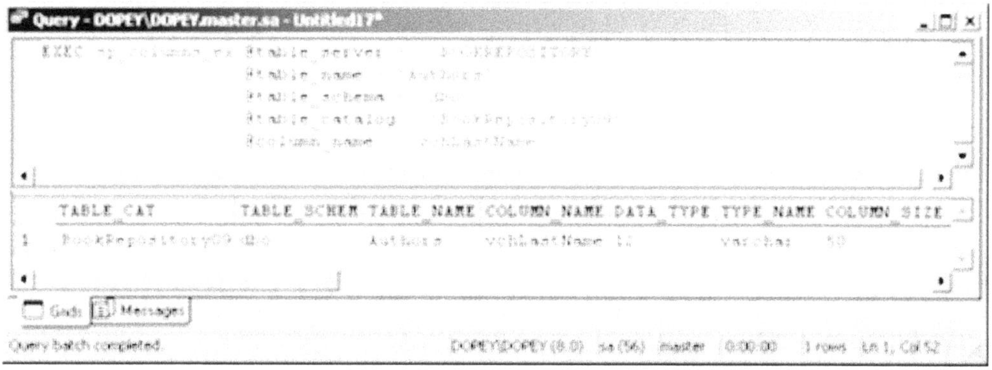


# 9.7 How to… Return Column Privileges for a Linked Server Table using sp_column_privileges_ex

To list privileges for columns on a specific table for a linked server, use `sp_column_privileges_ex`. The syntax from *SQL Server Books Online* is as follows:

```
sp_column_privileges_ex [ @table_server = ] 'table_server'
                        [ , [ @table_name = ] 'table_name' ]
```

```
[ , [ @table_schema = ] 'table_schema' ]
[ , [ @table_catalog = ] 'table_catalog' ]
[ , [ @column_name = ] 'column_name' ]
```

| Parameter | Description |
|---|---|
| `[ @table_server = ]` | Linked server name |
| `[ @table_name = ]` | Table name |
| `[ @table_schema = ]` | Schema name (usually object owner) |
| `[ @table_catalog = ]` | Catalog name (usually database) |
| `[ @column_name = ]` | Column name |

**Example 9.7.1: Return permissions for a specific column**

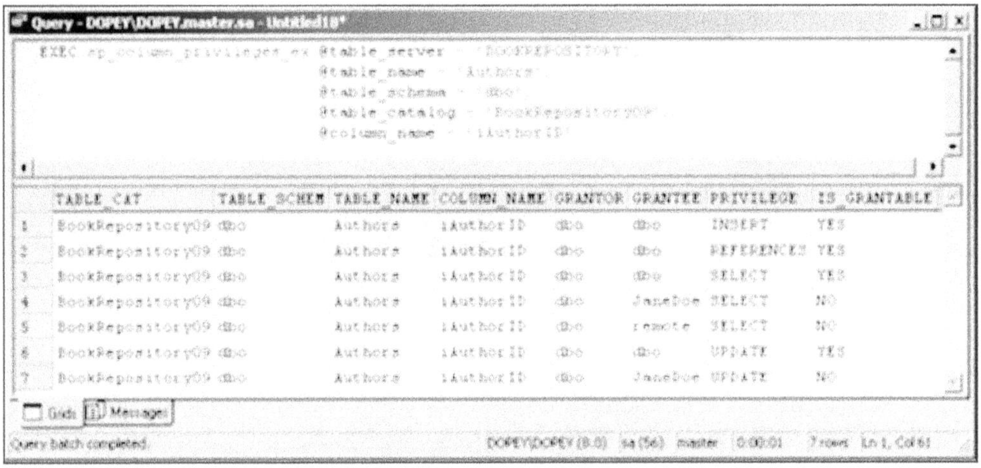


# 9.8 How to... List Linked Servers Defined on Your Local Server

To list all defined linked servers on your local server, execute `sp_linkedservers`.

The system stored procedure returns the following information:

| Column | Description |
|---|---|
| SRV_NAME | Linked server name |
| SRV_PROVIDERNAME | OLE DB provider name |
| SRV_PRODUCT | Database product name |

| Column | Description |
|---|---|
| SRV_DATASOURCE | OLE DB data source name |
| SRV_PROVIDERSTRING | OLE DB provider string |
| SRV_LOCATION | OLE DB location |
| SRV_CAT | OLE DB catalog |

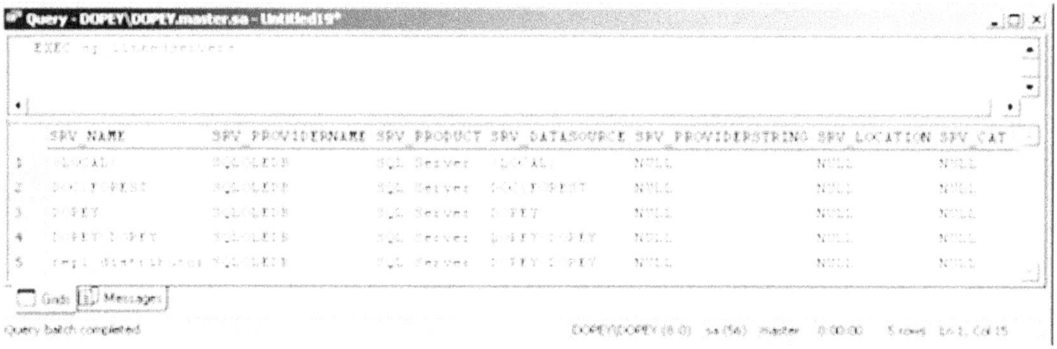


# 9.9 How to... Troubleshoot Linked Servers and Distributed Queries

As with many SQL Server issues and bugs, making use of Internet references will ensure you have the latest information. The chances are that if you encounter an error, someone else has encountered that error too. Make use of Microsoft's Knowledge Base site http://support.microsoft.com/, along with message boards and news groups.

The following are common errors in distributed queries for linked servers. Keep in mind that the error number is usually listed as Msg instead of error in the error text. For example, Query Analyzer will display error 7399 as Server: Msg 7399...:

> **Beginning with SQL Server 2000 Service Pack 3, error messages returned from a distributed query will return more detailed error information if the OLE DB Provider of the linked server supports the `IErrorRecords` OLE DB interface.**

| Error Number | Message | Description |
|---|---|---|
| 115 | '<Linked-Server Name>' is not a recognized OPTIMIZER LOCK HINTS option. | You may receive this error if running an `OPENQUERY` function within the context of a database with compatibility level 65 or lower (SQL Server 6.5). Change your local database compatibility to 70 (7.0) or greater. |

*Table continued on following page*

| Error Number | Message | Description |
|---|---|---|
| 7303 | Could not initialize data source object of OLE DB provider '%ls'. %ls | The linked server setup parameters may be incorrect or the login is invalid. |
| 7306 | Could not open table '%ls' from OLE DB provider '%ls'. %ls | Implies that the OLE DB provider doesn't support data modification statements. |
| 7314 | OLE DB provider '%ls' does not contain table '%ls'. The table either does not exist or the current user does not have permissions on that table. | Indicates the table does not exist, user permissions are insufficient, or the server is case-sensitive and another case should be used for the object name. |
| 7321 | An error occurred while preparing a query for execution against OLE DB provider '%ls'. %ls | This error suggests a query string syntax error. Make sure you are using the proper syntax for the OLE DB provider being accessed.<br><br>This error also occurs if you are using a four-part name, with an OLE DB connection to DB2 on an AS/400 platform. If the OLE DB property Nested Queries is enabled, you will receive error 7321. To resolve this problem, you can either disable Nested Queries or use `OPENQUERY` instead of a four-part name. See Microsoft Knowledge Base article Q278984 *PRB: Error 7321 Occurs When You Run a Query That Uses Four-Part Names Against DB2 on an AS/400 Computer*. |
| 7356 | OLE DB provider '%ls' supplied inconsistent metadata for a column. Metadata information was changed at execution time. | This occurs when inconsistent column meta data is returned between compilation and execution time for the query. To troubleshoot this, you need to determine which column or columns are responsible for the inconsistent meta data. For example, you can get this error if connecting to an Oracle table that did not specify nullability of a column. See Microsoft Knowledge Base Article Q251238 *PRB: Distributed Queries Return Error 7356 with MSDAORA* for more details. |

| Error Number | Message | Description |
|---|---|---|
| 7357 | Could not process object '%ls'. The OLE DB provider '%ls' indicates that the object has no columns. | This error suggests that you chose either invalid column names or table names, or that you have insufficient permissions to access the object. |
| 7391 | The operation could not be performed because the OLE DB provider '%ls' was unable to begin a distributed transaction. | Indicates that the OLE DB provider may not support distributed transactions for data modification statements.<br><br>This error also occurs when trying to connect a distributed transaction through a firewall. MS DTC uses dynamic port allocation to bind a distributed transaction, and the port can be blocked by the firewall. To select one port for use by MS DTC and prevent dynamic port allocation, follow the procedure in Microsoft Knowledge Base article Q250367 *INFO: Configuring Microsoft Distributed Transaction Coordinator (DTC) to Work Through a Firewall*. |
| 7392 | Could not start a transaction for OLE DB provider '%ls'.<br><br>or:<br><br>Only one transaction can be active on this session. | Indicates that the OLE DB provider does not support nested transactions. By selecting `SET XACT_ABORT ON`, SQL Server will not require nested-transaction support from the provider. |
| 7399 | OLE DB provider '%ls' reported an error. %ls<br><br>Cannot start your application. The workgroup information file is missing or opened exclusively by another user. | *SQL Server Books Online* suggests that this is specifically a Microsoft Access-related error, due either to the Microsoft Access database not being configured with an `Admin` account without a password, or your registry key not pointing to the correct Access workgroup file.<br><br>This message can also occur, however, after installing Oracle 8.x client software on the server. The error occurs if you try to connect with the Oracle OLE DB connection without first restarting the server after installing the Oracle 8.x client software. See Microsoft Knowledge Base Article Q277002 PRB: *Distributed Query Against Oracle 8.x Fails* for more details. |

*Table continued on following page*

| Error Number | Message | Description |
|---|---|---|
| 7403 | Could not locate registry entry for OLE DB provider '%ls'. | Either you used an incorrect OLE DB provider name when adding the linked server, or the OLE DB drivers are not registered correctly. |
| 7413 | Could not perform a Windows NT-authenticated login because delegation is not available. | The error indicates that mapping has not been performed to a remote login and password. This can occur when security delegation is not supported. |
| 8114 | Error converting data type %ls to %ls. | This error indicates that the OLE DB provider has returned a datetime value outside the supported range. Omit the column from your query, or add a `WHERE` clause that eliminates invalid or out-of-range dates. |
| 8501 | MS DTC on server '%.*ls' is unavailable. | Data modifications require the MSDTC service to be running locally, as well as provider support for distributed transactions. Start the MSDTC service on your local server. |
| 15028 | The server 'Servername' already exists. | This error is received when you attempt to add a new linked server. Server information for both linked servers and replication servers is kept in the `sysservers` table. If replication configuration has already added an entry for the server you are attempting to add, you may get this error.<br><br>To resolve this issue, you need only change server status to allow data access. The instructions for doing this are fully described in the Microsoft Knowledge Base article 275098, *PRB: Adding a Linked Server Causes Error 15028*. |
| Slow Response Time | Slow response time for a query with multiple OR clauses within a stored procedure or OLE DB for ODBC connection. | If you are using multiple `OR` clauses for fields in a composite index, the execution time may be sub-optimal as an index or table scan may occur instead of using the composite index.<br><br>This is a known bug and is referenced in Microsoft Knowledge Base Article Q223423, *BUG: Optimizer Uses Scan with Multiple OR Clauses on Composite Index*. This Knowledge Base article gives several suggestions for workarounds. |

# 10

# Failover Clustering

Microsoft Cluster Service (MSCS) is available for installation on Windows 2000 Advanced Server, Windows 2000 Datacenter Server, and Windows NT Enterprise Edition with Service Pack 5 (although this is not recommended). MSCS allows applications, such as SQL Server 2000 Enterprise Edition, to take advantage of high-availability **failover** functionality. A failover means that if one server, or **node**, fails, the applications on another server in the cluster will start up and take over for the failed node. There are two types of failovers, planned and those that occur as a result of a server hardware or software problem. Only applications that are **cluster-aware** can utilize the MSCS failover capabilities. Cluster-aware applications, such as SQL Server, will remain available even if one node encounters a failure. Windows 2000 Advanced Server supports two-node clustering, and Windows 2000 Datacenter supports four-node clustering.

MSCS achieves high availability by using a shared disk array. For SQL Server clustering, this shared disk array contains the database files (`.mdf`, `.ndf`, `.ldf`), along with backups, and other optional components. The shared disk can be a regular external SCSI disk or disk array, or a Storage Area Network (SAN) array. SAN arrays are sold by hardware and software vendors, and allow high-speed data transfer to external disk arrays via a fiber channel connection (and network card). Software RAID is not supported; only hardware RAID configurations are allowed. File encryption is also unsupported for the shared disk(s).

Binary installation files and executables are installed locally on both nodes of a two-node cluster, and are not placed on the shared disk. The SQL Server and SQL Server Agent services are also installed on each node of the cluster. For a SQL Server 2000 **virtual server**, the same service is installed on both nodes, but only one side is active at any time. Virtual server is another way of saying that the SQL Server instance is on a failover cluster. Clients and applications connect to the virtual server as they would for a nonclustered default or named instance of SQL Server. The SQL Server 2000 virtual server can exist or be controlled by either node within a cluster (but only **one** at a time):

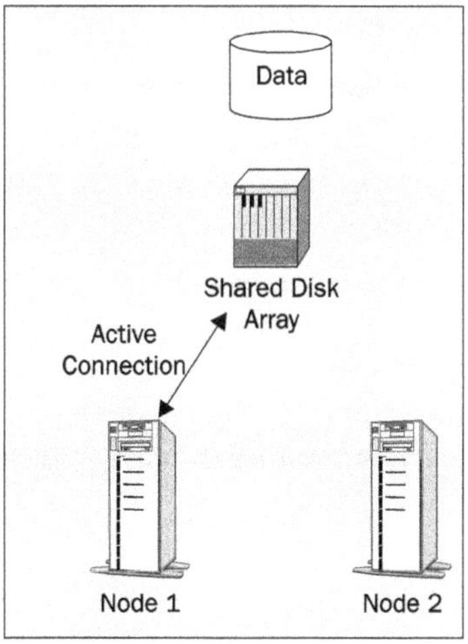

If a failure occurs on the active node, the second node will 'go live'; its services will start up and take over control of the files on the shared disk array for the SQL Server 2000 virtual server:

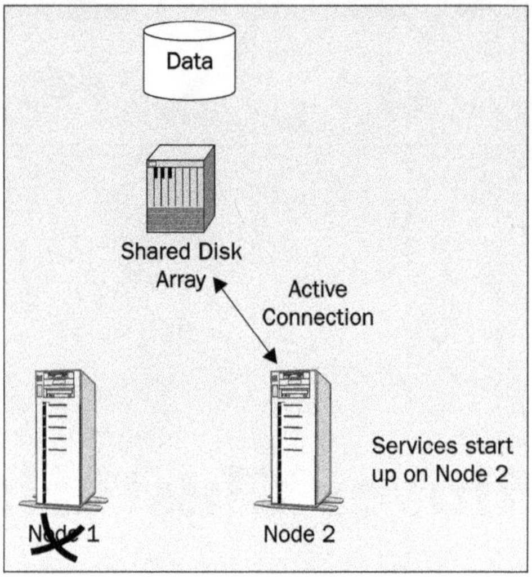


In a two-node cluster, two servers are connected using a private network (heartbeat) connection. The private network gives the two nodes a fast path for checking each other's status. Network connectivity for end users is established via a public IP address. End users connect to the SQL Server 2000 virtual server using the virtual server NetBIOS name. This name and TCP/IP address is defined prior to SQL Server installation, and is specified during installation.

A SQL Server 2000 virtual server is defined by a cluster group, which in turn is made up of separate resources. Resources included in a SQL Server 2000 virtual server group include a shared disk drive or drives, the virtual server name, the virtual server IP address, the SQL Server and SQL Server agent services and, optionally, the SQL Server Fulltext service. This group is treated as a single unit where, in the event of a node failure, all resources must be started or engaged on the failover node. Resources and groups are managed in Cluster Administrator, which will be reviewed later in this chapter.

A two-node cluster needs the following names and IP addresses:

| Type | Description |
|---|---|
| Physical server name and TCP/IP address for first node | Just like a normal server requirement, you have a name and associated IP address. |
| Physical server name and TCP/IP address for second node | ... |
| Cluster name and TCP/IP address | The cluster name is a virtual name and IP address used for adding MSCS, and is referenced in Cluster Administrator (more on this later on). |
| Heartbeat name and TCP/IP address for Node 1 | The heartbeat or **private** network connection between the two nodes for checking status and availability. These should be on the same subnet. |

| Type | Description |
|---|---|
| Heartbeat name and TCP/IP address for Node 2 | ... |
| SQL Server 2000 virtual server name and TCP/IP address | This is the name that SQL Server users will use to access the clustered instance. This instance can exist on either Node 1 or Node 2. Users should treat this instance like any regular SQL Server instance. If you are installing just one SQL Server instance on the cluster, this is an active/passive setup. |
| Second SQL Server 2000 virtual server name and TCP/IP address | If using two instances of SQL Server on one cluster, this is called an active/active setup. |

Failover clustering with SQL Server 2000 Enterprise Edition allows an **active/passive**, or **active/active** setup. Active/passive, also called **single instance**, means the failover cluster has one node that remains unused until a failover occurs. You can have a SQL Server named instance called `BookRepo\INS1` that is managed by Node1 by default, but can fail over to Node2:

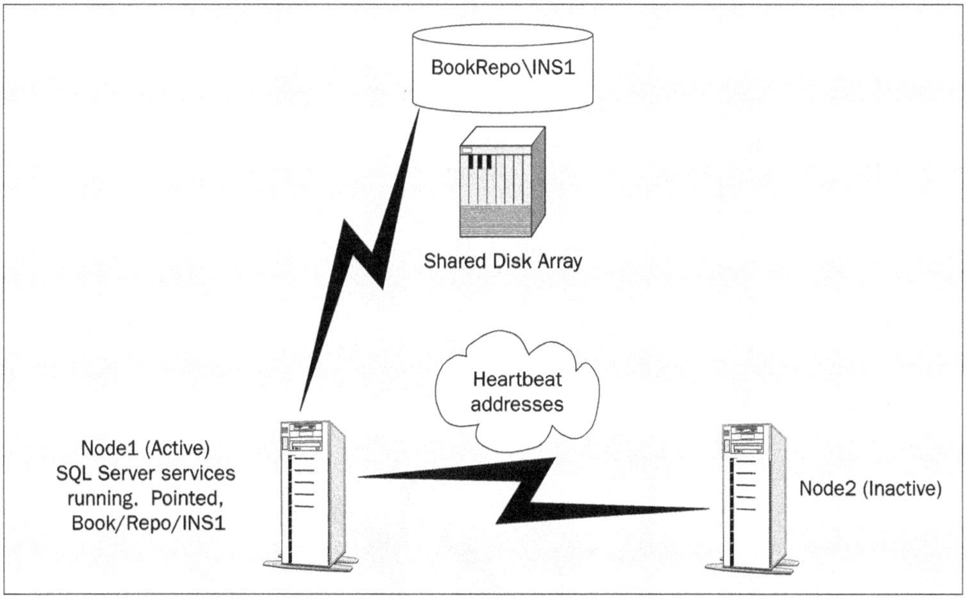


Active/active configuration, also called **multi-instance**, makes use of both nodes in a cluster. You can run two instances of SQL Server on the cluster. For example, Node1 can run `BookRepo\INS1` and Node2 can run `BookRepo\INS2`. Both instances are separate installations of SQL Server and can fail over to each other's node if one node fails. The advantage of active/active is that you have twice the SQL Server instances to work with, and the hardware does not go to waste:

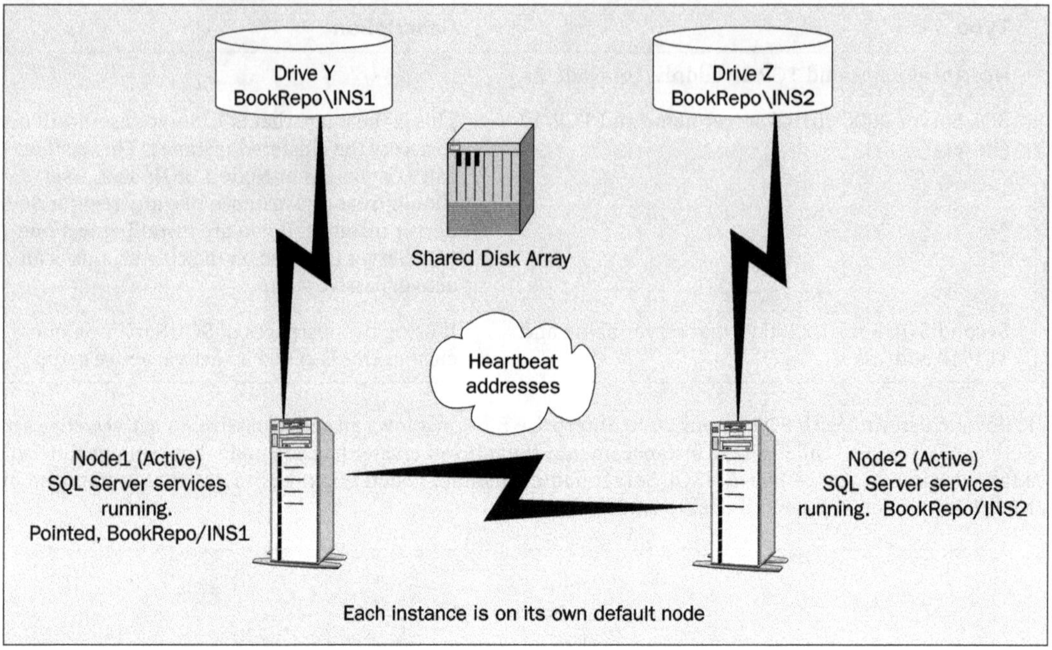


In the event of a failure in Node2, services for both instances of SQL Server would be running on Node1, pointing to the associated shared disk drives in order to keep both instances running.

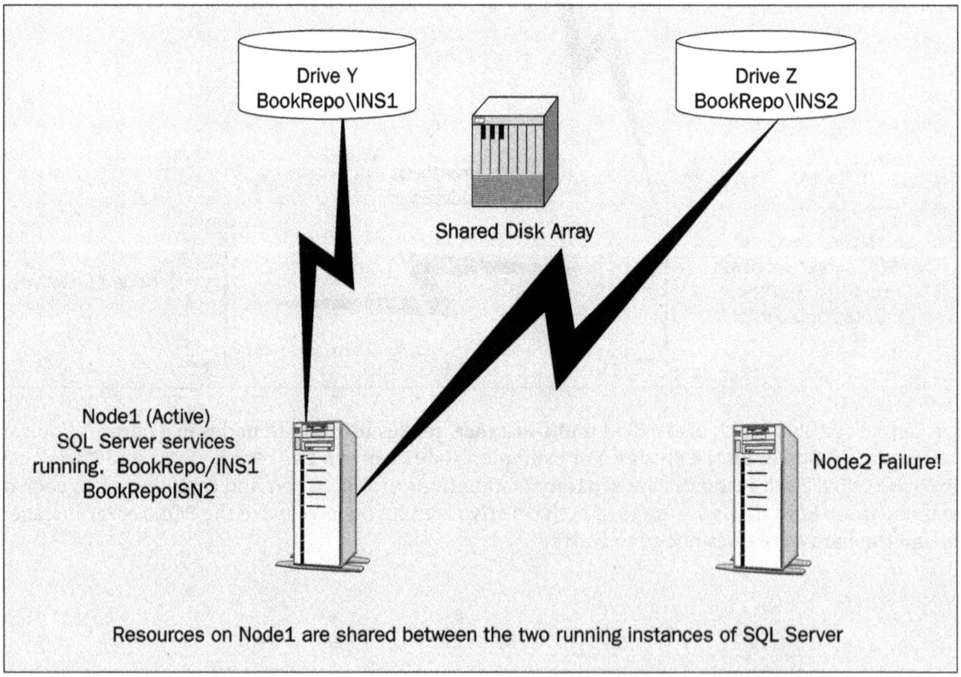

It is important to understand that MSCS allows **high availability**, but not total fault-tolerance. If one node fails with an existing SQL Server 2000 virtual server, that virtual server will restart and be controlled from the second node. Depending on how large your instances are, and the recovery time for your databases, failover can take anywhere from 15 seconds to several minutes. During a failover, any users currently connected will be disconnected as if the server were rebooted.

Also note that failover clustering is **not** the same as network load balancing (NLB). Workload is not distributed between the two nodes for one SQL Server instance. NLB is a Microsoft Windows product that balances incoming Internet Protocol traffic across multiple nodes, acting as one logical application, and allowing the application to scale out up to 32 nodes. NLB is used primarily for Web and media servers, as well as Terminal Services. Failover Clustering (the cluster service) on the other hand, is used primarily for database, file, print, and messaging servers.

Nor is a failover cluster a substitute for a disaster recovery plan. You must still produce a disaster recovery plan, in order to get mission-critical applications back online as quickly as possible (see Chapter 6).

# Cluster Meta Data

The Cluster Group manages failover and keeps track of groups and resources. This group uses a shared drive called the **quorum drive**, which manages the cluster and logging:

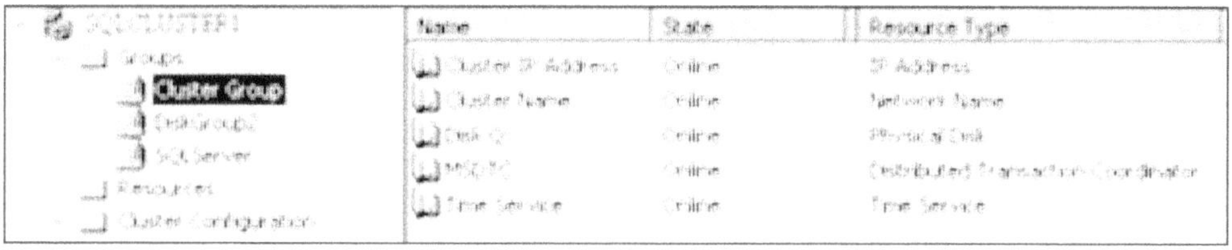

Do not use this quorum drive to install files on your SQL Server instances. The cluster group usually consists of the cluster IP address resource, cluster name resource, quorum drive resource, time service resource, and MS DTC service resource. Just like a SQL Server group, the Cluster Group is only managed by one node at a time, but can failover to the second node in the event of a problem.

# Cluster Administrator

Throughout this chapter, you will be using the Cluster Administrator. Cluster Administrator can be launched on either of the cluster nodes, or from your client.

> **If you are familiar with previous versions of failover clustering for SQL Server, please note that as an enhancement from SQL Server 2000 onwards, you can now use SQL Server Service Manager or SQL Server Enterprise Manager to start and stop SQL Server, without having to use Cluster Administrator to start and stop SQL Server services.**

If you have not installed the Administrative Tools from the Windows 2000 CD, you must do so in order to run Cluster Administrator from your client. To install these utilities, run `AdminPak.msi` from the I386 folder on the Windows 2000 Advanced Server CD.

To launch Cluster Administrator, go to Start | Programs | Administrative Tools | Cluster Administrator. A faster method is to go to Start | Run, type in cluadmin and OK.

Cluster Administrator allows you to:

- Add new groups (groups are logical groupings of resources).
- Add resources to groups (resources being disk drives, IP addresses, network names, services, and more...)
- Fail a group to another node. This means that the group and the resources it contains are taken offline on the existing node, and brought online on the other node.
- Take a group offline (if you need to add new resources or configure group properties).
- Configure resource properties and dependencies (resource dependencies help make sure that certain resources are necessary for others to run).
- Monitor the status of the nodes and resources (red X marks and yellow caution flags show issues with entities in Cluster Administrator).

This chapter will explain how to use Cluster Administrator in the context of installing and configuring a SQL Server 2000 Virtual Server. This chapter also assumes that MSCS has already been installed and configured.

# Pre-Installation Checklist for SQL Server Failover Clustering

- SQL Server 2000 Enterprise Edition is required.
- For active/passive, you need to install SQL Server once. For active/active, you install SQL Server twice, once for each virtual server name. Make sure your name and TCP/IP addresses are reserved for your virtual server name(s).
- Verify that you can ping each of the heartbeat DNS names for the cluster, both for the physical node names, and the cluster name. If you get a response problem, make sure that the nodes are running and IP addresses have been configured properly.
- Make sure that the shared disk drive letter mappings are the **same** on both nodes of the cluster.
- Make sure that the shared disk drive(s) are accessible.
- Make sure your hardware is listed on Microsoft's Hardware Compatibility List (HCL). The fact that you can get it to work does not mean that Microsoft will support you if you run into problems. Treat this warning seriously for your production environments.
- Make sure all operating system service packs and patches are installed first.
- Make sure NetBIOS is disabled for your private (heartbeat) network properties. Go to Start | Settings | Network | Dialup Connections. Double-click the private network connection. Click Properties. Select TCP/IP and select Properties. Click the Advanced button. On the WINS tab, make sure NetBIOS is disabled.
- Make sure your network cards being used for both public and private connections are not set to `auto detect`. Go to Start | Settings | Network | Dialup Connections. Double-click the network connection (make sure to do this for each network connection used). Click Properties. Click Configure. In the Advanced tab, click Advanced, and select Link Speed & Duplex. Make sure this is not set to Auto detect, but rather to the speed capabilities for the card.
- Determine ahead of time the naming convention for your virtual SQL Server name(s) and cluster name. With two physical names, two private heartbeat names, one cluster name, and one or more virtual SQL Server names, keeping track can get a little confusing!

- ❑ Do not install a failover cluster on a domain controller. Putting SQL Server instances on a domain controller is generally not recommended for nonclustered implementations in general. You may encounter performance contention if the domain controller is particularly busy, or security issues if you require a domain account for running the SQL Server and SQL Server Agent service accounts.

# 10.1 How to… Install a SQL Server 2000 Virtual Server

Prior to installing the SQL Server 2000 instance, you must install a **cluster aware** version of the Microsoft Distributed Transaction Coordinator (MS DTC) service.

- ❑ Open a command line window and type comclust. Press Enter. The MS DTC service will now be installed as 'cluster aware':

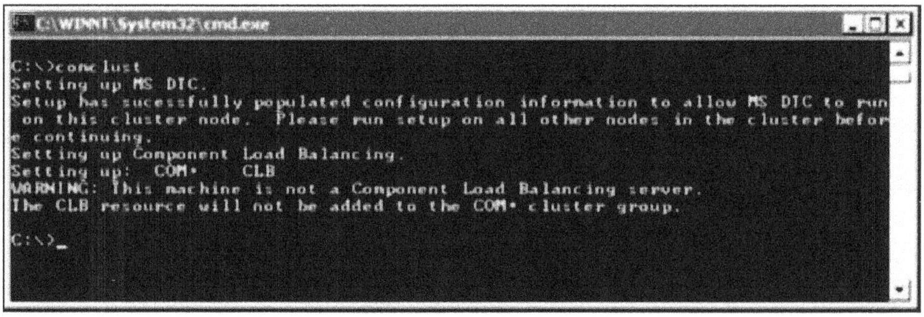


- ❑ Repeat step 1 on the second node.
- ❑ Check to make sure that the MS DTC service was added to the Cluster Group on your cluster. Go to Start | Run | and type cluadmin.
- ❑ Expand the Group folder and click the Cluster Group (this may have been named something else by your administrator after the MSCS installation, but this is the group with the quorum disk resources, cluster name, and IP address). Make sure MS DTC is in the group:

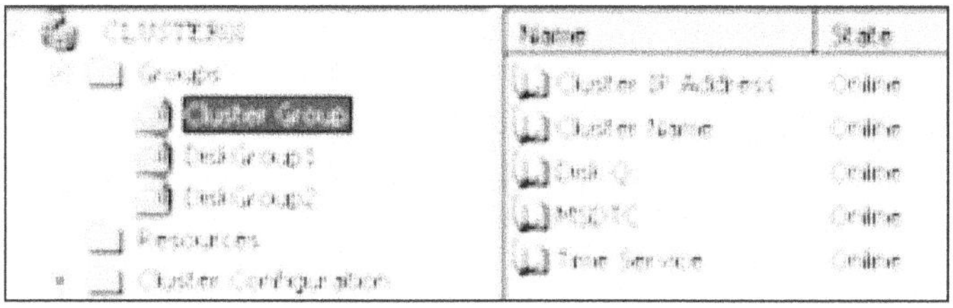


- ❑ While in Cluster Administrator, verify that the node from which you are installing SQL Server currently controls the shared disk(s) you plan to use for the SQL Server instance. If not, right-click the group containing the disk resources and select Move Group; this will move control of the group to the opposite node.
- ❑ Insert the SQL Server 2000 CD ROM on the installation node. Installing a SQL Server instance for clustering from a network drive can cause difficulties and does not always work. If the main splash screen doesn't automatically start up in a few seconds, double-click `autorun.exe` in the root directory of the CD.

- Select SQL Server 2000 Components.
- Select Install Database Server.
- Select Next.
- Type in the SQL Server 2000 virtual server name.
- Enter your name and company.
- Read the software license agreement and, if you agree to the terms, select Yes.
- Enter the SQL Server 2000 Enterprise Edition CD key.
- Enter the IP address for the SQL Server 2000 virtual server you reserved prior to installation. Select the network connection (public or private); your SQL Server instance should use the public connection.
- Select the shared disk that the data files should occupy. Do not use the quorum disk for your SQL Server data files; the Quorum disk belongs to the Cluster Group (or whatever you named the group that controls the failover cluster), which is the group that manages the cluster's groups and resources. If the SQL Server instance requires the cluster drive and the SQL Server group fails, this may also take the cluster down. This is because dependencies, such as a physical disk, require that all dependents (including SQL Server and the Cluster Service) exist in the same group. Sharing the Quorum disk with your Virtual SQL Server instance may cause I/O contention or performance issues.
- Select which nodes in the cluster will have SQL Server installed. The default for a two-node cluster should already have the two physical nodes selected.
- Select an administrator account with administrator permissions for **both** nodes in the cluster. This must be a domain account.
- Decide whether or not this will be a default instance or a named instance. If a named instance, uncheck Default and select an instance name. For active/passive, keeping Default checked is the norm, but for active/active, your server names may make more sense if you use an instance name.
- Select the installation type and directory location. Program files are placed on a local partition (during installation on **both** nodes) and the data files on a shared disk.
- Select which components to install.
- Select the domain account to be used for the SQL Server and SQL Server agent services. This must be an account that exists on **both** nodes in the cluster, with administrator permissions.
- Select the SQL Server instance collation.
- Select the TCP/IP port. If the port number is 0, a port will be dynamically chosen for you upon installation. If this is an externally facing SQL Server Instance (accessed over a firewall), you may wish to pre-define a TCP/IP port that will be opened to the firewall for such SQL Server Instances. If you are configuring a multi-instance cluster, you may need two such defined ports. Defining standard ports for single or multi-instance clusters will allow you to minimize the number of ports that must be opened on your firewall for each externally-facing failover cluster. The alternative is unique ports, selected randomly during the install, for each instance belonging to a Virtual Server or Named Instance.
- Select Next:

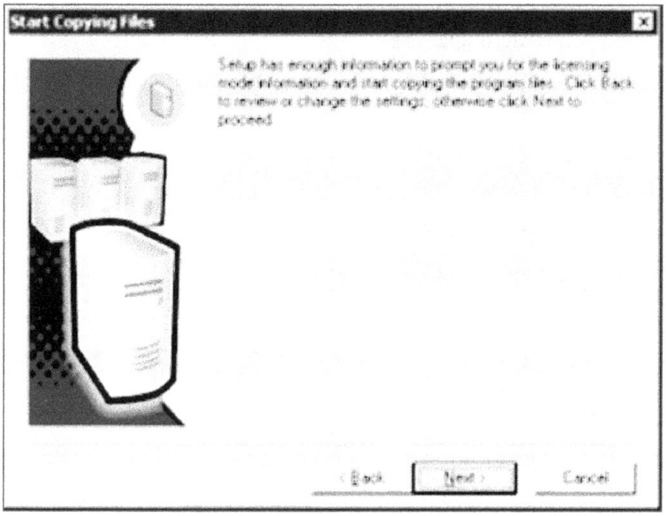


- Choose a licensing mode.
- As the installation begins, you will receive update dialog boxes indicating that operations are being performed on the cluster nodes, and that virtual server resources are being created:

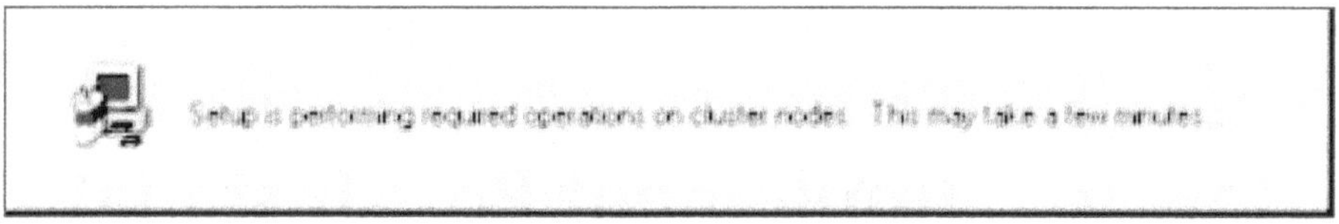

- Select Finish.
- Although you may not be prompted to do so, reboot the first node on which you installed the SQL Server 2000 Virtual Server, and then the second node too.
- To create an active/active configuration, repeat the steps to add a new SQL Server instance.

# 10.2 How to... Install a Service Pack for a SQL Server 2000 Virtual Server

As new service packs are released, make sure to read the instructions thoroughly to see if any changes in procedure have been added for clustered installs. The following example shows how to install service pack 2 for SQL Server 2000 for a SQL Server 2000 Virtual Server (see Chapter 1 for a review of downloading and installing a service pack):

- First, make sure you are installing the service pack from the node currently controlling the SQL Server instance group that you wish to upgrade.
- Double-click the `setup.bat` file in the installation path directory of the service pack files.
- Select Next.
- Select the virtual server name that you wish to upgrade.
- Select the authentication mode for the service pack setup.

  You will receive the following update:

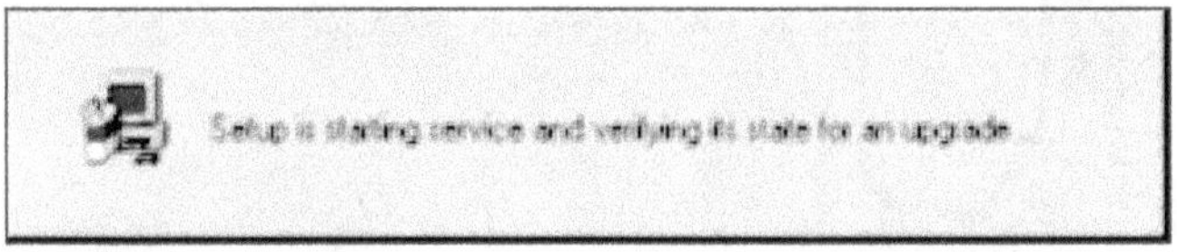

- Select the user name and password with administrator permissions for all nodes in the cluster.
- Installation will begin. System databases will be updated, and binary files on both nodes will be updated.
- You will be prompted to back up the `master` and `msdb` databases.
- Restart both nodes in the cluster. If you have an active/active topology, restart the first node, and then failover the non-upgraded instance to the restarted node and restart the second node. To fail over or fail back a group, simply right-click the group in Cluster Administrator and select Move Group. Fail back each SQL Server group to its default instance (node by which you want each SQL Server group to be controlled).

# 10.3 How to... Implement Post-Installation Steps

After installing a SQL Server virtual server, there are some remaining steps that must be performed:

- Start Cluster Administrator by selecting Start | Run and typing cluadmin.
- In Cluster Administrator, type in the cluster or server name. If you have already been in Cluster Administrator, any cluster connections you had open will immediately be brought up instead. If you want to access a new cluster, go to the File | Open Connection window:

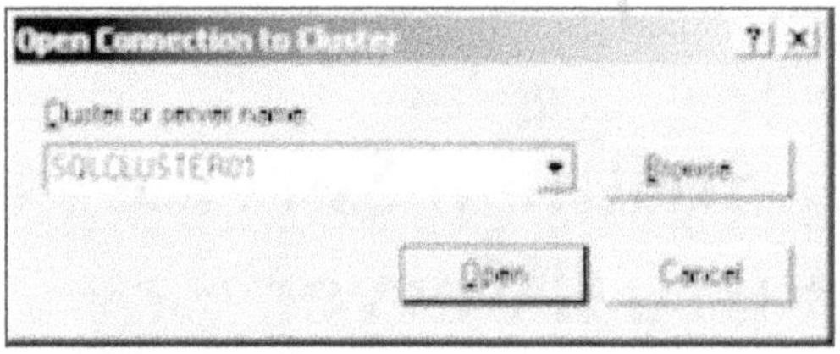


- Give the SQL Server 2000 virtual server group a more appropriate name (instead of Disk Group 1 or something not indicating SQL Server). To change the group name, expand Groups and click the group name once to enter a new name. Select Enter when complete.

# Adding Additional Disk Resources

After installing SQL Server, the only disk resource added to your SQL Server 2000 Virtual Server group will be the data file drive selected during installation. If you wish to use additional shared disk drives for SQL Server, they must be added to the SQL Server group.

- Open the group that currently holds the disk drives you wish to add to the SQL Server group, right-click each disk resource, select Change Group, and select the group to which to move it.
- You will be prompted to make sure you wish to move this resource to a new group, and then again, for which you should select Yes:
- If the original group is now empty, right-click the group in Cluster Administrator and select Delete.
- Next, you must make this physical disk a dependency of SQL Server so that SQL Server can use it. Dependencies ensure that resources are available before a specific resource can be taken online within a cluster group. First, the SQL Server 2000 virtual server group must be taken offline; do this by right-clicking the group in Cluster Administrator, and selecting Take Offline.
- In the right pane, with the Virtual SQL Server instance group selected in the left pane, right-click the SQL Server resource (the service) and select Properties.
- In the Dependencies tab, click the Modify button.
- Add the disk resource you wish the Virtual SQL Server instance to use, by clicking the available resources and selecting the right arrow to add to the Dependencies pane.
- Select OK in the Modify Dependencies dialog box, and OK again in the Properties dialog box for the service.
- Right-click the SQL Server group in the left pane of Cluster Administrator, and select Bring Online.

# Other Post-Installation Configurations to Monitor

- Watch out for fixed memory sizes defined on your SQL Server instances; make sure the total size used for an active/active cluster does not exceed the total memory resources of one node. For example, if you set a fixed 2.5GB size for each instance but the total memory per server is 4GB, you will have problems if two instances need to share a node.
- Keep the `BUILTIN\Administrators` account in SQL Server, as it is used by the cluster service account.
- If you plan on using replication on a clustered SQL Server instance, use a share name on the shared disk. Do not use a local disk on either of the physical server nodes.
- Always look for instructions specific to clustering. For example, if downloading the latest security patch, follow the instructions for a cluster and not the regular installation instructions. If explicit clustered installation instructions do not exist, do not assume that your changes will work, or that your new components will be cluster-aware.
- If you ever need to change an IP address for the Virtual SQL Server, you must do so using the SQL Server Enterprise Edition installation CD. See Microsoft Knowledge Base article Q244980, *HOWTO: Change the Network IP Addresses on a Virtual SQL Server*.
- To change the domain of a SQL Server Failover Cluster, reference the Microsoft Knowledge Base article 319016, *HOW TO: Change Domains for a SQL Server 2000 Failover Cluster*.

- Unlike a nonclustered instance of SQL Server 2000, renaming a Virtual Server on a failover cluster is not recommended. You must uninstall and reinstall the cluster with the new name. For more details, see the Microsoft Knowledge Base article 307336, *INF: How to Change a Clustered SQL Server Network Name*.
- Microsoft recommends that symmetric multiprocessing (SMP) systems should have one processor reserved for the operating system and cluster service, using processor affinity. You should consider this within the context of how intense CPU usage will be for your SQL Server 2000 virtual server (or servers for active/active).

# 10.4 How to... Troubleshoot a Failed SQL Server Virtual Server

When installing a new SQL Server 2000 virtual server, installation could take anywhere from 15 to 30 minutes, depending on the hardware used. If your installation takes longer than that, make sure the installation has not hung. Press the Alt-Tab key combination to make sure that there are no error messages in the background. For example, if attempting to install SQL Server from a network drive, you might receive a files not found error in the background (which is why installing from a CD-ROM drive is preferred).

For failed or interrupted installations, you can usually restart installation by removing the resources created so far via Cluster Administrator; these include the resources for SQL Server Name and SQL Server IP address. Do not delete the resource for the shared disk drive(s) you may be using. You may also need to delete binary files that were installed on the local disk on both nodes, before trying to reinstall the SQL Server clustered instance.

Before attempting to do a manual cleanup of the files and resources, attempt a regular uninstall first (see the next section). For more details on manual uninstalls of Virtual Servers, see the Microsoft Knowledge Base article 290991, *Manually Remove SQL Server 2000 Default, Named, or Virtual Instance*.

Some other troubleshooting tips to keep in mind:

- SQL Server 2000 clustering does not support SQLMail and SQLAgentMail.
- Examine the Sqlstp.log file in C:\WINNT directory for more detail about which errors occurred and how far the installation proceeded before failing.
- Check out the Microsoft Knowledge Base article Q321063 HOW TO: *Troubleshoot the 'Setup Failed to Perform Required Operations on the Cluster Nodes' Error*, for more in-depth information on troubleshooting failed installations. Other useful troubleshooting articles include article Q279642, *PRB: SQL Server 2000 Virtual Server Setup Error: 'The Drive Chosen for the Program Files Installation Path <C:>, Is Not a Valid Path on All the Nodes of the Cluster', Not Valid*; article Q235529, *MSCS Virtual Server Limitations in a Windows 2000 Domain Environment*; and article Q283794, *Problems Using Certificate with Virtual Name in Clustered SQL Servers*.

# 10.5 How to... Uninstall a SQL Server 2000 Virtual Server

To uninstall a SQL Server 2000 Virtual Server:

- From the SQL Server 2000 Enterprise Edition installation CD, select Setup.

- Select Next from the Welcome screen.
- Select the SQL Server 2000 Virtual Server you wish to uninstall.
- Select Upgrade, remove, or add components to an existing instance of SQL Server.
- Select the named instance to remove.
- Select Next to proceed with uninstalling the installation.
- Select a valid service account with administrator permissions to all nodes (installation will remove binary files from both nodes in the cluster).
- You will receive a prompt updating the progress of the operation.
- You will then receive a prompt after the instance has been removed successfully.
- Select Finish in the final dialog box. Reboot each node in the cluster.

# 11

# DTS

Data Transformation Services (DTS) is the most versatile tool included with SQL Server 2000. Most SQL Server professionals are first exposed to DTS via the DTS Import and Export Wizard; however, you can program DTS within the DTS Designer development environment in Enterprise Manager. DTS also exposes a Component Object Model (COM) that you can use via COM-enabled programming languages.

DTS is often used for moving data between heterogeneous or homogeneous data sources. It is also used to transform the data; meaning that the data is changed in some manner from how it was stored on the original server. The core DTS functionality offers the ability to:

- Transfer (import and export) schemas and data between SQL Server instances and heterogeneous data sources.
- Execute Transact-SQL commands against a SQL Server instance.
- Execute batch files or other valid executables.
- Transform data.
- Import files from an FTP site.
- Use Microsoft Message Queuing to exchange messages between DTS packages (a package is a saved DTS definition with one or more connections, DTS tasks, DTS transformations, and workflow constraints associated with it).
- Send mail.
- Execute ActiveX script tasks using VBScript, JScript, or PerlScript (PerlScript is not available by default).
- Create workflow dependencies, ensuring that certain actions take place after a successful, failed, or completed event. Workflow also defines the order of execution and allows steps to execute in sequential or parallel order.

Also, because DTS has an exposed COM Object Model, programming languages, such as Visual Basic or C++, can create or invoke DTS packages as part of an application.

The SQL Server 2000 client installation adds the necessary components for creating DTS packages. You can save your DTS packages to:

- A **SQL Server** instance. The package is saved in the `sysdtspackages` table in the `msdb` database. Saving your DTS packages in this way gives you more recoverability of your packages in the event of loss or damage (assuming you are backing up your `msdb` database on a scheduled basis).
- A **Structured Storage File** using the `*.dts` file extension.
- A **Visual Basic** `*.bas` file. This option is helpful if you wish to delve into the code and object models used to generate the DTS package programmatically.
- To **Meta Data Services**, which allows you to store and manage meta data about information systems and applications. Beginning with SQL Server 2000 Service Pack 3, this option is disabled by default and will not appear in the Location drop-down list in the Save DTS Packages dialog box. This option is also disabled after the service pack installation in the save, schedule, and replication pages of the DTS Import/ExportWizard. To enable this option, in Enterprise Manager, expand the Server Registration, right click the Data Transformation Services folder, and in the Package Properties dialog, select the checkbox Enable Save To Meta Data Services.

DTS packages can be executed manually from DTS Designer, programmatically using the DTS Object Model (with the `dtsrun` command-line utility), via the `dtsrunui` utility, or scheduled as a SQL Server Agent job.

This chapter will review how to create a DTS Package using DTS Designer, how to execute a DTS Package via `dtsrun`, and other concepts that are necessary for DTS Package development.

# 11.1 How to... Use DTS Designer

To launch DTS Designer, in Enterprise Manager:

- Expand the Server group and registration.
- Expand the Data Transformation Services folder.
- Right-click Local Packages, and select New Package.

This will open the DTS Designer workspace:

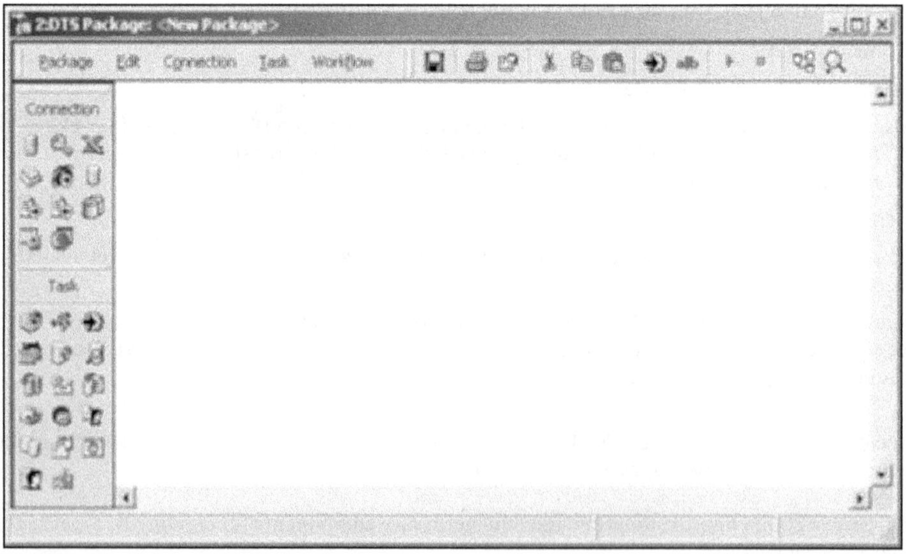

Within DTS Designer, you can create a DTS package. The building blocks of a DTS package are:

- **Connection** objects. These define connections to data sources.
- **Task** objects. These define actions to take within the package.
- **Workflow** definitions. Workflow definitions help determine the order in which tasks are executed, and whether or not they should be executed. This is accomplished through **precedent constraints**.

# 11.2 How to... Add and Configure a Connection Object

To add a connection object to your package, click the Connection menu and select a connection type. If you are familiar with the connection icon, you can drag the connection icon from the left-hand toolbar to your DTS workspace instead of using the Connection menu.

SQL Server 2000 includes many connection types with the standard SQL Server installation, but you can use other connections, depending on the OLE DB drivers installed on your workstation or server. If you are developing your DTS package from your workstation and you plan to save the package to a SQL Server instance, make sure the SQL Server computer shares the same OLE DB drivers (otherwise the package may not run properly from the server).

## Connection Properties

Connection properties show different field options depending on the data source selected:

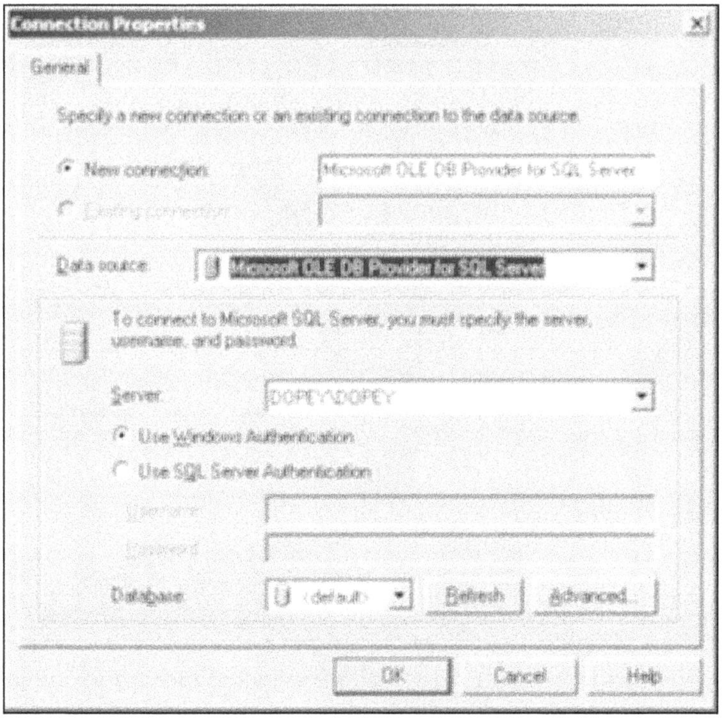

Below is a table reviewing the connection properties common fields:

| Name | Description |
|---|---|
| New connection | User-defined connection description. |
| Existing connection | Allows you to select an existing connection from your DTS package (used if you want to represent the same connection visually, or use it for multiple transformation tasks). For example, you could use the same JoeProd connection object to create two transformation tasks to the JoeRemote connection. Transformations are reviewed later on. |
| Data source | Data source driver type. |
| User/System DSN | User- or system-defined DSN. Select the New button to create a new DSN. The DSN list is from the workstation or server creating the package. |
| File DSN | Defined file DSN. The DSN list is from the workstation or server creating the package. |
| Use Windows authentication | Uses Windows authentication to connect to SQL Server. |
| Use SQL Server authentication | Uses SQL authentication to connect to SQL Server. |
| Username | User login name. |
| Password | Connection password. |
| File name | File path and directory, if using a file-based data provider. |
| | 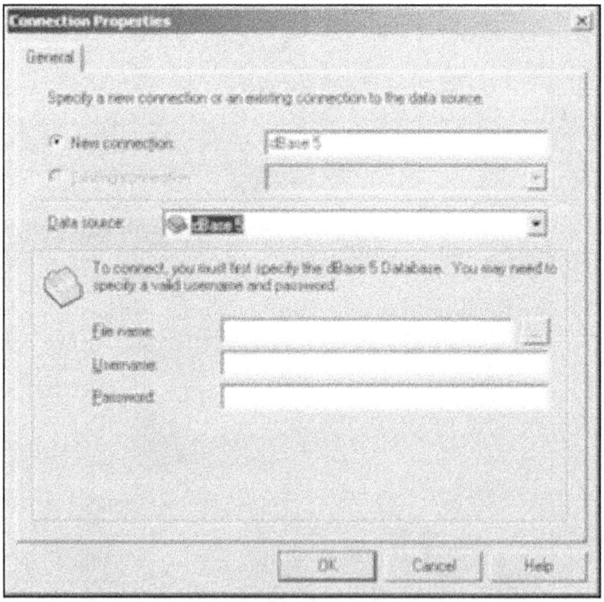 |

| Name | Description |
|---|---|
| Advanced | Shows advanced options for the data source. Options listed depend on the OLE DB driver: |

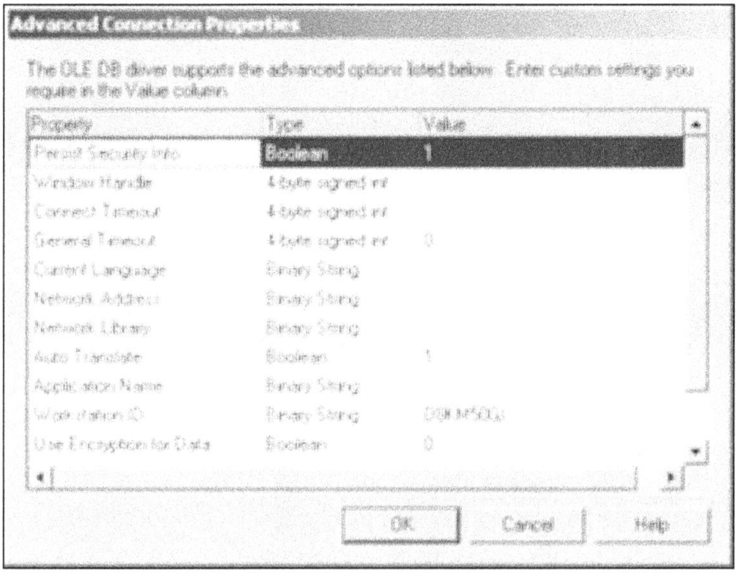


Select OK when you have finished configuring the single connection. You will see your new connection in the DTS Designer workspace.

Create as many connections as you will need for your DTS package; remember to label them descriptively, so you can distinguish them within the DTS Designer:

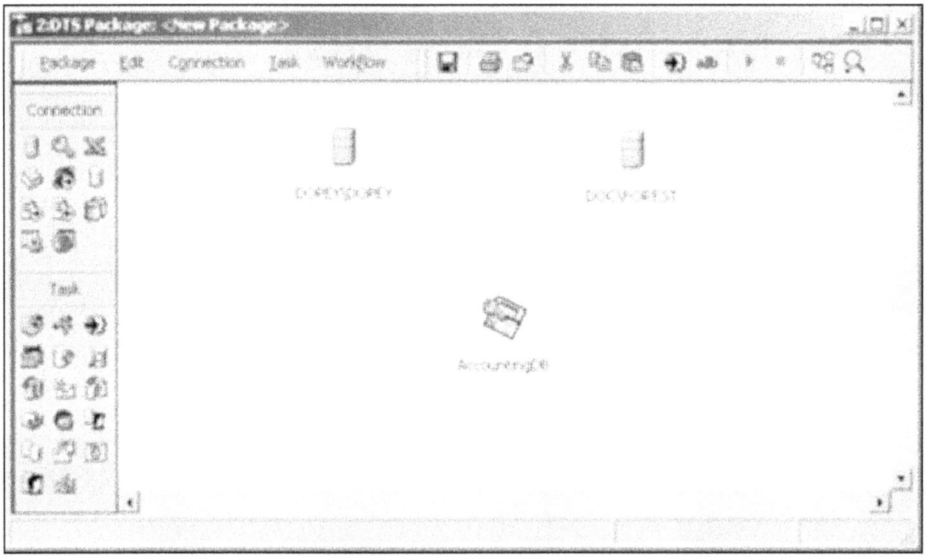

Each connection type installed with SQL Server has its associated icon:

| Icon | Connection Type |
|---|---|
|  | Microsoft OLE DB Provider for SQL Server |
|  | Microsoft Access |
|  | Microsoft Excel 97-2000 |
|  | Dbase 5 |
|  | HTML File (Source) |
|  | Paradox 5.x |
|  | Text File (Source) |
|  | Text File (Destination) |
| 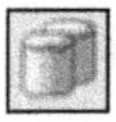 | Microsoft ODBC Driver for Oracle |
|  | Microsoft Data Link (Microsoft Data Link refers to `*.udl` files; these files define OLE DB connections) |
|  | Other (ODBC Data Source) |

# 11.3 How to… Add a New Task

To add a task to your DTS package, select one from the Task menu. If you are familiar with the Task icon, you can drag the Task icon from the left-hand tool bar to your DTS workspace instead of using the Task menu.

# 11.4 How to… Configure the File Transfer Protocol Task

The File Transfer Protocol task allows you to download data from an Internet site or directory to a destination directory. This task only allows you to **download** files, but not **upload** files:

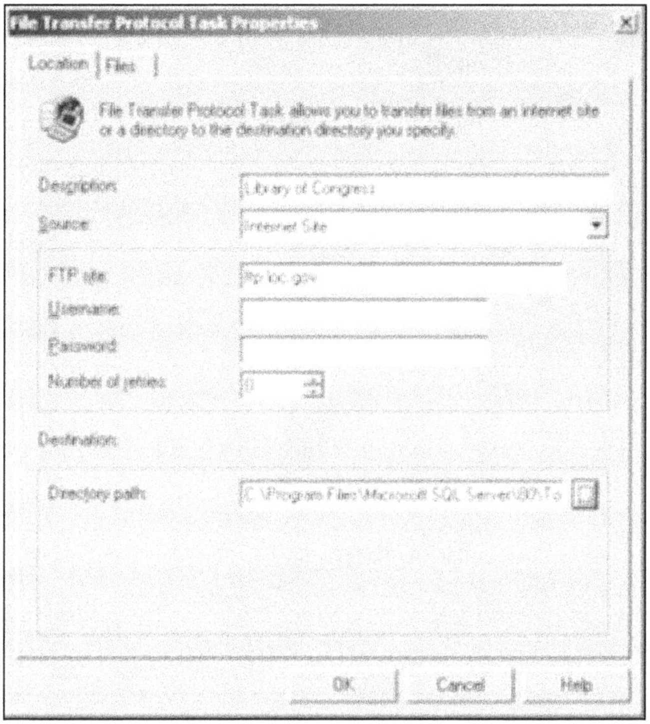


The Location tab fields are:

| Name | Description |
|---|---|
| Description | User-defined task description. |
| Source | Select a Directory or Internet Site. |
| Directory path | Appears as an option when Directory is selected. Selects the directory path of the file to download. |
| FTP site | Appears when an Internet Site is selected for the source. Selects the FTP address. |
| Username | Sets the username required for the FTP site. |
| Password | Sets the password for the FTP site. |
| Number of retries | Sets how many times a connection will be attempted after a connection failure. |
| Directory path | Specifies the location for the download of the destination files. |

The Files tab allows you to select which files to download. You can move between directories by double-clicking on those rows in the Source pane with <DIR>. To select a specific file to download, select the file to transfer and click the > button:

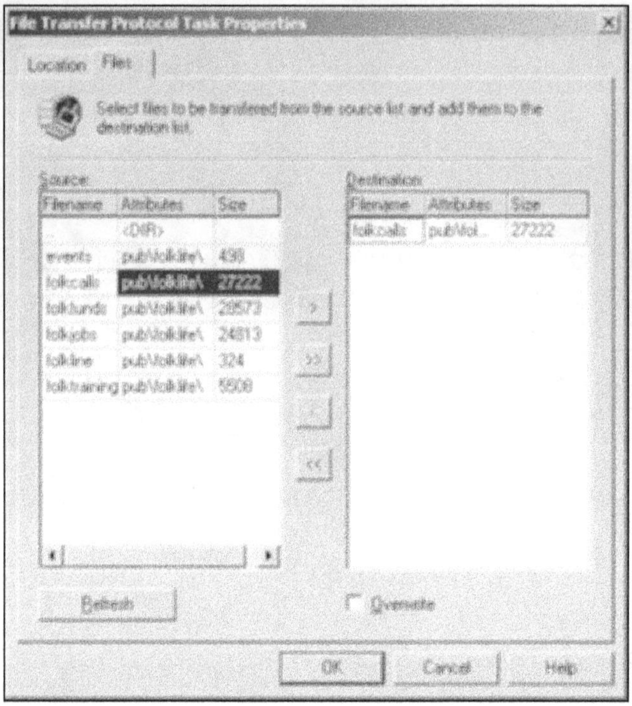


There is a known bug that occurs when you enter the address of an FTP site that points to a directory with an empty folder. Once you connect to an empty folder for a site, the options to move back to the FTP root directory, or move up one level, are no longer available. To avoid the problem, you need to put a placeholder file in the empty folders on the FTP site. If you are already caught in the middle of the problem, you must switch back to the Location tab, perform a dummy edit of the FTP Site text box, and then move back to the Files tab. Otherwise, you must click Cancel, and re-enter the task. For more information see Microsoft Knowledge Base article *Q300365, PRB: DTS FTP Task Does Not Allow User to Return to Parent Directory from an Empty Folder*.

# 11.5 How to... Configure the ActiveX Script Task

The **ActiveX script task** allows you to execute VBScript, PerlScript, or Jscript tasks within your DTS package (PerlScript is **not** available by default, and will only be seen if Perl is installed on the machine from which you are configuring the ActiveX Script Task). Scripts allow you to perform tasks including:

- Manipulating and analyzing data sources.
- Executing COM objects.
- Creating DTS packages or steps programmatically.
- Writing your own error handlers.

Here are the ActiveX script task properties:

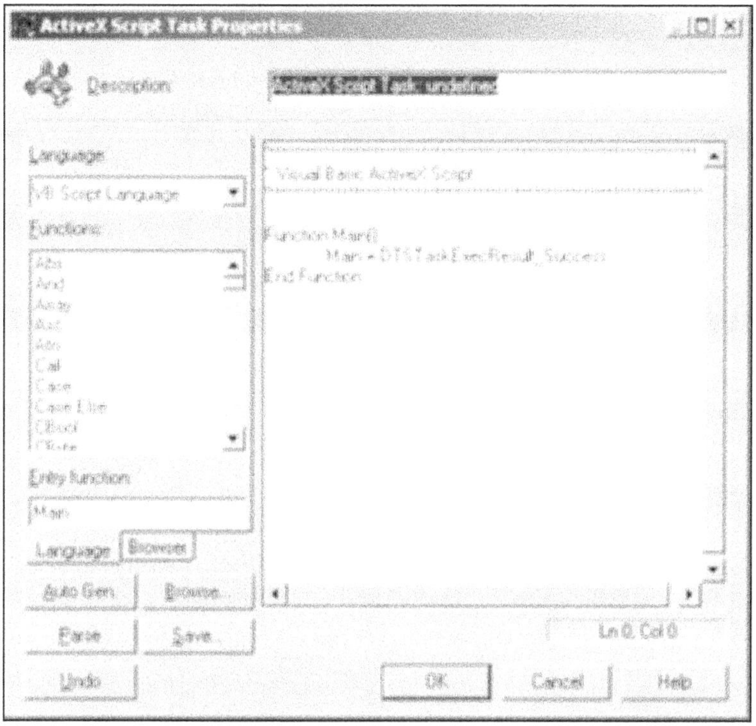


| Name | Description |
|---|---|
| Description | Set your user-friendly task description. |
| Language | Select the scripting language type you prefer to use. |
| Functions | Select scripting functions for use in the script window. Double-click the function to make it appear in the script window. |
| Script window | ActiveX scripting window. |
| Auto Gen. | Generates appropriate base function calls depending on the selected scripting language. |
| Parse | Checks the validity of your code. |
| Undo | Lets you undo the last action taken in the script window. |
| Browse | Allows you to import a valid script file into the script window. |
| Save | Allows you to save the script window code to an outside file. |

The Browser tab lists tasks, steps, and global variable constants. Double-click the value to move it to the script window, for use in your code.

Some tips to keep in mind when using ActiveX Script tasks:

- Make sure that any COM objects or OLE DB providers referenced in your code are available on the server where the package is saved and executed.
- If you are referencing third-party drivers or Dynamic Link Libraries within your ActiveX task, make sure the drivers or DLLs support free threading (parallelism); otherwise, your ActiveX task may hang when scheduled as a job, or when you run it from the command-line utility `dtsrun`. If they do not support free threading, one workaround is to select Execute on main package thread within the Workflow Property tab (reviewed later on), for each ActiveX task that does not support free threading. See the Microsoft Knowledge Base Article *Q318819 PRB: A DTS Package Raises Exceptions or Stops Responding When You Run It as a Scheduled Job* for more information.

# 11.6 How to... Configure the Transform Data Task

The **transform data task** lets you export, transform, and import data. This task uses the **Data Pump Interface** as its engine. The Data Pump Interface programmatically exposes several phases of a data row transformation process, and is also used as the engine for the Data Driven Query and Parallel Data Pump tasks. (The Parallel Data Pump task is exposed via the DTS Object Model only, not through DTS Designer.)

To use the transform data task, click the task icon or select it from the Task menu. You will be asked to select a source and a destination connection. After selecting these connections, you will see a black arrow form from source to destination:

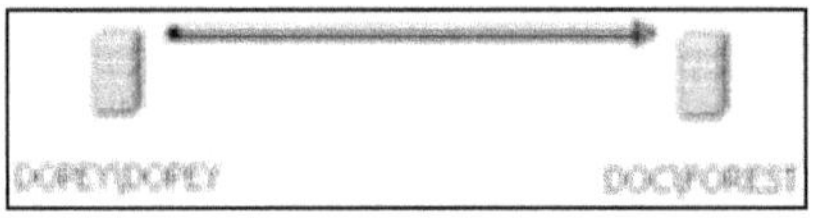

Double-click the arrow to access the Transform Data Task Properties dialog box.

## The Source Tab

The first thing you will see is the Source tab:

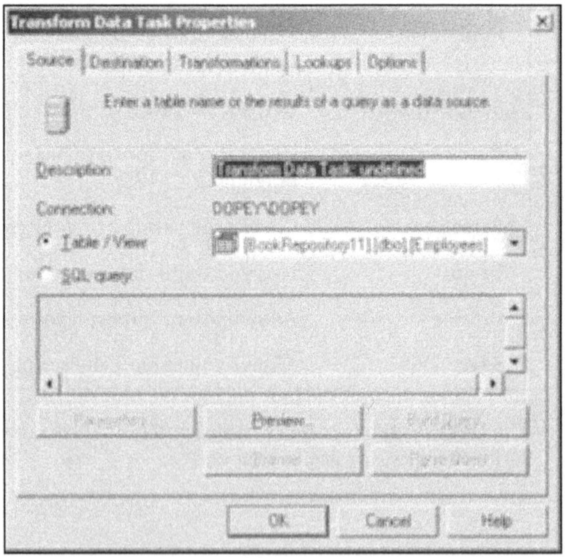

| Name | Description |
|---|---|
| Description | Set your user-friendly task description. |
| Connection | Cannot be edited, but specifies your source server. |
| Table / View | Select this bullet for exporting data from a table or view. Select the table or view from the drop box. Tables show the icon and views show the icon before the object name. |
| SQL query | Select this bullet if you wish to use extract data from an SQL query. |
| Parameters | You can use question marks as placeholders for parameters using global variables. For example, you can map a global variable to a value in the `WHERE` clause:<br>`SELECT vchBookName, iBookID`<br>`FROM Books WHERE vchBookName = ?`<br>Click the Parameters button to map the question mark to a specific defined global variable (or create one within the dialog box). |
| Preview | Click the Preview button to view the result set from your `SELECT` statement. For example:<br>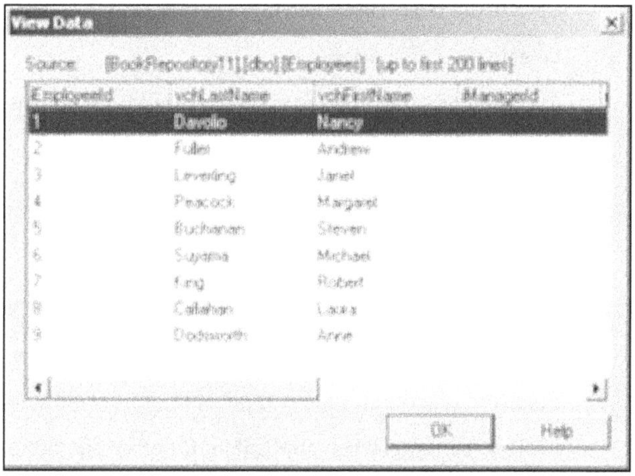 |
| Build Query | Click the Build Query button to create a `SELECT`, `INSERT` (`FROM/INTO`), `UPDATE`, `DELETE`, or `CREATE TABLE` statement based on the Data Transformations Query designer. All tables and views are shown in the left-hand pane, from which you can click and drag to the query menu. The interface allows those unfamiliar with SQL to create basic statements visually. For those more experienced with Transact-SQL, you may prefer bypassing this functionality altogether, as creating queries with multiple `JOIN` or `UNION` statements may prove unwieldy within the graphical interface. More complicated operations in Transact-SQL may also be inadvertently overlaid when options are selected via the graphical interface. |
| Browse | Allows you to import a `.sql` file into your SQL query window. |
| Parse Query | Checks the query for valid syntax. |

# The Destination Tab

The Destination tab is as follows:

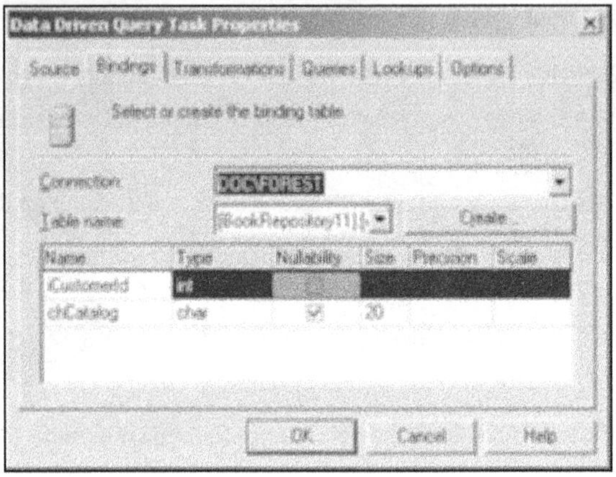


| Name | Description |
|---|---|
| Connection | Selects the destination server. |
| Table name | Selects the destination table. |
| Create | Creates a table for the source data, should the table not already exist. The CREATE TABLE is generated dynamically based on the source table; however, you can modify the statement if you wish. |
| Name | Name of the column. |
| Type | Data type of the column. |
| Nullability | Whether or not the column allows NULL values. |
| Size | Size of column (when applicable). |
| Precision | Precision of column (when applicable; for example, NUMERIC data type). |
| Scale | Scale of column (when applicable; for example, NUMERIC data type). |

# The Transformations Tab

The Transformations tab is as follows:

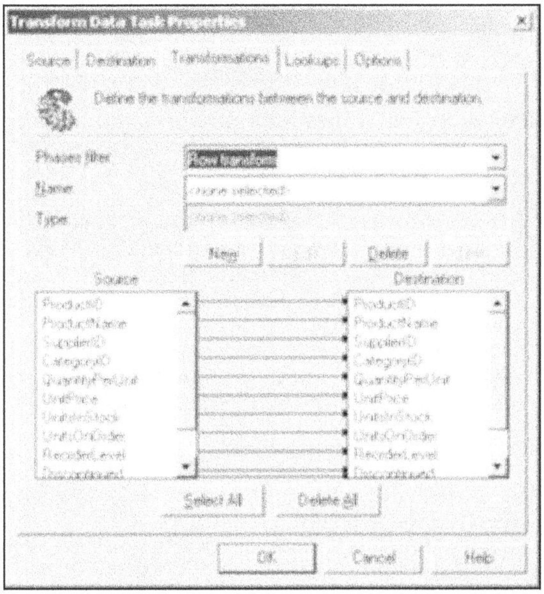

| Name | Description |
|---|---|
| Phases filter | Select a specific data pump phase for which to add a transformation.<br><br>(If Show multi-phase pump in DTS Designer is not enabled in the package properties, you will not see this option. Unfortunately, this option is not configured within a DTS package. To enable this option, right-click the Data Transformation Services folder in the SQL Server Enterprise Manager console tree, and select Properties. In the Designer section, select the Show multi-phase pump in DTS Designer check box.)<br><br>The phases are:<br><br>**Pre source data**: This phase is executed before the first retrieval of the source data. Useful for writing header rows to a file, or preparing variables, objects, or settings prior to other phases.<br><br>**Row transform**: This is the default phase, and is where column mapping and transformations can be applied between the source and destination rows.<br><br>**Insert success**: Phase that is fired when an `INSERT` operation succeeds.<br><br>**Insert failure**: Phase that is fired when an `INSERT` operation fails.<br><br>**Transform failure**: Phase that is fired when a specific transformation fails. |

*Table continued on following page*

| Name | Description |
|---|---|
| | **Batch complete**: Phase fires when the batch succeeds or fails. The number of rows affected is defined by Insert batch size field on the Options tab.<br><br>**Pump complete**: Phase that is fired when all rows have been processed.<br><br>**Post source data**: Phase that allows you to work with the destination data after it has been transformed and inserted (good for footer rows and final steps).<br><br>The default phase is Row transform and, by selecting different phases, you will see that the default transformation arrows disappear. This means there are no default settings for the different phases, and that you can specify various transformations based on different phases of the data pump. |
| Name | Lists all the defined transformations for the selected phase. By default, one transformation can exist for each column mapping in the table. |
| New | Create a new transformation. |
| Edit | Select the transformation you wish to edit (by clicking the black arrow) and select the Edit button. |
| Delete | Select the transformation you wish to delete by clicking the black arrow and selecting the Delete button. |
| Test | If you wish to test a specific transformation, highlight the transformation black arrow, and select Test. SQL Server will output the results to a temporary text file, and the dialog box will indicate the success or failure of the transformation.<br><br>Click the View Results button to see the text file transformation results. |
| Black arrows | Created by clicking a source column and dragging to the destination column. You will be prompted to select a transformation type, and be presented with the transformation dialog box. |
| Source | Shows the source data column names. |
| Destination | Destination table column names. |
| Select all | Selects all defined transformations. |
| Delete all | Removes all transformations. |

The Create New Transformation dialog box is presented when you click the New button or click a source column and drag it to the Destination column:

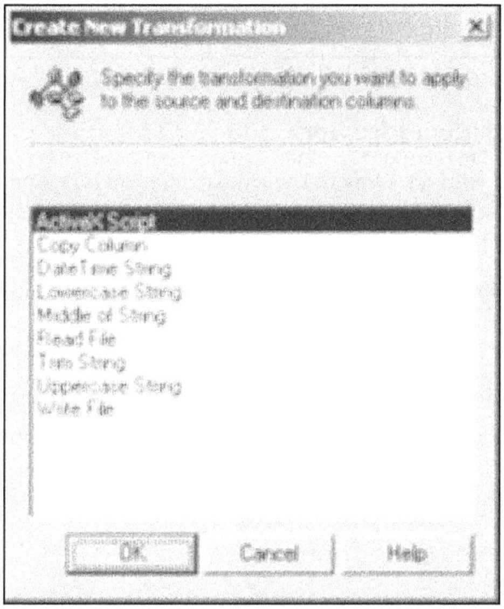


Selecting any of these transformation types will bring up the same three-tab dialog box (four-tab dialog if you have the Show multi-phase pump option enabled). By selecting the Properties button on the General tab, you can configure the transformation properties specific to the transformation type you select.

Let's first review the tabs that are the same across all transformation types, starting with the Transformation Options General tab:

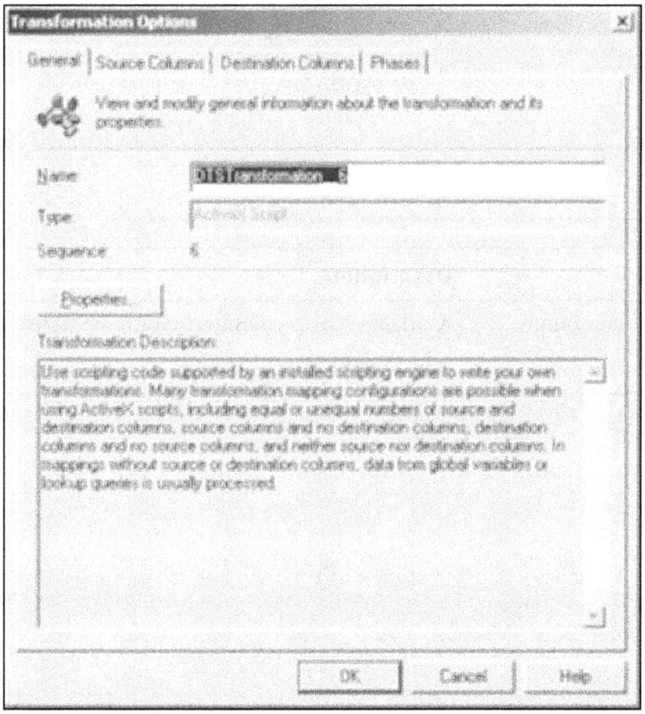

| Name | Description |
|---|---|
| Name | User-defined name of the specific transformation task. |
| Type | The transformation type. |
| Properties | This is your gateway to the transformation type-specific properties. For example, if you selected ActiveX transformations, this will bring up the ActiveX Script Transformation Properties dialog box. |
| Transformatio n description | Describes the transformation type. |

The Transformation Options Source Columns tab:

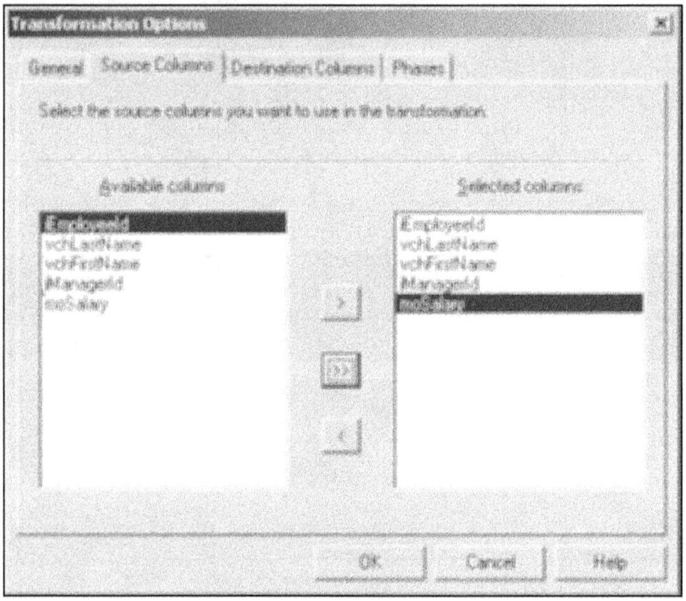


| Name | Description |
|---|---|
| Available columns | Available source columns that can be transformed. |
| Selected columns | Columns that are selected for transformation. |

The Transformation Options Destination Columns tab:

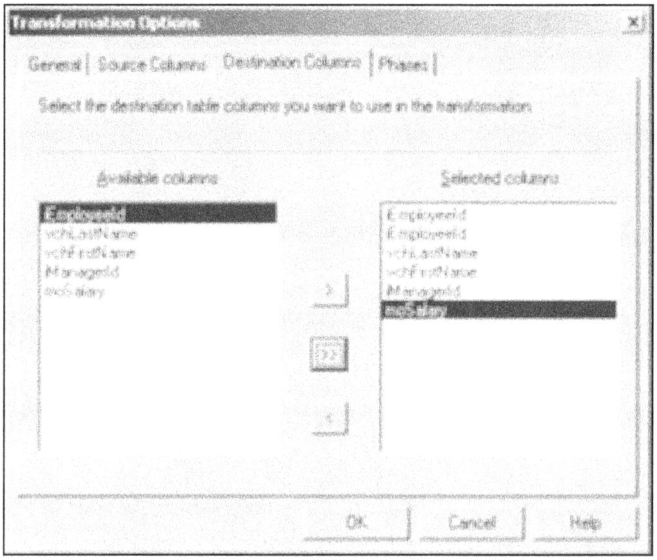

| Name | Description |
|---|---|
| Available columns | Available destination columns that can be used for the destination column. |
| Selected columns | Columns that are selected as destination columns. |

The Transformation Options Phases tab:

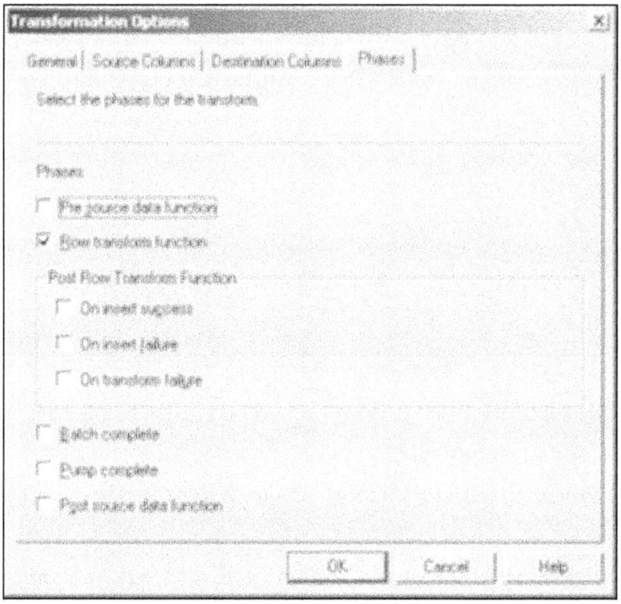

| Name | Description |
|---|---|
| Phases | Select the checkboxes of the phases to which this transformation applies. |

As stated earlier, the actual transformation is configured via the Properties button on the General tab of the Transformation Options dialog box.

## The ActiveX Transformation

The ActiveX script transformation allows you to use a scripting language to transform every row of the source data. After selecting Properties on the General tab of the Transformation Options dialog box, you will be presented with the ActiveX Script Transformation Properties dialog box. This is the same dialog box used for ActiveX tasks, only the column and destination syntax is already included in your script window. You can apply functions or other programmatic changes to the source or destination columns according to your requirements:

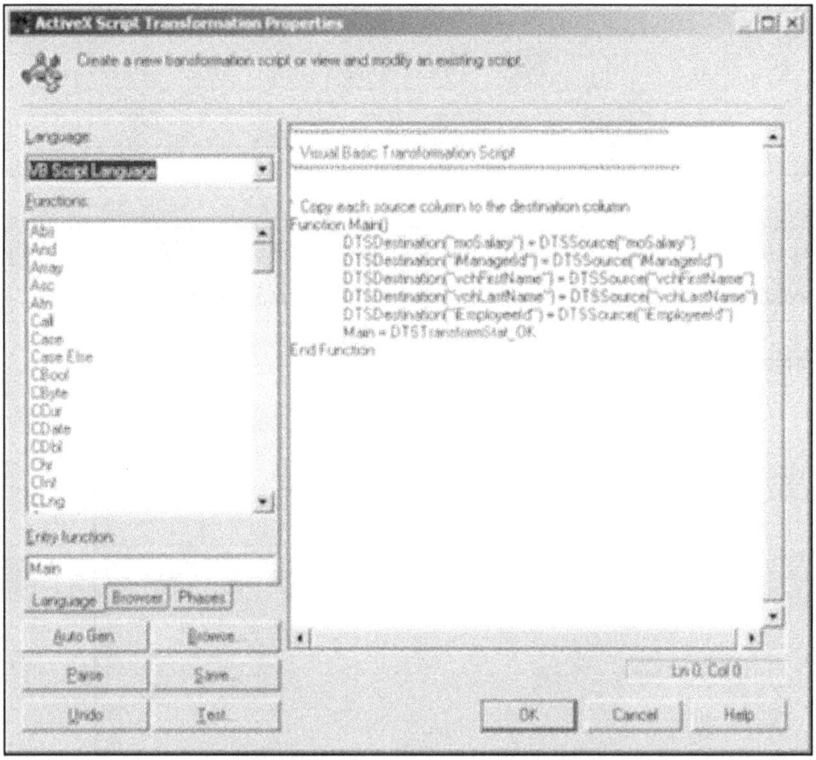


## The Copy Column, Lowercase String, and Uppercase String Transformations

The **copy column** transformation copies the source data to the destination data table without any transformations.

The **lowercase string** transformation converts all column data to lowercase characters for the string data type.

The **uppercase string** transformation converts all column data to uppercase characters for the string data type.

Properties for the copy column, lowercase string, and uppercase string transformations use the Column Order dialog box. This dialog box allows you to map each source and destination column, in the event that columns are not in the same order between the source or destination, or the destination table has fewer columns than the source table:

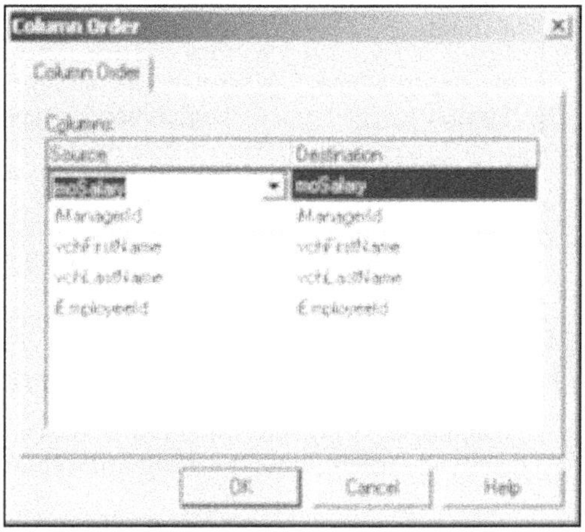


## The Date Time String Transformation

The **date time string** transformation allows you to choose the date format that is used to convert a source date into a new destination format. This is useful when you wish to migrate DATETIME or SMALLDATETIME data type source columns into destination VARCHAR or CHAR columns. For example, you may wish to extract only the year of an employee's hire date, rather then the full date for each employee record.

In the screenshot below, the source date includes the more detailed date and time format, whereas the destination table will only store the actual year (within a CHAR(4) data type column). Keep in mind that using a DATETIME or SMALLDATETIME destination column will cause the data to be stored as a full date, without regard to the date format; whereas, using a CHAR or VARCHAR data type destination column will reflect the date format chosen:

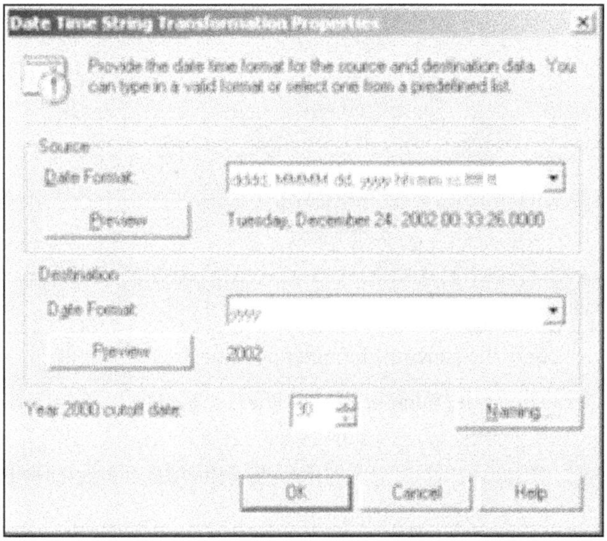

| Name | Description |
|---|---|
| Source Date Format | Select the predefined date formats for the source data from the dropdown combo box; or type in your own format. |
| Destination Date Format | Select the predefined date formats for the destination data from the dropdown combo box; or type in your own format. |
| Year 2000 cutoff date | Specify the 2000 cutoff date for interpreting two-digit year values as four-digit year values. |
| Naming | Click the Naming button to define definitions for string months and days of the week. |

## The Middle of String Transformation

The **middle of string** transformation allows you to take a substring (a chunk of a string) from the source column and insert it into the destination column, rather than inserting the entire string:

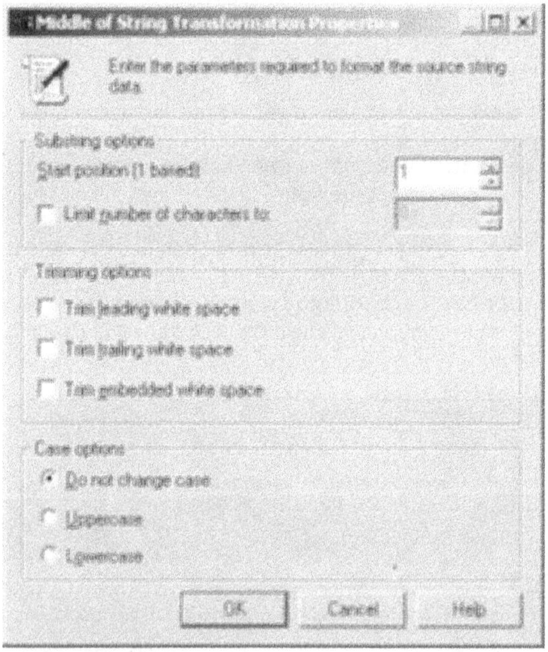


| Name | Description |
|---|---|
| Start position | Sets the starting character position. |
| Limit number of characters to | Limits the number of characters copied from the starting character position onward. |
| Trim leading white space | Removes white space preceding the first character of the string data. |

| Name | Description |
|---|---|
| Trim trailing white space | Removes white space after last character of string data. |
| Trim embedded white space | Removes any white space within the substring. |
| Case options | If Do not change case is selected, the case of the string remains the same. If Uppercase is selected, the substring is converted to uppercase after the trim operations. If Lowercase is selected, the substring is converted to lowercase after the trim operations. |

## The Read File Transformation

The **read file** transformation allows you to copy file contents based on file names in the source data file. These must be a valid file name. The Read File Transformation Properties dialog box allows you to select the valid directory and file type to search for the source column name. You can specify an error if the file is not found by selecting the checkbox:

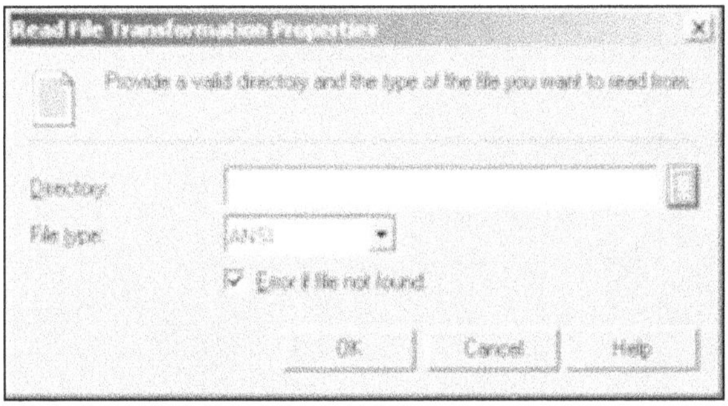


## The Trim String Transformation

The **trim string transformation** allows you to remove white space and change column case on the source data being transferred to the destination table. Note that the source data is not changed, but is transformed prior to being inserted at the destination:

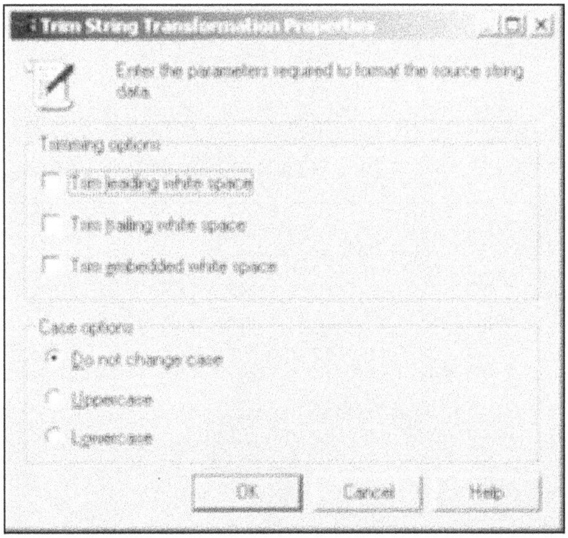

| Name | Description |
|---|---|
| Trim leading white space | Removes white space from the beginning of the string data. |
| Trim trailing white space | Removes white space from the end of the string data. |
| Trim embedded white space | Removes any white space from the string. |
| Case options | If Do not change case is selected, the case of the string remains the same. If Uppercase is selected, the string is converted to uppercase after the trim operations. If Lowercase is selected, the string is converted to lowercase after the trim operations. |

## The Write File Transformation

The **write file transformation** takes the source column data and writes it to a file, using a name from a second source column; there are no destination columns used for this type of transformation. This transformation type is useful for outputting data in a single column that must be shared with other non-SQL Server data sources (for example, a list of order numbers, dates, or IDs that an application or other database system may act on):

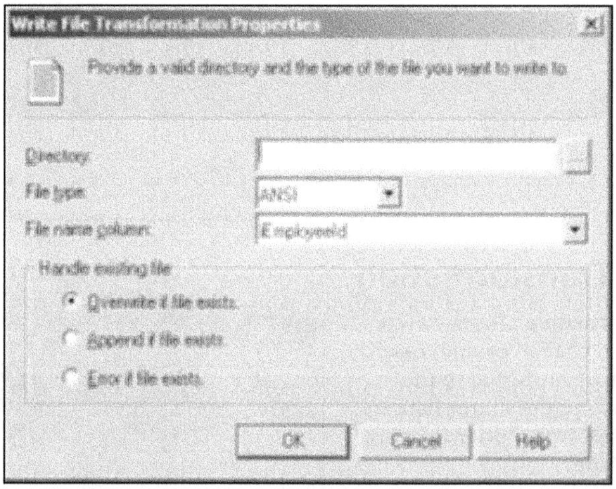


| Name | Description |
|---|---|
| Directory | Selects the destination directory for the output file. |
| File type | Selects the file type for the output file. |
| File name column | Selects which column sets the file name. |
| Handle existing file | Selects what action to take if a file already exists, either overwriting the file, appending to the file, or raising an error. |

# The Lookups Tab

Once you have defined the specifics of your transformation or transformations, select the Lookups tab in Transform Data Task Properties. This tab allows you to define a lookup query, which returns a value based on source column values.

For example, if you have an integer column that specifies the month, you can cross-reference this numeric value with a table that has integer and month name description as a VARCHAR field. Thus, we can transfer this text description of the month to the destination table, rather than the integer value.

Be warned that lookups can slow down your transformation significantly:

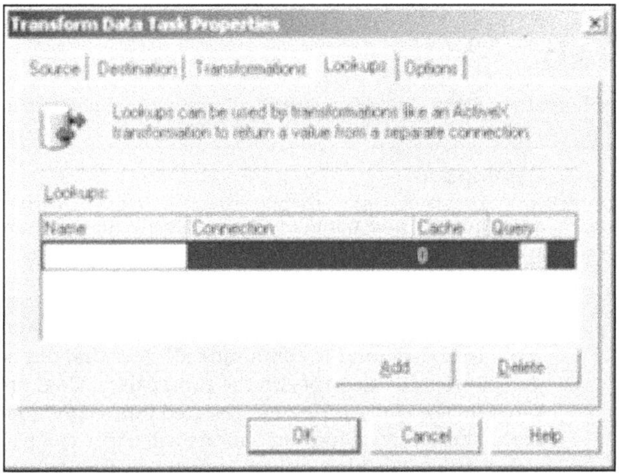


| Name | Description |
|---|---|
| Name | User-defined name for the lookup. |
| Connection | Connection of the lookup table, defining context of the lookup query. |
| Cache | For large transformations, you can keep a small number of lookup rows in the cache, improving lookup performance. |
| Query | Brings up the Data Transformation Services Query Designer, to help build the lookup query. |

The steps for using a lookup query are as follows:

- In the Lookups tab, define the name of the lookup, the connection used for the lookup query, and the cache; then define the lookup query using a question mark or question marks for those values you wish to look up based on the source transformation data. For example:

```
SELECT   RegionDesc
FROM     RegionDesc
WHERE RegionCode = ?
```

This query states that the RegionDesc field should be returned based on the RegionCode used.

- Reference the lookup query, based on the name you selected, within your ActiveX transformations. For example:

```
Function Main()
DTSDestination('RegionCode')=DTSLookups('Region').Execute(DTSSource('RegionCode'))
Main = DTSTransformStat_OK
End Function
```

The above VBScript uses the DTSLookups object to reference our lookup from the Lookup tab and uses the RegionCode source column value as a parameter.

# The Options Tab

The Options tab for the Transform Data Task Properties allows you to specify the following settings:

| Name | Description |
|---|---|
| Exception file name: | Sets the path and name of the exception file where exception records are written; this will create the file dynamically if it does not already exist. |
| File type | Select 7.0 format to save the exception file in 7.0 format. The Error text option will record errors during the task. Source error rows will generate a separate exception file containing all rows that did not get written to the destination due to errors on the source data. Dest error rows will generate a separate file containing rows rejected due to problems with the destination data. These error handling options will assist you in determining what data is problematic, giving you an opportunity to catch or resolve issues, and migrate missing data. |
| File format | Lets you set the row and column delimiters (how to separate rows and columns). Also specifies how text is qualified (that is, double or single quotes, or none). |
| Max error count | Number of errors before the task terminates. When Fast Load is selected, either row or batch failures are counted towards this number. |
| Fetch buffer size | Sets number of rows being fetched at the data source. |
| First row | Specifies first row of data to begin moving from the source (good for data sets that include column headers). |
| Last row | Specifies the last row of data to transfer. |
| Use fast load | If selected, specifies that the transformation uses bulk-copy processing. This can be used for the Microsoft OLE DB Provider for SQL Server only. |
| Keep NULL values | Preserves NULL values at the destination column. Used only when Use fast load is enabled. |
| Check constraints | If selected, constraints on the destination table are checked. This slows down performance, but enforces data integrity. |

| Name | Description |
| --- | --- |
| Table lock | Places a table lock instead of row-level locks on the destination table; this reduces concurrency, but improves the transformation task speed. |
| Enable identity insert | Allows the insert of explicit values into the destination `IDENTITY` column. |
| Always commit final batch | This option commits batches, even if an error occurs after the batch commit. This prevents re-loading of the successfully transformed rows. |
| Insert batch size: | If set to 0, all data is loaded in one batch. If set to 1, data is loaded one row at a time. Values greater than 1 specify the number of rows per batch. If you select 0, one failure will cause the entire load to be cancelled. If selecting 1, each row failure counts against the max error count. If a value greater than 1, one row failure fails the entire batch and the entire loading (however, previously loaded batches are committed or rolled back). |

Keep in mind that the transform data task gives much functionality and flexibility, but can incur significant performance overhead. You may decide to configure simple bulk insert operations to staging tables on the destination server, transforming the data via an ActiveX script once it has been transferred. This often reduces the performance bottleneck of mixing data imports with transformations.

# Configuring the Execute Process Task

The **execute process task** allows you to execute any Win32 executable or batch file from within a DTS package. Watch out for executing programs or batch files that require user feedback (dialog boxes, prompts); these programs may cause your DTS package to hang:

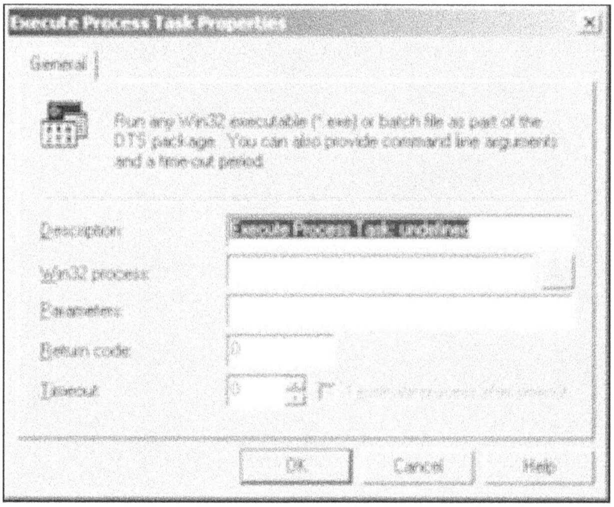

| Name | Description |
|---|---|
| Description | User-defined description of the task. |
| Win32 process | Name of the .exe, .bat, .com, or .cmd file to execute. |
| Parameters | Command-line parameters required for the executable or batch file, separating parameters by a space. |
| Return code | This specifies the return code for a successful execution. |
| Timeout | Sets the number of seconds allowed for the process to execute successfully, defaulting to 0 (no time limit). |
| Terminate process after timeout | If selected, terminates the process after a timeout. |

# 11.7 How to... Configure the Execute SQL Task

The **execute SQL task** allows you to execute valid Transact-SQL statements within a DTS package. You can execute SELECT, INSERT, DELETE, UPDATE, and stored procedure queries; you can also create and drop database objects and perform other DDL statements. In addition, this task can be used to populate global variables, and can make use of parameterized queries that use global variables in the Transact-SQL statement:

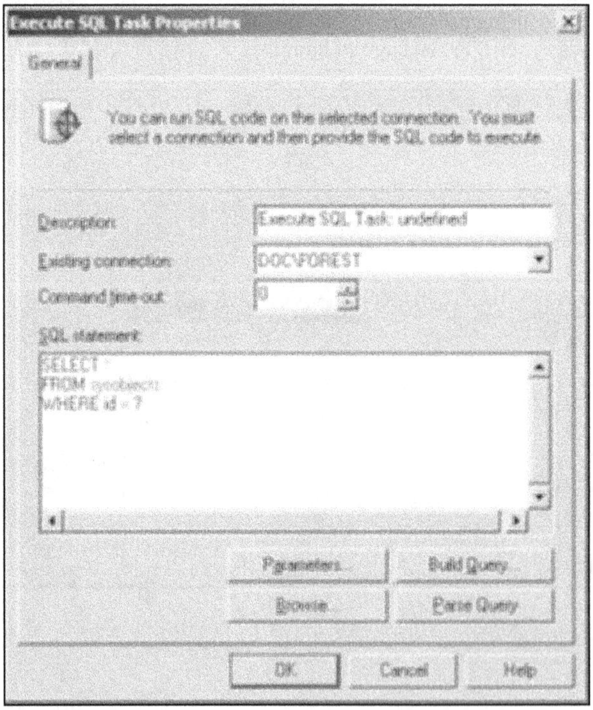

| Name | Description |
|---|---|
| Description | User-defined description of the task. |
| Existing connection | Select the connection against which the SQL statement will run. |
| Command timeout | The maximum number of seconds the query can take before timing out. When 0, there is no timeout limit. |
| SQL Statement | Define your Transact-SQL statements (use `GO` to separate multiple queries). |
| Parameters | Select this button to show the Parameter Mapping dialog box, allowing you to map global variables to your question mark placeholders in the query.<br>You can also map the output of your query to a global variable: |

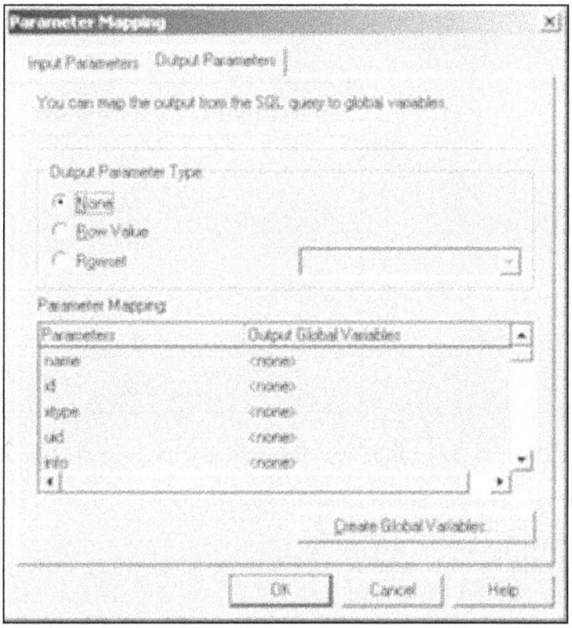


| Name | Description |
|---|---|
| Build Query | Build a query using the DTS Query Designer. |
| Browse | Import a .sql file into the SQL statement window. |
| Parse Query | Checks the syntax of the SQL statement. |

# 11.8 How to... Configure the Data Driven Query Task

Whereas the transform data and bulk insert tasks (covered later) are optimized for `INSERT` operations, the **data driven query task** is optimized for `UPDATE` and `DELETE` operations.

The data driven query task takes a query result set and goes through it row by row, performing actions based on the row and column values. The action taken could be a table UPDATE, DELETE, INSERT, SELECT, or execution of a stored procedure.

For example, you could define a query that checks the gender of each customer row from a customers table (source table) and updates the type of clothing catalog they should receive in the catalogs table (binding or destination table).

The data driven query task is powerful but can be confusing at first. This next table will walk through the settings of each tab for a specific example. In the example, we will have a table called customers, which contains iCustomerId and chGender columns:

```
CREATE TABLE customer
  (iCustomerId int NOT NULL IDENTITY (1,1),
   chGender char(1) NOT NULL)
```

The table contents are as follows:

| iCustomerId | chGender |
|---|---|
| 1 | M |
| 2 | M |
| 3 | F |
| 4 | F |
| 5 | F |
| 6 | M |

Next, we have the catalog table, which specifies what type of clothing catalog each customer should be sent:

```
CREATE TABLE clothingcatalog
  (iCustomerId int NOT NULL,
   chCatalog char(20) NULL)
```

The requirements of this data driven query task are as follows:

- The chGender of each customer in the customer table will determine the chCatalog column of the clothingcatalog table. The chCatalog field should be updated to reflect the appropriate catalog.

We begin with two connections and a data driven query task. The customer table is located on DOPEY\DOPEY server and the clothingcatalog is located on the DOC\FOREST server.

The following are settings for the Data Driven Query Task Properties:

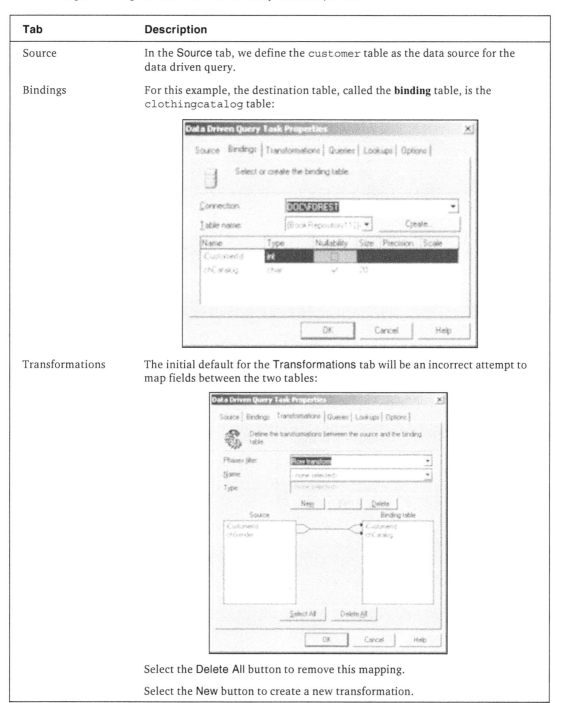

| Tab | Description |
|---|---|
| Source | In the Source tab, we define the `customer` table as the data source for the data driven query. |
| Bindings | For this example, the destination table, called the **binding** table, is the `clothingcatalog` table:<br>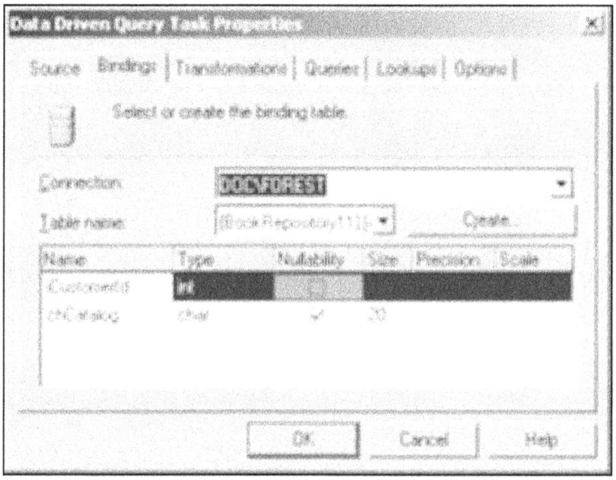<br> |
| Transformations | The initial default for the Transformations tab will be an incorrect attempt to map fields between the two tables:<br>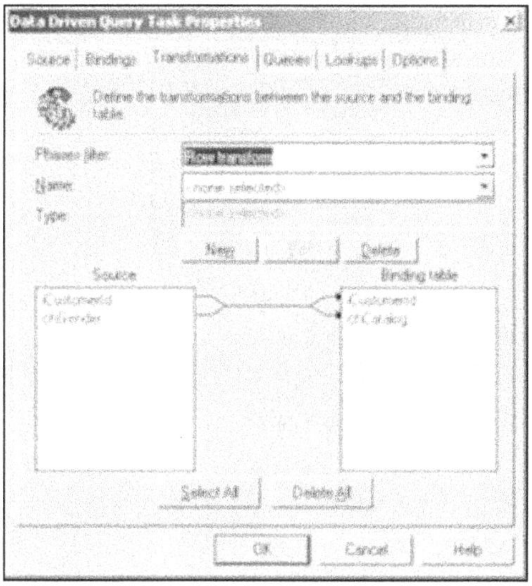<br><br>Select the Delete All button to remove this mapping.<br>Select the New button to create a new transformation. |

*Table continued on following page*

| Tab | Description |
|---|---|
| | Select ActiveX Script.<br><br>Select Properties to display the ActiveX Script Transformation Properties dialog box. This example uses a `Case` statement to check for `chGender` (VBScript's `Case` syntax is similar to a Transact-SQL `CASE` statement).<br><br>When the `chGender` is `M` for a row in the `customer` table, the `clothingcatalog` value is 'Tom's Suits Catalog'. When the `chGender` is `F`, the catalog is 'Mary's Professional Clothing Catalog'. Both `Case` statements use the `DTSTransformStat_UpdateQuery` constant, which instructs the ActiveX script that it should run an `UPDATE` query. Other DTS constants for data driven queries are included in *SQL Server Books Online*, in the *DTSTransformStatus* section:<br><br>`Function Main()`<br><br>`  Select Case DTSSource("chGender")`<br><br>`    Case "M"`<br>`      DTSDestination("chCatalog").Value = "Tom's Suits Catalog"`<br>`      DTSDestination("iCustomerId") = DTSSource("iCustomerId")`<br>`      Main = DTSTransformStat_UpdateQuery`<br><br>`    Case "F"`<br>`      DTSDestination("chCatalog").Value = "Mary's Professional Clothing Catalog"`<br>`      DTSDestination("iCustomerId") = DTSSource("iCustomerId")`<br>`      Main = DTSTransformStat_UpdateQuery`<br><br>`  End Select`<br><br>End Function |

| Tab | Description |
|---|---|
| Queries | The data driven query task allows you to define `INSERT`, `UPDATE`, `DELETE`, and `SELECT` queries. In this example, an `UPDATE` query is defined by setting the `chCatalog` field based on the `iCustomerId`. Notice the lower pane, where **Destination** and **Parameter** settings are defined. There is one parameter for each question mark used in the query:<br>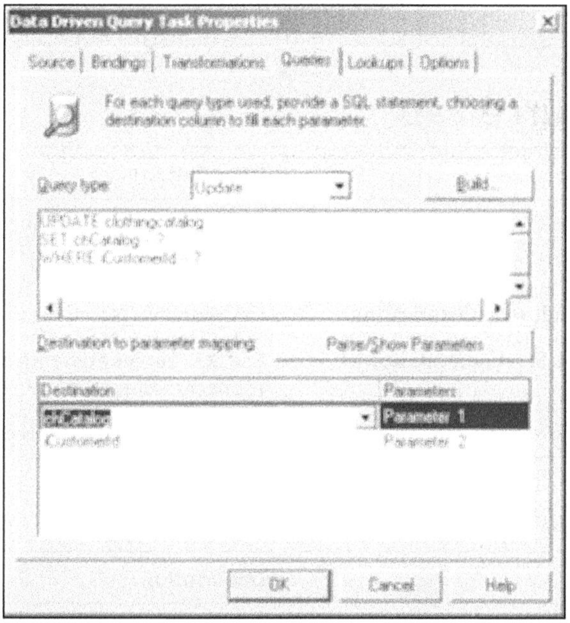<br>You can configure different destination columns by selecting the row and the correct column from the drop down list box. |

This example does not use the **Lookups** or **Options** tabs; however, note that these tabs are functionally equivalent to the **Lookups** and **Options** tabs of the **Transform Data Task** dialog box.

After executing this DTS package, you should see the number of rows impacted by the data driven query, displayed in the **Executing DTS Package** dialog box.

The `clothingcatalog` table will now have gender specific catalogs listed for each `iCustomerId`:

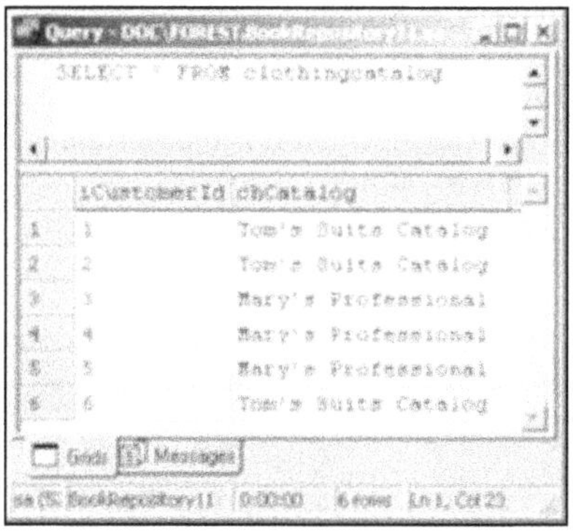

# 11.9 How to... Configure the Copy SQL Server Objects Task

If you have used the DTS Import and DTS Export Wizard, you will be familiar with the **copy sql server objects task**. As the name implies, this task allows us to transfer SQL Server objects between SQL Server instances. Specifically, you can transfer database objects from one instance of SQL Server version 7.0 to another, transfer objects from one instance of SQL Server version 7.0 to an instance of SQL Server 2000, or objects from one instance of SQL Server 2000 to another SQL Server 2000 instance.

## The Source Tab

| Name | Description |
|---|---|
| Description | User-defined description of the task. |
| Server | Select the source server. |
| Use Windows authentication | Use Windows NT authentication to connect. |
| Use SQL Server authentication | Use SQL Server authentication (username and password) to connect to the source server. |
| Database | Select the source database from which to transfer objects. |

## The Destination Tab

| Name | Description |
|---|---|
| Server | Select the source server. |
| Use Windows authentication | Use Windows NT authentication to connect. |
| Use SQL Server authentication | Use SQL Server authentication (username and password) to connect to the source server. |
| Database | Select the source database from which to transfer objects. |

## The Copy Tab

| Name | Description |
|---|---|
| Create destination objects (tables, views, stored procedures, constraints, and so on) | Creates schema for objects at destination. |
| Drop destination objects first | Drops schema objects on the destination server with the same name on the source. |
| Include all dependent objects | Includes schema-dependent objects, such as a table referenced by a view. |
| Include extended properties | Copies extended properties to destination. |

| Name | Description |
|---|---|
| Copy data | Copies data to tables. |
| Replace existing data | Removes destination data and replaces with the source data. |
| Append data | Adds data to table, but does not delete existing data. |
| Use collation | Check this box to ensure no loss of data due to collation differences between the two SQL Server instances. |
| Copy all objects | If selected, copies all objects in the source database. Click Select Objects and select the objects you wish to transfer manually. |
| Use default options | If selected, uses default options. If not selected, select the Options button and configure options manually. |

# 11.10 How to... Configure the Send Mail Task

The **send mail task** allows you to send e-mail from a DTS package. You must have a valid MAPI client configured on the workstation or server from which this task originated. You can configure send mail tasks to send notification of events based on the completion of the DTS package, or based on individual task outcomes or results. For example, you could send an e-mail if a specific task failed, send an e-mail to indicate that the package has begun running, or e-mail progress reports:

| Name | Description |
|---|---|
| Description | User-defined description of task. |
| Profile name | The selected mail profile name. |
| Password | Mail profile login. |
| To | E-mail address of the addressee. |
| CC | Carbon copy list. |
| Subject | Subject for e-mail. |
| Message | The e-mail message. |
| Attachments | Click the Add button to search for a specific file, or type the path and filename in the text box. |

If you are opening a send mail task from a saved DTS package, you may not see the profile listed in the task that was originally saved with the task; this is because the profile configured on your workstation may not match what is configured on the server. To get around this, perform a disconnected edit; this allows you to view the correct value for the profile. A disconnected edit allows you to view the properties saved with the DTS package, even if your workstation or client does not contain the same OLE DB drivers or settings.

To perform a disconnected edit within the DTS package in DTS designer:

- From the Package menu, select Disconnected Edit.

- ☐ Expand the **Tasks** node and select the `DTSTask_DTSSendMailTask_N` (where `N` is the number of the task – if more than one mail task exists on your box, this will be an incremented number). The right-hand pane will show the send mail task settings, which you can configure or change, even without the profile setting loaded on your workstation:

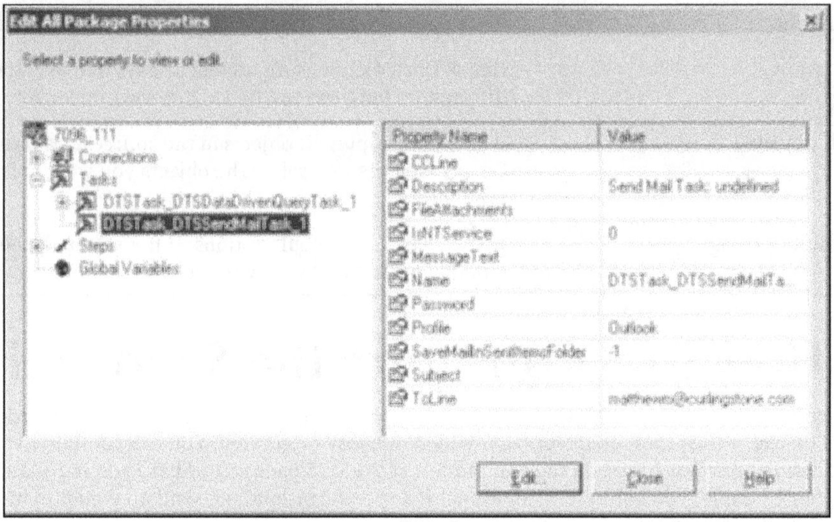


For more information on this bug, see Microsoft Knowledge Base article Q288438 *BUG: DTS Send Mail Task Does Not Display Correct Mail Profile Name in DTS Designer*. See Chapter 4's *Configuring SQL Mail and SQL Agent Mail* for a review of the core functionality that controls this DTS task. Keep in mind that this task cannot run on a failover cluster, as SQL Mail's MAPI interface is not cluster-aware.

# 11.11 How to... Configure the Bulk Insert Task

The **bulk insert task** allows us to import text files at high speed into SQL Server. Depending on the scenario, bulk insert can be the fastest method of importing data (even faster than `BCP`). As a trade-off however, the bulk insert task is more limited in functionality than `BCP` or the transform data task. The source data can only be imported from a text file, and the destination for the data must be a SQL Server table or view. Also, only members of the `sysadmin` server role can execute the bulk insert task, and they must also have read permissions to the source file.

## The General Tab

| Name | Description |
|---|---|
| Description | User-defined task description. |
| Existing connection | Selects the SQL Server connection for which to import data. |
| Destination table | Selects the destination table for the imported table. |
| Source data file | Type in the path and file name of the file to import. |
| Use format file | Specifies that a format file will be used for the text file (similar to format files for `BCP`). |

| Name | Description |
|---|---|
| Generate | This button allows you to generate a format file based on your file selections. |
| Specify format | Instead of using a format file, you can select a row delimiter and column delimiter (requires less complicated data source formats). |

## The Options Tab

| Name | Description |
|---|---|
| Check constraints | If selected, table constraints are checked upon import, potentially slowing down the import process, but enforcing data integrity. |
| Enable identity insert | Allows explicit values to be inserted into an identity column. |
| Sorted data | If selected, indicates that the data source file has been sorted on a specific column. Enter the destination column name (for the sorted column) in the text box. |
| Keep nulls | Allows the retention of null values. |
| Table lock | Places a table lock during the bulk insert, reducing concurrency at the destination table but improving import speed. |
| Code page | If `CHAR`, `VARCHAR`, or `TEXT` columns have character values greater than 127 or less than 32, specify the appropriate code page. |
| Insert batch size | If selected, specifies how many rows are in a batch. If set to 0, all data is loaded in one batch, if set to one, each row is defined as a batch. |
| Only copy selected rows. | If selected, you can specify a start and stop row in the source result set. |

# 11.12 How to... Configure the Execute Package Task

The **execute package task** allows you to execute an external DTS package from within a package; this enables you to re-use packages and adopt modular DTS package programming.

## The General Tab

| Name | Description |
|---|---|
| Description | User-defined description of the task. |
| Location | Sets the location of the DTS package (SQL Server, Meta Data Services (disabled by default in SQL Server 2000 SP3), structured storage file). |
| Package name | Name of package to execute. |
| Password | Password (if required) for package. |
| Server and authentication method | For SQL Server and Meta Data Services packages, specify the server and authentication method. |

To keep the packages flexible, take advantage of **inner** and **outer** global variables.

The Inner Package Global Variables tab sets the global variables for the package being called. The setting is based on global variables defined in the name, type, and value of the execute package task.

Outer package global variables pass a global variable to the called package from the calling package. If both packages have a global variable called `gvBooks`, the calling package (parent) can pass the value of the global variable to the child package. If the child package does not have the `gvBooks` global variable, then the variable is created temporarily during the scope of the package execution.

Some issues to be aware of when using the execute package task:

- If you are using Visual Basic 6.0 to instantiate a package, the execute package task may cause problems when you attempt to use event handlers for the called (child) package. You must either do without the event handling for the child package, or remove the execute package task from the instantiated package call.
- You may also run into issues when saving a DTS package that uses an execute package task to a Visual Basic file. If you modify or delete packages, but try to re-use the file, the file may fail as it hard codes the package ID. For more details, see Microsoft Knowledge Base article Q299354 *PRB: DTS Execute Package Task May Fail to Execute Child Package* for more information.

# 11.13 How to... Configure the Message Queue Task

The **message queue task** allows you to exchange messages between DTS packages. The messages can be formatted as strings, global variables, or data files. The Microsoft Message Queue functionality comes with the Windows 2000 operating system, but is not installed by default. You must install it from the installation CD.

# The Message Queue Task Properties for Sending a Message

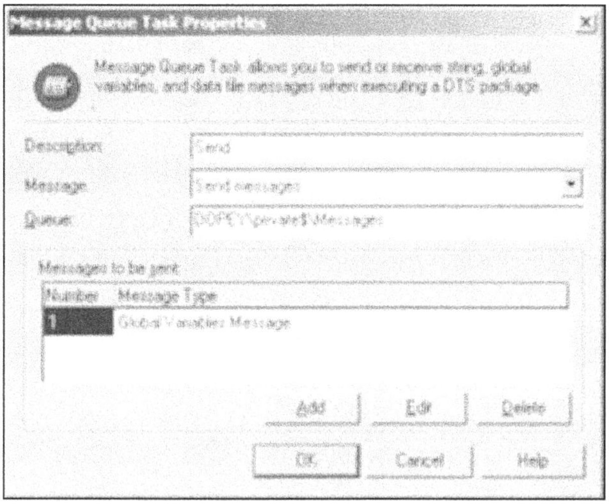


| Name | Description |
| --- | --- |
| Description | User-defined description of the task. |
| Message | Defines whether the task will send or receive a message. |
| Queue | Points to a defined Message Queue directory, using the format `computer_name\queue_type$\queue_name`, for sending or receiving messages. |
| Messages to be sent | Lists message number and message type. |
| Add | Adds a new message. |
| Edit | Edits an existing message. |
| Delete | Deletes an existing message. |

# The Message Queue Message Properties

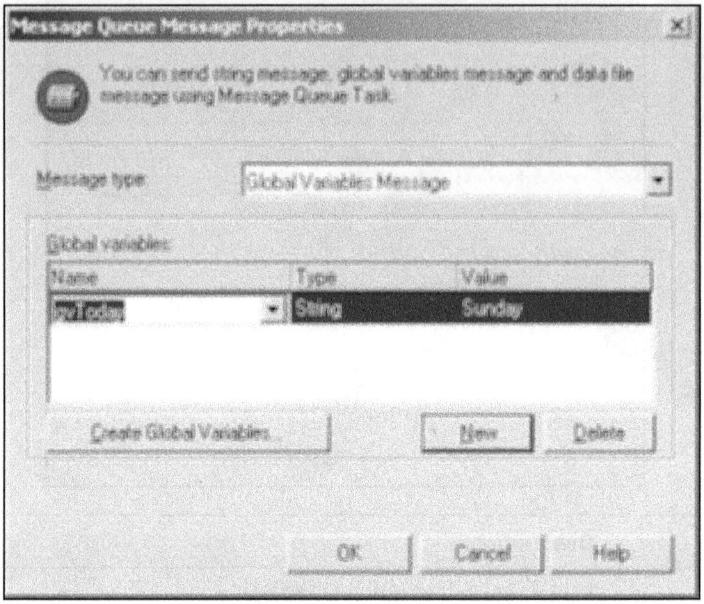


| Name | Description |
|---|---|
| Message type | Select the message type, data file message, global variables message, or string message. |
| String message | Defines a string text message. |
| Global variables message | Defines which global variables from the current package will be sent as a message. You can also create new global variables at the package level. |
| File name | Allows you to define a path and file name. |

# The Message Queue Task Properties for Receiving a Message

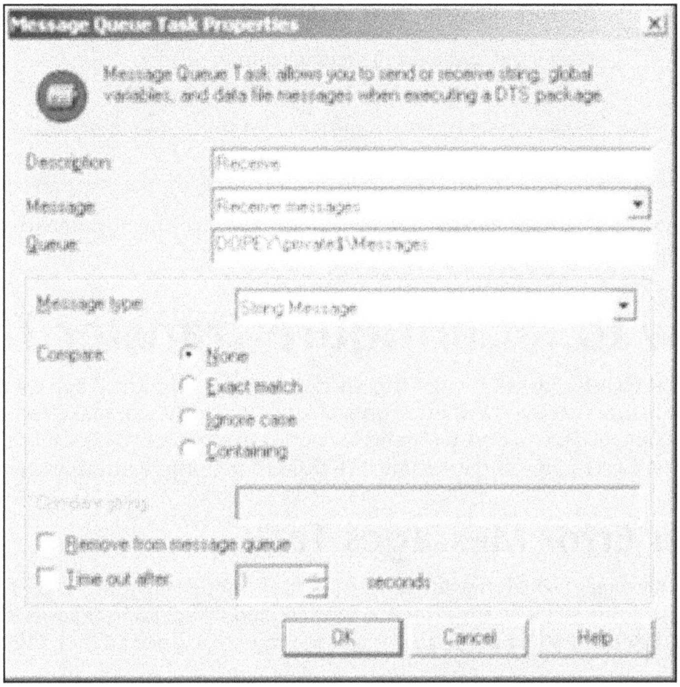


| Name | Description |
|---|---|
| Description | User-defined description of the task. |
| Message | Defines whether the task will send or receive a message. |
| Queue | Points to a defined Message Queue directory, using the format `computer_name\queue_type$\queue_name`, for sending or receiving messages. |
| Message type | Defines the message type to receive: global variable message, string message, or data file message. |
| Only receive message from a specific package or version | Displayed when global variable messages are selected; this field allows you to filter which messages are received by the task. If you select No filter, SQL Server will not apply any filters. From package selects a specific package to receive from. From version only accepts messages from a specific package version. |
| Identifier | Displayed when global variable messages are selected. Lists the GUID of the package or package version. |
| Compare and Compare String | Displayed when receiving a string message.<br><br>Defines a comparison to the Compare String. Can be None (no filter), Exact match, Ignore Case, or Containing. |

*Table continued on following page*

| Name | Description |
|---|---|
| Save file as: | Displayed when receiving a data file message. Saves the received data file. |
| Overwrite | Displayed when receiving a data file message. When selected, will overwrite a file with the same name as the received file. |
| Remove from message queue | If selected, removes the message upon receipt. |
| Timeout after | Selects number of seconds before the task times out, waiting to receive a message. |

For more information on Message Queuing, see Microsoft's Message Queue home page, http://www.microsoft.com/msmq/default.htm.

# 11.14 How to... Configure Transfer Tasks

DTS includes several **transfer tasks** for migrating various database objects. When using these tasks to migrate databases to a new SQL Server 2000 instance (from a 7.0 or 2000 source), make sure to perform tasks in the proper order. For example, issue a transfer logins task prior to a transfer database task. Also, note that the Copy Database Wizard uses many of these same DTS tasks to perform the transfer operations.

## The Transfer Error Messages Task

The **transfer error messages task** allows you to transfer user-defined error messages from the source server to the destination server; this includes any error message created by `sp_addmessage`. The destination server must be version SQL Server 2000, but the source can be either SQL Server 7.0 or 2000:

- The Source and Destination tabs define the server connection and authentication methods.
- The Error Messages tab allows you to select which errors to transfer to the destination server.

## The Transfer Database Task

The **transfer database task** allows you to copy or move a SQL Server 7.0 or 2000 database to a SQL Server 2000 instance:

- The Source and Destination tabs define the server connection and authentication methods.
- The Databases tab allows you to select which databases are copied or moved (removed from the source server and copied to the destination).
- The File locations tab allows you to select the destination drives of the data and log files for the copied or moved databases. Select the Modify button to select a new location.

  The Modify button will bring up the Database files dialog, where you can select the specific destination file location. If you see red X marks by your logical file, this indicates there is a name conflict, or space issue on the destination server:

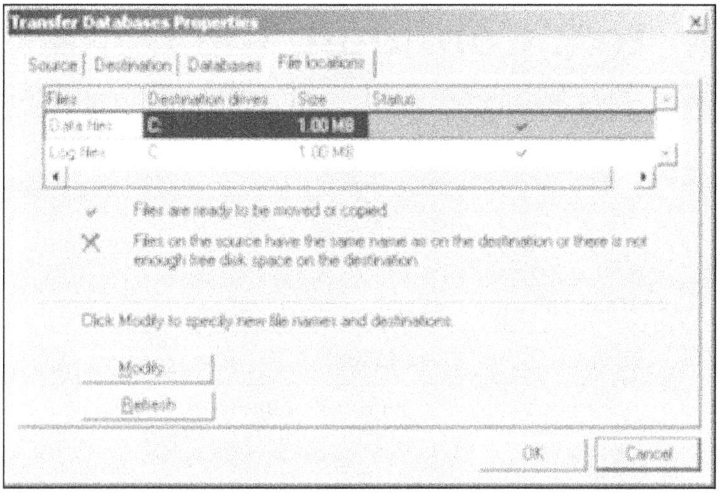

## The Transfer Master Stored Procedures Task

The **transfer master stored procedures task** is used to copy stored procedures from the `master` database on a SQL Server 7.0 or 2000 instance to the master database of a SQL Server 2000 instance:

- The Source and Destination tabs define the server connection and authentication methods.
- The Stored Procedures tab allows you to select all stored procedures, or specific stored procedures, from the source `master` database.

## The Transfer Jobs Task

The **transfer jobs task** allows you to transfer some or all SQL Server Agent jobs from a SQL Server 7.0 or SQL Server 2000 instance, to a SQL Server 2000 instance:

- The Source and Destination tabs define the server connection and authentication methods.
- The Jobs tab allows you to select all or some jobs to transfer from the source instance.

## The Transfer Logins Task

The **transfer logins task** allows you to transfer logins (Windows and SQL authentication) and passwords (for SQL authentication) from a SQL Server 7.0 or 2000 instance to a destination SQL Server 2000 instance:

- The Source and Destination tabs define the server connection and authentication methods.
- The Logins tab allows you to migrate all logins on the SQL Server instance, or only those logins associated with a specific database or databases.

# 11.15 How to... Configure the Dynamic Properties Task

The **dynamic properties task** allows you to set package properties at package runtime, based on the values of a `.ini` file, Transact-SQL query, global variable, data file, constant, or environment variable. This functionality makes the process of migrating DTS packages to new servers much easier, as task properties no longer need to be hard-coded with the server name, database name, login, password, and file locations.

## The General Tab

| Name | Description |
|---|---|
| Description | User-defined description of the task. |
| Change list | Lists defined dynamic properties. |
| Add | Adds a new dynamic property. |
| Edit | Edits an existing dynamic property. |
| Delete | Deletes an existing dynamic property. |

The Dynamic Properties Task: Package Properties dialog box (accessed with the Add button) allows you to select which package properties should be dynamically set. The connection, task, global variable, and step properties can all be set via dynamic properties.

In the example below, the DOPEY\DOPEY connection and OLE DB Properties nodes are expanded, and the Data Source is selected.

Click the Property value in the right-hand pane and select the Set button to modify how this property is dynamically configured:

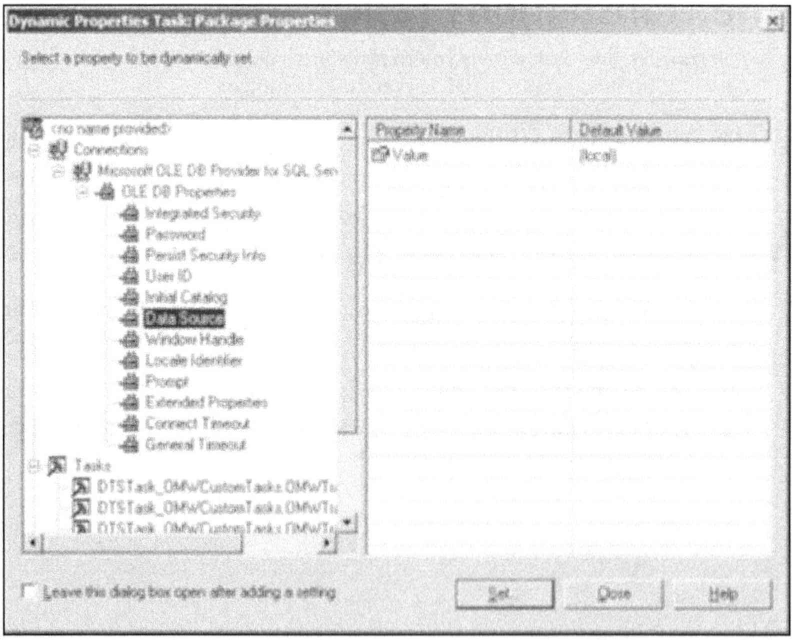

In the Add/Edit Assignment dialog, you can associate a specific property with a `.ini` file setting, Transact-SQL query, global variable, environmental variable, constant, or data file.

In this example, we will use a `.ini` file will to define the server name. If you are moving the package to a new server, you must make sure that the `.ini` file exists in the same location on the new server as on the original.

The `.ini` file requires a header for the file, and one or more name/value pairs:

```
[DTS Package 1 Variables]
ServerName=DOPEY\DOPEY
```

You can then reference the `.ini` file, and set the property based on the name/value pair. In the previous example of an `.ini` file, setting a Data Source property of a connection object to use the `ServerName` `.ini` value will set the Data Source to DOPEY\DOPEY:

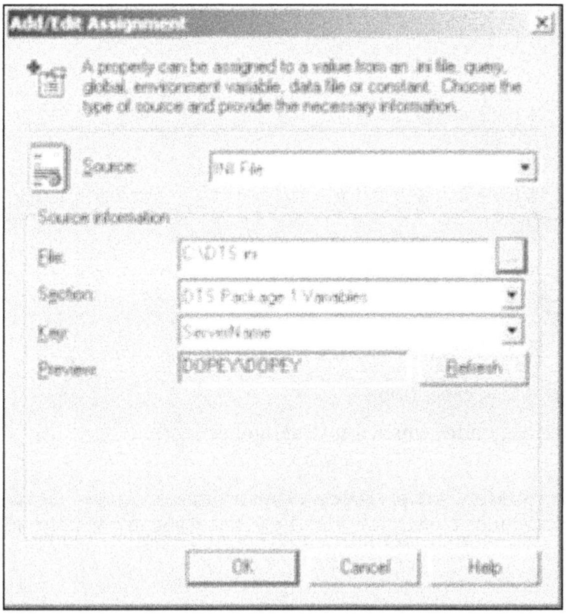


Make sure to have your dynamic properties task assigned as the first task to run in your DTS package; otherwise, your runtime variables may not be set in time.

Overleaf is an example of making sure that the DTS properties task runs first, running the next task when the dynamic properties task succeeds.

The direction of the workflow arrows specifies the order of runtime. Note that, since the connection icon is not a task, it cannot be part of a workflow (unless connected to it via a transform data task):

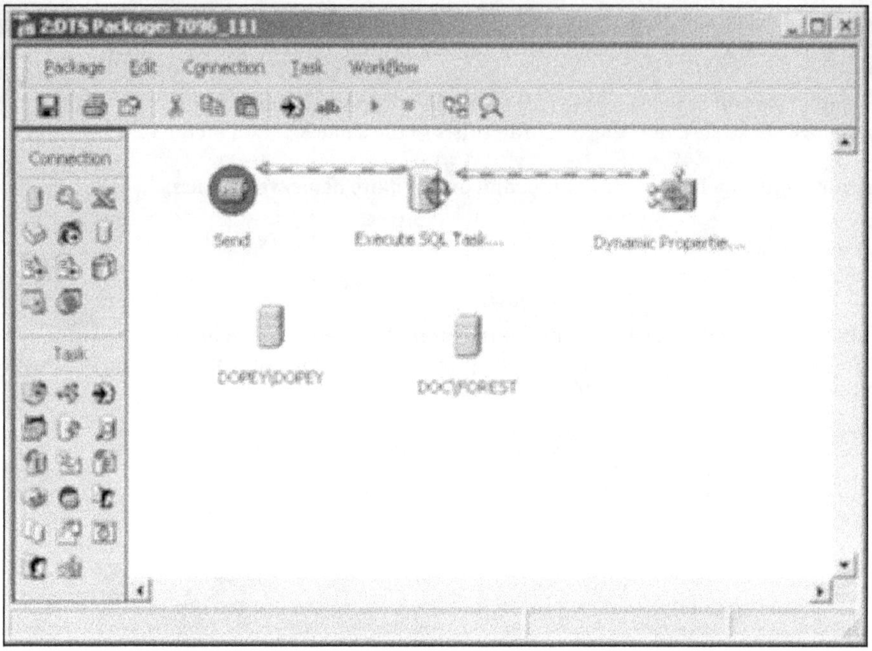


# Configuring Workflow

Workflow in DTS serves two purposes in a DTS package:

- It defines the order of task execution.
- It defines the conditions under which a task should execute.

The elements that define workflow are **precedence constraints**. An arrow between two tasks in the DTS Designer represents a precedence constraint, and the color of the arrow helps identify the type of constraint that we are using.

The **on success** arrow is green and white. On success means that the first task must succeed for the second task (the task with the arrow pointing at it) to execute:

The **on failure** arrow is red and white. On failure means that if the first task has failed, a second task (the task with the arrow pointing at it) will run in response.

The **on completion** arrow is blue and white. On completion means that the second task will run under either a successful or failed execution of the first task.

To create a precedence constraint, select two tasks you wish to join using the constraint. Hold the *Ctrl* key down and select the task you wish to run **first** and click the second task (the one with the arrow pointing at it) to run **second**.

Select the Workflow menu and select which constraint you want.

Once the precedence constraint is defined, you can change the constraint type by double-clicking the arrow. You can then select the new precedence type from the drop-down list, or switch the source and destination steps to change the order of execution.

To remove a precedence constraint, click the arrow and press the delete key.

Some tips to note about workflow and precedence constraints:

- You can choose multiple precedence constraints for each task. You can have multiple tasks executing in parallel. Remember that when using multiple precedent constraints pointing to one task, all source tasks pointing to the destination task must meet the defined conditions for the destination task to run. For example, below is an error task that is indicated by multiple execute SQL tasks:

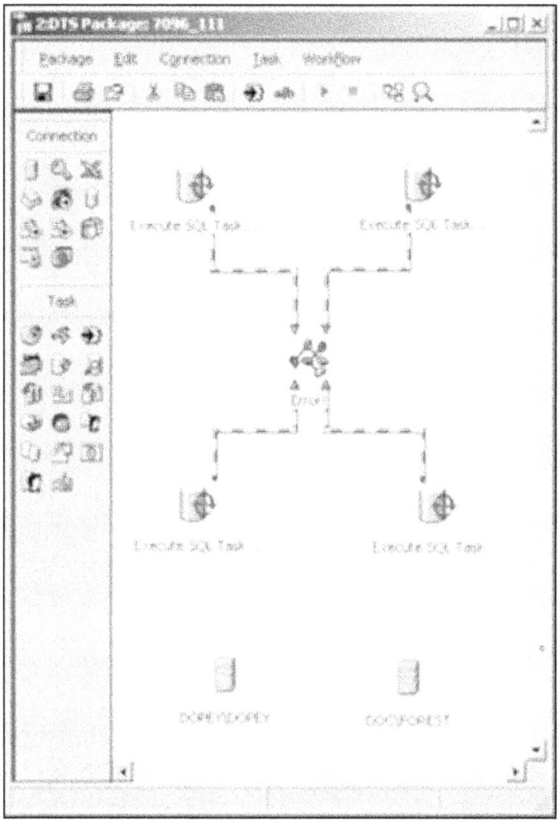


  Many DTS developers try to re-use one Error ActiveX task to handle errors for multiple tasks. Unfortunately, the above workflow configuration means that all the execute SQL tasks must fail before the final ActiveX error task is executed. Remember that precedence constraints work like the AND clause, and not like the OR clause.

- Precedence constraints have a programmatic interface, just like DTS connections and tasks. You can use ActiveX to program more complicated workflow and precedence constraint handling (such as skipping a task or switching constraint types). To access these advanced functions, right-click the destination task being referenced by a precedent constraint and select Workflow | Workflow Properties.

On the Precedence tab, you can configure source step, precedence type, and destination steps:

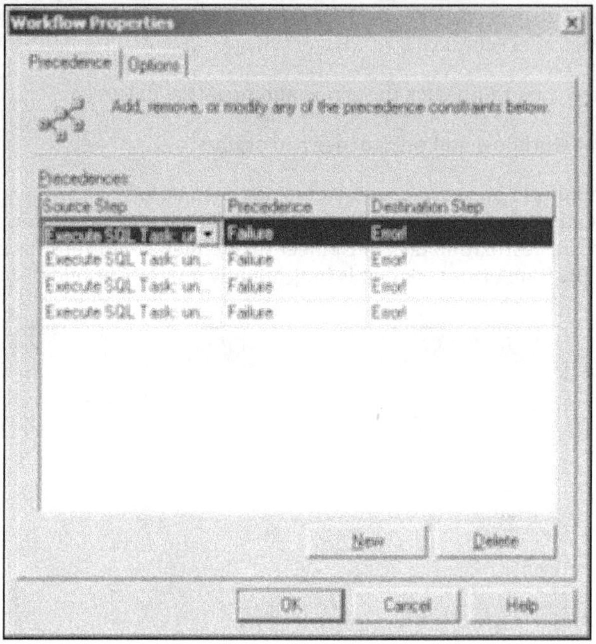


On the Options tab, you can configure the advanced workflow options for the task:

| Name | Description |
|---|---|
| Join transaction if present | When selected, the task steps join an existing transaction, which can either commit or rollback. |
| Commit transaction on successful completion of this step | When selected, the step completion triggers a transaction commit. |
| Rollback transaction on failure | When selected, the step failure will trigger the package transaction to rollback. |
| Execute on main package thread | If selected, the task will be forced to execute on the main package thread (rather than using a spawned thread). Should be used for providers that do not support parallel task execution. |
| DSO rowset provider | Allows OLE DB rowset data to be exposed to external consumers. |
| Close connection on completion | Select this option to close an OLE DB provider connection after completion of the package. |
| Disable this step | Disables this job step at runtime. |
| Fail package on step failure | Terminates DTS package if the specified step fails. |

| Name | Description |
|---|---|
| Task priority | Sets the priority of the task process. |
| Use ActiveX script | If selected, an ActiveX script can be used to manage the workflow properties. |
| Properties | Select the Properties button to bring up the Workflow ActiveX Script Properties dialog. From here, you can programmatically work with the precedent constraints, using logic to skip or change the nature of the defined workflow. Be aware that much of this logic will not be represented visually in your package, which can cause confusion if you have not documented the steps properly. |

# Understanding the DTS Package Execution Context

DTS development can be frustrating without a solid understanding of DTS package execution context. **Execution context** means 'Where is the package executing?' or, more specifically, 'Who spawned the DTS package executable process?'.

Execution context also refers to the security mode used to run the package. Both the originator of execution (workstation or server) and the security context can determine whether or not your package will succeed:

| If you execute a DTS package from... | It will run under the context of... |
|---|---|
| Your workstation using DTS designer | DTS runs within the context of **your workstation** |
| Your workstation using the `dtsrun` command line utility | DTS runs within the context of **your workstation** |
| Scheduled as a job on a SQL Server instance. | DTS runs within the context of the **SQL Server computer** |
| Executed via a stored procedure on a SQL Server instance | DTS runs within the context of the **SQL Server computer** |

When developing a DTS package from your workstation that you plan to save and execute from a SQL Server computer, make sure to program your package in such a way as to avoid referencing settings available on your workstation but not on the server.

For example, you may reference a system DSN, OLE DB driver, or mapped drive that does not exist on the SQL Server computer, but which is available on your workstation. When you execute the DTS package via DTS designer from your workstation, everything works fine; however, once scheduled as a job, the DTS package may fail if it encounters settings that do not exist on the SQL Server computer.

Security used to execute a DTS package is also important. DTS packages that are scheduled as a SQL Server Agent job must be run under certain owner permissions to work. Below is a table reviewing combinations of execution and security context:

| Execution Context | Security Context |
|---|---|
| Scheduled as a job, and owned by a member of the sysadmin server role | Runs under the security context of the SQL Agent service account. The SQL Agent service can run under a local system account; but, if configured as such, the DTS package cannot perform operations that require non-local permissions (such as using VBScript to copy a file from one server to another). Using a domain account for the SQL Agent service means that the package, when scheduled as a job and owned by a sysadmin member, will adopt the permissions of that account. |
| Scheduled as a job, and not a member of the sysadmin role | The package is run under the SQL Agent Proxy account security context. If no rights or permissions are assigned to this account, the package will not run. See Chapter 4 for a review on how to configure the SQL Agent Proxy account. This proxy account requires read and write access to the c:\documents and settings\<proxyaccount>\local settings\temp directory. This account also requires login access to SQL Server and, depending on the package, access to databases and objects. If possible, **do** consider running DTS packages under a non-sysadmin owner, to minimize security or permission issues.<br><br>Beginning with SQL Server 2000 Service Pack 3, DTS has been enhanced to use the system Temp folder if the user Temp folder is unavailable. |
| Manually executed using the dtsrun command-line utility | The security context is that of the Windows account with which you are currently logged on. |
| Executed via xp_cmdshell and dtsrun, via a member of the sysadmin group | The security context is that of the domain account used to start the SQL Server service. If the SQL Server service is using a local system account, the DTS package will not be able to access connections or file paths outside of the SQL Server computer. |
| Executed using xp_cmdshell and dtsrun, via a user who is not a member of the sysadmin group | The security context is that of the SQL Agent Proxy account. |
| Executing a DTS package with a connection that uses authentication | The authentication used for the connection(s) is the same as the domain account used to log in to the client or server to execute the package. If executed from a job, the connection authentication used is the same as the SQL Server Agent service account if a member of the sysadmin group owns the job. For non-sysadmin job owners, the SQL Agent Proxy account is used for connection authentication. Be wary of setting a SQL Agent Proxy account, as this opens up potential security permissions to non-sysadmin users. (See Chapter 4 for a review of the SQL Agent proxy account). |

# 11.16 How to... Configure Package Properties

Several important DTS settings are made at the package level. Such properties include the amount of logging done for the package, the maximum number of tasks that can run in parallel, and the definition of global variables for use by your tasks.

To configure package properties:

- Make sure no icons within DTS Designer are highlighted. If tasks are highlighted, click on the white space of the designer area. From the Package menu in DTS Designer, select Properties:

## The General Tab

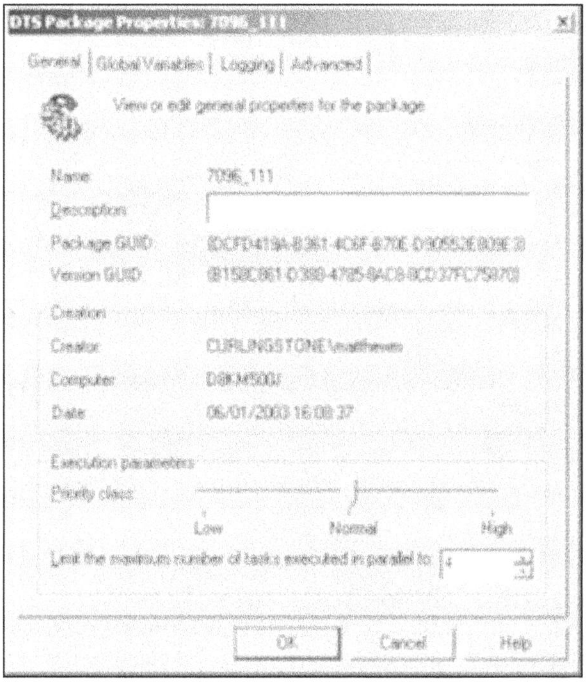


| Name | Description |
|---|---|
| General | User-defined description of the package. |
| Priority class | Select Low, Normal, or High using the slide bar. Only set this task to high if you have a good reason to do so. Setting a package to a high priority can bump more important processes, or impede your server performance. |
| Limit the maximum number of tasks executed in parallel to: | Multiple tasks within a DTS package can be run in parallel, meaning they can execute simultaneously. Experiment with this value to find the best trade-off between speed and overall system performance. Be careful not to set this value too high, or performance of the package could be adversely affected. |

# The Global Variables Tab

The Global Variables tab allows you to add, remove, and modify global variables. Global variables allow you to store values for re-use throughout the DTS package; they can even be used to transfer data from package to package.

Global variables are often used for packages that must be migrated from server to server, using server name, database name, login, and password variables so that data can be changed more easily by referencing the global variables (rather than scattered and hard-coded settings throughout the package tasks).

The Explicit Global Variables checkbox, when selected, specifies that ActiveX scripts must declare each global variable explicitly, and that global variables must be defined either in the Global Variables tab or the Execute SQL Task settings.

To create a new global variable, select the New button. Enter in the Name, Type, and Value for the global variable.

# The Logging Tab

The Logging tab includes options for logging package step activity:

| Name | Description |
|---|---|
| Log package execution to SQL Server | Log information for each step that has executed during the package execution. The information is saved to the `msdb` database. |
| Fail package on first error | Directs the package to stop on the first step failure. |
| Write completion status to event log | Writes package status to the Windows 2000 application log. |
| Error file | Chooses a file to log step status and error information. The file will be created dynamically if it does not exist, and can use the `.txt` format. |

# The Advanced Tab

The Advanced tab allows you to enable meta data lineage functionality, transactions, and OLE DB service components (allows services like session pooling, depending on the OLE DB provider). The Lineage and Scanning options are only useful if you plan to store your packages in the Meta Data Services node:

| Name | Description |
|---|---|
| Use transactions | Enables transactions within the context of your package. |
| Commit on successful package completion | When selected, each individual SQL statement is treated as a transaction, automatically committing statements that complete successfully, and rolling back statements that fail. When unchecked, the first SQL statement submitted within the package is treated as an implicit transaction, which must either be committed or rolled back in order to take effect. |
| Transaction isolation level | The locking mode of your transaction will be determined by the transaction isolation level, with Chaos allowing dirty reads (most concurrency, no locks) to Serialization guaranteeing that no dirty, phantom, or non-repeatable reads (least concurrency, strictest locking method). |

# 11.17 How to... Set the Package Owner and User Password

When you save your package for the first time, or if you select a Save As operation, you can define a **package owner password** and **package user password**.

> **This is unrelated to the authentication method used when connecting to SQL Server.**

If you set an owner password, users will require this password to run or edit the package. This is useful for larger environments with multiple developers, ensuring that your package cannot be edited or executed by the wrong users. You can have an owner password without specifying a user password.

If you set the user password, the owner password must also be set. Users with the user password can run the package, but cannot open or edit the package without the owner password. This is useful for keeping your source code safe (particularly if the package contains sensitive properties or logic), whilst still allowing users to execute the package.

Set the owner or user password in the Save or Save As dialog box:

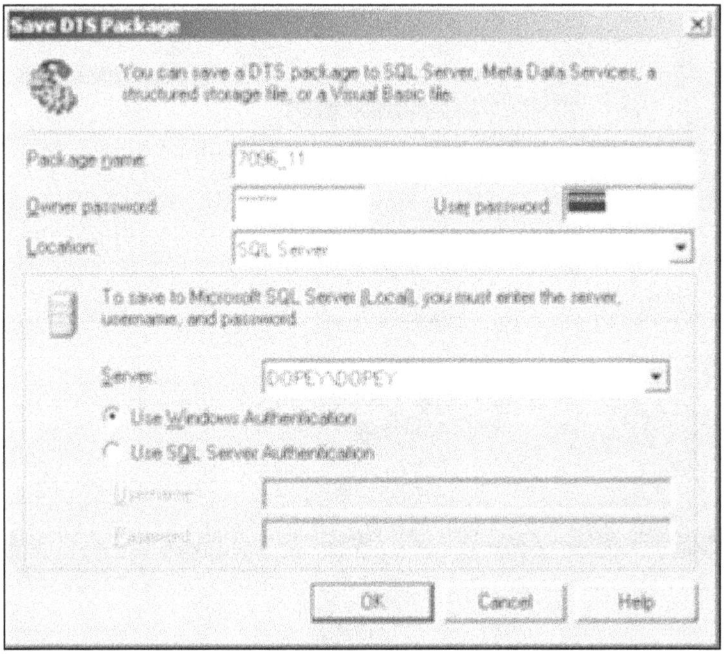

# 11.18 How to... Schedule a DTS Package

To create a scheduled job for your DTS package, you can use two methods:

## Method 1: Create a Job Automatically via the DTS Tree View

- Expand the Data Transformation Services folder and select Local Packages. Right-click the package you wish to schedule as a job and select Schedule Package.
- Select the schedule for the new DTS package job.
- The newly created job will have the same name as the DTS package; you can configure it with additional settings as you wish.

For example, you may want to change the package owner to a login other than your own connection's login:

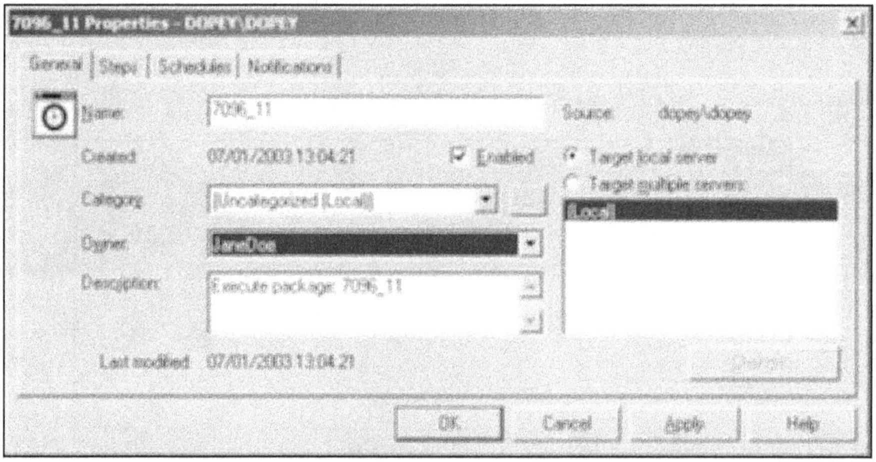


The scheduled DTS package uses one step:

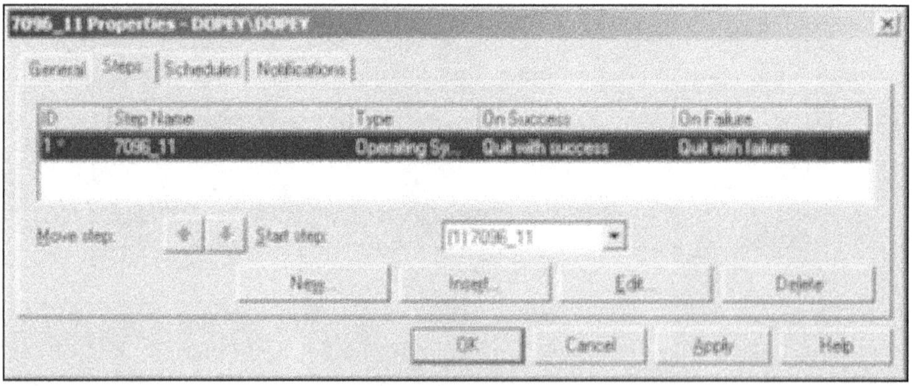

This step uses the `dtsrun` utility, to execute the package. The `/~Z` indicates that the package connection information is both encrypted and in hexadecimal:

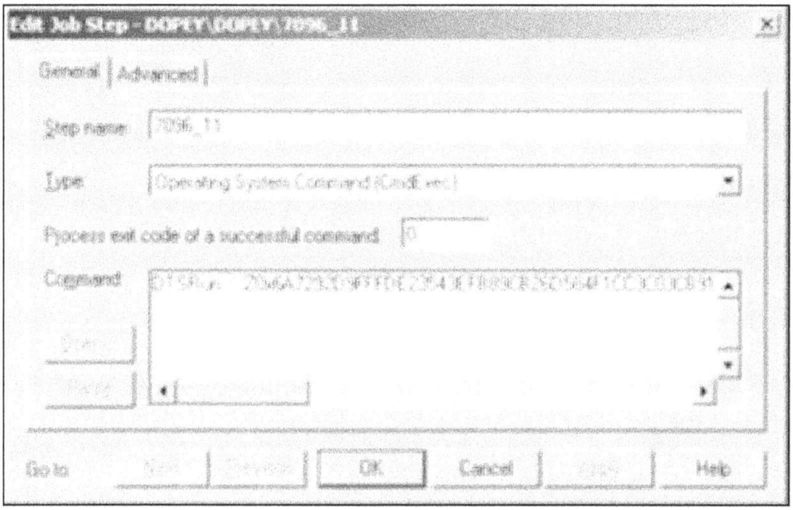

# Method 2: Scheduling a Job Using dtsrun

The second method involves creating your own `dtsrun` step in a job. Rather than use an encrypted string, if creating a `dtsrun` command yourself, you can use the following syntax:

```
dtsrun /Sserver_name /Uuser_nName /Ppassword /Npackage_name /Mpackage_password
```

For example, creating a job step that runs the `DTS_BookRepo` package:

```
dtsrun /SDOPEY\DOPEY /Usa /Psqlfun /NDTS_BookRepo
```

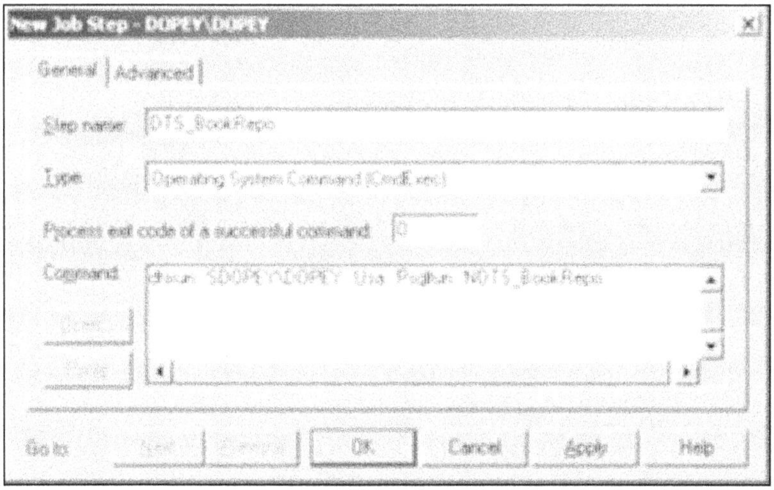

Remember to use the job type Operating System Command (CmdExec) for your `dtsrun` utility call.

# 11.19 How to... Use dtsrun

The dtsrun utility is used to execute a DTS package. The command syntax from *SQL Server Books Online* is as follows:

```
dtsrun
[/?] |
[
   [
     /[~]S server_name[\instance_name]
     { {/[~]U user_name [/[~]P password]} | /E }
   ]
   {
     {/[~]N package_name }
     | {/[~]G package_guid_string}
     | {/[~]V package_version_guid_string}
   }
   [/[~]M package_password]
   [/[~]F filename]
   [/[~]R repository_database_name]
   [/A global_variable_name:typeid=value]
   [/L log_file_name]
   [/W NT_event_log_completion_status]
   [/Z] [/!X] [/!D] [/!Y] [/!C]
]
```

| Parameter | Description |
|---|---|
| /? | Displays all dtsrun options. |
| ~ | Indicates that the parameter will use hexadecimal encrypted values. This is used for /S, /U, /P, /N, /G, /V, /M, /F, and /R. |
| /S | Server name (using named instances is allowed using servername\instancename). |
| /U | SQL authentication login. |
| /P | SQL authentication password. |
| /E | Use Windows NT authentication instead of SQL authentication. |
| /N | Package name. If spaces exist in the name, use double quotations. |
| /G | The package ID of the DTS package. You can find the package ID in the id column of the sysdtspackages table, or in the Package GUID field in the General tab of the DTS Package Properties. |
| /V | The version ID assigned when the package was first saved or executed, and each time it is modified. You can find the version ID in the versionid column of the sysdtspackages table, or in the Version GUID field in the General tab of the DTS Package Properties. |
| /M | Package user password. |
| /F | If referencing a structured storage file for the DTS package, this is the file name and path. |

| Parameter | Description |
|---|---|
| /R | If referencing a package stored in SQL Server Meta Data Services, specifies the repository database name. If no name, the default database is used. |
| /A | Sets global variables from the command line for the package. |
| /L | Sets the package log file name and path. |
| /W | If set to True, will log the package completion status to the Windows Application Log. |
| /Z | Indicates that the dtsrun command line is encrypted via SQL Server 2000 encryption. (To generate an encrypted dtsrun string, use the /!Y switch.) |
| /!X | Stops the package running. Used for creating an encrypted command line only. |
| /!D | Deletes the DTS package from SQL Server. |
| /!Y | Displays the dtsrun command in encrypted format. |
| /!C | Copies the command to the clipboard. |

## Example 11.19.1: Executing a package located in SQL Server's msdb database

Keep in mind that you can schedule dtsrun executions in a job via xp_cmdshell or the CmdExec window. For this example, we will execute dtsrun from a command prompt:

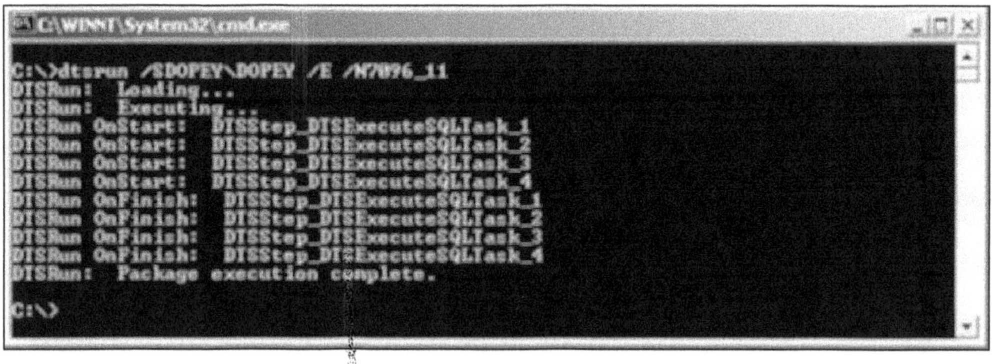


## Example 11.19.2: Executing a package from SQL Server Meta Data Services

### Example 11.19.3: Executing a package from a structured storage file

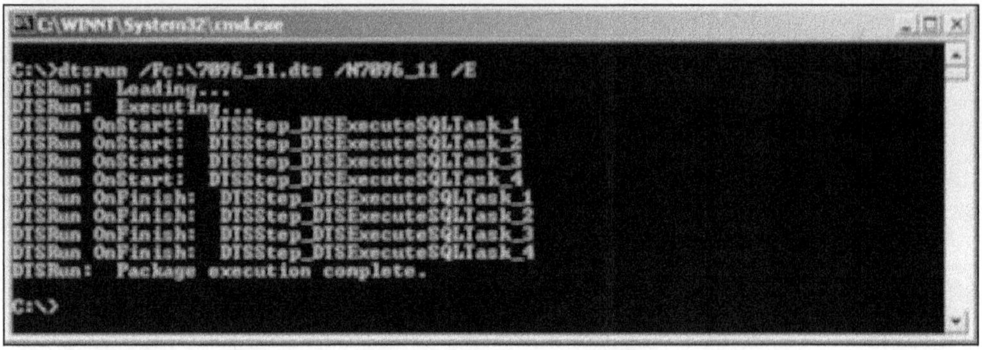


### Example 11.19.4: Creating an encrypted dtsrun string

### Example 11.19.5: Setting a global variable for the package

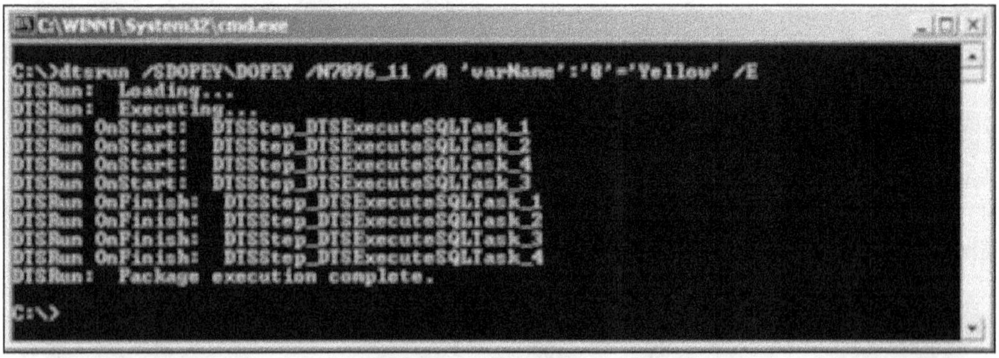


Notice that for the `/A` global variable setting, each parameter is placed in quotes. `'varName'` is the global variable name, `'8'` stands for the global variable data type, and `'Yellow'` is the assigned value for the global variable. The integer values for each global variable data type are as follows:

| Global Variable Data Type | Integer |
|---|---|
| Integer (small) | 2 |
| Integer | 3 |
| Real (4-byte) | 4 |
| Real (8-byte) | 5 |
| Currency | 6 |
| Date | 7 |
| String | 8 |
| Boolean | 11 |
| Decimal | 14 |
| Integer (1-byte) | 16 |
| Unsigned int (1-byte) | 17 |
| Unsigned int (2-byte) | 18 |
| Unsigned int (4-byte) | 19 |
| Integer (8-byte) | 20 |
| Unsigned int (8-byte) | 21 |
| Int | 22 |
| Unsigned int | 23 |
| HRESULT | 25 |
| Pointer | 26 |
| LPSTR | 30 |
| LPWSTR | 31 |

# 11.20 How to... Generate a dtsrun String Dynamically via dtsrunui

The `dtsrunui` utility allows you to execute DTS packages from the user interface; but one excellent side benefit is its ability to create a `dtsrun` string for you dynamically. To use `dtsrunui`:

- Select the Start menu and select Run. Enter `dtsrunui`.
- From the dialog box, select the package name you wish to execute using the Run button, or schedule using the Schedule button. Select Advanced to script the `dtsrun` string:

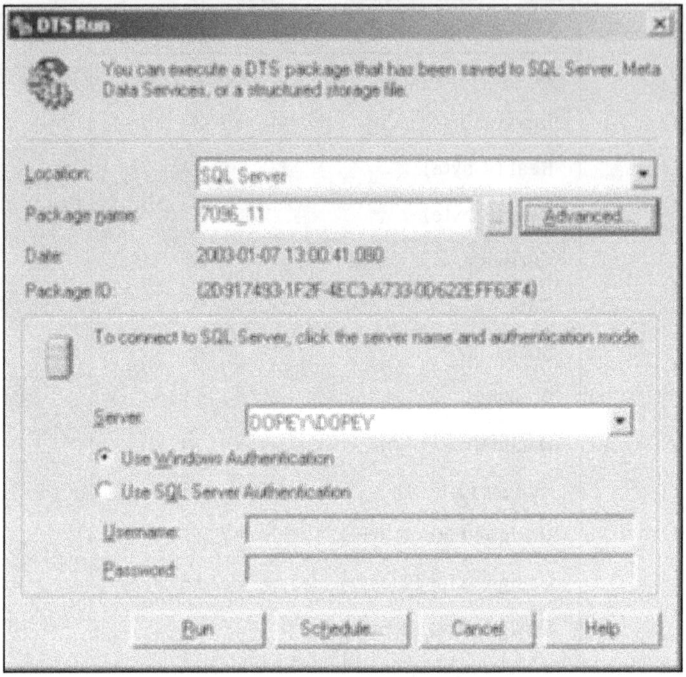


- ❑ Select any extra options you would like for your `dtsrun` string, such as encryption or SQL Server 7.0 format.
- ❑ Select the Generate button and the string will be created.
- ❑ Copy this string for your use.

# 11.21 How to... Register a Custom Task

**Custom tasks** are tasks created by developers or third-party software vendors for use by SQL Server DTS. Custom tasks can be used programmatically within a DTS package, or built in such a way as to be compatible with DTS Designer.

Custom tasks can be created using Microsoft Visual Basic, Visual C++, or any COM-compliant programming language. *SQL Server Books Online* includes detailed instructions on how to develop a DTS custom task in these languages.

Once your custom DTS task `.dll` file is compiled, you can register it on your workstation or SQL Server computer. Make sure to test your custom task thoroughly, before using it in a production environment.

To register a custom DTS task so it appears in your workstation or server DTS Designer Task menu:

- ❑ From DTS Designer, select the Task menu and select Register Custom Task.
- ❑ Select the Task description (label for the custom task), the location of the task `.dll` file, and the Icon location.
- ❑ Select OK to add the custom task.

This task will now appear in its alphabetic order in the Task menu. It can then be used within DTS Designer.

To remove a custom task:

- Select the Task menu and select Unregister Custom Task.
- In the Unregister Custom Task dialog box, only custom tasks will be listed.
- Select the task you wish to remove from the drop down box, and select OK.

# 11.22 How to... Transfer DTS Packages between Servers

To move a DTS package from SQL Server to a new SQL Server instance:

- From within the DTS package in DTS Designer, select Package and Save As.
- Select the name of the package, the location of the package, and the new server's name. At this time, you can also add an owner or user password.

Of course, having to transfer hundreds of DTS packages can make this an unattractive method.

One method that works, but is not **officially** supported, is transferring the contents of the `sysdtspackages` table. This method may not work in future versions, and should be used only when other options are time-prohibitive.

- From the destination server, create a linked server to the source server (See Chapter 9 for instructions on adding a linked server).
- Import the DTS packages to a local temporary table by using a `SELECT` statement from the `sysdtspackages` table on the linked server source:

```
SELECT *
INTO #tmpDTSPackages
FROM sourceserver.msdb.dbo.sysdtspackages
```

- Examine the table to make sure only the DTS packages you wish to migrate are included. Note that each time a DTS package is saved or changed, a new DTS package version is added to the `sysdtspackages` table, so you may see multiple versions for each package.
- If you are sure that all rows include packages you wish to transfer to the local destination server, run a query to insert the DTS packages from the temporary table to the `msdb.dbo.sysdtspackages`:

```
USE msdb

INSERT msdb.dbo.sysdtspackages
SELECT *
FROM #tmpDTSPackages
```

# 11.23 How to... Troubleshoot DTS Packages

With all the potential moving parts in SQL Server DTS, expect to get unusual error messages now and then. Some basic tips to help you navigate DTS issues include:

- Use the same SQL Server version when editing DTS packages. Do not use SQL Server 2000 to edit a SQL Server 7.0 package as, under certain circumstances and versions, the package could be corrupted.
- Make sure your OLE DB provider connections work independently of the package; if they do not work outside DTS, they will not work within DTS.
- Remember that DTS runs under the context of the computer/server that spawned it. If you are running DTS within DTS designer or `dtsrun` from your workstation, it is running based on your workstation's context. If you schedule the package as a job and the job executes the package, it is running under the server's context. Errors **will** occur if you reference drives or data sources that exist on your workstation, but not on the server.
- Utilize the dynamic properties task as much as possible if you plan to migrate DTS packages from a development environment to your production environment. Many hours can be wasted tracking down why a certain task is not doing anything, when in fact it is performing the action correctly, just on the wrong server. Use dynamic properties for server names, logins, file directories, and any variable that can change between servers. Do not hardcode server-specific variables.
- When testing and troubleshooting your DTS package, if the package is stored in SQL Server, make sure that you back up your `msdb` database. Saving your DTS packages as you develop them to backup servers, or as `.dts` files is good practice. Recreating a large and artful package from scratch can be a frustrating experience. Integrate DTS package recovery with your disaster recovery plan (see Chapter 6 for more information on creating a DRP).
- Storing `.dts` files within archiving utilities, such as Visual Source Safe (VSS), is an excellent way to maintain DTS package version control.

If users without system administration privileges need to modify packages created by other users, they must be either the owner of the DTS package, or a member of the `sysadmin` fixed server role. To reassign the owner, you can use the undocumented stored procedure `sp_reassign_dtspackageowner`, which has the following syntax:

```
sp_reassign_dtspackageowner [@name=] 'name',
        [@id=] 'id',
        [@newloginname=] 'newloginname'
```

This procedure may not be supported in the future, but if not hopefully Microsoft will find a replacement for it.

For specific error messages, two excellent resources are:

- http://www.sqldts.com/ (has a detailed troubleshooting section)
- http://support.microsoft.com/

Lastly, document your DTS packages as much as possible. DTS Designer allows you to add text annotations by pressing the  button and typing in your text. This self-documenting feature can make the package purpose more obvious to yourself and others:

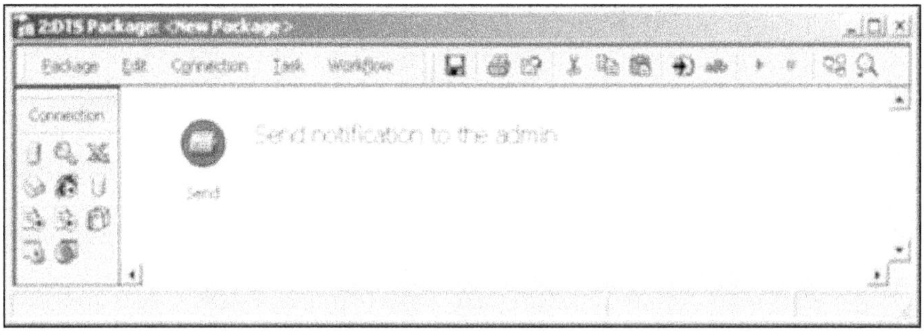


Right-click the text annotation to modify the font and properties.

# 12

# Log Shipping

In previous chapters, you've seen how to distribute copies of data using replication and how to maintain high availability with SQL Server failover clustering.

**Log shipping**, another high-availability option available for SQL Server 2000, is used for maintaining a second copy or **warm standby** of your database or databases. Using SQL Server 2000 Enterprise Edition, you can create and configure log shipping by using the SQL Server Maintenance Plan Wizard. Log shipping copies transaction log backups from the source database to a different server, and then restores each transaction log to a standby database. This standby database can be used as a warm standby, in the event of a failure on the source server or database. Log shipping can also be used to generate a remote copy of a database for use by reporting applications, and is valuable in the event of a site disaster.

There are three components involved in the log shipping process: the **primary server**, the **secondary server**, and the **monitoring server**. The primary server is the server that hosts the database that you wish to preserve in the event of a failure. The secondary server is the server that hosts the database that will be used as backup in the event of a failure on the primary server. The monitoring server is the server that watches the log shipping process and reports any problems with data transfer between the primary server and the secondary server.

## The Log Shipping Process

Log shipping allows you to keep a closely synchronized copy of a selected database. The following process achieves this:

- An initial full backup is performed for the primary database.
- The secondary database, on a secondary server, is created from this initial full backup. This can also be a restore over an existing database. This secondary database is kept in either **standby** or **no recovery** mode, so that transaction logs can continue to be applied to it. Standby mode allows read access during periods when transaction logs are not being restored to the secondary database. No recovery mode does not allow user access.
- Transaction log backups are performed on a scheduled basis on the primary database.
- Transaction log backups are copied to a secondary server.

- Transaction log backups are restored to the secondary database.
- Periodically, logins are transferred to the secondary server from the primary server, in the event that the secondary database must be used (converted from a secondary database to a primary database):

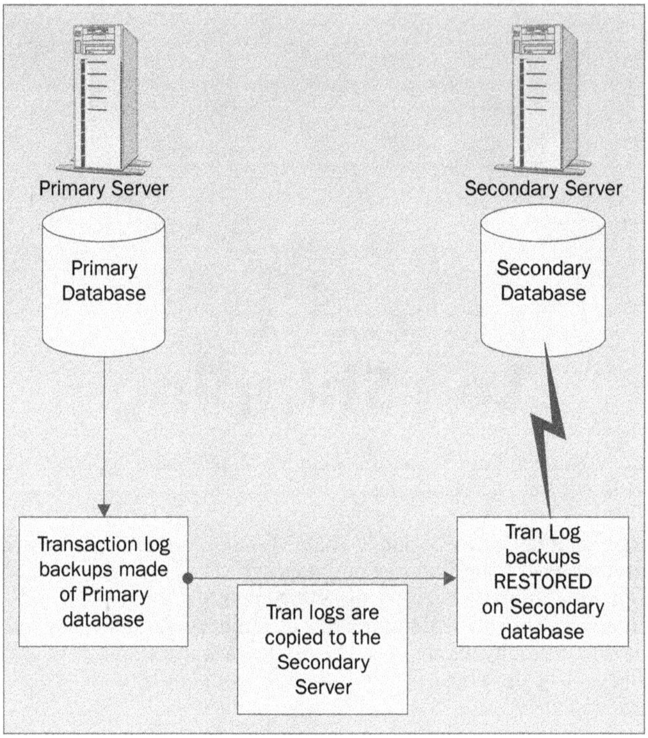


Unlike replication, log shipping reflects any data, object, or schema changes within the primary database on the warm standby when the latest transaction log(s) are applied. Log shipping is also beneficial for distributing warm standbys to remote or off-site servers. If an outage or disaster occurs at your site, you should be able to continue business against your database with relatively little down time.

Log shipping can also be less costly than a failover cluster solution. Although log shipping via the SQL Server Maintenance Plan Wizard requires Enterprise Edition, log shipping does **not** have as stringent requirements for hardware (or as complex a setup) as failover clustering. If the source and destination servers can run SQL Server (Enterprise Edition), chances are you can implement log shipping. The same cannot be said of failover clustering (where all components should be listed on the Hardware Compatibility List).

The disadvantages of log shipping are that switching the database roles is a manual process; you must run certain stored procedures and ensure that the latest logins have been transferred from the primary to the secondary server (we'll see more on this later in the chapter). There is also a risk of data loss, depending on the frequency with which copying transaction logs from the primary database to the secondary database takes place.

Log shipping prior to SQL Server 2000 was always a manual or third-party software solution that was not built in to the SQL Server tool suite. SQL Server 2000 Enterprise and Developer editions (although Developer cannot be used in a production environment) now includes the following features and support:

- Log shipping setup with the Database Maintenance Plan Wizard.

- Log shipping monitoring with Log Shipping Monitor. Log Shipping Monitor includes alerts for problems with the log shipping process.
- Log shipping configuration modification, using the database maintenance plan properties.
- System stored procedures for changing log shipping roles.

Monitoring should be performed by a separate server from the primary and secondary servers. By maintaining a separate monitoring server, if either log shipping server encounters a failure, the monitoring server can fire an alert. Although the primary or secondary server can also act as a monitoring server, this is not recommended because a failure of the monitoring server along with the log shipping process will not trigger an alert.

Unfortunately, the supported version of log shipping is not yet available with versions older than SQL Server 2000. The *Back Office Resource Kit* provides a simple log shipper tool for SQL Server 7.0, which provides a cut-down version of log shipping. However if anything goes wrong with the Resource Kit's version of log shipping, you will most likely have to rebuild everything from scratch; whereas SQL Server 2000's supported log shipping has more fault-tolerance (you can solve most log shipping problems without rebuilding the entire log shipping scenario). See Microsoft Knowledge Base article - 275146, *INF: Frequently Asked Questions - SQL Server 7.0 - Log Shipping*, for information on SQL Server 7.0 log shipping. Other unsupported log shipping solutions can be found on such code-sharing sites such as http://www.swynk.com/.

This chapter will describe how to set up log shipping using the Database Maintenance Plan Wizard, how to configure and monitor log shipping, and how to perform a database role change and role reversal.

# Checklist... Log Shipping Pre-Configuration Recommendations and Best Practices

The following are pre-configuration requirements for setting up log shipping in the Database Maintenance Plan Wizard:

- Both SQL Server instances must be running either SQL Server Enterprise or SQL Server Developer Editions. (Developer Edition cannot be used in a production environment.)The user who configures log shipping must be a member of the `sysadmin` server role to have permission to modify the database to log ship.
- Identify which servers will act as the **primary server**, **secondary server**, and **monitoring server**. The primary server is the SQL Server instance containing the database for which you wish to configure log shipping. This secondary server is the SQL Server instance that contains the database that receives the initial database restore and continuous transaction log restores from the source server. The monitoring server monitors the status of log shipping, keeping status and history in the `msdb` system database. Select a stable monitoring server, as you cannot change certain log shipping configurations when the monitoring server is unavailable. The performance impact of monitoring log shipping is usually not significant; **do**, however, select a server that has capacity.
- The `MSSQLServer` and `SQLServerAgent` services must be configured with a Windows authentication account with `sysadmin` permissions on **all** participating servers (primary, secondary, and monitoring).
- Create a shared network file share on both the primary and secondary servers. The primary server share will hold the source database's transaction logs; the secondary server share will contain the transaction logs backups (copied from the primary), which will be restored to the secondary server database. The SQL Server Agent service account must have read and write permissions to these file shares. To configure a share, right-click the folder, selecting Properties | Sharing | Share this folder. Click the Permissions button to grant permissions to the SQL Server Agent service account.

- The database being log shipped must use the full or bulk-logged recovery model. The simple recovery model is not supported.
- Create one database maintenance log shipping plan for each log shipped database.
- Make sure that the log shipped database does not have other backup jobs or maintenance plans running against it. Redundant backups can nullify the log shipping process or cause problems with your log shipping pair.
- Do not use other maintenance plan options within your log shipping maintenance plan. For example, do not include an integrity or optimization job with your log shipping maintenance plan; keep your plan simple and use it only for log shipping.
- Keep in mind that you can log ship one primary database to multiple secondary servers and databases.
- Do not hard code the server name in your applications referencing the database. Create your applications in such a way as to make it easy to switch database servers, ensuring that you can take advantage of a log shipping.

# 12.1 How to... Set up Log Shipping with the Database Maintenance Plan Wizard

The following steps detail how to set up log shipping with the Database Maintenance Plan Wizard. These steps will not review the dialog boxes unrelated to log shipping:

- From Enterprise Manager on the primary server, start a new Database Maintenance Plan Wizard.
- Select the source database and check the Ship the transaction logs to other SQL Servers (Log Shipping) check box. You must configure each database separately; if you select multiple databases, you cannot set up log shipping. If you have selected only one database and cannot select the Ship the transaction logs to other SQL Servers (Log Shipping) checkbox, make sure that the database is using the full recovery model:

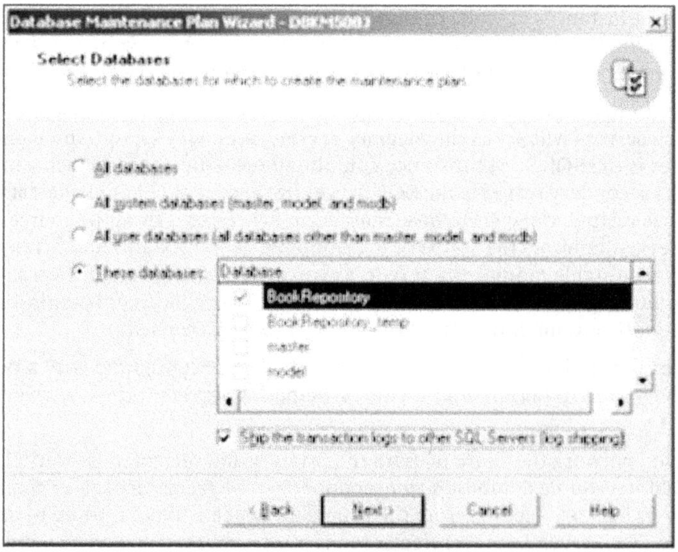


- Skip past the dialog boxes that are unrelated to log shipping.

- On the Specify Transaction Log Backup Disk Directory dialog, specify the transaction log backup directory to back up to on the primary server. Also, select how long transaction log backups should be maintained in the Remove files older than field. Be careful not to delete files prematurely; for example, specifying a 3- or 4-day period would allow you to recover from a problem encountered over the weekend or an extended holiday. If you are performing tape backups of your backup files, consider the frequency of the backups when determining how many days to keep on the server. If a problem occurs with the log shipping process and the source transaction log backups are deleted before the copy process is fixed, log shipping may fail:

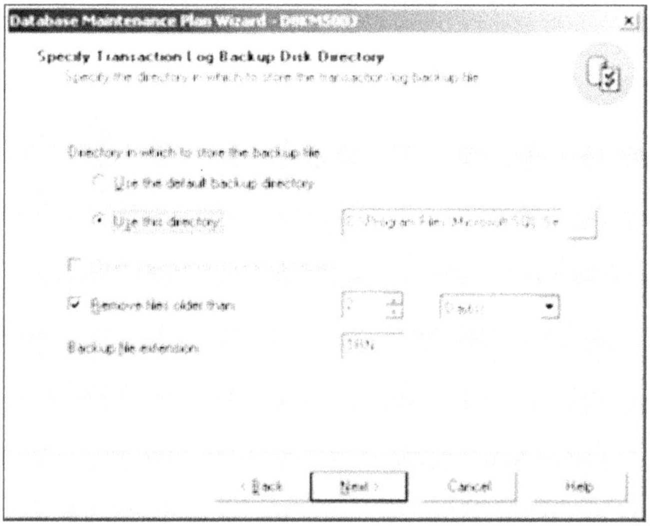


- Specify the name of the share used for log shipping on your primary log shipping server on the next screen, and click Next:

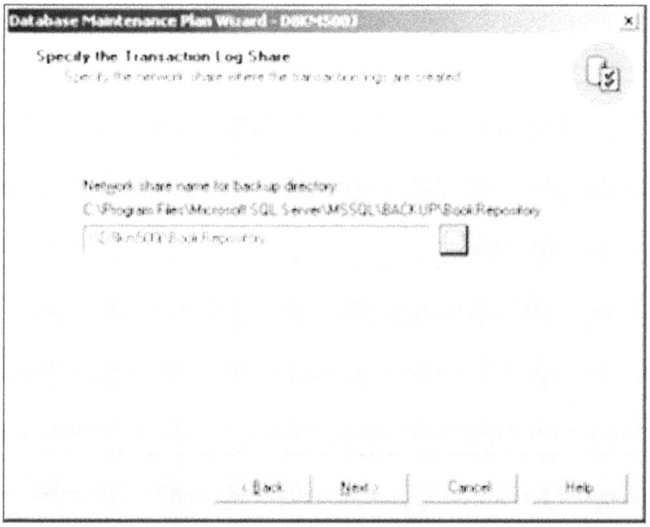


- Click the Add button to add a destination server for log shipping.

- Under Server Name, select the name of the secondary server. Select the Transaction Log Destination Directory. For the secondary server, determine whether a new database must be created or whether to use an existing database; if you select a new database specify the location of the data and log file.
- Under the Database Load State section, determine whether the database will be placed in no recovery mode or standby mode. No recovery mode means that users cannot access the database until it is recovered. SQL Server Enterprise Manager will show the database in a 'loading' status. Standby mode allows users to have read-only access to the database; however, users will be kicked out of the database during restores if Terminate users in database is selected. Otherwise, if users are in your database during a restore attempt, the restore will fail.
- Select the Allow database to assume primary role checkbox if you want the secondary server to have the option of becoming the primary log shipping server. This provides you with the flexibility to perform a role reversal between the primary and secondary servers. If you select this, you must set a transaction log backup directory share name:

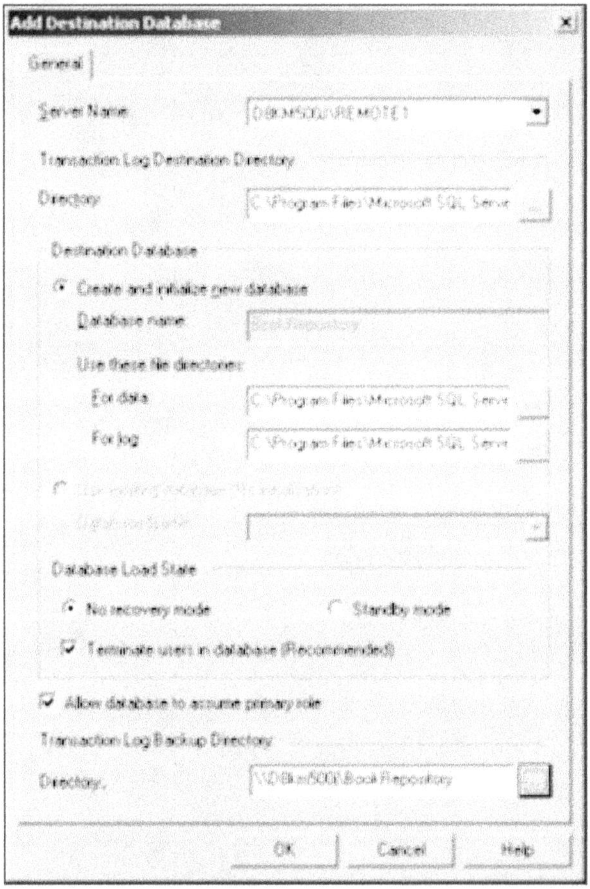


- If you opted to create a new database, you must decide whether this database is created with the most recent backup file for the primary database or with an immediate full primary database backup.
- Select the frequency of transaction log backups in the Backup Schedule section of the resulting Log Shipping Schedules screen.

- The Copy/load frequency section determines how often the primary server transaction logs are copied to the secondary server and restored on the secondary database. Configure this value to a time frequency that is acceptable for your data recovery needs. For example, if you can afford to lose 15 minutes of data, consider a copy/load frequency of 15 minutes. When Copy/load frequency is set to 0, Load delay is also set to 0; the load delay determines how long the log shipping plan waits after a transaction log is copied to the secondary server before restoring on the secondary database. Set this load delay to a larger value for slower networks, or for transaction logs that take a longer time to copy fully to the secondary server.

- The File retention period determines how long transaction log backups are kept on the destination server:

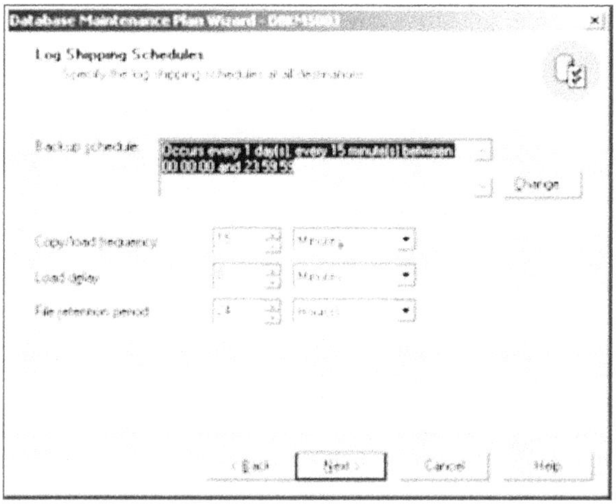


- The Log Shipping Thresholds dialog box controls alert thresholds with the backup alert and out of sync alert:
  - The backup alert threshold triggers an alert if the time since the last primary server database transaction log backup exceeds the value specified.
  - The out of sync alert threshold triggers an alert if the time between the last primary server database transaction log backup and the last secondary server database transaction log restore exceeds the value specified. These alerts only show up in the SQL log and Log Shipping Monitor, so be sure to configure the SQL Server agent alert running on the monitoring server to perform a net send or email to yourself or other production support DBAs:

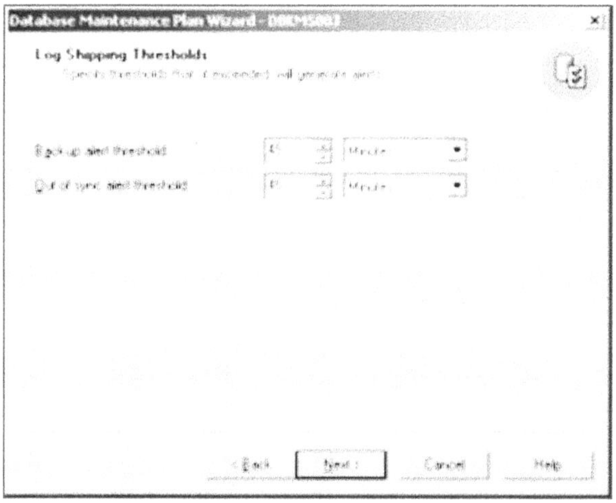

- Specify the central monitoring server; this should **not** be the same as your primary or secondary servers. If you must select one of the log shipping pairs, use the secondary server for monitoring.
- Also, the SQL Server edition for monitoring can be the Standard Edition of SQL Server 2000; it does not have to be Enterprise Edition. Regarding the form of security used by the Monitor server, Microsoft recommends that Windows NT authentication be used. If SQL Server authentication is selected, the `log_shipping_monitor_probe` SQL Login is used to monitor log shipping, and must be used for other database maintenance plans. You must select a password for this login when it is first created:

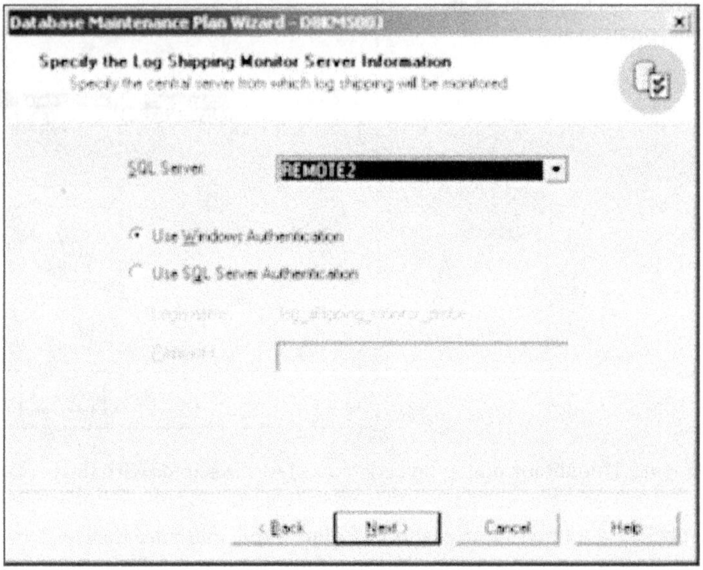


- In the remaining dialog boxes, choose whether or not to generate reports and maintain history.
- When you reach the dialog box for naming the database maintenance plan, make sure to give it a name that reflects its use in log shipping and the database name.

After configuring your log shipping maintenance plan, you need to perform two more steps to ensure that your secondary database can be used as a primary database in the event of a primary server failure, upgrade, or other such event.

# Login Transfer

The last two tasks focus on ensuring that primary server logins exist on the secondary server. If your primary server is gone, you obviously cannot retrieve the original logins; so, it is important that you execute the following steps as soon as possible after creating your log shipping maintenance plan:

- Create a transfer logins task in a DTS package and schedule it to run frequently (or as frequently as new logins are created or modified). See the previous chapter for details on how to create such a package. Make sure you configure the package to transfer logins from the primary server to the secondary server, specifically for the Logins for selected databases option:

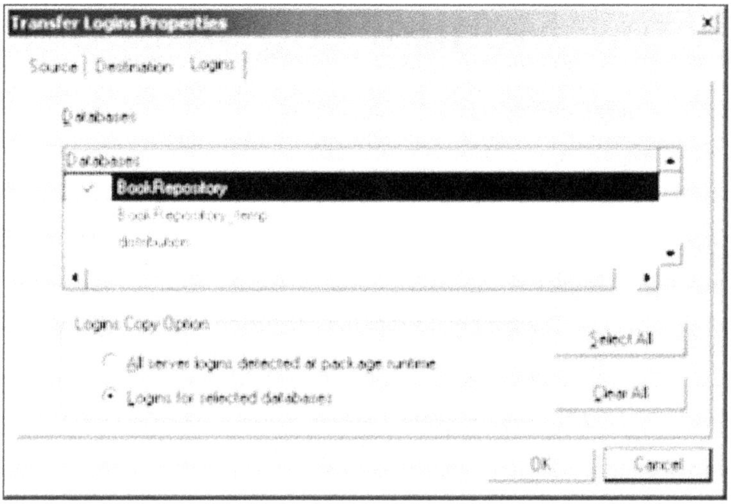

- Secondly, you must create a job to BCP OUT the sysxlogins table from the primary server to a destination directory on the secondary server. This will be necessary to resolve login SIDs between the primary and secondary server during the role change (**primary role change** means that the secondary server is brought online and is used as the primary database). Also note that SID differences between sysxlogins and sysusers can be resolved using the sp_change_users_login system stored procedure (reviewed later on). To configure the BCP job:
  - Begin by creating a new SQL Server Agent job on the primary server. Make sure sa or a login with sysadmin permissions owns the job.
  - Create a job step that performs a BCP OUT operation for the sysxlogins table in the master database. You can use BCP OUT to move the file directly to the secondary server file share. Use the Operating System Command (CmdExec) job type. The graphic below shows the command for BCP OUT:

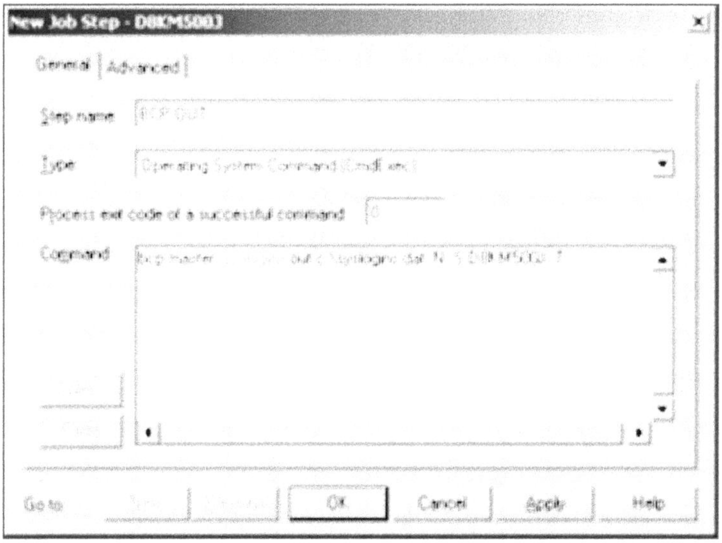

# 12.2 How to... Monitor Log Shipping Status

Log Shipping Monitor can be used to check the status of log shipping and to edit specific information that pertains to the primary and secondary server. To monitor the status of log shipping, carry out the following steps; remember that the monitor server is defined as part of the database maintenance plan:

- Expand the server group and server registration of the monitoring server. Expand the Management folder and select Log Shipping Monitor.
- You will see a list of one or more log shipping pairs (primary and destination log shipping configurations). Double-click on the entry to view the log shipping pair properties.
- The Status tab of the Log Shipping Pair Properties dialog box displays primary and secondary log shipping database status:
  - From this dialog box, you can monitor the last backup file created, last file copied, and last file loaded to the log shipping secondary database. The screenshot below shows a `first_file_000000000000.trn` value; this means that the initial copy and load has not yet been communicated to the monitoring server. This data will not be refreshed until you exit the properties and re-open them again.
  - If the initial copy and loads have already run and the `first_file_000000000000.trn` continues to appear in the fields, you may have a problem referred to in Microsoft Knowledge Base article Q292586, *PRB: Backup, Copy, and Load Job Information Is Not Updated on the Log Shipping Monitor*. This problem is seen when the `msdb..log_shipping_primaries` table (the table used to store information about backups performed on the primary server) on the monitor server isn't updated, or if the `msdb..log_shipping_secondaries` table (the table used to store information on the last file copied to the secondary server, as well as the last transaction log restored) is not updated with each copy/load of the transaction log. If this occurs, and you have configured log shipping monitoring to use Windows NT authentication, be sure that the SQL Server service accounts on the primary and secondary servers have `SELECT` and `UPDATE` privileges for the `log_shipping_primaries` and `log_shipping_secondaries` tables on the monitor server's `msdb` database. If you chose SQL Server authentication for the log shipping monitor, make sure that the `log_shipping_monitor_probe` login on the monitoring server has `SELECT` and `UPDATE` privileges for the `msdb..log_shipping_primaries` and `msdb..log_shipping_secondaries` tables:

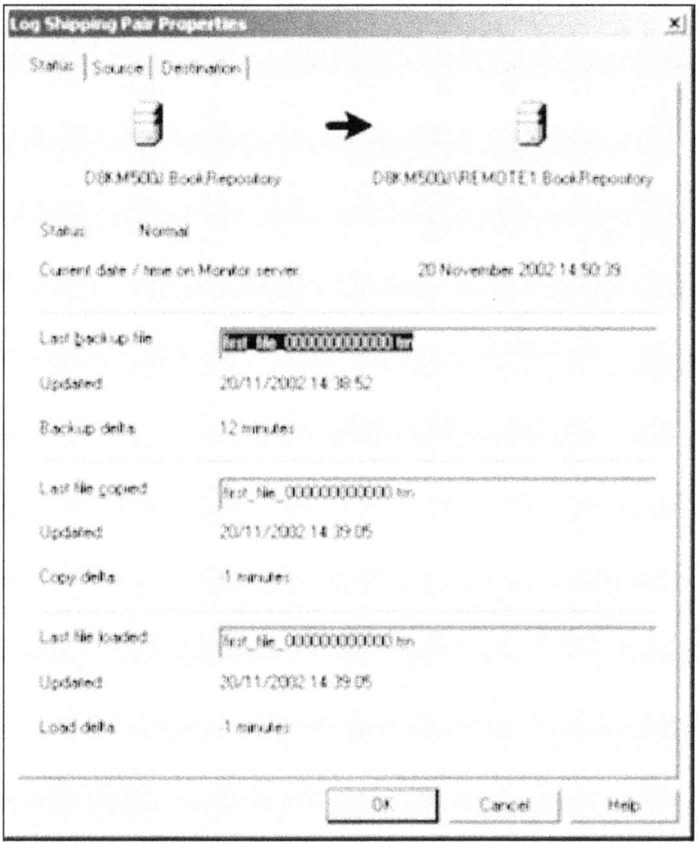


- ❑ On the Source tab, you can change the backup failure alert threshold, change the backup alert error number, or disable the backup alert:
  - ❑ You can also specify that alert generation is suppressed between certain time periods and on selected days. For example, if you expect intermittent network outages over the weekend (network upgrade), you could temporarily suppress alerts during that time.
  - ❑ Click the View Backup Schedule button to view the backup schedule.
- ❑ The Destination tab allows you to configure the alert threshold, alert number, and whether or not the alert is enabled:
  - ❑ You can also suppress alert generation between certain time periods and on specific days.
  - ❑ Select the View Copy Schedule and View Load Schedule buttons to view the frequency of copy and load (restore) operations.

You can also view more information on errors that occur while performing log shipping operations, by performing these steps:

- ❑ Expand the server group and server registration of the monitoring server. Expand the Management folder and select Log Shipping Monitor.
- ❑ You will see a list of one or more log shipping pairs (primary and destination log shipping configurations). Right-click the pair you wish to monitor, and select View Backup History to view backup history or View Copy/Restore History for history on the copy and restore jobs.

# 12.3 How to... Configure Log Shipping Properties

You can modify the properties of your log shipping pair by double-clicking your log shipping maintenance plan in Enterprise Manager, under the Management folder and Database Maintenance Plan node:

- On the Log Shipping tab, select Add to create a new Log Shipping pair, Delete to remove an existing pair, and Edit to edit an existing Log Shipping pair:

> **Note that if you delete the last Log Shipping pair, you must reconfigure log shipping from scratch.**

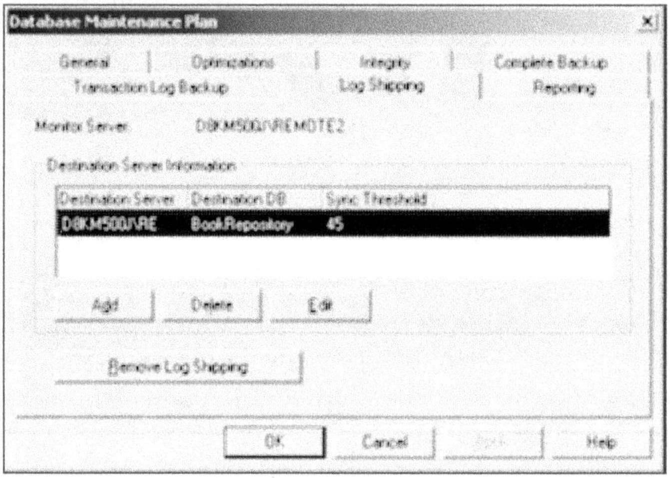


- From the General tab of the Edit Destination Database dialog box (accessed with the Edit button from above), you can modify the transaction log destination directory and future destination share directory (if you enabled the secondary server to assume a primary role during setup).
- On the Initialize tab, you can change the secondary database load state and enable the Terminate users in database option, for when a restore operation begins. You can also configure the copy and load frequencies:

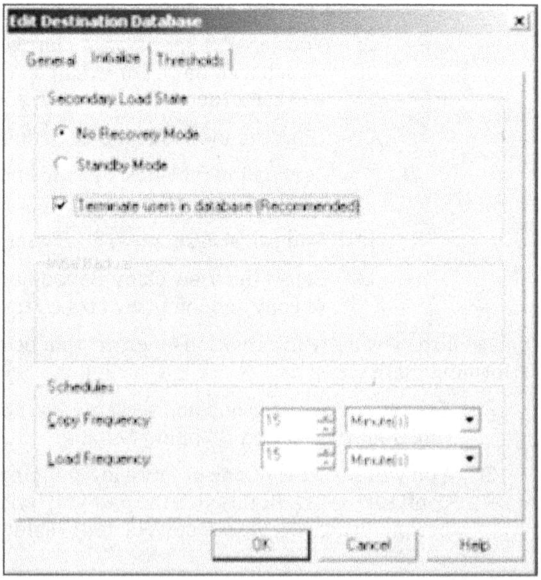

Lastly, on the Thresholds tab, you can configure the Out of Sync, Load Time Delay, File Retention Period, and History Retention Period values.

# 12.4 How to... Create a Primary Role Change for the Secondary Server

The purpose of log shipping is to provide a warm standby copy of the primary server database, for use in the event of a failure on the primary database.

Enabling a secondary database for use by users is called a **primary role change**. A primary role change removes the primary server from log shipping and sets up the secondary server database for use as the primary server.

The primary role change assumes and requires that you followed the earlier log shipping installation steps of scheduling a job to transfer logins and BCP OUT the master.dbo.syslogins table to the secondary server.

To issue a primary role change:

- Execute the sp_change_primary_role stored procedure from the primary server; this assumes that your primary server is available. If it is not available, you can run this procedure later, after the server becomes available again. You can continue with the rest of the steps even if the primary server is not available.

  The sp_change_primary_role stored procedure removes the primary server from the log shipping plan. The following is an example of running sp_change_primary_role:

```
EXEC msdb.dbo.sp_change_primary_role
     @db_name = 'BookRepository',
     @backup_log = 1,
     @terminate = 0,
     @final_state = 2,
     @access_level = 1
GO
```

| Parameter | Description |
|---|---|
| @db_name | Database to be removed from log shipping. |
| @backup_log | This parameter defaults to 1 and issues a final transaction log backup of the primary server database. |
| @terminate | This parameter defaults to 1 and specifies that all pending transactions in the primary server database be rolled back. The database is also placed in single user mode for the duration of the stored procedure. If you use the value 0, make sure there are no active connections to the database (the procedure requires exclusive access). |
| @final_state | This parameter specifies the final recovery state of the primary server database, the default value is 1, which places the database in RECOVERY mode, the value 2 places the database in NO RECOVERY mode, and the value 3 places the database in STANDBY mode. |

*Table continued on following page*

| Parameter | Description |
|---|---|
| @access_level | This parameter sets the user access status for the primary server database. The default is 1, which is MULTI_USER mode; otherwise, selecting 2 gives RESTRICTED_USER, and 3 sets SINGLE_USER. |

- From the secondary server, execute the sp_change_secondary_role stored procedure. This procedure converts the secondary database to the primary database. The following is an example of executing sp_change_secondary_role:

```
EXEC msdb.dbo.sp_change_secondary_role
    @db_name = 'BookRepository',
    @do_load = 1,
    @force_load = 1,
    @final_state = 1,
    @access_level = 1,
    @terminate = 1,
    @stopat = NULL
GO
```

| Parameter | Description |
|---|---|
| @db_name | Secondary database to convert to a primary database. |
| @do_load | The default for this parameter is 1, which means that any pending transaction logs should be copied from the primary server and restored, prior to converting the secondary database into a primary database. |
| @force_load | If do_load is set to 1 and force_load is set to 1, all transaction logs are restored in spite of load delay settings specified during the Log Shipping setup. If do_load is not selected, this option is ignored. |
| @final_state | This parameter specifies the final recovery state of the converted database, the default value is 1, which places the database in RECOVERY mode, the value 2 places the database in NO RECOVERY mode, and the value 3 places the database in STANDBY mode. |
| @access_level | This parameter sets the user access status for the converted database. The default is 1, which is MULTI_USER mode; otherwise, selecting 2 gives RESTRICTED_USER, and 3 gives SINGLE_USER. |
| @terminate | Set this option to 1 if setting @final_state to STANDBY mode. |
| @keep_replication | If set to 1, specifies that replication settings are preserved when restoring pending transaction logs to the secondary (converted) database; the default is 0. This option will only be used if do_load is set to 1. |
| @stopat | This parameter operates just like the STOPAT clause of a RESTORE LOG command, allowing you to restore the transaction logs as of a specified point in time. This parameter takes a valid datetime data type. |

- You may receive an error when running sp_change_secondary_role, reporting something along the lines of:

Exclusive access could not be obtained because the database is in use.

You can avoid this error by ensuring that no outstanding transaction log restores are pending. If there are pending transaction log restores, manually run the RESTORE SQL Server agent job and then run sp_change_secondary_role. You can also change the @terminate parameter to 0, but you must make sure that no other users are in the database prior to executing sp_change_secondary_role again.

- On the monitoring server, execute the sp_change_monitor_role stored procedure. This stored procedure configures the current secondary database and server as the primary database and server:

```
EXEC msdb.dbo.sp_change_monitor_role
    @primary_server = 'D8KM500J',
    @secondary_server = 'REMOTE1',
    @database = 'BookRepository',
    @new_source = 'REMOTE1'
GO
```

| Parameter | Description |
|---|---|
| @primary_server | Specifies the name of the old primary server (being replaced). |
| @secondary_server | Specifies the name of the old secondary server (being converted to primary). |
| @database | The name of the secondary database. |
| @new_source | The name of the new primary server. |

- From the new primary server, you must now ensure that logins and user access are restored to the new primary database. As instructed earlier, you should BCP OUT the sysxlogins table and copy it to the secondary server periodically.
- Use the sp_resolve_logins stored procedure to resolve logins on the new primary server that were logins on the old demoted primary server. For example:

```
EXEC sp_resolve_logins
    @dest_db = 'BookRepository',
    @dest_path = 'j:\mssql\backup\BookRepository\',
    @filename = 'syslogins.dat'
GO
```

| Parameter | Description |
|---|---|
| @dest_db | This sets the new primary database. |
| @dest_path | The path to the location to which the old demoted primary server's bcp out file was copied. |
| @filename | The file name of the syslogins bcp out file. |

- Lastly, you must resolve the master database syslogins table with the primary database's sysusers table, by executing sp_change_users_login for each user in the database. As you will recall from previous chapters, this stored procedure fixes orphaned database users (users with SIDs that do not relate to SIDs in syslogins).

sp_change_users_login performs a fix for the tstShip login, associating syslogins and sysusers, based on the login and user name:

```
USE BookRepository
GO
EXEC sp_change_users_login 'Auto_fix', 'tstShip'
```

This completes the primary role change. The new primary database can now be used for production purposes. A primary role change is not the same as a **role reversal**. In a role reversal, the new primary database begins log shipping to another secondary database (or databases). To perform a role reversal:

- ❑ Remove the log shipping database maintenance plan from the new primary server. To do this, open the database maintenance plan and select the Remove Log Shipping button from the Log Shipping tab.
- ❑ Select Yes at the confirmation dialog box.
- ❑ Check the secondary server and, if this server was previously a demoted primary, make sure the log shipping database maintenance plan is also deleted.
- ❑ Create a new log shipping plan from the new primary server, repeating steps reviewed earlier in the chapter for creating a log shipping pair. At this point, you can choose the demoted server as a secondary server, or an entirely new server instance as the new secondary server.

# 12.5 How to... Troubleshoot Log Shipping

Although SQL Server 2000's Maintenance Plan Wizard and Log Shipping Monitor functionality has automated a lot of the setup, log shipping is still not fully automated, in that you must perform several manual steps to carry out a primary role change. With that said, the functionality as it stands today provides a robust and viable high-availability solution. Those bugs that do occur are well known. An excellent resource for common questions and errors is Microsoft's Knowledge Base article 314515, *INF: Frequently Asked Questions – SQL Server 2000 – Log Shipping*.

The following table also details known errors and issues involving log shipping:

| Error Number | Symptoms | Description |
|---|---|---|
| 3154 | You see the error message:<br>The backup set holds a backup of a database other than the existing '%1s' database. | This error occurs when multiple databases are configured for log shipping; those database transaction logs are shipped to the same folder. Furthermore, the database names may only differ by a t_log in the name. For example, you would see this error if you had a database named BookRepository and BookRepository_tlog, both log shipped to the same folder. The workaround is to avoid naming your database with a t_log, or creating a separate folder for each tran log backup database. See Microsoft Knowledge Base article 3154, *BUG: Error 3154 Reported in Log Shipping Restore Job Sporadically*, for more information. |

| rror Number | Symptoms | Description |
|---|---|---|
| No error number | Backup, Copy, and Load Job information is not updated within the log shipping monitor. | This was referenced earlier in the chapter, and is resolved by making sure that the SQL Server service accounts on the primary and secondary servers have `SELECT` and `UPDATE` privileges for the `log_shipping_primaries` and `log_shipping_secondaries` tables on the monitor server's `msdb` database (if you chose to monitor using Windows authentication). If you chose SQL Server authentication for the log shipping monitor, make sure that the `log_shipping_monitor_probe` login on the monitoring server has `SELECT` and `UPDATE` privileges for the `msdb..log_shipping_primaries` and `msdb..log_shipping_secondaries` tables. See Microsoft Knowledge Base article 292586, *PRB: Backup, Copy, and Load Job Information Is Not Updated on the Log Shipping Monitor*, for more information. |
| No error number | You click the Delete button on the Log Shipping tab of the Maintenance plan in order to delete the secondary server of a plan with only one destination server. This removes the log shipping pair entirely. | To add a destination to a log shipping pair while keeping the current setup, add the new destination **first**, and then delete the old secondary server. |
| No error number | After configuring log shipping via the Maintenance Plan Wizard, if you select `NORECOVERY` mode in the Add Destination Database dialog box, the database will actually be created in `STANDBY` mode. | Once the first tran log backup is applied, the recovery status is reverted to `NORECOVERY`. There is nothing further that you need to do. |
| No error number | After designating a network share for storing your source or destination transaction log files, you cannot modify the network share to point to a new backup location via the GUI. The old share, rather than new share, is still used. | To resolve this, you can drop the old share, and then share a new folder with the same share name. If this isn't an option, you can run the following script on the secondary servers (after backing up the `msdb` database on all secondary servers):<br>`USE msdb`<br>`GO`<br>`UPDATE log_shipping_plans`<br>`SET source_dir =`<br>`'\\new_computer_name\new_sharename'`<br>`WHERE source_dir =`<br>`'\\old_computer_name\old_sharename'`<br>See Microsoft's Knowledge Base article 314570, *PRB: Cannot Modify Backup Network Share After You Change the Transaction Log Backup Folder* for more details. |

Before relying on a log shipping solution, perform a dry-run setup. Configure log shipping between two servers, monitor the status, and attempt a failover. Try to script out as much of the primary role change process as possible. Make sure you are transferring logins frequently and ensure that you are keeping up with user additions. Try to determine how long the entire role change process takes and document the process well.

# 13

# Other Utilities

Before proceeding, there are some additional features and utilities with which you should be familiar as a SQL Server DBA or developer. This chapter covers:

- **Query utilities**
  Using osql; utilizing Query Analyzer features such as the Object Browser and Analyzer Templates.
- **Connectivity utilities**
  Using the Server Network Utility and Client Network Utility.
- **Server documentation**
  Using the SQLDIAG command line tool to document server state and SQL Server settings.
- **Full-text indexing**
  Creating a full-text index and querying the indexed columns.
- **Custom error messages**
  Creating custom SQL Server error messages for use by your applications.

## 13.1 How to... Use osql

Both **isql** and **osql** are command line utilities that allow you to issue valid Transact-SQL statements against SQL Server. isql is the older of the two, and uses the DB-Library API (application programming interface) to communicate with SQL Server. DB-Library was developed for earlier versions of SQL Server (pre-version 7.0). When using isql against SQL Server 2000, your client connection is limited to pre-SQL Server version 7.0 connectivity. Features such as named instances or Unicode input files are not supported with isql, although named instances **can** be connected to with isql if you configure a client alias (described later in this chapter).

The osql utility uses ODBC to communicate with SQL Server, and is able to take advantage of all SQL Server 2000 features. Use osql for your SQL Server 2000 connectivity. As isql is provided for backward compatibility, only osql is reviewed in this chapter, although isql and osql have quite similar syntax.

The syntax for osql from *SQL Server Books Online* is as follows:

```
osql
    [-?] |
    [-L] |
    [
        {
            {-U login_id [-P password]}
            | -E
        }
        [-S server_name[\instance_name]] [-H wksta_name] [-d db_name]
        [-l time_out] [-t time_out] [-h headers]
        [-s col_separator] [-w column_width] [-a packet_size]
        [-e] [-I] [-D data_source_name]
        [-c cmd_end] [-q "query"] [-Q "query"]
        [-n] [-m error_level] [-r {0 | 1}]
        [-i input_file] [-o output_file] [-p]
        [-b] [-u] [-R] [-O]
    ]
```

| Parameter | Description |
|---|---|
| `-?` | Lists all osql switches. |
| `-L` | Lists locally configured servers and servers broadcasting on the network. |
| `-U login_id` | SQL Server authentication login. |
| `-P password` | SQL Server authentication password. |
| `-E` | Windows authentication used to log in to SQL Server instead of SQL Server authentication. |
| `-S server_name[\instance_name]` | SQL Server instance name. |
| `-H wksta_name` | Name of workstation (displayed in `sysprocesses.hostname`, if specified). |
| `-d db_name` | Database context to use. |
| `-l time_out` | Number of seconds before a connection login attempt times out. Default is eight seconds. |
| `-t time_out` | Number of seconds before a command execution times out (default is no timeout). |
| `-h headers` | Specifies the number of rows to print between column headings. If selecting `-1`, no headers are printed. No space is allowed between the `-h` and `-1` value. |
| `-s col_separator` | Sets the column-separator character; the default is a blank space. The special character must be enclosed in double quotation marks. |
| `-w column_width` | Sets the maximum character screen width, defaulting to 80 characters. |

| Parameter | Description |
|---|---|
| -a packet_size | Configures the network packet size (from 512 through 65,535). A packet size of 8192 is the fastest setting for bulk copy operations. |
| -e | Echoes the input. |
| -I | Enables the QUOTED_IDENTIFIER option. |
| -D data_source_name | Name of a valid ODBC data source name. |
| -c cmd_end | Sets a Transact-SQL command terminator (default is GO, on its own line). |
| -q "query" | Executes a query on osql startup, but **does not exit** osql after completion. This is an important switch to be aware of, as your osql batch behavior may not act as you intended if you wanted to close your connection after a query execution. If you use the -q switch, **you should not use the GO statement**. Use double quotation marks around the query, and single quotation marks around anything within the query. |
| -Q "query" | Executes a query and **immediately exits** the osql connection. Use double-quotation marks around the query, and single-quotation marks around anything within the query. |
| -n | Hides numbering and prompt symbols from input lines. |
| -m error_level | Sets the base-line error level. Error levels lower than the specified level will not be displayed. Designating -1 specifies that all headers are returned with messages. |
| -r | If 0 is specified, error messages with a severity level of 17 or higher are redirected to the screen. If 1 is specified, all message output is redirected. |
| -i input_file | References a batch file containing valid Transact-SQL statements. |
| -o output_file | References an output file for returned output from SQL Server. |
| -p | Displays performance statistics. |
| -b | If -b is chosen, any error message with a severity level of 10 or greater will cause osql to exit. |
| -u | Causes output file to be stored in Unicode format. |
| -R | If -R is chosend, the SQL Server ODBC driver will use client settings for converting currency and datetime data to character data. |
| -O | Deactivates specific osql features in order to mimic isql features. |

# Tips for Using osql

- The osql utility parameters are **case-sensitive**.
- The osql utility can be run from a command prompt, or from within a batch file.
- To exit osql from a command prompt, use `EXIT` or `QUIT`.
- Use `GO` to execute all statements entered after the last `GO` execution.
- Use *CTRL+C* to end a query without exiting osql.
- Use `RESET` to clear all statements entered, and `ED` to call the editor. This calls an interactive DOS editor, such as the one below:

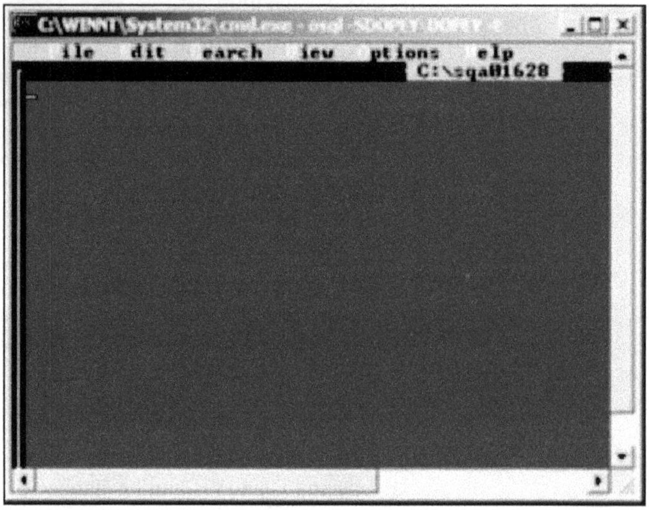


- You can change the default editor by issuing a `SET EDITOR=application_name`. For example, entering the following at the command line would call notepad for editing purposes:

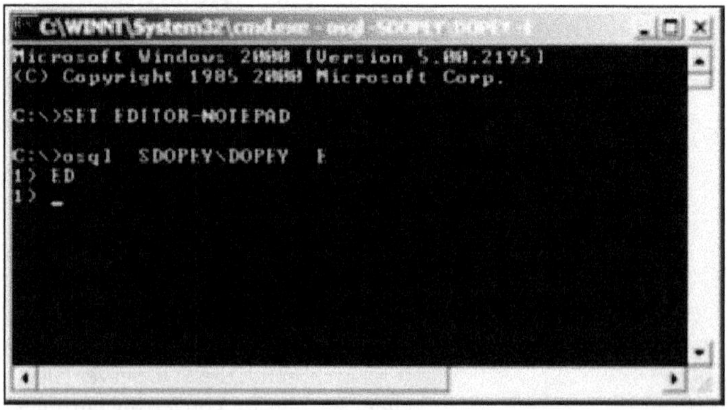

- Use the `!!` command syntax to execute an operating-system command. For example, running `!! TIME` displays and allows you to set the current system time:

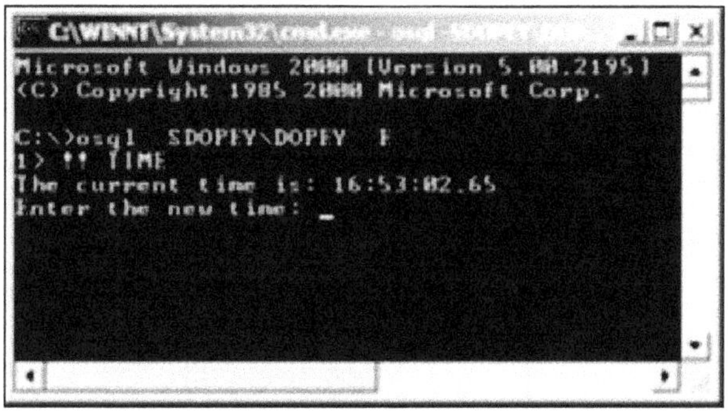


### Example 13.1.1: Listing all local servers and servers broadcasting on the network

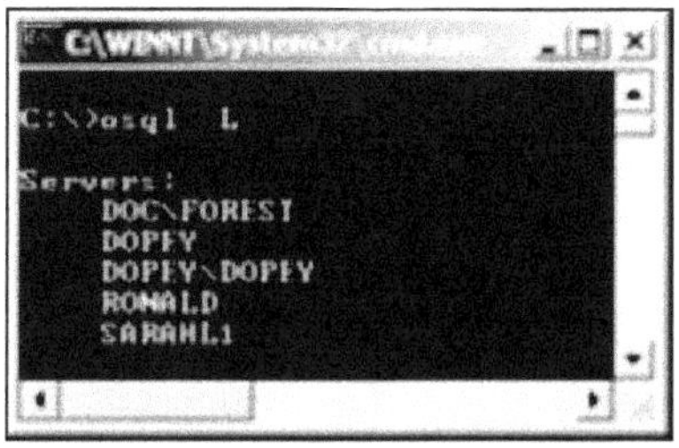


### Example 13.1.2: Executing a stored procedure on a SQL Server instance

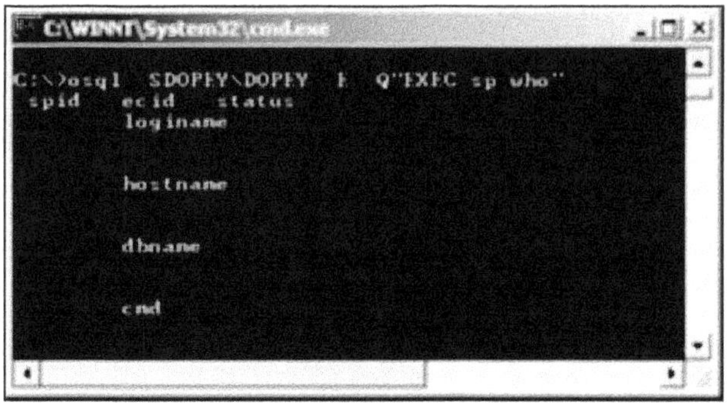


Notice that the upper case `Q` was used, meaning that after the results are returned, the osql session ends.

### Example 13.1.3: Outputting query results to a text file

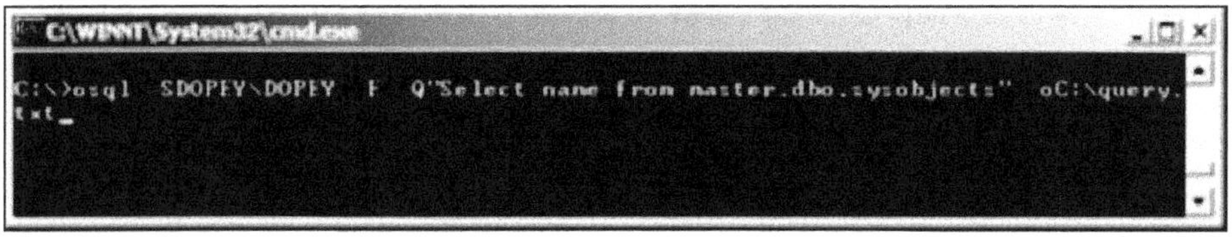

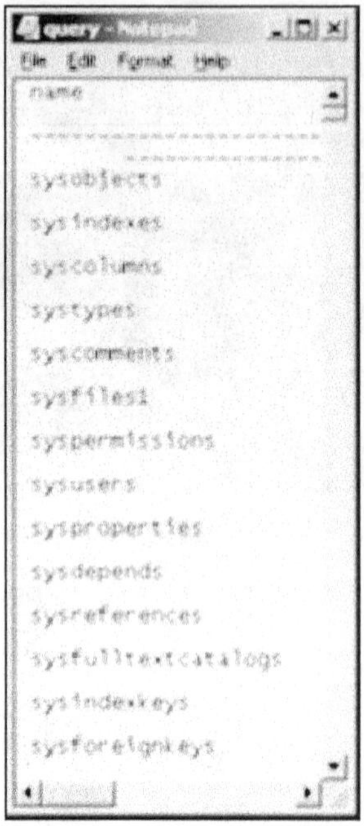


### Example 13.1.4: Executing a query from an .sql file

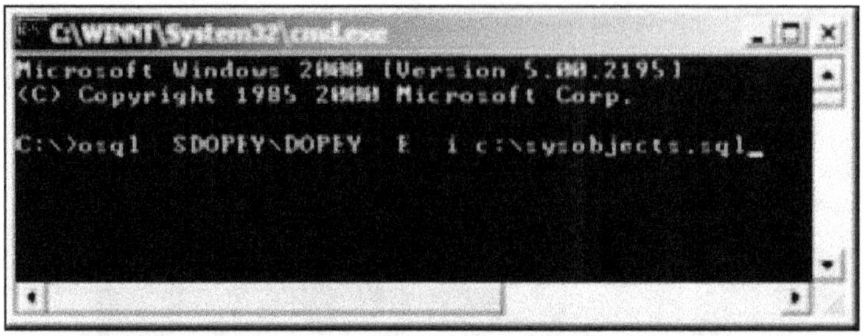


### Example 13.1.5: Working in an interactive osql session

The first line opens up a session, designating the server name, and Windows authentication:

```
osql -S SDOPEY\DOPEY -E
```

The next two lines create two `PRINT` statements. These will not be executed until you specify the batch with the `GO` keyword:

```
1> PRINT 'This is the first line of my interactive session'
2> PRINT 'Notice that nothing is done until I designate G O'
3> GO
```

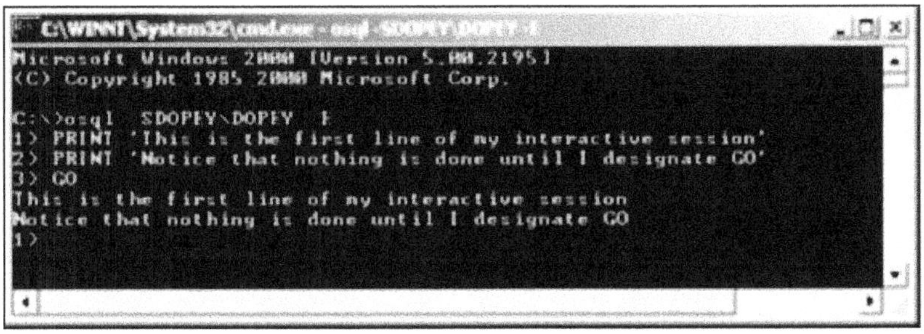


To exit the session, type `EXIT`.

# 13.2 How to... Use Query Analyzer Templates

Templates assist with producing pre-defined syntax blocks within your SQL Query Analyzer query editor window.

## To Use a Template

- Within SQL Server Analyzer, select the Edit | Insert Template.
- From the Insert Template dialog box, select the folder containing the template you wish to use:

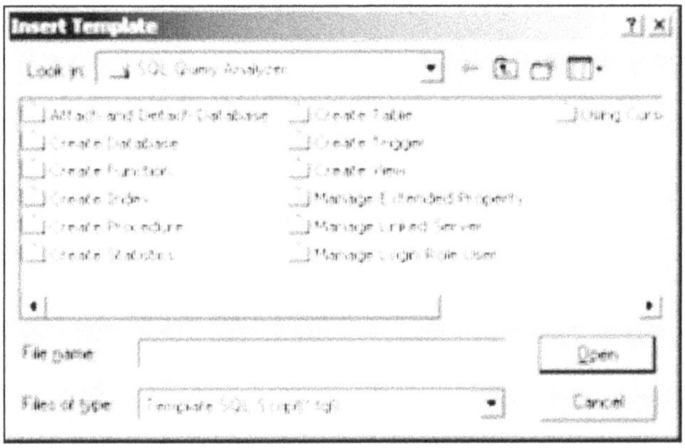


- Then select the specific `*.tql` file (file format for template files).
- Select the Open button.
- The template is then loaded into the query window:

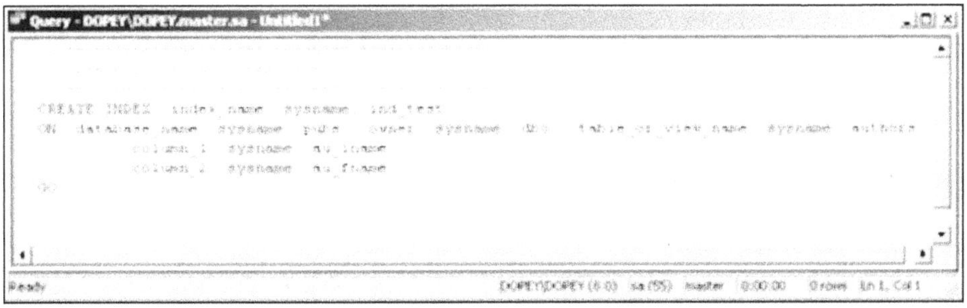

- Select Edit | Replace Template Parameters...
- In the Replace Template Parameters dialog box, you can specify values for each parameter; this can be a real timesaver for larger syntax statements. Select Replace All when finished:

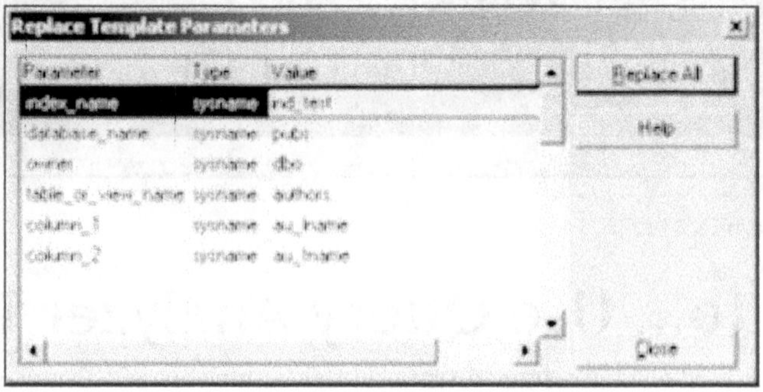


- The query template will then be filled in with the values you specified:

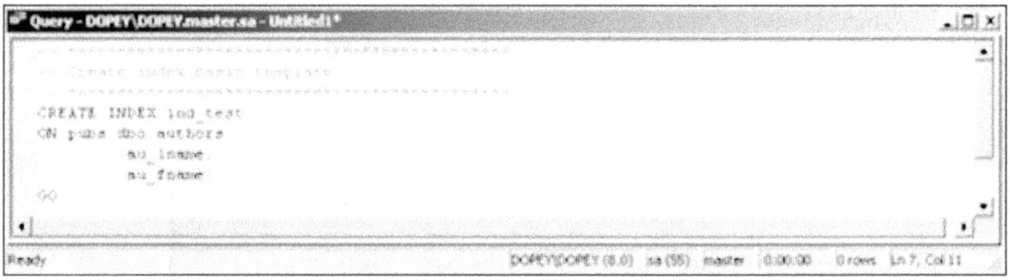


- You can also create your own template files. To do so, you must use the following syntax block for any object you wish to parameterize:

```
<parameter_name, data_type, value>
```

| Parameter | Value |
|---|---|
| parameter_name | Name of the script parameter (must be unique within the script). |
| data_type | Data type of the parameter. |
| value | Value is the default value if the Replace Template Parameters dialog box is used to edit parameters. |

In the following example, a template is created for a simple SELECT query. This query holds a template parameter placeholder for a table name:

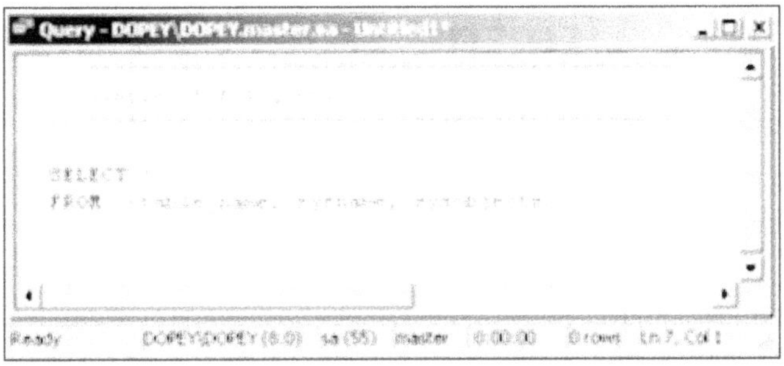


To save this template for re-use later, go to the File menu, select Save As, and select the template name and file type of Template SQL Files (*.tql):

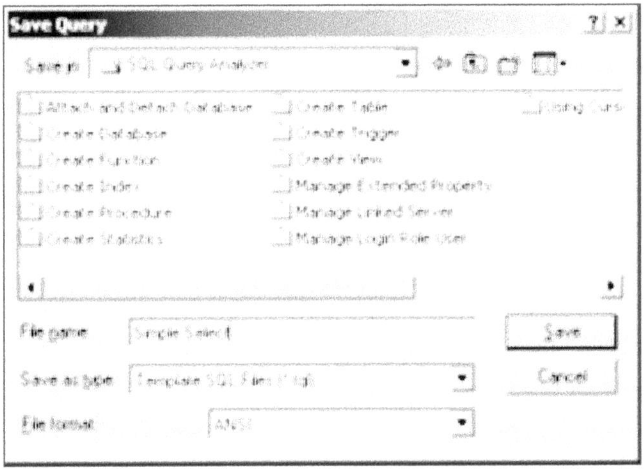


You can then select the template file in the future, and instantiate the Replace Template Parameters (as shown in the previous example):

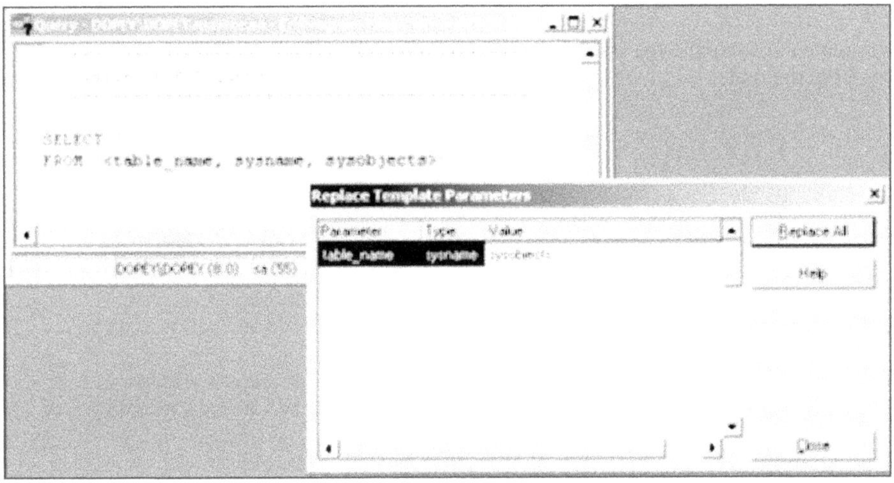

# 13.3 How to... Use the Query Analyzer Object Browser

Remembering object names and their exact spellings can be a major time-consumer for database developers. If you have ever had to switch back and forth between Enterprise Manager and SQL Query Analyzer to retrieve an object name, you will appreciate the features provided by the Query Analyzer Object Browser.

To access the Object Browser, select Tools | Object Browser | Show/Hide (toggles visibility of the Object Browser).

The Object Browser can also be made visible simply by clicking the toolbar button: 

The left-hand pane displays the hierarchical database objects.

To copy an object name to the query window, simply expand the database from which you wish to copy the name, expand the object type, and click-and-drag the object to the query editor window.

You can place **all** object names in the query window simply by dragging and dropping the **entire** folder:

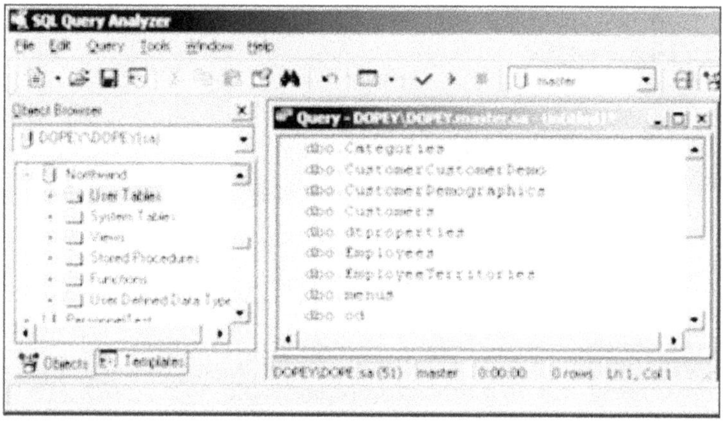


To browse table data, expand the User Tables folder and select Open. The query window will be populated with rows from the table:

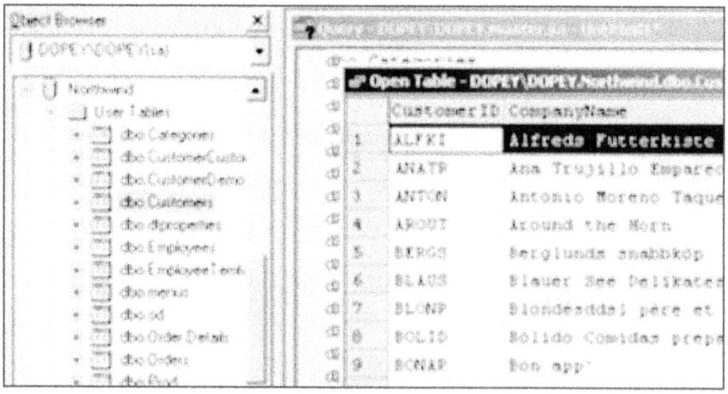

To execute a stored procedure, expand the Stored Procedures folder for the selected database, right-click the selected stored procedure, and click Open.

This will open the Execute Procedure dialog box, which allows you to select the value of each parameter for the stored procedure. You can either Copy the procedure to the clipboard or Execute the procedure from the dialog box:

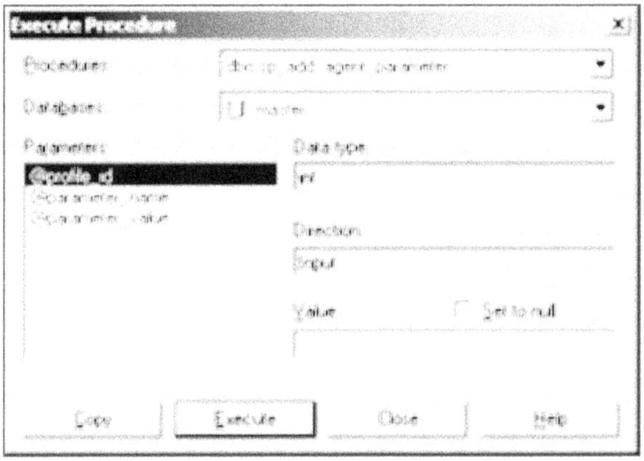


The Copy button places the procedure's syntax, along with any applicable parameters specified in the Execute Procedure dialog box, onto the clipboard. You can then paste the result into the Query Analyzer window, or elsewhere.

To place the entire contents of a stored procedure in the query window, right-click the stored procedure (in this case, `pr_Insert_Books`), and select Edit.

This will create an `ALTER PROCEDURE` command, allowing you to modify the stored procedure:

To delete an object (equivalent to the DROP Transact-SQL statement), right-click and select Delete.

There are several options for scripting a database object. Depending on the object type, you can script an object's CREATE, ALTER, DROP, SELECT, INSERT, UPDATE, DELETE, and EXECUTE statements.

For example, the scripting of an INSERT statement for a table object:

```
INSERT INTO [BookRepository13].[dbo].[ClothingCatalog]([CustomerId], [Catalog])
VALUES(<CustomerId,int,>, <Catalog,char(20),>)
```

You can decide if the scripting should be placed in a file, in a new query window, or copied to the clipboard. You can modify scripting options by right-clicking the object and selecting Scripting Options. This will allow you to determine whether headers are included in the script, the version of the script (7.0 compatible), object owner qualification, and other options:

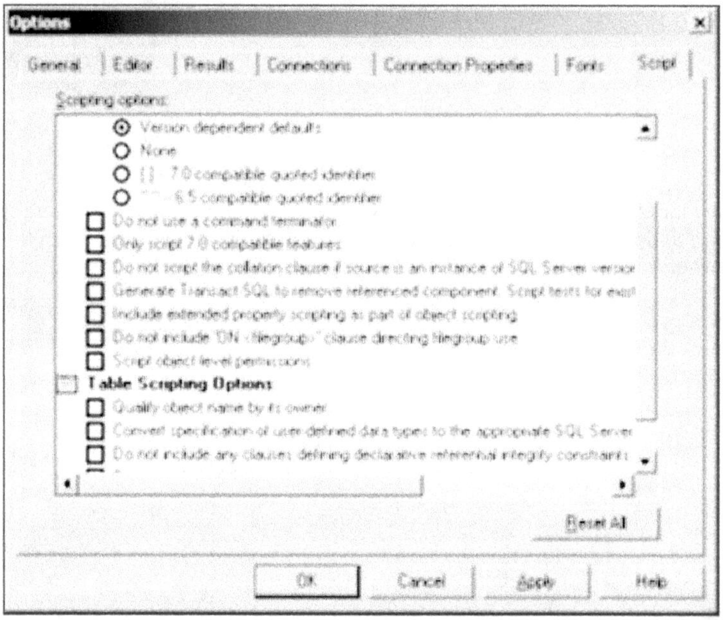


The Object Browser also allows you to define extended properties for objects. Extended properties are name/value pairs that allow you to store meta data regarding the specific database object. To add an extended property for an object, right-click the object and select Extended Properties....

In the Extended Property dialog box, you can add new name/value pairs by selecting the Add button: 

To remove an extended property, select the delete button: 

Lastly, the object browser allows you to work with templates (the same type of templates mentioned in the previous section). Select the Templates tab to retrieve the list of templates:

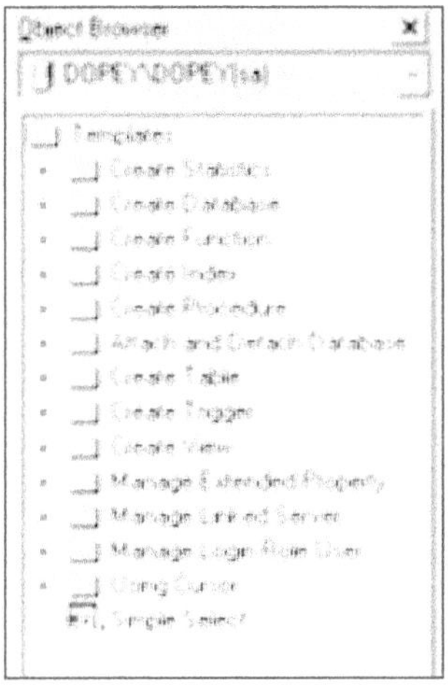

Expand the template folder and right-click the template you wish to use, select Open to transfer the template to the query editor, or click-and-drag the template into the query editor window.

# 13.4 How to... Use the Query Analyzer Keyboard Shortcuts

Within Query Analyzer, you can create custom keyboard shortcuts that may be used to execute frequently utilized stored procedures. To configure shortcuts, within Query Analyzer go to Tools | Customize. In the Custom tab, you can configure stored procedures to be executed based on shortcut keyboard combinations. For example, *Alt+F1* is configured to execute `sp_help`. Select Apply when finished or, to reset all changes, select Reset All:

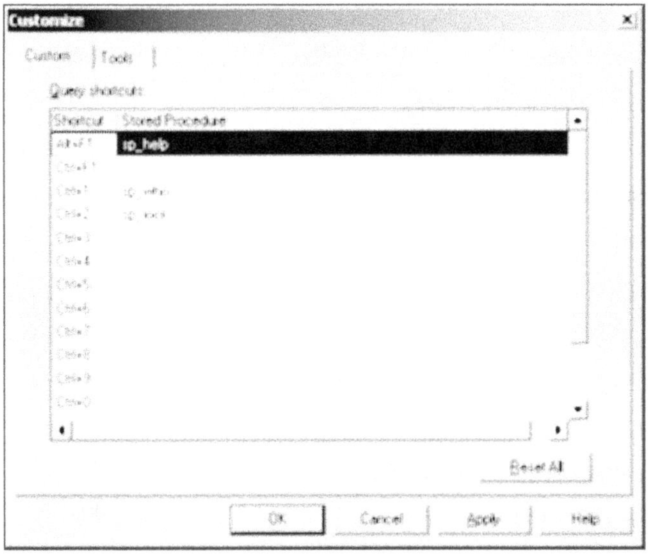

Query Analyzer also comes with a number of pre-defined menu shortcuts. These include, as listed in *SQL Server Books Online*:

| Activity | Shortcut |
|---|---|
| Bookmarks: Clear all bookmarks | *CTRL-SHIFT-F2* |
| Bookmarks: Insert or remove a bookmark (toggle) | *CTRL+F2* |
| Bookmarks: Move to next bookmark | *F2* |
| Bookmarks: Move to previous bookmark | *SHIFT+F2* |
| Cancel a query | *ALT+BREAK* |
| Connections: Connect | *CTRL+O* |
| Connections: Disconnect | *CTRL+F4* |
| Connections: Disconnect and close child window | *CTRL+F4* |
| Database object information | *ALT+F1* |
| Editing: Clear the active Editor pane | *CTRL+SHIFT+DEL* |
| Editing: Comment out code | *CTRL+SHIFT+C* |
| Editing: Copy. You can also use *CTRL+INSERT* | *CTRL+C* |
| Editing: Cut. You can also use *SHIFT+DEL* | *CTRL+X* |
| Editing: Decrease indent | *SHIFT+TAB* |
| Editing: Delete through the end of a line in the Editor pane | *CTRL+DEL* |
| Editing: Find | *CTRL+F* |
| Editing: Go to a line number | *CTRL+G* |
| Editing: Increase indent | *TAB* |
| Editing: Make selection lowercase | *CTRL+SHIFT+L* |
| Editing: Make selection uppercase | *CTRL+SHIFT+U* |
| Editing: Paste. You can also use *SHIFT+INSERT* | *CTRL+V* |
| Editing: Remove comments | *CTRL+SHIFT+R* |
| Editing: Repeat last search or find next | *F3* |
| Editing: Replace | *CTRL+H* |
| Editing: Select all | *CTRL+A* |
| Editing: Undo | *CTRL+Z* |
| Execute a query. You can also use *CTRL+E* | *F5* |
| Help for SQL Query Analyzer | *F1* |
| Help for the selected Transact-SQL statement | *SHIFT+F1* |

| Activity | Shortcut |
|---|---|
| Navigation: Switch between query and result panes | *F6* |
| Navigation: Switch panes | *Shift+F6* |
| Navigation: Window Selector | *CTRL+W* |
| New Query window | *CTRL+N* |
| Object Browser (show/hide) | *F8* |
| Object Search | *F4* |
| Parse the query and check syntax | *CTRL+F5* |
| Print | *CTRL+P* |
| Results: Display results in grid format | *CTRL+D* |
| Results: Display results in text format | *CTRL+T* |
| Results: Move the splitter | *CTRL+B* |
| Results: Save results to file | *CTRL+SHIFT+F* |
| Results: Show Results pane (toggle) | *CTRL+R* |
| Save | *CTRL+S* |
| Templates: Insert a template | *CTRL+SHIFT+INSERT* |
| Templates: Replace template parameters | *CTRL+SHIFT+M* |
| Tuning: Display estimated execution plan | *CTRL+L* |
| Tuning: Display execution plan (toggle ON/OFF) | *CTRL+K* |
| Tuning: Index Tuning Wizard | *CTRL+I* |
| Tuning: Show client statistics | *CTRL+SHIFT+S* |
| Tuning: Show server trace | *CTRL+SHIFT+T* |
| Use database | *CTRL+U* |

# 13.5 How to... Use SQLDIAG

`SQLDIAG` is a command line utility that gathers diagnostic information and outputs it to a text file. The stored information can provide a valuable server snapshot, which can come in handy during recovery or troubleshooting operations. If you ever need to contact Microsoft Product Support, you most probably will be asked to provide the output of a `SQLDIAG` operation for the SQL Server instance that has encountered problems.

`SQLDIAG` outputs operating system, hardware, SQL Server open connections, current locking, current databases, SQL Instance configuration settings, driver and registry listings, SQL error logs, and more. With such useful information, scheduling a job to run `SQLDIAG` periodically (and copying the output to a different server) would provide valuable disaster recovery data.

The syntax from *SQL Server Books Online* is as follows:

```
sqldiag
    [-?] |
    [-I instance_name]
    [ [-U login_ID] [-P password] | [-E] ]
    [-O output_file]
    [-X] [-M] [-C]
```

| Parameter | Value |
|---|---|
| `-?` | Displays parameter usage. |
| `-I instance_name` | SQL Server 2000 instance to report on. |
| `-U login id` | SQL Authentication login id (case-sensitive). |
| `-P password` | SQL Authentication password. |
| `-E` | Use Windows Authentication to connect to the SQL Server instance. |
| `-O output_file` | Name and path of the output file. The default name is `sqldiag.txt`. It is stored by default in the `\mssql\log` folder. |
| `-X` | Excludes the SQL error logs from the output. |
| `-M` | Adds the DBCC stackdump to the output. |
| `-C` | Adds cluster information to the trace. |

`SQLDIAG` can be run from `xp_cmdshell`, from a command prompt on the server itself, or scheduled within a SQL Server Agent job. `SQLDIAG` is stored in the `install_directory\Program files\Microsoft SQL Server\MSSQL\BINN` directory. This directory is **not** added by default to the Windows path setting, so you cannot execute without first navigating to the `BINN` directory.

## Example 13.5.1: Executing SQLDIAG from a command line

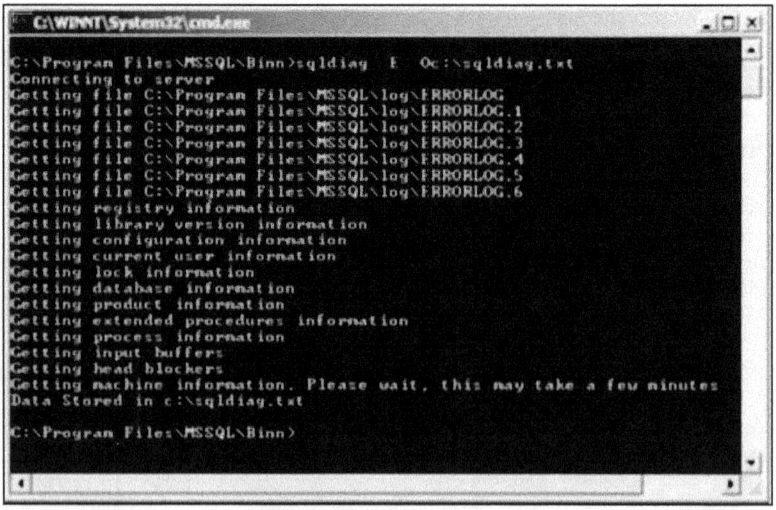

If you wish to run SQLDIAG for a virtual SQL Server on a failover cluster, you must perform extra steps for SQLDIAG to run properly. Microsoft Knowledge Base article Q233332 *INF: How To Run SQLDIAG On a Clustered/Virtual SQL Server* reviews how to add a new cluster resource to the SQL instance group, in order to instantiate SQLDIAG.

# 13.6 How to... Check the Port Number of a Named Instance using the Server Network Utility

The **Server Network Utility** is used to specify the network protocol on which the SQL Server instance will listen for client requests. This utility looks similar to the **Client Configuration utility**; however, Client Configuration utility controls how applications connect to SQL Server, whereas the Server Network Utility is used to set the network libraries for SQL Server 2000.

Java developers often need the SQL Server port number for producing JDBC connections to the SQL Server instance. For SQL Server named instances, the port number is not the default 1433. For SQL Server virtual servers and named instances, the TCP/IP port is chosen dynamically during installation or selected explicitly by the administrator.

Firewall engineers are also concerned with the TCP/IP port used by SQL Server, as port numbers must be explicitly opened for SQL Server instances that require Internet or cross-network access. The UDP port 1434 also needs to be open in order to retrieve the names of named instances on the server, as well as to determine the TCP port they are using.

## Verifying the TCP/IP Port

- In Enterprise Manager, expand Server group, right-click the server registration and select Properties (you can also launch the Server Network Utility by going to Start | Programs | Microsoft SQL Server and selecting Server Network Utility).
- Select the Network Configuration... button.
- Under the Enabled protocols section, select TCP/IP | Properties button:

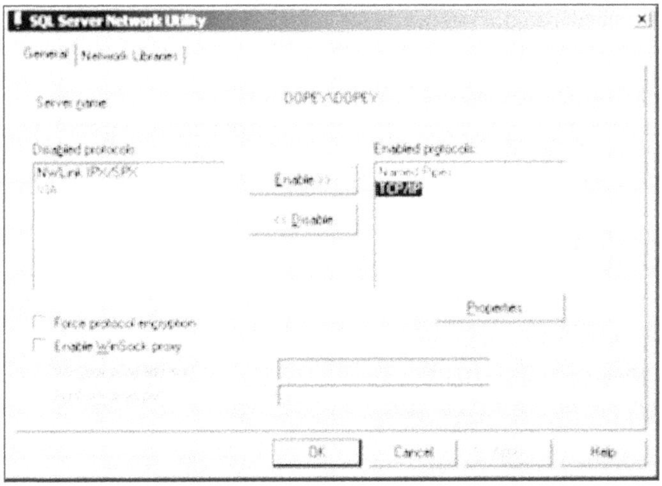

- The TCP/IP dialog box will show the Default port number. You can always change the port from this dialog box, but be aware that the SQL Server service must be restarted in order for the change to take effect. You can also view the port number by looking at the SQL Error Log. Look towards the beginning of the SQL Error log for `'SQL Server listening` on `XXX.XXX.XXX.XXX` (TCP/IP address)`:` `1433` (port number).' For example:

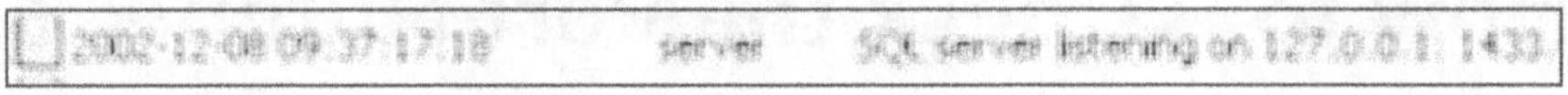


  Be careful when changing the port number if existing applications are already using the SQL Server instance, or if the new port is not opened to the firewall (if that is your requirement).

  The Hide Server option is used to hide an instance of SQL Server, meaning clients looking to list instances of SQL Server present on the network (via a **broadcast**) will be unable to get a response from this hidden instance:

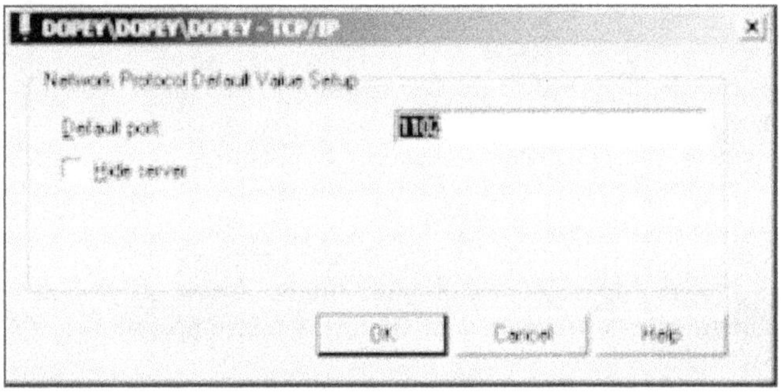


# 13.7 How to... Create a Client-Side Alias using the Client Network Utility

The Client Network Utility is used to set and display the default Net-Library and connection information on clients used to connect to SQL Server. Clients attempting to connect to SQL Server with Microsoft Data Access Components (MDAC) versions 2.5 or earlier will be unable to connect to a SQL Server named instance. If your clients are unable or unwilling to upgrade to MDAC 2.6 (or later), you can have them create a **client-side alias** referencing the named instance instead.

Client-side aliases are also useful for associating names with SQL Server instance IP addresses, where name resolution may not be possible on your network. For example, if you are attempting to connect to a SQL Server instance on a different domain (perhaps a server in a different company), you may find that the SQL Server IP address is available for connectivity, but the name is not. Associating the IP address with a friendly name is easier than having to remember the IP address.

## Creating a Client-Side Alias

- From the client machine, select Start | Programs | Microsoft SQL Server | Client Network Utility.
- From the Alias tab, select the Add button.
- From the Add Network Library Configuration select a server alias name, and the appropriate network library. For example, for a named instance, one can specify TCP/IP and the server IP address under Server name:

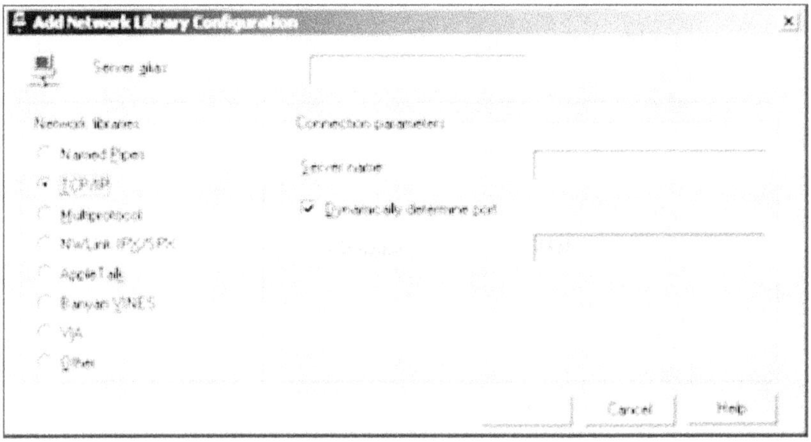

# 13.8 How to... Configure Full-Text Indexing

Full-text indexing allows you to issue intelligent word and phrase searches against character string and image data. The supported searchable data types are `TEXT`, `NTEXT`, `VARCHAR`, `NVARCHAR`, `CHAR`, `NCHAR`, and `IMAGE`. When designating `IMAGE` data, full-text searches can operate against `*.doc`, `*.xls`, `*.ppt`, `*.txt`, and `*.htm` file extensions.

Full-text indexes are **not** the same as table indexes, and belong to full-text catalogs. Only one full-text index is allowed per table, and that index can only belong to one full-text catalog. One database can have multiple full-text catalogs. These catalogs are stored outside SQL Server as files on the server:

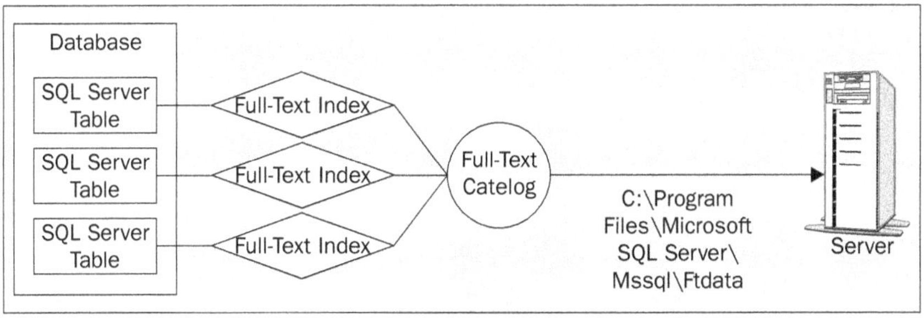


When setting up full-text indexing for a specific **base table**, a primary or candidate key is required to identify the row uniquely. `NULL` values are not allowed for this key. One or more string or image columns can be identified for full-text indexing. If you include an image column in your full-text index, a binding column is also required to specify the type of file stored in the image column.

The Microsoft Search service is responsible for managing full-text indexing, full-text catalogs, and the Transact-SQL searches on columns with full-text indexes defined. The Microsoft Search service is installed by default with **typical** installation of SQL Server 2000 Standard and Enterprise editions. The service can be found in your Service Control panel under MSSEARCH and defaults to the local system account for logging on. Keep this service configured as a local system account. A domain account is not necessary. **One** MSSEARCH service is used to manage all instances of SQL Server on the computer:

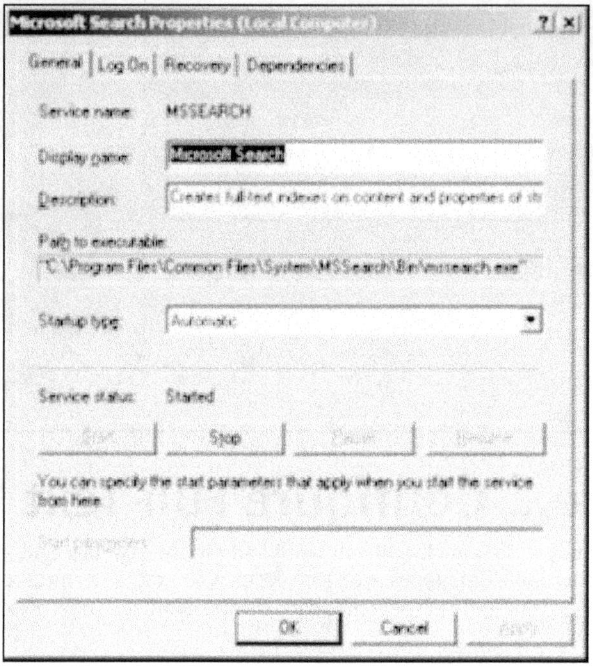


It is also important to understand that full-text indexes are not always updated automatically. Population of the index and catalog must be scheduled to reflect changes to the base table data. SQL Server 2000 did add functionality for automatic updates to the index, and this will be reviewed in more detail later in this chapter (under the discussion of Change Tracking).

# Creating Full-Text Indexing in Enterprise Manager

- ❑ Expand Server group and the registration of the SQL Server instance to which you wish to add full-text indexing. Select Tools | Full-Text Indexing.
- ❑ elect Next in the Full-Text Indexing Wizard introduction dialog box:

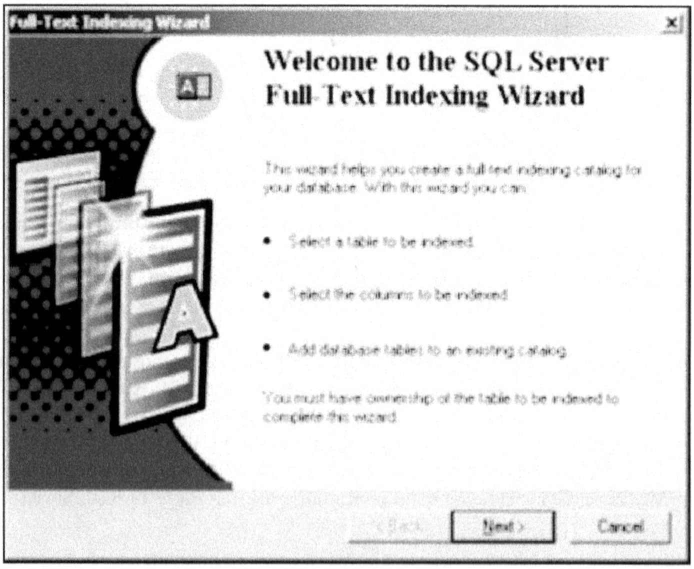

- ❑ Select the database to which you wish to add full-text indexing.
- ❑ Select the table to which you wish to add a full-text index.
- ❑ Select the unique index for the table:

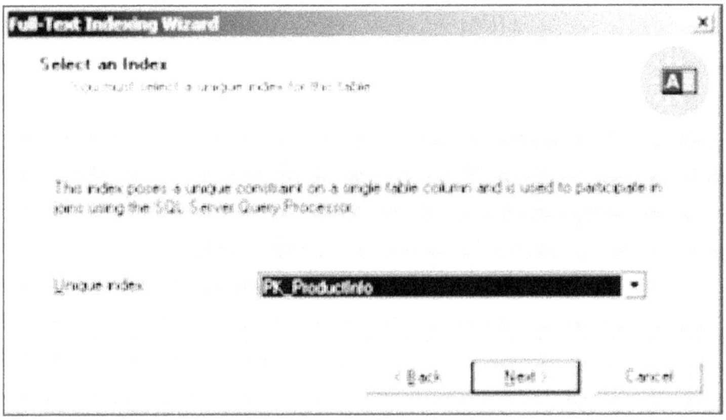


- ❑ Select the columns to be indexed. For image columns, select the Document type column (column that defines what document type is stored in the image column). Select a language for parsing the string and image columns (in this example, English [United States]):

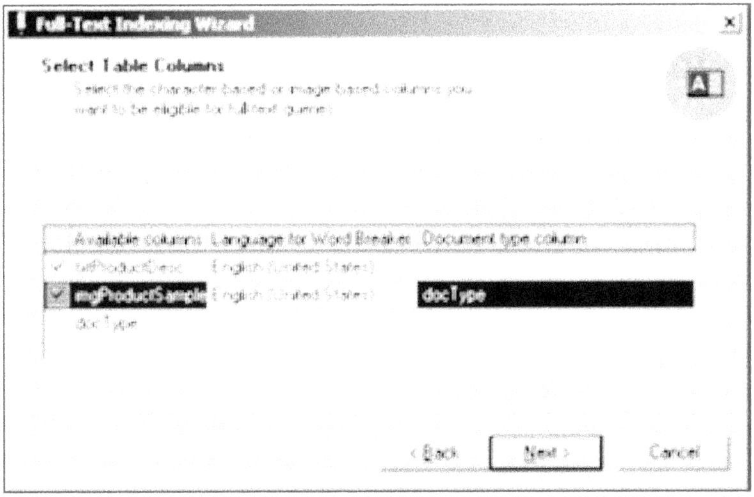


- ❑ If there is no existing catalog for the database, you must create a new one; otherwise, select from existing database catalogs. If you are designating a table with many rows and large `TEXT` or `IMAGE` data types, you may want to assign the table its own catalog. Give the unique Name if creating a new catalog, and the Location path of the catalog files:

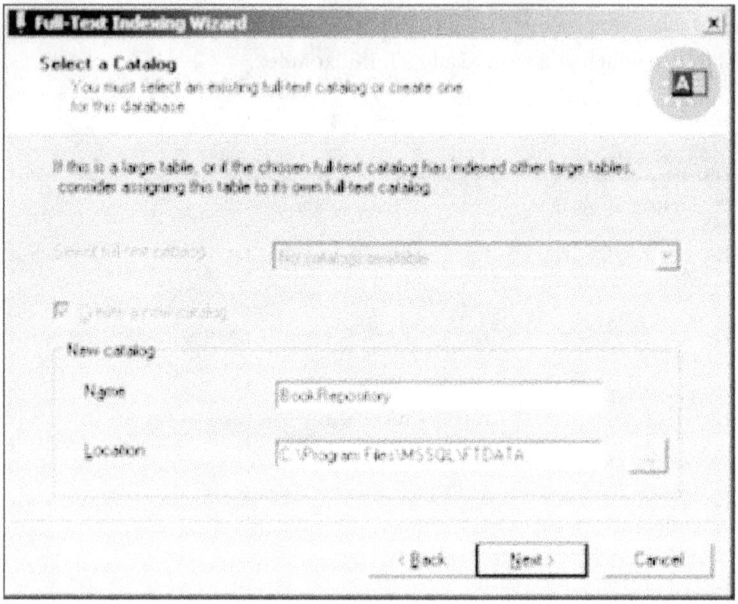


- From the Select or Create Population Schedules (Optional) dialog box, you can add new schedules for populating the catalog (which can contain multiple indexes), or for the population of the specific table:

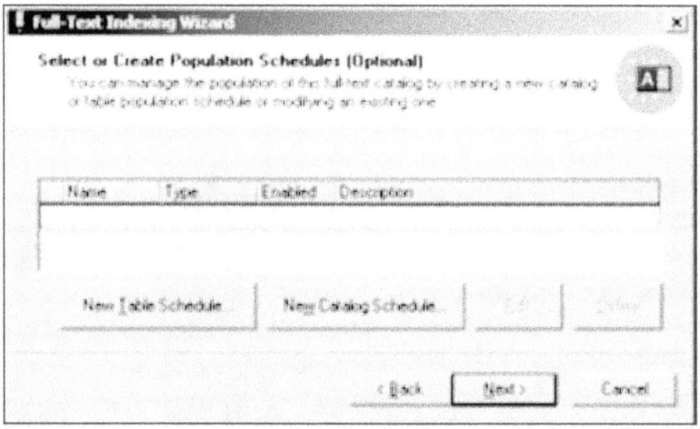


- The New Full-Text Indexing Table Schedule and Catalog Schedule dialog boxes allow you to create a SQL Server job to run updates to your full-text table index or catalog. The Job type allows you to define a Full population job, Incremental population job, or Update index job. A Full population rebuilds all entries in the full-text table. Incremental population will update all entries in a full-text index for a table with time-stamped rows. Update index refers to Change Tracking updates.
- Change Tracking, introduced in SQL Server 2000, allows you to maintain a record of modified rows in a system table. You can then schedule index changes via Background, On demand, or Scheduled methods. Background propagates row changes, as they occur on the base table rows, to the full-text index. On demand stores all tracked changes, and propagates them when an Update Index (on this current dialog box) is run. Scheduled means that SQL Agent runs the update index option periodically.

> **Monitor the server performance impact of using Change Tracking when background updates are enabled, as the performance implications can be severe. For scheduled updates, consider running during slow or off-periods (when SQL Server resource utilization is lower).**

- Although you can schedule Change Tracking updates via this dialog box, you can only create a full-text index that uses Change Tracking with the `sp_fulltext_table` system stored procedure (this will be reviewed later):

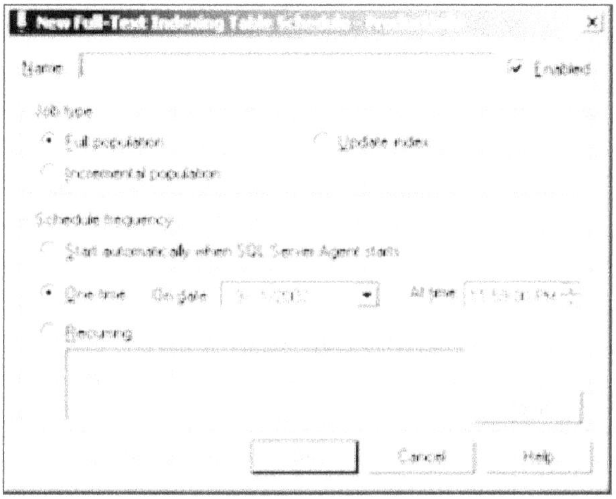


- You can also choose multiple schedules:

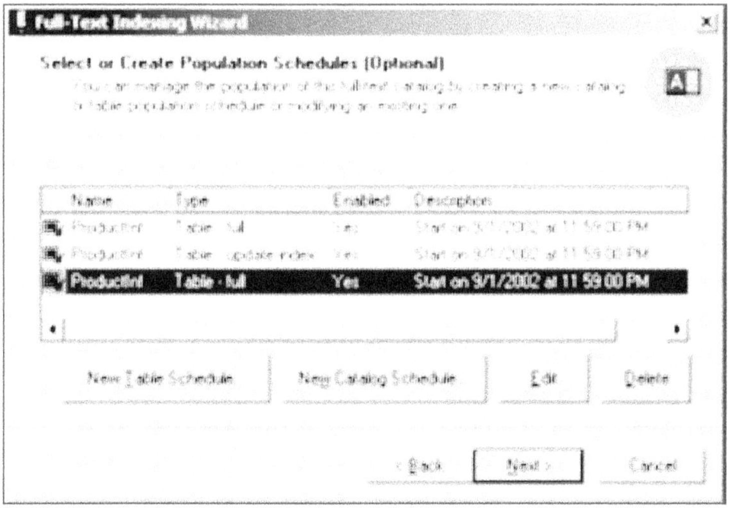


- Select Finish at the final dialog box.
- Once the full-text index is built, you can see it listed in Enterprise Manager under the Databases folder, the selected database, and the Full-Text Catalogs node.

- To populate the full-text catalog (if not populated already from your SQL Server Agent job), right-click the full-text index and select Start Full Population. From this menu, you can create a New Full-Text Catalog, Rebuild Catalog, Stop Population, Start Incremental Population, manage Schedules, or Delete the catalog.
- To manage properties of the catalog, double-click the catalog entry.
- The Status tab displays information on the catalog location, status, number of items, size, and last population time. Select the Refresh button to refresh the information:

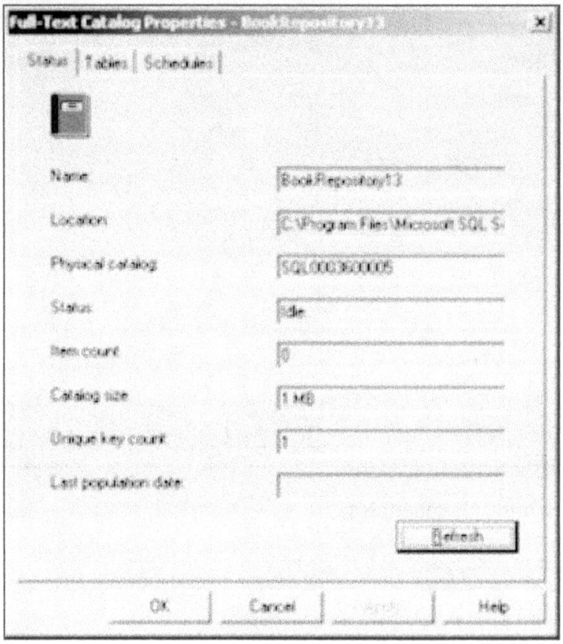


- The Tables tab displays all tables in the database enabled for full-text indexing.
- The Schedules tab allows you to add, edit, or delete SQL Server Agent scheduled jobs for the full-text catalog.
- Full-text indexing Full and Incremental population can have a performance impact on your server, so make sure to schedule updates during server quiet periods. If you find that full-text indexing is taking a toll on performance, make sure that the mssearch.exe is not being starved of memory or, in turn, starving SQL Server of memory. If so, consider reducing the number of full-text indexed columns, or configuring fixed upper and lower SQL Server instance memory limits.
- Right-click Full-Text Catalogs to create a New Full-Text Catalog, Rebuild All Catalogs, Repopulate All Catalogs, or Remove All Catalogs.

# 13.9 How to... Use Full-Text Index Stored Procedures

Full-text indexing can be configured more easily via the Enterprise Manager wizards. More advanced control, however, is available with the full-text index system stored procedures.

# Enabling a Database for Full-Text Indexes

- The sp_fulltext_database system stored procedure enables or disables a database's ability to use full-text indexing. To enable a database to use full-text indexing, execute the following syntax, where dbname is the name of the database you wish to enable:

```
USE dbname
EXEC sp_fulltext_database 'enable'
```

- If this database is already enabled and you execute the above stored procedure, full-text catalogs will be dropped and recreated. You must then repopulate the catalog.
- To disable full-text indexing for a database, execute the following syntax, where dbname is the name of the database you wish to disable full-text indexing for:

```
USE dbname
EXEC sp_fulltext_database 'disable'
```

# Adding a New Full-Text Catalog

- The sp_fulltext_catalog allows you to add or drop a full-text catalog, as well as start and stop indexing for a specific catalog.
- The syntax from *SQL Server Books Online* is as follows:

```
sp_fulltext_catalog [ @ftcat = ] 'fulltext_catalog_name' ,
    [ @action = ] 'action'
    [ , [ @path = ] 'root_directory' ]
```

| Parameter | Value |
|---|---|
| @ftcat = 'fulltext_catalog_name' | Name of the full-text catalog. |
| @action='action' | Action to perform. This can be one of the following keywords:<br><br>Create: creates a new full-text catalog.<br><br>Drop: drops a full-text catalog. The catalog must not contain any indexes.<br><br>start_incremental: starts an incremental population for each index.<br><br>start_full: starts a full population for each index.<br><br>Stop: stops index population for the catalog.<br><br>Rebuild: rebuilds the catalog and reassociates all full-text catalog and indexing references. |
| @path='root_directory' | When the action specified is Create, sets the path of the full text catalog. |

### Example 13.9.1: Creating a new full-text catalog

```
USE BookRepository13
EXEC sp_fulltext_catalog 'BookRepo_Cat', 'create'
```

# Enabling a Base Table for Full-Text Indexing

Once a catalog is defined for the database, you can enable a base table or tables for full-text indexing. To do so, use the `sp_fulltext_table` system stored procedure. The syntax from *SQL Server Books Online* is as follows:

```
sp_fulltext_table [ @tabname = ] 'qualified_table_name'
     , [ @action = ] 'action'
     [ , [ @ftcat = ] 'fulltext_catalog_name'
     , [ @keyname = ] 'unique_index_name' ]
```

| Parameter | Value |
|---|---|
| `@tabname= 'qualified_table_name'` | Name of table in full-text enabled database. This must be a base table. |
| `@action = 'action'` | Specifies the action to perform. This can be one of the following keywords:<br>`Create`: creates the full-text index for the table.<br>`Drop`: drops the full-text index for the table.<br>`Deactivate`: deactivates the full-text index, keeping index metadata, but stopping population.<br>`Activate`: activates the ability of the full-text index to be used and populated.<br>`start_change_tracking`: starts incremental population of the full-text index (if the table has a timestamp); otherwise, a full population is performed.<br>`stop_change_tracking`: stops tracking changes on table.<br>`update_index`: moves tracked changes to full-text index.<br>`start_background_updateindex`: immediately propagates tracked changes to the full-text index as they are detected.<br>`stop_background_updateindex`: stops changes from being immediately propagated.<br>`start_full`: starts a full-text index full population for the table.<br>`start_incremental`: starts a full-text index incremental population.<br>`Stop`: stops full and incremental populations. |

| Parameter | Value |
|---|---|
| @ftcat = 'fulltext_catalog_name' | Catalog that owns the new full-text index. (Used for the Create action). |
| @keyname = 'unique_index_name' | Sets the valid single-key-column with unique non-NULL index for the selected table (used for the create action). |

### Example 13.9.2: Enabling full-text indexing for a table

The sp_fulltext_table requires sysadmin permissions in order to execute:

```
USE BookRepository13
EXEC sp_fulltext_table  'Books', 'create', 'BookRepository13', 'pk_bookid'
```

## Adding Columns to the Full-Text Index

After enabling a table for full-text indexing, you are ready to add columns to the index using the sp_fulltext_column system stored procedure. The syntax from *SQL Server Books Online* is as follows:

```
sp_fulltext_column [ @tabname = ] 'qualified_table_name' ,
    [ @colname = ] 'column_name' ,
    [ @action = ] 'action'
    [ , [ @language = ] 'language' ]
    [ , [ @type_colname = ] 'type_column_name' ]
```

| Parameter | Value |
|---|---|
| @tabname = 'qualified_table_name' | Table name where the column is contained. |
| @colname = 'column_name' | Name of the string or image column. |
| @action= 'action' | Takes either the ADD or DROP value. The ADD value adds the column to the full-text index. The DROP value removes a column from the full-text index. |
| @language='language' | Sets the language of the column. The default is the server's default full-text language. |
| @type_colname='type_column_name' | Defines the character column used to indicate the type of file kept in the image column. For example, if indexing an image column, a second column named type could contain the value doc, meaning it contains a MS Word document. The full-text index will then use a .doc filter to index the contents. |

### Example 13.9.3: Adding a column to a full-text index

```
USE BookRepository13
EXEC sp_fulltext_column 'Books', 'BookDescription', 'add'
```

After adding columns to indexed tables, and tables to catalogs, you can activate the full-text index using sp_fulltext_table:

```
EXEC sp_fulltext_table 'Books','activate'
```

You can now fully populate the catalog by executing the sp_fulltext_catalog stored procedure:

```
EXEC sp_fulltext_catalog 'BookRepo_Cat', 'start_full'
```

This will perform a full population on all full-text indexes in the catalog. You are now ready to begin querying your full-text indexes.

## Final Thoughts on Full-Text Indexing

- Unless you have enabled your index with start_change_tracking, your index will become out-of-date as changes are applied to the source data. Unlike table indexes (clustered and nonclustered), full-text indexes are external files that must be populated and refreshed periodically. Be sure to schedule population jobs to run periodically, but watch out for the associated performance overhead.
- UPDATETEXT and WRITETEXT do not trigger change tracking for a full-text index.
- If you prefer using system stored procedures for managing full-text indexes, use the procedures sp_help_fulltext_catalogs, sp_help_fulltext_columns, and sp_help_fulltext_tables for gathering full-text index meta data (information about configuration).
- Because full-text catalogs use files external to SQL Server, migrating and copying full-text indexes to new servers requires special steps. For details on how to handle this, see Microsoft Knowledge Base article Q240867 INF: *How to Move, Copy, and Back Up Full-Text Catalog Folders and Files*.
- When implementing full-text indexing on a failover cluster for a virtual SQL Server instance, make sure the cluster service, SQL Server service, and SYSTEM account have full control access to the directories containing the full-text index catalog files.

# 13.10 How to... Query a Full-Text Index

Full-text indexes can be queried with the CONTAINS, FREETEXT, FREETEXTTABLE, and CONTAINSTABLE Transact-SQL commands.

## Using the CONTAINS Predicate

Use CONTAINS to search for case-insensitive phrases or words. CONTAINS can be used for a word or phrase, a word near to another word, inflectional versions of a word (for example: gave, given, gives), and a prefix of a word or phrase. The syntax for CONTAINS in SQL Server Books Online is rather lengthy so, rather than review it here, several examples of how CONTAINS is used within a query will be presented instead (including which parameters are used, and why):

### Example 13.10.1: Using CONTAINS to find a phrase

```
USE BookRepository13
GO
SELECT *
FROM ProductInfo
WHERE CONTAINS(
                txtProductDesc, '"fast answers"'
                )
GO
```

The above example uses `CONTAINS (txtProductDesc, '"fast answers"')` in the `WHERE` clause. The first parameter `txtProductDesc` specifies the full-text indexed field to search. The second parameter `'"fast answers"'` gives the search string.

### Example 13.10.2: Using CONTAINS to find inflectional versions of a single word

Much more complicated and intelligent search terms are allowed with `CONTAINS`. You can create a query to search for **inflectional** versions of a word. For example, if the word 'fast' is searched using the `INFLECTIONAL` keyword:

```
USE BookRepository13
GO
Select * from ProductInfo
WHERE Contains(txtProductDesc, 'FORMSOF (INFLECTIONAL, fast)')
```

This would return every row with versions of the word `fast` in the `txtProductDesc`. The following query returned results for `fastest`, `faster`, and `fast`:

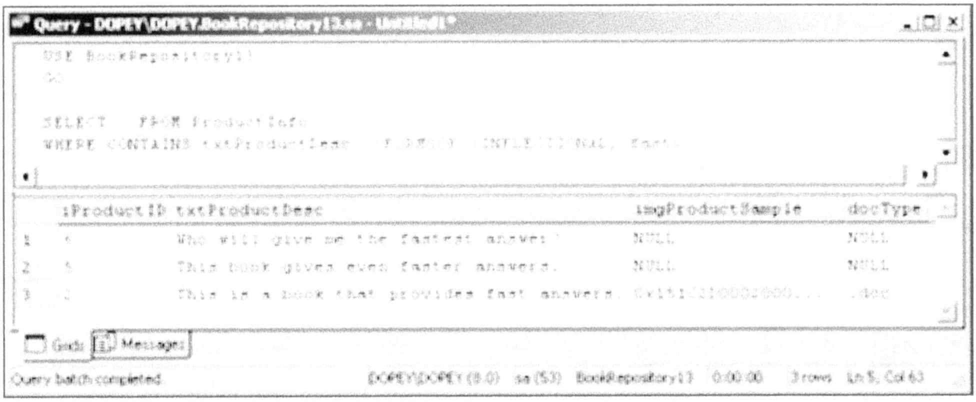


### Example 13.10.3: Using CONTAINS for finding words in close proximity to each other

`CONTAINS` allows the proximity term `NEAR`. `NEAR` is used for gauging words with proximity to each other. For example:

```
SELECT * FROM ProductInfo
WHERE CONTAINS (txtProductDesc, ' sql NEAR server')
```

### Example 13.10.4: Using CONTAINS with the wildcard symbol

`CONTAINS` supports use of the `*` wildcard symbol. The asterisk is the equivalent of saying 'ends with', essentially helping you find a word chunk. The asterisk will be applied to **all** words in your search term, not just the word next to the asterisk.

The example below searches for all terms that begin with `serv`:

```
SELECT * FROM ProductInfo
WHERE CONTAINS (txtProductDesc, '"serv*"')
```

The above query would return rows with `txtProductDesc` values containing `server` or `serves`. If using the asterisk as a wildcard, your search term **must** be contained in double quotes; otherwise your search statement will be searching for a literal asterisk value.

### Example 13.10.5: Using the CONTAINS with AND and OR operators

When using the AND and OR operators, make sure to enclose the search terms in quotations. The following is an example of using the AND clause:

```
SELECT * FROM ProductInfo
WHERE CONTAINS (txtProductDesc, '"SQL" AND "SERVER"')
```

Next is an example of using the OR clause:

```
SELECT * FROM ProductInfo
WHERE CONTAINS (txtProductDesc, '"SQL" OR "SERVER"')
```

### Example 13.10.6: Searching all columns with CONTAINS

The previous examples showed how to search a single full-text indexed column. You can, however, use the asterisk symbol to search **all** indexed columns for a table. For example:

```
SELECT * FROM ProductInfo
WHERE CONTAINS (*, '"SQL SERVER"')
```

## Using the CONTAINSTABLE Function

The CONTAINSTABLE function allows you to rank your results in order of relevance and frequency. Rank is determined by the number of occurrences of your search term in the column, as well as the proximity of search terms.

### Example 13.10.7: Display results using CONTAINSTABLE

The following example searches for occurrences of the word 'SQL'. The first parameter for CONTAINSTABLE is the full-text index **table name**. The second parameter is the **searchable column**. The third parameter is the search term, while the last is optional, and specifies the **number of rows to return** (the example below asks for the 'top 10' matches):

```
SELECT * FROM
CONTAINSTABLE (ProductInfo, txtProductDesc, '"SQL"', 10)
```

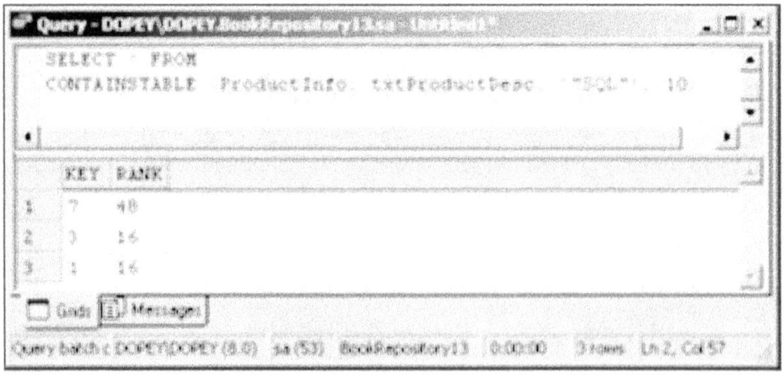


Notice that the results return the KEY value of the row and the ranking number. To include other row data with the result sets, you can join the KEY data to the original table. For example:

```
SELECT * FROM
CONTAINSTABLE (ProductInfo, txtProductDesc, '"SQL"', 10) AS  a,
ProductInfo  b
WHERE a.[KEY] = b.iProductID
```

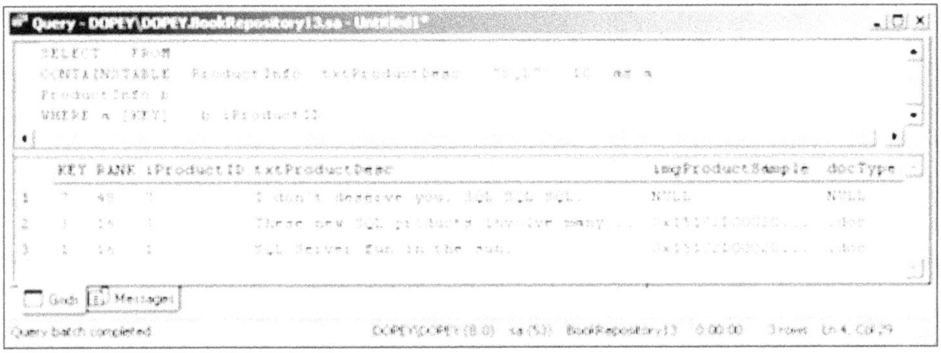

# Using the FREETEXT Predicate

The FREETEXT predicate allows you to perform fuzzy searches. FREETEXT breaks apart phrases, removes common words, and returns information based more on meaning than exact wording. The results are then weighted accordingly.

## Example 13.10.8: Using FREETEXT

The FREETEXT statement takes two parameters, the first being either a specific column designation or asterisk (for all searchable columns), and the second designating the search string. The following searches for the term 'fastest database':

```
SELECT * FROM ProductInfo
WHERE FREETEXT (txtProductDesc, 'fastest database' )
```

Notice that the results return includes different versions of 'fast' and various combinations of the words:

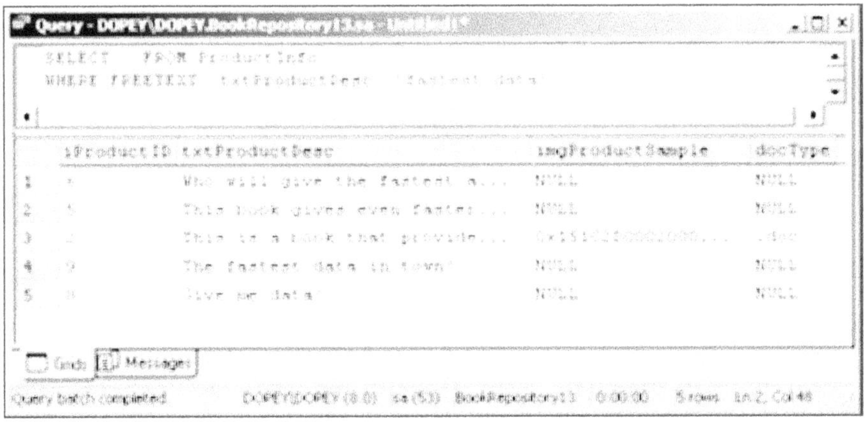

# Using the FREETEXTTABLE Function

FREETEXTTABLE, like CONTAINSTABLE, returns the row ranking for the search string. Unlike CONTAINSTABLE, FREETEXTTABLE attempts searches that match the meaning of the free text search condition, rather than using the exact or similar wording of the search condition.

## Example 13.10.9: Using FREETEXTTABLE

Just like CONTAINSTABLE, FREETEXTTABLE returns the row key (unique identifier) and the ranking number of the row. The FREETEXTTABLE takes the **table name** as its first parameter, **column name** for the second parameter, and **search string** for the third parameter. An optional fourth parameter allows you to limit the top N rows (for example, to return only the top 10 rows):

```
SELECT * FROM
FREETEXTTABLE (ProductInfo, txtProductDesc, 'fastest data' )
```

This returns:

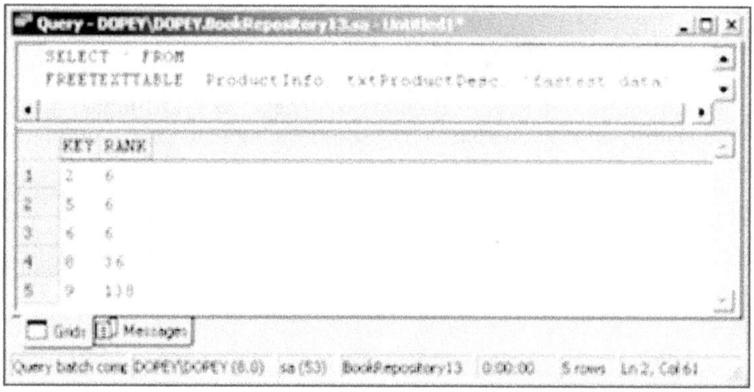


Like CONTAINSTABLE, you can join the results to more descriptive columns from the full-text indexed table:

```
SELECT * FROM
FREETEXTTABLE (ProductInfo, txtProductDesc, 'fastest data' )a,
ProductInfo b
WHERE a.[KEY] = b.iProductId
```

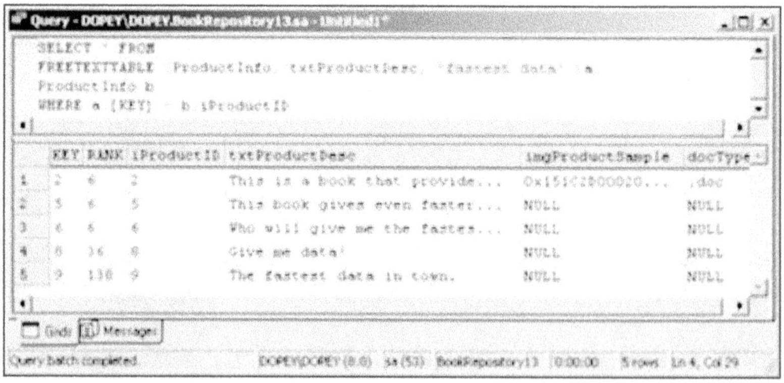

# 13.11 How to… Create Custom Messages

You can create user-defined SQL Server messages, for use by applications, stored procedures, and Transact-SQL scripts. User-defined errors are useful when you need to return consistent error messages, regardless of which object caused the error. Placeholders, discussed later, help you customize the error displayed for the particular object (for example, Table or View). Only members of the sysadmin and serveradmin fixed server roles can add, modify, or delete user-defined SQL Server messages. To add new messages using Enterprise Manager:

- Expand the Server group and right-click the server registration. Select All Tasks | Manage SQL Server Messages.
- Select the Messages tab. Select the New button to add new system messages:

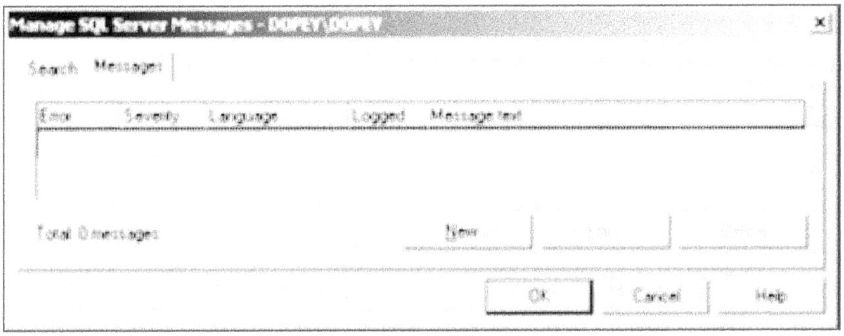


- In the New SQL Server Message dialog box, select the Error number, Severity level, Message text, Language, and whether or not the error should Always write to Windows eventlog:

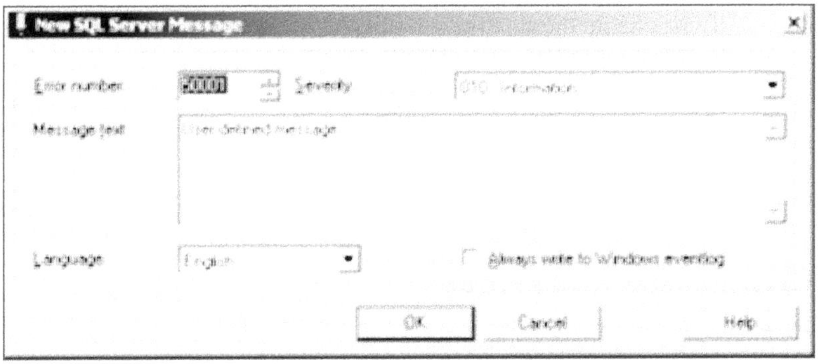


- Message text messages can make use of placeholder symbols. These symbols are then replaced by values when invoking `RAISERROR`. `RAISERROR` is a Transact-SQL command that allows you to return user-defined error messages. `RAISERROR` is reviewed in Chapter 16. The placeholder symbols are as follows:

| Symbol | Data Type |
|---|---|
| %d, %ld, or %D | Decimal, Integer |
| %x | Hexadecimal number |
| %ls or %.*ls | Character string |
| %c | Single character |
| %lf | Double, Float |

- You can also add user-defined error messages via the sp_addmessage stored procedure. Only members of the sysadmin and serveradmin fixed servers roles can execute this procedure. The syntax from *SQL Server Books Online* is as follows:

```
sp_addmessage [ @msgnum = ] msg_id ,
    [ @severity = ] severity ,
    [ @msgtext = ] 'msg'
    [ , [ @lang = ] 'language' ]
    [ , [ @with_log = ] 'with_log' ]
    [ , [ @replace = ] 'replace' ]
```

| Parameter | Description |
|---|---|
| @msgnum | The integer ID of the message. All user-defined error messages start after 50,001. |
| @severity | The SMALLINT severity level of the message. |
| @lang | The sysname language for the message. |
| @with_log | If set to true, the message is written to the Windows NT application log when the message is invoked. The default is false. |
| @replace | If the value is replace, the new message overwrites the existing error message if the msgnum already exists. |

The unique identifier for a user-defined error message is both message number **and** language. This means you set the same message number for various languages.

## Example 13.11.1: Using sp_addmessage

In this example, a message number of 55,000 is added with a severity level of 12. The language is set to US English, and will be logged to the Windows NT application log when invoked:

```
USE master
EXEC dbo.sp_addmessage @msgnum = 55000,
                       @severity = 12,
                       @msgtext = N'There are no books left!',
                       @lang = 'us_english',
                       @with_log = 'true'
```

To drop a user-defined message, use the sp_dropmessage system stored procedure. The sp_dropmessage procedure takes two parameters, message number and language.

### Example 13.11.2: Using sp_dropmessage

```
USE master
EXEC sp_dropmessage @msgnum = 55000,
                    @lang = 'us_english'
```

Use `sp_altermessage` to configure whether or not your user-defined message logs to the Windows 2000 application event log. This procedure is not used to change other error message attributes. For details on using this, see Chapter 4.

# 14

# DDL

DDL stands for Data Definition Language. DDL is used to define and manage all the objects in a SQL Server database. This chapter will review database object usage, syntax, and design practices. Chapter 1 detailed how to script the DDL of database objects using Enterprise Manager; this is often the method that new DBAs and developers use to become familiar with database object syntax. This chapter will provide you with the information required to generate the syntax independently of Enterprise Manager. We begin by reviewing the core unit of every database – the database table.

## 14.1 How to... Create a Table

Tables are used to store data in the database and make up the base upon which most database objects depend. Tables are defined with one or more columns. Each column for the table has a defined data type, which determines what kind of data is stored within this column.

These columns also have a pre-determined **nullability**; nullability defines whether a column can contain a NULL value. A NULL value means that the value is unknown. Once a table is created, it can start receiving data in the form of rows.

For example, if we had a table that holds the details of employees, we could have a column each for employee IDs, names, and department. Each row represents one employee:

| | Employee Number | Name | Department |
|---|---|---|---|
| **Type** | Integer | Text | Text |
| **Row 1** | 1 | Joseph Sack | IT |
| **Row 2** | 2 | Matthew Moodie | Editorial |
| **Row 3** | 3 | Tim Briggs | Editorial |

To create a new table in the database, use the CREATE TABLE command. Below is the simple form of the Transact-SQL syntax for CREATE TABLE:

```
CREATE TABLE <database_name.owner.table_name> (
  <column_name_1> <datatype_for_column_1> nullability,
  <column_name_N> <datatype_for_column_N> nullability)
```

| Parameter | Description |
|---|---|
| database_name.owner.table_name | Name of database, object owner, and new table name. These three elements are separated by periods. Only the table name is required; however, including at least the two-part object name is good practice, particularly if you are not the owner of the database. |
| column_name_N | Name of the column in the table. You are limited to 1,024 columns for one table. |
| datatype_for_column_N | The column's data type; see Chapter 3 for a review of data type storage. A table row size (combined size of defined columns for the table) cannot exceed 8,060 bytes. |
| nullability | Whether the column allows NULL values. If "NULL", NULL values are permitted; if "NOT NULL", NULL values are not permitted. |

## Example 14.1.1: Creating a table

This example creates a table called ImportBooks for the BookRepository14 database. The table defines three columns:

| Column Name | Data Type | Nullability |
|---|---|---|
| iImportId | INT | NOT NULL |
| vchBookTitle | VARCHAR(50) | NULL |
| dtShipDate | DATETIME | NULL |

Notice that the column names use a naming convention that denotes the data type of the column, that is, i denotes an INT data type, vch denotes a VARCHAR data type, and so on. This naming convention is called the **Hungarian Notation**. By using a predefined naming convention, you can, potentially, speed up your development by knowing at all times what data type is held in each column (without having always to look it up). This naming convention is often used by C and Visual Basic developers.

**One disadvantage of using this naming convention arises if the data type needs to change. For example, if you change iImportId to a float data type, you would also need to change the name of the column, and any references to it. Another argument against using this notation is the opinion that developers should know the data type beforehand, in spite of the name. In the end, it is a matter of preference; if the benefits of using this notation outweigh the drawbacks for your environment, use what method you prefer (Hungarian Notation versus column names without the notation).**

With naming conventions dealt with, here's how to create the table:

```
CREATE TABLE BookRepository14.dbo.ImportBooks
  (iImportId int NOT NULL,
   vchBookTitle varchar (50) NULL,
   dtShipDate datetime NULL)
```

You can use the following data types for SQL Server 2000:

| Data Type | Value Range |
|---|---|
| BIGINT | Whole number from -2 ^ 63 (-9,223,372,036,854,775,808) through 2 ^ 63-1 (9,223,372,036,854,775,807). |
| BINARY | Fixed-length binary data with a maximum of 8000 bytes. |
| BIT | Whole number, either 0 or 1. |
| CHAR | Fixed-length character data with maximum length of 8000 characters. |
| DATETIME | Date and time from January 1, 1753 through December 31, 9999. 1753 was the year following the adoption of the Gregorian calendar, which produced a difference of 12 days from the previous calendar. Beginning with 1753 sidesteps all sorts of calculation problems. |
| DECIMAL or NUMERIC (no real difference between the two) | Range from -10 ^ 38 +1 through 10 ^ 38-1. Decimal uses precision and scale. Precision determines maximum total number of decimal digits both left and right of the decimal point. Scale determines maximum decimal digits to the right of the decimal point. |
| FLOAT | Floating precision numeral from -1.79E + 308 through 1.79E +308. |
| IMAGE | Variable-length binary data from 0 through 2 31 -1. |
| INT | Whole number from -2 ^ 31 (-2,147,483,648) through 2 ^ 31-1 (2,147,483,647). |
| MONEY | Monetary value between -2 ^ 63 (-922,337,203,685,477.5808) through 2 ^ 63-1 (+922,337,203,685,477.5807). |
| NCHAR | Fixed-length Unicode character data with a maximum length of 4000 characters. |
| NTEXT | Variable-length Unicode character data with a maximum length of 1,073,741,823 characters. |
| NVARCHAR | Variable-length Unicode character data with maximum length of 4000 characters. |
| REAL | Floating precision number from -3.40E + 38 through 3.40E +38. |

| Data Type | Value Range |
|---|---|
| SMALLDATETIME | Date and time from January 1, 1900, through June 6, 2079. |
| SMALLINT | Whole number from -32,768 through 32,767. |
| SMALLMONEY | Monetary value between -214,748.3648 through +214,748.3647. |
| SQL_VARIANT | A data type that can store all data types except TEXT, NTEXT, TIMESTAMP, and another SQL_VARIANT. |
| TEXT | Variable-length data with maximum length of 2,147,483,647 characters. |
| TIMESTAMP | Database-wide unique number that is updated when a row gets updated. |
| TINYINT | Whole number from 0 through 255. |
| UNIQUEIDENTIFIER | Stores a GUID (globally unique identifier). |
| VARBINARY | Variable-length data with a maximum of 8000 bytes. |
| VARCHAR | Variable-length character data with a maximum length of 8000 characters. |

Some basic guidelines when selecting data types for your columns:

- Store character data types in character type columns (CHAR, NCHAR, VARCHAR, NVARCHAR, TEXT, NTEXT), numeric data in numeric type columns (INT, BIGINT, TINYINT, SMALLMONEY, MONEY, DECIMAL/NUMERIC, FLOAT), and date and time data in SMALLDATE or DATETIME data types. For example, although you can store numeric and datetime information in character-based fields, doing so may slow down your performance when attempting to use the column values within mathematical or other Transact-SQL functions.
- If your character data type columns will be using the **same or similar** number of characters consistently, use fixed-length data types (CHAR, NCHAR). Fixed-length columns consume the same amount of storage for each row, whether or not they are fully utilized. If you expect that the length of your character columns will vary significantly from row to row, use variable-length data types (VARCHAR, NVARCHAR). Variable-length columns have some storage overhead tacked on; however, they will only consume storage for characters used.
- Choose the **smallest** numeric or character data type required to store the data. You may be tempted to select data types for columns that use more storage than is necessary, resulting in wasted storage. Conserving column space can increase the number of rows that can fit on a data page, reduce total storage needed in the database and, potentially, improve index performance (smaller index keys).

# 14.2 How to... Create a Table with a Primary Key

A **primary key** defines a column, or set of columns, that uniquely identifies all rows in the table. A primary key is a type of **constraint**. Constraints place limitations on what data can be entered into a column or columns. A primary key enforces **entity integrity**, meaning that rows are guaranteed to be unambiguous and unique. Best practices for database normalization dictate that every table should have a primary key to prevent duplicate data.

A primary key column or set of columns cannot contain or allow NULL values. A set of columns used to define the primary key is called a **composite key**.

Only one primary key is allowed for each table. When a primary key is chosen, an underlying table **index** is created, defaulting to a CLUSTERED index (index types are reviewed later); you can explicitly choose a NONCLUSTERED index instead. An index created on a primary key counts against the total indexes allowed for a table, the limit being 1 clustered index and up to 249 nonclustered indexes.

You can specify a primary key within the column definition of a CREATE TABLE command. The CONSTRAINT constraint_name syntax defines the logical name of the primary key constraint and index. CONSTRAINT constraint_name is optional, and the system will instead assign your constraint a less user-friendly name than one you would otherwise choose:

```
CREATE TABLE <databasename.owner.table_name> (
 <column_ name_1> <datatype_for_column_1> Nullability
CONSTRAINT constraint_name PRIMARY KEY CLUSTERED,
 <column_name_2> <datatype_for_column_2> Nullability)
```

> **This first example of CREATE TABLE uses what is called a column constraint, which is specified as part of the column definition, and applies to that single column.**

Alternatively, you can define the primary key after the column definitions, specifying a primary key for one or more columns:

```
CREATE TABLE <databasename.owner.table_name> (
 <column_name_1> <datatype_for_column_1> Nullability,
 <column_name_2> <datatype_for_column_2> Nullability,
 CONSTRAINT <table_constraint_name> PRIMARY KEY CLUSTERED (column_1, column_2) )
```

> **This previous example uses a table constraint, which must be used when declaring a constraint on more than one column.**

### Example 14.2.1: Creating a single column primary key

In the following example, the iImportId column is set as the primary key for the table. This statement also explicitly states that the index must be a CLUSTERED index:

```
CREATE TABLE BookRepository14.dbo.ImportBooks
  (iImportId int NOT NULL PRIMARY KEY CLUSTERED,
   vchBookTitle varchar (50) NULL,
   dtShipDate datetime NULL)
```

### Example 14.2.2: Creating a composite primary key

The following example shows how to create a primary key on two columns (a composite primary key). Notice that the index type this time is NONCLUSTERED:

```
CREATE TABLE BookRepository14.dbo.ImportBooks
  (iImportId int NOT NULL,
   vchBookTitle varchar (50) NOT NULL,
   dtShipDate datetime NULL,
   CONSTRAINT pk_ImportBooks PRIMARY KEY NONCLUSTERED
    (iImportId, vchBookTitle))
```

Rather than specifying the PRIMARY KEY clause after a column name definition, the CONSTRAINT clause is used instead. CONSTRAINT comes at the end of the column definitions section of a CREATE TABLE statement, followed by the constraint name, in this case, pk_ImportBooks. The type of constraint is specified after the name, along with the index type. Lastly, the two fields comprising the composite primary key are listed, separated by commas within parenthesis.

# 14.3 How to... Create a Unique Constraint

You can only have one primary key on each table. If you wish to enforce uniqueness in other non-key columns, you can use a UNIQUE constraint. You can choose multiple UNIQUE constraints for each table and are allowed to set a UNIQUE constraint for columns that allow NULL values (although only one NULL value is allowed per column). Like primary keys, UNIQUE constraints enforce entity integrity by ensuring that rows can be uniquely identified.

The basic syntax for adding a UNIQUE constraint is:

```
CREATE TABLE <table_name> (
<column_name_1> <datatype_for_column_1> NOT NULL,
<column_name_2> <datatype_for_column_2> NOT NULL,
CONSTRAINT <table_constraint_name> UNIQUE NONCLUSTERED (c1) )
```

The UNIQUE constraint, like a primary key constraint, creates an underlying table index. This index can be CLUSTERED or NONCLUSTERED; however, you may not create the index as CLUSTERED if such an index already exists for the table.

The UNIQUE constraint can apply to one or more columns.

### Example 14.3.1: Creating a UNIQUE constraint on a single column

```
CREATE TABLE BookRepository14.dbo.ImportBooks
  (iImportId int NOT NULL,
   vchBookTitle varchar (50) NULL,
   dtShipDate datetime NULL,
   CONSTRAINT unq_ImportBooks UNIQUE NONCLUSTERED (vchBookTitle))
```

# 14.4 How to... Create a Computed Column

A column defined within a CREATE TABLE statement can be derived from a computation, and is called a **computed column**. Columns can be a freestanding calculation or can involve other columns defined in the table. Computed columns are not actually stored in the table and have special requirements above and beyond regular columns. You can use computed columns for computed values that are frequently accessed in reporting or update queries. By using computed columns instead of placing calculations in the SELECT query itself, you redistribute the overhead to the table level. Be sure to test the performance and overhead of using computed columns versus other solutions (such as computations in your SELECT query).

Computed columns:

- Cannot use sub-queries in the computation
- Cannot be used with a DEFAULT definition
- Cannot be use for a FOREIGN KEY definition
- Cannot be the target of an INSERT
- Cannot be the target of an UPDATE

Computed columns:

- Can use other columns in the table for the computation
- Can use deterministic functions or variables
- Can use mathematical operators such as *, /, +, and -
- Can be referenced in SELECT expressions and elements within a SELECT statement (WHERE, ORDER BY, GROUP BY, HAVING)
- Can define, or be a part of, a primary key
- Can define, or be a part of, a unique constraint

### Example 14.4.1: Creating a table with a computed column

In the following example, a calculated column called moTotalPrice is computed from the sum of the moBookPrice and moTaxes columns:

```
CREATE TABLE BookRepository14.dbo.BookSales
  (iBookId int NOT NULL,
   moBookPrice money NOT NULL,
   moTaxes money NOT NULL,
   moTotalSales money NOT NULL,
   moTotalPrice as (moBookPrice + moTaxes))
```

Developing this example, the following INSERT statement is performed against the BookSales table:

```
INSERT BookSales (iBookId, moBookPrice, moTaxes) VALUES (2, 55.00, 1.50)
```

Notice that the moTotalPrice calculated column is not included in the INSERT statement. Below, a SELECT statement is performed against the table:

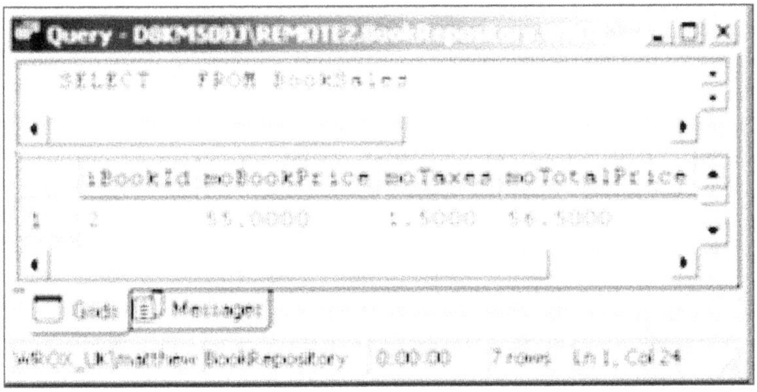


The total of 55.00 and 1.50 is computed into the new column, represented in the moTotalPrice as 56.50.

# 14.5 How to... Place a Table on a Filegroup

The CREATE TABLE statement allows you to specify a non-default filegroup for storing your table. If you do not specify a filegroup, the default filegroup is used. Use filegroups for very large databases, by separating tables onto separate arrays, so that they can be backed up separately. Filegroups can also sometimes provide performance enhancements based on the array type and the file placement. The syntax for placing a table on a named filegroup is as follows:

```
CREATE TABLE <table_name> (
  <column_name_1> <datatype_for_column_1> Nullability,
  <column_name_2> <datatype_for_column_2> Nullability)
  ON <file_group_name>
```

### Example 14.5.1: Placing a table on a non-default filegroup

This example places a table called BookImport on a filegroup named FG3:

```
CREATE TABLE BookImport(
  iBookId int NOT NULL,
  vchBookName varchar(10) NULL,
  dtImportDate datetime NULL)
  ON FG3
```

# 14.6 How to... Place Text or Images on a Separate Filegroup

In the previous topic, a table was placed into a different filegroup from the default; you can also specify that IMAGE, NTEXT, and TEXT data type columns are stored in a separate filegroup. The syntax for placing such column types on their own filegroup is as follows:

```
CREATE TABLE <table_name> (
  <column_name_1> <datatype_for_column_1> Nullability,
  <column_name_2> <datatype_for_column_2> Nullability)
  TEXTIMAGE_ON <file_group_name>
```

This syntax is only valid if an NTEXT, IMAGE, or TEXT type column is defined for the table.

### Example 14.6.1: Placing an image type column on its own filegroup

In this example, the column imgBookCover is placed on the filegroup named FG2 by using the TEXTIMAGE_ON clause:

```
CREATE TABLE BookCover (
  iBookId int NOT NULL,
  imgBookCover image NULL)
  TEXTIMAGE_ON FG2
```

# 14.7 How to... Create a Table with a Foreign Key Reference

**Foreign key** constraints establish and enforce relationships between tables. This relationship is defined to maintain **referential** integrity, which means that every value in the foreign key column must exist in the corresponding column for the referenced table. Foreign key constraints also help define **domain** integrity, in that they define the range of potential and allowed values for a specific column or columns.

The referenced table column or columns must be part of a primary key or unique constraint. The referenced and referencing columns should also be of the same data type. Also, you cannot define foreign key constraints across databases or servers (for that, use triggers).

For example, the column `iBookId` in the `BookSales` table has a foreign key reference to the `iBookId` primary key column in the `Books` table:

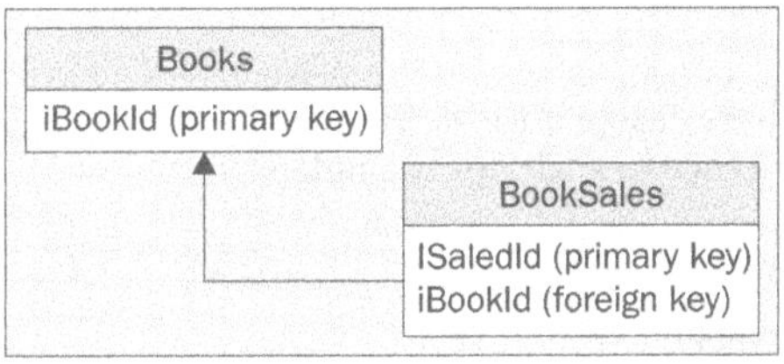


This means that the `iBookId` column in `BookSales` can only use values that exist in the `iBookId` table of the `Books` table.

The basic syntax for defining a foreign key reference is as follows:

```
CREATE TABLE <table_name> (
  <column_name_1> <datatype_for_column_1> Nullability,
  <column_name_2> <datatype_for_column_2> Nullability,
  CONSTRAINT <constraint_name>
    FOREIGN KEY (<local_column_name>)
    REFERENCES <ref_table> (<ref_column> ,...n)
```

| Parameter | Description |
|---|---|
| `CONSTRAINT <constraint_name>` | The name of the foreign key constraint for the table. If a name is not specified, a system-generated name is produced instead. If possible, get into the habit of creating explicit names for constraints, as the system names can get pretty unwieldy. |
| `FOREIGN KEY (<local_column_name>)` | The name of the local column that is referring to the primary key table. |
| `REFERENCES <ref_table> (<ref_column>,...n)` | The name of the table and specific columns being referenced. The referenced columns must be a primary key or unique constraint. |

### Example 14.7.1: Creating a foreign key reference

The following example creates a foreign key reference for the BookCatalog table, referencing the Books table primary key, iBookId:

```
CREATE TABLE BookCatalog
  (iCatalogId int NOT NULL PRIMARY KEY CLUSTERED,
   iBookId int NOT NULL,
   vchCatalogDescription varchar(100) NULL,
   CONSTRAINT fk_BookId
     FOREIGN KEY (iBookId)
     REFERENCES Books (iBookId))
```

# 14.8 How to... Set Recursive Foreign Key References

A common scenario for a database design is the definition of a recursive foreign key reference. This is when a table defines a foreign key reference to itself; for example:

- A manager is an employee
- Every employee has a manager

One table can define these requirements. For example, the Employees table has iEmployeeId as the primary key, along with an iManagerId foreign key column. This is possible, as only employees can be managers of other employees:

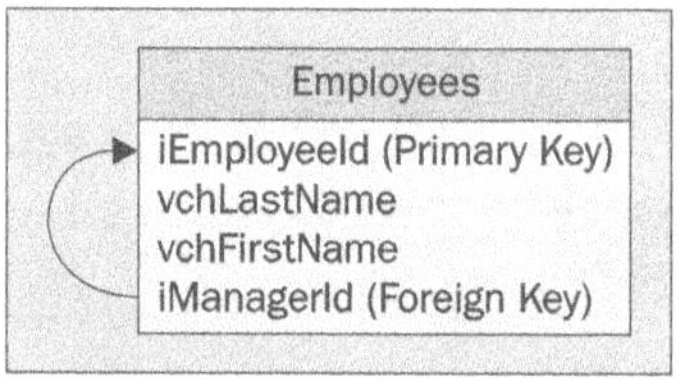


### Example 14.8.1: Defining a recursive relationship

Based on the previous example of iEmployeeId and iManagerId, the example below creates a foreign key reference to the primary key of its own table:

```
CREATE TABLE Employees
  (iEmployeeId int NOT NULL PRIMARY KEY,
   vchLastName varchar(100) NULL,
   vchFirstName varchar(100) NULL,
   iManagerId int NOT NULL,
   CONSTRAINT fk_ManagerId
   FOREIGN KEY (iManagerId)
   REFERENCES Employees (iEmployeeId))
```

# 14.9 How to... Create a Cascading Change with ON DELETE

Foreign keys restrict what values can be placed in the foreign key column. If the associated unique or primary key does not exist, the value is not allowed. This restriction is bi-directional. If an attempt is made to delete a primary key, but a row referencing this specific key exists in the foreign key table, an error will be returned. All referencing foreign key rows must be deleted prior to deleting the primary key or unique value in question.

> **There is an exception to this rule: when defining a foreign key, you can also specify that certain updates occur when changes are made in the primary key table. This is called a cascading change, and is a new feature in SQL Server 2000.**

The two types of cascading changes are ON DELETE and ON UPDATE. When ON DELETE is used, if someone attempts to delete a primary key or unique value, referencing rows in the foreign key table will also be deleted. Cascading updates and deletes can sometimes have a negative effect on performance; so **do** test this behavior before deploying it in a production environment. The syntax for ON DELETE is as follows:

```
CREATE TABLE <table_name> (
  <column_name_1> <datatype_for_column_1> Nullability,
  <column_name_2> <datatype_for_column_2> Nullability,
  CONSTRAINT <constraint_name>
  FOREIGN KEY (<local_column_name>)
  REFERENCES <ref_table> (<ref_column> ,...n)
  ON DELETE <CASCADE or NO ACTION>
```

If CASCADE is selected, deletions will carry over to the referencing rows in the foreign key table. If NO ACTION is specified, an error will occur if an attempt is made to delete a primary key or unique value row with existing references in the foreign key table. This is the default and is equivalent to not using ON DELETE or ON UPDATE.

### Example 14.9.1: Creating a foreign key reference with ON DELETE CASCADE

```
CREATE TABLE BookCatalog
  (iCatalogId int NOT NULL PRIMARY KEY CLUSTERED,
   iBookId int NOT NULL,
   vchCatalogDescription varchar(100) NULL,
   CONSTRAINT fk_BookId
   FOREIGN KEY (iBookId)
   REFERENCES Books (iBookId) ON DELETE CASCADE)
```

# 14.10 How to... Create a Cascading Change with ON UPDATE

ON UPDATE, if enabled with CASCADE, will allow updates made to the primary key or unique value at the primary key table to be migrated to any referencing foreign key rows in the foreign key table. For example, if the primary key iBookId is changed from 10 to 15, any referencing values in the foreign key table would be updated with 15. Test the performance of cascading updates within a test environment; if the performance is not ideal, try integrating updates within the application tier, within a stored procedure, or using triggers.

The syntax for ON UPDATE is almost identical to ON DELETE:

```
CREATE TABLE <table_name> (
  <column_name_1> <datatype_for_column_1> Nullability,
  <column_name_2> <datatype_for_column_2> Nullability,
  CONSTRAINT <constraint_name>
  FOREIGN KEY (<local_column_name>)
  REFERENCES <ref_table> (<ref_column> ,...n)
  ON UPDATE <CASCADE or NO ACTION>
```

### Example 14.10.1: Creating a foreign key reference using ON UPDATE and ON DELETE

The following example enables cascading of both DELETE and UPDATE operations to the primary key or unique constraint values, to the foreign key column that references them:

```
CREATE TABLE BookCatalog
  (iCatalogId int NOT NULL PRIMARY KEY CLUSTERED,
   iBookId int NOT NULL,
   vchCatalogDescription varchar(100) NULL,
   CONSTRAINT fk_BookId
   FOREIGN KEY (iBookId)
   REFERENCES Books (iBookId)
     ON UPDATE CASCADE
     ON DELETE CASCADE)
```

# 14.11 How to... Use CHECK Constraints

CHECK constraints define what data format is allowed for a column. This is a form of domain integrity, in that the entry of a specific column or columns is restricted to a set of allowed values. Where data types define what type of data can be stored in a column, CHECK constraints define the format and allowed values for that column. CHECK constraints are defined by an **expression**.

The syntax for a CHECK constraint is as follows:

```
CREATE TABLE <table_name> (
<column_name_1> <datatype_for_column_1> Nullability,
<column_name_2> <datatype_for_column_2> Nullability,
CONSTRAINT <column_constraint_name> CHECK(<column_name_N> expression))
```

### Example 14.11.1: Applying a CHECK constraint to a table column

In the following example, a CHECK constraint will be added to the chGender column, restricting the value to either M or F:

```
CREATE TABLE EmployeeGender (
  iEmployeeId INT NOT NULL,
  chGender CHAR(1) NOT NULL,
  CONSTRAINT chkGender CHECK (chGender = 'M' or chGender = 'F'))
```

After applying the above constraint, should the user enter the letter Z, for example, the following message will be returned:

```
Server: Msg 547, Level 16, State 1, Line 1
INSERT statement conflicted with COLUMN CHECK constraint 'chkGender'. The conflict occurred in
database 'BookRepository', table 'EmployeeGender', column 'chGender'.
The statement has been terminated.
```

You can apply multiple `CHECK` constraints to one column. `CHECK` constraints are evaluated in the order of creation. The expression used in the `CHECK` constraint definition must evaluate to `true` or `false` (a Boolean expression).

The `CHECK` clause also works with the `NOT FOR REPLICATION` clause, which enables rows that are inserted in replication to bypass the `CHECK` constraint. This maintains the key values originally defined on the publisher table (assuming you are defining the `CHECK` constraint for a subscriber table).

### Example 14.11.2: Applying a CHECK constraint using NOT FOR REPLICATION

The following example demonstrates how to use a `CHECK` constraint with `NOT FOR REPLICATION`. This example also demonstrates how to apply constraints to multiple columns in the table. For example, the `moBookPrice` column is limited to a value greater than 0.00 and less than 100.00. The `iBookId` column is also limited to a value greater than 0:

```
CREATE TABLE Books (
  iBookId int NOT NULL ,
  vchBookName varchar (255) NULL ,
  moBookPrice money NOT NULL ,
  CONSTRAINT chkPrice CHECK NOT FOR REPLICATION
  (moBookPrice < 100.00 AND moBookPrice > 0.00 AND iBookId > 0))
```

# 14.12 How to... Use the DEFAULT Property During Table Creation

If you do not know the value of a column in a row when it is first inserted into a table, you can use a `DEFAULT` value to fill that row with an anticipated or non-`NULL` value.

The syntax for using a `DEFAULT` property is as follows:

```
CREATE TABLE <table_name> (
<column_name_1> <datatype_for_column_1> Nullability,
<column_name_2> <datatype_for_column_2> Nullability
DEFAULT <default_value>)
```

For example, let's say we have a table used by a library to track the due-date status of library books. When a person first takes a book out, that book is not yet overdue. It may be overdue later, but it is never overdue when first taken out. The following example sets the `DEFAULT` for the `chOverDue` flag to `No`:

```
CREATE TABLE BookStatus
  (iBookId int NOT NULL,
   iPatronId int NOT NULL,
   chOverDue char(3) NOT NULL DEFAULT 'No')
```

If you inserted a row, for example:

```
INSERT BookStatus (iBookId, iPatronId) VALUES (1, 2)
```

Notice that the chOverDue value wasn't specified, even though the table definition specifies NOT NULL. This is fine, because a DEFAULT is defined for the chOverDue column. Performing a SELECT against this table shows the DEFAULT value set for the column:

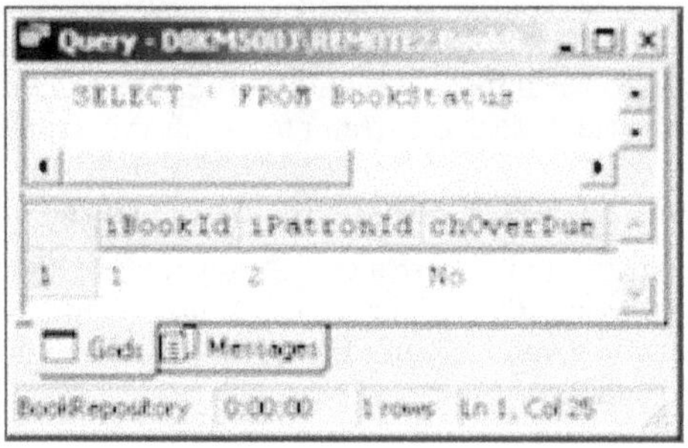


# 14.13 How to... Use the IDENTITY Property During Table Creation

The IDENTITY property allows you to define an automatically incrementing numeric value for a specific column or columns. An IDENTITY column is most often used for surrogate primary key columns, as they are more compact than non-numeric data type candidate keys; **surrogate** keys are also called **artificial** keys, meaning they are independent of the data itself and are used to enforce uniqueness. A big advantage to surrogate primary keys is that they do not need to change. If you use business data to define your key, such as first name and last name, these values can change. Surrogate keys do not have to change, as their only meaning is within the context of the table itself.

When a new row is inserted into a table with an IDENTITY column, the column is inserted with a unique incremented value. The data type for an identity column can be INT, TINYINT, SMALLINT, BIGINT, DECIMAL, or NUMERIC. Tables may only have one identity column defined, and the defined IDENTITY column cannot have a DEFAULT or rule settings associated with it.

The syntax for the IDENTITY property within a CREATE TABLE is as follows:

```
CREATE TABLE <table_name> (
<column_name_1> <datatype_for_column_1> Nullability,
<column_name_2> <datatype_for_column_2> Nullability
  IDENTITY (seed, increment) <NOT FOR REPLICATION>)
```

The IDENTITY property takes two values, seed and increment. seed defines the starting number for the IDENTITY column; increment defines the value added to the previous IDENTITY column to get the value for the next row added to the table. The default for both seed and increment is 1.

For example, defining an IDENTITY (1, 1) would provide the following numeric increments for consecutive rows:

| Number |
|---|
| 1 |
| 2 |
| 3 |
| 4 |
| 5 |

However, an IDENTITY (5, 10) would begin with the number 5 and increment by 10 for each consecutive row added:

| Number |
|---|
| 5 |
| 15 |
| 25 |
| 35 |
| 45 |

Like the DEFAULT property, the IDENTITY property allows the NOT FOR REPLICATION clause; when new rows are inserted, the IDENTITY column automatically increments, based on the seed and increment values defined.

When replicating from the publisher to the subscriber, it is important for the subscriber to reflect data as it exists on the publisher; if new values are generated at the subscriber, data integrity can be compromised. NOT FOR REPLICATION preserves the original values of the publisher IDENTITY column data when replicated to the subscriber, thus retaining any values referenced by foreign key constraints (prevents the breaking of relationships between tables that may use the IDENTITY column as a primary key and foreign key reference).

## Example 14.13.1: Defining an IDENTITY property for a new table

In this example, we define an IDENTITY column for the iBookId integer data type column:

```
CREATE TABLE Books
  (iBookId int NOT NULL IDENTITY (1,1),
   vchBookName varchar (255) NULL ,
   moBookPrice money NOT NULL)
```

If iBookId should also be a primary key, you could use the following syntax:

```
CREATE TABLE Books
  (iBookId int NOT NULL IDENTITY (1,1)PRIMARY KEY CLUSTERED,
   vchBookName varchar (255) NULL ,
   moBookPrice money NOT NULL)
```

You do not have to mention an IDENTITY column explicitly in an INSERT statement, because SQL Server automatically increments the iBookId. For example:

```
INSERT Books (vchBookName, moBookPrice) VALUES ('Dune', 9.99)
```

The previous example does not insert an explicit value into iBookId, as this is handled automatically. If you performed a SELECT against Books, you would see that the value was assigned for iBookId:

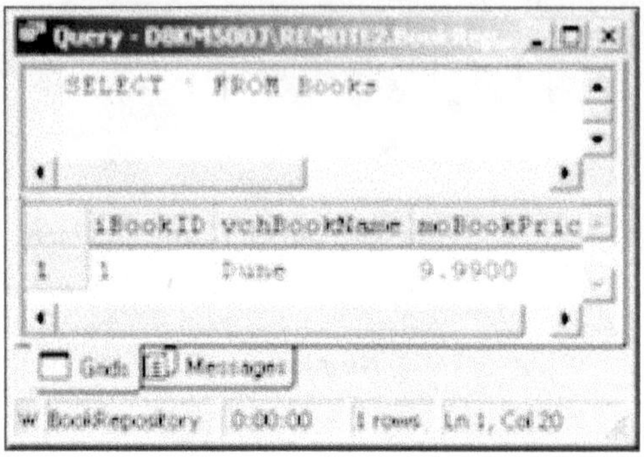

### Example 14.13.2: Inserting an explicit value into an IDENTITY column

If for some reason you have to insert an explicit value into an IDENTITY column, you could use the SET IDENTITY_INSERT clause to enable updates. For example, the following batch inserts an explicit value of 12 into the IDENTITY column, by using SET IDENTITY_INSERT:

```
SET IDENTITY_INSERT Books ON
GO

INSERT Books (iBookId, vchBookName, moBookPrice)
  VALUES (12, 'I Claudius', 6.99)
GO

SET IDENTITY_INSERT Books OFF
GO
```

Make sure to set the IDENTITY_INSERT option OFF when you have finished. In this example, you will see the break in the sequence:

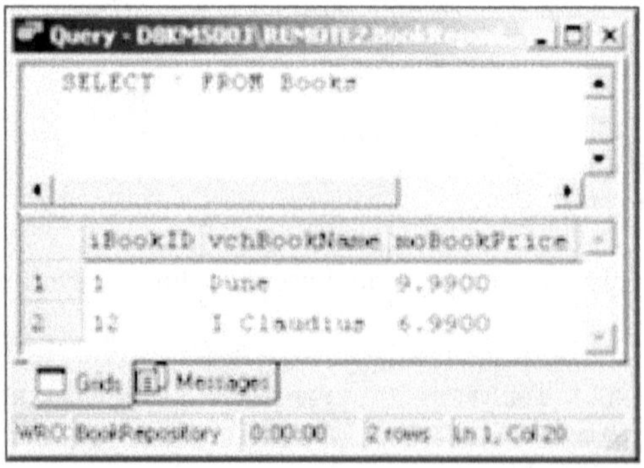

If you proceed with a new INSERT, for example:

```
INSERT Books (vchBookName, moBookPrice) VALUES ('Dicionary of SQL', 11.99)
```

You will see that the future rows will continue from the highest value set in the table:

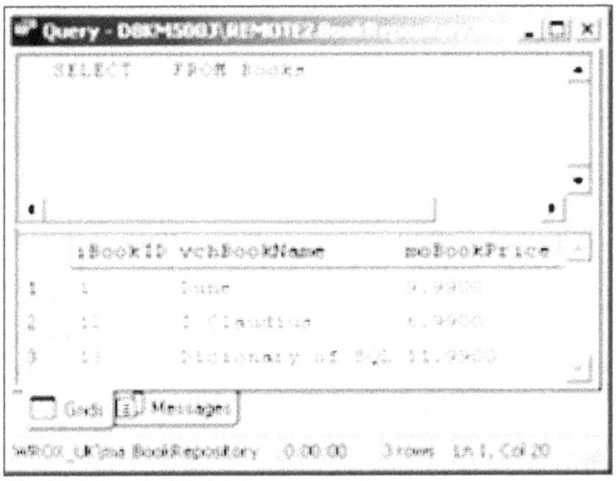

# 14.14 How to... Use DBCC CHECKIDENT to View and Correct IDENTITY Seed Values

To check the current maximum IDENTITY value for a table, use the DBCC CHECKIDENT command. For example, the following syntax checks the current and maximum IDENTITY value for the Books table:

```
DBCC CHECKIDENT (Books, NORESEED)
```

Returns:

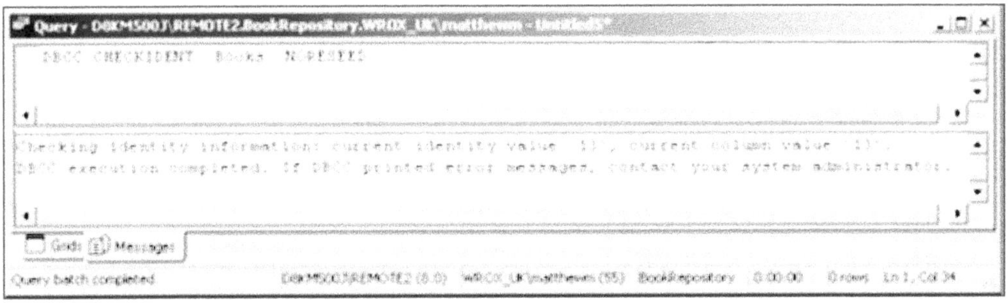

If the current maximum column value is less then the current IDENTITY value, using the following syntax will set the current identity value to the lowest column value:

```
DBCC CHECKIDENT (Books, RESEED)
```

If you wish to set the IDENTITY seed value explicitly, use the following syntax:

```
DBCC CHECKIDENT (Books, RESEED, 50)
```

The third parameter is the number with which you wish to reseed the `IDENTITY` value. `IDENTITY` values are not corrected if the column was created or altered with `NOT FOR REPLICATION`.

# 14.15 How to... Use ROWGUIDCOL

Unlike the `IDENTITY` column, which guarantees uniqueness within the defined table, the `ROWGUIDCOL` property ensures uniqueness across all databases in the **world**. This unique ID is generated by a combination of the `ROWGUIDCOL` property, the `UNIQUEIDENTIFIER` data type, and the `NEWID()` function. You could use the `UNIQUE` constraint to ensure that the value is unique within the table (although the ID is unique, it is not prevented from being copied to other rows).

Only one `ROWGUIDCOL` column may be defined for a table.

They syntax for `ROWGUIDCOL` is as follows:

```
CREATE TABLE <table_name>
   (<column_name_1> uniqueidentifier ROWGUIDCOL
      CONSTRAINT <constraint_name> DEFAULT NEWID(),
    <column_name_2> <datatype_for_column_2> Nullability)
```

## Example 14.15.1: Defining a column with a ROWGUIDCOL property

In this example, we will create a table called `BookShipment`, where the shipment ID is defined by the `ROWGUIDCOL` property:

```
CREATE TABLE BookShipment
   (unqShipmentID uniqueidentifier ROWGUIDCOL
      CONSTRAINT defID DEFAULT NEWID(),
    vchShipmentDescription varchar(100) NULL)
```

The following `INSERT` statement references all values but the `ROWGUIDCOL` column; this is because this column is populated with a `NEWID()` by default:

```
INSERT BookShipment (vchShipmentDescription)
  VALUES ('10 SQL Server Fast Answers for DBA and Developer')
```

A `NEWID()` value is generated for `unqShipmentID` upon `INSERT`:

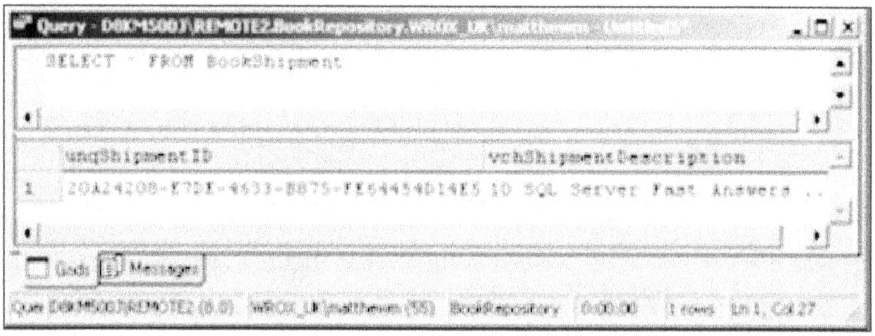


To reference a `ROWGUIDCOL` column explicitly in a query, you can use the `ROWGUIDCOL` keyword. For example:

```
SELECT ROWGUIDCOL FROM BookShipment
```

# 14.16 How to... Specify Column Collation

The Windows or SQL collation can be explicitly defined for columns with the data type of CHAR, NCHAR, VARCHAR, NVARCHAR, TEXT, and NTEXT (for a review of collations, see Chapter 2). The following is syntax for selecting column level collation:

```
CREATE TABLE <table_name>
  (<column_name_1> <datatype_for_column_1> COLLATE Windows_or_SQL_collation
     Nullability,
  <column_name_2> <datatype_for_column_2> COLLATE Windows_or_SQL_collation
     Nullability )
```

### Example 14.16.1: Defining a column's collation

In the following example, the vchBookName column is defined with an accent-sensitive collation. Column collations can be different from the default server collation column (although be careful if you are joining columns that have different collations within a query, as errors may be raised):

```
CREATE TABLE Books
  (iBookId int NOT NULL ,
   vchBookName varchar (255) COLLATE Latin1_General_CI_AI NULL,
   iAuthorId int NULL)
```

# 14.17 How to... Add a Column to an Existing Table

Using ALTER TABLE, you can add a new column to an existing table. The syntax is as follows:

```
ALTER TABLE <tablename> ADD <column_definition>
```

### Example 14.17.1: Adding a column

For example, adding a new column called chCover to the Books table:

```
ALTER TABLE Books ADD chCover char(4) NULL
```

When adding a new column, the column must either accept NULL values or have a DEFAULT constraint defined. For example:

```
ALTER TABLE Books ADD chCover char(4) NOT NULL
  CONSTRAINT cnsCoverType DEFAULT 'Soft'
```

The previous example creates the new chCover column without allowing NULL values; instead, a DEFAULT constraint is defined for the new column. In both examples, the new column is added as the last column of the table.

# 14.18 How to... Drop a Column and Constraints from a Table

Use ALTER TABLE with the DROP COLUMN clause to drop a column from a table. The syntax is as follows:

```
ALTER TABLE <table_name> DROP COLUMN <column_definition>
```

You cannot drop a column if:

- Any constraints or rules are referencing the column; this includes PRIMARY KEY, FOREIGN KEY, UNIQUE, and CHECK constraints. This also includes DEFAULT properties defined for the column.
- The column is participating in replication.
- The column is used in an index.

To remove a constraint, you can use the following syntax:

```
ALTER TABLE <table_name> DROP CONSTRAINT <constraint_name>
```

### Example 14.18.1: Removing a constraint

For example, to remove the chCover column we added in the previous example, we must first drop the DEFAULT definition defined for chCover:

```
ALTER TABLE Books DROP CONSTRAINT cnsCoverType
```

You can then remove the chCover column:

```
ALTER TABLE Books DROP COLUMN chCover
```

# 14.19 How to... Change a Column Definition

You can change a column definition using ALTER TABLE and ALTER COLUMN; this includes changing the column data type, nullability, and collation. The syntax is as follows:

```
ALTER TABLE <table_name>
  ALTER COLUMN <column_name> <datatype> <nullability> <collation>
```

The limits for changing a column definition include:

- The column cannot be of the data types TEXT, NTEXT, IMAGE, or TIMESTAMP.
- The column cannot be used in a PRIMARY KEY, FOREIGN KEY, CHECK, or UNIQUE constraint. If the column data type is of variable length, the column can have the data type length increased for CHECK or UNIQUE constraints.
- The column data type may only have length, precision, or scale changed for a column defined with a DEFAULT property.
- The column, if referenced by a CREATE STATISTICS statement, must DROP STATISTICS first. This does not include automatically generated statistics.
- The column may not be changed if currently replicated in a publication.

- ❑ The column cannot be changed if used in an index, unless expanding the column size of a VARCHAR, NVARCHAR, or VARBINARY data type.
- ❑ If you are changing to a new data type, the new data type must be compatible and convertible from the old type. The new data type may not be a timestamp. If the column is an IDENTITY column, the new data type must support the IDENTITY property.
- ❑ Collation changes may not be made to CHAR, NCHAR, VARCHAR, NVARCHAR, TEXT, and NTEXT columns if constraints reference the column needing to be changed. Changes also cannot be made if the column is SCHEMABOUND (more on this later), has an index defined for it, a full-text index (for a review of full-text indexes, see Chapter 13), or CREATE STATISTICS defined.

### Example 14.19.1: Increasing the size of a column

The following example increases the size of the data type for the vchBookName column from VARCHAR(255) to VARCHAR(500):

```
ALTER TABLE Books
ALTER COLUMN vchBookName varchar(500) NULL
```

### Example 14.19.2: Restrict NULL values

In this next example, the same column is changed to restrict the storage of NULL values:

```
ALTER TABLE Books
ALTER COLUMN vchBookName varchar(500) NOT NULL
```

If you attempt to insert a NULL value into a NOT NULL column, you will receive the error Cannot insert the value NULL into column '%.*ls', table '%.*ls'; column does not allow nulls. %ls fails.

### Example 14.19.3: Adding a collation

Lastly, we will modify the vchBookName column to use a collation that is accent-sensitive:

```
ALTER TABLE Books
ALTER COLUMN vchBookName varchar(500)COLLATE Latin1_General_CI_AS NOT NULL
```

# 14.20 How to... Remove the ROWGUIDCOL Property

You can remove the ROWGUIDCOL property from a column by using the following syntax:

```
ALTER TABLE <table_name>
ALTER COLUMN <column_name> DROP ROWGUIDCOL
```

### Example 14.20.1: Dropping a ROWGUIDCOL property

For example, the following syntax removes the ROWGUIDCOL property from the unqShipmentID column in the BookShipment table:

```
ALTER TABLE BookShipment
ALTER COLUMN unqShipmentID DROP ROWGUIDCOL
```

# 14.21 How to... Add a Primary Key Constraint to an Existing Table

You can add a primary key constraint to an existing table (without a current primary key defined) by using the following syntax:

```
ALTER TABLE <table_name>
ADD CONSTRAINT <constraint_name> PRIMARY KEY [CLUSTERED | NONCLUSTERED]
  (<column_1>[,]<column_N...>)
```

### Example 14.21.1: Adding a primary key

For example, adding a primary key for `iBookId` to the `Books` table:

```
ALTER TABLE Books
ADD CONSTRAINT pk_BookId PRIMARY KEY CLUSTERED (iBookId)
```

# 14.22 How to... Add a Foreign Key Constraint to an Existing Table

You can add a foreign key constraint to an existing table and column by using the following syntax:

```
ALTER TABLE <table_name>
ADD CONSTRAINT <constraint_name> FOREIGN KEY
  (<local_column>[,]<local_column_n>)
REFERENCES <referenced_table>(<ref_column>[,]<ref_column_n>)
ON DELETE {CASCADE | NO ACTION}
ON UPDATE {CASCADE | NO ACTION}
```

### Example 14.22.1: Adding a foreign key

The following example adds a foreign key reference to the `Authors` table `iAuthorId` column, from the local table `iAuthorId` column of the `Books` table:

```
ALTER TABLE Books
ADD CONSTRAINT fk_AuthorId FOREIGN KEY (iAuthorId)
REFERENCES Authors(iAuthorId)
```

This example adds the same constraint, including cascading deletes and updates:

```
ALTER TABLE Books
ADD CONSTRAINT fk_AuthorId FOREIGN KEY (iAuthorId)
REFERENCES Authors(iAuthorId)
ON DELETE CASCADE
ON UPDATE CASCADE
```

# 14.23 How to... Add a DEFAULT Constraint to an Existing Table

If you did not include a DEFAULT property during the table and column creation, you can use the following syntax for adding a DEFAULT constraint to the existing table:

```
ALTER TABLE <table_name>
ADD CONSTRAINT <constraint_name>
DEFAULT <default_value>
[WITH VALUES]
```

The WITH VALUES clause is optional and, if used, it will update all NULL values for the column with the new DEFAULT value. If not specified, existing NULL values (prior to the DEFAULT definition) will be maintained.

### Example 14.23.1: Adding a default value

The following is an example of adding a default value to the vchBookType column of the Books table:

```
ALTER TABLE Books
ADD CONSTRAINT defBookType
DEFAULT 'Hard'
FOR chCover
WITH VALUES
```

# 14.24 How to... Add a CHECK Constraint to an Existing Table

To add a CHECK constraint to an existing table, use the following syntax:

```
ALTER TABLE <table_name>
ADD CONSTRAINT <constraint_name>
CHECK [NOT FOR REPLICATION] (<expression>)
```

The NOT FOR REPLICATION clause is optional, and means that data published to the table will not be validated by the CHECK constraint.

### Example 14.24.1: Adding a CHECK constraint

The following example adds a CHECK constraint to the Books table, restricting the types of books allowed in the chCover field:

```
ALTER TABLE Books
ADD CONSTRAINT chkBookType
CHECK NOT FOR REPLICATION (chCover = 'Hard' or chCover = 'Soft')
```

# 14.25 How to... Add a UNIQUE Constraint to an Existing Table

To add a UNIQUE constraint to an existing table, use the following syntax:

```
ALTER TABLE <table_name>
ADD CONSTRAINT <constraint_name>
UNIQUE [ CLUSTERED | NONCLUSTERED ]
(<column_1_name>[,]<column_N>)
```

### Example 14.25.1: Adding a UNIQUE constraint

The following example adds a UNIQUE constraint for the iBookId column in the Books table:

```
ALTER TABLE Books
ADD CONSTRAINT unqBookId
UNIQUE NONCLUSTERED (iBookId)
```

# 14.26 How to... Disable and Enable Constraints

You can disable validation of data against newly added or re-enabled CHECK or FOREIGN KEY constraints. The syntax for disabling and enabling this checking is as follows:

```
ALTER TABLE <table_name>
[NOCHECK or CHECK] CONSTRAINT [ALL or <constraint_name> [,] <constraint_name_n...>]
```

### Example 14.26.1: Disabling and enabling constraints

The following example disables all foreign key and CHECK constraint checking for the Books table:

```
ALTER TABLE Books
NOCHECK CONSTRAINT ALL
```

To re-enable checking:

```
ALTER TABLE Books
CHECK CONSTRAINT ALL
```

# 14.27 How to... Drop a Table

To remove a table from the database, use the DROP TABLE command:

```
DROP TABLE <table_name>
```

### Example 14.27.1: Dropping a table

For example:

```
DROP TABLE Authors
```

You cannot drop a table that is referenced by a foreign key constraint. If you drop a table being referenced by a view or stored procedure, these objects must either be dropped or changed to reference a different table. Also, you cannot drop a table being published for replication; you must drop the article from the publication first.

# 14.28 How to... Create a Temporary Table

Temporary tables are defined just like regular tables, only they are stored in the `tempdb` database. Temporary tables are often used to store temporary results, for use in queries, updates, and stored procedures. They can be used to return or pass a set of results from a called procedure to a calling stored procedure.

Developers often use temporary tables to avoid Transact-SQL cursors (producing results sets, looping through rows, and deleting the rows when finished). Some developers would argue that temporary tables should be avoided altogether (just as cursors should be avoided), due to the performance overhead that they sometimes incur, including excessive transaction logging, and locking of database objects. It is difficult to generalize that temporary tables should always be avoided but, rather, they should be viewed as one tool of many available to the SQL Server developer.

There are two different temporary table types: local and global. **Local** temporary tables are available for use by the current user connection that created them. They are defined by adding a single pound (#) sign at the beginning of the table name. For example:

```
CREATE TABLE #Authors
  (iAuthorID int NOT NULL,
   vchLastName varchar(100) NULL,
   vchFirstName varchar(100) NULL)
```

Multiple connections can create the same named temporary table for local temporary tables without encountering conflicts. The internal representation of the local table is given a unique name so as not to conflict with other temporary tables with the same name created by other connections in the `tempdb` database. For example, if three connections create the `#Authors` table, you will see three versions of the table in the `tempdb.dbo.sysobjects` table. Each object will have a slightly varying number appended to the name, so preventing a naming conflict. This number is transparent to the user and they do not have to concern themselves with it.

Local temporary tables are dropped by using the `DROP` statement or are automatically removed when the user connection is closed.

The second type of temporary table is the **global** temporary table. Global temporary tables are defined with two pound signs (##) at the beginning of a table name. For example:

```
CREATE TABLE ##Authors
  (iAuthorID int NOT NULL,
   vchLastName varchar(100) NULL,
   vchFirstName varchar(100) NULL)
```

Once a connection creates a global temporary table, any user with access to the current database can access the table. You cannot create simultaneous versions of a global temporary table, as this will generate a naming conflict.

Global temporary tables are removed if explicitly dropped by `DROP TABLE` or, automatically, after the last connection exits and the global temporary table is no longer referenced by any connections.

Temporary tables are defined like regular tables, and can have indexes, constraints (but not foreign key constraints), and other related elements just like regular tables.

# 14.29 How to... Create a Table Variable

SQL Server 2000 has introduced the **table variable**, which can sometimes work more efficiently than a temporary table, as SQL Server automatically clears it after it has been used; you do not need to `DROP` a table variable explicitly.

Table variables can incur less locking and logging than a temporary table, because they are only available for the duration of the batch, function, or stored procedure where they are used. Table variables can also reduce recompilations of a stored procedure, compared to the temporary table counterparts.

The syntax for creating a table variable is as follows:

```
DECLARE @<variable_name> TABLE (<table_definition>)
```

## Example 14.29.1: Creating and working with a table variable

In the following example, a table variable called `@Authors` will be created to process rows from the permanent table `Authors`:

```
DECLARE @Authors TABLE
   (iAuthorId int NOT NULL ,
    vchLastName varchar (50)  NULL ,
    vchFirstName varchar (50)  NULL)

INSERT @Authors SELECT * FROM Authors
```

> **If you are using a table variable within a batch, don't use the `GO` statement prior to the table variable; the `GO` statement signals the end of a batch and will remove the table variable from memory. Also, you cannot use the `INSERT EXEC` syntax to insert rows into table variables.**

# 14.30 How to... Set Table Options with sp_tableoption

The system stored procedure `sp_tableoption` allows you to set options for a specific user-defined table. The syntax for `sp_tableoption` is as follows:

```
sp_tableoption @TableNamePattern =  <'table_name'> ,
               @OptionName = <'option_name>' ,
               @OptionValue =  <'value>'
```

The configurable options are:

| Option | Description |
|---|---|
| `pintable` | When enabled, the entire table is placed into RAM. This is the same as issuing a `DBCC PINTABLE` command, which will be discussed later in the chapter. |
| `table lock on bulk load` | When enabled, bulk load operations against the table will obtain a bulk update lock instead of row locks. This reduces concurrency, but can increase the performance of the bulk load operation. |
| `text in row` | When enabled, `TEXT`, `NTEXT`, and `IMAGE` strings are stored in the data row. For smaller `BLOB` data types, this can result in faster row access, as `BLOB` data is stored in the data page. You can either set this option `ON`, or specify the number of bytes to limit in row storage, from 24 to 7000 bytes. |

### Example 14.30.1: Enabling table lock on bulk load

```
sp_tableoption 'Employees',
               'table lock on bulk load', 'ON'
```

### Example 14.30.2: Enabling text in row for TEXT, NTEXT, and IMAGE columns up to 750 bytes

```
sp_tableoption 'Books',
               'text in row', '750'
```

# 14.31 How to... Display Constraint Information for a Table Using sp_helpconstraint

Use the system stored procedure `sp_helpconstraint` to list all constraints defined for a specified table. This procedure takes two parameters: the table name and whether or not the table name should be included in the output. Either leave the second parameter blank to display the table name or use `nomsg` to prevent the table name from being returned in the output.

### Example 14.31.1: Listing constraints for a specific table

```
EXEC sp_helpconstraint 'Books'
```

The output includes the type of constraints, constraint names, cascading attributes (cascaded delete or update), the status of the constraints (enabled or disabled), and columns referenced by the constraints.

# 14.32 How to... Use DBCC PINTABLE to Place a Table's Data Pages Into Memory

The DBCC PINTABLE command allows you to place a table's data pages into the buffer cache (memory). Once the table's data pages are **pinned** to the buffer cache, SQL Server prevents them from being flushed (removed) from memory. Since reading from memory is faster than reading from physical disk, you will see a significant performance benefit for frequently accessed tables.

This operation should only be used for smaller tables that are referenced frequently, and only if you can establish true performance improvements for doing so (without hurting system-wide performance).

The syntax for DBCC PINTABLE is as follows:

```
DBCC PINTABLE ( database_id , table_id )
```

## Example 14.32.1: Enabling PINTABLE for a table

```
USE BookRepository14

DECLARE @dbid INTEGER
SET @dbid = DB_ID('BookRepository14')

DECLARE @tableid INTEGER
SET @tableid = OBJECT_ID('dbo.Books')

DBCC PINTABLE (@dbid, @tableid)
```

The above example sets two variables, @dbid and @tableid, and populates them with the ID values of the BookRepository14 database and the Books table. The DBCC PINTABLE then takes the two parameters and issues the following warning after execution:

```
Warning: Pinning tables should be carefully considered. If a pinned table is larger, or grows larger, than
the available data cache, the server may need to be restarted and the table unpinned.
DBCC execution completed. If DBCC printed error messages, contact your system administrator.
```

To remove a table from memory, use the DBCC UNPINTABLE command.

## Example 14.32.2: Disabling PINTABLE functionality for a table

```
DECLARE @dbid INTEGER
SET @dbid = DB_ID('BookRepository14')

--Determine id number for the dbo.Books table
DECLARE @tableid INTEGER
SET @tableid = OBJECT_ID('dbo.Books')

USE BookRepository
DBCC UNPINTABLE (@dbid, @tableid)
```

# Performance Impact of Constraints

Constraints help maintain database integrity in a number of ways; however, such protections introduce performance drawbacks. Adding constraints can slow down the process of bulk imports, as well as other high-speed operations that need to occur against your user-defined tables. Use constraints intelligently, making sure that you don't add any redundant functionality. If you are doing bulk insert operations, you may want to consider temporarily dropping constraints (and indexes too) as a means of decreasing the load time.

If you have a choice between triggers and constraints, choose constraints if the functionality will meet your application needs. Constraints operate against the data before a change is made and are generally faster and less of a performance drain. Triggers, which we will review later in this chapter, generally should be used for more complex business logic and data-driven decision-making. There are also cases where constraints cannot be used; for example, when you require referential integrity for cross-database or cross-server tables.

# Views, Updateable Views, Indexed Views, Partitioned Views

Views allow you to create a virtual representation of a table using a `SELECT` statement as a definition. You can then reference the view with a `SELECT` query in the same way as you would with a table. The defining `SELECT` statement can join one or more tables and can include one or more columns. Views are generally used to provide de-normalized data. Rather than forcing a user to join several tables to generate a result set, a view can be defined to present a rowset in a simple manner.

For example, let's say we have three tables: `Books`, `BookOrders`, and `Orders`. The user needs the `vchBookName` and `dtOrderdate` fields; if you wish to prevent them from querying all three tables, you can generate the `SELECT` statement within a view definition, simplifying the query definition:

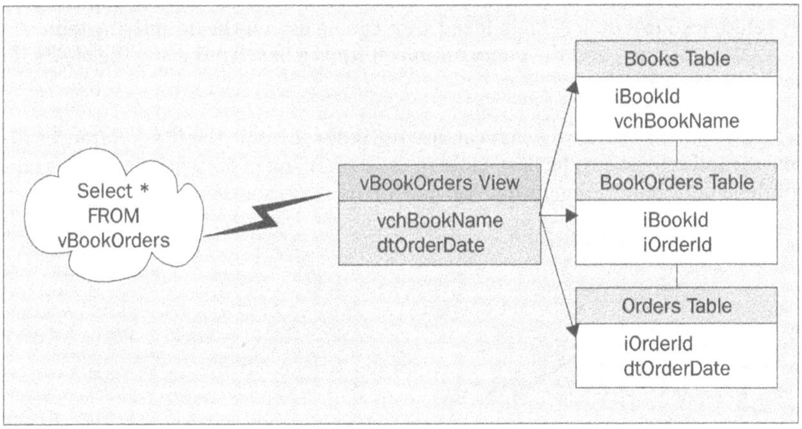


Views are also useful for managing security and protecting sensitive data. If you wish to obscure the database's schema from the end user, you can grant permissions exclusively to views, rather than the underlying table. You can also use views to expose just those columns you wish the end user to see, by including just the necessary columns in the view definition.

Views can allow updates and indexing under some circumstances.

# Regular Views

You define a regular view with a SELECT statement. If the appropriate permissions are granted, users can access views using SELECT statements; views allow up to 1024 defined columns. Views are also updateable if they meet the following conditions:

- They have no aggregate functions or the TOP, GROUP BY, UNION, or DISTINCT clauses in their definition. Aggregate functions are only allowed in sub-queries used in the FROM, WHERE, or HAVING clauses (see Chapter 15 for a review of SELECT queries and sub-queries).
- They don't contain computed values or values based on functions.
- Any non-nullable columns on the base table must be included in the view definition.

UPDATE and INSERT operations against a view must affect only one underlying table referenced in the view definition. DELETE operations are only allowed if the view references one table in the FROM clause that defines the view. If you cannot meet the requirements mentioned earlier, you can also use INSTEAD OF triggers to update views. We will review triggers later in the chapter.

# Indexed Views

A view is no more efficient than the underlying SELECT query used to define it. One way you can improve the performance of a frequently accessed view is to add an index to it. You must first create a unique clustered index on the view. Once this view has been built, the data that makes up the view is stored in much the same way as a clustered index for a table is stored. You can also create additional nonclustered indexes, as you would for a regular table. Prior to creating nonclustered indexes on the view, you must first define the clustered index. The underlying (base) tables are not impacted physically by the creation of indexed views, as the view is treated like a separate database object.

You can create indexed views in any edition of SQL Server 2000; however, in SQL Server 2000 Enterprise Edition, indexed views are more versatile, as they can be used within a query execution plan even if the view is not directly referenced in a query. An indexed view can be used if the underlying table or tables are referenced in a SELECT query, and the query optimizer finds a benefit to using the view's index over any table indexes it may have to choose from.

The diagram below shows two queries that can use the indexed view; the first references the view in the FROM clause, and the second references the base table in the FROM clause. Both queries can use the view, even though one of them does not even mention the view in the FROM clause:

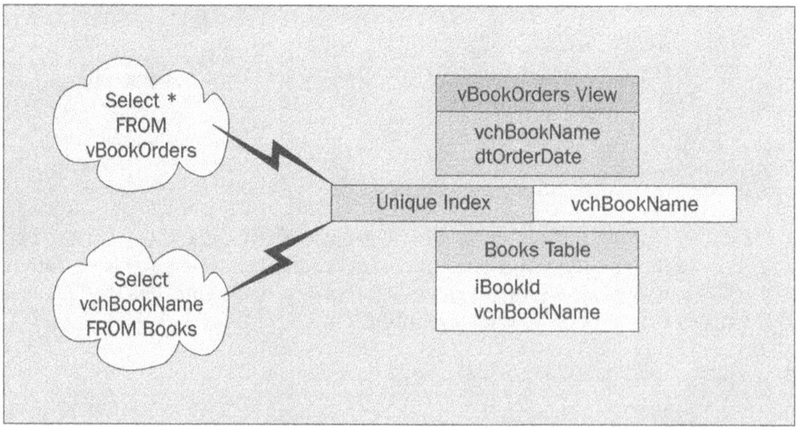

There are some drawbacks and limitations to indexed views. Indexed views require SQL Server Enterprise or Developer Editions. They are also more useful for static data (reporting or data warehousing data), than data that is frequently updated; this is because base tables with frequent updates will trigger frequent index updates against the view, potentially reducing the benefit of query performance against data update speed.

## INSTEAD OF Trigger View

`INSTEAD OF` triggers facilitate updates against views and are more a technique than a type of view. If your view schema does not permit direct updates, you can use `INSTEAD OF` triggers to handle `INSERT`, `UPDATE`, and `DELETE` activity against the view; this is particularly useful for views that reference multiple tables. For example, one update against a view can be used to update multiple base tables. `INSTEAD OF` triggers will be reviewed in more detail later in this chapter.

## Partitioned Views

A partitioned view is used to represent one logical table made up of horizontally partitioned tables. These tables can be located across separate SQL Server instances – this is a **distributed** partition view.

The example below shows a partitioned view called `vBookSales`. The `vBookSales` view is defined by joining three tables, `BookSales_WI`, `BookSales_MN`, and `BookSales_NY`, with a `UNION` clause. Each table has the same schema but each has a unique `CHECK` constraint limiting the values that are allowed in the base table (Wisconsin sales, Minnesota sales, and New York sales). The columns used for each table making up the view must share the same data type, size, and collation. The `CHECK` constraints defined for the smaller tables must not allow an overlap in table values:

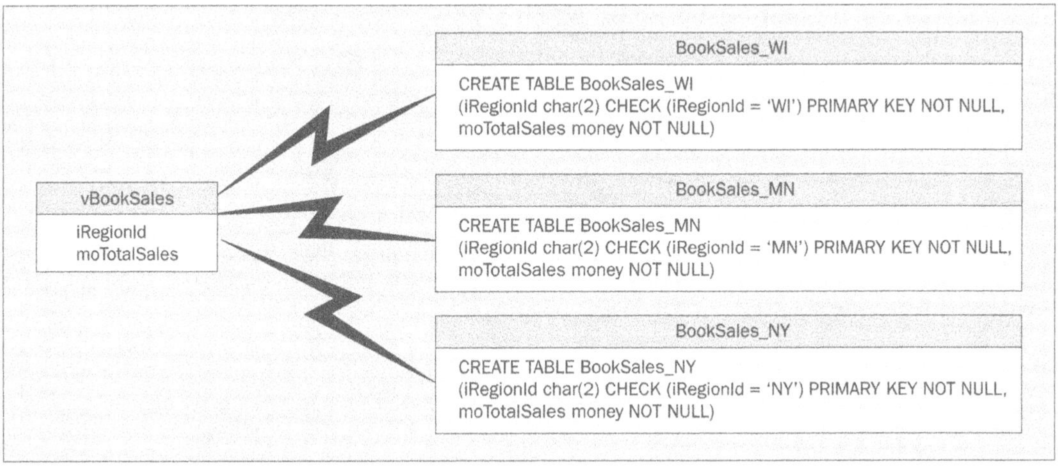


Partitioned views can be used for both updates and read activity. If you define the view across multiple servers, each view must be defined on each member server to be accessed by each participating SQL Server instance. Each SQL Server instance must have a linked server entry added for the other participating servers. Using the **lazy schema validation** option for each linked server entry ensures good performance for the distributed partitioned view, as the instances will not request meta data (information about view schema itself, columns, data types) for the view until they actually need it.

> **All types of views require careful planning and are no more efficient than the `SELECT` query that defines them.**

Some final tips on views, before looking at how to create, update, and remove them:

- Do not nest views more than one level deep; specifically, do not define a view that calls another view, and so on. This can lead to confusion when you attempt to tune inefficient queries, not to mention a performance overhead for each level that is nested.
- Use stored procedures if possible. Stored procedures can offer a performance boost, as the execution plan is re-usable. Stored procedures can reduce network traffic, provide business logic, and have fewer restrictions than a view. Stored procedures can be used for `INSERT`, `UPDATE`, `DELETE`, and `SELECT` statements in addition to much more complex application requirements (see Chapter 16 for more on this).
- Tune your views as you would tune a `SELECT` query. Poorly performing views can have a huge impact on server performance.

# 14.33 How to... Create a View

The basic syntax for creating a view is:

```
CREATE VIEW <view_name>
  {WITH ENCRYPTION | WITH SCHEMABINDING | WITH VIEW_METADATA }
  AS
  <select_statement>
  {WITH CHECK OPTION }
GO
```

## Example 14.33.1: Creating a view based on a SELECT statement

```
CREATE VIEW vBooks AS
  SELECT vchBookName, iAuthorID
  FROM Books
GO
```

## Example 14.33.2: Using the WITH CHECK OPTION on a view

You can use `WITH CHECK OPTION` to make sure any `INSERT` activity in the view does not include a value that cannot be read from that view. For example, the following view is defined so that the user can only `SELECT` books by authors with an `iAuthorID` equal to 1 or 10:

```
CREATE VIEW vBooks AS
  SELECT vchBookName, iAuthorID FROM Books WHERE iAuthorID IN (1, 10)
  WITH CHECK OPTION
GO
```

The following `INSERT` statement against the view will be allowed:

```
INSERT vBooks (vchBookName, iAuthorId) VALUES ('Dune', 1)
```

However, an `INSERT` such as the following will not be allowed:

```
INSERT vBooks (vchBookName, iAuthorId) VALUES ('An Affair to Remember', 22)
```

You would receive an error like this:

```
Server: Msg 550, Level 16, State 1, Line 1
The attempted insert or update failed because the target view either specifies WITH CHECK OPTION or
spans a view that specifies WITH CHECK OPTION and one or more rows resulting from the operation did
not qualify under the CHECK OPTION constraint.
The statement has been terminated.
```

### Example 14.33.3: Using WITH ENCRYPTION

If you do not wish your view **definition** to be viewable, you can use the `WITH ENCRYPTION` extension. For example:

```
CREATE VIEW vAuthors WITH ENCRYPTION AS
  SELECT vchFirstName, vchLastName
  FROM dbo.Authors
GO
```

If you attempt to view the definition in Enterprise Manager (in the Views node of the database), you will see the following output for encrypted objects:

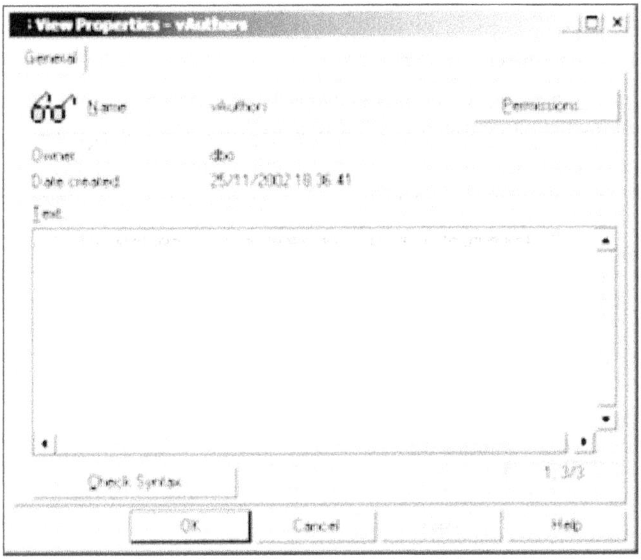


# 14.34 How to... Create an Indexed View

If you intend to create indexes for your view, the view must be **schemabound**. The `WITH SCHEMABINDING` clause binds the view definition to the schema of the underlying base tables. `SCHEMABINDING` restricts what changes can be made to the base tables while the view is schemabound to it. You cannot drop a schemabound base table without first dropping the view referencing the table `WITH SCHEMABINDING`. You can `ALTER` columns in a schemabound table; but changes to columns of the base tables referenced in the view are not allowed. The syntax for `SCHEMABINDING` is:

```
CREATE VIEW <view_name>
  WITH SCHEMABINDING
  AS
  <select_statement>
GO
```

The requirements for creating the indexable views are also more stringent than regular views:

- ANSI_NULLS must be ON during the CREATE VIEW statement. ANSI_NULLS must also be ON for the CREATE TABLE statements used to create the base tables referenced by the view.
- Column expressions returning a float data type value cannot be the unique key for an indexed view.
- If GROUP BY is specified, the keywords HAVING, CUBE, and ROLLUP are not allowed.
- In the FROM clause, outer and self-joins are not allowed.
- Functions referenced in the view definition must be deterministic, just like columns for a table using functions. Deterministic means that the calculation must always return the same result and cannot use functions or commands that return varied values.
- Only base tables are allowed for the view definition. No nested view references are allowed. These base tables must belong to the same database and have the same owner. These tables must also use the two-part name syntax, owner.table_name.
- QUOTED_IDENTIFIER must be ON during the CREATE VIEW statement.
- The SCHEMABINDING clause (reviewed later) is required. This ensures that certain updates are not allowed to the referenced base tables. If any user-defined functions are used (more on functions later), they must also be created with SCHEMABINDING.
- The GROUP BY clause requires a COUNT_BIG(*) aggregate function (returns the BIGINT data type).
- The SELECT statement may not include the asterisk symbol (for all columns) and must explicitly state all columns. Columns must be unique and, if repeated, must use an aliased name.
- The view definition cannot use derived tables, functions that return table variables, or sub-queries. Nor are certain functions and keywords allowed, such as UNION, TOP, ORDER BY, DISTINCT, COUNT, AVG, MAX, MIN, STDEV, VAR, STDEVP, VARP, COMPUTE, COMPUTE BY, CONTAINS, FREETEXT, and SUM (for nullable expressions).

## Example 14.34.1: Creating an indexed view

In this example, a view is first defined for the Books table, using the WITH SCHEMABINDING keywords:

```
CREATE VIEW vBooks WITH SCHEMABINDING AS
  SELECT vchBookName, iAuthorId
  FROM dbo.Books
GO
```

The first index for the view must be a UNIQUE CLUSTERED index:

```
CREATE UNIQUE CLUSTERED INDEX idx_vBooks_BookName
  ON vBooks (vchBookName)
```

You can then create additional nonclustered indexes for the view, for example:

```
CREATE NONCLUSTERED INDEX idx_vBooks_iAuthorID
  ON vBooks (iAuthorId)
```

# 14.35 How to... Create a Partitioned View

The syntax for creating a partitioned view is as follows:

```
CREATE VIEW <view_name> AS
  <select_statement_horizontal_partition_1>
  UNION ALL
  <select_statement_horizontal_partition_N>
GO
```

Updateable partitioned views (INSERT, UPDATE, DELETE) have more stringent requirements than read-only partitioned views. The table below reviews restrictions by modification type:

| Requirement | INSERT | UPDATE | DELETE |
|---|---|---|---|
| SQL Server 2000 Enterprise or Developer Editions. | Required | Required | Required |
| Any INSERT statements against the view must include all columns. | Required | | |
| CHECK constraints allow only the operators: <,>, =, >=, <=, AND, OR, and BETWEEN. | Required | Required | Required |
| CHECK constraints must be defined on the same columns and cannot allow overlapping values in the member tables. | Required | Required | Required |
| Columns from each table must be in the SELECT list. The wildcard symbol is not allowed. | Required | Required | Required |
| Horizontally partitioned tables are combined using UNION ALL in the view definition. | Required | Required | Required |
| If the inserted value falls outside the range of allowed values for the CHECK constraint, it is an invalid update against the view. | Required | | |
| Only one constraint is allowed on the CHECK constraint column. | Required | Required | Required |
| Referenced tables in the view definition cannot be referenced more than once within the same view. | Required | Required | Required |
| Referenced tables must have primary key constraints defined on an identical number of columns. | Required | Required | Required |
| Self-joins are not allowed. | Required | Required | Required |
| The CHECK constraint column must be part of the primary key of the table (and, therefore, cannot allow NULL values). Computed columns are not allowed either for the CHECK constraint column. | Required | Required | Required |
| The DEFAULT keyword is not allowed for updates. | Required | Required | |

*Table continued on following page*

| Requirement | INSERT | UPDATE | DELETE |
|---|---|---|---|
| The IDENTITY column cannot be modified. | | Required | |
| The IDENTITY column is not allowed for updates. | Required | | |
| The member table columns must be in the same ordinal position in the SELECT list and cannot be referenced more than once in the same list. Data types and collation must be the same for columns in each of the member tables. | Required | Required | Required |
| The primary key cannot be changed if the participating table contains TEXT, IMAGE, or NTEXT columns. | | Required | |
| The TIMESTAMP column is not allowed for updates. | Required | Required | |

Distributed partitioned views require MS DTC to be running and the XACT_ABORT SET option to be set ON.

### Example 14.35.1: Creating a distributed partition view

In this example, the base table definitions will first be defined:

```
CREATE TABLE BookSales_WI
   (chRegionID char(2) CHECK (chRegionId = 'WI') PRIMARY KEY NOT NULL,
    iStoreID int NOT NULL,
    moTotalSales money NOT NULL)

CREATE TABLE BookSales_MN
   (chRegionID char(2) CHECK (chRegionId = 'MN') PRIMARY KEY NOT NULL,
    iStoreID int NOT NULL,
    moTotalSales money NOT NULL)

CREATE TABLE BookSales_NY
   (chRegionID char(2) CHECK (chRegionId = 'NY') PRIMARY KEY NOT NULL,
    iStoreID int NOT NULL,
    moTotalSales money NOT NULL)
```

These tables could be defined on three separate SQL Server instances, or on the same instance. When defining a distributed partitioned view, you must define the view using the four-part name for the associated remote servers, and the three-part name for the view on the local server. If we had three SQL Server instances, WIServer, MNServer, and NYServer, each with a BookRepository14 database that contained their associated member table, you would define the view as follows on the WIServer:

```
CREATE VIEW vBookSales AS
  SELECT chRegionId, iStoreID, moTotalSales
  FROM BookRepository.dbo.BookSales_WI
UNION ALL
  SELECT chRegionId,iStoreID, moTotalSales
  FROM MNServer.BookRepository.dbo.BookSales_MN
UNION ALL
  SELECT chRegionId,iStoreID, moTotalSales
   FROM NYServer.BookRepository.dbo.BookSales_NY
```

On MNServer, you would define vBookSales view without the four-part name on the BookSales_MN, and use the four-part name with the other two member tables:

```
CREATE VIEW vBookSales AS
  SELECT chRegionId,iStoreID, moTotalSales
  FROM WIServer.BookRepository.dbo.BookSales_WI
UNION ALL
  SELECT chRegionId, iStoreID, moTotalSales
  FROM BookRepository.dbo.BookSales_MN
UNION ALL
  SELECT chRegionId,iStoreID, moTotalSales
  FROM NYServer.BookRepository.dbo.BookSales_NY
```

The same applies to the NYServer:

```
CREATE VIEW vBookSales AS
  SELECT chRegionId, iStoreID, moTotalSales
  FROM WIServer.BookRepository.dbo.BookSales_WI
UNION ALL
  SELECT chRegionId,iStoreID, moTotalSales
  FROM MNServer.BookRepository.dbo.BookSales_MN
UNION ALL
  SELECT chRegionId, iStoreID, moTotalSales
  FROM BookRepository.dbo.BookSales_NY
```

# 14.36 How to... Change a View

You can use the ALTER VIEW command to change an existing view definition, without dropping the existing view. The syntax is as follows:

```
ALTER VIEW <view_name>
  {WITH ENCRYPTION | WITH SCHEMABINDING | WITH VIEW_METADATA}
AS
  <select_statement>
  {WITH CHECK OPTION }
GO
```

### Example 14.36.1: Change the view definition

In the following example, the vBooks view will be changed to display all columns, instead of just a subset of the columns (vchBookName, iAuthorId) defined in the original view definition:

```
ALTER VIEW vBooks AS
  SELECT * FROM Books
GO
```

# 14.37 How to... Drop a View

To drop a view, use the following syntax:

```
DROP VIEW <view_name>
```

### Example 14.37.1: Dropping a view

In this example, the vBooks view is dropped:

```
DROP VIEW vBooks
```

# 14.38 How to... Refresh Meta Data for a Specific View

If the underlying table schema for the SELECT query definition of the view undergoes changes, you can use the sp_refreshview stored procedure to refresh the view's meta data. The syntax is:

```
EXEC sp_refreshview '<view_name>'
```

### Example 14.38.1: Refreshing the meta data for a view

```
EXEC sp_refreshview 'vBookSales'
```

# Stored Procedures

A stored procedure allows you to group one or more statements as a logical unit and store this unit as an object in a SQL Server database. Stored procedures are used to execute Transact-SQL commands and can often produce faster execution times than ad hoc queries from a workstation. Stored procedures can be called from the SQL Server instance itself, from a workstation, or from an application. Stored procedures are also helpful for Internet-based applications, as they allow for the offloading of business logic to the database server for data-specific routines.

The key to a stored procedure's good performance is SQL Server's ability to store a pre-compiled execution plan for commands used within the stored procedure (which has also been parsed to ensure there are no syntax errors). This stored execution plan can then be re-used for future stored procedure calls, instead of running an ad hoc query or batch without an execution plan.

Network performance can also be improved when you use a stored procedure, as the Transact-SQL statements from the stored procedure are invoked on the server itself, reducing Transact-SQL calls over the network. This leaves only the stored procedure call and parameters and returned results (when applicable) to be transferred over the network.

Stored procedures also allow you to store data-related business logic outside the application. Applications can be programmed to call only stored procedures for Transact-SQL activity, rather then sending explicit statements and batches; this reduces network packets, particularly if the batches are run frequently.

# 14.39 How to... Create Stored Procedures

To create a stored procedure, use the following syntax:

```
CREATE PROCEDURE <procedure_name> [ ; number]
  <@param1> <datatype_for_param1> [VARYING]
    = <default_value_for_param1> [OUTPUT],
  <@param_N> <datatype_for_param_N> [VARYING]
    = <default_value_for_param_N> [OUTPUT]

  [ WITH { RECOMPILE | ENCRYPTION | RECOMPILE, ENCRYPTION } ]
  [ FOR REPLICATION ]

  AS <SQL_commands>
```

| Parameter | Description |
|---|---|
| `procedure_name` | Name of the stored procedure. |
| `; number` | Optional integer, allowing you to use the same name as an existing procedure, but with different functionality. |
| `@param1` | Stored procedures allow parameters, which are used within the stored procedure to take the place of constants. Parameters must begin with the `@` sign as the first character. You are allowed up to 2,100 parameters for one stored procedure. If you do not choose a default value for the parameter, you must provide a value when calling the procedure. |
| `datatype_for_param1` | The data type of the parameter. |
| `VARYING` | Applies to cursor parameters, specifying result sets supported as an output parameter. |
| `= default_value_for_param1` | The default value for the parameter. |
| `OUTPUT` | Specifies that the parameter return information to the calling procedure. |
| `WITH { RECOMPILE \| ENCRYPTION \| RECOMPILE , ENCRYPTION }` | `WITH RECOMPILE` specifies that the execution plan for the procedure is recompiled each time it is executed.<br><br>`WITH ENCRYPTION` encrypts the stored procedure definition, so it cannot be read in Enterprise Manager or within `syscomments`. |
| `FOR REPLICATION` | Indicates that the stored procedure cannot be executed on the subscriber in a replication topology. The procedure can only be executed during replication. |
| `SQL_commands` | One or more SQL statements. |

### Example 14.39.1: Creating a basic stored procedure

In the following example, a stored procedure is created to return data from the Books table:

```
CREATE PROCEDURE pr_Return_Books AS
  SELECT iBookId, vchBookName FROM Books
GO
```

To execute the stored procedure, run the following:

```
EXEC pr_Return_Books
```

### Example 14.39.2: Creating a stored procedure to INSERT new rows into a table

The next example creates a stored procedure that updates the Books table. The procedure defines two parameters, @BookName and @AuthorId; these values are then passed to the INSERT statement within the procedure:

```
CREATE PROCEDURE pr_Insert_Books
  @BookName varchar(255),
  @AuthorId int AS

  INSERT Books (vchBookName, iAuthorId) VALUES (@BookName, @AuthorId)
GO
```

To execute the stored procedure, you would be required to supply both parameters, for example:

```
EXEC pr_Insert_Books 'SQL Fun', 4
```

Since defaults are not defined for the parameters in the procedure, if you run the procedure without specifying values, you will receive the following error for this example:

Server: Msg 201, Level 16, State 3, Procedure pr_Insert_Books, Line 0
Procedure 'pr_Insert_Books' expects parameter '@BookName', which was not supplied.

### Example 14.39.3: Using OUTPUT parameters

You can use OUTPUT parameters to put data into variables for use by the calling process or procedure. If a parameter is not modified with the OUTPUT keyword, it is not available to the calling procedure. In this following example, the iAuthorId integer value is returned to a variable:

```
CREATE PROCEDURE pr_Return_iAuthorid
  @BookName varchar(255),
  @AuthorId int OUTPUT AS

  SELECT @AuthorId = iAuthorId FROM Books WHERE vchBookName = @BookName
GO
```

The following example shows how to use this new procedure to put the value of iAuthorId into an integer variable:

```
DECLARE @CapturedAuthorId int

EXEC pr_Return_iAuthorid 'SQL Fun', @CapturedAuthorId OUTPUT

PRINT @CapturedAuthorId
```

The previous example creates an integer variable for holding the value of iAuthorId. Next, the pr_Return_iAuthorId stored procedure is called, specifying a specific book and using the declared @CapturedAuthorId variable. OUTPUT is also used, meaning that the variable should receive its value from the procedure call. Lastly, the @CapturedAuthorId is printed.

## Tips on Stored Procedures

Here are some tips on using stored procedures:

- Use SET NOCOUNT ON at the beginning of your stored procedure to minimize the number of messages that are sent back to the client that called the stored procedure.
- Put all temporary table definitions at the beginning of your procedure, instead of interspersing temporary table creations and queries throughout the procedure (combined with references to your temporary table). This spreading out of DDL and DML is called **interleaving**. When a temporary object is referenced for the first time, SQL Server recompiles the stored procedure; by placing all DDL definitions at the beginning of the procedure, this first recompile will capture all temporary tables that will be created for the entire procedure, rather than recompiling each time a new temporary procedure is encountered. Recompiles occur during certain DDL activities and can have a negative impact on performance.
- If you are certain that a useful execution plan will not be used for your stored procedure due to extremes in the data accessed in your procedure, use WITH RECOMPILE to force SQL Server to recompile your stored procedure.
- Avoid naming your procedures with the sp_ prefix. Using sp_ can cause a small amount of overhead, as SQL Server may interpret this procedure as a system stored procedure. As such, use your own naming convention; for naming, use keywords within the procedure to suggest its purpose; for example pr_Insert_xxxxx, pr_Report_xxxxx, or pr_Update_xxxx.
- A stored procedure will not be a magic bullet or substitute for proper query tuning.

# 14.40 How to... Modify Stored Procedures

To modify a procedure's definition, use the ALTER PROCEDURE command. The ALTER PROCEDURE command's parameters are identical to the CREATE PROCEDURE command's parameters, except that ALTER PROCEDURE modifies existing stored procedures.

### Example 14.40.1: Changing a stored procedure

In this example, the pr_Return_Books stored procedure is modified to include a PRINT statement and an INSERT statement to record the user connection and date the table was read:

```
ALTER PROCEDURE pr_Return_Books AS

  PRINT 'List of books...'

  SELECT iBookId, vchBookName FROM Books
  INSERT BookAudit VALUES (USER, GETDATE())
GO
```

# 14.41 How to... Drop Stored Procedures

To drop a stored procedure, use the following syntax:

```
DROP PROCEDURE <procedure_name>
```

### Example 14.41.1: Dropping a stored procedure

```
DROP PROCEDURE pr_Return_Books
```

# 14.42 How to... Run Stored Procedures at Startup

The sp_procoption stored procedure allows you to set a stored procedure to run automatically when the SQL Server service is started or restarted.

**The startup stored procedure cannot allow any parameters.**

The syntax is:

```
sp_procoption @ProcName = <'procedure_name'>,
  @OptionName = 'startup',
  @OptionValue = <'true'_or_'false'>
```

### Example 14.42.1: Enabling a stored procedure to run during SQL Server startup

The following example configures the pr_Clean_Up procedure to run automatically during SQL Server startup:

```
EXEC sp_procoption @ProcName = 'pr_Clean_Up',
  @OptionName = 'startup',
  @OptionValue = 'true'
```

# 14.43 How to... Force a Stored Procedure to Recompile

When table data referenced from within a stored procedure undergoes significant changes, or new indexes are added to the referenced tables, your current stored procedure execution plan may not run as efficiently as it once did.

By recompiling a stored procedure, you optimize the execution plan for the current database state. You can use the system stored procedure sp_recompile to mark a stored procedure for recompilation the next time someone executes it. The sp_recompile procedure can also be used to recompile triggers.

The syntax is as follows:

```
sp_recompile @objname = <'object_name'>
```

### Example 14.43.1: Recompiling a stored procedure

```
EXEC sp_recompile @objname = 'pr_Calcdate'
```

After executing this example, the following output is produced:

Object 'pr_Calcdate' was successfully marked for recompilation.

# 14.44 How to... Print the Text of the Stored Procedure

To display the text definition of an unencrypted stored procedure, use the `sp_helptext` system stored procedure. This procedure can also be used to display the text definition for a default, user-defined function, trigger, view, or rule. The syntax is as follows:

```
sp_helptext @objname = <'object_name'>
```

### Example 14.44.1: Displaying the text definition of a stored procedure

```
sp_helptext @objname = 'pr_Insert_Books'
```

This example would return the following:

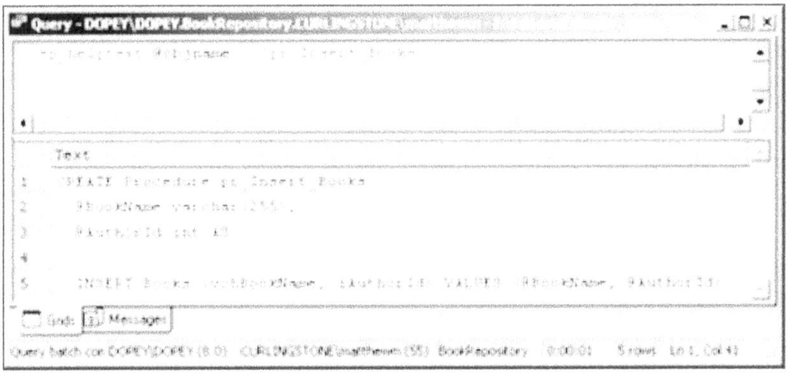


# 14.45 How to... Force a Flush of the Procedure Cache

Stored procedure execution plans are kept in the part of the memory pool called the **procedure cache**. If you are looking to test the initial compilation times of a stored procedure, you can use the `DBCC FREEPROCCACHE` command to clear all execution plans from the procedure cache.

Executing this command will cause all procedures to recompile, as well as any Transact-SQL statements that may be using existing execution plans.

> **Do not run this command on production databases, as it affects the entire procedure cache.**

### Example 14.45.1: Clearing the procedure cache

The DBCC FREEPROCCACHE takes no parameters:

```
DBCC FREEPROCCACHE
```

Executing this command returns the following output:

DBCC execution completed. If DBCC printed error messages, contact your system administrator.

# 14.46 How to... Add an Extended Stored Procedure

Extended stored procedures allow you to extend the functionality of SQL Server by referencing functionality from dynamic link libraries (DLLs).

Database users call extended stored procedures and pass parameters to them, just as with regular stored procedures. Extended stored procedures are defined by referencing a DLL file and are not defined with Transact-SQL statements like a regular stored procedure. Because a DLL is loaded and used from within SQL Server, there is an increased risk of memory leaks or performance issues (depending on the DLL). If a DLL misbehaves, SQL Server can crash.

To add an extended stored procedure, use the system stored procedure `sp_addextendedproc`. The syntax is as follows:

```
sp_addextendedproc @functname = <'procedurename'>,
                   @dllname = <'dll_name'>
```

Place the DLL file you wish to add into the SQL Server instance `Binn` directory; the DLL name is limited to 255 characters. The extended stored procedure can only be added to the `master` database.

### Example 14.46.1: Adding an extended stored procedure

The following example adds the extended stored procedure `xp_scrubdata`:

```
USE master
EXEC sp_addextendedproc xp_scrubdata, 'scrubdata.dll'
```

To reference the extended stored procedure, call it as you would a regular stored procedure, including any parameters that may be required:

```
EXEC master.dbo.xp_scrubdata
```

# 14.47 How to... Show the Name of the DLL Associated with an Extended Stored Procedure

You can list the DLL references for a single or for all extended stored procedures for your SQL Server instance by executing `sp_helpextendedproc`.

### Example 14.47.1: Listing all extended stored procedures for a SQL Server instance

```
USE master
EXEC sp_helpextendedproc
```

### Example 14.47.2: Listing an extended stored procedure DLL file for a single procedure

The following syntax shows the DLL file for the `xp_subdirs` extended stored procedure:

```
USE master
EXEC sp_helpextendedproc 'xp_subdirs'
```

# 14.48 How to... Unload the Extended Stored Procedure DLL from Memory

When an extended stored procedure is executed, the DLL file is loaded into memory, and is not removed until the SQL Server instance is restarted. To force the DLL from memory without restarting the SQL Server instance, use the `DBCC dllname (FREE)` command.

### Example 14.48.1: Removing a DLL reference from memory

In this example, we remove the DLL for the extended stored procedure `xp_subdirs` from memory by executing:

```
DBCC xp_subdirs (FREE)
```

It is important to realize the DLL references can take up valuable memory address space within SQL Server; this can impact the amount of space available for use by the buffer cache and procedure cache.

# 14.49 How to... Remove an Extended Stored Procedure

Use the `sp_dropextendedproc` system stored procedure to drop an extended stored procedure. This procedure takes one parameter – the extended stored procedure name.

### Example 14.49.1: Dropping an extended stored procedure

```
USE master
EXEC sp_dropextendedproc 'xp_scrubdata'
```

# User-Defined Functions

System functions are not new to SQL Server; however, **user-defined functions** (UDFs) were introduced in SQL Server 2000. UDFs allow you to encapsulate logic and subroutines into one function that can then be used within your queries and DML statements.

UDFs, like stored procedures, accept parameters and are defined with Transact-SQL. UDFs, unlike stored procedures, must always return a scalar value or a table, and cannot contain output parameters. UDFs can return all data types, with the exception of the `CURSOR`, `TIMESTAMP`, `TEXT`, `NTEXT`, and `IMAGE` data types.

UDFs can be defined as:

- **Scalar UDFs**
  Return one value, and cannot return table data types.
- **Inline UDFs**
  Return a table data type, and do not explicitly define the returned table, but rather use a single SELECT statement for defining the returned rows and columns.
- **Multistatement UDFs**
  Allow you to generate a table result set, based on Transact-SQL operations within the UDF definition. Multistatement UDFs allow assignment, flow-of-control, DECLARE and SELECT variable assignments, extended stored procedure executions, and **local** table variable DML statements.

  Multistatement UDFs have more restrictions on what is allowed within the UDF definition. Only local cursor operations are allowed within the multistatement UDF definition and they can only be used to assign values to local variables, and they cannot return data to the client.

UDFs can be **deterministic** or **non-deterministic**. A deterministic UDF always returns the same value given the same parameters. Non-deterministic UDFs return a different value or values when executed with the same parameters across multiple executions. Within the UDF definition itself, non-deterministic built-in functions, such as @@CONNECTIONS or GETDATE(), are not allowed (however, they are allowed as parameter values for the UDF call itself).

Extended stored procedure calls are also classed as non-deterministic for the purpose of defining UDFs, because they can cause unpredictable results within the database. You should not reference extended stored procedures that attempt to return result sets.

On a different note, UDFs can also use schemabinding (as described in the review of views earlier in the chapter). Like schemabinding with views, UDF schemabinding prevents you from changing the underlying objects referenced by the UDF, thus preventing changes that could hurt your user-defined function.

For example, if someone changed the data type of a column in a table referenced by the UDF, and the UDF used this column in a calculation, the conversion could break or cause the UDF not to function properly. If you wish to restrict changes to objects referenced from within the UDF, you can define the function with SCHEMABINDING. You can only use this option if objects referenced within the UDFs are also schemabound, and exist within the same database as the UDF.

Schemabound tables can still have columns added or dropped on the base tables, so long as the columns are not referenced by the function. Other objects, such as tables, must exist in the same database of the UDF, and REFERENCES permissions must be granted for all objects referenced in the UDF definition.

UDFs are more flexible than stored procedures, in that they can be utilized in the following ways:

- Within the SELECT clause of a query.
- Used as an expression within a WHERE clause of a query, as a table.
- Within the FROM clause. A function call can also be joined with other tables.
- Used to return one value.
- Used to return a table.
- Used as a substitute for a sub-query.

Some suggested UDF definition practices:

- If you can use an inline UDF instead of a multistatement UDF, do so; as inline UDFs generally run faster than comparable multistatement UDFs.
- If you attempt to create a UDF that returns the result of a CASE statement, which in turn uses a sub-query, you may get an error message if you do not explicitly assign the value to a local variable. Assigning the CASE value to the variable, and returning that variable with the RETURN @variable syntax, solves this. For more details on this bug, see the Microsoft Knowledge Base article 275199, *BUG: UDF that Returns the Results of a CASE with a Correlated Subquery Returns Error Message 107*.
- You cannot make four-part linked server query calls within a UDF. You must instead use the OPENQUERY syntax to access data within a UDF from a linked server.

# 14.50 How to... Create Scalar User-Defined Functions

Scalar UDFs return one value, which can be any data type other than a table, TEXT, NTEXT, IMAGE, or TIMESTAMP. The syntax for a scalar UDF is as follows:

```
CREATE FUNCTION <ownername.scalar_function_name>
  (<@param1>,
  <@paramN...>)
  RETURNS <function_data_type>
  WITH [ENCRYPTION | SCHEMABINDING] AS
BEGIN
  <function_body>
  <RETURN value>
END
GO
```

| Parameter | Description |
|---|---|
| ownername.scalar_function_name | Two-part name of the UDF, with owner first, and then function name. |
| @param1, @paramN... | Parameters for the UDF, allowing up to 1,024 individual parameters. Defaults may be defined, but the function call must include the DEFAULT keyword in place of the parameter. |
| RETURNS <function_data_type> | Can return any data type, with the exception of table, TEXT, NTEXT, IMAGE, or TIMESTAMP. |
| WITH [ENCRYPTION \| SCHEMABINDING] | If used, ENCRYPTION encrypts the text definition of the UDF. When SCHEMABINDING is chosen, underlying and referenced database objects cannot undergo certain changes. |
| <function_body> | Transact-SQL statements for generating the RETURN value for the function. |
| RETURN <value> | The command within the body of the definition that sets the function RETURN value. |

### Example 14.50.1: Creating a scalar user-defined function

The following example creates a user-defined function, called `taxRate`. It takes an input parameter, called `State`, and returns a numeric value, based on the state parameter. So, if the state code of `MN` is provided, a value of .07 is returned:

```
CREATE FUNCTION taxRate (@State nvarchar(2)) RETURNS numeric (2,2) AS
BEGIN
  DECLARE @TaxRate numeric (2,2)
    SELECT @TaxRate = case @State
    WHEN 'MN' Then .07
    WHEN 'WI' Then .05
    WHEN 'WA' Then 0
    WHEN 'NY' Then .11
  ELSE 0
END

RETURN @TaxRate
END
```

You can then instantiate the UDF in a number of ways; for example, you can call the UDF in a `PRINT` statement:

```
PRINT dbo.taxRate('MN')
```

The `PRINT` function returns:

0.07

You can also use the UDF within a `SELECT` statement (or other DML commands).

In this example, the `BookSales` table is referenced in the `FROM` clause. The `taxRate` function takes the `nvchState` column as the input parameter, to determine the tax rate for each row. That value is then multiplied by the value in the `moTotalSales` column to generate total state taxes:

```
SELECT iBookId as 'Book Id',
  moTotalSales as 'Gross Sales',
  moTotalSales * dbo.taxRate('MN')as 'State Taxes'
FROM BookSales
```

In both cases, use the two-part function name, `ownername.scalar_function_name`, to call the UDF.

# 14.51 How to... Create Inline User-Defined Functions

Inline UDFs allow you to return a table result set similar to a view, only the returned results are dynamically generated based on the specified parameters (and the result set is not updateable).

The syntax is as follows:

```
CREATE FUNCTION <owner.inline_function_name>
  (<@param1,
   <@paramN>)
  RETURNS TABLE
  WITH [ENCRYPTION | SCHEMABINDING]
  AS
  RETURN <select statement>
GO
```

| Parameter | Description |
|---|---|
| `owner.inline_function_name` | The two-part name of the UDF, with owner first and then function name. |
| `@param1, @paramN` | Parameters for the UDF, allowing up to 1,024 individual parameters. Defaults may be defined in the definition, but the function call must include the `DEFAULT` keyword in place of the parameter. |
| `RETURNS TABLE` | Required designation for an inline UDF. |
| `WITH [ENCRYPTION \| SCHEMABINDING]` | If `ENCRYPTION` is used, SQL Server encrypts the text definition of the UDF. When `SCHEMABINDING` is chosen, underlying and referenced database objects cannot undergo certain changes. |
| `RETURN <select statement>` | One valid `SELECT` statement. |

### Example 14.51.1: Creating an inline UDF

The following UDF returns a table rowset of books published by an author specified in the parameter:

```
CREATE FUNCTION BooksByAuthor
  (@AuthorId int)
RETURNS TABLE
  AS
  RETURN SELECT vchBookName FROM Books WHERE iAuthorId = @Authorid
GO
```

Once it's created, you can reference the UDF as you would a table. The following example returns all books written by the author with ID `1`:

```
SELECT * FROM dbo.BooksByAuthor (1)
```

# 14.52 How to... Create Multistatement User-Defined Functions

Like inline UDFs, multistatement UDFs return a table rowset. Multistatement UDFs are not constrained to one `SELECT` statement, but rather allow you to use more complicated Transact-SQL statements to define the table output. The syntax is as follows:

```
CREATE FUNCTION <owner.multistatement_function_name>
  (<@param1>,
   <@paramN>)
  RETURNS <@table_variable_name> TABLE
    (<column_name_1> <data_type_for_column1>,
     <column_name_N> <data_type_for_columnN>)
  WITH [ENCRYPTION | SCHEMABINDING]
  AS
  BEGIN
    <Transact-SQL batches>
    RETURN
  END
GO
```

| Parameter | Description |
|---|---|
| `owner.multistatement_function_name` | Two-part name of the UDF, with owner first and then function name. |
| `@param1, @paramN` | Parameters for the UDF, allowing up to 1,024 individual parameters. Defaults may be defined in the definition, but the function call must include the `DEFAULT` keyword in place of the parameter. |
| `RETURNS <@table_variable_name>`<br>`TABLE (<column_name_1> <data_type_for_column1>,`<br>`<column_name_N> <data_type_for_columnN>)` | Definition of the table variable column and associated data types. Unlike inline UDFs, the multistatement UDF must have its columns defined explicitly. |
| `WITH [ENCRYPTION \| SCHEMABINDING]` | If `ENCRYPTION` is used, SQL Server encrypts the text definition of the UDF. When `SCHEMABINDING` is chosen, underlying and referenced database objects cannot undergo certain changes. |
| `<Transact-SQL batches>` | Transact-SQL statements that generate the result set. |

## Example 14.52.1: Creating a multistatement UDF

The following example creates a multistatement UDF that extracts book names based on the supplied author ID, and then adds a header row to the resultant table:

```
CREATE FUNCTION dbo.AddRowHeader (@BookId int)
  RETURNS @KeyValues TABLE (vchBookName varchar(500))
  AS
  BEGIN
    INSERT @KeyValues SELECT vchBookName FROM Books WHERE iBookId = @BookId

    INSERT @KeyValues VALUES (' Books Header ------------')
    RETURN
  END
GO
```

The function can then be referenced as follows:

```
SELECT * FROM dbo.AddRowHeader(1) ORDER BY vchBookName
```

This example returns the book names for author ID `1` and then orders the field. Since the header row has a leading space, it will appear first in the row set.

# 14.53 How to... Modify User-Defined Functions

To change an existing UDF, use the `ALTER FUNCTION` command. You cannot change the function types; for example, you cannot change a scalar function to an inline function.

### Example 14.53.1: Changing an existing user-defined function

The following example adds extra fields to be returned when the `BooksByAuthor` UDF is called:

```
ALTER FUNCTION BooksByAuthor (@AuthorId int)
  RETURNS TABLE
  AS
  RETURN
    SELECT vchBookName, iAuthorid, iBookId FROM Books
      WHERE iAuthorId = @Authorid
```

# 14.54 How to... Drop User-Defined Functions

Use the `DROP FUNCTION` command to drop a UDF. Specify the owner and function two-part name.

### Example 14.54.1: Dropping a UDF

The following example drops the `BooksByAuthor` UDF:

```
DROP FUNCTION BooksByAuthor
```

# Indexes

Indexes assist with query processing by speeding up data access against tables and views. Indexes are defined by selecting an index key, which is made up of one or more columns from the table or view.

If indexes do not exist for a table, that table is called a **heap**; meaning the data pages are stored in no particular order. A heap referenced in queries results in a table scan. A table scan occurs when all rows in the table are evaluated against the required end-result (instead of just a subset of the data). For example, let's say we have a table called `Employees`; if you wanted to issue a query against this table for all those employees with a last name of `Smith`, in the absence of an index, **all rows** would need to be read and evaluated by the query processor. Hence, we can use indexes to prevent this from happening.

SQL Server 2000 provides two types of indexes, **clustered** and **nonclustered**. SQL Server uses a **B-Tree** data structure for each clustered and nonclustered index. When an index is used, SQL Server navigates from the B-Tree structure's root and traverses down to the leaf nodes. For a table with a clustered index, the leaf nodes are the data pages themselves:

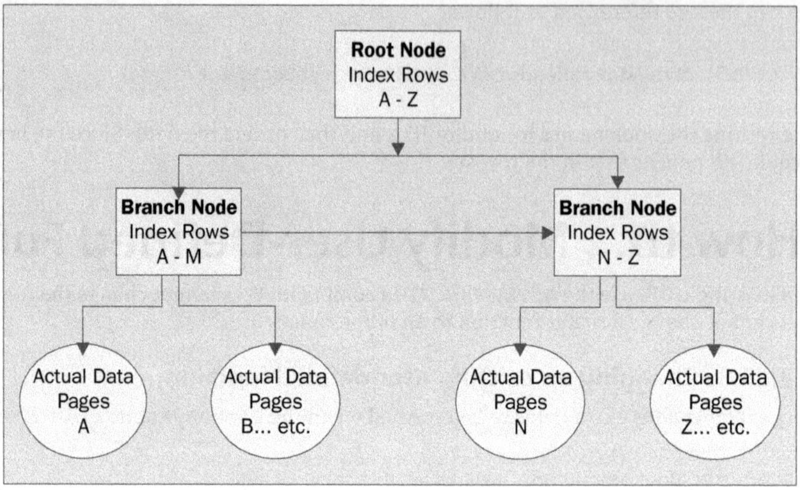


Clustered indexes determine the physical order of data in a table. Since data pages can only be physically stored in one way, for one table, you can only have one clustered index for each table. Because clustered indexes physically arrange data pages in order of the index key (or keys) during index creation, clustered indexes have the benefit of reducing data page fragmentation. After a clustered index is created, data pages are physically contiguous, which can assist with the speed of queries.

Nonclustered indexes store index pages separately from the physical data, with pointers to the physical data located in the index pages and nodes. Nonclustered index columns are stored in the order of the index key column values. You can have up to 249 nonclustered indexes on each table or indexed view.

For nonclustered indexes, the leaf node level is the index key coupled to a bookmark. The nonclustered index bookmark points to the B-Tree structure of the table's clustered index (if one exists). If the base table is a heap, the nonclustered index bookmark points to the table row's Row-ID (row identifier):

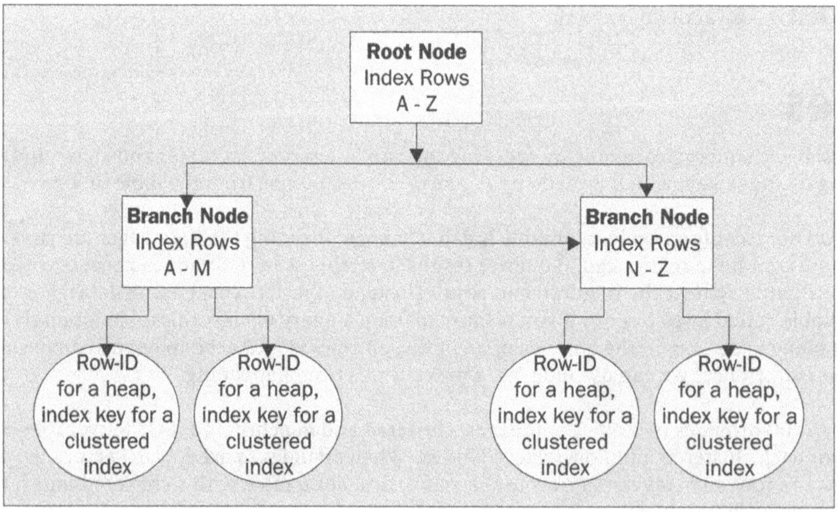

# To Index or not to Index?

Indexes should be added to a table based on the anticipated query activity for the tables in your database. Do not add indexes without proper evidence that database queries will benefit. Since the query optimizer does not always choose the best execution plan, you should perform tests to make sure your indexes are actually being used. Indexes take up space, and should not be added 'just in case'. Tools for testing the effectiveness of your indexes are reviewed in Chapter 17.

Indexes can slow down data loads significantly, and may not make sense for tables that are used expressly for data imports and staging. If your table will not be queried and is used as an intermediate staging ground, leaving indexes off the table may be a better choice. The same goes for very small tables where, no matter what, the query optimizer always performs a table scan.

Keep in mind that heaps become naturally fragmented over time and, if data updates are frequent enough, even small tables can begin to take up more space than necessary. There are those who believe that a clustered index should exist for every table in the database, period. One technique for reducing bulk load operations on a table is to remove the index during the load and add the index once the load is finished.

# Selecting a Clustered Index

Clustered index selection is a critical choice, as you can only have one clustered index for each table. In general, good candidates for clustered indexes include columns that are queried often in range queries. Range queries use the `BETWEEN` keyword and the greater than (>) and less than (<) operators. Other columns to consider are those used to order large result sets, those used in aggregate functions, and those that are whose contents are distinct (such as primary or unique keys).

Frequently updated columns and non-unique columns are not a good choice for the clustered index key. Lastly, choose a smaller clustered index key over a wider column, reducing the size of the index needed and improving I/O operations.

Every table should have a clustered index, unless you have a very compelling reason not to have one (very small tables, with relatively static data, may not need one).

# Selecting a Nonclustered Index

When selecting columns for nonclustered indexes, look for those columns that are referenced frequently in the `WHERE` clause. Search for columns involved in searchable arguments using operators such as =, <, >, `IN`, `EXISTS`, and `LIKE`. These operators encourage index utilization and help narrow the search for th e query processor.

Nonclustered indexes are good for queries that pull smaller result sets on unique data. Index columns are used frequently in `JOIN` and `ORDER BY` clauses.

# 14.55 How to... Create an Index

Earlier in the chapter, constraints were reviewed as one method of creating an index on a table. The other method is to use the `CREATE INDEX` command. The syntax from SQL Server Books Online is as follows:

```
CREATE [ UNIQUE ] [ CLUSTERED | NONCLUSTERED ] INDEX index_name
    ON { table | view } ( column [ ASC | DESC ] [ ,...n ] )
[ WITH < index_option > [ ,...n] ]
[ ON filegroup ]

< index_option > :: =
```

```
    { PAD_INDEX |
        FILLFACTOR = fillfactor |
        IGNORE_DUP_KEY |
        DROP_EXISTING |
    STATISTICS_NORECOMPUTE |
    SORT_IN_TEMPDB
}
```

| Parameter | Description |
|---|---|
| UNIQUE | If used, the index key or keys must be 100% unique (no two rows are alike). Exactly one null value is allowed, if the key column allows nulls. |
| CLUSTERED | Creates a clustered index. |
| NONCLUSTERED | Creates a nonclustered index. |
| index_name | The unique name of the index being created. |
| { table \| view } | The name of the table or view to which you are adding the index. |
| ( column [ ASC \| DESC ] [ ,...n ] ) | The column or columns used for the index key. The default ordering for the columns is ascending; however, you can use DESC to sort the index in descending order.<br><br>Total index key length for all columns cannot exceed 900 bytes for fixed columns. If a combination of variable length and fixed columns is less than 900 bytes, but could potentially exceed that (due to variable length columns), a warning will be issued (but the index will be created). |
| [ WITH < index_option > [ ,...n] ] | Specifies one or more options (which are specified after [ON filegroup]). |
| PAD_INDEX | PAD_INDEX is used if FILLFACTOR is specified. PAD_INDEX specifies the space to leave open on each index page. If not selected, SQL Server makes sure the index page has enough empty space for one row. |
| FILLFACTOR = fillfactor | The FILLFACTOR percentage determines how full the leaf level of the index pages should be when the index is first created. Tables with high update-to-read ratios should consider modifying the FILLFACTOR to leave space for new rows; otherwise, excessive page splitting could occur. A page split operation occurs when an index page becomes full and SQL Server must split the rows of the index page to a new index page to make room for new rows.<br><br>Specifying both 0 and 100% translates to a leaf page that is 100% full. When a fill factor is too low, database queries can suffer, as more data pages must be read to fulfill the query request. |
| IGNORE_DUP_KEY | This option can be used for unique clustered and unique nonclustered indexes. When set, warnings are issued when a duplicate row is added to the table, but the transaction is allowed. If IGNORE_DUP_KEY is not used, an error is raised and the transaction is rolled back. |

| Parameter | Description |
|---|---|
| DROP_EXISTING | When chosen, an existing index is dropped and rebuilt. The advantage over selecting an explicit DROP and CREATE is that nonclustered indexes are only rebuilt if the keys are different. |
| STATISTICS_NORECOMPUTE | When set, statistics are not automatically recomputed after the index is finished. An explicit UPDATE STATISTICS must be executed. |
| SORT_IN_TEMPDB | This option sorts results for the index build in tempdb, instead of in the table's database, potentially reducing the creation time (depending on the physical location of tempdb), but increasing the amount of space needed in tempdb for the sorting operation. |
| [ON filegroup] | This option lets you specify a specific filegroup for your index pages to be stored. If you are using a CLUSTERED index, keep in mind that the data pages will be stored on the filegroup you specify. |

### Example 14.55.1: Create a clustered index

This example creates a clustered index for the iBookId column in the Books table:

```
CREATE CLUSTERED INDEX idx_BookID ON Books (iBookId)
```

### Example 14.55.2: Create a nonclustered index

This example creates a nonclustered index, using two columns, on the Books table:

```
CREATE NONCLUSTERED INDEX idx_Name_Author ON Books (vchBookName, iAuthorId)
```

### Example 14.55.3: Specify a fill factor

This example creates a nonclustered index, specifying a fill factor of 75% and leaving space on the index page (PAD_INDEX):

```
CREATE NONCLUSTERED INDEX idx_Name_Author ON Books (vchBookName, iAuthorId)
WITH FILLFACTOR = 75, PAD_INDEX
```

### Example 14.55.4: Placing the index on a different file group and sorting in tempdb

This example creates a nonclustered index, sets the sort operations to occur in tempdb, while placing the index itself on the FG2 filegroup:

```
CREATE NONCLUSTERED INDEX idx_Name_Author ON Books (vchBookName, iAuthorId)
WITH SORT_IN_TEMPDB
ON FG2
```

# 14.56 How to... Drop an Index

Use the DROP INDEX syntax to remove a non-constraint generated index. The syntax is as follows:

```
DROP INDEX <table.index_name or view.index_name>
```

### Example 14.56.1: Dropping an index

The following example drops the idx_Name_Author index from the Books table:

```
DROP INDEX Books.idx_Name_Author
```

# 14.57 How to... Display Indexes Defined for a Table

To display all indexes defined for a table, use the system stored procedure sp_helpindex. This procedure takes one parameter; the table or view name for which to list all indexes.

### Example 14.57.1: List all indexes for a table

In this example, all indexes will be listed for the Books table:

```
EXEC sp_helpindex 'Books'
```

In this example, sp_helpindex returns the index name, description, and index keys for the Books table:

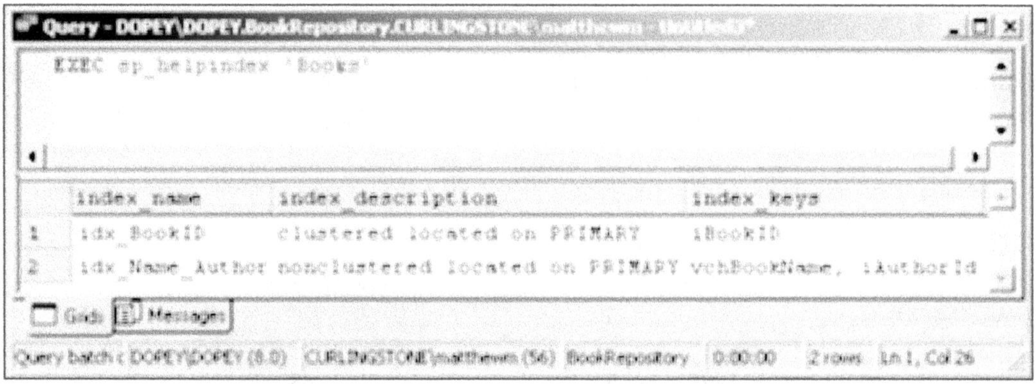


# Triggers

Triggers respond to user INSERT, UPDATE, or DELETE operations against a table or a view. When a data modification event occurs, the trigger performs a set of actions defined within the trigger. Triggers are defined in Transact-SQL and allow a full range of activities to be performed, much like stored procedures. Triggers are useful for complicated data validation routines and cleanup operations.

A trigger can be defined specifically as FOR UPDATE, FOR INSERT, FOR DELETE, or any combination of the three. UPDATE triggers respond to modifications against one or more columns within the table; INSERT triggers respond to new data being added to the database; and DELETE triggers respond to data being deleted from the database.

There are two types of triggers, AFTER triggers and INSTEAD OF triggers. AFTER triggers execute after the data modification has been completed against the table. INSTEAD OF triggers execute instead of the original data modification. INSTEAD OF triggers are allowed for both tables and views.

Multiple triggers can be defined for one table. The order in which they are fired can be configured using the sp_settriggerorder stored procedure (reviewed later in the chapter).

The **nested triggers** server option will determine if triggers can cause other triggers to fire (cascading triggers). If enabled, triggers can cascade in a chain of up to 32 firings.

Watch out for **recursive** trigger firing. Recursive trigger firing occurs when a trigger fires and that firing causes an action to fire the same table trigger again. This can also occur when a trigger fires, which in turn impacts a different table, causing that table's trigger to fire and perform an action against the original table. If the database option RECURSIVE_TRIGGERS is set OFF (the default), such behavior is prevented.

SQL Server creates two "virtual" tables specifically for triggers, the deleted and inserted tables. These two tables capture before and after pictures of the modified data. The following table shows what tables each update type impacts:

| Operation | inserted Table Holds... | deleted Table Holds... |
|---|---|---|
| INSERT | Inserted rows | n/a |
| UPDATE | New rows (rows with updates) | Old rows (pre-update) |
| DELETE | n/a | Deleted rows |

The inserted and deleted tables can be used within your trigger to validate and use the before and after data modifications. They will store data for both single row and multi-row updates. Be sure to program your triggers with both types of updates (single and multi-row) in mind. For example, a DELETE operation can impact just one row or fifty rows – so make sure the trigger is programmed to handle this accordingly.

When working with triggers, keep in mind the following:

- Triggers should be written to run quickly. Long-running triggers can slow down data modification operations significantly.
- Non-logged updates do not cause the trigger to fire (for example WRITETEXT, bulk insert operations).
- Constraints usually run faster than a trigger; so, if your business requirements can be fulfilled by a constraint, use constraints instead.
- Do not return result sets from a SELECT statement within your trigger.
- You can only create triggers on tables that you own (or are the sysadmin for).
- If cascading referential integrity for DELETE or UPDATE is defined for the base table, you cannot define an INSTEAD OF DELETE or INSTEAD OF UPDATE on that table.
- Avoid Transact-SQL cursors within your triggers. Cursors can incur significant performance overhead, particularly if updates cause the trigger to fire repeatedly.
- AFTER triggers run after the data modification has already occurred, so they cannot be used to prevent a constraint violation.

# 14.58 How to... Create a Trigger

A trigger is created using the CREATE TRIGGER command. The syntax is as follows:

```
CREATE TRIGGER <trigger_name>
  ON <table_name or view_name>
  [ WITH ENCRYPTION ]
  [ (FOR  or AFTER) DELETE, INSERT, UPDATE |
```

```
    INSTEAD OF DELETE, INSERT, UPDATE ]
    [WITH APPEND]
    [NOT FOR REPLICATION]
    AS
    BEGIN
      <transact_sql_statements>
    END
  GO
```

| Parameter | Description |
|---|---|
| <trigger_name> | Unique name of the trigger. |
| <table_name or view_name> | Table or view name. |
| [ WITH ENCRYPTION ] | Encrypts the Transact-SQL trigger definition. |
| [ (FOR or AFTER) DELETE, INSERT, UPDATE \| INSTEAD OF DELETE, INSERT, UPDATE ] | You can use FOR or AFTER interchangeably and on tables. After choosing FOR or AFTER, you can select one or more modification types from DELETE, INSERT, or UPDATE.<br>If you are defining an INSTEAD OF trigger, use INSTEAD OF, rather than FOR or AFTER. You can then use one or more modification types. |
| [WITH APPEND] | WITH APPEND is included for backward compatibility only, and should only be used if you are using compatibility level 65 or lower. It specifies that a trigger of an existing type is to be added (that is, there is already an INSERT trigger defined for the table). |
| [NOT FOR REPLICATION] | Specifies that the trigger should not be executed when a replication modification is performed against the table. |

### Example 14.58.1: Creating an AFTER trigger for INSERT

The following example creates an AFTER trigger on the Books table. It uses the virtual table inserted to get a count of inserted rows in the Books table. Assuming each row specifies a unique book, this count is then added to the existing total books count:

```
CREATE TRIGGER trg_BookAudit ON Books FOR INSERT
  AS
  BEGIN
    UPDATE Inventory
      SET iTotalBooks = iTotalBooks + (SELECT COUNT(*) FROM inserted)
  END
GO
```

### Example 14.58.2: Creating an AFTER trigger for UPDATE

The following example creates a trigger on the Books table for UPDATE modifications. The first section uses the IF UPDATE() function, available for triggers, to evaluate if a column has or has not been modified. In this case, if vchBookName was not modified, the trigger is ended with a RETURN statement.

The trigger then updates a table called AuditUpdates, which records the old vchBookName value or values and the new vchBookName value or values. Notice that this trigger is written in such a way as to insert single or multiple row updates into the AuditUpdates table:

```
CREATE TRIGGER trg_Books_Update ON Books FOR UPDATE
  AS
  IF NOT UPDATE(vchBookName)
    RETURN
BEGIN

    INSERT AuditUpdates SELECT 'Books', USER, GETDATE(),
           'vchBookName', deleted.vchBookName, inserted.vchBookName
    FROM inserted, deleted WHERE inserted.iBookId = deleted.iBookId
  END
GO
```

The IF UPDATE (column) function tests to see if an INSERT or UPDATE has occurred against a specific column. You can specify multiple evaluations using IF UPDATE (column) separated with AND or OR.

The IF (COLUMNS_UPDATED()) function tests to see which columns were updated by an INSERT or UPDATE trigger. The COLUMNS_UPDATED() function returns a VARBINARY bit pattern, which can be used to determine the inserted or updated columns. Using this function can get a little complicated, and may be difficult to use for tables with more than 32 columns. For a summary of this function, see Microsoft Knowledge Base article Q232195, *INF: Proper Use of the COLUMNS_UPDATED() Function*.

### Example 14.58.3: Creating an AFTER trigger for DELETE

This example creates a trigger that restricts books with a title containing "SQL" from being deleted from the table. The ROLLBACK TRANSACTION command will cancel the DELETE operation. Note that if multiple rows are deleted in one transaction, with some containing "SQL" and others not, the entire transaction is rolled back (no partial deletes are performed):

```
CREATE TRIGGER trg_Books_Delete ON Books FOR DELETE
  AS

IF EXISTS (SELECT * FROM deleted WHERE vchBookName LIKE '%SQL%')
  BEGIN
    RAISERROR ('SQL-related books should not be deleted.', 16, 1)
    ROLLBACK TRANSACTION
  END
GO
```

### Example 14.58.4: Creating an INSTEAD OF trigger

The following INSTEAD OF trigger is defined for the vBookAuthors view. When an INSERT operation is issued against the view columns, the trigger will fire and create an INSERT operation against the Books table and the Authors table:

```
CREATE TRIGGER trg_BookAuthor_INSTEAD ON vBookAuthors INSTEAD OF INSERT
  AS

  INSERT Books (vchBookName, iAuthorId)
    SELECT inserted.vchBookName, inserted.iAuthorId FROM inserted

  INSERT Authors (iAuthorId, vchLastName, vchFirstName)
    SELECT inserted.iAuthorId, inserted.vchLastName, inserted.vchFirstName
      FROM inserted
GO
```

# 14.59 How to... Alter a Trigger

Use the ALTER TRIGGER command to change the definition of an existing trigger. The parameters for ALTER TRIGGER are the same as for CREATE TRIGGER.

### Example 14.59.1: Changing an existing trigger

The following example modifies the trg_Books_Delete trigger by adding a new RAISERROR statement to warn users to contact management. Also, if a new SQL-related book is inserted, a PRINT statement will be returned commenting on this choice of topic:

```
ALTER TRIGGER trg_Books_Delete ON Books FOR DELETE, INSERT
  AS

  IF EXISTS (SELECT * FROM deleted WHERE vchBookName LIKE '%SQL%')
    BEGIN
      RAISERROR ('SQL-related books should not be deleted. Contact management if
this book MUST be deleted.', 16, 1)
      ROLLBACK TRANSACTION
    END
  ELSE
  IF EXISTS (SELECT * FROM inserted WHERE vchBookName LIKE '%SQL%')
     BEGIN
       PRINT 'Another SQL book?  Well... okay.'
     END

GO
```

# 14.60 How to... Drop a Trigger

Use the DROP TRIGGER command to drop a trigger. This command takes one parameter, the trigger's name.

### Example 14.60.1: Dropping a trigger

```
DROP TRIGGER trg_Books_Delete
```

# 14.61 How to... Monitor the Nesting Level within a Trigger

Use the TRIGGER_NESTLEVEL function within a trigger to determine the levels of nesting for a particular trigger. The value returned will show the number of levels deep from which a trigger is being fired. For example, if Trigger A calls Trigger B and Trigger B calls Trigger C, the nesting level is 3.

If you wish to restrict nesting level to a certain level, you could use the following in your trigger code:

```
IF (TRIGGER_NESTLEVEL()) > 2
  RETURN
```

# 14.62 How to... Specify the Firing Order of AFTER Triggers

For tables with multiple triggers, you can choose the first and last triggers that should be fired by using the sp_settriggerorder system stored procedure. The syntax is as follows:

```
sp_settriggerorder @triggername = <'triggername'>,
                   @order = <'first_last_none'>,
                   @stmttype = <'UPDATE_INSERT_DELETE'>
```

| Parameter | Description |
|---|---|
| @triggername = <'triggername'> | Name of the trigger for which you wish to choose the firing order. |
| @order = <'first_last_none'> | Select first, last, or none. When none is chosen, the trigger fires in no particular order. |
| @stmttype = <'UPDATE_INSERT_DELETE'> | Select the transaction type for which the trigger was defined, UPDATE, INSERT, or DELETE. If the type you specify differs from the trigger definition, the sp_settriggerorder statement will fail. |

### Example 14.62.1: Setting the trigger order

```
EXEC sp_settriggerorder @triggername = 'trg_Books_Delete',
                        @order =  'first',
                        @stmttype =  'DELETE'
```

# 14.63 How to... List Triggers for Table

Use the sp_helptrigger stored procedure to list all triggers for a specific table. The sp_helptrigger procedure takes the name of the table or view you wish to examine as its first parameter. Its second parameter is optional, allowing you to narrow down the result set to one type of trigger (DELETE, INSERT, or UPDATE).

### Example 14.63.1: Listing triggers for a table

```
sp_helptrigger 'Books'
```

This example returns the following result set:

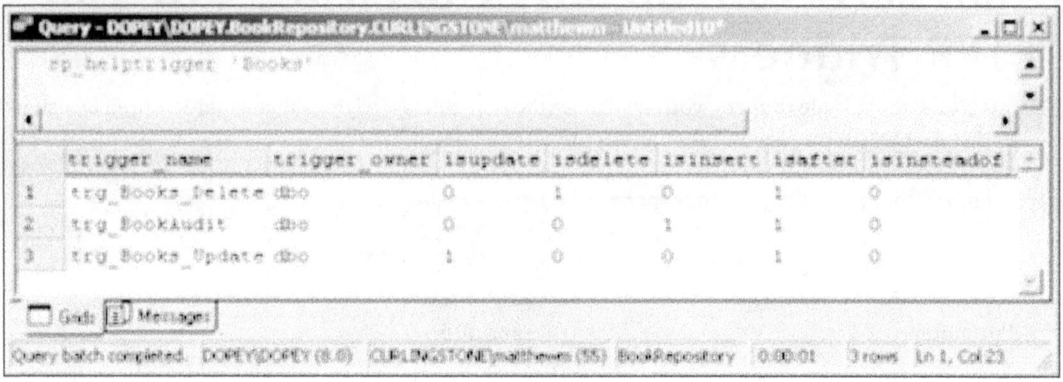

| | trigger_name | trigger_owner | isupdate | isdelete | isinsert | isafter | isinsteadof |
|---|---|---|---|---|---|---|---|
| 1 | trg_Books_Delete | dbo | 0 | 1 | 0 | 1 | 0 |
| 2 | trg_BookAudit | dbo | 0 | 0 | 1 | 1 | 0 |
| 3 | trg_Books_Update | dbo | 1 | 0 | 0 | 1 | 0 |

This displays the trigger name, owner, type of trigger (DELETE, INSERT, or UPDATE), and whether or not it is an AFTER or an INSTEAD OF trigger.

### Example 14.63.2: Listing only INSERT triggers for a table

```
sp_helptrigger 'Books', 'INSERT'
```

Note that specifying one type of trigger does not mean triggers with multiple types will not also be returned. For instance, this example returns trg_BookAudit (INSERT) and trg_Books_Delete (DELETE and INSERT):

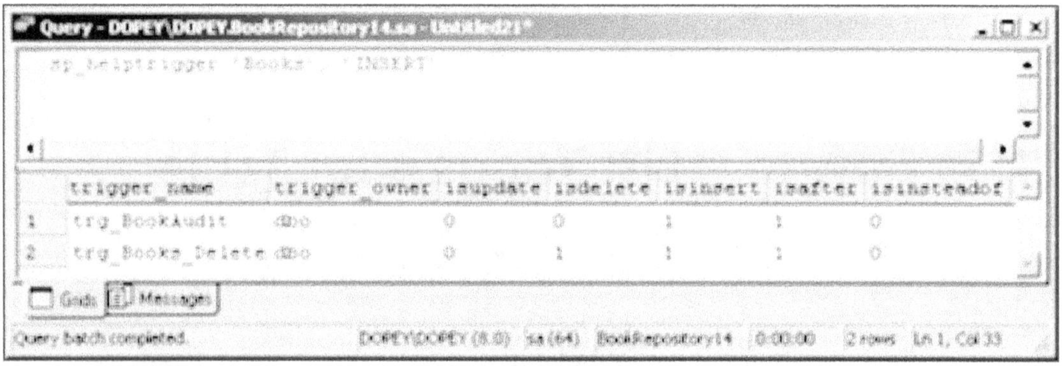

| | trigger_name | trigger_owner | isupdate | isdelete | isinsert | isafter | isinsteadof |
|---|---|---|---|---|---|---|---|
| 1 | trg_BookAudit | dbo | 0 | 0 | 1 | 1 | 0 |
| 2 | trg_Books_Delete | dbo | 0 | 1 | 1 | 1 | 0 |

# 14.64 How to... Enable and Disable Table Triggers

Use the ALTER TABLE command to disable or enable triggers defined for a table. A disabled trigger still exists, but is not fired when an INSERT, UPDATE, or DELETE operation occurs.

### Example 14.64.1: Disable all triggers for a table

```
ALTER TABLE Books
DISABLE TRIGGER ALL
```

### Example 14.64.2: Disable a specific trigger for a table

```
ALTER TABLE Books
DISABLE TRIGGER trg_BookAudit
```

### Example 14.64.3: Enable all triggers for a table

```
ALTER TABLE Books
ENABLE TRIGGER ALL
```

# Working with Database Objects

The last section of this chapter will review general techniques for working with database objects in general.

# 14.65 How to... Change the Name of a User-Created Database Object

To rename a database object, use the `sp_rename` system stored procedure. Use this procedure with caution, as changing object names can break references to the object referenced in triggers, stored procedures, views, or anything else that may be expecting the original name. The syntax is as follows:

```
sp_rename @objname = <'object_name'>,
          @newname = <'new_name'>,
          @objtype = <'object_type'>
```

| Parameter | Description |
|---|---|
| `@objname = <'object_name'>` | Name of object that you wish to rename. |
| `@newname = <'new_name'>` | New name of object. |
| `@objtype = <'object_type'>` | Object type – defaulting to `NULL`. If set, selections are `column`, `database`, `index`, `object`, or `userdatatype`. |

### Example 14.65.1: Renaming a trigger

This example renames the `trg_BookAudit` trigger to `trg_BookAudit_INSERT`:

```
EXEC sp_rename 'trg_BookAudit', 'trg_BookAudit_INSERT'
```

After running, the following output is generated in Query Analyzer:

Caution: Changing any part of an object name could break scripts and stored procedures.
The object was renamed to 'trg_BookAudit_INSERT'.

### Example 14.65.2: Renaming a table column

The following example renames a column in the `Authors` table. Note that the first parameter uses the `tablename.columnname` syntax, while the second parameter just references the column name. Do not use the `tablename.columnname` syntax for the second parameter, or SQL Server will create the new column with this value as the **literal** name:

```
EXEC sp_rename 'Authors.vchIndicator', 'vchIndicator', 'column'
```

# 14.66 How to... Display Information About a Database Object

Use the `sp_help` system stored procedure to return helpful information about a database object. This procedure takes one parameter, the object name.

## Example 14.66.1: List all objects for a database

The following syntax lists all objects for the database, including tables, views, user-defined functions, user-defined data types, constraints, stored procedures, and defaults:

```
EXEC sp_help
```

## Example 14.66.2: List information for a specific object

The following example lists information about the `Books` table:

```
EXEC sp_help 'Books'
```

This returns the table creation date, columns, data types, identity properties, filegroup location, and indexes:

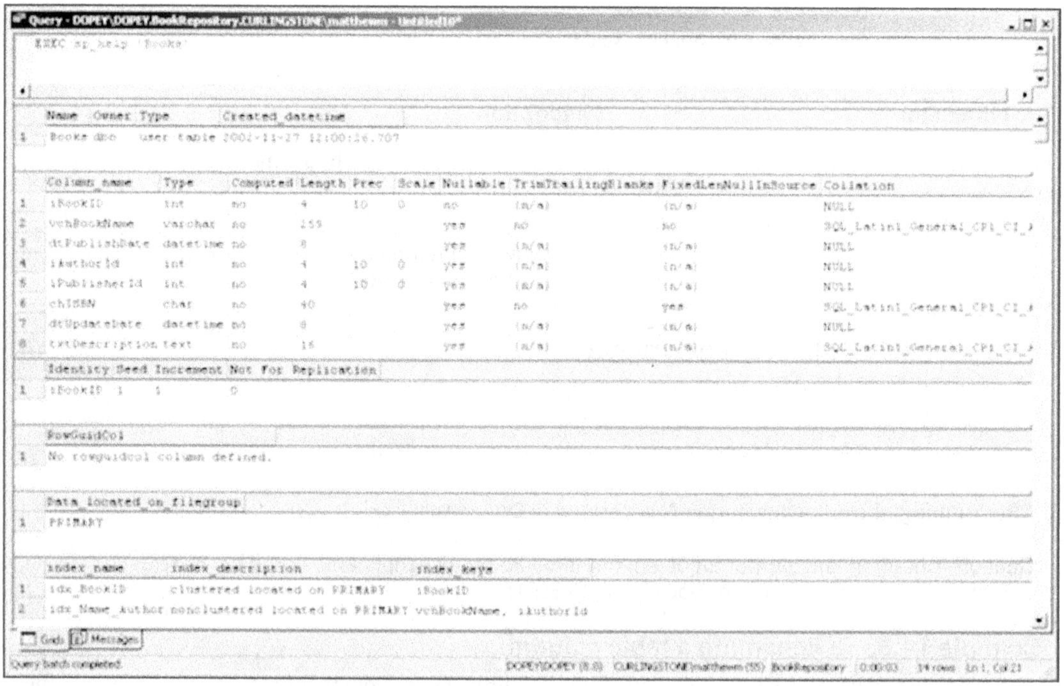

| | Name | Owner | Type | Created_datetime |
|---|---|---|---|---|
| 1 | Books | dbo | user table | 2002-11-27 12:00:16.707 |

| | Column_name | Type | Computed | Length | Prec | Scale | Nullable | TrimTrailingBlanks | FixedLenNullInSource | Collation |
|---|---|---|---|---|---|---|---|---|---|---|
| 1 | iBookID | int | no | 4 | 10 | 0 | no | (n/a) | (n/a) | NULL |
| 2 | vchBookName | varchar | no | 255 | | | yes | no | no | SQL_Latin1_General_CP1_CI_A |
| 3 | dtPublishDate | datetime | no | 8 | | | yes | (n/a) | (n/a) | NULL |
| 4 | iAuthorId | int | no | 4 | 10 | 0 | yes | (n/a) | (n/a) | NULL |
| 5 | iPublisherId | int | no | 4 | 10 | 0 | yes | (n/a) | (n/a) | NULL |
| 6 | chISBN | char | no | 40 | | | yes | no | yes | SQL_Latin1_General_CP1_CI_A |
| 7 | dtUpdateDate | datetime | no | 8 | | | yes | (n/a) | (n/a) | NULL |
| 8 | txtDescription | text | no | 16 | | | yes | (n/a) | (n/a) | SQL_Latin1_General_CP1_CI_A |

| | Identity | Seed | Increment | Not For Replication |
|---|---|---|---|---|
| 1 | iBookID | 1 | 1 | 0 |

| | RowGuidCol |
|---|---|
| 1 | No rowguidcol column defined. |

| | Data_located_on_filegroup |
|---|---|
| 1 | PRIMARY |

| | index_name | index_description | index_keys |
|---|---|---|---|
| 1 | idx_BookID | clustered located on PRIMARY | iBookID |
| 2 | idx_Name_Author | nonclustered located on PRIMARY | vchBookName, iAuthorId |

# 14.67 How to... Display Information on Database Object Dependencies

When you create objects such as foreign key constraints, views, stored procedures, and triggers, you create **dependencies** on other database objects. Dependencies cause problems if you change the referenced objects without changing the object doing the referencing. For example, changing a table name without changing its name in a UDF will cause the UDF to break.

Use the sp_depends system stored procedure to reveal dependencies for an object. This procedure is limited to reporting dependencies within the database only. This procedure takes only one parameter, the object's name.

## Example 14.67.1: Showing dependencies for a table

```
EXEC sp_depends 'Books'
```

This call returns a list of objects referring to or depending on the Books table:

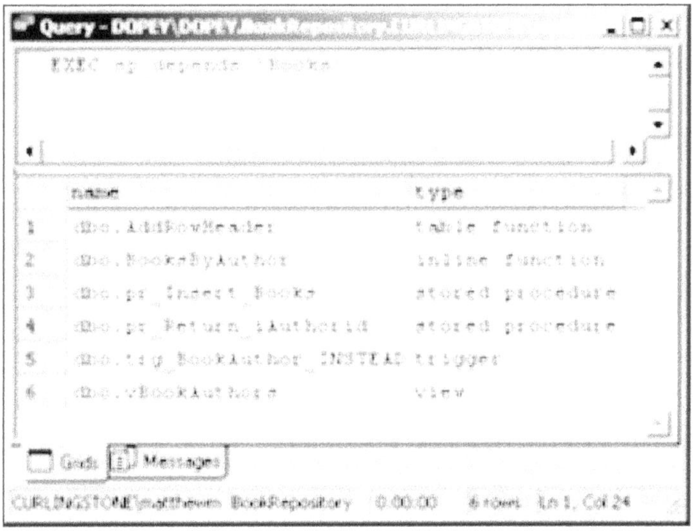


sp_depends will not list dependencies on objects that involve **deferred name resolution**. Deferred name resolution means that the object may or may not exist when the stored procedure is first compiled; however, it must exist when first executed. If the object does not exist in the stored procedure when it is initially run, the stored procedure may fail with an error. For example, the following procedure pr_ReadBogusTable references a table called meow that does not exist:

```
CREATE PROCEDURE pr_ReadBogusTable AS
SELECT *
FROM meow
```

However, if you attempt to execute this procedure:

```
EXEC pr_ReadBogusTable
```

The following error will be returned:

```
Server: Msg 208, Level 16, State 1, Procedure pr_ReadBogusTable, Line 3
Invalid object name 'meow'.
```

So the lesson for deferred name resolution is that you should check your object references carefully, prior to compiling your stored procedure; ensure that the object exists, or is created within the procedure itself.

Regarding the deferred object resolution bug with `sp_depends`, see Microsoft Knowledge Base article 201846, *BUG: Reference to Deferred Object in Stored Procedure Will Not Show in Sp_depends*, for more information.

> **One last gotcha – if a stored procedure or view depends on a table that is dropped, you must drop and recreate the stored procedure or view for the changes to be properly reflected in `sysdepends`. This bug may be fixed in the future.**

# 14.68 How to... Change an Object Owner

To change the owner of a database object, use the `sp_changeobjectowner` system stored procedure. This procedure takes two parameters, the first is the object and the second specifies the new object owner.

### Example 14.68.1: Change the owner of a table object

This example changes the table `Books`, owned by `JackSmith`, to be owned by `dbo`:

```
EXEC sp_changeobjectowner 'JackSmith.Books', 'dbo'
```

This command returns the following output:

```
Caution: Changing any part of an object name could break scripts and stored procedures.
```

# 14.69 How to... Query the Meta Data of Database Objects

The `OBJECTPROPERTY` function allows you to query meta data properties of your database objects. The syntax is as follows:

```
SELECT OBJECTPROPERTY (object_id , property_name)
```

| Parameter | Description |
|---|---|
| `object_id` | Database `object_id`. This value can be retrieved by using the function `OBJECT_ID('object_name')`. |
| `property_name` | Name of property you wish to retrieve. |

### Example 14.69.1: Checking if the table has an INSERT trigger

The following call to `OBJECTPROPERTY` uses the `OBJECT_ID()` function for the first parameter and `HasInsertTrigger` for the property being validated:

```
SELECT OBJECTPROPERTY (OBJECT_ID('Books'), 'HasInsertTrigger')
```

This function returns `1` if the `Books` table has an `INSERT` trigger and `0` if not.

See SQL Server Books Online for a comprehensive listing of available object properties.

# 15

# DML

Data Manipulation Language (DML) provides a means of retrieving and modifying data within the database. DML statements include SELECT, INSERT, UPDATE, and DELETE. This chapter will review the syntax and usage of each of these operations. We will also explore the basic techniques often performed with DML statements, including the use of table aliases, self joins, subqueries, derived tables, UNION, COMPUTE, CUBE, ROLLUP, TRUNCATE, and query hints.

## 15.1 How to... Use a Simple SELECT Statement

The SELECT statement allows you to retrieve data from the database. The full syntax of a SELECT statement is quite lengthy, and trying to understand it in its entirety can be intimidating. Instead of presenting the entire SELECT statement syntax in one piece, this chapter will break the syntax down into meaningful definitions and examples.

Let's begin with the syntax of a basic query. A *query* is the act of retrieving a row, or rows via a SELECT statement:

```
SELECT <select_list>
FROM <data_source>
```

| Parameter | Description |
|---|---|
| <select_list> | The list of columns you wish to see in your query output. |
| <data_source> | The source of your data, be it a table, view, user-defined function, or table variable. |

Before proceeding with the SELECT examples, you should note that many of the syntax examples presented in this chapter display query result sets in Query Analyzer using **grid format**. You can change the format of your Query Analyzer result sets by going to the Query menu and selecting Results in Grid. Results in Grid is generally faster than text mode, as text mode requires SQL Server to pre-parse the result columns of the output prior to placing them in the text format. If you prefer your query results as text, select Results in Text.

## Example 15.1.1: A simple SELECT query

By default, the maximum number of characters per column for Query Analyzer result output is 256. You can increase this value up to 8192 characters, by select Tools | Options | Results and increasing the Maximum characters per column value.

The following query selects all columns from the `Leaders` table; this is achieved by using the asterisk sign (`*`), which symbolizes all columns. The `FROM` clause is used to specify the data source, which in this case is `dbo.Leaders`. Notice that the two-part name is used first, being `owner.table_name`:

```
SELECT *
FROM dbo.Leaders
```

This example returns:

| | ID | vchTitle | vchCountry | vchLastName | vchFirstName |
|---|---|---|---|---|---|
| 1 | 1 | President | Afghanistan | Karzai | Hamid |
| 2 | 2 | President | Albania | Moisiu | Alfred |
| 3 | 3 | Prime Minister and First Lord of the Treasury | United Kingdom | Blair | Tony |
| 4 | 4 | President | USA | Bush | George |
| 5 | 5 | President of the Government | Spain | Aznar | Jose Maria |
| 6 | 6 | Prime Minister | Sweden | Persson | Goran |
| 7 | 7 | Prime Minister | Australia | Howard | John |
| 8 | 8 | Prime Minister | Belgium | Verhofstadt | Guy |
| 9 | 9 | President | Brazil | Cardoso | Fernando Henrique |
| 10 | 10 | President | China | Zemin | Jiang |
| 11 | 11 | Prime Minister | Thailand | Thaksin | Chinnawat |
| 12 | 12 | Prime Minister | Japan | Koizumi | Junichiro |
| 13 | 13 | President | Ireland | McAleese | Mary |
| 14 | 14 | President | Russia | Putin | Vladimir |
| 15 | 15 | Prime Minister | Canada | Chretien | Jean |

## Example 15.1.2: A simple SELECT returning three columns

In general, avoid using the asterisk sign in your Transact-SQL programming. Unnecessary columns can increase the overhead of the query. The next example queries the `Leaders` table, this time only returning the `vchCountry`, `vchLastName`, and `vchFirstName` columns:

```
SELECT vchCountry,
       vchLastName,
       vchFirstName
FROM Leaders
```

This returns:

| | vchCountry | vchLastName | vchFirstName |
|---|---|---|---|
| 1 | Afghanistan | Karzai | Hamid |
| 2 | Albania | Moisiu | Alfred |
| 3 | United Kingdom | Blair | Tony |
| 4 | USA | Bush | George W. |
| 5 | Spain | Aznar | Jose Maria |
| 6 | Sweden | Persson | Goran |
| 7 | Australia | Howard | John |
| 8 | Belgium | Verhofstadt | Guy |
| 9 | Brazil | Cardoso | Fernando Henrique |
| 10 | China | Jemin | Jiang |
| 11 | Thailand | Thaksin | Chinnawat |
| 12 | Japan | Koizumi | Junichiro |
| 13 | Ireland | McAleese | Mary |
| 14 | Russia | Putin | Vladimir |
| 15 | Canada | Chretien | Jean |
| 16 | Scotland | McConnell | Jack |

# 15.2 How to... Use DISTINCT to Remove Duplicate Values

The DISTINCT keyword is used to remove duplicate values from the set of selected columns, so that only unique rows appear in the result set. The syntax is as follows:

```
SELECT [ALL | DISTINCT] <select_list>
FROM <data_source>
```

The default behavior of a SELECT statement is to use the ALL keyword, meaning that duplicate rows will be retrieved and displayed if they exist. If you use the DISTINCT keyword, only unique rows will be returned for your query.

## Example 15.2.1: Removing duplicates from a one column query

In this first query, vchTitle is displayed from the Leaders table without specifying the DISTINCT keyword:

```
SELECT vchTitle
FROM dbo.Leaders
```

This returns:

| | vchTitle |
|---|---|
| 1 | President |
| 2 | President |
| 3 | Prime Minister and First Lord of the Treasury |
| 4 | President |
| 5 | President of the Government |
| 6 | Prime Minister |
| 7 | Prime Minister |
| 8 | Prime Minister |
| 9 | President |
| 10 | President |
| 11 | Prime Minister |
| 12 | Prime Minister |
| 13 | President |
| 14 | President |
| 15 | Prime Minister |
| 16 | First Minister |

To only show unique rows, add the DISTINCT keyword prior to the column listing:

```
SELECT DISTINCT vchTitle
FROM dbo.Leaders
```

This returns only unique vchTitle rows:

| | vchTitle |
|---|---|
| 1 | First Minister |
| 2 | President |
| 3 | President of the Government |
| 4 | Prime Minister |
| 5 | Prime Minister and First Lord of the Treasury |

### Example 15.2.2: Removing duplicates from a multi-column query

This example shows unique rows for a multi-column query:

```
SELECT DISTINCT City,
        Country,
        PostalCode
FROM Customers
```

### Example 15.2.3: Using DISTINCT with other AGGREGATE functions

You can also use DISTINCT for a column that is used within an AGGREGATE function. AGGREGATE functions will be covered in more detail in Chapter 16.

The following query calculates the average freight cost from the orders table:

```
SELECT AVG(Freight)
FROM ORDERS
```

To return the average of unique freight costs, you could run the following query instead:

```
SELECT AVG(DISTINCT Freight)
FROM ORDERS
```

# 15.3 How to... Use Column Aliases

In the previous example, you may have noticed that the column name for the average freight cost query output was No column name. For column computations or aggregate functions, you can use a **column alias** to name the columns of your query output explicitly. These types of columns are called **derived columns**. You can also use column aliases to rename columns that already have a name.

Aliases are defined by using the AS clause; the syntax for specifying an alias is as follows:

```
SELECT [ALL | DISTINCT] <column_1> AS 'column_name_1',
     <column_N...> AS 'column_name_N...'
FROM <data_source>
```

## Example 15.3.1: Using the AS clause to name a derived column

In this example, we will execute the query from the example in the last section, but this time we will include a column alias:

```
SELECT AVG(DISTINCT Freight)AS 'Average Freight Cost'
FROM ORDERS
```

This query returns:

| | Average Freight Cost |
|---|---|
| 1 | [illegible] |

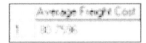

## Example 15.3.2: Using the AS clause to rename a named column

In this example, the Leaders table is queried for the vchLastName and vchFirstName table. To get the result set to return friendlier column headings, we use the AS clause to rename vchLastName as Last Name and vchFirstName as First Name:

```
SELECT vchLastName as 'Last Name',
       vchFirstName as 'First Name'
FROM Leaders
```

This query returns the aliased column names (showing only the first few rows for the example):

| | Last Name | First Name |
|---|---|---|
| 1 | Karzai | Hamid |
| 2 | Moisiu | Alfred |
| 3 | Blair | Tony |

# 15.4 How to... Use the TOP Keyword

The `TOP` keyword allows you to limit the number of rows returned in your query result set. The syntax is as follows:

```
SELECT  [ALL | DISTINCT]
        TOP n [PERCENT]
<column_1>,
<column_N…>
FROM <data_source>
```

The `TOP` keyword can limit either the number of rows, or the percentage of rows returned for the query. Use the `TOP` keyword instead of `SET ROWCOUNT`, as `TOP` is usually faster.

### Example 15.4.1: Limiting the number of rows returned

The following query returns the first five rows from the employee table. (Keep in mind that the first five rows could be *any* five rows from the table. To guarantee that a particular five rows are returned, use the `ORDER BY` clause, reviewed later in the chapter.):

```
SELECT TOP 5 *
FROM employee
```

### Example 15.4.2: Limiting the percentage of rows returned

The following query returns the top 10% of rows in the employee table query result set:

```
SELECT TOP 10 PERCENT
       emp_id,
       fname,
       lname
FROM employee
```

# 15.5 How to... Use the WITH TIES Clause to Return Repeating Values in the TOP Clause

The `WITH TIES` clause works with the `TOP` keyword and the `ORDER BY` clause (reviewed later in the chapter), to retrieve any rows with equivalent values to the last value returned.

### Example 15.5.1: Using WITH TIES

In this first example, the query will select the top 5 rows from the `leaders` table, displaying the `vchTitle` column in the results. The `ORDER BY` clause is used to order the result set in ascending order (the default ordering), for the `vchTitle` column:

```
SELECT TOP 5
      vchTitle
FROM leaders
ORDER BY vchTitle
```

This returns:

| | vchTitle |
|---|---|
| 1 | Governor General |
| 2 | Governor General |
| 3 | President |
| 4 | President |
| 5 | President |

In these query results, the fifth row is the title `President`; what if there were additional rows with the `President` value? Since the result set was ordered by `vchTitle`, there could have been extra `President` values in rows 6, 7, and 8. Using `WITH TIES` will show all occurrences of the last row value specified in the `ORDER BY` clause:

```
SELECT TOP 5 WITH TIES
      vchTitle
FROM leaders
ORDER BY vchTitle
```

This returns:

| | vchTitle |
|---|---|
| 1 | Governor General |
| 2 | Governor General |
| 3 | President |
| 4 | President |
| 5 | President |
| 6 | President |
| 7 | President |
| 8 | President |
| 9 | President |

Although the query specified that only the top 5 rows would be returned, `WITH TIES` will include any other rows with a value equal to the last row. This may be useful for numeric values, for example, returning the highest salaries in the company; you could display the top 5 salaries for the company, along with any recurrences of the last row value specified in the `ORDER BY` clause.

# 15.6 How to... Create a Table using INTO

The `INTO` clause allows you to create a table based on the results of a query result set. The columns you select will determine the schema of the table. This is a great technique for quickly 'copying' the base schema and data of an existing table. When you use `INTO`, you are not required to pre-define the new table's schema explicitly (for example, you do not need to issue a `CREATE TABLE` statement). The schema is reproduced, but constraints, indexes, and other separate objects dependent on the source table are not copied. The syntax is as follows:

```
SELECT  [ALL | DISTINCT]
            TOP n [PERCENT]
<column_1>,
<column_N...>
INTO <new_table_name>
FROM <data_source>
```

## Example 15.6.1: Creating a table based on the query result set

The following query creates a table called `employee_backup`:

```
SELECT emp_id,
          fname,
          lname,
          hire_date
INTO employee_backup
FROM employee
```

When the query is executed, rows are not returned; only a notification of the number of rows affected is provided:

(43 row(s) affected)

You can then perform a query from the new table:

```
SELECT * FROM employee_backup
```

This returns the following (showing a partial result set in this example):

| | emp_id | fname | lname | hire_date |
|---|---|---|---|---|
| 1 | PMA42628M | [illegible] | Accorti | 1992-08-27 00:00:00.000 |
| 2 | PSA89086M | Pedro | Afonso | 1990-12-24 00:00:00.000 |
| 3 | VPA30890F | Victoria | Ashworth | 1990-09-13 00:00:00.000 |
| 4 | H-B39728F | Helen | Bennett | 1989-09-21 00:00:00.000 |
| 5 | L-B31947F | Lesley | Brown | 1991-02-13 00:00:00.000 |
| 6 | F-C16315M | Francisco | Chang | 1990-11-03 00:00:00.000 |
| 7 | PTC11962M | Philip | Cramer | 1989-11-11 00:00:00.000 |
| 8 | A-C71970F | Ana | Cruz | 1991-10-26 00:00:00.000 |
| 9 | AMD15433F | Ann | Devon | 1991-07-16 00:00:00.000 |
| 10 | ARD36773F | Anabela | Domingues | 1993-01-27 00:00:00.000 |

## Example 15.6.2: Creating a table without rows

You may at some point wish to generate an empty table, based on columns defined in a query, for use within another process (for example, an intermediate load table used within a stored procedure). If you wish to create a table based on a query, without populating the new table with any rows, add a `WHERE` clause (reviewed later in the chapter) to qualify a condition that will always provide zero rows.

The following query creates a table called `employee_schema_only`, and adds a `WHERE` clause qualifying a search condition where `1 = 0`. Since the value `1` will never equal the value `0`, rows are not returned; an empty table is created, however:

```
SELECT  emp_id,
        fname,
        lname,
        hire_date
INTO employee_schema_only
FROM employee
WHERE 1 = 0
```

This returns:

(0 row(s) affected)

Using the `TOP` keyword, you can produce the same results; for example, using `TOP 0` (returning `0` rows):

```
SELECT  TOP 0
        emp_id,
        fname,
        lname,
        hire_date
INTO employee_schema_only
FROM employee
```

If you select from `employee_schema_only`, you will see the column headers, but no data:

```
SELECT * FROM employee_schema_only
```

This returns:

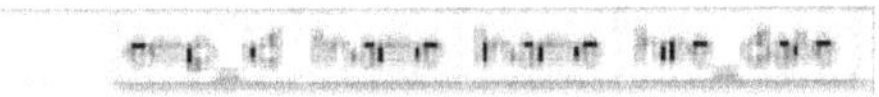

| emp_id | fname | lname | hire_date |
| --- | --- | --- | --- |

# 15.7 How to... Use the FROM Clause

The `FROM` clause specifies the data source for your query. This data source could include one or more tables, views, or derived tables (reviewed later in the chapter). The most basic syntax for the `FROM` clause is as follows:

```
SELECT  <select_list>
FROM <data_source>
```

You have already seen multiple examples of the `FROM` clause; most examples have used just one table or view for the data source. The next few sections will show you how to use multiple tables, views, or derived tables in one query. A total of 256 tables or views can be used in one query, for one `FROM` clause.

# 15.8 How to... Use Table JOINs

The `JOIN` clause allows you to combine multiple tables or views into one result set. The `JOIN` clause combines a column or columns from one table with another table, evaluating whether there is a match or whether a search condition is met.

With the `JOIN` clause, you can join primary and foreign key, composite key, and any other data type compatible columns. Joined columns do not need to have the same name, only compatible data types.

The basic syntax for the `JOIN` clause is as follows:

```
SELECT  <select_list>
FROM <table_1> <INNER or LEFT OUTER or RIGHT OUTER or FULL OUTER or CROSS> JOIN
<table_2> ON <search conditions>…
```

## Example 15.8.1: Using an INNER JOIN

The `INNER JOIN` operates by matching common values in two tables; only rows that are equivalent in both tables are retrieved. In this example, we will attempt to join rows in the `employee` and `jobs` tables from the `pubs` database:

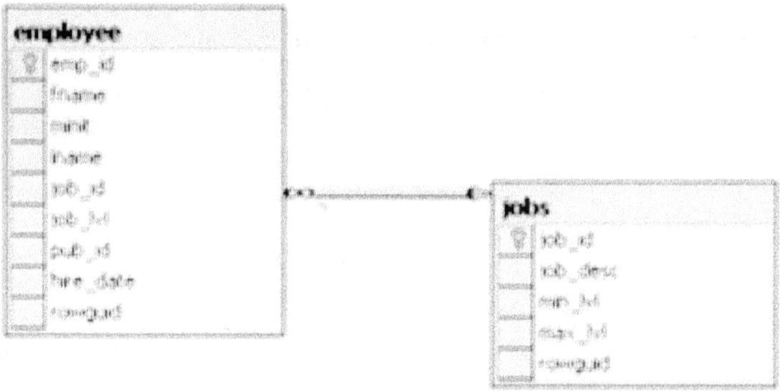


The `job_id` column in the employee table has a foreign key reference to the primary key of the jobs table; this is a column that can be used in a `JOIN` operation between the two tables. In the following query, the employee ID, first name, last name, and job description will be retrieved; all columns except the job description can be retrieved from the employee table. The employee table contains the job ID, which can be used to retrieve the associated job description from the jobs table:

```
SELECT employee.emp_id,
       employee.fname,
       employee.lname,
       jobs.job_desc
FROM employee
       INNER JOIN jobs
    ON employee.job_id = jobs.job_id
```

The results are as follows (showing the first few rows):

| | emp_id | fname | lname | job_desc |
|---|---|---|---|---|
| 1 | PMA42628M | Jam | Accorti | Sales Representative |
| 2 | PSA89086M | Pedro | Afonso | Designer |
| 3 | VPA30890F | Victoria | Ashworth | Managing Editor |
| 4 | H-B39728F | Helen | Bennett | Editor |
| 5 | L-B31947F | Lesley | Brown | Marketing Manager |
| 6 | F-C16315M | Francisco | Chang | Chief Financial Officer |
| 7 | PTC11962M | Philip | Cramer | Chief Executive Officer |
| 8 | A-C71970F | Aria | Cruz | Productions Manager |
| 9 | AMD15433F | Ann | Devon | Business Operations Manager |
| 10 | ARD36773F | Anabela | Domingues | Public Relations Manager |

Notice that the query uses the `tablename.columnname` qualification. This is not necessary if the column names in the two tables are unique; however, adding the table name or table alias name (described later on) can improve readability, and help ensure that you retrieve the intended columns from the correct tables.

`INNER` joins are the default `JOIN` type; you can use just the `JOIN` keyword, instead of `INNER JOIN`. Do not join columns that contain `NULL` values, since `NULL` values are not joinable. To reiterate before showing more examples, `INNER JOIN` statements only return rows where there is a matching column in each table used in the `JOIN`.

### Example 15.8.2: Using multiple INNER JOIN statements

You can use multiple `JOIN` statements for one query. This next example will take the previous query, and add information about the publisher name associated with the employee. The employee table has the `pub_id`, which is a foreign key reference to the `pub_id` primary key in the `publishers` table:

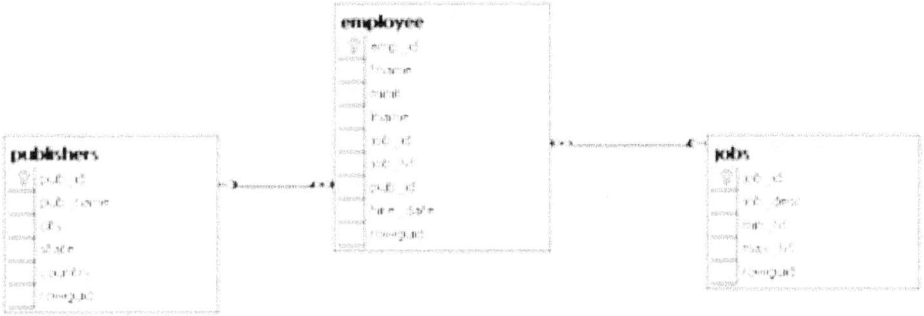


```
SELECT employee.emp_id,
         employee.fname,
         employee.lname,
         jobs.job_desc,
         publishers.pub_name
FROM employee
         INNER JOIN jobs
               ON employee.job_id = jobs.job_id
         INNER JOIN publishers
               ON employee.pub_id = publishers.pub_id
```

Notice that there is no comma between the `INNER JOIN` clauses. In this previous example, the `job_id` from the employee table was joined to the `jobs` table, and the `pub_id` of the `employees` table was used to join to the `publishers` table.

This previous query returns the following results (first few rows displayed):

| | emp_id | fname | lname | job_desc | pub_name |
|---|---|---|---|---|---|
| 1 | [illegible] | [illegible] | [illegible] | Sales Representative | Binnet & Hardley |
| 2 | [illegible] | Pedro | [illegible] | Designer | Algodata Infosystems |
| 3 | [illegible] | Victoria | [illegible] | Managing Editor | Binnet & Hardley |
| 4 | [illegible] | Helen | Bennett | Editor | Binnet & Hardley |
| 5 | [illegible] | Lesley | Brown | Marketing Manager | Binnet & Hardley |
| 6 | [illegible] | Francisco | Chang | Chief Financial Officer | Scootney Books |
| 7 | [illegible] | Philip | Cramer | Chief Executive Officer | Scootney Books |
| 8 | [illegible] | Ana | Cruz | Productions Manager | Algodata Infosystems |
| 9 | [illegible] | Ann | Devon | Business Operations Manager | Scootney Books |

You may notice that the output rows are in no particular order; you can use the ORDER BY clause to sort the results. For example, by last name:

```
SELECT employee.emp_id,
       employee.fname,
       employee.lname,
       jobs.job_desc,
       publishers.pub_name
FROM employee
       INNER JOIN jobs
             ON employee.job_id = jobs.job_id
       INNER JOIN publishers
             ON employee.pub_id = publishers.pub_id
ORDER BY employee.lname
```

## Example 15.8.3: Using LEFT and RIGHT OUTER JOIN statements

LEFT and RIGHT OUTER JOIN statements, like INNER JOIN statements, return rows that match the conditions of the join search condition. Unlike INNER JOINs, LEFT OUTER JOINs return unmatched rows from the first table of the join pair, and RIGHT OUTER JOINs return unmatched rows from the second table of the join pair.

Let's say that we wish to display all stores and their associated sales. If we produce an INNER JOIN using stor_id from the stores and sales table, only those rows that have a match for the stor_id will be returned; we will not see stores that exist in the stores table but do not have orders in the sales table:

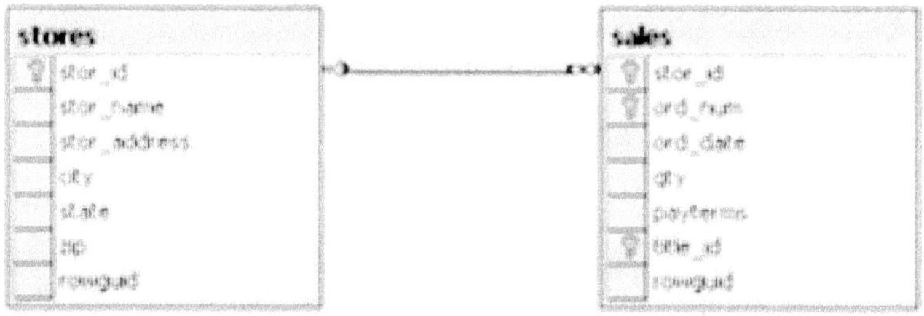


Using a LEFT OUTER JOIN will allow us to show all stores, whether or not the stores had associated sales:

```
SELECT   stores.stor_id,
         stores.stor_name,
         sales.ord_num,
         sales.ord_date,
         sales.qty
FROM     stores
LEFT OUTER JOIN sales
    ON stores.stor_id = sales.stor_id
```

The LEFT table in this case is the stores table. Since it is listed first in the FROM clause, it will be used as the table to display matched **and** unmatched rows. The output will show all those orders with the associated store info, as well as NULL values for those stores without associated orders in the sales table:

| | stor_id | stor_name | ord_num | ord_date | qty |
|---|---|---|---|---|---|
| 9 | 7131 | Doc-U-Mat: Quality Laundry and Books | N914008 | 1994-09-14 00:00:00.000 | 20 |
| 10 | 7131 | Doc-U-Mat: Quality Laundry and Books | N914014 | 1994-09-14 00:00:00.000 | 25 |
| 11 | 7131 | Doc-U-Mat: Quality Laundry and Books | P3087a | 1993-05-29 00:00:00.000 | 20 |
| 12 | 7131 | Doc-U-Mat: Quality Laundry and Books | P3087a | 1993-05-29 00:00:00.000 | 25 |
| 13 | 7131 | Doc-U-Mat: Quality Laundry and Books | P3087a | 1993-05-29 00:00:00.000 | 15 |
| 14 | 7131 | Doc-U-Mat: Quality Laundry and Books | P3087a | 1993-05-29 00:00:00.000 | 25 |
| 15 | 7896 | Fricative Bookshop | QQ2299 | 1993-10-28 00:00:00.000 | 15 |
| 16 | 7896 | Fricative Bookshop | TQ456 | 1993-12-12 00:00:00.000 | 10 |
| 17 | 7896 | Fricative Bookshop | X999 | 1993-02-21 00:00:00.000 | 35 |
| 18 | 8000 | [illegible] | NULL | NULL | NULL |

The RIGHT OUTER JOIN clause works in the same way as the LEFT OUTER JOIN, except that unmatched rows from the right table (second table in a join pair) are displayed.

The next example displays the publisher name from the publishers table, and associated employees in the employee table. Using RIGHT join, any publishers unmatched with an employee will be displayed:

```
SELECT publishers.pub_name,
       employee.fname,
       employee.lname
FROM   employee
RIGHT OUTER JOIN publishers
    ON employee.pub_id = publishers.pub_id
ORDER BY pub_name
```

This returns:

| | pub_name | fname | lname |
|---|---|---|---|
| 17 | Binnet & Hardley | Paul | Henriot |
| 18 | Binnet & Hardley | Elizabeth | Lincoln |
| 19 | Binnet & Hardley | Martine | Rance |
| 20 | Binnet & Hardley | Daniel | Tonini |
| 21 | Five Lakes Publishing | Rita | Muller |
| 22 | Fun in the Sun Publishing | NULL | NULL |
| 23 | GGG&G | Janine | Labrune |
| 24 | Lucerne Publishing | Carlos | Hernadez |

Any unmatched right table rows will show NULL values for the unmatched table columns.

### Example 15.8.4: Using a FULL OUTER JOIN

The FULL OUTER JOIN clause returns unmatched rows on both the LEFT and RIGHT tables. This is an excellent method for finding orphaned or missing rows, as you can identify missing associations and data between two tables.

This example searches for unmatched rows between the stores and sales tables. Using the stor_id column as the join column, a WHERE clause is used to determine any unmatched rows in either the sales or stores tables:

```
SELECT  stores.stor_id,
         stores.stor_name,
         sales.ord_num,
         sales.ord_date,
         sales.qty
FROM    stores
FULL OUTER JOIN sales
            ON stores.stor_id = sales.stor_id
WHERE sales.ord_num IS NULL OR
      stores.stor_id IS NULL
```

This returns rows displaying one unmatched row from the `stores` table, and one from the `sales` table. Values from unmatched sides will show up as `NULL`:

| | stor_id | stor_name | ord_num | ord_date | qty |
|---|---|---|---|---|---|
| 1 | 1111 | Rock a doodle doo | NULL | NULL | NULL |
| 2 | NULL | NULL | P723 | 2002-04-22 00:00:00.000 | 22 |

## Example 15.8.5: Using a CROSS JOIN

A `CROSS JOIN` results in a Cartesian product when a `WHERE` clause is not specified. A Cartesian product produces a result set based on every possible combination of rows from the left table multiplied by the rows in the right table. If the stores table has 7 rows, and the sales table has 22 rows, you will receive 154 rows as your output (each possible combination of row displayed). For example, the following query will display 154 row combinations:

```
SELECT  stores.stor_id,
     stores.stor_name,
     sales.ord_num,
     sales.ord_date
FROM    stores
CROSS JOIN sales
```

If you include a `WHERE` clause to join two columns, the `CROSS JOIN` will act like a regular `INNER JOIN`. Not **all** `WHERE` clauses will cause the `CROSS JOIN` to behave like an `INNER JOIN`. `WHERE` clauses must join columns between two tables referenced in the `CROSS JOIN`. For example, this example adds a `WHERE` clause between the `stor_id` columns of the `sales` and `stores` tables:

```
SELECT  stores.stor_id,
     stores.stor_name,
     sales.ord_num,
     sales.ord_date
FROM    stores
CROSS JOIN sales
WHERE stores.stor_id = sales.stor_id
```

This is the same as the `INNER` join syntax of:

```
SELECT  stores.stor_id,
     stores.stor_name,
     sales.ord_num,
     sales.ord_date
FROM    stores INNER JOIN
    sales ON
    stores.stor_id = sales.stor_id
```

### Example 15.8.6: Not using the JOIN clause

You can also avoid using the `JOIN` clause by simply listing the tables you wish to use in your query, and qualifying a join in the `WHERE` clause. (This type of `JOIN` syntax is not ANSI compliant). The following query lists `iAuthorId`, `vchLastName`, and `vchFirstname` from the `Authors` table. In addition to this, the `vchBookName` is listed from the `Books` table. Notice that the `FROM` clause lists both tables, with a table alias, and separated by a comma. The `JOIN` operation takes place when the `iAuthorId` columns are matched in the `WHERE` clause, `A.iAuthorID = B.iAuthorID`:

```
SELECT   A.iAuthorId,
          A.vchLastName,
          A.vchFirstName,
          B.vchBookName
FROM     Authors A,
          Books B
WHERE    A.iAuthorId = B.iAuthorId
```

# 15.9 How to... Use Table Aliases and Self Joins

Table aliases improve query readability and reduce column ambiguity by specifying which column in the query belongs to which table. To define a table alias, you can use two methods:

### Method 1

```
FROM <table_name> AS <alias_name>
```

### Method 2

```
FROM <table_name> <alias_name>
```

### Example 15.9.1: Using a table alias for a two table query

This example creates an alias for the employee table, using `E` as the alias name. For the `Jobs` table, the query uses `J` as the alias name. This reduces the amount of typing for each fully-qualified column name in the query, improving readability:

```
SELECT E.emp_id,
         E.fname,
         E.lname,
         J.job_desc
FROM employee E
         INNER JOIN jobs J
               ON E.job_id = J.job_id
ORDER BY E.lname
```

### Example 15.9.2: Self joins with aliases

Table aliases are necessary for **self join** operations. A self join occurs when a table joins with itself to produce a query result set. Since you cannot reference the same table name twice within a query, you can use an alias to do this instead. Self joins are often used to represent recursive relationships. For example, a table called `Company` can include a column called `ParentCompanyID`; since the parent and child companies are distinct rows in the same table, you would depend on a self join to return data where both the child and parent company are represented within the same row.

This example lists the name of the publishers from the publishers table; this query also lists the name of the parent company publisher (which is an ID reference to the same table, publisher_id). To achieve this, the publishers table is first aliased as Pub, and then aliased again for the Parent records:

```
SELECT Pub.pub_id as 'Publisher ID',
        Pub.pub_name as 'Publisher',
        Parent.pub_name as 'Parent Company'
FROM   publishers AS Pub
        LEFT OUTER JOIN publishers AS Parent
      ON Pub.parent_co = Parent.pub_id
```

Since a LEFT OUTER JOIN is used to join the parent_co field to the pub_id field, you will see all publishers from the left table, even if there is no associated parent company:

| | Publisher ID | Publisher | Parent Company |
|---|---|---|---|
| 1 | 0736 | New Moon Books | Five Lakes Publishing |
| 2 | 0877 | Binnet & Hardley | NULL |
| 3 | 1389 | Algodata Infosystems | NULL |
| 4 | 1622 | Five Lakes Publishing | Five Lakes Publishing |
| 5 | 1756 | Ramona Publishers | NULL |
| 6 | 9901 | GGG&G | Scootney Books |
| 7 | 9952 | Scootney Books | Scootney Books |
| 8 | 9998 | Fun in the Sun Publishing | NULL |
| 9 | 9999 | Lucerne Publishing | NULL |

# 15.10 How to... Use Derived Tables

A **derived table** is a subquery in the FROM clause that is used as a data source. Derived tables are defined with table aliases, so they may be referenced within the query. The syntax is as follows:

```
SELECT [ALL | DISTINCT]
          TOP n [PERCENT]
          <column_1>,
          <column_N...>
FROM    (sub_query) AS <alias_name>
```

## Example 15.10.1: Using a derived table

This example uses a derived table that is a query against the jobs table:

```
SELECT *
FROM (SELECT job_desc,
                min_lvl
       FROM jobs) as MyJobs
WHERE MyJobs.min_lvl > 1
```

Derived tables can sometimes perform significantly better than temporary tables, as you eliminate the steps needed for SQL Server to create and allocate the temporary table. Make sure to test your temporary table solution against a derived table, to determine which performs better (see Chapter 17 for a review of how to gauge a query's performance).

# 15.11 How to... Use the WHERE Clause to Specify Rows Returned in the Result Set

The WHERE clause is used to restrict rows returned in your query result set. The WHERE clause uses search conditions, which in turn use predicates; a predicate is an expression that evaluates to TRUE, FALSE or UNKNOWN. The number of search conditions allowed for one query is unlimited. The syntax is as follows:

```
SELECT [ALL | DISTINCT]
        TOP n [PERCENT]
        <column_1>,
        <column_N...>
INTO   <new_table_name>
FROM   <data_source>
WHERE  <search_condition or search_conditions>
```

Search conditions are separated by the logical operators AND, OR, and NOT. For example, this pseudo-code snippet ensures that any rows returned by the query evaluate to TRUE. If search conditions 1 AND 2 are TRUE, the row or rows will be returned:

```
WHERE <search condition 1> AND
  <search condition 2>
```

The next pseudo-code snippet demonstrates the OR operator; if either search condition is TRUE, the associated rows will be returned:

```
WHERE <search condition 1> OR
        <search condition 2>
```

The last operator used for separating search conditions is NOT. This pseudo-code snippet demonstrates NOT, specifying that only rows evaluating to NOT be TRUE should be returned:

```
WHERE NOT <search condition 1>
```

You can use multiple operators (AND, OR, NOT) in one WHERE clause; it is important, however, to embed your ANDs and ORs properly in brackets. The AND operator limits the result sets, and the OR operator expands the conditions for which rows will be returned. Using both AND and OR operators in the same WHERE clause without the use of brackets can cause confusion. Let's say that we have the following query that uses both AND and OR operators:

```
SELECT vchTitle,
       vchLastName,
       vchFirstName
FROM   Leaders
WHERE  vchLastName = 'Karzai' OR
         vchLastName = 'Blair' OR
         vchLastName = 'Aznar' AND
         vchFirstName = 'Jose Maria'
```

This query requests that either the last name returned be `Karzai`, `Blair`, or `Aznar`. The `AND` operator, however, follows the `Aznar` search condition, specifying that the first name column is `Jose Maria`; so the intentions of this query are ambiguous. Did the query writer intend the results to return anyone named `Jose Maria Karzai`? Or `Jose Maria Blair`? Or was `Jose Maria` intended for `Aznar` only? This query would have returned the following results:

| | vchTitle | vchLastName | vchFirstName |
|---|---|---|---|
| 1 | President | Karzai | Hamid |
| 2 | Prime Minister and First Lord of the Treasury | Blair | Tony |
| 3 | President of the Government | Aznar | Jose Maria |

Let's take the same query, but add brackets to clarify what we mean. The query below requests the rows that have the last name `Karzai`, `Blair`, or `Aznar`. In addition to this, any of those three last names must have `Jose Maria` as the first name:

```
SELECT vchTitle,
       vchLastName,
       vchFirstName
FROM   Leaders
WHERE  (vchLastName = 'Karzia' OR
         vchLastName = 'Blair' OR
         vchLastName = 'Aznar') AND
         vchFirstName = 'Jose Maria'
```

By adding parentheses, you group search conditions as one unit. This returns the following results:

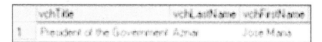

| | vchTitle | vchLastName | vchFirstName |
|---|---|---|---|
| 1 | President of the Government | Aznar | Jose Maria |

Only one row is returned, as only one row satisfies the conditions in brackets, as well as the last clause connected with the `AND` operator.

The search conditions themselves can use various operators. The basic syntax for a search condition is as follows:

```
<left_predicate> <operator> <right_predicate or subquery or value>
```

Below is a table listing valid predicates within a search condition:

| Operator | Description |
|---|---|
| != | Tests two expressions not being equal to each other. |
| !> | Tests that the left condition is not greater than the expression to the right. |
| < | Tests the left condition as less than the right condition. |
| <= | Tests the left condition as less than or equal to the right condition. |
| <> | Tests two expressions not being equal to each other. |
| = | Tests equality between two expressions. |

| Operator | Description |
|---|---|
| > | Tests the left condition being greater than the expression to the right. |
| >= | Tests the left condition being greater than or equal to the expression to the right. |
| ALL | When used with a comparison operator and subquery, ALL compares a scalar value against a single column set of values (provided via a subquery). |
| ANY | When used with a comparison operator and subquery, if any retrieved values satisfy the search condition, the rows will be retrieved. |
| BETWEEN | Specifies an inclusive range of values. Used with the AND clause between the beginning and ending values. |
| CONTAINS | Does a fuzzy search for words and phrases. |
| ESCAPE | Takes the character used prior to a wildcard character to specify that the literal value of the wildcard character should be searched, rather than use the character as a wildcard. |
| EXISTS | When used with a subquery, EXISTS tests for the existence of rows in the subquery. |
| FREETEXT | Searches character-based data for words using meaning, rather than for literal values. |
| IN | Provides an inclusive list of values for the search condition. |
| IS NOT NULL | Evaluates whether the value is not null. |
| IS NULL | Evaluates whether the value is null. |
| LIKE | Tests character string for pattern matching. |
| NOT BETWEEN | Specifies a range of values not to include. Used with the AND clause between the beginning and ending values. |
| NOT IN | Provides a list of values for which not to return rows. |
| NOT LIKE | Tests character string, excluding those with pattern matches. |
| SOME | When used with a comparison operator and subquery, if any retrieved values satisfy the search condition, the rows will be retrieved. |

## Example 15.11.1: Using the = operator

The following example uses the = operator to list all leaders with the last name Karzai:

```
SELECT vchTitle,
       vchLastName,
       vchFirstName
FROM   Leaders
WHERE vchLastName = 'Karzai'
```

This returns:

| | vchTitle | vchLastName | vchFirstName |
|---|---|---|---|
| 1 | President | Karzai | Hamid |

## Example 15.11.2: Using the != operator

This example requests rows where the last name is not equal to `Karzai`:

```
SELECT vchTitle,
       vchLastName,
       vchFirstName
FROM   Leaders
WHERE vchLastName != 'Karzai'
```

This returns (partial result set):

| | vchTitle | vchLastName | vchFirstName |
|---|---|---|---|
| 1 | President | Moisiu | Alfred |
| 2 | Prime Minister and First Lord of the Treasury | Blair | Tony |
| 3 | President | Bush | George |
| 4 | President of the Government | Aznar | Jose Maria |
| 5 | Prime Minister | Persson | Goran |
| 6 | Prime Minister | Howard | John |
| 7 | Prime Minister | Verhofstadt | Guy |
| 8 | President | Cardoso | Fernando Henrique |
| 9 | President | Zemin | Jiang |
| 10 | Prime Minister | Thaksin | Chinnavat |
| 11 | Prime Minister | Koizumi | Junichiro |
| 12 | President | McAleese | Mary |
| 13 | President | Putin | Vladimir |
| 14 | Prime Minister | Chretien | Jean |

## Example 15.11.3: Using the < and <= operators

This example seeks to show all rows from the `OrderDetails` table, where the `UnitPrice` is less than `2.0`:

```
SELECT *
FROM OrderDetails
WHERE UnitPrice < 2.00
```

This returns no rows, as no `UnitPrice` is less than `2.0`. However, if you run the same query, using `<=`, you will see many unit price values equal to `2.0`:

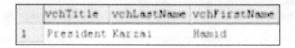

```
SELECT *
FROM OrderDetails
WHERE UnitPrice <= 2.00
```

This returns:

| | OrderID | ProductID | UnitPrice | Quantity | Discount |
|---|---|---|---|---|---|
| 1 | 10252 | 33 | 2.0000 | 25 | 5.0000001E-2 |
| 2 | 10269 | 33 | 2.0000 | 60 | 5.0000001E-2 |
| 3 | 10271 | 33 | 2.0000 | 24 | 0.0 |
| 4 | 10273 | 33 | 2.0000 | 20 | 0.0 |
| 5 | 10341 | 33 | 2.0000 | 8 | 0.0 |
| 6 | 10382 | 33 | 2.0000 | 60 | 0.0 |
| 7 | 10410 | 33 | 2.0000 | 49 | 0.0 |
| 8 | 10414 | 33 | 2.0000 | 50 | 0.0 |
| 9 | 10415 | 33 | 2.0000 | 20 | 0.0 |
| 10 | 10454 | 33 | 2.0000 | 20 | 0.2 |
| 11 | 10473 | 33 | 2.0000 | 12 | 0.0 |

## Example 15.11.4: Using the ALL, ANY, and SOME operators

The ALL and ANY operators work in conjunction with other operators. SOME and ANY are functionally equivalent. In this example, the query selects rows from the Orders table where the OrderId column equals ANY OrderId found in the OrderDetails table:

```
SELECT *
FROM Orders
WHERE OrderID = ANY (SELECT OrderId
    FROM OrderDetails)
```

In the next example, the ALL keyword is used to return rows from the Orders table, where the value of the OrderId column is greater than all OrderId values in the OrderDetails table:

```
SELECT *
FROM Orders
WHERE OrderID > ALL (SELECT OrderId
           FROM OrderDetails)
```

## Example 15.11.5: Using the BETWEEN operator

The following query returns rows from the Orders table where the OrderDate is between 7/1/1996 and 7/16/1996. The BETWEEN clause includes values that are in the beginning and end range (so it is more like the operator >= and <=, than > and <). Notice that the query example uses the ANSI/ISO standard date format, YYYY/MM/DD:

```
SELECT *
FROM Orders
WHERE OrderDate BETWEEN
    '1996/07/01' AND '1996/07/16'
```

### Example 15.11.6: Using the ESCAPE operator

This query searches for any ShipAddress with an underscore value in it. As an underscore is also a wildcard value, use the ESCAPE operator to define it as an escape character. If an ESCAPE character precedes the underscore, it is treated as a literal value. This example also demonstrates how to use the LIKE operator, for searching pattern matches on character-type columns:

```
SELECT *
FROM Orders
WHERE ShipAddress LIKE '%/_%' ESCAPE '/'
```

Wildcards are used to search for chunks or pattern matches within strings. The wildcards used for queries in Transact-SQL are as follows:

| Wildcard | Usage |
|---|---|
| % | Represents a string of zero or more characters. |
| _ | Represents a single character. |
| [] | Specifies a single character, from a selected range or list. |
| [^] | Specifies a single character not within the specified range. |

The following is an example of returning all ShipAddress values with a second letter of N:

```
SELECT DISTINCT ShipAddress
FROM Orders
WHERE ShipAddress LIKE '_N%'
```

This returns:

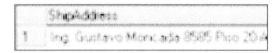


This next query lists all ShipAddress values that begin with the letter A or B:

```
SELECT DISTINCT ShipAddress
FROM Orders
WHERE ShipAddress LIKE '[AB]%'
```

This returns:

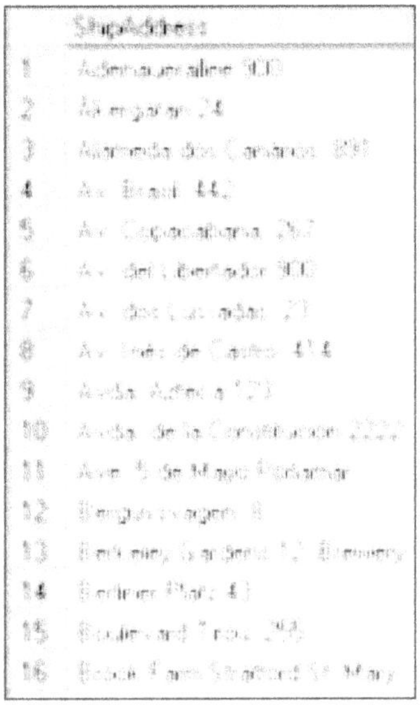

### Example 15.11.7: Using the IS NULL operator

This next example returns all rows from the `Orders` table where the `RequiredDate IS NULL`. Remember that a `NULL` value is, by definition, an unknown value, and not a blank or space value. Use `IS NULL` instead of `= 'NULL'`, as the character string `NULL` will be sought instead (assuming the column uses a character datatype):

```
SELECT *
FROM Orders
WHERE RequiredDate IS NULL
```

`IS NULL` is also needed when you wish to evaluate options that are not equal to a specified value or values, including those values that are `NULL`. For example, the next query returns any `ShipRegion` not equal to `RJ`. `NULL` values will **not** be returned in the result set:

```
SELECT ShipRegion
FROM Orders
WHERE ShipRegion <> 'RJ'
ORDER BY ShipRegion
```

To include `NULL` values with this query, you must add the `IS NULL` value to the `WHERE` clause. (Since the `ORDER BY` orders `ShipRegion` in the default ascending order, `NULL`s will appear first in the results, as they are treated as the lowest order.):

```
SELECT ShipRegion
FROM Orders
WHERE ShipRegion <> 'RJ'OR
ShipRegion IS NULL
ORDER BY ShipRegion
```

### Example 15.11.8: Using the IN operator

This query returns rows from the `Leaders` table where the `vchCountry` has the value of either `Spain` or `Sweden`. You can list many values in the `IN` (or `NOT IN`) clause; you can also choose a single column subquery instead of explicit values:

```
SELECT *
FROM Leaders
WHERE vchCountry IN ('Spain', 'Sweden')
```

# 15.12 How to... Use the GROUP BY Clause

The `GROUP BY` clause is used to select which column or columns are used for grouping rows together as units. `GROUP BY` is mostly used when aggregate functions are referenced in the `SELECT` statement (aggregate functions are reviewed in the next chapter). The syntax for `GROUP BY` is as follows:

```
SELECT [ALL | DISTINCT]
         TOP n [PERCENT]
         <column_1>,
         <column_N...>
INTO     <new_table_name>
FROM    <data_source>
WHERE   <seach_condition or search_conditions>
GROUP BY [ ALL ] column_1, column_N...
    WITH { CUBE | ROLLUP }
```

### Example 15.12.1: Using GROUP BY

The following query performs a count of all customers who live in each city (each row in the `Customers` table represents an individual customer). By performing `COUNT(*)` the query retrieves the number of rows. By selecting `GROUP BY City`, the results are grouped by city, with the row counts calculated for each city. The results are further narrowed down, specifying that the city must be Buenos Aires, Bruxelles, or Sao Paulo:

```
SELECT City,
         COUNT(*)as 'Total Customers'
FROM Customers
WHERE City IN ('Buenos Aires', 'Bruxelles', 'Sao Paulo')
GROUP BY City
```

The query results are seen below; the number was generated by the number of rows in the table for each associated city:

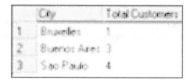

| | City | Total Customers |
|---|---|---|
| 1 | Bruxelles | 1 |
| 2 | Buenos Aires | 3 |
| 3 | Sao Paulo | 4 |

### Example 15.12.2: Using ALL with GROUP BY

This next example uses the `GROUP BY ALL` clause. By choosing the `ALL` clause, all row values are used in the grouping, even if they were not qualified to appear via the `WHERE` clause. For example, running the same query as in the previous example, except with the `ALL` clause, returns the following results:

```
SELECT City,
        COUNT(*)as 'Total Customers'
FROM Customers
WHERE City IN ('Buenos Aires', 'Bruxelles', 'Sao Paulo')
GROUP BY ALL City
```

This returns (partial result set shown):

| | City | Total Customers |
|---|---|---|
| 1 | Aachen | 0 |
| 2 | Albuquerque | 0 |
| 3 | Anchorage | 0 |
| 4 | Århus | 0 |
| 5 | Barcelona | 0 |
| 6 | Barquisimeto | 0 |
| 7 | Bergamo | 0 |
| 8 | Berlin | 0 |
| 9 | Bern | 0 |
| 10 | Boise | 0 |
| 11 | Bräcke | 0 |
| 12 | Brandenburg | 0 |
| 13 | Bruxelles | [illegible] |
| 14 | Buenos Aires | [illegible] |
| 15 | Butte | 0 |
| 16 | Campinas | 0 |
| 17 | Caracas | 0 |
| 18 | Charleroi | 0 |
| 19 | Cork | 0 |
| 20 | Cowes | 0 |

Notice that Total Customers are zero for those cities not specified in the `WHERE` clause. This does not mean they have zero rows, but rather that data is not displayed for them.

## Example 15.12.3: Using CUBE

When working with the `GROUP BY` clause, you can use `WITH CUBE` to add rows to your result that summarize total values based on the columns in the `GROUP BY` clause. For example, the following query displays the total unit price per city from the `Orders` and `OrderDetails` table:

```
SELECT Orders.ShipCity,
         SUM(OrderDetails.UnitPrice)
FROM   OrderDetails,
       Orders
WHERE  Orders.OrderId = OrderDetails.OrderId AND
         ShipCity IN ('Torino', 'Berlin', 'Vancouver')
GROUP BY Orders.ShipCity
WITH CUBE
```

Because the query groups by `ShipCity`, an extra row will be displayed, showing the total for all `ShipCity` `UnitPrices`. The ShipCity column displays a `NULL` value for the totaled row:

| | ShipCity | (No column name) |
|---|---|---|
| 1 | Berlin | 320.8500 |
| 2 | Torino | 244.0000 |
| 3 | Vancouver | 71.8000 |
| 4 | NULL | 636.6500 |

If you added extra columns to the query, including them in the `GROUP BY` clause, `CUBE` would attempt to aggregate values for each grouping combination. `CUBE` is often used for reporting purposes, providing an easy method of reporting totals by grouped column.

## Example 15.12.4: Using ROLLUP

`WITH ROLLUP` is used in conjunction with `GROUP BY` to add hierarchical summaries based on the ordering of columns in the `GROUP BY` clause. For example, the following query retrieves the `City`, `Product Id`, and total `Unit Price` from the `OrderDetails` and `Orders` tables. Qualifications (search conditions) are added to the `WHERE` clause, specifying which products should be listed, and from which cities:

```
SELECT Orders.ShipCity,
         OrderDetails.ProductId,
         SUM(OrderDetails.UnitPrice) as 'Total Price'
FROM   OrderDetails,
         Orders
WHERE  Orders.OrderId = OrderDetails.OrderId AND
         ShipCity IN ('Torino', 'Berlin', 'Vancouver')AND
         OrderDetails.ProductID IN (77, 71, 51)
GROUP BY Orders.ShipCity,
           OrderDetails.ProductId
WITH ROLLUP
```

The `WITH ROLLUP` produces aggregates for each change in `City`. So, after the two rows listed for Berlin, a total is produced, with a `NULL` value placeholder in the `ProductId` column. Notice that the final row is a grand total:

| | ShipCity | ProductId | Total Price |
|---|---|---|---|
| 1 | Berlin | 71 | 21.5000 |
| 2 | Berlin | 77 | 13.0000 |
| 3 | Berlin | NULL | 34.5000 |
| 4 | Torino | 51 | 53.0000 |
| 5 | Torino | 77 | 13.0000 |
| 6 | Torino | NULL | 66.0000 |
| 7 | Vancouver | 77 | 10.4000 |
| 8 | Vancouver | NULL | 10.4000 |
| 9 | NULL | NULL | 110.9000 |

If the GROUP BY clause ordered ProductId instead of ShipCity, the results would have looked like this:

| | ProductId | ShipCity | Total Price |
|---|---|---|---|
| 1 | [illegible] | Toronto | [illegible] |
| 2 | [illegible] | NULL | [illegible] |
| 3 | [illegible] | Berlin | [illegible] |
| 4 | [illegible] | NULL | [illegible] |
| 5 | [illegible] | Berlin | [illegible] |
| 6 | [illegible] | Toronto | [illegible] |
| 7 | [illegible] | Vancouver | [illegible] |
| 8 | [illegible] | NULL | [illegible] |
| 9 | NULL | NULL | [illegible] |

Now, for every change in ProductID, a total row is created, with a NULL placeholder in the ShipCity column.

# 15.13 How to... Use the HAVING Clause

When coupled with the GROUP BY clause, HAVING allows you to qualify or define a search condition for the grouped or aggregated columns. The syntax for the HAVING clause is as follows:

```
SELECT [ALL | DISTINCT]
         TOP n [PERCENT]
         <column_1>,
         <column_N…>
INTO     <new_table_name>
FROM    <data_source>
WHERE   <seach_condition or search_conditions>
GROUP BY [ ALL ] column_1, column_N…
    WITH { CUBE | ROLLUP }
HAVING <search_condition>
```

## Example 15.13.1: Using the HAVING clause

This example returns the product ID and total unit price from the OrderDetails table. By using the HAVING clause, only those totals (by product ID) that exceed 1000 are returned:

```
SELECT ProductId,
        SUM(UnitPrice)as 'Total Price'
FROM OrderDetails
GROUP BY ProductId
HAVING SUM(UnitPrice) > 1000
```

This returns:

| | ProductId | Total Price |
|---|---|---|
| 1 | 69 | 1036.8000 |
| 2 | 62 | 2227.8000 |
| 3 | 38 | 5902.4000 |
| 4 | 29 | 3713.3800 |
| 5 | 60 | 1638.8000 |
| 6 | 20 | 1215.0000 |
| 7 | 28 | 1385.2000 |
| 8 | 59 | 2761.0000 |
| 9 | 43 | 1205.2000 |
| 10 | 51 | 1971.6000 |
| 11 | 72 | 1217.4000 |
| 12 | 18 | 1612.5000 |
| 13 | 17 | 1349.4000 |
| 14 | 56 | 1770.8000 |

One key clarification is needed regarding the HAVING clause; HAVING qualifies the grouped or aggregated data, after the data has been grouped or aggregated. Use the WHERE clause to qualify what rows are returned *before* the data is aggregated or grouped.

# 15.14 How to... Use the ORDER BY Clause

The ORDER BY clause orders query results. The default sorting order of ORDER BY is ascending, which can be explicitly specified as ASC. Choose DESC to return the results in reverse order. You can use one or more columns in your ORDER BY clause, so long as the columns do not exceed 8,060 bytes in total. The syntax for ORDER BY is as follows:

```
SELECT [ALL | DISTINCT]
         TOP n [PERCENT]
         <column_1>,
         <column_N...>
INTO    <new_table_name>
FROM   <data_source>
WHERE  <seach_condition or search_conditions>
GROUP BY [ ALL ] column_1, column_N...
    WITH { CUBE | ROLLUP }
HAVING <search_condition>
ORDER BY <order_expression> <ASC or DESC>
```

## Example 15.14.1: Using ORDER BY

This example uses the query from the previous example, ordering the output in numeric order by ProductId:

```
SELECT ProductId,
        SUM(UnitPrice)as 'Total Price'
FROM OrderDetails
GROUP BY ProductId
HAVING SUM(UnitPrice) > 1000
ORDER BY ProductId
```

This returns:

| | ProductId | Total Price |
|---|---|---|
| 1 | 17 | 1349.4000 |
| 2 | 18 | 1612.5000 |
| 3 | 20 | 1215.0000 |
| 4 | 28 | 1385.2000 |
| 5 | 29 | 1713.3800 |
| 6 | 38 | 5902.4000 |
| 7 | 43 | 1205.2000 |
| 8 | 51 | 1971.6000 |
| 9 | 56 | 1770.8000 |
| 10 | 59 | 2761.0000 |
| 11 | 60 | 1638.8000 |
| 12 | 62 | 2227.8000 |
| 13 | 69 | 1036.8000 |
| 14 | 72 | 1217.4000 |

To output the results from highest to lowest, add the DESC clause:

```
SELECT ProductId,
        SUM(UnitPrice)as 'Total Price'
FROM OrderDetails
GROUP BY ProductId
HAVING SUM(UnitPrice) > 1000
ORDER BY ProductId DESC
```

Query results can be ordered by a column not displayed in the result set. For example, the next query displays the last name and first name of world leaders; the results, however, are sorted in order of vchCountry:

```
SELECT vchLastName,
vchFirstName
FROM Leaders
ORDER BY vchCountry
```

This returns (first few rows displayed):

| | vchLastName | vchFirstName |
|---|---|---|
| 1 | Karzai | Hamid |
| 2 | Moisiu | Alfred |
| 3 | Howard | John |
| 4 | Verhofstadt | Guy |
| 5 | Cardoso | Fernando Henrique |
| 6 | Chretien | Jean |
| 7 | Zemin | Jiang |

What you do not see is vchCountry; nevertheless, the first three leaders shown belong to Afghanistan, Albania, and Australia.

# 15.15 How to... Use Subqueries

A subquery is a SELECT statement nested inside another SELECT, INSERT, UPDATE, or DELETE statement. Subqueries can be nested inside other subqueries up to 32 levels deep. For the subquery, you cannot include ORDER BY (unless used in conjunction with a TOP clause), COMPUTE BY, or FOR BROWSE.

Subqueries can be used to return:

- A single value
- An asterisk (*) for correlated subqueries (described later)
- A list of values against which to be evaluated via an IN, NOT IN, ANY, SOME, or ALL operator

Subqueries can also be used in place of an expression in a SELECT clause. You cannot return NTEXT, TEXT, or IMAGE data types in a subquery SELECT list. The GROUP BY and HAVING clauses are only allowed if the subquery returns a single value; and DISTINCT is not allowed if GROUP BY is specified. The INTO and COMPUTE clauses are not allowed at all.

## Example 15.15.1: Using a subquery for a single value

This query returns the name of a book from the Books table, based on the maximum iBookId from the BookSales table. The subquery returns a single value, which is used to set the value of the outer query (an outer query is the calling query, and the inner query is the subquery):

```
SELECT    vchBookName
FROM BOOKS
WHERE     iBookId =
           (SELECT MAX(iBookId)
          FROM BookSales)
```

## Example 15.15.2: Using a subquery for an IN list

This example retrieves all book names for those books with a matching iBookId in the Books and BookSales tables; this time, the subquery supplies a list of multiple values (book IDs). Multiple value subqueries can be used with outer queries with the IN or NOT IN operator:

```
SELECT    vchBookName
FROM BOOKS
WHERE    iBookId IN
        (SELECT iBookId
      FROM BookSales)
```

The ANY operator is equivalent to the IN clause. The next query returns the same results, but with using the = and ANY operator:

```
SELECT    vchBookName
FROM BOOKS
WHERE    iBookId = ANY
     (SELECT iBookId FROM BookSales)
```

You can use the ALL operator to compare against ALL values of the subquery. The following query only returns vchBookName values from the Books table where the iBookId is greater than all values in the BookSales table:

```
SELECT   vchBookName
FROM BOOKS
WHERE   iBookId > ALL
     (SELECT iBookId FROM BookSales)
```

### Example 15.15.3: Using a subquery in place of an expression

You can use a subquery in place of an expression; this type of subquery should only return one row and one column. This example query displays iBookId and moBookPrice from the BookSales table. A subquery is used for the third column, displaying total book sales from the BookOrders table:

```
SELECT  iBookId,
         moBookPrice,
         (SELECT SUM(moBookSales) FROM BookOrders) AS 'Total Sales'
FROM BookSales
```

### Example 15.15.4: Using a correlated subquery

A correlated subquery depends on the outer query for its values. The subquery is repeatedly executed for each row selected by the outer query. In this example, the ProductID and ProductName columns are returned from the Products table, for those rows with a matching CategoryID in the Categories table:

```
SELECT  ProductID,
         ProductName
FROM    Products
WHERE  CategoryID IN
              (SELECT Categories.CategoryId
              FROM Categories
              WHERE Products.CategoryID = Categories.CategoryID)
```

Notice that the full table name is used to qualify the CategoryId. Use aliases to distinguish columns within a correlated subquery. Make sure that your correlated subqueries are truly necessary, as most can be re-written to use the JOIN clause instead. For example, the previous query could also be fulfilled more simply like this:

```
SELECT     ProductID,
            ProductName
FROM      Products P
INNER JOIN Categories C ON
    C.CategoryId = P.CategoryId
```

Keep in mind that correlated subqueries can also be used in the HAVING clause of an outer calling query. For example, this query returns iRegionId and moTotalSales from BookSales_NY, where the minimum value of the moTotalSales is greater than all moTotalSales values from the BookSales_MN table:

```
SELECT iRegionId,
        moTotalSales
FROM   BookSales_NY
GROUP BY iRegionId,
           moTotalSales
HAVING MIN(moTotalSales) > ALL
    (SELECT MAX(moTotalSales)
                   FROM BookSales_MN)
```

### Example 15.15.5: Checking for the existence of a row or rows

You can use the EXISTS or NOT EXISTS keywords to validate whether the subquery returns a row (rather than a particular column). The following example selects the vchBookName from the Books table, where there is a row match from the BookSales table:

```
SELECT vchBookName
FROM Books B
WHERE EXISTS
        (SELECT *
         FROM BookSales S
        WHERE B.iBookId = S.iBookId)
```

Again, this is a query that could best be performed by a JOIN operation. For example:

```
SELECT vchBookName
FROM Books B
INNER JOIN BookSales S ON
    B.iBookId = S.iBookId
```

# 15.16 How to... Use UNION to Combine Result Sets

The UNION operator is used to combine the results of two or more SELECT statements into a single result set. Each SELECT statement being merged must have the same number of columns, with the same or compatible data types in the same order. The syntax is as follows:

```
SELECT <columns>
FROM <data source, sources>
WHERE <query specification>
UNION <ALL>
SELECT <columns>
FROM <data source, sources>
WHERE <query specification>
```

The default behavior of the UNION operator is to remove all duplicate rows, and display column names based on the first result set. If the ALL clause is added, duplicate rows are not removed.

### Example 15.16.1: Using the UNION operator

The following example takes all rows from the Orders_Hawaii and Orders_Georgia, and combines them into one result set. Any duplicate rows are removed automatically:

```
SELECT OrderId, OrderDate, ShipRegion
FROM Orders_Hawaii
UNION
SELECT OrderId, OrderDate, ShipRegion
FROM Orders_Georgia
```

This returns (partial result set):

| | OrderId | OrderDate | ShipRegion |
|---|---|---|---|
| 1 | 10248 | 1996-07-04 00:00:00.000 | Georgia |
| 2 | 10248 | 1996-07-04 00:00:00.000 | Hawaii |
| 3 | 10249 | 1996-07-05 00:00:00.000 | Georgia |
| 4 | 10249 | 1996-07-05 00:00:00.000 | Hawaii |
| 5 | 10250 | 1996-07-08 00:00:00.000 | Georgia |
| 6 | 10250 | 1996-07-08 00:00:00.000 | Hawaii |
| 7 | 10251 | 1996-07-08 00:00:00.000 | Georgia |

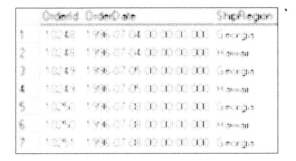

## Example 15.16.2: Using the UNION ALL operator

When ALL is added to the UNION operator, duplicates are not removed from the results. Let's say we have three tables with overlapping order numbers; if we used UNION to display all three result sets as one result set, using ALL would display the duplicate values:

```
SELECT OrderId
FROM Orders_Hawaii
UNION ALL
SELECT OrderId
FROM Orders_Georgia
UNION ALL
SELECT OrderId
FROM Orders
ORDER BY OrderId
```

Notice that the last SELECT query uses the ORDER BY clause to sort the results for the entire result set. Make sure to refer to the column name in the first SELECT statement for use in the ORDER BY clause. For example, if the first table is OrderID, and the second table uses the Orderidentity as the column name, and you wish to order the results by this column, reference the OrderID not Orderidentity. The results of the previous example (top few rows displayed) display the duplicates:

| | OrderId |
|---|---|
| 1 | 10248 |
| 2 | 10248 |
| 3 | 10248 |
| 4 | 10249 |
| 5 | 10249 |
| 6 | 10249 |
| 7 | 10250 |
| 8 | 10250 |
| 9 | 10250 |
| 10 | 10251 |

# 15.17 How to... Use COMPUTE in a SELECT Statement

`COMPUTE` creates aggregate function totals at the end of a query result set for specific columns listed in the `SELECT` statement. If using `ORDER BY`, you can also create aggregate function totals by the column being ordered. The syntax for `COMPUTE` is as follows:

```
SELECT <columns>
FROM <data source, sources>
WHERE <query specification>
ORDER BY <columns>
COMPUTE
  <AVG | COUNT | MAX | MIN | STDEV | STDEVP | VAR | VARP | SUM >
      ( expression )
  BY <expression or expressions>
```

### Example 15.17.1: Including computations for the entire result set

The following query lists `stor_id`, `ord_num`, and `qty` from the sales table. At the end of the result set, the average and sum of the `qty` field will be calculated:

```
SELECT stor_id,
       ord_num,
       qty
FROM   sales
COMPUTE AVG(qty), SUM(qty)
```

This returns:

| | stor_id | ord_num | qty |
|---|---|---|---|
| 1 | 6380 | 6871 | 5 |
| 2 | 6380 | 722a | 3 |
| 3 | 7066 | A2976 | 50 |
| 4 | 7066 | QA7442.3 | 75 |
| 5 | 7067 | D4482 | 10 |
| 6 | 7067 | P2121 | 40 |
| 7 | 7067 | P2121 | 20 |
| 8 | 7067 | P2121 | 20 |
| 9 | 7131 | N914008 | 20 |
| 10 | 7131 | N914014 | 25 |
| 11 | 7131 | P3087a | 20 |
| 12 | 7131 | P3087a | 25 |

| | avg | sum |
|---|---|---|
| 1 | 23 | 515 |

### Example 15.17.2: Listing computations for each change in a column grouping

This next example lists `stor_id`, `ord_num`, and `qty` from the `sales` table, but this time computes average and sum `qty` for each unique `stor_id`. Notice that the `ORDER BY` clause is included, which is required to use `COMPUTE BY stor_id`:

```
SELECT stor_id,
         ord_num,
         qty
FROM   sales
WHERE stor_id IN (6380, 7066, 7067)
ORDER BY stor_id
COMPUTE AVG(qty), SUM(qty)
BY stor_id
```

This returns:

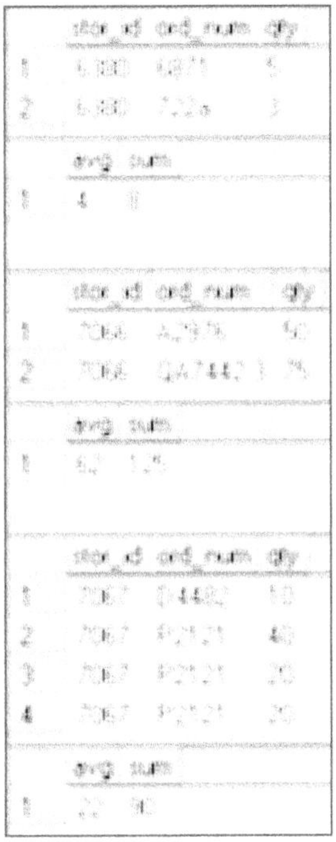

| | stor_id | ord_num | qty |
|---|---|---|---|
| 1 | 6380 | 6871 | 5 |
| 2 | 6380 | 722a | 3 |

| | avg | sum |
|---|---|---|
| 1 | 4 | 8 |

| | stor_id | ord_num | qty |
|---|---|---|---|
| 1 | 7066 | A2976 | 50 |
| 2 | 7066 | QA7442.3 | 75 |

| | avg | sum |
|---|---|---|
| 1 | 62 | 125 |

| | stor_id | ord_num | qty |
|---|---|---|---|
| 1 | 7067 | D4482 | 10 |
| 2 | 7067 | P2121 | 40 |
| 3 | 7067 | P2121 | 20 |
| 4 | 7067 | P2121 | 20 |

| | avg | sum |
|---|---|---|
| 1 | 22 | 90 |

The average and sum values of `qty` are computed for each unique `stor_id` value.

# 15.18 How to... Use the FOR Clause

The `FOR` clause is used to specify `BROWSE` or `XML` options. When `FOR BROWSE` is chosen, locks are `NOT` held while the `SELECT` statement accesses data. A table is **browse compliant** when it includes a `TIMESTAMP` column, a unique index, and uses `FOR BROWSE` in the `SELECT` statement.

`FOR XML` is completely unrelated to `BROWSE` mode, and is used to return a relational result set in hierarchical `XML` format.

The syntax for the `FOR` clause is as follows:

```
SELECT [ALL | DISTINCT]
         TOP n [PERCENT]
         <column_1>,
         <column_N…>
```

```
INTO      <new_table_name>
FROM     <data_source>
WHERE   <seach_condition or search_conditions>
GROUP BY [ ALL ] column_1, column_N...
    WITH { CUBE | ROLLUP }
HAVING <search_condition>
ORDER BY <order_expression> <ASC or DESC>
FOR <BROWSE | XML > { RAW | AUTO | EXPLICIT }
      < , XMLDATA >
      <, ELEMENTS >
      <, BINARY BASE64 >
```

Chapter 18 will discuss FOR XML and its associated keywords in more detail.

# 15.19 How to... Use the INSERT Statement

The INSERT statement adds rows into a table. The simple form of the syntax is as follows:

```
INSERT <INTO> <table_name or view_name> (<column_list>)
VALUES (<comma separated value list>)
```

The INTO keyword is optional for use in the INSERT statement. After choosing the table name for the new rows, you must include a column listing for the table in brackets if you do not plan on supplying all column values for the INSERT. A comma must separate each column; otherwise, column lists are unnecessary if your INSERT statement provides all values. You should use column lists for your production code, however, particularly if the base schema undergoes periodic changes; doing so will allow you to add new columns to the base table without changing the referencing code.

After the VALUES keyword (in brackets), include a comma-separated list of the values to insert. The VALUES keyword must be provided in the same order as the listed columns or, if no columns are listed, the same order of the columns in the table.

## Example 15.19.1: Adding data to a table via the INSERT statement

In this example, a single row will be inserted into the Books table:

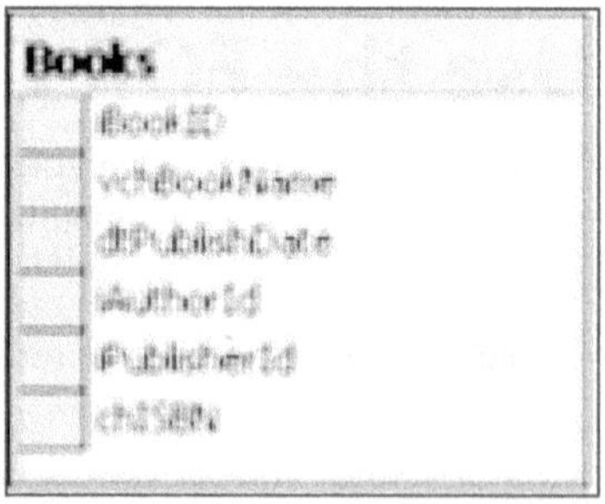


Because iBookId is an IDENTITY column, an INSERT statement cannot add its value explicitly. Since not all values are provided, table columns must be explicitly listed within brackets. After the VALUES keyword, each supplied value is listed too, in column order, with the appropriate data type:

```
INSERT Books (vchBookName,
              dtPublishDate,
              iAuthorId,
              iPublisherId,
              chISBN)
VALUES ('Love in the age of SQL',
        '2/2/02',
        2,
        33,
        '023482-32422')
```

## Example 15.19.2: Inserting DEFAULT values

Use the `DEFAULT` or `DEFAULT VALUES` keywords to skip entering a literal value for your `INSERT` statement, inserting the `DEFAULT` table definition values instead.

For example, the `Fruits` table has a default value for the `chFoodType` column, using `fruit` when the value is not set:

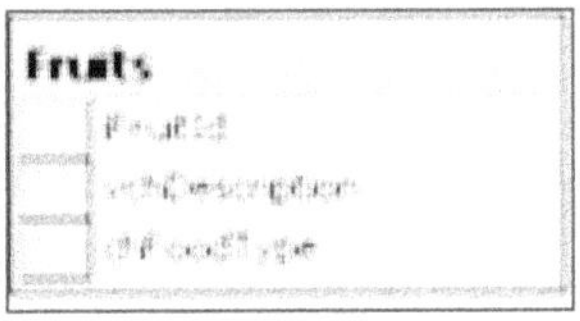

To insert the `DEFAULT` value automatically, the next example uses the following syntax (the `iFruitID` is an `IDENTITY` column and is not used in the `INSERT` statement):

```
INSERT Fruits (vchDescription, chFoodType)
VALUES ('Apple', DEFAULT)
```

If the `vchDescription` also used a `DEFAULT`, you could use the `DEFAULT VALUES` to create a row without any provided values. This is useful for when you need to insert a row before you have all the required information:

```
INSERT Fruits
DEFAULT VALUES
```

## Example 15.19.3: Inserting data from a SELECT statement

Previous examples showed how to insert one single row of data; by using the `INSERT...SELECT` statement, you can insert multiple rows into a table based on a `SELECT` query from a table, table variable, or view. The `SELECT` statement must return columns in the same order and data type compatibility as the `INSERT` column list. When the column list is not specified, the `SELECT` statement must provide all values of the table into which the data is being inserted.

This example inserts one or more rows into the `fruits` table, using a `SELECT` query from the `exotic_fruits` table:

```
INSERT fruits (vchDescription, chFoodType)
SELECT vchDescription,
       chFoodType
FROM exotic_fruits
WHERE chFoodType = 'exotic'
```

### Example 15.19.4: Inserting data from a stored procedure call

You can add rows to a table based on the output of a stored procedure. The stored procedure can only be used if it returns data via a `SELECT` or `READTEXT` from within the procedure definition. (`READTEXT` and other text and image functions will be reviewed in Chapter 16.)

The following example creates a table to contain the results of the `sp_helprolemember` stored procedure. An `INSERT` statement is used to contain the returned results from the stored procedure:

```
CREATE TABLE RoleMembers
    (DbRole varchar(50) NOT NULL,
     MemberName varchar(100) NOT NULL,
     MemberSID varbinary(80) NULL)

INSERT RoleMembers
EXEC sp_helprolemember

SELECT *
FROM RoleMembers
```

This example returns something like the following (although the output you receive will depend on the roles defined in the current database, and the members of those roles):

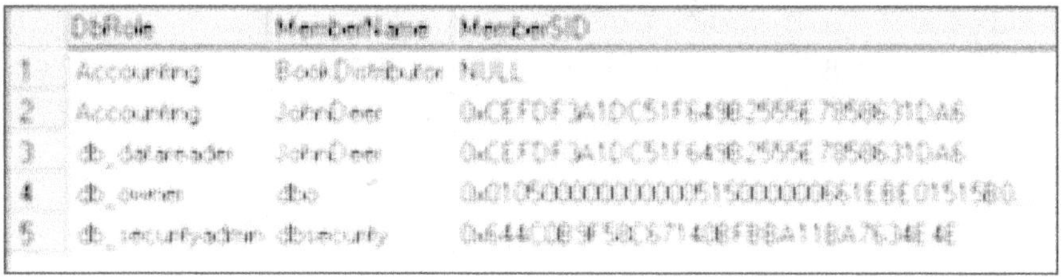

| | DbRole | MemberName | MemberSID |
|---|---|---|---|
| 1 | Accounting | BookDistributor | NULL |
| 2 | Accounting | JohnDoe | [illegible] |
| 3 | db_datareader | JohnDoe | [illegible] |
| 4 | db_owner | dbo | [illegible] |
| 5 | db_securityadmin | dbsecurity | [illegible] |

# 15.20 How to... Use the UPDATE Statement

The `UPDATE` statement is used to modify data in a table. With the `UPDATE` statement, you can apply changes to a single column or multiple columns, and to a single row or multiple rows.

The `UPDATE` statement works in a similar manner to the `SELECT` statement, in that you can update rows with a `FROM` clause and associated `WHERE` clause search conditions.

The basic syntax is as follows:

```
UPDATE <table_name or view name>
SET <column name> = <expression or default>
FROM <table or view name>
WHERE <search condition>
```

The `FROM` and `WHERE` clauses are not mandatory; you will find, however, that they are usually implemented to specify the rows to be modified.

### Example 15.20.1: Updating values in a table

Our first example updates the dtUpdateDate column of the Books table for all rows. The GETDATE() function is used for the value; a literal date value, however, could also have been provided. All rows are affected, as a WHERE clause was not used:

```
UPDATE Books
SET dtUpdateDate = GETDATE()
```

### Example 15.20.2: Updating values in a table using the WHERE clause

This example updates the Books table, updating the dtPublishDate column when the iBookId equals 2. Notice that a WHERE clause is used instead of a FROM clause; a WHERE clause without a FROM clause means that the table used in the WHERE clause is the same as the table being updated:

```
UPDATE Books
SET dtPublishDate = '2/2/2002'
WHERE iBookId = 1
```

### Example 15.20.3: Update multiple columns

To update multiple columns within the same UPDATE query, separate each column/value pair with a comma. Taking the previous example, the dtPublishDate and dtUpdateDate columns will be updated this time:

```
UPDATE Books
SET dtPublishDate = '2/2/2002',
  dtUpdateDate = GETDATE()
WHERE iBookId = 1
```

### Example 15.20.4: Performing UPDATEs based on other tables

An UPDATE can be performed on a table using values derived from another table. To do this, you can use the same FROM and WHERE clauses that you would with a SELECT statement, including joins and search conditions.

This example updates the vchDescription column of the Fruits table. The vchDescription column is changed to the vchDescription column of the exotic_fruits table, for those rows that have a matching iFruitId (between the two tables):

```
UPDATE Fruits
SET vchDescription = exotic_fruits.vchDescription
FROM Fruits,
   Exotic_Fruits
WHERE Fruits.iFruitId = Exotic_Fruits.iFruitId
```

This next query updates the nuTotalBooksSold field for all rows in the Authors table, using the total count of books sold in the BookSales table. Notice that the iAuthorId is joined between the Authors and BookSales tables:

```
UPDATE Authors
SET nuTotalBooksSold = (SELECT COUNT(*)
       FROM BookSales
       WHERE Authors.iAuthorId =
       BookSales.iAuthorId)
```

# 15.21 How to... Use the DELETE Statement

Use the DELETE statement to remove one or more rows from a table. The simple syntax is as follows:

```
DELETE <FROM> <table_name or view name >
FROM <outside table or view to join against>
WHERE <search condition>
```

The WHERE clause works similarly to the SELECT statement WHERE clause, applying a search condition to those rows impacted by the DELETE operation. The DELETE clause is also similar to the UPDATE clause, in that the clause can remove records based on its own search condition, or a search condition from another table.

### Example 15.21.1: Delete rows from a table

The following example deletes all rows from the exotic_fruits table; this is because a WHERE clause is not specified to narrow down the rows that must be removed:

```
DELETE exotic_fruits
```

### Example 15.21.2: Delete rows based on search criteria

This example deletes any rows where the vchDescription is equal to Apple:

```
DELETE exotic_fruits
WHERE vchDescription ='Apple'
```

### Example 15.21.3: Delete rows based on search criteria from another table

This example removes rows based on search criteria from a different table (a table from which nothing is being deleted). Rows are deleted from Authors whenever a match is found between the iAuthorId of the Authors and BookSales table:

```
DELETE Authors
FROM Authors A,
   BookSales B
WHERE A.iAuthorId = B.iAuthorId
```

# 15.22 How to... TRUNCATE a TABLE

The TRUNCATE TABLE statement, like the DELETE statement, can delete rows from a table. TRUNCATE TABLE deletes rows faster than DELETE, because it is minimally logged. The TRUNCATE operation *can* be rolled back if used within a transaction. Unlike DELETE, however, TRUNCATE TABLE must be used to remove all rows in the table (no WHERE clause), and cannot be run against columns actively referenced by a foreign key constraint. The syntax is:

```
TRUNCATE TABLE <table_name>
```

For example:

```
TRUNCATE TABLE authors
```

# 15.23 How to... Use Hints

Microsoft provides query, join, and table **hints** that can be used to override SELECT, INSERT, UPDATE, and DELETE processing behavior. Because hints override SQL Server commands, their use is not recommended unless you have significant query-tuning experience, and good reasons for using them. Hints can improve performance in the short term, but underlying objects can undergo changes that minimize the improvements. Furthermore, new service packs and SQL Server editions could nullify any positive effects. If you choose to use hints, document where you used them so you can evaluate their usage later on. Be sure to test the performance of your queries with and without the query hints (see Chapter 17 for more details on examining query performance).

## Table Hints

Below is a list of table hints. Those hints grouped together in the same cell can only have one selection from the group used per query; you cannot, for example, use both NOLOCK and HOLDLOCK for the same query. Table hints can be used for SELECT, INSERT, UPDATE, and DELETE queries. Specify table hints by using the WITH clause:

| Hint Name | Description |
|---|---|
| FASTFIRSTROW | This hint optimizes the query to pull the first row of the result set very quickly. Whether or not this hint will work depends on the size of your table, indexing used, and the type of data you are returning. Test your results with and without the hint, to be sure that the hint is necessary. Use this hint in order to begin returning results to the client faster, not to improve the speed of the entire result set. |
| INDEX = | Overrides SQL Server's index choice and forces a specific index for the table to be used. You are advised to use the INDEX (index_number_1, index_number_N) syntax instead, as INDEX = may not be available in future editions of SQL Server. |
| NOEXPAND | When an indexed view is referenced, the query optimizer will treat the view like a table with a clustered index. |
| HOLDLOCK<br>SERIALIZABLE<br>REPEATABLEREAD<br>READCOMMITTED<br>READUNCOMMITTED<br>NOLOCK | Selecting one of these hints determines the isolation level for the table. For example, specifying NOLOCK means that the operation (SELECT, for example) will place no locking on the table. |
| ROWLOCK<br>PAGLOCK<br>TABLOCK<br>TABLOCKX<br>NOLOCK | Determines the granularity of locking for the table; for example, selecting ROWLOCK to force only row locks for a query. |
| READPAST | Skips locked rows, and does not read them. |

*Table continued on following page*

| Hint Name | Description |
|---|---|
| UPDLOCK | The hint will force update locks instead of shared locks to be generated (not compatible with NOLOCK or XLOCK). |
| XLOCK | This hint forces exclusive locks on the resources being referenced (not compatible with NOLOCK or UPDLOCK). |

### Example 15.23.1: Using a locking table hint

This example selects all rows of the Books table, without placing any locks (but risking dirty reads). Notice that the WITH keyword is used, with the hint placed in parentheses. You can use multiple hints for one query, separated by commas, so long as they do not belong to the same category grouping:

```
SELECT *
FROM Books
WITH (NOLOCK)
```

### Example 15.23.2: Using multiple hints

This example uses three hints, thus producing no locks, optimizing speed for the first row, and forcing a specific index to be used:

```
SELECT *
FROM products
WITH (NOLOCK, FASTFIRSTROW,INDEX(1))
```

## Join Hints

Join hints force the internal JOIN operation used to join two tables in a query:

| Hint Name | Description |
|---|---|
| LOOP<br>MERGE<br>HASH<br>REMOTE | Each hint type specifies which method will be used to join the rows of two tables. LOOP joins operate best when one table is small and the other is large, with indexes on the joined columns. MERGE joins are optimal for medium or large tables that are sorted on the joined column. HASH joins are optimal for large, unsorted tables. REMOTE forces the join operation to occur at the site of the table referenced on the right (the second table referenced in a JOIN clause). For performance benefits, the left table should be the local table, and should have fewer rows than the remote right table. |

### Example 15.23.3: Forcing a MERGE join

This next example forces a MERGE join for a query. Notice that the MERGE hint precedes the JOIN keyword:

```
SELECT *
FROM Employees E
  INNER MERGE JOIN EmployeeTerritories T ON
    E.EmployeeID = T.EmployeeID
```

# Query Hints

Query hints can be used for SELECT, UPDATE, or DELETE operations (but not for an INSERT operation). Query hints are set with the OPTION clause:

| Hint Name | Description |
|---|---|
| <HASH or ORDER> GROUP | When used in conjunction with the GROUP BY clause, specifies whether hashing or ordering is used for GROUP BY and COMPUTE aggregations. |
| <MERGE or HASH or CONCAT> UNION | Selects the strategy used to join all result sets for UNION operations. |
| FAST *integer* | Speeds up the retrieval of rows for the top *integer* value chosen. |
| FORCE ORDER | When used, table joins are performed in the order in which the tables appear. |
| ROBUST PLAN | Creates a query plan with the assumption that the row size of a table will be at maximum width. |
| MAXDOP *integer* | This determines the max degree of parallelism for your query (overriding the server level setting). |
| KEEP PLAN | The recompile threshold for the query is **relaxed** when this hint is used. |
| KEEPFIXED PLAN | When this hint is used, the query optimizer is forced not to recompile due to statistics or indexed column changes. Only schema changes or sp_recompile will cause the query plan to be recompiled. |
| EXPAND VIEWS | This hint keeps the query optimizer from using indexed views when the base table is referenced. |

### Example 15.23.4: Using query hints

This query example uses two query hints, forcing the GROUP BY clause to use a HASH method, and using a ROBUST PLAN option:

```
SELECT ProductName,
       COUNT(*)
FROM   Products
GROUP BY ProductName
OPTION (HASH GROUP, ROBUST PLAN)
```

# 16

# Transact-SQL Techniques

Transact-SQL, an extension to the SQL database programming language, is a powerful language offering many features. Transact-SQL provides the SQL Server developer with several useful functions, conditional processing methods, advanced transaction control, exception and error handling, scrollable cursors, and much more. This chapter explores how to utilize Transact-SQL techniques within your SQL statements, batches, and procedures.

## 16.1 How to... Use Aggregate Functions

Aggregate functions return **one** value based on calculations against one ore more values. Aggregate functions can be used within SELECT, COMPUTE, COMPUTE BY, and HAVING clauses, but cannot be used in a WHERE clause. They can be used to calculate the summary values of the non-null values in a particular column, and can be applied to all the rows in a table, producing a single value (a scalar aggregate).

The general syntax for using aggregate functions is:

```
Aggregate_function ([ALL | DISTINCT] expression)
```

| Parameter | Description |
|---|---|
| Aggregate_function | The name of the function. |
| ALL | When used, the aggregate function is applied to ALL values. |
| DISTINCT | When used, the aggregate function is applied to only unique instances of values. |
| expression | The expression can use any numeric data type except BIT, with no aggregate functions or sub-queries allowed. |

The aggregate functions available with Transact-SQL are:

- AVG
- BINARY_CHECKSUM

- CHECKSUM
- CHECKSUM_AGG
- COUNT
- COUNT_BIG
- GROUPING
- MAX
- MIN
- SUM
- STDEV
- STDEVP
- VAR
- VARP

# AVG

Calculates the average of non-NULL values.

### Example 16.1.1: Using AVG

The following query calculates the average book price for all books in the BookSales table:

```
SELECT AVG(moBookPrice)as 'Average Price'
FROM dbo.BookSales
```

# BINARY_CHECKSUM

This function can detect changes to a row of a table or a list of expressions by returning a binary checksum value computation. Order of columns can impact the result.

### Example 16.1.2: Using BINARY_CHECKSUM

The first example displays two versions of the word Hello; they are the same word, but in different character cases (the second HELLO is in uppercase):

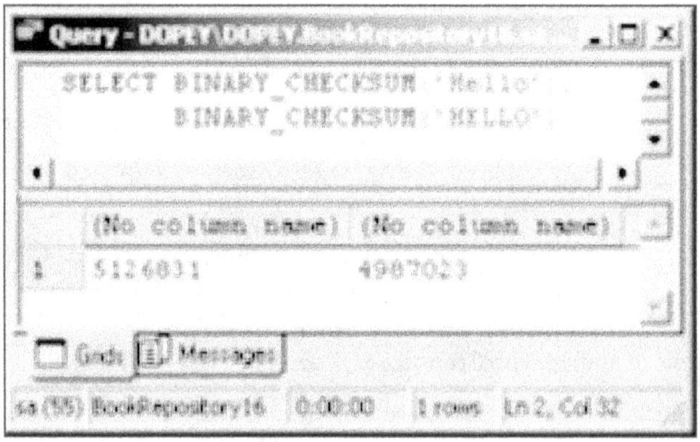


This returns two different values.

Now, if we re-run this query using the same case for both expressions:

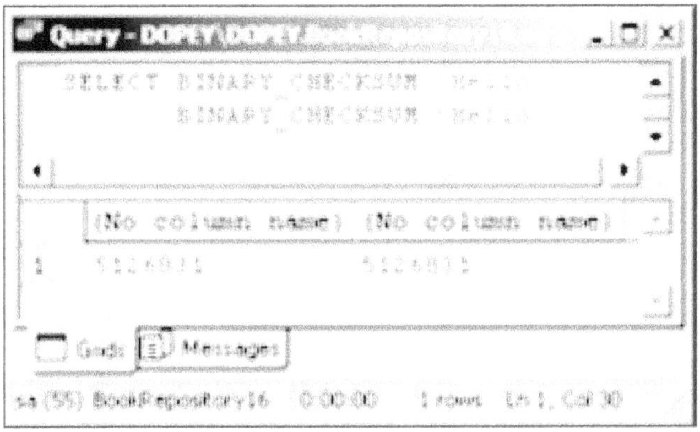


The same number will be returned.

You can also execute BINARY_CHECKSUM against all columns in a table. In this next query, the BINARY_CHECKSUM is calculated on the Books table, for the row with an iBookId of 3:

```
SELECT BINARY_CHECKSUM(*)
FROM Books
WHERE iBookId = 3
```

Now an update is executed against that same row:

```
UPDATE Books
SET dtUpdateDate = GETDATE()
WHERE iBookID = 3
```

If the BINARY_CHECKSUM query is run against the row again, a different value will be returned because the column has been changed. **Most** variances, when comparing string values, will be detected using BINARY_CHECKSUM; however, there is no guarantee that every change to a row will result in a different BINARY_CHECKSUM value. It is possible (albeit not very likely) that two different rows will have the same checksum value.

# CHECKSUM

Calculates a row or expression's value for use in a hash index. Hash indexes can be used for character columns that are too wide to index optimally. CHECKSUM is implemented by creating a CHECKSUM column that references a specific character column, upon which an index can then be placed. The query can now reference the CHECKSUM value index to retrieve the wide character row. CHECKSUM is **mostly** unique, so any query should reference both the CHECKSUM column (so the index is used) and the character column. See the following example for more detail.

## Example 16.1.3: Using CHECKSUM

In this example, we will add a computed column to the Leaders table, which will calculate CHECKSUM for the vchTitle column. To add the column, the following syntax will be used:

```
ALTER TABLE Leaders
ADD hash_job_desc AS CHECKSUM(vchTitle)
```

Selecting the results from the table, you will see the new CHECKSUM column:

Next, an index can be added to the hash_job_desc. Since the computed column uses an integer data type, it will be a smaller (and potentially more efficient) index than if placed on the vchTitle column:

```
CREATE NONCLUSTERED INDEX idx_hash_vchTitle
       ON Leaders(hash_job_desc)
```

This new hash_job_desc can now be used in a query searching for vchTitle matches, especially since it is now indexed:

```
SELECT *
FROM LEADERS
WHERE hash_job_desc= CHECKSUM('President') AND
      vchTitle = 'President'
```

The vchTitle column is **still** searched in the WHERE clause; this is because the CHECKSUM is not 100% guaranteed to be unique for each value. However, CHECKSUM will usually be accurate, and will, therefore, hold a performance benefit over an attempt to create indexes on larger character columns.

By viewing the execution plan, you will see that the new index was used properly (more on the execution plan in Chapter 17).

To enable the execution plan viewing, execute the following statement:

```
SET SHOWPLAN_TEXT ON
```

Then run the query:

```
SELECT *
FROM LEADERS
WHERE hash_job_desc= CHECKSUM('President') AND
      vchTitle = 'President'
```

This returns the following output, which notes that the `idx_has_vchTitle` index **was** used:

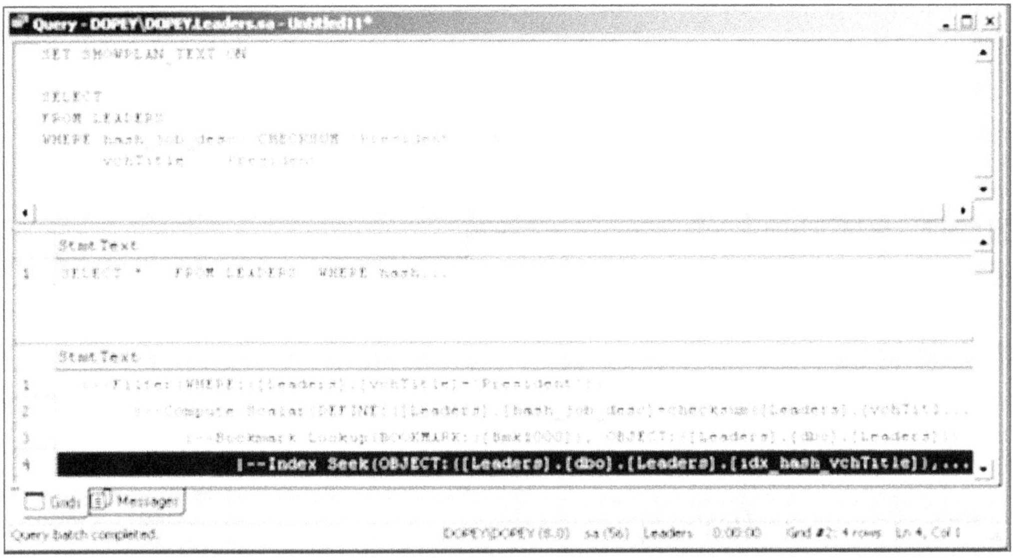


# CHECKSUM_AGG

This aggregate function is used to return a `CHECKSUM` value for an entire grouping of columns. It returns one value for either the entire table, or a specific column to evaluate whether changes have occurred. The data type for the function must be either a `BINARY_CHECKSUM` function result or an integer data type.

## Example 16.1.4: Using CHECKSUM_AGG

This next example calculates the `CHECKSUM_AGG` for the entire `Leaders` table:

```
SELECT CHECKSUM_AGG (BINARY_CHECKSUM(*))
FROM Leaders
```

This returns a number. We will update the `Leaders` table:

```
UPDATE Leaders
SET vchFirstName = 'George W.'
WHERE ID = 4
```

Re-executing the `CHECKSUM_AGG` will now return a new number, indicating that a change has been made somewhere in the table.

# COUNT

`COUNT` returns an `INT` data type with the count of rows in a group. If there is no other column grouping, then the entire table (or query) is considered to be one group, and `COUNT` will return the number of rows in the query or table. `COUNT` is the only aggregate function that does **not** ignore `NULL` values. (However `COUNT DISTINCT <expression>` does ignore `NULL`s, counting the number of non-null values of the `<expression>`.)

### Example 16.1.5: Using COUNT

The following query retrieves the row count from the `Leaders` table:

```
SELECT COUNT(*)
FROM Leaders
```

This returns a number, 16 in this case.

# COUNT_BIG

`COUNT_BIG` works just like `COUNT`, only `COUNT_BIG` returns a `BIGINT` data type value.

# GROUPING

`GROUPING` works in conjunction with `CUBE` or `ROLLUP`, to evaluate whether the row is either an actual row from the table, or the result of a `CUBE` or `ROLLUP` operator. `GROUPING` returns the value `0` for a regular row, and `1` when a result of `CUBE` or `ROLLUP`.

### Example 16.1.6: Using GROUPING and SUM

This next query retrieves the `SUM` of the quantity column of the `Sales` table, grouped by each `stor_id`. The `GROUPING` aggregate function is also used, against the column in the `GROUP BY` clause (`stor_id`):

The last row displays a `1` for the `Grouping?` field, because it is not an actual row of the table, but rather a result of the `WITH CUBE` clause.

# MAX

This function returns the highest value in a group of non-`NULL` values.

# MIN

This function returns the lowest value in a group of non-NULL values.

### Example 16.1.7: Using MIN and MAX

The following query displays the minimum and maximum quantity values from the Sales table:

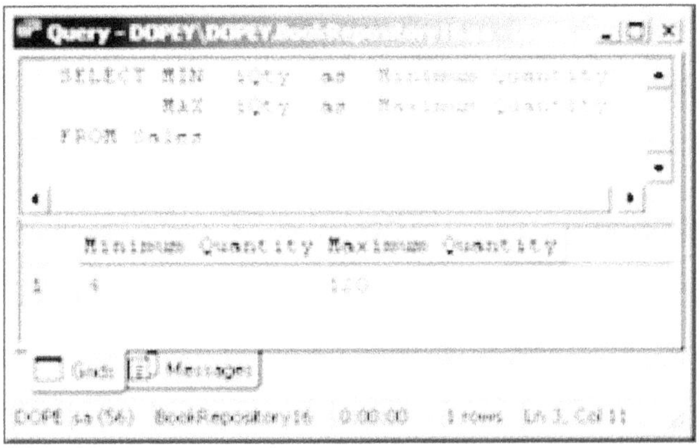


# SUM

SUM returns the total of all non-NULL values in an expression.

# STDEV

STDEV returns the standard deviation of all values provided in the expression. STDEV evaluates a population **sample**.

# STDEVP

STDEVP returns the standard deviation for **all** values in the provided expression. STDEV evaluates a population, not just a sample of the population.

### Example 16.1.8: Using STDEV and STDEVP

This example shows the standard deviation of a sample of the quantity field, and the entire population of the quantity field, from the Sales table:

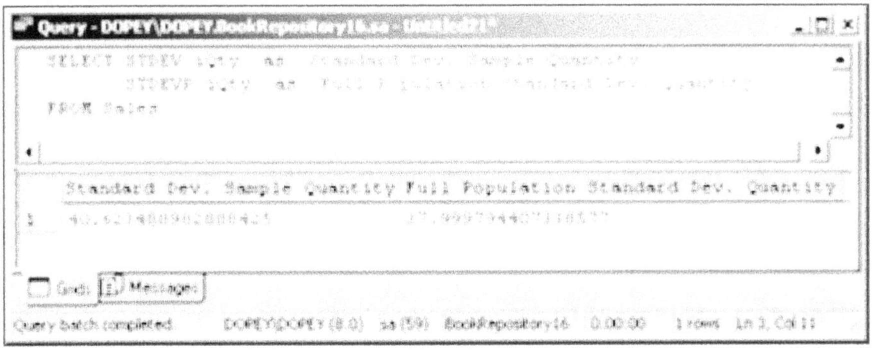

## VAR

VAR returns the variance of the provided values in an expression. VAR uses a sample of the provided population.

## VARP

VARP returns the variance of the provided values for the entire data population provided.

### Example 16.1.9: Using VAR and VARP

The following query computes the sample and full population variance of the quantity field, from the Sa les table:

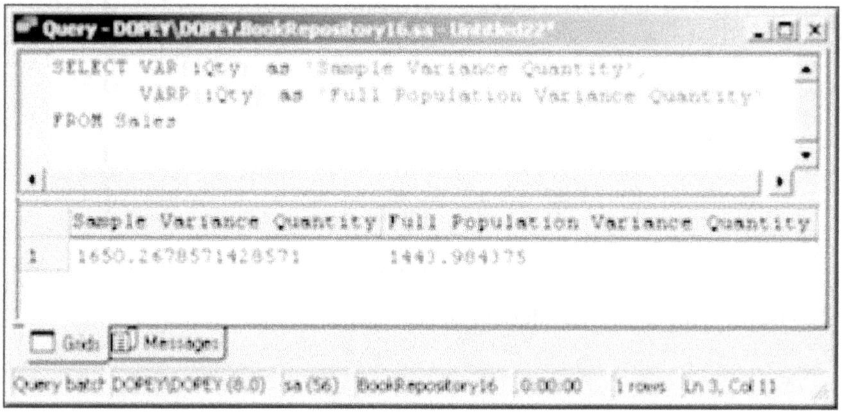


# 16.2 How to... Use String Functions

String functions perform operations against a character data type, and return a value depending on the function type used. String functions are **scalar** functions, meaning they operate on **one** value, and return a **single** value. String functions can be used anywhere an expression is permitted, including within the SELECT and WHERE clauses. String functions can also be nested within other string functions.

The general syntax for string functions is:

```
function_name (arguments)
```

## ASCII

ASCII takes the leftmost character of a character expression and returns the ASCII code. The syntax is:

```
ASCII (<string>)
```

The string can be either the CHAR or VARCHAR data type.

### Example 16.2.1: Using ASCII

This example selects the values of letters A and Z in ASCII code:

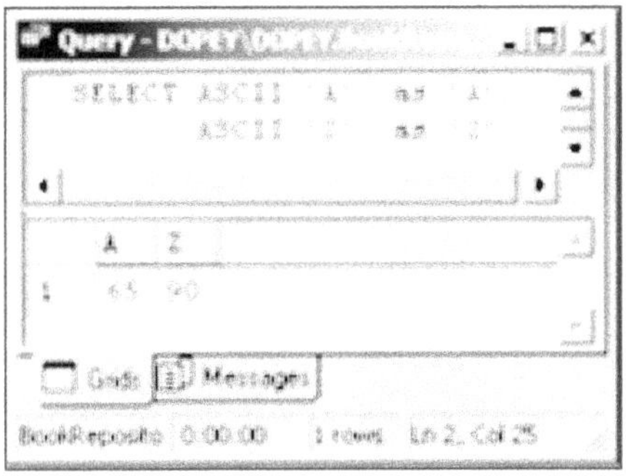

# CHAR

`CHAR` converts an integer value for an ASCII code to a character value instead. The syntax is:

```
ASCII (<integer_value>)
```

## Example 16.2.2: Using CHAR

In this case, we do the reverse of the previous example, seeking the character values for the numbers 65 and 90:

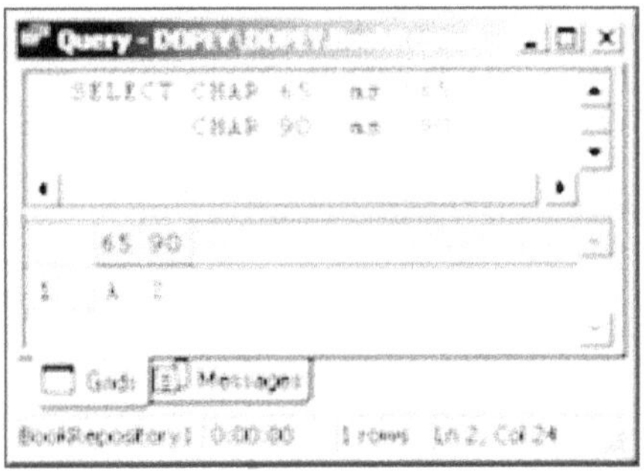

# CHARINDEX

The `CHARINDEX` function returns the position of a string you wish to find within another string. The syntax is:

```
CHARINDEX (<string_you_wish_to_find> , <string_you_are_searching_in>,
<integer_value_starting_position>)
```

The string to be searched can be any of the character type data types, including `CHAR`, `NCHAR`, `VARCHAR`, `NVARCHAR`, `TEXT`, and `NTEXT`.

## Example 16.2.3: Using CHARINDEX

This example searches for the string `Find Me` within a longer string. The starting position is the first character (`1`):

```
SELECT CHARINDEX ('Find Me' , 'Where will you find me?' , 1)
```

This returns 16, meaning the string `find me` is found on the sixteenth character of the larger string.

# PATINDEX

The PATINDEX function works just like CHARINDEX, except that PATINDEX can also use wildcards. PATINDEX returns the start position of the first occurrence of the search pattern, and does not use a starting position integer value. The syntax for PATINDEX is:

```
PATINDEX (<string_you_wish_to_find>, <string_you_are_searching_in>)
```

The string to be searched can be any of the character type data types, including CHAR, NCHAR, VARCHAR, NVARCHAR, TEXT, and NTEXT.

### Example 16.2.4: Using PATINDEX

This example searches for Find within the larger string. Notice that wildcards are used, and no starting position is specified:

```
SELECT PATINDEX ('%Find%' , 'Where will you find me?')
```

This returns 16.

# DIFFERENCE and SOUNDEX

The two functions, DIFFERENCE and SOUNDEX, both work with character strings to evaluate those that 'sound similar'. SOUNDEX assigns the strings a 4-digit code, and DIFFERENCE evaluates the level of similarity between the SOUNDEX output for two separate strings. DIFFERENCE returns a value of zero to four, with four indicating the closest match in similarity. The syntax for SOUNDEX is:

```
SOUNDEX (<expression_to_evaluate>)
```

This function allows CHAR, NCHAR, VARCHAR, and NVARCHAR data type expressions.

The syntax for DIFFERENCE is:

```
DIFFERENCE (<expression_1>, <expression_2>)
```

The expression can be the data type of CHAR, NCHAR, VARCHAR, or NVARCHAR.

### Example 16.2.5: Using SOUNDEX

This example performs the SOUNDEX function against two words, Rock and Out:

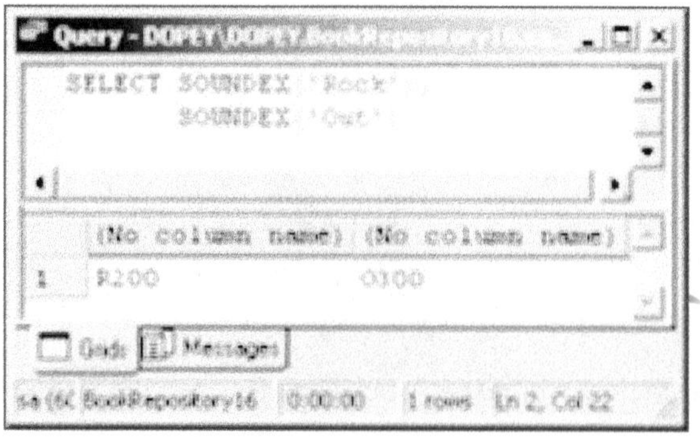

Now, if we run a query showing `Rock` and `Rack`, you will see that the code is identical, as vowels are disregarded when calculating the `SOUNDEX` value:

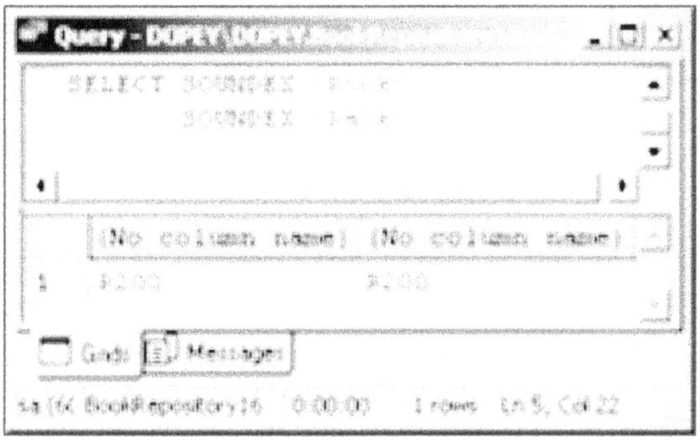


### Example 16.2.6: Using DIFFERENCE

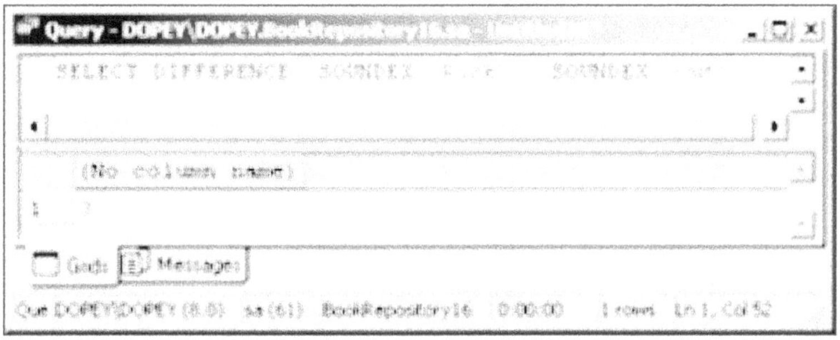


# LEFT and RIGHT

The `LEFT` function returns a part of a character string, beginning at the specified number of characters from the left. The `RIGHT` function is similar to the `LEFT` function, only it returns a part of a character string, beginning at the specified number of characters from the right.

The syntax for `LEFT` is:

```
LEFT (<character_expression>, <integer_start_position>)
```

The expression can be the data type of `CHAR`, `NCHAR`, `VARCHAR`, or `NVARCHAR`.

The syntax for `RIGHT` is:

```
RIGHT (<character_expression>, <integer_start_position>)
```

The expression can be the data type of `CHAR`, `NCHAR`, `VARCHAR`, or `NVARCHAR`.

### Example 16.2.7: Using LEFT and RIGHT

This first example extracts the **first** five characters of the string `Hello There`:

```
SELECT LEFT('Hello There', 5)
```

This returns Hello.

This next example extracts the **last** five characters of the string Hello There:

```
SELECT RIGHT('Hello There', 5)
```

This returns There.

# LEN

This function returns the number of characters of a string expression, excluding any blanks after the last character (trailing blanks). The syntax for LEN is:

```
LEN (<string>)
```

The string can be the data type of CHAR, NCHAR, VARCHAR, or NVARCHAR.

## Example 16.2.8: Using LEN

This example returns the number of characters for the string Blueberry:

```
SELECT LEN('Blueberry')
```

This returns 9.

This second example shows the impact on length of leading and trailing blanks:

```
SELECT LEN('    Blueberry                         ')
```

This returns 13, as the trailing blanks aren't counted.

# LOWER and UPPER

The LOWER function returns a character expression in lowercase. The UPPER function returns a character expression in uppercase. The syntax for LOWER is:

```
LOWER (<string_to_put_in_lowercase>)
```

The syntax for UPPER is:

```
UPPER (<string_to_put_in_uppercase>)
```

The string expression for both UPPER and LOWER can be the data type of CHAR, NCHAR, VARCHAR, or NVARCHAR.

## Example 16.2.9: Using UPPER and LOWER

The following example shows the result of using UPPER and LOWER on the string Hello There:

```
SELECT UPPER('Hello There')
```

This returns HELLO THERE.

```
SELECT LOWER('Hello There')
```

This returns hello there.

# LTRIM and RTRIM

The LTRIM function returns a string with **leading blanks** (blanks before the starting characters) removed. The RTRIM function returns a string with **trailing blanks** removed. The syntax for LTRIM is:

```
LTRIM (<string_to_trim_leading_blanks>)
```

The syntax for RTRIM is:

```
RTRIM (<string_to_trim_trailing_blanks>)
```

The string expression for both LTRIM and RTRIM can be the data type of CHAR, NCHAR, VARCHAR, or NVARCHAR.

### Example 16.2.10: Using LTRIM and RTRIM

For this example, let's first insert a value into the Books table, with leading and trailing blanks for the value of txtDescription:

```
INSERT INTO Books (vchBookName, txtDescription)
  VALUES (' SQL II: The Sequel ', 'A sequel to the classic bestseller')
```

Next, if we run the following SELECT statement, and attempt to pull any rows with the value SQL II: The SQL, none will be returned; this is because it was inserted with leading and trailing blanks:

```
SELECT *
FROM Books
WHERE vchBookName = 'SQL II: The Sequel'
```

To remove both leading and trailing blanks, use LTRIM and RTRIM together:

```
SELECT *
FROM Books
WHERE LTRIM(RTRIM(vchBookName)) = 'SQL II: The Sequel'
```

This returns the expected result.

# NCHAR and UNICODE

The NCHAR function takes an integer value specifying a Unicode character, and converts it to its character equivalent. The syntax for NCHAR is:

```
NCHAR (<integer_value_for_Unicode_character>)
```

The UNICODE function does the reverse of NCHAR, and returns the Unicode integer value for the first character of the character or input expression. The syntax for UNICODE is:

```
UNICODE (<expression_to_convert_to_integer>)
```

### Example 16.2.11: Using NCHAR and UNICODE

This first example returns the Unicode integer value for the letter Z:

```
SELECT UNICODE('Z')
```

This returns 90.

Now we can perform the opposite, returning the Unicode character value for the integer value 90:

```
SELECT NCHAR(90)
```

This returns Z.

## REPLACE and STUFF

The REPLACE function replaces all instances of a given string within a specified string, and replaces it with a new string, returning the value of the modified string:

```
REPLACE (<string_to_be_searched>, <string_to_replace>, <replacement_string>)
```

The string to be searched can be a CHAR, NCHAR, VARCHAR, or NVARCHAR, and the BINARY data type.

The STUFF function deletes a specified length of characters and inserts the given string at a specified starting point. The syntax for STUFF is as follows:

```
STUFF (<character_string>, <integer_start>, <integer_deletion_length>,
<string_to_stuff_into_other_string>)
```

The character string can be a CHAR, NCHAR, VARCHAR, or NVARCHAR, or the BINARY data type.

### Example 16.2.12: Using REPLACE and STUFF

In this example, the REPLACE function is used to remove the There from Hello There!, and replace it with Friend:

```
SELECT REPLACE ('Hello There!', 'There', 'Friend')
```

This returns Hello Friend!

In this example using STUFF, the string below will have eight characters deleted, beginning with the 19th character. The replacement string will be the word bun,:

```
SELECT STUFF ('Hold the pickles, lettuce, and mayo',
19, 8, 'bun,')
```

This returns Hold the pickles, bun, and mayo.

## QUOTENAME

The QUOTENAME function takes an input string, and returns it as a valid SQL Server-delimited Unicode identifier. The syntax for QUOTENAME is:

```
QUOTENAME (<character_string>, <delimiter_character>)
```

The character string can be CHAR, NCHAR, VARCHAR, NVARCHAR, or NTEXT (but not TEXT).

The second parameter determines the delimiter used, with a choice of a single quotation mark, left or right bracket (default), or double quotation mark.

### Example 16.2.13: Using QUOTENAME

This example places quotes around a string, as a quotation mark was used for the second parameter:

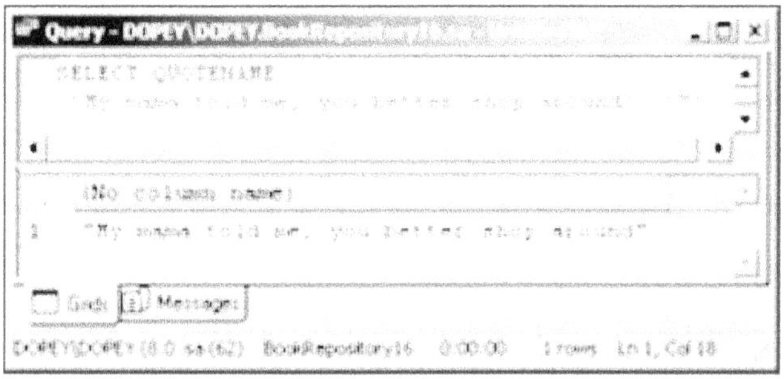

# REPLICATE

The REPLICATE function repeats a given character expression a given number of times. The syntax for REPLICATION is:

```
REPLICATE (<string_expression>, <integer_times_to_repeat>)
```

The string expression can be a CHAR, NCHAR, VARCHAR, NVARCHAR, or BINARY data type.

### Example 16.2.14: Using REPLICATE

This example returns the string specified in the first parameter eight times:

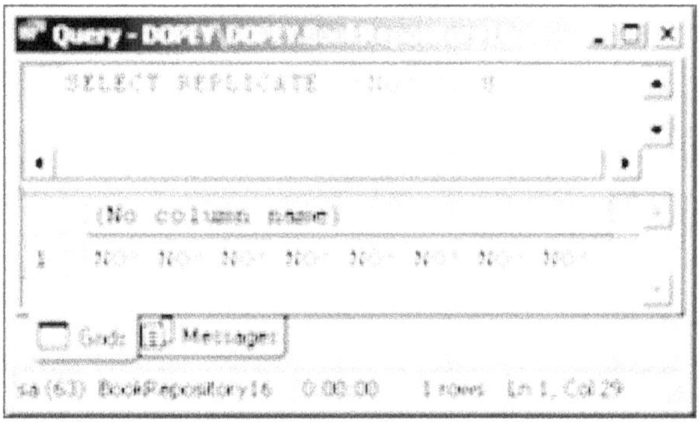

# REVERSE

The REVERSE function takes a character expression, and outputs the expression with each character position displayed in reverse order. The syntax for REVERSE is:

```
REVERSE (<expression_to_reverse>)
```

The string expression can be CHAR, NCHAR, VARCHAR, or NVARCHAR.

### Example 16.2.15: Using REVERSE

This next example reverses the word `!PLEH`:

```
SELECT REVERSE ('!PLEH')
```

This returns HELP!

## SPACE

The `SPACE` function returns a string of repeated blank spaces, based on the integer you use for the input parameter. The syntax for `SPACE` is:

```
SPACE (<integer_number_of_blank_spaces>)
```

### Example 16.2.16: Using SPACE

This example places ten blank spaces between two strings:

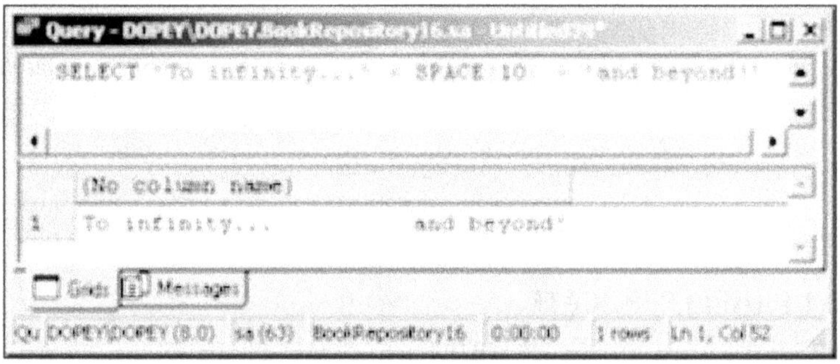


## STR

The `STR` function returns numeric data as character data. Unlike `NCHAR` or `ASCII` functions, `STR` represents the numbers as a string, so they may be inserted as a character data type or printed in a `PRINT` statement. `STR` is equivalent to the `CAST` and `CONVERT` functions, only it is limited to converting numeric values to the `CHAR` data type. The syntax for `STR` is as follows:

```
STR (<numeric_value_to_convert>, <optional_total_length_of_number>,
<optional_numer_of_places_right_of_the_decimal_point>)
```

### Example 16.2.17: Using STR

In this first example, the following statement will attempt to print a sentence concatenating two strings, and the number `59`:

```
PRINT 'Mom is ' + 59 +' years old'
```

This will return the following error:

Server: Msg 245, Level 16, State 1, Line 1
Syntax error converting the varchar value 'Mom is ' to a column of data type int.

Now let's try it again, but this time using the STR function to convert the number 59 to its string equivalent:

```
PRINT 'Mom is ' + STR(59) + ' years old'
```

This returns: Mom is         59 years old.

# SUBSTRING

The SUBSTRING function returns a defined chunk of a specified character (CHAR, NCHAR, VARCHAR, NVARCHAR), BINARY, TEXT, or NTEXTSTRING. The syntax for SUBSTRING is:

```
SUBSTRING (<expression_to_take_a_chunk_out_of>, <integer_start_position>,
<number_of_characters_to_take>)
```

## Example 16.2.18: Using SUBSTRING

This example takes a chunk out of the string defined in the first parameter, beginning at the 7th character, and taking out six characters from that point:

```
SELECT SUBSTRING
('I sure could use a vacation!', 7, 6)
```

This returns could.

# CONVERT and CAST

CONVERT and CAST are not exclusively defined as string functions, as they can be used to **convert multiple data types** from one type to another, not just character data types. The syntax for CAST is as follows:

```
CAST (<expression_to_convert> AS <data_type> (<optional_length>))
```

The syntax for CONVERT is:

```
CONVERT (<data_type> (<optional_length>), <expression_to_covert>,
<optional_style>)
```

The optional_style parameter is used for conversions from DATETIME or SMALLDATETIME to character data types using a specified integer value.

## Example 16.2.19: Using CAST and CONVERT

This first example uses CAST to convert a number into a CHAR(2) data type:

```
SELECT CAST(10 as char(2)) + ' more days until New Year''s Day!'
```

This returns: 10 more days until New Year's Day!

This next example uses CONVERT to convert a date (using the GETDATE() function) into a CHAR(25) data type:

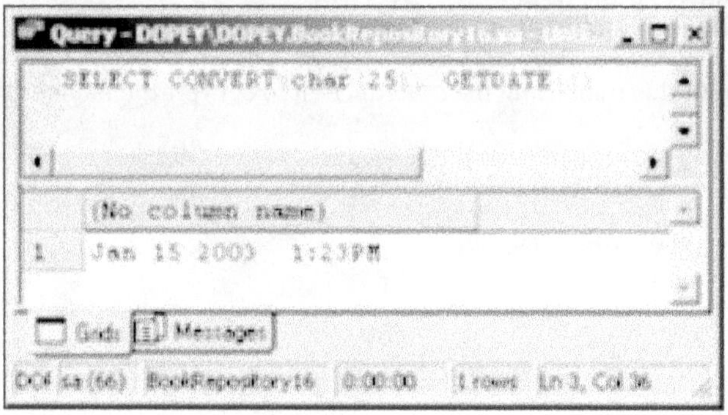


Styles can affect how your dates are presented when in character format. For example, using the style number 101 returns the mm/dd/yy format:

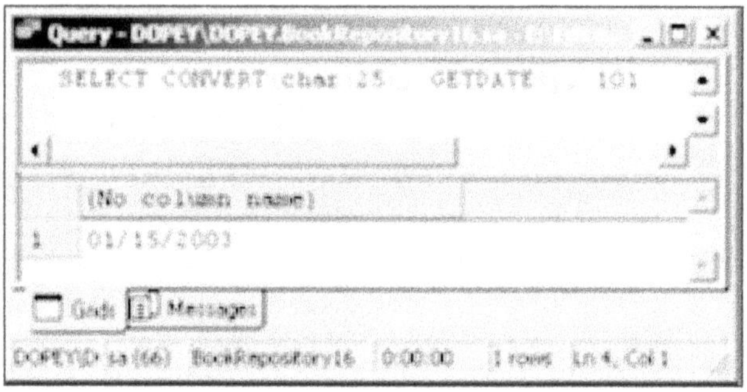


The different style options are as follows, as paraphrased from *SQL Server Books Online*:

| Without century (yy) | With century (yyyy) | Standard |
|---|---|---|
| - | 0 or 100 | Default |
| 1 | 101 | USA |
| 2 | 102 | ANSI |
| 3 | 103 | British/French |
| 4 | 104 | German |
| 5 | 105 | Italian |
| 6 | 106 | - |
| 7 | 107 | - |
| 8 | 108 | - |
| - | 9 or 109 | Default + milliseconds |
| 10 | 110 | USA |

| Without century (yy) | With century (yyyy) | Standard |
|---|---|---|
| 11 | 111 | JAPAN |
| 12 | 112 | ISO |
| - | 13 or 113 | Europe default + milliseconds |
| 14 | 114 | - |
| - | 20 or 120 | ODBC canonical |
| - | 21 or 121 | ODBC canonical (with milliseconds) |
| - | 126 | ISO8601 |
| - | 130 | Kuwaiti |
| - | 131 | Kuwaiti |

# 16.3 How to... Use Date Functions

Date functions are used to convert, manipulate, present, and calculate differences of DATETIME or SMALLDATETIME data types. Recall from Chapter 14 that the DATETIME data type date ranges are from January 1, 1753 through December 31, 9999. SMALLDATETIME ranges from January 1, 1900, through June 6, 2079.

## DATEADD

This function returns a new date that is incremented or decremented based on the interval and number specified. The syntax is:

```
DATEADD (<part_of_date_for_new_value>, <integer_increment_or_decrement>,
<date_to_modify>)
```

The first parameter takes either the following abbreviations, or the value listed in bold:

- yy or yyyy for Year
- qq or q for Quarter
- mm or m for Month
- dy or y for Dayofyear (day of year)
- dd or d for Day
- wk or ww for Week
- hh for Hour
- mi or n for Minute
- ss or s for Second
- ms for Millisecond

### Example 16.3.1: Using DATEADD

This example adds two years to the date 1/1/2001:

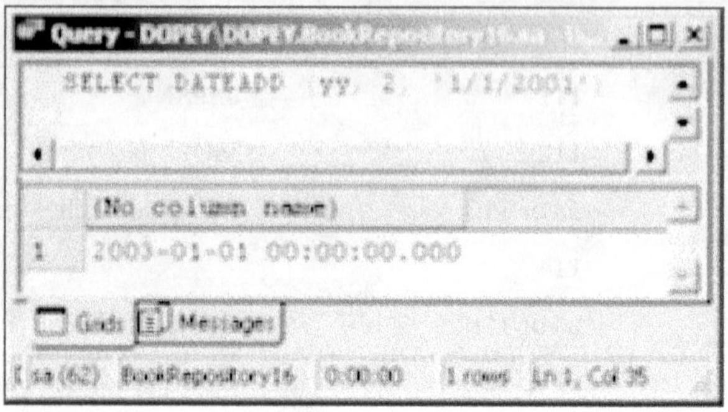


This next example subtracts 30 days from the date 10/31/2002:

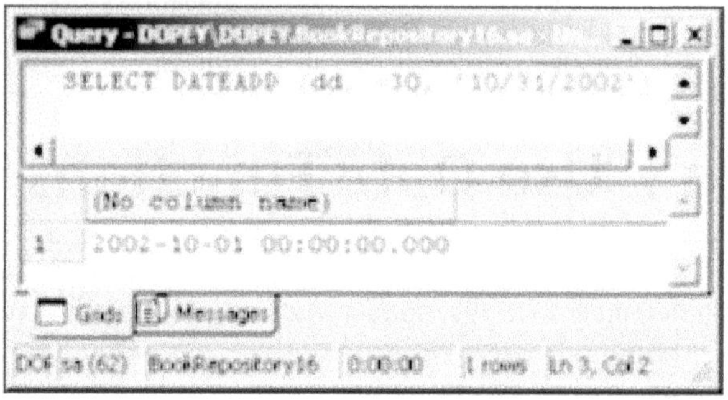


# DATEDIFF

This function subtracts the first date from the second date, to produce a value in the format of the increment specified. The syntax for DATEDIFF is:

```
DATEDIFF (<part_of_date_for_new_value>, <first_date>, <second_date>)
```

The first parameter takes the same date values as DATEADD (mm, mi, ss, and so on).

## Example 16.3.2: Using DATEDIFF

This example returns the difference in days between 10/31/2002 and 6/1/2002:

```
SELECT DATEDIFF(dd, '10/31/2002','6/1/2002')
```

It returns -152.

# DATENAME

This function returns a string value for the part of a date specified in the first parameter; the second parameter gives the date to base the string value on. The syntax is:

```
DATENAME (<part_of_date_for_new_value>, <date>)
```

The first parameter takes the same date values as DATEADD and DATEDIFF (mm, mi, ss, and so on). DATENAME is specific to the login language setting; so if, for example, the language is set to DEUTSCH, the previous example would return Januar.

### Example 16.3.3: Using DATENAME

This example returns the name of the month, based on the date 1/1/2002:

```
SELECT DATENAME (month, '1/1/2002')
```

It returns January.

## DATEPART

This function returns an integer value for the part of a date specified in the first parameter. The second parameter sets the date to base the string value on. The syntax is:

```
DATEPART (<part_of_date_for_new_value>, <date>)
```

### Example 16.3.4: Using DATEPART

This example returns the integer value for the given month in the 5/1/2002 date:

```
SELECT DATEPART (month, '5/1/2002')
```

It returns 5.

## DAY

This function returns an integer value for the given day in the date provided for the first and only parameter. The syntax is:

```
DAY (<date>)
```

### Example 16.3.5: Using DAY

This example returns the day integer value for the date 1/16/02:

```
SELECT DAY ('1/16/02')
```

It returns16.

## GETDATE

This function returns the current system date and time, based on SQL Server server time value. The syntax is:

```
GETDATE ()
```

### Example 16.3.6: Using GETDATE()

This example returns the current system date and time:

```
SELECT GETDATE()
```

## GETUTCDATE

This function returns the Coordinated Universal Time (UTC) (formerly known as Greenwich Mean Time), based on the current local time of the SQL Server instance time value. The syntax is:

```
GETUTCDATE()
```

### Example 16.3.7: Using GETUTCDATE()

This example returns the Universal Time Coordinate value:

```
SELECT GETUTCDATE()
```

## MONTH

This function returns the integer representing the month of the provided date for the first and only parameter. The syntax is:

```
MONTH (<date>)
```

### Example 16.3.8: Using MONTH

This example returns the integer value for the given month in the date `7/31/02`:

```
SELECT MONTH ('7/31/02')
```

It returns 7.

## YEAR

This function returns the integer representing the year of the provided date for the first and only parameter. The syntax is:

```
YEAR (<date>)
```

### Example 16.3.9: Using YEAR

This example returns the integer value for the given year in the date `3/10/1973`:

```
SELECT YEAR ('3/10/1973')
```

It returns 1973.

# 16.4 How to... Use Display Information with @@ Functions

The `@@` functions are used to return information. Unlike the previous functions, these `@@` functions (called global variables in previous versions of SQL Server) do not take or expect parameters.

# @@CONNECTIONS

Returns the number of connections made to the SQL Server instance since it was last started.

### Example 16.4.1: Displaying total connections made since the SQL Server instance was last started

```
SELECT @@CONNECTIONS
```

# @@CPU_BUSY

Shows the number of busy CPU milliseconds since the SQL Server instance was last started.

# @@DATEFIRST

Returns the value of the specified first day of the week for the SQL Server instance (based on `SET DATEFIRST`).

# @@DBTS

Returns the current system timestamp value. Timestamp has nothing to do with dates or time but, rather, is used for insert and update tracking in a timestamp column of a table. `@@DBTS` returns the last-used timestamp value for the database.

# @@ERROR

Returns the last error integer value for the last Transact-SQL statement executed within the scope of the current connection.

### Example 16.4.2: Displaying the error-message number of the last Transact-SQL statement

First, a statement is executed that generates a divide by zero error:

```
SELECT 1/0
```

This returns:

```
Server: Msg 8134, Level 16, State 1, Line 1
Divide by zero error encountered.
```

If `@@ERROR` is executed immediately afterwards:

```
SELECT @@ERROR
```

This returns the last error number, 8134.

# @@IDENTITY

Executing `SELECT @@IDENTITY` after an `INSERT`, `SELECT INTO`, or bulk copy statement for a table with an identity column defined, will return the last-used identity value generated by the very last insert.

Do be careful when using `@@IDENTITY` within your application, as `@@IDENTITY` will return the current `IDENTITY` value across any scope in the current session. For example, if an `INSERT` occurs against a table with an `IDENTITY` column, and this table `INSERT` causes the table trigger to fire, which in turn `INSERT`s into a different table with an `IDENTITY` column, `@@IDENTITY` will return the last `IDENTITY` value of the **second** table.

## @@IDLE

Displays the total idle time of the SQL Server instance, since the instance was last started, in milliseconds.

## @@BUSY

Displays the number of milliseconds spent performing `I/O` operations since the SQL Server instance was last started.

## @@LANGID

Returns a `SMALLINT` data type value representing the local language identifier for the current database.

## @@LANGUAGE

Returns the name of the language currently in use.

## @@LOCK_TIMEOUT

Returns the current connection lock timeout setting in milliseconds.

## @@MAX_CONNECTIONS

Returns the maximum number of simultaneous user connections to the SQL Server instance.

## @@MAX_PRECISION

Returns the maximum precision level for decimal and numeric data types for the SQL Server instance.

## @@NESTLEVEL

Returns the current nesting level for the stored procedure context (when a stored procedure calls another stored procedure, and so on, up to 32 levels).

## @@OPTIONS

Returns an integer value representing the current connection `SET` options.

## @@PACK_RECEIVED

Returns the total input packets read from the network since the SQL Server instance was last started. You can monitor whether the number increments or stays the same, thus surmising whether there is a network availability issue.

## @@PACK_SENT

Returns the total output packets sent to the network since the SQL Server instance was last started.

## @@PACKET_ERRORS

Displays the total network packet errors that have occurred since the SQL Server instance last started.

## @@PROCID

Displays the current procedure's stored procedure identifier.

## @@REMSERVER

Once connected to a remote server, this function returns the remote server's name.

## @@ROWCOUNT

This function returns the number of rows affected by the last Transact-SQL statement.

## @@SERVERNAME

Displays the local server name.

## @@SERVICENAME

Displays the registry key name of the SQL Server Service instance.

## @@SPID

Returns the current connection's server process identifier (the SPID you see when you execute `sp_who` or `sp_who2`).

## @@TEXTSIZE

Displays the maximum bytes of `TEXT` or `IMAGE` data that a `SELECT` statement can return for the current connection.

## @@TIMETICKS

Displays the number of microseconds per tick. A tick is a unit of measurement set to a specified number of milliseconds (31.25 milliseconds for Windows 2000).

## @@TOTAL_ERRORS

Displays read/write errors encountered since the SQL Server instance was last started.

## @@TOTAL_READ

Displays the number of non-cached disk reads by the SQL Server instance since it was last started.

## @@TOTAL_WRITE

Displays the number of disk writes by the SQL Server instance since it was last started.

### Example 16.4.3: Displaying total disk read and write activity since the SQL Server instance was last started

```
SELECT @@TOTAL_READ,
       @@TOTAL_WRITE
```

## @@TRANSCOUNT

Displays active transactions for the current connection.

## @@VERSION

Displays version information for your current SQL Server instance.

# 16.5 How to... Use Mathematical Functions

Mathematical functions return values often needed for operations on numeric data. The general form for mathematical functions is:

```
function_name(arguments)
```

## ABS

Calculates the absolute value. The syntax is:

```
ABS (<numeric_value>)
```

### Example 16.5.1: Using ABS

```
SELECT ABS(-19)
```

Returns:

19

```
SELECT ABS(19)
```

Also returns:

19

## ACOS

Calculates the angle, the cosine of which is the specified argument, in radians. The syntax is:

```
ACOS (<float_value>)
```

### Example 16.5.2: Using ACOS

```
SELECT ACOS(.5)
```

Returns:

1.0471975511965976

# ASIN

Calculates the angle, the sine of which is the specified argument, in radians. The syntax is:

```
ASIN (<float_value>)
```

### Example 16.5.3: Using ASIN

```
SELECT ASIN(.75)
```

Returns:

0.848062078981481

# ATAN

Calculates the angle, the tangent of which is the specified argument, in radians. The syntax is:

```
ATAN (<float_value>)
```

### Example 16.5.4: Using ATAN

```
SELECT ATAN(50)
```

Returns:

1.550798992821746

# ATN2

Calculates the angle, the tangent of which is between two float expressions, in radians. The syntax is:

```
ATN2(<float_value_1>, <float_value_2>)
```

### Example 16.5.5: Using ATN2

```
SELECT ATN2(40,100)
```

Returns:

0.3805063771123649

# CEILING

Calculates the smallest integer greater than or equal to the provided argument. The syntax is:

```
CEILING (<numeric_value>)
```

### Example 16.5.6: Using CEILING

```
SELECT CEILING(1.5)
```

Returns:

2

# COS

Calculates the cosine. The syntax is:

```
COS (<float_value>)
```

### Example 16.5.7: Using COS

```
SELECT COS(12)
```

Returns:

0.84385395873249214

# COT

Calculates the cotangent. The syntax is:

```
COT(<float_value>)
```

### Example 16.5.8: Using COT

```
SELECT COT(100)
```

Returns:

-1.7029569194264691

# DEGREES

Converts radians to degrees. The syntax is:

```
DEGREES (<numeric_value>)
```

### Example 16.5.9: Using DEGREES

```
SELECT DEGREES(1.5)
```

Returns:

85.943669269623484000

# EXP

Calculates the exponential value of a provided argument. The syntax is:

```
EXP(<float_value>)
```

### Example 16.5.10: Using EXP

```
SELECT EXP(10)
```

Returns:

22026.465794806718

## FLOOR

Calculates the largest integer less than or equal to the provided argument. The syntax is:

```
FLOOR(<numeric_value>)
```

### Example 16.5.11: Using FLOOR

```
SELECT FLOOR (2.5)
```

Returns:

2

## LOG

Calculates the natural logarithm. The syntax is:

```
LOG (<float_value>)
```

### Example 16.5.12: Using LOG

```
SELECT LOG(2)
```

Returns:

0.69314718055994529

## LOG10

Calculates the Base-10 logarithm. The syntax is:

```
LOG (<float_value>)
```

### Example 16.5.13: Using LOG10

```
SELECT LOG10(20)
```

Returns:

1.3010299956639813

# PI

Returns the Pi constant. This function takes no parameters:

```
PI ()
```

### Example 16.5.14: Using PI

This next example displays the value (partial result) of `PI`:

```
SELECT PI()
```

This returns 3.1415926535897931

# POWER

Returns the value of the first argument to the power of the second argument. The syntax is:

```
POWER (<numeric_value>, <power_to_raise_numeric_value>)
```

### Example 16.5.15: Using POWER

This next example displays 15 to the power of 3:

```
SELECT POWER(15, 3)
```

Returns:

3375

# RADIANS

Converts degrees to radians. The syntax is:

```
RADIANS (<numeric_value>)
```

### Example 16.5.16: Using RADIANS

```
SELECT RADIANS(.5)
```

Returns:

.008726646259971650

# RAND

Produces a random float type value ranging from 0 and 1. The syntax is:

```
RAND (<tinyint_smallint_or_int_seed>)
```

### Example 16.5.17: Using RAND

If `RAND` is run without a value, a random number between 0 and 1 will be generated each time:

```
SELECT RAND()
```

Returns any number from 0 to 1.

Using a defined number as the parameter of `RAND()` will return the same value. For example:

```
SELECT RAND(.75)
```

Always returns:

0.94359739042414437

# ROUND

Rounds a provided argument's value to a specified precision. The syntax is:

```
ROUND(<numeric_value>, <precision_value>, <optional_function>)
```

When a positive number, the precision value specifies the number of decimal places to which to round the numeric value. When a negative number, the precision value is rounded on the left side of the decimal point. The last parameter is optional and, when set, truncates the numeric value based on the `TINYINT`, `SMALLINT`, or `INT` value provided.

### Example 16.5.18: Rounding to the nearest hundred

```
SELECT ROUND(450, -2)
```

Returns:

500

### Example 16.5.19: Rounding to the nearest ten

```
SELECT ROUND(455, -1)
```

Returns:

460

# SIGN

Returns `-1` for negative values, `0` for zero values, and `1` if the provided argument is positive. The syntax for `SIGN` is:

```
SIGN (<numeric_value>)
```

### Example 16.5.20: Testing a negative value

```
SELECT SIGN(-5)
```

Returns:

-1

### Example 16.5.21: Testing a positive value

```
SELECT SIGN(5)
```

Returns:

1

# SIN

Calculates sine for a given angle in radians. The syntax for `SIN` is:

```
SIN (<float_value>)
```

### Example 16.5.22: Using SIN

```
SELECT SIN ( 90 )
```

Returns:

0.89399666360055785

# SQUARE

Calculates the square of a provided expression. The syntax is:

```
SQUARE (<float_value>)
```

### Example 16.5.23: Using SQUARE

```
SELECT SQUARE(15)
```

Returns:

225.0

# SQRT

Calculates the square root. The syntax for SQRT is:

```
SQRT (<float_value>)
```

### Example 16.5.24: Using SQRT

```
SELECT SQRT(6)
```

Returns:

2.4494897427831779

## TAN

Calculates the tangent. The syntax for TAN is:

```
TAN (<float_value>)
```

### Example 16.5.25: Using TAN

```
SELECT TAN(1)
```

Returns:

1.5574077246549023

# 16.6 How to... Use Security functions

Security functions are used to return information about user and role security. They can be used independently of any other expression (although preceded by a SELECT statement at the very least, along with the proper parameters where applicable), or used within a Transact-SQL expression.

## HAS_DBACCESS

Use HAS_DBACCESS to see whether the current user connection has access to the specified database. The syntax is:

```
HAS_DBACCESS (<database_name>)
```

### Example 16.6.1: Using HAS_DBACCESS

```
SELECT HAS_DBACCESS ('BookRepository16')
```

This returns 1.

## IS_MEMBER

Use IS_MEMBER to validate whether the current user login has membership to the specified Windows NT group or SQL Server role. The function will return 1 if the conditions evaluate to TRUE. The syntax is:

```
IS_MEMBER(<group_or_role_name>)
```

### Example 16.6.2: Using IS_MEMBER

```
SELECT IS_MEMBER('db_owner')
```

This returns 1.

## IS_SRVROLEMEMBER

Use IS_SRVROLEMEMBER to validate whether the current user login is a member of the specified SQL Server server role. The function will return 1 if the conditions evaluate to TRUE. The syntax is:

```
IS_SRVROLEMEMBER (<server_role>, <optional_login_to_validate>)
```

### Example 16.6.3: Using IS_SRVROLEMEMBER

First, we will check whether the current connection is a member of sysadmin:

```
SELECT IS_SRVROLEMEMBER ('sysadmin')
```

This returns 1.

Next, the login JaneDoe will be verified, to see whether it is also a member of sysadmin:

```
SELECT IS_SRVROLEMEMBER ('sysadmin', 'JaneDoe')
```

This returns 0.

# SUSER_SID

SUSER_SID returns the security identification number for the specified user login. The syntax is:

```
SUSER_SID(<login>)
```

### Example 16.6.4: Using SUSER_SID

# SUSER_SNAME

Provided with a security identification number (SID), SUSER_SNAME will return the associated login name. The syntax is:

```
SUSER_NAME(<sid>)
```

### Example 16.6.5: Using SUSER_SNAME

```
SELECT SUSER_SNAME (0x0FB1CBDCE9FC67419FED0DC3D2FED4A4)
```

This returns JaneDoe.

# USER_ID

The `USER_ID` function returns the database identification number for a provided user. The syntax is:

```
USER_ID (<user_name>)
```

### Example 16.6.6: Using USER_ID

```
SELECT USER_ID ('JackSmith')
```

This returns something like 10.

# USER_NAME

This function returns a database user's user name when provided with the user identification number. The syntax is:

```
USER_NAME (<integer_id>)
```

### Example 16.6.7: Using USER_NAME

```
SELECT USER_NAME (10)
```

This returns JackSmith.

# 16.7 How to... Use Meta Data Functions

Meta data functions are used to return data about the database and the objects within. They can be used independently of any other expression (although preceded by a `SELECT` statement at the least, along with the proper parameters where applicable), or used within a Transact-SQL expression.

# COL_LENGTH

This function returns the defined maximum length of a specific table column in bytes (but not the actual length). The syntax is:

```
COL_LENGTH (<table_name>, <column_name>)
```

The first parameter requires the column's table, and the second parameter expects the name of the column for which the number of bytes is to be returned.

### Example 16.7.1: Using COL_LENGTH

This example returns the column length in bytes for the `lname` column from the `Employee` table. Variable length columns will display bytes based on the maximum possible length for the column:

```
SELECT COL_LENGTH ('Employee','lname')
```

It returns 30.

# DB_ID

This function returns the database integer ID for the specified database name. The syntax is:

```
DB_ID ( <database_name>)
```

### Example 16.7.2: Using DB_ID

```
SELECT DB_ID('BookRepository')
```

This returns 11.

# DB_NAME

This function returns the database name, given the database integer ID. The syntax is:

```
DB_NAME(<integer_db_id>)
```

### Example 16.7.3: Using DB_NAME

```
SELECT DB_NAME(11)
```

This returns BookRepository.

# FILE_ID

FILE_ID returns the file identification number for a specified logical file name in the current database context. The syntax is:

```
FILE_ID(<logical_file_name>)
```

### Example 16.7.4: Using FILE_ID

```
SELECT FILE_ID('BookRepo_Dat')
```

This returns 1.

# FILE_NAME

FILE_NAME returns the logical file name for the current database context, given the file identification number. The syntax is:

```
FILE_NAME(<integer_file_id>)
```

### Example 16.7.5: Using FILE_NAME

```
SELECT FILE_NAME(1)
```

This returns BookRepo_Dat.

# FILEGROUP_ID

FILEGROUP_ID returns the filegroup identification number when provided with the filegroup name. The syntax is:

```
FILEGROUP_ID (<filegroup_name>)
```

### Example 16.7.6: Using FILEGROUP_ID

In this example, the filegroup ID will be returned for the filegroup name FG3:

```
SELECT FILEGROUP_ID ('FG3')
```

It returns 3.

# FILEGROUP_NAME

FILEGROUP_NAME returns the filegroup name when provided with the filegroup identification number. The syntax is:

```
FILEGROUP_NAME(<filegroup_id>)
```

### Example 16.7.7: Using FILEGROUP_NAME

```
SELECT FILEGROUP_NAME (3)
```

This returns FG3.

# FILEPROPERTY

This function returns property values when provided with the file name and property name. The syntax is:

```
FILEPROPERTY (<logical_file_name>, <property>)
```

The valid properties are:

- IsReadOnly: checks whether the file is read-only. Returns 1 for TRUE, and 0 for FALSE.
- IsPrimaryFile: checks whether the file is the primary database file. Returns 1 for TRUE, and 0 for FALSE.
- IsLogFile: checks whether the file is a transaction log file. Returns 1 for TRUE, and 0 for FALSE.
- SpaceUsed: returns the amount of space used for the file, given as the number of 8KB pages allocated to the file.

### Example 16.7.8: Using FILEPROPERTY

This query checks to see whether the BookRepo_Dat file is the primary data file of the database:

```
SELECT FILEPROPERTY ('BookRepo_Dat','IsPrimaryFile')
```

It returns 1.

## OBJECT_ID

OBJECT_ID returns the database object identifier number, as assigned in the sysobjects database. The syntax is:

```
OBJECT_ID (<object_name>)
```

### Example 16.7.9: Using OBJECT_ID

```
SELECT OBJECT_ID ('Employees')
```

This returns 117575457.

## OBJECT_NAME

OBJECT_NAME returns the object name when provided with the object identifier number. The syntax is:

```
OBJECT_NAME(<object_identifier_number>)
```

### Example 16.7.10: Using OBJECT_NAME

```
SELECT OBJECT_NAME(117575457)
```

This returns Employees.

# 16.8 How to... Use System Functions

System functions are used to return information on an array of SQL Server settings and user connection context properties. Some system functions are also used to process arguments independently of system or connection settings (like COALESCE or ISNULL, for example). They can be used independently of any other expression (although preceded by a SELECT statement, and used with the proper parameters where applicable), or used within a Transact-SQL expression.

## APP_NAME

This function returns the name of the application for the current SQL Server connection. The syntax is:

```
APP_NAME ()
```

### Example 16.8.1: Using APP_NAME() from Query Analyzer

```
SELECT APP_NAME()
```

This returns SQL Query Analyzer.

## COALESCE

This function returns the first non-NULL value from the provided arguments. The syntax is:

```
COALESCE (<expression_1>, <expression_N>...)
```

### Example 16.8.2: Using COALESCE

This first example returns the first non-NULL expression from a list of two values (one hello and the other NULL):

```
SELECT COALESCE ('Hello', NULL)
```

This returns Hello.

Now if we run this SELECT statement again, only including two NULL values in the list prior to hello, the function still returns the first non-NULL value:

```
SELECT COALESCE (NULL, NULL, 'Hello')
```

Again, therefore, this returns Hello.

## CURRENT_TIMESTAMP

This function returns the date and time, exactly like the GETDATE() function.

### Example 16.8.3: Using CURRENT_TIMESTAMP

```
SELECT CURRENT_TIMESTAMP
```

## CURRENT_USER

This function displays the current user for the current connection.

### Example 16.8.4: Using CURRENT_USER

```
SELECT CURRENT_USER
```

This returns dbo.

## DATALENGTH

This function returns the number of bytes used for an expression. The syntax is as follows:

```
DATALENGTH(<expression>)
```

### Example 16.8.5: Using DATALENGTH

```
SELECT DATALENGTH('My Momma told me, "you better shop around".')
```

This returns 43.

## GETANSINULL

GETANSINULL returns information on the nullability settings of a specific database. When a database permits null values, and nullability is not explicitly defined, this function will return 1. The syntax is:

```
GETANSINULL (<database_name>)
```

### Example 16.8.6: Using GETANSINULL

```
SELECT GETANSINULL ('BookRepository')
```

This returns 1.

# HOST_ID

HOST_ID returns the workstation identification number for the current connection. This function does not accept parameters. The syntax is:

```
HOST_ID()
```

### Example 16.8.7: Using HOST_ID

```
SELECT HOST_ID()
```

This returns 1488.

# HOST_NAME

HOST_NAME returns the workstation name for the current connection. This function does not accept parameters. The syntax is:

```
HOST_NAME()
```

### Example 16.8.8: Using HOST_NAME

```
SELECT HOST_NAME()
```

This returns JOEPROD.

# IDENT_CURRENT

This function displays the last identity value generated for a specified table, regardless of session or scope context (unlike @@IDENTITY or SCOPE_IDENTITY) The syntax is:

```
IDENT_CURRENT('<table_name>')
```

### Example 16.8.9: Using IDENT_CURRENT

```
SELECT IDENT_CURRENT('Books')
```

Returns the value of the most recently generated IDENTITY value in the Books table.

# IDENT_INCR

This function displays the increment value for the IDENTITY column of a specific table or referencing view. The syntax is:

```
IDENT_INCR('<table_or_view>')
```

### Example 16.8.10: Using IDENT_INCR

```
SELECT IDENT_INCR('Books')
```

Returns the increment value for the IDENTITY column of the Books table.

## IDENT_SEED

This function displays the defined seed value for the IDENTITY column of a specific table or referencing view. The syntax is:

```
IDENT_SEED('<table_or_view>')
```

### Example 16.8.11: Using IDENT_SEED

```
SELECT IDENT_SEED('Books')
```

Returns the defined seed value for the IDENTITY column of the Books table.

## ISDATE and ISNUMERIC

ISDATE establishes whether an expression is a valid DATETIME value. The syntax for ISDATE is:

```
ISDATE (<expression>)
```

ISNUMERIC establishes whether or not an expression is a valid numeric data type value. The syntax is:

```
ISNUMERIC (<expression>)
```

Both ISNUMERIC and ISDATE return a 1 if the expression evaluates to TRUE.

### Example 16.8.12: Using ISDATE

```
SELECT ISDATE('I am not a date')
```

This returns 0.

```
SELECT ISDATE('12/1/2002')
```

This returns 1.

### Example 16.8.13: Using ISNUMERIC

```
SELECT ISNUMERIC('I am not a number.')
```

This returns 0.

```
SELECT ISNUMERIC(29.75)
```

This returns 1.

# ISNULL

ISNULL validates whether an expression is NULL and, if so, replaces the NULL value with an alternative value. The syntax is as follows:

```
ISNULL (<expression_to_validate>, <replacement_value>)
```

### Example 16.8.14: Using ISNULL

This example returns the value Missing Data, whenever a NULL value is encountered in the chISBN column of the Books table:

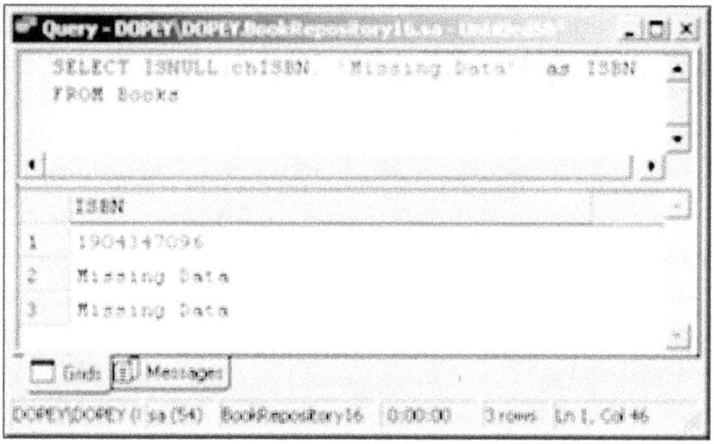


# NULLIF

NULLIF returns a null value when the two provided expressions are the same value; otherwise, the first expression is returned. The syntax is:

```
NULLIF (<expression_1>, <expression_2>)
```

### Example 16.8.15: Using NULLIF

```
SELECT NULLIF (1, 1)
```

This returns NULL.

```
SELECT NULLIF (47, 1)
```

This returns 47.

# ROWCOUNT_BIG

This function works in a similar way to @@ROWCOUNT, except that the returned data type is BIGINT. The syntax is:

```
ROWCOUNT_BIG()
```

### Example 16.8.16: Using ROWCOUNT_BIG

This example creates a temp table and inserts one row into the created table. ROWCOUNT_BIG returns how many rows were affected by the last transaction:

```
CREATE TABLE #TempFun
 (iFunId int NOT NULL)

INSERT #TempFun
VALUES (1)

SELECT ROWCOUNT_BIG()
```

It returns 1.

## SCOPE_IDENTITY

This function works in a similar way to @@IDENTITY, except it is only sensitive to the current scope's last inserted IDENTITY value. If the last INSERT operation impacts another table with an IDENTITY column (by a trigger), that second table IDENTITY value will not be reflected in SCOPE_IDENTITY.

### Example 16.8.17: Using SCOPE_IDENTITY

```
SELECT SCOPE_IDENTITY()
```

This returns the last IDENTITY column value for the last INSERT operation into an IDENTITY type table. This function does not reflect IDENTITY values from tables impacted by trigger firings from the original scope's INSERT operation.

## SESSION_USER

This returns the current session's username for the database.

### Example 16.8.18: Using SESSION_USER

```
SELECT SESSION_USER
```

This returns dbo.

## STATS_DATE

STATS_DATE returns the date of the last statistics update for the table and index. The syntax is:

```
STATS_DATE (<table_id>, <index_id>)
```

### Example 16.8.19: Using STATS_DATE

This example returns the last statistics update for the books table index ID number 1:

```
SELECT STATS_DATE (OBJECT_ID('Books'), 1)
```

It returns 2002-09-26 14:22:37.880.

## SYSTEM_USER

This function returns the login name or user name for the current user connection. The syntax is:

```
SYSTEM_USER
```

### Example 16.8.20: Using SYSTEM_USER

```
SELECT SYSTEM_USER
```

This returns sa.

## USER

This function returns the user database name for the current user context. The syntax is:

```
USER
```

### Example 16.8.21: Using USER

```
SELECT USER
```

This returns dbo.

# 16.9 How to... Use IMAGE, TEXT, and NTEXT Functions

Transact-SQL is generally not used for importing and presenting IMAGE and BINARY data types. Most application developers use programming language classes and extensions, such as TextCopy from MFC (Microsoft Foundation Class) C++, ADO's stream object, and Java classes for handling binary filestreams.

That said, you **can** use Transact-SQL functions for updating, retrieving, and searching IMAGE, TEXT, and NTEXT data. Make sure to test the performance of using Transact-SQL commands against those provided with programming languages. Text and image functions use the following general form:

```
function_name(arguments)
```

## TEXTPTR

The TEXTPTR function returns a text-pointer value for use with the READTEXT, WRITETEXT, and UPDATETEXT functions. This text-pointer relates to a specific IMAGE, TEXT, or NTEXT column. The syntax is:

```
TEXTPTR (<column_name>)
```

### Example 16.9.1: Using TEXTPTR

This example sets a variable with the pointer value to the HomePage NTEXT column of the Suppliers table. The pointer is **not used** in this example, but will be used in the next four function examples:

```
USE Northwind
GO
DECLARE @Pointer varbinary(16)
SELECT @Pointer = TEXTPTR(HomePage)
FROM Suppliers
```

# TEXTVALID

In order for a pointer to be used for an IMAGE, NTEXT, or TEXT column, that pointer must be **valid** (current and useable). Use the TEXTVALID function to determine a pointer's usability. If the pointer is valid, an integer value of 1 will be returned; otherwise, 0 will be returned. The syntax for TEXTVALID is:

```
TEXTVALID ('<table.column_name>', <text_pointer_variable>)
```

## Example 16.9.2: Using TEXTVALID

This example checks the validity of HomePage pointers:

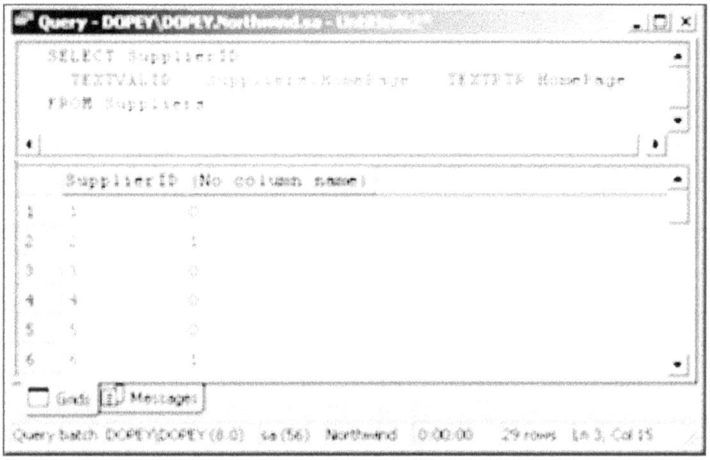

Those values with a 0 value are invalid pointers (and happen to be NULL values).

# READTEXT

The READTEXT function allows IMAGE, TEXT, or NTEXT values to be read or returned. The syntax is as follows:

```
READTEXT <table.column_name> <text_pointer> <offset> <read_size>
<optional_HOLDLOCK>
```

| Parameter | Description |
|---|---|
| <table.column_name> | The first parameter is the name of the table and column name from which to read. |
| <text_pointer> | The second parameter is the text pointer. |
| <offset> | The third parameter is the beginning point from which to read the bytes or characters. |
| <read_size> | The read_size parameter determines how much of the IMAGE, TEXT, or NTEXT column to read, beginning from the offset value. |
| <optional_HOLDLOCK> | The last parameter is the HOLDLOCK hint, which locks the text value during the read and end of transaction. No updates are then allowed against the column. |

### Example 16.9.3: Using READTEXT

This example populates the text pointer for the `HomePage` column of the `SupplierID` row with an ID of `6`. The first 90 characters are then read with the `READTEXT` function:

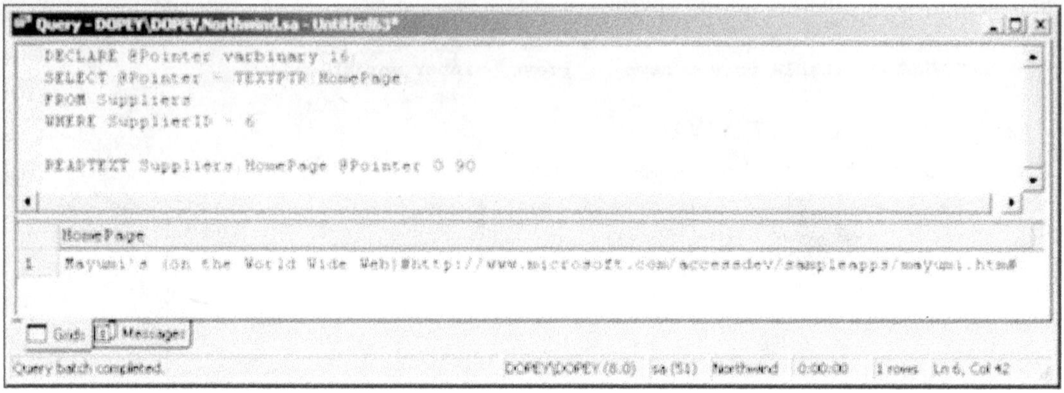


# WRITETEXT

The `WRITETEXT` function allows an `IMAGE`, `TEXT`, or `NTEXT` column to be overwritten with a new value. When the database recovery model is simple or bulk-logged, this operation is non-logged. The syntax is as follows:

```
WRITETEXT <table.column_name> <text_pointer> <optional_WITH_LOG> <data_to_overwrite
column with>
```

| Parameter | Description |
|---|---|
| `<table.column_name>` | The first parameter is the name of the table and column name from which to read. |
| `<text_pointer>` | The second parameter is the text pointer. |
| `<offset>` | The third parameter is the beginning point from which to read the bytes or characters. |
| `<read_size>` | The `read_size` parameter determines how much of the `IMAGE`, `TEXT`, or `NTEXT` column to read, beginning from the offset value. |
| `<optional_HOLDLOCK>` | The last parameter is the `HOLDLOCK` hint, which locks the text value during the read and end of transaction. No updates are then allowed against the column. |

### Example 16.9.4: Using WRITETEXT

If your `TEXT`, `IMAGE`, or `NTEXT` column contains a `NULL` value, it will not return a valid pointer value. If this occurs, you cannot use `WRITETEXT` to add initial data to this column. One solution is to add an initial `DEFAULT` value for the column, or put in a dummy column. In this example, the `Supplier` row, with an ID of `1`, will have a new value inserted into the `NTEXT` value. Since the value is `NULL`, if you attempt to run this code:

```
DECLARE @Pointer varbinary(16)
SELECT @Pointer = TEXTPTR(HomePage)
FROM Suppliers
WHERE SupplierID = 1

WRITETEXT Suppliers.HomePage @Pointer 'No Home Page yet.'
```

you will get the following error:

Server: Msg 7133, Level 16, State 2, Line 6
NULL textptr (text, ntext, or image pointer) passed to WriteText function.

So, first we will initialize the column:

```
UPDATE Suppliers
SET HomePage = ' '
WHERE SupplierID = 1
```

Had this been a `BINARY` column, you could have used:

```
UPDATE ExampleImages
SET HomePageGraphic = 0x0
WHERE ImageId = 1
```

If you re-run the initial `WRITETEXT` statement, the new value will insert, since the pointer is now valid.

# UPDATETEXT

The `UPDATETEXT` function allows you to update a **portion** of an `IMAGE`, `TEXT`, or `NTEXT` column. The syntax is as follows:

```
UPDATETEXT <table.column_name> <text_pointer> <NULL_or_Insert_offset>
<NULL_or_delete_length> <optional_WITH_LOG> <inserted_data>
```

| Parameter | Description |
|---|---|
| `<table.column_name>` | The first parameter is the name of the table and column name from which to read. |
| `<text_pointer>` | The second parameter is the text pointer. |
| `<NULL_or_Insert_offset>` | The optional insert offset parameter indicates the number of bytes to skip in the column before inserting the new data (for `NTEXT`, this offset is the number of characters). |
| `<NULL_or_delete_length>` | The delete length parameter determines the amount of data to delete from the column, beginning at the offset position (`NTEXT` indicates number of characters, and `IMAGE` and `TEXT` indicate number of bytes). |
| `<optional_WITH_LOG>` | The `WITH LOG` parameter is no longer used in SQL Server 2000. |
| `<inserted_data>` | The inserted data parameter is the data to insert into the column. You can also use another table and column source, as well as text pointer for `TEXT`, `NTEXT`, or `IMAGE` columns. |

### Example 16.9.5: Using UPDATETEXT

This example appends the statement `But coming soon!` to the end of an existing `NTEXT` column. The function begins at the 17th character, and since `0` is set for the delete parameter, no text is removed in its place:

```
DECLARE @Pointer varbinary(16)
SELECT @Pointer = TEXTPTR(HomePage)
FROM Suppliers
WHERE SupplierID = 1

UPDATETEXT Suppliers.HomePage @Pointer 17 0 ' But coming soon!'
```

# 16.10 How to... Use Information Schema Views

Information schema views provide system views for accessing database object meta data, such as tables, columns, privileges, and constraints. Whenever possible, you should use information schema views instead of accessing SQL Server database system tables directly. Accessing system tables directly can cause problems when Microsoft decides to change the system table structure, or naming, or columns, along with the damage that can be done if incorrect updates are made.

In each case, the view must be prefaced by `INFORMATION_SCHEMA.view_name`. The view will only return data from database objects to which the current user has access. For example, the `CONSTRAINT_COLUMN_USAGE` view will only display columns with constraints for those tables that the user has permissions to view.

The information schema views are as follows:

| Information Schema View Name | Description |
|---|---|
| CHECK_CONSTRAINTS | Lists all CHECK constraints in the database. |
| COLUMN_DOMAIN_USAGE | Lists one row for each column in the database that has a user-defined data type. |
| COLUMN_PRIVILEGES | Lists privileges granted to each column. |
| COLUMNS | Lists all columns for all tables in the current database that are accessible to the current user. |
| CONSTRAINT_COLUMN_USAGE | Lists each column that has a constraint defined on it. |
| CONSTRAINT_TABLE_USAGE | Lists one row for each table with a constraint defined on it. |
| DOMAIN_CONSTRAINTS | Lists one row for each user-defined data type in the database that is currently referenced or in use by a column. |
| DOMAINS | Displays user-defined data types accessible in the current database. |
| KEY_COLUMN_USAGE | Returns one row for each column that is part of a key. |
| PARAMETERS | Returns one row for each parameter defined in a user-defined function or stored procedure in the database. |

| nformation Schema View Name | Description |
|---|---|
| REFERENTIAL_CONSTRAINTS | Lists one row for each foreign key constraint defined in the database. |
| ROUTINE_COLUMNS | Lists one row for each column returned by a table-valued function. |
| ROUTINES | Lists one row for each stored procedure and function in the database. |
| SCHEMATA | Lists each database to which the current user has permissions. |
| TABLE_CONSTRAINTS | Lists one row for each table constraint defined in the current database. |
| TABLE_PRIVILEGES | Lists one row for each table permission granted to the user within the current database. |
| TABLES | Lists one row for each table. |
| VIEW_COLUMN_USAGE | Lists each column used within a view definition. |
| VIEW_TABLE_USAGE | Lists each table used or referenced from a view. |
| VIEWS | Lists each view in the database. |

### Example 16.10.1: Using the COLUMNS information schema view

This example returns all `NTEXT` columns for the `Northwind` database:

# Normalization in a Nutshell

Normalization is a methodology used to ensure that data held in your database is unique, appropriately organized, and logically related. Normalization comprises 'normal forms', which are rules that determine the level of normalization. Normalization applies to *relational* databases, but not necessarily to non-relational databases (such as star schemas or other types of design used for analytical processing and data warehouse reporting).

We will discuss the first three normal forms.

# First Normal Form (1NF)

To comply with the First Normal Form, a cell, which is a cross-section of a column and row, must contain only **one** value. In other words, a cell must be **atomic**.

For example, lets review the `BookOrders` table:

| dtOrderDate | vchBooks | iBookIDs |
|---|---|---|
| 2/20/02 | 'SQL Fun', 'Windows XP Fun' | 1, 3 |
| 4/20/02 | 'My Sunset SQL', 'Cheers to SQL', 'Joy in the land of Normalization' | 2, 4, 5 |

This table has three columns, `dtOrderDate`, `vchBooks`, and `iBookIDs`. This table is not in 1NF, as it contains multiple books in one cell of the `vchBooks` column, and multiple IDs in one cell of the `iBookIDs` column.

**Repeating groups**, which occur when a cell or cells have multiple occurrences of the same type of data, are forbidden.

Primary keys defined for a table help enforce the first normal form. We could change the `BookOrders` table to something like this:

| iOrderid (pk) | iBookID (pk) | iQuantity | dtOrderDate | vchBook |
|---|---|---|---|---|
| 1 | 1 | 1 | 2/20/02 | SQL Fun |
| 1 | 3 | 1 | 2/20/02 | Windows XP Fun |
| 2 | 2 | 1 | 4/20/02 | My Sunset SQL |
| 2 | 4 | 1 | 4/20/02 | Cheers to SQL |
| 2 | 5 | 1 | 4/20/02 | Joy in the Land of Normalization |

We have added the `iOrderID` identifier to the table. The `iOrderID` and `iBookID` are defined as the primary key (also called a composite primary key, as it uses more than one column) as they uniquely identify the row. The `iQuantity` field was added, as one may purchase one or more of the same book in a single order. Each unique book order is given its own row. No duplicate rows exist, and no single cell contains more than one value of the same type.

# Second Normal Form (2NF)

A table must obey the First Normal Form before complying with the Second Normal Form. The Second Normal Form stipulates that a table can only store data that relates to the table purpose and use, defined by the primary key. The primary key is used to identify uniquely the described entity. Foreign key references are allowed, but not the data that describes the foreign key from another table (we'll discuss this in the 3NF review).

2NF seeks to avoid what is called a **partial dependency**. Partial dependencies occur when an attribute (column) within a table relies on only part of a composite primary key. In our previous example, the `vchBook` column is **not** dependent on both `iOrderID` and `iBookID`, but is instead dependent on only the `iBookID` column.

To rectify this, you can split this table into two tables. A second table, named Books, can be created with iBookID and vchBook columns. The vchBook column can be taken out of BookOrders, since it is only partially dependent on the primary key.

Here is the BookOrders table:

| iOrderid (pk) | iBookID (pk) | iQuantity | dtOrderDate |
|---|---|---|---|
| 1 | 1 | 1 | 2/20/02 |
| 1 | 3 | 1 | 2/20/02 |
| 2 | 2 | 1 | 4/20/02 |
| 2 | 4 | 1 | 4/20/02 |
| 2 | 5 | 1 | 4/20/02 |

And the Books table:

| iBookID (pk) | vchBook |
|---|---|
| 1 | SQL Fun |
| 3 | Windows XP Fun |
| 2 | My Sunset SQL |
| 4 | Cheers to SQL |
| 5 | Joy in the Land of Normalization |

# Third Normal Form (3NF)

Tables must obey the First and Second Normal Forms to be in 3NF. In addition to this, **transitive dependencies** may not exist for a table. A transitive dependency occurs when a non-key column depends on, or determines the value of, another non-key column. If you update data involved in a transitive dependency, you could encounter problems if the related data is not also updated. Preventing transitive dependencies will help prevent such update anomalies.

The next example shows a version of the Books table that is not in 3NF:

| iBookId (pk) | vchBookName | iPublisherID | vchPublisherName |
|---|---|---|---|
| 1 | SQL Server 2000 Fast Answers | 1 | Curlingstone |

The iBookID column is the primary key of the Books table; the remaining columns should all be attributes that relate to this primary key. However, vchPublisherName does not depend on iBookID, but rather depends on iPublisherID (a non-key attribute). This is an example of a transitive dependency.

To rectify, we could split the table into two tables, such as Books:

| iBookId (pk) | vchBookName | iPublisherID |
|---|---|---|
| 1 | SQL Server 2000 Fast Answers | 1 |

and Publisher:

| iPublisherID (pk) | vchPublisherName |
|---|---|
| 1 | Curlingstone |

A new table, Publisher, is created with the iPublisherID as primary key. The vchPublisherName column is then removed from Books, and added as a dependency of iPublisherID.

Normalized databases assist with query performance, data integrity, and stability. It is possible to be **too** normalized, especially in cases where decision-making support (reporting) or data warehousing is required. Normalization usually involves the creation of multiple tables, which can lead to larger queries involving more complexity. A little bit of de-normalization can sometimes help query performance (views and stored procedures are often used to de-normalize the data for reporting purposes).

# 16.11 How to... Use CASE

The Transact-SQL CASE expression allows a value to be returned conditionally. The value returned is based on the value of the specified column or other expression. The syntax is as follows:

```
CASE <optional_input_value>
  WHEN <expression_1> THEN <result_1>
  WHEN <expression_N> THEN <result_N>
  ELSE <end_result>
END
```

| Parameter | Description |
|---|---|
| CASE <optional_input_value> | The optional input_value parameter is used for the analysis of what value to return. |
| WHEN <expression_N> THEN <result_N> | The <expression_N> parameter is the expression used against the input_value where, if TRUE, the result_N value is returned. |
| ELSE <end_result> | The ELSE <end_result> parameter is used if none of the WHEN expressions evaluate to TRUE. |

## Example 16.11.1: Using CASE

This example lists the country from the leaders table, and then analyzes that same column in a CASE statement. For various values, either Western or Eastern is returned. Otherwise, if none of the defined expressions evaluate to TRUE, the ELSE statement is used to present I will tell you later... as a string:

You can also use the CASE statement without the initial input expression. For example:

```
SELECT vchCountry,
  CASE
    WHEN vchCountry = 'USA' THEN 'Western'
    WHEN vchCountry = 'Japan' THEN 'Eastern'
    ELSE 'I will tell you later...'
  END
FROM Leaders
```

This syntax includes the actual column name in the expression to be evaluated to TRUE, instead of using it as an input value in the initial CASE declaration. Also note that if an initial input expression is not provided, the expressions in the WHEN clause can still use any valid Boolean expression of arbitrary complexity. CASE is not limited to column=value expressions. For example, the following CASE statement evaluates three expressions. The first evaluating to TRUE will return the associated value. In this example, 1<>2 is TRUE and, therefore, One is the loneliest number is returned:

```
SELECT CASE
  WHEN 1<>2 THEN 'One is the loneliest number'
  WHEN 2<>2 THEN 'Two is better'
  WHEN 3<>3 THEN 'Three is a crowd'
END
```

# BEGIN and END

The BEGIN and END Transact-SQL keywords are used to group a block of Transact-SQL statements into one logical unit. You will most often see BEGIN and END used with control-of-flow Transact-SQL statements. Control-of-flow statements are reviewed next.

# 16.12 How to... Use IF...ELSE

The IF...ELSE keywords allow you to evaluate expressions and, when TRUE, execute an action or batch of statements. This is called conditional processing, or control-of-flow language, because it controls the flow of Transact-SQL execution. The syntax for using IF...ELSE is as follows:

```
IF <expression_1>
  <Single_or_Batch_of_statements_if_TRUE>
    <expression_N>
  <Single_or_Batch_of_statements_if_TRUE>
ELSE
  <Single_or_Batch_of_statements_if_TRUE>
```

The first expression will evaluate whether the result is TRUE or FALSE. If the statement is TRUE, the single Transact-SQL statement or batch of statement is executed. If not, the next expression is evaluated. If none of the expressions evaluate to TRUE, the ELSE statement executes the single Transact-SQL statement or batch of statements.

## Example 16.12.1: Using IF...ELSE

This example checks to see whether the current database user is dbo and, if so, prints the appropriate statement:

```
IF (SELECT CURRENT_USER)= 'dbo'
  BEGIN
    PRINT 'I am dbo!'
  END
ELSE
  BEGIN
    PRINT 'I am not dbo. '
  END
```

## Example 16.12.2: Using IF...ELSE with query expressions

In the next example, an IF...ELSE block is used to analyze how many tables are in the current database. Depending on the number of tables, a SELECT query with the TOP keyword will be used in order to decide what TOP number should be returned:

```
IF (SELECT COUNT(*) FROM INFORMATION_SCHEMA.TABLES)> 10 AND
   (SELECT COUNT(*) FROM INFORMATION_SCHEMA.TABLES)< 20
  BEGIN
    SELECT TOP 11 *
    FROM INFORMATION_SCHEMA.TABLES
  END
IF (SELECT COUNT(*) FROM INFORMATION_SCHEMA.TABLES)> 20
  BEGIN
    SELECT TOP 20 *
    FROM INFORMATION_SCHEMA.TABLES
  END
ELSE
  BEGIN
    SELECT TOP 10 *
    FROM INFORMATION_SCHEMA.TABLES
  END
```

The ELSE statement is not required for every IF statement. For example, the following IF statement is perfectly fine without an associated ELSE statement:

```
IF (SYSTEM_USER) = 'sa'
BEGIN
  PRINT 'Hurrah!'
END
```

# 16.13 How to... Use WHILE, BREAK, and CONTINUE

The WHILE keyword is used to analyze a condition, and where this condition is TRUE, execute a statement block repeatedly until the statement is no longer TRUE. The BREAK condition is used to exit the WHILE loop from within the WHILE statement, if you choose to do so, and the CONTINUE keyword restarts the WHILE loop. The syntax is as follows:

```
WHILE <expression_being_evaluated_TRUE_or_FALSE>
  <SQL_statement_block>
```

## Example 16.13.1: Using WHILE

This first example evaluates a condition that will always be TRUE. For example, the value 1 will never be equal to 0, and therefore 1<>0 will **always** be TRUE. The PRINT statement will continue to execute until you stop the query:

```
WHILE 1 <> 0
  BEGIN
    PRINT 'Help me! I cannot stop!'
  END
```

## Example 16.13.2: Using WHILE to loop through a result set

This next example creates a local variable for holding the iCustomerID column value from the Customers table. The WHILE statement will print each iCustomerId while the @CustomerID is not NULL. Since each loop in the WHILE statement increments the value of the @CustomerID, eventually the WHILE statement will stop processing after it prints each iCustomerID from the Customers table:

```
USE Northwind

DECLARE @CustomerID nchar(5)

SELECT @CustomerID = MIN(CustomerId)
FROM Customers

WHILE @CustomerID IS NOT NULL
  BEGIN

    PRINT @CustomerID

    SELECT @CustomerID = MIN(CustomerId)
    FROM Customers
    WHERE CustomerID > @CustomerID
  END
```

### Example 16.13.3: Using BREAK

Here, we use the previous example but add an IF statement. When the @CustomerId value is equal to CACTU, the WHILE loop is exited with a BREAK command:

```
DECLARE @CustomerID nchar(5)

SELECT @CustomerID = MIN(CustomerId)
FROM Customers

WHILE @CustomerID IS NOT NULL
  BEGIN

    PRINT @CustomerID

    If (@CustomerID)='CACTU' BREAK

    SELECT @CustomerID = MIN(CustomerId)
    FROM Customers
    WHERE CustomerID > @CustomerID
  END
```

If the CONTINUE keyword had been used instead of BREAK, the WHILE loop would be restarted, and any statements after the CONTINUE would be ignored. The following statement runs eternally, as the CACTU value keeps on being encountered; but the local variable assignment after the CONTINUE stops being run. Therefore, after stopping the query, you will see that the CACTU value is printed over and over again:

```
DECLARE @CustomerID nchar(5)

SELECT @CustomerID = MIN(CustomerId)
FROM Customers

WHILE @CustomerID IS NOT NULL
  BEGIN

    PRINT @CustomerID

    IF (@CustomerID)= 'CACTU'
BEGIN
        CONTINUE
      END

    SELECT @CustomerID = MIN(CustomerId)
    FROM Customers
    WHERE CustomerID > @CustomerID
  END
```

This returns (partial result set):

```
ALFKI
ANATR
ANTON
AROUT
BERGS
```

```
BLAUS
BLONP
BOLID
BONAP
BOTTM
BSBEV
CACTU
CACTU
CACTU
CACTU
CACTU
CACTU
CACTU
CACTU
CACTU
CACTU
CACTU
CACTU
CACTU
CACTU
...
```

# 16.14 How to... Use RETURN

The RETURN keyword exits the query or procedure immediately after being called. As with BREAK, no further processing is performed in the procedure or batch. The RETURN statement can be used to return integer values, which can be used with stored procedures to indicate success or failure, or just used to return a value to the calling procedure or client.

The syntax for RETURN is:

```
RETURN <optional_integer_value>
```

### Example 16.14.1: Using RETURN in a batch

```
PRINT 'This is before the batch.'

SELECT TOP 1 *
FROM INFORMATION_SCHEMA.Tables

RETURN

PRINT 'This statement never prints'
```

The last PRINT statement does not run.

### Example 16.14.2: Using RETURN with a stored procedure

The following stored procedure validates the current user, to check whether she or he is logged in as dbo to the database. If not, the procedure is exited with a RETURN code of 1. If the user **is** dbo, the procedure is exited with a RETURN code of 0 (which is usually used by programmers to indicate that no errors occurred):

```
CREATE PROCEDURE ValidatePermissions
AS

IF (CURRENT_USER) <> 'dbo'
BEGIN
RETURN 1
END
ELSE
RETURN 0
```

To capture the return code, create a variable, and assign the value of that variable based on the stored procedure call:

```
DECLARE @ReturnCode int
EXEC @ReturnCode = ValidatePermissions
PRINT @ReturnCode
```

This returns a `PRINT` statement of 0 for a `dbo` user.

# 16.15 How to... Use RAISERROR

The `RAISERROR` command allows you to return either a user-defined error message (from the `sysmessages` table), or an error message produced from a string. The syntax for `RAISERROR` is:

```
RAISERROR (<message_id_OR_message_string>,
                         <severity_level>,
                         <message_state>,
                         <arguments_N> )
WITH <LOG_or_NOWAIT_or_SETERROR>
```

| Parameter | Description |
|---|---|
| `<message_id_OR_message_string>` | The first parameter seeks either a message ID of 50,000 or greater, or an ad hoc message string with up to 400 characters. |
| `<severity_level>` | The `severity_level` parameter allows levels 0 through 18 for regular users, and 19 through 25 for `sysadmin` members. |
| `<message_state>` | Allows an integer value, between 1 and 127, to indicate a messages invocation state. |
| `<arguments_N>` | The `<arguments_N>` parameter allows one or more arguments that are used to formulate the message string. For example, you can use placeholder parameters in your message string, so that varying object names of string values can be used in the error message, depending on the situation. These placeholder parameters are then replaced by values when invoking `RAISERROR`. You can use up to twenty substitution parameters. The parameters are as follows: |

| Parameter | Description | |
|---|---|---|
| <arguments_N> | **Symbol** | **Data Type** |
| | %d, %ld, or %D | Decimal, integer |
| | %x | Hexadecimal number |
| | %ls or %.*ls | Character string |
| | %c | Single character |
| | %lf | Double, float |
| WITH <LOG_or_NOWAIT_or_SETERROR> | The WITH LOG option is required for levels 19 through 25. The WITH LOG option logs the error to the application log. The WITH NOWAIT option sends the messages to the client, and WITH SETERROR sets @@ERROR's value to either the message_id value or 50,000. The WITH LOG option can only be executed by members of the sysadmin role. | |

### Example 16.15.1: Using an existing message ID in RAISERROR

First, a new error will be added to sysmessages:

```
sp_addmessage 60002, 16, 'Warning, you have gone too far this time!'
```

This example then raises our new error:

```
RAISERROR (60002, 16, 1)
```

This returns:

Server: Msg 60002, Level 16, State 1, Line 1
Warning, you have gone to far this time!

### Example 16.15.2: Using a message string

```
RAISERROR ('Your use of RETURN is foolish...', 16, 1)
```

This returns:

Server: Msg 50000, Level 16, State 1, Line 1
Your use of RETURN is foolish...

### Example 16.15.3: Using substitution parameters

First a new message will be created that uses substitution:

```
EXEC sp_addmessage @msgnum = 60012, @severity = 16,
   @msgtext = N'You cannot make this change if you are %s.'
```

Next, to instantiate the RAISERROR with the parameter (the percentage sign is the placeholder in the message text):

```
RAISERROR (60012, 16, 1, 'JaneDoe')
```

This returns:

```
Server: Msg 60012, Level 16, State 1, Line 1
You cannot make this change if you are JaneDoe.
```

# Transact-SQL Cursors

SQL Server is a set-processing product, meaning that operations made against the database operate optimally when performed against a **set of results**, rather than a single row. For example, an UPDATE statement could be used to update 100 rows at the same time. You should tune your database activity (SELECT, INSERT, UPDATE, and DELETE) to take advantage of set-processing behavior.

Transact-SQL **cursors** allow you to process and work with individual rows from a result set. SQL Server also uses API cursor functions, which expose cursor-like functionality to programming languages (ADO, OLE DB, JDBC, ODBC, DB-Library). The underlying behavior of Transact-SQL cursors and API cursors is identical. Transact-SQL cursors, however, are generally used within scripts, stored procedures, or triggers.

The lifecycle of a Transact-SQL cursor is as follows:

- A cursor is defined in a SQL statement that returns a valid result set. This result set is defined as either **updateable** or **read-only**.
- The cursor is then populated, after which the rows can be fetched one row at a time, or as a block. The rows can be fetched forward or backward within the result set (scrolling).
- Depending on the cursor type, the data can be modified during the scrolling (forward or backward behavior) or read and used with other operations.
- After the cursor has been used, it should be closed and de-allocated from memory.

Transact-SQL cursors can impact server performance negatively by consuming resources, such as memory, excessively. You may often find that set-processing methods are much faster than their Transact-SQL cursor counterparts. Cursors should only be used if a set-processing alternative cannot be used in their place. Used wisely, cursors can be quite useful; on the other hand, using cursors indiscriminately can have a severe impact on performance.

# 16.16 How to... Create and use Transact-SQL Cursors

The first step in using a Transact-SQL cursor is to create the cursor by using the DECLARE statement. There are two different versions of the DECLARE syntax block, the ANSI SQL-92 syntax, and the Transact-SQL extended syntax. You **cannot** mix the two forms of syntax:

ANSI SQL-92 DECLARE:

```
DECLARE <cursor_name> <INSENSITIVE> <SCROLL> CURSOR
FOR <select_statement>
<FOR> <READ_ONLY_or_UPDATE> <OF column_name_N...>
```

| Parameter | Description |
|---|---|
| cursor_name | Name of the Transact-SQL cursor. |
| INSENSITIVE | When used, a copy of the data will be used from a temporary table in tempdb. No modifications are allowed to the data. |
| SCROLL | Enables all fetch operations, such as FIRST, LAST, PRIOR, NEXT, RELATIVE, and ABSOLUTE. These operations control the movement of the cursor through the result set. This option is not allowed if FAST_FORWARD is set. |
| select_statement | SELECT statement that defines the result set of the cursor. The keywords COMPUTE, COMPUTE BY, INTO, and FOR BROWSE are not allowed. |
| <FOR> <READ_ONLY_or_UPDATE> <OF column_name_N...> | When READ_ONLY is chosen, no updates can be made via the cursor. The UPDATE clause specifies which columns can be modified within the cursor. If columns are not chosen with the UPDATE clause, all columns are then updateable by default. |

Transact-SQL Extended syntax:

```
DECLARE <cursor_name> CURSOR
    <LOCAL_or_GLOBAL>
    <FORWARD_ONLY_or_SCROLL>
    <STATIC_or_KEYSET_or_DYNAMIC_or_FAST_FORWARD>
    <READ_ONLY or SCROLL_LOCKS or OPTIMISTIC>
    <TYPE_WARNING>
FOR <select_statement>
<FOR UPDATE> <OF column_name_N...>
```

| Parameter | Description |
|---|---|
| cursor_name | Name of the Transact-SQL cursor. |
| LOCAL or GLOBAL | If LOCAL is specified, the cursor can only be referenced from within the context of the procedure, batch, or trigger. A LOCAL cursor can be passed to an OUTPUT parameter. GLOBAL cursors can be referenced by any connection. The default type is LOCAL. |
| FORWARD_ONLY | FORWARD_ONLY restricts the cursor to allow moving forward from the first row to the last rows using FETCH NEXT. |
| STATIC or KEYSET or DYNAMIC or FAST_FORWARD | STATIC makes a temporary copy of the data used in the cursor. No modifications are allowed for STATIC. KEYSET stores only the primary key values in tempdb, and allows modifications to the non-key data. DYNAMIC reflects data against the actual data source, and allows you to scroll forward and backward in the cursor, while being able to make data changes. FAST_FORWARD specifies that the cursor can only move forward from the first row to the last row, and is read-only. |

| Parameter | Description |
|---|---|
| READ_ONLY or SCROLL_LOCKS or OPTIMISTIC | READ_ONLY prevents modifications to the data via the cursor. SCROLL_LOCKS locks rows as they are read, to ensure data modifications succeed (updates or deletes). OPTIMISTIC allows updates and deletes, does not place locks on the cursor data, but rejects modifications if changes have been made between the time the row was last read and the cursor modification was requested. |
| TYPE_WARNING | Sends a warning message to the client if the cursor is implicitly converted from one type to another. |
| select_statement | SELECT statement that defines the result set of the cursor. The keywords COMPUTE, COMPUTE BY, INTO, and FOR BROWSE are not allowed. |
| <FOR UPDATE> <OF column_name_N...> | When READ_ONLY is set, no updates can be made via the cursor. The UPDATE clause specifies which columns can be modified within the cursor. If no columns are chosen with the UPDATE clause, all columns are then updateable by default. |

DECLARE CURSOR permissions default to any user who has SELECT permissions on the views, tables, and columns used in the cursor.

### Example 16.16.1: Using DECLARE CURSOR

This example selects the spid from the sysprocesses table, using a FORWARD_ONLY cursor type:

```
DECLARE spid_cursor CURSOR
FORWARD_ONLY
FOR SELECT spid
  FROM master.dbo.sysprocesses
```

## Opening a Cursor

After a cursor is declared, it can then be opened, using the OPEN keyword. The syntax for OPEN is:

```
OPEN <optional_GLOBAL> <cursor_name_or_cursor_variable_name>
```

The GLOBAL parameter defines the cursor as a global cursor. The next parameter is the name of the cursor or the cursor variable (reviewed later).

### Example 16.16.2: Using OPEN

This next example opens the spid_cursor cursor:

```
OPEN spid_cursor
```

# Fetching a Cursor

Once a cursor is opened, you can use the FETCH command to retrieve a specific row from the cursor. The syntax for FETCH is:

```
FETCH <NEXT_or_PRIOR_or_FIRST_or_LAST_or_ABSOLUTE(n)_or_RELATIVE(n)>
FROM <optional_GLOBAL> <cursor_name_or_cursor_variable_name>
INTO <@variable_1>, <@variable_N…>
```

| Parameter | Description |
|---|---|
| NEXT | Returns the next result row after the current row. This is the default FETCH type. |
| PRIOR | Returns the result row preceding the current row. |
| FIRST | Returns the first row of the cursor. |
| LAST | Returns the last row of the cursor. |
| ABSOLUTE | Returns the row from the front of the cursor, where N is the number from the first row to the current row. If the number is negative, the row is located from the end of the cursor. |
| RELATIVE | Moves to the new row based on the current row, with positive N moving forward in the cursor, and negative moving backward in the cursor. |
| GLOBAL | Use GLOBAL if the cursor is a global cursor. |
| cursor_name_or_cursor_variable_name | The name of the cursor or cursor variable. |
| INTO <@variable_1>, <@variable_N…> | You can populate local variable or parameter values using the INTO statement to populate the local variables in the order they are returned in the SELECT statement that defines the cursor. |

### Example 16.16.3: Using FETCH

This example first creates the @spid local variable for use with populating the individual spid from the spid_cursor cursor. Once the variable is populated, it is printed with the PRINT statement, and the DBCC INPUTBUFFER is run against the specific spid:

```
DECLARE @spid smallint

FETCH NEXT
FROM spid_cursor
INTO @spid

PRINT 'Spid #: ' + STR(@spid)

EXEC ('DBCC INPUTBUFFER (' + @spid + ')')
```

At this point, you can use a series of Transact-SQL commands for working with the individual row in the cursor. When you wish to repeat this action for each spid in the spid_cursor, you may use the various @@ functions available for cursors.

This next example uses @@cursor_rows to determine the number of rows currently populated in the cursor that was last opened. The @@fetch_status will be used with a WHILE statement to validate the status of the cursor. The @@fetch_status function returns 0 if the last FETCH was successful, -1 if the FETCH failed or reached the end of the result set, and -2 if the row fetched was missing.

This example uses @@cursor_rows to determine whether the actions within the BEGIN and END block should be invoked (only if rows are greater than 0). Then a WHILE statement is invoked, looping until the @@fetch_status is equal to 0. Once the FETCH reaches past the last row, the WHILE loop is broken. This statement will continue to print each spid, and each DBCC INPUTBUFFER, for each spid returned in the original DECLARE statement:

```
DECLARE @spid smallint

IF @@cursor_rows > 0
  BEGIN

    WHILE @@fetch_status = 0
      BEGIN
        FETCH NEXT
        FROM spid_cursor
        INTO @spid

        PRINT 'Spid #: ' + STR(@spid)

        EXEC ('DBCC INPUTBUFFER (' + @spid + ')')

      END
  END
```

# Closing a Cursor

Once you have finished using a cursor, use the CLOSE and DEALLOCATE cursors. CLOSE closes an open cursor by releasing the result set and freeing up any allocated locks held on the underlying table rows. The cursor can still be re-opened with OPEN in this state. The syntax for CLOSE is:

```
CLOSE <optional_GLOBAL> <cursor_name_or_cursor_variable_name>
```

If the cursor is a global cursor, use the GLOBAL keyword prior to the cursor name.

## Example 16.16.4: Using CLOSE

```
CLOSE spid_cursor
```

# Deallocating a Cursor

Finally, use DEALLOCATE to remove any reference to the defined cursor. If you do not wish to open the cursor again, use DEALLOCATE. The syntax is:

```
DEALLOCATE <optional_GLOBAL> <cursor_name_or_cursor_variable_name>
```

If the cursor is a global cursor, use the GLOBAL keyword prior to the cursor name.

### Example 16.16.5: Using DEALLOCATE

```
DEALLOCATE spid_cursor
```

## System Stored Procedures and Cursors

There are also system stored procedures that can be used when working with cursors. The sp_cursor_list procedure is used to return all cursors currently visible to the connection. The sp_describe_cursor returns the attributes of a cursor. The sp_describe_cursor_columns returns the attributes of the columns in the result set, and the sp_describe_cursor_tables procedure returns information on the base tables referenced by the cursor definition.

As was noted in the syntax examples, a cursor can be a regular Transact-SQL cursor, or a **cursor data type variable**. Cursor data types contain a reference to a cursor.

### Example 16.16.6: Using a system stored procedure on cursors

This final example creates a local variable of the cursor data type, and populates it with our previous example. Notice that the syntax is almost identical to that of a regular cursor, but the scope of the variable is only held during the batch run time, whereas a cursor can be held open for the connection to use in separate batches (and, for GLOBAL variables, separate connections):

```
DECLARE @spid_cursor cursor

SET @spid_cursor =  CURSOR
FORWARD_ONLY
   FOR     SELECT spid
                FROM master.dbo.sysprocesses

OPEN @spid_Cursor
DECLARE @spid smallint

FETCH NEXT
FROM @spid_cursor
INTO @spid

PRINT 'Spid #: ' + STR(@spid)
EXEC ('DBCC INPUTBUFFER (' + @spid + ')')

CLOSE @spid_cursor
DEALLOCATE @spid_cursor
```

# 16.17 How to... Create Extended Properties

SQL Server has adopted the Microsoft Access concept of attaching properties to database objects, and extended it to allow multiple user-defined extended properties to be attached to various objects within the database. Extended properties allow you to add meta data about the database and database objects. Such meta data can be used to include user-friendly business- or application-specific information about user-defined database objects. The extended property is made up of a name/value pair, where the value is a SQL_VARIANT data type, with up to 7500 bytes of data. Extended properties are not allowed on system objects.

To add an extended property, use the sp_addextendedproperty stored procedure. The syntax is:

```
sp_addextendedproperty
  <property_name>,
  <property_value>,
  <level_0_object_type>,
  <level_0_object_name>,
  <level_1_object_type>,
  <level_1_object_name>,
  <level_2_object_type>,
  <level_2_object_name>
```

The `property_name` parameter is the name of the extended property being added. The `property_value` is the value for the property. The next parameters indicate level names and types, based on objects that allow extended properties. Level 0 objects are as follows:

| Level 0 |
|---|
| User |
| User-defined data types |

Level 1 objects are owned by the `User` object in Level 0:

| Level 1 |
|---|
| Table |
| View |
| Schema-bound view |
| Stored procedure |
| Rule |
| Default |
| Function |
| Schema-bound function |

Level 2 objects are as follows:

| Level 1 owner(s) | Level 2 |
|---|---|
| Table | Column |
| View | |
| Schema-bound view | |
| Function | |
| Schema-bound function | |

| Level 1 owner(s) | Level 2 |
|---|---|
| Table | Index |
| Schema-bound view | |
| Table | Constraint |
| Function | |
| Schema-bound function | |
| Table | Trigger |
| View | INSTEAD OF trigger |
| Schema-bound view | |
| Stored procedure | Parameter |
| Function | |
| Schema-bound function | |

Use `sp_updateextendedproperty` to update the value of an existing extended property. The syntax is almost identical to `sp_addextendproperty`, but an existing property is modified instead of a new property being created.

Use `sp_dropextendedproperty` to drop an extended property. This procedure is also almost identical to `sp_updateextendedproperty` and `sp_addextendedproperty`, only the property referenced is dropped, and the property value is not included (only the property name).

To list extended properties use the `fn_listextendedproperty` function. The syntax is:

```
SELECT *
FROM
::fn_listextendedproperty (
  <level_0_object_type>,
  <level_0_object_name>,
  <level_1_object_type>,
  <level_1_object_name>,
  <level_2_object_type>,
  <level_2_object_name>)
```

Like the stored procedures, this function requires the level types and names. Unlike the stored procedures, all values must be embedded in single quotes.

## Example 16.17.1: Adding an extended property to a table column

This next example creates an extended property, called `User Friendly Description`, with a value of `Customer Identifier`. This is defined for the `CustomerID` on the `Customers` table:

```
USE Northwind

sp_addextendedproperty 'User Friendly Description', 'Customer Identifier',
                       'user', dbo, 'table', Customers,
                       'column', CustomerID
GO
```

### Example 16.17.2: Modifying an extended property

```
sp_updateextendedproperty 'User Friendly Description', 'Customer ID for the
Customers Table',
                         'user', dbo, 'table', Customers, 'column', CustomerID
GO
```

### Example 16.17.3: Dropping an extended property

```
sp_dropextendedproperty 'User Friendly Description',
                         'user', dbo, 'table', Customers, 'column', CustomerID
GO
```

### Example 16.17.4: Using ::fn_listextendedproperty

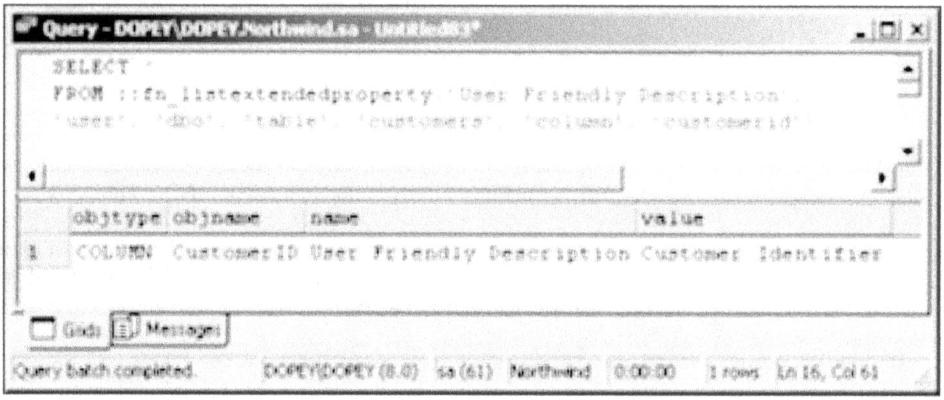


# Managing Extended Properties in the Object Browser

You can also manage extended properties in the Object Browser window of Query Analyzer. To add a new property in the Object Browser, follow these steps:

- Expand the nodes until you reach the object to which you wish to add an extended property.
- Right-click the object and select Extended Properties.
- In the Extended Properties dialog box, type in the name/value pair and select Apply
- Select the  button to add new extended properties, and the  button to delete them:

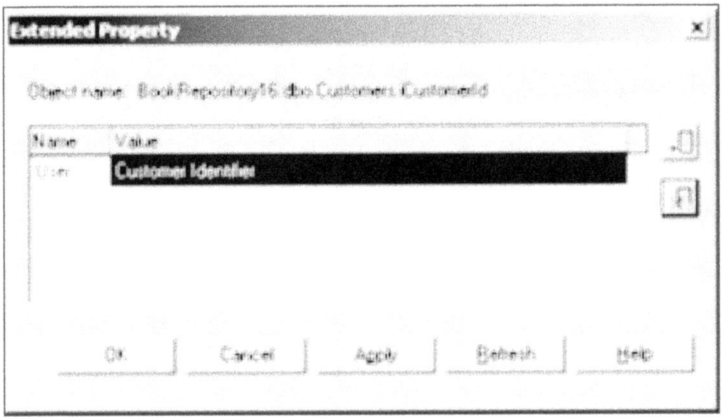


# 16.18 How to... Create a Script that Creates a Script

As a DBA or developer, you may some day need to execute a Transact-SQL script that has to be run against several objects within a database, or databases within a SQL Server instance. One beneficial time-saving technique involves using a SELECT query to write that script for you.

### Example 16.18.1: Writing a SELECT statement that generates a script

In this example, a script is needed to set all user databases to the FULL recovery model. This query uses concatenation to generate the ALTER DATABASE string, using the name column from the master.dbo.sysdatabases table:

```
SELECT 'ALTER DATABASE ' + name +
' SET RECOVERY FULL'
FROM master.dbo.sysdatabases
WHERE name NOT IN ('master', 'tempdb', 'model', 'msdb')
```

This returns (varying according to the databases on your server):

```
ALTER DATABASE BookRepository SET RECOVERY FULL
ALTER DATABASE Northwind SET RECOVERY FULL
ALTER DATABASE pubs SET RECOVERY FULL
```

You can then execute the batch of commands to set all your user databases to the same recovery model. This technique can be used in numerous ways: creating scripts against tables or objects from the information schema views, or system tables. Be careful when scripting an action against multiple objects or databases; be sure the change is what you intended, and that you are fully aware of the script's outcome.

# 16.19 How to... Use sp_executesql

Unlike stored procedures, regular ad hoc SQL batches and statements usually cause SQL Server to generate a new execution plan each time they are run. The only time an execution plan will be reused for an ad hoc query is if there is an exact match to a previously executed query. The sp_executesql stored procedure allows you to create and use a reusable execution plan, where the only items that change are the query parameters. This is a worthy solution, when given a choice between ad hoc statements and stored procedures. The sp_executesql procedure has the same behavior as EXECUTE with regard to batches, the scope of names, and database context.

The syntax for sp_executesql is as follows:

```
sp_executesql N'<@SQL_Statement_or_Batch>',
              N'<@Parameter_Name_1> <Datatype_1>',
              N'<@Parameter_Name_N> <Datatype_N>'
```

| Parameter | Description |
|---|---|
| N'<@SQL_Statement_or_Batch> | The N'<@SQL_Statement>' parameter is the Unicode string containing the Transact-SQL statement or batch of statements. |
| N'<@Parameter_Name_N> <Datatype_N>' | This indicates one or more parameters embedded in the SQL statement. The <@Parameter_Name_N> parameter defines the SQL_Statement parameter name, and the <Datatype_N> defines the data type of the parameter. |

### Example 16.19.1: Using sp_executesql

This example uses sp_executesql to create a re-usable execution plan for selecting a row from the Leaders table based on the country. The vchCountry value is the only changing parameter:

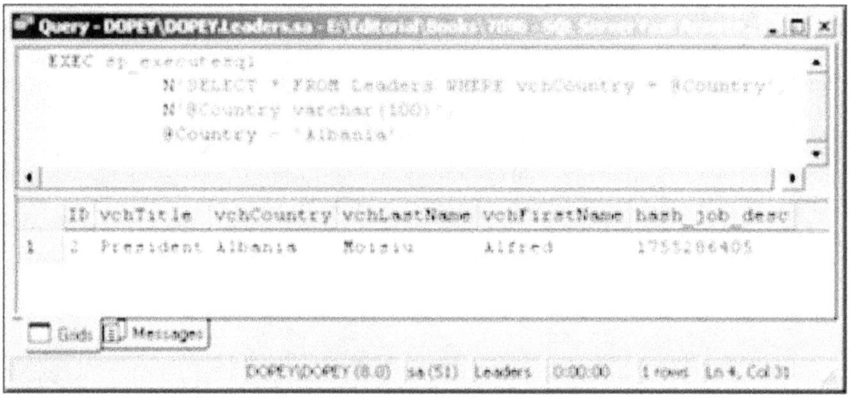


If you must use ad hoc queries instead of stored procedure calls, investigate and compare the query runtimes of ad hoc statements and sp_executesql. Sometimes ad hoc queries may still perform faster than their sp_executesql counterparts. The sp_executesql is not a magic bullet for all types of queries, so make sure to test all scenarios.

# 16.20 How to... Use String Concatenation

String concatenation is the process of attaching two or more characters, binaries, or columns into one expression using the plus sign (+). Concatenation with a NULL value will return a NULL value (and not a concatenated value), unless SET CONCAT_NULL_YIELDS_NULL OFF is configured.

### Example 16.20.1: Using string concatenation in a PRINT statement

```
PRINT 'Fun ' + 'with' + ' concatenation!'
```

This returns:

Fun with concatenation!

### Example 16.20.2: Using concatenation with table columns in a SELECT query

This example displays the `name` and `id` columns from the `sysobjects` table. Notice that the `STR` function is used with `id` to convert the integer value to a character type. `LTRIM` is then used to strip leading blanks from the column:

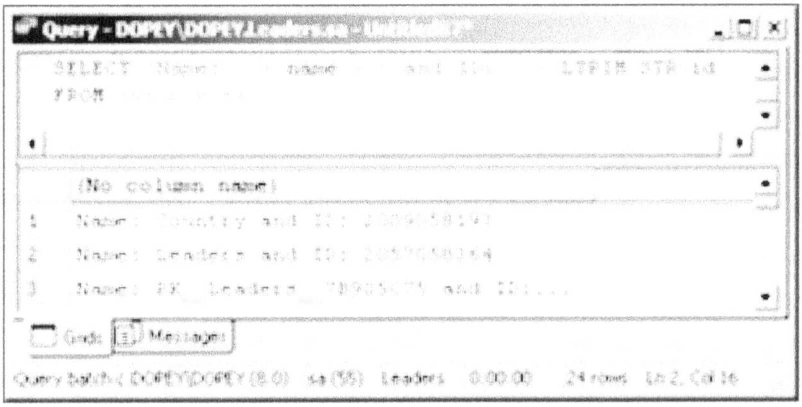

# Batches

A batch is a set of Transact-SQL statements submitted and executed together. Batches are optimized and compiled into a single execution plan. The `GO` keyword signals the end of a batch in a group of Transact-SQL Statements within Query Analyzer, isql, or osql. All statements in a trigger, stored procedure, `EXECUTE` statement call, and `sp_executesql` stored procedure call are also defined as their own batches. Batches have several purposes, but they all have one thing in common – they are used when a specific action has to happen either before or separately from everything else in your script.

Batches are not to be confused with transactions; although batches are submitted and executed together, an error within the batch will **not** begin a rollback of statements leading up to the error (although it will halt the continuation of statements following the batch). Only if a transaction is used along with a batch will you see such rollback behavior.

Also keep in mind that syntax errors, or any error type that keeps the entire batch from compiling, will prevent **all** statements within the batch. Runtime errors (errors which occur during execution), on the other hand, will cause the statement raising the error to fail, and possibly those statements afterwards within the batch (although constraint violation errors may allow other statements to execute after the failed statement).

# 16.21 How to... Use EXEC

Throughout this book you have seen multiple occurrences of the `EXEC` command (short for `EXECUTE`) within query examples. `EXEC` is used to execute functions, stored procedures, extended stored procedures, and character strings within a Transact-SQL batch.

With `EXEC`, you can use strings as Transact-SQL batches by embedding them in parentheses after the `EXEC` statement. Strings must be less than 8,000 bytes; however multiple 8,000 byte strings can be concatenated together into one `EXEC` statement. `EXEC` is often used to create dynamic Transact-SQL statements, generated at run time and summarized in a string to be executed. The syntax for doing so is:

```
EXEC (<string or concatenated strings>)
```

### Example 16.21.1: Using EXEC to execute a string as a Transact-SQL batch

First let's try to insert values into a table using a variable called `@TableName`. The `@TableName` variable will be set to the value `Books`, and then an `INSERT` will be performed against the table name variable:

```
DECLARE @TableName
SELECT @TableName = 'Books'

INSERT @TableName (vchBookName, chISBN)
VALUES ('Data Modeling for Everyone', '1904347002')
```

After attempting to execute this, you will get the following error:

Server: Msg 137, Level 15, State 2, Line 4
Must declare the variable '@TableName'.

Now let's try this same batch, but using concatenated strings and `EXEC`:

```
DECLARE @TableName sysname
SELECT @TableName = 'Books'

EXEC('INSERT ' + @TableName + '(vchBookName, chISBN)
VALUES (''Data Modeling for Everyone'',''1904347002'')')
```

This inserts the row, and returns:

(1 row(s) affected)

# 16.22 How to... Bind a Connection to Other Transactions using sp_bindsession and sp_getbindtoken

With the stored procedures `sp_getbindtoken` and `sp_bindsession`, you can bind a connection to other open transactions, so long as the transactions exist on the same SQL Server instance. Once a connection is bound, two or more connections can join and participate in the same transaction until the transaction is either rolled back or committed. This is one of the few methods of inter-connection communication between separate connections.

`sp_getbindtoken` returns a unique **bind token** used for identification of the open transaction; This token is used for binding other connections to it. The syntax is:

```
sp_getbindtoken  <@variable_to_grab_token> = <return_value> OUTPUT,
<@optional_for_xp_flag>
```

The first parameter is the return value bind token generated for the transaction. The second parameter, `@optional_for_xp_flag`, if equal to `1`, will create a bind token that can be passed to an extended stored procedure for call back into the server.

`sp_bindsession` binds or unbinds the connection. The syntax is:

```
sp_bindsession <bind_token or NULL>
```

### Example 16.22.1: Binding a transaction to another connection

The first session begins a transaction, creates a table, and returns a bind token:

```
BEGIN TRAN FunTransaction
CREATE TABLE FunValue (vchFunCode varchar (10) NOT NULL)
DECLARE @Token varchar (255)
EXEC sp_getbindtoken @Token OUTPUT
PRINT @Token
```

Now a second session binds itself to the open transaction, enters some data into the new table, and commits the transaction:

```
EXEC sp_bindsession 'f@1I2@j0iQ?0LcXjR5XV3=5---.aC---'
GO

INSERT FunValue
VALUES ('Fun SQL')

COMMIT TRAN FunTransaction
```

Note that the value passed to `sp_bindsession` is the same as `@Token`.

# 16.23 How to... Use COM Automation sp_oa Procedures

SQL Server includes OLE automation extended stored procedures that allow you to access DLL component functionality (ActiveX). Use these extended stored procedures to access functionality that may not exist within SQL Server or the Transact-SQL language.

Only DLL files registered on the SQL Server instance server can be referenced. Be cautious when creating ActiveX objects, as some can cause performance or system difficulties (such as memory leaks). By default, automation objects are loaded in-process, which means they are loaded within the memory space of SQL Server. You can load an object out-of-process by specifying the integer value 4 during the `sp_OACreate` call. Out-of-process means that the object uses memory space separate from SQL Server's executable memory, with the result that it may run more safely, but may run slower than if run in-process.

Before using these procedures, apply the latest service pack for SQL Server 2000. There are memory leak errors associated with using the `sp_OA` procedures in pre-SP1 versions of SQL Server. For more details on the bug itself, see Microsoft Knowledge Base article 282229, *FIX: SP_OA Procedures Leak Memory and Cause Various Errors*.

You may also encounter problems when attempting to pass a non-string data type by reference, thus receiving a type mismatch error. When a value is passed by reference, the actual variable is passed; in contrast, when a value is passed by value, you pass a copy of the variable, not the variable itself. When using the `sp_OAMethod` procedure, Microsoft recommends that you use a string variable when passing variables by reference, and that any variables should first be initialized (essentially setting a default value for the variable). For more information on this, see Microsoft Knowledge Base article 173848, *BUG: Sp_OA Procedures May Produce "Bad Variable Type" or "Type Mismatch" Error*.

The `sp_OA` extended stored procedures are as follows.

# sp_OACreate

This stored procedure creates the OLE object instance. The syntax is:

```
sp_OACreate <programmatic_id or class_identifier>,
                                         <object_token> OUTPUT,
                                         <optional_execution_context>
```

| Parameter | Description |
|---|---|
| <programmatic_id or class_identifier> | The first parameter requires either the programmatic ID of the OLE object, or the class identifier. |
| <object_token> OUTPUT | The second parameter is the object token which should return an integer value to a local variable. This variable will be used with other sp_OA procedures for working with the object. |
| <optional_execution_context> | The last parameter is optional, and determines in which context the object should be instantiated. The default is in-process, which is the value 1. To run out-of-process, use the value 4. |

# sp_OAGetProperty

This procedure retrieves a property value. The syntax is:

```
sp_OAGetProperty <object_token>,
                                  <property_name>,
                                  <optional_property_value> OUTPUT,
                                  <optional_index>
```

| Parameter | Description |
|---|---|
| <object_token> | The object_token parameter uses the OLE object integer value captured by sp_OACreate for the specified object. |
| <property_name> | The property_name parameter is the name of the object property to return. |
| <optional_property_value> OUTPUT | If specified, the optional_property_value can output the returned value to an OUTPUT local variable. |
| <optional_index> | The optional_index parameter is for those properties with index parameters. |

# sp_OASetProperty

This procedure sets a property value. The syntax is:

```
sp_OASetProperty <object_token>,
                                 <property_name>,
                                  <new_property_value>,
                                  <optional_index>
```

| Parameter | Description |
|---|---|
| <object_token> | The object_token parameter holds the object integer value created during sp_OACreate. |
| <property_name> | The property_name parameter holds the name of the property to modify. |
| <new_property_value> | The new_property_value parameter holds the value to set for the property. |
| <optional_index> | The last option is used for those properties that utilize index parameters. |

# sp_OAMethod

This procedure calls a method. The syntax is:

```
sp_OAMethod  <object_token>,
                        <method_name>,
                        <optional_return_value> OUTPUT,
                        <@optional_parameter_name = parameter OUTPUT,
                         <...N>
```

| Parameter | Description |
|---|---|
| <object_token> | The object_token parameter holds the object integer value created during sp_OACreate. |
| <method_name> | The method_name is the method name being called for the object. |
| <optional_return_value> OUTPUT | If there is a return value for the method call, use a local variable to capture the data in the optional_return_value parameter. |
| <@optional_parameter_name = parameter OUTPUT,<br><...N> | If the method requires one or more parameters, use the parameters in the fourth parameter and beyond (depending on the number of parameters). |

# sp_OADestroy

This stored procedure destroys an object. The syntax is:

```
sp_OADestroy <object_token>
```

The object_token parameter holds the object integer value created during sp_OACreate.

# sp_OAGetErrorInfo

This retrieves the most recent error information concerning sp_OA object access. The syntax is:

```
sp_OAGetErrorInfo <object_token>,
                                  <optional_source> OUTPUT,
                                  <optional_description> OUTPUT,
                                  <optional_helpfile> OUTPUT,
                                  <optional_helpid> OUTPUT
```

| Parameter | Description |
|---|---|
| <object_token> | The object_token parameter holds the object integer value created during sp_OACreate. |
| <optional_source> OUTPUT | The optional_source returns error source information to a local variable that can hold the OUTPUT. |
| <optional_description> OUTPUT | The optional_description returns a description of the error to a local variable that can hold the OUTPUT. |
| <optional_helpfile> OUTPUT | The optional_helpfile returns help file information to a local variable that can hold the OUTPUT. |
| <optional_helpid> OUTPUT | The optional_helpid returns the help file context id to a local variable that can hold the OUTPUT. |

# sp_OAStop

This procedure stops the OLE Automation environment for the SQL Server instance. When sp_OACreate is first called, the OLE Automation environment is instantiated, and is not stopped until the SQL Server instance is stopped or sp_OAStop is called. Do not call this procedure while other users are calling sp_OA procedures, as this could cause errors for actively running sp_OA calls.

## Example 16.23.1: Creating a script file for stored procedures using the sp_OA procedures

This example uses the sp_OA procedures to instantiate the SQLDMO ActiveX object. This script will create a file in the c:\temp directory, with all the stored procedures of the pubs databases scripted out:

```
DECLARE @ObjectToken_SQLDMO int
DECLARE @ObjectToken_Transfer int
DECLARE @Databases int
DECLARE @DB int

-- Create the SQLDMO.SQLServer and SQLDMO.Transfer Objects
EXEC sp_OACreate 'SQLDMO.SQLServer', @ObjectToken_SQLDMO OUTPUT
EXEC sp_OACreate 'SQLDMO.Transfer', @ObjectToken_Transfer OUTPUT

-- Set the properties of the SQLDMO.SQLServer objects
-- Use NT Authentication to connect
EXEC sp_OASetProperty @ObjectToken_SQLDMO ,'LoginSecure','True'

-- Call the method to connect to SQL Server
```

```
EXEC sp_OAMethod @ObjectToken_SQLDMO,'Connect',null,'JOEPROD'

-- Retrieve the property for the Databases collection, create an object variable
EXEC sp_OAGetProperty @ObjectToken_SQLDMO,'Databases',@Databases OUTPUT

-- Set the selected database to the Pubs database
EXEC sp_OAMethod @Databases, 'Item', @DB OUTPUT, 'Pubs'

-- Configure the properties, defining what objects to script
EXEC sp_OASetProperty @ObjectToken_Transfer, 'CopySchema',1
EXEC sp_OASetProperty @ObjectToken_Transfer, 'CopyAllObjects',0
EXEC sp_OASetProperty @ObjectToken_Transfer, 'CopyAllStoredProcedures', 1
EXEC sp_OASetProperty @ObjectToken_Transfer, 'CopyData',0

-- Script the pubs database stored procedures
EXEC sp_OAMethod @DB,'ScriptTransfer',NULL,@ObjectToken_Transfer, 8 ,
'c:\temp\pubs_procs.txt'

-- Cleanup all defined objects
EXEC sp_OADestroy @DB
EXEC sp_OADestroy @Databases
EXEC sp_OADestroy @ObjectToken_Transfer
EXEC sp_OADestroy @ObjectToken_SQLDMO
```

### Example 16.23.2: Using error handling for sp_OA procedures

The previous example lacked error handling; you can add error handling by capturing the result of the stored procedure in an integer variable, in this case `@ErrorHandler`. By performing a capture of the return result of a stored procedure, if the value is any number other than `0`, you can analyze the number using the `sp_OAGetErrorInfo` extended stored procedure.

The following example shows the beginning of the script, with error handling included:

```
DECLARE @ObjectToken_SQLDMO int
DECLARE @ObjectToken_Transfer int
DECLARE @Databases int
DECLARE @DB int
DECLARE @ErrorHandler int
DECLARE @Source varchar(30)
DECLARE @Desc varchar (200)

-- Create the SQLDMO.SQLServer and SQLDMO.Transfer Objects
EXEC @ErrorHandler = sp_OACreate 'SQLDMO.SQLServer', @ObjectToken_SQLDMO OUTPUT
IF @ErrorHandler <> 0
  BEGIN
    EXEC sp_OAGetErrorInfo null, @strSource OUT, @strDesc OUT
    SELECT 'Result' =  convert (binary(4), @ErrorHandler), source =
           @strSource, description = @strDesc
    END
```

# 16.24 How to... Remove All Clean Buffers from the Buffer Pool

If you wish to test the performance of queries with a cleared buffer cache (no cached query plans), you can run the DBCC DROPCLEANBUFFERS procedure to remove all clean buffers from the buffer pool. This has the same impact on query performance as restarting your SQL Server instance, without you actually having to do so. (DBCC FREEPROCCACHE, reviewed in Chapter 14, has a similar impact by removing all elements from the procedure cache.) To execute, simply run the following statement in Query Analyzer:

```
DBCC DROPCLEANBUFFERS
```

This returns:

DBCC execution completed. If DBCC printed error messages, contact your system administrator.

# 16.25 How to... Use WAITFOR

The WAITFOR function specifies a length of time or time to wait, suspending activity prior to executing code following the WAITFOR statement. WAITFOR is useful for making sure a certain period of time passes before running a chunk of code. The syntax is as follows:

```
WAITFOR  <DELAY 'time'> or TIME <'time_to_wait_until'>
```

### Example 16.25.1: Using a time DELAY

This example delays the execution of the PRINT statement for ten seconds:

```
WAITFOR DELAY '00:00:10'
PRINT 'I waited 10 seconds!'
```

### Example 16.25.2: Using a TIME interval

This next example waits until a specific time before executing a PRINT statement:

```
WAITFOR TIME '19:14'
PRINT 'Well I waited until 7:14 PM!'
```

# 17

# Performance Tuning

This chapter reviews techniques for identifying and troubleshooting performance problems in your SQL Server environment. Performance problems range from physical component bottlenecks (memory, physical I/O), to query tuning and design flaws (indexes, normalization, locking). Performance tuning is a holistic field, often requiring the configuration and design of multiple areas. This chapter will examine the tools necessary to identify and troubleshoot these areas.

As you review the various tools and techniques available for performance tuning, keep in mind that modeling and testing your database on a test environment can often help reduce performance problems in your production environment. If it is within your budget, investing in a test environment that simulates your production environment will help you performance-tune database and server issues more effectively.

Implementing performance improvements on a production environment is certainly possible without a test environment, but often not without causing business interruptions or outages. Without a test environment, you are often unable to foresee whether or not the changes will help. Of course, many applications will encounter performance problems that could not have been anticipated, but this is where a test environment can again benefit, as you can test solutions prior to moving the change to the production environment.

## 17.1 How to... Use System Monitor to Identify Hardware Bottlenecks

The Windows 2000 System Monitor (formerly known as Performance Monitor) is used to identify hardware and software bottlenecks on your SQL Server computer. A bottleneck is defined as an area or resource within your computer that is impeding performance. Areas where bottlenecks can occur include RAM (memory), CPU (processor), I/O (disk read and write activity), and network throughput.

SQL Server query performance problems (which could be anything from blocking, deadlocks, query performance, table or index scans) can often accentuate a hardware bottleneck. For example, if your query is performing an index scan against millions of rows, you may see both high CPU and I/O related counters. As another example, you may have an application that makes thousands of connections to the server, resulting in lower available memory.

This section will show you how to use System Monitor to identify potential hardware bottlenecks.

To launch System Monitor:

- Select Start | Programs | Administrative Tools | Performance

An alternative method for launching System Monitor is:

- Select Start | Run
- Type `perfmon`
- Select OK.

The Performance dialog box shows the System Monitor node, which can be used to view the various defined **counters**. Counters display the measurements of specific conditions on your SQL Server machine. Under Performance Logs and Alerts, you will see the Counter Logs node, which the following examples will use. A counter log allows you to measure activity and defined counters over a period of time:

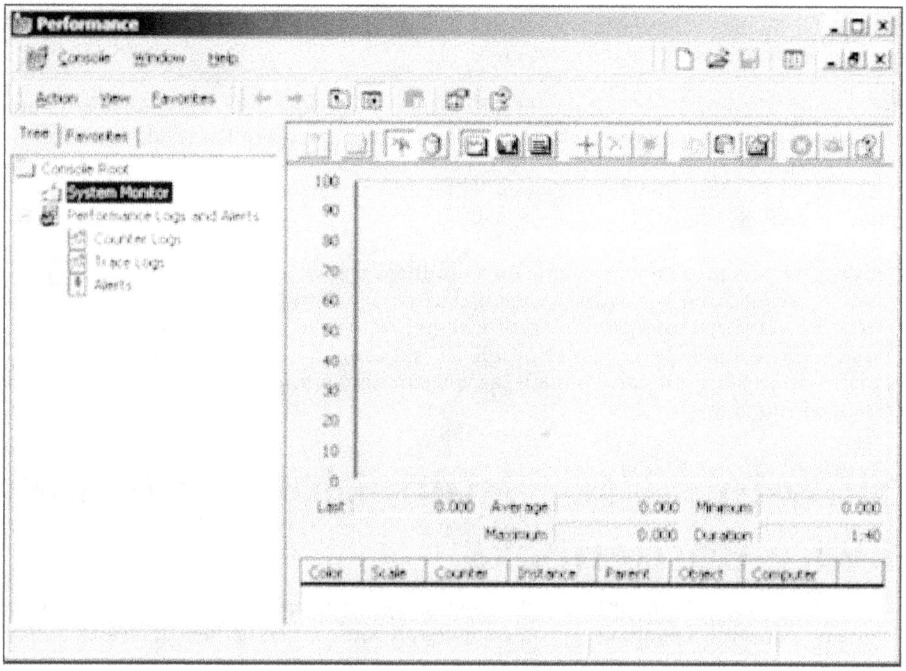

To set up a counter log, first click the Counter Log node:

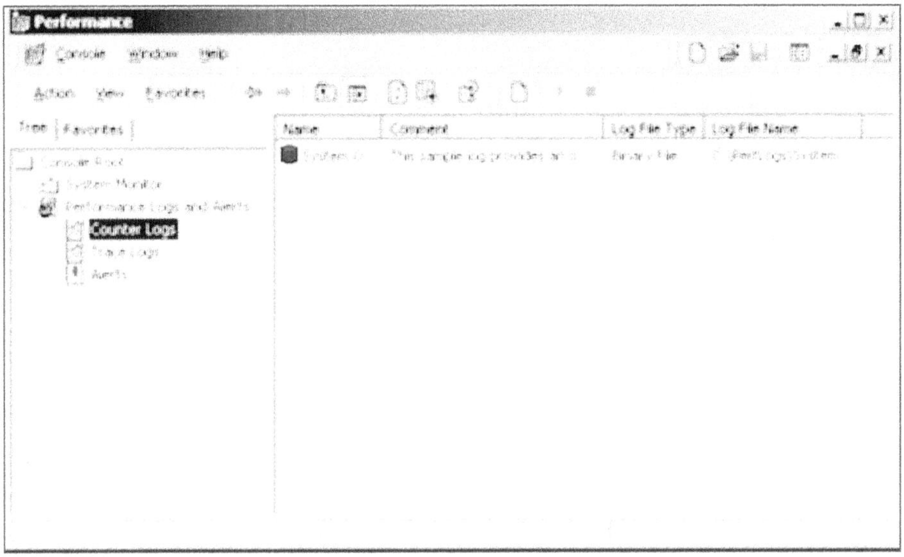

A counter log executes the log tracking of either the local machine or remote machines. To ensure that the counter log can access the machine, make sure to configure the Performance Logs and Alerts service in Service Manager to run with a domain account with administrator access to the remote machine. If the Local System account is set for the service, only the local machine will be accessible via the counter logs.

To configure the service account:

- ❑ Select Start | Programs | Administrative Tools | Services
- ❑ Double-click Performance Logs and Alerts:

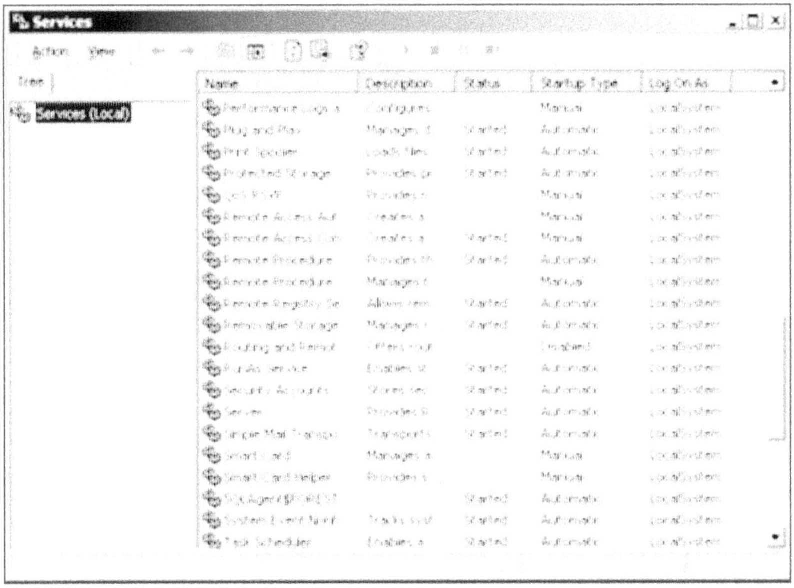

Configure the Log on as selection accordingly:

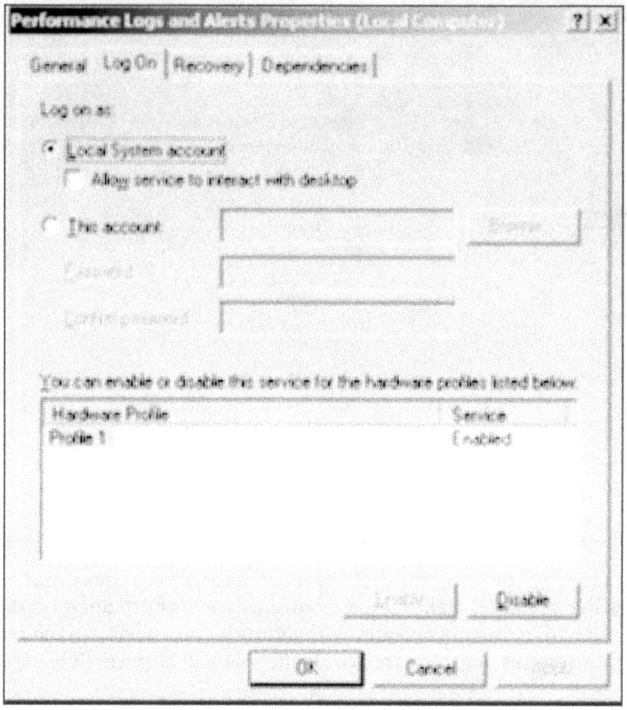


To create a new counter log from System Monitor, follow these steps:

- Right-click Counter Logs and select New Log Settings.
- Select the name of your new counter log. Counter logs are re-usable, so choose a name that indicates the server, or the purpose of the counter log.
- In the General tab, select the Add button to begin adding counters.
- After this introduction to System Monitor, the various counters and their uses will be reviewed. The counters listed will depend on what is installed on the machine being monitored. When a SQL Server instance is installed, the installation process adds the associated SQL Server object counters to the machine.
- If the performance objects for which you are searching do not show up as an option in the drop-down box, you may be encountering the problem described in the Microsoft Knowledge Base article 248933, *PRB: Performance Object Is Not Displayed in Performance Monitor*. This problem occurs because of the performance monitor DLL being marked as 'disabled'. Resolution requires registry values, so be sure to read the article carefully.
- Choose the name of the server for which you wish to track counters. Select the Performance object drop-down list, and associated counters. Select All instances or Selected instances from list: according to the counter you choose (for example, you may see multiple CPUs for a processor performance object, and choose to track one, some, or all in your counter log):

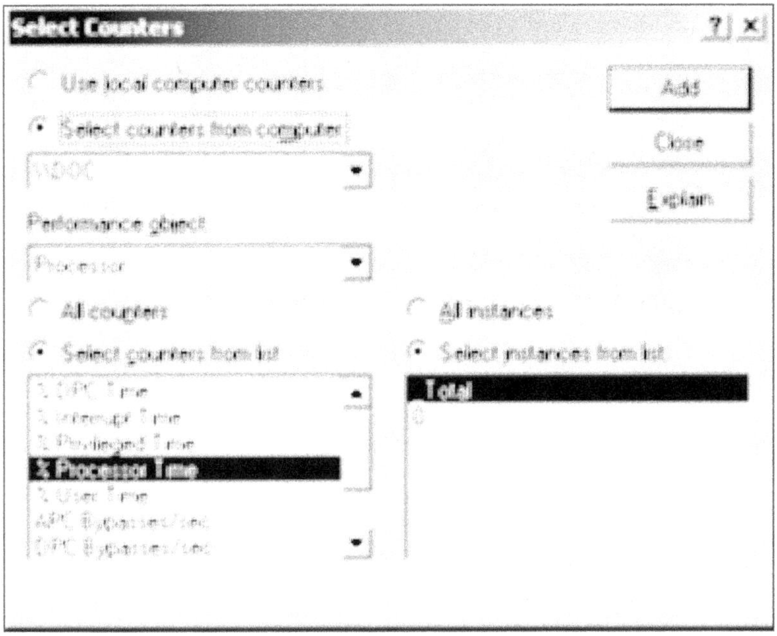


- For an explanation of the counter you are currently selecting, click the Explain button; this will create a new window with the counter description:

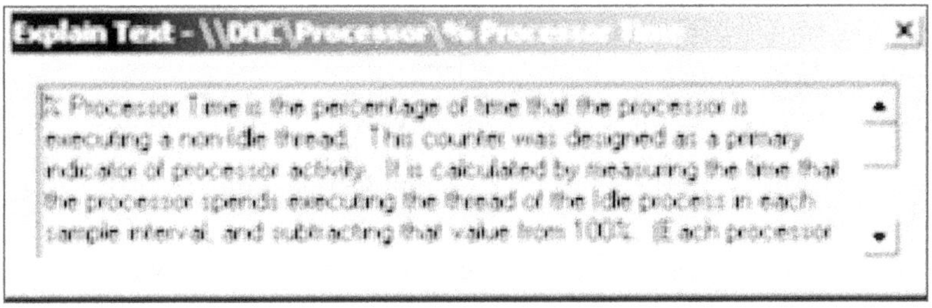


- When you have finished adding various counters, select the Close button.
- Back at the General tab, make sure to verify which counters were selected. Change the Interval to 1 second, so that information is sampled more frequently. Some counters default to measurement of values every 15 seconds. By using this setting, you may miss spikes or performance problems that occur between measurements. When averaging your results, the total average of the counter over a period of time may be misrepresented:

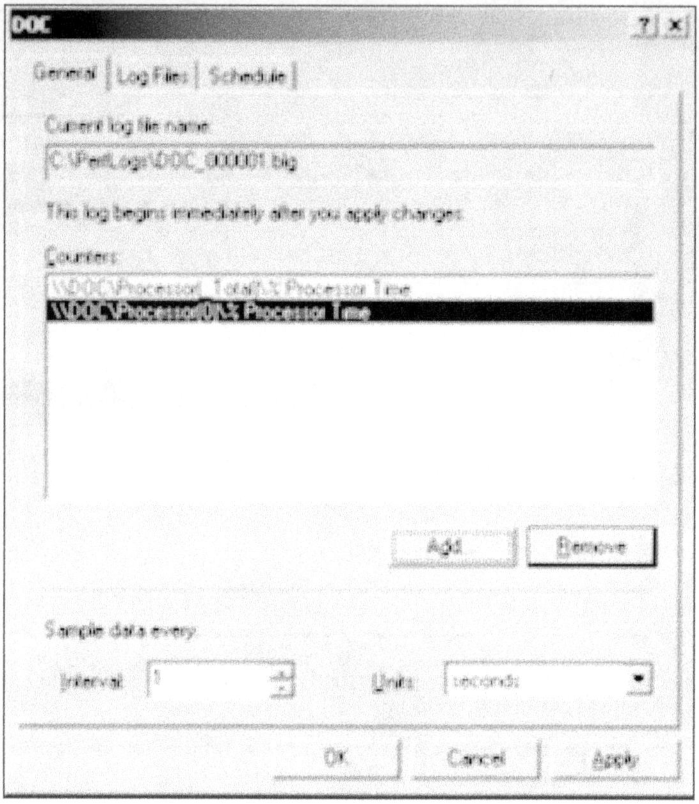


- ❑ In the Log Files tab, select the Location and File name of the counter log. Log file names will automatically increment each time the counter log is restarted, beginning with the file format of `C:\PerfLogs\filename_000001.blg`, and incrementing `0000N.blg` for each start of the counter log.
- ❑ If you wish to export your counter log information to a spreadsheet, change the Log file type from Binary File to Text File CSV or Text File TSV format.
- ❑ If you are measuring the performance of another server from a Windows XP client, you may encounter problems when attempting to open the default `.blg` (binary performance log) file type format produced by the Windows XP System Monitor within Windows 2000. The format of `.blg` files was changed in Windows XP. You can use the `relog.exe` utility to convert the Windows XP `.blg` file to a Windows 2000 `.tsv` or `.csv` format; otherwise, you can just open the `.blg` log from the Windows XP client. For more information on using `relog.exe`, see the Microsoft Knowledge Base article 305858, *Windows 2000 Cannot Open Windows XP .blg Log Files*.
- ❑ Configure the Log file size if you wish to limit the total size of the counter log:

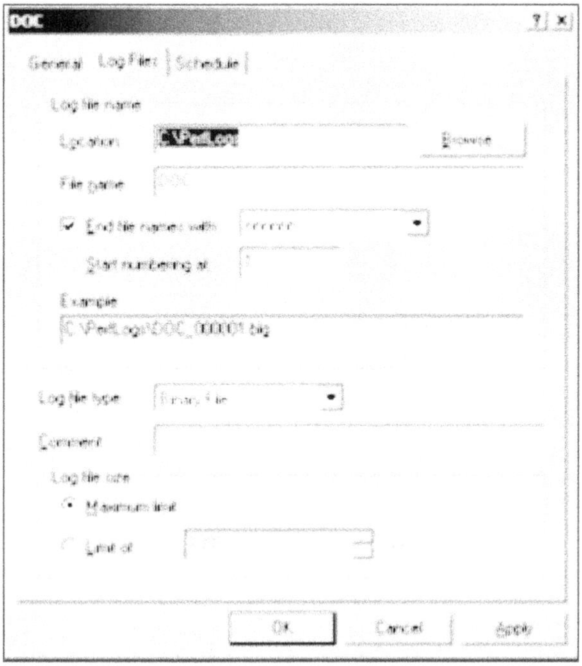


- On the Schedule tab, you can schedule the counter log to start manually, or at a defined time. The stop time can also be scheduled.
- Lastly, you can trigger a command file to be executed when the counter log file closes. Select OK when you have finished configuring your counter log:

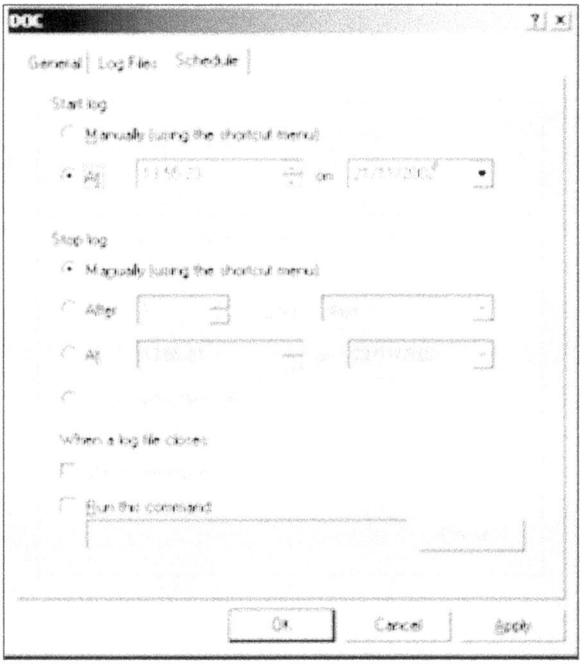

- You will now see your new counter log in the right-hand pane of System Monitor. Depending on how you scheduled the counter log, it may turn from red to green, indicating that it has started recording. If the log fails with an error, be sure to check the service account of the Performance Logs and Alerts service.

The log counter can also be started manually. To do this:

- Right-click the log counter and select Start:

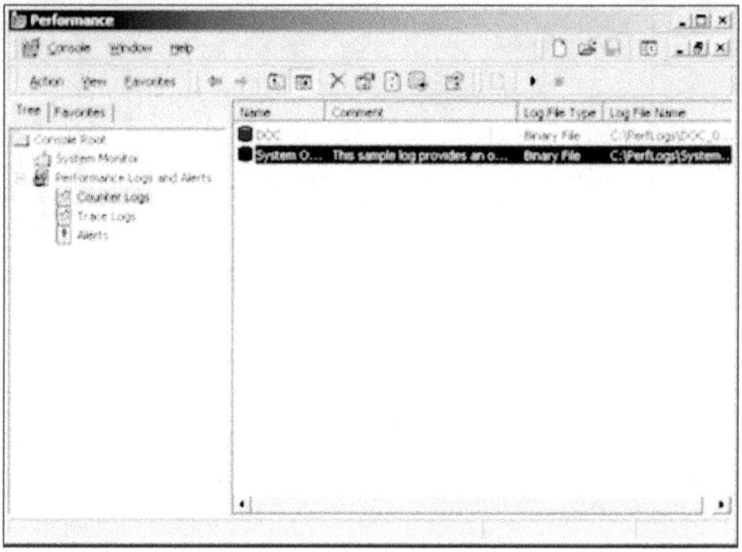


- Run your counter logs during representative time periods. Run the trace during busy periods, or at times when you suspect bottlenecks are occurring.
- To stop the log, right-click the counter log and select Stop.
- To view the results of the counter log, click the System Monitor node in the left-hand pane of System Monitor:

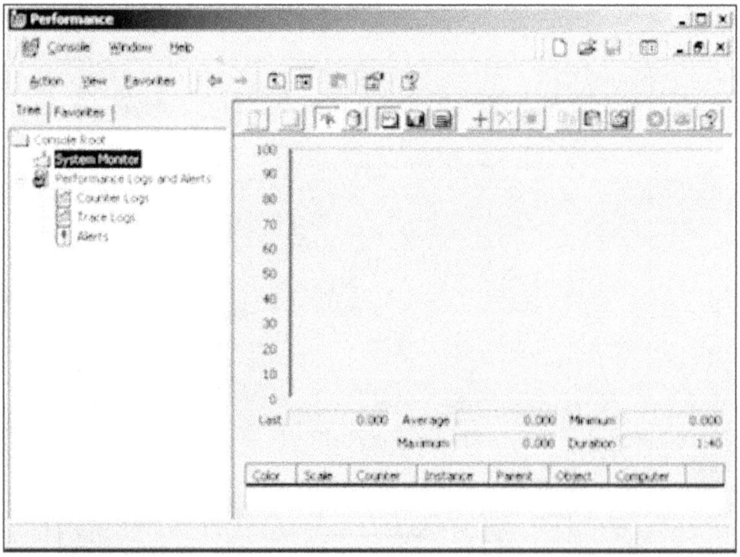

Click the properties icon on the right-hand pane toolbar.

In the System Monitor Properties dialog box, click the Source tab, and select the Log file option, pointing to the counter log that you have created.

Click the Time Range button if you wish to see the time range that the counter log covers. From the Range slider bar, you can configure varying start and stop times:

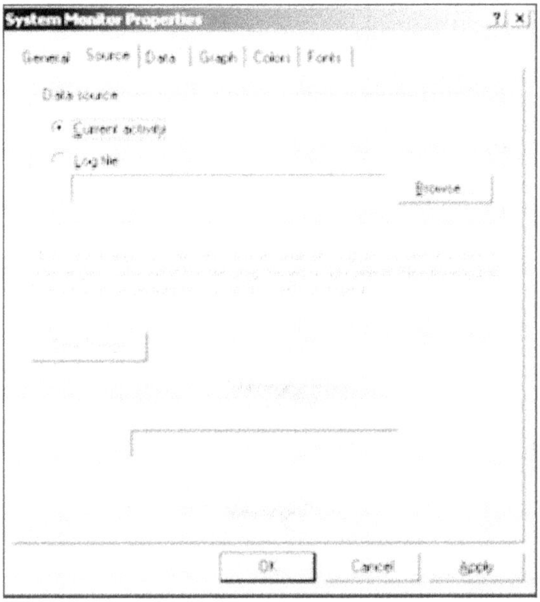


- In the Data tab, use the Add button to add the various counters you selected in the counter log.
- Only those counters that you included in the counter log will be selectable via the Performance object drop-down box. Select the Add button for each counter you wish to view. Select Close when finished:

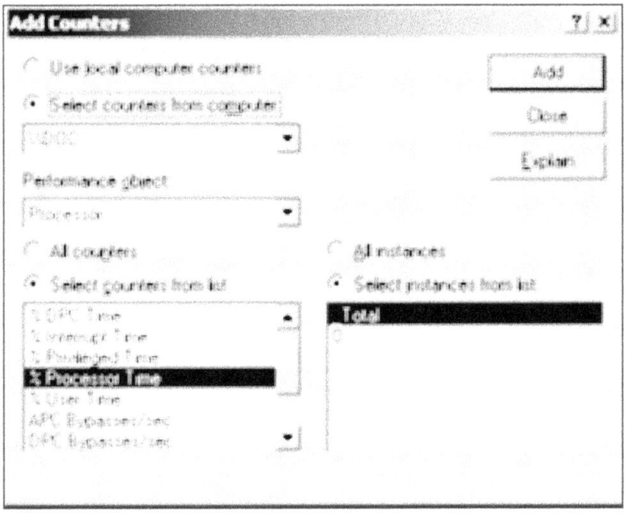

- Check in the Data tab that you selected all counters you wish to view, and select OK when finished.

- Back at the System Monitor main screen, select the  icon to see a graph of the various counters over time:

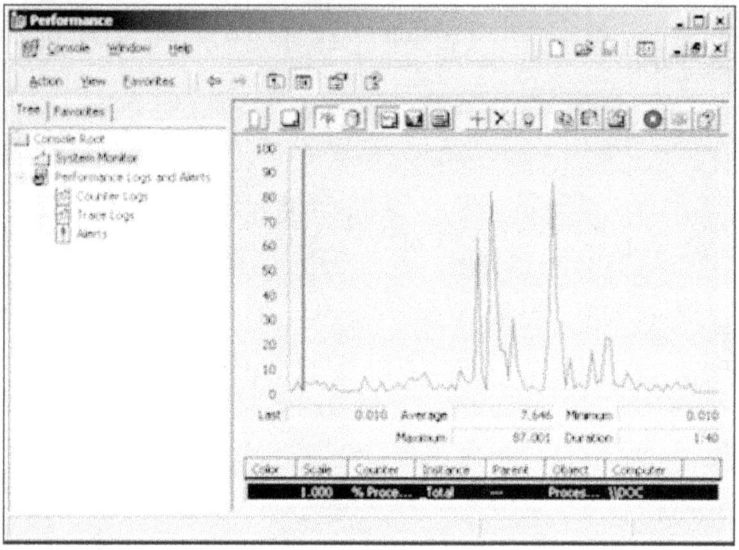


- Select the  icon to view a bar chart of the results. Select the  icon to view the report view (where you can view average, minimum, and maximum values of the counters more easily):

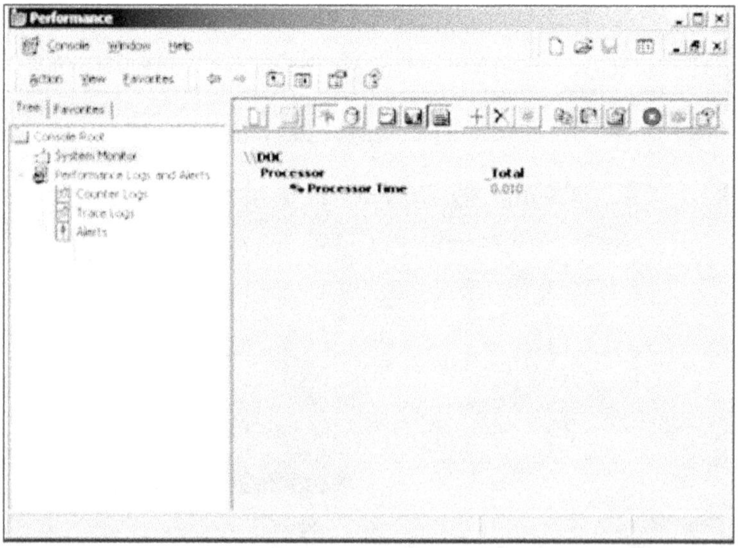


- To configure average, minimum, and maximum values, select the  icon. In the Report and histogram data section, select the average, minimum, or maximum values. When measuring activity, take all these values into consideration to surmise whether a bottleneck exists:

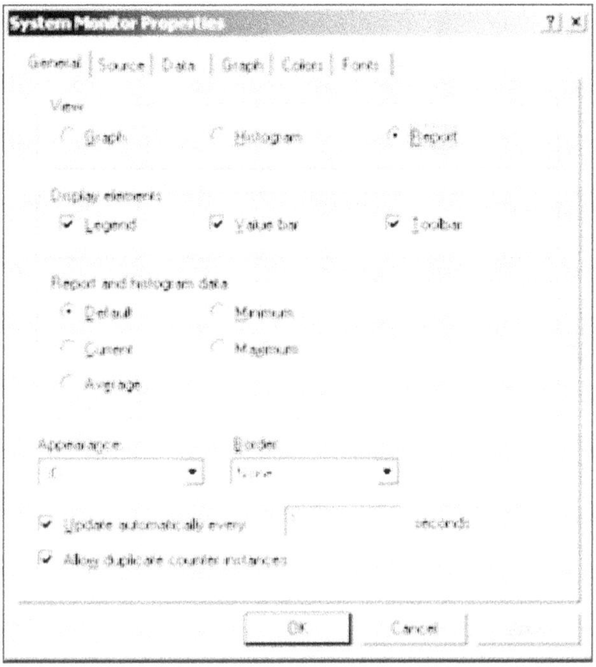


# Detecting Bottlenecks With Counters

As mentioned earlier, bottlenecks can be detected using various counters. The following table lists various counters, which can help identify resource bottlenecks:

| Performance Object | Counter | Description and Bottleneck Type |
|---|---|---|
| Memory | Pages/Sec | If only SQL Server is running on your machine, this counter should remain relatively low. Pages/sec measures pages per second that are paged in or out of memory to disk (the paging file). **Paging** occurs when an application requires a data page that is not in memory, and is forced to copy the required page into memory, and copy another page back to the disk. Paging negatively impacts system performance by causing excessive I/O activity. If you see extended periods of 20 or longer, also take a look at the Buffer Cache hit ratio counter (described further on). If the Buffer Cache hit ratio is less than optimal, you may have a memory bottleneck (or SQL Server's memory management may be mis-configured). Extended periods of 20 or longer suggest a paging issue. Pages/sec can spike for short durations without indicating a problem. |

*Table continued on following page*

| Performance Object | Counter | Description and Bottleneck Type |
|---|---|---|
| Memory | Pages/Sec | If a memory bottleneck is suggested, you may want to consider either adding more memory (be sure to consider how much memory your SQL Server edition can utilize), or otherwise consider offloading some of the database activity to a separate SQL Server instance. The same solutions apply to other memory counters that suggest memory bottlenecks. |
| Memory | Available Mbytes | This counter indicates the amount of RAM in MBs available on the SQL Server machine. If the server is a dedicated machine (only running SQL Server), and SQL Server is using its maximum allowed memory for its edition, this number can be relatively low. Otherwise, if SQL Server (or other applications) is starving the OS of memory (leaving less than the required amount available for use by the operating system), this suggests a memory bottleneck. |
| Network interface | Bytes total/sec | This measures bytes received and sent from the server to the network. Monitor this counter to see how it increases or decreases. The relative increases (relative to previous numbers) may suggest excessive network overload, although network bottlenecks are increasingly rare with the latest network technology available.<br><br>If you think you have a network bottleneck, consider investigating further your network card settings, and physical location of the machine within the network (with routers, switches, and physical lines considered). |
| PhysicalDisk or LogicalDisk | Avg. Disk Queue Length | PhysicalDisk measures counters at the physical drive level (array level, not disks within a RAID array), whereas LogicalDisk measures counters at the logical drive letter level. Avg. Disk Queue Length measures I/O read or write activity that needs to wait before being able to fulfil its request. If the value of this counter repeatedly exceeds 2, you may have an I/O bottleneck. You must divide the number of this counter by the number of physical drives in the array. If you have 10 disks that make up Physical Disk 0, then a counter value of 10 translates to a value of 1, meaning you do not exceed 2. If the counter value was 30, then the value divided by 10 disks equals 3, which, if continuously found in the counter log, suggests an I/O bottleneck. |

| Performance Object | Counter | Description and Bottleneck Type |
|---|---|---|
| PhysicalDisk or LogicalDisk | Avg. Disk Queue Length | I/O bottlenecks can be tackled by a variety of solutions. File placement of your database files across multiple arrays can sometimes reduce I/O contention. Performance tuning your query activity can also assist with I/O, by reducing the number of rows and columns, and the method by which they are retrieved (table scans, index scans, index seeks). You can also scale out database activity to other SQL Server instances in order to reduce I/O activity; this solution applies to the other counters that are used to identify I/O issues. |
| PhysicalDisk or LogicalDisk | % Disk time | This counter measures the percentage of time the disk is busy servicing I/O requests. Consistent periods exceeding 90% suggest an I/O bottleneck. |
| Processor | % Processor time | This counter displays total CPU utilization over all available processors. Consistently high values over 85% can indicate issues; this should also be weighed against the end-user experience, however. If end-user queries are processing quickly and with no problems, then you can assume that your server is well utilized (but keep an eye on CPU to make sure it doesn't get worse). When a CPU gets 'pegged' at 100% for extended periods of time, this may be an indicator of poorly written queries. If you have ruled out all other bottleneck types, you may need to upgrade the speed of your processors, or increase the number of processors on your system. |
| SQLServer | Buffer cache hit ratio | This displays the percentage of SQL Server requests that locate a page in the buffer cache (memory) instead of having to perform an I/O operation. This number should be as close to 100% as possible, with a RAM (memory) bottleneck suggested when the counter dips below 85-95%. This number may be lower for data warehouse or data mart OLAP databases, as these types of applications may extract millions of rows of data periodically, which couldn't possibly fit entirely into the procedure cache. The guidelines of 85-95% primarily relate to OLTP-type databases. |
| SQLServer | Latches:<br>Average latch wait time (ms) | Latches are lightweight SQL Server resource locks. Very high latch waits per second suggest an I/O bottleneck when coupled with other counters that suggest issues. |
| SQLServer | Memory Manager Object:<br>Total server memory (KB) | This counter is good for monitoring how much memory SQL Server needs to use. This presumes that you have configured the SQL Server instance to use dynamic versus fixed memory. |

*Table continued on following page*

| Performance Object | Counter | Description and Bottleneck Type |
|---|---|---|
| SQLServer | Access Methods:<br>Page splits/sec | This indicates the amount of page splitting occurring in your database per second. Determine the ideal fill factor for your indexes so that page splitting is reduced, but not at the expense of read requests from queries. |
| SQLServer | Access Methods:<br>Full scans/sec | This records the number of table or index scans. The lower the number, the better (unless you are seeing table scans against very small tables). Improving your table indexing, and query construction, can help lower this number. |
| System | Processor queue length | This displays the number of threads waiting in the processor queue for an available processor. If the value of this counter exceeds 2, when divided by the number of processors on the system, you may have a CPU bottleneck. For example, if you have 2 processors, and consistently see a value of 8, divide that number by two for a value of 4. This value exceeds 2, and suggests a CPU bottleneck. |

This table reviews some of the key counters to monitor; there are, however, hundreds of other system counters that can be used to troubleshoot and monitor your environment. For more information on counters specific to SQL Server, see *SQL Server Books Online's* topic *Using SQL Server Objects*. For a review of operating system counters, see Microsoft's Knowledge Base article 146005, *Optimizing Windows NT for Performance*. This article reviews additional counters you can monitor for both 2000 Server and NT Server alike.

# Query Tuning Best Practices

A query is generally considered **good** when it runs with a response time appropriate to the end-user and the requirements of the application, and performs the intended action. Good queries depend on well-designed schemas and construction. For example, inappropriate or excessive use of cursors can increase the duration of the query and consume server resources, as against set-based non-cursor solutions. An effective indexing strategy is also important (indexing is discussed later in this chapter). Be sure to design your query effectively, rather than depending on indexes to improve your query performance; indexing should be secondary to good query design. There are certain behaviors that will help you create effective and efficient queries:

- When creating a `SELECT` query, ask yourself whether you need each column referenced in the query (`SELECT` clause). Minimizing the number of columns returned by your query can, potentially, improve performance, thus reducing memory overhead and the amount of data that must travel across your network.
- Use the `WHERE` clause to narrow down the number of rows returned. Design your query to return only those rows you need (use `WHERE` clauses that narrow down your result set). Do not return all rows "just in case". This can consume unnecessary CPU cycles to retrieve the data, memory, and network bandwidth.
- Use a `WHERE` clause whenever necessary. The `WHERE` clause provides the Query Optimizer with the information it needs to retrieve the required rows; even adding potentially redundant `WHERE` clauses can help give information that the optimizer needs. Indexes thrive on `WHERE` clause expressions, and the query processor will be more likely to use indexes if `WHERE` clauses are included (see the indexing section of this chapter to review what types of operators in a `WHERE` clause expression are more likely to be used).

- If a query is to be run frequently, be sure that it does not hold (lock) resources too long. A query that is run monthly has different query design requirements from one run every second.
- Take advantage of the various tools provided by SQL Server to tune your queries. Such tools reviewed in this chapter include the graphical showplan, `SHOWPLAN_ALL`, `SHOWPLAN_TEXT`, `STATISTICS IO`, `STATISTICS PROFILE`, SQL Profiler, and `STATISTICS TIME`. Each provides valuable performance information about individual statements and batches.
- When you test your query in the test environment (you should always have a test environment), make sure the referenced tables have the same schema, indexing, and data rows. The query optimizer takes into account the distribution of data values (via statistics), so do not use 'dummy data', but rather data that accurately reflects that stored in the production environment. Query performance can change vastly due to differences in the previously mentioned requirements.
- Make sure any columns involved in `JOIN` operations have indexes on them.
- Decide whether the `DISTINCT` clause is necessary in your query. Is your data naturally unique? If so, get rid of `DISTINCT`. Test and compare the performance.
- `ORDER BY` adds more performance overhead by forcing the ordering of the result set; if `ORDER BY` is unnecessary, remove it. Alternatively, you could choose to sort the data via the client-side code.
- Cursors and temporary tables should be used wisely. Sub-queries or derived table references can sometimes be used as faster alternatives. Both cursors and temporary tables have their advantages, but always use them prudently. Always compare the performance of alternatives.
- Do not underestimate the power of stored procedures. Stored procedures can sometimes yield an exponential performance increase over a regular ad hoc query call from an application. If you cannot use a stored procedure, try `sp_executesql` instead.

# 17.2 How To... Use SQL Profiler to Capture Activity

SQL Profiler is a tool with which both the DBA and developer should become intimately familiar. SQL Profiler requires `sysadmin` privileges on the SQL Server instance. SQL Profiler allows you to capture SQL statements and activity as they occur against the SQL Server instance. This enables you to capture long-running queries, queries that consume CPU resources, events such as table scans, security audit events, errors, and warnings.

> **To get more accurate results, avoid running SQL profiler when System Monitor counter logs are being generated.**

SQL Profiler is the tool installed with the SQL Server suite that provides a GUI for configuring a client-side trace of activity against your SQL Server instance.

Chapter 5 described how to set up a SQL Profiler trace to detect deadlock events. Save the output to a file or a table, then save the trace as a template so it can be re-used.

This section will review the other events that can be tracked using SQL Profiler, and will provide an example of tracing long-running queries.

The following tables review the different categories of events that SQL Profiler can trace for a SQL Server 2000 instance:

## Cursor Category

| Event | Description |
|---|---|
| CursorClose | Closing of a Transact-SQL cursor |
| CursorExecute | Transact-SQL cursor execution |
| CursorImplicitConversion | A specific cursor type is converted to a new cursor type |
| CursorOpen | A Transact-SQL cursor is opened |
| CursorPrepare | A Transact-SQL cursor is prepared for use |
| CursorRecompile | A Transact-SQL cursor is recompiled due to a schema change |
| CursorUnprepare | A prepared Transact-SQL cursor is deleted |

## Database Category

| Event | Description |
|---|---|
| DataFileAutoGrow | Captures when a data file has grown automatically |
| DataFileAutoShrink | Captures when a data file has shrunk automatically |
| LogFileAutoGrow | Captures when a log file has grown automatically |
| LogFileAutoShrink | Captures when a log file has shrunk automatically |

## Errors and Warnings Category

| Event | Description |
|---|---|
| Attention | Captures client attention events |
| ErrorLog | Captures error events logged in the SQL Server error log |
| EventLog | Captures events logged in the Windows application log |
| Exception | Captures an exception that has occurred in SQL Server |
| Execution Warnings | Captures warnings that occurred during a statement or procedure execution |
| Hash Warnings | Captures hashing operation errors |
| Missing Column Statistics | Logged when column statistics for a query optimizer do not exist |
| Missing Join Predicate | Warns when a query is missing a join predicate (no join can mean an implicit Cartesian product) |
| OLEDB Errors | Captures OLE DB errors |
| Sort Warnings | Captures when sort operations do not fit in memory for queries (ORDER BY, for example) |

# Locks Category

| Event | Description |
|---|---|
| `Lock:Acquired` | Lock on a resource has been acquired |
| `Lock:Cancel` | Lock on a resource has been cancelled |
| `Lock:Deadlock` | A deadlock has occurred |
| `Lock:Deadlock Chain` | Events leading up to the deadlock |
| `Lock:Escalation` | Captures when a finer-grained lock converts to a coarser-grained lock |
| `Lock:Released` | A resource lock has been released |
| `Lock:Timeout` | A resource lock request has timed out, due to another transaction holding the resource |

# Objects Category

| Event | Description |
|---|---|
| `AutoStats` | Records when statistics have been automatically created or updated |
| `Object:Created` | Records when an object has been created (for example, a table, index, or database) |
| `Object:Closed` | Records when an open object has been closed |
| `Object:Deleted` | Records when an object has been deleted |
| `Object:Opened` | Records when an object has been accessed via a query |

# Performance Category

| Event | Description |
|---|---|
| `Degree of Parallelism 1-4` | These are four different events, used to track different types of parallelism in SQL Server version 7.0. In SQL Server 2000, however, `Degree Of Parallelism 1` will track `SELECT`, `INSERT`, `UPDATE`, and `DELETE` statements and their associated degree of parallelism. |
| `Execution Plan` | Records the plan tree of a Transact-SQL statement. |
| `ShowPlan All` | Displays the query plan and full compile-time details. |
| `ShowPlan Statistics` | Displays the query plan with runtime details. |
| `ShowPlan Text` | Displays the query plan tree. |

## Scans Category

| Event | Description |
|---|---|
| Scan:Started | Captures a table or index scan starting |
| Scan:Stopped | Captures the end of a table or index scan |

## Security Audit Category

| Event | Description |
|---|---|
| Audit Add DB User Event | Records user additions and removals |
| Audit Add Login to Server Role Event | Records addition or removal of logins to fixed server roles |
| Audit Add Member to DB Role Event | Records addition or removal of members to database roles (fixed or user-defined) |
| Audit Add Role Event | Captures an add or drop of database roles |
| Audit Addlogin Event | Captures an add or drop of a SQL Server login |
| Audit App Role Change Password Event | Captures an application role password change |
| Audit Backup/Restore Event | Captures BACKUP and RESTORE operations |
| Audit Change Audit Event | Captures AUDIT modifications |
| Audit DBCC Event | Captures DBCC command calls |
| Audit Login Event | Captures login events |
| Audit Login Change Password Event | Captures password change events (although not the new password itself) |
| Audit Login Change Property Event | Captures default database or default language changes to a login |
| Audit Login Failed Event | Captures a failed login attempt |
| Audit Login GDR Event | Captures grant, revoke, and deny actions for Windows account logins |
| Audit Logout Event | Captures logout events |
| Audit Object Derived Permission Event | Captures CREATE, ALTER, or DROP commands |
| Audit Object GDR Event | Captures permission grants via GRANT, DENY, or REVOKE |
| Audit Object Permission Event | Captures successful or unsuccessful use of object permissions |
| Audit Server Starts and Stops Event | Returns shut down, start, and pausing of services |
| Audit Statement GDR Event | Returns permission events for GRANT, DENY, and REVOKE |
| Audit Statement Permission Event | Records statement permissions use |

## Server Category

| Event | Description |
|---|---|
| `Server Memory Change` | Captures server memory fluctuations by 1MB increments, or by 5% increments (whichever is greater) of the maximum server memory |

## Sessions Category

| Event | Description |
|---|---|
| `Existing Connection` | Lists all user connections prior to the trace starting |

## Stored Procedure Category

| Event | Description |
|---|---|
| `RPC Output Parameter` | Shows output parameter information for previously executed remote procedure calls |
| `RPC:Completed` | Captures when an RPC has completed |
| `RPC:Starting` | Captures when an RPC has started |
| `SP:CacheHit` | Records when a procedure was found in the cache |
| `SP:CacheInsert` | Records when a new item is inserted into the procedure cache |
| `SP:CacheMiss` | Records when a stored procedure was not found in the procedure cache |
| `SP:CacheRemove` | Captures when a stored procedure has been removed from cache |
| `SP:Completed` | Captures when a stored procedure has completed |
| `SP:ExecContextHit` | Records the version of a stored procedure found in the cache |
| `SP:Recompile` | Records when a procedure has recompiled |
| `SP:Starting` | Records when a procedure call has started |
| `SP:StmtCompleted` | Captures when a statement within a stored procedure has completed |
| `SP:StmtStarting` | Captures when a statement within a stored procedure has started |

## Transactions Category

| Event | Description |
|---|---|
| `DTCTransaction` | Captures when MS DTC transactions occur between two or more databases |
| `SQLTransaction` | Captures `BEGIN`, `COMMIT`, `SAVE`, and `ROLLBACK TRANSACTION` statements |
| `TransactionLog` | Captures when transactions are written to the transaction log |

# T-SQL Category

| Event | Description |
|---|---|
| `Exec Prepared SQL` | Records when a prepared SQL statement or statements have been executed |
| `Prepare SQL` | Records when a SQL statement or statements have been prepared for use |
| `SQL:BatchCompleted` | Captures a Transact-SQL batch completion |
| `SQL:BatchStarting` | Captures when a Transact-SQL batch begins |
| `SQL:StmtCompleted` | Captures when a Transact-SQL statement has completed |
| `SQL:StmtStarting` | Captures when a Transact-SQL statement has begun |
| `Unprepare SQL` | Records when a SQL statement or statements have been unprepared |

# User Configurable Category

| Event | Description |
|---|---|
| `UserConfigurable 0-9` | 10 separate events whose value is user-defined |

### Example 17.2.1: Capturing long-duration queries

One method for ensuring that your queries perform well in your database is to measure how long they take to run. The various completion events below capture remote procedure calls, stored procedures, and SQL statements and batches. The `SP:Completed` event records the total time the stored procedure took to execute, whereas the `SP:StmtCompleted` displays the time of an individual statement call within the stored procedure:

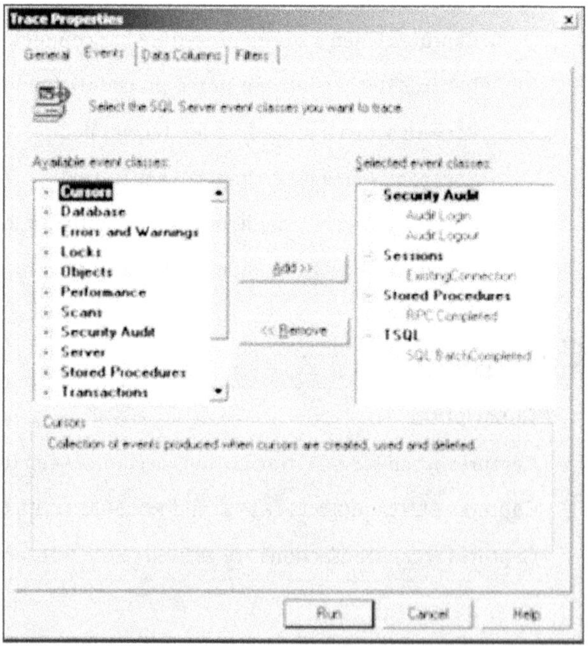

In the Data Columns tab, this example groups the `Duration` column, so that results are ordered by the length of time each event took to execute. `EventClass` and `TextData` are also critical, so that you can ascertain what type of event took so long (and correct it):

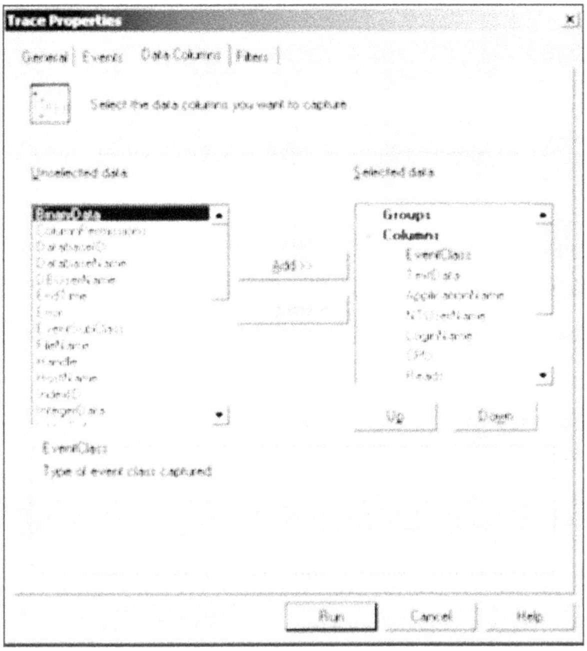


Lastly, in the Filters column, Duration is filtered to be greater than or equal to 2000 milliseconds (2 seconds). Configure an appropriate number for your purposes and environment:

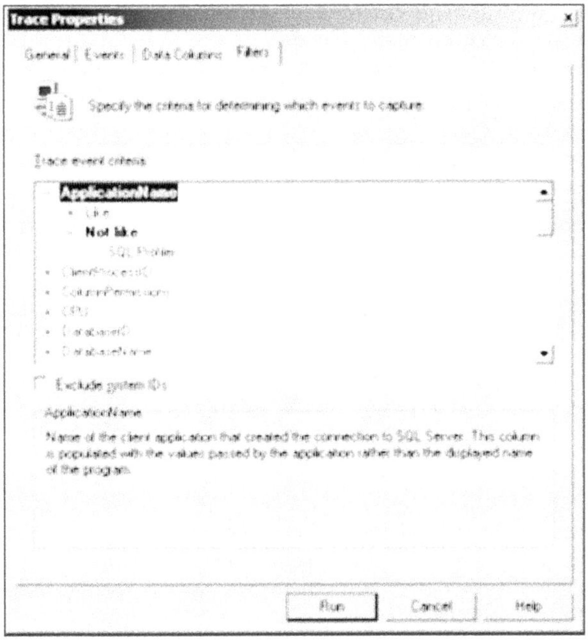

Click the Run button to start the trace. The output will capture statements that exceed 2 seconds. From the output window, you can analyze which queries should be tuned. Click on the row with the highest duration, or other rows, to view the offending Transact-SQL statement in the lower pane. You can copy this to Query Analyzer to investigate further (investigative techniques are reviewed later on the chapter):

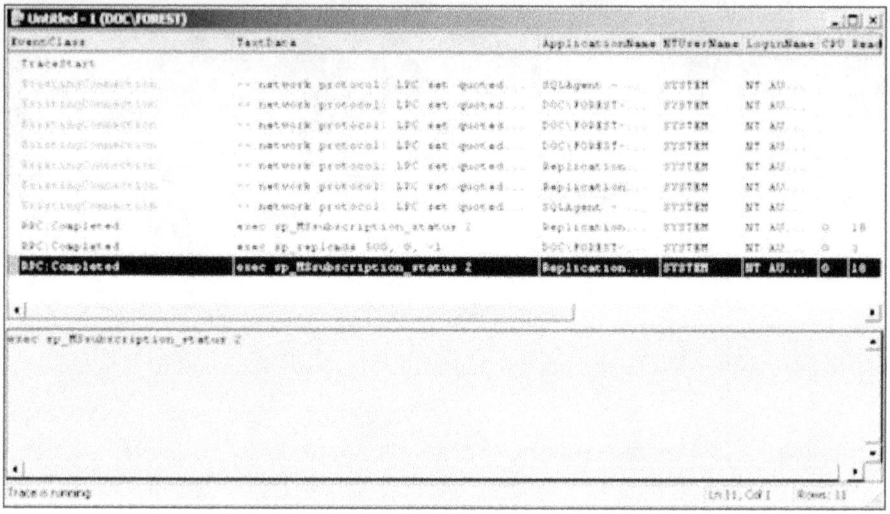


There are various reasons why the duration of a query may be excessive:

- Some queries may perform poorly because they are written in an incorrect or inefficient manner. Check the construction of your query, to make sure it is returning what it was intended to return (and no more). Then verify the execution plan, as well as the type of table access that is occurring (table scan, index scan, index seek). Indexing and execution plan analysis is reviewed later in the chapter. Also, some queries may be well constructed, indexed properly, but still may take a long time to run due to the volume of records being returned, or the complexity of the query. If this query is causing performance problems with other activity, consider running it during off hours only, or offloading the query to a separate copy of the database (using replication or log shipping, for example).
- Other queries may run long due to poor indexing of the underlying tables. If the query is performing excessive scans, place it in Query Analyzer, and investigate what indexes are being used (or not) using graphical showplan, `SHOWPLAN_ALL`, or `SHOWPLAN_TEXT`. You can also run the query through the Index Tuning Wizard, to discover any obvious (or otherwise) indexing suggestions.
- Some queries may run long because they are being blocked by other queries. You may often see queries that run in a few milliseconds when run from Query Analyzer but, when involved in the application, run for much longer. At this point, you should investigate the locking occurring on your server (is the transaction being blocked?). You should also take a look at the execution plan (reviewed later), to ensure that the same plan is always being used, or is equally effective each time the query is executed.

# 17.3 How to... Script a Server-Side Profiler Trace

A client-side Profiler trace originates from the SQL Profiler application and, when the application is stopped, the trace is stopped. This means that you cannot log off from your workstation with the SQL Profiler trace still running unless you stop the trace first. You can always run SQL Profiler from the server, and then disconnect (if logged on with terminal services). There is, however, a better way: **server-side traces**.

Server-side traces are defined using system stored procedures. The functionality is the same as running a trace via SQL Profiler, except that the events, columns, and filters are defined via stored procedures. The SQL Profiler GUI uses the same procedures to generate the trace data; much (but not all) of the control, however, remains at the client running SQL Profiler. The trace runs *server-side*, meaning it runs as a process *entirely* on the server, without any GUI, such as SQL Profiler. The advantage of server-side traces is that they don't need a GUI to run, and can be started and stopped programmatically.

A disadvantage of server-side traces is that they are more complex than using a GUI, and are disconcerting to some, as you can forget that they are running on your SQL Server instance! Traces **do** incur some performance overhead, both from the process of running the trace, and the disk space used to store the table or file output. Server-side traces should be used with care for these reasons.

SQL Server 2000 improved on the procedures used to produce a server-side Profiler trace, reducing the number of procedures needed to manage the trace definition, and increasing the re-usability of existing procedures.

The system stored procedures used to configure and utilize server-side traces are as follows:

## sp_trace_create

This procedure creates the trace definition. The syntax is:

```
sp_trace_create <trace_id> OUTPUT,
                @options = <option_value>,
                @tracefile = <'trace_file'>,
                @maxfilesize = <max_file_size>,
                @stoptime = <'stop_time'>
```

| Parameter | Description |
|---|---|
| `<trace_id>` | Declares a local variable to contain the value returned as an `OUTPUT` parameter. This value is set to the unique number assigned to the trace by SQL Server. |
| `@options = <option_value>` | This can be the sum of one or more integer values that set the configuration of the trace. The valid integer values are:<br>`1` = Trace produces a rowset.<br>`2` = Creates a file rollover when the max file size is reached.<br>`4` = Used for C2-compliant security, specifying that if the trace cannot be written to, that SQL Server should shut down.<br>`8` = Sets the trace as a **black box trace**. A black box trace records the last 5MB of activity for the SQL Server instance. This value is not compatible with other options. |
| `@tracefile = <'trace_file'>` | Specifies the path and file name of the trace file. |
| `@maxfilesize = <max_file_size>` | Sets the maximum file size in MBs. If the rollover option is not chosen, the trace will stop running after reaching the limit. |
| `@stoptime = <'stop_time'>` | Sets the date and time to stop the trace. |

### Example 17.3.1: Using sp_trace_create

This example creates the initial trace definition. The second parameter uses no options and, therefore, is 0. Also notice that the Unicode N is included for the trace file location, and that a local variable is used to capture the trace integer identifier:

```
DECLARE @TraceID int

EXEC sp_trace_create @TraceId OUTPUT , 0, N'C:\temp\mytrace'
PRINT @TraceID
```

This returns 1.

# sp_trace_setevent

This procedure adds or removes events or event columns from a trace. The trace must be defined first, and must not be running. The syntax is:

```
sp_trace_setevent <trace_id>,
                  @eventid = <event_id>,
                  @columnid = <column_id>,
                   @on = <on>
```

| Parameter | Description | |
|---|---|---|
| <trace_id> | Integer value of the trace. | |
| <event_id> | event_id is associated with the specific events that a trace can track (see the previous section for descriptions of each event). The event numbers are as follows: | |
| | 10 | RPC:Completed |
| | 11 | RPC:Starting |
| | 12 | SQL:BatchCompleted |
| | 13 | SQL:BatchStarting |
| | 14 | Login |
| | 15 | Logout |
| | 16 | Attention |
| | 17 | ExistingConnection |
| | 18 | ServiceControl |
| | 19 | DTCTransaction |
| | 20 | Login Failed |
| | 21 | EventLog |
| | 22 | ErrorLog |
| | 23 | Lock:Released |

| | | |
|---|---|---|
| <event_id> | event_id is associated with the specific events that a trace can track (see the previous section for descriptions of each event). The event numbers are as follows: | |
| | 24 | Lock:Acquired |
| | 25 | Lock:Deadlock |
| | 26 | Lock:Cancel |
| | 27 | Lock:Timeout |
| | 28 | DOP Event |
| | 33 | Exception |
| | 34 | SP:CacheMiss |
| | 35 | SP:CacheInsert |
| | 36 | SP:CacheRemove |
| | 37 | SP:Recompile |
| | 38 | SP:CacheHit |
| | 39 | SP:ExecContextHit |
| | 40 | SQL:StmtStarting |
| | 41 | SQL:StmtCompleted |
| | 42 | SP:Starting |
| | 43 | SP:Completed |
| | 46 | Object:Created |
| | 47 | Object:Deleted |
| | 50 | SQL Transaction |
| | 51 | Scan:Started |
| | 52 | Scan:Stopped |
| | 53 | CursorOpen |
| | 54 | Transaction Log |
| | 55 | Hash Warning |
| | 58 | Auto Update Stats |
| | 59 | Lock:Deadlock Chain |
| | 60 | Lock:Escalation |
| | 61 | OLEDB Errors |
| | 67 | Execution Warnings |
| | 68 | Execution Plan |

*Table continued on following page*

| Parameter | Description | |
|---|---|---|
| <event_id> | event_id is associated with the specific events that a trace can track (see the previous section for descriptions of each event). The event numbers are as follows: | |
| | 69 | Sort Warnings |
| | 70 | CursorPrepare |
| | 71 | Prepare SQL |
| | 72 | Exec Prepared SQL |
| | 73 | Unprepare SQL |
| | 74 | CursorExecute |
| | 75 | CursorRecompile |
| | 76 | CursorImplicitConversion |
| | 77 | CursorUnprepare |
| | 78 | CursorClose |
| | 79 | Missing Column Statistics |
| | 80 | Missing Join Predicate |
| | 81 | Server Memory Change |
| | 82-91 | User Configurable (0-9) |
| | 92 | Data File Auto Grow |
| | 93 | Log File Auto Grow |
| | 94 | Data File Auto Shrink |
| | 95 | Log File Auto Shrink |
| | 96 | Show Plan Text |
| | 97 | Show Plan ALL |
| | 98 | Show Plan Statistics |
| | 100 | RPC Output Parameter |
| | 101 | Reserved |
| | 102 | Audit Statement GDR |
| | 103 | Audit Object GDR |
| | 104 | Audit Add/Drop Login |
| | 105 | Audit Login GDR |
| | 106 | Audit Login Change Property |
| | 107 | Audit Login Change Password |
| | 108 | Audit Add Login to Server Role |

| | | |
|---|---|---|
| <event_id> | event_id is associated with the specific events that a trace can track (see the previous section for descriptions of each event). The event numbers are as follows: | |
| | 109 | Audit Add DB User |
| | 110 | Audit Add Member to DB |
| | 111 | Audit Add/Drop Role |
| | 112 | App Role Pass Change |
| | 113 | Audit Statement Permission |
| | 114 | Audit Object Permission |
| | 115 | Audit Backup/Restore |
| | 116 | Audit DBCC |
| | 117 | Audit Change Audit |
| | 118 | Audit Object Derived Permission |
| <column_id> | This specifies which column id is included with the event. The integer values associated with the column selections are as follows: | |
| | 1 | TextData |
| | 2 | BinaryData |
| | 3 | DatabaseID |
| | 4 | TransactionID |
| | 6 | NTUserName |
| | 7 | NTDomainName |
| | 8 | ClientHostName |
| | 9 | ClientProcessID |
| | 10 | ApplicationName |
| | 11 | SQLSecurityLoginName |
| | 12 | SPID |
| | 13 | Duration |
| | 14 | StartTime |
| | 15 | EndTime |
| | 16 | Reads |
| | 17 | Writes |
| | 18 | CPU |
| | 19 | Permissions |

*Table continued on following page*

| Parameter | Description |
|---|---|
| <column_id> | This specifies which column id is included with the event. The integer values associated with the column selections are as follows:<br>20 `Severity`<br>21 `EventSubClass`<br>22 `ObjectID`<br>23 `Success`<br>24 `IndexID`<br>25 `IntegerData`<br>26 `ServerName`<br>27 `EventClass`<br>28 `ObjectType`<br>29 `NestLevel`<br>30 `State`<br>31 `Error`<br>32 `Mode`<br>33 `Handle`<br>34 `ObjectName`<br>35 `DatabaseName`<br>36 `Filename`<br>37 `ObjectOwner`<br>38 `TargetRoleName`<br>39 `TargetUserName`<br>40 `DatabaseUserName`<br>41 `LoginSID`<br>42 `TargetLoginName`<br>43 `TargetLoginSID`<br>44 `ColumnPermissionsSet` |
| <on> | When set to `1`, this parameter turns the event on. If the `column_id` parameter is null, all columns are cleared and the event is turned on. If the `column_id` parameter is not null, the column is turned on for the specific event. If the `<on>` parameter is set to `0`, and the `column_id` is `NULL`, the event is turned off and all columns are cleared. If the `column_id` is not `NULL`, the column is turned off for the specified event. |

### Example 17.3.2: Using sp_trace_setevent

This example continues work with the new trace, with the integer id of 1. This trace will track SQL:StmtCompleted, event 41, and will include the columns EventClass, SPID, CPU, Duration, IntegerData, Reads, Writes, and TextData. Notice that sp_trace_setevent is called for each event/column combination. Notice also that a local variable is defined for @on, to be a data type of BIT. The @on variable is then assigned as 1, and used for the last parameter:

```
DECLARE @on bit
SELECT @on = 1

EXEC sp_trace_setevent @TraceID, 41, 1, @on
EXEC sp_trace_setevent @TraceID, 41, 12, @on
EXEC sp_trace_setevent @TraceID, 41, 13, @on
EXEC sp_trace_setevent @TraceID, 41, 16, @on
EXEC sp_trace_setevent @TraceID, 41, 17, @on
EXEC sp_trace_setevent @TraceID, 41, 18, @on
EXEC sp_trace_setevent @TraceID, 41, 25, @on
```

# sp_trace_setfilter

This procedure applies a filter to a stopped trace. The syntax is:

```
sp_trace_setfilter <trace_id>,
              @columnid = <column_id>,
              @logical_operator = <logical_operator>,
              @comparison_operator = <comparison_operator>,
              @value = <value>
```

| Parameter | Description |
|---|---|
| <trace_id> | The ID of the trace |
| @columnid = <column_id> | The column ID for which to apply the filter |
| @logical_operator = <logical_operator> | Specifies either AND (0) or OR (1) |
| @comparison_operator = <comparison_operator> | Selects the comparison operator. The integer values translate to the following operators:<br>0 =<br>1 <><br>2 ><br>3 <<br>4 >=<br>5 <=<br>6 LIKE<br>7 NOT LIKE |
| @value = <value> | value is the value to be used for the filter expression |

### Example 17.3.3: Using sp_trace_setfilter

This example adds a filter to our existing trace `1`; we then filter the `Duration` column to include only values >= 500 milliseconds. Notice that the `BIGINT` variable is required for plugging in the 500 milliseconds value:

```
DECLARE @value bigint
SELECT @value = 500

EXEC sp_trace_setfilter 1, 13, 0, 4, @value
```

## sp_trace_setstatus

This procedure is used to start, stop, or delete a trace defined for the SQL Server instance. The syntax is:

```
sp_trace_setstatus <trace_id>,
               @status = <status>
```

| Parameter | Description |
|---|---|
| `<trace_id>` | The ID of the trace |
| `@status = <status>` | Select `0` to stop a trace, `1` to start the trace, and `2` to close and delete the trace definition |

### Example 17.3.4: Using sp_trace_setstatus to start a trace

Now that the columns, events, file location, and filters are defined, the trace will be started:

```
EXEC sp_trace_setstatus 1, 1
```

Assuming the previous trace procedure examples were executed, you will now have a trace actively running on the server. To see all traces running on the SQL Server instance, use the following query:

```
SELECT * FROM :: fn_trace_getinfo(default)
```

This returns property settings for all traces (active or not) configured on the SQL Server instance:

| | traceid | property | value |
|---|---|---|---|
| 1 | 1 | 1 | 1 |
| 2 | 1 | 2 | NULL |
| 3 | 1 | 3 | 5 |
| 4 | 1 | 4 | NULL |
| 5 | 1 | 5 | 1 |

The property column uses `1` to set trace options, `2` to display filename, `3` for maxsize settings, `4` for `StopTime`, and `5` for trace status. The filename is `C:\temp\mytrace.trc`, the maxsize is 5MB, no setting for `StopTime`, and a trace status of `1` means that the trace is running.

To stop the trace, execute the following statement (assuming the trace ID is `1`):

```
EXEC sp_trace_setstatus 1, 0
```

If you do not intend to use the trace again, then execute the following statement (this also assumes that the trace ID is `1`):

```
EXEC sp_trace_setstatus 1, 2
```

Once the reference to the trace is removed, you can open the trace as it is running by opening the `*.trc` file defined for your trace:

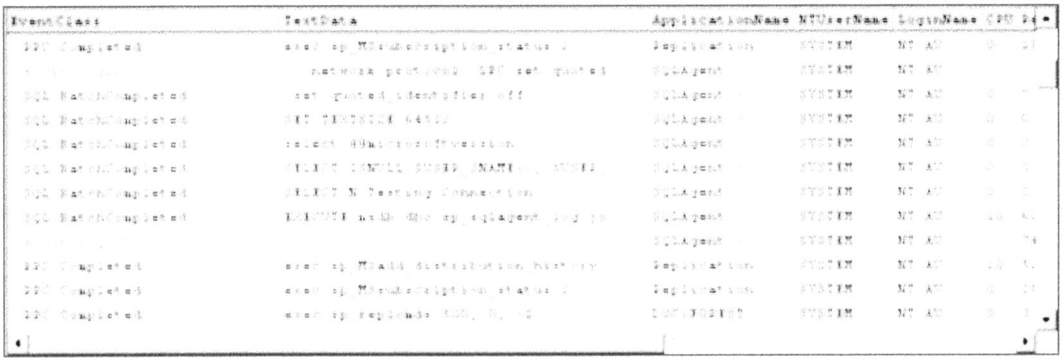

You can also return the results of the trace by executing the `fn_trace_gettable` function. This function takes the file name for the first parameter, and the number of rollover files for the second parameter (grouping all files into one result set in Query Analyzer):

```
SELECT * FROM ::fn_trace_gettable('c:\temp\mytrace.trc', default)
GO
```

This returns (partial result set):

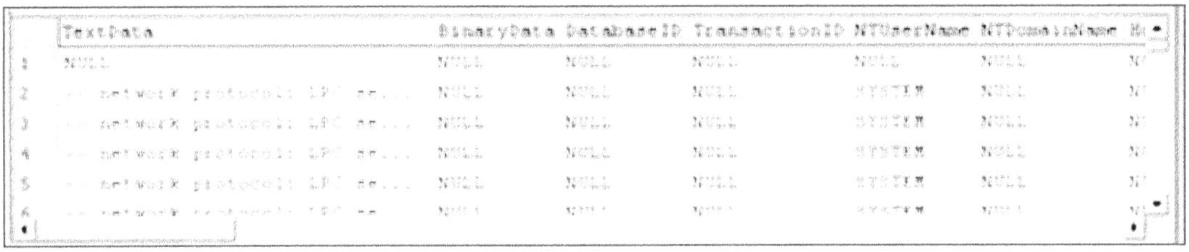

# Some Final Tips

- Do not try to open the trace file until the reference has been removed with `EXEC sp_trace_setstatus @TraceId, 2`. If you try to open the file prior to the trace being deleted, you will get a 0 bytes error.
- You cannot automatically overlay an existing `*.trc` file. Rename, move, or delete the existing file if you wish to use the same trace file name.
- If you wish to output the trace results to a table, unlike the SQL Profiler client, you cannot output results *directly* to a SQL Server table. You must first output the results to a file, and then use `fn_trace_gettable` to output those results to a table (using `SELECT..INTO`).

# 17.4 How to... Use SHOWPLAN_ALL, SHOWPLAN_TEXT

Use SHOWPLAN_ALL and SHOWPLAN_TEXT to return detailed information about an execution plan for a statement or batch. SHOWPLAN_ALL produces output without actually executing the statement or batches in Query Analyzer. Keep in mind that the statement needs be set OFF before any other command can be executed on the current user connection.

SHOWPLAN_ALL output is intended for use by applications that can handle the multi-column output (like Query Analyzer), whereas SHOWPLAN_TEXT is used for returning output that is more readable to applications like osql.exe (MS-DOS applications).

The syntax for SHOWPLAN_ALL is:

```
SET SHOWPLAN_ALL <ON_or_OFF>
```

## Example 17.4.1: Using SHOWPLAN_ALL

```
SET SHOWPLAN_ALL ON
GO

SELECT TOP 10 *
FROM Orders
```

This returns (separated for ease of viewing):

| | StmtText | StmtId | NodeId | Parent | PhysicalOp | LogicalOp | Argument |
|---|---|---|---|---|---|---|---|
| 1 | SELECT TOP 10 * FROM t_L... | 1 | 1 | 0 | NULL | NULL | 1 |
| 2 | \|--Top(10) | 1 | 2 | 1 | Top | Top | NULL |
| 3 | \|--Table Scan(OBJECT... | 1 | 4 | 2 | Table Scan | Table Scan | OBJECT:([BookReposit |

The StmtText column displays the text of the Transact-SQL statement used, and then the description of operations performed. Operators describe the methods used by the query processor to retrieve the rows or perform other Transact-SQL commands or operations. StmtID indicates the number of statements in the executed batch. NodeID indicates the node of the current query. Parent sets the node ID of the parent step. PhysicalOp notes the physical algorithm operation being performed:

| LogicalOp | Argument | DefinedValues | E |
|---|---|---|---|
| NULL | 1 | NULL | 1 |
| Top | NULL | NULL | [illegible] |
| Table Scan | OBJECT:([BookRepository].[d... | [t_LastOrder].[rowguid], [t... | 1 |

LogicalOp displays the relational algebraic operator of the node (showing the physical operation if there is no associated logical operation). Argument displays the supplementary information about the operation (which varies with the physical operator). DefinedValues shows values or expressions used by the query, and used by the query processor:

| EstimateRows | EstimateIO | EstimateCPU | AvgRowSize | TotalSubtreeCost | OutputList |
|---|---|---|---|---|---|
| 1.0 | NULL | NULL | NULL | 0.0374583 | NULL |
| 1.0 | 0.0 | 0.0000001 | 31 | 0.0374583 | [t_LastOrder].[rowguid], [t. |
| 1.0 | 3.7578501E-2 | 7.9600002E-5 | 31 | 3.7658099E-2 | [t_LastOrder].[rowguid], [t. |

EstimateRows displays rows output by the operator. EstimateIO displays I/O cost for the operator, and EstimateCPU displays estimated CPU cost for the operator. AvgRowSize displays the average row size in bytes for the rows being passed via the operator. TotalSubtreeCost displays the cumulative cost of the operation and all prior operations. Outputlist displays the list of columns being output by the current operation:

| Warnings | Type | Parallel | EstimateExecutions |
|---|---|---|---|
| NULL | SELECT | 0 | NULL |
| NULL | PLAN_ROW | 0 | 1.0 |
| NULL | PLAN_ROW | 0 | 1.0 |

Warnings displays any warning messages affecting the current operation. Type shows the type of node of the specific operation (type shows `SELECT`, `INSERT`, `UPDATE`, `DELETE`, and `EXECUTE` for Transact-SQL statements and `PLAN_ROW` for execution plan subnodes). Parallel displays 0 if the operator is not running in parallel, and 1 if it is running in parallel. EstimateExecutions displays the number of times the operator will be executed during query runtime.

The syntax for `SHOWPLAN_TEXT` is:

```
SET SHOWPLAN_TEXT <ON_or_OFF>
```

## Example 17.4.2: Using SHOWPLAN_TEXT

```
SET SHOWPLAN_TEXT ON
GO

SELECT TOP 10 *
FROM Orders
```

This returns two result sets:

| | StmtText | StmtId | NodeId | Parent | PhysicalOp | LogicalOp | Argument | DefinedValues | Estimate |
|---|---|---|---|---|---|---|---|---|---|
| 1 | SET SHOWPLAN_TEXT ON | 2 | 1 | 0 | NULL | NULL | 1 | NULL | NULL |

| | StmtText | StmtId | NodeId | Parent | PhysicalOp | LogicalOp | Argument |
|---|---|---|---|---|---|---|---|
| 1 | SELECT TOP 10 * FROM O... | 3 | 1 | 0 | NULL | NULL | 1 |
| 2 | \|--Top(10) | 3 | 2 | 1 | Top | Top | NULL |
| 3 | \|--Table Scan(OBJECT... | 3 | 4 | 2 | Table Scan | Table Scan | OBJECT:([BookRepos |

These results show the operation of the top 10 rows, and then the clustered index scan operation. As a general rule, table scan operations should be avoided, unless performed against small tables with few rows. Index scans are next in line, usually performing better than table scans, but not usually ideal. Lastly we have **index seeks**, which should operate better then their scan counterparts.

# 17.5 How to... Use Graphical Showplan

Now that SHOWPLAN_ALL and SHOWPLAN_TEXT have been reviewed, meet their visual counterpart, the **graphical showplan**. The graphical showplan, executed from Query Analyzer, displays and represents the execution plan (or estimated execution plan) with icons and arrows representing the various methods used for the data retrieval.

To display the estimated query execution plan:

- ❑ In Query Analyzer, select Query | Display Estimated Execution Plan. This will perform an operation to estimate the execution plan, and present the graphical execution plan:

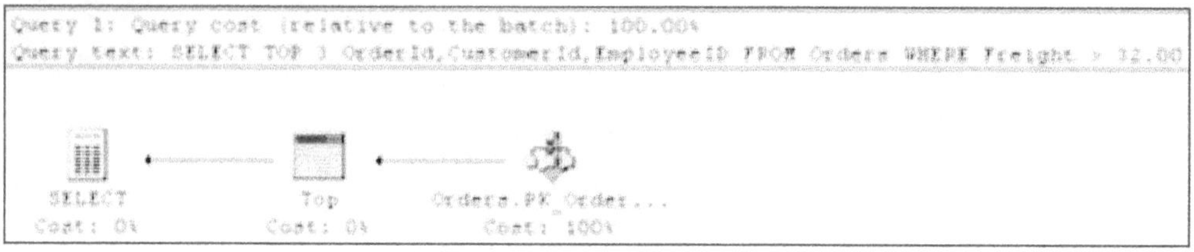


Read the execution output from right to left, and top to bottom (signifying the order of operations). For complex query plans, you may see several chunks divided by the query process. Arrows indicate the order of execution for each operator.

Each icon represents either a logical or physical operator. A physical operator represents a physical process used to work with the statement; a logical operator either displays the name of the physical process, or represents a relational operation used for statement processing (such as use of functions).

By waving your mouse cursor over the selected icons, you can reveal more information about each of the operations used to execute the query. This is called a **tool tip**:

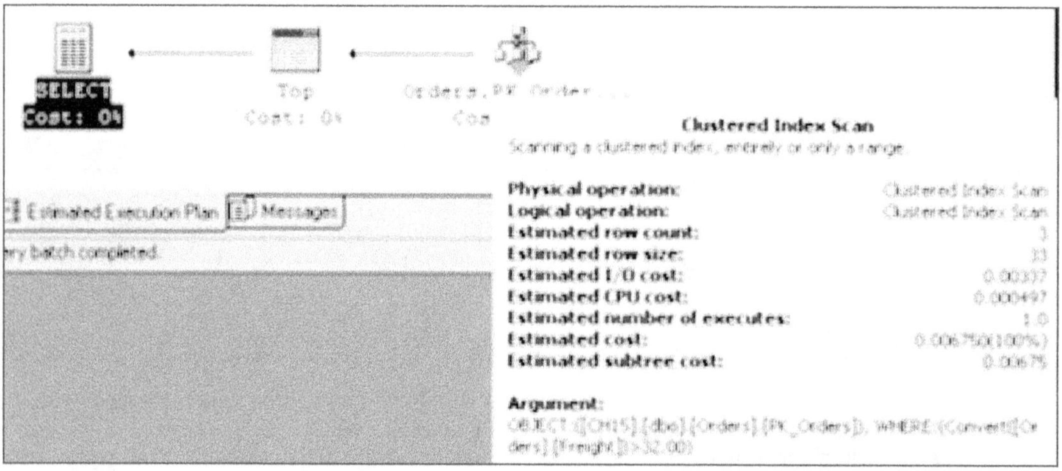

The following table summarizes the information:

| Tool Tip | Description |
|---|---|
| Physical operation | Indicates the type of physical operator used. When highlighted in red, the query optimizer has issued a warning regarding missing statistics or join predicates. |
| Logical operation | Either the same as the physical operator, or listed after the physical operator and separated by a forward slash. |
| Estimated row count | Number of rows output by the operator. |
| Estimated row size | Size of the row. |
| Estimated I/O cost | Total I/O activity for the operation. |
| Estimated CPU cost | Total CPU activity for the operation. |
| Estimated number of executes | Number of times the operation was executed during the query. |
| Estimated subtree cost | Cost calculated by the query optimizer for execution of the operation in relation to all prior operations in the subtree. |
| Argument | Any predicates or parameters used by the query. |

The following table displays logical and physical operators you may see in your query plans:

| Operator | Icon | Description |
|---|---|---|
| Assert |  | Performs verification of a condition, such as validating referential integrity or constraints. |
| Bookmark Lookup |  | Uses a row ID or clustering key to look up a corresponding row in a table or clustered index. Bookmark lookups cause extra I/O and are less efficient than a clustered index seek, if an index lookup can provide access to all columns referenced in the query (covered index or indexed view). |
| Clustered Index Delete |  | Deletes rows from a clustered index. |
| Clustered Index Insert |  | Inserts rows into a clustered index. |
| Clustered Index Scan |  | Scans the clustered index of a specific table or view. Index scans are usually better than table scans, but less effective in most cases than index seeks. These usually occur because there are too many rows to retrieve compared to the total table rows. This may also be caused by a `WHERE` clause expression on a column with little uniqueness. |

*Table continued on following page*

| Operator | Icon | Description |
|---|---|---|
| Clustered Index Seek |  | Uses seek to retrieve rows from a clustered index. This is an ideal operation for retrieving rows. |
| Clustered Index Update |  | Updates clustered index rows. |
| Collapse |  | Removes unnecessary intermediate changes from a row update, thus optimizing the process. |
| Compute Scalar |  | Evaluates an expression to produce a scalar value. Scalar values operate on a single value and return a single value. |
| Concatenation | 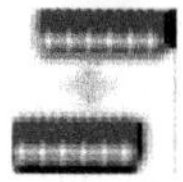 | Concatenation scans multiple inputs, returning each row scanned. |
| Constant Scan |  | Introduces a constant row into a query. |
| Deleted Scan |  | Scans the *deleted* trigger table. |
| Dynamic Cursor |  | Dynamic cursor operation; sees all changes made by other users. |
| Fetch Query Cursor |  | Retrieves rows when a cursor fetch is issued. |
| Filter |  | Adds a filter condition for application to a SQL query. |
| Hash Match |  | Builds a hash table. |
| Hash Match Root |  | Co-ordinates the operation of all hash match team operators (described next). |
| Hash Match Team |  | Part of a team of hash operators sharing a hash function and portioning method. |
| Index Delete | 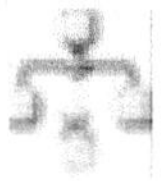 | Deletes rows from a nonclustered index. |

| Operator | Icon | Description |
|---|---|---|
| Index Insert |  | Inserts rows into a nonclustered index. |
| Index Scan |  | Performs a scan against a nonclustered index. |
| Index Seek | 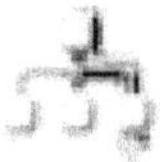 | Performs a seek operation against a nonclustered index (ideal operation compared to scan activity). |
| Index Spool |  | Scans input rows, placing a copy of each row into a spool file stored in `tempdb`, and then building an index based on the rows. This operation type causes extra I/O when creating the worktable, and should be avoided if possible. |
| Index Update |  | Updates rows within a nonclustered index. |
| Inserted Scan |  | Scans a trigger's `inserted` table. |
| Keyset cursor |  | Cursor operator that can view updates, but not insert operations. |
| Log Row Scan |  | Scans the transaction log. |
| Merge Join |  | Performs a merge join operation between two tables or other row sources. |
| Nested Loop |  | Performs a nested loop join operation between two tables or other row sources. |
| Parallelism |  | Indicates that parallelism is being used within the query. |
| Parameter Table Scan |  | Used for `INSERT` queries within a stored procedure, or when scanning a table that is acting as a parameter for a query. |
| Population Query Cursor |  | Populates a cursor's work table when the cursor is opened. |

*Table continued on following page*

| Operator | Icon | Description |
|---|---|---|
| Refresh Query Cursor |  | Fetches current row data for the cursor. |
| Remote Delete |  | Deletes rows from a remote object. |
| Remote Insert | 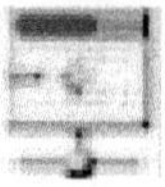 | Inserts rows into a remote object. |
| Remote Query |  | Queries a remote data source. |
| Remote Scan | 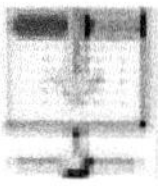 | A scan of a remote object. |
| Remote Update |  | An update of rows of a remote object. |
| Row Count Spool |  | Used to check for the existence of rows rather than the data contained within them. This operation type causes extra I/O when creating the worktable, and should be evaluated and avoided if possible. |
| Sequence | 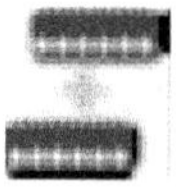 | A wide update execution plan, updating different objects. |
| Snapshot Query Cursor | 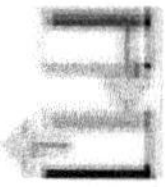 | Cursor operator that cannot see changes made by other users. |
| Sort |  | A row sort operation. |
| Stream Aggregate |  | Groups columns and calculates aggregate expressions. |
| Table Delete |  | Deletes row from a table. |
| Table Insert |  | Inserts rows into a table. |

| Operator | Icon | Description |
|---|---|---|
| Table Scan |  | Scans the tables for row retrieval (the least desirable table retrieval operation, unless the number of rows in the table is small). Scans involve every row of the table being read. |
| Table Spool |  | Scans input and places a copy of each row into a `tempdb` spool table. This operation type causes extra I/O when creating the worktable, and should be evaluated and avoided if possible. |
| Table Update |  | Updates rows in a table. |
| Top |  | Performs the top operation of a query. |

To show the actual execution plan, follow these steps:

- From the Query menu, select Show Execution Plan.
- After you execute the query, click the Execution Plan tab:

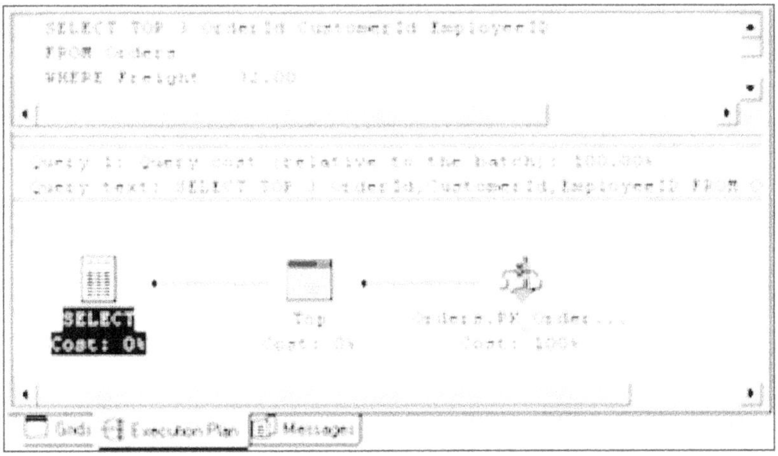


When running various queries, you may notice black arrows of varying sizes between scan or seek operations. These arrows represent row retrievals, and the size denotes the number of rows and the cost of handling them in the retrieval process. For example, the following displays a query that returns one row:

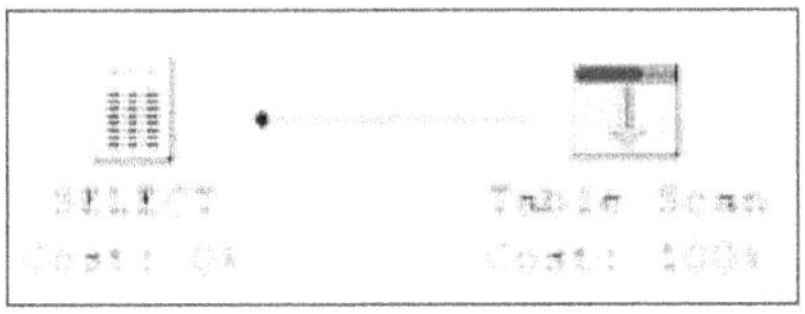

Next, we have a query that retrieves several thousand rows:

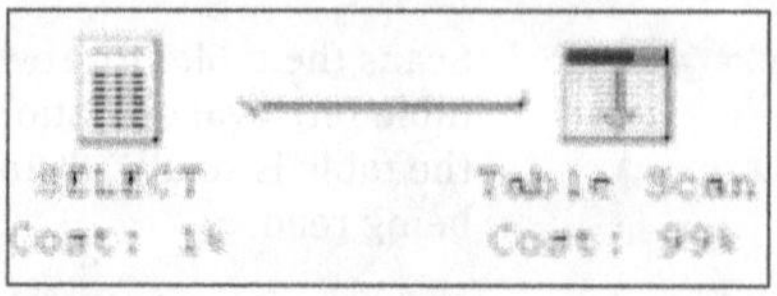


You can also right-click a scan or seek operator to access more index or statistics functionality. Select Create Missing Statistics... to add missing statistics when applicable. Select Manage Indices to add, remove, or modify indexes for the table or view. Select Manage Statistics to manage statistics for the table affected.

# 17.6 How to... Use SET STATISTICS IO

When enabled, `STATISTICS IO` returns disk activity (I/O) generated by the executed statement or statements. The syntax for `STATISTICS IO` is:

```
SET STATISTICS IO <ON_or_OFF>
```

## Example 17.6.1: Using STATISTICS IO

```
SET STATISTICS IO ON

SELECT TOP 3 OrderId, CustomerId, EmployeeID
FROM Orders
WHERE Freight > 32.00
```

This returns the resultset first:

| | OrderId | CustomerId | EmployeeID |
|---|---|---|---|
| 1 | 10248 | VINET | 5 |
| 2 | 10250 | HANAR | 4 |
| 3 | 10251 | VICTE | 3 |

Then, on the Messages results tab (if using Grids output):

(3 row(s) affected)

Table 'Orders'. Scan count 1, logical reads 2, physical reads 0, read-ahead reads 0.

The results show the name of the table(s) involved in the query, the number of scans, logical reads (from memory), physical reads (from disk), and data pages placed in the data cache by the query.

Look to improve queries with high physical or logical read values (pay attention to both values, even if physical is `0` and logical is not, or vice versa).

# 17.7 How to... Use SET STATISTICS TIME

When enabled, the `STATISTICS TIME` command returns the number of milliseconds taken to parse, compile, and execute each statement executed in the batch. Use this command to understand what phase of the query takes the most time (parse and compile versus execution time), and tune the query accordingly. The syntax is:

```
SET STATISTICS TIME <ON_or_OFF>
```

### Example 17.7.1: Using STATISTICS TIME

```
SET STATISTICS TIME ON

SELECT TOP 3 OrderId, CustomerId, EmployeeID
FROM Orders
WHERE Freight > 32.00
```

This returns the query result set, and the total time in milliseconds (in the form of text messages):

| | OrderId | CustomerId | EmployeeID |
|---|---|---|---|
| 1 | 10248 | VINET | 5 |
| 2 | 10250 | HANAR | 4 |
| 3 | 10251 | VICTE | 3 |

SQL Server parse and compile time:
CPU time = 0 ms, elapsed time = 0 ms.

SQL Server Execution Times:
CPU time = 0 ms, elapsed time = 0 ms.

(3 row(s) affected)

SQL Server Execution Times:
CPU time = 0 ms, elapsed time = 0 ms.

## 17.8 How to... Use SET STATISTICS PROFILE

After executing a query with `STATISTICS PROFILE` enabled, the original query result set will be returned, along with a second result set detailing the execution steps of the query.

The syntax for `STATISTICS PROFILE` is:

```
SET STATISTICS PROFILE <ON_or_OFF>
```

### Example 17.8.1: Using SET STATISTICS PROFILE

This example enables `STATISTICS PROFILE`, and then executes a query against the `Orders` table:

```
SET STATISTICS PROFILE ON

SELECT TOP 3 OrderId, CustomerId, EmployeeID
FROM Orders
WHERE Freight > 32.00
```

This returns the result set first:

| | OrderId | CustomerId | EmployeeID |
|---|---|---|---|
| 1 | 10248 | VINET | 5 |
| 2 | 10250 | HANAR | 4 |
| 3 | 10251 | VICTE | 3 |

It then returns the details of the execution plan (separated for ease of viewing). The results displayed include the same columns as the `SHOWPLAN_ALL` command, and two new columns: Rows and Executes. Rows indicates the number of rows affected by the operators, and Executes the number of times the operator was executed.

You can then review the output just as you would with `SHOWPLAN` or the graphical showplan, reviewing the query execution plan (data access, index, and operations used), and verifying whether there are opportunities for improvement. For example, if you identify a table scan that involves several rows, you could first investigate whether or not the query is written properly and, if not, correct it. You could then verify the indexes on the table, and determine whether the appropriate index or indexes exist.

| | Rows | Executes |
|---|---|---|
| 1 | 3 | 1 |
| 2 | 3 | 1 |
| 3 | 3 | 1 |

<table>
<tr><th>StmtText</th></tr>
<tr><td>SELECT TOP 3 OrderId, CustomerId, EmployeeID FROM Orders</td></tr>
<tr><td>|--Top(3)</td></tr>
<tr><td>|--Clustered Index Scan(OBJECT:([BookRepository].[dbo].[Orders].[PK_Orders]))</td></tr>
</table>

| StmtId | NodeId | Parent | PhysicalOp | LogicalOp |
|---|---|---|---|---|
| 1 | 1 | 0 | NULL | NULL |
| 1 | 2 | 1 | Top | Top |
| 1 | 4 | 2 | Clustered Index Scan | Clustered Index Scan |

| Argument |
|---|
| NULL |
| NULL |
| OBJECT:([BookRepository].[d... |

| DefinedValues |
|---|
| NULL |
| NULL |
| [Orders].[EmployeeID], [Ord... |

| EstimateRows | EstimateIO | EstimateCPU | AvgRowSize |
|---|---|---|---|
| 3.0 | NULL | NULL | NULL |
| 3.0 | 0.0 | 3.0000001E-7 | 25 |
| 3.0 | 0.01878925 | 4.0899999E-5 | 25 |

| TotalSubtreeCost | OutputList | Warnings |
|---|---|---|
| 3.7660901E-2 | NULL | NULL |
| 3.7660901E-2 | [Orders].[EmployeeID], [Ord... | NULL |
| 3.7660301E-2 | [Orders].[EmployeeID], [Ord... | NULL |

| Type | Parallel | EstimateExecution |
|---|---|---|
| SELECT | 0 | NULL |
| PLAN_ROW | 0 | 1.0 |
| PLAN_ROW | 0 | 1.0 |

# 17.9 How to… Use Query Analyzer's Server Trace and Client Statistics

Use Query Analyzer's **Server Trace** to track event, duration, CPU cycles, reads, and writes involved for an executed batch or query. To enable Server Trace in Query Analyzer, select Query menu | Show Server Trace.

In this example, a batch of various operations will be performed:

```
CREATE TABLE #Temp (iID int NOT NULL)

INSERT #Temp
VALUES (1)

UPDATE #Temp
SET iID = 2

SELECT *
FROM #Temp

DELETE #Temp

DROP TABLE #Temp
```

After executing this query, click the Trace results tab to view the server-side statistics. In this example, you will see various `SQL:StmtCompleted` events that were triggered while executing the batch. The output includes Duration, CPU, Reads, and Writes just like the SQL Profiler trace:

| Text | Event Class | Duration | CPU | Reads | Writes |
|---|---|---|---|---|---|
| CREATE TABLE #Temp (i... | SQL:StmtCompleted | 0 | 0 | 11 | 0 |
| INSERT #Temp VALUES... | SQL:StmtCompleted | 0 | 0 | 10 | 0 |
| UPDATE #Temp SET iID... | SQL:StmtCompleted | 0 | 0 | [illegible] | 0 |
| SELECT * FROM #Temp | SQL:StmtCompleted | 10 | 10 | 6 | 0 |
| DELETE #Temp | SQL:StmtCompleted | 0 | 0 | 8 | 0 |
| DROP TABLE #Temp | SQL:StmtCompleted | 0 | 0 | 42 | 0 |

Use the Client Statistics function of Query Analyzer to show various settings and values during query or batch runtime. Reviewing Query Analyzer Client Statistics can be very helpful for performance tuning queries, stored procedures, and scripts. Client Statistics returns three result sets, the first being **application profile statistics**, the second **network statistics**, and the third **result set time statistics**.

To use Client Statistics in Query Analyzer, go to Query | Show Client Statistics. In this example, a simple `SELECT` query will be executed:

```
SELECT *
FROM Orders
```

After executing, select the Client Statistics results tab:

| Counter | Value | Average |
|---|---|---|
| **Application Profile Statistics** | | |
| Timer resolution (millise... | 0 | 0 |
| Number of INSERT, UPDATE,... | 0 | 0 |
| Rows effected by INSERT, ... | 0 | 0 |
| Number of SELECT statements | 1 | 1 |
| Rows effected by SELECT s... | 3 | 3 |
| Number of user transactions | 1 | 1 |

Various statistics regarding the number of statements executed in the batch, fetch times, packages sent and received, and cumulative processing time will be returned.

# Checklist: Index Best Practices

Indexing your database involves planning your index strategy ahead of time, testing your implementation, and then re-evaluating your index strategy continually over time. There are certain techniques that can increase the likelihood of your indexes being effective. Effective indexes are used by the query processor, improve query performance, and reduce I/O. This section will review the dos and don'ts of index practices.

## Dos of Indexing Your Database Tables

- ❑ When possible, test your indexing in a test environment. Never implement new index changes in a production environment without testing first. There are many reasons for this; the index change could hurt performance of the query you wish to improve, or impact the performance of unrelated queries. Smaller companies or operations may not have the hardware to do this. If you must perform tests on a production SQL Server instance, consider the following options:
    - ❑ If storage permits, create a test database on the production server. Test your queries and indexes against this test database. If storage does not permit, try moving just those tables you need for testing to a test database on the production server.
    - ❑ Test your index and queries during off-peak production hours.
- ❑ Make one change at a time. Implement a single change, test it, keep or undo it, then make another change and start again.
- ❑ Test all related queries that the index may affect. Performance may improve for one query, but deteriorate for others.
- ❑ Over time, continually monitor your query performance to ensure that the indexes are still effective. The number of rows in a table, the distribution of data, and query behavior can change over time. As these variables change, so might the usefulness of your indexes.
- ❑ If fragmentation is a problem (`DBCC SHOWCONTIG`, reviewed next, can identify this) and, if your maintenance window is large enough, consider rebuilding your indexes on a scheduled basis. Index fragmentation can occur quickly, depending on the frequency and number of updates made against your tables. Page splits can occur depending on your table row size and the number of updates. Page space can also go unused, meaning more pages must be retrieved by a query to fulfill a request (more I/O). Rebuilding indexes (especially with higher fill factors) can reduce I/O and improve query response time. High fill factors can also cause `INSERT` activity to suffer, if page splits occur frequently.
- ❑ Create indexes on tables based on the query activity for your application. Only create indexes that are necessary. Indexes take up space, and add overhead to `INSERT`, `UPDATE`, and `DELETE` operations.

- Read-only or reporting databases with minimal data change activity can sometimes utilize more indexes without the same consequences as transaction-processing databases. Remember always to weigh up the effect of your index on query performance against the effect on table updates (`INSERT`, `UPDATE`, `DELETE` operations), as indexes can make updates slower. If your read-only database is loaded periodically, consider dropping all indexes on the table, and re-adding them after the data load (to decrease the load time).
- Unless you have a compelling reason not to do so, always add a clustered index. As reviewed in Chapter 14, a table without a clustered index is called a **heap**, meaning that the data pages are stored in no particular order. Clustered indexes are ordered according to the clustered key. For tables with many rows, queries against the table will result in a table scan operation, possibly causing performance problems. Data held in a heap is not re-organized when indexes are rebuilt; for high-update tables, fragmentation can become significant. If you have a clustered index defined for the table, and periodically execute index rebuilds, you can reduce the table fragmentations. Clustered indexes are useful for *range* queries, queries that use the operators `BETWEEN`, >, >=, <, <=. Clustered indexes are also ideal for large result sets (particularly ordered result sets).Your clustered index should ideally have the following attributes:
    - The index key or key width should take up as few bytes as possible. Remember that each nonclustered index also contains the clustered index key.
    - Your nonclustered index should be placed on columns used in expressions that retrieve small, or one-row result sets. The following column types are good for indexing:
        - Columns used to `JOIN` two tables.
        - Columns used in the `WHERE` clause.
        - Columns that are used for expressions that **do not** use the following operators, which make it more difficult for the query optimizer to perform an index seek (although the query optimizer can often find a way):
            - `<>`
            - `!=`
            - `!<`
            - `!>`
            - `IN`
            - `NOT`
            - `NOT IN`
            - `NOT LIKE`

          When these operators are used, the SQL Server query optimizer is sometimes forced to scan all the pages of the index to find the required values. Avoiding such operators allows the query optimizer to traverse the index branches more effectively.
- Index columns that determine a preferred sort order, specified in `ORDER BY` or `GROUP BY`.
- Index key column order is important. When creating an index, the leftmost column defined for a composite index key is the one that is used for an expression in a `WHERE` clause. The remaining columns in the index key lend themselves to faster retrieval of other columns needed by the query.
- Use a covering index to reduce I/O in your query. A covering index includes all columns referenced within the query (`SELECT`, `WHERE`, `ORDER BY`, `GROUP BY`, and so on) within the index. Use covered queries for frequently executed queries, but only if the size and overhead is not significant.
- Use a 100% fill factor for indexes on read-only tables; this decreases I/O and improves query performance.

### Example: Comparison of queries using the NOT LIKE operator and the < and > operators

```
SELECT vchLastName
FROM leaders
WHERE vchLastName NOT LIKE ('Bush')
```

Looking at the graphical showplan, you can see that an index scan was used, even though the `vchLastName` column (for our example) has a nonclustered index on it:

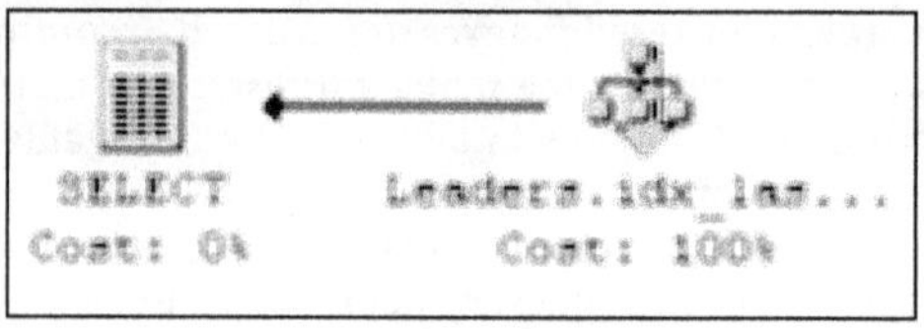


Now let's try the query using the `<` and `>` operators instead:

```
SELECT vchLastName
FROM leaders
WHERE vchLastName < 'Bush' OR vchLastName > 'Bush'
```

This time, our nonclustered index on `vchLastName` is used:

When `NOT` is used, the SQL Server query optimiser usually has to scan all the index pages to locate the required values. Using the < and > operators, as in the second instance above, enables the query optimizer to traverse the index branches more effectively.

### Example: The importance of index key column order

Let's say we have the following index defined on the `Leaders` table:

Notice that `vchLastName` is the leftmost column in the index, and that `vchFirstName` is the second column of the composite index. If we ran the following query, we would see an index seek operation:

```
CREATE INDEX idxLeaders_LName_FName ON
 Leaders (vchLastName, vchFirstName)
SELECT vchLastName
FROM Leaders
WHERE vchLastName = 'Howard'
```

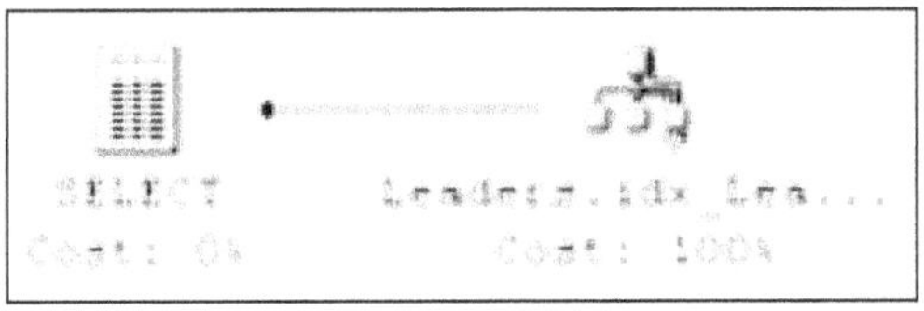

Now, if we run this query qualifying only the `vchFirstName` column, the same index cannot be used, as `vchFirstName` is not the leftmost column (and a scan is performed instead of a seek against the index of the previous query):

```
SELECT *
FROM Leaders
WHERE vchFirstName = 'Goran'
```

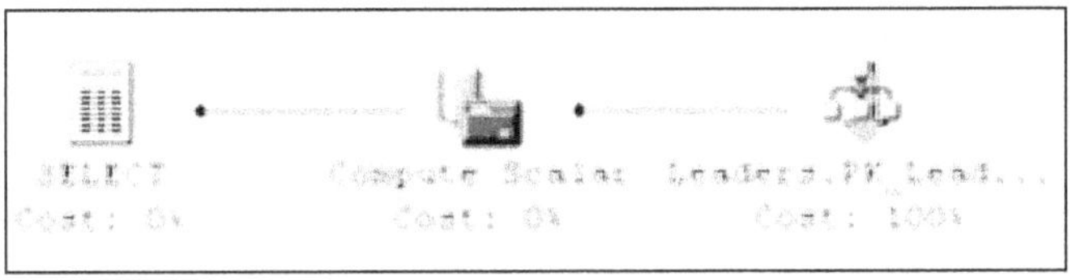

Keep in mind that if you qualified both `vchLastName` and `vchFirstName` in your query, the proper index can be used.

# The Don'ts of Indexing

- SQL Server lets you create duplicate indexes (indexes on the same columns). This creates unnecessary overhead and space usage, and you should remove duplicate indexes when you find them. You should also remove indexes that are never used. Keep in mind that it is not easy to determine which indexes are not being used, unless your application code base is such that you can review the execution plan of all queries that could be run against the database.
- Do not add indexes for columns with low uniqueness. Pay attention to the cardinality of the column being indexed; cardinality of a column refers to how many distinct values exist within the column. If a table column has 100% cardinality, it means that all values are 100% unique. Columns with higher cardinality (uniqueness) are more likely to be used when defined as index keys, than columns that have a lower cardinality.
- Some operators used within expressions make indexes less likely to be used; this is because these types of operators expand a range of potential rows, rather than narrow down the field of retrieval. Such operators include:
    - `<>`
    - `!=`
    - `!<`
    - `!>`
    - `NOT`
    - `NOT IN`
    - `NOT LIKE`
    - `OR`
- For clustered indexes, avoid columns that are updated too frequently.

# 17.10 How to... Display fragmentation using DBCC SHOWCONTIG

The DBCC SHOWCONTIG command reveals the level of fragmentation for a specific table and its indexes. This DBCC command is key to determining whether your table or index has internal or external fragmentation.

**Internal fragmentation** concerns how full an 8K page is. When a page is under-utilized, more I/O operations may be necessary to fulfil a query request than if the page were full, or almost full.

**External fragmentation** concerns how contiguous the extents are. There are eight 8K pages per extent, making each extent 64K. Several extents can make up the data of a table or index. If the extents are not physically close to each other, and are not in order, query access can suffer.

They syntax for DBCC SHOWCONTIG is:

```
DBCC SHOWCONTIG
  (<table_name> or <table_id> or <view_name> or <view_id>,
   <optional_index_name> or <optional_index_id>)
WITH <FAST>,
      <TABLERESULTS>,
      <ALL_INDICES>,
      <ALL_LEVELS>
```

| Parameter | Description |
|---|---|
| <table_name> or <table_id> or <view_name> or <view_id> | The name of the view or table, or the ID of the view or table (retrieved via OBJECT_ID), for which to display fragmentation. |
| <optional_index_name> or <optional_index_id> | The optional name or ID of the index to check fragmentation. If the index is not specified, the DBCC command analyzes the base index for the table or view. |
| <FAST> | When specified, a fast scan of the index is performed, skipping the leaf or data level index pages. FAST cannot be used with ALL_LEVELS. |
| <TABLERESULTS> | When specified, the DBCC results are displayed as a rowset. |
| <ALL_INDICES> | Returns results for all indexes on the specified table or view. |
| <ALL_LEVELS> | When set, output for each index level will be processed. Otherwise, only the index leaf level or table level is processed. |

### Example 17.10.1: Using DBCC SHOWCONTIG

This example executes DBCC SHOWCONTIG for the SupplierBooks table:

```
DBCC SHOWCONTIG ('SupplierBooks')
```

This returns:

```
DBCC SHOWCONTIG scanning 'SupplierBooks' table...
Table: 'SupplierBooks' (619149251); index ID: 1, database ID: 5
TABLE level scan performed.
- Pages Scanned................................: 37
- Extents Scanned..............................: 6
- Extent Switches..............................: 33
- Avg. Pages per Extent........................: 6.2
- Scan Density [Best Count:Actual Count].......: 14.71% [5:34]
- Logical Scan Fragmentation ..................: 48.65%
- Extent Scan Fragmentation ...................: 33.33%
- Avg. Bytes Free per Page.....................: 3339.0
- Avg. Page Density (full).....................: 58.75%
DBCC execution completed. If DBCC printed error messages, contact your system administrator.
```

The following table analyzes the output:

| Output | Description |
|---|---|
| - Pages Scanned : 37 | Indicates the number of 8K pages scanned (data or index) for the `DBCC SHOWCONTIG` analysis. |
| - Extents Scanned : 6 | Displays the number of 64K blocks scanned for the table or index. |
| - Extent Switches : 33 | Indicates the number of times the `DBCC` execution moved from one extent to another during the analysis. Extent switches are an indicator of external fragmentation when the number is higher. |
| - Avg. Pages per Extent : 6.2 | Indicates the number of 8K pages per extent in the page chain. |
| - Scan Density [Best Count:Actual Count] : 14.71% [5:34] | Deals with the ideal number of extent changes compared to the actual extent changes; the closer to 100%, the better. |
| - Logical Scan Fragmentation : 48.65% | Deals with out-of-order 8K pages for the leaf level of an index (not a heap or text page). |
| - Extent Scan Fragmentation : 33.33% | Covers the percentage of out of order extents in the leaf level of the index (not relevant to heaps). |
| - Avg. Bytes Free per Page : 3339.0 | Indicates internal fragmentation, displaying the average of free space available for an 8K page. The higher the number, the less utilized the pages are; low numbers indicate less or no internal fragmentation. |
| - Avg. Page Density (full) : 58.75% | Indicates how full the pages are, with the row size taken into account. This number displays the internal fragmentation average, with lower numbers indicating more fragmentation. |

If you encounter internal or external fragmentation, rebuilding indexes on a specified frequency will help manage this issue. Internal fragmentation is controlled by how you design your index fill factor, how large your row size is, and the frequency of update, insert, and delete activities (which can cause page splits).

Rebuilding indexes can help re-order and alleviate internal fragmentation; the effect may not last long, however, depending on the amount and type of activity against the table. If your maintenance schedule window is large enough, do schedule index rebuilds for your databases. Heaps (tables without indexes) do not provide as many options when you attempt to alleviate fragmentation, reinforcing the need to have a clustered index for each table in your database.

Here are the results of the same DBCC operation on the same table, but after the clustered index has been rebuilt:

```
-- First rebuilding the clustered index called SupplierBooks1

DBCC DBREINDEX ('SupplierBooks', 'SupplierBooks1')

-- Next, re-running DBCC SHOWCONTIG

DBCC SHOWCONTIG ('SupplierBooks')
```

```
DBCC SHOWCONTIG scanning 'SupplierBooks' table...
Table: 'SupplierBooks' (619149251); index ID: 1, database ID: 5
TABLE level scan performed.
- Pages Scanned................................: 22
- Extents Scanned..............................: 3
- Extent Switches..............................: 2
- Avg. Pages per Extent........................: 7.3
- Scan Density [Best Count:Actual Count].......: 100.00% [3:3]
- Logical Scan Fragmentation ..................: 0.00%
- Extent Scan Fragmentation ...................: 33.33%
- Avg. Bytes Free per Page.....................: 95.6
- Avg. Page Density (full).....................: 98.82%

DBCC execution completed. If DBCC printed error messages, contact your system administrator.
```

As you can see, the extent switches have been reduced to 2 (down from 33), and the average page density is 98%. Scan Density shows 100%, which is the best possible contiguity. The rebuild of the clustered index has improved both internal and external fragmentation.

# 17.11 How to... Use the Index Tuning Wizard

The Index Tuning Wizard is an excellent tool provided by Microsoft, which is used to provide indexing suggestions based on a query or batch of queries. Use the Index Tuning Wizard to give you suggestions for improvements, but do not use this tool as your 'one-stop shop' for index planning and creation. The Index Tuning Wizard can review the actual queries being run in your database, so its recommendations are based on how your database is really being used.

You should create your indexes through planning, testing, and the best practices reviewed in the previous section. Use Index Tuning Wizard as a quick reference.

To demonstrate the Index Tuning Wizard, we begin by showing the estimated execution plan for the following query:

```
SELECT iBookId,
       iSupplier,
       iSupplyId
FROM SupplierBooks
WHERE iSupplier = 7
```

The estimated execution plan is as follows:

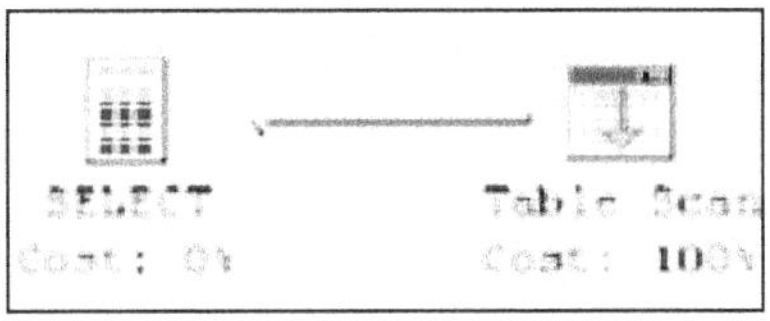


The query performs a table scan, and does not use any indexes. To analyze this query using the Index Tuning Wizard, from Query Analyzer, follow these steps:

- With the query you wish to analyze in the Query window, select Query | Index Tuning Wizard.
- Select Next in the welcome window.
- Select the database you wish to analyze. You can also select Keep all existing indices to tune the workload with your given environment in mind. Select the Tuning mode for your given query, with Thorough being the most time-consuming. Select Next when you have finished.
- Select the **workload** to be analyzed; this can be a file containing SQL statements, a SQL Server trace table or, in this example, a SQL Query Analyzer selection. Click the Advanced Options button to configure limits on the index suggestions.
- Next, select the table or tables used in the query you are analyzing. Select Next. You will then see a progress dialog box, as the query is analyzed.
- Once the analysis is complete, the Wizard will suggest adding zero or more indexes to your tables used in the queries. An estimated improvement in performance will also be noted; in this case, an index on `SupplierBooks`' `iBookID` column is suggested:

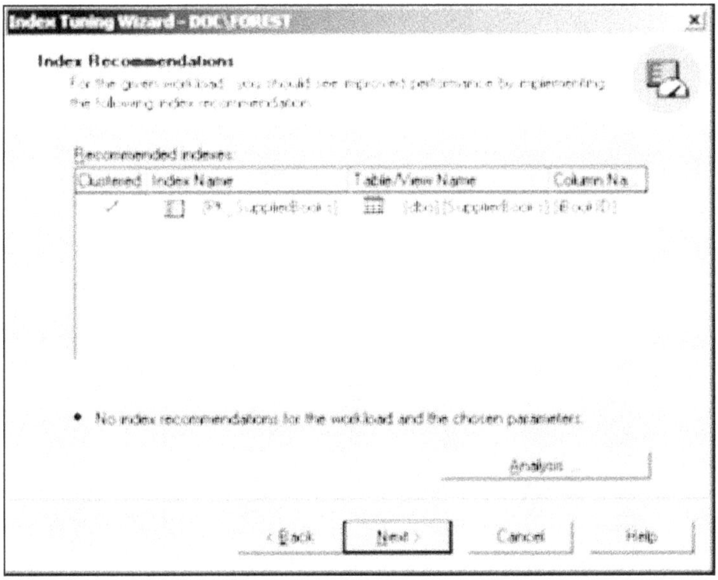


- Selecting the Analysis button displays reports about the indexes, tables, views, and query. You can select the various report choices from the drop-down box, as well as saving the results as a `.txt` file. Select Close to return to the Index Recommendations dialog box:

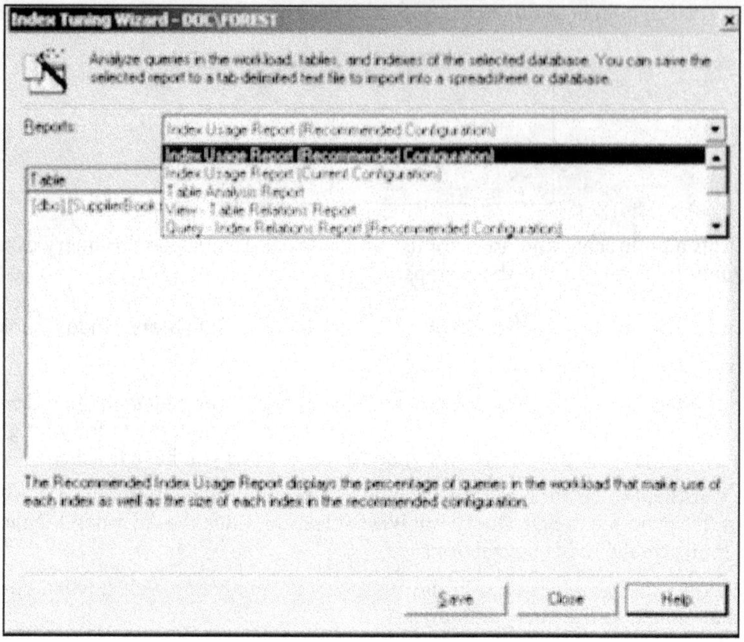

- In the Schedule Index Update Job dialog box, you can choose to apply your changes immediately, schedule another time (for example, if your new indexes will be very large), or save the index creation to a script file. In this example, we will apply the recommendation. In a test or production environment, however, do not blindly accept every recommendation made by the Index Tuning Wizard; instead, save the recommendations using the Save script file checkbox and review each recommendation. Based on your knowledge of the database and how it is used, either accept or reject the recommendations. Select Next when finished.
- Select Finish to complete the change. This should return a dialog box with the message The Index Tuning Wizard has successfully completed.

Now, if we re-run the original query, a different query execution plan is generated, using an index seek instead of a table scan:

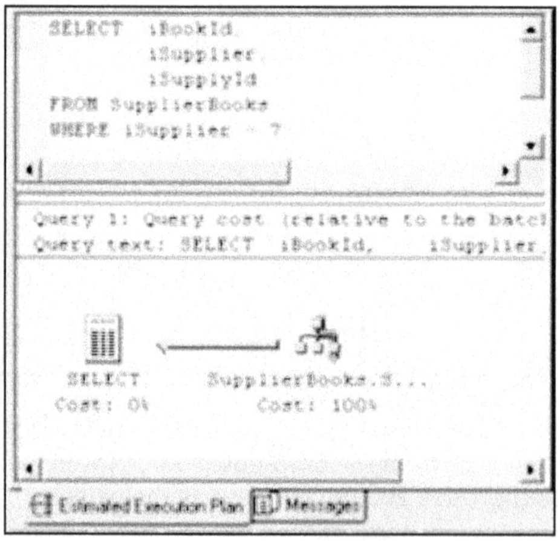

# 17.12 How to... Use CREATE STATISTICS

Statistics are critical for proper query processing and performance. Table and index statistics, which can be created manually with CREATE STATISTICS or generated automatically via SQL Server, determine and track a column's selectivity and distribution of values.

Cardinality refers to a key value's uniqueness, with a higher column cardinality translating to higher uniqueness. Distribution statistics determine the efficiency of an index when used to retrieve data based on the column in question.

In addition, statistics track the number of rows in a user table, data pages used by the table, and also DML activity affecting keys of the table since statistics were last updated. Statistics are automatically regenerated (Chapter 3 explored how to enable the database property AUTO_UPDATE_STATISTICS), and are based on table activity or the settings of the statistics when they were originally created.

The syntax for CREATE STATISTICS is:

```
CREATE STATISTICS <name_of_statistics>
ON <table_or_view> (<column_1>, <column_N>)
WITH <FULLSCAN> or <SAMPLE number PERCENT or ROWS>,
<NORECOMPUTE>
```

| Parameter | Description |
|---|---|
| <name_of_statistics> | Name given to the statistics generated. |
| <table_or_view> | The name of the table or view for which to add statistics. The view must be an indexed view, with a clustered index already defined. |
| (<column_1>, <column_N>) | Defines one or more columns from the table or view for which statistics are to be created. |
| WITH <FULLSCAN> or <SAMPLE number PERCENT or ROWS> | When FULLSCAN is chosen, all rows in the table are read in order to gather statistics. If SAMPLE is set, either a number of rows or a percentage of rows will be generated (if PERCENT, use a number between 0 and 100). |
| <NORECOMPUTE> | When NORECOMPUTE is specified, statistics will not be automatically recomputed based on table activity and changes. There is never usually a good reason to do this, as the overhead for updating statistics is generally minimal. |

### Example 17.12.1: Using CREATE STATISTICS

This example creates statistics for two columns in the Books table:

```
CREATE STATISTICS Books_stats
  ON Books (vchBookName, iAuthorId)
  WITH FULLSCAN
GO
```

### Example 17.12.2: Using sampling

This next example creates statistics on two columns from the `Books` table, except it bases the statistics on a sample of 100 rows from the table:

```
CREATE STATISTICS Books_stats
  ON Books (vchBookName, iAuthorId)
  WITH SAMPLE 100 ROWS
GO
```

### Example 17.12.3: Dropping statistics

To remove statistics, use `DROP STATISTICS`. For example:

```
DROP STATISTICS Books.Books_stats
```

Finally, keep in mind that statistics count towards your total index limit for a table.

# 17.13 How to... Display Columns with Statistics with sp_helpstats

The `sp_helpstats` system stored procedure lists all statistics for a specific table. The syntax is:

```
sp_helpstats <object_name>,
             <ALL_or_STATS>
```

| Parameter | Description |
|---|---|
| <table_name> | Sets the table name for which to list statistics. |
| <ALL_or_STATS> | The `ALL` parameter lists statistics for the table and indexes. `STATS` lists statistics not associated with indexes (`STATS` is the default). |

### Example 17.13.1: Using sp_helpstats

This example lists both table and index statistics for the `Books` table:

```
EXEC sp_helpstats 'Books', 'ALL'
```

This returns:

| | statistics_name | statistics_keys |
|---|---|---|
| 1 | _WA_Sys_iAuthorId_76CBA758 | iAuthorId |
| 2 | Books_stats | vchBookName, iAuthorId |
| 3 | idx_BookId | BookID |
| 4 | idx_Name_Author | vchBookName, iAuthorId |

The `_WA` statistics for the `iAuthorId` represents system-generated statistics; system-generated statistics are often created when needed by SQL Server during query processing. The remaining indexes listed in the output are related to the table, and its associated indexes.

# 17.14 How to... Show Current Distribution Statistics for a Table DBCC SHOW_STATISTICS

Once you know the name of the statistics you wish to investigate, you can view the distribution and statistics details via the `DBCC SHOW_STATISTICS` command. The syntax is:

```
DBCC SHOW_STATISTICS (<'table_name'>, <'statistics_name'>)
```

## Example 17.14.1: Using DBCC SHOW_STATISTICS

This example displays statistics information for the `PK_Leaders` primary key index statistics from the `Leaders` table:

```
DBCC SHOW_STATISTICS ( 'Leaders' ,'PK_Leaders')
```

This returns a few different result sets. The first of these is:

| | Updated | Rows | Rows Sampled | Steps | Density | Average key length |
|---|---|---|---|---|---|---|
| 1 | Nov 25 2002 3:11PM | 4 | 4 | 4 | 0.25 | 9.75 |

This shows when the statistics were last updated, how many rows make up the statistics, the number sampled, the distribution steps, the density (selectivity), and the average key length.

The second result set returns:

| | All density | Average Length | Columns |
|---|---|---|---|
| 1 | 0.25 | 9.75 | vchCountry |

This shows the selectivity of a set of columns (when there is more than one column), the average length of the columns (when there is more than one column), and the column names.

The last result set returns:

| | RANGE_HI_KEY | RANGE_ROWS | EQ_ROWS | DISTINCT_RANGE_ROWS | AVG_RANGE_ROWS |
|---|---|---|---|---|---|
| 1 | Russia | 0.0 | 1.0 | 0 | 0.0 |
| 2 | Sweden | 0.0 | 1.0 | 0 | 0.0 |
| 3 | United Kingdom | 0.0 | 1.0 | 0 | 0.0 |
| 4 | United States | 0.0 | 1.0 | 0 | 0.0 |

This shows the range of values for the columns, the range of rows, the distinctiveness, and the average range of rows. The `EQ_ROWS` column shows the number of columns equal to the `RANGE_HI_KEY` values.

From the values returned for the statistics, you can determine whether the uniqueness of the values would be useful for query processing.

# 17.15 How to... Update Statistics against all User-Defined Tables using sp_updatestats

The sp_updatestats procedure runs UPDATE STATISTICS against all user-defined tables in the current database context. Use this when you wish to force all statistics to update after a major data refresh, or after upgrading from a different version of SQL Server to SQL Server 2000.

The syntax for sp_updatestats is:

```
sp_updatestats <'resample'>
```

The sole parameter, 'resample', is optional. This parameter causes statistics to be recreated using the old statistics sampling ratio.

## Example 17.15.1: Using sp_updatestats

This example updates statistics for the entire database:

```
EXEC sp_updatestats
```

# 18

# XML

Microsoft introduced built-in XML support with SQL Server 2000. This chapter will provide a brief overview of XML itself, as well as SQL Server 2000 XML support and related technologies. For a detailed overview of the topics touched on here, see *SQL Server 2000 XML Distilled* by Kevin Williams et al *(ISBN 1-904347-08-8)*,

## XML

XML stands for Extensible Markup Language. XML is used primarily to make documents self-describing. Self-describing data is easier to interpret when it is moved from one business unit to another, or from one company to another.

XML looks similar to HTML, in that it makes use of tags. Unlike HTML however, XML tags do not have predefined meanings. In XML, you define your own tags. Tags in HTML describe the format of the data, whereas XML tags describe the data itself. For example, in HTML, the following block means that the string `Welcome!` is presented in bold characters:

```
<b> Welcome! </b>
```

In XML, the tag `<b>` doesn't have a predefined meaning.

XML is **not** a programming language. **XML is a data format**. XML presents data hierarchically, and not in a relational format.

The following is an example of relational data from the `Leaders` table versus a hierarchical XML document.

Relational data:

| | | | | |
|---|---|---|---|---|
| 1 | President | Afghanistan | Karzai | Hamid |
| 2 | President | Albania | Moisiu | Alfred |
| 3 | Prime Minister | United Kingdom | Blair | Tony |

Hierarchical XML data:

```
<?xml version="1.0" encoding="ISO-8859-1"?>
<TheWorld>
  <Leaders ID="1">
    <vchTitle>President</vchTitle>
    <vchCountry>Afghanistan</vchCountry>
    <vchLastName>Karzai</vchLastName>
    <vchFirstName>Hamid</vchFirstName>
  </Leaders>
  <Leaders ID="2">
    <vchTitle>President</vchTitle>
    <vchCountry>Albania</vchCountry>
    <vchLastName>Moisiu</vchLastName>
    <vchFirstName>Alfred</vchFirstName>
  </Leaders>
  <Leaders ID="3">
    <vchTitle>Prime Minister</vchTitle>
    <vchCountry>United Kingdom</vchCountry>
    <vchLastName>Blair</vchLastName>
    <vchFirstName>Tony</vchFirstName>
  </Leaders>
</TheWorld>
```

We can use XML to share data more easily by formatting company data in shared dialects and schemas. XML data can be transferred across the Internet, rendered in web pages, stored in XML files, and converted to various file types. This flexibility translates into a format that allows you to separate data from presentation, as well as keeping the data platform independent.

# The Anatomy of an XML Document

In the previous section's example of an XML document, the first line was:

```
<?xml version="1.0" encoding="ISO-8859-1"?>
```

This is the XML **declaration**. For an XML document to be **well-formed** (meaning it follows the rules of an XML document), the declaration should always be included. If the document does not include a header, it will not be well formed and, therefore, does not adhere to all the basic XML syntax rules. Most XML parsers (involved in consuming, translating, or transforming the document) will expect a document to be well-formed. The declaration defines the XML version of the document (for now always 1.0, defined by the World Wide Web Consortium (W3C)). The encoding, which can differ, defines the XML character set.

The previous example also included **elements** and **attributes**. Elements are called **tags** in HTML. The following XML chunk has an element called `<vchTitle>` and a closing element called `</vchTitle>` (notice the forward slash to mark the end of the element):

```
<vchTitle>President</vchTitle>
```

The next example shows the use of an attribute. The element is `<Leaders>`, and the `ID="3"` is the attribute describing the `<Leaders>` element. Attributes are normally used to describe elements, or provide additional information about elements:

```
<Leaders ID="3">
```

There are no fixed rules on when to use attributes and when to use elements; if an item occurs many times, it must be an element, since attributes cannot occur more than once for one element.

A well-formed XML document must have a **root element**. The XML document hierarchy is made up of parent and child elements, all of which must be within the root element; the root element is the parent of all elements within a document.

In the following example `<TheWorld>` is the root element, and all children tags exist within the `<TheWorld>` opening and closing (`</TheWorld>`) elements:

```
<TheWorld>
  ...
</TheWorld>
```

Elements within other elements are called **child** elements; for example, the `<Leaders></Leaders>` elements were child elements of the `<TheWorld>` root element, and `<vchTitle>` and other elements are child elements of the `<Leaders>` parent. Child and parent elements must always be properly nested, meaning that their open and closing tags should not overlap, but rather should always be contained within one another, beginning with the root node.

Other requirements for an XML document are that each opening element be associated with a closing element; always use closing tags in XML. XML parsers are much less forgiving than HTML parsers (usually a web browser) regarding this. Also, be aware that elements are case-sensitive, and that attribute values must always appear within double quotes (for example `ID="3"`, not `ID=3`).

# XML Technologies

There are a number of XML-related technologies. Some of these technologies are used for displaying XML, like XHTML (HTML 5.0), XSL (Extensible Stylesheet Language), and XSLT (XSL Transformations. Others are used to model and map the XML document, such as DTD (Document Type Definition) or XML Schema. DOM (Document Object Model) and SAX (Simple API for XML) are used to manipulate the contents of an XML document programmatically, and XPath (XML Path language), XLINK (XML Linking Language), and XQL (XML Query Language) are used to query the contents of an XML document.

**SOAP** (Simple Object Access Protocol) is used to transfer arbitrary XML documents between systems. This latest version of SQLXML includes SOAP functionality. Shortly after SQL Server 2000 was released, Microsoft began offering free downloads of **SQLXML** (XML for SQL Server), which further extended interoperability between XML and SQL Server 2000. At the time of writing, SQLXML is currently at version 3.0 SP1 (service pack 1). SOAP with SQLXML enables SQL Server stored procedures, user-defined functions, and other SQLXML technologies (described next), to be exposed as web services. Such web services can then be accessed from multiple platforms or programming languages, by using the SOAP protocol.

In addition to the aforementioned XML-related technologies, there are multiple methods available for importing, exporting, and manipulation of XML data as it relates to SQL Server 2000:

- **OPENXML**
  Reviewed in more detail later, OPENXML uses Transact-SQL extensions and system stored procedures to load an XML document into the SQL Server 2000 memory space. The source XML document must be stored in a `CHAR`, `NCHAR`, `VARCHAR`, `NVARCHAR`, `TEXT`, or `NTEXT` table column within a table in SQL Server. Once the document is in memory, we can use a rowset view of the XML data. We can use the results of this rowset within other Transact-SQL operations (such as importing the results into a table). OPENXML uses the Microsoft XML parser, called Microsoft XML Core Services (MSXML), for parsing the document.

- **MSXML**
  MSXML can be used with or independently of SQL Server, and is available as a free download from the Microsoft site. MSXML includes an XML parser, XSLT engine, DOM APIs, XSD (XML Schema definition language), XPATH, and SAX. At the time of writing, MSXML is currently at version 4.0, SP1. Using a programming language such as Visual Basic 6.0, and ADO (Microsoft's data access interface), you can export or load data to or from SQL Server by accessing the DOM exposed by MSXML. MSXML also includes two programming classes that enable HTTP access.
- **Microsoft XML OLE DB Simple Provider**
  ADO can also work with the Microsoft XML OLE DB Simple Provider, which can be used to read XML documents into a recordset, and then used for importing into SQL Server 2000. For more information on this provider, see Microsoft Knowledge Base article 271722, *HOWTO: Access Hierarchical XML Data with the XML OLE DB Simple Provider*.
- **SQLXML XML Bulk Load Utility**
  SQLXML version 1.0 introduced the XML Bulk Load utility, which allows high-speed bulk loads of data packaged inside XML tags into SQL Server. Unlike `OPENXML`, the entire XML document is **not** loaded into memory, so XML Bulk Load can be used to load very large documents. XML Bulk Load is a stand-alone COM object, and can be referenced and invoked by COM compliant programming languages.
- **FOR XML**
  The `FOR XML` clause is reviewed in the next section, and is used within the Transact-SQL statement to output data in XML hierarchical format.
- **SQLXML Client-side XML Processing**
  SQLXML 3.0 SP1 includes client-side XML processing, which converts a relational result set to a hierarchical XML document format on the **client** side. If you call a `SELECT FOR XML` query, with client-side XML formatting enabled, only the `SELECT` statement (without the FOR XML) is passed to SQL Server. The rowset is then converted to an XML document by SQLXML on the client workstation.
- **XML Schema Definition (XSD) Annotated Schemas**
  XSD is an extension of the W3C XML Schema specification. Microsoft added **annotated schemas**, which allow you to avoid complicated `XML FOR EXPLICIT` clause statements by binding the XSD definition directly to the database schema. This binding is also called **XML views**, allowing these views to be queried by the XML Path language (XPath). You should consider using XSD, instead of `FOR XML`, if you are more familiar with XML and XPath than Transact-SQL. XPath is not as expressive as Transact-SQL (for example, XPath lacks wildcards, has limited data types, and doesn't have a `UNION` clause).
- **Direct URL Queries**
  Internet Information Services 5.0 includes XML and SQL Server 2000 integration features. In conjunction with IIS, you can embed SQL queries directly into URL strings. SQL Server can then return the results as an XML document, and display the results in the browser.
- **XML Templates**
  Also in conjunction with IIS 5.0, XML templates contain SQL statements that incoming URL requests can invoke. Templates are more secure and flexible than direct URL queries, and are not limited in size or complexity. XML templates are stored on the server itself.
- **SQLXML Updategrams**
  Introduced in SQLXML version 1.0, updategrams allow you to modify data in SQL Server by using special XML tags. With updategrams, you use an XML grammar to specify before and after images for fragments of the modified data. Updategrams implement an XML-to-SQL mapping that eliminates the need to write Transact-SQL update queries. This may be beneficial for those developers unfamiliar with Transact-SQL and more comfortable with XML and related XML languages.
- **SQLXML Diffgrams**
  Diffgrams are similar to updategrams but they can be generated automatically from an ADO.NET `Dataset` object (ADO.NET is the next generation data access model for Microsoft's .NET Framework). Aside from ADO.NET, diffgrams can also be used with ADO version 2.6.

- **SQLXML Managed Classes**
  Introduced in SQLXML version 2.0, the SQLXML managed classes consist of .NET objects (classes) that allow programmers unfamiliar with traditional SQL to use XML templates or server-side XPath queries against SQL Server instead. To use these classes, the .NET framework and SQLXML free download must be installed on the machine where you plan to use them.

Some excellent references on the Web include:

- SQXML SQL Server 2000 (a Kevin Williams site) at http://www.sqlxml.org/
- PerfectXML at www.PerfectXML.com/SQLXML.asp
- Microsoft's XML Web Services page at http://www.microsoft.com/sql/techinfo/xml/default.asp

Kevin Williams' book, *SQL Server 2000 XML Distilled (ISBN 1-904347-08-8)*, is also a great place for more information.

# 18.1 How to... Use FOR XML

The Transact-SQL SELECT statement FOR XML clause allows you to convert relational rowset data into hierarchical XML output.

FOR XML has three modes which impact how the hierarchical data is formatted: AUTO, RAW, and EXPLICIT.

AUTO mode returns each table used in the FROM clause of the query as an element, and each column referenced in the SELECT clause as an attribute associated with the element. AUTO mode is ideal for queries using complex JOIN operations, easing the conversion to hierarchical format.

The GROUP BY clause and aggregate functions are not allowed in conjunction with FOR XML AUTO.

The following is an example of using FOR XML AUTO clause:

```
SELECT TOP 2
  Leaders.ID,
  Leaders.vchTitle,
  Leaders.vchCountry,
  Leaders.vchLastName,
  Country.iPopulation
FROM Leaders, Country
WHERE Leaders.vchCountry = Country.vchName
FOR XML AUTO
```

This returns:

```
<Leaders ID="1" vchTitle="President"
         vchCountry="Afghanistan" vchLastName="Karzai">
  <Country iPopulation="26668251"/>
</Leaders>
<Leaders ID="2" vchTitle="President"
         vchCountry="Albania" vchLastName="Moisiu">
  <Country iPopulation="3119000"/>
</Leaders>
```

AUTO mode can also be specified with elements; when adding elements, this AUTO mode maps columns to elements instead of attributes. For example:

```
SELECT TOP 2
           Leaders.ID,
           Leaders.vchTitle,
           Leaders.vchCountry,
           Leaders.vchLastName,
           Country.iPopulation
FROM Leaders, Country
WHERE Leaders.vchCountry =
               Country.vchName
FOR XML AUTO, ELEMENTS
```

This returns:

```
<Leaders>
  <ID>1</ID>
  <vchTitle>President</vchTitle>
  <vchCountry>Afghanistan</vchCountry>
  <vchLastName>Karzai/vchLastName>
  <Country>
    <iPopulation>26668251</iPopulation>
  </Country>
  </Leaders>
<Leaders>
  <ID>2</ID>
  <vchTitle>President</vchTitle>
  <vchCountry>Albania</vchCountry>
  <vchLastName>Moisiu</vchLastName>
  <Country>
    <iPopulation>3119000</iPopulation>
  </Country>
</Leaders>
```

RAW mode generates one row element for each row of the query result set, and includes the column data as the row element's attributes. RAW mode does not support retrieval of binary data.

The following is an example of using the FOR XML RAW clause:

```
SELECT TOP 2
  Leaders.ID,
  Leaders.vchTitle,
  Leaders.vchCountry,
  Leaders.vchLastName,
  Country.iPopulation
FROM Leaders, Country
WHERE Leaders.vchCountry = Country.vchName
FOR XML RAW
```

This returns:

```
<row ID="1" vchTitle="President" vchCountry="Afghanistan"
     vchLastName="Karzaia" iPopulation="26668251"/>

<row ID="2" vchTitle="President" vchCountry="Albania"
     vchLastName="Moisiu" iPopulation="3119000"/>
```

By adding the XMLDATA keyword to the FOR XML clause, a schema data type definition is prepended to the XML output. This is useful for returning the data types of each column. For example:

```
SELECT TOP 2
  Leaders.ID,
  Leaders.vchTitle,
  Leaders.vchCountry
FROM Leaders, Country
FOR XML AUTO, XMLDATA
```

This returns two XML blocks, the first defining the schema of the XML document (defining the elements, attributes, and associated data types), and the second defining the XML document itself:

```
<Schema name="Schema4" xmlns="urn:schemas-microsoft-com:xml-data"
        xmlns:dt="urn:schemas-microsoft-com:datatypes">
  <ElementType name="Leaders" content="empty" model="closed">
    <AttributeType name="ID" dt:type="i4"/>
    <AttributeType name="vchTitle" dt:type="string"/>
    <AttributeType name="vchCountry" dt:type="string"/>
    <attribute type="ID"/>
    <attribute type="vchTitle"/><attribute type="vchCountry"/>
  </ElementType>
</Schema>

<Leaders xmlns="x-schema:#Schema4" ID="1" vchTitle="President"
         vchCountry="Afghanistan"/>
<Leaders xmlns="x-schema:#Schema4" ID="1" vchTitle="President"
         vchCountry="Afghanistan"/>
```

The BINARY BASE64 keyword is used with FOR XML AUTO, and FOR XML EXPLICIT (described next), when binary information needs to be embedded in the XML document as base64-encoded format.

For example, the picture column from the Categories table is output using FOR XML AUTO and BINARY BASE64 (results not shown, as the BINARY BASE64 output of one row alone takes up several pages):

```
SELECT TOP 1
  CategoryID,
  picture
FROM Categories
FOR XML AUTO, BINARY BASE64
```

EXPLICIT mode is the most complex mode to learn, but offers the most control. Using FOR XML EXPLICIT, you can specify exactly which columns are elements or attributes in your query result set. You can specify nesting, and use subqueries and UNION queries to create sophisticated XML hierarchies.

EXPLICIT format is based on the concept of a **universal table**, which contains information about the hierarchical structure of the XML document. The keywords TAG and PARENT are used in a FOR XML EXPLICIT SELECT statement. TAG is used to define the tag number of the current element, and the PARENT column stores the tag number of the parent element (which is always NULL for the top level of the hierarchy).

After the TAG and PARENT values are defined in the SELECT statement, the elements and attributes must then be defined via the XML identifier syntax:

```
ElementName!TagNumber!AttributeName!Directive
```

XML parameters include:

- **ElementName**
  The `ElementName` defines the generic identifier of the element.
- **TagNumber**
  `TagNumber` defines the nesting value of the element within the XML tree.
- **AttributeName**
  `AttributeName` is the name of the XML attribute if `Directive` is not specified, otherwise it is the name of the contained element when `optionalDirective` is defined as `xml`, `cdata`, or `element`.
- **Directive**
  The `Directive` field controls the XML format returned. Permitted values include:

| Directive Value | Description |
|---|---|
| `xml` | Directs the column to act as a contained element, without entity encoding taking place (conversion of special characters to its entity associated value). |
| `cdata` | Non-entity encoded data. |
| `element` | Generates a contained element with a specified name, with entity encoding applied to the contents of the element. |
| `ID, IDREF, IDREFS` | These three types all facilitate XML intra-document links. |
| `hide` | The attribute will not be displayed, but can still be used for ordering. |
| `xmltext` | Wraps the contents of the column in a single tag, to be consumed or parsed later on, or used for overflow data. |

## Example 18.1.1: Using FOR XML EXPLICIT

In this example, the top two rows are returned from the `Leaders` table. The `ID` field and `vchLastName` columns are defined as attributes of the `Leaders` parent element, and the `vchCountry` column is defined as an element:

```
SELECT TOP 2
  1 as TAG,
  NULL as PARENT,
  ID as [Leaders!1!Leaders!id],
  vchCountry as [Leaders!1!vchCountry!element],
  vchLastName as [Leaders!1!vchLastName]
FROM dbo.Leaders
FOR XML EXPLICIT
```

This returns:

```
<Leaders Leaders="1" vchLastName="Karzaia">
  <vchCountry>Afghanistan</vchCountry>
</Leaders>

<Leaders Leaders="2" vchLastName="Moisiu">
  <vchCountry>Albania</vchCountry>
</Leaders>
```

For multiple levels in the XML tree use the `UNION ALL` operator with additional `SELECT` statements.

# 18.2 How to... Use sp_makewebtask to Output XML Documents

You can use FOR XML to output your relational data as hierarchical data; but how do you get it out of SQL Server? This chapter briefly reviewed various technologies that can assist you with outputting data into XML format and files (URL queries, templates, SQLXML); however, there is one easy method that is built-in to SQL Server 2000, the sp_makewebtask procedure.

You can use the sp_makewebtask procedure to produce an HTML or XML document. This procedure has a total of 33 parameters, but for our purposes, we will only need to use three of them. The user executing this procedure must have SELECT permissions for the query from which you will be returning data (using FOR XML in this case), CREATE PROCEDURE permissions in the database where the query is run, and permissions to write the generated HTML document to the selected location.

The syntax of sp_makewebtask using just the 3 parameters (see *Microsoft SQL Server Books Online* for the full array of choices) is as follows:

```
sp_makewebtask [@outputfile =] 'outputfile',
               [@query =] 'query'
               [, [@templatefile =] 'templatefile']
```

| Parameter | Description |
|---|---|
| @outputfile ='outputfile' | The location of the HTML or XML file to be generated (UNC names are allowed for remote computers). Depending on your security context, your SQL Server service account, SQL Server Agent, or proxy accounts should be configured to have permissions to write to this location. |
| @query = 'query' | The Transact-SQL query used to output the results. |
| @templatefile = 'templatefile' | Template files are used to generate the HTML or XML document, and contain placeholders and formatting instructions. The <%insert_data_here%> tag is used to indicate where query results should be added to an HTML table. <%begindetail%> and <%enddetail%> tags are used to define a complete row format (see SQL Server Books Online for a review of the formatting options).<br><br>For our upcoming example, create a template file in Notepad called C:\temp\leaders.tpl, the contents of which should be:<br><br><leaders><br>  <%begindetail%><br>  <%insert_data_here%><br>  <%enddetail%><br></leaders><br><br>Notice that we have placed a <leaders> root tag to make this a well-formed document. |

### Example 18.2.1: Using sp_makewebtask to generate an XML document

Once you have created a template file, as shown in the syntax table above, you can execute the sp_makewebtask stored procedure in Query Analyzer, with the following example parameters:

```
sp_makewebtask @outputfile = 'C:\temp\leaders.xml',
  @query = 'SELECT * FROM Leaders FOR XML AUTO',
  @templatefile = 'C:\temp\leaders.tpl'
```

This produces a Leaders.xml file with the results of the SELECT * FROM LEADERS in XML format. If you open this file with Microsoft Internet Explorer (version 5 or higher), you will see something similar to this:

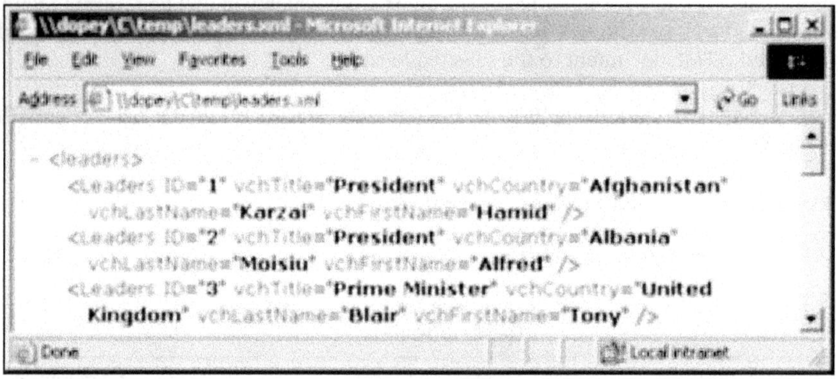


# 18.3 How to... Use OPENXML

The OPENXML Transact-SQL command allows us to query XML documents stored in a table column like a relational table. OPENXML allows retrieval of both elements and attributes from an XML document fragment. The generated rowset can then easily be used within other SQL statements (sub-query or INSERT statement, for example).

The sp_xml_preparedocument system stored procedure is used in conjunction with OPENXML to move the XML document into memory. The document is stored in the internal cache of SQL Server, using up to one eighth of the total available SQL Server memory. The procedure reads the XML document and parses it internally using the MSXML (Microsoft XML) parser.

The sp_xml_preparedocument stored procedure is responsible for returning a handle that we can use to access the internal representation of the XML document. The handle can be used for the duration of the user connection to SQL Server, or until the handle is de-allocated using sp_xml_removedocument.The sp_xml_removedocument procedure is used to clear the document from memory once finished.

The syntax for sp_xml_preparedocument is as follows:

```
sp_xml_preparedocument hdoc OUTPUT
[, xmltext]
[, xpath_namespaces]
```

| Parameter | Description |
|---|---|
| hdoc OUTPUT | This is an integer OUTPUT parameter value that indicates the handle of the newly created XML document. |
| xmltext | This is the field containing the XML document. This column data type can be CHAR, NCHAR, VARCHAR, NVARCHAR, TEXT, or NTEXT. |
| xpath_namespaces | This parameter specifies the namespace declarations used in the row and column XPath expressions. This value defaults to <root xmlns:mp="urn:schemas-microsoft-com:xml-metaprop">. A **namespace** is a collection of element type and attribute names that is significant to the consuming parser or XML-related technology (in this case Xpath). |

The syntax for sp_xml_removedocument is as follows:

```
sp_xml_removedocument hdoc
```

This procedure takes only one parameter, hdoc, which is the integer handle of the XML document loaded into memory with sp_xml_preparedocument. Always remember to de-allocate your XML documents using sp_xml_removedocument when you have finished using them; otherwise, the memory will not be de-allocated until the user session that loaded the document disconnects.

OPENXML uses XPath, which is a general-purpose query language for addressing, sorting, and filtering elements of an XML document, including the text within them.

OPENXML is used in the FROM clause, or anywhere else a rowset provider (table or view) is allowed.

The syntax is:

```
OPENXML (idoc, rowpattern, flags)
[WITH (SchemaDeclaration or TableName)]
```

| Parameters | Description |
|---|---|
| idoc | Integer document handle of the XML document. |
| rowpattern | XPath pattern used for identification of nodes to be processed as rows. |
| flags | Indicates XML data and relational rowset mapping.<br>0 creates attribute-centric mapping.<br>1 applies attribute-centric mapping first, and then element-centric mapping for columns not yet processed.<br>2 uses element-centric mapping.<br>8 specifies that consumed data should not be copied to the overflow property @mp:xmltext. |
| WITH (SchemaDeclaration or Tablename) | When WITH (SchemaDeclaration) is used, the actual syntax is made up of a column name (rowset name), column type (valid data type), column pattern (optional XPath pattern), and optional meta data properties (meta data about the XML nodes).<br>If Tablename is used instead of a SchemaDeclaration, a table must already exist for holding the rowset data. |

## Example 18.3.1: Using OPENXML

This example extracts the `ID` and `vchLastName` fields from an XML document (held in a `VARCHAR` local variable), and presents the data in a columnar report format.

The beginning of this example declares an integer variable `@idoc` for use by the `sp_xml_preparedocument` system stored procedure. The `@doc VARCHAR(1000)` local variable is used to populate the XML document string. A memory reference is then created to the `@doc` XML string, outputting the reference in memory value to the `@idoc` integer variable.

Lastly, `OPENXML` is used with `@idoc`, along with an XPath statement pattern, to return the values of the `ID` and `vchLastName` columns as a relational result set:

```
DECLARE @idoc int
DECLARE @doc varchar(1000)
SELECT @doc =
'<TheWorld>
<Leaders ID="1" vchLastName="Karzai
">
  <vchCountry>Afghanistan</vchCountry>
</Leaders>

<Leaders ID="2" vchLastName="Moisiu">
  <vchCountry>Albania</vchCountry>
</Leaders>
</TheWorld>'

EXEC sp_xml_preparedocument @idoc OUTPUT, @doc

SELECT *
FROM OPENXML (@idoc, '/TheWorld/Leaders',1)
WITH (ID int, vchLastName varchar(100))
```

This returns:

OPENXML works best with smaller documents (1MB or less), since documents are loaded into memory. Documents can only consume up to 1/8 the total available SQL Server memory. Concurrent loading of the same document by different user sessions may cause the memory limit to be reached, as well as the loading of a single document that exceeds the maximum memory available.

# Index

## A Guide to the Index

The index is arranged in word-by-word order (so that New York would appear before Newark). Acronyms are listed unexpanded and the ellipsis (...) and asterisk (*) have their usual meanings, indicating omissions and variant endings respectively.

# B

## C

# E

# F

# G

## H



## I

## J

## K



## L

# M

# N

# O

## Q



## R

## T

# U

# X



# Y



# Z

Apress®

# License Agreement (Single-User Products)

THIS IS A LEGAL AGREEMENT BETWEEN YOU, THE END USER, AND APRESS. BY OPENING THE SEALED DISK PACKAGE, YOU ARE AGREEING TO BE BOUND BY THE TERMS OF THIS AGREEMENT. IF YOU DO NOT AGREE TO THE TERMS OF THIS AGREEMENT, PROMPTLY RETURN THE UNOPENED DISK PACKAGE AND THE ACCOMPANYING ITEMS (INCLUDING WRITTEN MATERIALS AND BINDERS AND OTHER CONTAINERS) TO THE PLACE YOU OBTAINED THEM FOR A FULL REFUND.

## APRESS SOFTWARE LICENSE

1. GRANT OF LICENSE. Apress grants you the right to use one copy of this enclosed Apress software program (the "SOFTWARE") on a single terminal connected to a single computer (e.g., with a single CPU). You may not network the SOFTWARE or otherwise use it on more than one computer or computer terminal at the same time.

2. COPYRIGHT. The SOFTWARE copyright is owned by Apress and is protected by United States copyright laws and international treaty provisions. Therefore, you must treat the SOFTWARE like any other copyrighted material (e.g., a book or musical recording) except that you may either (a) make one copy of the SOFTWARE solely for backup or archival purposes, or (b) transfer the SOFTWARE to a single hard disk, provided you keep the original solely for backup or archival purposes. You may not copy the written material accompanying the SOFTWARE.

3. OTHER RESTRICTIONS. You may not rent or lease the SOFTWARE, but you may transfer the SOFTWARE and accompanying written materials on a permanent basis provided you retain no copies and the recipient agrees to the terms of this Agreement. You may not reverse engineer, decompile, or disassemble the SOFTWARE. If SOFTWARE is an update, any transfer must include the update and all prior versions.

4. By breaking the seal on the disc package, you agree to the terms and conditions printed in the Apress License Agreement. If you do not agree with the terms, simply return this book with the still-sealed CD package to the place of purchase for a refund.

# DISCLAIMER OF WARRANTY

NO WARRANTIES. Apress disclaims all warranties, either express or implied, including, but not limited to, implied warranties of merchantability and fitness for a particular purpose, with respect to the SOFTWARE and the accompanying written materials. The software and any related documentation is provided "as is." You may have other rights, which vary from state to state.

NO LIABILITIES FOR CONSEQUENTIAL DAMAGES. In no event shall be liable for any damages whatsoever (including, without limitation, damages from loss of business profits, business interruption, loss of business information, or other pecuniary loss) arising out of the use or inability to use this Apress product, even if Apress has been advised of the possibility of such damages. Because some states do not allow the exclusion or limitation of liability for consequential or incidental damages, the above limitation may not apply to you.

# U.S. GOVERNMENT RESTRICTED RIGHTS

The SOFTWARE and documentation are provided with RESTRICTED RIGHTS. Use, duplication, or disclosure by the Government is subject to restriction as set forth in subparagraph (c) (1) (ii) of The Rights in Technical Data and Computer Software clause at 52.227-7013. Contractor/manufacturer is Apress, 2560 Ninth Street, Suite 219, Berkeley, California, 94710.

This Agreement is governed by the laws of the State of California.

Should you have any questions concerning this Agreement, or if you wish to contact Apress for any reason, please write to Apress, 2560 Ninth Street, Suite 219, Berkeley, California, 94710.

**Data drives everything.**

Share information, exchange ideas, and discuss any database programming or administration issues.

**Unfortunately, it is.**

Talk about the Apress line of books that cover software methodology, best practices, and how programmers interact with the "suits."

**Try living without plumbing (and eventually IPv6).**

Talk about networking topics including protocols, design, administration, wireless, wired, storage, backup, certifications, trends, and new technologies.

**Ugly doesn't cut it anymore, and CGI is absurd.**

Help is in sight for your site. Find design solutions for your projects and get ideas for building an interactive Web site.

**We've come a long way from the old Oak tree.**

Hang out and discuss Java in whatever flavor you choose: J2SE, J2EE, J2ME, Jakarta, and so on.

**Lots of bad guys out there—the good guys need help.**

Discuss computer and network security issues here. Just don't let anyone else know the answers!

**All about the Zen of OS X.**

OS X is both the present and the future for Mac apps. Make suggestions, offer up ideas, or boast about your new hardware.

**Cool things. Fun things.**

It's after hours. It's time to play. Whether you're into LEGO® MINDSTORMS™ or turning an old PC into a DVR, this is where technology turns into fun.

**Source code is good; understanding (open) source is better.**

Discuss open source technologies and related topics such as PHP, MySQL, Linux, Perl, Apache, Python, and more.

**No defenestration here.**

Ask questions about all aspects of Windows programming, get help on Microsoft technologies covered in Apress books, or provide feedback on any Apress Windows book.

HOW TO PARTICIPATE:

Go to the Apress Forums site at **http://forums.apress.com/**.

Click the New User link.

www.ingramcontent.com/pod-product-compliance
Lightning Source LLC
Chambersburg PA
CBHW081446050326
40690CB00015B/2702
*9781590595923*